THE BOOK OF THE STATES

2009 EDITION
VOLUME 41

The Council of State Governments
Lexington, Kentucky

Headquarters: (859) 244-8000
Fax: (859) 244-8001
Internet: www.csg.org

Sharing capitol ideas.

Headquarters:
David Adkins, Executive Director/CEO
2760 Research Park Drive, P.O. Box 11910
Lexington, KY 40578-1910
Phone: (859) 244-8000
Internet: www.csg.org

Eastern:
Wendell M. Hannaford, Director
100 Wall Street, 20th Floor
New York, NY 10005
Phone: (212) 482-2320
Internet: www.csgeast.org

Midwestern:
Michael H. McCabe, Director
701 E. 22nd Street, Suite 110
Lombard, IL 60148
Phone: (630) 925-1922
Internet: www.csgmidwest.org

Southern:
Colleen Cousineau, Director
P.O. Box 98129
Atlanta, GA 30359
Phone: (404) 633-1866
Internet: www.slcatlanta.org

Western:
Kent Briggs, Director
1107 9th Street, Suite 730
Sacramento, CA 95814
Phone: (916) 553-4423
Internet: www.csgwest.org

Washington, D.C.:
Christopher Whatley, Director
444 N. Capitol Street, NW, Suite 401
Washington, D.C. 20001
Phone: (202) 624-5460
Internet: www.csg.org

Manufactured in the United States of America

Publication Sales Department
1(800) 800-1910

Paperback Price: $99.00
ISBN # 978-0-87292-759-9

Hard Cover Price: $125.00
ISBN # 978-0-87292-758-2

Foreword

Walk into almost any library in America and there is a good chance you will find this book on the shelf. Librarians understand the utility of this resource because it provides accurate, concise, easily accessible, up-to-date information on a variety of key data points. We hope you will also find it a useful tool in answering your questions about the states and territories.

The Book of the States was first published in 1935 in the midst of the Great Depression. As state leaders searched for answers to the challenges they faced then, The Council of State Governments, under the leadership of our founder, Henry Toll, developed this resource as a tool to empower state leaders to achieve their goal of making a difference. What was needed then is needed now. The Council of State Governments is proud to present this 2009 edition with the hope that it will be a resource for this generation of state leaders as they seek to change the world for the better.

The authors and staff who contributed their work to create this book did so as an extension of their calling to advance the common good. Information empowers both political leaders and citizens alike to effectively participate in making the choices that determine our future. On behalf of The Council of State Governments, I want to commend all of the contributors for their commitment to make this volume a powerful source of knowledge. Additionally, CSG has an ongoing commitment to improve this resource. To that end, we welcome your suggestions on how to enhance future editions of *The Book of the States*.

We recognize one of the most valuable roles The Council of State Governments can play in advancing excellence in state government is to be a fair, honest and impartial broker of information. CSG accomplishes that goal in many formats and forums including the publication of this book. That tradition was sustained through the work of my predecessor, Daniel M. Sprague, who dedicated three decades of service to CSG, and also by CSG East Director Alan Sokolow, who dedicated four decades of service to CSG, before their retirements at the end of 2008. With appreciation for all they did to support the important work of state government leaders, we dedicate this edition of *The Book of the States* to Dan and Alan with profound gratitude. Their legacy of service lives on in these pages and in the countless lives they touched through their work.

May 2009

David Adkins
Executive Director/CEO
The Council of State Governments

The Council of State Governments is the premier multibranch organization forecasting policy trends for the community of states, commonwealths and territories on a national and regional basis. CSG alerts state elected and appointed officials to emerging social, economic and political trends; offers innovative state policy responses to rapidly changing conditions; and advocates multistate problem-solving to maximize resources and competitiveness. CSG promotes excellence in decision-making and leadership skills and champions state sovereignty.

Staff Acknowledgements

The staff wishes to thank the authors who shared their expertise and insights, the hundreds of individuals in the states who responded to surveys conducted by The Council of State Governments, national organizations of state officials, federal agencies and think tank organizations who made their most recent data and information available for this volume.

The Book of the States 2009

Managing Editor **Audrey S. Wall** ▪ *Associate Editor* **Heather M. Perkins**

Graphic Designer **Chris Pryor** ▪ *Graphic Designer* **Lisa K. Eads**

Graphic Designer **Jessica T. Downey** ▪ *Graphic Designer* **Rebecca Field**

Copy Editor **Mary Branham** ▪ *Copy Editor* **Mikel Chavers**

Research Assistant **Kasey D. Cooke** ▪ *Research Assistant/Intern* **Chelsea Clark**

Table of Contents

Chapter Nine

The Book of the States: The Information Source for the States since 1935

By Jack Penchoff

For 74 years, *The Book of the States* has remained a constant, reliable compendium of information and data for state officials, academicians and students interested in how state government works.

First published in 1935, *The Book of the States* had been an integral part of The Council of State Governments founder Henry Toll's plans for a new league of states. Section 1, Article VI of the 1933 Articles of Organization that established CSG reads: "*The Book of the States*. It shall be the policy of the Council to publish a handbook of the state governments, known as *The Book of the States*, at least once every two years."

Toll envisioned the book as a series of 30 to 40 handbooks on such topics as health, education and taxation. These handbooks would be bound together in one book.

In the first volume he outlined a format that has remained essentially unchanged since Volume 1. "When this plan is carried out, this book will become an essential working tool for every state legislator, as well as for every important official of every state," he wrote "It also will be an essential reference book in every newspaper office, in every political science department, in every public library."

The Book of the States was published every two years until 2002 when it became an annual publication. And through the years, other directories have spun off the publication. For example, the first of CSG's Leadership Directories was printed as a standalone publication in 1947. Until then, the information in those directories was contained in *The Book of the States*.

The Book of the States was a critical part of Toll's vision for CSG, which he saw as a facilitator for greater cooperation among the states.

CSG was organized in 1933 with the recognition that for states to cooperate, all branches of government need to be involved.

President Franklin Roosevelt also recognized the need for greater government cooperation. In a letter to Toll dated Feb. 17, 1935, FDR wrote: "I think to all students of government that there is urgent need for better machinery of cooperation between federal, state and local governments in many fields."

In its first couple of editions, *The Book of the States* contained a list of uniform state laws. While acknowledging that not every possible law was listed, "they are, however, the products of thought, study and research of trained minds, and will provide information for all legislators interested in these subjects."

But as the threat of World War II grew, a group of state and federal officials met in August 1940 to review and compile state laws related to internal security. The result of the meeting was *A Legislative Program for Defense*. The committee reconvened after the U.S. entered World War II and broadened its mission to produce *Suggested State War Legislation*. The military focus gave way after 1946 to *Suggested State Legislation*, an annual volume of draft legislation about topics of major governmental interest, which continues to be published more than 60 years later.

And while *The Book of the States* has been the genesis for several spinoffs such as *Suggested State Legislation* and the Leadership Directories, there's been no problem filling the void in subsequent volumes.

The Book of the States continues to provide state officials with the most current data available. A dedicated staff annually compiles information of comparable state data that fits into more than 600 pages. Much of the data is similar to that developed for earlier volumes. However, as CSG has responded to changes that impact state government, so has *The Book of the States*.

The 500 page 1943–44 edition, for example, contains tables, charts and articles on State Councils of Defense, a directory of federal war agencies and a table on the distribution of war supply contracts by agency and state.

More recent editions have valuable information on topics that were not envisioned 65 years ago. This edition of *The Book of the States* contains tables on statewide ballot propositions, state tax collections, demographic trends, and emergency management budgets and staffing. As the challenges and complexities of state government evolve, so do the pages of what the CSG staff affectionately refers to as *BOS*.

Jack Penchoff is director of Communications at The Council of State Governments and is the senior editor of *State News* magazine.

Chapter One

STATE CONSTITUTIONS

State Constitutional Developments in 2008

By John Dinan

Fewer state constitutional amendments were proposed and approved in 2008 than in recent even-numbered years. Several amendments, however, generated considerable attention. Voters in three more states approved same-sex marriage bans, including the first measure to overturn a state court ruling that had legalized the practice. Two more affirmative action bans were proposed; one was approved, the other defeated, marking the first popular rejection of such a measure. Other notable amendments addressed abortion, voting rights, redistricting, gambling and investment of public funds in the stock market. Meanwhile, voters in three states rejected automatically referred measures on whether to call constitutional conventions.

State constitutional amendment activity was higher in 2008 than in recent odd-numbered years but somewhat lower than comparable presidential or mid-term election years. Several amendments attracted significant attention. California became the first state to approve a same-sex marriage ban that overturned a state court ruling legalizing the practice. Colorado voters became the first in the country to reject an affirmative action ban after recent approvals in several other states. And California voters approved an amendment entrusting state legislative redistricting to a citizens' commission.

In other notable developments, 2008 marked the conclusion of the second meeting of the Florida Taxation and Budget Reform Commission, one of two Florida commissions that convene every 20 years and submit amendments directly to voters. Meanwhile, voters in Connecticut, Hawaii and Illinois declined to approve convention referendums submitted pursuant to constitutional requirements for periodic submission of these questions. Finally, state court rulings prevented a number of amendments from appearing on state ballots or from taking effect.

Constitutional Amendment and Revision Methods

Constitutional amendments were proposed in 30 states in 2008. The number of states considering amendments jumped considerably from the eight states that considered amendments in 2007, but it was slightly lower than the 34 states that considered amendments in 2006 (the last even-numbered year) and the 33 states that considered amendments in 2004 (the last presidential election year). Of the 111 amendments submitted to voters in 2008, 67 were approved. This compares to 34 amendments proposed and 33 approved in 2007, 166 amendments proposed and 125 approved in 2006, and 140 amendments proposed and 98 approved in 2004. Colorado voters considered more amendments (14) than any other state. Alabama voters approved the highest number of amendments (eight), all but one of which were local amendments.

Legislative Proposals and Constitutional Initiatives

All but four of the 111 amendments considered in 2008 were proposed by legislatures or through the initiative process. Legislatures proposed 78 amendments, and voters approved 52 of these measures, for a passage rate of 66.7 percent. Twenty-nine amendments were proposed via the initiative process, and 12 were approved, for a passage rate of 41.4 percent. These rates are generally in line with the passage rates for legislative-proposed and voter-initiated amendments in recent years.

Constitutional Conventions and Revision Commissions

None of the 111 amendments considered in 2008 were proposed via constitutional convention; four amendments were proposed by a revision commission. The U.S. Virgin Islands held the only constitutional convention in 2008. The 30 convention delegates began meeting in October 2007 for the purpose of drafting a territorial constitution and continued to meet in 2008 with an eye toward completing their work before the statutory deadline of October 1, 2008. When it became clear the convention would not finish by then, the territorial legislature extended the deadline to May 1, 2009.[1] If the convention agrees on a draft constitution by this new date, the document would be submitted to the territorial governor and then the U.S. president and Congress before it is voted on by residents of the territory.

Citizens in three states—Connecticut, Hawaii, and Illinois—voted on whether to call conventions pursuant to constitutional requirements that this question be submitted periodically. In Connecticut and

Illinois, the question must be submitted every 20 years; in Hawaii, the question is submitted every decade. All three states rejected a convention, with at least three-fifths of voters opposing the measure in each state.

In Hawaii, the lieutenant governor and attorney general were the main proponents of calling a convention, and the Republican Party endorsed the effort. However, the Democratic Party and Hawaii Alliance (a coalition of union and teachers groups) opposed a convention and campaigned aggressively against it. This generated a greater degree of attention to the convention referendum than the last few times it appeared on the ballot.

In Illinois, then-Lt. Gov. Pat Quinn favored a convention call, and the Chamber of Commerce, Farm Bureau and AFL-CIO opposed the measure. Supporters and critics argued not only about the merits of a convention but also about the wording of the referendum. In fact, in the months before the election, Quinn and the Chicago Bar Association filed suit against the secretary of state and State Board of Elections, arguing that the ballot stated incorrectly that failure to vote on the referendum would count as a "no" vote and that the ballot stated inappropriately and unnecessarily that the last convention referendum in 1988 failed by a large margin. A Cook County circuit judge in October 2008 agreed with plaintiffs' concerns about the ballot wording and ordered election officials to distribute a handout at the polls correcting the misleading ballot statements. But the judge also ruled that there was not enough time to order the ballots be rewritten. The Chicago Bar Association vowed after the referendum's defeat to take the case to the state Supreme Court, with the intent of either securing a re-vote in 2010 or at least resolving these questions before the next automatic convention referendum in 2028.[2]

In Connecticut, the debate about the convention referendum became entwined with public reaction to an Oct. 10, 2008, state Supreme Court ruling legalizing same-sex marriage. Prior to the court ruling, convention support and opposition generally followed the patterns seen in other states, with some Republican legislators, Gov. Jodi Rell and taxpayers' groups in support, and Democratic politicians, unions and teachers in opposition. Once the court issued its ruling, however, same-sex marriage opponents lent their support to a convention on the grounds that it might provide an opportunity to overturn the court decision.[3]

Although voters in 2008 rejected each of these convention referendums—as they have with convention questions around the country in recent decades—several of the 14 states with periodic convention question requirements have votes scheduled in coming years. Votes are scheduled in Maryland, Michigan and Montana in 2010, and in Alaska and Ohio in 2012.

Meanwhile, Alabama Citizens for Constitutional Reform continued to press the state legislature to submit a convention call to voters, and the group secured more legislative support—at least in the House—than in previous years. A majority of House members supported a motion filed late in the 2008 legislative session to consider a bill calling for a convention, but the bill received less than the three-fifths vote needed to debate the bill at that point in the session.[4]

Constitutional commissions were operating in 2008 in Utah and Florida. The Utah Constitutional Revision Commission is the only commission with an ongoing charge to recommend constitutional amendments for legislative consideration. Although this commission did not submit any new recommendations in 2008, one of its 2007 recommendations clarifying the gubernatorial succession process was approved by voters in the November 2008 election.

The Florida Taxation and Budget Reform Commission is one of two Florida commissions that convene every 20 years and can submit constitutional amendments for voter ratification. Commissions in other states must submit any recommended amendments to the legislature, which then decides whether to submit them to the people. However, the Florida Constitution Revision Commission and the Florida Taxation and Budget Reform Commission are uniquely empowered to submit constitutional changes directly to voters. The Constitution Revision Commission was established by the 1968 Florida Constitution and directed to meet in the tenth year after adoption of the constitution and then every twentieth year thereafter; it last met in 1997–1998. The Taxation and Budget Reform Commission, whose charge is confined to recommending tax, revenue, and fiscal measures, was created by a 1988 amendment and met initially in 1990. Then, by virtue of a 1998 amendment, it was directed to meet next in 2007–2008 and every twentieth year thereafter. This commission is comprised of 25 voting members—11 appointed by the governor and seven each by the Senate president and House speaker—and four nonvoting ex-officio members who are legislators appointed by House and Senate leaders.

The 2007–2008 Florida Taxation and Budget Reform Commission recommended seven constitutional

Table A: State Constitutional Changes by Method of Initiation: 2004–05, 2006–07 and 2008

Method of initiation	Number of states involved			Total proposals			Total adopted			Percentage adopted		
	2004–2005	2006–2007	2008	2004–2005	2006–2007	2008	2004–2005	2006–2007	2008	2004–2005	2006–2007	2008
All methods	40	37	30	166	200(a)(d)	111(e)	112	158(b)(d)	67(e)	67.5	78.0(c)	60.4
Legislative proposal	38	36	28	127	167(a)(d)	78(e)	95	147(b)(d)	52(e)	74.8	86.8(c)	66.7
Constitutional												
initiative	13	12	10	39	33	29	17	11	12	43.6	33.3	41.4
convention	...	...	...	...	...	...	...	...	...	...	...	...
commission	...	...	1	...	...	4	...	...	3	...	...	75.0

Source: Based on surveys conducted in previous years by Janice May and updated by John Dinan for the years 2005–2008.

Key:

(a) Excludes Delaware, where proposals are not submitted to voters.

(b) Includes Delaware.

(c) In calculating the percentages, the amendments adopted in Delaware (where proposals are not submitted to voters) are excluded (two amendments were adopted in 2007).

(d) Excludes one Alabama amendment that was proposed by the legislature and appeared on the ballot but was determined by the governor's office prior to the vote not to have received enough votes in the legislature to properly appear on the ballot, and thus even though the amendment was approved by voters in November 2006 and the vote totals were certified by the state canvassing board, the governor did not proclaim the results for the amendment and so it has not received an official amendment number.

(e) Excludes one New Mexico amendment approved by voters in November 2008 but declared invalid by the state supreme court on single-subject grounds in December 2008.

changes, but the Florida Supreme Court prevented three of these proposals from appearing on the ballot. The court found the language of one proposal that would have reduced state property taxes and increased the sales tax and other revenue sources misleading. The court also ruled that the commission strayed from its mission when it recommended two other proposals designed to preserve school voucher programs from judicial invalidation.[5] Voters in November 2008 approved three of the four amendments that remained on the ballot. The approved amendments give tax breaks to owners of working waterfront property, homeowners who make energy efficiency or hurricane protection improvements, and landowners who donate land for conservation purposes. The rejected amendment would have allowed counties to hold referendums on increasing local sales taxes to support community colleges.

Constitutional Changes

Voters in 2008 considered several high-profile amendments regarding individual rights, most notably pertaining to same-sex marriage, affirmative action and abortion. Voters also considered amendments targeting governing institutions; the most notable to pass was a California redistricting reform measure. Also notable was voter approval of an Arkansas amendment instituting annual legislative sessions. As for policy amendments, many of them this year dealt with taxes and gambling, and a number of these measures passed. Other policy amendments sought to permit government investment in stocks, and all but one of these were defeated.

Individual Rights

Voters in Florida, Arizona and California approved same-sex marriage bans in 2008, and the actions were notable for different reasons. The Florida vote was notable because the amendment secured the necessary 60 percent of the vote, required after a 2006 amendment increasing to three-fifths the percentage of the popular vote required for ratifying amendments. The Arizona approval was significant because voters there had previously rejected a same-sex marriage amendment, albeit worded differently. Adoption of the California measure marked the first time voters approved a same-sex marriage ban after a state court had already legalized the practice; the California Supreme Court had legalized the practice in a May 15, 2008, decision. In the aftermath of the November 2008 vote in favor of the amendment overturning the state Supreme Court ruling, same-sex marriage supporters promptly challenged the legitimacy of the amendment. The California Supreme Court declined to enjoin enforcement of the amendment, but agreed to hear arguments in early 2009 about whether the amendment was an invalid revision of the constitution, whether it violated the separation of powers doctrine, and what effect it would have on same-sex marriages performed before November. Passage of the Florida, Arizona and California measures brings to 30 the number of same-sex marriage amendments, all enacted since 1998. Of these amendments, Hawaii's provision *authorizes* the legislature to reserve marriage for opposite-sex couples; the other 29 *prohibit* same-sex marriage and in some cases civil unions.

Table B: Substantive Changes in State Constitutions: Proposed and Adopted: 2004–05, 2006–07 and 2008

	Total proposed			*Total adopted*			*Percentage adopted*		
Subject matter	*2004–2005*	*2006–2007*	*2008*	*2004–2005*	*2006–2007*	*2008*	*2004–2005*	*2006–2007*	*2008*
Proposals of statewide applicability	138	172(a)	102(d)	94	134(b)(e)	60(d)	68.1	76.7(c)	58.8
Bill of Rights	16	30(e)	15	15	26(e)	11	93.8	86.7	73.3
Suffrage & elections	14	7	10	6	4	6	42.9	57.1	60.0
Legislative branch	14	12	12	6	7	7	42.8	58.3	58.3
Executive branch	5	1	5	4	1	4	80.0	100.0	80.0
Judicial branch	10	8(a)	1	5	6(b)	0	50.0	50.0(c)	0.0
Local government	4	1	3	3	0	0	75.0	0.0	0.0
Finance & taxation	33	65	32	23	51	15	69.7	78.5	46.9
State & local debt	7	10	3	6	9	3	85.7	90.0	100.0
State functions	14	5	1	8	4	1	57.1	80.0	100.0
Amendment & revision	1	1	0	1	1	0	100.0	100.0	0.0
General revision proposals	0	0	0	0	0	0	0.0	0.0	0.0
Miscellaneous proposals	20	32	20	17	25	13	85.0	78.1	65.0
Local amendments	28	28(f)	9	18	24(f)	7	64.3	85.7	77.8

Source: Based on surveys conducted in previous years by Janice May and updated by John Dinan for the years 2005–2008.

Key:

(a) Excludes Delaware, where amendments do not require popular approval.

(b) Includes Delaware.

(c) In calculating the percentages, the amendments adopted in Delaware (where proposals are not submitted to voters) are excluded.

(d) Excludes one New Mexico amendment approved in November 2008 but declared invalid by the state supreme court in December 2008.

(e) Includes amendments restricting the use of eminent domain, regardless of whether these protections were actually inserted in the bill of rights or in other articles.

(f) Excludes one Alabama amendment that was proposed by the legislature and appeared on the ballot but was determined by the governor's office prior to the vote not to have received enough votes in the legislature to properly appear on the ballot, and thus even though the amendment was approved by voters in November 2006 and the vote totals were certified by the state canvassing board, the governor did not proclaim the results for the amendment and so it has not received an official amendment number.

Affirmative action bans were considered by voters in Nebraska and Colorado in 2008. Nebraska voters approved a ban, while voters in Colorado became the first to defeat such a measure. Since 1996, Ward Connerly, working through the American Civil Rights Institute and operating primarily in states with the constitutional initiative process, has secured passage of constitutional affirmative action bans in California and Michigan and a statutory ban in Washington. Connerly and his organization had planned to qualify constitutional bans in as many as five Western states in 2008, but supporters were unable to secure enough signatures in Oklahoma and Missouri and encountered difficulty with the validity of signatures in Arizona. Despite the mixed success in 2008, efforts are under way to qualify affirmative action bans for the ballot in Missouri and perhaps other states in 2010.

Voters in California and Colorado rejected anti-abortion amendments. In California, voters defeated a parental notification amendment appearing on the ballot for the third time in four years. Colorado voters were the first in the country to vote on a "personhood" amendment stipulating that fetuses are persons from the moment of conception and entitled to the same rights as all other people. Anti-abortion advocates have tried in recent years to qualify such personhood amendments for state ballots and succeeded for the first time in Colorado, only to see the measure soundly defeated. Advocates are continuing their efforts to qualify personhood amendments for the ballot in other states, including Montana.

Voters in six states considered amendments expanding or clarifying voting eligibility and processes. Arkansas and Iowa voters approved amendments deleting outdated language denying the vote to any "idiot or insane person" and inserting different language or establishing a different procedure for determining mental competence. Maryland voters authorized early voting, thereby overturning a 2006 state Supreme Court decision invalidating an early voting statute. Connecticut voters permitted 17-year-olds to vote in primary elections if they will turn 18 by the general election. And Oregon voters approved an amendment lowering from 21 to 18 the minimum age for voting in school board elections. Nevada voters were the only ones to defeat a voting-related amendment in 2008, but this defeat does not have any practical significance. Nevada's constitution requires a voter to live in the state for six months, but that requirement was rendered unenforceable by a 1972 U.S. Supreme Court ruling that 30 days is the maximum allowable residency requirement. The vote leaves this defunct language in the state constitution.

Table C: State Constitutional Changes by Legislative, Initiative, and Commission Proposal: 2008

State	Legislative proposal			Constitutional initiative			Commission proposal		
	Number proposed	Number adopted	Percentage adopted	Number proposed	Number adopted	Percentage adopted	Number proposed	Number adopted	Percentage adopted
Alabama	10	8	80.0%	...	...	...	...	...	...
Arizona	1	1	100.0	3	1	33.3	...	...	...
Arkansas	2	2	100.0	1	1	100.0	...	...	...
California	...	...	...	9	4	44.4	...	...	...
Colorado	4	2	50.0	10	2	20.0	...	...	...
Connecticut	1	1	100.0	...	...	...	...	...	...
Florida	2	1	50.0	1	1	100.0	4	3	75.0
Georgia	3	2	66.7	...	...	...	...	...	...
Hawaii	1	0	0.0	...	...	...	...	...	...
Iowa	1	1	100.0	...	...	...	...	...	...
Louisiana	7	3	42.9	...	...	...	...	...	...
Maryland	2	2	100.0	...	...	...	...	...	...
Michigan	...	...	...	1	1	100.0	...	...	...
Minnesota	1	1	100.0	...	...	...	...	...	...
Missouri	2	2	100.0	...	...	...	...	...	...
Montana	1	0	0.0	...	...	...	...	...	...
Nebraska	2	1	50.0	1	1	100.0	...	...	...
Nevada	2	1	50.0	1	1	100.0	...	...	...
New Jersey	2	1	50.0	...	...	...	...	...	...
New Mexico	4(a)	2(a)	50.0	...	...	...	...	...	...
New York	1	1	100.0	...	...	...	...	...	...
North Dakota	2	0	0.0	...	...	...	...	...	...
Ohio	3	3	100.0	1	0	0.0	...	...	...
Oklahoma	4	4	100.0	...	...	...	...	...	...
Oregon	5	5	100.0	1	0	0.0	...	...	...
South Carolina	3	1	33.3	...	...	...	...	...	...
South Dakota	4	1	25.0	...	...	...	...	...	...
Utah	5	4	80.0	...	...	...	...	...	...
Wisconsin	1	1	100.0	...	...	...	...	...	...
Wyoming	2	1	50.0	...	...	...	...	...	...
Totals	78	52	66.7	29	12	41.4	4	3	75.0

Source: Survey conducted by John Dinan in December 2008.

(a) Excludes one amendment approved by voters but declared invalid by the state supreme court.

Regarding other rights-related amendments in 2008, Oregon and California voters approved measures expanding victims' rights provisions in various ways. Oklahoma voters became the latest to approve an amendment guaranteeing an individual right to hunt, trap and fish.

Nevada voters also gave second approval, as required for all citizen-initiated amendments there, to an amendment banning use of eminent domain for economic development purposes. A number of amendments tightening restrictions on the eminent domain power were proposed in the aftermath of the U.S. Supreme Court's 2005 ruling in *Kelo v. City of New London*. The second passage of the Nevada amendment is the latest in a series of eminent domain measures approved in the last three years. California voters in June 2008 defeated an initiated amendment that would have imposed significant new restrictions on eminent domain and phased out rent-control policies. Instead, California voters approved a rival initiated amendment enacting modest restrictions on the use of eminent domain to take single-family homes and transfer them to private entities.

Governing Institutions

California voters adopted the most important institutional amendment in 2008 when they approved an initiated measure eliminating legislative responsibility for drawing state legislative and board of equalization districts. Reformers in several states have sought unsuccessfully in recent years to enact legislative redistricting reforms through initiative processes; that includes a failed 2005 California amendment that would have entrusted all redistricting to a three-member panel of retired judges. In 2008, California voters narrowly approved a redistricting reform amendment and thereby entrusted future legislative redistricting—but not congressional redistricting—to a 14-person citizens' commission. Utah voters approved a redistricting amendment that requires the legislature to undertake a decennial redistricting no later than the next annual session following release of census data.

In other actions targeting legislatures, Arkansas voters approved an amendment allowing legislative sessions in even-numbered years, making it the 45th state to move to annual sessions. California voters in February 2008 rejected an initiated amendment intended to alter the current legislative term limits—six years for delegates and eight years for senators—by allowing legislators to serve up to 12 years in either the House or Senate and up to 12 years of legislative service altogether. South Dakota voters rejected an amendment to repeal legislative term limits. Voters there extended from 35 to 40 days the limit on legislative sessions in even-numbered years, thereby permitting 40-day sessions in both odd and even years, but rejected an amendment increasing the travel reimbursement rate for legislators. Utah voters approved an amendment pushing back the start of the legislative session by one week. Colorado voters defeated an amendment lowering from 25 to 21 the minimum age to serve in the state legislature. Louisiana voters approved an amendment requiring the governor and legislative leaders to give seven days notice, rather than the current five days, before calling a special session. Voters there also ratified an amendment allowing the House speaker or Senate president to appoint a temporary replacement for any legislator called up for military service for more than six months.

Regarding the executive branch, the most important development was Wisconsin voters' approval in April 2008 of an amendment eliminating the "Frankenstein veto." Wisconsin governors have long wielded a partial veto power that is among the most powerful of any state executive. Until passage of a 1990 amendment, Wisconsin governors wielded what was dubbed the "Vanna White veto," which involved crossing out letters within words of legislation and thereby altering legislators' intent. Even after this 1990 amendment and continuing until passage of this 2008 amendment, Wisconsin governors wielded a "Frankenstein veto," by crossing out words in legislation and stitching together the remaining words to create a new sentence from multiple sentences.

Utah, New Mexico and Hawaii also considered amendments related to the executive branch. In Utah, voters approved an amendment making clear that if the governorship becomes vacant, the lieutenant governor assumes the office for the remainder of the four-year term. New Mexico voters approved an amendment stipulating that in case of a vacancy in the lieutenant governorship, the governor appoints a replacement subject to Senate confirmation. Another ratified New Mexico amendment requires Cabinet secretaries to be confirmed at the start of each gubernatorial term, which means that they must be reconfirmed at the start of a governor's second term. Hawaii voters rejected an amendment lowering from 30 to 25 the minimum age to serve as governor or lieutenant governor.

Four amendments in 2008 targeted direct democratic institutions, but only one passed: an Ohio amendment requiring initiative and referendum petitions to be submitted 125 days before the election, replacing the previous 60-day requirement for statutory measures and 90-day rule for constitutional measures. Colorado, Wyoming and Arizona voters defeated amendments that generally sought to make it more difficult to enact ballot initiatives. Colorado voters rejected an amendment that would have differentiated between the signature requirements for qualifying statutory and constitutional initiatives by reducing the requirement for statutory measures but increasing this requirement and adding a geographic distribution requirement for constitutional measures. Wyoming voters rejected an amendment seeking to tighten the geographic distribution requirement for qualifying initiatives and referendums. Arizona voters defeated an amendment making it more difficult to approve initiated measures seeking increases in taxes or spending; under the proposal, such measures would require approval by a majority of *registered* voters in the entire state.

Voters considered various other amendments affecting state and local governing institutions in 2008. Louisiana voters agreed to impose a three-term limit on officials serving on various state commissions. In New Mexico, a majority of voters supported two amendments regarding school board elections, but because of supermajority requirements and court rulings, neither will be added to the state constitution. One amendment would have permitted school board elections to be held at the same time as other nonpartisan elections. The measure failed because it did not receive a three-fourths supermajority statewide and did not secure two-thirds majority support in all counties—it failed in two counties—as required for passage of New Mexico amendments affecting certain suffrage and education provisions. The other amendment would have increased the size of certain school boards—only Albuquerque would currently be affected—and provided for voting by mail in these elections; the New Mexico Supreme Court in December 2008 invalidated this amendment because it addressed two different issues.[6] In a separate vote, New

Mexico voters rejected an amendment allowing county commissioners to increase their salaries mid-term.

By far the most far-reaching institutional amendment was proposed in Michigan via the initiative process, but kept off of the ballot by an August 2008 state appeals court decision holding that the changes were so numerous and sweeping that they amounted to a constitutional revision that could only be proposed by a convention. Among other things, the amendment would have reduced the size of the state House, Senate, Supreme Court and Appeals Court, and cut the salaries of these and other state officials. It would have also entrusted the task of state legislative redistricting to a nine-member panel and prevented state courts from reviewing the work of this panel.[7]

Policy

Voters in 2008 considered and rejected most amendments designed to increase taxes, but they approved several amendments granting tax exemptions and rendered a mixed verdict on amendments altering procedures for considering tax changes.

Minnesota voters were the only ones in 2008 to approve an amendment increasing taxes; the measure raises the sales tax by three-eighths of 1 percent and dedicates the revenue to environmental protection and arts funding. Colorado voters rejected two tax amendments: one to increase the sales tax by one-fifth of 1 percent to pay for services for the developmentally disabled, and one to increase severance taxes on oil and gas companies. Florida voters rejected a commission-submitted amendment to allow localities to hold referendums on increasing the local sales tax to fund community colleges.

But voters approved several amendments granting tax exemptions. Florida voters in January 2008 approved an amendment doubling the homestead exemption from property taxes. Voters there also approved, in November 2008, commission-submitted amendments giving tax breaks to landowners who donate land for conservation purposes, homeowners who make energy-efficiency or hurricane-protection improvements, and owners of working waterfront property. Oklahoma voters granted household personal property tax exemptions to disabled veterans. Georgia voters approved an amendment giving tax breaks to large landowners who agreed to conserve forest land.

Voters in several states considered amendments to change procedures for increasing or reducing taxes. The most significant was in Oregon, where voters eliminated the double-majority requirement for local property tax elections; property tax increases were previously approved only if at least half of registered voters participated in the election. Arizona voters approved an initiated amendment prohibiting any future tax on the sale or transfer of real property. Nevada voters approved an amendment requiring the legislature to make certain findings and meet certain criteria before exemptions are granted. The amendment was intended to achieve uniformity in granting exemptions from property, sales and use taxes. Several other tax-related amendments were circulated in Nevada but kept off of the ballot for various reasons. One Nevada amendment sought to require two-thirds voter approval for initiatives seeking to raise taxes, but the secretary of state found problems with affidavits signed by signature-gatherers and kept it off of the ballot. Another Nevada amendment would have imposed a 2 percent cap on the annual increase in property taxes; however, after much legal wrangling, the state Supreme Court sided with challenges to the legitimacy of the affidavit forms relied on by petitioners. Colorado voters defeated a complex amendment that, among other things, would have repealed the requirement in the Taxpayer Bill of Rights—the TABOR law—that state revenues in excess of a certain amount be refunded to taxpayers.

Gambling amendments appeared on the ballot in four states and were approved in all but one. Arkansas voters approved an initiated amendment eliminating a longstanding constitutional prohibition on lotteries; it is the 43rd state since 1964 to authorize a lottery. Maryland voters approved an amendment allowing up to 15,000 slot machines in five locations around the state. Colorado voters ratified an initiated amendment allowing casinos to extend their hours and permitting residents of the three cities with casinos to hold referendums on increasing the bet limit from $5 to as much as $100. The only gambling amendment defeated at the polls was an Ohio initiative that would have authorized a privately owned casino in the southwest part of the state.[8] It is the fourth gaming measure rejected in the state since 1990.

Voters considered six amendments empowering state or local governments to invest in the stock market, but the only one approved was a Nebraska amendment considered in May 2008, before the financial crisis that sent the stock market tumbling. The five amendments appearing on the November 2008 ballot were all rejected. South Carolina voters declined to permit the state government or local governments to invest pension funds in equities. Voters in Louisiana, Montana and Utah also rejected amendments permitting investment of public funds in equities.

Although fiscal amendments were the dominant policy amendments in 2008, voters in Colorado considered three amendments targeting unions and approved one of them. Voters approved an amendment prohibiting campaign donations from public employee unions and other entities with no-bid government contracts of at least $100,000. They rejected amendments to make Colorado a right-to-work state and to prohibit deduction of union dues from public employees' paychecks.

Looking ahead, the possibility that Congress will amend the National Labor Relations Act to eliminate the role of the secret ballot in union organizing has already prompted one effort to qualify a state amendment to maintain the secret ballot. Opponents of the pending congressional legislation are circulating an Arkansas constitutional amendment that would guarantee the "right of individuals to vote by secret ballot." The proposal would be framed to provide greater protection for this right than at the federal level, thereby seeking to insulate the amendment from federal challenge.

Voters considered a wide range of other policy amendments. Michigan voters approved an initiated amendment eliminating certain restrictions on embryonic stem cell research, following the path of recent stem cell research amendments approved in other states. Missouri voters approved an amendment requiring that all public meetings be conducted in English. South Carolina voters approved eliminating a defunct constitutional provision establishing 14 as the age of consent for unmarried women because it had been superseded by a statute increasing the age to 16. However, because of a unique South Carolina requirement that amendments receive legislative approval both before submission to voters (by a two-thirds legislative vote) and after voter ratification (by a majority legislative vote), this amendment did not take effect until it was approved in the 2009 legislative session. Oklahoma voters approved an amendment allowing winemakers to sell wine directly to restaurants and liquor stores. Arizona voters rejected an initiated amendment that would prohibit enactment of any universal health care legislation that limits an individual's right to obtain health care through private medical plans and providers.

Conclusion

Several trends emerge from a review of state constitutional developments in 2008. First, although voters considered fewer amendments in 2008 than in recent even-numbered years, they were asked to vote on a number of high-profile measures concerning individual rights and public policy. Amendments regarding same-sex marriage, affirmative action, abortion, embryonic stem cell research and eminent domain all appeared on the ballot in 2008, as they have repeatedly in recent years. The constitutional initiative process again was generally the means of qualifying these controversial amendments for the ballot.

Second, in passing judgment on several fiscal policy amendments, voters were apparently influenced by the economic downturn in the second half of the year. Of the six amendments seeking to permit investment of public funds in the stock market, the only amendment approved was considered in a spring primary election; voters defeated all five amendments appearing on the fall general election ballot. Amendments to increase taxes prevailed in only one case—in Minnesota—whereas amendments granting tax exemptions were approved in a number of states.

Third, state courts in 2008 disqualified a number of amendments. In Florida, Michigan and Nevada, state courts kept amendments from appearing on the ballot, whether because they exceeded the charge of the commission that recommended them or included misleading language, as in Florida, or were so sweeping that they amounted to a constitutional revision as in Michigan, or were qualified with invalid signature affidavits as in Nevada. Meanwhile, the New Mexico Supreme Court invalidated an amendment already approved by voters on the ground that it improperly combined two different subjects. And the California Supreme Court agreed to hear challenges to the legitimacy of a same-sex marriage ban that overturned a court decision issued earlier in 2008; a ruling is expected later in 2009.

Finally, in a continuation of a longstanding trend, voters were again reluctant to call constitutional conventions, as demonstrated by the defeat of periodic convention referendums in Hawaii, Illinois and Connecticut in 2008. As a result, another year went by without a convention being called in one of the 50 states, although delegates to a Virgin Islands convention continued their work of drafting a territorial constitution.

Notes

[1]Bill Kossler, "Senate Extends Deadline for Constitutional Convention to May 2009," *St. Thomas Source*, Sept. 30, 2008.

[2]Rupay Shenoy, "Bar assn. wants Ill. Sup. Ct. to review con-con," *Associated Press State and Local Wire*, Nov. 6, 2008.

[3]Ken Dixon, "State debates constitutional convention," *Connecticut Post Online*, Oct. 27, 2008.

[4] Kim Chandler, "House rejects constitution rewrite," *Birmingham News*, May 2, 2008, p. 6B.

[5] Alex Leary and Ron Matus, "Tax Cut, Voucher Plans Tossed," *St. Petersburg Times*, Sept. 4, 2008, p. 1A.

[6] Andrea Schoellkopf, "Justices Strike Down APS Board Expansion," *Albuquerque Journal*, Dec. 12, 2008, p. C1.

[7] Charlie Cain, "Reform ballot proposal rejected," *Detroit News*, Aug. 21, 2008.

[8] Michael Sangiacomo, "Ohio voters reject gambling issue for a fourth time," *Cleveland Plain Dealer*, Nov. 5, 2008, p. X8.

Acknowledgements

The Council of State Governments and the author would like to thank the following individuals for their contribution.

Alabama .... Mark S. Berte
Alaska .... Jerry McBeath
Arizona .... Toni McClory
Arkansas .... Art English
Colorado .... Richard B. Collins
Florida .... Rebecca Mae Salokar
Georgia .... Ed Jackson
Hawaii .... Anne Feder Lee
Illinois .... Ann Lousin
James Nowlan
Sam Gove
Kentucky .... Michael W. Hail
Louisiana .... Warren M. Billings
Maryland .... Dan Friedman
Michigan .... Robert A. Sedler
Minnesota .... Mary Jane Morrison
Mississippi .... John W. Winkle III
Montana .... Fritz Snyder
Nebraska .... Anthony B. Schutz
Nevada .... Eric Herzik
New Hampshire .... Richard A. Hesse
New Mexico .... K. Seckler
North Dakota .... Dana Michael Harsell
Ohio .... Steven H. Steinglass
Pennsylvania .... Joel Fishman
Rhode Island .... Mel A. Topf
South Carolina .... Cole Blease Graham Jr.
South Dakota .... Michael Card
Texas .... Lawrence Miller
Utah .... Robert H. Rees
Washington .... Hugh D. Spitzer
Wisconsin .... Michael R. Fine
Wyoming .... Robert B. Keiter

About the Author

John Dinan is associate professor of political science at Wake Forest University. He is the author of *The American State Constitutional Tradition* and *The Virginia State Constitution: A Reference Guide*, as well as various articles about state constitutions.

Table 1.1
GENERAL INFORMATION ON STATE CONSTITUTIONS
(As of January 1, 2009)

State or other jurisdiction	Number of constitutions*	Dates of adoption	Effective date of present constitution	Estimated length (number of words)**	Number of amendments: Submitted to voters	Number of amendments: Adopted
Alabama	6	1819, 1861, 1865, 1868, 1875, 1901	Nov. 28, 1901	365,000 (a)(c)	1,103	807
Alaska	1	1956	Jan. 3, 1959	15,988 (b)	41	29
Arizona	1	1911	Feb. 14, 1912	45,909 (b)	258	143
Arkansas	5	1836, 1861, 1864, 1868, 1874	Oct. 30, 1874	59,500 (b)	193	95 (d)
California	2	1849, 1879	July 4, 1879	54,645	879	518
Colorado	1	1876	Aug. 1, 1876	74,522 (b)	329	154
Connecticut	4	1818 (f), 1965	Dec. 30, 1965	17,256 (b)	31	30
Delaware	4	1776, 1792, 1831, 1897	June 10, 1897	19,000	(e)	140
Florida	6	1839, 1861, 1865, 1868, 1886, 1968	Jan. 7, 1969	57,017 (b)	148	115
Georgia	10	1777, 1789, 1798, 1861, 1865, 1868, 1877, 1945, 1976, 1982	July 1,1983	39,526 (b)	89 (g)	68 (g)
Hawaii	1 (h)	1950	Aug. 21, 1959	21,440 (b)	129	108
Idaho	1	1889	July 3, 1890	24,232 (b)	206	119
Illinois	4	1818, 1848, 1870, 1970	July 1, 1971	15,751 (b)	17	11
Indiana	2	1816, 1851	Nov. 1, 1851	10,379 (b)	78	46
Iowa	2	1846, 1857	Sept. 3, 1857	11,500 (b)	58	53 (i)
Kansas	1	1859	Jan. 29, 1861	12,296 (b)	123	93 (i)
Kentucky	4	1792, 1799, 1850, 1891	Sept. 28, 1891	23,911 (b)	75	41
Louisiana	11	1812, 1845, 1852, 1861, 1864, 1868, 1879, 1898, 1913, 1921, 1974	Jan. 1, 1975	69,773 (b)	221	154
Maine	1	1819	March 15, 1820	16,276 (b)	203	171 (j)
Maryland	4	1776, 1851, 1864, 1867	Oct. 5, 1867	41,622 (b)	259	223 (k)
Massachusetts	1	1780	Oct. 25, 1780	36,700 (l)	148	120
Michigan	4	1835, 1850, 1908, 1963	Jan. 1, 1964	35,858 (b)	67	29
Minnesota	1	1857	May 11, 1858	11,740 (b)	215	120
Mississippi	4	1817, 1832, 1869, 1890	Nov. 1, 1890	24,323 (b)	158	123
Missouri	4	1820, 1865, 1875, 1945	March 30,1945	42,600 (b)	172	111
Montana	2	1889, 1972	July 1, 1973	14,028 (b)	55	30
Nebraska	2	1866, 1875	Oct. 12, 1875	34,645 (b)	347 (m)	226 (m)
Nevada	1	1864	Oct. 31, 1864	31,944 (b)	229	136
New Hampshire	2	1776, 1784	June 2, 1784	9,200	287 (n)	145
New Jersey	3	1776, 1844, 1947	Jan. 1, 1948	22,956 (b)	78	43
New Mexico	1	1911	Jan. 6, 1912	27,200	288 (y)	157 (y)
New York	4	1777, 1822, 1846, 1894	Jan. 1, 1895	51,700	293	218
North Carolina	3	1776, 1868, 1970	July 1, 1971	16,532 (b)	42	34
North Dakota	1	1889	Nov. 2, 1889	19,074 (b)	264	149 (o)
Ohio	2	1802, 1851	Sept. 1, 1851	50,557 (b)	279	166
Oklahoma	1	1907	Nov. 16, 1907	74,075 (b)	344 (p)	179 (p)
Oregon	1	1857	Feb. 14, 1859	54,083 (b)	484 (q)	243 (q)
Pennsylvania	5	1776, 1790, 1838, 1873, 1968 (r)	1968 (r)	27,711 (b)	36 (r)	30 (r)
Rhode Island	3	1842 (f) 1986 (s)	Dec. 4, 1986	10,908 (b)	11 (s)	10 (s)
South Carolina	7	1776, 1778, 1790, 1861, 1865, 1868, 1895	Jan. 1, 1896	32,541 (b)	682 (t)	493 (t)
South Dakota	1	1889	Nov. 2, 1889	27,675 (b)	227	214
Tennessee	3	1796, 1835, 1870	Feb. 23, 1870	13,300	61	38
Texas	5 (u)	1845, 1861, 1866, 1869, 1876	Feb. 15, 1876	90,000	631 (v)	456
Utah	1	1895	Jan. 4, 1896	19,366	163	111
Vermont	3	1777, 1786, 1793	July 9, 1793	10,286 (b)	211	53
Virginia	6	1776, 1830, 1851, 1869, 1902, 1970	July 1, 1971	21,601 (b)	51	43
Washington	1	1889	Nov. 11, 1889	34,300 (b)	174	101
West Virginia	2	1863, 1872	April 9, 1872	26,000	121	71
Wisconsin	1	1848	May 29, 1848	18,660 (b)	194	145 (i)
Wyoming	1	1889	July 10, 1890	29,300	125	98
American Samoa	2	1960, 1967	July 1, 1967	6,000	15	7
No. Mariana Islands	1	1977	Jan. 9, 1978	11,000	57	53 (w)(x)
Puerto Rico	1	1952	July 25, 1952	9,281	6	6

See footnotes at end of table.

GENERAL INFORMATION ON STATE CONSTITUTIONS—Continued (As of January 1, 2009)

Source: Based on surveys conducted in previous years by Janice May and updated by John Dinan in 2005-2008.

*The constitutions referred to in this table include those Civil War documents customarily listed by the individual states.

** Estimated word lengths are in some cases taken from the 2007 edition.

(a) The Alabama constitution includes numerous local amendments that apply to only one county. An estimated 70 percent of all amendments are local. A 1982 amendment provides that after proposal by the legislature to which special procedures apply, only a local vote (with exceptions) is necessary to add them to the constitution.

(b) Computer word count.

(c) The total number of Alabama amendments includes one that is commonly overlooked.

(d) Eight of the approved amendments have been superseded and are not printed in the current edition of the constitution. The total adopted does not include five amendments proposed and adopted since statehood.

(e) Proposed amendments are not submitted to the voters in Delaware.

(f) Colonial charters with some alterations served as the first constitutions in Connecticut (1638, 1662) and in Rhode Island (1663).

(g) The Georgia constitution requires amendments to be of "general and uniform application throughout the state," thus eliminating local amendments that accounted for most of the amendments before 1982.

(h) As a kingdom and republic, Hawaii had five constitutions.

(i) The figure includes amendments approved by the voters and later nullified by the state supreme court in Iowa (three), Kansas (one), Nevada (six) and Wisconsin (two).

(j) The figure does not include one amendment approved by the voters in 1967 that is inoperative until implemented by legislation.

(k) Two sets of identical amendments were on the ballot and adopted in the 1992 Maryland election. The four amendments are counted as two in the table.

(l) The printed constitution includes many provisions that have been annulled. The length of effective provisions is an estimated 24,122 words (12,400 annulled in Massachusetts, and in Rhode Island before the "rewrite" of the constitution in 1986, it was 11,399 words (7,627 annulled).

(m) The 1998 and 2000 Nebraska ballots allowed the voters to vote separately on "parts" of propositions. In 1998, 10 of 18 separate propositions were adopted; in 2000, 6 of 9.

(n) The constitution of 1784 was extensively revised in 1792. Figure shows proposals and adoptions since the constitution was adopted in 1784.

(o) The figures do not include submission and approval of the constitution of 1889 itself and of Article XX; these are constitutional questions included in some counts of constitutional amendments and would add two to the figure in each column.

(p) The figures include five amendments submitted to and approved by the voters which were, by decisions of the Oklahoma or U.S. Supreme Courts, rendered inoperative or ruled invalid, unconstitutional, or illegally submitted.

(q) One Oregon amendment on the 2000 ballot was not counted as approved because canvassing was enjoined by the courts.

(r) Certain sections of the constitution were revised by the limited convention of 1967-68. Amendments proposed and adopted are since 1968.

(s) Following approval of the eight amendments and a "rewrite" of the Rhode Island Constitution in 1986, the constitution has been called the 1986 Constitution. Amendments since 1986 total eight proposed and eight adopted. Otherwise, the total is 106 proposals and 60 adopted.

(t) In 1981 approximately two-thirds of 626 proposed and four-fifths of the adopted amendments were local. Since then the amendments have been statewide propositions.

(u) The Constitution of the Republic of Texas preceded five state constitutions.

(v) The number of proposed amendments to the Texas Constitution excludes three proposed by the legislature but not placed on the ballot.

(w) By 1992, 49 amendments had been proposed and 47 adopted. Since then, one was proposed but rejected in 1994, all three proposals were ratified in 1996 and in 1998, of two proposals one was adopted.

(x) The total excludes one amendment ruled void by a federal district court.

(y) The total excludes one amendment approved by voters in November 2008 but later declared invalid on single subject grounds by the state supreme court.

Table 1.2
CONSTITUTIONAL AMENDMENT PROCEDURE: BY THE LEGISLATURE
Constitutional Provisions

State or other jurisdiction	Legislative vote required for proposal (a)	Consideration by two sessions required	Vote required for ratification	Limitation on the number of amendments submitted at one election
Alabama	3/5	No	Majority vote on amendment	None
Alaska	2/3	No	Majority vote on amendment	None
Arizona	Majority	No	Majority vote on amendment	None
Arkansas	Majority	No	Majority vote on amendment	3
California	2/3	No	Majority vote on amendment	None
Colorado	2/3	No	Majority vote on amendment	None (b)
Connecticut	(c)	(c)	Majority vote on amendment	None
Delaware	2/3	Yes	Not required	No referendum
Florida	3/5	No	3/5 vote on amendment (d)	None
Georgia	2/3	No	Majority vote on amendment	None
Hawaii	(e)	(e)	Majority vote on amendment (f)	None
Idaho	2/3	No	Majority vote on amendment	None
Illinois	3/5	No	(g)	3 articles
Indiana	Majority	Yes	Majority vote on amendment	None
Iowa	Majority	Yes	Majority vote on amendment	None
Kansas	2/3	No	Majority vote on amendment	5
Kentucky	3/5	No	Majority vote on amendment	4
Louisiana	2/3	No	Majority vote on amendment (h)	None
Maine	2/3 (i)	No	Majority vote on amendment	None
Maryland	3/5	No	Majority vote on amendment	None
Massachusetts	Majority (j)	Yes	Majority vote on amendment	None
Michigan	2/3	No	Majority vote on amendment	None
Minnesota	Majority	No	Majority vote in election	None
Mississippi	2/3 (k)	No	Majority vote on amendment	None
Missouri	Majority	No	Majority vote on amendment	None
Montana	2/3 (i)	No	Majority vote on amendment	None
Nebraska	3/5	No	Majority vote on amendment (f)	None
Nevada	Majority	Yes	Majority vote on amendment	None
New Hampshire	3/5	No	2/3 vote on amendment	None
New Jersey	(l)	(l)	Majority vote on amendment	None (m)
New Mexico	Majority (n)	No	Majority vote on amendment (n)	None
New York	Majority	Yes	Majority vote on amendment	None
North Carolina	3/5	No	Majority vote on amendment	None
North Dakota	Majority	No	Majority vote on amendment	None
Ohio	3/5	No	Majority vote on amendment	None
Oklahoma	Majority	No	Majority vote on amendment	None
Oregon	(o)	No	Majority vote on amendment (p)	None
Pennsylvania	Majority (p)	Yes (p)	Majority vote on amendment	None
Rhode Island	Majority	No	Majority vote on amendment	None
South Carolina	2/3 (q)	Yes (q)	Majority vote on amendment	None
South Dakota	Majority	No	Majority vote on amendment	None
Tennessee	(r)	Yes (r)	Majority vote in election (s)	None
Texas	2/3	No	Majority vote on amendment	None
Utah	2/3	No	Majority vote on amendment	None
Vermont	(t)	Yes	Majority vote on amendment	None
Virginia	Majority	Yes	Majority vote on amendment	None
Washington	2/3	No	Majority vote on amendment	None
West Virginia	2/3	No	Majority vote on amendment	None
Wisconsin	Majority	Yes	Majority vote on amendment	None
Wyoming	2/3	No	Majority vote in election	None
American Samoa	2/3	No	Majority vote on amendment (u)	None
No. Mariana Islands	3/4	No	Majority vote on amendment	None
Puerto Rico	2/3 (v)	No	Majority vote on amendment	3

See footnotes at end of table.

CONSTITUTIONAL AMENDMENT PROCEDURE: BY THE LEGISLATURE — Continued
Constitutional Provisions

Source: Surveys conducted in previous years by Janice May and updated by John Dinan in 2005–2008.

Key:

(a) In all states not otherwise noted, the figure shown in the column refers to the proportion of elected members in each house required for approval of proposed constitutional amendments.

(b) Legislature may not propose amendments to more than six articles of the constitution in the same legislative session.

(c) Three-fourths vote in each house at one session, or majority vote in each house in two sessions between which an election has intervened.

(d) Three-fifths vote on amendment, except amendment for "new state tax or fee" not in effect on Nov. 7, 1994 requires two-thirds of voters in the election.

(e) Two-thirds vote in each house at one session, or majority vote in each house in two sessions.

(f) Majority vote on amendment must be at least 50 percent of the total votes cast at the election (at least 35 percent in Nebraska); or, at a special election, a majority of the votes tallied which must be at least 30 percent of the total number of registered voters.

(g) Majority voting in election or three-fifths voting on amendment.

(h) If five or fewer political subdivisions of the state are affected, majority in state as a whole and also in affected subdivisions) is required.

(i) Two-thirds of both houses.

(j) Majority of members elected sitting in joint session.

(k) The two-thirds must include not less than a majority elected to each house.

(l) Three-fifths of all members of each house at one session, or majority of all members of each house for two successive sessions.

(m) If a proposed amendment is not approved at the election when submitted, neither the same amendment nor one which would make substantially the same change for the constitution may be again submitted to the people before the third general election thereafter.

(n) Amendments concerning certain elective franchise and education matters require three-fourths vote of members elected and approval by three-fourths of electors voting in state and two-thirds of those voting in each county.

(o) Majority vote to amend constitution, two-thirds to revise ("revise" includes all or a part of the constitution).

(p) Emergency amendments may be passed by two-thirds vote of each house, followed by ratification by majority vote of electors in election held at least one month after legislative approval. There is an exception for an amendment containing a supermajority voting requirement, which must be ratified by an equal supermajority.

(q) Two-thirds of members of each house, first passage; majority of members of each house after popular ratification.

(r) Majority of members elected to both houses, first passage; two-thirds of members elected to both houses, second passage.

(s) Majority of all citizens voting for governor.

(t) Two-thirds vote senate, majority vote house, first passage; majority both houses, second passage. As of 1974, amendments may be submitted only every four years.

(u) Within 30 days after voter approval, governor must submit amendment(s) to U.S. Secretary of the Interior for approval.

(v) If approved by two-thirds of members of each house, amendment(s) submitted to voters at special referendum; if approved by not less than three-fourths of total members of each house, referendum may be held at next general election.

Table 1.3
CONSTITUTIONAL AMENDMENT PROCEDURE: BY INITIATIVE
Constitutional Provisions

State or other jurisdiction	*Number of signatures required on initiative petition*	*Distribution of signatures*	*Referendum vote*
Arizona	15% of total votes cast for all candidates for governor at last election.	None specified.	Majority vote on amendment.
Arkansas	10% of voters for governor at last election. governor in each of 15 countries.	Must include 5% of voters for	Majority vote on amendment.
California	8% of total voters for all candidates for governor at last election.	None specified.	Majority vote on amendment.
Colorado	5% of total legal votes for all candidates for secretary of state at last general election.	None specified.	Majority vote on.
Florida	8% of total votes cast in the state in the last election for presidential electors.	8% of total votes cast in each of 1/2 of the congressional districts.	Three-fifths vote on amendment except amendment for "new state tax or fee" not in effect Nov. 7, 1994 requires 2/3 of voters voting in election.
Illinois (a)	8% of total votes cast for candidates for governor at last election.	None specified.	Majority voting in election or 3/5 voting on amendment.
Massachusetts (b)	3% of total votes cast for governor at preceding biennial state election (not less than 25,000 qualified voters.	No more than 1/4 from any one county.	Majority vote on amendment which must be 30% of total. ballots cast at election.
Michigan	10% of total voters for all candidates at last gubernatorial election.	None specified.	Majority vote on amendment.
Mississippi (c)	12% of total votes for all candidates for governor in last election	No more than 20% from any one congressional district	Majority vote on amendment and not less than 40% of total vote cast at election
Missouri	8% of legal voters for all candidates for governor at last election	The 8% must be in each of 2/3 of the congressional districts in the state.	Majority vote on amendment.
Montana	10% of qualified electors, the number of qualified voters to be determined by number of votes cast for governor in preceding election in each county and in the state.	The 10% to include at least 10% of qualified voters in one-half of the counties.	Majority vote on amendment.
Nebraska	10% of total votes for governor at last election.	The 10% must include 5% in each of 2/5 of the counties.	Majority vote on amendment which must be at least 35% of total vote at the election.
Nevada	10% of voters who voted in entire state in last general election.	None in effect after a U.S. District Court ruling in 2004 invalidated the requirement.	Majority vote on amendment in two consecutive general elections
North Dakota	4% of population of the state.	None specified.	Majority vote on amendment.
Ohio	10% of total number of electors who voted for governor in last election.	At least 5% of qualified electors in each of 1/2 of counties in the state	Majority vote on amendment.
Oklahoma	15% of legal voters for state office receiving highest number of voters at last general state election.	None specified.	Majority vote on amendment.
Oregon	8% of total votes for all candidates for governor at last election at which governor was elected for four-year term.	None specified.	Majority vote on amendment except for supermajority equal to supermajority voting requirement contained in proposed amendment.
South Dakota	10% of total votes for governor in last election.	None specified.	Majority vote on amendment.
No. Mariana Islands	50% of qualified voters of commonwealth.	In addition, 25% of qualified voters in each senatorial district.	Majority vote on amendment if legislature approved it by majority vote; if not, at least 2/3 vote in each of two senatorial districts in addition to a majority vote.

Source: Surveys conducted in previous years by Janice May and updated by John Dinan in 2005–2008.

Key:

(a) Only Article IV, the Legislature Article, may be amended by initiative petition.

(b) Before being submitted to the electorate for ratification, initiative measures must be approved at two sessions of a successively elected legislature by not less than one-fourth of all members elected, sitting in joint session.

(c) Before being submitted to the electorate, initiated measures are sent to the legislature, which has the option of submitting an amended or alternative measure alongside of the original measure.

Table 1.4
PROCEDURES FOR CALLING CONSTITUTIONAL CONVENTIONS
Constitutional Provisions

State or other jurisdiction	*Provision for convention*	*Legislative vote for submission of convention question (a)*	*Popular vote to authorize convention*	*Periodic submission of convention question required (b)*	*Popular vote required for ratification of convention proposals*
Alabama	Yes	Majority	ME	No	Not specified
Alaska	Yes	No provision (c)(d)	(c)	10 years (c)	Not specified (c)
Arizona	Yes	Majority	(e)	No	MP
Arkansas	No	No			
California	Yes	2/3	MP	No	MP
Colorado	Yes	2/3	MP	No	ME
Connecticut	Yes	2/3	MP	20 years (f)	MP
Delaware	Yes	2/3	MP	No	No provision
Florida	Yes	(g)	MP	No	3/5 voting on proposal
Georgia	Yes	(d)	No	No	MP
Hawaii	Yes	Not specified	MP	9 years	MP (h)
Idaho	Yes	2/3	MP	No	Not specified
Illinois	Yes	3/5	(i)	20 years; 1988	MP
Indiana	No	No			
Iowa	Yes	Majority	MP	10 years; 1970	MP
Kansas	Yes	2/3	MP	No	MP
Kentucky	Yes	Majority (j)	MP (k)	No	No provision
Louisiana	Yes	(d)	No	No	MP
Maine	Yes	(d)	No	No	No provision
Maryland	Yes	Majority	ME	20 years; 1970	MP
Massachusetts	No		No	Not specified	
Michigan	Yes	Majority	MP	16 years; 1978	MP
Minnesota	Yes	2/3	ME	No	3/5 voting on proposal
Mississippi	No	No			
Missouri	Yes	Majority	MP	20 years; 1962	Not specified (l)
Montana	Yes (m)	2/3	MP	20 years	MP
Nebraska	Yes	3/5	MP (o)	No	MP
Nevada	Yes	2/3	ME	No	No provision
New Hampshire	Yes	Majority	MP	10 years	2/3 voting on proposal
New Jersey	No	No			
New Mexico	Yes	2/3	MP	No	Not specified
New York	Yes	Majority	MP	20 years; 1957	MP
North Carolina	Yes	2/3	MP	No	MP
North Dakota	No	No			
Ohio	Yes	2/3	MP	20 years; 1932	MP
Oklahoma	Yes	Majority	(e)	20 years	MP
Oregon	Yes	Majority	(e)	No	No provision
Pennsylvania	No	No			
Rhode Island	Yes	Majority	MP	10 years	MP
South Carolina	Yes	(d)	ME	No	No provision
South Dakota	Yes	(d)	(d)	No	(p)
Tennessee	Yes (q)	Majority	MP	No	MP
Texas	No	No			
Utah	Yes	2/3	ME	No	MP
Vermont	No	No			
Virginia	Yes	(d)	No	No	MP
Washington	Yes	2/3	ME	No	Not specified
West Virginia	Yes	Majority	MP	No	Not specified
Wisconsin	Yes	Majority	MP	No	No provision
Wyoming	Yes	2/3	ME	No	Not specified
American Samoa	Yes	(r)	No	No	ME (s)
No. Mariana Islands	Yes	Majority (t)	2/3	10 years	MP and at least 2/3 in each of 2 senatorial districts
Puerto Rico	Yes	2/3	MP	No	MP

See footnotes at end of table.

PROCEDURES FOR CALLING CONSTITUTIONAL CONVENTIONS — Continued
Constitutional Provisions

Source: Surveys conducted in previous years by Janice May and updated by John Dinan in 2005-2008.

Key:

MP — Majority voting on the proposal.

ME — Majority voting in the election.

(a) In all states not otherwise noted, the entries in this column refer to the proportion of members elected to each house required to submit to the electorate the question of calling a constitutional convention.

(b) The number listed is the interval between required submissions on the question of calling a constitutional convention; where given, the date is that of the first required submission of the convention question.

(c) Unless provided otherwise by law, convention calls are to conform as nearly as possible to the act calling the 1955 convention, which provided for a legislative vote of a majority of members elected to each house and ratification by a majority vote on the proposals. The legislature may call a constitutional convention at any time.

(d) In these states, the legislature may call a convention without submitting the question to the people. The legislative vote required is two-thirds of the members elected to each house in Georgia, Louisiana, South Carolina and Virginia; two-thirds concurrent vote of both branches in Maine; three-fourths of all members of each house in South Dakota; and not specified in Alaska, but bills require majority vote of membership in each house. In South Dakota, the question of calling a convention may be initiated by the people in the same manner as an amendment to the constitution (see Table 1.3) and requires a majority vote on the question for approval.

(e) The law calling a convention must be approved by the people.

(f) The legislature shall submit the question 20 years after the last convention, or 20 years after the last vote on the question of calling a convention, whichever date is last.

(g) The power to call a convention is reserved to the people by petition.

(h) The majority must be 50 percent of the total voted cast at a general election or at a special election, a majority of the votes tallied which must be at least 30 percent of the total number of registered voters.

(i) Majority voting in the election, or three-fifths voting on the question.

(j) Must be approved during two legislative sessions.

(k) Majority must equal one-fourth of qualified voters at last general election.

(l) Majority of those voting on the proposal is assumed.

(m) The question of calling a constitutional convention may be submitted either by the legislature or by initiative petition to the secretary of state in the same manner as provided for initiated amendments (see Table 1.3).

(n) Two-thirds of all members of the legislature.

(o) Majority must be 35 percent of total votes cast at the election.

(p) Convention proposals are submitted to the electorate at a special election in a manner to be determined by the convention. Ratification by a majority of votes cast.

(q) Conventions may not be held more often than once in six years.

(r) Five years after effective date of constitutions, governor shall call a constitutional convention to consider changes proposed by a constitutional committee appointed by the governor. Delegates to the convention are to be elected by their county councils. A convention was held in 1972.

(s) If proposed amendments are approved by the voters, they must be submitted to the U.S. Secretary of the Interior for approval.

(t) The initiative may also be used to place a referendum convention call on the ballot. The petition must be signed by 25 percent of the qualified voters or at least 75 percent in a senatorial district.

Chapter Two

FEDERALISM AND INTERGOVERNMENTAL RELATIONS

State-Federal Relations: Agendas for Change and Continuity

By John Kincaid

The current economic crisis and the new Democratic majority in the federal government will produce significant policy changes relevant to state-federal relations, but, overall, American federalism will continue its contemporary coercive course in an evolutionary manner because that course has involved expansions of federal power that were augmented by crises in the past and by change-minded presidents supported by partisan majorities in Congress.

The 2008 election of Barack Obama to the White House was as much, or more, a voter rejection of policies associated with President George W. Bush as it was a voter affirmation of Obama's policy positions and embrace of an historic opportunity to elect a black American to the presidency. Obama's victory also was driven by the severe economic crisis that began to develop in mid-2008—a crisis that will take a heavy toll on state and local government budgets and, thereby, on public services.

Obama's election—along with the strengthened Democratic majorities in both houses of Congress, increased Democratic control of state legislatures (both chambers in 27 states), and increased Democratic governorships (to 28)—have placed state-federal relations firmly in Democratic hands after more than three decades in which intergovernmental relations were either dominated by Republicans or contested by Democrats and Republicans.

This historic change in partisan control of the federal system signals major changes to come in state-federal relations, but will those changes be revolutionary or evolutionary? Most likely they will be both. There will be revolutionary changes in some policies that involve state-federal relations because many Democratic policy preferences differ significantly from those of Republicans, but over the long-term, the changes are likely to produce evolutionary enhancements of coercive federalism rather than a revolutionary New Federalism.[1]

Evolutionary Federalism

Several factors point to evolution rather than revolution. First, federalism played virtually no role in the 2008 presidential and congressional elections. Unlike Presidents Richard M. Nixon and Ronald Reagan, for example, no viable, prospective, presidential candidate articulated a New Federalism. The only campaign issues that attracted some attention to federalism were gay marriage and federal crackdowns on medicinal marijuana. Both candidates treated same-sex marriage as an issue to be decided by the states. They differed on drug enforcement. Obama pledged to stop federal raids on medicinal marijuana outlets; McCain vowed to enforce federal drug laws.

Second, most of the criticism of President Bush focused on the war in Iraq, the Guantánamo Bay detention camp, domestic facets of the war on terrorism, "tax cuts for the rich," global warming and other issues not central to state-federal relations. Otherwise, Bush's overall intergovernmental record was not criticized as much as his records in those other policy arenas. Consequently, the public pressure for change was not as white hot as it was in other policy areas.

In February 2007, for example, a national poll, conducted by the author and a colleague, asked: "Considering President George W. Bush's response to New York City after 9/11 in 2001, his response to New Orleans after Hurricane Katrina in 2005, and his support for the NCLB education law, overall, would you say that President Bush's policies for our state and local governments have been very helpful, somewhat helpful, not very helpful, or not at all helpful?" Despite Bush's low job-approval ratings of only 32 percent to 37 percent at that time, 16.3 percent of the respondents termed Bush's intergovernmental actions as "very helpful," while 35.4 percent said "somewhat helpful," 23.5 percent responded "not very helpful," and 24.8 percent declared "not at all helpful." In short, 51.7 percent fell on the positive side. Notable, though, is that 70.5 percent of Democrats fell on the negative side, while 81.2 percent of Republicans fell on the positive side of the question. In turn, 78.9 percent of black respondents fell on the negative side, while 63.3 percent of Hispanics and 55.8 percent of whites fell on the positive side.[2]

In terms of the three issues posed in the question, the Obama administration will certainly revise but probably not revolutionize domestic anti-terrorism policies, in part because it recognizes the political necessity of preventing another 9/11. President

Obama needs to repair but not necessarily revolutionize the emergency-response system so as not to repeat President Bush's botched response to Katrina, and, even during the campaign, Obama signaled his support for some of the core principles of the No Child Left Behind Act of 2002.

Third, the constitutional, legal, fiscal and political institutional inertia of coercive federalism built up over the last 40-some years is a formidable barrier to revolutionary change.

Fourth, the development of coercive federalism since the 1960s has been supported by both parties because the scope of federal policymaking is so comprehensive and so intergovernmental that incumbents of both parties in Congress and the White House need to bring state and local governments into alignment with their policy preferences in order to achieve their national policy objectives. President Obama and congressional Democrats will be no different, as reflected, for example, in the provision of the American Recovery and Reinvestment Act of 2009 that authorizes a state legislature, via a "concurrent resolution," to accept federal stimulus money for its state if the governor declines to accept it. This provision—inserted into the Recovery Act because several governors, led by Republican Gov. Mark Sanford of South Carolina, threatened not to accept stimulus funds—overrides constitutional rules, legislative procedures, and established norms in many states.

Fifth, President Obama's intergovernmentally relevant responses to the severe economic crisis affecting the nation and the world have thus far been consistent with long-term patterns in state-federal relations. For example, most of the $506.5 billion in funds to be spent under the Recovery Act will go to state and local governments, with most of it going to the states; most of the money will reach state and local governments through existing intergovernmental program structures; and most of the money will finance social welfare such as Medicaid and unemployment compensation.

Impacts on Dimensions of Coercive Federalism

The various facets of coercive federalism could be affected by the partisan change in state-federal relations in the following ways.

Grants-in-Aid

There will be a substantial increase in federal aid to state and local governments in the short term, an increase already evident in the Recovery Act. Under Bush, federal grants-in-aid increased by 63.2 percent in nominal dollars (to $466.6 billion in 2008) and by 31.2 percent in constant (2008) dollars (compared to 60.5 percent and 30.7 percent respectively under Clinton). Aside from the economic crisis, Obama had pledged during his campaign to increase federal funding for various programs, such as K-12 education. Congressional Democrats have supported higher spending as well; consequently, there is likely to be a long-term increase in federal aid, although at levels below the temporary bump provided by the Recovery Act. At the same time, an important question for the states is whether they will be locked into higher long-term spending as a result of program expansions produced by the momentary influx of the Recovery Act funds.

One characteristic of federal aid in the era of coercive federalism is that aid has shifted substantially from places to people; 64.4 percent of federal aid is now dedicated for payments to individuals (i.e., social welfare).[3] Among the long-term consequences of this shift are that (1) place-oriented aid for infrastructure, economic development, education and the like has declined sharply; (2) increased aid for social welfare has locked state budgets into programs ripe for escalating federal regulation and matching state costs; and (3) local governments have experienced a steep decline in federal aid. Medicaid, which accounts for almost 45 percent of all federal aid, is the leading example.

This trend will experience a brief interruption due to Recovery Act money dedicated to infrastructure, school construction and other place-based programs, but, if the national economy recovers, these funds will contract in less than a decade under pressures of federal deficit reduction and growing social welfare spending. Indeed, even in the Recovery Act, the single largest category of spending is for Medicaid ($90 billion), followed by unemployment compensation and other social welfare programs.

The effects of the shift of aid from places have been felt strongly, for instance, in the declining revenues for surface transportation. The Obama administration has said it is unwilling to increase the federal motor fuels tax and to consider a new financing scheme based on charging drivers by the mile. Consequently, in order to maintain surface-transportation infrastructure, states will be compelled to increase revenues through higher taxes, more tolls, and privatization.

Another characteristic of federal aid is coercive conditions of aid intended to accomplish through spending power federal objectives that cannot be achieved through Congress's constitutionally delegated powers. A leading example of such conditioned aid is No Child Left Behind, commonly called NCLB, which mandates all U.S. elementary- and secondary-school students reach proficiency in reading and mathematics by 2014. In 2005, the National Conference of State Legislatures blasted NCLB as flawed, under-funded, stifling of state innovation and unconstitutional.

Nevertheless, key elements of NCLB, especially its testing and performance-accountability requirements, are likely to endure, in part because the public has supported the idea of such requirements for decades, and the public's reception of NCLB was generally positive. Moreover, a number of leading black and Hispanic civil rights organizations generally support NCLB. Even the Rev. Al Sharpton co-authored an editorial "staunchly" supporting "NCLB's core concept that schools should be held accountable for boosting student performance."[4] The act also is supported by editorially liberal newspapers such as the *New York Times* and *Washington Post* and by many education reformers, Democratic and Republican. Furthermore, Obama has signaled his intention not only to retain but also to strengthen the key testing and accountability provisions of NCLB while also defusing some teacher concerns by revising certain rules and increasing funding for education. Consequently, NCLB is likely to mark a major change in federal-state-local relations in public education, a substantial augmentation of coercive federalism, and a lasting legacy of the Bush administration.

Earmarking, another characteristic of federal aid under coercive federalism, shows every sign of continuing under the Democrats' intergovernmental regime. Earmarking is popular, in part, because of the shift of federal aid from places to people. Faced with declining federal aid for place-based functions, members of Congress scramble to find money for public facilities and other tangible projects in their states and districts for which they can claim personal credit. In turn, state and local officials have been forced to lobby for earmarks as second-best sources of place-based funding, although members of Congress frequently ignore those officials and earmark money for projects that conflict with the needs and plans of state and local governments.

In summary, federal grants-in-aid will continue to shift toward people, the federal government will continue to attach intrusive policy conditions to federal aid, and earmarking will not come to an end. Otherwise, a revolutionary change in this field would be federal assumption of Medicaid's long-term care costs or enactment of a universal federal health care plan that would federalize or abolish Medicaid.

Mandates

Mandates—direct federal orders—also characterize coercive federalism. However, the 1995 Unfunded Mandates Reform Act reduced mandate enactments. Only seven intergovernmental mandates having costs above the act's threshold have been enacted since 1995. One was a complex Bush-supported tax mandate that will affect local governments in 2011.

President Bush, however, forged creative circumventions of the Unfunded Mandates Reform Act by developing *de facto* mandates, such as the REAL ID Act of 2005. Technically, REAL ID is not a mandate because states can opt out of it, but it is a *de facto* mandate in the sense that a state's withdrawal would have catastrophic consequences for its residents, namely, driver's licenses that could not be used for such activities as boarding an airplane, riding Amtrak trains, purchasing a firearm, opening a bank account, applying for federal benefits, and entering a federal building.

In January 2008, President Obama said he does not support the Real ID program "because it is an unfunded mandate, and not enough work has been done with the states to help them implement the program."[5] Otherwise, Obama has not commented on REAL ID. He voted for REAL ID but did not cast a vote on REAL ID funding in July 2007; consequently, his position is unclear, although his 2008 statement suggests a willingness to implement REAL ID under funding conditions more favorable to the states.

The new secretary of Homeland Security, former Arizona Gov. Janet Napolitano, signed a bill in June 2008 barring Arizona's participation in REAL ID. However, as Homeland Security secretary, she has said she will examine "realistic options" for REAL ID implementation, including state experimentation, such as Washington's version of the Western Hemisphere Travel Initiative under which it issues driver's licenses with enhanced security features. Her office also agreed to participate in a working group organized by the National Governors Association to review REAL ID's implementation.

Democratic dominance of the intergovernmental system might curb mandates in many areas; however, there are many policy fields, such as environmental protection and business regulation, in which Democratic federal officials will be eager to ensure state and local compliance. The Unfunded Mandates Reform Act, moreover, was not enacted by Congress when Democrats were in the majority. Instead, Republicans, who had made mandate relief a part of their 1994 "Contract with America," enacted the mandate reform act when they took over Congress in 1995.

Hence, it is not clear whether, overall, the new Democratic intergovernmental regime will be friendly or unfriendly to mandates. It is likely that Democrats will support more funding for federal mandates.

Preemption

Federal preemptions of state laws under the U.S. Constitution's supremacy clause are another characteristic of coercive federalism. President Bush furthered this trend. Under the new Democratic regime, there is likely to be heightened debate and conflict over preemption, coupled with rollbacks of some preemptions and preemption practices of the Republican years. U.S. Rep. Henry Waxman, D-Calif., complained in June 2006, for example, that during the previous five years, Congress had voted at least 57 times to preempt state laws. Of those votes, 27 yielded preemption bills signed by Bush.

The pace of preemption under Bush was consistent with that of presidents since Lyndon B. Johnson, but the objects of preemption differed from the policy preferences of most Democrats because most of Bush's preemptions displaced state business-regulation and consumer-protection laws in response to business preferences to be regulated (or de-regulated) by the federal government rather than by the states. Consequently, congressional Democrats will likely repeal some Bush statutory preemptions.

Bush also used executive rule-making to advance preemption when Congress dragged its feet. For the first time in its 33-year history, for example, the Consumer Product Safety Commission issued a rule in 2006 on mattress flammability that preempted state laws that set higher standards and included language in the preamble to protect mattress manufacturers from state court lawsuits when their mattresses conform to the new federal standard. President Obama, therefore, will likely reverse some of Bush's administrative preemptions and reduce the use of administrative preemption.

Obama, however, is not averse to preemption. For example, he voted for the Class Action Fairness Act of 2005, which was strongly supported by Bush. This law moved from state to federal courts most class action lawsuits involving at least 100 plaintiffs, two-thirds of whom live in different states, seeking $5 million or more in damages. Federal judges will apply state consumer protection laws in such cases, but federal procedural law will govern the cases. This act, lamented Sen. Harry Reid, D-Nev., "turns federalism upside down by preventing state courts from hearing state law claims."[6]

Furthermore, the need to reinvigorate the national economy and to remedy regulatory deficiencies that contributed to the home mortgage debacle and massive financial institution failures will put strong pressure on Congress and the president to engage in broad-ranging preemption. In addition, governors, more often than state legislators, have supported federal preemptions intended to clear state-law barriers from national markets.

At the same time, though, trial lawyers represented by the American Justice Association, as well as many consumer and civil rights groups, are pushing hard to roll back preemptions enacted not only during the Bush years but also in prior years extending back to President Reagan. These interests are likely to find many allies among congressional Democrats.

Battles over preemption will be intensified by the U.S. Supreme Court's March 2009 decision in *Wyeth* v. *Levine* (No. 06-1249) in which the justices, by a 6-3 vote, upheld a Vermont jury's award of $6.7 million to musician Diana Levine, whose arm had to be amputated after an anti-nausea drug was injected into her artery. Wyeth, the drug's manufacturer, had argued that it was immunized from state lawsuits because the federal Food and Drug Administration had approved Wyeth's warning labels on the drug, which included a warning against intra-arterial injection. The Bush administration supported Wyeth's argument.

This case involved implied preemption, namely, preemption based not on a federal statute but on a conflict between a federal regulation and a state law. The court held that, absent explicit congressional preemption, it would not find an implied preemption. As Justice John Paul Stevens wrote in the majority opinion:

"State tort suits uncover unknown drug hazards and provide incentives for drug manufacturers to disclose safety risks promptly. They also serve a distinct compensatory function that may motivate injured persons to come forward with information. …

Wyeth has not persuaded us that failure-to-warn claims like Levine's obstruct the federal regulation of drug labeling. Congress has repeatedly declined to pre-empt state law, and the FDA's recently adopted position that state tort suits interfere with its statutory mandate is entitled to no weight. Although we recognize that some state-law claims might well frustrate the achievement of congressional objectives, this is not such a case.

We conclude that it is not impossible for Wyeth to comply with its state and federal law obligations and that Levine's common-law claims do not stand as an obstacle to the accomplishment of Congress' purposes in the FDCA."

This case will intensify conflict between business groups that will now want explicit federal statutory preemption of state laws governing such matters as product labeling and consumer groups that want to retain state authority to regulate such matters in addition to, and in a stricter manner than, federal regulation. The *Wyeth* ruling also will motivate pharmaceutical companies to lobby state legislatures and governors to emulate the states that have already granted deference to the FDA when determining the validity of drug-label warnings, especially when the drug's manufacturer is not guilty of wrongdoing.

Taxation

Another characteristic of coercive federalism has been federal constraints on state taxation and borrowing, beginning especially with limits imposed on tax-exempt private activity bonds in 1984. Judicial and statutory prohibitions of state taxation of Internet services and mail-order sales are prominent constraints. In October 2007, President Bush signed a seven-year extension of the moratorium on state-local taxation of Internet access.

During the transition, Obama was asked to decide whether to support a temporary sales tax holiday for which the states would be compensated with federal money. According to Joe Klein, Obama's economic advisers loved the idea. But Obama rejected it. "He thought it would provide a temporary benefit, that it had no substantial or lasting policy impact."[7] Tellingly, Obama rejected the idea for policy reasons, not federalism reasons.

Key questions are whether Obama will support repeal or at least expiration of the Internet-access tax moratorium and also support congressional approval of an interstate compact upholding the Streamlined Sales and Use Tax Agreement. Support for these state tax policies might be construed as violations of Obama's promise not to increase taxes for 95 percent of Americans. Another question is whether he will support an elimination or reduction of federal income tax deductions for state and local taxes and for mortgage interest and medical expenses. State and local officials have generally opposed elimination or reduction of these deductions. This issue has a partisan electoral dimension because the average state and local tax payment in blue (Democratic) states was $7,487 in 2005 compared to $4,834 in red (Republican) states. State and local tax deductions as a percentage of average income was 5.9 percent in the blue states and 3.7 percent in the red states.[8] Obama's pledge to increase taxes on incomes of $250,000 or more will likely reduce the value of those deductions while retaining their value for those taxpayers who have lower incomes and who itemize their deductions.

Although Democratic federal officials will be sensitive to the tax needs of their fellow Democrats in the states, they are not likely to allow those needs to stand in the way of fiscally and politically important federal objectives.

Federalization of Criminal Law

Another feature of coercive federalism is the federalization of criminal law. The number of federal criminal laws increased from about 4,000 in 2000 to about 4,450 by 2007.[9] More than half these laws have been enacted since the mid-1960s. These laws cover a wide range of behavior. Another aspect of this federalization has been U.S. Department of Justice efforts to enforce federal death-penalty statutes, even in states lacking capital punishment.

The federalization of criminal law is likely to continue because members of both political parties in Washington, D.C., like to look tough on crime and because the current financial debacle is likely to generate new federal criminal statutes. Given Democratic proclivities, however, there is likely to be less emphasis on enforcing the death penalty under federal law.

Demise of Intergovernmental Institutions

Coercive federalism has been marked, too, by the demise of executive and congressional intergovernmental institutions established during the era of cooperative federalism. Most notable was the death of the U.S. Advisory Commission on Intergovernmental Relations in 1996 after 37 years of operation. Committees dedicated to intergovernmental relations disappeared from Congress.

It is unlikely that the new Democratic regime will revive the bipartisan advisory commission or intergovernmental committees in Congress. A key question, however, is whether the White House Office for Intergovernmental Affairs and Public Liaison will play a more elevated political and policy role than it did under President Bush. This office's location in the White House is a sign of enhanced importance, and it is headed by Obama's close confidant, Valerie B. Jarrett. However, she is senior adviser to the president as well as assistant to the president for both intergovernmental affairs and public liaison. Consequently, her intergovernmental affairs responsibilities could easily be reduced by the political pressures of her other responsibilities.

Another question is whether Obama will revive Reagan's federalism executive order (EO 12612), which President Bill Clinton revoked in 1998 (EO 13085) but then revived in weaker form in 1999 (EO 13132) after state officials objected to his 1998 order. This order lay fallow under Bush; however, the new administration has not signaled an intention to revive the order. State officials seem to have lost faith in the efficacy of such an order, but the American Association for Justice—formerly the Association of Trial Lawyers of America—is pressing the administration to resurrect the order, especially to reduce federal-agency preemptions of state tort laws.

Decline of Political Cooperation

There has been a decline, too, in federal-state cooperation in major intergovernmental programs such as Medicaid and surface transportation. Congress earmarks and alters programs more in response to national and regional interest groups than to elected state and local officials, who themselves are viewed as interest groups.

This facet of coercive federalism is likely to be alleviated to some degree by the dominance of Democrats in the state-federal intergovernmental arena. In particular, for example, even though the National Governors Association and the National Conference of State Legislatures are officially bipartisan, Democratic majorities in those organizations and in other organizations representing state officials will facilitate more intense contacts and smoother negotiations between state officials and Democratic federal officials. The state membership of the National Association of Attorneys General also consists of 31 Democrats, and that organization plays important intergovernmental roles on matters involving federal preemption, business and trade regulation, and criminal law. The prevalence of Democrats in both the federal and state arenas is likely also to reduce the number of dueling federal and state policies that became prominent during the Bush years.[10]

Conclusion

During a period of severe economic crisis, perhaps even depression, it might seem odd to suggest that the course of American federalism through this crisis and during a new presidential administration committed to change will likely be evolutionary rather than revolutionary and, thus, largely stick to a course that is some 40 years old. However, the fundamental underlying feature of coercive federalism is expansion of federal power, and major expansions occurred during the Great Depression under Franklin D. Roosevelt's New Deal and during the tumultuous decade of the 1960s under Lyndon B. Johnson's Great Society and Creative Federalism. Both of those expansions laid the foundations for coercive federalism; consequently, during the current crisis, there is not likely to be a contraction of federal power.

Notes

[1]For background, see John Kincaid, "State-Federal Relations: Federal Dollars Down, Federal Power Up," *The Book of the States* (Lexington, KY: Council of State Governments, 2006), 19-25; John Kincaid, "State-Federal Relations: Defense, Demography, Debt, and Deconstruction as Destiny," *The Book of the States* (Lexington, KY: The Council of State Governments, 2005), 25-30; John Kincaid, "Trends in Federalism: Continuity, Change and Polarization," *The Book of the States* (Lexington, KY: Council of State Governments, 2004), 21-27; John Kincaid, "State-Federal Relations: Continuing Regulatory Federalism," *The Book of the States* (Lexington, KY: Council of State Governments, 2002), 25-32; John Kincaid, "From Cooperation to Coercion in American Federalism: Housing, Fragmentation, and Preemption, 1780-1992," *Journal of Law and Politics* 9 (Winter 1993): 333-433.

[2]John Kincaid and Richard L. Cole, "Public Opinion on Issues of Federalism in 2007: A Bush Plus?" *Publius: The Journal of Federalism* 38 (Summer 2008): 469-487.

[3]For explication, see John Kincaid, "The State of U.S. Federalism, 2000–2001," *Publius: The Journal of Federalism* 31 (Summer 2001): 1-69.

[4]Joel I. Klein and Al Sharpton, "Charter Schools Can Close the Education Gap," *Wall Street Journal*, January 12, 2009, p. A24.

[5]Anne Broache and Declan McCullagh, "Technology Voters' Guide: Barack Obama," *CNET News*, January 2, 2008, *http://news.cnet.com/Technology-Voters-Guide-Barack-Obama---page-2/2100-1028_3-6224109-2.html*, accessed March 3, 2009.

[6]Stephen Labatan, "Senate Approves Measure to Curb Big Class Actions," *New York Times*, February 11, 2005, p. A20.

[7]Joe Klein, "Obama Promises New Destiny, Work Begins Today," *Time*, January 21, 2009, *http://www.time.com/time/politics/article/0,8599,1872924,00.html*, accessed March 4, 2009.

[8]John Maggs, "Limping Toward Tax Reform," *National Journal* 37 (October 22, 2005): 3280.

[9]John S. Baker, Jr., "Revisiting the Explosive Growth of Federal Crimes," *Legal Memorandum* 26, Washington, DC: Heritage Foundation, 16 June, p. 1.

[10]John Kincaid, "State-Federal Relations: Dueling Policies," *The Book of the States* (Lexington, KY: Council of State Governments, 2008), 19–24.

About the Author

John Kincaid is the Robert B. and Helen S. Meyner Professor of Government and Public Service and director of the Meyner Center for the Study of State and Local Government, Lafayette College, Easton, Pa. He is former editor of *Publius: The Journal of Federalism*; former executive director of the U.S. Advisory Commission on Intergovernmental Relations; and co-editor of *Constitutional Origins, Structure, and Change in Federal Countries* (2005), *Interaction in Federal Systems* (2008), and *Local Government in Federal Systems* (2008).

Trends in Congressional Preemption

By Joseph F. Zimmerman

Congress first enacted statutes preempting regulatory powers of states and their political subdivisions in 1790, but the impact of subsequent preemption acts with a few exceptions was relatively minor until 1965 when a sharp increase in such statutes occurred and many statutes involved fields traditionally regulated by the states. Most preemption statutes involve civil rights, commerce, communications, environmental protection, finance, health, telecommunications and transportation. This article focuses principally upon the preemption bills signed into law by President George W. Bush.

The United States Constitution established the world's first federal system by delegating specific powers to Congress, reserving unspecified powers to the states, and empowering Congress and state legislatures to employ concurrent powers, including taxation. The drafters recognized the potential for conflicts between congressional acts and state acts and included Article VI, which declares congressional acts and treaties made with foreign nations "shall be the supreme law of the land." Not all conflicting state laws are invalid. The U.S. Supreme Court on a number of occasions opined a conflict between a congressional statute and a state statute is not of a sufficient magnitude to trigger the supremacy of the law clause.

Most of the delegated domestic powers in Article I, Section 8 are latent broad ones that Congress may exercise at its will to remove regulatory powers completely or partially from the states and local governments in a given field. Additional preemption powers have been delegated to Congress by the 13th, 14th, 15th, 19th, 24th and 26th Amendments to the Constitution. The necessary and proper clause does not delegate a power to Congress, but does supplement the delegated powers by empowering the national legislature to enact statutes necessary to effectuate the delegated powers.

Congress first preempted state powers in 1790 by enacting the *Copyright Act* and the *Patent Act* (1 Stat. 124, 1 Stat. 109). Although the national legislature is not specifically authorized to regulate immigration, two delegated powers—"establish a uniform rule of naturalization" and regulate commerce with foreign nations—serve as the constitutional basis for the resultant congressional preemption power to regulate immigration.

A preemption statute can range in length from less than one page to hundreds of pages and may be simple or exceptionally complex. Congress in recent decades has included one or more preemption statutes in omnibus budget reconciliation acts and appropriations acts that are hundreds of pages in length and in other preemption acts. As a result, the total number of preemption acts (currently 608) is higher than the total number of preemption bills signed into law by the various presidents. The amount of regulatory authority removed from states in a field by a preemption act ranges from little to all.

The subject matter of preemption acts has varied over the years. Nineteenth century acts focused principally on bankruptcy, false claims, civil rights, voting rights and interstate commerce. The early decades of the 20th century witnessed supersession acts relating to bankruptcy, firearms, health and safety, interstate commerce, labor relations, securities and transportation. Beginning in 1957, preemption acts covered age discrimination, animal welfare, civil rights, consumer protection, drug abuse, economic deregulation of specified industries, endangered species, environmental protection, hazardous materials, highway safety, housing, medical devices and voting rights among others. Congress enacted the first anti-terrorism act in 1994 and 18 other similar acts from 2001 to 2008, following the Sept. 11, 2001, terrorist attacks on the country.

State government officials do not always oppose a preemption bill as they recognize some problems require a national solution. For example, states cooperatively were unable to solve the problem involving commercial vehicle drivers who, holding operator licenses issued by several sister states, continue to drive with a license issued by one state after suspension or revocation by another state of their respective license for a serious motor vehicle violation. In consequence, states supported enactment of the *Commercial Motor Vehicle Safety Act of 1986* (100 Stat. 3207) authorizing states to continue to issue commercial driver's licenses and making possession of more than one such license a federal crime. State and local government officers, however, strongly object to unfunded mandates contained in preemption laws. To date, Congress has enacted five preemption relief acts; the most recent one is the *Safe Drinking Water Act Amendments of 1996* (110 Stat. 1613).

Preemption Types

There are three types of preemption statutes: complete, partial, and contingent in terms of their effect. Each type may include a sunset clause. A complete preemption act, also known as field preemption, removes from states all regulatory powers in a specified field and may assign a national government department or agency responsibility for regulation unless the act is a complete economic deregulation one such as the *Bus Regulatory Reform Act of 1982* (96 Stat. 1104). Congress may authorize a state to play a role related to a completely preempted field in emergency situations. The *Atomic Energy Act of 1946* (60 Stat. 755) is a complete preemption act, yet the Nuclear Regulatory Commission has limited resources and relies upon state and local governments for an immediate response to a problem in the event of a radioactive discharge at a nuclear power plant. Congress also authorizes states to enforce national regulatory standards contained in several complete preemption statutes.

Four complete preemption statutes authorize a limited turn-back of regulatory authority to individual states upon their application to the administering federal department or agency. The first such statute is the *Atomic Energy Act of 1959* (73 Stat. 688). One complete preemption act offers state governments a choice. The *Electronic Signatures in Global and National Commerce Act of 2000* (114 Stat. 464) exempts a state from preemption if it adopts "the *Uniform Electronic Transactions Act* as approved and recommended for enactment ... by the National Conference of Commissioners on Uniform State Laws in 1999."

A partial preemption statute assumes one of five forms:

- States may lose their regulatory authority only in part of the field.
- A statute may include a savings clause stipulating a state law is not preempted "unless there is a direct and positive conflict" between it and the concerned federal law such as the clause contained in the *Gun Control Act of 1968* (82 Stat. 1226).
- A statute may establish minimum regulatory standards and/or authorize a national department or agency to promulgate minimum standards. The *Water Quality Act of 1965* (79 Stat. 903) (now *Clean Water Act*), authorizes states to continue to regulate the field provided each state submits a plan to the U.S. Environmental Protection Agency containing regulatory standards meeting or exceeding the national standards, and evidence the state has the necessary qualified personnel and equipment to enforce the standards. If the plan is approved, the agency delegates regulatory primacy to the states under which only the state regulates and the roles of the agency are to monitor state performance and provide grants and technical assistance. Congress enacted five minimum standards preemption acts.
- A statute may establish maximum regulatory standards in a specified field that may not be exceeded by states. The first and only such standards are contained in the *Gramm-Leach-Bliley Financial Services Modernization Act of 1999* (113 Stat. 1338), which established 13 maximum insurance regulatory standards.
- The *Hazardous Materials Transportation Safety and Security Reauthorization Act of 2005* (119 Stat. 1895) established the first procedural standard by allowing a state to establish procedures to conduct background checks for drivers hauling hazardous materials that are more stringent than the federal procedures, as long as there is a state appeals process similar to the federal one.

A number of preemption acts contain both complete and partial preemption provisions. An example is the *Energy Policy Act of 2005* (119 Stat. 615), which contains two complete preemption provisions and one partial preemption provision. States lobby Congress for relief from costly mandates contained in a number of preemption statutes, but no relief act has been enacted since the *Safe Drinking Water Act Amendments of 1996* (110 Stat. 1613).

The third type is labeled a contingent preemption statute because such a statute applies to a state and/or a local government only if a specified condition(s) exists in the unit. This type dates to the *Voting Rights Act of 1965* (79 Stat. 437), which applies the suspensive law to a governmental unit only if two conditions exist: A voting device such as a literacy test has been used and fewer than 50 percent of the voters cast ballots in the preceding presidential election.

Preemption Trends

Congress, as noted, enacted two complete preemption acts in 1790, but subsequently enacted supersession acts at a slow pace for years. Only 29 such acts had been enacted 110 years later. Congress subsequently enacted preemption statutes at the following pace: 14

from 1900 to 1909, 22 from 1910 to 1919, 17 from 1920 to 1929, 31 from 1930 to 1939, 16 from 1940 to 1949, 24 from 1950 to 1959, 47 from 1960 to 1969, 102 from 1970 to 1979, 93 from 1980 to 1983, 87 from 1990 to 1999 and 124 from 2000 to 2008. The data reveal that a Democratic Party-controlled Congress enacted the largest number—102—of preemption statutes during a single decade. A Republican Party-controlled Congress, however, enacted 133 preemption acts in 12 years from 1995 to 2006.

The change in party control of Congress in 2007 resulted in the enactment of only 25 preemption statutes by January 1, 2009, including two temporary extensions of the *Andean Trade Preference Act* (121 Stat. 235 and 122 Stat. 646), extension of the *Internet Tax Freedom Act* to 2014 (121 Stat. 1024), reauthorization of the *Terrorism Risk Insurance Program* (121 Stat. 1839), two renewals of import restrictions on products from Burma (121 Stat. 264 and 122 Stat. 2649) and enactment of the *United States-Peru Trade Promotion Agreement Implementation Act* (121 Stat. 1455).

Congress enacted only a few acts removing major powers from the states prior to the 20th century including the *Interstate Commerce Act of 1887* (24 Stat. 379) and the *Bankruptcy Act of 1898* (30 Stat. 544). Beginning with the *Food and Drug Act of 1906* (34 Stat. 768), Congress enacted important supersession acts on a regular—although slow—basis until 1964 when the pace of enactment increased sharply. Twenty-six supersession acts that have the greatest impact on the states were enacted from 1964 to 1999. These statutes include, among others, the *Civil Rights Act of 1964* (78 Stat. 241), *Water Quality Act of 1965* (79 Stat. 903) (now *Clean Water Act*), *Air Quality Act of 1967* (81 Stat. 485) (now *Clean Air Act*), *Occupational Safety and Health Act of 1970* (84 Stat. 1590), *Fair Labor Standards Act of 1974* (88 Stat. 55), *Safe Drinking Water Act of 1974* (88 Stat. 1676), *Surface Mining Control and Reclamation Act of 1977* (91 Stat. 445), *Comprehensive Environmental Response, Compensation, and Liability Act of 1980* (94 Stat. 2767), *Riegle-Neal Interstate Banking and Branching Efficiency Act of 1994* (108 Stat. 2338), *Telecommunications Act of 1996* (110 Stat. 56), and *Gramm-Leach-Bliley Financial Services Modernization Act of 1999* (113 Stat. 1338).

The Bush Preemption Record

President George W. Bush signed 123 preemption bills into law from 2001 to 2008 and did not veto a supersession bill. Eighteen antiterrorism acts, including the *USA Patriot Act* (115 Stat. 396), were responses to the 2001 terrorists' attacks on the World Trade Center in New York City and the Pentagon in Arlington, Va. These acts removed relatively little regulatory authority from the states.

Thirteen preemption acts pertain to banking, commerce, energy and finance, including three acts affecting the jurisdiction of courts. The *Public Company Accounting and Reform and Corporate Responsibility Act of 2002* (116 Stat. 746) was the congressional response to financial abuses by large corporations, including Enron, which filed for bankruptcy protection. Banks successfully lobbied Congress to enact the *Check Clearing for the 21st Century Act of 2003* (117 Stat. 1190) authorizing electronic truncation (substitute checks) to expedite check clearance by eliminating the return of paper checks to the banks of origin. Large companies lobbied successfully for enactment of the *Class Action Fairness Act of 2005* (119 Stat. 4) to address abuses associated with class action lawsuits. The *Protection of Lawful Commerce in Arms Act of 2005* (119 Stat. 2005) prohibits bringing qualified civil liability actions in federal or state courts against dealers, distributors, importers and manufacturers of firearms. And the *Fair Minimum Wage Act of 2007* (121 Stat. 188) increased the national minimum wage over a two-year period.

Thirty-seven acts relate to environmental protection, health and safety. They include: the *Partial Birth Abortion Ban Act of 2003* (117 Stat. 1201), *Food Allergen Labeling and Consumer Protection Act of 2004* (118 Stat. 906), *Dietary Supplement and Nonprescription Drug Consumer Protection Act of 2006* (120 Stat. 3469), *Federal Employee Dental and Vision Benefits Enhancement Act of 2004* (118 Stat. 4001) and the *Maritime Pollution Prevention Act of 2008* (122 Stat. 2611). The employee dental and vision benefits act nullifies only a state or local law or regulation pertaining to dental and vision benefits, insurance plans or contracts of federal employees.

Foreign commerce and taxation are the subjects of 13 preemption acts. President Bush was a strong advocate of international open markets and signed free trade agreements with Chile (2003), Singapore (2003), Australia (2004), Morocco (2004), Dominican Republic-Central America (2005), Bahrain (2006) and Peru (2007). He also signed two bills extending the *Andean Trade Preference Act* to Feb. 29, 2008, and to Dec. 31, 2008, respectively. In addition, he signed bills in 2001, 2004 and 2007 extending the prohibition of state and local government taxation of access to the Internet.

President Bush signed four intellectual property bills: The *Anti-Counterfeiting Act of 2004* (118 Stat. 3912), which prohibits trafficking in counterfeit labels, illicit labels and counterfeit documentation or packaging; the *Fraudulent Online Indentity Sanctions Act of 2004* (118 Stat. 3916); and the *Artists' Rights and Theft Prevention Act of 2003* (119 Stat. 218). The free trade agreements also contain new intellectual property provisions ratifying a series of international instruments pertaining to a procedure for settling domain names disputes, extension of the terms of copyright protection, and prevention of circumvention of technological measures used by copyright holders to restrict unauthorized acts.

Seven telecommunications preemption acts were signed by the president. The *Controlling the Assault of Non-Solicited Pornography and Marketing Act of 2003* (CAN-SPAM, 117 Stat. 2716) supersedes the regulatory powers of state and local governmental units relative to the regulation of using electronic mail to send commercial messages. The *Satellite Home Viewer Extension and Reauthorization Act of 2004* (118 Stat. 3393) contains licensing provisions for satellite carriers and allows them to retransmit signals of any station outside the local market of the subscriber.

Congress enacted three transportation statutes containing preemption provisions. The *National Defense Authorization Act for Fiscal Year 2002* (115 Stat. 1012) preempts the authority of the states over specified transportation projects. The *Real Interstate Driver Equity Act of 2002* (116 Stat. 2342) forbids state and local governments or interstate agencies to require a license or impose a fee for a motor vehicle providing prearranged ground transportation services. The *Sanitary Food Transportation Act of 2005* (119 Stat. 1912) removes a state or local government requirement if compliance with it is not possible or "is an obstacle to accomplishing and carrying out this section or a regulation prescribed under this section."

Conclusions and Recommendations

Enactment of 608 preemption statutes may suggest states have been reduced significantly in importance as the result of losing regulatory powers completely or partially in many fields, but the number of preemption statutes enacted during a given time period is not an accurate measure of the amount and importance of regulatory powers removed from state governments. Several preemption statutes did not immediately affect states as they had not legislated in the concerned areas as illustrated by the *Copyright Act of 1790* and the *Patent Act of 1790*. Furthermore, many supersession statutes remove little authority from states and other statutes simply extend the sunset clause in an existing preemption statute. State retention of several important regulatory powers is attributable in part to Congress enacting five minimum standards acts allowing states to exercise regulatory primacy.

Congress has employed its preemption powers since 1978 both to regulate and to deregulate. Most notably, preemption statutes provide for substantial deregulation of the financial, communications and transportation industries while other statutes simultaneously regulate state and local governments as polities. Nevertheless, states retain important regulatory powers and since 1965 have been exercising more broadly and frequently their reserved powers in response to congressional enactment of five minimum standards preemption acts. The national financial crisis, attributable to credit default swaps and derivatives backed by subprime mortgages, ensures congressional regulation through preemption of previously unregulated credit default swaps and other activities of the financial services industry.

Recommendations

Congress should give serious consideration to innovative preemption statutes preserving state powers to an extent while generally achieving harmonious regulations throughout the nation. One innovative opt-out provision dates to the *Johnson Act of 1951* (64 Stat. 1134) criminalizing the act of transporting a gambling device into a state while authorizing the state legislature to enact a statute exempting the state from the provision.

The *Riegle-Neal Interstate Banking and Branching Efficiency Act of 1994* (108 Stat. 2352) contains a opt-out provision authorizing a state legislature to enact a law prohibiting interstate branching within the state otherwise authorized by the act, and an opt-in provision authorizing interstate branching through *de novo* branches provided the law applies equally to all banks and permits out-of-state banks to establish branches *de novo* in the state. These provisions allow the state legislature to tailor the national law in accordance with local conditions.

Similarly, Congress could enact additional contingent preemption statutes that date to the *Voting Rights Act of 1965* (79 Stat. 437). The act is a suspensive law applicable to a state only if two specified conditions exist.

The *Electronic Signatures in Global and National Commerce Act of 2000* (114 Stat. 464) is a third alternative approach. The act exempts a state from preemption provided its legislature enacts the *Uniform Electronic Transaction Act* drafted by the National

Conference of Commissioners on Uniform State Laws, composed of state officers.

A fourth alternative approach is congressional encouragement of states to enter into interstate regulatory compacts by granting consent-in-advance and providing grants-in-aid to states to facilitate compact drafting and implementation.

In sum, changes in the global economy, inventions and technological innovations, as well as lobbying by business, civil rights, environmental, telecommunications and other interest groups will result in Congress continuously preempting completely or partially the regulatory powers of state and local governments unless state legislatures initiate additional actions to harmonize their regulatory laws and implementing administrative rules and regulations. Harmonization can be achieved by enactment of reciprocity statutes, uniform state laws and interstate compacts that create a commission with regulatory powers.

About the Author

Joseph F. Zimmerman is a professor of political science at Rockefeller College of the State University of New York at Albany. He is the author of more than 30 books and numerous articles.

The Branches of Government: Can We Build Bridges?

By Rep. Kim Koppelman

CSG's Interbranch Working Group grew out of the realization that many state issues require the input and perspective of the judicial, legislative and executive branches of government. By bringing officials together from all three branches to help solve complex public problems, it has become the catalyst to share best practices and identify and monitor divisive issues across the states.

When the founders of our states and nation sought to formulate a representative republic, they fashioned a government made up of three branches—legislative, executive and judicial.

We all learned that in civics or government classes, but in today's world, how well do these three branches really function? How well do they relate with one another? Do they relate at all?

If the answer is "not much" or "not very well," what impact does that have on the quality of our government?

Are the taxpayers getting the government they deserve, or can we do better, if the branches work better together or at least better understand one another? What would that mean for the quality of state government in America?

Most of the time, when the branches of government interact, something is at stake. It might be a legislative hearing on the budget of an executive branch agency or the courts, or perhaps a battle over a governor's program or initiative with which legislators disagree, or actions by a court that curtail the authority or second-guess actions of one of the other branches.

Easing the Tension

While necessary in our system of checks and balances, these interactions can be tense and clearly adversarial.

What if the branches could talk with one another when nothing was at stake, but just in an effort to improve not only the working relationship between them, but also the understanding of how each branch could do its job better, by considering the role of the other branches and the impact it has?

When an organization like The Council of State Governments raises such questions, it becomes clear that CSG is in a unique position not only to ask the question, but to address the deficiencies that exist and the clear communication gap.

One venue where such questions were asked a few years ago was CSG's Public Safety and Justice Task Force, which I was privileged to co-chair. One of its members at the time was Joseph Lambert, then Kentucky Supreme Court's chief justice. As we began discussing these issues, it became apparent that in many, if not all, states, there was room to improve how the branches of government worked together.

The next logical question was, what could be done to improve the understanding between branches of state government? It quickly became obvious that no organization was in a position to address this problem as well as CSG.

A Unifying History

As the only organization representing all three branches of government in all the states, CSG already had a history of bringing officials from different branches together. It just seemed that the organization could do an even better job of this, by making it a focus, and that state governments and the officials who serve in them would benefit from the process.

Discussions led to brainstorming, which gave way to planning. The concept quickly grew into the CSG Interbranch Working Group, which has met regularly at national meetings for the past few years.

In 2008, as CSG chair, I was pleased and honoured to be able to plan and host our first national Interbranch Summit of the States, which was held in North Dakota's capital city, Bismarck, June 22-24.

The summit was a groundbreaking event that brought together leaders from all three branches of state government, from throughout the nation, to discuss how the branches do their respective work, the impact that has on the other branches, and the ultimate quality of government delivered for the people.

The legislative branch was well-represented by lawmakers and legislative leaders from several states. Executive branch officials—from governor to state treasurer—were represented, including lieutenant governors, secretaries of state, and attorneys general, while Supreme Court justices and judges at other levels ably provided the judiciary's perspective.

Surprising revelations surfaced in seemingly simple exercises. One telling example was following the progression of a statute through the branches. Sen. Bart Davis of Idaho, CSG's chair-elect, and Colorado Appeals Judge Russel Carparelli tracked the progression of a bill from its passage, to an executive branch agency drafting policies for its enforcement and, finally, a court's attempts to apply the statute and interpret the legislature's original intent.

Summit participants grappled with understanding issues from the perspective of a branch of government other than their own. Legislators' perspectives on administrative rules and court decisions, for example, helped executive branch officials and judges better understand the intent of those who draft laws.

A judge's explanation of the difficulty of discerning legislative intent and the means judges use to try to do so helped legislators think about how they could make their intent clearer for those who must enforce and interpret the laws they pass.

Rave Reviews

In the weeks and months after the summit, comments like "This was really valuable," "We must do this again" and "Others need to experience this" were common.

The Interbranch Summit of the States and the Interbranch Working Group have launched perhaps the most meaningful effort in many years to bring those in state government together.

It has returned CSG to its interbranch roots and sought to renew founder Henry Toll's vision of creating a "community of the states."

Many good state-government organizations exist, but most are monolithic. Legislators meet with other legislators. Executive branch officials gather with counterparts from other states. Judges get together.

But never before has there been such a unique opportunity for officials from all branches to gather together, understand one another better and seek to put what they learn into practice to improve government in their states.

About the Author

Rep. Kim Koppelman of North Dakota served as the 2008 CSG national chair. He co-founded and co-chaired the CSG Interbranch Working Group, along with former Kentucky Supreme Court Chief Justice Joseph Lambert.

Interstate Compacts in 2009 and Beyond: Opportunities for an Increased Diversity of Use

By Keith A. Scott

As our world shrinks and the enormity of specific policy issues grows, multiple states are finding themselves facing similar, if not identical, situations. While states must act to address current and emerging problems, they are not required to act alone. In fact, states may find that acting in cooperation with their neighbors affords significant opportunities for creative problem solving, economies of scale and the bolstering of state rights over a range of topics. Interstate compacts are not new, nor are they unfamiliar to the modern policymaker. However, the innovative ways in which interstate compacts may be used are evolving before us – seeking to tackle a host of issues not previously addressed by this interstate mechanism. As states struggle with nearly unparalleled financial downturns and revenue declines, interstate compacts are an efficient tool to promote cooperative regional or national action.

Background

States have historically used interstate compacts to settle boundary disputes. Examples include the Maryland-Virginia Compact of 1785, the Virginia-Kentucky Boundary (Kentucky & Virginia Jurisdiction Act of 1789), and the Virginia-North Carolina Boundary Agreement of 1791. In some instances, these compacts have been modified or updated,[1] and other compacts pertaining to boundaries have become the subject of legal actions. But these early examples of interstate cooperation not only proved to be effective methods for individual states to form lasting relationships on common issues, they also pioneered more comprehensive and diverse compacts.

The use of interstate compacts became more widespread, particularly in the 20th century, after states gained a protected right to use them.[2] On average, each state is a member of 27 different interstate compacts. While some of these are boundary compacts, many have been used in the areas of corrections, natural resources, energy, transportation or other regulatory fields.[3] To a lesser extent, compacts as a form of multistate cooperation, have also been used to address other key topics, such as education, emergency management, mental health and multistate taxation.

While interstate compacts have been used to resolve multi-state problems shared among a group

Table A: Interstate Compact Membership

State	*Number of compacts*	*State*	*Number of compacts*	*State*	*Number of compacts*	*State*	*Number of compacts*
Eastern Region		**Midwestern Region**		**Southern Region**		**Western Region**	
Connecticut	30	Illinois	25	Alabama	30	Alaska	20
Delaware	22	Indiana	26	Arkansas	29	Arizona	28
Maine	32	Iowa	21	Florida	27	California	27
Massachusetts	27	Kansas	35	Georgia	24	Colorado	36
New Hampshire	33	Michigan	23	Kentucky	23	Hawaii	14
New Jersey	33	Minnesota	23	Louisiana	23	Idaho	26
New York	31	Nebraska	32	Maryland	34	Montana	25
Pennsylvania	29	North Dakota	19	Mississippi	25	Nevada	21
Rhode Island	25	Ohio	25	Missouri	30	New Mexico	32
Vermont	30	South Dakota	18	North Carolina	21	Oregon	28
District of Columbia	34	Wisconsin	15	Oklahoma	26	Utah	27
Regional total	326	Regional total	262	South Carolina	18	Washington	30
				Tennessee	24	Wyoming	25
				Texas	24	Regional total	339
				Virginia	52		
				West Virginia	27		
				Regional total	437		

Source: National Center for Interstate Compacts.

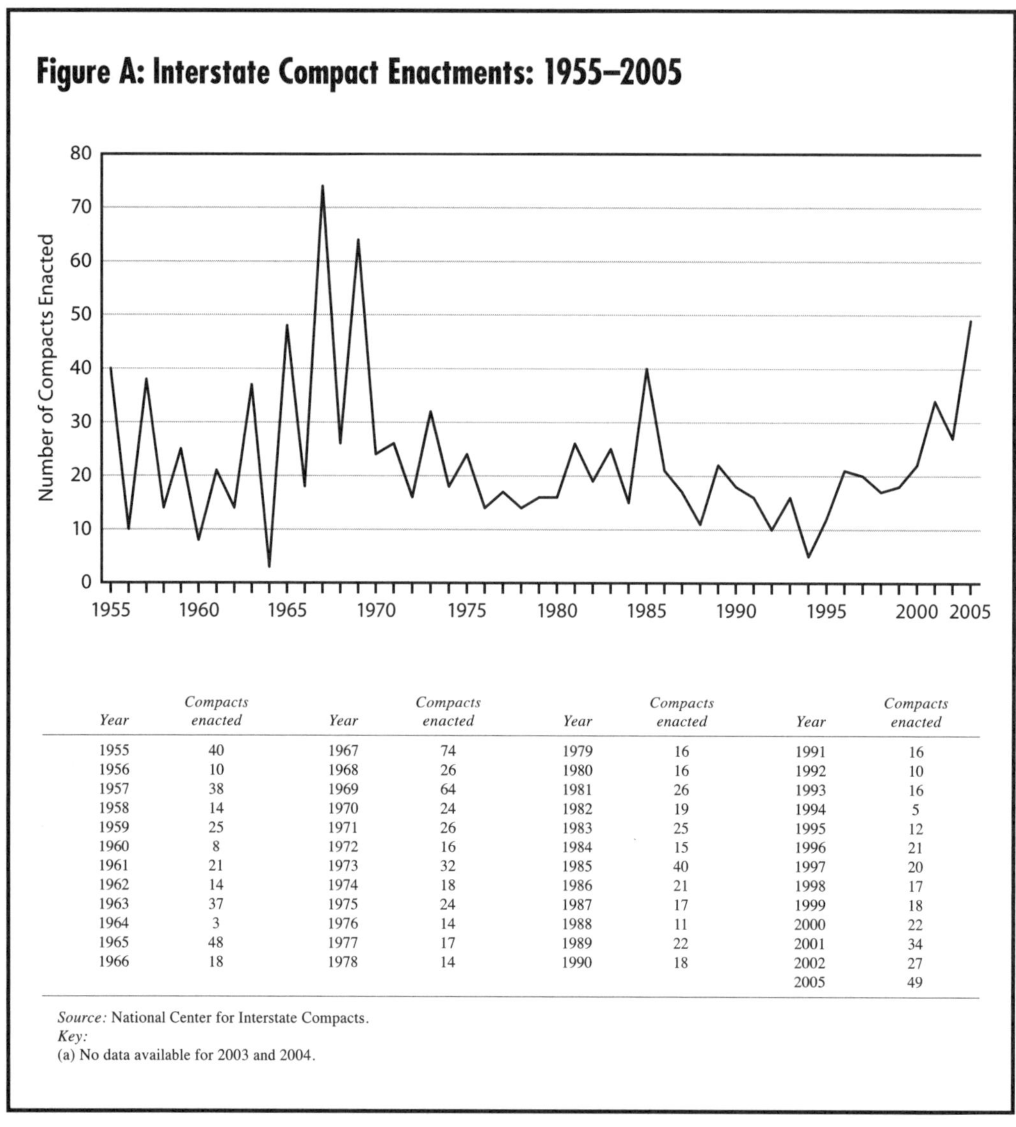

Figure A: Interstate Compact Enactments: 1955–2005

Year	*Compacts enacted*	*Year*	*Compacts enacted*	*Year*	*Compacts enacted*	*Year*	*Compacts enacted*
1955	40	1967	74	1979	16	1991	16
1956	10	1968	26	1980	16	1992	10
1957	38	1969	64	1981	26	1993	16
1958	14	1970	24	1982	19	1994	5
1959	25	1971	26	1983	25	1995	12
1960	8	1972	16	1984	15	1996	21
1961	21	1973	32	1985	40	1997	20
1962	14	1974	18	1986	21	1998	17
1963	37	1975	24	1987	17	1999	18
1964	3	1976	14	1988	11	2000	22
1965	48	1977	17	1989	22	2001	34
1966	18	1978	14	1990	18	2002	27
						2005	49

Source: National Center for Interstate Compacts.
Key:
(a) No data available for 2003 and 2004.

of jurisdictions, not every issue area is replete with agreements. In fact, some areas of public policy have been addressed purposefully via other interstate mechanisms, such as uniform state laws or formal/informal memorandums of understanding. This lack of use may be tied to the speed of development and implementation often associated with interstate compacts—typically five to seven years, though more recent efforts have been completed on far shorter schedules.

Although no state is a member of fewer than 14 interstate compacts—most states are members of many more. These instruments have facilitated interstate cooperation since well before the promulgation of the U.S. Constitution. Furthermore, the states' collective right to enter into compact agreements has been protected by that venerable document of fundamental laws and principles since 1789. Typically, states rely on three very different methods for multistate cooperation: interstate compacts, uniform laws and memorandums of understanding. The latter two, while sufficient for many purposes, do not have the same soundness of properties as compacts and therefore are not as complete and reliable.

Uniform laws, also referred to as *uniform state laws*, have been around since the late 1800s. Their purpose is to seek enactment of identical laws among several states on a particular issue. That objective is similar to interstate compacts, but in practice, uniform state laws miss the mark of uniformity on a frequent basis.[4] They often result in many different versions of the same law. Because they are not contractual agreements like interstate compacts, states enacting the laws are free to enact unilateral changes to their version of the law. If that law creates an unfavorable impact on another state or states, there is generally no enforcement mechanism available to the aggrieved state.

Memorandums of understanding generally are the least binding agreement as compared to both uniform state laws and interstate compacts. They frequently amount to a written agreement with no real legal enforceability. Therefore, while they express the intent of the parties, they often are not ideal instruments for legally memorializing binding multilateral agreements.

New Uses for Interstate Compacts

While several successful efforts have been undertaken to educate policymakers about the purpose and benefits of compacts, use of the tool in new areas is often slow to develop. While compacts have historically helped resolve multistate matters pertaining to boundary disputes, natural resources, corrections, multistate taxation, education and other important issues, they can be used to address a great number of problems states face today, including energy and infrastructure, prescription drug monitoring, and thoroughbred horse racing.

Energy and Infrastructure

States continue to experience a variety of issues under the broad umbrella of infrastructure. The ability to provide, for instance, adequate electrical power to the residents of one state sometimes depends on the willingness of neighboring states to permit the siting of transmission lines through their boundaries. The solution is typically not just a matter of where to place the lines as a function of geographical convenience, but rather may also have to do with environmental safety issues, as well as preservation of natural resources and the preferences of the residents of that state.

Finding a means of interstate cooperation is essential and failure to do so may mean that the transmission lines never get sited. This lack of state cooperation then raises the specter of federal intervention with national regulatory bodies controlling how electricity is distributed. An interstate compact that encompasses these factors and issues may present states with the best opportunity to determine their own state-driven solutions to the problem. The federal Energy Policy Act of 2005[5] specifically granted states the ability to craft regional interstate compacts related to transmission line siting—a rare pre-emptive permission and 'nudge' from Congress, but states have thus far not seriously pursued such agreements.

Prescription Drug Monitoring

Dangers derived from the use of illicit drugs are not restricted to the population of illegal drugs that fill the evening news. Drugs that are commonly prescribed for medical purposes can also be problematic if they are not carefully dispensed and monitored in terms of who is receiving them and where they are being distributed. Some states are experiencing difficulty with policing this activity and certain classes of drugs are finding their way into the wrong hands, posing a substantial danger of misuse and drug overdoses - impacting families, schools, places of employment as well as the medical community.

One solution successfully implemented in many states is the prescription drug monitoring program – intrastate databases tracking the dispensing of specific classed drugs and that alert officials to nefarious activities. While rarely 'live' or instantaneous in nature, the programs are effective at tracking dispensing, physician prescription writing habits, and patient abuse – essentially seeking to eliminate 'doctor shopping,' which is the seeking of multiple doctors for multiple prescriptions that can be filled from several pharmacies.

While states have done an excellent job in creating these systems within their boundaries, interstate cooperation that permits the sharing of this data across state lines is virtually non-existent. Small scale pilot projects have shown promise, but no effort has been undertaken on a multi-state or national scale allowing information systems to interface on a regular and accurate basis. There has been some rumbling of activity at the federal level, but this too has not proceeded far. States are in a unique position to facilitate and control such a national effort by being both the primary innovators of intrastate prescription data monitoring and the creators/beneficiaries of the interstate compact mechanism.

Thoroughbred Horse Racing

The thoroughbred horse racing industry has been the subject of increased scrutiny since the unfortunate death of *Eight Belles* at the 2008 Kentucky

Derby. Since that time, the industry has taken upon itself the responsibility to look critically at the horse racing business and in doing so has identified several areas for potential reform. Despite previous efforts to standardize issues such as wagering and the medication of horses, this activity has occurred in a disparate fashion at the state level with many of the 35 industry states adopting different versions of such rules.

Despite saber-rattling to the contrary, federal intervention in this area is not necessarily expected and may depend on how well states seek to manage it themselves. Unlike other areas of interstate cooperation, the regulatory nature and need for constant cooperation between states in thoroughbred horse racing may serve as an ideal model for interstate compacts. Because there are divergent interests residing in the different states where horse racing takes place, it has become increasingly more difficult to establish uniformity. This is precisely where interstate compacts can assist as effective tools for identifying commonalities and creating cooperation and multi-state governance of an issue.

Conclusion

Interstate compacts have demonstrated their adaptability for more than two hundred years – taking on both traditional and non-traditional issues. Having evolved from a simple contract to an in-depth tool for policy regulation, interstate compacts have emerged as an instrument uniquely suited for the rapidly changing world occupied by state governments. It is then incumbent upon state officials to think about interstate compacts as potential solutions to non-traditional and emerging policy areas, such as energy infrastructure, prescription drug monitoring and thoroughbred horse racing. The issues of today, and the interstate responses crafted, help states not only solve current policy dilemmas, but strengthen the common bonds between states and solidify the role of the states in governing critical issues within our federalist system.

Notes

[1]For example, in 1958, the legislatures of Maryland and Virginia revisited the 1785 compact to remedy portions that had become obsolete. This culminated in the formation of the Potomac River Compact of 1958. *ssl.csg.org/compactlaws/potomacriverof1958.html.*

[2]U.S. Constitution, Article I, Section 10, Clause 3.

[3]*http://www.csg.org/programs/ncic/database/search.aspx.*

[4]*http://www.law.cornell.edu/uniform/uniform.html.*

[5]Energy Policy Act of 2005, Title XII (Electricity), Subtitle B, Sec. 1221; *http://www.doi.gov/iepa/EnergyPolicyActof2005.pdf*

About the Author

Keith A. Scott is the director of the National Center for Interstate Compacts at The Council of State Governments.

Table 2.1
SUMMARY OF STATE INTERGOVERNMENTAL EXPENDITURES: 1944–2007
(In thousands of dollars)

			To local governments						
					For specified purposes				
Fiscal year	Total	To Federal government (a)	Total	For general local government support	Education	Public welfare	Highways	Health	Miscellaneous and combined
1944	$1,842,000	. . .	$1,842,000	$274,000	$861,000	$368,000	$298,000	. . .	$41,000
1946	2,092,000	. . .	2,092,000	357,000	953,000	376,000	339,000	. . .	67,000
1948	3,283,000	. . .	3,283,000	428,000	1,554,000	648,000	507,000	. . .	146,000
1950	4,217,000	. . .	4,217,000	482,000	2,054,000	792,000	610,000	. . .	279,000
1952	5,044,000	. . .	5,044,000	549,000	2,523,000	976,000	728,000	. . .	268,000
1953	5,384,000	. . .	5,384,000	592,000	2,737,000	981,000	803,000	. . .	271,000
1954	5,679,000	. . .	5,679,000	600,000	2,930,000	1,004,000	871,000	. . .	274,000
1955	5,986,000	. . .	5,986,000	591,000	3,150,000	1,046,000	911,000	. . .	288,000
1956	6,538,000	. . .	6,538,000	631,000	3,541,000	1,069,000	984,000	. . .	313,000
1957	7,440,000	. . .	7,440,000	668,000	4,212,000	1,136,000	1,082,000	. . .	342,000
1958	8,089,000	. . .	8,089,000	687,000	4,598,000	1,247,000	1,167,000	. . .	390,000
1959	8,689,000	. . .	8,689,000	725,000	4,957,000	1,409,000	1,207,000	. . .	391,000
1960	9,443,000	. . .	9,443,000	806,000	5,461,000	1,483,000	1,247,000	. . .	446,000
1962	10,906,000	. . .	10,906,000	839,000	6,474,000	1,777,000	1,327,000	. . .	489,000
1963	11,885,000	. . .	11,885,000	1,012,000	6,993,000	1,919,000	1,416,000	. . .	545,000
1964	12,968,000	. . .	12,968,000	1,053,000	7,664,000	2,108,000	1,524,000	. . .	619,000
1965	14,174,000	. . .	14,174,000	1,102,000	8,351,000	2,436,000	1,630,000	. . .	655,000
1966	16,928,000	. . .	16,928,000	1,361,000	10,177,000	2,882,000	1,725,000	. . .	783,000
1967	19,056,000	. . .	19,056,000	1,585,000	11,845,000	2,897,000	1,861,000	. . .	868,000
1968	21,950,000	. . .	21,950,000	1,993,000	13,321,000	3,527,000	2,029,000	. . .	1,080,000
1969	24,779,000	. . .	24,779,000	2,135,000	14,858,000	4,402,000	2,109,000	. . .	1,275,000
1970	28,892,000	. . .	28,892,000	2,958,000	17,085,000	5,003,000	2,439,000	. . .	1,407,000
1971	32,640,000	. . .	32,640,000	3,258,000	19,292,000	5,760,000	2,507,000	. . .	1,823,000
1972	36,759,246	. . .	36,759,246	3,752,327	21,195,345	6,943,634	2,633,417	. . .	2,234,523
1973	40,822,135	. . .	40,822,135	4,279,646	23,315,651	7,531,738	2,953,424	. . .	2,741,676
1974	45,941,111	$341,194	45,599,917	4,803,875	27,106,812	7,028,750	3,211,455	. . .	3,449,025
1975	51,978,324	974,780	51,003,544	5,129,333	31,110,237	7,136,104	3,224,861	. . .	4,403,009
1976	57,858,242	1,179,580	56,678,662	5,673,843	34,083,711	8,307,411	3,240,806	. . .	5,372,891
1977	62,459,903	1,386,237	61,073,666	6,372,543	36,964,306	8,756,717	3,631,108	. . .	5,348,992
1978	67,287,260	1,472,378	65,814,882	6,819,438	40,125,488	8,585,558	3,821,135	. . .	6,463,263
1979	75,962,980	1,493,215	74,469,765	8,224,338	46,195,698	8,675,473	4,148,573	. . .	7,225,683
1980	84,504,451	1,746,301	82,758,150	8,643,789	52,688,101	9,241,551	4,382,716	. . .	7,801,993
1981	93,179,549	1,872,980	91,306,569	9,570,248	57,257,373	11,025,445	4,751,449	. . .	8,702,054
1982	98,742,976	1,793,284	96,949,692	10,044,372	60,683,583	11,965,123	5,028,072	. . .	9,228,542
1983	100,886,902	1,764,821	99,122,081	10,364,144	63,118,351	10,919,847	5,277,447	. . .	9,442,292
1984	108,373,188	1,722,115	106,651,073	10,744,740	67,484,926	11,923,430	5,686,834	. . .	10,811,143
1985	121,571,151	1,963,468	119,607,683	12,319,623	74,936,970	12,673,123	6,019,069	. . .	13,658,898
1986	131,966,258	2,105,831	129,860,427	13,383,912	81,929,467	14,214,613	6,470,049	. . .	13,862,386
1987	141,278,672	2,455,362	138,823,310	14,245,089	88,253,298	14,753,727	6,784,699	. . .	14,786,497
1988	151,661,866	2,652,981	149,008,885	14,896,991	95,390,536	15,032,315	6,949,190	. . .	16,739,853
1989	165,415,415	2,929,622	162,485,793	15,749,681	104,601,291	16,697,915	7,376,173	. . .	18,060,733

See footnotes at end of table.

SUMMARY OF STATE INTERGOVERNMENTAL EXPENDITURES: 1944–2007—Continued
(In thousands of dollars)

			To local governments						
					For specified purposes				
Fiscal year	*Total*	*To Federal government (a)*	*Total*	*For general local government support*	*Education*	*Public welfare*	*Highways*	*Health*	*Miscellaneous and combined*
1990	175,027,632	3,243,634	171,783,998	16,565,106	109,438,131	18,403,149	7,784,316	. . .	19,593,296
1991	186,398,234	3,464,364	182,933,870	16,977,032	116,179,860	20,903,400	8,126,477	. . .	20,747,101
1992	201,313,434	3,608,911	197,704,523	16,368,139	124,919,686	25,942,234	8,480,871	. . .	21,993,593
1993	214,094,882	3,625,051	210,469,831	17,690,986	131,179,517	31,339,777	9,298,624	. . .	20,960,927
1994	225,635,410	3,603,447	222,031,963	18,044,015	135,861,024	30,624,514	9,622,849	. . .	27,879,561
1995	240,978,128	3,616,831	237,361,297	18,996,435	148,160,436	30,772,525	10,481,616	. . .	28,926,886
1996	252,079,335	3,896,667	248,182,668	20,019,771	156,954,115	31,180,345	10,707,338	10,790,396	18,530,703
1997	264,207,209	3,839,942	260,367,267	21,808,828	164,147,715	35,754,024	11,431,270	11,772,189	15,453,241
1998	278,853,409	3,515,734	275,337,675	22,693,158	176,250,998	32,327,325	11,648,853	12,379,498	20,037,843
1999	308,734,917	3,801,667	304,933,250	25,495,396	192,416,987	35,161,151	12,075,195	13,611,228	26,173,293
2000	327,069,829	4,021,471	323,048,358	27,475,363	208,135,537	40,206,513	12,473,052	15,067,156	19,690,737
2001	350,326,546	4,290,764	346,035,782	31,693,016	222,092,587	41,926,990	12,350,136	16,518,461	21,454,592
2002	364,789,480	4,370,330	360,419,150	28,927,053	227,336,087	47,112,496	12,949,850	20,816,777	23,276,887
2003	382,781,397	4,391,095	378,390,302	30,766,480	240,788,692	49,302,737	13,337,114	20,241,742	23,953,537
2004	389,706,202	4,720,728	384,985,474	31,027,535	248,356,196	42,802,564	13,972,060	20,366,508	28,460,611
2005	408,528,723	4,675,517	403,853,206	28,284,852	263,171,516	46,859,165	14,486,020	17,656,423	33,395,230
2006	428,924,716	6,503,840	422,420,876	29,984,822	279,403,028	53,891,394	15,230,034	18,127,028	25,784,570
2007	457,376,669	4,701,360	452,675,309	30,945,612	298,883,069	56,945,447	14,844,331	19,436,156	31,620,694

Source: U.S. Department of Commerce, U.S. Census Bureau, Governments Division, March 2009. 2007 Survey of State Government Finances. Data users who create their own estimates using data from this report should cite the U.S. Census Bureau as the source of the original data only. The data in this table are based on information from public records and contain no confidential data. Although the data in this table come from a census of governmental units and are not subject to sampling error, the census results do contain nonsampling error. Additional information on nonsampling error, response rates, and definitions may be found at *http://www.census.gov/govs/www/surveymethodology07.html*.

Key:

. . . — Not available. Detail may not add to totals due to rounding.

(a) Represents primarily state reimbursements for the supplemental security July income program. This column also duplicates some funds listed under "Public welfare" and "All other" columns.

Table 2.2
STATE INTERGOVERNMENTAL EXPENDITURES, BY STATE: 2000–2007
(In thousands of dollars)

	Expenditure amounts							
State	*2007*	*2006*	*2005*	*2004*	*2003*	*2002*	*2001*	*2000*
United States	$457,376,669	$428,924,716	$403,467,210	$389,706,202	$382,781,397	$364,789,480	$350,326,546	$327,069,829
Alabama	6,088,940	5,000,116	4,494,345	4,164,719	4,074,005	4,095,562	3,892,653	3,908,350
Alaska	1,365,793	1,217,110	1,145,159	1,049,706	1,091,391	1,055,596	986,921	1,026,962
Arizona	9,860,543	8,606,646	8,069,461	7,544,080	6,936,753	6,968,635	6,439,144	5,940,651
Arkansas	4,300,048	3,866,226	3,869,400	3,233,499	3,210,582	3,071,214	2,941,918	2,725,242
California	92,415,603	88,317,088	80,948,431	80,132,150	84,468,847	74,687,370	69,747,365	65,389,054
Colorado	6,000,582	5,621,254	5,187,799	4,860,577	4,666,350	4,295,239	3,909,362	3,702,849
Connecticut	3,831,974	3,428,482	3,513,039	3,396,810	3,030,485	3,734,962	3,252,917	3,362,551
Delaware	1,194,559	1,129,736	945,950	922,710	903,476	822,544	788,160	856,008
Florida	19,680,891	19,345,077	17,328,518	16,473,396	14,460,722	14,053,858	15,010,631	14,073,445
Georgia	10,515,856	9,753,253	9,521,119	9,335,405	9,016,458	8,644,827	8,383,261	7,179,698
Hawaii	138,054	157,863	147,201	134,452	125,434	130,387	124,448	157,902
Idaho	1,931,829	1,606,232	1,519,654	1,496,785	1,449,076	1,407,058	1,363,445	1,277,688
Illinois	14,259,666	13,946,155	14,212,799	13,303,609	13,369,662	13,090,976	12,770,065	12,050,100
Indiana	8,178,674	8,081,787	7,993,289	7,963,397	6,760,945	6,556,774	7,052,415	6,735,704
Iowa	3,892,136	3,881,967	3,642,335	3,529,971	3,442,552	3,326,499	3,284,057	3,211,878
Kansas	3,869,984	3,596,388	3,281,217	2,878,801	2,925,220	2,971,413	2,953,527	2,853,333
Kentucky	4,469,153	4,384,427	3,915,278	3,967,334	3,693,634	3,559,669	3,620,278	3,280,144
Louisiana	6,262,247	5,654,409	4,588,748	4,410,251	4,329,053	4,168,290	3,800,785	3,721,576
Maine	1,276,381	1,217,377	1,093,027	1,049,160	1,051,164	1,009,582	976,233	912,376
Maryland	7,568,283	6,916,136	5,801,050	5,632,520	5,358,342	5,235,506	5,003,670	4,355,724
Massachusetts	9,364,680	6,814,813	6,475,520	6,202,583	6,435,841	6,283,972	6,886,054	6,240,692
Michigan	19,423,935	19,407,575	18,679,748	19,035,055	19,851,778	19,067,058	18,145,167	17,201,031
Minnesota	10,686,237	10,867,738	10,108,813	9,638,153	9,618,471	8,271,462	8,196,532	7,610,072
Mississippi	5,086,220	4,826,721	4,005,786	3,880,446	3,665,580	3,456,588	3,354,226	3,248,019
Missouri	5,626,071	5,386,306	5,485,698	5,260,101	5,159,094	5,073,185	4,802,371	4,528,746
Montana	1,175,674	1,088,009	1,005,091	955,378	938,000	910,845	863,553	760,511
Nebraska	1,793,817	1,721,265	1,770,897	1,695,613	1,784,749	1,820,137	1,684,159	1,585,847
Nevada	3,826,539	3,667,299	3,272,860	2,948,274	2,648,660	2,432,909	2,271,654	2,250,330
New Hampshire	1,408,445	1,385,014	1,245,235	1,278,988	1,283,091	1,178,642	1,040,566	1,053,267
New Jersey	10,667,575	11,060,423	11,394,615	9,813,688	8,997,417	9,320,357	9,081,634	8,639,491
New Mexico	4,144,807	3,745,089	3,608,081	3,031,473	2,951,328	2,768,420	2,561,979	2,447,354
New York	50,525,675	45,615,561	43,731,212	44,112,115	40,874,514	38,982,253	34,712,602	31,273,000
North Carolina	12,646,039	11,260,558	10,675,563	10,326,743	10,356,152	9,450,766	9,309,537	9,301,095
North Dakota	741,535	735,705	701,125	613,513	1,190,923	585,521	569,034	589,807
Ohio	17,755,241	17,131,020	16,368,355	15,730,201	15,249,395	15,052,078	14,594,220	12,932,081
Oklahoma	4,067,276	3,857,145	3,748,031	3,715,417	3,395,494	3,377,045	3,486,043	3,089,257
Oregon	5,047,346	4,947,578	4,764,615	4,637,052	4,071,501	4,212,673	4,027,505	3,919,771
Pennsylvania	15,189,027	13,650,400	13,307,866	12,156,969	11,943,470	12,787,590	13,120,752	11,369,795
Rhode Island	1,009,313	998,505	908,479	868,929	828,198	749,034	711,439	677,552
South Carolina	4,870,680	4,699,299	4,246,231	4,159,942	4,155,920	4,241,010	4,168,449	3,806,116
South Dakota	652,117	633,891	614,371	576,215	514,949	506,347	480,960	448,131
Tennessee	6,161,614	5,910,319	5,705,768	5,301,665	4,952,923	4,477,936	4,582,883	4,364,404
Texas	21,915,924	19,264,517	17,489,900	17,032,016	17,332,957	16,680,780	17,204,468	16,231,378
Utah	2,601,367	2,384,403	2,189,527	2,112,921	2,165,151	2,170,884	2,100,657	1,977,703
Vermont	1,415,922	1,357,660	1,266,715	981,307	938,085	918,858	919,865	931,604
Virginia	10,438,607	10,019,166	9,720,400	8,819,067	8,352,635	8,369,313	7,869,121	7,132,350
Washington	8,644,100	7,820,778	7,228,017	6,911,826	6,785,341	6,806,350	6,576,757	6,370,710
West Virginia	2,074,429	2,077,950	2,015,637	1,942,069	1,544,758	1,453,707	988,322	1,359,668
Wisconsin	9,744,914	9,561,057	9,200,766	9,285,137	9,478,166	9,523,191	8,895,941	8,170,504
Wyoming	1,570,347	1,301,223	1,314,469	1,204,014	952,705	974,608	818,841	838,308

Source: U.S. Department of Commerce, U.S. Census Bureau, Governments Division, March 2009. 2007 Survey of State Government Finances. Data users who create their own estimates using data from this report should cite the U.S. Census Bureau as the source of the original data only. The data in this table are based on information from public records and contain no confidential data. Although the data in this table come from a census of governmental units and are not subject to sampling error, the census results do contain nonsampling error. Additional information on nonsampling error, response rates, and definitions may be found at *http://www.census.gov/govs/www/surveymethodology07.html*.

Note: Includes payments to the federal government, primarily state reimbursements for the supplemental security income program.

Table 2.3
STATE INTERGOVERNMENTAL EXPENDITURES, BY FUNCTION AND BY STATE: 2007
(In thousands of dollars)

			Specified functions				
State	*Total*	*General local government support*	*Education*	*Public welfare*	*Highways*	*Health*	*Miscellaneous and combined*
United States	$457,376,669	$30,945,612	$298,883,069	$56,945,447	$14,844,331	$19,436,156	$36,322,054
Alabama	6,088,940	212,512	4,741,967	57,641	216,692	21,380	838,748
Alaska	1,365,793	27,718	890,167	55,706	2,807	42,952	346,443
Arizona	9,860,543	1,924,779	5,848,934	953,704	719,608	68,208	345,310
Arkansas	4,300,048	316,893	3,628,759	0	164,505	673	189,218
California	92,415,603	838,549	50,799,670	24,376,058	2,452,487	8,846,072	5,102,767
Colorado	6,000,582	73,693	3,837,678	1,095,736	300,434	81,040	612,001
Connecticut	3,831,974	121,539	2,620,074	463,724	2,096	261,197	363,344
Delaware	1,194,559	0	1,060,122	9,296	9,646	22,473	93,022
Florida	19,680,891	1,993,378	14,760,438	49,519	583,200	1,450	2,292,906
Georgia	10,515,856	423,075	9,320,101	481,599	0	82,251	208,830
Hawaii	138,054	101,106	0	305	0	9,973	26,670
Idaho	1,931,829	202,987	1,556,943	0	131,192	1,776	38,931
Illinois	14,259,666	1,743,977	8,346,029	1,661,256	727,065	154,188	1,627,151
Indiana	8,178,674	2,602,720	4,858,975	231,821	30,024	38,962	416,172
Iowa	3,892,136	138,059	2,834,446	100,764	443,251	99,987	275,629
Kansas	3,869,984	75,308	3,414,220	13,538	171,606	29,299	166,013
Kentucky	4,469,153	0	3,681,665	117,871	188,436	142,545	338,636
Louisiana	6,262,247	194,533	4,027,540	95,694	92,704	0	1,851,776
Maine	1,276,381	121,221	1,058,776	19,599	26,167	0	50,618
Maryland	7,568,283	109,450	5,643,296	1,508	554,141	613,522	646,366
Massachusetts	9,364,680	1,829,476	5,990,073	404,663	184,648	18,228	937,592
Michigan	19,423,935	1,087,349	13,000,763	2,825,238	1,237,818	229,090	1,043,677
Minnesota	10,686,237	1,450,652	7,032,132	588,989	717,282	134,630	762,552
Mississippi	5,086,220	759,873	3,094,365	156,338	202,712	41,186	831,746
Missouri	5,626,071	3,913	4,860,621	46,172	302,582	24,230	388,553
Montana	1,175,674	228,220	800,989	28,701	27,989	13,730	76,045
Nebraska	1,793,817	297,991	1,248,341	29,225	0	68,265	149,995
Nevada	3,826,539	1,171,684	2,379,354	88,959	103,727	12,395	70,420
New Hampshire	1,408,445	77,135	1,077,243	103,871	29,674	30,105	90,417
New Jersey	10,667,575	1,956,835	6,703,954	888,297	223,231	35,379	859,879
New Mexico	4,144,807	1,288,275	2,803,615	0	25,132	0	27,785
New York	50,525,675	1,592,864	26,727,683	12,185,959	10,926	4,631,869	5,376,374
North Carolina	12,646,039	148,876	8,825,954	2,556,290	228,394	223,101	663,424
North Dakota	741,535	119,125	470,153	16,453	76,636	7,957	51,211
Ohio	17,755,241	2,017,204	10,865,722	2,130,217	969,869	1,027,953	744,276
Oklahoma	4,067,276	119,488	3,178,641	48,125	261,474	179,257	280,291
Oregon	5,047,346	153,922	3,583,516	316,523	465,589	124,658	403,138
Pennsylvania	15,189,027	38,168	9,042,987	2,145,701	606,364	983,057	2,372,750
Rhode Island	1,009,313	94,542	885,200	27,575	0	0	1,996
South Carolina	4,870,680	1,077,528	3,352,152	59,063	90,415	26,707	264,815
South Dakota	652,117	58,318	503,357	4,089	36,660	1,445	48,248
Tennessee	6,161,614	541,065	4,087,488	589,603	324,232	1,266	617,960
Texas	21,915,924	194,959	19,750,987	600,880	155,217	195,628	1,018,253
Utah	2,601,367	0	2,390,589	22,528	57,327	31,928	98,995
Vermont	1,415,922	22,538	1,312,909	102	55,899	0	24,474
Virginia	10,438,607	970,444	6,590,156	670,324	387,555	307,815	1,512,313
Washington	8,644,100	94,737	6,758,088	9,169	647,990	225,250	908,866
West Virginia	2,074,429	84,341	1,758,311	21,610	1,272	50,221	158,674
Wisconsin	9,744,914	1,745,354	5,968,830	595,394	596,754	289,385	549,197
Wyoming	1,570,347	499,239	909,096	50	902	3,473	157,587

Source: U.S. Department of Commerce, Bureau of the Census, Governments Division, March 2009. 2007 Survey of State Government Finances. Data users who create their own estimates using data from this report should cite the U.S. Census Bureau as the source of the original data only. The data in this table are based on information from public records and contain no confidential data. Although the data in this table come from a census of governmental units and are not subject to sampling error, the census results do contain nonsampling error. Additional information on nonsampling error, response rates, and definitions may be found at *http://www.census.gov/govs/www/surveymethodology07.html*.

Note: Detail may not add to total due to rounding.

Table 2.4
STATE INTERGOVERNMENTAL EXPENDITURES, BY TYPE OF RECEIVING GOVERNMENT AND BY STATE: 2007
(In thousands of dollars)

State	Total intergovernmental expenditure	Federal	School districts	Other local governments
United States	$457,376,669	$4,701,360	$243,163,369	$209,511,940
Alabama	6,088,940	0	4,722,830	1,366,110
Alaska	1,365,793	0	0	1,365,793
Arizona	9,860,543	0	5,420,220	4,440,323
Arkansas	4,300,048	32	3,628,733	671,283
California	92,415,603	3,550,225	47,721,223	41,144,155
Colorado	6,000,582	3,236	3,829,062	2,168,284
Connecticut	3,831,974	0	24,841	3,807,133
Delaware	1,194,559	1,010	1,055,340	138,209
Florida	19,680,891	0	14,346,550	5,334,341
Georgia	10,515,856	0	9,320,101	1,195,755
Hawaii	138,054	305	0	137,749
Idaho	1,931,829	6	1,556,943	374,880
Illinois	14,259,666	205	8,276,106	5,983,355
Indiana	8,178,674	0	4,858,975	3,319,699
Iowa	3,892,136	0	2,831,072	1,061,064
Kansas	3,869,984	502	3,411,933	457,549
Kentucky	4,469,153	2,184	3,681,665	785,304
Louisiana	6,262,247	0	4,026,303	2,235,944
Maine	1,276,381	13,484	0	1,262,897
Maryland	7,568,283	0	0	7,568,283
Massachusetts	9,364,680	193,360	834,401	8,336,919
Michigan	19,423,935	30,712	12,999,775	6,393,448
Minnesota	10,686,237	0	7,021,853	3,664,384
Mississippi	5,086,220	0	3,076,069	2,010,151
Missouri	5,626,071	24	4,860,621	765,426
Montana	1,175,674	227	800,821	374,626
Nebraska	1,793,817	29,225	1,248,341	516,251
Nevada	3,826,539	6,224	2,379,354	1,440,961
New Hampshire	1,408,445	0	406	1,408,039
New Jersey	10,667,575	0	4,889,638	5,777,937
New Mexico	4,144,807	0	2,803,615	1,341,192
New York	50,525,675	629,000	13,617,246	36,279,429
North Carolina	12,646,039	0	0	12,646,039
North Dakota	741,535	0	470,153	271,382
Ohio	17,755,241	2,750	10,865,722	6,886,769
Oklahoma	4,067,276	45,045	3,177,961	844,270
Oregon	5,047,346	0	3,579,026	1,468,320
Pennsylvania	15,189,027	160,366	9,042,987	5,985,674
Rhode Island	1,009,313	27,575	53,112	928,626
South Carolina	4,870,680	0	3,317,746	1,552,934
South Dakota	652,117	0	502,557	149,560
Tennessee	6,161,614	0	244,095	5,917,519
Texas	21,915,924	0	19,553,643	2,362,281
Utah	2,601,367	0	2,390,515	210,852
Vermont	1,415,922	102	1,312,909	102,911
Virginia	10,438,607	691	18,189	10,419,727
Washington	8,644,100	4,870	6,757,850	1,881,380
West Virginia	2,074,429	0	1,756,026	318,403
Wisconsin	9,744,914	0	5,968,830	3,776,084
Wyoming	1,570,347	0	908,011	662,336

Source: U.S. Department of Commerce, U.S. Census Bureau, Governments Division, March 2009. 2007 Survey of State Government Finances. Data users who create their own estimates using data from this report should cite the U.S. Census Bureau as the source of the original data only. The data in this table are based on information from public records and contain no confidential data. Although the data in this table come from a census of governmental units and are not subject to sampling error, the census results do contain nonsampling error. Additional information on nonsampling error, response rates, and definitions may be found at *http://www.census.gov/govs/www/surveymethodology07.html*.

Note: Detail may not add to total due to rounding.

Table 2.5
STATE INTERGOVERNMENTAL REVENUE FROM FEDERAL AND LOCAL GOVERNMENTS: 2007
(In thousands of dollars)

State	Total intergovernmental revenue	From federal government					From local governments				
		Total	Education	Public welfare	Health & hospitals	Highways	Total	Education	Public welfare	Health & hospitals	Highways
United States	$430,202,361	$409,751,859	$73,399,424	$233,432,273	$20,511,606	$35,186,919	$20,450,502	$2,718,203	$10,336,137	$830,958	$1,901,086
Alabama	7,732,269	6,952,453	1,451,104	3,879,023	297,741	601,722	779,816	14,727	682,347	44,198	25,781
Alaska	2,288,253	2,283,391	295,309	824,845	57,275	388,041	4,862	4,862	0	0	0
Arizona	8,122,068	7,768,145	1,366,135	5,317,620	268,208	373,243	353,923	45,333	182,542	55,810	32,601
Arkansas	4,286,094	4,266,327	716,563	2,416,959	103,862	391,929	19,767	8,313	0	650	0
California	49,889,749	47,250,580	10,848,673	26,090,503	2,154,138	2,942,708	2,639,169	191,070	895,746	3,559	736,086
Colorado	4,732,975	4,654,549	1,186,839	1,954,982	702,973	424,703	78,426	11,271	194	985	25,422
Connecticut	4,167,175	4,154,039	416,605	2,631,616	292,025	351,444	13,136	925	0	0	0
Delaware	1,241,741	1,196,071	155,209	652,609	89,140	102,790	45,670	45,670	0	0	0
Florida	19,239,807	18,942,878	3,207,223	10,113,915	1,459,871	2,158,316	296,929	10,259	0	145,954	0
Georgia	13,005,370	12,766,455	2,221,782	5,823,638	1,044,989	2,688,421	238,915	159,534	0	0	41,164
Hawaii	2,063,945	2,060,092	535,984	928,358	114,952	109,460	3,853	0	0	0	0
Idaho	1,842,758	1,828,156	312,065	877,960	128,823	297,304	14,602	675	6,668	58	7,095
Illinois	14,234,320	13,726,288	2,691,518	8,216,164	510,106	1,018,745	508,032	35,490	391,063	0	61,051
Indiana	7,941,998	7,766,607	1,503,220	4,499,002	244,864	875,374	175,391	12,269	76,867	6,396	43,964
Iowa	4,378,744	4,152,034	840,426	2,408,859	138,861	368,185	226,710	996	176,941	25,715	15,575
Kansas	3,156,389	3,116,714	654,127	1,582,724	84,543	371,979	39,675	8,000	0	0	31,675
Kentucky	6,338,156	6,305,939	1,218,515	3,661,305	205,888	597,908	32,217	25,580	0	0	0
Louisiana	12,417,474	12,327,714	1,629,453	4,731,454	303,376	680,507	89,760	17,451	0	3,203	0
Maine	2,393,954	2,383,360	247,026	1,527,313	71,604	169,354	10,594	894	0	37	9,422
Maryland	7,199,413	6,926,021	1,350,647	3,337,330	783,135	622,898	273,392	29,678	23,761	85,541	17,734
Massachusetts	9,617,501	9,228,262	1,338,308	5,985,377	451,738	407,077	389,239	4,641	0	0	164
Michigan	13,083,153	12,806,628	2,638,778	6,900,897	826,442	889,571	276,525	21,939	77,944	59,535	41,975
Minnesota	6,680,661	6,570,590	1,126,335	4,065,909	201,604	610,880	110,071	5,896	39,006	24,660	29,693
Mississippi	9,103,302	8,960,692	1,203,200	4,013,295	164,630	954,826	142,610	5,451	46,916	0	42,882
Missouri	8,005,044	7,846,433	1,127,282	4,325,712	922,619	839,856	158,611	831	107,454	13,919	26,382
Montana	1,813,956	1,805,683	310,874	771,108	80,701	336,454	8,273	78	4,587	0	2,364
Nebraska	2,532,557	2,471,102	164,842	1,741,316	52,567	238,613	61,455	42,991	890	392	12,713
Nevada	2,091,256	1,948,322	429,027	947,545	115,983	294,011	142,934	12,197	97,034	1,522	26,353
New Hampshire	1,775,088	1,555,946	240,054	693,601	27,566	163,120	219,142	3,397	192,049	180	13,000
New Jersey	11,462,648	10,897,477	1,600,674	5,796,624	385,558	1,561,153	565,171	201,079	2,526	47,053	156,760
New Mexico	4,219,834	4,116,885	798,371	2,544,546	168,710	295,810	102,949	31,591	0	71,358	0
New York	47,324,109	39,594,539	4,767,343	29,055,941	1,565,804	1,623,934	7,729,570	298,890	5,862,135	0	0
North Carolina	13,231,264	12,459,398	1,948,587	8,397,880	441,770	755,864	771,866	102,813	576,589	23,460	35,109
North Dakota	1,227,870	1,195,983	275,194	472,810	32,316	238,036	31,887	1	5,979	1,976	17,637
Ohio	16,691,614	16,189,482	2,225,597	10,627,053	577,787	1,219,159	502,132	36,288	189,538	37,837	68,783
Oklahoma	5,406,356	5,279,021	1,019,131	2,510,224	881,784	485,923	127,335	575	2,700	832	34,519
Oregon	4,653,941	4,609,380	1,166,569	2,078,257	346,650	311,291	44,561	9,217	0	0	30,654
Pennsylvania	16,323,614	15,850,909	2,794,301	9,850,534	599,417	1,394,303	472,705	110,212	0	995	20,889
Rhode Island	2,086,752	1,962,853	278,015	997,389	206,055	261,045	123,899	3,413	0	0	0
South Carolina	7,097,636	6,691,204	1,200,063	4,219,204	229,516	547,963	406,432	68,859	256,066	10,279	11,392

See footnotes at end of table.

STATE INTERGOVERNMENTAL REVENUE FROM FEDERAL AND LOCAL GOVERNMENTS: 2007—Continued
(In thousands of dollars)

State	Total intergovernmental revenue	From federal government					From local governments				
		Total	Education	Public welfare	Health & hospitals	Highways	Total	Education	Public welfare	Health & hospitals	Highways
South Dakota	1,276,075	1,255,519	207,986	498,771	68,204	252,979	20,556	11,392	0	4,539	4,063
Tennessee	8,341,938	8,245,935	1,237,854	5,229,057	289,987	793,629	96,003	28,967	0	4,707	30,767
Texas	28,277,613	27,374,244	6,215,577	15,027,027	1,195,754	2,213,655	903,369	449,030	403,046	51,252	0
Utah	3,076,320	3,072,612	749,836	1,539,163	119,393	279,562	3,708	3,643	0	0	0
Vermont	1,379,970	1,375,164	217,188	766,425	51,993	162,087	4,806	0	0	0	4,806
Virginia	6,883,654	6,408,106	1,504,691	3,450,861	213,164	613,152	475,548	329,411	0	62,188	65,869
Washington	7,892,810	7,581,632	1,798,180	3,417,317	886,280	730,419	311,178	138,943	0	23,247	91,838
West Virginia	3,256,627	3,186,283	525,195	1,851,607	131,087	392,312	70,344	2,033	0	0	0
Wisconsin	6,769,288	6,607,759	1,286,700	3,841,697	186,698	604,027	161,529	13,767	30,797	16,090	80,878
Wyoming	1,947,258	1,776,003	155,249	338,947	33,455	181,177	171,255	157,661	4,752	2,831	4,026

Source: U.S. Department of Commerce, U.S. Census Bureau, March 2009. 2007 Survey of State Government Finances. Data users who create their own estimates using data from this report should cite the U.S. Census Bureau as the source of the original data only. The data in this table are based on information from public records and contain no confidential data. Although the data in this table come from a census of governmental units and are not subject to sampling error, the census results do contain nonsampling error. Additional information on nonsampling error, response rates, and definitions may be found at *http://www.census.gov/govs/www/surveymethodology07.html*.

Note: Detail may not add to total due to rounding.

Table 2.6
SUMMARY OF FEDERAL GOVERNMENT EXPENDITURE, BY STATE AND OUTLYING AREA: FISCAL YEAR 2006
(In millions of dollars)

State and outlying area	Total	Retirement and disability	Other direct payments	Grants	Procurement	Salaries and wages
United States	$2,454,998	$739,328	$569,380	$494,148	$408,665	$243,478
Alabama	43,928	14,490	9,913	7,510	8,329	3,686
Alaska	9,250	1,237	673	3,077	2,172	2,092
Arizona	46,355	14,644	8,392	8,779	10,625	3,914
Arkansas	21,500	8,323	5,608	4,639	1,333	1,598
California	253,906	70,007	62,300	54,947	43,271	23,382
Colorado	34,423	9,948	6,074	6,035	7,522	4,844
Connecticut	30,617	8,470	6,592	5,438	8,368	1,749
Delaware	5,853	2,382	1,322	1,371	250	528
Florida	142,705	52,698	41,457	22,452	14,830	11,269
Georgia	64,551	20,059	13,315	11,802	10,103	9,271
Hawaii	13,491	3,534	1,790	2,308	2,148	3,711
Idaho	9,950	3,502	1,764	2,005	1,715	964
Illinois	82,221	28,267	24,010	16,070	6,805	7,068
Indiana	43,766	15,645	12,067	8,088	5,355	2,612
Iowa	21,835	7,674	6,919	3,957	1,972	1,312
Kansas	21,523	7,007	5,796	3,358	2,755	2,607
Kentucky	37,605	11,861	7,656	6,927	7,298	3,863
Louisiana	69,731	10,551	23,978	22,833	9,534	2,836
Maine	10,979	3,977	2,102	2,683	1,249	969
Maryland	75,498	15,624	11,149	15,674	21,804	11,247
Massachusetts	57,222	15,456	13,910	13,171	10,930	3,755
Michigan	67,352	25,750	18,992	12,927	5,853	3,830
Minnesota	31,908	11,276	8,383	7,055	2,681	2,513
Mississippi	42,250	8,061	9,118	15,986	7,020	2,066
Missouri	52,266	15,612	12,387	8,601	11,112	4,555
Montana	8,011	2,681	1,800	2,026	531	973
Nebraska	13,927	4,403	4,567	2,528	1,034	1,395
Nevada	14,603	5,689	2,573	2,573	2,274	1,495
New Hampshire	8,875	3,390	1,646	1,743	1,411	686
New Jersey	61,267	20,778	16,306	11,295	8,403	4,483
New Mexico	20,938	5,252	2,796	4,652	6,030	2,209
New York	152,934	45,302	40,674	45,276	11,872	9,810
North Carolina	62,011	22,957	13,295	13,009	4,669	8,082
North Dakota	6,313	1,611	2,051	1,415	429	806
Ohio	80,774	28,832	20,785	16,518	8,875	5,764
Oklahoma	29,077	10,184	6,717	5,598	2,876	3,703
Oregon	23,586	9,542	5,250	5,455	1,332	2,007
Pennsylvania	103,265	36,416	28,899	20,197	10,849	6,904
Rhode Island	8,766	2,836	2,247	2,238	601	844
South Carolina	33,833	12,268	6,813	6,261	4,997	3,494
South Dakota	7,991	2,044	3,072	1,483	623	769
Tennessee	50,596	16,470	12,106	9,556	8,851	3,614
Texas	166,618	47,034	36,942	30,483	35,618	16,543
Utah	15,714	4,674	2,411	3,179	3,150	2,301
Vermont	5,274	1,593	974	1,368	870	470
Virginia	103,062	22,921	13,388	7,590	41,915	17,248
Washington	48,177	16,180	8,362	8,975	8,134	6,525
West Virginia	16,209	6,519	3,525	3,549	1,158	1,458
Wisconsin	34,561	13,459	8,550	7,155	3,323	2,074
Wyoming	5,170	1,324	794	2,069	431	552
Dist. of Columbia	40,358	2,037	2,760	4,175	14,225	17,161
American Samoa	246	48	10	152	31	5
Fed. States of Micronesia	100	1	8	91	0	0
Guam	1,380	250	92	289	401	348
Marshall Islands	191	1	2	78	110	0
No. Mariana Islands	177	27	14	126	2	8
Palau	37	1	3	34	0	0
Puerto Rico	16,232	6,355	3,402	4,789	673	1,013
U.S. Virgin Islands	621	182	84	285	11	58
Undistributed	23,418	18	794	244	17,925	4,437

Source: U.S. Department of Commerce, Bureau of the Census, Consolidated Federal Funds Report for Fiscal Year 2006, April 2008.

Note: All amounts are aggregates. Detail may not add to total due to rounding. Total expenditure does not include data on contingent liabilities (loans and insurance). For additional information see the complete report at *http://www.census.gov/govs/www/cffr06.html*.

Table 2.7
FEDERAL GOVERNMENT EXPENDITURE FOR DIRECT PAYMENTS FOR INDIVIDUALS FOR RETIREMENT AND DISABILITY, FOR SELECTED PROGRAMS, BY STATE AND OUTLYING AREA: FISCAL YEAR 2006
(In thousands of dollars)

State and outlying area	Total	Social Security payments: Retirement insurance payments	Survivors insurance payments	Disability insurance payments	Supplemental security income payments	Federal retirement and disability benefits: Civilian	Military	Veterans benefits: Payments for service connected disability	Other benefit payments	Other
United States	$739,328,443	$349,779,006	$106,946,943	$99,450,082	$37,669,880	$59,250,631	$35,944,288	$26,120,010	$7,703,251	$16,464,353
Alabama	14,490,475	5,509,239	2,105,998	2,495,405	853,295	1,463,563	940,533	581,477	262,401	278,564
Alaska	1,236,799	430,747	146,466	145,377	38,496	193,146	149,157	106,716	10,032	16,662
Arizona	14,643,900	7,111,556	1,837,787	1,837,271	549,411	1,214,843	1,014,127	646,490	146,204	286,209
Arkansas	8,322,655	3,455,953	1,178,736	1,487,327	466,594	561,627	409,929	425,506	130,524	206,461
California	70,007,005	33,490,532	9,567,097	8,859,092	5,570,903	5,075,540	3,535,452	2,171,319	602,602	1,134,468
Colorado	9,947,739	4,334,474	1,277,359	1,085,172	306,683	1,081,569	1,000,382	486,760	109,246	266,095
Connecticut	8,469,632	5,063,617	1,237,866	1,028,561	303,907	349,660	177,734	170,169	40,879	97,238
Delaware	2,381,804	1,190,804	320,309	325,594	73,745	205,301	132,343	68,412	17,123	48,174
Florida	52,697,727	26,545,159	6,643,124	5,792,521	2,343,685	3,997,395	3,721,804	2,062,695	616,121	975,224
Georgia	20,059,145	8,307,458	2,779,512	2,914,446	1,040,991	1,880,355	1,525,324	861,185	303,752	446,121
Hawaii	3,533,873	1,620,976	358,594	296,581	121,723	593,403	308,535	144,902	27,388	61,771
Idaho	3,502,321	1,649,153	475,860	434,623	118,807	317,585	207,708	160,806	33,668	104,112
Illinois	28,267,122	14,626,486	4,649,493	3,560,524	1,562,979	1,545,503	578,418	545,087	171,693	1,026,939
Indiana	15,644,675	8,169,823	2,581,428	2,177,929	564,882	806,965	342,890	388,353	102,431	509,975
Iowa	7,673,746	4,201,994	1,291,627	886,838	227,730	457,821	160,927	195,282	66,745	184,782
Kansas	7,006,619	3,470,848	1,051,608	798,389	212,307	554,586	363,186	218,666	66,221	270,808
Kentucky	11,860,650	4,566,989	1,849,369	2,354,273	963,497	774,725	405,349	451,723	142,577	352,148
Louisiana	10,550,683	4,075,108	2,091,736	1,771,491	823,837	603,265	430,404	396,499	167,984	190,360
Maine	3,976,854	1,747,434	515,859	640,278	168,887	331,549	193,936	255,017	50,390	73,505
Maryland	15,623,898	5,890,339	1,785,765	1,436,769	531,363	3,997,498	1,015,461	420,574	108,874	437,257
Massachusetts	15,456,435	7,940,439	2,151,779	2,366,502	863,914	997,773	303,576	489,083	124,068	219,301
Michigan	25,750,143	13,536,752	4,321,839	4,017,270	1,289,579	976,481	388,844	579,082	186,355	453,941
Minnesota	11,275,523	6,083,836	1,699,690	1,349,720	412,063	608,746	241,903	444,683	96,408	338,473
Mississippi	8,061,182	3,118,782	1,212,576	1,538,316	631,293	594,238	419,418	277,723	121,805	147,031
Missouri	15,611,773	7,375,499	2,341,993	2,372,973	622,155	1,220,581	574,023	503,140	174,079	427,330
Montana	2,680,529	1,202,740	374,972	304,778	79,159	293,848	133,308	141,442	29,846	120,436
Nebraska	4,403,324	2,166,248	656,580	468,293	116,926	292,981	243,879	198,838	48,867	210,711
Nevada	5,688,820	2,714,280	653,763	684,902	180,220	516,753	505,602	249,659	61,759	121,881
New Hampshire	3,390,062	1,724,085	425,562	499,132	73,042	287,949	175,426	131,851	29,883	43,133
New Jersey	20,778,485	11,840,409	3,048,990	2,605,323	843,165	1,275,314	321,376	430,071	107,424	306,412

See footnotes at end of table.

FEDERAL GOVERNMENT EXPENDITURE FOR DIRECT PAYMENTS FOR INDIVIDUALS FOR RETIREMENT AND DISABILITY, FOR SELECTED PROGRAMS, BY STATE AND OUTLYING AREA: FISCAL YEAR 2006—Continued
(In thousands of dollars)

State and outlying area	Total	Social Security payments: Retirement insurance payments	Social Security payments: Survivors insurance payments	Social Security payments: Disability insurance payments	Social Security payments: Supplemental security income payments	Federal retirement and disability benefits: Civilian	Federal retirement and disability benefits: Military	Veterans benefits: Payments for service connected disability	Veterans benefits: Other benefit payments	Other
New Mexico	5,251,830	2,040,661	656,022	669,089	281,113	659,144	404,727	357,331	69,054	114,688
New York	45,301,926	24,088,450	6,480,534	6,663,985	3,467,709	2,132,504	502,980	950,633	292,345	722,786
North Carolina	22,956,727	10,608,067	2,910,604	3,606,440	994,919	1,652,454	1,453,752	1,077,264	280,229	372,997
North Dakota	1,611,481	772,428	295,733	155,660	36,234	139,628	65,900	69,484	16,207	60,209
Ohio	28,831,780	14,211,244	5,191,118	3,604,467	1,476,526	1,721,023	698,387	718,061	278,783	932,172
Oklahoma	10,183,884	4,281,323	1,468,565	1,335,186	423,846	1,112,624	544,382	661,263	195,401	161,293
Oregon	9,541,567	4,829,397	1,297,202	1,146,473	332,774	793,590	362,691	465,903	116,217	197,320
Pennsylvania	36,416,259	18,420,843	5,847,694	4,609,475	1,857,404	2,444,284	766,857	830,773	312,337	1,326,592
Rhode Island	2,835,691	1,445,292	345,937	423,057	160,563	203,723	107,183	99,278	26,923	23,735
South Carolina	12,268,274	5,344,868	1,592,247	1,954,483	531,092	989,710	945,449	530,133	180,585	199,706
South Dakota	2,043,830	978,348	313,138	203,841	63,313	219,325	105,535	102,241	29,730	28,359
Tennessee	16,469,876	7,271,239	2,422,941	2,636,841	851,754	1,310,123	815,654	602,057	217,523	341,744
Texas	47,033,566	20,089,637	7,461,377	5,733,861	2,558,059	3,749,195	3,461,234	2,400,851	681,831	897,520
Utah	4,673,699	2,089,586	607,241	452,126	125,078	845,623	247,419	141,965	31,345	133,315
Vermont	1,592,633	827,250	226,876	225,487	63,362	99,600	55,084	57,282	13,661	24,031
Virginia	22,921,202	8,049,607	2,453,850	2,521, 831	726,157	4,067,862	3,494,218	887,579	224,770	495,328
Washington	16,179,648	7,402,008	1,993,989	1,880,677	675,834	1,561,472	1,294,932	845,312	167,856	357,569
West Virginia	6,519,161	2,441,056	1,093,379	1,301,853	426,534	407,598	154,527	279,317	83,512	331,386
Wisconsin	13,458,577	7,514,121	2,099,309	1,693,803	500,856	591,582	262,279	442,675	109,006	244,945
Wyoming	1,323,676	619,486	181,680	141,604	31,779	136,285	79,296	58,315	11,986	63,246
Dist. of Columbia	2,037,205	450,560	140,428	162,165	125,230	1,015,785	57,387	38,785	17,011	29,854
American Samoa	48,352	12,553	12,726	11,923	0	1,772	3,335	4,803	1,072	167
Fed. States of Micronesia	821	211	127	16	0	265	32	169	0	0
Guam	250,023	79,875	34,960	19,984	0	55,104	40,615	15,683	2,814	988
Marshall Islands	798	505	187	29	0	44	0	10	22	2
No. Mariana Islands	27,088	6,614	5,166	1,755	4,506	6,570	1,549	813	95	20
Palau	795	263	162	13	0	146	145	26	40	0
Puerto Rico	6,355,179	2,636,964	1,153,214	1,736,038	0	247,033	92,350	275,183	184,375	30,021
Virgin Islands	181,624	104,787	27,202	22,250	0	15,904	5,435	3,610	1,172	1,265
Undistributed	17,670	0	0	0	0	95	0	0	0	17,575

Source: U.S. Department of Commerce, Bureau of the Census, Consolidated Federal Funds Report for Fiscal Year 2006, April 2008.

Note: Reported amounts represent obligations of federal funds during the fiscal year. Detail may not add to total due to rounding. For additional information see the complete report at *http://www.census.gov/govs/www/cffr.html*.

Table 2.8
FEDERAL GOVERNMENT EXPENDITURE FOR DIRECT PAYMENTS OTHER THAN FOR RETIREMENT AND DISABILITY, FOR SELECTED PROGRAMS, BY STATE AND OUTLYING AREA: FISCAL YEAR 2006
(In thousands of dollars)

State and outlying area	Total	Medicare benefits: Hospital insurance	Medicare benefits: Supplementary medical insurance	Excess earned income tax credits	Unemployment compensation	Food stamp payments	Housing assistance	Agricultural assistance	Federal employees life and health insurance	Other
United States	$569,379,676	$187,896,268	$161,197,316	$37,593,035	$28,173,231	$30,258,849	$9,253,628	$28,466,357	$21,204,497	$65,336,494
Alabama	9,912,702	3,519,673	2,621,536	992,498	196,767	593,700	201,445	615,201	361,337	810,546
Alaska	672,732	157,025	112,355	58,644	104,562	85,985	12,203	12,904	2,172	126,882
Arizona	8,392,343	2,712,245	2,620,327	695,307	181,482	626,262	60,446	131,246	300,566	1,064,462
Arkansas	5,607,696	1,877,403	1,475,971	516,473	220,116	414,385	39,922	614,975	123,336	325,113
California	62,299,718	20,565,153	19,889,444	3,884,896	3,998,693	2,363,070	700,530	1,325,676	1,668,262	7,903,995
Colorado	6,074,191	1,876,238	1,650,902	402,328	282,044	321,030	97,860	445,392	310,208	688,188
Connecticut	6,592,166	2,725,135	2,300,141	253,774	518,338	239,084	163,579	12,383	137,653	242,080
Delaware	1,321,857	478,102	411,408	98,205	87,893	70,177	27,777	28,399	49,434	70,461
Florida	41,457,066	14,192,726	14,919,585	2,649,212	702,728	1,684,350	250,147	658,656	1,043,596	5,356,066
Georgia	13,315,387	4,378,547	3,530,141	1,682,644	501,463	1,098,316	244,908	573,027	596,736	709,606
Hawaii	1,790,455	556,342	560,225	129,187	86,406	147,847	27,422	5,448	177,927	99,651
Idaho	1,764,197	541,367	463,684	165,616	95,877	100,168	10,628	190,128	75,253	121,476
Illinois	24,010,223	8,543,906	6,707,872	1,465,401	1,579,551	1,503,199	529,424	2,107,469	545,827	1,027,573
Indiana	12,067,271	3,833,366	3,001,381	726,488	667,923	648,115	202,871	960,030	267,546	1,759,551
Iowa	6,919,377	1,651,495	1,615,955	260,549	289,551	244,226	33,093	2,284,600	171,257	368,652
Kansas	5,796,113	1,647,531	1,510,113	286,367	183,230	188,318	56,405	1,580,983	141,758	201,408
Kentucky	7,656,057	2,721,020	2,095,243	573,862	347,221	645,359	130,688	467,366	196,579	478,721
Louisiana	23,977,582	3,992,382	2,670,701	998,056	681,955	1,031,648	108,576	405,846	530,797	13,557,621
Maine	2,102,367	783,246	634,763	122,362	100,101	169,291	29,563	36,242	93,235	133,564
Maryland	11,149,173	3,400,791	3,044,985	548,727	355,865	336,097	180,717	92,144	2,910,945	278,902
Massachusetts	13,910,352	6,094,697	4,238,796	450,128	1,232,937	421,541	449,261	15,383	36,191	971,418
Michigan	18,992,009	6,724,394	6,278,104	1,097,864	1,805,021	1,238,789	156,131	400,930	307,310	983,467
Minnesota	8,383,405	2,463,226	2,040,194	385,236	621,790	295,404	129,064	1,444,186	276,146	728,159
Mississippi	9,117,775	2,077,362	1,481,210	765,999	218,832	507,104	79,634	1,237,840	155,180	2,594,615
Missouri	12,387,064	4,104,425	3,344,119	742,044	357,970	740,065	135,707	773,373	1,463,517	725,844
Montana	1,800,102	473,987	415,244	109,027	57,430	89,956	22,163	388,879	79,854	163,562
Nebraska	4,567,471	861,861	792,043	176,966	83,933	124,317	36,894	1,469,251	116,707	905,499
Nevada	2,572,606	884,916	840,773	265,492	218,090	124,333	29,941	9,227	100,597	99,236
New Hampshire	1,646,006	644,541	497,664	84,618	64,730	57,880	33,918	8,919	124,487	129,248
New Jersey	16,305,981	6,248,660	5,657,059	778,956	1,669,017	455,859	397,343	21,816	476,938	600,334

See footnotes at end of table.

FEDERAL GOVERNMENT EXPENDITURE FOR DIRECT PAYMENTS OTHER THAN FOR RETIREMENT AND DISABILITY, FOR SELECTED PROGRAMS, BY STATE AND OUTLYING AREA: FISCAL YEAR 2006—Continued
(In thousands of dollars)

State and outlying area	Total	Medicare benefits: Hospital insurance	Medicare benefits: Supplementary medical insurance	Excess earned income tax credits	Unemployment compensation	Food stamp payments	Housing assistance	Agricultural assistance	Federal employees life and health insurance	Other
New Mexico	2,795,890	781,968	737,026	338,221	99,684	253,366	24,727	104,764	165,789	290,344
New York	40,674,226	14,984,690	13,003,497	2,341,964	2,096,788	2,239,982	1,241,888	170,231	795,860	3,799,326
North Carolina	13,294,639	4,431,834	3,492,936	1,381,755	640,346	920,977	186,707	984,157	398,602	857,324
North Dakota	2,050,620	376,995	335,548	58,487	34,133	46,220	13,628	981,452	48,334	155,823
Ohio	20,784,723	7,865,338	6,629,691	1,322,692	1,041,247	1,290,223	481,592	657,123	528,211	968,607
Oklahoma	6,717,057	2,513,319	1,759,356	539,888	132,252	467,306	55,053	415,007	348,583	486,293
Oregon	5,250,410	1,713,144	1,609,039	343,539	430,682	483,746	45,953	117,513	237,851	268,943
Pennsylvania	28,899,383	11,775,797	9,609,069	1,235,856	1,931,529	1,182,259	415,290	191,874	754,252	1,803,457
Rhode Island	2,246,527	853,162	650,963	106,459	192,940	80,929	97,364	2,574	90,802	171,334
South Carolina	6,813,022	2,166,087	1,812,341	792,437	302,313	589,432	136,544	214,094	223,289	576,485
South Dakota	3,072,304	414,236	355,601	85,628	18,951	66,155	15,625	940,518	29,833	1,145,756
Tennessee	12,105,578	4,339,201	2,834,719	954,328	383,289	976,014	209,657	288,277	299,843	1,820,249
Texas	36,941,824	11,822,771	8,870,382	4,247,360	1,029,043	2,939,333	307,517	3,466,937	1,197,550	3,060,930
Utah	2,410,814	739,240	584,179	231,706	90,208	143,717	20,244	45,224	238,069	318,226
Vermont	973,964	335,395	248,985	49,483	77,259	60,295	12,681	24,534	32,779	132,554
Virginia	13,387,908	3,454,943	3,001,220	817,454	302,070	525,715	166,066	220,811	1,376,224	3,523,405
Washington	8,362,083	2,764,217	2,558,218	548,153	688,155	594,597	108,912	292,425	244,974	562,432
West Virginia	3,525,447	1,467,169	1,174,935	233,068	120,363	266,405	53,933	17,892	3,182	188,500
Wisconsin	8,550,278	2,881,145	2,520,659	464,819	728,798	346,650	71,300	633,924	235,681	667,303
Wyoming	794,112	244,585	194,146	49,084	27,089	26,309	7,420	56,308	143,131	46,041
Dist. of Columbia	2,760,045	522,201	459,960	81,094	87,447	104,154	94,648	297,018	864,488	249,034
American Samoa	9,711	0	0	0	0	5,600	0	0	0	4,111
Fed. States of Micronesia	8,128	0	0	0	0	0	0	0	0	8,128
Guam	91,550	996	806	0	0	54,545	3,424	41	20,043	11,695
Marshall Islands	1,798	0	0	0	0	0	0	0	0	1,798
No. Mariana Islands	13,627	0	0	0	0	8,449	1,141	0	0	4,037
Palau	2,545	0	0	0	0	0	-2	0	0	2,546
Puerto Rico	3,401,925	698,561	1,317,627	2,634	202,397	0	175,246	24,844	85,776	894,841
U.S. Virgin Islands	84,372	17,512	14,476	0	4,735	20,595	23,176	895	0	2,984
Undistributed	793,720	0	0	0	0	0	705,634	0	0	88,086

Source: U.S. Department of Commerce, Bureau of the Census, Consolidated Federal Funds Report for Fiscal Year 2006, April 2008.

Note: These amounts generally represent obligations incurred during the fiscal year. Detail may not add to total due to rounding. For additional information see the complete report at *http://www.census.gov/govs/www/cffr.html*.

Table 2.9
FEDERAL GOVERNMENT EXPENDITURE FOR GRANTS, BY AGENCY, BY STATE AND OUTLYING AREA: FISCAL YEAR 2006
(In thousands of dollars)

State and outlying area	*Total*	*Dept. of Agriculture*	*Appalachian Regional Commission*	*Dept. of Commerce*	*Corporation for National and Community Service*	*Corporation for Public Broadcasting*	*Dept. of Defense*	*Dept. of Education*
United States	$494,147,576	$25,556,578	$61,641	$1,810,347	$844,416	$156,883	$3,839,233	$37,755,763
Alabama	7,510,144	424,394	4,725	106,885	9,302	2,847	118,380	577,925
Alaska	3,077,330	91,724	0	105,571	4,671	1,484	42,618	301,942
Arizona	8,779,235	482,150	0	7,934	8,052	4,131	74,634	833,310
Arkansas	4,639,336	329,614	0	6,350	7,671	1,754	63,497	363,833
California	54,946,643	3,146,172	0	106,763	104,578	9,952	349,287	4,505,032
Colorado	6,035,250	263,589	0	70,034	-332	381	40,004	489,019
Connecticut	5,438,338	175,418	0	14,673	6,072	125	40,697	339,819
Delaware	1,370,948	76,728	0	7,392	2,298	0	16,425	117,787
Florida	22,451,928	1,206,097	0	55,916	27,600	10,614	128,902	1,828,555
Georgia	11,801,518	843,472	3,415	17,431	20,922	5,357	69,374	1,005,468
Hawaii	2,307,993	113,360	0	37,581	3,686	0	87,358	235,704
Idaho	2,005,307	127,036	0	6,171	4,095	1,736	33,917	166,251
Illinois	16,070,478	864,255	0	14,460	20,209	6,382	92,237	1,459,253
Indiana	8,087,822	400,290	0	8,197	10,524	3,829	62,162	632,451
Iowa	3,957,098	239,113	0	6,211	7,765	3,792	48,307	322,480
Kansas	3,358,269	223,704	0	6,165	7,979	1,950	50,051	360,119
Kentucky	6,926,671	397,817	10,777	14,237	8,202	2,164	25,311	544,630
Louisiana	22,833,262	486,265	0	22,573	52,038	1,685	317,120	1,381,126
Maine	2,682,519	97,194	0	18,441	5,541	87	25,491	155,882
Maryland	15,673,821	320,626	1,945	57,126	31,600	3,572	143,010	584,352
Massachusetts	13,170,970	377,174	25	45,587	43,012	534	134,672	742,966
Michigan	12,926,970	667,787	0	27,263	19,726	8,543	58,678	1,103,657
Minnesota	7,055,343	387,884	0	8,772	20,777	1,696	49,646	496,714
Mississippi	15,985,910	393,743	6,581	225,105	19,266	2,177	135,265	808,460
Missouri	8,600,622	438,136	0	9,875	10,838	5,740	44,999	617,848
Montana	2,026,142	104,139	0	4,302	8,113	1,322	33,956	197,382
Nebraska	2,527,536	171,013	0	3,636	5,457	3,013	10,951	226,531
Nevada	2,573,107	126,372	0	4,985	4,965	1,640	18,490	210,129
New Hampshire	1,742,533	63,985	0	61,854	5,130	1,375	37,780	140,918
New Jersey	11,295,472	476,523	0	23,355	9,447	3,439	79,345	894,689
New Mexico	4,652,039	246,610	0	10,530	7,851	3,937	31,404	407,579
New York	45,276,093	1,557,817	2,353	51,691	49,108	5,361	140,961	2,590,994
North Carolina	13,008,524	744,860	3,216	37,623	9,864	5,325	105,884	985,232
North Dakota	1,415,422	111,991	0	4,254	2,218	0	32,888	154,661
Ohio	16,518,305	749,520	5,131	144,993	17,366	5,140	82,068	1,135,798
Oklahoma	5,597,727	403,974	0	16,124	7,390	2,636	30,842	535,567
Oregon	5,454,868	281,435	0	55,958	18,530	1,511	45,705	436,402
Pennsylvania	20,196,551	747,228	5,205	25,504	28,902	4,792	362,730	1,199,636
Rhode Island	2,238,380	69,339	0	16,919	5,641	0	14,796	144,718
South Carolina	6,260,921	355,397	2,178	54,829	6,005	3,138	43,464	544,680
South Dakota	1,483,330	100,104	0	4,210	2,439	1,856	21,252	173,390
Tennessee	9,555,672	485,724	3,212	8,769	11,006	1,532	53,660	714,311
Texas	30,482,761	2,306,817	0	50,571	43,041	7,245	145,229	3,170,238
Utah	3,178,579	184,916	0	3,536	9,299	4,597	21,299	293,979
Vermont	1,367,553	63,991	75	5,102	3,873	0	20,837	103,610
Virginia	7,589,537	455,476	2,648	47,173	18,822	1,835	74,379	792,213
Washington	8,975,353	452,558	0	82,004	32,946	4,611	45,120	665,590
West Virginia	3,549,023	175,152	9,886	25,666	6,636	1,893	27,056	236,437
Wisconsin	7,155,186	375,842	2	21,253	23,374	4,953	46,895	615,448
Wyoming	2,069,327	46,919	0	677	2,256	1,036	12,290	114,316
Dist. of Columbia	4,175,208	161,963	266	21,695	31,735	0	33,263	301,189
American Samoa	151,703	8,987	0	1,653	4,834	537	0	28,624
Fed. States of Micronesia	90,920	3,016	0	0	0	0	0	5,905
Guam	289,265	21,043	0	2,852	5,913	0	1,303	49,660
Marshall Islands	78,479	314	0	0	0	0	0	2,190
No. Mariana Islands	126,346	10,123	0	12	550	0	0	17,799
Palau	33,731	405	0	0	0	0	0	3,532
Puerto Rico	4,788,644	1,898,201	0	10,199	4,913	3,627	6,218	650,630
U.S. Virgin Islands	285,313	21,084	0	1,705	700	0	7,128	37,203
Undistributed	244,300	0	0	0	0	0	0	0

See footnotes at end of table.

FEDERAL GOVERNMENT EXPENDITURE FOR GRANTS, BY AGENCY, BY STATE AND OUTLYING AREA: FISCAL YEAR 2006—Continued
(In thousands of dollars)

State and outlying area	Election Assistance Commission	Dept. of Energy	Environmental Protection Agency	Equal Employment Opportunity Commission	Dept. of Health and Human Services	Dept. of Homeland Security	Dept. of Housing and Urban Development	Institute of Museum and Library Services
United States	$58,266	$2,288,362	$3,837,564	$32,098	$283,179,805	$12,802,074	$36,600,100	$227,224
Alabama	0	57,308	48,312	0	4,049,749	191,484	382,978	3,022
Alaska	0	16,311	104,952	196	1,329,144	21,708	139,553	1,649
Arizona	0	18,562	77,545	503	5,638,241	13,866	399,342	5,481
Arkansas	0	6,652	36,679	0	2,815,132	58,090	154,486	1,895
California	0	248,582	289,970	2,549	34,448,727	243,463	3,660,230	20,331
Colorado	0	59,260	60,145	319	2,659,426	24,393	299,062	4,560
Connecticut	0	36,902	50,899	863	3,452,918	19,601	414,046	3,114
Delaware	7,447	21,623	29,105	423	690,283	8,689	53,368	1,039
Florida	0	28,831	122,135	1,599	11,692,693	2,245,177	1,077,449	9,973
Georgia	0	40,838	80,630	163	6,506,627	41,270	651,591	5,087
Hawaii	7,447	7,932	28,644	142	1,056,974	26,181	141,399	1,723
Idaho	0	14,782	44,179	335	1,026,071	5,285	60,751	1,336
Illinois	0	79,921	129,181	1,605	9,176,804	38,725	1,228,317	10,692
Indiana	0	44,482	61,614	550	4,804,317	25,307	321,797	3,760
Iowa	0	16,323	30,725	848	2,445,614	8,962	157,757	3,205
Kansas	0	12,247	38,726	375	1,838,835	52,906	114,129	3,001
Kentucky	0	13,181	57,627	211	4,214,292	46,634	296,206	2,577
Louisiana	0	9,284	72,667	55	5,742,870	5,626,443	6,623,893	3,351
Maine	0	5,056	39,524	250	1,823,893	10,474	125,091	1,618
Maryland	0	30,940	83,566	649	12,506,218	23,066	521,653	3,897
Massachusetts	0	139,611	93,067	1,704	8,765,705	64,178	1,020,445	6,333
Michigan	35,925	112,635	129,989	869	7,948,087	23,341	603,631	7,075
Minnesota	0	53,503	67,373	604	4,533,319	31,391	350,094	4,046
Mississippi	0	26,600	45,542	0	4,251,659	2,102,420	5,253,733	1,991
Missouri	0	27,258	80,614	851	5,629,976	39,638	363,400	4,904
Montana	7,447	17,622	49,099	294	843,546	4,864	71,203	1,875
Nebraska	0	6,587	39,637	599	1,442,022	11,958	109,432	1,742
Nevada	0	90,810	40,870	755	1,034,852	14,572	149,608	2,448
New Hampshire	0	4,483	36,278	132	903,007	38,949	103,114	1,238
New Jersey	0	36,589	88,129	488	6,815,912	20,847	855,167	5,648
New Mexico	0	81,217	45,225	314	2,484,964	6,343	138,814	2,395
New York	0	172,759	235,164	2,470	31,958,958	131,395	2,858,261	15,359
North Carolina	0	40,059	89,184	76	8,728,778	28,235	516,476	6,911
North Dakota	0	26,122	33,078	171	519,349	14,879	61,096	896
Ohio	0	104,615	87,645	2,008	11,043,080	44,735	900,456	7,288
Oklahoma	0	15,201	69,166	403	2,987,284	28,075	292,490	2,589
Oregon	0	21,288	54,943	533	3,044,230	29,549	283,696	2,280
Pennsylvania	0	161,272	129,360	2,187	13,010,324	109,169	973,237	10,811
Rhode Island	0	5,547	29,693	225	1,452,998	3,332	110,971	1,107
South Carolina	0	25,011	38,425	682	3,704,723	27,820	211,551	3,441
South Dakota	0	4,220	30,952	172	613,780	28,344	73,919	1,181
Tennessee	0	33,501	47,559	289	6,213,203	63,233	347,726	3,850
Texas	0	84,687	221,209	1,017	16,139,505	1,077,176	1,534,092	12,232
Utah	0	19,503	36,028	400	1,695,308	16,072	109,576	2,382
Vermont	0	5,653	33,260	72	794,173	1,345	62,608	1,444
Virginia	0	60,444	85,932	236	3,789,013	27,536	500,070	5,229
Washington	0	44,587	112,314	725	5,313,748	30,268	518,635	4,082
West Virginia	0	16,511	60,473	231	2,052,147	8,099	122,407	1,628
Wisconsin	0	46,598	91,863	1,206	4,365,954	10,627	283,681	4,406
Wyoming	0	8,666	21,682	107	369,347	706	21,019	1,732
Dist. of Columbia	0	24,067	67,248	190	1,649,111	40,053	241,932	4,088
American Samoa	0	173	2,733	0	15,295	2,800	1,404	120
Fed. States of Micronesia	0	0	0	0	450	825	0	0
Guam	0	181	5,664	0	38,887	623	32,897	115
Marshall Islands	0	0	0	0	112	0	0	0
No. Mariana Islands	0	174	4,115	0	10,259	839	3,888	130
Palau	0	0	0	0	103	0	0	54
Puerto Rico	0	1,161	42,696	445	1,060,275	−11,892	451,878	2,592
U.S. Virgin Islands	0	431	4,531	7	37,536	−1,992	13,436	271
Undistributed	0	0	0	0	0	0	230,960	0

See footnotes at end of table.

FEDERAL GOVERNMENT EXPENDITURE FOR GRANTS, BY AGENCY, BY STATE AND OUTLYING AREA: FISCAL YEAR 2006—Continued
(In thousands of dollars)

State and outlying area	Dept. of the Interior	Dept. of Justice	Dept. of Labor	NASA	National Archives and Records Admin.	National Endowment for the Arts	National Endowment for the Humanities	National Science Foundation
United States	$4,397,866	$5,582,772	$8,355,690	$939,342	$4,898	$96,016	$116,448	$5,060,612
Alabama	30,912	91,759	121,496	39,590	158	971	666	40,906
Alaska	75,417	41,089	54,678	3,272	0	822	872	28,720
Arizona	66,712	92,744	127,175	14,863	52	1,562	1,442	99,411
Arkansas	13,410	32,232	84,392	1,169	10	636	838	14,956
California	211,917	669,916	520,438	155,756	777	9,048	8,358	743,413
Colorado	201,617	70,591	108,278	45,979	0	2,528	1,262	252,539
Connecticut	2,994	49,396	106,175	3,589	122	1,394	1,791	50,685
Delaware	1,069	23,416	22,713	3,939	4	676	1,101	26,056
Florida	27,706	272,543	245,780	30,019	0	1,924	2,615	138,812
Georgia	12,416	192,860	177,641	16,165	97	2,763	2,466	97,205
Hawaii	27,396	33,992	42,677	16,596	6	896	1,021	42,942
Idaho	40,431	29,165	41,826	7,127	0	801	710	11,871
Illinois	24,063	222,337	370,170	13,942	207	2,900	5,644	211,926
Indiana	16,956	60,776	168,932	7,639	27	987	2,123	88,476
Iowa	5,696	47,285	74,787	5,210	270	754	849	41,431
Kansas	10,289	39,768	55,862	2,702	0	703	810	33,093
Kentucky	64,015	76,548	115,433	6,143	44	1,096	1,258	32,381
Louisiana	42,593	172,933	464,505	5,860	25	1,595	1,803	41,669
Maine	4,456	24,200	47,130	5,097	175	900	1,513	18,682
Maryland	7,254	121,191	179,948	112,938	160	2,483	2,927	112,856
Massachusetts	11,254	118,483	184,007	48,829	344	3,850	8,420	358,578
Michigan	13,685	123,637	383,592	17,150	0	1,617	2,988	158,411
Minnesota	12,013	58,738	122,327	2,931	0	3,440	1,947	69,401
Mississippi	16,693	127,218	184,402	4,221	0	1,115	1,689	22,343
Missouri	14,166	105,781	139,964	11,622	5	2,368	3,722	70,864
Montana	99,284	32,256	32,057	8,874	10	967	547	25,853
Nebraska	4,985	49,217	36,026	2,880	0	787	1,098	26,310
Nevada	268,832	64,251	49,955	1,858	0	671	540	13,043
New Hampshire	6,125	40,464	27,769	11,117	0	763	778	19,524
New Jersey	3,442	133,495	212,135	12,575	270	1,390	2,632	122,966
New Mexico	635,359	39,516	55,593	3,928	10	1,234	1,596	38,316
New York	11,646	457,350	445,658	30,103	244	14,998	11,814	390,988
North Carolina	13,023	102,979	293,765	7,358	132	1,340	3,606	119,614
North Dakota	46,115	27,250	25,558	10,506	7	691	552	10,704
Ohio	19,730	116,152	312,167	26,059	71	1,860	2,874	90,008
Oklahoma	20,478	79,376	79,731	8,574	0	991	840	30,898
Oregon	156,581	60,932	151,018	4,986	6	1,145	1,209	61,459
Pennsylvania	54,853	169,663	373,222	19,856	0	2,756	5,123	206,924
Rhode Island	1,460	24,595	38,660	5,003	130	948	621	33,755
South Carolina	3,398	62,975	134,249	3,835	122	937	846	35,525
South Dakota	56,295	26,226	24,712	2,054	9	670	560	10,238
Tennessee	10,466	70,231	157,039	7,690	119	944	2,193	41,015
Texas	43,254	445,394	672,858	63,944	309	2,641	3,275	205,656
Utah	234,302	30,671	62,376	6,317	7	1,036	657	42,800
Vermont	2,371	29,276	21,941	2,142	0	904	1,106	6,102
Virginia	30,508	135,689	223,175	54,071	377	1,428	4,986	101,222
Washington	36,777	117,904	218,720	9,466	0	2,112	1,588	130,959
West Virginia	42,223	63,979	62,867	26,004	0	641	572	8,776
Wisconsin	10,940	87,216	172,963	6,608	209	1,046	1,811	137,757
Wyoming	1,154,613	18,662	24,984	1,030	10	690	677	9,794
Dist. of Columbia	12,183	150,973	154,727	17,883	374	2,789	3,355	313,025
American Samoa	65,720	7,773	1,881	0	0	253	243	0
Fed. States of Micronesia	79,512	51	1,162	0	0	0	0	0
Guam	84,867	6,241	4,925	0	0	241	325	33
Marshall Islands	62,813	51	0	0	0	0	0	0
No. Mariana Islands	51,373	4,710	1,635	0	0	298	315	0
Palau	22,540	0	347	0	0	0	0	0
Puerto Rico	3,050	25,900	129,192	2,274	0	745	967	18,165
U.S. Virgin Islands	87,421	2,759	8,293	0	0	271	306	1,558
Undistributed	6,199	-4	0	0	0	0	0	0

See footnotes at end of table.

FEDERAL GOVERNMENT EXPENDITURE FOR GRANTS, BY AGENCY, BY STATE AND OUTLYING AREA: FISCAL YEAR 2006—Continued
(In thousands of dollars)

State and outlying area	Small Business Admin.	Social Security Admin.	Dept. of State	State Justice Institute	Tennessee Valley Authority (a)	Dept. of Transportation	Dept. of the Treasury (b)	Dept. of Veterans Affairs	Other
United States	$195,163	$13,910	$250,237	$2,207	$376,146	$58,218,271	$815,046	$580,960	$91,639
Alabama	11,672	0	1,544	0	93,428	1,089,808	59	9,620	244
Alaska	800	0	253	28	0	708,934	176	0	748
Arizona	2,262	0	3,614	4	0	800,438	481	3,835	891
Arkansas	2,354	0	1,013	0	0	640,814	110	1,577	170
California	11,661	2,386	31,775	64	0	5,403,269	1,548	25,872	14,808
Colorado	1,191	1,254	3,674	18	0	1,365,204	123	9,149	1,983
Connecticut	2,130	0	2,491	0	0	629,289	469	31,553	1,112
Delaware	650	0	643	1	0	257,298	46	18	713
Florida	6,388	0	5,762	7	0	3,257,901	10,857	13,957	2,113
Georgia	2,463	0	4,720	10	6,114	1,978,333	2,146	11,970	2,505
Hawaii	500	0	1,337	0	0	391,527	576	0	398
Idaho	894	0	580	1	0	373,404	136	5,887	530
Illinois	7,948	0	10,583	286	357	2,053,901	2,683	19,826	1,666
Indiana	2,423	0	3,766	5	0	1,350,524	513	4,341	1,054
Iowa	3,499	296	3,031	7	0	468,917	206	12,946	812
Kansas	1,056	0	1,788	26	0	496,723	109	4,445	709
Kentucky	8,457	0	1,469	0	33,027	937,261	332	14,196	1,145
Louisiana	2,931	0	1,859	1	0	1,742,500	1,528	12,528	1,561
Maine	740	0	705	2	0	260,454	167	9,266	490
Maryland	2,233	669	4,424	221	0	804,272	1,887	6,092	2,046
Massachusetts	2,358	4,751	18,784	0	0	953,821	399	17,659	4,421
Michigan	5,062	2,339	4,614	286	0	1,443,103	2,665	19,862	755
Minnesota	2,063	0	4,372	4	0	743,033	594	26,576	2,086
Mississippi	18,875	500	877	2	20,222	2,301,791	700	11,407	1,310
Missouri	1,654	0	3,279	3	0	944,358	444	27,077	1,239
Montana	1,931	0	923	4	0	474,288	32	3,451	499
Nebraska	602	0	2,006	0	0	361,619	87	8,958	383
Nevada	1,969	0	602	25	0	463,247	40	7,436	140
New Hampshire	1,580	0	661	32	0	229,724	135	4,284	1,334
New Jersey	3,282	0	4,065	2	0	1,464,791	2,593	21,746	510
New Mexico	4,182	0	1,891	18	0	398,784	68	3,307	1,052
New York	10,392	1,714	37,754	183	0	4,006,799	10,495	65,443	7,861
North Carolina	5,698	0	4,816	22	1,850	1,143,965	2,865	4,339	1,429
North Dakota	1,585	0	245	1	0	328,321	30	1,969	286
Ohio	5,135	0	7,171	6	0	1,586,217	451	14,311	6,250
Oklahoma	2,019	0	1,880	0	0	948,534	118	31,838	711
Oregon	1,587	0	3,199	10	0	731,463	728	2,959	1,526
Pennsylvania	6,931	0	10,030	14	0	2,546,227	3,573	25,989	1,033
Rhode Island	1,555	0	1,292	2	0	268,274	151	5,319	1,330
South Carolina	1,564	0	2,440	3	0	985,648	316	7,541	179
South Dakota	795	0	341	0	0	302,338	75	2,847	353
Tennessee	5,079	0	1,798	124	221,017	1,041,832	2,324	4,363	1,862
Texas	7,028	0	10,067	61	0	4,198,438	11,699	21,809	3,270
Utah	719	0	1,243	5	0	398,289	373	2,415	473
Vermont	2,897	0	581	9	0	199,589	108	2,959	1,525
Virginia	8,831	0	5,535	343	131	1,152,727	3,096	4,680	1,731
Washington	3,493	0	4,309	5	0	1,129,337	902	11,681	911
West Virginia	3,862	0	366	21	0	592,768	87	2,084	552
Wisconsin	3,815	0	2,907	0	0	820,341	299	15,354	1,819
Wyoming	500	0	240	0	0	256,151	25	927	273
Dist. of Columbia	3,514	0	26,709	330	0	530,336	380,976	0	1,234
American Samoa	297	0	0	0	0	8,376	0	0	0
Fed. States of Micronesia	0	0	0	0	0	0	0	0	0
Guam	500	0	0	11	0	32,835	149	0	0
Marshall Islands	0	0	0	0	0	13,000	0	0	0
No. Mariana Islands	0	0	0	0	0	19,068	0	1,060	0
Palau	0	0	0	0	0	6,750	0	0	0
Puerto Rico	1,055	0	137	0	0	119,224	364,296	2,232	463
U.S. Virgin Islands	500	0	71	0	0	62,093	0	0	0
Undistributed	0	0	0	0	0	0	0	0	7,145

Source: U.S. Department of Commerce, Bureau of the Census, Consolidated Federal Funds Report for Fiscal Year 2006, April 2008.

(a) Payments in lieu of taxes have been categorized as "grants."

(b) Includes Treasury payments to recipients that are separate from the government of the District of Columbia and Washington Metropolitan Transit Authority (WMATA), as well as distributions to state and local governments of seized cash assets and proceeds from the sale of other seized assets.

Table 2.10
FEDERAL GOVERNMENT EXPENDITURE FOR PROCUREMENT CONTRACTS, BY AGENCY, BY STATE AND OUTLYING AREA: FISCAL YEAR 2006
(In thousands of dollars)

State and outlying area	Dept. of Defense and nondefense Total	Department of Defense				
		Total	Army	Navy	Air Force	Other defense
United States	$408,664,580	$265,730,889	$83,410,784	$72,534,173	$59,651,560	$50,134,372
Alabama	8,329,134	6,735,003	3,157,297	368,960	460,317	2,748,430
Alaska	2,171,578	1,670,792	747,062	59,778	467,829	396,123
Arizona	10,625,210	9,393,824	2,723,364	2,622,644	913,913	3,133,903
Arkansas	1,332,943	883,227	510,926	21,913	174,977	175,411
California	43,270,738	32,131,268	5,420,955	7,203,687	14,295,835	5,210,791
Colorado	7,521,707	4,114,693	879,993	111,506	2,257,484	865,710
Connecticut	8,367,983	7,784,917	1,937,722	3,954,212	1,248,886	644,096
Delaware	250,300	130,905	47,659	7,007	49,281	26,958
Florida	14,829,719	10,801,789	3,644,983	2,910,459	3,166,178	1,080,168
Georgia	10,103,277	5,545,836	2,031,051	586,240	2,448,585	479,961
Hawaii	2,147,829	1,863,310	533,348	504,619	344,418	480,925
Idaho	1,714,520	165,761	99,293	6,154	43,138	17,175
Illinois	6,805,297	3,284,062	1,198,550	370,312	742,852	972,348
Indiana	5,354,952	4,579,745	3,342,376	547,914	199,926	489,530
Iowa	1,972,348	948,206	287,787	139,385	433,918	87,115
Kansas	2,754,696	1,697,922	698,784	16,264	853,419	129,456
Kentucky	7,297,719	5,388,425	1,002,974	617,008	325,868	3,442,575
Louisiana	9,533,644	4,990,077	3,501,977	688,195	84,438	715,467
Maine	1,248,854	1,074,420	106,677	629,599	11,107	327,036
Maryland	21,803,858	10,245,393	4,159,927	3,536,256	1,063,865	1,485,345
Massachusetts	10,929,536	9,010,720	2,249,268	3,910,368	1,724,820	1,126,264
Michigan	5,853,081	3,900,252	2,988,794	323,419	225,501	362,538
Minnesota	2,680,739	1,534,157	486,694	544,236	75,017	428,210
Mississippi	7,019,655	5,719,791	1,133,602	3,813,462	642,022	130,704
Missouri	11,112,012	9,430,656	3,901,575	3,536,844	1,286,251	705,986
Montana	531,017	247,921	134,702	2,922	73,817	36,480
Nebraska	1,033,895	720,150	123,621	11,523	375,347	209,658
Nevada	2,273,844	742,596	217,107	239,114	232,001	54,373
New Hampshire	1,410,698	1,178,851	611,429	267,286	204,512	95,623
New Jersey	8,403,324	6,245,751	2,776,371	1,657,899	306,205	1,505,276
New Mexico	6,029,507	1,059,642	443,795	74,146	424,377	117,324
New York	11,871,812	8,087,810	2,246,063	3,719,368	980,018	1,142,361
North Carolina	4,669,103	2,743,859	994,756	753,076	256,071	739,957
North Dakota	429,323	237,676	87,229	1,797	74,761	73,889
Ohio	8,874,962	6,001,049	1,684,314	641,132	2,091,084	1,584,519
Oklahoma	2,875,659	2,064,140	643,273	179,428	765,693	475,746
Oregon	1,332,094	570,318	426,163	57,186	15,170	71,798
Pennsylvania	10,848,651	7,601,280	3,379,254	2,172,157	487,548	1,562,320
Rhode Island	601,327	452,781	38,690	381,819	2,128	30,144
South Carolina	4,997,372	2,107,479	646,286	891,669	288,451	281,073
South Dakota	622,805	387,018	85,528	52,991	50,614	197,886
Tennessee	8,850,714	2,788,690	664,301	147,061	1,677,379	299,949
Texas	35,617,605	27,083,092	6,729,415	7,002,364	9,469,457	3,881,856
Utah	3,149,684	2,290,967	550,789	68,076	1,481,212	190,890
Vermont	870,173	751,733	246,304	468,610	13,248	23,571
Virginia	41,915,022	29,725,283	6,809,412	11,178,380	3,417,174	8,320,317
Washington	8,134,467	4,795,598	686,466	1,663,758	1,180,328	1,265,046
West Virginia	1,157,727	375,139	227,916	34,724	34,950	77,550
Wisconsin	3,323,058	2,166,713	952,183	489,154	67,671	657,705
Wyoming	430,748	164,342	18,336	779	54,714	90,513
Dist. of Columbia	14,225,192	3,922,466	1,340,365	1,532,074	398,042	651,986
American Samoa	30,891	13,673	1,503	0	0	12,171
Fed. States of Micronesia	128	0	0	0	0	0
Guam	401,144	388,125	728	294,936	72,906	19,554
Marshall Islands	109,867	109,867	109,867	0	0	0
No. Mariana Islands	1,829	1,414	151	1,343	0	-80
Palau	0	0	0	0	0	0
Puerto Rico	672,882	369,810	92,875	51,222	1,259	224,453
U.S. Virgin Islands	11,415	973	961	8	5	0
Undistributed (a)	17,925,314	7,309,530	3,647,993	1,467,729	1,615,571	578,238

Source: U.S. Department of Commerce, Bureau of the Census, Consolidated Federal Funds Report for Fiscal Year 2006, April 2008.

FEDERAL GOVERNMENT EXPENDITURE FOR PROCUREMENT CONTRACTS, BY AGENCY, BY STATE AND OUTLYING AREA: FISCAL YEAR 2006—Continued
(In thousands of dollars)

	Nondefense agencies							
State and outlying area	Total	Dept. of Agriculture	Dept. of Commerce	Dept. of Education	Dept. of Energy	Environmental Protection Agency	General Services Admin.	Dept. of Health and Human Services
United States	$142,933,691	$4,473,867	$2,096,898	$1,063,826	$22,468,300	$1,559,229	$11,890,210	$11,015,019
Alabama	1,594,130	39,971	2,105	116	1,694	8,122	128,010	48,129
Alaska	500,786	50,065	45,692	0	653	2,091	50,801	9,702
Arizona	1,231,386	39,628	2,992	268	15,563	998	85,992	68,568
Arkansas	449,716	43,408	63	95	855	256	31,413	48,161
California	11,139,471	353,336	101,759	34,883	2,497,251	64,946	752,763	593,958
Colorado	3,407,014	157,451	36,953	6,111	824,114	36,064	177,866	54,693
Connecticut	583,066	3,409	1,592	53,683	2,119	3,733	34,974	13,979
Delaware	119,394	6,602	1,065	170	121	16,177	9,181	2,461
Florida	4,027,930	25,570	56,496	537	41,281	20,085	342,978	18,107
Georgia	4,557,441	78,252	33,783	1,121	11,443	69,882	485,931	2,517,315
Hawaii	284,519	4,760	13,975	2,414	1,057	15	32,837	4,393
Idaho	1,548,759	57,073	1,077	103	1,180,997	269	18,904	4,249
Illinois	3,521,235	183,310	4,367	14,844	774,696	28,210	192,554	71,357
Indiana	775,207	25,657	8,129	80	1,927	2,504	55,588	31,728
Iowa	1,024,142	240,580	6,237	81,959	29,385	2,246	19,114	171,635
Kansas	1,056,774	123,061	1,385	576	47	18,567	52,715	7,714
Kentucky	1,909,294	20,830	7,904	247	80,550	11,469	144,700	11,884
Louisiana	4,543,567	116,469	6,363	375	157,895	3,719	187,255	27,584
Maine	174,434	13,818	1,867	107	3	1,852	13,325	852
Maryland	11,558,464	77,011	520,344	305,576	266,595	112,950	689,860	3,634,797
Massachusetts	1,918,816	15,225	35,488	30,955	2,551	79,415	256,290	103,275
Michigan	1,952,829	58,426	3,908	1,516	1,015	29,133	838,663	151,557
Minnesota	1,146,582	304,380	2,810	1,236	7,882	7,495	96,921	67,081
Mississippi	1,299,864	31,458	91,285	104	273	1,105	248,416	11,077
Missouri	1,681,356	251,751	4,676	356	478,180	13,585	190,950	67,866
Montana	283,096	51,944	764	117	9,234	353	22,778	28,061
Nebraska	313,745	58,193	2,639	252	2,663	6,288	40,788	6,226
Nevada	1,531,249	6,143	7,911	535	1,078,128	7,916	31,328	11,904
New Hampshire	231,847	9,960	2,149	3,634	1,547	2,548	20,191	4,243
New Jersey	2,157,573	11,232	13,950	31,828	82,865	83,161	201,182	51,200
New Mexico	4,969,864	21,097	1,516	127	4,307,476	1,950	132,722	100,461
New York	3,784,002	37,346	14,606	18,208	718,054	29,022	591,634	97,296
North Carolina	1,925,244	56,806	13,488	45,987	228,186	67,280	114,289	259,002
North Dakota	191,646	25,894	223	88	7,050	836	13,183	30,833
Ohio	2,873,913	21,097	5,590	311	908,893	220,220	245,813	160,902
Oklahoma	811,520	13,427	4,838	2,411	11,968	10,676	134,581	59,474
Oregon	761,776	151,888	10,581	6,617	3,292	9,848	90,401	26,328
Pennsylvania	3,247,372	70,581	30,726	10,107	566,596	131,239	218,066	472,967
Rhode Island	148,546	10	1,141	1,308	1,223	9,248	19,506	5,074
South Carolina	2,889,893	19,659	27,607	210	1,774,663	743	46,318	167,900
South Dakota	235,786	14,252	1,105	11,083	5,866	6	9,611	38,466
Tennessee	6,062,024	46,383	1,064	177	2,807,221	1,199	120,886	24,767
Texas	8,534,514	180,611	19,710	34,331	510,148	63,022	509,836	171,320
Utah	858,717	33,343	2,210	196	1,475	2,146	40,948	24,100
Vermont	118,440	888	247	143	18	1,292	14,424	696
Virginia	12,189,739	173,590	588,611	53,235	565,736	214,321	1,999,847	556,061
Washington	3,338,869	81,673	49,142	735	2,170,764	31,495	184,009	48,898
West Virginia	782,588	57,859	20,128	1,122	112,134	659	45,782	15,620
Wisconsin	1,156,345	125,093	3,526	2	2,902	37,307	55,974	97,192
Wyoming	266,406	12,177	174	0	5,741	178	7,585	820
Dist. of Columbia	10,302,726	243,817	122,891	300,055	108,687	55,083	1,716,755	373,244
American Samoa	17,218	16,399	93	0	0	0	61	0
Fed. States of Micronesia	128	0	0	0	0	0	0	0
Guam	13,020	228	154	0	0	0	7,539	0
Marshall Islands	0	0	0	0	0	0	0	0
No. Mariana Islands	415	29	0	−7	0	0	−99	0
Palau	0	0	0	0	0	0	0	0
Puerto Rico	303,072	2,175	383	88	0	41	27,249	1,230
U.S. Virgin Islands	10,441	3	40	0	0	0	3,485	4
Undistributed (a)	10,615,785	608,567	157,377	3,494	97,622	36,259	85,535	438,607

See footnotes at end of table.

FEDERAL GOVERNMENT EXPENDITURE FOR PROCUREMENT CONTRACTS, BY AGENCY, BY STATE AND OUTLYING AREA: FISCAL YEAR 2006—Continued
(In thousands of dollars)

	Nondefense agencies—continued							
State and outlying area	*Dept. of Homeland Security*	*Dept. of Housing and Urban Development*	*Dept. of the Interior*	*Dept. of Justice*	*Dept. of Labor*	*NASA*	*National Archives and Records Admin.*	*National Science Foundation*
United States	$14,952,036	$938,803	$4,862,143	$5,006,868	$1,325,671	$11,319,554	$150,309	$209,915
Alabama	112,722	4,141	24,828	24,923	468	557,457	0	0
Alaska	85,939	45	85,738	7,705	10,153	20,581	60	0
Arizona	178,520	2,350	276,995	41,160	10,434	82,146	0	18
Arkansas	13,064	397	29,798	23,569	23	4,145	1,925	0
California	600,066	4,272	471,807	259,127	92,631	1,809,850	8,761	2,608
Colorado	439,768	51,433	288,245	30,467	8,334	756,120	2,371	15,915
Connecticut	60,223	1,281	4,291	44,343	8,921	60,253	0	183
Delaware	3,885	95	860	1,942	2,081	7,516	0	0
Florida	389,057	43,514	122,302	148,769	10,395	880,742	0	115
Georgia	292,900	59,168	38,073	174,987	3,845	26,728	7,416	0
Hawaii	25,605	15	41,029	4,215	167	16,339	0	0
Idaho	7,803	178	53,071	3,818	9	8,078	22	616
Illinois	89,594	2,847	34,904	45,539	24,395	28,500	115	734
Indiana	49,925	2,674	18,580	30,965	17,416	108,429	7	23
Iowa	9,673	189	8,236	5,917	11,288	9,051	2,432	0
Kansas	4,027	4,828	10,336	28,139	5,845	3,565	4,432	0
Kentucky	65,659	319	13,092	47,811	25,093	7,183	26	0
Louisiana	3,089,943	23,602	67,292	59,792	4,056	376,719	385	0
Maine	9,024	140	6,747	2,278	13,020	5,714	0	0
Maryland	1,000,833	127,515	201,637	239,916	103,560	1,314,526	72,053	10,343
Massachusetts	117,103	−381	59,465	41,923	35,856	159,558	4,938	1,036
Michigan	29,048	615	28,917	37,205	27,078	26,533	1,949	793
Minnesota	19,276	8,699	14,364	37,892	7,833	13,595	382	6
Mississippi	458,764	208	21,543	15,178	2,923	194,593	0	0
Missouri	55,409	350	16,906	33,064	28,123	15,132	6,151	364
Montana	1,035	0	47,128	2,741	5,518	15,034	0	32
Nebraska	2,768	28	9,926	3,675	742	3,360	0	4
Nevada	43,036	518	79,525	6,771	30,844	4,229	0	11
New Hampshire	7,231	3,238	4,646	4,155	4	25,057	0	37
New Jersey	131,945	1,356	33,837	72,572	25,183	59,261	124	21
New Mexico	82,908	973	119,208	6,554	9,293	59,402	0	24
New York	179,686	31,181	32,818	145,720	51,423	92,763	4,380	817
North Carolina	66,133	233	20,936	121,019	53	12,775	7	1,141
North Dakota	4,261	−2	12,012	11,131	5,591	12,657	0	0
Ohio	87,356	2,873	29,100	34,446	62,566	200,592	46	7
Oklahoma	11,619	41,945	31,298	55,434	13,767	45,024	0	759
Oregon	19,044	501	89,337	15,351	30,282	9,148	0	0
Pennsylvania	41,282	72,808	89,020	101,380	35,350	35,293	253	183
Rhode Island	7,454	226	2,362	2,788	4,777	6,757	0	0
South Carolina	35,632	22	7,174	37,469	885	3,900	30	0
South Dakota	2,007	64	50,670	9,461	541	2,265	4	0
Tennessee	103,961	938	17,409	21,203	8,190	52,054	1,521	74
Texas	771,389	161,105	97,823	314,692	122,271	2,891,365	9,812	741
Utah	1,622	726	80,328	2,785	1,933	472,341	0	0
Vermont	26,338	0	1,506	253	6,731	3,474	0	0
Virginia	3,002,026	62,815	872,023	714,532	119,962	514,389	3,064	79,506
Washington	116,904	5,085	111,215	13,282	13,343	26,766	763	520
West Virginia	29,600	4	16,930	86,637	10,742	62,178	404	37
Wisconsin	44,929	996	17,571	64,158	1,365	25,281	20	0
Wyoming	3,751	4	32,592	2,399	1	1,692	0	0
Dist. of Columbia	2,433,489	200,943	395,354	1,092,251	271,228	116,383	5,061	89,164
American Samoa	9	0	0	0	0	0	0	0
Fed. States of Micronesia	0	0	0	0	0	0	0	0
Guam	1,249	0	650	0	0	0	0	0
Marshall Islands	0	0	0	0	0	0	0	0
No. Mariana Islands	0	0	160	0	0	0	0	0
Palau	0	0	0	0	0	0	0	0
Puerto Rico	16,510	1,630	7,381	14,677	18,147	2,333	0	0
U.S. Virgin Islands	194	0	518	1,292	0	0	0	0
Undistributed (a)	468,835	10,102	612,631	657,397	20,992	70,724	11,394	4,083

See footnotes at end of table.

FEDERAL GOVERNMENT EXPENDITURE FOR PROCUREMENT CONTRACTS, BY AGENCY, BY STATE AND OUTLYING AREA: FISCAL YEAR 2006—Continued
(In thousands of dollars)

	Nondefense agencies—continued							
State and outlying area	*U.S. Postal Service (b)*	*Small Business 0Admin.*	*Social Security Admin.*	*Dept. of State*	*Dept. of Transportation*	*Dept. of the Treasury*	*Dept. of Veterans Affairs*	*Other nondefense (c)*
United States	$15,142,998	$87,132	$780,180	$1,596,882	$5,197,975	$3,933,739	$16,349,337	$6,512,799
Alabama	194,246	253	5,587	36,005	4,172	4,329	84,353	312,499
Alaska	39,615	0	25	21,100	53,333	986	16,325	178
Arizona	242,738	0	486	3,352	27,219	885	148,558	2,516
Arkansas	127,050	4	512	60	782	1,587	122,314	235
California	1,647,180	3,893	31,046	23,927	293,312	674,007	790,250	27,838
Colorado	258,005	1,008	744	5,053	65,839	6,408	122,696	61,356
Connecticut	205,066	2	8,510	5,187	7,418	2,201	56,361	5,337
Delaware	41,895	0	19	495	232	960	22,779	859
Florida	836,969	506	1,935	19,550	581,061	13,194	438,758	36,006
Georgia	406,974	819	5,651	4,599	57,084	49,935	181,340	50,195
Hawaii	57,891	313	393	472	61,356	1,713	15,219	343
Idaho	56,433	0	601	417	2,435	121,095	31,077	434
Illinois	752,450	771	13,609	22,338	54,450	198,229	910,829	72,590
Indiana	293,173	19	801	1,600	18,257	3,700	84,964	19,063
Iowa	174,495	998	539	49	7,524	204,254	32,346	5,995
Kansas	171,935	8	1,060	253	18,735	809	596,779	1,958
Kentucky	180,474	22	338	2,611	6,479	9,154	81,170	1,192,278
Louisiana	186,454	42	307	1,660	146,262	618	76,590	10,184
Maine	81,156	0	89	30	5,425	65	18,663	261
Maryland	322,118	10,545	491,641	101,932	810,385	808,659	188,454	147,213
Massachusetts	415,084	198	2,723	3,337	236,457	25,770	282,448	10,102
Michigan	525,540	469	8,352	5,508	13,398	24,922	134,519	3,765
Minnesota	302,124	257	335	11,299	22,658	6,058	187,243	26,758
Mississippi	106,009	5	428	123	2,509	2,726	103,818	7,319
Missouri	358,931	403	7,294	12,110	26,628	6,501	103,832	2,794
Montana	51,033	0	264	22	27,619	994	18,082	342
Nebraska	108,008	0	197	330	6,799	121	50,518	10,220
Nevada	102,944	0	78	285	20,347	748	96,353	1,694
New Hampshire	81,735	0	162	36,196	6,490	571	12,206	5,845
New Jersey	573,228	184	8,909	11,939	651,261	9,204	76,242	26,890
New Mexico	76,577	0	164	845	13,651	976	33,142	797
New York	1,113,866	987	20,709	19,551	79,937	179,725	301,165	23,108
North Carolina	407,366	58	1,026	33,291	60,402	2,496	174,485	238,783
North Dakota	41,054	0	340	67	3,847	8,415	13,903	261
Ohio	587,448	872	1,726	6,780	32,515	18,298	232,469	13,994
Oklahoma	160,835	0	85	6,985	119,501	4,356	77,080	5,456
Oregon	166,422	0	764	5,965	42,035	2,555	79,999	1,415
Pennsylvania	703,436	5,295	7,929	31,035	42,515	59,551	384,647	137,114
Rhode Island	64,487	0	37	80	273	2,954	18,610	230
South Carolina	158,966	2	526	21,664	35,104	21	529,420	21,977
South Dakota	45,651	0	82	218	5,109	160	37,382	1,783
Tennessee	295,060	14	382	594	21,421	122,285	696,608	1,718,612
Texas	984,387	5,078	1,282	12,101	219,944	51,083	1,355,739	46,725
Utah	111,671	4	26,478	391	8,684	11,639	49,489	−13,795
Vermont	43,128	0	25	39	898	318	17,759	262
Virginia	405,946	14,535	37,125	521,866	575,838	316,868	308,597	489,245
Washington	291,809	27	1,833	2,827	51,352	10,031	120,427	5,971
West Virginia	95,918	0	48	1,123	1,443	131,900	82,622	9,698
Wisconsin	279,532	0	1,086	7,886	13,124	622	370,139	7,639
Wyoming	25,694	0	128	0	15,814	2,003	14,866	140,786
Dist. of Columbia	112,100	31,710	11,313	518,927	432,486	705,716	186,359	779,708
American Samoa	206	0	125	0	199	0	125	0
Fed. States of Micronesia	0	0	0	126	0	2	0	0
Guam	2,205	0	33	5	489	35	433	0
Marshall Islands	0	0	0	0	0	0	0	0
No. Mariana Islands	224	0	0	0	109	0	0	0
Palau	0	0	0	0	0	0	0	0
Puerto Rico	63,459	300	56	0	1,122	863	144,769	659
U.S. Virgin Islands	4,597	0	29	0	255	10	6	10
Undistributed (a)	0	7,531	74,217	72,677	183,982	120,453	6,034,013	839,292

See footnotes at end of table.

FEDERAL GOVERNMENT EXPENDITURE FOR PROCUREMENT CONTRACTS, BY AGENCY, BY STATE AND OUTLYING AREA: FISCAL YEAR 2006—Continued

Source: U.S. Department of Commerce, Bureau of the Census, Consolidated Federal Funds Report for Fiscal Year 2006, April 2008.

Note: Statistics covering federal government procurement contracts, are provided by the U.S. Postal Service (USPS) for Postal Service procurement and by the Federal Procurement Data Center (FPDC) within the General Services Administration for procurement actions of nearly all other federal agencies, including the U.S. Department of Defense. Data on the procurement contracts of the Federal Aviation Administration (FAA) are obtained directly from that agency. Amounts provided by the USPS represent actual outlays for contractual commitments, while amounts provided by the FPDC represent the value of obligations for contract actions, and do not reflect actual federal government expenditures. In general, only current-year contract actions are reported for data provided by the FPDC; however, multiple-year obligations may be reflected for contract actions of less than three years' duration.

(a) For all agencies, this line includes procurement purchases made using government-issued purchase cards.

(b) Data shown for U.S. Postal Service represent actual outlays for contractual commitments, while all other amounts shown represent the value of contract actions, and do not reflect federal government expenditures. Nonpostal data generally involve only current actions; however, multiple obligations may be reflected for contract actions of less than three years' duration. Negative amounts represent the deobligation of prior-year contracts.

(c) Includes Fiscal Year 2000 procurement data for the Tennessee Valley Authority, which did not provide Fiscal Year 2006 procurement data.

Table 2.11
FEDERAL GOVERNMENT EXPENDITURE FOR SALARIES AND WAGES, BY AGENCY, BY STATE AND OUTLYING AREA: FISCAL YEAR 2006
(In thousands of dollars)

			Department of Defense							
					Military services					
									Army	
State and outlying area	Total	Nondefense civilian (a)	Total	Other defense civilian	Total	Active military	Inactive military	Civilian	Total	Active military
United States	$243,477,854	$149,092,887	$94,384,967	$4,869,391	$89,515,576	$56,076,489	$10,309,983	$23,129,104	$36,722,979	$20,081,264
Alabama	3,685,934	1,954,269	1,731,665	78,674	1,652,991	569,010	323,668	760,313	1,275,433	318,038
Alaska	2,091,636	756,500	1,335,136	12,355	1,322,781	1,110,957	49,961	161,863	682,020	564,552
Arizona	3,914,326	2,499,965	1,414,361	54,130	1,360,231	988,064	68,707	303,460	413,756	227,677
Arkansas	1,597,515	1,038,594	558,921	4,861	554,060	239,529	201,668	112,863	262,667	4,160
California	2,380,726	13,161,757	10,219,969	366,162	9,853,807	6,867,014	660,546	2,326,247	1,148,155	351,287
Colorado	4,843,710	2,845,195	1,998,515	146,656	1,851,859	1,385,576	120,474	345,809	956,129	776,008
Connecticut	1,748,585	1,218,856	529,729	45,329	484,400	332,517	81,827	70,056	83,402	1,035
Delaware	527,946	264,289	263,657	2,653	261,004	164,925	37,929	58,150	31,743	315
Florida	11,268,890	6,764,119	4,504,771	131,670	4,373,101	2,981,817	341,721	1,049,563	501,018	116,220
Georgia	9,271,282	4,211,151	5,060,131	102,597	4,957,534	3,389,947	417,753	1,149,834	3,206,393	2,477,976
Hawaii	3,710,961	590,961	3,120,000	45,117	3,074,883	2,302,847	151,745	620,291	1,190,183	929,402
Idaho	963,569	656,620	306,949	1,766	305,183	183,991	72,606	48,586	86,425	918
Illinois	7,068,182	5,212,608	1,855,574	76,259	1,779,315	1,051,183	253,758	474,374	485,914	24,621
Indiana	2,611,636	1,808,908	802,728	180,096	622,632	50,898	325,316	246,418	378,435	21,000
Iowa	1,312,328	1,061,754	250,574	2,808	247,766	27,964	171,199	48,603	190,383	9,120
Kansas	2,607,276	1,309,891	1,297,385	15,834	1,281,551	889,660	201,183	190,708	1,052,631	736,222
Kentucky	3,863,479	1,608,320	2,255,159	41,270	2,213,889	1,837,451	195,495	180,943	2,160,468	1,810,703
Louisiana	2,835,782	1,694,884	1,140,898	16,174	1,124,724	694,143	213,759	216,822	670,851	368,104
Maine	968,820	533,561	435,259	18,503	416,756	120,494	46,442	249,820	56,758	10,752
Maryland	11,246,967	8,011,225	3,235,742	82,517	3,153,225	1,543,652	170,867	1,438,706	997,788	349,297
Massachusetts	3,754,582	3,115,808	638,774	71,592	567,182	156,754	162,097	248,331	234,008	12,873
Michigan	3,829,549	3,191,536	638,013	96,043	541,970	72,771	200,523	268,676	405,090	17,835
Minnesota	2,512,705	2,045,241	467,464	14,055	453,409	48,548	326,760	78,101	361,572	14,078
Mississippi	2,065,738	1,004,435	1,061,303	11,026	1,050,277	486,587	240,066	323,624	354,049	18,744
Missouri	4,554,898	2,919,216	1,635,682	78,844	1,556,838	723,735	583,169	249,934	1,215,452	497,970
Montana	973,165	724,537	248,628	1,368	247,260	146,235	57,373	43,652	66,709	720
Nebraska	1,394,626	763,450	631,176	13,693	617,483	370,865	107,682	138,936	144,635	6,120
Nevada	1,494,817	895,744	599,073	5,847	593,226	454,457	55,720	83,049	64,213	4,365
New Hampshire	686,020	559,122	126,898	10,574	116,324	53,193	31,523	31,608	44,651	130
New Jersey	4,483,444	3,362,329	1,121,115	47,968	1,073,147	327,314	159,175	586,658	606,916	44,950
New Mexico	2,209,036	1,338,669	870,367	23,547	846,820	505,378	72,537	268,905	182,319	19,980
New York	9,809,826	7,941,220	1,868,606	83,250	1,785,356	1,154,161	300,831	330,364	1,433,321	959,258
North Carolina	8,081,863	2,824,980	5,256,883	80,584	5,176,299	4,372,597	277,907	525,795	2,439,632	1,995,309
North Dakota	806,064	401,514	404,550	2,412	402,138	281,641	56,702	63,795	60,073	1,035
Ohio	5,764,378	3,849,464	1,914,914	456,846	1,458,068	446,008	240,236	771,824	270,084	24,255
Oklahoma	3,702,997	1,501,567	2,201,430	53,047	2,148,383	1,160,016	152,985	835,382	907,238	643,365
Oregon	2,007,059	1,716,125	290,934	1,508	289,426	49,199	128,472	111,755	190,183	7,650
Pennsylvania	6,903,900	5,246,205	1,657,695	424,913	1,232,782	161,921	410,026	660,835	675,258	48,384
Rhode Island	844,236	413,131	431,105	4,907	426,198	136,077	60,929	229,192	64,681	4,905
South Carolina	3,493,595	1,227,641	2,265,954	47,003	2,218,951	1,696,223	207,426	315,302	827,581	556,951
South Dakota	768,993	540,500	228,493	1,528	226,965	128,497	57,821	40,647	61,891	1,035
Tennessee	3,614,484	2,990,142	624,342	37,385	586,957	145,512	235,262	206,183	352,374	13,590
Texas	16,542,742	9,130,096	7,412,646	187,674	7,224,972	5,254,027	675,960	1,294,985	4,415,288	3,214,430
Utah	2,301,214	1,171,793	1,129,421	44,625	1,084,796	245,002	212,721	627,073	286,497	13,095
Vermont	469,622	363,842	105,780	2,542	103,238	11,934	72,465	18,839	79,496	945
Virginia	17,248,076	5,941,381	11,306,695	1,515,369	9,791,326	6,770,183	270,631	2,750,512	2,222,404	1,131,523
Washington	6,525,254	2,907,548	3,617,706	41,126	3,576,580	2,416,778	216,610	943,192	1,433,528	1,050,752
West Virginia	1,458,036	1,274,226	183,810	1,024	182,786	28,073	97,464	57,249	129,494	1,440
Wisconsin	2,073,595	1,714,917	358,678	5,741	352,937	40,501	234,117	7,319	273,771	8,810
Wyoming	552,192	342,982	209,210	1,139	208,071	140,149	30,701	37,221	35,255	180
Dist. of Columbia	17,160,707	15,133,429	2,027,278	64,602	1,962,676	1,113,104	80,569	769,003	863,522	664,860
American Samoa	5,417	4,640	777	0	777	727	0	50	50	0
Micronesia	0	0	0	0	0	0	0	0	0	0
Guam	348,369	39,843	308,526	5,336	303,190	233,475	18,986	50,729	10,987	1,890
Marshall Islands	0	0	0	0	0	0	0	0	0	0
No. Mariana Islands	7,993	7,944	49	0	49	38	0	11	11	0
Palau	0	0	0	0	0	0	0	0	0	0
Puerto Rico	1,013,271	793,823	219,448	6,842	212,606	11,504	167,196	33,906	178,156	2,430
U.S. Virgin Islands	58,253	53,832	4,421	0	4,421	1,666	717	2,038	2,038	0
Undistributed	4,436,589	4,436,589	0	0	0	0	0	0	0	0

Source: U.S. Department of Commerce, Bureau of the Census, Consolidated Federal Funds Report for Fiscal Year 2006, April 2008.

FEDERAL GOVERNMENT EXPENDITURE FOR SALARIES AND WAGES, BY AGENCY, BY STATE AND OUTLYING AREA: FISCAL YEAR 2006—Continued
(In thousands of dollars)

	Department of Defense—continued									
	Military services—continued									
	Army—continued		*Navy*				*Air Force*			
State and outlying area	*Inactive military*	*Civilian*	*Total*	*Active military*	*Inactive military*	*Civilian*	*Total*	*Active military*	*Inactive military*	*Civilian*
United States	$9,240,860	$7,400,855	$29,478,212	$20,746,229	$471,554	$8,260,429	$23,314,385	$15,248,996	$597,569	$7,467,820
Alabama	311,559	645,836	25,952	17,572	6,326	2,054	351,606	233,400	5,783	112,423
Alaska	39,738	77,730	6,881	5,297	768	816	633,880	541,108	9,455	83,317
Arizona	55,200	130,879	240,707	212,818	7,369	20,520	705,768	547,569	6,138	152,061
Arkansas	181,973	76,534	4,393	2,437	1,742	214	287,000	232,932	17,953	36,115
California	558,681	238,187	7,129,821	5,497,751	60,449	1,571,621	1,575,831	1,017,976	41,416	516,439
Colorado	96,212	83,909	46,270	35,961	8,002	2,307	849,460	573,607	16,260	259,593
Connecticut	69,706	12,661	372,689	322,899	3,375	46,415	28,309	8,583	8,746	10,980
Delaware	25,015	6,413	2,124	942	1,060	122	227,137	163,668	11,854	51,615
Florida	274,161	110,637	2,079,753	1,562,235	34,692	482,826	1,792,330	1,303,362	32,868	456,100
Georgia	383,936	344,481	563,936	387,666	11,789	164,481	1,187,205	524,305	22,028	640,872
Hawaii	132,229	128,552	1,400,545	1,000,411	3,922	396,212	484,155	373,034	15,594	95,527
Idaho	69,927	15,580	6,009	1,783	1,298	2,928	212,749	181,290	1,381	30,078
Illinois	223,505	237,788	756,404	675,822	18,378	62,204	536,997	350,740	11,875	174,382
Indiana	309,555	47,880	170,089	11,905	4,853	153,331	74,108	17,993	10,908	45,207
Iowa	154,995	26,268	8,682	5,703	2,823	156	48,701	13,141	13,381	22,179
Kansas	174,876	141,533	8,574	6,863	1,685	26	220,346	146,575	24,622	49,149
Kentucky	190,658	159,107	25,087	10,453	3,112	11,522	28,334	16,295	1,725	10,314
Louisiana	200,337	102,410	105,569	54,405	8,163	43,001	348,304	271,634	5,259	71,411
Maine	39,138	6,868	336,571	100,610	4,603	231,358	23,427	9,132	2,701	11,594
Maryland	162,191	486,300	1,564,402	716,075	3,742	844,585	591,035	478,280	4,934	107,821
Massachusetts	138,297	82,838	41,331	26,433	2,766	12,132	291,843	117,448	21,034	153,361
Michigan	172,929	214,326	33,226	25,061	7,356	809	103,654	29,875	20,238	53,541
Minnesota	306,595	40,899	26,129	18,187	7,274	668	65,708	16,283	12,891	36,534
Mississippi	228,553	106,752	303,273	196,960	3,353	102,960	392,955	270,883	8,160	113,912
Missouri	542,876	174,606	115,604	62,246	34,246	19,112	225,782	163,519	6,047	56,216
Montana	52,550	13,439	1,881	1,154	727	0	178,670	144,361	4,096	30,213
Nebraska	92,509	46,006	27,660	23,732	3,291	637	445,188	341,013	11,882	92,293
Nevada	48,785	11,063	63,550	49,640	2,928	10,982	465,463	400,452	4,007	61,004
New Hampshire	28,576	15,945	45,232	41,655	868	2,709	26,441	11,408	2,079	12,954
New Jersey	148,704	413,262	141,982	32,548	3,353	106,081	324,249	249,816	7,118	67,315
New Mexico	60,025	102,314	11,119	6,739	2,327	2,053	653,382	478,659	10,185	164,538
New York	265,574	208,489	134,088	109,779	18,221	6,088	217,947	85,124	17,036	115,787
North Carolina	253,965	190,358	2,233,754	1,946,763	8,582	278,409	502,913	430,525	15,360	57,028
North Dakota	46,378	12,660	1,167	478	585	104	340,898	280,128	9,739	51,031
Ohio	207,322	38,507	44,981	28,189	13,670	3,122	1,143,003	393,564	19,244	730,195
Oklahoma	134,661	129,212	109,008	100,189	5,276	3,543	1,132,137	416,462	13,048	702,627
Oregon	108,734	73,799	19,595	13,818	4,864	913	79,648	27,731	14,874	37,043
Pennsylvania	375,718	251,156	433,136	75,640	13,585	343,911	124,388	37,897	20,723	65,768
Rhode Island	52,558	7,218	335,911	117,930	4,467	213,514	25,606	13,242	3,904	8,460
South Carolina	192,969	77,661	892,447	720,850	6,874	164,723	498,923	418,422	7,583	72,918
South Dakota	47,550	13,306	806	197	579	30	164,268	127,265	9,692	27,311
Tennessee	221,078	117,706	147,075	98,804	10,154	38,117	87,508	33,118	4,030	50,360
Texas	612,778	588,080	474,492	389,058	33,814	51,620	2,335,192	1,650,539	29,368	655,285
Utah	205,712	67,690	11,858	6,689	3,848	1,321	786,441	225,218	3,161	558,062
Vermont	70,230	8,321	1,621	1,373	219	29	22,121	9,616	2,016	10,489
Virginia	232,915	857,966	6,221,642	4,598,491	29,497	1,593,654	1,347,280	1,040,169	8,219	298,892
Washington	180,389	202,387	1,712,325	1,035,803	18,442	658,080	430,727	330,223	17,779	82,725
West Virginia	92,818	35,236	19,009	14,374	1,573	3,062	34,283	12,259	3,073	18,951
Wisconsin	221,731	43,230	13,734	7,303	5,743	688	65,432	24,388	6,643	34,401
Wyoming	28,695	6,380	453	53	400	0	172,363	139,916	1,606	30,841
Dist. of Columbia	47,006	151,656	821,216	219,844	32,868	568,504	277,938	228,400	695	48,843
American Samoa	0	50	727	727	0	0	0	0	0	0
Micronesia	0	0	0	0	0	0	0	0	0	0
Guam	8,742	355	176,660	144,263	0	32,397	115,543	87,322	10,244	17,977
Marshall Islands	0	0	0	0	0	0	0	0	0	0
No. Mariana Islands	0	11	38	38	0	0	0	0	0	0
Palau	0	0	0	0	0	0	0	0	0	0
Puerto Rico	159,346	16,380	6,789	1,378	1,653	3,758	27,661	7,696	6,197	13,768
U.S. Virgin Islands	0	2,038	235	235	0	0	2,148	1,431	717	0
Undistributed	0	0	0	0	0	0	0	0	0	0

See footnotes at end of table.

FEDERAL GOVERNMENT EXPENDITURE FOR SALARIES AND WAGES, BY AGENCY, BY STATE AND OUTLYING AREA: FISCAL YEAR 2006—Continued
(In thousands of dollars)

State and outlying area	Total (a)	Nondefense agencies							
		Dept. of Agriculture	Dept. of Commerce	Dept. of Education	Dept. of Energy	Environmental Protection Agency	Federal Deposit Insurance Corporation	General Services Admin.	Dept. of Health and Human Services
United States	$149,092,887	$6,091,676	$2,824,964	$389,882	$1,461,721	$1,592,304	$460,028	$1,039,445	$4,772,383
Alabama	1,954,269	73,702	7,374	92	0	3,065	2,488	3,928	3,853
Alaska	756,500	60,348	37,467	0	209	2,504	0	2,874	25,126
Arizona	2,499,965	107,542	12,310	0	19,043	301	2,407	4,421	220,351
Arkansas	1,038,594	119,427	3,029	115	3,363	0	1,811	1,619	25,117
California	13,161,757	490,254	73,014	14,692	40,640	82,774	27,102	76,486	95,939
Colorado	2,845,195	223,900	95,994	5,472	60,404	62,827	3,109	28,935	35,919
Connecticut	1,218,856	11,866	4,456	0	165	609	2,229	941	1,942
Delaware	264,289	15,322	740	0	0	0	983	119	850
Florida	6,764,119	110,449	60,605	577	0	7,194	5,793	7,868	23,534
Georgia	4,211,151	169,184	14,393	15,185	7,317	94,556	16,702	56,638	524,759
Hawaii	590,961	31,932	22,094	0	349	467	0	3,382	1,941
Idaho	656,620	150,832	7,322	0	32,433	2,114	0	1,035	3,053
Illinois	5,212,608	110,431	17,075	13,632	31,313	110,872	24,157	58,431	53,417
Indiana	1,808,908	55,651	58,274	118	247	173	3,130	2,583	2,186
Iowa	1,061,754	134,624	5,053	87	896	329	5,410	1,262	1,198
Kansas	1,309,891	68,181	11,169	0	0	43,559	2,707	1,157	12,379
Kentucky	1,608,320	69,707	7,739	0	3,060	281	4,607	983	1,205
Louisiana	1,694,884	168,536	10,726	0	7,236	935	3,624	2,812	9,561
Maine	533,561	18,373	5,949	0	0	0	0	381	1,606
Maryland	8,011,225	279,277	851,876	0	132,361	8,125	2,287	12,296	2,565,733
Massachusetts	3,115,808	29,129	42,864	7,187	1,359	63,661	17,095	21,456	42,295
Michigan	3,191,536	81,827	19,023	0	0	28,161	2,978	5,849	8,563
Minnesota	2,045,241	123,035	9,092	184	73	6,964	4,829	2,479	24,006
Mississippi	1,004,435	119,571	16,163	0	0	2,208	2,322	936	1,066
Missouri	2,919,216	277,844	32,577	7,449	9,242	1,041	19,565	65,401	30,478
Montana	724,537	180,014	8,086	0	11,638	2,903	882	1,268	51,784
Nebraska	763,450	97,053	6,150	0	1,458	0	3,279	1,096	6,497
Nevada	895,744	25,826	7,551	0	29,073	13,303	0	1,782	4,510
New Hampshire	559,122	24,058	2,574	0	166	0	2,404	1,470	603
New Jersey	3,362,329	34,226	18,137	0	1,484	18,807	3,030	15,555	11,350
New Mexico	1,338,669	122,113	5,267	0	101,226	205	1,589	2,638	145,635
New York	7,941,220	71,899	25,851	7,701	13,748	64,818	18,541	55,472	67,402
North Carolina	2,824,980	130,956	34,141	0	142	110,341	4,519	3,398	71,006
North Dakota	401,514	56,135	4,364	0	4,767	0	2,644	851	20,890
Ohio	3,849,464	63,419	11,057	2,404	12,754	51,542	2,421	6,911	46,858
Oklahoma	1,501,567	63,325	23,017	0	9,070	4,827	4,414	3,442	82,207
Oregon	1,716,125	252,671	22,154	0	123,757	9,930	1,794	3,514	12,528
Pennsylvania	5,246,205	107,928	16,482	8,073	32,904	74,565	5,754	46,609	68,163
Rhode Island	413,131	3,468	3,989	0	0	6,283	0	728	529
South Carolina	1,227,641	58,512	20,455	0	37,853	0	1,536	1,848	2,226
South Dakota	540,500	58,244	6,142	0	14,156	81	2,257	901	61,052
Tennessee	2,990,142	76,102	9,369	0	62,937	634	10,069	3,010	7,970
Texas	9,130,096	244,280	44,561	10,131	18,201	76,527	49,403	82,391	56,131
Utah	1,171,793	109,367	8,528	0	1,739	167	4,166	2,006	3,182
Vermont	363,842	19,745	2,570	0	0	0	0	377	473
Virginia	5,941,381	155,211	708,480	97	1,695	116,620	571	128,835	7,982
Washington	2,907,548	136,491	96,802	5,263	178,456	45,676	3,841	35,748	51,289
West Virginia	1,274,226	49,779	3,126	0	25,840	2,031	1,061	1,504	27,604
Wisconsin	1,714,917	108,481	8,024	0	0	166	5,472	1,402	3,490
Wyoming	342,982	51,771	3,840	0	5,081	0	0	510	5,517
Dist. of Columbia	15,133,429	650,635	291,612	291,001	423,866	465,452	174,208	269,592	231,533
American Samoa	4,640	389	1,033	0	0	0	0	0	42
Micronesia	0	0	0	0	0	0	0	0	0
Guam	39,843	3,298	1,902	0	0	206	0	0	59
Marshall Islands	0	0	0	0	0	0	0	0	0
No. Mariana Islands	7,944	619	0	0	0	112	0	0	0
Palau	0	0	0	0	0	0	0	0	0
Puerto Rico	793,823	33,890	3,322	349	0	4,253	838	2,194	7,631
U.S. Virgin Islands	53,832	827	0	73	0	135	0	121	163
Undistributed	4,436,589	0	0	0	0	0	0	0	0

See footnotes at end of table.

FEDERAL GOVERNMENT EXPENDITURE FOR SALARIES AND WAGES, BY AGENCY, BY STATE AND OUTLYING AREA: FISCAL YEAR 2006—Continued
(In thousands of dollars)

	Nondefense agencies—continued							
State and outlying area	Dept. of Homeland Security	Dept. of Housing and Urban Development	Dept. of the Interior	Dept. of Justice	Dept. of Labor	NASA	National Archives and Records Admin.	National Science Foundation
United States	$9,838,425	$846,675	$4,425,809	$11,467,691	$1,358,501	$1,805,236	$167,193	$130,535
Alabama	51,347	5,937	8,927	76,343	10,345	241,824	0	50
Alaska	46,313	2,885	144,768	13,119	1,114	0	413	206
Arizona	366,903	8,316	254,590	142,022	4,072	198	0	0
Arkansas	23,873	4,466	18,195	58,001	3,405	0	1,685	0
California	1,206,398	54,854	420,555	680,494	74,124	197,997	6,750	131
Colorado	121,704	26,177	506,147	140,229	32,007	965	2,001	369
Connecticut	61,909	5,556	3,590	57,455	5,276	96	0	0
Delaware	3,979	293	2,458	12,474	755	0	0	0
Florida	718,941	20,329	78,163	428,480	39,466	188,630	87	50
Georgia	289,983	33,799	68,181	190,816	44,942	64	5,024	0
Hawaii	83,990	2,036	30,028	29,376	1,758	0	0	0
Idaho	22,362	1,045	128,014	16,927	2,365	0	0	0
Illinois	249,490	36,944	15,253	243,118	65,608	107	2,139	0
Indiana	56,702	6,065	14,445	85,851	8,093	121	0	0
Iowa	18,668	2,449	7,972	22,094	2,824	0	1,000	0
Kansas	21,366	13,433	23,275	62,404	4,190	0	3,035	0
Kentucky	51,500	4,736	20,910	145,151	30,500	0	0	0
Louisiana	141,290	7,489	70,238	124,496	6,928	1,268	0	0
Maine	50,952	340	11,580	8,942	1,925	0	0	0
Maryland	241,464	11,436	46,451	316,961	6,731	301,092	69,964	0
Massachusetts	181,637	18,327	72,371	106,992	38,709	0	5,208	151
Michigan	200,316	13,186	25,020	118,771	8,781	127	1,584	0
Minnesota	93,616	7,775	50,483	97,078	4,196	94	0	0
Mississippi	54,682	4,120	24,848	57,521	3,566	27,331	0	0
Missouri	105,747	8,846	44,361	106,398	27,634	0	28,917	0
Montana	69,638	773	122,717	14,159	2,103	121	0	0
Nebraska	53,927	2,993	27,311	18,674	2,601	0	0	0
Nevada	75,878	2,197	117,713	35,453	2,642	0	0	0
New Hampshire	18,044	3,199	5,639	14,334	2,933	0	0	0
New Jersey	245,248	10,871	20,883	219,589	15,531	98	0	0
New Mexico	102,591	2,425	271,258	40,464	2,523	5,969	89	0
New York	636,077	42,543	58,337	401,203	52,016	2,999	2,401	0
North Carolina	128,368	7,811	34,977	127,251	5,715	0	0	0
North Dakota	32,825	554	48,501	8,158	1,462	0	0	0
Ohio	115,217	19,481	17,240	111,971	35,429	159,802	2,998	0
Oklahoma	38,549	10,304	61,741	86,710	4,130	0	0	0
Oregon	63,109	4,190	191,388	56,557	3,539	113	0	35
Pennsylvania	181,370	33,367	69,659	339,031	76,538	0	2,885	0
Rhode Island	33,322	2,229	3,514	10,113	1,819	0	0	0
South Carolina	51,411	5,257	13,254	111,126	2,674	0	0	0
South Dakota	8,099	508	82,693	18,056	1,176	0	0	0
Tennessee	61,086	11,232	37,826	85,327	7,868	0	0	0
Texas	1,189,161	47,769	68,134	638,710	65,931	328,611	6,261	0
Utah	33,815	2,002	113,331	31,323	8,964	1,122	0	0
Vermont	106,243	373	3,869	8,001	383	0	0	0
Virginia	620,725	7,660	303,114	857,406	40,549	202,606	0	129,398
Washington	231,849	14,962	148,576	83,407	20,908	33	1,615	35
West Virginia	26,055	1,682	46,320	248,890	36,417	3,710	0	0
Wisconsin	34,704	5,578	39,348	52,952	7,822	123	0	0
Wyoming	6,576	211	98,727	8,904	1,585	0	0	0
Dist. of Columbia	1,041,733	299,588	314,303	1,876,983	523,137	140,015	23,137	110
American Samoa	871	0	646	0	0	0	0	0
Micronesia	0	0	0	0	0	0	0	0
Guam	14,117	69	1,353	4,858	73	0	0	0
Marshall Islands	0	0	0	0	0	0	0	0
No. Mariana Islands	2,932	0	670	1,645	75	0	0	0
Palau	0	0	0	0	0	0	0	0
Puerto Rico	131,393	6,008	7,376	68,775	2,644	0	0	0
U.S. Virgin Islands	18,360	0	4,568	8,567	0	0	0	0
Undistributed	0	0	0	2,537,581	0	0	0	0

See footnotes at end of table.

FEDERAL GOVERNMENT EXPENDITURE FOR SALARIES AND WAGES, BY AGENCY, BY STATE AND OUTLYING AREA: FISCAL YEAR 2006—Continued
(In thousands of dollars)

	Nondefense agencies—continued							
State and outlying area	*U.S. Postal Service*	*Small Business Admin.*	*Social Security Admin.*	*Dept. of State*	*Dept. of Transportation*	*Dept. of the Treasury*	*Dept. of Veterans Affairs*	*All other nondefense (a)*
United States	$56,301,998	$428,145	$4,389,271	$1,152,940	$5,606,254	$7,210,432	$14,409,089	$8,795,789
Alabama	722,212	3,302	154,580	0	25,269	33,306	239,145	242,311
Alaska	147,291	863	2,978	95	111,447	6,115	26,351	1,280
Arizona	902,505	1,904	37,442	733	52,732	44,310	295,923	20,736
Arkansas	472,373	3,373	30,228	0	19,947	16,651	227,090	3,810
California	6,124,250	45,935	425,378	12,181	481,046	777,182	1,365,880	132,980
Colorado	959,268	11,660	47,914	969	141,019	110,060	186,734	40,084
Connecticut	762,440	1,141	26,470	1,688	18,750	48,678	140,315	6,488
Delaware	155,767	538	6,278	0	3,228	11,096	47,299	1,042
Florida	3,111,871	10,025	154,188	19,431	278,151	209,804	1,006,987	38,384
Georgia	1,513,137	22,065	112,490	199	252,142	345,272	349,184	66,547
Hawaii	215,239	1,464	6,593	1,416	34,014	9,629	35,993	4,878
Idaho	209,820	769	7,995	0	11,065	8,569	50,205	524
Illinois	2,797,627	6,736	216,781	4,458	240,863	184,474	566,191	155,028
Indiana	1,090,023	1,417	50,511	0	111,271	55,904	192,539	11,043
Iowa	648,775	1,673	22,952	0	17,791	16,495	145,368	1,975
Kansas	639,257	1,346	23,443	0	99,452	103,328	162,004	5,593
Kentucky	671,008	2,672	49,559	428	40,382	242,892	179,818	74,593
Louisiana	693,241	8,269	51,499	6,165	30,845	36,220	239,418	8,631
Maine	301,738	1,325	12,315	98	14,640	7,831	66,069	1,262
Maryland	1,197,643	2,058	926,184	3,366	52,215	404,260	207,880	330,145
Massachusetts	1,543,290	3,121	82,370	3,205	117,763	223,482	353,787	41,121
Michigan	1,953,968	2,512	89,094	472	71,348	140,132	343,937	16,986
Minnesota	1,123,303	2,161	32,453	169	114,613	57,519	272,726	11,925
Mississippi	394,142	4,565	38,626	0	14,751	16,033	191,804	12,399
Missouri	1,334,512	6,115	154,222	69	99,218	200,509	334,795	14,848
Montana	189,741	840	7,802	185	13,920	7,131	37,107	1,462
Nebraska	401,576	1,209	12,235	0	14,966	18,466	90,289	2,726
Nevada	382,748	1,402	12,660	0	34,986	23,824	120,815	2,620
New Hampshire	303,892	1,189	9,679	9,692	92,296	13,664	38,383	1,471
New Jersey	2,131,274	2,862	64,948	884	162,527	105,003	199,981	12,131
New Mexico	284,716	1,319	48,122	350	68,393	10,974	115,707	4,596
New York	4,141,379	23,711	284,807	18,304	292,250	528,872	965,393	110,185
North Carolina	1,514,596	3,434	68,966	2,274	47,657	66,015	366,650	17,379
North Dakota	152,641	1,110	5,869	0	11,093	6,543	42,342	765
Ohio	2,184,145	3,637	102,901	0	148,519	178,615	524,342	25,057
Oklahoma	597,988	1,300	31,731	0	265,074	37,038	169,087	4,306
Oregon	618,761	1,384	30,107	0	26,103	39,253	203,749	3,006
Pennsylvania	2,615,389	4,672	259,542	3,672	88,593	445,710	631,041	116,236
Rhode Island	239,765	947	10,525	0	9,487	10,786	57,665	1,376
South Carolina	591,040	1,114	37,857	33,265	23,280	17,437	175,539	5,550
South Dakota	169,732	721	6,165	0	6,993	5,998	96,582	944
Tennessee	1,097,040	1,498	62,796	0	110,713	202,967	389,586	743,602
Texas	3,659,974	120,203	202,600	14,609	432,086	598,480	1,010,866	83,021
Utah	415,194	1,449	11,894	0	71,701	247,381	99,890	4,331
Vermont	160,353	1,083	3,843	0	4,972	5,053	44,856	442
Virginia	1,509,316	10,054	133,366	2,727	244,947	113,703	294,743	122,195
Washington	1,084,951	3,886	95,195	4,170	194,044	85,443	294,348	17,754
West Virginia	356,625	890	28,775	0	12,914	183,534	209,804	3,829
Wisconsin	1,039,305	1,978	43,562	0	25,079	39,802	275,052	6,966
Wyoming	95,531	1,000	2,533	0	5,769	4,126	50,691	402
Dist. of Columbia	416,792	85,044	23,452	1,007,177	722,395	875,546	511,216	4,337,323
American Samoa	764	0	161	0	508	0	64	0
Micronesia	0	0	0	0	0	0	0	0
Guam	8,198	285	577	0	3,996	0	684	24
Marshall Islands	0	0	0	0	0	0	0	0
No. Mariana Islands	834	0	205	489	175	0	0	13
Palau	0	0	0	0	0	0	0	0
Puerto Rico	235,944	2,501	23,118	0	16,050	28,986	164,483	24,702
U.S. Virgin Islands	17,091	414	735	0	806	331	692	20
Undistributed	0	0	0	0	0	0	0	1,896,742

Source: U.S. Department of Commerce, Bureau of the Census, Consolidated Federal Funds Report for Fiscal Year 2006, April 2008. For additional information see the complete report at *http://www.census.gov/govs/www/cffr.html.*

Note: Department of Defense data represent salaries, wages and compensation, such as housing allowances; distributions by state are based on duty station. State details for all other federal government agencies are estimates, based on place of employment.

(a) The "undistributed" amount includes the salaries and wages for the Federal Judiciary that could not be geographically allocated.

Table 2.12
FEDERAL GOVERNMENT DIRECT LOAN PROGRAMS—VOLUME OF ASSISTANCE PROVIDED BY STATE AND OUTLYING AREA: FISCAL YEAR 2006
(In thousands of dollars)

		Department of Agriculture			
State and outlying area	Total	Commodity loans—price supports	Other agriculture loans	Federal direct student loans	Other direct loans
United States	$23,766,996	$5,097	$4,389,837	$10,158,223	$9,213,839
Alabama	410,633	0	70,124	182,274	158,235
Alaska	21,091	0	17,348	0	3,743
Arizona	324,181	0	39,703	271,864	12,614
Arkansas	132,637	0	115,401	2,716	14,520
California	1,394,223	439	137,085	1,157,679	99,019
Colorado	262,623	617	49,168	201,901	10,938
Connecticut	102,043	0	14,502	74,870	12,671
Delaware	88,559	0	22,634	60,745	5,181
Florida	1,266,958	0	183,764	185,724	897,469
Georgia	722,900	0	111,520	576,776	34,604
Hawaii	11,287	0	7,048	349	3,890
Idaho	118,424	328	59,166	58,694	236
Illinois	848,169	0	113,053	704,949	30,167
Indiana	322,179	0	78,805	226,871	16,503
Iowa	637,054	0	190,925	441,895	4,234
Kansas	223,945	2,408	89,989	128,600	2,948
Kentucky	155,668	0	117,208	30,806	7,655
Louisiana	5,233,451	0	215,859	3,548	5,014,044
Maine	100,408	0	71,259	23,269	5,879
Maryland	385,460	0	33,629	341,338	10,492
Massachusetts	836,419	0	26,466	727,363	82,590
Michigan	661,942	0	165,491	492,187	4,264
Minnesota	396,227	2	142,201	251,009	3,014
Mississippi	2,106,828	0	167,463	2,772	1,936,593
Missouri	382,437	0	113,083	238,610	30,744
Montana	33,143	479	32,030	0	635
Nebraska	195,962	149	110,034	84,828	951
Nevada	135,324	0	20,104	109,821	5,399
New Hampshire	80,960	0	28,413	25,528	27,018
New Jersey	397,482	0	33,127	333,453	30,902
New Mexico	-6,833	1	21,523	-31,376	3,018
New York	1,268,142	0	79,586	1,076,544	112,012
North Carolina	451,707	0	178,932	261,326	11,449
North Dakota	69,599	53	68,298	0	1,248
Ohio	784,754	0	100,663	653,696	30,395
Oklahoma	221,654	153	109,132	100,995	11,374
Oregon	331,649	2	54,719	274,204	2,724
Pennsylvania	193,718	0	110,021	35,789	47,908
Rhode Island	118,048	0	9,250	101,874	6,924
South Carolina	178,879	0	73,556	102,378	2,945
South Dakota	98,195	27	102,312	-4,874	731
Tennessee	-626,318	0	116,178	-770,898	28,402
Texas	906,950	199	270,810	209,221	426,720
Utah	51,267	1	51,820	-1,144	591
Vermont	28,889	0	31,909	-3,125	106
Virginia	486,377	0	104,238	351,273	30,867
Washington	385,847	233	75,539	294,612	15,464
West Virginia	300,986	0	67,217	233,040	730
Wisconsin	344,854	0	124,437	215,117	5,301
Wyoming	13,130	5	11,715	683	727
Dist. of Columbia	124,384	0	0	120,084	4,300
American Samoa	0	0	0	0	0
Fed. States of Micronesia	1,965	0	1,965	0	0
Guam	6,608	0	7,443	-1,105	270
Marshall Islands	1,141	0	1,141	0	0
No. Mariana Islands	1,744	0	1,473	0	271
Palau	57	0	57	0	0
Puerto Rico	37,900	0	36,375	-687	2,213
U.S. Virgin Islands	3,085	0	2,925	160	0
Undistributed	0	0	0	0	0

See footnotes at end of table.

FEDERAL GOVERNMENT DIRECT LOAN PROGRAMS—VOLUME OF ASSISTANCE PROVIDED BY STATE AND OUTLYING AREA: FISCAL YEAR 2006—Continued

Source: U.S. Department of Commerce, Bureau of the Census, Consolidated Federal Funds Report for Fiscal Year 2006, April 2008.

Note: Amounts represent dollar volume of direct loans made during the fiscal year. The CFDA defines "Direct Loans" as "Financial assistance provided through the lending of federal monies for a specific period of time, with a reasonable expectation of repayment. Such loans may or may not require the payment of interest." The CFDA defines "Guaranteed/Insured Loans" as "Programs in which the federal government makes an arrangement to indemnify a lender against part or all of any defaults by those responsible for the repayment of loans." Loan program amounts reflect the volume of loan activities. These amounts represent either direct loans made to certain categories of borrowers, or the federal government contingent liability for loans guaranteed. Loan data does not represent actual expenditures associated with the loan programs. Any actual outlays under these programs, appear in the direct payments categories in the CFFR. Federal government contingent liability can vary by program, and caution should be used in comparing one federal loan program to another, or in interpreting the data presented to reflect actual federal outlays over time.

The following also should be noted:

1. Amounts guaranteed do not necessarily represent future outlays.

2. All amounts reflect the dollar value of loans provided during the fiscal year, and not the cumulative totals of such activity over the life of the program.

3. Direct loans are not reported on a net basis, as in the federal budget, but rather are shown in terms of total amounts loaned.

4. Programs otherwise similar can vary in the share of the total liability that the federal government guarantees or insures. Certain veterans guaranteed loan programs are guaranteed only up to a stated maximum dollar value, for example. In these cases, the federal government contingent liability is less than the total value of the loan or insured policy agreement.

Table 2.13
FEDERAL GOVERNMENT GUARANTEED LOAN PROGRAMS—VOLUME OF COVERAGE PROVIDED BY STATE AND OUTLYING AREA: FISCAL YEAR 2006
(In thousands of dollars)

State and outlying area	*Total*	*Mortgage insurance for homes*	*Federal Family Education Loan program*	*Veterans housing guaranteed and insured loans— VA home loans*	*Mortgage insurance— condominiums*	*U.S.D.A. guaranteed loans*	*Small business loans*	*Other guaranteed loans*
United States	$159,814,291	$52,556,609	$54,254,646	$23,500,000	$2,851,222	$10,446,652	$15,632,913	$572,249
Alabama	2,802,431	950,260	755,821	401,703	7,495	515,150	172,003	0
Alaska	642,635	203,986	60,030	196,031	70,315	81,832	30,440	0
Arizona	6,380,684	913,405	3,705,979	1,092,983	42,302	91,429	534,587	-2
Arkansas	1,775,791	634,300	487,763	184,839	2,424	376,006	90,460	0
California	9,791,991	806,224	4,176,297	1,308,560	75,395	267,870	3,147,993	9,653
Colorado	4,903,208	1,994,631	1,098,912	906,727	292,787	177,894	432,258	0
Connecticut	1,887,846	794,105	589,606	80,667	192,500	34,499	193,640	2,828
Delaware	463,773	209,397	90,991	103,994	3,114	25,114	31,164	-1
Florida	8,243,961	2,133,804	2,925,623	1,825,199	197,771	176,703	952,228	32,633
Georgia	6,342,834	3,204,978	1,354,758	962,461	95,370	135,272	589,995	0
Hawaii	348,024	84,809	126,060	66,959	12,517	32,952	24,726	0
Idaho	934,805	437,621	89,995	179,472	2,904	96,308	128,505	0
Illinois	6,581,824	2,122,643	2,746,382	594,707	234,573	360,995	513,555	8,970
Indiana	4,222,250	1,875,654	1,532,704	388,442	29,902	147,493	248,054	0
Iowa	1,566,561	378,460	698,456	123,009	19,374	211,561	135,702	0
Kansas	1,549,408	540,953	533,366	226,526	4,142	144,400	100,021	0
Kentucky	2,564,322	788,545	715,935	249,075	29,210	682,091	99,466	0
Louisiana	1,962,188	641,485	810,510	212,461	7,072	197,371	93,290	0
Maine	591,220	161,646	221,973	59,952	5,541	79,058	63,049	0
Maryland	3,338,534	1,286,521	571,266	1,086,271	136,662	44,516	213,296	0
Massachusetts	2,162,140	483,395	1,225,296	102,322	42,287	29,794	279,046	0
Michigan	4,566,808	1,972,791	1,425,823	391,642	84,767	301,966	380,069	9,750
Minnesota	3,528,201	806,831	1,481,562	247,928	161,412	386,064	444,209	195
Mississippi	1,544,762	627,245	496,847	193,315	1,153	121,883	104,319	0
Missouri	3,912,113	1,393,324	1,451,620	452,630	34,030	310,791	269,719	0
Montana	689,887	265,677	185,042	69,115	8,132	108,723	53,198	0
Nebraska	1,253,082	347,601	397,947	255,078	2,124	169,727	80,605	0
Nevada	1,307,224	401,956	84,725	572,441	23,857	8,856	215,389	0
New Hampshire	604,688	107,893	296,299	61,979	21,738	21,120	95,660	-1
New Jersey	3,465,057	1,892,331	682,276	256,281	218,297	4,623	403,743	7,508
New Mexico	1,189,549	506,616	251,462	279,395	8,800	56,616	84,214	2,446
New York	7,003,643	1,783,720	4,075,693	204,731	20,578	111,364	639,002	168,554
North Carolina	4,893,739	1,841,239	1,141,710	1,193,148	53,744	293,395	370,503	0
North Dakota	593,082	152,336	195,009	53,840	5,961	138,747	47,190	0
Ohio	6,368,288	2,606,732	1,963,453	704,174	128,857	410,364	486,708	68,000
Oklahoma	2,207,489	928,244	620,999	291,384	6,464	226,091	134,306	0
Oregon	1,710,942	506,871	561,480	362,570	12,761	97,250	170,423	0
Pennsylvania	6,701,728	1,478,093	3,862,874	505,599	40,028	236,587	447,557	130,991
Rhode Island	539,988	148,279	283,009	25,225	6,084	1,569	75,822	0
South Carolina	2,055,504	610,511	717,559	336,171	6,425	277,645	107,193	0
South Dakota	635,756	111,254	227,427	66,114	1,081	187,843	42,037	0
Tennessee	3,643,150	1,580,508	1,080,833	551,308	32,604	258,225	139,675	-2
Texas	14,119,549	6,486,737	3,593,136	2,223,759	47,133	490,354	1,268,681	9,750
Utah	2,335,647	1,171,477	435,070	292,219	138,423	47,939	250,521	0
Vermont	390,639	26,975	256,631	21,574	4,477	38,793	42,190	0
Virginia	6,422,004	1,446,038	1,044,117	1,903,198	107,646	1,632,302	288,720	-17
Washington	3,684,916	1,283,423	626,789	1,181,949	84,364	88,778	419,612	0
West Virginia	501,249	160,120	171,172	61,538	129	80,073	28,215	0
Wisconsin	2,441,072	660,361	901,673	298,955	22,680	247,874	309,529	0
Wyoming	408,093	177,188	124,997	55,020	1,931	22,143	26,814	0
Dist. of Columbia	975,757	44,810	767,325	8 ,790	5,891	0	27,941	121,000
American Samoa	338	0	0	0	0	0	338	0
Fed. States of Micronesia	0	0	0	0	0	0	0	0
Guam	41,203	316	6,267	1,888	0	29,176	3,556	0
Marshall Islands	0	0	0	0	0	0	0	0
No. Mariana Islands	650	0	0	0	0	650	0	0
Palau	0	0	0	0	0	0	0	0
Puerto Rico	1,017,464	380,224	326,098	24,777	55,914	130,204	100,247	0
U.S. Virgin Islands	5,258	2,722	0	319	80	609	1,527	0
Undistributed	-663	-658	0	0	0	0	0	-5

See footnotes at end of table.

FEDERAL GOVERNMENT GUARANTEED LOAN PROGRAMS—VOLUME OF COVERAGE PROVIDED BY STATE AND OUTLYING AREA: FISCAL YEAR 2006—Continued

Source: U.S. Department of Commerce, Bureau of the Census, Consolidated Federal Funds Report for Fiscal Year 2006, April 2008.

Note: Amounts represent dollar volume of loans guaranteed during the fiscal year. The CFDA defines "Guaranteed/Insured Loans" as "Programs in which the federal government makes an arrangement to indemnify a lender against part or all of any defaults by those responsible for the repayment of loans." Loan and program amounts reflect the volume of loan activities. These amounts represent the federal government contingent liability for loans guaranteed. Loans and insurance data do not represent actual expenditures associated with the loan or insurance programs. Any actual outlays under these programs, such as insurance claims paid by the federal government, appear in the direct payments categories in the CFFR. Federal government contingent liability can vary by program, and caution should be used in comparing one federal loan or insurance program to another, or in interpreting the data presented to reflect actual federal outlays over time.

The following also should be noted:

1. Amounts guaranteed or insured do not necessarily represent future outlays.

2. All amounts reflect the dollar value of loans or insurance coverage provided during the fiscal year, and not the cumulative totals of such activity over the life of the program.

3. Direct loans are not reported on a net basis, as in the federal budget, but rather are shown in terms of total amounts loaned.

4. Programs otherwise similar can vary in the share of the total liability that the federal government guarantees or insures. Certain veterans guaranteed loan programs are guaranteed only up to a stated maximum dollar value, for example. In these cases, the federal government contingent liability is less than the total value of the loan or insured policy agreement.

Table 2.14
FEDERAL GOVERNMENT INSURANCE PROGRAMS — VOLUME OF COVERAGE PROVIDED BY STATE AND OUTLYING AREA: FISCAL YEAR 2006
(In thousands of dollars)

	Insurance programs by volume of coverage provided					
State and outlying area	*Total*	*Flood insurance*	*Crop insurance*	*Foreign investment insurance*	*Life insurance for veterans*	*Other insurance*
United States	$1,065,893,710	$1,008,653,027	$53,760,910	$1,269,046	$1,775,489	$435,239
Alabama	9,165,508	8,829,866	309,905	0	24,473	1,264
Alaska	499,130	489,323	340	0	2,497	6,970
Arizona	6,786,441	6,588,620	155,318	68	40,204	2,232
Arkansas	2,194,086	1,640,895	533,432	0	15,250	4,508
California	63,199,398	58,751,236	4,184,209	10,149	180,656	73,147
Colorado	3,940,030	3,246,459	629,743	1,681	28,807	33,340
Connecticut	6,963,363	6,812,050	121,492	0	28,009	1,812
Delaware	5,454,981	4,535,153	51,274	859,000	5,542	4,012
Florida	422,486,677	417,921,144	4,368,404	17,364	162,203	17,563
Georgia	18,479,532	17,532,754	875,045	45	40,987	30,702
Hawaii	8,259,031	8,165,226	76,074	0	15,559	2,172
Idaho	1,952,226	1,436,296	507,480	0	7,968	483
Illinois	12,045,623	6,313,328	5,651,009	0	73,381	7,905
Indiana	5,743,751	3,394,796	2,320,304	0	26,701	1,950
Iowa	6,540,325	1,219,056	5,298,152	0	21,993	1,124
Kansas	3,197,181	1,207,953	1,954,559	1,399	17,554	15,716
Kentucky	2,823,961	2,357,029	442,846	0	17,781	6,304
Louisiana	83,905,036	83,407,594	436,012	27,264	20,442	13,725
Maine	1,456,209	1,387,383	59,085	0	9,742	0
Maryland	11,506,521	11,205,070	252,545	2,867	37,375	8,665
Massachusetts	9,191,213	9,074,668	58,897	6,210	46,896	4,542
Michigan	4,755,039	3,642,515	1,053,200	177	48,604	10,543
Minnesota	5,041,892	1,390,231	3,610,489	0	36,947	4,225
Mississippi	12,948,929	12,448,325	482,944	0	12,500	5,160
Missouri	4,153,896	2,991,844	1,110,619	0	33,927	17,506
Montana	1,149,897	495,660	636,337	0	7,303	10,597
Nebraska	4,556,419	1,553,229	2,984,963	0	13,322	4,905
Nevada	3,601,329	3,572,141	15,741	0	12,213	1,235
New Hampshire	1,199,767	1,180,304	9,300	0	9,474	690
New Jersey	41,012,699	40,829,931	115,567	0	60,711	6,490
New Mexico	2,047,489	1,943,983	87,218	0	13,726	2,562
New York	26,699,669	26,255,971	276,574	50,525	114,405	2,193
North Carolina	26,917,570	25,677,793	1,189,988	0	47,210	2,580
North Dakota	3,156,230	763,117	2,381,137	0	4,543	7,433
Ohio	6,425,727	4,778,487	1,569,435	0	64,922	12,882
Oklahoma	2,200,512	1,725,968	448,097	0	20,550	5,897
Oregon	6,633,765	5,572,365	1,030,944	2,000	22,922	5,534
Pennsylvania	10,247,620	9,874,630	274,755	215	91,683	6,337
Rhode Island	3,000,690	2,989,607	2,067	0	7,310	1,706
South Carolina	39,025,488	38,563,504	427,873	6,445	25,618	2,047
South Dakota	2,235,731	422,495	1,806,325	0	5,864	1,046
Tennessee	3,912,370	3,117,604	759,142	0	27,309	8,314
Texas	128,969,225	126,250,495	2,566,260	26,703	104,204	21,563
Utah	823,728	779,918	17,036	0	11,212	15,563
Vermont	502,129	483,315	13,982	0	4,109	724
Virginia	20,550,431	20,142,662	344,696	3,375	51,814	7,884
Washington	7,095,357	5,933,515	1,107,949	0	39,583	14,310
West Virginia	2,099,807	2,076,266	10,519	0	9,983	3,039
Wisconsin	2,852,050	1,748,476	1,054,007	0	38,322	11,245
Wyoming	500,494	409,156	87,621	0	3,295	422
Dist. of Columbia	440,523	181,253	0	253,560	3,242	2,469
American Samoa	47	47	0	0	0	0
Fed. States of Micronesia	0	0	0	0	0	0
Guam	38,770	38,770	0	0	0	0
Marshall Islands	0	0	0	0	0	0
No. Mariana Islands	73	73	0	0	0	0
Palau	0	0	0	0	0	0
Puerto Rico	4,974,276	4,970,131	0	0	4,145	0
U.S. Virgin Islands	333,109	332,612	0	0	497	0
Undistributed	737	737	0	0	0	0

See footnotes at end of table.

FEDERAL GOVERNMENT INSURANCE PROGRAMS—VOLUME OF COVERAGE PROVIDED BY STATE AND OUTLYING AREA: FISCAL YEAR 2006—Continued

Source: U.S. Department of Commerce, Bureau of the Census, Consolidated Federal Funds Report for Fiscal Year 2006, April 2008.

Note: Amounts represent dollar volume of the face value of insurance coverage provided during the fiscal year. Detail may not add to total due to rounding. The CFDA defines "Insurance" as "Financial assistance provided to assure reimbursement for losses sustained under specified conditions. Coverage may be provided directly by the federal government or through private carriers and may or may not involve the payment of premiums." All data on insurance programs of the federal government, with the exception of data on flood insurance, come from the FAADS. National Flood Insurance data (CFDA number 97.022), reflecting insurance in force on September 30, 2006, are from FEMA, Department of Homeland Security. Insurance program amounts reflect the volume of insurance activities. Insurance data do not represent actual expenditures associated with the loan or insurance programs. Any actual outlays under these programs, such as insurance claims paid by the federal government, appear in the direct payments categories in the CFFR. Federal government contingent liability can vary by program, and caution should be used in comparing one federal loan or insurance program to another, or in interpreting the data presented to reflect actual federal outlays over time.

The following also should be noted:

1. Amounts insured do not necessarily represent future outlays.
2. All amounts reflect the dollar value of insurance coverage provided during the fiscal year, and not the cumulative totals of such activity over the life of the program.
3. Programs otherwise similar can vary in the share of the total liability that the federal government guarantees or insures.

Table 2.15
PER CAPITA AMOUNTS OF FEDERAL GOVERNMENT EXPENDITURE, BY MAJOR OBJECT CATEGORY, BY STATE AND OUTLYING AREA: FISCAL YEAR 2006
(In dollars)

State and outlying area	United States resident population— July 1, 2006 (a)	Total	Retirement and disability	Other direct payments	Grants	Procurement	Salaries and wages
United States totals*	299,398,484	$8,058.14	$2,446.39	$1,887.02	$1,630.13	$1,300.98	$793.62
Alabama	4,599,030	9,551.66	3,150.77	2,155.39	1,632.98	1,811.06	801.46
Alaska	670,053	13,804.99	1,845.82	1,004.00	4,592.67	3,240.90	3,121.60
Arizona	6,166,318	7,517.45	2,374.82	1,361.00	1,423.74	1,723.10	634.79
Arkansas	2,810,872	7,648.92	2,960.88	1,995.00	1,650.50	474.21	568.33
California	36,457,549	6,964.42	1,920.23	1,708.83	1,507.14	1,186.88	641.34
Colorado	4,753,377	7,241.71	2,092.77	1,277.87	1,269.68	1,582.39	1,019.00
Connecticut	3,504,809	8,735.63	2,416.57	1,880.89	1,551.68	2,387.57	498.91
Delaware	853,476	6,857.67	2,790.71	1,548.79	1,606.31	293.27	618.58
Florida	18,089,888	7,888.68	2,913.10	2,291.73	1,241.13	819.78	622.94
Georgia	9,363,941	6,893.53	2,142.17	1,421.99	1,260.32	1,078.96	990.10
Hawaii	1,285,498	10,494.85	2,749.03	1,392.81	1,795.41	1,670.81	2,886.79
Idaho	1,466,465	6,784.97	2,388.27	1,203.03	1,367.44	1,169.15	657.07
Illinois	12,831,970	6,407.54	2,202.87	1,871.13	1,252.38	530.34	550.83
Indiana	6,313,520	6,932.16	2,477.96	1,911.34	1,281.03	848.17	413.66
Iowa	2,982,085	7,322.02	2,573.28	2,320.32	1,326.96	661.40	440.07
Kansas	2,764,075	7,786.68	2,534.89	2,096.95	1,214.97	996.61	943.27
Kentucky	4,206,074	8,940.54	2,819.89	1,820.24	1,646.83	1,735.04	918.55
Louisiana	4,287,768	16,262.76	2,460.65	5,592.09	5,325.21	2,223.45	661.37
Maine	1,321,574	8,307.83	3,009.18	1,590.81	2,029.79	944.97	733.08
Maryland	5,615,727	13,443.98	2,782.17	1,985.35	2,791.06	3,882.64	2,002.76
Massachusetts	6,437,193	8,889.26	2,401.11	2,160.93	2,046.07	1,697.87	583.26
Michigan	10,095,643	6,671.37	2,550.62	1,881.21	1,280.45	579.76	379.33
Minnesota	5,167,101	6,175.17	2,182.18	1,622.46	1,365.44	518.81	486.29
Mississippi	2,910,540	14,516.30	2,769.65	3,132.67	5,492.42	2,411.81	709.74
Missouri	5,842,713	8,945.57	2,672.01	2,120.09	1,472.03	1,901.86	779.59
Montana	944,632	8,480.50	2,837.64	1,905.61	2,144.90	562.14	1,030.21
Nebraska	1,768,331	7,875.70	2,490.10	2,582.93	1,429.33	584.67	788.67
Nevada	2,495,529	5,851.74	2,279.60	1,030.89	1,031.09	911.17	599.00
New Hampshire	1,314,895	6,749.83	2,578.20	1,251.82	1,325.23	1,072.86	521.73
New Jersey	8,724,560	7,022.33	2,381.61	1,868.97	1,294.68	963.18	513.89
New Mexico	1,954,599	10,712.33	2,686.91	1,430.42	2,380.05	3,084.78	1,130.17
New York	19,306,183	7,921.50	2,346.50	2,106.80	2,345.16	614.92	508.12
North Carolina	8,856,505	7,001.73	2,592.08	1,501.12	1,468.81	527.19	912.53
North Dakota	635,867	9,928.03	2,534.31	3,224.92	2,225.97	675.18	1,267.66
Ohio	11,478,006	7,037.30	2,511.92	1,810.83	1,439.13	773.21	502.21
Oklahoma	3,579,212	8,123.95	2,845.29	1,876.69	1,563.96	803.43	1,034.58
Oregon	3,700,758	6,373.29	2,578.27	1,418.74	1,473.99	359.95	542.34
Pennsylvania	12,440,621	8,300.61	2,927.21	2,322.99	1,623.44	872.03	554.95
Rhode Island	1,067,610	8,211.01	2,656.11	2,104.26	2,096.63	563.25	790.77
South Carolina	4,321,249	7,829.49	2,839.06	1,576.63	1,448.87	1,156.46	808.47
South Dakota	781,919	10,220.06	2,613.86	3,929.18	1,897.04	796.51	983.47
Tennessee	6,038,803	8,378.54	2,727.34	2,004.63	1,582.38	1,465.64	598.54
Texas	23,507,783	7,087.80	2,000.77	1,571.47	1,296.71	1,515.14	703.71
Utah	2,550,063	6,162.20	1,832.78	945.39	1,246.47	1,235.14	902.41
Vermont	623,908	8,453.08	2,552.67	1,561.07	2,191.92	1,394.71	752.71
Virginia	7,642,884	13,484.67	2,999.03	1,751.68	993.02	5,484.19	2,256.75
Washington	6,395,798	7,532.57	2,529.73	1,307.43	1,403.32	1,271.85	1,020.24
West Virginia	1,818,470	8,913.75	3,584.97	1,938.69	1,951.65	636.65	801.79
Wisconsin	5,556,506	6,219.86	2,422.13	1,538.79	1,287.71	598.05	373.18
Wyoming	515,004	10,038.86	2,570.22	1,541.95	4,018.08	836.40	1,072.21
Dist. of Columbia	581,530	69,400.30	3,503.18	4,746.18	7,179.69	24,461.67	29,509.58
American Samoa	57,794	4,257.76	836.62	168.03	2,624.89	534.50	93.72
Fed. States of Micronesia	108,004	925.85	7.60	75.25	841.82	1.18	0.00
Guam	171,019	8,071.33	1,461.96	535.32	1,691.42	2,345.61	2,037.02
Marshall Islands	60,451	3,158.65	13.21	29.75	1,298.23	1,817.46	0.00
No. Mariana Islands	82,459	2,145.12	328.51	165.26	1,532.23	22.18	96.93
Palau	20,579	1,801.39	38.64	123.65	1,639.09	0.00	0.00
Puerto Rico	3,927,776	4,132.59	1,618.01	866.12	1,219.17	171.31	257.98
U.S. Virgin Islands	108,605	5,717.76	1,672.34	776.87	2,627.07	105.10	536.37
Undistributed	N.A.	0.00	0.00	0.00	0.00	0.00	0.00

Source: U.S. Department of Commerce, Bureau of the Census, Consolidated Federal Funds Report for Fiscal Year 2006, April 2008.

Note: U.S. total population and per capita figures in the top row include only the 50 states and the District of Columbia; the U.S. Outlying Areas represented at the bottom of the table are excluded from this figure.

N.A. — Not applicable

(a) All population figures represent resident population as of July 1, 2006.

Table 2.16
PERCENT DISTRIBUTION OF FEDERAL GOVERNMENT EXPENDITURE, BY MAJOR OBJECT CATEGORY, BY STATE AND OUTLYING AREA: FISCAL YEAR 2006
(In dollars)

State and outlying area	*Percent distribution of United States resident population— July 1, 2006 (a)*	*Total*	*Retirement and disability*	*Other direct payments*	*Grants*	*Procurement*	*Salaries and wages*
United States	100%	100%	100%	100%	100%	100%	100%
Alabama	1.5	1.8	2.0	1.7	1.5	2.0	1.5
Alaska	0.2	0.4	0.2	0.1	0.6	0.5	0.9
Arizona	2.0	1.9	2.0	1.5	1.8	2.6	1.6
Arkansas	0.9	0.9	1.1	1.0	0.9	0.3	0.7
California	12.0	10.3	9.5	10.9	11.1	10.6	9.6
Colorado	1.6	1.4	1.3	1.1	1.2	1.8	2.0
Connecticut	1.2	1.2	1.1	1.2	1.1	2.0	0.7
Delaware	0.3	0.2	0.3	0.2	0.3	0.1	0.2
Florida	6.0	5.8	7.1	7.3	4.5	3.6	4.6
Georgia	3.1	2.6	2.7	2.3	2.4	2.5	3.8
Hawaii	0.4	0.5	0.5	0.3	0.5	0.5	1.5
Idaho	0.5	0.4	0.5	0.3	0.4	0.4	0.4
Illinois	4.2	3.3	3.8	4.2	3.3	1.7	2.9
Indiana	2.1	1.8	2.1	2.1	1.6	1.3	1.1
Iowa	1.0	0.9	1.0	1.2	0.8	0.5	0.5
Kansas	0.9	0.9	0.9	1.0	0.7	0.7	1.1
Kentucky	1.4	1.5	1.6	1.3	1.4	1.8	1.6
Louisiana	1.4	2.8	1.4	4.2	4.6	2.3	1.2
Maine	0.4	0.4	0.5	0.4	0.5	0.3	0.4
Maryland	1.8	3.1	2.1	2.0	3.2	5.3	4.6
Massachusetts	2.1	2.3	2.1	2.4	2.7	2.7	1.5
Michigan	3.3	2.7	3.5	3.3	2.6	1.4	1.6
Minnesota	1.7	1.3	1.5	1.5	1.4	0.7	1.0
Mississippi	1.0	1.7	1.1	1.6	3.2	1.7	0.8
Missouri	1.9	2.1	2.1	2.2	1.7	2.7	1.9
Montana	0.3	0.3	0.4	0.3	0.4	0.1	0.4
Nebraska	0.6	0.6	0.6	0.8	0.5	0.3	0.6
Nevada	0.8	0.6	0.8	0.5	0.5	0.6	0.6
New Hampshire	0.4	0.4	0.5	0.3	0.4	0.3	0.3
New Jersey	2.9	2.5	2.8	2.9	2.3	2.1	1.8
New Mexico	0.6	0.9	0.7	0.5	0.9	1.5	0.9
New York	6.4	6.2	6.1	7.1	9.2	2.9	4.0
North Carolina	2.9	2.5	3.1	2.3	2.6	1.1	3.3
North Dakota	0.2	0.3	0.2	0.4	0.3	0.1	0.3
Ohio	3.8	3.3	3.9	3.7	3.3	2.2	2.4
Oklahoma	1.2	1.2	1.4	1.2	1.1	0.7	1.5
Oregon	1.2	1.0	1.3	0.9	1.1	0.3	0.8
Pennsylvania	4.1	4.2	4.9	5.1	4.1	2.7	2.8
Rhode Island	0.4	0.4	0.4	0.4	0.5	0.1	0.3
South Carolina	1.4	1.4	1.7	1.2	1.3	1.2	1.4
South Dakota	0.3	0.3	0.3	0.5	0.3	0.2	0.3
Tennessee	2.0	2.1	2.2	2.1	1.9	2.2	1.5
Texas	7.7	6.8	6.4	6.5	6.2	8.7	6.8
Utah	0.8	0.6	0.6	0.4	0.6	0.8	0.9
Vermont	0.2	0.2	0.2	0.2	0.3	0.2	0.2
Virginia	2.5	4.2	3.1	2.4	1.5	10.3	7.1
Washington	2.1	2.0	2.2	1.5	1.8	2.0	2.7
West Virginia	0.6	0.7	0.9	0.6	0.7	0.3	0.6
Wisconsin	1.8	1.4	1.8	1.5	1.4	0.8	0.9
Wyoming	0.2	0.2	0.2	0.1	0.4	0.1	0.2
Dist. of Columbia	0.2	1.6	0.3	0.5	0.8	3.5	7.0
American Samoa	0.0	0.0	0.0	0.0	0.0	0.0	0.0
Fed. States of Micronesia	0.0	0.0	0.0	0.0	0.0	0.0	0.0
Guam	0.1	0.1	0.0	0.0	0.1	0.1	0.1
Marshall Islands	0.0	0.0	0.0	0.0	0.0	0.0	0.0
No. Mariana Islands	0.0	0.0	0.0	0.0	0.0	0.0	0.0
Palau	0.0	0.0	0.0	0.0	0.0	0.0	0.0
Puerto Rico	1.3	0.7	0.9	0.6	1.0	0.2	0.4
U.S. Virgin Islands	0.0	0.0	0.0	0.0	0.1	0.0	0.0
Undistributed	0.0	1.0	0.0	0.1	0.0	4.4	1.8

Source: U.S. Department of Commerce, Bureau of the Census, Consolidated Federal Funds Report for Fiscal Year 2006, April 2008.

Note: Detail may not add to total because of rounding. Values for the 50 states, the District of Columbia, and the U.S. Outlying Areas were used in calculating these distributions.

(a) All population figures represent resident population as of July 1, 2006.

Table 2.17
FEDERAL GOVERNMENT EXPENDITURE FOR DEFENSE DEPARTMENT AND ALL OTHER AGENCIES, BY STATE AND OUTLYING AREA: FISCAL YEAR 2006

State and outlying area	Federal expenditure (millions of dollars)		Per capita federal expenditure (dollars) (a)		Percent distribution of federal expenditure		Exhibit: Dept. of Energy, defense-related activities (millions of dollars) (b)
	Dept. of Defense	All other federal agencies	Dept. of Defense	All other federal agencies	Dept. of Defense	All other federal agencies	
United States	399,899	2,055,099	1,306.00	6,752.14	100%	100%	16,064
Alabama	9,526	34,403	2,071.22	7,480.45	2.4	1.7	0
Alaska	3,198	6,052	4,772.31	9,032.68	0.8	0.3	0
Arizona	11,897	34,458	1,929.34	5,588.11	3.0	1.7	0
Arkansas	1,916	19,585	681.49	6,967.44	0.5	1.0	0
California	46,236	207,670	1,268.21	5,696.21	11.6	10.1	1,233
Colorado	7,154	27,269	1,504.95	5,736.76	1.8	1.3	522
Connecticut	8,533	22,084	2,434.68	6,300.95	2.1	1.1	0
Delaware	543	5,310	636.61	6,221.06	0.1	0.3	0
Florida	19,157	123,548	1,059.00	6,829.68	4.8	6.0	15
Georgia	12,201	52,350	1,302.94	5,590.59	3.1	2.5	0
Hawaii	5,379	8,112	4,184.53	6,310.32	1.3	0.4	0
Idaho	714	9,236	487.11	6,297.85	0.2	0.4	780
Illinois	5,810	76,411	452.80	5,954.74	1.5	3.7	320
Indiana	5,788	37,979	916.69	6,015.48	1.4	1.8	0
Iowa	1,408	20,427	472.16	6,849.87	0.4	1.0	0
Kansas	3,409	18,114	1,233.16	6,553.52	0.9	0.9	0
Kentucky	8,074	29,530	1,919.66	7,020.88	2.0	1.4	18
Louisiana	6,878	62,852	1,604.21	14,658.55	1.7	3.1	0
Maine	1,729	9,250	1,308.37	6,999.46	0.4	0.5	0
Maryland	14,640	60,858	2,606.89	10,837.08	3.7	3.0	66
Massachusetts	10,088	47,134	1,567.10	7,322.16	2.5	2.3	0
Michigan	4,986	62,366	493.86	6,177.51	1.2	3.0	0
Minnesota	2,293	29,615	443.80	5,731.37	0.6	1.4	0
Mississippi	7,336	34,914	2,520.42	11,995.88	1.8	1.7	0
Missouri	11,685	40,581	1,999.99	6,945.58	2.9	2.0	408
Montana	664	7,347	702.72	7,777.78	0.2	0.4	0
Nebraska	1,606	12,321	908.29	6,967.41	0.4	0.6	0
Nevada	1,866	12,737	747.64	5,104.10	0.5	0.6	762
New Hampshire	1,519	7,356	1,155.19	5,594.64	0.4	0.4	0
New Jersey	7,768	53,499	890.31	6,132.01	1.9	2.6	0
New Mexico	2,366	18,572	1,210.55	9,501.78	0.6	0.9	3,927
New York	10,600	142,334	549.07	7,372.43	2.7	6.9	433
North Carolina	9,560	52,450	1,079.48	5,922.25	2.4	2.6	0
North Dakota	741	5,572	1,165.36	8,762.67	0.2	0.3	0
Ohio	8,696	72,078	757.66	6,279.64	2.2	3.5	613
Oklahoma	4,841	24,237	1,352.47	6,771.47	1.2	1.2	0
Oregon	1,270	22,316	343.08	6,030.21	0.3	1.1	0
Pennsylvania	10,389	92,876	835.05	7,465.56	2.6	4.5	381
Rhode Island	1,006	7,760	942.16	7,268.85	0.3	0.4	0
South Carolina	5,362	28,471	1,240.93	6,588.57	1.3	1.4	1,731
South Dakota	742	7,249	949.33	9,270.73	0.2	0.4	0
Tennessee	4,282	46,314	709.14	7,669.40	1.1	2.3	1,370
Texas	38,102	128,516	1,620.83	5,466.97	9.5	6.3	506
Utah	3,689	12,025	1,446.67	4,715.52	0.9	0.6	0
Vermont	933	4,341	1,496.11	6,956.97	0.2	0.2	0
Virginia	44,601	58,461	5,835.57	7,649.10	11.2	2.8	0
Washington	9,753	38,423	1,524.96	6,007.61	2.4	1.9	1,914
West Virginia	741	15,469	407.23	8,506.53	0.2	0.8	4
Wisconsin	2,835	31,726	510.13	5,709.73	0.7	1.5	0
Wyoming	465	4,705	903.17	9,135.69	0.1	0.2	12
Dist. of Columbia	6,040	34,318	10,387.07	59,013.23	1.5	1.7	1,047
American Samoa	18	228	307.74	3,950.03	0.0	0.0	0
Fed. States of Micronesia	0	100	0.30	925.56	0.0	0.0	0
Guam	739	642	4,318.64	3,752.69	0.2	0.0	0
Marshall Islands	110	81	1,817.46	1,341.19	0.0	0.0	0
No. Mariana Islands	3	174	36.52	2,108.59	0.0	0.0	0
Palau	0	37	7.05	1,794.34	0.0	0.0	0
Puerto Rico	688	15,544	175.12	3,957.47	0.2	0.8	0
U.S. Virgin Islands	18	603	165.35	5,552.42	0.0	0.0	0
Undistributed	7,310	16,108	0.00	0.00	1.8	0.8	0

Source: U.S. Department of Commerce, Bureau of the Census, Consolidated Federal Funds Report for Fiscal Year 2006, April 2008.

Note: Detail may not add to total due to rounding. For additional information see the complete report at *http://www.census.gov/govs/www/cffr.html.*

(a) All population figures represent resident population as of July 1, 2006.

(b) These data are presented for illustrative purposes only. They were compiled from preliminary FY 2006 state budget allocation tables that were prepared for submission to Congress and that were found on the Department of Energy Web site.

Table 2.18
STATE RANKINGS FOR PER CAPITA AMOUNTS OF FEDERAL GOVERNMENT EXPENDITURE: FISCAL YEAR 2006

State	Total	Retirement and disability	Other direct payments	Grants	Procurement	Salaries and wages
Alabama	11	2	10	19	9	20
Alaska	3	49	49	3	3	1
Arizona	31	40	43	32	11	31
Arkansas	29	5	16	17	48	37
California	38	48	29	25	20	30
Colorado	33	46	45	43	14	11
Connecticut	16	36	22	24	6	45
Delaware	41	12	35	21	50	33
Florida	25	7	8	47	32	32
Georgia	40	45	40	44	23	12
Hawaii	7	15	42	16	13	2
Idaho	42	38	47	34	21	29
Illinois	45	43	24	45	45	39
Indiana	39	33	19	41	30	48
Iowa	32	24	7	38	37	47
Kansas	28	28	14	48	25	14
Kentucky	13	11	26	18	10	15
Louisiana	1	34	1	2	7	28
Maine	20	3	31	13	27	25
Maryland	5	13	17	5	2	4
Massachusetts	15	37	9	12	12	36
Michigan	44	27	21	42	42	49
Minnesota	48	44	30	35	47	46
Mississippi	2	14	4	1	5	26
Missouri	12	18	11	27	8	23
Montana	17	10	20	10	44	9
Nebraska	26	32	5	31	41	22
Nevada	50	42	48	49	28	35
New Hampshire	43	22	46	37	24	41
New Jersey	36	39	25	39	26	42
New Mexico	6	17	39	6	4	6
New York	24	41	12	7	39	43
North Carolina	37	21	38	28	46	16
North Dakota	10	29	3	8	36	5
Ohio	35	31	27	30	35	44
Oklahoma	23	8	23	23	33	8
Oregon	46	23	41	26	49	40
Pennsylvania	21	6	6	20	29	38
Rhode Island	22	19	13	11	43	21
South Carolina	27	9	32	29	22	18
South Dakota	8	20	2	15	34	13
Tennessee	19	16	15	22	16	34
Texas	34	47	33	38	15	27
Utah	49	50	50	46	19	17
Vermont	18	26	34	9	17	24
Virginia	4	4	28	50	1	3
Washington	30	30	44	33	18	10
West Virginia	14	1	18	14	38	19
Wisconsin	47	35	37	40	40	50
Wyoming	9	25	36	4	31	7

Source: U.S. Department of Commerce, Bureau of the Census, Consolidated Federal Funds Report for Fiscal Year 2006, April 2008.

Note: States are ranked from largest per capita amount of federal funds (1) to smallest per capita amount of federal funds (50). Rankings are based upon per capita amounts shown in Table 2.10. Federal funds for loans and insurance coverage are excluded from consideration in this table. Also excluded are per capita amounts from the District of Columbia and the U.S. Outlying Areas.

Chapter Three

STATE LEGISLATIVE BRANCH

2008 Legislative Elections

By Tim Storey

Democrats have been on a roll in legislative elections and increased their numbers again in 2008. Buoyed by the strong campaign of President Barack Obama in many key states, Democratic gains last year leave them at their best political position in legislatures in well over a decade. Democrats control 24 legislatures, Republicans control 14 and 8 are divided between the two parties.

For the third consecutive election cycle, Democrats made gains in legislatures in 2008 elections. Democrats now hold more than 55 percent of all legislative seats for the first time since getting crushed by Republicans in 1994. Democrats netted just shy of 100 seats in 2008 padding their 350 seat gains over the past four years. The gains were far from a landslide and definitely limited because the party has come off of two consecutive election cycles where they increased their numbers.

Nationally, it's been a rough four years for Republican legislative candidates. After the 2004 election, there were almost exactly the same number of Republican and Democratic state legislators. Now, there are 862 more Democratic legislators than Republicans, and Democrats control a majority of all state legislatures.

Courtesy of 2008 gains, Democratic legislators fill 4,084 of the nation's 7,382 state legislative seats with Republicans holding 3,222. Third party candidates, including the country's only current Green Party legislator in Arkansas, control 17 legislative seats, or less than one percent. Candidates run for the Nebraska Senate in nonpartisan elections, so those 49 senate seats are considered nonpartisan. As is always the case, a handful of seats are vacant pending special elections or appointments.

President Obama's convincing Electoral College win spelled good news for many Democratic legislative candidates. At the top of the ticket, Obama, a former Illinois state senator, won the Electoral College vote 365-173 and defeated Arizona Senator John McCain by more than 9.4 million votes garnering 52.9 percent of all votes cast for president. Obama's coattails and vaunted campaign field operation undoubtedly helped Democrats gain seats, and in some cases majority control, in legislatures in some highly contested battleground states such as Nevada, Ohio and Wisconsin. However, in states like Oklahoma and Tennessee that did not see substantial campaign activity from either McCain or Obama, Republicans picked up seats and took majority control, and in fact, an anti-Obama backlash in those states may have helped Republican candidates. Oklahoma was the only state in the country where Senator McCain won every county.

With redistricting just around the proverbial corner, Republicans are hoping for a big comeback in 2010 when traditionally, the party controlling the White House loses big in legislative races. The GOP can also take solace in the fact that the last time a party gained seats in four consecutive elections was in the 1930s. Winning four election cycles in a row has only happened twice in the past 110 years. But 2008, like 2006 and 2004, belonged to the Democrats.

Post-2008 Numbers

A total of 5,824 of the nation's 7,382 state legislative seats were scheduled for elections last year in 44 states. Six states did *not* have regular legislative elections in 2008. Louisiana, Mississippi, New Jersey and Virginia hold state-level elections in odd-numbered years, so they had only special elections to fill vacancies in 2008. In Maryland and Alabama, all legislators serve four-year terms and were last elected in 2006, so they also did not have any elections. Michigan and Minnesota only had state house elections last year; no senate seats were up in those two states. More than 10,000 candidates ran in the general election for legislative seats in 2008, and as usual, about 35 percent of the races were uncontested.

Prior to the 2008 election, Democrats controlled the legislative branch in 23 states while Republicans had majority control in both chambers in 14 states. In 12 states, partisan control was divided with neither party controlling both the house/assembly and senate. The legislature of Nebraska is unicameral and nonpartisan. Elections in 2008 led to Democrats adding four to the number of states in their column—all states that were previously divided. At 27 states, Democrats now control more than half of all legislatures for the first time since before the 1992 election

Figure A: State Legislative Party Control, 2009

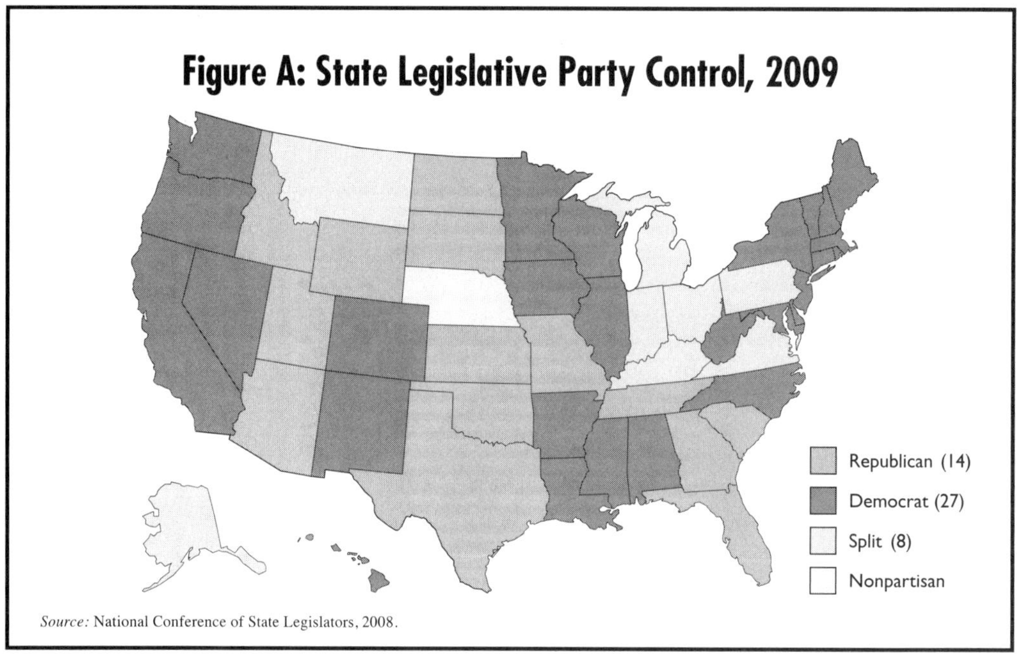

Source: National Conference of State Legislators, 2008.

when they had the majority of both chambers in 30 states. Republicans emerged from the election controlling both houses of the legislature in 14 states. Only eight legislatures have divided control which is the lowest number of split legislatures in 25 years.

Democrats gained legislative seats in 31 of the 44 states with 2008 elections, and Republicans picked up seats in nine states. There were three states (Kansas, Missouri and Washington) where the overall partisan numbers were the same before and after the election.

There were only 11 governor's races in 2008. Missouri was the only state where the party of the governor changed in the election going from Republican to Democrat. However, Republicans regained control of the governor's office in Arizona after Democrat Gov. Janet Napolitano resigned to become the Secretary of the Department of Homeland Security under President Obama thus making Republican Secretary of State Jan Brewer Arizona's governor. Democrats still hold the majority of governors with a 28 Democrat-22 Republican advantage. There are 17 states in all regions of the country where Democrats control all of state government. Republicans control the governor and the legislature in nine states, and 23 states have divided control.

In terms of legislative chambers, the post-2008 numbers looked good for Democrats. Headed into 2009 sessions, Democrats had numerical majorities in 60 chambers. Republicans claim an outright majority in 36 legislative bodies and two wound up tied. The election left the Alaska Senate, the nation's smallest legislative body, tied at 10 Democrats to 10 Republicans and the Montana House, the nation's most competitive legislative body, tied at 50 Democrats to 50 Republicans.

New Majorities

Since 1900, an average of 12 legislative chambers change hands in every election cycle and just like in 2006, this was an average year. Twelve chambers switched hands in this election cycle including two that went from tied to Democratic control. In the 2008 elections, Democrats supplemented their pick-up of the Virginia Senate in 2007 by adding five chambers to their control column. Republicans earned the majority in four legislative bodies. As noted above, two chambers went from GOP control to being tied—the Alaska Senate and the Montana House.

The Montana House, now tied 50 Democrats to 50 Republicans, has been the most competitive chamber in the country for the past 20 years. Party control in the Montana House has shifted nine times since 1980—more than any other legislative body. Montana takes the prize for political competitiveness in legislative elections because in addition to the House, the next most competitive chamber in the

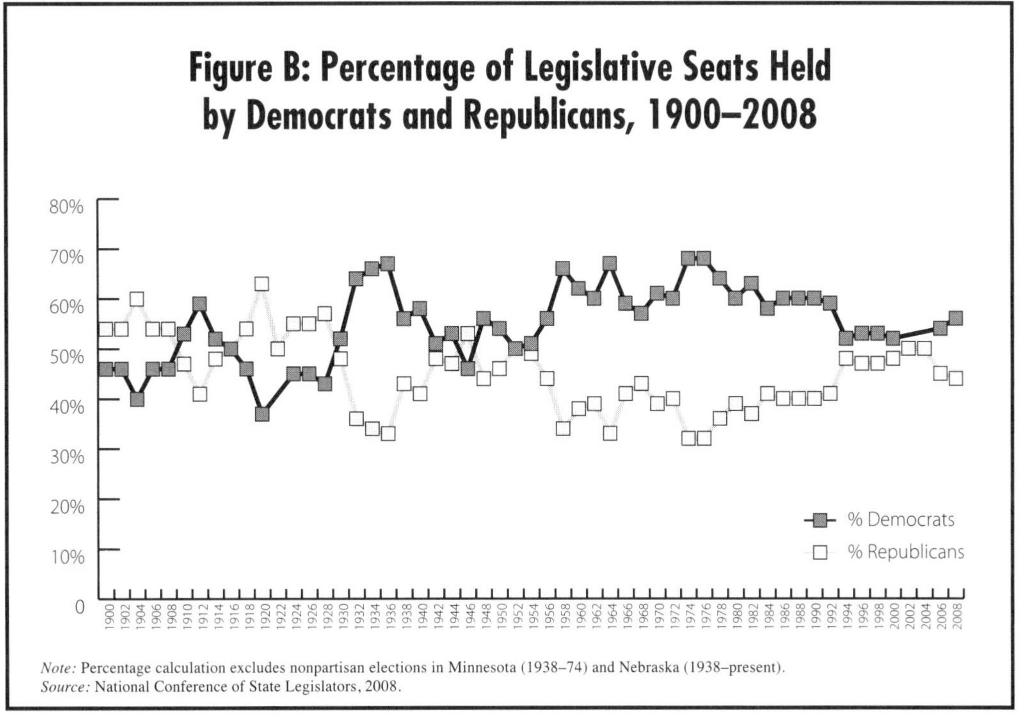

Figure B: Percentage of Legislative Seats Held by Democrats and Republicans, 1900–2008

Note: Percentage calculation excludes nonpartisan elections in Minnesota (1938–74) and Nebraska (1938–present).
Source: National Conference of State Legislators, 2008.

country over the past 30 years is the Montana Senate. It has switched eight times since 1980 and is now held by Republicans after four years of a Democratic majority. Under Montana law, the party holding the governor's office gets to organize and choose the leaders when there is a tie in the legislature. Since the state has a Democratic governor, the Montana House Speaker is Democratic Rep. Bob Bergren. At least one state legislative body has been tied with an even number of Democrats and Republicans for the past 25 years. During that time, both the Alaska Senate and Montana House were tied twice before, so those two chambers are now tied for the third time in 25 years.

The other tied legislative body following last year's elections is the Alaska Senate. A coalition including all 10 Democratic and three Republican senators voted to elect Republican Sen. Gary Stevens as the Senate President in Alaska. Democrats gained seats in both chambers of the Alaska Legislature even though the state's popular governor, Sarah Palin, was at the top of the GOP ticket as the vice-presidential candidate.

The coalition vote for Alaska Senate President where the leader needed a substantial block of the opposite, or minority, party to get elected was one of several such arrangements coming off the 2008 election. There are similar, coalition style, leadership arrangements in four additional chambers—the Louisiana House, the New Mexico Senate, the Tennessee House and the Texas House. It is not unusual for there to be coalition leadership in one or two legislatures every year, but five chambers at once is unusually high.

In addition to taking the Montana Senate, the other bright spots for the GOP were in two southern states, Oklahoma and Tennessee. Before the election, the Oklahoma Senate was tied 24 Democrats to 24 Republicans and had been operating with co-Senate leaders for two years under a power sharing agreement. In a state where Republican presidential candidate U.S. Sen. John McCain ran very strong, the party grabbed two Senate seats emerging with a 26 Republican to 22 Democrat majority. It is the first time since Oklahoma became a state in 1907 that Republicans have controlled the Sooner State Senate.

Technically, the Tennessee Senate was also tied at 16-16 with one independent prior to last fall's election although Republicans had functional control over the body under a coalition vote including the lone independent. Tennessee was another state where

McCain ran strong helping Republicans there win three additional seats and earn a 19 Republican to 14 Democrat majority. The Tennessee House results were far closer. In the 2008 election, 50 Republican candidates won Tennessee House seats giving the party a numerical majority in the House for the first time since reconstruction. However, in a contentious vote for the House Speaker, all 49 Democratic Representatives joined to elect Republican Kent Williams as the new Speaker. The Tennessee State Republican Party subsequently expelled Williams from the state party.

Democrats picked up chambers from Republicans in five states including several in large states that had been controlled by the GOP for decades. Perhaps the biggest prize for Democrats was the New York Senate. Barack Obama won New York by a 25 percent margin and that helped Democrats pry away two state Senate seats and get a majority of 32 Democrats to 30 Republicans. It is the first time Democrats have controlled the Empire State Senate since 1966. Looking at overall control of state government including the Assembly and the governor's office in New York, it is the first time that Democrats have controlled the state since 1935 when Herman H. Lehman was the governor.

Another state that shifted demonstrably to all-Democratic control was Delaware where the party won the House after picking up six seats. With Delaware's favorite son, U.S. Sen. Joe Biden, running at the top of the ticket for vice-president, Democrats swept into power including a victory over long-time House Speaker Terry Spence. Before losing his re-election race, Spence had served as speaker for 20 years and had the distinction of being the longest serving House speaker in the country.

In Ohio, term limits helped open the door for Democrats to take the House for the first time since losing it in 1994. Of the 21 representatives termed-out in 2008, 17 of them were Republican, so it was a golden opportunity for the Democrats who took advantage of record spending in the state by the Obama campaign to flip the numbers from 53 Republicans to 46 Democrats before the election to a 53 Democrat to 46 Republican advantage.

Also for the first time since 1994, Democrats took over the Wisconsin legislature by winning the Assembly 52 Democrats to 47 Republicans with one independent. Democrats won the Wisconsin Senate in 2006.

Democrats unified control in Nevada by winning a 12 Democrat to 9 Republican majority in the Senate, the second-smallest state legislative body in the United States. Republicans controlled the Nevada Senate for 16 years although never by more than three seats.

Regional Breakdown

Republicans renewed their success in the southern part of the United States in the 2008 election cycle although not by much. The party netted 6 legislative seats in the 15 southern states. Since 1982, Republicans have steadily gained seats in the south in every election except for 2006 when Democrats won 24 seats. Republicans now hold 14 of the 30 legislative chambers in the south. Republican gains in the region were hampered by a strong Democratic showing in Texas House races where Republicans held on to a 76 Republican to 74 Democrat majority. One Texas House Republican incumbent won re-election by 19 votes out of more than 40,000 cast or the chamber would have been tied.

With the addition of the Delaware House and New York Senate, Democrats now dominate the northeastern part of the country. The only legislative body north of Virginia and east of Ohio held by Republicans is the Pennsylvania Senate. Democrats now hold more than 65 percent of all legislative seats in the eastern states which is the highest percentage Democrats have enjoyed in that region, formerly dominated by the Republican Party, since at least 1900. The best region for the GOP is the Midwest where they command just more than half of all legislative seats. In the west, Democrats have increased their share of seats to more than 53 percent.

Diversity of Legislators

The 2008 legislative elections brought about the most diverse picture of state legislatures in history. Women now make up nearly a quarter of state legislatures increasing to 24.2 percent—the highest level ever. Another historic first for the country occurred in New Hampshire when women candidates won more than half of the races for the Granite State Senate. It is the first time in U.S. history that a legislative body has a majority of women members.

The number of African-American legislators also surged in the election. Nine percent of state legislators are African-American. And in another historic first, the Colorado Senate and House both elected African-American presiding officers—Senate President Peter Groff and House Speaker Terrance Carroll. It is the first time in American history that two black legislators presided over a legislature in the same state at the same time. The number of Latino state legislators also increased in 2008 with Latino legislators now making up more than 3 percent of legislatures. Most Latino legislators serve in five states: New Mexico, California, Texas, Florida and Nevada.

Conclusion

Overall legislative turnover was down slightly in 2008 to 17.3 percent with more than 1,100 new state legislators taking office in 2009. The turnover numbers may spike up in 2010 because the national parties will be pouring money into state legislative races at unprecedented levels in advance of redistricting. That could lead to more volatility. It is also possible that some current members will want to retire before 2010 rather than face a rancorous redistricting process.

Even though 2008 was another Democratic year in legislative elections, Republicans have plenty of reasons to be optimistic about the all-important 2010 pre-redistricting election. Since 1900, the party holding the White House has lost seats in legislatures in every presidential mid-term election except for two—in 1934 during the depression and in 2002 in an election dominated by the events of Sept. 11, 2001. That means that the party out of the White House has gained seats in 25 out of the last 27 mid-term election cycles which is a daunting trend for Democrats to break. And if Democrats could manage to net seats in 2010, it would be the fourth consecutive election cycle to go their way, and that hasn't happened since Democrats did it in 1936. Unless legislative election trends going back over a century break, 2010 could be a resurgent year for the GOP just in time for legislative and congressional redistricting.

About the Author

Tim Storey is a senior fellow in the Legislative Management Program of the Denver, Colo.-based National Conference of State Legislatures. He specializes in the areas of elections and redistricting as well as legislative organization and management. He has staffed NCSL's Redistricting and Elections Committee since 1990 and authored numerous articles on the topics of elections and redistricting. Every two years, he leads NCSL's StateVote project to track and analyze legislative election results. He graduated from Mars Hill College in North Carolina and received his master's degree from the University of Colorado's Graduate School of Public Affairs.

Table 3.1
NAMES OF STATE LEGISLATIVE BODIES AND CONVENING PLACES

State or other jurisdiction	Both bodies	Upper house	Lower house	Convening place
Alabama	Legislature	Senate	House of Representatives	State House
Alaska	Legislature	Senate	House of Representatives	State Capitol
Arizona	Legislature	Senate	House of Representatives	State Capitol
Arkansas	General Assembly	Senate	House of Representatives	State Capitol
California	Legislature	Senate	Assembly	State Capitol
Colorado	General Assembly	Senate	House of Representatives	State Capitol
Connecticut	General Assembly	Senate	House of Representatives	State Capitol
Delaware	General Assembly	Senate	House of Representatives	Legislative Hall
Florida	Legislature	Senate	House of Representatives	The Capitol
Georgia	General Assembly	Senate	House of Representatives	State Capitol
Hawaii	Legislature	Senate	House of Representatives	State Capitol
Idaho	Legislature	Senate	House of Representatives	State Capitol
Illinois	General Assembly	Senate	House of Representatives	State House
Indiana	General Assembly	Senate	House of Representatives	State House
Iowa	General Assembly	Senate	House of Representatives	State Capitol
Kansas	Legislature	Senate	House of Representatives	State Capitol
Kentucky	General Assembly	Senate	House of Representatives	State Capitol
Louisiana	Legislature	Senate	House of Representatives	State Capitol
Maine	Legislature	Senate	House of Representatives	State House
Maryland	General Assembly	Senate	House of Delegates	State House
Massachusetts	General Court	Senate	House of Representatives	State House
Michigan	Legislature	Senate	House of Representatives	State Capitol
Minnesota	Legislature	Senate	House of Representatives	State Capitol
Mississippi	Legislature	Senate	House of Representatives	State Capitol
Missouri	General Assembly	Senate	House of Representatives	State Capitol
Montana	Legislature	Senate	House of Representatives	State Capitol
Nebraska	Legislature	(a)		State Capitol
Nevada	Legislature	Senate	Assembly	Legislative Building
New Hampshire	General Court	Senate	House of Representatives	State House
New Jersey	Legislature	Senate	General Assembly	State House
New Mexico	Legislature	Senate	House of Representatives	State Capitol
New York	Legislature	Senate	Assembly	State Capitol
North Carolina	General Assembly	Senate	House of Representatives	State Legislative Building
North Dakota	Legislative Assembly	Senate	House of Representatives	State Capitol
Ohio	General Assembly	Senate	House of Representatives	State House
Oklahoma	Legislature	Senate	House of Representatives	State Capitol
Oregon	Legislative Assembly	Senate	House of Representatives	State Capitol
Pennsylvania	General Assembly	Senate	House of Representatives	Main Capitol Building
Rhode Island	General Assembly	Senate	House of Representatives	State House
South Carolina	General Assembly	Senate	House of Representatives	State House
South Dakota	Legislature	Senate	House of Representatives	State Capitol
Tennessee	General Assembly	Senate	House of Representatives	State Capitol
Texas	Legislature	Senate	House of Representatives	State Capitol
Utah	Legislature	Senate	House of Representatives	State Capitol
Vermont	General Assembly	Senate	House of Representatives	State House
Virginia	General Assembly	Senate	House of Delegates	State Capitol
Washington	Legislature	Senate	House of Representatives	State Capitol
West Virginia	Legislature	Senate	House of Delegates	State Capitol
Wisconsin	Legislature	Senate	Assembly (b)	State Capitol
Wyoming	Legislature	Senate	House of Representatives	State Capitol
Dist. of Columbia	Council of the District of Columbia	(a)		Council Chamber
American Samoa	Legislature	Senate	House of Representatives	Maota Fono
Guam	Legislature	(a)		Congress Building
No. Mariana Islands	Legislature	Senate	House of Representatives	Civic Center Building
Puerto Rico	Legislative Assembly	Senate	House of Representatives	The Capitol
U.S. Virgin Islands	Legislature	(a)		Capitol Building

Source: The Council of State Governments, *Directory I — Elective Officials 2008.*

Key:

(a) Unicameral legislature. Except in the District of Columbia, members go by the title Senator.

(b) Members of the lower house go by the title Representative.

Table 3.2
LEGISLATIVE SESSIONS: LEGAL PROVISIONS

State or other jurisdiction	Regular sessions: Year	Regular sessions: Legislature convenes: Month	Regular sessions: Legislature convenes: Day	Regular sessions: Limitation on length of session (a)	Special sessions: Legislature may call	Special sessions: Legislature may determine subject	Special sessions: Limitation on length of session
Alabama	Annual	Jan. Mar. Feb.	2nd Tues. (b) 1st Tues. (c)(d) 1st Tues. (e)	30 L in 105 C	No	Yes (f)	12 L in 30 C
Alaska	Annual	Jan.	3rd Tues. (g)	121 C; 90 Statutory (g)	By petition, 2/3 members, each house	Yes	30 C
Arizona	Annual	Jan.	2nd Mon.	(h)	By petition, 2/3 members, each house	Yes	None
Arkansas	Annual	Jan. Feb.	2nd Mon. 2nd Mon.	60 C (i) 30C	No	No (j)	None
California	Biennium (k)	Jan.	1st Mon. (d)	None	No	No	None
Colorado	Annual	Jan.	No later than 2nd Wed.	120 C	By petition, 2/3 members, each house	Yes (l)	None
Connecticut	Annual	Jan. Jan.	Wed. after 1st Mon. (odd-years) Wed. after 1st Mon. (even-years)	(m)	By petition, 2/3 members, each house (n)	Yes	None
Delaware	Annual	Jan.	2nd Tues.	June 30	Joint call, presiding officers, both houses	No	None
Florida	Annual	Mar.	1st Tues. after 1st Mon. (o)	60 C (i)	Joint call, presiding officers, both houses or by petition	Yes	20 C (i)
Georgia	Annual	Jan.	2nd Mon.	40 L	By petition, 3/5 members, each house	No (p)	40 L
Hawaii	Annual	Jan.	3rd Wed.	60 L (i)	By petition, 2/3 members, each house	Yes	30 L (i)
Idaho	Annual	Jan.	Mon. on or nearest 9th day	None	No	No	20 C
Illinois	Annual	Jan.	2nd Wed.	None (q)	Joint call, presiding officers, both houses	Yes (l)	None
Indiana	Annual	Jan.	2nd Mon. (r)	odd-61 C or Apr. 29; even-30 C or Mar. 14	No	Yes	30 L or 40 C
Iowa	Annual	Jan.	2nd Mon.	None	By petition, 2/3 members, each house	Yes	None
Kansas	Annual	Jan.	2nd Mon.	odd-None; even-90 C (i)	Petition to governor of 2/3 members, each house	Yes	None
Kentucky	Annual	Jan.	1st Tues after 1st Mon.	even-60 L; odd-30 L (s)	No	No	None
Louisiana	Annual	Mar. (even-years) Apr. (odd-years)	last Mon. (even-years) last Mon. (odd-years)	even-60 L in 85 C; odd-45 L in 60 C	By petition, majority, each house	Yes	30 C
Maine	(t)	Dec. (even-years); January (subsequent even-year)	1st Wed. (quadrennial election year) Wed. after 1st Tues.	Calendar days set by statute (u)	Joint call, presiding officers of both houses with the consent of a majority of the members of each political party	Yes	None
Maryland	Annual	Jan.	2nd Wed.	90 C	By petition, majority, each house	Yes	30 C
Massachusetts	Biennium	Jan.	1st Wed.	(v)	By petition (w)	Yes	None
Michigan	Annual	Jan.	2nd Wed.	None	No	No	None
Minnesota	Biennium	Feb.	Feb. 12, 2008	120 L	No (x)	Yes	None

See footnotes at end of table.

LEGISLATIVE SESSIONS: LEGAL PROVISIONS — Continued

State or other jurisdiction	Regular sessions				Special sessions		
		Legislature convenes					
	Year	Month	Day	Limitation on length of session (a)	Legislature may call	Legislature may determine subject	Limitation on length of session
Mississippi	Annual	Jan.	Tues. after 1st Mon.	125 C (y); 90 C (y)	No	No	None
Missouri	Annual	Jan.	Wed. after 1st Mon.	May 30	By petition, 3/4 members, each house	Yes (l)	30 C (z)
Montana	Biennial-odd year	Jan.	1st Mon.	90 L	By petition, majority, each house	Yes	None
Nebraska	Annual	Jan.	Wed. after 1st Mon.	odd-90 L; even-60 L	By petition, 2/3 members, each house	Yes	None
Nevada	Biennial-odd year	Feb.	1st Mon.	120 C	No	No	None (aa)
New Hampshire	Annual	Jan.	Wed. after 1st Tues.	45 L	By petition, 2/3 members, each house	Yes	15 L (bb)
New Jersey	Biennium	Jan.	2nd Tues. of even year	None	By petition, majority, each house (cc)	Yes	None
New Mexico	Annual	Jan.	3rd Tues.	odd-60 C; even-30 C	By petition, 3/5 members, each house (l)	Yes (l)	30 C
New York	Annual	Jan. (dd)	Wed. after 1st Mon.	None	By petition, 2/3 members, each house	Yes (l)	None
North Carolina	(ee)	Jan.	3rd Wed. after 2nd Mon. (odd-years)	None	By petition, 3/5 members, each house	Yes	None
North Dakota	Biennial-odd year	Jan.	Tues. after Jan. 3, but not later than Jan. 11	80 L in the biennium	Yes (ff)	Yes	None (ff)
Ohio	Biennium	Jan.	1st Mon. (gg)	None	Joint call, presiding officers, both houses	Yes	None
Oklahoma	Annual	Feb.	1st Mon.	last Fri. in May	By petition, 2/3 members, each house	Yes	None
Oregon	Biennial-odd year	Jan.	2nd Mon.	None	By petition, majority, each house	Yes	None
Pennsylvania	Biennium (hh)	Jan.	1st Tues.	None	Governor may call	No	None
Rhode Island	Annual	Jan.	1st Tues.	None	Joint call, presiding officers, both houses	Yes	None
South Carolina	Biennium	Jan.	2nd Tues.	(ii)	By vote, 2/3 members, each house	Yes	None
South Dakota	Annual	Jan.	2nd Tues.	odd-40 L; even-40 L	By petition, 2/3 members, each house	Yes (jj)	None
Tennessee	Biennium (kk)	Jan.	2nd Tues.	90 L (ll)	By petition, 2/3 members, each house	Yes	30 L (ll)
Texas	Biennial-odd year	Jan.	2nd Tues.	140 C	No	No	30 C
Utah	Annual	Jan.	4th Mon.	45 C	No	No	30 C
Vermont	Annual	Jan.	Wed. after 1st Mon.	None	No	Yes	None
Virginia	Annual	Jan.	2nd Wed.	odd-30 C (i); even-60 C (i)	(tt)	Yes	None (mm)
Washington	Annual	Jan.	2nd Mon.	odd-105 C; even-60 C	By vote, 2/3 members, each house	Yes	30 C
West Virginia	Annual	Jan	2nd Wed.	60 C (i)	By petition, 3/5 members, each house	Yes (l)	None

See footnotes at end of table.

LEGISLATIVE SESSIONS: LEGAL PROVISIONS — Continued

State or other jurisdiction	Regular sessions				Special sessions		
	Year	Legislature convenes		Limitation on length of session (a)	Legislature may call	Legislature may determine subject	Limitation on length of session
		Month	Day				
Wisconsin	Biennium	Jan.	1st Mon.	None	(nn)	No	None
Wyoming	Biennium	Jan.(odd years) Feb. (even-years) (even-years)	2nd Tues. (odd-years) 2nd Mon.	odd-40 L; even-20 L;	By petition, majority members, each house bienniumn-60 L	Yes	20 L
Dist. of Columbia	(oo)	Jan.	2nd day	None	. . .	. . .	. . .
American Samoa	Annual	Jan. July	2nd Mon. 2nd Mon.	45 L 45 L	No	No	None
Guam	(pp)	Jan.	2nd Mon.	None (pp)	Only the governor may call	No	None (pp)
No. Mariana Islands	Annual	(rr)	(d)(rr)	90 L (qq)	Upon request of presiding officers, both houses	Yes (l)	10 C
Puerto Rico	Annual (rr)	Jan. Aug.	2nd Mon. 3rd Mon.	5 mo. 4 mo.	No	No	20 C
U.S. Virgin Islands	Annual	Jan. (ss)	2nd Mon. (ss)	None	No, governor calls	No	None

Source: The Council of State Governments' survey, February 2009.

Key:

Annual — holds legislative sessions every year.

Biennial — odd year–holds legislative sessions every other year.

Biennium — holds legislative sessions in a two-year term of activity.

C — Calendar day

L — Legislative day (in some states called a session day or workday; definition may vary slightly, however, generally refers to any day on which either house of legislature is in session).

(a) Applies to each year unless otherwise indicated.

(b) General election year (quadrennial election year).

(c) Year after quadrennial election.

(d) Legal provision for organizational session prior to stated convening date. Alabama– in the year after quadrennial election, second Tuesday in January for 10 C. California–in the even-numbered general election year, first Monday in December for an organizational session, recess until the first Monday in January of the odd-numbered year. No. Mariana Islands–in year after general election, second Monday in January.

(e) Other years.

(f) By 2/3 vote each house.

(g) Convening date is statutory. Length of session is 121 calendar days, 90 by statute.

(h) No constitutional or statutory provision; however, by legislative rule regular sessions shall be adjourned sine die no later than Saturday of the week during which the 100th day from the beginning of each regular session falls.The Speaker/President may by declaration authorize the extension of the session for a period not to exceed seven additional days. Thereafter the session can be extended only by a majority vote of the House/Senate.

(i) Session may be extended by vote of members in both houses. Arkansas–2/3 vote. Florida–3/5 vote, session may be extended by vote of members in each house. Hawaii– petition of 2/3 membership for maximum 15-day extension. Kansas–2/3 vote. Virginia–2/3 vote for 30 C extension. West Virginia– may be extended by the governor.

(j) After governor's business has been disposed of, members may remain in session up to 15 C days by a 2/3 vote of both houses.

(k) Regular sessions begin after general election, in December of even-numbered year. In California, in the even-numbered general election year, first Monday in December for an organizational session, recess until the first Monday in January of the odd-numbered year.

(l) Only if legislature convenes itself. In Illinois, governor may call a special session and determine its subject. The Constitution does not mention limiting the subject(s) of a special session called by legislative leaders. In New York, special sessions may also be called by the governor. Legislature may determine subject only if it has convened itself. In New Mexico, special sessions may only be called by the governor and subjects are limited to issues included in governor's proclamation; extraordinary session may only be called by the legislature and have no limitations on subject.

(m) Odd-numbered years–not later than Wednesday after first Monday in June; even-numbered years–not later than Wednesday after first Monday in May.

(n) Notice sent to secretary of state.

(o) A regular session of the legislature shall convene on the first Tuesday after the first Monday of each odd-numbered year, and on the first Tuesday after the first Monday in March, or such other date as may be fixed by law, of each even-numbered year.

(p) If three-fifths of the General Assembly certifies to governor that an emergency exists, governor must convene a special session for all purposes.

(q) Constitution encourages adjournment by May 31.

(r) Legislators may reconvene at any time after organizational meeting; however, second Monday in January is the final date by which regular session must be in process.

(s) During the odd-year session, the members convene for four days, then break until February.

(t) Regular session begins after general election in even-numbered years. Session which begins in December of general election year runs into the following year (odd-numbered); second session begins in next even-numbered year. The second session is limited to budgetary matters; legislation in the governor's call; emergency legislation; legislation referred to committee for study.

(u) Statutory adjournment for the First Regular Session (beginning in December of even-numbered years and continuing into the following odd-numbered year) is the third Wednesday of June; statutory adjournment for the Second Regular Session (beginning in January of the subsequent even-numbered year) is the third Wednesday in April. The statutes provide for up to two extensions of up to five legislative days each for each session.

LEGISLATIVE SESSIONS: LEGAL PROVISIONS — Continued

(v) Legislative rules say formal business must be concluded by Nov. 15th of the 1st session in the biennium, or by July 31st of the 2nd session for the biennium.

(w) Joint rules provide for the submission of a written statement requesting special session by a specified number of members of each chamber.

(x) Special session is called by the governor.

(y) 90 C sessions every year, except the first year of a gubernatorial administration during which the legislative session runs for 125 C.

(z) 30 C if called by legislature; 60 C if called by governor.

(aa) No limit, however legislators are only paid up to 20 calendar days during a special session.

(bb) Limitation is on legislative pay and mileage.

(cc) Or by joint call, presiding officers, both houses.

(dd) Session officially begins on the first Wednesday following the first Monday of the new legislative term (commencing the first of the year), and lasts until the legislature completes its business and adjourns sine die. However, over the past several years, both houses have adopted the tactic of declaring a recess at the call of the leaders, in order to facilitate easy recall of the legislature to override vetoes, etc. Over time the custom has become to formally adjourn both houses just before the new session opens. This leads to the rather interesting convention that when the governor calls the legislature into session, it is considered "special" or "executive," even though the regular session is ongoing.

(ee) Legal provision for session in odd-numbered year; however, legislature may divide, and in practice has divided, to meet in even-numbered years as well.

(ff) Legislative Council may reconvene the Legislature assembly. However, a reconvened session may not exceed the number of days available (80) but not used by the last regular session.

(gg) Unless Monday is a legal holiday; in second year, the General Assembly convenes on the same date.

(hh) Sessions are two years and begin on the 1st Tuesday of January of the odd-numbered year. Session ends on November 30 of the even-numbered year. Each calendar year receives its own legislative number.

(ii) The regular session ends the first Thursday in June (June 7, 2007); it can be extended with a two-thirds majority vote.

(jj) Legislators must address topic for which the special session was called.

(kk) Each General Assembly convenes for a First and Second Regular Session over a two-year period.

(ll) 90 legislative days over a two-year period. During special sessions members will be paid up to 30 legislative days; further days will be without pay or per diem.

(mm) No limitation, but the convening of the new General Assembly following an election would by operation end the special session.

(nn) The Legislature may call itself into Extraordinary Session on any subject by a majority vote of the organizing committees of each house, by joint resolution, or by a petition of a majority of each house.

(oo) Each Council period begins on January 2 of each odd-numbered year and ends on January 1 of the following odd-numbered year.

(pp) Legislature meets on the first Monday of each month following its initial session in January. One legislative day or one special session day may become several calendar days. Special sessions may address only one subject.

(qq) 60 L before April 1 and 30 L after July 31.

(rr) Legislature meets twice a year. During general election years, the legislature only convenes on the January session.

(ss) The legislature convenes in January on the second Monday, March, June and September, the third Wednesday.

(tt) The Constitution provides that the governor must call a special session upon "application" of 2/3 of the members of each house.

Table 3.3
THE LEGISLATORS: NUMBERS, TERMS, AND PARTY AFFILIATIONS: 2009

State or other jurisdiction	*Senate*						*House/Assembly*						*Senate and House/ Assembly totals*
	Democrats	*Republicans*	*Other*	*Vacancies*	*Total*	*Term*	*Democrats*	*Republicans*	*Other*	*Vacancies*	*Total*	*Term*	
State and territory totals	1,074	906	12	11	2,072*	. . .	3,079	2,375	25	6	5,505	. . .	7,577*
State totals	1,021	890	2	9	1,971*	. . .	3,041	2,346	18	6	5,411	. . .	7,382*
Alabama	19	13	. . .	3	35	4	62	43	. . .	. . .	105	4	140
Alaska	10	10	. . .	. . .	20	4	18	22	. . .	. . .	40	2	60
Arizona	12	18	. . .	. . .	30	2	24	36	. . .	. . .	60	2	90
Arkansas	27	8	. . .	. . .	35	4	71	28	1 (e)	. . .	100	2	135
California	25	14	. . .	1	40	4	51	29	. . .	. . .	80	2	120
Colorado	21	14	. . .	. . .	35	4	38	27	. . .	. . .	65	2	100
Connecticut	24	12	. . .	. . .	36	2	114	36	. . .	1	151	2	187
Delaware	16	5	. . .	. . .	21	4	24	17	. . .	. . .	41	2	62
Florida	14	26	. . .	. . .	40	4	44	76	. . .	. . .	120	2	160
Georgia	22	34	. . .	. . .	56	2	73	107	. . .	. . .	180	2	236
Hawaii	23	2	. . .	. . .	25	4	45	6	. . .	. . .	51	2	76
Idaho	7	28	. . .	. . .	35	2	18	52	. . .	. . .	70	2	105
Illinois	37	22	. . .	. . .	59	(a)	70	48	. . .	. . .	118	2	177
Indiana	17	33	. . .	. . .	50	4	52	48	. . .	. . .	100	2	150
Iowa	32	18	. . .	. . .	50	4	56	44	. . .	. . .	100	2	150
Kansas	9	31	. . .	. . .	40	4	49	76	. . .	. . .	125	2	165
Kentucky	15	21	1 (b)	1	38	4	65	35	. . .	. . .	100	2	138
Louisiana	22	15	. . .	2	39	4	51	50	3 (b)	1	105	4	144
Maine	20	15	. . .	. . .	35	2	95	55	1 (c)	. . .	151	2	186
Maryland	33	14	. . .	. . .	47	4	104	36	1 (b)	. . .	141	4	188
Massachusetts	35	5	. . .	. . .	40	2	142	16	1 (b)	1	160	2	200
Michigan	16	21	. . .	1	38	4	67	43	. . .	. . .	110	2	148
Minnesota	46 (d)	21	. . .	. . .	67	4	87 (d)	47	. . .	. . .	134	2	201
Mississippi	27	25	. . .	. . .	52	4	74	48	. . .	. . .	122	4	174
Missouri	11	23	. . .	. . .	34	4	74	89	. . .	. . .	163	2	197
Montana	23	27	. . .	. . .	50	4	50	50	. . .	. . .	100	2	150
Nebraska	Nonpartisan election				49	4	Unicameral						49
Nevada	12	9	. . .	. . .	21	4	28	14	. . .	. . .	42	2	63
New Hampshire	14	10	. . .	. . .	24	2	224	175	. . .	1	400	2	424
New Jersey	23	16	. . .	1	40	4 (f)	48	32	. . .	. . .	80	2	120
New Mexico	27	15	. . .	. . .	42	4	45	25	. . .	. . .	70	2	112
New York	32	30	. . .	. . .	62	2	108	41	1 (b)	. . .	150	2	212
North Carolina	30	20	. . .	. . .	50	2	68	52	. . .	. . .	120	2	170
North Dakota	21	26	. . .	. . .	47	4	36	58	. . .	. . .	94	4	141
Ohio	12	21	. . .	. . .	33	4	53	46	. . .	. . .	99	2	132
Oklahoma	22	26	. . .	. . .	48	4	40	61	. . .	. . .	101	2	149
Oregon	18	12	. . .	. . .	30	4	36	24	. . .	. . .	60	2	90
Pennsylvania	21	29	. . .	. . .	50	4	104	99	. . .	. . .	203	2	253
Rhode Island	33	4	1 (b)	. . .	38	2	69	6	. . .	. . .	75	2	113
South Carolina	19	27	. . .	. . .	46	4	52	71	. . .	1	124	2	170
South Dakota	14	21	. . .	. . .	35	2	24	46	. . .	. . .	70	2	105
Tennessee	14	19	. . .	. . .	33	4	49	50	. . .	. . .	99	2	132
Texas	12	19	. . .	. . .	31	4	74	76	. . .	. . .	150	2	181
Utah	8	21	. . .	. . .	29	4	22	53	. . .	. . .	75	2	104
Vermont	23	7	. . .	. . .	30	2	95	48	7 (g)	. . .	150	2	180
Virginia	21	19	. . .	. . .	40	4	45	53	2 (b)	. . .	100	2	140
Washington	31	18	. . .	. . .	49	4	61	36	. . .	1	98	2	147
West Virginia	26	8	. . .	. . .	34	4	71	29	. . .	. . .	100	2	134
Wisconsin	18	15	. . .	. . .	33 (h)	4	52	46	1 (b)	. . .	99 (h)	2	132
Wyoming	7	23	. . .	. . .	30	4	19	41	. . .	. . .	60	2	90
Dist. of Columbia (i)	11	0	2 (b)	. . .	13	4	Unicameral						13
American Samoa	Nonpartisan election				18 (j)	4	Nonpartisan election				20 (j)	2	38
Guam	10	5	. . .	. . .	15	2	Unicameral						15
No. Mariana Islands	2	4	3 (k)	. . .	9	4	1	12	7 (l)	. . .	20	2	29
Puerto Rico	22 (m)	7 (n)	. . .	2	31 (p)	4	37 (m)	17 (n)	. . .	. . .	54 (p)	4	85
U.S. Virgin Islands	10	. . .	5 (o)	. . .	15	2	Unicameral						15

See footnotes at end of table.

THE LEGISLATORS: NUMBERS, TERMS, AND PARTY AFFILIATIONS: 2009—Continued

Source: The Council of State Governments, February 2009.

**Note:* Senate and combined body (Senate and House/Assembly) totals include Unicameral legislatures.

Key:

. . . — Does not apply.

(a) The entire Senate comes up for election in every year ending in "2" with districts based on the latest decennial census. Senate districts are divided into three groups. One group elects senators for terms of four years, four years and two years; the second group for terms of four years, two years and four years; the third group for terms of two years, four years and four years.

(b) Independent.

(c) Unenrolled.

(d) Democratic-Farmer-Labor.

(e) Green Party.

(f) All 40 Senate terms are on a 10-year cycle which is made up of a two-year term, followed by two consecutive four-year terms, beginning after the decennial census.

(g) Independent (2); Progressive (5).

(h) All House seats contested in even-numbered years; in the Senate, 17 seats contested in gubernatorial years; 16 seats contested in presidential years.

(i) Council of the District of Columbia.

(j) Senate: senators are not elected by popular vote, but by county council chiefs. House: 21 seats; 20 are elected by popular vote and one is an appointed, nonvoting delegate from Swains Island.

(k) Covenant Party.

(l) Covenant (4); Independent (3).

(m) New Progressive Party.

(n) Popular Democratic Party.

(o) Independent (3); Independent Citizens Movement (2).

(p) Constitutionally, the Senate consists of 27 seats and the House consists of 51 seats. However, extra at-large seats can be granted to the opposition to limit any party's control to 2/3. After the 2008 election, extra seats for the minority party were added in both the Senate and House.

Table 3.3A
THE LEGISLATORS: NUMBERS, TERMS, AND PARTY AFFILIATIONS BY REGION: 2009

	Senate						*House/Assembly*						*Senate and House/ Assembly*
State	*Democrats*	*Republicans*	*Other*	*Vacancies*	*Total*	*Term*	*Democrats*	*Republicans*	*Other*	*Vacancies*	*Total*	*Term*	*totals*
State totals	1,021	890	2	9	1,971*	. . .	3,041	2,346	18	6	5,411	. . .	7,382*
Eastern Region													
Connecticut	24	12	. . .	. . .	36	2	114	36	. . .	1	151	2	187
Delaware	16	5	. . .	. . .	21	4	24	17	. . .	. . .	41	2	62
Maine	20	15	. . .	. . .	35	2	95	55	1 (a)	. . .	151	2	186
Massachusetts	35	5	. . .	. . .	40	2	142	16	1 (g)	1	160	2	200
New Hampshire	14	10	. . .	. . .	24	2	224	175	. . .	1	400	2	424
New Jersey	23	16	. . .	1	40	4 (b)	48	32	. . .	. . .	80	2	120
New York	32	30	. . .	. . .	62	2	108	41	1	. . .	150	2	212
Pennsylvania	21	29	. . .	. . .	50	4	104	99	. . .	. . .	203	2	253
Rhode Island	33	4	1 (g)	. . .	38	2	69	6	. . .	. . .	75	2	113
Vermont	23	7	. . .	. . .	30	2	95	48	7 (c)	. . .	150	2	180
Regional total	241	133	1	1	376	. . .	1,023	525	10	3	1,561	. . .	1,937
Midwestern Region													
Illinois	37	22	. . .	. . .	59	(d)	70	48	. . .	. . .	118	2	177
Indiana	17	33	. . .	. . .	50	4	52	48	. . .	. . .	100	2	150
Iowa	32	18	. . .	. . .	50	4	56	44	. . .	. . .	100	2	150
Kansas	9	31	. . .	. . .	40	4	49	76	. . .	. . .	125	2	165
Michigan	16	21	. . .	1	38	4	67	43	. . .	. . .	110	2	148
Minnesota	46 (e)	21	. . .	. . .	67	4	87 (e)	47	. . .	. . .	134	2	201
Nebraska	Nonpartisan election				49	4	Unicameral						49
North Dakota	21	26	. . .	. . .	47	4	36	58	. . .	. . .	94	4	141
Ohio	12	21	. . .	. . .	33	4	53	46	. . .	. . .	99	2	132
South Dakota	14	21	. . .	. . .	35	2	24	46	. . .	. . .	70	2	105
Wisconsin	18	15	. . .	. . .	33 (f)	4	52	46	1 (g)	. . .	99 (f)	2	132
Regional total	222	229	0	1	501	. . .	546	502	1	0	1,049	. . .	1,550
Southern Region													
Alabama	19	13	. . .	3	35	4	62	43	. . .	. . .	105	4	140
Arkansas	27	8	. . .	. . .	35	4	71	28	1 (h)	. . .	100	2	135
Florida	14	26	. . .	. . .	40	4	44	76	. . .	. . .	120	2	160
Georgia	22	34	. . .	. . .	56	2	73	107	. . .	. . .	180	2	236
Kentucky	15	21	1 (g)	1	38	4	65	35	. . .	. . .	100	2	138
Louisiana	22	15	. . .	2	39	4	51	50	3 (g)	1	105	4	144
Maryland	33	14	. . .	. . .	47	4	104	36	1 (g)	. . .	141	4	188
Mississippi	27	25	. . .	. . .	52	4	74	48	. . .	. . .	122	4	174
Missouri	11	23	. . .	. . .	34	4	74	89	. . .	. . .	163	2	197
North Carolina	30	20	. . .	. . .	50	2	68	52	. . .	. . .	120	2	170
Oklahoma	22	26	. . .	. . .	48	4	40	61	. . .	. . .	101	2	149
South Carolina	19	27	. . .	. . .	46	4	52	71	. . .	1	124	2	170
Tennessee	14	19	. . .	. . .	33	4	49	50	. . .	. . .	99	2	132
Texas	12	19	. . .	. . .	31	4	74	76	. . .	. . .	150	2	181
Virginia	21	19	. . .	. . .	40	4	45	53	2 (g)	. . .	100	2	140
West Virginia	26	8	. . .	. . .	34	4	71	29	. . .	. . .	100	2	134
Regional total	334	317	1	6	658	. . .	1,017	904	7	2	1,930	. . .	2,588
Western Region													
Alaska	10	10	. . .	. . .	20	4	18	22	. . .	. . .	40	2	60
Arizona	12	18	. . .	. . .	30	2	24	36	. . .	. . .	60	2	90
California	25	14	. . .	1	40	4	51	29	. . .	. . .	80	2	120
Colorado	21	14	. . .	. . .	35	4	38	27	. . .	. . .	65	2	100
Hawaii	23	2	. . .	. . .	25	4	45	6	. . .	. . .	51	2	76
Idaho	7	28	. . .	. . .	35	2	18	52	. . .	. . .	70	2	105
Montana	23	27	. . .	. . .	50	4	50	50	. . .	. . .	100	2	150
Nevada	12	9	. . .	. . .	21	4	28	14	. . .	. . .	42	2	63
New Mexico	27	15	. . .	. . .	42	4	45	25	. . .	. . .	70	2	112
Oregon	18	12	. . .	. . .	30	4	36	24	. . .	. . .	60	2	90
Utah	8	21	. . .	. . .	29	4	22	53	. . .	. . .	75	2	104
Washington	31	18	. . .	. . .	49	4	61	36	. . .	1	98	2	147
Wyoming	7	23	. . .	. . .	30	4	19	41	. . .	. . .	60	2	90
Regional total	224	211	0	1	436	. . .	455	415	0	1	871	. . .	1,307

Source: The Council of State Governments, February 2009.

**Note:* Senate and combined body (Senate and House/Assembly) totals include Unicameral legislatures.

Key:

. . . — Does not apply.

(a) Unenrolled.

(b) All 40 Senate terms are on a 10-year cycle which is made up of a two-year term, followed by two consecutive four-year terms, beginning after the decennial census.

(c) Independent (2); Progressive (5).

(d) The entire Senate comes up for election in every year ending in "2" with districts based on the latest decennial census. Senate districts are divided into three groups. One group elects senators for terms of four years, four years and two years; the second group for terms of four years, two years and four years; the third group for terms of two years, four years and four years.

(e) Democratic-Farmer-Labor.

(f) All House seats contested in even-numbered years; in the Senate, 17 seats contested in gubernatorial years; 16 seats contested in presidential years.

(g) Independent.

(h) Green Party.

Table 3.4
MEMBERSHIP TURNOVER IN THE LEGISLATURES: 2008

State or other jurisdiction	Senate: Total number of members	Senate: Number of membership changes	Senate: Percentage change of total	House/Assembly: Total number of members	House/Assembly: Number of membership changes	House/Assembly: Percentage change of total
Alabama	35	1	3	105	1	1
Alaska	20	3	15	40	6	15
Arizona	30	8	27	60	21	35
Arkansas	35	6	17	100	34	34
California	40	11	28	80	29	36
Colorado	35	10	29	65	19	29
Connecticut	36	5	14	151	26	17
Delaware	21	3	14	41	10	24
Florida	40	7	18	120	36	30
Georgia	56	5	9	180	21	12
Hawaii	25	4	16	51	6	12
Idaho	35	6	17	70	11	16
Illinois	59	5	8	118	13	11
Indiana	50	8	16	100	16	16
Iowa	50	9	18	100	18	18
Kansas	40	10	25	125	20	16
Kentucky	38	3	8	100	9	9
Louisiana	39	3	8	105	2	2
Maine	35	10	29	151	53	35
Maryland	47	1	2	141	1	1
Massachusetts	40	5	13	160	16	10
Michigan	38	0	0	110	46	42
Minnesota	67	2	3	134	23	17
Mississippi	52	15	29	122	20	16
Missouri	34	6	18	163	44	27
Montana	50	14	28	100	38	38
Nebraska	49	16	33		Unicameral	
Nevada	21	3	14	42	8	19
New Hampshire	24	6	25	400	141	35
New Jersey	40	1	3	80	1	1
New Mexico	42	8	19	70	11	16
New York	62	8	13	150	8	5
North Carolina	50	7	14	120	18	15
North Dakota	47	5	11	94	10	11
Ohio	33	9	21	99	35	35
Oklahoma	48	6	13	101	17	17
Oregon	30	7	23	60	17	28
Pennsylvania	50	7	14	203	27	13
Rhode Island	38	8	21	75	16	21
South Carolina	46	9	20	124	24	19
South Dakota	35	16	46	70	34	49
Tennessee	33	6	18	99	23	23
Texas	31	2	6	150	23	15
Utah	29	6	21	75	14	19
Vermont	30	3	10	150	34	23
Virginia	40	9	23	100	4	4
Washington	49	3	6	98	17	17
West Virginia	34	7	21	100	19	19
Wisconsin	33	2	6	99	14	14
Wyoming	30	4	13	60	14	23
Dist. of Columbia	13	1	8		Unicameral	
American Samoa	18	12	67	21	11	52
Guam	15	5	33		Unicameral	
No. Mariana Islands	9	10	111	18	1	6
Puerto Rico	28	14	11	51	21	41
U.S. Virgin Islands	15	7	47		Unicameral	

Source: The Council of State Governments, February 2009.

Table 3.5
THE LEGISLATORS: QUALIFICATIONS FOR ELECTION

State or other jurisdiction	House/Assembly					Senate				
	Minimum age	U.S. citizen (years) (a)	State resident (years) (b)	District resident (years)	Qualified voter (years)	Minimum age	U.S. citizen (years) (a)	State resident (years) (b)	District resident (years)	Qualified voter (years)
Alabama	21	. . .	3 (c)	1	. . .	25	. . .	3 (c)	1	. . .
Alaska	21	★	3	1	★	25	★	3	1	★
Arizona	25	★	3	1	. . .	25	★	3	1	. . .
Arkansas	21	★	2	1	★	25	★	2	1	★
California	18	3	3	1	★	18	3	3	1	★
Colorado	25	★	1	1	★	25	★	1	1	★
Connecticut	18	★	★	★	★	18	★	★	★	★
Delaware	24	★	3	1	★	27	★	3 (c)	1	★
Florida	21	. . .	2	2	. . .	21	. . .	2	2	. . .
Georgia	21	★	2 (c)	1	★	25	★	2 (c)	1	★
Hawaii	18	★	3	★	★	18	★	3	★	★
Idaho	21	★	30 days	1	★	21	★	30 days	1	★
Illinois	21	★	2	2 (n)	. . .	21	★	2	2 (n)	. . .
Indiana	21	★	2	1	★	25	2	2	1	. . .
Iowa	21	★	1	60 days	. . .	25	★	1	. . .	. . .
Kansas	18	★	★(c)	★	★	18	★	★(c)	★	★
Kentucky	24	★	2 (c)	1	★	30	★	6 (c)	1	★
Louisiana	18	★	2	1	★	18	★	2	1	★
Maine	21	5	1	3 mo.	. . .	25	5	1	3 mo.	. . .
Maryland	21	. . .	1 (c)	6 mo. (f)	. . .	25	. . .	1 (c)	6 mo. (f)	. . .
Massachusetts	18	. . .	. . .	1	★	18	. . .	5	5	★
Michigan	21	★	★	(d)	★	21	★	★	(d)	★
Minnesota	18	. . .	1	6 mo.	★	21	. . .	1	6 mo.	★
Mississippi	21	. . .	4 (c)	2	★	25	. . .	4 (c)	2	★
Missouri	24	★	★	1	2	30	★	★	1	3
Montana	18	. . .	1	6 mo. (g)	. . .	18	. . .	1	6 mo. (g)	. . .
Nebraska	U	U	U	U	U	21	★	★(c)	1	★
Nevada	21	★	1 (c)	30 days (l)	★	21	★	1 (c)	30 days (l)	★
New Hampshire	18	. . .	2 (c)	★	★	30	. . .	7 (c)	★	★
New Jersey	21	★	2 (c)	1	★	30	★	2 (c)	1	★
New Mexico	21	★	★	★	★	25	★	★	★	★
New York	18	★	5	1 (h)	. . .	18	★	5	1 (h)	. . .
North Carolina	21	. . .	. . .	1	. . .	25	. . .	2	1	. . .
North Dakota	18	. . .	1	★	★	18	. . .	1	★	★
Ohio	18	★	30 days	1	★	18	★	30 days	1	★
Oklahoma	21	★	★(c)	★	★	25	★	★(c)	★	★
Oregon	21	★	. . .	1	. . .	21	★	★	1	. . .
Pennsylvania	21	. . .	4 (c)	4	. . .	25	. . .	4 (c)	4	. . .
Rhode Island	18	★	30 days	30 days	★	18	★	30 days	30 days	★
South Carolina	21	. . .	. . .	★(e)	. . .	25	. . .	. . .	★(e)	. . .

See footnotes at end of table.

THE LEGISLATORS: QUALIFICATIONS FOR ELECTION—Continued

State or other jurisdiction	House/Assembly					Senate				
	Minimum age	U.S. citizen (years) (a)	State resident (years) (b)	District resident (years)	Qualified voter (years)	Minimum age	U.S. citizen (years) (a)	State resident (years) (b)	District resident (years)	Qualified voter (years)
South Dakota	21	★	2	★	★	21	★	2	★	★
Tennessee	21	★	(c)	1	★	30	★	3	1	★
Texas	21	★	2	1	★	26	★	5	1	★
Utah	25	★	3 (c)	6 mo.	. . .	25	★	3 (c)	6 mo.	. . .
Vermont	18	★	2	1	. . .	18	★	2	1	. . .
Virginia	21	★	★	★	★	21	★	★	★	★
Washington	18	★	. . .	. . .	★	18	★	. . .	. . .	★
West Virginia	18	1	1 (c)	1	★	25	5	5 (c)	1	★
Wisconsin	18	★	1	★(m)	★(m)	18	★	1	★(m)	★(m)
Wyoming	21	★	★(c)	1	★	25	★	★(c)	1	★
Dist. of Columbia	U	U	U	U	U	18	. . .	1	★	★
American Samoa	25	★(i)	5	1	. . .	30 (j)	★ (i)	5	1	. . .
Guam	U	U	U	U	U	25	★	5	. . .	★
No. Mariana Islands	21	. . .	3	(d)	★	25	. . .	5	(d)	★
Puerto Rico	25	★	2	1 (k)	. . .	30	★	2	1 (k)	. . .
U.S. Virgin Islands	U	U	U	U	U	21	. . .	3 (c)	3	★

Source: The Council of State Governments survey, February 2009.

Note: Many state constitutions have additional provisions disqualifying persons from holding office if they are convicted of a felony, bribery, perjury or other infamous crimes.

Key:

U — Unicameral legislature; members are called senators, except in District of Columbia.

★ — Formal provision; number of years not specified.

. . . — No formal provision.

(a) In some states candidate must be a U.S. citizen to be an elector, and must be an elector to run.

(b) In some states candidate must be a state resident to be an elector, and must be an elector to run.

(c) State citizenship requirement. In Tennessee- must be a citizen for three years.

(d) Must be a qualified voter of the district; number of years not specified.

(e) At the time of filing.

(f) If the district was established for less than six months, residency is length of establishment of district.

(g) Shall be a resident of the county if it contains one or more districts or if the district contains all or parts of more than one county.

(h) After redistricting, candidate must have been a resident of the county in which the district is contained for one year immediately preceding election.

(i) Or U.S. national.

(j) Must be registered matai.

(k) The district legislator must live in the municipality he/she represents.

(l) 30 days prior to close of filing for declaration of candidacy.

(m) Ten days prior to election.

(n) In the first election after a redistricting, a candidate may be elected from any district that contains a part of the district in which (s)he resided at the time of redistricting, and may be re-elected if a resident of the district (s)he represents for 18 months before re-election.

Table 3.6
SENATE LEADERSHIP POSITIONS: METHODS OF SELECTION

State or other jurisdiction	President	President pro tem	Majority leader	Assistant majority leader	Majority floor leader	Assistant majority floor leader	Majority whip	Majority caucus chair	Minority leader	Assistant minority leader	Minority floor leader	Assistant minority floor leader	Minority whip	Minority caucus chair
Alabama (b)	(a)	ES	(b)	. . .	(b)	. . .	. . .	. . .	(b)	. . .	(b)	. . .	. . .	. . .
Alaska	ES	. . .	EC	. . .	. . .	. . .	EC	EC	EC	. . .	. . .	. . .	EC	EC
Arizona	ES	AP	EC	. . .	. . .	. . .	EC	. . .	EC	EC	. . .	. . .	EC	. . .
Arkansas	(a)	ES	EC	. . .	. . .	. . .	EC	. . .	EC	. . .	. . .	. . .	EC	. . .
California	(a)	ES	EC	. . .	. . .	. . .	EC	EC	EC	EC	EC	. . .	EC	EC
Colorado	ES	ES	EC	EC	. . .	. . .	. . .	EC	EC	EC	. . .	. . .	. . .	EC
Connecticut (c)	(a)	ES	AP	AP	AP	AP	AP	AP	EC	AL	AL	AL	AL	AL
Delaware	(a)	ES	EC	. . .	. . .	. . .	EC	. . .	EC	. . .	. . .	. . .	EC	. . .
Florida	EC/ES	AP	AP	AL	AP or AL	AP or AL	AP or AL	AP or AL	EC	AL	AL	AL	AL	AL
Georgia	(a)	ES	EC	. . .	. . .	. . .	EC	EC	EC	. . .	. . .	. . .	EC	EC
Hawaii (d)	ES	ES (e)	EC	. . .	EC	. . .	EC	EC (f)	EC	. . .	EC	. . .	. . .	. . .
Idaho	(a)	ES	EC	EC	. . .	. . .	. . .	EC	EC	EC	. . .	. . .	. . .	EC
Illinois (g)	ES	. . .	AP (g)	AP/5	. . .	. . .	AP/3	AP	EC	AL/5	. . .	. . .	AL	AL
Indiana	(a)	ES	. . .	. . .	AT	AT	AT	EC	EC	. . .	EC	(h)	(h)	EC
Iowa	ES	ES	EC	EC	. . .	. . .	. . .	. . .	EC	EC	. . .	. . .	. . .	. . .
Kansas	ES	ES (e)	EC	EC	. . .	. . .	EC	EC	EC	EC	. . .	. . .	EC	EC
Kentucky (i)	ES	ES	. . .	. . .	EC	. . .	EC	EC	. . .	. . .	EC	. . .	EC	. . .
Louisiana	ES	ES	. . .	. . .	. . .	. . .	. . .	. . .	. . .	. . .	. . .	. . .	. . .	. . .
Maine	ES	AP	EC	EC	(j)	(j)	(k)	. . .	EC	EC	(l)	(l)	(m)	. . .
Maryland	ES	ES	AP (n)	AP (n)	(n)	(n)	AP	. . .	EC (o)	. . .	(o)	. . .	EC	. . .
Massachusetts	EC	. . .	AP	AP	. . .	. . .	. . .	(p)	EC	. . .	. . .	. . .	. . .	(p)
Michigan (q)	(a)	ES	EC	EC	EC	EC	EC	EC	EC	EC	EC	EC	EC	EC
Minnesota	ES	ES	EC	EC	. . .	. . .	AL /7	. . .	EC	EC	. . .	. . .	EC/5	. . .
Mississippi	(a)	ES	. . .	. . .	. . .	. . .	. . .	. . .	. . .	. . .	. . .	. . .	. . .	. . .
Missouri	(a)	ES	. . .	. . .	EC	EC	EC	EC	EC	. . .	. . .	. . .	. . .	EC
Montana	ES	ES	. . .	. . .	ES	. . .	ES	. . .	. . .	. . .	ES	. . .	ES	. . .
Nebraska (U)	(a)	ES (r)	. . .	. . .	. . .	. . .	. . .	. . .	. . .	. . .	. . .	. . .	. . .	. . .
Nevada (s)	(a)	ES	. . .	. . .	EC	EC	EC	. . .	. . .	. . .	EC	EC	EC	. . .
New Hampshire	ES	AP	AP	AP	. . .	. . .	AP	. . .	EC	AL	. . .	. . .	AL	. . .
New Jersey	ES	ES	MA	MA	MA	MA	MA	MA	MI	MI	MI	MI	MI	MI
New Mexico	(a)	ES	EC (t)	. . .	EC (t)	. . .	EC	EC	EC (t)	. . .	EC (t)	. . .	EC	EC
New York (u)	(a)	ES	EC	AT (v)	AT (v)	. . .	AT	AT (v)	EC	AT (v)	AT (v)	. . .	AL	AL (v)
North Carolina	(a)	ES	EC	. . .	. . .	. . .	EC	EC	EC	. . .	. . .	. . .	EC	EC
North Dakota	(a)	ES	EC	EC	. . .	. . .	. . .	EC	EC	EC	. . .	. . .	. . .	EC
Ohio (w)(x)	ES (x)	ES	. . .	. . .	ES	ES	ES	. . .	ES (x)	ES	. . .	. . .	ES	. . .
Oklahoma	(a)	ES	EC	EC	EC	EC	EC	EC	EC	EC	EC	EC	EC	EC
Oregon	ES	ES	EC	EC	. . .	. . .	EC	. . .	EC	EC	. . .	. . .	EC	. . .
Pennsylvania	ES	ES	EC	EC	EC	EC	EC	EC	EC	EC	EC	EC	EC	EC
Rhode Island (y)	ES	ES	EC	AL	. . .	. . .	AL	. . .	EC	AL	. . .	. . .	AL	. . .
South Carolina	(a)	ES	EC	. . .	. . .	. . .	. . .	. . .	EC	. . .	. . .	. . .	. . .	. . .
South Dakota	(a)	ES	EC	EC	. . .	. . .	EC	. . .	EC	EC	. . .	. . .	EC	. . .
Tennessee	ES	AP	EC	. . .	EC	EC	. . .	EC	EC	. . .	EC	. . .	. . .	EC
Texas	(a)	ES	. . .	. . .	. . .	. . .	. . .	. . .	. . .	. . .	. . .	. . .	. . .	. . .
Utah	ES	. . .	EC	. . .	. . .	EC (z)	EC	. . .	EC	. . .	. . .	EC (z)	EC	EC (z)
Vermont	(a)	ES	EC	EC	EC (aa)	EC (aa)	EC (aa)	EC (aa)	EC	EC	EC (aa)	EC (aa)	EC (aa)	EC (aa)

See footnotes at end of table.

SENATE LEADERSHIP POSITIONS: METHODS OF SELECTION — Continued

State or other jurisdiction	President	President pro tem	Majority leader	Assistant majority leader	Majority floor leader	Assistant majority floor leader	Majority whip	Majority caucus chair	Minority leader	Assistant minority leader	Minority floor leader	Assistant minority floor leader	Minority whip	Minority caucus chair
Virginia	(a)	ES	EC (bb)	. . .	EC (bb)	. . .	. . .	EC	EC	. . .	EC	. . .	. . .	EC
Washington (cc)	(a)	ES	EC	EC	EC	EC	EC	EC	EC	EC	EC	EC	EC	EC
West Virginia	ES	AP	AP	. . .	. . .	. . .	AP	. . .	EC	. . .	. . .	. . .	AL	. . .
Wisconsin	ES (dd)	EC	EC	EC	. . .	. . .	. . .	EC	EC	EC	. . .	. . .	. . .	EC
Wyoming	ES	ES (e)	. . .	. . .	EC	. . .	EC	EC	. . .	. . .	EC	. . .	EC	EC
Dist. of Columbia (U)	(ee)	(ff)	. . .	. . .	. . .	. . .	. . .	. . .	. . .	. . .	. . .	. . .	. . .	. . .
American Samoa	ES	ES	. . .	. . .	. . .	. . .	. . .	. . .	. . .	. . .	. . .	. . .	. . .	. . .
Guam (U)(gg)	ES (r)	ES (e)	EC	EC	EC	EC	EC	. . .	EC	EC	EC	EC	EC	. . .
No. Mariana Islands	ES (hh)	. . .	(hh)	. . .	ES (ii)	. . .	. . .	. . .	EC	. . .	. . .	. . .	. . .	. . .
Puerto Rico	ES (p)	EC	EC	. . .	EC (jj)	. . .	. . .	(kk)	EC (p)	. . .	EC (jj)	. . .	. . .	(p)
U.S. Virgin Islands (U)	ES	. . .	ES	. . .	. . .	. . .	. . .	ES	ES	. . .	. . .	. . .	. . .	ES

Source: The Council of State Governments' survey, January 2009.

Note: In some states, the leadership positions in the Senate are not empowered by the law or by the rules of the chamber, but rather by the party members themselves. Entry following slash indicates number of individuals holding specified position.

Key:

ES — Elected or confirmed by all members of the Senate.
EC — Elected by party caucus.
AP — Appointed by president.
AT — Appointed by president pro tempore.
AL — Appointed by party leader.
MA — Elected by majority party.
MI — Elected by minority party.
(U) — Unicameral legislative body.
. . . — Position does not exist or is not selected on a regular basis.

(a) Lieutenant governor is president of the Senate by virtue of the office.

(b) Majority leader and majority floor leader appointed by president pro tempore and the Senate Democratic Caucus. Minority leader and minority floor leader elected by active members of the minority party. Additional leadership positions: deputy president pro tempore- appointed by Committee on Assignments and Dean of Senate- appointed by Committee on Assignments.

(c) Position titles are as follows: chief deputy president pro tem, two deputy presidents pro tem, a chief assistant president pro tem, three assistant presidents pro tem, three deputy majority leaders (AP); a minority leader pro tem, two chief deputy minority leaders, a deputy minority leader-at-large, and three deputy minority leaders (AL).

(d) An additional position of President Emeritus exists.

(e) Official title is vice president. In Guam, vice speaker.

(f) Official title is majority caucus leader.

(g) The president can appoint a majority leader, and has done so in the current General Assembly. Additional leadership positions: the minority leader appoints a deputy minority leader and four assistant minority leaders

(h) Appointed by minority leader.

(i) In each chamber, the membership elects Chief Clerk; Assistant Clerk; Enrolling Clerk; Sergeant-at-Arms; Doorkeeper; Janitor; Cloakroom Keeper; and Pages.

(j) Same position as majority leader.

(k) Same position as assistant majority leader.

(l) Same position as minority leader.

(m) Same position as assistant minority leader.

(n) Majority leader also serves as majority floor leader; deputy majority leader is official title and serves as assistant majority floor leader. There is also an assistant deputy majority leader, a majority whip, deputy majority whip, and two assistant majority whips.

(o) Minority leader also serves as the minority floor leader.

(p) President and minority floor leader are also caucus chairs. In Puerto Rico, president and minority leader. In Oregon, majority leader and minority leader.

(q) Senate Rule 1.104 provides that the president pro tempore (ES), assistant president pro tempore (ES), and the associate president pro tempore (ES) are elected by a majority of the Senate. The rules also provide for the selection of additional positions: assistant majority caucus whip (EC), assistant minority caucus whip (EC), assistant majority caucus chairperson (EC), and assistant minority caucus chairperson (EC).

(r) Official title is speaker. In Guam the Speaker is elected on the Floor by majority and minority members on Inauguration Day.

(s) Additional leadership positions: Assistant Majority and Minority Whips, elected by caucus.

(t) Majority leader also serves as majority floor leader. Minority leader also serves as minority floor leader.

(u) Additional positions appointed by the majority leader: Senate Finance Comm. Chair, Vice President pro tem, Majority Program Development Comm. Chair, Majority Steering Comm. Chair, two assistant majority leaders, various deputies and assistants. Additional positions appointed by the minority leader: Senate Finance Comm. ranking member, Minority Policy Comm. Chair, Minority Program Development Chair, three additional assistant minority leaders, various deputies and assistants.

(v) The assistant majority leader bears the title of senior assistant majority leader; majority floor leader bears the title of deputy majority leader for legislative operations; majority caucus chair bears the title of majority conference chair; assistant minority leader bears the title deputy minority leader; minority floor leader bears the title assistant minority leader for floor operations; minority caucus chair bears the title minority conference chair.

(w) While the entire membership actually votes on the election of leaders, selections generally have been made by the members of each party prior to the date of this formal election.

(x) In Ohio president acts as majority leader and caucus chair; minority leader also acts as minority caucus chair; the fourth ranking minority leadership position is assistant minority whip (ES).

(y) Additional positions include deputy president pro tempore.

(z) Official title for majority floor leader is known as the assistant majority whip; the assistant minority floor leader is known as the assistant minority whip and the minority caucus chair is known as minority caucus manager.

(aa) Majority leader serves as majority floor leader and majority caucus chair. Assistant majority leader serves as assistant majority floor leader and majority whip. Minority leader serves as minority floor leader and minority caucus chair. Assistant minority leader serves as assistant minority floor leader and minority whip.

(bb) Majority party and Minority party in Senate elect caucus officers.

(cc) Washington Senate also has the leadership position of vice-president pro tem.

(dd) Caucus nominee elected by whole membership.

(ee) Chair of the Council, which is an elected position.

(ff) Appointed by the chair; official title is chair pro tem.

(gg) Additional positions include: Parliamentarian, elected by majority caucus and Senior Senator, elected by majority caucus.

(hh) Speaker also serves as majority leader.

(ii) Official title is floor leader.

(jj) Official title is alternate floor leader.

(kk) Official title is caucus chair.

Table 3.7
HOUSE/ASSEMBLY LEADERSHIP POSITIONS: METHODS OF SELECTION

State or other jurisdiction	Speaker	Speaker pro tem	Majority leader	Assistant majority leader	Majority floor leader	Assistant majority floor leader	Majority whip	Majority caucus chair	Minority leader	Assistant minority leader	Minority floor leader	Assistant minority floor leader	Minority whip	Minority caucus chair
Alabama	EH	EH	EC	. . .	. . .	. . .	. . .	. . .	EC	. . .	. . .	. . .	. . .	. . .
Alaska	EH	. . .	EC	. . .	. . .	. . .	EC	EC	EC	. . .	. . .	. . .	EC	EC
Arizona	EH	AS	EC	. . .	. . .	. . .	EC	. . .	EC	. . .	. . .	EC	EC	. . .
Arkansas	EH	AS	EC	. . .	. . .	. . .	EC	. . .	EC	. . .	. . .	. . .	EC	. . .
California	EH	AS	AS	AS	AS	. . .	AS	EC	EC	. . .	EC	. . .	EC	EC
Colorado (a)	EH	AS	EC	EC	. . .	. . .	EC	EC	EC	EC	. . .	. . .	EC	EC
Connecticut	EH	AS/4 (b)	EC	EC/4 (b)	. . .	AS	AS	AS	EC	AL	AL	AL	AL	AL
Delaware	EH	. . .	EC	. . .	. . .	. . .	EC	. . .	EC	. . .	. . .	. . .	EC	. . .
Florida	EH	EH	AS	AS	AS	AS	AS	AS	EC	EC	AL	AL	AL	AL
Georgia	EH	EH	EC	. . .	. . .	. . .	EC	EC	EC	. . .	. . .	. . .	EC	EC
Hawaii (c)	EH	EH (d)	EC	. . .	EC	EC	EC	. . .	EC	EC	EC	EC	EC	. . .
Idaho	EH	. . .	EC	EC	. . .	. . .	. . .	EC	EC	EC	. . .	. . .	. . .	EC
Illinois	EH	. . .	AS (e)	AS (e)	. . .	. . .	. . .	AS (e)	EC	AL (e)	. . .	. . .	. . .	AL (e)
Indiana	EH	AL	EC	AL	AL	AL	AL	AL	EC	AL	EC	AL	AL	AL
Iowa	EH	EH	EC	EC	. . .	. . .	. . .	. . .	EC	EC	. . .	. . .	. . .	. . .
Kansas (f)	EH	EH	EC	EC	. . .	. . .	EC	EC	EC	EC	. . .	. . .	EC	EC
Kentucky (g)	EH	EH	. . .	. . .	EC	. . .	EC	EC	. . .	. . .	EC	. . .	EC	EC
Louisiana	EH	EH	. . .	. . .	. . .	. . .	. . .	. . .	. . .	. . .	. . .	. . .	. . .	. . .
Maine	EH	AS (h)	EC (h)	EC (h)	(h)	(h)	(h)	. . .	EC (h)	EC (h)	(h)	(h)	(h)	. . .
Maryland (bb)	EH	EH (i)	AS (j)	AS (j)	(j)	AS	AS	(k)	EC (l)	EC	EC (l)	EC (l)	EH	(k)
Massachusetts	EC	. . .	AS	AS	. . .	. . .	. . .	. . .	EC	AL	. . .	. . .	. . .	. . .
Michigan (n)	EH	EH	. . .	. . .	EC	EC	EC	EC	EC	EC	EC	EC	EC	EC
Minnesota	EH	AS	EC	EC	. . .	. . .	. . .	. . .	EC	AL	. . .	. . .	. . .	. . .
Mississippi	EH	EH	. . .	. . .	. . .	. . .	. . .	. . .	. . .	. . .	. . .	. . .	. . .	. . .
Missouri	EH	EH	. . .	. . .	EC	EC	EC	EC	. . .	. . .	EC	EC	EC	EC
Montana	EH	EH	. . .	. . .	. . .	. . .	EH	. . .	. . .	. . .	EH	. . .	EH	. . .
Nebraska	(o)													
Nevada	EH	EH	. . .	. . .	EC	EC	EC	. . .	. . .	. . .	EC	EC	EC	. . .
New Hampshire	EH	AS (d)	AS	AS	. . .	. . .	AS	. . .	AS	AL	. . .	. . .	AL	. . .
New Jersey	EH	EH	MA	MA	MA	MA	MA	MA	MI	MI	MI	MI	MI	MI
New Mexico	EH	. . .	EC	. . .	EC (m)	. . .	EC	EC	EC	. . .	EC (m)	. . .	EC	EC
New York (p)	EH	AS	AS	AS	. . .	. . .	AS	AS (q)	EC	AL	. . .	. . .	AL	AL (q)
North Carolina	EH	EH	EC	. . .	. . .	. . .	EC	EC	EC	. . .	. . .	. . .	EC	EC
North Dakota	EH	. . .	EC	EC	. . .	. . .	. . .	EC	EC	EC	. . .	. . .	. . .	EC
Ohio (r)	EH (k)	EH	. . .	. . .	EH	EH	EH	. . .	EH (k)	EH	. . .	. . .	EH	. . .
Oklahoma	EH	EH	AS	AS	AS	AS	AS	AS	EC	EC	EC	EC	EC	EC
Oregon	EH	EH	EC	EC	. . .	. . .	EC	. . .	EC	EC	. . .	. . .	EC	. . .
Pennsylvania	EH	EH	EC	EC	EC	EC	EC	EC	EC	EC	EC	EC	EC	EC
Rhode Island	EH	EH	EC	AL	. . .	. . .	AL	. . .	EC	AL	. . .	. . .	AL	. . .
South Carolina	EH	EH	EC	. . .	. . .	. . .	. . .	. . .	EC	. . .	. . .	. . .	. . .	. . .
South Dakota	EH	EH	EC	EC	. . .	. . .	EC	. . .	EC	EC	. . .	. . .	EC	. . .
Tennessee	EH	EH	EC	EC	EC	. . .	EC	EC	EC	EC	EC	EC	EC	EC
Texas	EH	AS	. . .	. . .	. . .	. . .	. . .	. . .	. . .	. . .	. . .	. . .	. . .	. . .
Utah	EH	AS	EC	EC (s)	. . .	. . .	EC	. . .	EC	. . .	. . .	EC (s)	EC	EC (s)
Vermont	EH	. . .	EC	EC	(t)	(t)	(t)	(t)	EC	EC	(t)	(t)	(t)	(t)

See footnotes at end of table.

HOUSE/ASSEMBLY LEADERSHIP POSITIONS: METHODS OF SELECTION—Continued

State or other jurisdiction	Speaker	Speaker pro tem	Majority leader	Assistant majority leader	Majority floor leader	Assistant majority floor leader	Majority whip	Majority caucus chair	Minority leader	Assistant minority leader	Minority floor leader	Assistant minority floor leader	Minority whip	Minority caucus chair
Virginia (u)	EH	. . .	EC (v)	. . .	EC (v)	. . .	EC	EC	EC (w)	. . .	EC (w)	. . .	AL	EC
Washington	EH	EH	EC	EC	EC	EC	EC	EC	EC	EC	EC	EC	EC	EC
West Virginia	EH	AS	AS	AS	. . .	. . .	AS	AS	EC	. . .	. . .	. . .	. . .	. . .
Wisconsin	EH (x)	EH (x)	EC	EC	. . .	. . .	. . .	EC	EC	EC	. . .	. . .	. . .	EC
Wyoming	EH	EH	. . .	. . .	EC	. . .	EC	EC	. . .	. . .	EC	. . .	EC	EC
Dist. of Columbia	(o)													
American Samoa	EH	EH (d)	. . .	. . .	. . .	. . .	. . .	. . .	. . .	. . .	. . .	. . .	. . .	. . .
Guam	(o)													
No. Mariana Islands	EH (y)	. . .	(y)	. . .	EH (z)	. . .	. . .	. . .	EC	. . .	. . .	. . .	. . .	. . .
Puerto Rico	EH (k)	EH (d)	EC	. . .	EC (aa)	. . .	. . .	. . .	EC (k)	. . .	EC	. . .	. . .	(k)
U.S. Virgin Islands	(o)													

Source: The Council of State Governments' survey, January 2009.

Note: In some states, the leadership positions in the House are not empowered by the law or by the rules of the chamber, but rather by the party members themselves. Entry following slash indicates number of individuals holding specified position.

Key:

EH — Elected or confirmed by all members of the House.
EC — Elected by party caucus.
AS — Appointed by speaker.
AL — Appointed by party leader.
MA — Elected by majority party.
MI — Elected by minority party.
. . . — Position does not exist or is not selected on a regular basis.

(a) Additional positions include deputy majority whip (EC) and assistant majority caucus chair (EC).

(b) Official titles: speaker pro tem - deputy speaker; assistant majority leader - deputy majority leader.

(c) Other positions in Hawaii include speaker emeritus.

(d) Official title is deputy speaker. In Hawaii, American Samoa and Puerto Rico, vice speaker.

(e) The two deputy majority leaders appointed by the speaker are among eight assistant majority leaders; and the two deputy Republican (minority) leaders appointed by the Republican (minority) leader are among the eight assistant leaders. (The term "Minority" is in the state constitution, but has not been recently used by the leadership of the Republican (Minority) party.)

(f) Additional positions include minority agenda chair (EC) and minority policy chair (EC).

(g) In each chamber, the membership elects chief clerk; assistant chief clerk; enrolling clerk; sergeant-at-arms; doorkeeper; janitor; cloakroom keeper; and pages.

(h) Speaker pro tem each occurrence. Majority leader also serves as majority floor leader; assistant majority leader also serves as assistant majority floor leader and majority whip; minority leader also serves as minority floor leader; assistant minority leader also serves as assistant minority floor leader and minority whip.

(i) There is also a deputy speaker pro tem.

(j) Majority leader also serves as majority floor leader. Official title of assistant majority leader is deputy majority leader. There are also an assistant majority floor leader, majority whip, chief deputy majority whips, and deputy majority whips.

(k) Speaker and minority leader are also caucus chairs.

(l) Minority leader also serves as the minority floor leader. There are also a minority whip, assistant minority leader, a chief deputy minority whip, an assistant minority whip, and several deputy minority whips.

(m) Majority leader also serves as majority floor leader; minority leader also serves as minority floor leader.

(n) Other positions include: two associate speakers pro tempore (EH); majority caucus chair (EC); assistant majority whip (EC); assistant associate minority floor leader (EC); minority assistant caucus chair (EC); assistant minority whip (EC).

(o) Unicameral legislature; see entries in Table 3.6, "Senate Leadership Positions — Methods of Selection."

(p) Additional majority positions appointed by the speaker: deputy speaker (AS), deputy majority leader, Ways and Means Committee chair, Democratic Program Committee chair, Democratic Steering Committee chair, various deputies and assistants. Additional minority positions appointed by the minority leader: deputy minority leader, Ways and Means Committee ranking member, Republican Steering Committee chair, Republican Program Committee chair, various deputies and assistants.

(q) Official titles: the majority caucus chair is majority conference chair; minority caucus chair is minority conference chair.

(r) While the entire membership actually votes on the election of leaders, selections generally have been made by the members of each party prior to the date of this formal election. Additional positions include assistant majority whip, the 6th ranking majority leadership position (EH) and assistant minority whip, the 4th ranking minority leadership position (EH).

(s) Assistant majority leader is known as majority assistant whip; assistant minority floor leader known as minority assistant whip; minority caucus chair known as minority caucus manager.

(t) Majority leader also serves as majority floor leader; assistant majority leader also serves as assistant majority floor leader and majority whip; minority leader also serves as minority floor leader; assistant minority leader also serves as assistant minority floor leader and minority whip.

(u) The majority caucus also has a secretary, who is appointed by the speaker; the minority caucus has 2 vice-chairs, 1 vice-chair/treasurer and an interim sergeant-at-arms.

(v) The title of majority leader is not used in Virginia; the title is majority floor leader.

(w) The title of minority leader is not used in Virginia; the title is minority floor leader.

(x) Caucus nominee elected by whole membership.

(y) Speaker also serves as majority leader.

(z) Official title is floor leader.

(aa) Official title is alternate floor leader.

(bb) There is a parliamentarian for the majority appointed by the Speaker and a minority parliamentarian elected by the minority party caucus.

Table 3.8
METHOD OF SETTING LEGISLATIVE COMPENSATION

State	Method
Alabama	Constitutional Amendment 57
Alaska	Alaska Stat. §24.10.100 , §24.10.101
Arizona	Art. V, §12; A.R.S. §41-1901 thru 41-1904. Commission recommendations are put on the ballot for a vote of the people.
Arkansas	Amendment 70, Ark. Stat. Ann. §10-2-212 et seq.
California	Art. IV, §4; Proposition 112; Cal. Gov. Code §8901 et seq.
Colorado	Colorado Stat. 2-2-301(1)
Connecticut	Conn. Gen. Stat. Ann. §2-9a; The General Assembly takes independent action pursuant to recommendations of a Compensation Commission.
Delaware	Del. Code Ann. Title 29, §710 et seq.; §§3301-3304, are implemented automatically if not rejected by resolution.
Florida	§11.13(1), Florida Statutes; Statute provides members same percentage increase as state employees.
Georgia	Ga. Code Ann. §45-7-4 and §28-1-8; Statute authorizes annual cost of living adjustment via General Appropriations Act.
Hawaii	Art. III, §9; Commission recommendations take effect unless rejected by concurrent resolution or the governor. Any change in salary that becomes effective does not apply to the legislature to which the recommendation was submitted.
Idaho	Idaho Code 67-406a and 406b
Illinois	25 ILCS 120; Salaries set by Compensation Review Board. 25 ILCS 115; Tied to employment cost index, wages and salaries for state and local government workers.
Indiana	Ind. Code Ann. §2-3-1-1
Iowa	Iowa Code Ann. §2.10; Iowa Code Ann. §2A.1 thru 2A.5
Kansas	Kan. Stat. Ann. §46-137a et seq.; §75-3212
Kentucky	Ky. Rev. Stat. Ann. §6.226-229; the Kentucky committee has not met since 1995. The most recent pay raise was initiated and passed by the General Assembly.
Louisiana	La. Rev. Stat. 24:31 & 31.1
Maine	Maine Constitution Article IV, Part Third, §7 and 3 MRSA, §2 and 2-A; Increase in compensation is presented to the legislature as legislation; the legislature must enact and the governor must sign into law; takes effect only for subsequent legislatures.
Maryland	Art. III, §15; Commission meets before each four-year term of office and presents recommendations to the General Assembly for action. Recommendations may be reduced or rejected.
Massachusetts	Mass. Gen. Laws Ann. ch. 3, §§9,10 ; In 1998, the voters passed a legislative referendum that starting with the 2001 session, members will receive an automatic increase or decrease according to the median household income for the commonwealth for the preceding 2-year period.
Michigan	Art. IV §12; Compensation Commission recommends, legislature by majority vote must approve or reduce for change to be effective the session immediately following the next general election.
Minnesota	Minn. Stat. Ann §3.099 et seq.; §15A.082; By May 1 in odd-numbered years the Council submits salary recommendations to the presiding officers.
Mississippi	Miss. Code Ann. 5-1-41
Missouri	Art. III, §§16, 34; Mo. Ann. Stat. §21.140; Recommendations are adjusted by legislature or governor if necessary.
Montana	Mont. Laws 5-2-301; Tied to executive broadband pay plan.
Nebraska	Neb. Const. Art. III, §7; Neb. Rev. Stat. 50-123.01
Nevada	§218.210-§218.225
New Hampshire	Art. XV, part second
New Jersey	Art. IV, Sec IV 7 & 8; NJSA 52:10A-1; NJSA 52:14-15.111 to 52:14-15.114
New Mexico	Art. IV. §10; 2-1-8 NMSA

See footnotes at end of table.

METHOD OF SETTING LEGISLATIVE COMPENSATION—Continued

State	Method
New York	Art. 3, §6; Consolidated Laws of NY Ann. 32-2-5a
North Carolina	N.C.G.S. 120-3
North Dakota	Statutes 54-03-10 and 54-03-20; Legislative Compensation Commission 54-03-19.1
Ohio	Art. II, §31; Ohio Rev. Code Ann. title 1 ch. 101.27 thru 101.272
Oklahoma	Okla. Stat. Ann. title 74, §291 et seq.; Art V, §21; Title 74, §291.2 et seq.; Legislative Compensation Board.
Oregon	Or. Rev. Stat. §171.072; Requires commission to establish salaries of specified elective officers and members of Legislative Assembly. Provides that salaries established by the commission take effect unless bill is enacted that rejects salaries.
Pennsylvania	Pa. Cons. Stat. Ann. 46 PS §5; 65 PS §366.1 et seq. Legislators receive annual cost of living increase that is tied to the Consumer Price Index.
Rhode Island	Art. VI, §3
South Carolina	S.C. Code Ann. 2-3-20 and the annual General Appropriations Act
South Dakota	Art. III, §6 and Art. XXI, §2; S.D. Codified Laws Ann. §20402 et seq.
Tennessee	Art. II, §23; Tenn. Code Ann. §3-1-106 et seq.
Texas	Art. III, §24; In 1991 a constitutional amendment was approved by voters to allow Ethics Commission to recommend the salaries of members. Any recommendations must be approved by voters to be effective. The provision has yet to be used.
Utah	Art. VI, §9; Utah Code Ann. §36-2-2, et seq.
Vermont	Vt. Stat. Ann. tit 32, §1051 and §1052
Virginia	Art. IV, §5; Va. Code Ann. §30-19.11 thru §30-19.14
Washington	Art. II, §23; §43.03.060; Wash. Rev. Code Ann. §43.03.028; Salary Commission sets salaries of legislature and other state officials based on market study and input from citizens.
West Virginia	Art. 6, §33; W. Va. Code §4-2A-1 et seq.; Submits by resolution and must be concurred by at least four members of the commission. The Legislature must enact the resolution into law and may reduce, but shall not increase, any item established in such resolution.
Wisconsin	Sections 20.923 and 230.12, Wis. Statutes, created by Chapter 90, Laws of 1973, and amended by 1983 Wis. Act 27 and Wis. Act 33, provide the current procedure for setting salaries of elected state officials. Generally, compensation is determined as part of the state compensation plan for non-represented employees and is approved by vote of the joint committee on employment relations. Per diem authorized under 13.123 (1), Wis. Statutes, and Leg. Joint Rule 85. 20.916(8) State Statutes and Joint Committee on Employment Relations (JCOER) establishes the max. amount, according to the recommendations of the Director of the Office of State Employment Relations. The leadership of each house then determines, within that maximum, what amount to authorize for the session.
Wyoming	Wyo. Stat. §28-5-101 thru §28-5-105

Source: National Conference of State Legislatures 2008 and update January 2009.

Table 3.9
LEGISLATIVE COMPENSATION AND LIVING EXPENSE ALLOWANCES DURING SESSIONS

State	Salaries: Regular sessions: Per diem salary	Salaries: Regular sessions: Limit on days	Salaries: Annual salary	Mileage cents per mile	Session per diem rate
Alabama	$10 C	. . .	. . .	10/mile for a single roundtrip per session. 50.5/mile interim cmte. attendance.	$3,958/month plus $50/day for three days during each week that the legislature actually meets during any session (U).
Alaska	. . .	. . .	$24,012	50.5/mile for approved travel.	$189 or $234/day (depending on the time of year) tied to federal rate. Legislators who reside in the Capitol area receive 75% of the federal rate.
Arizona	. . .	. . .	$24,000	44.5/mile on actual miles.	$35/day for the 1st 120 days of regular session and for special session and $10/day thereafter. Members residing outside Maricopa County receive an additional $25/day for the 1st 120 days of reg. session and for special session and an additional $10/day thereafter (V). Set by statute.
Arkansas	. . .	. . .	$15,060	50.5/mile.	$136/d (V) plus mileage tied to federal rate.
California	. . .	. . .	$116,208	Members are provided a vehicle. Mileage is not reimbursed.	$170/day for each day they are in session.
Colorado	. . .	. . .	$30,000	46/mile or 48/mile for 4wd. vehicle. Actual miles paid.	$45/day for members living in the Denver metro area. $99/day for members living outside Denver (V). Set by the legislature.
Connecticut	. . .	. . .	$28,000	48.5/mile.	No per diem is paid.
Delaware	. . .	. . .	$42,750	40/mile.	$7,334 expense allowance annually.
Florida	. . .	. . .	$30,336	44.5/mile for business travel.	$126/day for House and $133 for Senate (V) tied to federal rate. Earned based on the number of days in session. Travel vouchers are filed to substantiate.
Georgia	. . .	. . .	$17,342	Set by legislature, tied to federal rate	$173/d (U) set by the Legislative Services Committee.
Hawaii	. . .	. . .	$48,708	. . .	$150/day for members living outside Oahu during session; $120/day for members living outside Oahu during interim while conducting legislative business; $10/day for members living on Oahu during the interim while conducting official legislative business.
Idaho	. . .	. . .	$16,116	One roundtrip per wk. at state rate.	$122/day for members establishing second residence in Boise; $49/day if no second residence is established and up to $25/day travel (V) set by Compensation Commission.
Illinois	. . .	. . .	$67,836	48.5/mile, tied to federal rate.	$132/per session day.
Indiana	. . .	. . .	$22,616	50.5/mile	$138/day (U) tied to federal rate.
Iowa	. . .	. . .	$25,000	39/mile	$118/day (U). $88.50/day for Polk County legislators (U) set by the legislature to coincide with federal rate. State mileage rates apply.
Kansas	$88.66 C	. . .	. . .	47/mile, set by Dept. of Admin.	$109/d (U) tied to federal rate.
Kentucky	$186.73 C	. . .	. . .	50.5/mile	$119.90/d (U) tied to federal rate. (110% federal per diem rate).
Louisiana	. . .	. . .	$16,800 plus add. $6,000/yr. (U) expense allowance.	55.5/mile, tied to federal rate.	$145/d (U) tied to federal rate.
Maine	. . .	. . .	$13,526 for first regular session; $9,874 for second regular session.	40/mile	$38/day housing, or mileage and tolls in lieu of housing (at rate of $0.44/mile up to $38/day) plus $32/day for meals. Per diem limits are set by statute.

See footnotes at end of table.

LEGISLATIVE COMPENSATION AND LIVING EXPENSE ALLOWANCES DURING SESSIONS — Continued

State	Salaries: Regular sessions: Per diem salary	Salaries: Regular sessions: Limit on days	Salaries: Annual salary	Mileage cents per mile	Session per diem rate
Maryland	. . .	. . .	$43,500	50.5/mile, $500 allowance for in district travel as taxable income, members may decline the allowance.	Lodging $96/day; meals $32/day (V) tied to federal rate and compensation commission. $225/day for out of state travel. Includes meals and lodging.
Massachusetts	. . .	. . .	$58,237.15	Between $10 and $100, determined by distance from State House.	From $10/day-$100/day, depending on distance from State House (V) set by the legislature.
Michigan	. . .	. . .	$79,650	50/mile.	$12,000 yearly expense allowance for session and interim (V) set by compensation commission.
Minnesota	. . .	. . .	$31,140.90	House: range of $100-$850 for in district mileage, plus additional amount for 11 largest districts. Senate: a reasonable allowance. Both bodies: mileage reimbursement to Capitol as needed	Senators receive $96/day and Representatives receive $77/legislative day (U) set by the legislature/Rules Committee.
Mississippi	. . .	. . .	$10,000	48.5/mile; determined by Federal Register and Legislature.	$109/day (U) tied to federal rate.
Missouri	. . .	. . .	$35,915	45.5/mile	$87.20/d tied to federal rate. Verification of per diem is by roll call.
Montana	$82.64L	. . .	. . .	50.5/mile; Rate is based on IRS rate. Reimbursement for actual mileage traveled in connection with legislative business	$103.64/d (U).
Nebraska	. . .	. . .	$12,000	50.5/mile, tied to federal rate.	$109/day outside 50-mile radius from Capitol; $39/day if member resides within 50 miles of Capitol (V) tied to federal rate.
Nevada	$137.90/d max. of 60 days of session for holdover Senators, $146.90/d for all other legislators.	60 days	. . .	Federal rate, currently 50.5/mile	Federal rate for Capitol area (U). Legislators who live more than 50 miles from the capitol, if require lodging, will be paid at HUD single-room rate for Carson City area for each month of session.
New Hampshire		2 yr. term	$200	Round trip home to State House @ 38¢/mile for first 45 miles and 19¢/mile thereafter; or members will be reimbursed for actual expenses and mileage will be paid at the maximum IRS mileage rate	No per diem is paid.
New Jersey	. . .	. . .	$49,000	. . .	No per diem is paid.
New Mexico	. . .	. . .	. . .	50.5/mile, tied to federal rate.	$144/d (V) tied to federal rate and the constitution.
New York	. . .	. . .	$79,500	50.5/mile.	Varies (V) tied to federal rate.
North Carolina	. . .	. . .	$13,951	29¢/mile, 1 round trip/week during session; 1 round trip for attendance at interim cmte. mtgs.	$104/d (U) set by statute. $559/m expense allowance.
North Dakota	$135 C	. . .	. . .	45¢/mile; one round trip/week during session.	Lodging reimbursement up to $900/m (V).
Ohio	. . .	. . .	$60,584	40¢/mile; one round trip/week from home to Statehouse for legislators outside Franklin County only	No per diem is paid.

See footnotes at end of table.

LEGISLATIVE COMPENSATION AND LIVING EXPENSE ALLOWANCES DURING SESSIONS — Continued

State	Salaries: Regular sessions: Per diem salary	Salaries: Regular sessions: Limit on days	Salaries: Annual salary	Mileage cents per mile	Session per diem rate
Oklahoma	...	...	$38,400	50.5/mile, tied to federal rate.	$132/d (U) tied to federal rate.
Oregon	...	...	$21,612	48.5/mile.	$109/d (U) tied to federal rate.
Pennsylvania	...	...	$78,315	50.5/mile, tied to federal rate.	$158/day (V) tied to federal rate. Can receive actual expenses or per diem.
Rhode Island	...	...	$13,089	40.5/mile to and from session.	No per diem is paid.
South Carolina	...	...	$10,400	34.5/mile.	$119/day for meals and housing for each statewide session day and committee meeting; tied to federal rate.
South Dakota	...	2 yr. term	$12,000	32¢/mile for one round trip from Pierre to home each weekend. One trip is also paid at 5¢/mile. During the interim, 32¢/mile for scheduled committee meetings.	$110/L (U) set by the legislature.
Tennessee	...	...	$19,009	35/mile.	$171/L (U) tied to the federal rate.
Texas	...	...	$7,200	50.5¢/mile set by General Appropriations bill; an allowance for single, twin and turbo engines at $1.07/mile is also given	$139/d (U) set by Ethics Commission.
Utah	$130 C	...	...	48.5/mile, rnd. trip from home to capitol.	$90/day (U) lodging allotment for each calendar day, tied to federal rate, $54/day meals (U).
Vermont	...	...	$625.36/wk. during session; $118 per day for special sessions or interim cmte. meeting	Federal mileage rate, now about 48.5¢/mile, state employee reimbursement rate	Federal per diem rate for Montpelier is $93/day for lodging and $54/day for meals for non-commuters; commuters receive $54/day for meals plus mileage.
Virginia	...	...	Senate: $18,000, House: $17,640	50.5/mile.	House: $135/day (U) tied to federal rate. Senate: $169 (U) tied to federal rate.
Washington	...	...	$42,106	50.5/mile.	$90/day
West Virginia	...	...	$20,000	48.5/mile based on Dept. of Admin. travel regs.	$131/d (U) during session set by compensation commission.
Wisconsin	...	...	$49,943	46.5¢/mile for in-district business mileage plus one round trip/week to Capitol	Current authorized amount is up to $88 per day ($44 per day for legislators living in Dane County). Per diem authorized under 13.123 (1), Wis Statutes, and Leg. Joint Rule 85. 20.916(8) State Statutes and Joint Committee on Employment Relations (JCOER) establishes the max. amount at 90% of the federal per diem rate for Madison. The leadership of each house then determines, within that maximum, what amount to authorize for the session. Current amount of $88 is approximately 64% of the federal per diem rate for Madison.
Wyoming	$150 L	...	...	35/mile.	$85/day (V) set by the legislature, includes travel days for those outside of Cheyenne.

Source: National Conference of State Legislatures, March 2009 for salaries and session per diems; March 2008 for mileage rates.

Key:
C — Calendar day
L — Legislative day
(U) — Unvouchered
(V) — Vouchered
d — day
w — week
m — month
y — year
. . . — Not applicable
N.R.— Not reported

Table 3.10
LEGISLATIVE COMPENSATION: OTHER PAYMENTS AND BENEFITS

State	Legislator's compensation for office supplies, district offices and staffing	Phone allowance	Transportation offered to legislators	Insurance benefits				
				Health	Dental	Optical	Disability insurance	Life insurance benefits
Alabama	None, although annual appropriation to certain positions may be so allocated.	Yes (a)	No	S.A., O.P.	S.A., O.P.	N.A.	N.A.	N.A.
Alaska	Senators receive $10,000/y and Representatives receive $8,000/y for postage, stationery and other legislative expenses. Staffing allowance determined by rules and presiding officers, depending on time of year.	Yes (a)	No	S.P.P.	S.P.P.	O.P.; unless included in Health Ins.	Optional; if selected is included in health insurance	Small policy available; additional is optional at legislator's expense.
Arizona	None.	Yes (b)	(c)	S.P.P.	S.P.P.	O.P.	S.P.P.—through the retirement system.	State pays 15K policy; additional amount is paid by legislator.
Arkansas	Legislators may receive reimbursement of up to $14,400 annually for legislative expenses incurred. Standing subcommittee chairs and committee chairs may receive additional annual expense reimbursements of up to $1,800 and $3,600, respectively. Legislators who formally decline to receive per diem and mileage reimbursements may receive additional annual expense reimbursements of up to $10,200.	No	No	S.A.	O.P.	O.P.	O.P.	State provides $10,000 coverage with option to purchase greater amount.
California	Based on the size of their districts.	Yes (a)	(d)	S.P.P.	S.P	S.P.	S.P.	S.P.
Colorado	None.	Yes (a)	No	S.P.P.	S.P.P.	N.A.	N.A.	State pays full amount for $12,000 policy; additional is optional at legislator's expense.
Connecticut	Senators receive $5,500 and Representatives receive $4,500 in unvouchered expense allowance.	Yes (e)	No	S.P.P.	S.P.P.	Some health insurance plans include discounts on eyewear.	O.P.	O.P.
Delaware	Reimbursement provided for office expenses.	Yes (a)	No	S.P.P.—After three months the state pays entire amount for basic plan.	O.P.	O.P.	N.A	O.P.
Florida	Senate $2,921/m for district office expenses. House $2,324/m for district office expenses. Speaker $3,246 and Senate President $3,567	Yes (a)	(f)	S.P.	S.P.	O.P.	S.P.	S.P.

See footnotes at end of table.

LEGISLATIVE COMPENSATION: OTHER PAYMENTS AND BENEFITS — Continued

				Insurance benefits				
State	Legislator's compensation for office supplies, district offices and staffing	Phone allowance	Transportation offered to legislators	Health	Dental	Optical	Disability insurance	Life insurance benefits
Georgia	$7,000/y reimbursable expense account. If the member requests and provides receipts, the member is reimbursed for personal services, office equipment, rent, supplies, transportation, telecommunications, etc.	No	No	S.A, S.P.P.	O.P.	O.P.	O.P.	O.P.
Hawaii	There is no set dollar amount for office supplies. All supplies are provided by the House Supply Room. Any item not carried in the Supply Room may be purchased with statutory legislative allowance funds which are currently $7,500/y. House members do not have district offices. With the exception of the Speaker's Office and Majority and Minority Leadership offices, the House Finance, Judiciary and Consumer Protection offices, each House Majority and Minority member is allowed 1 permanent full-time Office Manager. During the session each Majority member receives $6,000/m for temporary staff salaries, and each Minority member receives $5,500/m.	Yes (a)	(g)	S.P.P.	S.P.P.	S.P.P.	S.P.P.	O.P.
Idaho	$1,700/y for unvouchered constituent expense. No staffing allowance.	Yes (h)	No	S.P.P.	S.P.P.	N.A.	S.P.P.	O.P.
Illinois	Senators receive $83,063/y and Representatives $69,409/y for office expenses, including district offices and staffing.	No	No	S.P.P.	S.P.P.	S.P.P.	S.P.	O.P.
Indiana	40% of per diem for district offices during interim only. No staffing allowance.	Yes	No	S.P., legislator pays dep. portion	S.P.	S.P., legislator pays dep. portion	N.A.	O.P.
Iowa	$300/m to cover district constituency postage, travel, telephone and other expenses. No staffing allowance.	No	No	S.P.P.	S.P.P.	N.A.	S.P.	State pays first $20,000, additional at legislator expense.
Kansas	$6,910/y which is taxable income to the legislators. Staffing allowances vary for leadership who have their own budget. Legislators provided with secretaries during session only.	Yes (i)	No	S.P.P.	S.P., legislator pays dep. portion	O.P.	S.P.	150% of annual salary if part of KPERS. Additional insurance is optional at legislator's expense.
Kentucky	$1,756.75 for district expenses during interim.	No	Yes	S.P., legislator pays dep. portion	O.P.	O.P.	O.P.	State pays $20,000; extra available at legislator's expense.

See footnotes at end of table.

LEGISLATIVE COMPENSATION: OTHER PAYMENTS AND BENEFITS—Continued

State	Legislator's compensation for office supplies, district offices and staffing	Phone allowance	Transportation offered to legislators	Insurance benefits: Health	Dental	Optical	Disability insurance	Life insurance benefits
Louisiana	$500/m; Senators and Representatives receive an additional $,1500 supplemental allowance for vouchered office expenses, rent, travel mileage in district. Senators and Representatives staff allowance $2,000/m starting salary up to $3,000 with annual increases.	Yes (j)	No	S.P.P.	S.P.P.—Senators pay 100%	O.P.	O.P.	State pays half; legislator pays half.
Maine	None. However, supplies for staff offices are provided and paid for out of general legislative account.	Yes (k)	No	S.A.	S.A.	O.P.	N.A.	O.P.
Maryland	Members, $18,265/y for normal office expenses with limits on postage, telephone and publications, and an additional $1,400 to $2,000 for certain leadership positions. Members must document expenses. Members receive an additional allowance for district office staff salaries. Senators receive one administrative assistant.	No	No	S.A.	S.A., O.P.	Covered under medical plan	N.A.	Term insurance; optional at legislator's expense.
Massachusetts	$7,200/y for office expenses.	No	No	S.P.P.	S.P.P.	S.P.P.	O.P.	$5,000 policy provided; Additional up to 8 times salary at legislator's expense.
Michigan	$61,359 per majority Senator for office budget $61,359 for minority Senator for office budget.	Yes (a)	No	Health, vision, life, cancer, prescription offered via cafeteria plan.			N.A.	Offered at different levels as part of cafeteria plan.
Minnesota	None.	$125/m; (V)	(l)	State pays —100% single; 85% family.	State pays—90% single; 50% family.	S.A.	O.P.	State pays premium for benefit of $35,000.
Mississippi	A total of $1,500/m out of session.	Yes	No	S.P.—legislator only premiums	O.P.	N.A.	None	S.P.P.
Missouri	$800/m to cover all reasonable and necessary business expenses.	Yes (m)	No	S.P.P.	O.P.	O.P.	S.P.	S.P.—Additional amounts are optional at legislator's expense.
Montana	None.	Yes (n)	No	S.P.	S.P.	O.P.	N.A.	State pays $14,000 term policy. Additional at legislator's expense.
Nebraska	No allowance; however, each member is provided with two full-time capitol staff year-round.	Yes (a)	No	O.P.	O.P.	O.P.	O.P.	O.P.
Nevada	None.	$2,800 allowance	(o)	O.P.	O.P.	O.P.	O.P.	O.P.

See footnotes at end of table.

LEGISLATIVE COMPENSATION: OTHER PAYMENTS AND BENEFITS—Continued

State	Legislator's compensation for office supplies, district offices and staffing	Phone allowance	Transportation offered to legislators	Insurance benefits: Health	Dental	Optical	Disability insurance	Life insurance benefits
New Hampshire	None.	No	No	O.P.	O.P.	N.A.	N.A	N.A.
New Jersey	$750 for supplies, 12 cartons of copy paper, equipment and furnishings supplied through a district office program. $110,000/y for district office personnel. State provides stationery for each legislator. 12,500 postage stamps for Assembly Members; 10,000 postage stamps for Senate Members.	None for Assembly	(p)	S.A.	S.A.	S.A.	N.A.	State pays 1 1/2 times salary. Also available additional coverage of 1 1/2 times salary which is optional at legislator's expense.
New Mexico	None.	No	No	N.A.	N.A.	N.A.	N.A	N.A.
New York	Staff allowance set by majority leader for majority members and by minority leader for minority members. Staff allowance covers both district and capitol; geographic location; seniority and leadership responsibilities will cause variations.	Yes (a)	(q)	S.P.P.	S.P.P.	No cost if participating provider used	S.P.	O.P.
North Carolina	Non-leaders receive $6,708/y for any legislative expenses not otherwise provided. Full-time secretarial assistance is provided during session.	Yes (r)	No	S.P.; O.P. family coverage	O.P.	O.P.	O.P.	O.P.
North Dakota	Home Internet connection.	Yes (s)	No	S.A., S.P.	O.P.	O.P.	O.P.	State pays for $1,300 term life policy.
Ohio	None.	Yes (a)	No	S.P.P.	S.P.	S.P.	N.A.	Amount equal to salary; premium paid by state. Member may purchase a supplemental policy, which is also offered to state employees.
Oklahoma	$350/y for unvouchered office supplies plus five rolls of stamps.	Yes (t)	No	$262.19 allowance per month for all benefits.	S.A.	S.A.	S.A.	S.A.
Oregon	Session office supplies, $15.50/d. Interim office allowance, $450–750/m depending on geographic size of district. Session staffing allowance, $4,292/m; Interim staffing allowance, $3,454/m.	Yes (u)	No	S.A.	S.A.	S.A.	O.P.	O.P.
Pennsylvania	Staffing is determined by leadership.	No	(v)	Medical/hospital, dental, vision, prescription. Employee pays 1% of salary for health benefits.				Equal to salary to maximum of $150,000.

See footnotes at end of table.

LEGISLATIVE COMPENSATION: OTHER PAYMENTS AND BENEFITS — Continued

State	Legislator's compensation for office supplies, district offices and staffing	Phone allowance	Transportation offered to legislators	Insurance benefits				
				Health	Dental	Optical	Disability insurance	Life insurance benefits
Rhode Island	None.	No	No	S.A.	S.A.	S.A.	O.P.	O.P.
South Carolina	Senate $3,400/y for postage, stationery and telephone. House $1,800/y for telephone and $600/y for postage. Legislators also receive $1,000/m for in district expenses that is treated as income.	Yes (a)	No	S.P.P.	S.P.P.	N.A.	S.P.P.	S.P.P.
South Dakota	None.	Yes (w)	No	N.A.	N.A.	N.A.	S.P. for accidental death/dismemberment ins. only	N.A.
Tennessee	$1,000/m for expenses in district (U).	Yes (x)	(y)	State pays 80%, legislator pays 20%	O.P.	N.A.	N.A.	State pays $15,000; Legislator pays $7,000.
Texas	Approved allowance for staff salaries, supplies, stationery, postage, district office rental, telephone expense, etc.	No	No	S.P.	O.P.	Included in health coverage	O.P.	O.P.
Utah	None.	No (z)	No	S.P.P.	S.P.P.	S.P.P.	S.P.	S.P.
Vermont	None.	(aa)	No	O.P.	N.A.	N.A.	N.A.	N.A.
Virginia	Legislators receive $1,250/m; leadership receives $1,750/m office expense allowance. Legislators receive a staffing allowance of $37,871/y; leadership receives $56,804/y.	Yes	No	S.P.P.	S.P.P.	S.P.P.	S.P.—only permanent disability retirement through retirement system	S.P.P.
Washington	$1,950/quarter for legislative expenses, for which the legislator has not been otherwise entitled to reimbursement. No staffing allowance.	Yes (a)	No	S.P.P.	S.P.	Included in medical	S.P.P.	S.P.P.
West Virginia	None.	Yes	No	O.P.	O.P.	O.P.	N.A.	O.P.
Wisconsin	$12,000 for 2 year session in the Assembly. District Office $45,000 for two year period for office expenses. In Senate, $54,063 office budget for 2 year session and $198,417 staff salary budget.	(bb)	No	S.A.	Some HMOs cover	O.P.	O.P.	O.P.
Wyoming	Up to $750 quarter through the constituent service allowance.	(cc)	No	N.A.	N.A.	N.A.	N.A.	N.A.

See footnotes at end of table.

LEGISLATIVE COMPENSATION: OTHER PAYMENTS AND BENEFITS—Continued

Source: National Conference of State Legislatures, March 2008 with update January 2009.
Key:
(U) — Unvouchered.
(V) — Vouchered.
d — day.
m — month.
w — week.
y — year.
N.A. — Not available.
S.P. — State pays full amount.
S.P.P.— State pays portion and legislator pays portion.
S.A.— Same as state employees.
O.P.— Optional at legislator's expense.
(a) Official state business only.
(b) Phone cards are allowed for certain districts.
(c) Access to motor pool for legislative trips only.
(d) Members are provided a vehicle, on which they pay a portion of the payment.
(e) Official business only; charges for personal calls are reimbursed by legislator.
(f) Rental cars for official business.
(g) Neighbor Island members are allowed 1 round trip from their home island every week—during session and during the interim. Additional trips are allowed when authorized by the Speaker.
(h) During session only.
(i) If monthly bill exceeds $200, leadership is notified.
(j) District office line with one extension.
(k) Pre-paid phone cards are issued to members of the Senate and the House.
(l) Car rental is available with prior approval. Mileage reimbursement is available when using personal vehicles.
(m) Phone cards issued but expenditures deducted from monthly expense allowance.
(n) Leadership positions only.
(o) Motor pool or private; legislative police shuttle to/from Reno airport.
(p) Automobiles for Speaker, Majority Leader and Minority Leader in the Assembly. None for Senate.
(q) Top leadership has access to vehicles.
(r) Allowance of $2,275 for postage, stationery and telephone.
(s) Only Legislative Council members or chairs of interim cmtes.
(t) Senate members receive phone credit card for state-related business use away from Capitol
(u) State-provided office and district office phone for legislative business only.
(v) Business mileage reimbursement or use fleet lease vehicle from Department of General Services.
(w) Telephone allowance: $600/6 m for legislators and $900/6 m for leadership.
(x) Phone cards for in-state long distance (only).
(y) In lieu of mileage, members residing greater than 100 miles from the seat of government may be reimbursed for coach class airline fare for attendance at session or committee meetings. Limited to one round trip per week during session.
(z) All members are issued Blackberry phones.
(aa) Leaders for legislative business.
(bb) Members office expenses, including phone expense, are limited to the amount of each legislator's office budget, as established by the cmte. on Senate and Assembly organizations.
(cc) Telephone credit card for official business only with a $2,000 limit during 2 yrs.

Table 3.11
ADDITIONAL COMPENSATION FOR SENATE LEADERS

State	Presiding officer	Majority leader	Minority leader	Other leaders and committee chairs
Alabama	$2/day plus $1,500/ mo. expense allowance	None	None	Committee chairs: Senate Finance and Taxation Cmte. Chair, $150/mo.
Alaska	$500	None	None	None
Arizona	Generally approved for additional interim per diem.			None
Arkansas	None	None	None	$3,600/yr for committee chairs; $1,800/yr. sub-cmte. chairs.
California	$133,639/yr. (a)	$124,923/yr. (a)	$133,639/yr. (a)	None
Colorado	All leaders receive $99/day salary during interim when in attendance at committee or leadership meetings.			
Connecticut	$10,689	$8,835	$8,835	Leaders: Dep. min. and maj. ldrs., $6,446/year; asst. maj. and min. ldrs. and maj. and min. whips $4,241/yr. Committee chairs: All cmte. chairs, $4,241.
Delaware	$19,983	$12,376	$12,376	Leaders: Maj. and min. whips $7,794. Committee chairs: Joint Finance Cmte. Chair, $11,459; Capital Improvement Chair and Vice-Chair $4,578; Sunset Cmte. Chair $4,578. Joint Finance Cmte. Chair $11,459
Florida	$12,348	None	None	None
Georgia	$71,599/yr. (b)	$200/mo.	$200/mo.	President pro tem, $400/mo; admin. flr. ldr., $200/mo; asst. admin. flr. ldr., $100/mo.
Hawaii	$7,500	None	None	None
Idaho	$4,000	None	None	None
Illinois	$26,471	$19,893	$26,471	Asst. maj. and min. ldr., $19,893; maj. and min. caucus chair, $19,893. All cmte. chairs and minority spokesperson $9,948.
Indiana	$7,000	Maj. floor ldr. $5,500; asst. maj. floor ldr. $3,500	Min. floor ldr. $6,000; min. asst. floor ldr. $5,000; min. ldr. pro tem. emeritus $1,500	Leaders: asst. pres. pro tem. $3,000; maj. cauc. chair $5,500; asst. maj. cauc. chair $1,500; maj. whip $4,000; asst. maj. whip $2,000; min. cauc. chair $5,000; asst. min. cauc. chair $1,000; mem. $2,000; tax & fiscal policy ranking min. mem.$2,000; min. whip $3,000; asst. min. whip $1,000. Committee Chairs: Appropriations Comm. Chair $5,500; Tax & Fiscal Policy Chair. $5,500; Ag. & Sm. Business Comm. Chair $1,000; Commerce, Public Policy & Interstate Chair $1,000; Corrections, Criminal, & Civil Matters Chair $1,000; Energy & Environmental Affairs Chair $1,000; Pensions & Labor Comm. Chair $1,000; Health & Provider Services Comm. Chair $1,000; Insurance & Financial Institutions Chair $1,000; Nat. Resource Comm. Chair $1,000
Iowa	$11,593	$11,593	$11,593	Pres. Pro Tem $1,243.
Kansas	$13,696.80/yr	$12,356.76/yr	$12,356.76/yr	Leaders: Asst. maj., min. ldrs., vice pres., $6,990.62/yr. Committee Chairs: Senate Ways and Means Cmte. $11,014.64.
Kentucky	$46.51/day	$36.73/day	$36.73/day	Leaders: Maj., min. caucus chairs and whips, $28.15/day. Committee Chairs: for standing cmtes. only $18.38/day

See footnotes at end of table.

ADDITIONAL COMPENSATION FOR SENATE LEADERS — Continued

State	Presiding officer	Majority leader	Minority leader	Other leaders and committee chairs
Louisiana	$32,000	None	None	Pres. Pro Tem $24,500. Joint Budget Cmte. $28,000/yr. for chair and vice-chair.
Maine	150% of base salary	125% of base salary	112.5% of base salary	None
Maryland	$13,000/yr.	None	None	None
Massachusetts	$35,000	$22,500	$22,500	Leaders: asst. maj. and min. ldr., (and 2nd and 3rd assistant), Pres. Pro Tem., each $15,000. Committee Chairs: $7,500-$15,000/yr.
Michigan	$5,513	$26,000	$22,000	Leaders: Maj. flr. ldr., $12,000; min. flr. ldr., $10,000. Committee Chairs: Appropriation Cmte. Chairs $7,000.
Minnesota	None	$43,596 (a)	$43,596 (a)	Majority whip, $35,291. Senate Tax Cmte. Chair $35,292.
Mississippi	Lt. Gov.—$60,000 (a) Pres. Pro Tem, $15,000	None	None	None
Missouri	None	None	None	None
Montana	$5/day during session	None	None	None
Nebraska	None	None	None	None
Nevada	$900	$900	$900	Leaders: Pres. Pro Tem, $900. Committee Chairs: Standing cmte. Chairs $900.
New Hampshire	$50/two-yr term	None	None	None
New Jersey	1/3 above annual salary	None	None	None
New Mexico	None	None	None	None
New York	$41,500	None	$34,500	Leaders: 22 other leaders with compensation ranging from $13,000 to $34,000. Committee Chairs: between $9,000 and $34,000.
North Carolina	$38,151 (a) and $16,956 expense allowance.	$17,048 (a) and $7,992 expense allowance	$17,048 (a) and $7,992 expense allowance	Dep. pro tem: $21,739 (a) and $10,032 expense allowance
North Dakota	None	$10/day during session; $270/m during term of office	$10/day during session; $270/m during term of office	Leaders: Asst. ldrs., $5/day during session. Committee Chairs: Substantive standing cmte. chairs $5/day.
Ohio	$87,698 (a)	President Pro Tem $80,016; Maj Flr Leader $75,371; Asst. Maj. Flr. Leader $70,733; Maj. Whip $66,094; Asst. Maj. Whip $61,452 (a)	$80,016 (a)	Committee Leaders: $6,500 for all committee chairs except Finance Chair, who receives $10,000. Vice-chairs receive $5,000 with the Vice-Chair of Finance receiving $5,500.
Oklahoma	$17,932	$12,364	$12,364	$12,364 for Appropriations and Budget Committee Chairs
Oregon	$19, 884/yr.	None	None	None
Pennsylvania	$42,732/yr.	$34,187/yr.	$34,187/yr.	Maj. and min. whip, $25,945; maj. and min. caucus chair, $16,177; maj. and min. caucus secretaries, $10,683, maj. and min. caucus admin., $10,683.
Rhode Island	Double the base salary	None	None	None
South Carolina	Lt. gov. holds this position	None	None	Leaders: President pro tem, $11,000. Committee Chairs: $600/ interim expense allowance for committee chairs of the Senate.
South Dakota	None	None	None	None

See footnotes at end of table.

ADDITIONAL COMPENSATION FOR SENATE LEADERS — Continued

State	Presiding officer	Majority leader	Minority leader	Other leaders and committee chairs
Tennessee	$54,369	None	None	None
Texas	None	None	None	None
Utah	$3,000	$2,000	$2,000	Leaders: Maj. whip, asst. maj. whip, min. whip and asst. min. whip, $2,000. Committee Chairs: $2,000 for Executive Appropriations Chair (Co-chair)
Vermont	Lt. gov $63,701/yr	None	None	None
Virginia	None	$200/d for interim business	$200/d for interim business	President pro tem $200/d for interim business
Washington	Lt. gov. holds this position	$49,280 ($4,000 additional to base salary)(a)	$45,280 ($4,000 additional to base salary)(a)	None
West Virginia	$50/day during session.	$25/day during session.	$25/day during session.	Up to 4 add'l people named by presiding officer receive $150 for a maximum of 30 days. $150/day (max. 30 days) for Finance and Judiciary chair.
Wisconsin	None	None	None	None
Wyoming	$3/day	None	None	None

Source: National Conference of State Legislatures, March 2008 with updates March 2009.
(a) Total annual salary for this leadership position.
(b) Salary of the lieutenant governor.

Table 3.12
ADDITIONAL COMPENSATION FOR HOUSE/ASSEMBLY LEADERS

State	Presiding officer	Majority leader	Minority leader	Other leaders and committee chairs
Alabama	$2/day plus $1,500/mo. expense allowance	None	None	$150/mo. for House Ways and Means chair
Alaska	$500	None	None	None
Arizona	None	None	None	None
Arkansas	None	None	None	$3,600/yr. for cmte. chairs; $1,800/yr. sub cmte. chairs.
California	$133,639 (a)	$124,923 (a)	$133,639 (a)	2nd ranking min. ldrs. receive $124,923 yr.
Colorado	----------------- All leaders receive $99/day salary during interim when in attendance at committee or leadership matters. --------------			
Connecticut	$10,689	$8,835	$8,835	Dep. spkr., dep. maj. and min. ldrs., $6,446/yr; asst. maj. and min. ldrs.; maj. and min whips, $4,241/yr.
Delaware	$19,893	$12,376	$12,376	Leaders: maj. and min. whips, $7,794. Committee Chairs: $11,459 for Joint Finance Committee Chair; $4,578 Capital Improvement Chair and Vice Chair; $4,578 Sunset Committee Chair.
Florida	$12,348	None	None	None
Georgia	$6,812/mo.	$200/mo.	$200/mo.	Governor's flr. ldr., $200/mo; asst. flr. ldr., $100/mo.; spkr. pro tem, $400/mo.
Hawaii	$7,500	None	None	None
Idaho	$4,000	None	None	None
Illinois	$26,471	$22,379	$26,471	Leaders: dpty. maj. and min., $19,066; asst. maj. and asst. min., maj. and min. conference chr. $19,405. Committee Chairs and Minority Spokespersons: $9,948.
Indiana	$6,500	$5,000	$5,500	Leaders: Speaker pro tem, $5,000; maj. caucus chair, $5,000; min. caucus chair, $4,500; asst. min. flr. leader, $3,500; asst. maj. flr. ldr., $1,000; maj. whip, $3,500; min. whip, $1,500. Committee Chairs: Appropriations Cmte. Chair $5,500; Tax & Fiscal Policy Chair. $5,500; Ag. & Sm. Business Cmte. Chair $1,000; Commerce, Public Policy & Interstate Chair $1,000; Corrections, Criminal, & Civil Matters Chair $1,000; Energy & Environmental Affairs Chair $1,000; Pensions & Labor Cmte. Chair $1,000; Health & Provider Services Cmte. Chair $1,000; Insurance & Financial Institutions Chair $1,000; Nat. Resource Cmte. Chair $1,000.
Iowa	$11,593	$11,593	$11,593	Speaker pro tem, $1,243
Kansas	$13,696.80/yr.	$12,356.76/yr.	$12,356.76/yr.	Leaders: asst. maj. and min. ldrs., spkr. pro tem, $6,990.62/yr. Committee Chairs: $11,014.64/year for House Appropriations Cmte.
Kentucky	$46.51/day	$36.73/day	$36.73/day	Leaders: maj. and min. caucus chairs & whips, $28.15/day. Committee Chairs: $18.38/day for standing committees only.
Louisiana	$32,000 (a)	None	None	Leaders: Speaker pro tem, $24,500 (a). Committee Chairs: $28,000/year for chairman and vice chairman of Joint Budget Cmte.
Maine	150% of base salary	125% of base salary	112.5% of base salary	None

See footnotes at end of table.

ADDITIONAL COMPENSATION FOR HOUSE/ASSEMBLY LEADERS — Continued

State	Presiding officer	Majority leader	Minority leader	Other leaders and committee chairs
Maryland	$13,000/year	None	None	None
Massachusetts	$35,000	$22,500	$22,500	Leaders: asst. maj. and min. ldr. (and 2nd and 3rd asst.), and spkr. pro tem, $15,000 each. Committee Chairs: $7,500–$15,000/year.
Michigan	$27,000	No position	$22,000	Leaders: Spkr. pro tem, $5,513; min. flr. ldr., $10,000; maj. flr. ldr., $12,000. Committee Chairs: $7,000 for Appropriation Committee chairs.
Minnesota	140% of base salary	140% of base salary	140% of base salary	$35,292 for Committee on Finance.
Mississippi	$60,000 (a)	None	None	Spkr. pro tem., $15,000
Missouri	$208.34/mo.	$125/mo.	$125/mo.	None
Montana	$5/day during session	None	None	None
Nebraska	None	None	None	None
Nevada	$900	$900	$900	Leaders: Speaker pro tem, $900. Committee Chairs: $900/flat amount for all standing committee chairs.
New Hampshire	$50/two-year term	None	None	None
New Jersey	1/3 above annual base salary	None	None	None
New Mexico	None	None	None	None
New York	$41,500	$34,500	$34,500	Leaders: 31 leaders with compensation ranging from $9,000 to $25,000. Committee Chairs: $9,000 to $34,000 set by statute.
North Carolina	$38,151 (a) and $16,956 expense allowance	$17,048 (a) and $7,992 expense allowance	$17,048 (a) and $7,992 expense allowance	Speaker pro tem, $21,739 and $10,032 expense allowance.
North Dakota	$10/day during legislative session.	$10/day during legislative session, $270/m during term of office.	$10/day during legislative session, $270/m during term of office.	Leaders: Asst. ldrs., $5/day during legislative sessions. Committee Chairs: $5/day for all substantive standing committees
Ohio	$94,437 (a)	Speaker pro tem $86,165; maj flr. leader $81,163; asst. maj. flr. leader $76,169; maj. whip $71,173; asst. maj. whip $66,175	Minority leader $86,165; asst. min. ldr. $78,668; min. whip $71,173; asst. min. whip $63,381	$6,500 for all committee chairs except Finance Chair, who receives $10,000. Vice chair receives $5,000 with the Vice Chair of Finance receiving $5,500.
Oklahoma	$17,932	$12,364	$12,364	Leaders: Speaker pro tem, $12,364. Committee Chairs: $12,364 for Appropriations and Budget Committee Chairs.
Oregon	Speaker receives additional $19,884/year in salary	None	None	None
Pennsylvania	$42,732/year	$34,187/year	$34,187/year	Maj. and min. whips, $25,945; maj. and min. caucus chairs, $16,177; maj. and min. caucus secretaries, $10,683; maj. and min. policy chairs, $10,683; maj. and min. caucus admin., $10,683.
Rhode Island	Speaker of the House receives double annual rate for Representatives.	None	None	None
South Carolina	$11,000/yr	None	None	Leaders: Speaker pro tem, $3,600/yr. Committee Chairs: $600/interim expense allowance for committee chairs of the House
South Dakota	None	None	None	None

See footnotes at end of table.

ADDITIONAL COMPENSATION FOR HOUSE/ASSEMBLY LEADERS — Continued

State	Presiding officer	Majority leader	Minority leader	Other leaders and committee chairs
Tennessee	$54,369 (a)	None	None	None
Texas	None	None	None	None
Utah	$3,000	$2,000	$2,000	Leaders: whips and asst. whips, $2,000. Committee Chairs: $2,000 for Executive Appropriations Chair (Co-chair).
Vermont	$680/week during session plus an additional $10,281.50 in salary.	None	None	None
Virginia	$18,681	None	None	None
Washington	$49,280, $8,000 additional to base salary (a)	None	$45,280, $4,000 additional to base salary (a)	None
West Virginia	$50/day during session	$25/day during session	$25/day during session	Leaders: up to four add'l people named by Presiding Officer receive $150 for a maximum of 30 days. Committee Chairs: The Chair of Finance & Judiciary may receive $150/day up to 30 days. Speaker may receive $150/day up to 80 days when not in session or interim committees not meeting.
Wisconsin	$25/month	None	None	None
Wyoming	$3/day	None	None	None

Source: National Conference of State Legislatures, March 2008 with updates February 2009.
(a) Total annual salary for this position.

Table 3.13
STATE LEGISLATIVE RETIREMENT BENEFITS

State or other jurisdiction	Participation	Plan name	Requirements for regular retirement	Employee contribution rate	Benefit formula
Alabama	None available.				
Alaska	Optional	Public Employees Retirement System	Age 60 with 10 yrs.	Employee 6.75%	2% (first 10 yrs.); or 2.25% (second 10 yrs.); or 2.5% (over 20 yrs.) x average salary over 5 highest consecutive yrs. x yrs. of service
Arizona	Mandatory—except that officials subject to term limits may opt out for a term of office.	Elected Officials Retirement System	Age 65, 5+ yrs. service; age 62, 10+ yrs. service; or 20 yrs. service; earlier retirement with an actuarial reduction of benefits. Vesting at 5 yrs.	Employee 7%	4% x years of credited service x highest 3 yr. average in the past 10 yrs. The benefit is capped at 80% of FAS. An elected official may purchase service credit in the plan for service earned in a non-elected position by buying it at an actuarially-determined amount.
Arkansas	Optional. Those elected before 7/1/99 may have service covered as a regular state employee but must have 5 years of regular service to do so.	Arkansas Public Employees Retirement System	Age 65, 10 yrs. service; or age 55, 12 yrs. service; or any age, 28 yrs. service; any age if serving in the General Assembly on 7/1/79; any age if in elected office on 7/1/79 with 17 and 1/2 yrs. of service. As a regular employee, age 65, 5 yrs. service, or any age and 28 yrs. Members of the contributory plan established in 2005 must have a minimum of 10 yrs. legislative service if they have only legislative state employment.	Non-contributory plan in effect for those elected before 2006. For those elected then and thereafter, a contributory plan that requires 5% of salary.	For service that began after 7/1/99: 2.07% x FAS x years of service. FAS based on three highest consecutive years or service. For service that began after July 1, 1991, $35 x years of service equals monthly benefit. For contributory plan, 2% x FAS x years of service.
California	Legislators elected after 1990 are not eligible for retirement benefits for legislative service.				
Colorado	Mandatory	Either Public Employees' Retirement Association or State Defined Contribution Plan. A choice is not irrevocable.	PERA: age 65, 5 yrs. service; age 50, 30 yrs. service; when age + service equals 80 or more (min. age of 55). DCP: no age requirement & vested immediately	Employee: 8%	PERA: 2.5% x FAS x yrs. of service, capped at 100% of FAS. DCP benefit depends upon contributions and investment returns.
Connecticut	Mandatory	State Employees Retirement System Tier IIA	Age 60, 25 yrs. credited service; age 62, 10–25 yrs. credited service; age 62, 5 yrs. actual state service. Reduced benefit available with earlier retirement ages.	2%	(.0133 x avg. annual salary) + (.005 x avg. annual salary in excess of "breakpoint" x credited service up to 35 years. 2003—$36,400 2007—$ 46,000 2004—$38,600 2008—$48,800 2005—$40,900 2009—$51,700 2006—$43,400 After 2009—increase breakpoint by 6% per year rounded to nearest $100.

See footnotes at end of table.

STATE LEGISLATIVE RETIREMENT BENEFITS — Continued

State or other jurisdiction	Participation	Plan name	Requirements for regular retirement	Employee contribution rate	Benefit formula
Delaware	Mandatory	State Employees Pension Plan	Age 60, 5 yrs. credited service	3% of total monthly compensation in excess of $6,000	2% times FAS times years of service before 1997 + 1.85% times FAS times years of service from 1997 on. FAS = average of highest 3 years.
Florida	Optional. Elected officials may opt out and may choose between DB and DC plans.	Florida Retirement System	Vesting in DB plan, 6 years: in DC plan, 1 year. DB plan: Age 62 with 6 years; 30 years at any age. DC plan: any age	No employee contribution. Employer contribution for 2004–2005 for legislators is 12.49% of salary.	DB plan: 3% x years of creditable service x average final compensation (average of highest 5 yrs). DC plan: Dependent upon investment experience.
Georgia	Optional: Choice when first elected.	Georgia Legislative Retirement System	Vested after 8 yrs.; age 62, with 8 yrs. of service; age 60 with reduction for early retirement.	Employee rate 3.75% + $7 month	$36 month for each year of service.
Hawaii	Mandatory	Public Employees Retirement System; elected officials' plan	Age 55 with 5 years of service, any age with 10 years service. Vesting at 5 years.	Main plan is non-contributory; 7.8% for elected officials' plan for annuity.	3.5 x yrs. of service as elected official x highest average salary plus annuity based on contributions as an elected official. Highest average salary = average of 3 highest 12- month periods as elected official.
Idaho	Mandatory		Age 65 with 5 yrs. service; reduced benefit at age 55 with 5 yrs. of service.	6.97%	Avg. monthly salary for highest 42 consecutive months x 2% x months of credited service.
Illinois	Optional	General Assembly Retirement System	Age 55, 8 yrs. service; or age 62, 4 yrs. service	8.5% for retirement; 2% for survivors; 1% for automatic increases; 11.5% total	3% of each of 1st 4 yrs.; 3.5% for each of next 2 yrs.; 4% for each of next 2 yrs.; 4.5% for each of the next 4 yrs.; 5% for each yr. above 12
Indiana	DB plan is optional for those serving on April 30, 1989. Defined contribution plan is optional for those serving on April 30, 1989 and mandatory for those elected or appointed since April 30, 1989.	Legislator's Retirement System and Defined Benefit (DB) Plan and Defined Contribution Plan (DC).	DB plan: Vesting at 10 yrs. Age 65 with 10 yrs. of legislative service; or if no longer in the legislature, these options apply: at least 10 yrs. service; no state salary; at age 55+ Rule of 85 applies; or age 60 with 15 yrs. of service. Early retirement with reduced benefit. Immediate vesting in the DC plan,	DC plan: 5% employee, 20% state (of taxable income). DB plan and employer contributions funded by appropriation.	DB benefit plan monthly benefit: Lesser of (a) $40 x years of General Assembly service completed before November 8, 1989 or (b) 1/12 of the average of the three highest consecutive years of General Assembly service salary. DC plan: numerous options for withdrawing accumulations in accord with IRS regulations. Loans are available. A participant in both plans may receive a benefit from both plans.
Iowa	Optional	Public Employees Retirement System	Age 65; age 62 with 20 yrs. service Rule of 88; reduced benefit at 55 with at least 4 years of service.	3.7% individual	2% times FAS x years of service for first 30 years, + 1% times FAS times years in excess of 30 but no more than 5 in excess of 30. FAS is average of 3 highest years.
Kansas	Optional	Public Employees Retirement System	Age 65, age 62 with 10 yrs. of service or age plus yrs. of service equals 85 pts.	4% of salary,(4% annualized salary for Legislators).	3 highest yrs. x 1.75% x yrs. service divided by 12.

See footnotes at end of table.

STATE LEGISLATIVE RETIREMENT BENEFITS — Continued

State or other jurisdiction	Participation	Plan name	Requirements for regular retirement	Employee contribution rate	Benefit formula
Kentucky	Optional. Those who opt out are covered by the state employees' plan	Kentucky Legislator's Retirement Plan	Age 65 with five years of service; any age with 30 years of service, and intermediate provisions. Early retirement with reduced benefits.	5% of creditable compensation, set by law at $27,500: not the same as actual salary. Revised to be payable on compensation reported on W-2 forms beginning in 2005.	2.75% of FAS (based on creditable compensation) x years of service. FAS is the average monthly earnings for the 60 months preceding retirement.
Louisiana	None available				
Maine	Mandatory	Maine State Retirement Plan	Age 60 (if 10 yrs. of service on 7/1/93) and age 62 (if less than 10 yrs. of service on 7/1/93). Reduced benefit available for earlier retirement.	7.65% legislators; employer contribution is actuarially determined.	2% of average final compensation (the average of the 3 high salary years) times years of service.
Maryland	Optional	State Legislator's Pension Plan	Age 60, with 8 yrs.; age 50, 8+yrs creditable service (early reduced retirement)	5% of annual salary	3% of legislative salary for each yr of service up to a max. of 22 yrs. 3 months. Benefits are recalculated when legislative salaries are changed.
Massachusetts	Optional after each election or re-election to the General Court.	State Retirement System legislator's plan	Age 55 with 6 years service; unreduced benefit at 65. Vesting at 6 years. Reduced benefits for retirement before age 65.	9%. Some legislators are grandfathered at lower rates.	2.5 times years of service times FAS. FAS = average of highest 36 months. Service credit is allowed for membership in other Massachusetts retirement plans.
Michigan	Optional	Legislative Retirement System (DB) for legislators elected before 3/31/97. Others may join the state defined contribution plan.	Age 55, 5 yrs. or age plus service equals 70	7%-13% for DB plan. For the DC plan, the state contributes 4% of salary. Members may contribute up to 3% of salary. The state will match the member's contribution in addition to the state 4% contribution.	For DB plans, various provisions, depending on when service started. For the DC plan, benefits depend upon contributions and earnings.
Minnesota	Mandatory	Legislators Retirement Plan before 7/1/97; Defined Contribution Plan (DCP) since then.	LRP: Age 62, 6 yrs. service and fully vested. DCP: age 55 and vested immediately. LRP members do not have Social Security coverage. DCP members have Social Security coverage.	LRP: 9%; DCP: 4% from member, 6% from state.	2.7% x high 5 yr. avg. salary x length of service (yrs.) DCP benefit depends upon contributions and investment return.
Mississippi	Mandatory	Legislators' plan within the Public Employees' Retirement System	Age 60 with 4 or more years of service, or 25 years of service.	Regular: 7.25% state 9.75% to 10.75% effective July 1, 2005; Supplement for legislative service: 3%/6.33%	Legislators who qualify for regular state retirement benefits also automatically qualify for the legislators' supplemental benefits. Regular: 2% times FAS times years of service up to and including 25 years of service + 2.5% times FAS times service in excess of 25 years FAS is based on the high 4 years. Supplement: 1% times FAS times years of legislative service through 25 years, + 1.25% times FAS times years of service in excess of 25.

See footnotes at end of table.

STATE LEGISLATIVE RETIREMENT BENEFITS — Continued

State or other jurisdiction	Participation	Plan name	Requirements for regular retirement	Employee contribution rate	Benefit formula
Missouri	Mandatory	Missouri State Employee Retirement System	Age 55; three full biennial assemblies (6 years) or Rule of 80. Vesting at 6 years of service.	Non-contributory	Monthly pay divided by 24 x years of creditable service, capped at 100% of salary. Benefit is adjusted by the percentage increase in pay for an active legislator.
Montana	Optional	Public Employees Retirement System. Either a DB or a DC plan is available.	Vesting at 5 years Age 60 with at least 5 years service; age 65 regardless of years of service; or 30 years of service regardless of age	6.9% for DB plan. Employer contribution of 4.19% plus employee contribution of 6.9 % for DC plan.	DB plan: 1/56 times years of service times FAS. Early retirement with reduced benefits is available. DC plan: Employee contributions and earnings are immediately vested. Employer contributions and earnings are vested after 5 years.
Nebraska	None available				
Nevada	Mandatory; but Chapter 380, Laws of 2005, allows legislators to withdraw from the system at will. The decision is final.	Legislator's Retirement System	Age 60, 10 yrs. service	15% of session salary	Number of years x $25 = monthly allowance
New Hampshire	None available				
New Jersey	Mandatory	Public Employees' Retirement System	Age 60; no minimum service requirement. Early retirement with no benefit reduction with 25 years of service. Vesting at 8 years.	5% of salary	3% x Final Average Salary x years of service. FAS = higher of three highest years or three final years. Benefit is capped at 2/3 of FAS, Other formulas apply if a legislator also has other service covered by the Public Employee Retirement System.
New Mexico	Optional	Legislative Retirement Plan	Plans 1A and 1B: Age 65 with 5 years of service; 64/8; 63/11; 60/12; or any age with 14 years of service. Plan 2: 65 with five years of service or at any age with 10 years of service.	Plan 1A: $100 per year for service after 1959 Plan 1B: $200 per year (now closed to new enrollments). Plan 2: $500/year	Plan 1A: $250 per year of service. Plan 1B: $500 per year of service after 1959. Plan 2: 11 percent of the IRS per diem rate in effect on December 31st of the year a legislator retires x 60 x the years of credited service. For a legislator who retired in 2003 the benefit would be $957 per year of credited service. Annual 3% COLA.
New York	Mandatory	New York State and Local Retirement System	Age 62 with 5 years of service; 55 with 30 years; reduced benefit available at 55/5. Vesting at 5 years.	3% for first 10 years of membership (Tier 4 provisions).	Tier 4: For less than 20 yrs. of service, pension =1/60th 30 for (1.66%) of final average salary (FAS) x years of service: for 20-years service, pension =1/50th (2%) of FAS x years of service; each year of service beyond 39, pension =3/200th (1.5%) of FAS.
North Carolina	Mandatory	Legislative Retirement System	Age 65 with 5 years of service; reduced benefit available at earlier ages.	7%	Highest annual compensation x 4.02% x years of service.
North Dakota	None available.				
Ohio	Optional	Public Employees Retirement System	Age 60 with 5 years service or 55 with 25 years service or at any age with 30 years service	8.5% of gross salary. A 10% contribution rate for legislators will be phased in over three years starting in 2006.	2.2% of final average salary times years of service up to and through 30 years of service. 2.5% starting with the 31st year of service and every year thereafter.

See footnotes at end of table.

STATE LEGISLATIVE RETIREMENT BENEFITS—Continued

State or other jurisdiction	Participation	Plan name	Requirements for regular retirement	Employee contribution rate	Benefit formula
Oklahoma	Legislators may retain membership as regular public employees if they have that status when elected; one time option to join Elected Officials' Plan.	Public Employee Retirement System, as regular member or elected official member. [Information here is for the Elected Officials' Plan.]	Elected Officials' Plan: Age 60 with 6 years service vesting at 6 years.	Optional contribution of 4.5%, 6%, 7.5%, 8.5%, 9%, or 10% of total compensation.	Avg. participating salary x length of service x computation factor depending on optional contributions ranging from 1.9% for a 4.5% contribution to 4% for a 10% contribution.
Oregon	Optional	Public Employee Retirement System legislator plan	Age 55, 30+ yrs. service, 5 years vesting.	16.317% of subject wages	1.67% x yrs. service and final avg. monthly salary
Pennsylvania	Optional	State Employees' Retirement System	Age 50, 3 yrs. service; any age with 35 years of service; early retirement with reduced benefit.	7.5%	3% x final avg. salary x credited yrs. of service (x withdrawal factor if under regular retirement age—50 for legislators).
Rhode Island	Legislators elected after January 1995 are ineligible for retirement benefits based on legislative service. (a)				
South Carolina	Mandatory, but members may opt out six months after being sworn into office.	South Carolina Retirement System	Age 60, 8 yrs. service; 30 yrs. of service regardless of age	10%	4.82% of annual compensation x yrs. service
South Dakota	None available.				
Tennessee	Optional		Age 55, 4 yrs. service	5.43%	$70 per month x yrs. service with a $1,375 monthly cap
Texas	Optional	Employee Retirement System: Elected Class Members	Age 60, 8 yrs. service; age 50, 12 yrs. service. Vesting at 8 years.	8%	2.3% x district judge's salary x length of service, with the monthly benefit capped at a the level of a district judge's salary, and adjusted when such salaries are increased. Various annuity options are available. Military service credit may be purchased to add to elective class service membership. In July 2005, a district judge's salary was set at $125,000, a year.
Utah	Mandatory	Governors' and Legislators' Retirement Plan	Age 62 with 10 years and an actuarial reduction; age 65 with 4 years of service for full benefits.	Non-contributory	$24.80/month (as of July 2004) x years of service; adjusted semi-annually according to consumer price index up to a maximum increase of 2%.
Vermont	None available. Deferred compensation plan available.				
Virginia	Mandatory		Age 50, 30 yrs. service (unreduced); age 55, 5 yrs. service; age 50, 10 yrs. service (reduced)	8.91% of creditable compensation	1.7% of average final compensation x yrs. of service

See footnotes at end of table.

STATE LEGISLATIVE RETIREMENT BENEFITS — Continued

State or other jurisdiction	Participation	Plan name	Requirements for regular retirement	Employee contribution rate	Benefit formula
Washington	Optional. If before an election the legislator belonged to a state public retirement plan, he or she may continue in that by making contributions. Otherwise the new legislator may join PERS Plan 2 or Plan 3.	See column to left. PERS plan 2 is a DB plan. PERS plan 3 is a hybrid DB/DC plan.	PERS plan 2: Age 65 with 5 years of service credit. Plan 3: Age 65 with 10 years of service credit for the DB side of the plan; immediate benefits (subject to federal restrictions) on the DC side of the plan. The member may choose various options for investment of contributions to the DC plan.	PERS plan 2: Employee contribution of 2.43% for 2002. Estimated at 3.33% for 2005–2007. Plan 3: No required member contribution for the DB component. The member may contribute from 5% to 15% of salary to the DC component.	PERS plan 2: 2% x years of service credit x average final compensation. Plan 3: DB is 1% x service credit years x average final compensation. DC benefit depends upon the value of accumulations.
West Virginia	Optional		Age 55, if yrs. of service+age equal 80	4.5% gross income	2% of final avg. salary x yrs. service. Final avg. salary is based on 3 highest yrs. out of last 10 yrs.
Wisconsin	Mandatory		Age 62 normal; age 57 with 30 years of service.	2.6% of salary in 2003, adjusted annually	Higher benefit of formula (2.165% x years of service x salary for service before 2000; 2% x years of service x salary for service 2000 and after) or money-purchase calculation.
Wyoming	None available				
Dist. of Columbia	Mandatory		Age 62, 5 yrs. service; age 55, 30 yrs. service; age 60, 20 yrs. service	Before 10/1/87, 7%; after 10/1/87, 5%	Multiply high 3 yrs. average pay by indicator under applicable yrs. or months of service.
Puerto Rico	Optional	Retirement System of the Employees of the Government of Puerto Rico	After 1990, age 65 with 30 years of service.	8.28%	1.5% of average earnings multiplied by the number of years of accredited service.
Guam	Optional		Age 60, 30 yrs. service; age 55, 15 yrs. service	5% or 8.5%	An amount equal to 2% of avg. annual salary for each of the first 10 yrs. of credited service and 2.5% of avg. annual salary for each yr. or part thereof of credited service over 10 yrs.
U.S. Virgin Islands	Optional		Age 60, 10 yrs. service	8%	At age 60 with at least 10 yrs. of service, at 2.5% for each yr. of service or at any time with at least 30 yrs. service

Source: National Conference of State Legislatures, January 2006 and updated January 2009.

Notes:

This table shows the retirement plans effective for state legislators elected in 2003, 2004 and thereafter. In general the table does not include information on closed plans, plans that continue in force for some legislators who entered the plans in previous years, but which have been closed to additional members. The information in this table was updated for all states and Puerto Rico in 2004 and updated for 2005 state legislation. Information for the District of Columbia, Guam and the Virgin Islands dates from 2002.

Key:

N.A. — Information not available

None available. — No retirement benefit provided.

(a) Constitution has been amended effective 1/95. Any legislator elected after this date is not eligible to join the State Retirement System, but will be compensated for $10,000/yr. with cost of living increases to be adjusted annually.

Table 3.14
BILL PRE-FILING, REFERENCE AND CARRYOVER

State or other jurisdiction	Pre-filing of bills allowed (b)	Bills referred to committee by:		Bill referral restricted by rule (a)		Bill carryover allowed (c)
		Senate	House/Assembly	Senate	House/Assembly	
Alabama	★(d)	(e)(f)	Speaker (f)	L, M	L, M	. . .
Alaska	★	President	Speaker	L, M	L, M	★
Arizona	★	President	Speaker	L	L	. . .
Arkansas	★	President (g)	Speaker	L	L	. . .
California	★(h)	Rules Cmte.	Rules Cmte.	L	L	★(h)
Colorado	★	President	Speaker	L, M (i)	L (i)	. . .
Connecticut	★	Pres. Pro Tempore	Speaker	M	M	. . .
Delaware	★	Pres. Pro Tempore	Speaker	L	L	★
Florida	★	President	Speaker	L, M	M	. . .
Georgia	★	President (f)	Speaker	. . .	. . .	★
Hawaii	(j)	(j)	Speaker	. . .	. . .	★
Idaho	. . .	President (e)	Speaker	L	L	. . .
Illinois	★	Rules Cmte.	Rules Cmte.	(k)	(k)	★
Indiana	★(l)	Pres. Pro Tempore	Speaker	(m)	. . .	. . .
Iowa	★	President	Speaker	M	M	★
Kansas	★	President	Speaker	L (n)	L (n)	★
Kentucky	★	Cmte. on Cmtes.	Cmte. on Cmtes.	L, M	L, M	. . .
Louisiana	★	President (o)	Speaker (o)	L	L	. . .
Maine	★	Secy. of Senate	Clerk of House	(p)	(p)	★
Maryland	★	President (q)	Speaker (q)	L	L	. . .
Massachusetts	★	Clerk	Clerk	M	M	★
Michigan	. . .	Majority Ldr.	Speaker	. . .	. . .	★
Minnesota	★(r)	President	Speaker	L, M	L, M	★(r)
Mississippi	★	President (e)	Speaker	L	L	. . .
Missouri	★	Pres. Pro Tempore	Speaker	L	L	. . .
Montana	★	President	Speaker	. . .	. . .	. . .
Nebraska	★	Reference Cmte. (s)	U	L	U	★(t)
Nevada	★	President (u)	Speaker (u)	L (v)	. . .	. . .
New Hampshire	★	President	Speaker	L	M	★
New Jersey	★	President	Speaker	L, M	L, M	★
New Mexico	★	(w)	Speaker	L, M	M (x)	. . .
New York	★	Pres. Pro Tempore	Speaker	M	M	★
North Carolina	. . .	Rules Chair	Speaker	M	M	★
North Dakota	★	President	Speaker	L	L	. . .
Ohio	★(y)	Reference Cmte.	Rules & Reference Cmte.	L (z)	L, M (aa)	★(bb)
Oklahoma	★	Majority Leader	Speaker	L	L	★(cc)
Oregon	★	President	Speaker	(dd)	(ee)	. . .
Pennsylvania	★	President Pro Tempore	Chief Clerk	M	M	. . .
Rhode Island	★	President	Speaker	M	M	. . .
South Carolina	★	President	Speaker	M	M	★(ff)
South Dakota	★	President Pro Tempore	Speaker	L	L	. . .
Tennessee	★	Speaker	Speaker	L, M	L, M	★(gg)
Texas	★	President	Speaker	L	L	. . .
Utah	★	President	Speaker	L	L	. . .
Vermont	(hh)	President	Speaker	M	M	★
Virginia	★	Clerk	Clerk (ii)	L, M (jj)	(kk)	★(ll)
Washington	★	(mm)	Speaker	L	L	★
West Virginia	★	President	Speaker	L, M	L, M	★(nn)
Wisconsin	. . .	President	Speaker	. . .	. . .	★(oo)
Wyoming	★	President	Speaker	M	M	. . .
American Samoa	. . .	. . .	. . .	. . .	. . .	. . .
Guam	★	Committee on Calendar Chairs	U	L, M (pp)	U	★
Puerto Rico	. . .	President	Secretary	M	M	. . .
U.S. Virgin Islands	. . .	Senate President in Pro-Forma meeting	U	L	U	★

See footnotes at end of table.

BILL PRE-FILING, REFERENCE AND CARRYOVER — Continued

Source: The Council of State Governments' survey, January 2009.

Key:

★ — Yes

. . . — No

L — Rules generally require all bills be referred to the appropriate committee of jurisdiction.

M — Rules require specific types of bills be referred to specific committees (e.g., appropriations, local bills).

U — Unicameral legislature.

(a) Legislative rules specify all or certain bills go to committees of jurisdiction.

(b) Unless otherwise indicated by footnote, bills may be introduced prior to convening each session of the legislature. In this column only: ★ — pre-filing is allowed in both chambers (or in the case of Nebraska, in the unicameral legislature); . . . — pre-filing is not allowed in either chamber.

(c) Bills carry over from the first year of the legislature to the second (does not apply in Alabama, Arkansas, Montana, Nevada, North Dakota, Oregon and Texas, where legislatures meet biennially). Bills generally do not carry over after an intervening legislative election.

(d) Except between the end of the last regular session of the legislature in any quadrennium and the organizational session following the general election and special sessions.

(e) Lieutenant governor is the president of the Senate.

(f) Senate bills by president with concurrence of president pro tem. House bills by president pro tem with concurrence of president, if no concurrence, referred to majority leader for assignment.

(g) Senate Chief Counsel makes recommendations to the presiding officer.

(h) Bills drafted prior to session. Introduction on the first day. Bills introduced in the first year of the regular session and passed by the house of origin on or before the January 31 constitutional deadline are carryover bills.

(i) In either house, state law requires any bill which affects the sentencing of criminal offenders and which would result in a net increase of imprisonment in state correctional facilities must be assigned to the appropriations committee of the house in which it was introduced. In the Senate, a bill must be referred to the Appropriations Committee if it contains an appropriation from the state treasury or the increase of any salary. Each bill which provides that any state revenue be devoted to any purpose other than that to which it is devoted under existing law must be referred to the Finance Committee.

(j) Pre-filing allowed only in the House, seven calendar days before the commencement of the regular session, in even-numbered years. Senate bills are referred to committee by the members of the majority leadership appointed by the president.

(k) In even-numbered years, the Rules Committee is to refer to substantive committees only appropriation bills implementing the budget, and bills deemed by the Rules Committee to be of an emergency nature or of substantial importance to the operation of government.

(l) Only in the Senate.

(m) At the discretion of president pro tempore.

(n) Appropriation bills are the only "specific type" mentioned in the rules to be referred to either House Appropriation Committee or Senate Ways and Means.

(o) Subject to approval or disapproval. Louisiana—majority members present.

(p) Maine Joint Rule 308 sections 1, 2, 3, "All bills and resolves must be referred to committee, except that this provision may be suspended by a majority vote in each chamber."

(q) The president and speaker may refer bills to any of the standing committees or the Rules Committees, but usually bills are referred according to subject matter.

(r) Pre-filing of bills allowed prior to the convening of the second year of the biennium. Bill carryover allowed if in second year of a two-year session.

(s) The Nebraska Legislature's Executive Board serves as the Reference Committee.

(t) Bills are carried over from the 90-day session beginning in the odd-numbered year to the 60-day session, which begins in even-numbered year. Bills that have not passed by the last day of the 60-day session are all indefinitely postponed by motion on the last day of the session. The odd-numbered year shall be carried forward to the even-numbered year.

(u) In the Senate, any member may make a motion for referral, but committee referrals are under the control of the majority floor leader. In the House, any member may make a motion for referral, and a chart is used to guide bill referrals based on statutory authority of committee, but committee referrals are under the control of the majority floor leader.

(v) Rules do not require specific types of bills be referred to specific committees.

(w) Sponsor and members.

(x) Speaker has discretion.

(y) Senate Rule 33: Between the general election and the time for the next convening session, a holdover member or member-elect may file bills for introduction in the next session with the clerk's office. Those bills shall be treated as if they were bills introduced on the first day of the session. House Rule 61: Bills introduced prior to the convening of the session shall be treated as if they were bills introduced on the first day of the session. Between the general election and the time for the next convening session, a member-elect may file bills for introduction in the next session with the clerk's office. The clerk shall number such bills consecutively, in the order in which they are filed, beginning with the number "1."

(z) Senate Rule 35: Unless a motion or order to the contrary, bills are referred to the proper standing committee. All Senate bills and resolutions referred by the Committee on Reference on or before the first day of April in an even-numbered year shall be scheduled for a minimum of one public hearing.

(aa) House Rule 37: All House bills and resolutions introduced, in compliance with House Rules, on or before the fifteenth day of May in an even-numbered year shall be referred to a standing select, or special committee, and shall be scheduled for a minimum of one public hearing. House Rule 65: All bills carrying an appropriation shall be referred to the Finance and Appropriations Committee for consideration and report before being considered the third time.

(bb) Bills carry over between the first and second year of each regular annual session, but not to the next biennial two-year General Assembly.

(cc) A legislature consists of two years. Bills from the first session can carry over to the second session only. 2007 will begin a new Legislature, the 51st, and no bills will carry over to 2007.

(dd) The president can refer bills to any standing or special committee and may also attach subsequent referrals to other committees following action by the first committee.

(ee) Rules specify bills shall be referred by the speaker to any standing or special committee and may also attach subsequent referrals to other committees following action by the first committee.

(ff) Allowed during the first year of the two-year session.

(gg) Bills and resolutions introduced in the First Regular Session may carry over to the Second Regular Session (odd-numbered year to even-numbered year) only.

(hh) Bills are drafted prior to session but released starting first day of session.

(ii) Under the direction of the speaker.

(jj) Jurisdiction of the committees by subject matter is listed in the Rules.

(kk) The House Rules establish jurisdictional committees. The speaker refers legislation to those committees as he/she deems appropriate.

(ll) Even-numbered year session to odd-numbered year session.

(mm) By the floor leader.

(nn) Pre-filing allowed only in the House in even-numbered years.

(oo) From odd-year to even-year, but not between biennial sessions.

(pp) Substantive resolutions referred to sponsor for public hearing.

Table 3.15
TIME LIMITS ON BILL INTRODUCTION

State or other jurisdiction	Time limit on introduction of bills	Procedures for granting exception to time limits
Alabama	House: no limit. Senate: 24th legislative day of regular session (a).	Unanimous vote to suspend rules
Alaska	35th C day of 2nd regular session.	Introduction by committee or by suspension of operation of limiting rule.
Arizona	House: 29th day of regular session; 10th day of special session. Senate: 22nd day of regular session; 10th day of special session.	House: Permission of rules committee. Senate: Permission of rules committee.
Arkansas	55th day of regular session (50th day for appropriations bills). Retirement and health care legislation affecting licensures shall be introduced during the first 15 days.	2/3 vote of membership of each house.
California	Deadlines established by the Joint Rules Committee.	House: Rules Committee grants exception with 3/4 vote of House. Senate: Approval of Rules Committee and 3/4 vote of membership.
Colorado	House: 22nd C day of regular session. Senate: 17th C day of regular session.	Committees on delayed bills may extend deadline.
Connecticut	10 days into session in odd-numbered years, 3 days into session in even-numbered years (b).	2/3 vote of members present.
Delaware	House: no limit. Senate: no limit.	
Florida	House: noon of the first day of regular session. Senate: noon first day of regular session (c)(d).	Existence of an emergency reasonably compelling consideration notwithstanding the deadline.
Georgia	Only for specific types of bills.	
Hawaii	Actual dates established during session.	Majority vote of membership.
Idaho	House: 20th day of session for personal bills; 36th day of session for all committees; beyond that only privileged cmtes. Senate: 12th day of session for personal bills; 36th day of session for all committees; beyond that only privileged cmtes.	House and Senate: speaker/president pro tempore may designate any standing committee to serve as a privileged committee temporarily.
Illinois	House: determined by speaker. Senate: determined by senate president.	House: the speaker may set deadlines for any action on any category of legislative measure, including deadlines for introduction of bills. Senate: At any time, the president may set alternative deadlines for any legislative action with written notice filed with the secretary.
Indiana	House: Mid-January. Senate: Date specific—set in Rules, different for long and short session. Mid-January.	House: 2/3 vote. Senate: If date falls on weekend/Holiday - extended to next day. Sine die deadline set by statute, does not change.
Iowa	House: Friday of 6th week of 1st regular session; Friday of 2nd week of 2nd regular session. Senate: Friday of 7th week of 1st regular session; Friday of 2nd week of 2nd regular session.	Constitutional majority.
Kansas	Actual dates established in the Joint Rules of the House and Senate every two years when the joint rules are adopted.	Resolution adopted by majority of members of either house may make specific exceptions to deadlines.
Kentucky	House: No introductions during the last 14 L days of odd-year session, during last 22 L days of even-year session. Senate: No introductions during the last 14 L days of odd-year session, during last 20 L days of even-year session.	None.
Louisiana	House: 10th C day of odd year sessions and 23rd C day of even-year sessions. Senate:10th C day of odd year sessions and 23rd C day of even-year sessions.	None.
Maine	House: Cloture dates established by the Legislative Council. Cloture for 1st session of 124th legislature was January 16, 2009 per Maine Legislative Council. Senate: Cloture dates established by the Legislative Council. Cloture for 1st session of 124th legislature was January 16, 2009 per Main Legislative Council.	House: Bills filed after cloture date must be approved by a majority of the Legislative Council. Senate: Appeals heard by Legislative Council. Six votes required to allow introduction of legislation.

See footnotes at end of table.

TIME LIMITS ON BILL INTRODUCTION—Continued

State or other jurisdiction	*Time limit on introduction of bills*	*Procedures for granting exception to time limits*
Maryland	House and Senate: No introductions during the last 35 days of regular session, unless 2/3 of the elected members of a chamber vote yes. Additional limitations involve committee action. Senate bills introduced after the 24th calendar day must be referred to the Senate Rules Committee and also Senate bills introduced after the 10th calendar day on behalf of the administration, i.e. the governor, must be referred to the Senate Rules Committee. House bills introduced during the last 59 calendar days (after the 31st day) are referred to the House Rules Committee. The Senate Rules and House Rules contain further provisions concerning the requirements for forcing legislation out of these committees.	House: 2/3 vote of elected members of each house.
Massachusetts	1st Wednesday in December even-numbered years, 1st Wednesday in November odd-numbered years.	2/3 vote of members present and voting.
Michigan	No limit.	
Minnesota	No limit	
Mississippi	14th C day in 90 day session; 49th C day in 125 day session (e).	2/3 vote of members present and voting.
Missouri	House: 60th L day of regular session. Senate: March 1.	Majority vote of elected members each house; governor's request for consideration of bill by special message.
Montana	General bills & resolutions: 10th L day; revenue bills: 17th L day; committee bills and resolutions: 36th L day; committee bills implementing provisions of a general appropriation act: 75th L day; committee revenue bills: 62nd L day; interim study resolutions: 75th L day (c).	2/3 vote of members.
Nebraska	10th L day of any session (f).	3/5 vote of elected membership.
Nevada	Actual dates established at start of session.	Waiver granted by majority leader of the Senate and speaker of the Assembly acting jointly.
New Hampshire	Determined by rules.	2/3 vote of members present.
New Jersey	No limit.	
New Mexico	House: 15 days in short session/even years, 30 days in long session/odd years. Senate: 15 days in short session/even years, 30 days in long session/odd years.	None. Statutory limit for legislators; governor not limited and can send bill with message.
New York	Assembly: for unlimited introduction of bills, the final day is the last Tuesday in May of the 2nd year of the legislative term; for introduction of 10 or fewer bills, last Tuesday in May. Senate: 1st Tuesday in March.	Assembly: By unanimous consent or by introduction by Rules Cmte. or by message from the Senate. Senate: Exceptions are granted by the president pro tem or by introduction by Rules Cmte. or by message from Assembly.
North Carolina	Actual dates established during session.	Senate: 2/3 vote of membership present and voting shall be required.
North Dakota	Proposed limits for 2009 session; House: January 19. Senate: January 26.	2/3 vote of the floor or by approval of Delayed Bills Committee.
Ohio	No limit.	
Oklahoma	Time limit set in rules.	2/3 vote of membership.
Oregon	House: 50th C day of session. Senate: 50th C day of session. Rules adopted every 2 years.	House: Bills approved by the speaker: appropriation or fiscal measures sponsored by the Cmte. on Ways and Means; measures drafted by the Legislative Counsel and introduced as members' priority drafting requests. Senate: Measures approved by the senate president: appropriation or fiscal measures sponsored by the Committee on Ways and Means; measures drafted by the Legislative Counsel and introduced as members' priority drafting requests.
Pennsylvania	No limit.	

See footnotes at end of table.

TIME LIMITS ON BILL INTRODUCTION—Continued

State or other jurisdiction	Time limit on introduction of bills	Procedures for granting exception to time limits
Rhode Island	Second week of February for Public Bills.	Sponsor must give one legislative day's notice.
South Carolina	House: Prior to April 15 of the 2nd yr. of a two-yr. legislative session; May 1 for bills first introduced in Senate. Rule 5.12. Senate: May 1 of regular session for bills originating in House. Rule 47.	House: 2/3 vote of members present and voting. Senate: 2/3 vote of membership.
South Dakota	Individual bills: 40-day session: 15th L day; 35-day session: 10th L day. Committee bills: 40-day session: 16th L day; 35-day session: 11th L day.	2/3 approval of members-elect.
Tennessee	General bills, 10th L day of regular session (g).	Unanimous approval by Delayed Bills Committee.
Texas	60th C day of regular session.	4/5 vote of members present and voting.
Utah	12:00 p.m. on 11th day of session.	Motion for request must be approved by a constitutional majority vote.
Vermont	House: 1st session—last day of February; 2nd session—last day of January. Senate: 1st session—53 C day; 2nd session—25 C days before start of session.	Approval by Rules Committee.
Virginia	Set by joint procedural resolution adopted at the beginning of the session (usually the second Friday of the session is the last day to introduce legislation that does not have any earlier deadline).	As provided in the joint procedural resolution (usually unanimous consent or at written request of the governor).
Washington	Until 10 days before the end of session unless 2/3 vote of elected members of each house.	2/3 vote of elected members of each house.
West Virginia	House: 45th C day. Senate: 41st C day.	2/3 vote of members present.
Wisconsin	No limit.	
Wyoming	House: 15th L day of session. Senate: 12th L day of session.	2/3 vote of elected members.
American Samoa	House: After the 25th L day of the fourth Regular Session. Senate: After the 15th L day.	
Guam	Public hearing on bill must be held no more than 120 days after date of bill introduction.	
Puerto Rico	1st session—within first 125 days; 2nd session—within first 60 days.	None.
U.S. Virgin Islands	No limit.	

Source: The Council of State Governments' survey, January 2009.

Key:

C — Calendar

L — Legislative

(a) Not applicable to local bills, advertised or otherwise.

(b) Specific dates set in Joint Rules.

(c) Not applicable to appropriations bills.

(d) Not applicable to local bills and joint resolutions. Florida: Not applicable to local bills (which have no deadline) or claim bills (deadline is August 1 of the year preceding consideration or within 60 days of a senator's election).

(e) Except Appropriation and Revenue bills (51st/86th C day) and Local & Private bills (83rd/118th C day).

(f) Except appropriations bills and bills introduced at the request of the governor, bills can be introduced during the first 10 legislative days of the session. Appropriation bills and bills introduced at the request of the governor can be introduced at any time during the session.

(g) Local bills have no cutoff.

Table 3.16
ENACTING LEGISLATION: VETO, VETO OVERRIDE AND EFFECTIVE DATE

State or other jurisdiction	Governor may item veto appropriation bills		Days allowed governor to consider bill (a)			Votes required in each house to pass bills or items over veto (c)	Effective date of enacted legislation (d)
			During session	After session			
	Amount	Other (b)	Bill becomes law unless vetoed	Bill becomes law unless vetoed	Bill dies unless signed		
Alabama	★ (e)	. . .	6 (f)		10A	Majority of elected body	Date signed by governor, unless otherwise specified.
Alaska	★	. . .	15	20P		2/3 elected (g)	90 days after enactment
Arizona	★	★	5	10A		2/3 elected (h)	90 days after adjournment
Arkansas	★	. . .	5	20A		Majority elected	91st day after adjournment
California	★(i)	. . .	12 (j)	30A		2/3 elected	(k)
Colorado	★(l)	. . .	10 (m)	30A (m)		2/3 elected	90 days after adjournment (n)
Connecticut	★	. . .	5	15P	(o)	2/3 elected	Oct. 1, unless otherwise specified.
Delaware	★	. . .	10	10P	30A	3/5 elected	Immediately
Florida	. . .	★	7 (m)(p)	15P (m)		2/3 present	60 days after adjournment
Georgia	★	★	. . .	40A		2/3 elected	Unless other date specified, July 1 for generals, date signed by governor for locals.
Hawaii (q)	★ (r)	. . .	10 (s)	45A (s)(p)	(p)	2/3 elected	Immediately
Idaho	★	. . .	5	10P		2/3 present	July 1
Illinois	★ (r)	. . .	60 (m)	60 (m)		3/5 elected (g)	Usually Jan. 1 of next year (t)
Indiana	. . .	. . .	7	7P		Majority elected	(u)
Iowa	★	★	3		30A	2/3 elected	July 1 (t)
Kansas	★	★	10 (m)		10P	2/3 membership	Upon publication or specified date after publication
Kentucky	★	. . .	10	90A		Majority elected	90 days after adjournment sine die. Unless the bill contains an emergency clause or special effective date.
Louisiana (q)	★	★	10 (m)	20P (m)		2/3 elected	Aug. 15
Maine	★	. . .	10		(v)	2/3 elected	90 days after adjournment unless enacted as an emergency.
Maryland	★ (w)	★	6 (x)	30P (y)	(z)	3/5 elected (aa)	June 1 (bb)
Massachusetts	★	★	10	10P	10A	2/3 present	90 days after enactment
Michigan	★	★	14		14P	2/3 elected and serving	90 days after adjournment
Minnesota	★	(i)	3P	14A, 3P	3A, 14P	2/3 elected—90 House; 45 Senate	Aug. 1 (cc)
Mississippi	★	. . .	5	15P (dd)		2/3 elected	July 1 unless specified otherwise.
Missouri	★	. . .	15	45A		2/3 elected	Aug. 28 (ee)
Montana (q)	★	★	10 (m)	25A (m)		2/3 present	Oct. 1 (cc)
Nebraska	★	. . .	5	5A, 5P	(ff)	3/5 elected	90 days following adjournment sine die. Unless bill contains an emergency clause.
Nevada	. . .	. . .	5 (gg)	10A (gg)		2/3 elected	Oct. 1, unless measure stipulates a different date.
New Hampshire	. . .	. . .	5	5P		2/3 present	60 days after enactment, unless otherwise noted.
New Jersey	★	. . .	45			2/3 elected	Dates usually specified
New Mexico	★	★	3 (hh)		20A	2/3 present	90 days after adjournment unless other date specified.
New York	★	. . .	10 (ii)	(ii)	30A	2/3 votes in each house	20 days after enactment
North Carolina	. . .	. . .	10	30A		3/5 elected	60 days after adjournment
North Dakota	★	. . .	3	15A		2/3 elected	(jj)
Ohio	★	★	10	10P	10A	3/5 elected (kk)	91st day after filing with secretary of state. (ll)

See footnotes at end of table.

ENACTING LEGISLATION: VETO, VETO OVERRIDE AND EFFECTIVE DATE — Continued

State or other jurisdiction	Governor may item veto appropriation bills: Amount	Governor may item veto appropriation bills: Other (b)	Days allowed governor to consider bill (a) — During session: Bill becomes law unless vetoed	After session: Bill becomes law unless vetoed	After session: Bill dies unless signed	Votes required in each house to pass bills or items over veto (c)	Effective date of enacted legislation (d)
Oklahoma	★	. . .	5 (mm)		15A (mm)	2/3 elected	90 days after adjournment unless specified in the bill.
Oregon	★	. . .	5	30A (s)		2/3 present	Jan. 1st of following year. (nn)
Pennsylvania	★	★	30	30A, 10P		Majority	60 days after signed by governor
Rhode Island	. . .	. . .	6	10P (oo)	(oo)	3/5 present	Immediately (pp)
South Carolina	★	. . .	5	(qq)		2/3 elected	Date of signature
South Dakota	★	. . .	5 (rr)	15P (rr)		2/3 elected	July 1
Tennessee	★	. . .	10	(ss)		Constitutional majority	40 days after enactment unless otherwise specified
Texas	★	. . .	10	20A		2/3 elected	90 days after adjournment
Utah	★	. . .	10P	20A		2/3 elected	60 days after adjournment of the session at which it passed.
Vermont	. . .	. . .	5		3A	2/3 present	July 1
Virginia	★	★(tt)	7 (m)	30A (uu)		2/3 present (vv)	July 1 (ww)
Washington	★	★	5	20A		2/3 present	90 days after adjournment
West Virginia	. . .	(i)	5	15A (xx)		Majority elected	90 days after enactment
Wisconsin	★	. . .	6	6P		2/3 present	Day after publication date unless otherwise specified
Wyoming	★	★	3	15A		2/3 elected	Specified in act
American Samoa	★	. . .	10		30A	2/3 elected	60 days after adjournment (yy)
Guam	★	★	10	10P	30P (zz)	10 votes to override	Immediately (bbb)
No. Mariana Islands	★	. . .	40 (m)(aaa)			2/3 elected	Immediately
Puerto Rico	★	. . .	10		30P	2/3 elected	Specified in act
U.S. Virgin Islands	★(ccc)	★(ccc)	10	10P	30A	2/3 elected	Immediately

Source: The Council of State Governments' survey, January 2009.

Key:

★ — Yes

. . . — No

A — Days after adjournment of legislature.

P — Days after presentation to governor.

(a) Sundays excluded, unless otherwise indicated.

(b) Includes language in appropriations bill.

(c) Bill returned to house of origin with governor's objections.

(d) Effective date may be established by the law itself or may be otherwise changed by vote of the legislature. Special or emergency acts are usually effective immediately.

(e) The governor may line item distinct items or item veto amounts in appropriation bills, if returned prior to final adjournment.

(f) Except bills presented within five days of final adjournment, Sundays are included.

(g) Different number of votes required for revenue and appropriations bills. Alaska–3/4 elected. Illinois–3/5ths members elected to override any gubernatorial change except a reduction in an item, which a majority of the members elected to each house can restore to its original amount.

(h) Several specific requirements of 3/4 majority.

(i) Line item veto.

(j) For a bill to become law during session, if 12th day falls on a Saturday, Sunday, or holiday, the period is extended to the next day that is not a Saturday, Sunday, or holiday.

(k) For legislation enacted in regular sessions: January 1 of the following year. Urgency legislation: immediately upon chaptering by Secretary of State.

Legislation enacted in Special Session: 91st day after adjournment of the special session at which the bill was passed.

(l) Must veto entire amount of any item; an item is an indivisible sum of money dedicated to a stated purpose.

(m) Sundays included.

(n) An act takes effect on the date stated in the act, or if no date is stated in the act, then upon signature of the governor. If no safety clause on a bill, the bill takes effect 90 days after sine die if no referendum petition has been filed. The state constitution allows for a 90 day period following adjournment when petitions may be filed for bills that do not contain a safety clause.

(o) Bill enacted if not signed /vetoed within time frames.

(p) The governor must notify the legislature 10 days before the 45th day of his intent to veto a measure on that day. The legislature may convene on the 45th day after adjournment to consider the vetoed measures. If the legislature fails to reconvene, the bill does not become law. If the legislature reconvenes, it may pass the measure over the governor's veto or it may amend the law to meet the governor's objections. If the law is amended, the governor must sign the bill within 10 days after it is presented to him in order for it to become law.

(q) Constitution withholds right to veto constitutional amendments.

(r) Governor can also reduce amounts in appropriations bills. In Hawaii, governor can reduce items in executive appropriations measures, but cannot reduce or item veto amounts appropriated for the judicial or legislative branches.

ENACTING LEGISLATION: VETO, VETO OVERRIDE AND EFFECTIVE DATE—Continued

(s) Except Sundays and legal holidays. In Hawaii, except Saturdays, Sundays, holidays and any days in which the legislature is in recess prior to its adjournment. In Oregon, if the governor does not sign the bill within 30 days after adjournment, it becomes law without the governor's signature, Saturdays and Sundays are excluded.

(t) Effective date for bills which become law on or after July 1. Illinois–Unless specified in the act. Exception: An act enacted by a bill passed after May 31 cannot take effect before June 1 of the following year unless it was passed by 3/5ths of the members elected to each house.

(u) Varies with date of the veto.

(v) "If the bill or resolution shall not be returned by the governor within 10 days (Sundays excepted) after it shall have been presented to the governor, it shall have the same force and effect as if the governor had signed it unless the Legislature by their adjournment prevent its return, in which case it shall have such force and effect, unless returned within 3 days after the next meeting of the same Legislature which enacted the bill or resolution; if there is no such next meeting of the Legislature which enacted the bill or resolution, the bill or resolution shall not be a law." (excerpted from Article IV, Part Third, Section 2 of the Constitution of Maine).

(w) The governor cannot veto the budget bill but may exercise a total veto or item veto on a supplementary appropriations bill. In practice this means the governor may strike items in the annual general capital loan bill. Occasionally the governor will also veto a bond bill or a portion of a bond bill.

(x) If a bill is presented to the governor in the first 83 days of session, the governor has only six days (not including Sunday) to act before the bill automatically becomes law.

(y) All bills passed at regular or special sessions must be presented to the governor no later than 20 days after adjournment. The governor has a limited time to sign or veto a bill after it is presented. If the governor does not act within that time, the bill becomes law automatically; there is no pocket veto. The time limit depends on when the presentment is made. Any bill presented in the last 7 days of the 90-day session or after adjournment must be acted on within 30 days after presentment. Bills vetoed after adjournment are returned to the legislature for reconsideration at the next meeting of the same General Assembly.

(z) The governor has a limited time to sign or veto a bill after it is presented. If the governor does not act within that time, the bill becomes law automatically; there is no pocket veto. The time limit depends on when the presentment is made.

(aa) Vetoed bills are returned to the house of origin immediately after that house has organized at the next regular or special session. When a new General Assembly is elected and sworn in, bills vetoed from the previous session are not returned. These vetoed bills are not subject to any further legislative action.

(bb) Unless otherwise provided, June 1 is the effective date for bond bills, July 1 for budget, tax and revenue bills. By custom October 1 is the usual effective date for other legislation. If the bill is an emergency measure, it may take effect immediately upon approval by the governor or at a specified date prior to June 1. For vetoed legislation, 30 days after the veto is overridden or on the date specified in the bill, whichever is later. An emergency bill passed over the governor's veto takes effect immediately.

(cc) Different date for fiscal legislation. Minnesota, Montana—July 1.

(dd) Bills vetoed after adjournment are returned to the legislature for reconsideration. Mississippi–returned within three days after the beginning of the next session.

(ee) If bill has an emergency clause, it becomes effective upon governor's signature.

(ff) Bills are carried over from the 90-day session beginning in the odd-numbered year to the 60-day session, which begins in even-numbered years. Bills that have not passed by the last day of the 60-day session are all indefinitely postponed by motion on the last day of the session.

(gg) The day of delivery and Sundays are not counted for purposes of calculating these periods.

(hh) Except bills going up in the last three days of session, for which the governor has 20 days.

(ii) If the legislature adjourns during the governor's consideration of a 10-day bill, the bill shall not become law without the governor's approval.

(jj) August 1 after filing with the secretary of state. Appropriations and tax bills July 1 after filing with secretary of state, or date set in legislation by Legislative Assembly, or by date established by emergency clause.

(kk) The exception covers such matters as emergency measures and court bills that originally required a 2/3 majority for passage. In those cases, the same extraordinary majority vote is required to override a veto.

(ll) Emergency, current appropriation, and tax legislation effective immediately. The General Assembly may also enact an uncodified section of law specifying a desired effective date that is after the constitutionally established effective date.

(mm) During session the governor has 5 days (except Sunday) to sign or veto a bill or it becomes law automatically. After session a bill becomes a pocket veto if not signed 15 days after sine die.

(nn) Unless emergency declared or date specific in text of measure.

(oo) Bills become effective without signature if not signed or vetoed.

(pp) Date signed, date received by secretary of state if effective without signature, date that veto is overridden, or other specified date.

(qq) Two days after the next meeting.

(rr) During a session, a bill becomes law if a governor signs it or does not act on it within five days. If the legislature has adjourned or recessed or is within 5 days of a recess or an adjournment, the governor has 15 days to act on the bill. If he does not act the bill becomes law.

(ss) Adjournment of the legislature is irrelevant; the governor has 10 days to act on a bill after it is presented to him or it becomes law without his signature.

(tt) If part of the item.

(uu) The governor has thirty days after adjournment of the legislature to act on any bills. The Constitution of Virginia provides that : "If the governor does not act on any bill, it shall become law without his signature."

(vv) Must include majority of elected members.

(ww) Unless a different date is stated in the bill. Special sessions–first day of fourth month after adjournment.

(xx) Five days for supplemental appropriation bills.

(yy) Laws required to be approved only by the governor. An act is required to be approved by the U.S. Secretary of the Interior only after it is vetoed by the governor; and so approved, takes effect 40 days after it is returned to the governor by the secretary.

(zz) After legislature adjourns sine die at end of two-year term.

(aaa) Twenty days for appropriations bills.

(bbb) U.S. Congress may annul.

(ccc) May item veto language or amounts in a bill that contains two or more appropriations.

Table 3.17
LEGISLATIVE APPROPRIATIONS PROCESS: BUDGET DOCUMENTS AND BILLS

State or other jurisdiction	Budget document submission							Budget bill introduction		
	Legal source of deadline		Submission date relative to convening							
	Constitutional	Statutory	Prior to session	Within one week	Within two weeks	Within one month	Over one month	Same time as budget document	Another time	Not until committee review of budget document
Alabama	★	★	(a)	...	...	...	...	★	...	...
Alaska	★	★	...	(a)	...	...	...	★	...	...
Arizona	...	★	★	...	...	...	...	...	...	★
Arkansas	...	★	★	...	...	...	...	...	...	★
California	★	...	...	...	...	...	...	★(b)	...	...
Colorado	...	★	★(a)	...	...	...	...	...	76th day by rule	...
Connecticut	...	★	...	...	...	(a)	...	★	...	...
Delaware	...	...	...	...	...	...	...	...	...	...
Florida	★	★	★	...	...	...	...	...	...	★
Georgia	★	...	...	(a)	...	...	...	★	...	...
Hawaii	...	★	30 days	...	...	...	...	...	★	...
Idaho	...	★	...	★	...	...	...	...	...	★
Illinois	...	★	...	...	...	...	★(a)	...	★(c)	...
Indiana	...	★	...	...	...	...	...	...	★	...
Iowa	...	★	...	...	...	(a)	...	...	...	★(d)
Kansas	...	★	...	...	★(e)	...	...	...	★	...
Kentucky	★	...	...	...	(a)	...	...	★	...	...
Louisiana	...	★	(f)	(f)	...	...	...	(g)	...	...
Maine	...	★	...	(a)	...	...	...	★	...	...
Maryland	★	...	...	★(e)	...	...	...	★(h)	...	...
Massachusetts	...	★	...	...	...	★	...	★	...	...
Michigan	...	★	...	...	...	★	...	★	...	...
Minnesota	...	★	...	...	...	(a)	...	...	...	★
Mississippi	...	★	★	...	...	...	...	...	★	...
Missouri	★	...	...	...	...	★	...	...	...	★
Montana	...	★	★	...	...	...	...	...	★	...
Nebraska	...	★	...	...	...	★	...	★(i)	...	...
Nevada	★	...	(a)	...	...	...	...	...	...	★
New Hampshire	...	★	...	...	...	...	(a)	★	...	...
New Jersey	...	★	...	...	...	...	...	...	...	★
New Mexico	...	★	...	...	...	(a)	...	...	★	...
New York	★	...	...	...	★(a)	...	...	...	★(j)	...
North Carolina	...	...	...	...	...	...	...	★	...	...
North Dakota	...	★	(k)	...	...	...	...	...	...	★
Ohio	...	★	...	...	...	★(d)(e)	...	★	...	...
Oklahoma	...	★	★	★	...	...	...	★	...	...
Oregon	...	★	...	...	...	...	★(l)	★(m)	...	...
Pennsylvania	★	...	...	...	...	...	★	...	...	★
Rhode Island	...	★	...	...	...	...	★	...	★	...
South Carolina	...	★	...	★	...	...	...	...	...	★(n)
South Dakota	...	★	...	...	...	...	★(o)	...	★(p)	...
Tennessee	...	★	...	...	★(a)(e)	★(a)(e)	...	★	...	...
Texas	...	★	...	6th day	...	...	...	...	★(q)	...
Utah	...	★	(a)	...	...	...	...	...	...	...
Vermont	...	...	...	(s)	...	...	...	...	...	★
Virginia	...	★	Dec. 20	...	...	...	...	★	...	...
Washington	★(t)	...	Dec. 20 (u)	...	...	...	...	★	...	...
West Virginia	★	...	...	★	...	...	...	★	...	...
Wisconsin	...	★	...	...	...	★(v)	...	★	...	...
Wyoming	...	★	Dec. 1	...	...	...	...	...	...	★
American Samoa	...	★	★	...	...	...	...	★	...	...
Guam	...	★	...	...	...	★(w)	...	★	...	...
No. Mariana Islands	...	★	(a)	...	...	...	...	...	(v)	★
Puerto Rico	...	★	...	...	...	★	...	...	...	★
U.S. Virgin Islands	...	★	May 30	...	...	...	...	...	★	...

See footnotes at end of table.

LEGISLATIVE APPROPRIATIONS PROCESS: BUDGET DOCUMENTS AND BILLS—Continued

Source: The Council of State Governments' survey, January 2009.

Key:

★ — Yes

. . . —No

(a) Specific time limitations: Alabama—five days; Alaska—December 15, fourth legislative day; Colorado—presented by November 1 to the Joint Budget Committee; Connecticut—not later than the first session day following the third day in February, in each odd-numbered year; Georgia—first five days of session; Illinois—third Wednesday in February; Iowa—no later than February 1; Kentucky—tenth legislative day; Maine—the governor shall transmit the budget document to the legislature not later than the Friday following the first Monday in January of the first regular legislative session ... A governor-elect elected to a first term of office shall transmit the budget document to the legislature not later than the Friday following the first Monday in February of the first regular legislative session (Maine Revised Statutes, Title 5, Chapter 149, Section 1666); Minnesota—by the fourth Tuesday in January each odd-numbered year; Nevada—no later than 14 days before commencement of regular session; New Hampshire—by February 15; New Mexico—by January 1 each year; New York—the executive budget must be submitted by the governor to the legislature by the second Tuesday following the opening of session (or February 1 for the first session following a gubernatorial election); Tennessee—on or before February 1 for sitting governor; Utah—must submit to the legislature by the calendared floor time on the first day of the annual session; No. Mariana Islands—no later than six months before the beginning of the fiscal year.

(b) Budget and Budget Bill are annual—to be submitted within the first 10 days of each calendar year.

(c) Deadlines for introducing bills in general are set by Senate president and House speaker.

(d) Executive budget bill is introduced and used as a working tool for committee.

(e) Later for first session of a new governor; Kansas—21 days; Maryland—10 days; New Jersey—February 15; Ohio—by March 15; Tennessee—March 1.

(f) The governor shall submit his executive budget to the Joint Legislative Committee on the budget no later than 45 days prior to each regular session; except that in the first year of each term, the executive budget shall be submitted no later than 30 days prior to the regular session. Copies shall be made available to the entire legislature on the first day of each regular session.

(g) Bills appropriating monies for the general operating budget and ancillary appropriations, bills appropriating funds for the expenses of the legislature and the judiciary must be submitted to the legislature for introduction no later than 45 days prior to each regular session, except that in the first year of each term, such appropriation bills shall be submitted no later than 30 days prior to the regular session.

(h) Appropriations bill other than the budget bill (supplementary) may be introduced at any time. They must provide their own tax source and may not be enacted until the budget bill is enacted.

(i) Governor's budget bill is introduced and serves as a working document for the Appropriations Committee. The governor must submit the budget proposal by January 15 of each odd-numbered year (Neb.Rev.Stat. sec.81-125). The statute extends this deadline to February 1 for a governor who is in his first year of office.

(j) Submission of the governor's budget bills to the legislature occurs with submission of the executive budget.

(k) Legislative Council's Budget Section hears the executive budget recommendations during legislature's December organizational session.

(l) By December 1 of even-numbered year unless new governor is elected; if new governor is elected, then February 1 of odd-numbered year.

(m) Legislature often introduces other budget bills during legislative session that are not part of the governor's recommended budget.

(n) The Ways and Means Committee introduces the Budget Bill within five days after the beginning of the session (S.C. Code 11-11-70).

(o) It is usually over a month. The budget must be delivered to the legislature not later than the first Tuesday after the first Monday in December.

(p) It must be introduced no later than the 16th legislative day.

(q) Within first 30 days of session.

(r) Legislative rules require budget bills to be introduced by the 43rd day of the session.

(s) No official submission dates. Occurs by custom early in the session.

(t) And Rules.

(u) For fiscal period other than biennium, 20 days prior to first day of session.

(v) Last Tuesday in January. A later submission date may be requested by the governor.

(w) Usually January before end of current fiscal year.

Table 3.18
FISCAL NOTES: CONTENT AND DISTRIBUTION

	Content						Distribution						
							Legislators						
										Appropriations Committee			
State or other jurisdiction	Intent or purpose of bill	Cost involved	Projected future cost	Proposed source of revenue	Fiscal impact on local government	Other	All	Available on request	Bill sponsor	Members	Chair only	Fiscal staff	Executive budget staff
Alabama	★	★	. . .	★	★	★(a)	. . .	★	★	. . .	. . .	. . .	. . .
Alaska	. . .	★	★	★	. . .	. . .	★	★	★	. . .	. . .	★	★
Arizona	★	★	★	★	★	★	★	★	★	★	. . .	★	★
Arkansas (b)	. . .	★	★	. . .	★	★	★	. . .	. . .	. . .	. . .	. . .	. . .
California	★	★	★	★	★	. . .	★	★	★	. . .	. . .	★	★
Colorado	★	★	★	★	★	. . .	★	. . .	. . .	. . .	. . .	. . .	. . .
Connecticut	★	★	★	★	★	. . .	(c)	. . .	. . .	. . .	. . .	. . .	. . .
Delaware	. . .	★	. . .	. . .	. . .	. . .	★	. . .	. . .	. . .	. . .	. . .	. . .
Florida	★	★	★	★	★	★	★	. . .	. . .	. . .	. . .	★	. . .
Georgia	. . .	★	★	. . .	★	. . .	★	★	. . .	. . .	. . .	. . .	. . .
Hawaii	. . .	. . .	. . .	. . .	. . .	★	. . .	. . .	. . .	. . .	★	★	★
Idaho	★	★	★	★	★	★(d)	★	. . .	. . .	. . .	. . .	(e)	(e)
Illinois	. . .	★	★	★	★	. . .	(f)	★	★	. . .	. . .	. . .	. . .
Indiana	★	★	★	★	★	. . .	★	. . .	. . .	. . .	. . .	★	★
Iowa	★	★	★	★	★	. . .	(g)						
Kansas	★	★	★	★	★	. . .	★	★	★	. . .	★	★	★
Kentucky	★	★	★	★	★	★	. . .	★	★	★	. . .	★	. . .
Louisiana	. . .	★	★	. . .	★	. . .	★	★	. . .	. . .	★(h)	. . .	. . .
Maine	. . .	★	★	★	★	. . .	. . .	★(i)	★	. . .	. . .	★	★
Maryland	★	★	★	★	★	★(j)	. . .	. . .	★(k)	. . .	. . .	. . .	. . .
Massachusetts	. . .	★(l)	★	. . .	. . .	★	★	. . .	. . .	. . .	★	. . .	. . .
Michigan	★	★	★	★	★	★(m)	★(n)	. . .	. . .	. . .	. . .	. . .	. . .
Minnesota	★	★	★	★	★	. . .	. . .	. . .	★	. . .	★	★	★
Mississippi	. . .	★	★	★	. . .	. . .	. . .	. . .	★(o)	. . .	. . .	. . .	. . .
Missouri	★	★	★	★	★	. . .	. . .	★	★	. . .	. . .	. . .	★
Montana	. . .	★	★	. . .	★	★(p)	★	. . .	. . .	. . .	. . .	★	★
Nebraska	. . .	★	★	★	★	. . .	★	★	. . .	. . .	. . .	★	★
Nevada	. . .	★	★	★	★	★	★	. . .	. . .	. . .	. . .	. . .	. . .
New Hampshire	★	★	. . .	★	★	. . .	. . .	★	. . .	★	. . .	★	★
New Jersey	. . .	★	. . .	★	★	. . .	★	. . .	. . .	. . .	. . .	★	★
New Mexico	★	★	★	★	★	. . .	. . .	★	★	★	. . .	(q)	(q)
New York	. . .	★	★	. . .	★	★(r)	. . .	★	★	★	. . .	★	. . .
North Carolina	. . .	★	★	. . .	★	★	(s)	. . .	. . .	. . .	. . .	. . .	. . .
North Dakota	. . .	. . .	★	★	★	★(t)	(u)	★	. . .	. . .	. . .	★	★
Ohio	★	★	★	★	★	. . .	(v)	. . .	. . .	. . .	. . .	. . .	. . .
Oklahoma	★	★	★	★	. . .	. . .	. . .	★	★	. . .	★	★	. . .
Oregon	★	★	★	★	★	. . .	★	. . .	. . .	. . .	. . .	★	★
Pennsylvania	. . .	★	★	★	★	. . .	. . .	. . .	. . .	★	★	★	. . .
Rhode Island	★	★	★	★	★	. . .	. . .	★	. . .	★	. . .	★	★
South Carolina	★	★	★	★	★	. . .	. . .	★	. . .	(w)	. . .	★	★
South Dakota	. . .	★	★	★	★	. . .	. . .	★	. . .	. . .	. . .	. . .	. . .
Tennessee	★	★	★	. . .	★	. . .	★	★	★	. . .	. . .	. . .	. . .
Texas	. . .	★	★	★	★	★(x)	★	★	★	★	. . .	. . .	★
Utah	. . .	★	★	★	★	★(y)	★	★	★	. . .	. . .	★	★
Vermont	(z)						. . .	★	. . .	★	. . .	. . .	. . .
Virginia	★	★	★	★	★	★(aa)	(bb)	. . .	★	. . .	★	★(cc)	. . .
Washington	. . .	★	★	★	★	★(dd)	★	★	★	★	★	★	. . .
West Virginia	. . .	★	★	★	★	. . .	. . .	. . .	. . .	★	. . .	. . .	. . .
Wisconsin	. . .	★	★	★	★	. . .	(ee)	. . .	. . .	. . .	. . .	(ee)	. . .
Wyoming	. . .	★	★	★	. . .	. . .	★	. . .	. . .	. . .	. . .	. . .	. . .
Guam	. . .	★	. . .	. . .	★	★(ff)	★	. . .	. . .	★	★	★	. . .
No. Mariana Islands	★	★	★	★	★	★	. . .	. . .	. . .	. . .	★	★	★
Puerto Rico	(gg)												
U.S. Virgin Islands	★	★	. . .	★	. . .	. . .	★	. . .	. . .	. . .	. . .	. . .	. . .

See footnotes at end of table.

FISCAL NOTES: CONTENT AND DISTRIBUTION — Continued

Source: The Council of State Governments' survey, January 2009.

Note: A fiscal note is a summary of the fiscal effects of a bill on government revenues, expenditures and liabilities.

Key:

★ — Yes

. . . — No

(a) Fiscal notes included on final passage calendar.

(b) Only retirement, corrections, revenue, tax and local government bills require fiscal notes. During the past session, fiscal notes were provided for education.

(c) The fiscal notes are printed with the bills favorably reported by the committees.

(d) Statement of purpose.

(e) Attached to bill, so available to both fiscal and executive budget staff.

(f) A summary of each fiscal note is attached to the summary of its bill in the printed Legislative Synopsis and Digest, and on the General Assembly's Web site. Fiscal notes are prepared for the sponsor and attached to the bill on file with the House clerk or Senate secretary.

(g) Fiscal notes are available to everyone.

(h) Prepared by the Legislative Fiscal Office when a state agency is involved and prepared by Legislative Auditor's office when a local board or commission is involved; copies sent to House and Senate staff offices respectively.

(i) Distributed to members of the committee of reference; also available on the Legislature's Web site.

(j) A fiscal note is now known as a fiscal and policy note to better reflect the contents. Fiscal and policy notes also identify any mandate on local government and include analyses of the economic impact on small businesses.

(k) In practice fiscal and policy notes are prepared on all bills and resolutions prior to a public hearing on the bills/resolutions. After initial hard copy distribution to sponsor and committee, the note is released to member computer system and thereafter to the legislative Web site.

(l) Fiscal notes are prepared only if cost exceeds $100,000 or matter has not been acted upon by the Joint Committee on Ways and Means.

(m) Other relevant data.

(n) At present, fiscal information is part of the bill analysis on the legislative Web site.

(o) And committee to which bill referred.

(p) Mechanical defects in bill.

(q) Fiscal impact statements prepared by Legislative Finance Committee staff are available to anyone on request and on the legislature's Web site.

(r) Bills impacting workers' compensation benefits must have an actuarial impact statement; bills proposing changes in state or local government retirement systems must have an actuarial note.

(s) Fiscal notes are posted on the Internet and available to all members.

(t) Notes required only if impact is $5,000 or more. Bills impacting workforce safety and insurance benefits or premiums have actuarial statements as do bills proposing changes in state and local retirement systems.

(u) Fiscal notes are available online to anyone from the legislative branch Web site.

(v) Fiscal notes are prepared for bills before being voted on in any standing committee or floor session. Upon distribution to the legislators preparing to vote, the fiscal notes are made public.

(w) Fiscal impact statements on proposed legislation are prepared by the Office of State Budget and sent to the House or Senate standing committee that requested the impact. All fiscal impacts are posted on the OSB Web page.

(x) Equalized education funding impact statement and criminal justice policy impact statement.

(y) Fiscal notes are to include cost estimates on all proposed bills that anticipate direct expenditures by any Utah resident and the cost to the overall Utah resident population.

(z) Fiscal notes are not mandatory and their content will vary.

(aa) Technical amendments, if needed. Fiscal notes do not provide statements or interpretations of legislative intent for legal purposes. A summary of the stated objective, effect, and impact may be included.

(bb) Fiscal impact statements are widely available because they are also posted on the Internet shortly after they are distributed. The Joint Legislative Audit Review Commission (JLARC) also prepares a review of the fiscal impact statement if requested by a standing committee chair. The review statement is also available on the Internet.

(cc) Legislative budget directors.

(dd) Impact on private sector.

(ee) The fiscal estimate is printed as an appendix to the bill; anyone that has a copy of the bill has a copy of the fiscal estimate.

(ff) Fiscal impact on local economy.

(gg) The Legislature of Puerto Rico does not prepare fiscal notes, but upon request the economics unit could prepare one. The Department of Treasury has the duty to analyze and prepare fiscal notes.

Table 3.19
BILL AND RESOLUTION INTRODUCTIONS AND ENACTMENTS: 2008 REGULAR SESSIONS

State	Duration of session**	Introductions		Enactments		Measures vetoed by governor	Length of session
		Bills	Resolutions*	Bills	Adoptions*		
Alabama	Feb. 5–May 19, 2008	1,606	979	205	300	6 (a)(c)	30L
Alaska	Jan. 15–Apr. 13, 2008	279	N.A.	118	N.A.	0 (c)	90C
Arizona	Jan. 14–Jun. 27, 2008	1,380	162	347	29	32 (a)	166C
Arkansas	No regular session in 2008						
California	Jan. 7–Sept. 19, 2008	2,062	253	763	167	414 (c)	124L
Colorado	Jan. 9–May 6, 2008	662	126	473	94	7(c)	119C
Connecticut	Feb. 6–May 7, 2008	6,649	174	187	N.A.	6 (a)	67L
Delaware	Jan. 8–June 30, 2008	140	98	94	84	1	45L
Florida	Mar. 4–May 2, 2008	2,551	239	1,629	N.A.	10	56C
Georgia	Jan. 14–Apr. 4, 2008	1,655	1,877	421	1,675	16(a)(c)	40L
Hawaii	Jan. 16–Apr. 1, 2008	2,748	1,086	244	279	54 (a)(c)	60L
Idaho	Jan. 7–Apr. 2, 2008	635	73	413	47	3 (c)	87C
Illinois	Jan. 2–May 31, 2008	3,723	2	324	N.A.	12 (a)(c)	(b)
Indiana	Jan. 8–Mar. 14, 2008	770	131	147	82	3(a)	(b)
Iowa	Jan. 14–Apr. 26, 2008	1,335 (d)	27	193	3	2 (c)	104C
Kansas	Jan. 14–May 7, 2008 (e)	702	168	184	103	7 (c)	90L
Kentucky	Jan. 8–Apr. 15, 2008	1,286	648	119	N.A.	1(c)	58L
Louisiana	Mar. 31–June 23, 2008	2,188	752	937	711	29	85C
Maine	Jan. 2- Mar. 31, 2008	255	14	139 (f)	N.A.	0	(b)
Maryland	Jan. 9–Apr. 7, 2008	2,641	10	702 (g)	0	45	90C
Massachusetts	Jan. 2–Dec. 31, 2008	N.A.	N.A.	535	6	N.A.	1368C
Michigan	Jan. 9–Dec. 27, 2008	N.A.	N.A.	586	N.A.	2 (c)	360C
Minnesota	Feb. 12 –May 18, 2008	3,236	3	192	0	32 (a)(c)	44C
Mississippi	Jan. 8–Apr. 19, 2008	2,666	441	453	371	3	102C
Missouri	Jan. 9–May 30, 2008	1,874	62 (h)	136	1 (h)	7	80L
Montana	No regular session in 2008						
Nebraska (U)	Jan. 9–Apr.17, 2008	471	185	397 (i)	185	4(a)(c)	60L
Nevada	No regular session in 2008						
New Hampshire	Jan. 2–June. 4, 2008	1,061	N.A.	397	N.A.	2	146C
New Jersey	Jan 8, 2008–Dec. 2008	N.A.	N.A.	134	8	0	N.A.
New Mexico	Jan. 15–Feb. 14, 2008	1,185	39	93	9	14 (c)	30C
New York	Jan. 9, 2008–Jan.7, 2009	18,296	(j)	651	4,595	177	364C
North Carolina	May 13–July 18, 2008	1,248	85	229	32	1(a)	68C
North Dakota	No regular session in 2008						
Ohio	Jan. 2–Dec. 30, 2008	365	37	130	8	3 (c)	(b)
Oklahoma	Feb. 4–May 23, 2008	3,470	92	620	50	20 (a)(c)	64L
Oregon	No regular session in 2008						
Pennsylvania	Jan. 1–Nov. 30, 2008	5,243	1,431	136	(k)	4	355L
Rhode Island	Jan. 1, 2008–Jan. 6, 2009	2,628	N.A.	569	388	49	65L
South Carolina	Jan. 8–Nov. 9, 2008 (l)	2,024	746	N.A.	N.A.	(a)(l)	308C(l)
South Dakota	Jan. 8–Mar. 17, 2008	524	33	275	26	6 (a)(c)	39L
Tennessee	Jan. 8–May 21, 2008	3,743	1,674	649	(n)	2	41L
Texas	No regular session in 2008						
Utah	Jan. 21–Mar. 5, 2008	694	50	399	36	1	45C
Vermont	Jan. 8–May 3, 2008	512	249	142	227	8	117C
Virginia	Jan. 19–Mar. 13, 2008	2,378	890	884	720	5 (m)	65C
Washington	Jan. 14–Mar. 9, 2008	1,747	40	328	10	3 (c)	60C
West Virginia	Jan. 9–Mar. 16, 2008	2,134	343	245	137	12	57C
Wisconsin	Jan. 3, 2007–Jan. 5, 2009	1,574	230	239	159	1 (c)	93L
Wyoming	Feb. 11–Mar. 7, 2008	270	11	123	2	1 (c)	20L

See footnotes at end of table.

BILL AND RESOLUTION INTRODUCTIONS AND ENACTMENTS: 2008 REGULAR SESSIONS — Continued

Source: The Council of State Governments' survey of legislative agencies and state Web sites, March 2009.

* Includes Joint and Concurrent resolutions.

**Actual adjournment dates are listed regardless of constitutional or statutory limitations. For more information on provisions, see Table 3.2, "Legislative Sessions: Legal Provisions."

Key:

C — Calendar day.

L — Legislative day (in some states, called a session or workday; definition may vary slightly; however, it generally refers to any day on which either chamber of the legislature is in session).

U — Unicameral legislature

N.A. — Not available.

(a) Number of vetoes overridden: Alabama—3; Arizona—1; Connecticut—2; Georgia—1; Hawaii—5; Illinois—27; Indiana—2; Minnesota—1; Nebraska—4; North Carolina—1; Oklahoma—1; South Carolina—16; South Dakota—1.

(b) Length of session: Illinois—Senate 64L and House 59L; Indiana— Senate 63L and House 68L; Maine— Senate 34C and House 35C; Ohio—Senate 250L and House 236L.

(c) Line item or partial vetoes. Alabama—1 partial or line item veto; Alaska—4 partial or line item vetoes; California—2 partial or line item vetoes; Colorado—1 partial or line item veto; Georgia—26 partial or line item vetoes; Hawaii—4 partial or line item vetoes; Idaho—3 partial or line item vetoes; Illinois—35 partial or line item vetoes; Iowa—7 partial or line item vetoes; Kansas—5 partial or line item vetoes; Kentucky—3 line item vetoes; Michigan—9 line item vetoes; Minnesota—2 partial or line item vetoes; Nebraska—1 partial or line item veto; New Mexico—6 partial or line item vetoes; Ohio—2 partial or line item vetoes; Oklahoma—1 partial or line item veto; South Dakota—1 partial or line item veto; Washington—25 partial vetoes; Wisconsin— 3 partial vetoes; Wyoming— 1 partial or line item veto.

(d) 602 formal study bills filed and assigned to standing committees.

(e) First adjournment was April 4, 2008; the Veto Session was April 30–May 7, 2009.

(f) Includes resolves and private and special laws.

(g) Exercising his option to neither sign nor veto legislation, the governor permitted 3 bills to become law without his signature. Those bills (Chapters 700,701,702) took effect pursuant to the provisions of Article II, Section 17(c) of the Maryland Constitution. Pursuant to Article III, Section 52 (6) of the constitution, the Annual Operating Budget Bill (Chapter 335) took effect upon passage.

(h) These are Joint Resolutions. Joint Resolutions amend the constitution.

(i) 217 of the bill enactments were bills introduced in 2007; 180 were bills introduced in 2008.

(j) There are no official statistics for resolution introductions.

(k) Pennsylvania does not track the number of resolutions that have been passed. In general, resolutions are chamber based and highlight a day or honor a person.

(l) Session convened on Jan. 8, 2008 and pursuant to the sine die resolution adjourned 11/9/2008. They were technically in session for 44 weeks (308 calendar days) but were only in attendance for the following: House—Jan. 8–June 5 (they took the week before Easter off). They returned June 25 and October 20–24 (only in attendance the 20-22); Senate—Jan. 8–June 5, they returned June 25 and October 20–24 (only in attendance 20, 22, 23). During the October 20–24 extended session one bill was introduced in the House (the budget rescission bill which was enacted). During the June 25 session they overrode 15 of the governor's vetoes and the governor vetoed one bill that was overridden during the Oct. 20–24 extended session.

(m) The governor proposed 41 separate amendments to the Budget Bill; the General Assembly accepted 34 and rejected 7 amendments. The governor subsequently notified the General Assembly that he had vetoed one item in the bill. The Clerk of the House, as Keeper of the Rolls of the Commonwealth, by letter informed the governor that the purported veto would not be published because it failed to comport with provisions of the Constitution of Virginia relating to item vetoes.

(n) Tennessee does not track the number of adopted resolutions.

Table 3.20
BILL AND RESOLUTION INTRODUCTIONS AND ENACTMENTS: 2008 SPECIAL SESSIONS

State or other jurisdiction	Duration of session**	Introductions		Enactments/adoptions		Measures vetoed by governor	Length of session
		Bills	Resolutions*	Bills	Resolutions*		
Alabama	May 27–May 31, 2008	215	134	20	34	0	5L
Alaska	June 3–July 2, 2008	2	N.A.	0	N.A.	0	30C
	July 9–Aug. 7, 2008	12	N.A.	3	N.A.	0	30C
Arizona	No special session in 2008						
Arkansas	Mar. 31–Apr. 2, 2008	6	2	5	2	0	3C
California	Sept. 11, 2007–Sept. 19, 2008	2	1	1	1	0	(a)
	Sept. 11, 2007–Nov. 30, 2008	5	0	1	0	0	(a)
	Jan.(a)–Nov. 16, 2008	52	2	7	1	1	(a)
	Nov. 6–Nov. 30, 2008 (a)	2	3	0	0	0	(a)
Colorado	No special session in 2008						
Connecticut	Jun. 11–Dec. 9, 2008	0	7	0	0	0	2L
	Jun. 11, 2008–(b)	4	5	4	0	0	(b)
	Aug. 22–Dec. 9, 2008	2	6	2	0	0	3L
	Nov. 24–Dec. 9, 2008	0	0	0	0	0	2L
	Nov. 24–Dec. 9, 2008	2	4	2	0	0	2L
	Jan. 2, 2009	0	0	0	0	0	1L
Delaware	No special session in 2008						
Florida	No special session in 2008						
Georgia	No special session in 2008						
Hawaii	July 8, 2008	0	5	14	5	0 (c)	1L
	July 30–July 31, 2008	0	0	0	1	0	2L
	Nov. 17–Nov. 18, 2008	0	0	0	2	0	2L
Idaho	No special session in 2008						
Illinois	(d)—Jan. 13, 2009						
Indiana	No special session in 2008						
Iowa	No special session in 2008						
Kansas	No special session in 2008						
Kentucky	Jun. 23–Jun. 27, 2008	1	N.A	1	1	0	5C
Louisiana	Feb. 10–Feb. 26, 2008	172	110	27	94	1	13L
	Mar. 9–Mar. 14, 2008	66	57	12	49	0	6L
Maine	April 1–Apr. 18, 2008	308	15	194	N.A.	2	13C
Maryland	No special session in 2008						
Massachusetts	No special session in 2008						
Michigan	No special session in 2008						
Minnesota	No special session in 2008						
Mississippi	May 21–Aug. 4, 2008	29	110	7	97	0	93C
Missouri	No special session in 2008						
Montana	No special session in 2008						
Nebraska (U)	Nov. 14–Nov. 21, 2008	2	11	2	11	0	7L
Nevada	June 27, 2008	10	8	7	8	0	1C
	Dec. 8, 2008	4	7	4	7	0	1C
New Hampshire	No special session in 2008						
New Jersey	No special session in 2008						
New Mexico	Aug. 15–Aug. 19, 2008	51	0	10	0	(e)	5C
New York	Nov. 18, 2008 (Assembly only)	0	N.A.	0	29	0	1C
	Dec. 15, 2008 (Senate only)	0	N.A.	0	367	0	1C
North Carolina	Mar. 20, 2008	4	1	0	1	0	1C
North Dakota	No special session in 2008						
Ohio	No special session in 2008						
Oklahoma	No special session in 2008						
Oregon	Feb. 4–Feb. 29, 2008	88	22	54	18	0	19C
Pennsylvania	Jan. 1–Nov. 19, 2008 (f)	100	9	N.A.	N.A.	0	111L(g)
Rhode Island	No special session in 2008						
South Carolina	No special session in 2008 (h)						
South Dakota	No special session in 2008						
Tennessee	No special session in 2008						
Texas	No special session in 2008						
Utah	Sept. 25–Sept. 26, 2008	9	1	9	1	0	1C
Vermont	No special session in 2008						

See footnotes at end of table.

BILL AND RESOLUTION INTRODUCTIONS AND ENACTMENTS: 2008 SPECIAL SESSIONS — Continued

State or other jurisdiction	Duration of session**	Introductions		Enactments/adoptions		Measures vetoed by governor	Length of session
		Bills	Resolutions*	Bills	Resolutions*		
Virginia	Mar. 13–Apr. 23, 2008	2	52	2	52	0	6C
	Jun. 23–Jul. 9, 2008	76	120	11	103	0	6C
Washington	No special sessions in 2008						
West Virginia	Mar. 16, 2008	15	4	9	4	0	1C
	Jun. 25–Jun. 28, 2008	38	7	19	6	0	N.A.
Wisconsin	Jan. 11–Feb. 1, 2007	1	1	0	1	0	30L
	Mar. 12–May 15, 2008	1	6	1	5	0(l)	24L
	Apr. 17–May 14, 2008	1	6	1	6	0	11L
Wyoming	No special session in 2008						
American Samoa	No special sessions in 2008						
Guam	No special sessions in 2008						
No. Mariana Islands	No special sessions in 2008						
Puerto Rico	No special sessions in 2008						
U.S. Virgin Islands	No special sessions in 2008						

Source: The Council of State Governments' survey of state legislative agencies, March 2009.

* Includes Joint and Concurrrent resolutions.

** Actual adjournment dates are listed regardless of constitutional or statutory limitations. For more information on provisions, see Table 3.2, "Legislative Sessions: Legal Provisions."

Key:

N.A. — Not available

C — Calendar day.

L — Legislative day (in some states, called a session or workday; definition may vary slightly.

U — Unicameral legislature.

(a) The 1st Extraordinary Session-Senate 38L and Assembly 34L; the 2nd Extraordinary Session- Senate 38L and Assembly 37L; the 3rd Extraordinary Session—the Senate convened on Jan. 14, 2008 for 38L and the Assembly convened on Jan. 10, 2008 for 44L; the 4th Extraordinary Session the Senate convened on Nov. 6–Nov 30, 2008 for 1L day and the Assembly did not meet.

(b) House session date was June 11, 2008 for one legislative day: the Senate session date was June 11 through Dec. 9, 2008 for a total of two legislative days.

(c) 14 vetoes were overidden by the legislature.

(d) There were a total of 8 Senate and House special sessions in 2008. They began on the following dates (note that some began on the same date): January 2, July 9, July 9, July 10, August 12, August 13, September 22, and September 22. All special sessions adjourned on January 13, 2009. The House met on a total of 10 regular special session days and the Senate on 23 regular special session days. A total of 13 bills and 40 resolutions were considered during these special sessions. All 40 resolutions were adopted; 2 bills were enacted; and 4 bills were vetoed and not overridden.

(e) 1 partial or line item veto.

(f) Information was only provided for the House.

(g) Special session and regular session days can be scheduled for the same day.

(h) Technically there was not a special session because the session was extended per the Sine Die Resolution. Extended sessions ran—June 25 and October 20–24. For additional information on the South Carolina 2008 legislative session see Table 3.19.

Table 3.21
STAFF FOR INDIVIDUAL LEGISLATORS

State or other jurisdiction	Senate			House/Assembly		
	Capitol			Capitol		
	Personal	Shared	District	Personal	Shared	District
Alabama	. . .	YR/2	(a)	. . .	YR/10	(a)
Alaska (b)	YR/SO	. . .	YR	YR/SO	. . .	YR
Arizona	YR (c)	. . .	. . .	. . .	YR (c)	. . .
Arkansas	. . .	YR	. . .	. . .	YR (d)	. . .
California	YR	. . .	YR	YR	. . .	YR
Colorado	(e)	(e)	. . .	(e)	(e)	. . .
Connecticut (f)	YR/36	. . .	. . .	. . .	YR/38	. . .
Delaware	(g)					
Florida	YR (h)	. . .	YR (h)	YR (h)	. . .	YR (h)
Georgia	. . .	YR/3, SO/68	. . .	. . .	YR/25, SO/113	. . .
Hawaii	YR	. . .	. . .	YR	. . .	. . .
Idaho	. . .	SO, YR (i)	. . .	. . .	SO, YR (i)	. . .
Illinois	. . .	YR/1(j)	YR (j)	YR	YR/2 (j)	YR (j)
Indiana	. . .	YR/2 (k)	. . .	. . .	YR	. . .
Iowa	SO	. . .	. . .	SO	. . .	. . .
Kansas	SO/1	. . .	. . .	(l)	SO/3	. . .
Kentucky	. . .	YR (m)	. . .	. . .	YR (m)	. . .
Louisiana	(n)	YR (o)	YR (n)	(n)	YR (o)	YR (n)
Maine	YR,SO (p)	YR/27, SO/7	YR	. . .	YR (q)	. . .
Maryland	YR, SO (r)	. . .	YR (r)	YR (r)	SO (r)	YR (r)
Massachusetts	YR	. . .	. . .	YR	. . .	. . .
Michigan	YR (s)	. . .	. . .	YR/2 (s)	. . .	. . .
Minnesota	YR (t)	Varies	. . .	YR/3	Varies	. . .
Mississippi	. . .	YR	. . .	. . .	YR	. . .
Missouri	YR	YR	. . .	YR	YR	. . .
Montana	. . .	SO	. . .	. . .	SO	. . .
Nebraska	YR (u)	. . .	. . .	Unicameral		
Nevada	SO (v)	YR	. . .	SO (s)(v)	YR	. . .
New Hampshire	. . .	YR	. . .	. . .	YR	. . .
New Jersey	YR (h)	. . .	YR (h)	YR (h)	. . .	YR (h)
New Mexico	SO (w)	. . .	. . .	. . .	SO/2	. . .
New York	YR (x)	. . .	YR (x)	YR (x)	. . .	YR (x)
North Carolina	YR (y)	YR	. . .	YR (y)	YR	. . .
North Dakota	. . .	SO (v)	. . .	. . .	SO (v)	. . .
Ohio	YR/2 (z)	. . .	(aa)	YR/1 (bb)	. . .	(aa)
Oklahoma	YR/1(cc)	YR (cc)	. . .	YR (cc)	YR/1 (cc)	. . .
Oregon	YR (dd)	YR	YR (ee)	YR (dd)	YR	YR (ee)
Pennsylvania	YR	. . .	YR	YR	. . .	YR
Rhode Island	. . .	YR (ff)	. . .	. . .	YR (ff)	. . .
South Carolina	. . .	YR/2	. . .	YR/4	. . .	. . .
South Dakota	(gg)	(gg)	. . .	(gg)	(gg)	. . .
Tennessee	YR/1	. . .	. . .	(hh)	YR/1	. . .
Texas	YR/6 (ii)	. . .	. . .	YR/3 (ii)	. . .	. . .
Utah	(jj)	. . .	. . .	(jj)	. . .	. . .
Vermont	YR/1 (kk)	. . .	. . .	YR/1 (kk)	. . .	. . .
Virginia	SO/1 (ll)	. . .	(ll)	SO (ll)	SO/2	(ll)
Washington	YR/1	. . .	YR/1	YR/1	. . .	YR/1
West Virginia	SO	. . .	. . .	. . .	SO/17	. . .
Wisconsin	YR (mm)	YR	YR (mm)	YR (mm)	YR	YR (mm)
Wyoming	. . .	. . .	. . .	. . .	. . .	. . .
American Samoa	. . .	. . .	. . .	. . .	. . .	. . .
Guam	. . .	. . .	. . .	Unicameral		
No. Mariana Islands	YR (nn)	(nn)	. . .	YR (nn)	(nn)	(mm)
Puerto Rico	YR (nn)	. . .	. . .	YR (nn)	. . .	. . .
U.S. Virgin Islands	YR (nn)	. . .	. . .	Unicameral		

See footnotes at end of table.

STAFF FOR INDIVIDUAL LEGISLATORS—Continued

Source: The Council of State Governments' survey, January 2009.

Note: For entries under column heading "Shared," figures after slash indicate approximate number of legislators per staff person, where available.

Key:

. . . — Staff not provided for individual legislators.

YR — Year-round.

SO — Session only.

IO — Interim only.

(a) Six counties have local delegation offices with shared staff.

(b)The number of staff per legislator varies depending on their position.

(c) Representatives share a secretary with another legislator; however, House leadership and committee chairs usually have their own secretarial staff. All legislators share professional research staff.

(d) The legislators share 21 staff people; 4.76 legislators per staff person.

(e) Senate: has 17 session only staff and 18 year round staff. There are no district staffers, and since the entire staff works for multiple senators, they are not listed as shared. There are five session only staff in the bill room who are jointly managed by the Colorado Senate and House. House: year-round staff consists of five majority caucus staff; four minority caucus staff; 6 chief clerk non-partisan staff. The Colorado session only staff consists of three majority caucus staff; two minority caucus staff; 23 chief clerk non-partisan staff. The Colorado House of Representatives may have up to 65 legislative aides who serve as the legislator's personal staff. The legislative aides are employed for a total of 330 hours per legislator during the session only and they can work only in the capitol, and not in the district office. All of the legislators may hire an aide.

(f) The numbers are for staff assigned to specific legislators. There is additional staff working in the leadership offices that also support the rank and file members.

(g) Staffers are a combination of full time, part time, shared, personal, etc. and their assignments change throughout the year.

(h) Personal and district staff are the same. In Florida, two out of the three district employees may travel to the capitol for sessions.

(i) Idaho has 2 year round full-time, 3 part-time year round employees and 32 session only employees in the Senate. The House has 2 full time and 1 part time person year round and 37 additional people during session .

(j) The only staff working for individual rank-and-file legislators are (1) one secretary in the Capitol complex for each two members and (1-2) district staff, whom legislators select and pay from a separate allowance for that purpose. Partisan staffers help individual legislators with many issues in addition to staffing committees.

(k) Leadership has one legislative assistant. During session, college interns are hired to provide additional staff- one for every two members. Leadership has one intern.

(l) One clerical staff person for three individual House members is the norm. Chairpersons are provided their own individual clerical staff person.

(m) The General Assembly is provided professional and clerical staff services by a centralized, non-partisan staff, with the exception of House and Senate leadership which employs partisan staff. No district staff provided.

(n) Each legislator may hire as many assistants as desired, but pay from public funds ranges from $2,000 to $3,000 per month per legislator.

Assistant(s) generally work in the district office but may also work at the capitol during the session.

(o) The six caucuses are assigned one full-time position each (potentially 24 legislators per one staff person).

(p) President's office: six year round; Majority office: 7 year round, 1 session only; Secretary's office: nine year round, five session only.

(q) The 151 House members do not have individual staff. There are 21 people who work year round in the two partisan offices, 12 of whom are legislative aides who primarily work directly with legislators.

(r) Senators have one year round administrative aide and one session only secretary. Delegates have one part-time year round administrative aide and a shared session only secretary. Legislators may increase staff and also hire student interns if their district office funds are used.

(s) Senate—majority, 5 staff per legislator; minority, 3 staff per legislator. House—2 staff per legislator.

(t) One to two staff persons per legislator.

(u) Two to five staff persons per legislator.

(v) Secretarial staff; in North Dakota, leadership only.

(w) One plus; clerical plus attendant or analyst.

(x) House/party leaders determine allowances/funds for members once allocations are made. Members have considerable independence in hiring personal and committee staffs.

(y) Part time during interim.

(z) Some leadership offices have more.

(aa) Some legislators maintain district offices at their own expense.

(bb) Some offices have more.

(cc) Senate; Pro Tem—5 staff persons; House: year round one to five, majority party only; minority party one staff person per legislator. Committee, fiscal and legal staffs are available to legislators on a year round basis.

(dd) Two staff persons per legislator during session.

(ee) Senate— Equivalent of one full-time staff. House—1 during interim.

(ff) The General Assembly has a total of 280 full time positions, 267 full-time shared staff and additional 13 full-time positions for the House.

(gg) The non-partisan Legislative Research Council serves all members of both houses year round. Committee secretaries and legislative interns and pages provide support during the sessions.

(hh) Several House members have year-round personal staff. It depends on seniority, duties (such as committee chairs), and committee assignments.

(ii) Average staff numbers are from staff member totals from each chamber.

(jj) Most legislators are assigned student interns during session who are temporarily employed by OLRGC. Some legislators provide their own personal interns (volunteer/financial arrangements made between them).

(kk) No personal staff except one administrative assistant for the Speaker and one for the Senate Pro Tempore.

(ll) Senate—One administrative assistant (secretary) provided to the members during the session by the Clerk's offices. Members also receive a set dollar allowance to hire additional legislative assistants who may serve year round at the capitol and in the district. House—Members also receive a set dollar allowance to hire additional legislative assistants who may serve year round at the capitol and in the district.

(mm) Staffing levels vary according to majority/minority status and leadership or committee responsibilities. Members may assign staff to work in the district office.

(nn) Individual staffing and staff pool arrangements are at the discretion of the individual legislator.

Table 3.22
STAFF FOR LEGISLATIVE STANDING COMMITTEES

State or other jurisdiction	Committee staff assistance				Source of staff services **							
	Senate		House/Assembly		Joint central agency (a)		Chamber agency (b)		Caucus or leadership		Committee or committee chair	
	Prof.	Cler.	Prof.	Cler.	Prof.	Cler.	Prof.	Cler.	Prof.	Cler.	Prof.	Cler.
Alabama	•	★	•	★	B	B	B	B	. . .	. . .	. . .	. . .
Alaska	★	★	★	★	B	B	. . .	. . .	. . .	. . .	B	B
Arizona	★	★	★	★	B	B	B	B	B	B	B	B
Arkansas	★	★	★	★	B	B	B	B	. . .	. . .	. . .	. . .
California	★	★	★	★	B	B	B	B	B	B	B	B
Colorado	★	. . .	★	. . .	B	. . .	B	B	B	B (c)	. . .	. . .
Connecticut	. . .	★	. . .	★	B	. . .	. . .	. . .	. . .	B	. . .	B
Delaware	•	★	•	★	B	. . .	B	. . .	B	. . .	. . .	B
Florida	★	★	★	★	B	B	B	B	B	B	B	B
Georgia	•	★	•	★	B	B	B	B	B	B	B	. . .
Hawaii	•	★	•	★	B	B	B	B	B	B	B	B
Idaho	. . .	★	. . .	★	B (d)	B (d)	. . .	. . .	. . .	B (e)	. . .	. . .
Illinois	★	★	★	★	. . .	. . .	B	B	B	B	. . .	. . .
Indiana	★	. . .	★	. . .	. . .	. . .	S	. . .	S	. . .	. . .	. . .
Iowa	★	. . .	★	. . .	B	. . .	(f)	B	B	. . .	. . .	. . .
Kansas	★	★	★	★	B	B (g)	B	B	B	B	B	B
Kentucky	★	★	★	★	B	B	. . .	. . .	B (h)	B (h)	. . .	. . .
Louisiana	★(i)	★	★(i)	★	B	B	B	B	B	B	B (j)	B (j)
Maine	★(k)	★(k)	★(k)	★(k)	B	B	B	B	B	B	. . .	B
Maryland	★(l)	★(l)	★(l)	★(l)	B	B	. . .	. . .	. . .	. . .	. . .	. . .
Massachusetts	★	★	★	★	. . .	. . .	. . .	. . .	. . .	. . .	. . .	. . .
Michigan	★	★	★	★	B	. . .	. . .	★	B	. . .	. . .	S
Minnesota	★	★	★	★	. . .	. . .	B	S	B	S	B	B
Mississippi	•	★	•	★	. . .	. . .	B	B	. . .	. . .	B	B
Missouri	★	. . .	★	. . .	B	. . .	B	. . .	S	S	B	. . .
Montana	★	★	★	★	B	. . .	. . .	B	. . .	. . .	. . .	. . .
Nebraska	★	★	U	U	(m)	. . .	(m)	. . .	(m)	. . .	(m)	. . .
Nevada	★	★	★	★	B	. . .	. . .	B	. . .	. . .	. . .	. . .
New Hampshire	•	★	★	★	B	B	B	B	. . .	H	. . .	H
New Jersey	★	★	★	★	B	B	B	B	. . .	. . .	. . .	. . .
New Mexico	★	★	★	★	. . .	. . .	B	B	. . .	. . .	. . .	. . .
New York	★	★	★	★	B	B	B	B	B	B	B	B
North Carolina	★	★(n)	★	★(n)	B	. . .	. . .	. . .	. . .	. . .	. . .	B (n)
North Dakota	•	★	•	★	B	B	. . .	. . .	. . .	. . .	. . .	. . .
Ohio	★	★	★	★	B	. . .	. . .	. . .	B	. . .	B	B
Oklahoma	★	★	★	★	. . .	. . .	B	B	. . .	. . .	B	B
Oregon	★	★	★	★	B	B	B	B	B	B	B	B
Pennsylvania	★	★	★	★	B	B	B	B	B	B	B	B
Rhode Island	•	★	•	★	B	B	. . .	B	. . .	. . .	B	. . .
South Carolina	★	★	★	★	B	B	B	B	B	B	B	B
South Dakota	★	★	★	★	B	. . .	. . .	(l)	. . .	(l)	. . .	(l)
Tennessee	★	★	★	★	B	. . .	B	B	. . .	. . .	. . .	B
Texas	★	★	★	★	B	B	. . .	B	. . .	. . .	B	B
Utah	★	★(r)	★	★(r)	B	B	. . .	B	B (s)	B	. . .	. . .
Vermont	★	•	★	•	B	B	. . .	. . .	. . .	. . .	. . .	. . .
Virginia	★	★	★	★	B	. . .	B	B	. . .	. . .	(o)	(o)
Washington	★	★	★	★	. . .	. . .	B	B	B	B	B	B
West Virginia	★	★	★	★	B	B	B	B	B	B	B	B
Wisconsin	★	★	★	★	B	. . .	. . .	. . .	. . .	. . .	(p)	B
Wyoming	. . .	★	. . .	★	. . .	. . .	. . .	B	. . .	. . .	. . .	. . .
American Samoa	•	★	•	★	B	B	B	B	. . .	. . .	B	. . .
Guam	★	★	U	U	. . .	. . .	S	S	. . .	. . .	. . .	. . .
No. Mariana Islands	★	★	★	★	B (q)	B (q)	B (q)	B (q)	B (q)	B (q)	B (q)	B (q)
Puerto Rico	★	★	★	★	B (q)	B (q)	B (q)	B (q)	B (q)	B (q)	B (q)	B (q)
U.S. Virgin Islands	★	★	U	U	S (q)	S (q)	S (q)	S (q)	S (q)	S (q)	S (q)	S (q)

See footnotes at end of table.

STAFF FOR LEGISLATIVE STANDING COMMITTEES — Continued

Source: The Council of State Governments' survey, January 2009.

** — Multiple entries reflect a combination of organizations and location of services.

Key:

★ — All committees

• — Some committees

. . . — Services not provided

B — Both chambers

H — House

S — Senate

U — Unicameral

(a) Includes legislative council or service agency or central management agency.

(b) Includes chamber management agency, office of clerk or secretary and House or Senate research office.

(c) Senate—there is secretarial staff for both majority and minority offices for the Senate in the Capitol. Most of the clerical work is done by caucus staff. House—the clerical and secretarial staff for the House is more centralized and is supervised by the Clerk of the House.

(d) Professional staff and clerical support is provided via the Legislative Services Office, a non-partisan office serving all members on a year round basis.

(e) Leadership in each party hire their respective support staff.

(f) The Senate secretary and House clerk maintain supervision of committee clerks.

(g) Senators and House chairpersons select their secretaries and notify the central administrative services agency; all administrative employee matters handled by the agency.

(h) Leadership employs partisan staff to provide professional and clerical services. However, all members, including leadership are also served by the centralized, non-partisan staff.

(i) House Appropriations and Senate Finance Committees have Legislative Fiscal Office staff at their hearings.

(j) Staff are assigned to each committee but work under the direction of the chair.

(k) Standing committees are joint House and Senate committees.

(l) The clerical support comes from employees who are hired to work only during the legislative sessions. They are employees of either the House or the Senate, and are not part of the central agency.

(m) Professional services are not provided, except that the staff of the Legislative Fiscal Office serves the Appropriations Committee. Individual senators are responsible for the process of hiring their own staff.

(n) Member's personal secretary serves as a clerk to the committee or subcommittee that the member chairs.

(o) The House Appropriations Committee and the Senate Finance Committees have their own staff. The staff members work under the direction of the chair.

(p) Standing committees are staffed by subject specialist from the Joint Legislative Council.

(q) In general, the legislative service agency provides legal and staff assistance for legislative meetings and provides associated materials. Individual legislators hire personal or committee staff as their budgets provide and at their own discretion.

(r) Clerical staff not assigned to Rules Cmtes.

(s) Refers only to Chief Deputy of the Senate and Chief of Staff in the House.

Table 3.23
STANDING COMMITTEES: APPOINTMENT AND NUMBER

State or other jurisdiction	Committee members appointed by:		Committee chairpersons appointed by:		Number of standing committees during regular 2008 session	
	Senate	House/Assembly	Senate	House/Assembly	Senate	House/Assembly
Alabama	CC	S	CC	S	25	25
Alaska	CC	CC	CC	CC	9	9
Arizona	P	S	P	S	13	18
Arkansas	(a)	(b)	(a)	S	9	10
California	CR	S	CR	S	22	29
Colorado	MjL	S	MjL	S	11	10
Connecticut	CC	CC	CC	CC	(c)	(c)
Delaware	PT	S	PT	S	26	27
Florida	P	S	P	S	20	18
Georgia	CC	S	CC	S	25	34
Hawaii	P	(e)	P	(d)	13	17
Idaho	PT (f)	S	PT	S	10	14
Illinois	P, MnL	S, MnL	P	S	25	57
Indiana	PT	S	PT	S	20	20
Iowa	MjL, MnL	S	MjL	S	17	19
Kansas	(g)	S	(g)	S	17	21
Kentucky	P	S	P	S	14	19
Louisiana	P	S ((h)	P	S	17	17
Maine	P	S	P	S	17 (v)	6 (v)
Maryland	P	S	P	S	8	9
Massachusetts	P	S	P	S	5 (c)	8 (c)
Michigan	MjL	S	MjL	S	19	24
Minnesota	CR	S	MjL	S	14	27
Mississippi	P	S	P	S	31	41
Missouri	PT (i)	S	PT	S	35	35
Montana	CC	S	CC	S	17	17
Nebraska	CC	U	E	U	14	U
Nevada	MjL	S	MjL	S	9	11
New Hampshire	P (k)	S (k)	P (k)	S (k)	14	21
New Jersey	CC	CC	CC	CC	13	23
New Mexico	CC	S	CC	S	9 (l)	15 (l)
New York	PT	S	PT	S	31	37
North Carolina	CC	CC	CC	CC	24	45
North Dakota	CC	CC	MjL	MjL	11	12 (j)
Ohio	P (m)	S (m)	P (m)	S (m)	14	20
Oklahoma	PT	S	PT	S	18	25
Oregon	P	S	P	S	12	16
Pennsylvania	PT	S	PT	S	21	23
Rhode Island	P	S	P	S	11	9
South Carolina	(n)	S	(o)	E	15	11
South Dakota	PT	S	PT	S	13	13
Tennessee	S	S	S	S	13	16
Texas	P	S (p)	P	S	20	41
Utah	P	S	P	S	12	15
Vermont	CC	S	CC	S	11	14
Virginia	E	S	(q)	S	11	14
Washington	P (r)	S	E (s)	S	15	21
West Virginia	P	S	P	S	18	15
Wisconsin	MjL	S	MjL	S	18	40
Wyoming	P	S	P	S	12	12
Dist. of Columbia	(t)	U	(t)	U	9	U
American Samoa	P	S	E	S	23	13
Guam	(u)	U	(u)	U	11	U
No. Mariana Islands	P	S	P	S	8	7
Puerto Rico	P	S	P	S	22	32
U.S. Virgin Islands	E	U	E	U	9	U

See footnotes at end of table.

STANDING COMMITTEES: APPOINTMENT AND NUMBER — Continued

Source: The Council of State Governments' survey, January 2009.

Key:

CC — Committee on Committees
CR — Committee on Rules
E — Election
MjL — Majority Leader
MnL — Minority Leader
P — President
PT — President pro tempore
S — Speaker
U — Unicameral Legislature

(a) Selection process based on seniority.

(b) Members of the standing committees shall be selected by House District Caucuses with each caucus selecting five members for each "A" standing committee and five members for each "B" standing committee.

(c) Substantive standing committees are joint committees. Connecticut, 18 (there are also three statutory and four select committees for the House and the Senate); Massachusetts, 26.

(d) By resolution with members of majority party designating the chair, vice-chairs and majority party members of committees, and members of minority party designating minority party members.

(e) By resolution, with members of majority party designating the chair, vice-chairs and majority party members of committees, and members of minority party designating minority party members.

(f) Committee members appointed by the Senate leadership under the direction of the president pro tempore, by and with the Senate's consent.

(g) Committee on Organization, Calendar and Rules.

(h) Speaker appoints only 12 of the 19 members of the Committee on Appropriations.

(i) Senate minority committee members chosen by minority caucus, but appointed by president pro tempore.

(j) The House had a Constitutional Revision Committee.

(k) Senate president and House speaker consult with minority leaders.

(l) Senate: includes eight substantive committees and one procedural committee. House: includes 12 substantive committees and three procedural committees.

(m) The minority leader may recommend for consideration minority party members for each committee.

(n) Appointment based on seniority (Senate Rule 19D).

(o) Appointed by seniority which is determined by tenure within the committee rather than tenure within the Senate. Also, chair is based on the majority party within the committee (Senate Rule 19E).

(p) For each standing substantive committee of the House, except for the appropriations committee, a maximum of one-half of the membership, exclusive of chair and vice-chair, is determined by seniority; the remaining membership of the committee is determined by the speaker.

(q) Senior member of the majority party on the committee is the chair.

(r) Lieutenant governor is president of the Senate.

(s) Recommended by the Committee on Committees, approved by the president, then confirmed by the senate.

(t) Chair of the Council.

(u) Members are appointed by the Chairperson; Chairperson is elected during majority caucus prior to inauguration.

(v) There are currently 17 Joint Standing Committees, two Joint Select Committees, and a joint Government Oversight Committee.

Table 3.24
RULES ADOPTION AND STANDING COMMITTEES: PROCEDURE

State or other jurisdiction	Constitution permits each legislative body to determine its own rules	Committee meetings open to public*		Specific, advance notice provisions for committee meetings or hearings	Voting/roll call provisions to report a bill to floor
		Senate	House/ Assembly		
Alabama	★	★	★	Senate: 4 hours, if possible House: 24 hours, except Rules & Local Legislations Committee. Exceptions after 27th legislative day and special sessions.	Senate: final vote on a bill is recorded. House: recorded vote if requested by member of committee and sustained by one additional committee member.
Alaska	. . .	★	★	For meetings, by 4 p.m. on the preceding Thurs.; for first hearings on bills, 5 days	Roll call vote on any measure taken upon request by any member of either house.
Arizona	★	★	★	Senate: Written agenda for each regular and special meeting containing all bills, memorials and resolutions to be considered shall be distributed to each member of the committee and to the Secretary of the Senate at least five days prior to the committee meeting House: The committee chair shall prepare an agenda and distribute copies to committee members, the Information Desk and the Chief Clerk's Office by 4 p.m. each Wednesday for all standing committees meeting on Monday of the following week and 4 p.m. each Thursday for all standing committees meeting on any day except Monday of the following week.	Senate: roll call vote. House: roll call vote.
Arkansas	★	★	★	Senate: 2 days House: 18 hours (2 hours with 2/3's vote of the committee)	Senate: roll call votes are recorded. House: report of committee recommendation signed by committee chair.
California	★	★	★	Senate: advance notice provisions exist. House: advance notice provisions exist.	Senate: roll call. House: roll call.
Colorado	★	★	★	Senate: final action on a measure is prohibited unless notice is posted one calendar day prior to its consideration. The prohibition does not apply if the action receives a majority vote of the committee. House: Meeting publicly announced while the House is in actual session as much in advance as possible.	Senate: final action by recorded roll call vote. House: final action by recorded roll call vote.
Connecticut	★	★	★	Senate: one day notice for meetings, five days notice for hearings. House: one day notice for meetings, five days notice for hearings.	Senate: roll call required. House: roll call required.
Delaware	★	★	★	Senate: agenda released one day before meetings House: agenda for meetings released four days before meetings	Senate: results of all committee reports are recorded. House: results of all committee reports are recorded.
Florida	★	★	★	Senate: during session—3 hours notice for first 50 days, 4 hours thereafter House: two days.	Senate: vote on final passage is recorded. House: vote on final passage is recorded.
Georgia	★	★	★	Senate: a list of committee meetings shall be posted by 10 a.m. the preceding Friday House: none	Senate: bills can be voted out by voice vote or roll call. House: bills can be voted out by voice vote or roll call.
Hawaii	★	★(a)	★(a)	Senate: 72 hours before 1st referral committee meetings, 48 hours before subsequent referral committee House: 48 hours	Senate: A quorum of committee members must be present before voting. House: A quorum of committee members must be present before voting.
Idaho	★	★(a)	★(a)	Senate: none House: per rule; chair provides notice of next meeting dates and times to clerk to be read prior to adjournment each day of session.	Senate: bills can be voted out by voice vote or roll call. House: bills can be voted out by voice vote or roll call.

See footnotes at end of table.

RULES ADOPTION AND STANDING COMMITTEES: PROCEDURE—Continued

State or other jurisdiction	Constitution permits each legislative body to determine its own rules	Committee meetings open to public* Senate	House/Assembly	Specific, advance notice provisions for committee meetings or hearings	Voting/roll call provisions to report a bill to floor
Illinois	★	★(b)	★(b)	Senate: 6 days House: 6 days	Senate: votes on all legislative measures acted upon are recorded. House: votes on all legislative matters acted upon are recorded.
Indiana	★	★	★	Senate: 48 hours House: prior to adjournment of the meeting day next preceding the meeting or announced during session	Senate: committee reports—do pass; do pass amended, Reported out without recommendation. House: majority of quorum; vote can be by roll call or consent.
Iowa	★	★	★	Senate: none House: none	Senate: final action by roll call. House: committee reports include roll call on final disposition.
Kansas	★	★	★	Senate: none House: none	Senate: vote recorded upon request of member. House: total for and against actions recorded.
Kentucky	★	★	★	Senate: none House: none	Senate: each member's vote recorded on each bill. House: each member's vote recorded on each bill.
Louisiana	★	★(a)	★(a)	Senate: no later than 1 p.m. the preceding day House: no later than 4 p.m. the preceding day	Senate: any motion to report an instrument is decided by a roll call vote. House: any motion to report an instrument is decided by a roll call vote.
Maine	★	★	★	Senate: must be advertised two weekends in advance. House: must be advertised two weekends in advance.	Senate: recorded vote is required to report a bill out of committee. House: recorded vote is required to report a bill out of committee.
Maryland	★	★	★	Senate: none (c) House: none (c)	Senate: the final vote on any bill is recorded. House: the final vote on any bill is recorded.
Massachusetts	★	★	★	Senate: 48 hours for public hearings House: 48 hours for public hearings	Senate: voice vote or recorded roll call vote at the request of 2 committee members. House: recorded vote upon request by a member.
Michigan	★	★	★	Senate and House: Notice shall be published in the journal in advance of a hearing. Notice of a special meeting shall be posted at least 18 hours before a meeting. Special provisions for conference committees.	Senate: committee reports include the vote of each member on any bill. House: the daily journal reports the roll call on all motions to report bills.
Minnesota	★	★	★	Senate: 3 days House: 3 days	Senate: not needed. House: not needed. House: recorded roll call vote upon request by a member.
Mississippi	★	★	★	Senate: none House: none	Senate: bills are reported out by voice vote or recorded roll call vote. House: bills are reported out by voice vote or recorded roll call vote.
Missouri	★	★	★	Senate: 24 hours House: 24 hours	Senate: yeas and nays are reported in journal. House: bills are reported out by a recorded roll call vote.
Montana	★	★	★	Senate: 3 legislative days House: none	Senate: every vote of each member is recorded and made public. House: every vote of each member is recorded and made public.
Nebraska	★	★	U	Seven calendar days notice before hearing a bill.	In executive session, majority of the committee must vote in favor of the motion made.

See footnotes at end of table.

RULES ADOPTION AND STANDING COMMITTEES: PROCEDURE—Continued

State or other jurisdiction	Constitution permits each legislative body to determine its own rules	Committee meetings open to public*: Senate	House/ Assembly	Specific, advance notice provisions for committee meetings or hearings	Voting/roll call provisions to report a bill to floor
Nevada	★	★	★	Senate: by rule—"adequate notice" shall be provided. (d) House: by rule—"adequate notice" shall be provided. (d)	Senate: recorded vote is taken upon final committee action on bills. House: recorded vote is taken upon final committee action on bills.
New Hampshire	★	★	★	Senate: 4 days House: no less than 4 days	Senate: committees may report a bill out by voice or recorded roll call vote. House: committees may report a bill out by voice or recorded roll call vote.
New Jersey	★	★	★	Senate: 5 days House: 5 days	Senate: the chair reports the vote of each member present on a motion to report a bill. House: the chair reports the vote of each member present on motions with respect to bills.
New Mexico	★	★	★	Senate: none House: none	Senate: vote on the final report of the committee taken by yeas and nays. Roll call vote upon request. House: vote on the final report of the committee taken by yeas and nays. Roll call vote upon request.
New York	★	★(a)	★(a)	Senate: Rules require that notice be given for public hearings, but the Rules are silent as to how long. House: 1 week for hearings, Thursday of prior week for meetings.	Senate: majority vote required House: majority vote required
North Carolina	(f)	★	★	Senate: none (e) House: none (e)	Senate: no roll call vote may be taken in any committee. House: roll call vote taken on any question when requested by member & sustained by one-fifth of members present.
North Dakota	★	★	★	Senate: hearing schedule printed Friday mornings. House: hearing schedule printed Friday mornings.	Senate: included with minutes from standing committee. House: included with minutes from standing committee.
Ohio	★	★	★	Senate: 2 days. In a case of necessity, the notice of hearing may be given in a shorter period by such reasonable method as prescribed by the Committee on Rules. House: 5 days. If an emergency requires consideration of a matter at a meeting not announced on notice, the chair may revise or supplement the notice at any time before or during the meeting to include the matter.	Senate: the affirmative votes of a majority of all members of a committee shall be necessary to report or to postpone further consideration of bills or resolutions. Every member present shall vote, unless excused by the chair. At discretion of chair the roll call may be continued for a vote by any member who was present at the prior meeting, but no later than 10 a.m. of next calendar day. House: the affirmative votes of a majority of all members of a committee shall be necessary to report or to postpone further consideration of bills or resolutions. Every member present shall vote, unless excused by the chair. At discretion of chair the roll call may be continued for a vote by any member who was present at the prior meeting, but no later than 12 noon one day following the meeting. Members must be present in order to vote on amendment.
Oklahoma	★	★	★	Senate: 3 day notice. House: 3 day notice.	Senate: roll call vote. House: roll call vote.
Oregon	★	★	★	Senate: At least 48 hrs. notice except at the end of session when President invokes 1 hr. notice when adjournment sine die is imminent. House: First public hearing on a measure must have at least 72 hours notice, all other meetings at least 48 hours notice except in case of emergency.	Senate: affirmative roll call vote of majority of members of committee and recorded in committee minutes. House: affirmative roll call vote of majority of members of committee and recorded in committee minutes.

See footnotes at end of table.

RULES ADOPTION AND STANDING COMMITTEES: PROCEDURE—Continued

State or other jurisdiction	Constitution permits each legislative body to determine its own rules	Committee meetings open to public*: Senate	Committee meetings open to public*: House/ Assembly	Specific, advance notice provisions for committee meetings or hearings	Voting/roll call provisions to report a bill to floor
Pennsylvania	★	★	★	Senate: written notice to members containing date, time, place and agenda House: written notice to members containing date, time, place and agenda	Senate: a majority vote of committee members. House: a majority vote of committee members.
Rhode Island	★	★	★	Senate: notice required. House: notice required.	Senate: majority vote of the members present. House: majority vote of the members present.
South Carolina	★	★	★	Senate: 24 hours House: 24 hours	Senate: before the expiration of five days from the date of reference, any bill, may be recalled from committee by the vote of three-fourths of the Senators present and voting House: favorable report out of committee (majority of committee members voting in favor).
South Dakota	★	★	★	Senate and House: at least one legislative day must intervene between the date of posting and the date of consideration in both houses.	Senate and House: a majority vote of the members-elect taken by roll call is needed for final disposition on a bill. This applies to both houses.
Tennessee	★	★	★	Senate: 6 days House: 72 hours	Senate: majority referral to Calendar and Rules Committee, majority of Calendar and Rules Committee referral to floor. House: majority referral to Calendar and Rules Committee, majority of Calendar and Rules Committee referral to floor.
Texas	★	★	★	Senate: 24 hours House: The House requires five calendar days notice before a public hearing at which testimony will be taken, and two hours notice or an announcement from the floor before a formal meeting (testimony cannot be taken at a formal meeting). 24 hour advance notice is required during special session	Senate: bills are reported by recorded roll call vote. House: committee reports include the record vote by which the report was adopted, including the vote of each member.
Utah	★	★	★	Senate: Not less than 24 hours public notice. House: Not less than 24 hours public notice.	Senate: Voice vote accepting the recommendation of the committee. House: Voice vote accepting the recommendation of the committee.
Vermont	★	★	★	Senate: none House: none	Senate: vote is recorded for each committee member for every bill considered. House: vote is recorded for each committee member for every bill considered.
Virginia	★	★(a)	★(a)	Senate: none House: none	Senate: recorded vote, except resolutions that do not have a specific vote requirement under the Rules. In these cases, a voice vote is sufficient. House: vote of each member is taken and recorded for each measure.
Washington	★	★	★	Senate: 5 days House: 5 days	Senate: bills reported from a committee carry a majority report which must be signed by a majority of the committee. House: every vote to report a bill out of committee is by yeas and nays; the names of the members voting are recorded in the report.
West Virginia	★	★	★	Senate: none House: none	Senate: majority of committee members voting. House: majority of committee members voting.
Wisconsin	★	★	★	Senate: Monday noon of the preceding week. House: Monday noon of the preceding week.	Senate: number of ayes and noes, and members absent or not voting are reported. House: number of ayes and noes are recorded.
Wyoming	★	★	★	Senate: by 3 p.m. of previous day House: by 3 p.m. of previous day	Senate: bills are reported out by recorded roll call vote. House: bills are reported out by recorded roll call vote.

See footnotes at end of table.

RULES ADOPTION AND STANDING COMMITTEES: PROCEDURE—Continued

State or other jurisdiction	Constitution permits each legislative body to determine its own rules	Committee meetings open to public*		Specific, advance notice provisions for committee meetings or hearings	Voting/roll call provisions to report a bill to floor
		Senate	House/ Assembly		
American Samoa	★	★(g)	★(g)	Senate: At least 3 calendar days in advance. House: At least 3 calendar days in advance.	Senate/House: There are four methods of ascertaining the decision upon any matter: by raising of hands; by secret ballot, when authorized by law; by rising; and by call of the members and recorded by the Clerk of the vote of each.
Guam	★	★	U	Five days prior to public hearings.	Majority vote of committee members.
Puerto Rico	★	★	★	Senate: Must be notified every Thurs., one week in advance. House: 24 hours advanced notice, no later than 4 p.m. previous day	Senate: bills reported from a committee carry a majority vote House: bills reported from a committee carry a majority vote by referendum or in an ordinary meeting.
U.S. Virgin Islands	★	★	U	Seven calendar days.	Bills must be reported to floor by Rules Committee.

Source: The Council of State Governments' survey, January 2009.

Key:

★ — Yes

* — Notice of committee meetings may also be subject to state open meetings laws; in some cases, listed times may be subject to suspension or enforceable only to the extent "feasible" or "whenever possible."

U — Unicameral.

(a) Certain matters may be discussed in executive session. (Other states permit meetings to be closed for various reasons, but their rules do not specifically mention "executive session.")

(b) A session of a house or one of its committees can be closed to the public if two-thirds of the members elected to that house determine that the public interest so requires. A meeting of a joint committee or commission can be closed if two-thirds of the members of both houses so vote.

(c) General directive in the Senate and House rules to the Department of Legislative Services to compile a list of the meetings and to arrange for distribution which in practice is done on a regular basis.

(d) Senate: This rule may be suspended for emergencies by a two thirds vote of appointed committee members. House: This rule may be suspended for emergencies by a two thirds vote of appointed committee members. In the Assembly this rule does not apply to committee meetings held on the floor during recess or conference committee meetings.

(e) If public hearing, five calendar days.

(f) Not referenced specifically, but each body publishes rules.

(g) Unless privileged information is being discussed with counsel or the security of the territory is involved.

Table 3.25
LEGISLATIVE REVIEW OF ADMINISTRATIVE REGULATIONS: STRUCTURES AND PROCEDURES

State or other jurisdiction	*Type of reviewing committee*	*Rules reviewed*	*Time limits in review process*
Alabama	Joint bipartisan, standing committee	P	If not approved or disapproved within 35 days of filing, rule is approved. If disapproved by committee, rule suspended until adjournment, next regular session or until legislature by resolution revokes suspension. Rule takes effect upon final adjournment unless committee's disapproval is sustained by legislature. The committee may approve a rule.
Alaska	Joint bipartisan, standing committee and Legislative Affairs Agency review of proposed regulations.	P,E	. . .
Arizona	Joint bipartisan	P,E	. . .
Arkansas	Joint bipartisan	P,E	. . .
California	. . .	P,E	Regulation review conducted by independent executive branch agency. The only existing rules that are reviewed are emergency regulations—all others are reviewed prior to implementation.
Colorado	Joint bipartisan	E	Rules continue unless the annual legislative Rule Reviews Bill discontinues a rule. The Rule Reviews Bill is effective upon the governor's signature.
Connecticut	Joint bipartisan, standing committee	P	Submittal of proposed regulation shall be on the first Tuesday of month; after first submittal committee has 65 days after date of submission. Second submittal: 35 days for committee to review/take action on revised regulation.
Delaware	Attorney General review	P	The attorney general shall review any rule or regulation promulgated by any state agency and inform the issuing agency in writing as to the potential of the rule or regulation to result in a taking of private property before the rule or regulation may become effective.
Florida	Joint bipartisan	P,E	. . .
Georgia	Standing committee	P	The agency notifies the Legislative Counsel 30 days prior to the effective dates of proposed rules.
Hawaii	Legislative agency	P,E	In Hawaii, the legislative reference bureau assists agencies to comply with a uniform format of style. This does not affect the status of rules.
Idaho	Germane joint subcommittees	P	Germane joint subcommittees vote to object or not object to a rule. They cannot reject a proposed rule directly, only advise an agency which may choose to adopt a rule subject to review by the full legislature. The legislature as a whole reviews rules during the first three weeks of session to determine if they comport with state law. The Senate and House may reject rules via resolution adopted by both. Rules imposing fees must be approved or are deemed approved unless rejected. Temporary rules expire at the end of session unless extended by concurrent resolution.
Illinois	Joint bipartisan	P,E	An agency proposing non-emergency regulations must allow 45 days for public comment. At least five days after any public hearing on the proposal, the agency must give notice of the proposal to the Joint Committee on Administrative Rules, and allow it 45 days to approve or object to the proposed regulations.
Indiana	Joint bipartisan	P	. . .
Iowa	Joint bipartisan	P,E	. . .
Kansas	Joint bipartisan	P	Agencies must give a 60-day notice to the public and the Joint Committee of their intent to adopt or amend specific rules and regulations, a copy of which must be provided to the committee. Within the 60-day comment period, the Joint Committee must review and comment, if it feels necessary, on the proposals. Final rules and regulations are resubmitted to the committee to determine whether further expression of concern is necessary.
Kentucky	Joint bipartisan statutory committee	P,E	45 days.
Louisiana (b)	Standing committee	P	All proposed rules and fees are submitted to designated standing committees of the legislature. If a rule or fee is unacceptable, the committee sends a written report to the governor. The governor has 10 days to disapprove the committee report. If both Senate and House committees fail to find the rule unacceptable, or if the governor disapproves the action of a committee within 10 days, the agency may adopt the rule change. (d)
Maine	Joint bipartisan, standing committee	P	One legislative session.

See footnotes at end of table.

LEGISLATIVE REVIEW OF ADMINISTRATIVE REGULATIONS: STRUCTURES AND PROCEDURES — Continued

State or other jurisdiction	Type of reviewing committee	Rules reviewed	Time limits in review process
Maryland	Joint bipartisan	P,E	Proposed regulations are submitted for review at least 15 days before publication. Publication triggers 45 day review period which may be extended by the committee, but if agreement cannot be reached, the governor may instruct the agency to modify or withdraw the regulation, or may approve its adoption.
Massachusetts (b)	Public hearing by agency	P	In Massachusetts, the General Court (Legislature) may by statute authorize an administrative agency to promulgate regulations. The promulgation of such regulations are then governed by Chapter 30A of the Massachusetts General Laws. Chapter 30A requires 21 day notice to the public of a public hearing on a proposed regulation. After public hearing the proposed regulation is filed with the state secretary who approves it if it is in conformity with Chapter 30A. The state secretary maintains a register entitled "Massachusetts Register" and the regulation does not become effective until published in the register. The agency may promulgate amendments to the regulations following the same process.
Michigan	Joint bipartisan	P	Joint Committee on Administrative Rules (JCAR) has 15 session days in which to consider the rule and to object to the rule by filing a notice of objection. If no objection is made, the rules may be filed and go into effect. If JCAR does formally object, bills to block the rules are introduced in both houses of the legislature simultaneously by the committee chair and placed directly on the Senate and House calendars for action. If the bills are not enacted by the legislature and presented to the governor within 15 session days, the rules may go into effect. Between legislative sessions the committee can meet and suspend rules promulgated during the interim between sessions.
Minnesota	Joint bipartisan, standing committee	P,E	Minnesota Statute Sec. 3.842, subd. 4a
Mississippi	(a)		
Missouri	Joint bipartisan, standing committee	P,E	The committee must disapprove a final order of rulemaking within 30 days upon receipt or the order of rulemaking is deemed approved.
Montana	Germane joint bipartisan committees	P	Prior to adoption.
Nebraska	Standing committee	P	If an agency proposes to repeal, adopt or amend a rule or regulation, it is required to provide the Executive Board Chair with the proposal at least 30 days prior to the public hearing, as required by law. The Executive Board Chair shall provide to the appropriate standing committee of the legislature, the agency proposal for comment.
Nevada	Ongoing statutory committee (Legislative Commission)	P	Proposed regulations are either reviewed at the Legislative Commission's next regularly scheduled meeting (if the regulation is received more than three working days before the meeting), or they are referred to the Commission's Subcommittee to Review Regulations. If there is no objection to the regulation, then the Commission will "promptly" file the approved regulation with the secretary of state. If the Commission or its subcommittee objects to a regulation, then the Commission will "promptly" return the regulation to the agency for revision. Within 60 days of receiving the written notice of objection to the regulation, the agency must revise the regulation and return it to the Legislative Counsel. If the Commission or its subcommittee objects to the revised regulation, the agency shall continue to revise and resubmit it to the Commission or subcommittee within 30 days after receiving the written notice of objection to the revised regulation.
New Hampshire	Joint bipartisan	P	Under APA, for regular rulemaking, the joint committee of administrative rules has 45 days to review a final proposed rule from an agency, Otherwise the rule is automatically approved. If JLCAR makes a preliminary or revised objection, the agency has 45 days to respond, and JLCAR has another 50 days to decide to vote to sponsor a joint resolution, which suspends the adoption process. JLCAR may also, or instead, make a final objection, which shifts the burden of proof in court to the agency. There is no time limit on making a final objection. If no JLCAR action in the 50 days to vote to sponsor a joint resolution, the agency may adopt the rule.
New Jersey	Joint bipartisan	. . .	. . .
New Mexico	(g)		
New York	Joint bipartisan commission	P,E	. . .

See footnotes at end of table.

LEGISLATIVE REVIEW OF ADMINISTRATIVE REGULATIONS: STRUCTURES AND PROCEDURES — Continued

State or other jurisdiction	Type of reviewing committee	Rules reviewed	Time limits in review process
North Carolina	Rules Review Commission; Public membership appointed by legislature	P,E	The Rules Review Commission must review a permanent rule submitted to it on or before the 20th of the month by the last day of the next month. The commission must review a permanent rule submitted to it after the 20th of the month by the last day of the second subsequent month.
North Dakota	Interim committee	E	The Administrative Rules Committee meets in each calendar quarter to consider rules filed in previous 90 days.
Ohio	Joint bipartisan	P,E (h)	The committee's jurisdiction is 65 days from date of original filing plus an additional 30 days from date of re-filing. Rules filed with no changes, pursuant to the five-year review, are under a 90 day jurisdiction.
Oklahoma	Standing committee (c)	P,E	The legislature has 30 legislative days to review proposed rules.
Oregon	Office of Legislative Counsel	E	Agencies must copy Legislative Counsel within 10 days of rule adoption.
Pennsylvania	Joint bipartisan, standing committee	E	Time limits decided by the president pro tempore and speaker of the House.
Rhode Island	(a)		
South Carolina	Standing committee (e)	P	General Assembly has 120 days to approve or disapprove. If not disapproved by joint resolution before 120 days, regulation is automatically approved. It can be approved during 120 day review period by joint resolution.
South Dakota	Joint bipartisan	P	Rules must be adopted within 75 days of the commencement of the public hearing; emergency rules must be adopted within 30 days of the date of the publication of the notice of intent. Many other deadlines exits; see SDCL 1-26-4 for further details.
Tennessee	Joint bipartisan	P	All permanent rules take effect 165 days after filing with the secretary of state. Emergency rules take effect upon filing with the secretary of state.
Texas	Standing committee	P	No time limit.
Utah	(f)	P,E	Except as provided in Subsection (2)(b), every agency rule that is in effect on February 28 of any calendar year expires May 1 of that year unless it has been reauthorized by the legislature. (UCA 63G-3-502)
Vermont	Joint bipartisan	P	The Joint Legislative Committee on Rules must review a proposed rule within 30 days of submission to the committee.
Virginia	Joint bipartisan, standing committee	P	Standing committees and the Joint Commission on Administrative Rules may object to a proposed or final adopted rule before it becomes effective. This delays the process for 21 days and the agency must respond to the objection. In addition or as an alternative, standing committees and the Commission may suspend the effective date of all or a part of a final regulation until the end of the next regular session, with the concurrence of the Governor.
Washington	Joint bipartisan	P,E	If the committee determines that a proposed rule does not comply with legislative intent, it notifies the agency, which must schedule a public hearing within 30 days of notification. The agency notifies the committee of its action within seven days after the hearing. If a hearing is not held or the agency does not amend the rule, the objection may be filed in the state register and referenced in the state code. The committee's powers, other than publication of its objections, are advisory.
West Virginia	Joint bipartisan	P,E	. . .
Wisconsin	Joint bipartisan, standing committee	P,E	The standing committee in each house has 30 days to conduct its review for a proposed rule. If either objects the Joint Committee for the Review of Administrative Rules has 30 days to introduce legislation in each house overturning the rules. After 40 days the bills are placed on the calendar. If either bill passes, the rules are overturned. If they fail to pass, the rules go into effect.
Wyoming	Joint bipartisan	P,E	An agency shall submit copies of adopted, amended or repealed rules to the legislative service office for review within five days after the date of the agency's final action adopting, amending or repealing those rules. The legislature makes its recommendations to the governor who within 15 days after receiving any recommendation, shall either order that the rule be amended or rescinded in accordance with the recommendation or file in writing his objections to the recommendation.

See footnotes at end of table.

LEGISLATIVE REVIEW OF ADMINISTRATIVE REGULATIONS: STRUCTURES AND PROCEDURES — Continued

State or other jurisdiction	*Type of reviewing committee*	*Rules reviewed*	*Time limits in review process*
American Samoa	Standing committee	E	. . .
Guam	Standing committe	P	45 Calendar days
Puerto Rico	(a)		
U.S. Virgin Islands	(a)		

Source: The Council of State Governments' survey, February 2009.

Key:

P — Proposed rules

E — Existing rules

. . . — No formal time limits

(a) No formal rule review is performed by both legislative and executive branches.

(b) Review of rules is performed by both legislative and executive branches.

(c) House has a standing committee to which all rules are generally sent for review. In the Senate rules are sent to standing committee which deals with that specific agency.

(d) If the committees of both houses fail to find a fee unacceptable, it can be adopted. Committee action on proposed rules must be taken within 5 to 30 days after the agency reports to the committee on its public hearing (if any) and whether it is making changes on proposed rules.

(e) Submitted by General Assembly for approval.

(f) Created by statute (63G-3-501).

(g) No formal review is performed by legislature. Periodic review and report to legislative finance committee is required of certain agencies.

(h) The Committee reviews proposed new, amended, and rescinded rules. The Committee participates in a five-year review of every existing rule.

Table 3.26
LEGISLATIVE REVIEW OF ADMINISTRATIVE RULES/REGULATIONS: POWERS

State or other jurisdiction	Reviewing committee's powers: Advisory powers only (a)	Reviewing committee's powers: No objection constitutes approval of proposed rule	Reviewing committee's powers: Committee may suspend rule	Legislative powers: Method of legislative veto of rules
Alabama	. . .	★	★	If not approved or disapproved within 35 days of filing, rule is approved. If disapproved by committee, rule suspended until adjournment, next regular session or until legislature by resolution revokes suspension. Rule takes effect upon final adjournment unless committee's disapproval is sustained by legislature. The committee may approve a rule.
Alaska	★	. . .	(b)	Statute
Arizona	★	N.A.	N.A.	N.A.
Arkansas	★	. . .	. . .	. . .
California	. . .	★	★	. . .
Colorado	. . .	★	. . .	Rules that the General Assembly has determined should not be continued are listed as exceptions to the continuation.
Connecticut	. . .	★	. . .	Statute CGS 4-170 (d) and 4-171; see footnote (c)
Delaware	N.A.	N.A.	N.A.	N.A.
Florida	★	. . .	. . .	Statute
Georgia	. . .	★	. . .	Resolution (d)
Hawaii	★	. . .	. . .	. . .
Idaho	. . .	★	. . .	Concurrent resolution. All rules are terminated one year after adoption unless the legislature reauthorizes the rule.
Illinois	. . .	(e)	★(f)	(f)
Indiana	★	. . .	. . .	(g)
Iowa	. . .	. . .	(h)	E-mail legislation
Kansas	★	. . .	. . .	Statute
Kentucky	. . .	★	★	Enacting legislation to void.
Louisiana	. . .	★	(i)	Concurrent resolution to suspend, amend or repeal adopted rules or fees. For proposed rules and emergency rules, see footnote (i).
Maine	. . .	★	. . .	(j)
Maryland	★ (k)	. . .	. . .	. . .
Massachusetts	. . .	. . .	. . .	The legislature may pass a bill which would supersede a regulation if signed into law by the governor.
Michigan	. . .	. . .	(l)	Joint Committe on Rules has 15 session days to approve the filing of a notice of objection. The filing of the notice of objection starts another 15 day session period that stays the rules and causes committee members to introduce legislation in boht houses of the legislature for enactment and presentment to the governor. Any member of the legislature, pursuant to statute, can introduce a bill at a session, which in effect amends or rescinds a rule.
Minnesota	★	. . .	. . .	(m)
Mississippi	(n)			
Missouri	. . .	★	★	Concurrent resolution passed by both houses of the General Assembly.
Montana	. . .	. . .	★ (o)	Statute
Nebraska	★	★	. . .	. . .
Nevada	N.A.	★	★	Proposed regulations are either reviewed at the Legislative Commission's next regularly scheduled meeting (if the regulation is received more than three working days before the meeting), or they are referred to the Commission's Subcommittee to Review Regulations. If there is no objection to the regulation, then the Commission will "promptly" file the approved regulation with the Secretary of State. If the Commission or its subcommittee objects to a regulation, then the Commission will "promptly" return the regulation to the agency for revision. Within 60 days of receiving the written notice of objection to the regulation, the agency must revise the regulation and return it to the Legislative Counsel. If the Commission or its subcommittee objects to the revised regulation, the agency shall continue to revise and resubmit it to the Commission or subcommittee within 30 days after receiving the written notice of objection to the revised regulation.

See footnotes at end of table.

LEGISLATIVE REVIEW OF ADMINISTRATIVE RULES/REGULATIONS: POWERS — Continued

State or other jurisdiction	Reviewing committee's powers: Advisory powers only (a)	Reviewing committee's powers: No objection constitutes approval of proposed rule	Reviewing committee's powers: Committee may suspend rule	Legislative powers: Method of legislative veto of rules
New Hampshire	★	(q)	. . .	(r)
New Jersey	★	★	★	(s)
New Mexico	N.A.	N.A.	N.A.	No formal mechanism exists for legislative review of administrative rules.
New York	★	. . .	. . .	Reviewing commission's powers are advisory; it may, via its chair, introduce legislation with regard to agency rulemaking.
North Carolina	★	★	★	. . .
North Dakota	. . .	★(t)	. . .	The Administrative Rules Committee can void a rule.
Ohio	★	. . .	. . .	Concurrent resolution. Committee recommends to the General Assembly that a rule be invalidated. The General Assembly invalidates a rule through adoption of concurrent resolution.
Oklahoma	★	★ (p)	★(p)	The legislature may disapprove (veto) proposed rules by concurrent or joint resolution. A concurrent resolution does not require the governor's signature. Existing rules may be disapproved by joint resolution. A committe may not disapprove; only the full legislature may do so. Failure of the legislature to disapprove constitutes approval.
Oregon	★	★	★	. . .
Pennsylvania	. . .	★	★	Written or oral.
Rhode Island	(n)			
South Carolina	. . .	★	. . .	. . .
South Dakota	. . .	★	★	The Interim Rules Review Committee may, by statute, suspend rules that have not become effective yet by an affirmative vote of the majority of the committee.
Tennessee	. . .	. . .	★	Bill approved by Constitutional majority of both hoses declaring rule invalid.
Texas	★	. . .	. . .	N.A.
Utah	★	. . .	. . .	All rules must be reauthorized by the legislature annually. This is done by omnibus legislation, which also provides for the sunsetting of specific rules listed in the bill.
Vermont	(u)			Statute
Virginia	. . .	. . .	(v)	The General Assembly must pass a bill enacted into law to directly negate the administrative rule.
Washington	★	★	★	N.A.
West Virginia	★	. . .	. . .	(w)
Wisconsin	. . .	★	★	The standing committee in each house has 30 days to conduct its review for a proposed rule. If either objects the Joint Committee for the Review of Administrative Rules has 30 days to introduce legislation in each house overturning the rules. After 40 days the bills are placed on the calendar. If either bill passes, the rules are overturned. If they fail to pass, the rules go into effect.
Wyoming	★	★	. . .	Action must be taken by legislative order adopted by both houses before the end of the next succeeding legislative session to nullify a rule.
American Samoa				The enacting clause of all bills shall be: Be it by the Legislature of American Samoa, and no law shall be except by bill. Bills may originate in either house, and may be amended or rejected by the other. The Governor may submit proposed legislation to the Legislature for consideration by it. He may designate any such proposed legislation as urgent, if he so considers it.
Guam	N.A	N.A	N.A	Legislation to disapprove rules and regulations.
U.S. Virgin Islands	(n)			

See footnotes at end of table.

LEGISLATIVE REVIEW OF ADMINISTRATIVE RULES/REGULATIONS: POWERS—Continued

Source: The Council of State Governments' survey, January 2009.
Key:
★ — Yes
. . . — No
N.A. — Not applicable

(a) This column is defined by those legislatures or legislative committees that can only recommend changes to rules but have no power to enforce a change.

(b) Authorized, although constitutionally questionable.

(c) Disapproval of proposed regulations may be sustained, or reversed by action of the General Assembly in the ensuing session. The General Assembly may by resolution sustain or reverse a vote of disapproval.

(d) The reviewing committee must introduce a resolution to override a rule within the first 30 days of the next regular session of the General Assembly. If the resolution passes by less than a two-thirds majority of either house, the governor has final authority to affirm or veto the resolution.

(e) The Administrative Procedure Act is not clear on this point, but implies that the Joint Committee should either object or issue a statement of no objections.

(f) Joint Committee on Administrative Rules can send objections to issuing agency. If it does, the agency has 90 days from then to withdraw, change, or refuse to change the proposed regulations. If the Joint Committee determines that proposed regulations would seriously threaten the public good, it can block their adoption. Within 180 days the Joint Cmte., or both houses of the General Assembly, can "unblock" those regulations; if that does not happen, the regulations are dead.

(g) None—except by passing statute.

(h) Committee may delay rules.

(i) If the committee determines that a proposed rule is unacceptable, it submits a report to the governor who then has 10 days to accept or reject the report. If the governor rejects the report, the rule change may be adopted by the agency. If the governor accepts the report, the agency may not adopt the rule. Emergency rules become effective upon adoption or up to 60 days after adoption as provided in the rule, but a standing committee or governor may void the rule by finding it unacceptable within 2 to 61 days after adoption and reporting such finding to agency within four days.

(j) No veto allowed. Legislation must be enacted to prohibit agency from adopting objectionable rules.

(k) Except for emergency regulations which require committee approval for adoption.

(l) Committee can suspend rules during interim.

(m) The Legislative Commission to Review Administrative Rules (LCRAR) ceased operating, effective July 1, 1996. The Legislative Coordinating Commission (LCC) may review a proposed or adopted rule. Contact the LCC for more information. See Minn. Stat. 3.842, subd. 4a.

(n) No formal mechanism for legislative review of administrative rules. In Virginia, legislative review is optional.

(o) A rule disapproved by the reviewing committee is reinstated at the end of the next session if a joint resolution in the legislature fails to sustain committee action.

(p) Full legislature may suspend rules.

(q) Failure to object or approve within 45 days of agency filing of final proposal constitutes approval.

(r) The legislature may permanently block rules through legislation. The vote to sponsor a joint resolution suspends the adoption of a proposed rule for a limited time so that the full legislature may act on the resolution, which would then be subject to governor's veto and override.

(s) Article V, Section IV of the Constitution, as amended in 1992, says the legislature may review any rule or regulation to determine whether the rule or regulation is consistent with legislative intent. The legislature transmits its objections to existing or proposed rules or regulations to the governor and relevant agency via concurrent resolutions. The legislature may invalidate or prohibit an existing or proposed rule from taking effect by a majority vote of the authorized membership of each house.

(t) Unless formal objections are made or the rule is declared void, rules are considered approved.

(u) JLCAR may recommend that an agency amend or withdraw a proposal. A vote opposing rule does not prohibit its adoption but assigns the burden of proof in any legal challenge to the agency.

(v) Standing committees and the The Joint Commission on Administrative Rules may suspend the effective date of all or a part of a final regulation until the end of the next regular legislative session with the concurrence of the governor.

(w) State agencies have no power to promulgate rules without first submitting proposed rules to the legislature which must enact a statute authorizing the agency to promulgate the rule. If the legislature during a regular session disapproves all or part of any legislative rule, the agency may not issue the rule nor take action to implement all or part of the rule unless authorized to do so. However, the agency may resubmit the same or a similar proposed rule to the committee.

Table 3.27
SUMMARY OF SUNSET LEGISLATION

State	Scope	Preliminary evaluation conducted by	Other legislative review	Other oversight mechanisms in law	Phase-out period	Life of each agency (in years)	Other provisions
Alabama	C	Dept. of Examiners of Public Accounts	Standing Cmte.	Perf. audit	No later than Oct. 1 of the year following the regular session or a time as may be specified in the Sunset bill.	(Usually 4)	Schedules of licensing boards and other enumerated agencies are repealed according to specified time tables.
Alaska	C	Budget & Audit Cmte	. . .	. . .	1/y	. . .	. . .
Arizona	C	Legislative staff	Joint Cmte.	. . .	6/m	10	. . .
Arkansas	D	. . .	. . .	. . .	. . .	. . .	. . .
California	S	St. Legis. Sunset Review Cmte. (a)	. . .	Perf. eval.	. . .	Varies	. . .
Colorado	R	Dept. of Regulatory Agencies	Legis. Cmtes. of Reference	Bills need adoption by the legislature.	1/y	up to 15	State law provides certain criteria that are used to determine whether a public need exists for an entity or function to continue and that its regulation is the least restrictive regulation consistent with the public interest.
Connecticut	S	Legis. Program Review & Investigations Cmte.	. . .	Programs or entities must be afffimatively re-established by legislature.	1/y (b)	5 years	(c)
Delaware	C	Agencies under review submit reports to Del. Sunset Comm. based on criteria for review and set forth in statute. Comm. staff conducts separate review.	. . .	Perf. audit	Dec. 31 of next succeeding calendar year	4	Yearly sunset review schedules must include at least nine agencies. If the number automatically scheduled for review or added by the General Assembly is less than a full schedule, additional agencies shall be added in order of their appearance in the Del. Code to complete the review schedule.
Florida	C	Cmte. charged with oversight of the subject area.	Jt. cmte. charged with oversight of the subject area.	. . .	4–6/y	10	. . .
Georgia	R	Dept. of Audits	Standing Cmtes.	Perf. audit	. . .	. . .	A performance audit of each regulatory agency must be conducted upon the request of the Senate or House standing committee to which an agency has been assigned for oversight and review. (d)
Hawaii	R	Legis. Auditor	Standing Cmtes.	Perf. eval.	None	Established by the legislature	Schedules various professional and vocational licensing programs for repeal. Proposed new regulatory measures must be referred to the Auditor for sunrise analysis.
Idaho	(e)	. . .	. . .	. . .	. . .	. . .	. . .
Illinois	R,S(f)	Governor's Office of Mgmt. and Budget	Cmte. charged with re-enacting law	(g)	. . .	Usually 10	. . .

See footnotes at end of table.

SUMMARY OF SUNSET LEGISLATION—Continued

State	Scope	Preliminary evaluation conducted by	Other legislative review	Other oversight mechanisms in law	Phase-out period	Life of each agency (in years)	Other provisions
Indiana	S	Non-partisan staff units	Interim cmte. formed to review	. . .	. . .	. . .	Smaller program review process now in place after about a dozen years of formal sunset program.
Iowa		No Program					
Kansas	(h)	. . .	. . .	. . .	. . .	. . .	. . .
Kentucky	R	Administrative Regulation Review Subcommittee	Joint committee with subject matter jurisdiction.	. . .	. . .	. . .	. . .
Louisiana	C	Standing cmtes. of the two houses with subject matter jurisdiction.	. . .	Perf. eval.	1/y	Up to 6	Act provides for termination of a department and all offices in a department. Also permits committees to select particular agencies or offices for more extensive evaluation. Provides for review by Jt. Legis. Cmte. on Budget of programs that were not funded during the prior fiscal year for possible repeal.
Maine	S	Joint standing cmte. of jurisdiction.	Office of Program Evaluation & Government Accountability	None	. . .	Generally 10	. . .
Maryland	R	Dept. of Legislative Services	Standing Cmtes.	Perf. eval.	. . .	Varies (usually 10)	. . .
Massachusetts		No Program					
Michigan	(e)	. . .	. . .	. . .	. . .	. . .	. . .
Minnesota	S (e)	. . .	. . .	. . .	. . .	. . .	. . .
Mississippi	(i)	. . .	. . .	. . .	. . .	. . .	. . .
Missouri	R	Oversight Division of Cmte. on Legislative Research	. . .	. . .	. . .	6, not to exceed total of 12	. . .
Montana	(e)	. . .	. . .	. . .	. . .	. . .	. . .
Nebraska	D (e)(j)	. . .	. . .	. . .	. . .	. . .	. . .
Nevada	(e)	. . .	. . .	. . .	. . .	. . .	. . .
New Hampshire	(k)	. . .	. . .	. . .	. . .	. . .	. . .
New Jersey	(e)	. . .	. . .	. . .	. . .	. . .	. . .
New Mexico	S	Legis. Finance Cmte.	. . .	Public hearing before termination	1/y	6	.
New York	(e)	. . .	. . .	. . .	. . .	. . .	. . .
North Carolina	(l)	. . .	. . .	. . .	. . .	. . .	. . .
North Dakota		No Program					

See footnotes at end of table.

SUMMARY OF SUNSET LEGISLATION — Continued

State	Scope	Preliminary evaluation conducted by	Other legislative review	Other oversight mechanisms in law	Phase-out period	Life of each agency (in years)	Other provisions
Ohio	C (m)	Sunset Review Cmte.	. . .	Perf. eval.	(n)	4	. . .
Oklahoma	S, D	Jt. Cmtes. With jurisdiction over sunset bills	Appropriations and Budget Cmte.	. . .	1/y	6	. . .
Oregon	D (o)	. . .	(o)	Perf. eval.	1/y	. . .	. . .
Pennsylvania	R	Leadership Cmte.	. . .	. . .	. . .	varies	. . .
Rhode Island	(p)	. . .	No	. . .	. . .	. . .	. . .
South Carolina	(q)	. . .	. . .	. . .	. . .	. . .	. . .
South Dakota	(r)	. . .	. . .	. . .	. . .	. . .	. . .
Tennessee	C	Office of the Comptroller	Government Operations Committees	. . .	1/y	up to 6 years	. . .
Texas	S	Sunset Advisory Commission staff	. . .	. . .	1/y	12	. . .
Utah	S	Interim cmtes.	Standing cmtes. as amendments may be made to bill	. . .	(v)	(v)	. . .
Vermont	(s)	Legis. Council staff	Senate and House Government Operations Cmtes.	. . .	. . .	. . .	. . .
Virginia	S (e)	. . .	. . .	. . .	. . .	. . .	Sunset provisions vary in length. The only standard sunset required by law is on bills that create a new advisory board or commission in the executive branch of government. The legislation introduced for these boards and commisions must contain a sunset provision to expire the entity after three years.
Washington	D	. . .	. . .	Perf. Eval.	1/y	. . .	. . .
West Virginia	S	Jt. Cmte. on Govt. Operations	Performance Evaluation and Research Division	Perf. audit	1/y	6	Jt. Cmte. on Govt. Operations composed of five House members, five Senate members and five citizens appointed by governor. Agencies may be reviewed more frequently.
Wisconsin	(e)	. . .	. . .	. . .	. . .	. . .	. . .
Wyoming	D (t)	Program evaluation staff who work for Management Audit Cmte.	. . .	Perf. eval. (u)	. . .	. . .	. . .

See footnotes at end of table.

SUMMARY OF SUNSET LEGISLATION—Continued

Source: The Council of State Governments' survey, January 2009.

Key:

C - Comprehensive
R - Regulatory
S - Selective
D - Discretionary
d — day
m — month
y — year
. . . — Not applicable

(a) Review by the Jt. Legislative Sunset Review Cmte. of professional and vocational licensing boards terminated on January 1, 2004. Sunset clauses are included in other selected programs and legislation.

(b) Upon termination a program shall continue for one year to conclude its affairs.

(c) Since the sunset law was enacted in 1977, only one five-year cycle has been carried out. P.A. 01-160 enacted the last sunset postponement. Per that legislation, 28 entities or programs are scheduled for termination on July 1, 2008, the first year of a five-year cycle, unless affirmatively reestablished by the legislature. This termination date means that 28 entities or programs will be the subjects of PRI performance audits during calendar 2007 in order for the committee to meet its obligation under the Connecticut sunset law. H.B. 6997 is pending to postpone the sunset cycle until 2010 to allow for this study.

(d) The automatic sunsetting of an agency every six years was eliminated in 1992. The legislature must pass a bill in order to sunset a specific agency.

(e) While they have not enacted sunset legislation in the same sense as the other states with detailed information in this table, the legislatures in Idaho, Michigan, Minnesota, Montana, Nebraska, Nevada, New Jersey, New York, Virginia and Wisconsin have included sunset clauses in selected programs or legislation.

(f) Many tax laws provide that tax breaks enacted since 1994 will last only five years after taking effect unless the laws creating those breaks establish other sunset periods.

(g) Governor is to read GOMB report and make recommendations to the General Assembly every even-numbered year.

(h) Sunset legislation terminated July 1992. Legislative oversight of designated state agencies, consisting of audit, review and evaluation, continues.

(i) Sunset Act terminated December 31, 1984.

(j) Sunset legislation is discretionary, meaning that senators are free to offer sunset legislation or attach termination dates to legislative proposals. There is no formal sunset commission. Nebraska. Revised Statutes section 50-1303 directs the Legislature's Government, Military and Veteran's Committee to conduct an evaluation of any board, commission, or similar state entity. The review must include, among other things, a recommendation as to whether the board, commission, or entity should be terminated, continued or modified.

(k) New Hampshire's Sunset Committee was repealed July 1, 1986.

(l) North Carolina's sunset law terminated on July 30, 1981. Successor vehicle, the Legislative Committee on Agency Review, operated until June 30, 1983.

(m) There are statutory exceptions.

(n) Authority for latest review (HB 548 of the 123rd General Assembly) expired December 31, 2004. H.B. 516 of the 125 General Assembly re-established the Sunset Review Cmte, but postpones its operation until the 128th General Assembly. The bill terminates the Sunset Review Law on December 31, 2010.

(o) Sunset legislation was repealed in 1993.No general law sunsetting rules or agencies.

(p) No standing sunset statutes or procedures at this time.

(q) Law repealed by 1998 Act 419, Part II, Sect. 35E.

(r) South Dakota suspended sunset legislation in 1979. Under current law, the Executive Board of the Legislative Research Council is directed to establish one or more interim committees each year to review state agencies so that each state agency is reviewed once every ten years.

(s) Sunsets are at the legislature's discretion. Their structure will vary on an individual basis.

(t)Wyoming repealed sunset legislation in 1988.

(u) The program evaluation process evolved out of the sunset process, but Wyoming currently does not have a scheduled sunset of programs.

(v) Default is ten years, although years may be decreased by legislative decisions.

Chapter Four

STATE EXECUTIVE BRANCH

The State of the States: Governors Mirror New Administration Priorities

By Katherine Willoughby

The full force of the fiscal tsunami has been felt by all 50 states. Governors are weary of the bad news and anxious about keeping state offices open, programs operating and support flowing to the public. Governors apprise residents in their states about their budget and policy direction each year through state of state addresses. This research assesses the 2009 addresses to determine the focus of state leaders' agendas in this down economy.[1] *Findings indicate that governors talked explicitly with citizens about managing; their mood is somber, sometimes even angry. Still, these state leaders are surprisingly hopeful of the role states play in the everyday life of Americans. Most governors remained on task by providing the public with plans and ideas for expanding education and economic opportunities, and supporting healthy, safe and environmentally sound communities. A majority of governors even discussed advancements necessary regarding government accountability and responsiveness while close to one-third emphasized the need for greater transparency—issues that have been specifically targeted by the new administration in Washington.*

The Politics

The majority of governors' seats are held by Democrats in 2009—29 governors are Democratic and 21 are Republican. The 2008 gubernatorial elections yielded a party change only in Missouri, from one-term Republican Matt Blunt to Democrat Jay Nixon. In Delaware, Democrat Jack Markell beat the Republican challenger and replaced Democrat Ruth Ann Minner, whose second term ended this year. In North Carolina, Democrat Beverly Perdue beat her Republican challenger to replace Mike Easley, who also completed his second term. Incumbent Democrat governors in Montana, New Hampshire, Washington and West Virginia were re-elected in 2008, while incumbent Republican governors in Indiana, North Dakota, Utah and Vermont were re-elected to the top spot in those states.

The election of President Barack Obama and the majority Democratic Congress undoubtedly pushed state legislatures to Democrat majorities as well. Today, both houses of the legislature are majority Democratic in 27 states, up from 23 in 2008; in 14 states both houses are majority Republican. Eight states have split legislatures in which the house and senate have different party majorities, down from a dozen states last year. Democrats gained three state houses from last year—33 state houses are majority Democratic and 16 are majority Republican. On the senate side, Democrats gained two states—29 are majority Democratic and 20 are majority Republican in 2009. (Nebraska has a unicameral, nonpartisan legislature.) Seventeen states can be labeled Democratic with a Democratic governor and majority Democratic legislature; eight states are Republican. The states break down in terms of party control accordingly:

- Eight with Republican governor and legislature
- One with Republican governor and unicameral legislature
- Two with Republican governor and split legislature
- 10 with Republican governor and Democratic legislature
- Six with Democratic governor and Republican legislature
- Six with Democratic governor and split legislature
- 17 with Democratic governor and legislature

The Fiscal Picture

In the recent past, states had begun to crawl out of the economic decline of 2002 and 2003. In fact, by 2006, most states increased funding for existing programs beyond inflationary amounts, created new programs, replenished budget stabilization or other contingency funds, lent increased support to local governments and many even increased pension contributions and cut taxes.[2] Unfortunately, however, by 2008, the entire nation's economy was beginning a free fall. And, according to McNichol and Lav, the

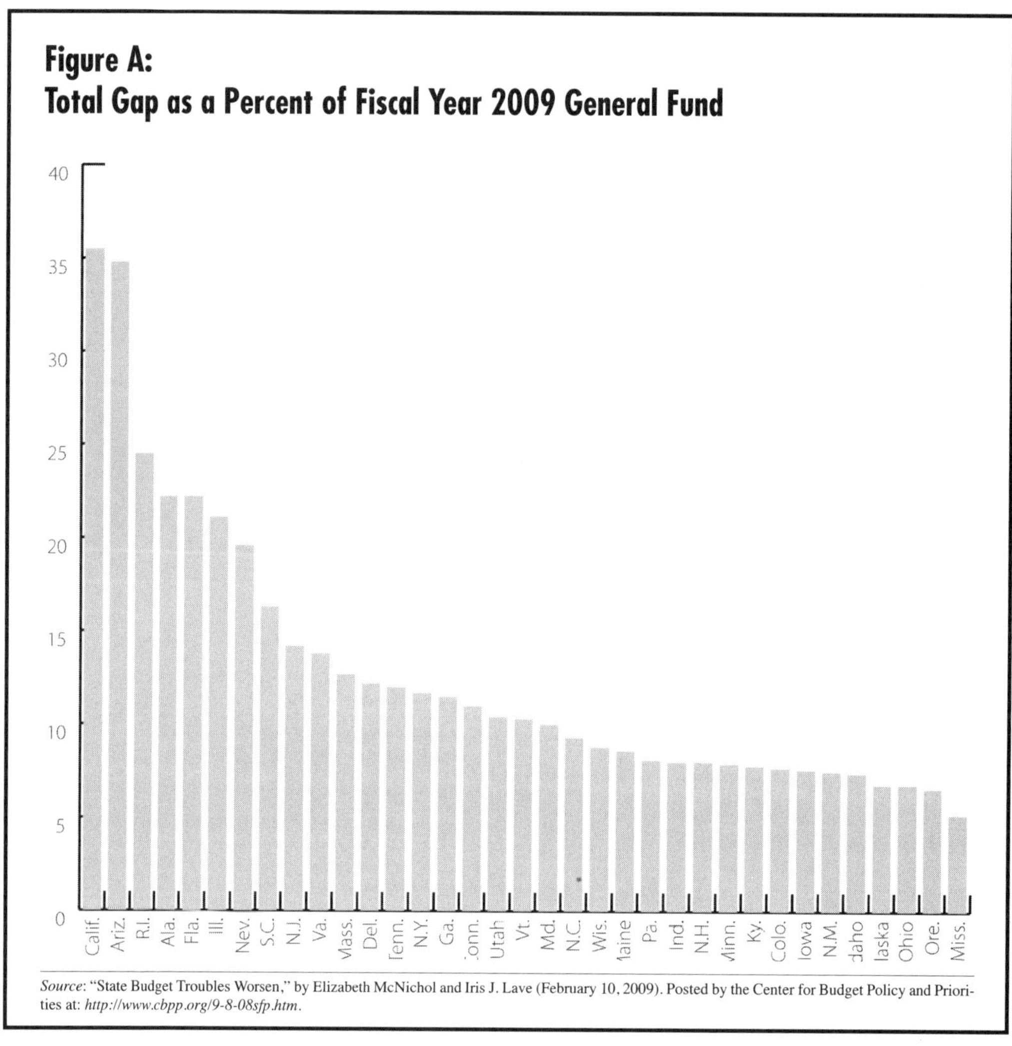

Figure A:
Total Gap as a Percent of Fiscal Year 2009 General Fund

Source: "State Budget Troubles Worsen," by Elizabeth McNichol and Iris J. Lave (February 10, 2009). Posted by the Center for Budget Policy and Priorities at: *http://www.cbpp.org/9-8-08sfp.htm*.

total state budget shortfall for 2009 is expected to close in on $100 billion. Estimated shortfalls for 2010 equal $145 billion and for 2011 state budget gaps are estimated at $180 billion. Figure A illustrates McNichol and Lav's tabulation of shortfalls greater than 5 percent in 2009 general fund budgets in 35 states. According to the authors, nine other states have total gaps under 5 percent of each state's fiscal 2009 general fund. Just six states—Montana, Nebraska, North Dakota, Texas, West Virginia and Wyoming—do not indicate a current year gap.[3] The revenue outlook is bleak; 28 percent of states have increased taxes and, according to a Center for Budget and Policy Priorities report, "governors in six more states have proposed new revenue measures."[4] Fiscal 2009 state budgets are being revisited, programs are being sliced and then cut again; to date, state programs and activities across the nation have been severely compromised. In the words of Connecticut Gov. Jodi Rell, "the cuts that must be made will be deep and they will affect every agency, every program and every service provided by state government."

What's on the Agenda?

Governors last year held "kitchen table" conversations with residents, keeping their budget and policy agendas short, not wanting to overreach with spending promises in the face of a deteriorating economy. This year, governors are even more direct with the bad news. "This fiscal year will be marked

Table A: Issues Expressed by Governors in State of the State Addresses, 2007–2009

Issue expressed by governors	*2007 percentage of governors mentioning issue (N=43)*	*2008 percentage of governors mentioning issue (N=42)*	*2009 percentage of governors mentioning issue (N=44)*
Education	100.0%	90.5%	86.4%
Economic development/tourism	79.5	81.0	79.5
Health care	86.4	83.3	79.5
Natural resources/energy	84.1	71.4	79.5
Tax/revenue initiative	84.1	59.5	65.9
Transportation/roads/bridges	52.3	59.5	65.9
Military troops/veteran recognition	68.2	73.8	63.6
Performace/accountability	72.7	42.9	52.3
Safety/corrections	75.0	59.5	50.0
Surplus/rainy day/reserves	70.5	54.8	45.5
Transparency	20.5	14.3	31.8
Local government	52.3	35.7	20.5
Pensions/OPEB	36.4	21.4	18.2
Ethics reform	13.6	11.9	15.9
Borders/illegal immigrants	11.4	16.7	6.8
Debt reduction	13.6	9.5	4.5

Source: Content analysis of 2007 and 2008 State of the State Addresses from Table C of Katherine G. Willoughby, 2008, "The State of the States: Governors Keep Agendas Short," *The Book of the States*, Vol. 40 (Lexington, KY: The Council of State Governments): 157–64; Content analysis of 2009 State of State Addresses conducted by Tanya Smilley and Soyoung Park, Ph.D. candidates, Public Policy, Andrew Young School of Policy Studies, Georgia State University, Atlanta, Georgia.

by thrift and sacrifice," said Oklahoma Gov. Brad Henry. Vermont Gov. Jim Douglas concurs that "The philosophy of sharing the sacrifice broadly must be part of any proposal we advance."

In the analysis of the content of governors' state of state addresses this year, as in the past, topics were considered addressed if the chief executive specifically discussed them as relevant to state operations and the budget *going forward*. That is, the governor needed to relay that the function, activity or issue is an important item in next year's—fiscal 2010—budget and policy direction. More often than not, the governor laid out relevant funding and/or programmatic issues related to the state function and/or agenda item in some detail. That is, just mentioning a state function or policy area like transportation in a speech did not generate a checkmark for this issue as an agenda item addressed by a governor. Further, a review by the governor of past accomplishments alone in any particular issue area did not count in the content analysis presented here. The only deviation from this protocol regards mention by a governor of military troops, family and veterans. A governor recognizing service on the part of these individuals and/or indicating thanks for this service, with or without recommending some future support to such personnel, received a check for this issue in Table A. In 2009, just slightly less than two-thirds of governors—10 percent less than the proportion of governors last year—recognize their military service personnel and/or veterans in state of state addresses to their residents.

Examination of governors' addresses in 2007, 2008 and 2009 suggests that as the economy worsened, state chief executives' consideration of the various issues did change. While primary agenda items remain education, health care, economic development, and natural resources and energy, gubernatorial mention of issues differed across years. Not surprisingly, given the political swing of the nation and states, Table A indicates that state chief executives honed in on issues important to the new administration in Washington, D.C. That is, a smaller percentage of governors than last year presented their concerns and initiatives regarding all state functional areas, except natural resources and energy, and transportation, roads and bridges. In line with President Obama's focus on green energy and capital investment—both to upgrade the nation's deteriorating transportation infrastructure as well as to pump up the economy—governors were more likely this year than last to specify initiatives in these areas. This research highlights the gubernatorial discussions of those topics receiving more attention this year than last year—including taxes and revenues, natural resources and energy, transportation, and performance, transparency and ethics.

Tax and Revenue Initiatives

The increased attention to revenues and tax issues by governors this year is not unusual. Perhaps no governor was more direct about his state's money problems than California Gov. Arnold Schwarzenegger. He held his state of state address to less than 10 minutes with a plea for collaboration and consensus within the legislature and across branches *before* he would deliver his budget and policy agenda to the state. Rather, according to the governor, "Addressing this emergency is the first and most important and greatest thing that we must do for the people of California. The $42 billion deficit is a rock upon our chest that we cannot breathe until we get it off. It doesn't make any sense for me to ... stand in front of you and talk about education or infrastructure, or water, or health care reform and all those things when we have this huge budget deficit."

Other governors discussing revenues in their addresses in 2009 called for holding steady on taxes (no increases), cutting taxes or expanding tax credits, or asked for new or changed dedicated revenues (such as highway taxes and fees), or recommended increases to tobacco taxes. Governors in Alabama, Arizona, Indiana, Iowa, Kansas, Missouri, Montana, Nebraska, Nevada, New Mexico, South Dakota and Vermont pushed for no tax increases. Those in Arkansas, Massachusetts, Minnesota, New York, North Dakota and Montana called for some sort of tax cut or cap (property taxes) or the elimination of a tax. For example, Montana Gov. Brian Schweitzer called for doing away with the business equipment tax for 90 percent of businesses in the state. Governors in Minnesota, New Jersey and Ohio discussed new and/or expanded tax credits. Finally, Nebraska's governor asserted both no tax increases and maintenance of the state's cash reserve. Gov. Dave Heineman said Nebraskans need tax relief and his budget continues to fund a $230 million property tax credit program, and he planned for zero revenue growth in fiscal 2010. The governor considers the state's cash reserve as a method for preventing tax increases; he plans on maintaining a strong reserve while using $40 million of the fund annually over the next two years.

Of governors pushing tax increases, most endorsed either increased or new earmarked revenues like highway and transportation related taxes and fees (Hawaii and Idaho) or increased taxes on tobacco products (Kentucky, New Hampshire, Pennsylvania, South Carolina, Virginia and West Virginia). Pennsylvania Gov. Ed Rendell asked for a tax on natural gas extraction, and South Carolina Gov. Mark Sanford called for increased taxes and fees associated with garbage (dumping within state borders) in addition to an increase in tobacco taxes. As a way to more strongly support local governments, Wyoming Gov. Dave Freudenthal asked residents to support elimination of the state's "sales and use tax exemption on wind energy projects. I've heard from any number of county commissioners that they are dealing with the impact of the development of wind energy, and they have no revenue. I acknowledge that it is appropriate for me to ask because I asked you (for) the exemption in the first place. And we did that because we wanted to signal that Wyoming is ready for business, particularly with regard to wind energy."

Natural Resources and Energy

A larger proportion of governors this year than last discussed natural resources and energy issues in their state of state addresses. Most governors sought to link into President Obama's push for conservation, the development of renewable and clean energy and to wean Americans from dependence on foreign oil, as evidenced in his stimulus package and budget proposals. Some governors were explicit, including Colorado Gov. Bill Ritter who said, "I'm working with our congressional delegation and the incoming Obama administration to ensure the federal recovery package includes funds for transmission lines and other clean-energy projects."

State chief executives presented numerous ideas for advancing "green" living. Several talked of their support for requirements regarding the construction of new homes, schools and/or state buildings that include using green products and that upon completion, they be energy efficient and/or supported with renewable energy sources. Many also suggested that state equipment be energy efficient. Others suggested creation of financing arms that would support both residential and business green projects. Some governors promoted green, tax free zones to boost renewable energy job creation. Several highlighted development and/or promotion of hybrid vehicles and/or the development of energy storage technologies.

Many governors discussed specific alternative energy sources including: solar, wind, offshore wind, wave, ethanol and biofuels. Kentucky Gov. Steve Beshear discussed advances in nuclear power. State leaders in Michigan, Oklahoma, New York, South Dakota, Virginia and West Virginia presented specific timelines and percentages for the reduction in the use of traditional energy by state employees or by the state entirely. Hawaii Gov. Linda Lingle explained a complex web of stakeholder support necessary to reduce her state's reliance on foreign oil:

"Last year we entered into a unique partnership with the federal Department of Energy called the Hawaii Clean Energy Initiative or HCEI. My administration and legislators will introduce several bills based on these HCEI recommendations. Implementing these policy changes will require a large measure of collaboration as we will need public funding, assistance from county governments, conservation by citizens, and investment by the business community. To successfully transition to a clean energy economy, we will need the involvement of our entire community, alignment of our efforts, and a continual focus on our objectives."

Likewise, Virginia Gov. Tim Kaine stated, "We will act by budget and legislation, but also through regulation, executive orders, creative partnerships and multi-state collaborations" (to promote green energy, energy conservation and environmental protection). Governors in Michigan, New Mexico, South Dakota and West Virginia laid out fairly comprehensive energy plans, too. For example, Michigan Gov. Jennifer Granholm asserted, "By the year 2020, Michigan will reduce our reliance on fossil fuels for generating electricity by 45 percent. We will do it through increased renewable energy, gains in energy efficiency and other new technologies." In New Mexico, Gov. Bill Richardson presented his plan for energy as including the following:

- make larger solar and geothermal energy providers eligible for the Advanced Energy Tax Credit;
- build a clean energy work force;
- construct a Green Grid to harness the power of solar and wind, and use smart electronics to deliver energy to consumers cheaper and more efficiently;
- pass the New Mexico Global Warming Solutions Act to start carbon trading in the region;
- extend the hybrid vehicle tax credit, and help keep fuel-efficient cars and trucks affordable;
- pursue a carbon storage enabling act, because before we move forward on clean coal or natural gas, we need a clear regulatory framework; and
- expand parks with creation of a new Pecos Canyon State Park.

Finally, South Dakota Gov. Mike Rounds presented a very detailed plan in which state government would change equipment and behaviors internal to state government to initiate energy savings—temperature controls, energy efficient vehicles, cleaning schedules, energy purchases, building materials and more would all be subjected to new requirements to foster less use of energy and a greater proportion of that used to be green.

He recommended an Energy Conservation Revolving Loan Fund to provide "low interest loans continually to schools, cities, counties, universities, tech schools and state agencies that have developed good ways to save tax dollars by becoming more energy efficient."

His plan also called for a reduction in the tax on biodiesel-blended fuel, an increase in wind energy production and requirements regarding the construction and operation of future power plants.

Several governors specified policy to influence behaviors in order to bring about more responsible use of energy. For example, in West Virginia, Gov. Joe Manchin III said, "My alternative and renewable energy bill will also require electric utility companies to provide net metering to residential, small business and industrial customers who generate their own electricity. This bill also requires the Public Service Commission to expand the availability of net metering to West Virginia electric customers. It will encourage private investment in renewable energy sources, including solar, wind, biomass, hydropower, waste heat recovery and even landfill gas. It is another step toward expanding our state's energy portfolio."

Transportation, Road and Bridges

On the whole, governors' plans regarding transportation, roads and bridges were not as thorough or comprehensive as those laid out for education, economic development, natural resources and energy. Most governors mentioning these issues brought up a past initiative not yet completed with an update on project progress going forward. Governors did seem to emphasize the link between financial support for transportation-related infrastructure, job creation and economic growth. That is, many mimicked President Obama regarding the usefulness of funding this government function both to modernize capital and to pump the economy. For example, in Pennsylvania, Rendell said, "the key to recovery lies in putting our citizens back to work through continued infrastructure investments, including the ongoing efforts to repair our bridges, roads and mass transit systems, improve our water quality and delivery systems, and expand our rail freight capacity." Rendell exclaimed that "public sector driven capital investment is clearly the best option we have these days for keeping Pennsylvanians employed." Likewise, Rhode Island Gov. Don Carcieri explained that investment in infrastructure promotes economic growth in the state. In Washington, Gov. Christine Gregoire was very positive, saying:

"My 'Washington Jobs Now' plan will stretch over the next two years — even as we undertake the largest transportation construction cycle in state history! We now have 1,400 transportation projects under way, or about to start, worth $3 billion. By combining this historic transportation package with my 'Washington Jobs Now' plan, we will provide nearly 20,000 jobs in the next two years."

Claiming transportation in the state as "intolerable," Hawaii's governor proposed, with legislators, a highway modernization program that "combines road building, highway and bridge safety improvements, anti-congestion traffic management, and a pavement maintenance program, in addition to safety legislation and increased public outreach and education." According to Lingle, the project will be supported with "existing funds and anticipated federal fiscal stimulus funding" with "longer-term projects paid for from increases in highway-related taxes and fees triggered at a future date if steady job growth indicates that our economy is growing again."

Other governors expressed some enthusiasm for expansion and advancement in this area of state function, including Maryland Gov. Martin O'Malley who exclaimed that, "perhaps best of all, we now have a new president who believes that America's transportation future is worth the investment." In North Dakota, Gov. John Hoeven discussed one time transportation related investments "to support projects statewide that will strengthen and enhance North Dakota's roads, bridges and water supply systems." Nevada Gov. Jim Gibbons called on the state legislature to support infrastructure building that does not require raising taxes, perhaps by endorsing public-private partnerships. According to Oregon Gov. Ted Kulongoski, "We will invest in the most green, sustainable, multi-modal, energy-efficient transportation system in the country." And in Ohio, Gov. Ted Strickland was positive about the state's transportation future. "We will work toward the restoration of passenger rail service between Cincinnati, Columbus and Cleveland," he said. "Our goal is to link Ohio's three largest cities by passenger rail for the first time in 40 years. This will be a first step toward a rail system that links neighborhoods within a city, and cities within our state."

Several governors provided detailed plans for managing transportation funds and projects in the current climate and into the future. New Hampshire Gov. John Lynch discussed the state's turnpike system purchase of a portion of Interstate 95, future open tolling on this interstate, a new E-Z pass, frequent user discount, a road improvement surcharge on vehicle registration, and federal transportation stimulus funds as the means with which the state will manage future transportation investment. On the other hand, Virginia Gov. Tim Kaine was very specific about cuts in transportation to support future initiatives:

"Our transportation agencies are reducing their administrative overhead to preserve scarce dollars for maintenance and construction. To balance its budget, VDOT will reduce central office staff and streamline operations around the state. Over the next two years, VDOT will reduce agency employment by about 1,000 employees, through retirements, attrition, and other restructuring. The Commonwealth Transportation Board has rewritten the six year construction plan to reflect the new, reduced financial projections, and the results are startling. Without a long-term commitment from the legislature to support transportation funding, and with a slump in existing revenue sources, dozens of road and bridge projects all across the Commonwealth have been taken out of the plan."

In South Dakota, Rounds was optimistic about meeting the state's future transportation needs, though he emphasized that "I have been taking steps now to ensure that South Dakota continues to maximize the dollars we receive from Washington under the current program. We will also work hard to ensure that rural states like South Dakota are well represented when Congress begins drafting a new highway funding program." Rounds did talk about reductions, delays and other measures to allow the state to manage transportation infrastructure needs into the future. Idaho Gov. Butch Otter mapped a three-point plan for transportation called Project 60 that has additional reporting requirements, recommends some tax and fee increases, a new excise tax on car rentals, elimination of the ethanol exemption from the fuel tax and shifting revenue to better support roads and bridges. Finally, the plan establishes "a task force on truck transportation to study the validity of—and perceived inequities in—Idaho's truck registration system." In Colorado, Ritter has been building support for a bill to "establish a new transportation vision for the future, a vision that creates jobs, a vision we can implement in stages, and a vision that's both bold and realistic about what we can afford."

Performance, Accountability and Transparency

President Barack Obama pledged to make the federal government more accountable, more transparent and more responsive to the American public. Toward that pledge, he quickly created a position for the nation's first chief performance officer and made an appointment shortly prior to his inauguration. He tasked this officer with ferreting out government waste and inefficiency, improving service delivery and advancing the public's trust and confidence in government. Although his choice, Nancy Killefer, stepped down within a month of her appointment in the face of unpaid taxes on household help, his message came through and undoubtedly influenced the governors in their 2009 state of state addresses. In fact, mention of performance and accountability by governors increased by almost 9.5 percent from 2008 to 2009. Governors' discussions about ethics increased by 4 percent. And, talk of transparency by governors increased the most of any of the issues listed in Table A, by 17.5 percent.

Indiana Gov. Mitch Daniels presented reform front and center in his state of state address:

"The largest and most momentous of our opportunities lies in the area of governmental reform. The cost in dollars, confusion and just plain bad government of our 150-year-old system is by now completely beyond dispute. The report so ably researched and written by former Governor Joe Kernan, Chief Justice Shepard, and five other outstanding citizens lays out the folly of too many politicians, too many layers, too many taxing units, all producing too little accountability and too few results. If there is anyone present who, given a blank slate, would draw up our system just as it is, please stand up now. I thought not. As intended at the outset, we have all had a full year to study the report and meditate on its recommendations. The public has spoken loudly, in referenda, in opinion surveys, and in the most recent general election, each time in clear favor of change. The hour for action has arrived."

Many governors expressing interest in these areas pushed Web connections and greater online presence by agencies and programs as a means to help government become more responsive, accountable and transparent. Consolidation, organizational restructuring and privatization were also mentioned by governors to streamline service delivery. In South Carolina, Sanford suggested state government be restructured to reduce the number of constitutionally elected officers. West Virginia's Manchin called for a modernization of the state court system. In New Hampshire, Gov. John Lynch proposed "sunsetting all commissions, committees and non-regulatory boards by the end of fiscal year 2011. We should then only re-enact those that are essential." Lynch called for consolidating licensing boards and commissions into state departments; a four-day work week for cleaning crews of state buildings; an expansion of electronic licensing and registrations; and, extending driver's licenses to 10 years as other efficiency measures.

Governors in Montana, Nevada, New Hampshire and Missouri called for greater efficiency in state operations through temporary salary cuts, salary freezes, personnel cuts, lapsing vacancies and/or increasing agency reporting requirements. Iowa Gov. Chet Culver suggested exploring the sale or lease of state assets, consolidation of state contracts and group purchasing agreements. In Idaho, Otter mentioned the state's zero-based budgeting system and the additional reporting and oversight requirements that highlight the relationship between funding and results in transportation as providing greater accountability to citizens.

Ethical concerns of governors were focused on campaign finance reform, reducing voter fraud, early voting processes and same day voter registration. Alabama Gov. Bob Riley plans to overhaul his state's ethics, including full disclosure of real and potential conflicts of interest of public officials and their spouses; full disclosure by lobbyists of spending on elected officials; and an ethics commission with subpoena power "to carry out its mission." Governors in Massachusetts and New Mexico called for ethics reform as well. In Utah, Gov. Jon Huntsman explained the purpose of a new "Commission on Strengthening Utah's Democracy, because without public support and participation we have no democracy." Arizona Gov. Janet Napolitano, who was later confirmed as secretary of the U.S. Department of Homeland Security, sought changes to the state's referendum and initiative processes—to support balance of power and to protect "the ability of the people to enact legislation." Napolitano also pushed efficiency and accountability by Arizona's 2-1-1 online component "which connects Arizonans with opportunities to serve. Arizonans can now go to AZ211.gov to donate resources or volunteer time to their communities and their state." Greater use of volunteers was endorsed by New York Gov. David Paterson, too.

Conclusion

Governors talked about a lot more than taxes, energy, transportation and performance in their state of state addresses this year. Table A shows most governors mentioned agendas related to—and sometimes even laid out elaborate plans to support and/or expand—education and health services, promote economic development and address public safety. It is interesting to note, however, that since last year, a greater proportion of governors addressed issues of immediate concern to President Obama, notably government performance and transparency and more specifically, transportation and infrastructure, and energy dependence. Also, examination of these discussions by state leaders indicates that a poor economy does not necessarily mean an across-the-board shutdown of operations, lack of innovation or loss of hope. Certainly, state of state addresses can be characterized as "pie in the sky"—they provide governors the bully pulpit to orient the public to a way of thinking about government presence and service. Still, assessment of these addresses reveals state leaders who, for the most part, are thinking holistically, realistically and yes, politically, about ways to keep state operations going and going in ways that are more responsive, better performing and transparent.

Notes

[1]Chief executives of state governments report annually or biennially to their legislatures regarding the fiscal condition of their state, commonwealth or territory. Governors often use their address to lay out their policy and budget agendas for their upcoming or continuing administration. The 2009 state of the state addresses were accessed from January through February 27, 2009 at *www.stateline.org*, *www.nga.org*, or at the state government homepage. This research considers those 44 states with transcripts available at this site as of February 27, 2009. Speeches not available by this date included those from Delaware, Florida, Illinois, Louisiana, Maine and North Carolina. All quotes and data presented here are from the addresses accessed on these websites, unless otherwise noted.

[2]Katherine Willoughby. "The State of the States: Governors Keep Agendas Short," in Keon Chi, ed. *The Book of the States*. Vol. 40 (Lexington, KY: Council of State Governments), 2008: 157 and Katherine Willoughby, (forthcoming). "Reaching and Maintaining Structural Balance: Leaders in the States," in *State and Local Fiscal Policy: Thinking Outside the Box?* Edward Elgar Press.

[3]Elizabeth C. McNichol, and Iris J. Lav, 2009. "State budget troubles worsen." Report available at Center for Budget and Policy Priorities (2009), *http://www.cbpp.org/9-8-08sfp.htm*.

[4]Nicholas Johnson, Phil Oliff and Jeremy Koulish. "Facing deficits, at least 40 states are imposing or planning cuts that hurt vulnerable residents," (2009). Report available at Center for Budget and Policy Priorities, *http://www.cbpp.org/3-13-08sfp.htm*.

About the Author

Katherine Willoughby is professor of public management and policy in the Andrew Young School of Policy Studies at Georgia State University in Atlanta. Her research concentrates on state and local government budgeting and financial management, public policy development and public organization theory. She has conducted extensive research in the area of state budgeting practices, with a concentration on performance measurement applicability at this level of government in the United States.

Gubernatorial Elections, Campaign Costs and Powers

By Thad Beyle

The 11 gubernatorial elections that took place in 2008 increased the Democratic to Republican governors' ratio to 29-to-21, but returned to the previous 28-22 ratio when former Arizona Gov. Janet Napolitano resigned in January after she was confirmed as the new secretary of Homeland Security in President Obama's cabinet. The cost of running for governor continues to be expensive. After several years of no forced gubernatorial exits from office, in March 2008 then-New York Gov. Eliot Spitzer resigned from office after he was linked to a prostitution ring. Then in January 2009 former Illinois Gov. Rod Blagojevich was impeached, convicted and removed from office.

Governors continue to be in the forefront of activity into the 21st century. With Republican governors across the country serving as his major supporters and guides, Texas Gov. George W. Bush sought and won the presidency in the 2000 election. He became the fourth of five presidents who had served as governor just prior to seeking and winning the presidency since the mid-1970s.[1]

But in 2008, another pattern re-emerged as first-term U.S. Sen. Barack Obama of Illinois won the Democratic nomination and then the general election for president. In selecting his cabinet, Obama turned to several governors to join him in major roles in Washington. Former Arizona Gov. Janet Napolitano was selected to become secretary of the U.S. Department of Homeland Security, and New Mexico Gov. Bill Richardson was selected to become the Secretary of the U.S. Department of Commerce. Napolitano was confirmed as Homeland Security secretary Jan. 21, and she resigned as governor and moved to Washington to take on this role. In early January, Richardson withdrew his name as a nominee as details surfaced surrounding a federal investigation into a state-level decision made to hire a particular consulting firm whose leader had made considerable contributions to his political campaigns. Richardson will remain as governor rather than move to Obama's administration. Another governor, Virginia Gov. Tim Kaine, was selected as national chairman of the Democratic Party, a role he can fill while serving out the last year of his single term allowed by Virginia law. Finally, on March 2, Obama selected Kansas Gov. Kathleen Seblius to serve as his secretary of Health and Human Services. She was confirmed April 28, 2009 and resigned the governorship. Fellow Democrat, Lt. Gov. Mark Parkinson was immediately sworn in.

However, the demands on the governors to propose state budgets and then keep them in balance during recent recessions—and in the current economic downturn—have made the governor's chair a hot seat in more ways than one. With no clear projections on just how long and deep the current recession will be, the 2009 and 2010 fiscal years look to be very difficult for state leaders. They face increasing demands for program services and support from those hurt by the economic decline, yet also face the continuing slide in tax and other revenues due to the economic decline.

2008 Gubernatorial Politics

The election cycle for governors has settled into a regular pattern. Over the past few decades, many states moved their elections to the off-presidential years in order to decouple the state and national campaigns. Now, only 11 states hold their gubernatorial elections in the same year as a presidential election. Two of these states—New Hampshire and Vermont—still have two-year terms for their governors, which means their elections alternate between presidential and non-presidential years.

Table A shows that in the year following a presidential election only two states have gubernatorial elections.[2] In the even years between presidential elections, 36 states hold their gubernatorial elections. In the year before a presidential election, three Southern states hold their gubernatorial elections.[3]

In the 2008 gubernatorial elections, eight incumbent governors sought re-election while three incumbents did not. All the incumbent governors seeking re-election won another term. Two of the three—former Delaware Gov. Ruth Ann Minner and former North Carolina Gov. Michael Easley—did not seek re-election because both were term-limited and had served the allowed two terms. Missouri Gov. Matt Blunt decided not to seek a second term following indications he would not be successful. For example, his positive job approval ratings in state-level polls in the early months of 2008 were in the low 40 per-

Table A: Gubernatorial Elections: 1970–2008

				Number of incumbent governors									
		Democratic winner		*Eligible to run*		*Actually ran*		*Won*		*Lost*			
Year	*Number of races*	*Number*	*Percent*	*Number*	*Percent*	*Number*	*Percent*	*Number*	*Percent*	*Number*	*Percent*	*In primary*	*In general election*
1970	35	22	63	29	83	24	83	16	64	8	36	1 (a)	7 (b)
1971	3	3	100	0	. . .	. . .	. . .	. . .	. . .	. . .	. . .	. . .	. . .
1972	18	11	61	15	83	11	73	7	64	4	36	2 (c)	2 (d)
1973	2	1	50	1	50	1	100	. . .	. . .	1	100	1 (e)	. . .
1974	35	27 (f)	77	29	83	22	76	17	77	5	24	1 (g)	4 (h)
1975	3	3	100	2	66	2	100	2	100	. . .	. . .	. . .	. . .
1976	14	9	64	12	86	8	67	5	63	3	33	1 (i)	2 (j)
1977	2	1	50	1	50	1	100	1	100	. . .	. . .	. . .	. . .
1978	36	21	58	29	81	23	79	16	73	7	30	2 (k)	5 (l)
1979	3	2	67	0	. . .	. . .	. . .	. . .	. . .	. . .	. . .	. . .	. . .
1980	13	6	46	12	92	12	100	7	58	5	42	2 (m)	3 (n)
1981	2	1	50	0	. . .	. . .	. . .	. . .	. . .	. . .	. . .	. . .	. . .
1982	36	27	75	33	92	25	76	19	76	6	24	1 (o)	5 (p)
1983	3	3	100	1	33	1	100	. . .	. . .	1	100	1 (q)	. . .
1984	13	5	38	9	69	6	67	4	67	2	33	. . .	2 (r)
1985	2	1	50	1	50	1	100	1	100	. . .	. . .	. . .	. . .
1986	36	19	53	24	67	18	75	15	83	3	18	1 (s)	2 (t)
1987	3	3	100	2	67	1	50	. . .	. . .	1	100	1 (u)	. . .
1988	12	5	42	9	75	9	100	8	89	1	11	. . .	1 (v)
1989	2	2	100	0	. . .	. . .	. . .	. . .	. . .	. . .	. . .	. . .	. . .
1990	36	19 (w)	53	33	92	23	70	17	74	6	26	. . .	6 (x)
1991	3	2	67	2	67	2	100	. . .	. . .	2	100	1 (y)	1 (z)
1992	12	8	67	9	75	4	44	4	100	. . .	. . .	. . .	. . .
1993	2	0	0	1	50	1	100	. . .	. . .	1	100	. . .	1 (aa)
1994	36	11 (bb)	31	30	83	23	77	17	74	6	26	2 (cc)	4 (dd)
1995	3	1	33	2	67	1	50	1	100	. . .	. . .	. . .	. . .
1996	11	7	64	9	82	7	78	7	100	. . .	. . .	. . .	. . .
1997	2	0	0	1	50	1	100	1	100	. . .	. . .	. . .	. . .
1998	36	11 (ee)	31	27	75	25	93	23	92	2	8	. . .	2 (ff)
1999	3	2	67	2	67	2	100	2	100	. . .	. . .	. . .	. . .
2000	11	8	73	7	88	6	86	5	83	1	17	. . .	1 (gg)
2001	2	2	100	0	. . .	. . .	. . .	. . .	. . .	. . .	. . .	. . .	. . .
2002	36	14	39	22	61	16	73	12	75	4	25	. . .	4 (hh)
2003	4 (ii)	1	25	2	50	2	100	. . .	. . .	2	100	. . .	2 (jj)
2004	11	6	55	11	100	8	73	4	50	4	50	2 (kk)	2 (ll)
2005	2	2	100	1	50	. . .	. . .	. . .	. . .	. . .	. . .	. . .	. . .
2006	36	20	56	31	86	27	87	25	93	2	7	1 (mm)	1 (nn)
2007	3	1	33	3	100	2	67	1	50	1	50	. . .	1 (oo)
2008	11	7	64	9	82	8	89	8	100	. . .	. . .	. . .	. . .
Totals:													
Number	533	293		411		323		245		78		20	58
Percent	100	55.0		77.1		78.6		75.9		24.1		25.6	74.4

Source: The Council of State Governments, *The Book of the States, 2008*, (Lexington, KY: The Council of State Governments, 2008), 166, updated.

Key:

(a) Albert Brewer, D-Ala.

(b) Keith Miller, R-Alaska; Winthrop Rockefeller, R-Ark.; Claude Kirk, R-Fla.; Don Samuelson, R-Idaho; Norbert Tieman, R-Neb.; Dewey Bartlett, R-Okla.; Frank Farrar, R-S.D.

(c) Walter Peterson, R-N.H.; Preston Smith, D-Texas.

(d) Russell Peterson, R-Del.; Richard Ogilvie, R-Ill.

(e) William Cahill, R-N.J.

(f) One independent candidate won: James Longley of Maine.

(g) David Hall, D-Okla.

(h) John Vanderhoof, R-Colo.; Francis Sargent, R-Mass.; Malcolm Wilson, R-N.Y.; John Gilligan, D-Ohio.

(i) Dan Walker, D-Ill.

(j) Sherman Tribbitt, D-Del.; Christopher "Kit" Bond, R-Mo.

(k) Michael Dukakis, D-Mass.; Dolph Briscoe, D-Texas.

(l) Robert F. Bennett, R-Kan.; Rudolph G. Perpich, D-Minn.; Meldrim Thompson, R-N.H.; Robert Straub, D-Oreg.; Martin J. Schreiber, D-Wis.

(m) Thomas L. Judge, D-Mont.; Dixy Lee Ray, D-Wash.

(n) Bill Clinton, D-Ark.; Joseph P. Teasdale, D-Mo.; Arthur A. Link, D-N.D.

(o) Edward J. King, D-Mass.

(p) Frank D. White, R-Ark.; Charles Thone, R-Neb.; Robert F. List, R-Nev.; Hugh J. Gallen, D-N.H.; William P. Clements, R-Texas.

(q) David Treen, R-La.

(r) Allen I. Olson, R-N.D.; John D. Spellman, R-Wash.

(s) Bill Sheffield, D-Alaska.

(t) Mark White, D-Texas; Anthony S. Earl, D-Wis.

(u) Edwin Edwards, D-La.

(v) Arch A. Moore, R-W.Va.

(w) Two Independent candidates won: Walter Hickel (Alaska) and Lowell Weiker (Conn.). Both were former statewide Republican office holders.

(x) Bob Martinez, R-Fla.; Mike Hayden, R-Kan.; James Blanchard, D-Mich.; Rudy Perpich, DFL-Minn.; Kay Orr, R-Neb.; Edward DiPrete, R-R.I.

(y) Buddy Roemer, R-La.

(z) Ray Mabus, D-Miss.

(aa) James Florio, D-N.J.

(bb) One Independent candidate won: Angus King of Maine.

(cc) Bruce Sundlun, D-R.I.; Walter Dean Miller, R-S.D.

(dd) James E. Folsom Jr., D-Ala.; Bruce King, D-N.M.; Mario Cuomo, D-N.Y.; Ann Richards, D-Texas.

(ee) Two Independent candidates won: Angus King of Maine and Jesse Ventura of Minnesota.

(ff) Fob James, R-Ala.; David Beasley, R-S.C.

(gg) Cecil Underwood, R-W.Va.

(hh) Don Siegelman, D-Ala.; Roy Barnes, D-Ga., Jim Hodges, D-S.C.; and Scott McCallum, R-Wis.

(ii) The California recall election and replacement vote of 2003 is included in the 2003 election totals and as a general election for the last column.

(jj) Gray Davis, D-Calif.; Ronnie Musgrove, D-Miss.

(kk) Bob Holden, D-Mo.; Olene Walker, R-Utah, lost in the pre-primary convention.

(ll) Joe Kernan, D-Ind.; Craig Benson, R-N.H.

(mm) Frank Murkowski, R-Alaska.

(nn) Robert Ehrlich, R-Md.

(oo) Ernie Fletcher, R-Ky.

cent range, and the poll just prior to the 2008 election saw his approval rating at 37 percent.

The party affiliations of the eight successful incumbents seeking another term were split evenly between the two major parties. The Democratic winners and their percent of the total vote were: Montana Gov. Brian Schweitzer (66.7 percent), New Hampshire Gov. John Lynch (70.2 percent), Washington Gov. Christine Gregoire (53.2 percent) and West Virginia Gov. Joe Manchin (73 percent). While three of these incumbent Democrats won easily, Gregoire's win was a rematch of her 2004 race with Republican Dino Rossi that she narrowly won by only 133 votes. This time around, she won by 194,014 votes.

The incumbent Republican winners were: Indiana Gov. Mitch Daniels (59.1 percent), North Dakota Gov. John Hoeven (76 percent), Utah Gov. Jon Huntsman (79.8 percent) and Vermont Gov. James Douglas (71.1 percent). Each won handily with Daniels receiving the lowest winning percentage of the vote.

Three new governors were elected in 2008: Delaware Gov. Jack Markell (67.5 percent), Missouri Gov. Jay Nixon (59.6 percent) and North Carolina Gov. Beverly Perdue, (50.3 percent). Perdue's win was the tightest contest in the 2008 elections. Overall, Democrats won seven and Republicans won four of the 11 elections in 2008. Thus, the ratio of Democratic to Republican governors shifted from 28 to 22 prior to the election to 29 to 21 post-election. But this ratio soon would change for several reasons, explained later under The New Governors and Gubernatorial Forced Exits sections.

Gubernatorial Elections

As can be seen in Table A, incumbents were eligible to seek another term in 411 (77.1 percent) of the 533 gubernatorial contests held between 1970 and 2008. In those contests, 323 eligible incumbents sought reelection (78.6 percent), and 245 of them succeeded (75.9 percent). Those who were defeated were more likely to lose in the general election than in their own party primary by a 2.9-to-1 ratio, although two of the four incumbent losses in 2004, and one of their losses in 2006, were tied to party primaries. Not since 1994 had an incumbent governor been defeated in his or her own party's primary.

Democratic candidates held a winning edge in the elections held from 1970 to 2008 (55 percent). In 204 of the races (38.3 percent), the results led to a party shift in which a candidate from a party other than the incumbent's party won. But these party shifts have evened out over the years so that neither of the two major parties has an edge in these party shifts. In three of the six party shifts in the 2006 elections, Democrats took over after lengthy absences from the governor's office. Democrats won seats for the first time since the 1986 elections in Massachusetts and Ohio, and for the first time since 1990 in New York. But there have been some interesting patterns in these shifts over the past 38 years of gubernatorial elections.

Between 1970 and 1992, Democrats won 200 of the 324 races for governor (62 percent). Then beginning in 1993 to 2003, Republicans leveled the playing field by winning 85 of the 145 races for governor (59 percent). Despite this Republican trend, Democrats won eight of the 11 gubernatorial races in 2000, when then-Gov. George W. Bush won the presidency in a very close race. Democrats later won six of the 11 when Bush won his second term in 2004. From 2004 to 2008 Democrats have won 36 of the 63 contests (57 percent).

Another factor in determining how many governors have served in the states is the number of newly elected governors who are truly new to the office and the number who are returning after complying with constitutional term limits or after holding other positions. Of new governors taking office over a decade, the average number of new governors elected in the states dropped from 2.3 new governors per state in the 1950s to 1.9 in the 1970s and to 1.1 in the 1980s. In the 1990s, the rate began to move up a bit to 1.4 new governors per state.

Into the first decade of the 21st century, there are new faces in the governors' offices. New governors were elected in 61 of the 116 elections held from 2000 to 2008 (54.6 percent). And two other governors succeeded to the office during 2004 and one each in 2005, 2006 and 2008. So, in 2009, 18 of the incumbent governors will be serving their first term (36 percent), while 26 will be serving their second term (52 percent). The beginning of the 21st century certainly proved to be a time of change in the governors' offices across the 50 states.

The New Governors

Over the 2004–2008 cycle of gubernatorial elections and resignations, there were several different routes to the governor's chair by the elected governors and by those governors who have ascended to the office. Fifteen new governors had previously held statewide office. These include:

- Seven lieutenant governors: Connecticut Gov. M. Jodi Rell, Nebraska Gov. Dave Heineman, Virginia Gov. Tim Kaine, former Idaho Gov. James

Table B: Total Cost of Gubernatorial Elections: 1977–2007 (in thousands of dollars)

Year	Number of races	Total campaign costs: Actual $	Total campaign costs: 2007$ (a)	Average cost per state (2007$)	Percent change in similar elections (b)
1977	2	12,312	42,166	21,083	N.A.
1978	36	102,342	324,894	9,025	N.A. (c)
1979	3	32,744	93,553	31,184	N.A.
1980	13	35,634	89,758	6,904	N.A.
1981	2	24,648	56,274	28,137	+33
1982	36	181,832	390,198	10,839	+20 (d)
1983	3	39,966	83,262	27,754	-11
1984	13	47,156	94,123	7,240	+5
1985	2	18,859	36,336	18,168	-35
1986	36	270,605	511,541	14,209	+31
1987	3	40,212	73,379	24,460	-12
1988	12 (e)	52,208	91,433	7,619	-3
1989	2	47,902	80,104	40,052	+120
1990	36	345,493	548,402	15,233	+7
1991	3	34,564	52,529	17,510	-28
1992	12	60,278	89,037	7,420	-3
1993	2	36,195	51,930	25,965	-35
1994	36	417,873	584,437	16,234	+7
1995	3	35,693	48,562	16,187	-8
1996	11 (f)	68,610	90,634	8,239	+2
1997	2	44,823	57,911	28,955	+12
1998	36	470,326	598,379	16,622	+2
1999	3	16,276	20,243	6,748	-58
2000	11	97,098	116,845	10,622	+29
2001	2	70,400	82,436	41,218	+42
2002	36	841,427	969,386	26,927	+62
2003	3	69,939	78,760	26,253	+289
2004	11	112,625	123,628	11,239	+6
2005	2	131,996	140,123	70,061	+70
2006	36	727,552	747,741	20,771	-23
2007	3	93,803	93,803	31,268	+19

Source: Thad Beyle.

Key:

N.A. — Not available.

(a) Developed from the Table, "Historical Consumer Price Index for All Urban Consumers (CPI-U)," Bureau of Labor Statistics, U.S. Department of Labor. Each year's actual expenditures are converted to the 2007$ value of the dollar to control for the effect of inflation over the period.

(b) This represents the percent increase or decrease in 2007$ over the last bank of similar elections, i.e., 1977 v. 1981, 1978 v. 1982, 1979 v. 1983, etc.

(c) The data for 1978 are a particular problem as the two sources compiling data on this year's elections did so in differing ways that excluded some candidates. The result is that the numbers for 1978 under-represent the actual costs of these elections by some unknown amount. The sources are: Rhodes Cook and Stacy West, "1978 Advantage," *CQ Weekly Report*, (1979): 1757–1758, and *The Great Louisiana Spendathon* (Baton Rouge: Public Affairs Research Council, March 1980).

(d) This particular comparison with 1978 is not what it would appear to be for the reasons given in note (c). The amount spent in 1978 was more than indicated here so the increase is really not as great as it appears.

(e) As of the 1986 election, Arkansas switched to a four-year term for the governor, hence the drop from 13 to 12 for this off-year.

(f) As of the 1994 election, Rhode Island switched to a four-year term for the governor, hence the drop from 12 to 11 for this off-year.

Risch, Kentucky Gov. Steve Beshear, New York Gov. David Paterson and North Carolina Gov. Beverly Perdue;

- Five attorneys general: Washington Gov. Christine Gregoire, Arkansas Gov. Mike Beebe, Florida Gov. Charlie Crist, former New York Gov. Eliot Spitzer and Missouri Gov. Jay Nixon;
- Two secretaries of state: West Virginia Gov. Joe Manchin and Iowa Gov. Chet Culver; and
- One state treasurer: Delaware Gov. Jack Markell.

Five governors were members or former members of Congress who returned to work within their state. These included U.S. Sen. Jon Corzine, who became governor in New Jersey, and U.S. congressmen: Idaho Gov. L.C. "Butch" Otter, Nevada Gov. Jim Gibbons, Ohio Gov. Ted Strickland and Louisiana Gov. Bobby Jindal. Montana Gov. Brian Schweitzer unsuccessfully sought a U.S. Senate seat in 2000 as the Democratic candidate and turned that around to win the governorship in 2004.

New Hampshire Gov. John Lynch and Utah Gov. Jon Huntsman were the two governors that came from the business sector. Two mayors or former mayors were elected in 2006: Alaska Gov. Sarah Palin was the former mayor of Wasilla, Alaska, and Maryland Gov. Martin O'Malley was the former mayor of Baltimore, Md.

Finally, three new governors followed a unique path compared to their counterparts: Mitch Daniels, former head of the Federal Office of Management and Budget, became the governor in Indiana; Bill Ritter, former Denver district attorney, became the governor in Colorado; and Deval Patrick, head of the Civil Rights Division of the U.S. Department of Justice in the Clinton Administration, became the governor of Massachusetts.

In the 423 gubernatorial races between 1977 and 2008, among the candidates were 110 lieutenant governors (31 won), 91 attorneys general (25 won), 30 secretaries of state (eight won), 27 state treasurers (seven won), and 16 auditors or comptrollers (three won). Looking at these numbers from a bettor's point of view, the odds of a lieutenant governor winning were 3.5 to 1, an attorney general winning was 3.6 to 1, a secretary of state winning was 3.8 to 1, a state treasurer winning was 3.9 to 1 and a state auditor or comptroller winning was 5.3 to 1.

One other unique aspect about the current governors is that eight women will be serving as governor into 2009—one less than in the last half of 2004, which was the all-time high for women governors serving at one time. Seven women were elected in their own right: Alaska Gov. Sarah Palin, former Arizona Gov. Janet Napolitano, Hawaii Gov. Linda Lingle, Kansas Gov. Kathleen Sebelius, Michigan Gov. Jennifer Granholm, North Carolina Gov. Beverly Perdue and Washington Gov. Christine Gregoire. The last one is Connecticut Gov. M. Jodi Rell, who as lieutenant governor became governor after the resignation of former Gov. John Rowland in 2004, and then was elected in her own bid to continue serving as governor in 2006.

In January 2009, when former Arizona Gov. Janet Napolitano was confirmed as secretary of the U.S. Department of Homeland Security and she resigned her governorship, she was succeeded by another woman as governor, Secretary of State Jan Brewer. Thus the number of women governors in the states will stay at eight. But because Napolitano, a Democrat, was succeeded by Brewer, a Republican, this succession will also change the Democratic-Republican gubernatorial ratio back to 28-to-22. When Kansas Gov. Kathleen Sebelius resigned after her confirmation as the secretary of Health and Human Services, her successor was Lt. Gov. Mark Parkinson, reducing the number of women governors serving to seven—but the ratio of Democratic to Republican governors remained the same at 28-to-22.

Women continue to hold their own in gubernatorial races. From 2004 to 2008, 10 of the 18 women running either as the incumbent or as the candidate of a major party won—a 55.6 percent success rate. There will be more soon.[4]

Cost of Gubernatorial Elections

Table C presents data on the costs of the most recent elections from 2004 through 2007. There is a great range in how much these races cost, from the 2006 race in California ($132.6 million in 2007 dollars), to the low-cost 2006 race in South Dakota ($1.3 million in 2007 dollars). Both races saw an incumbent Republican governor win re-election.

But looking at how much was spent by the candidates per general election vote, a slightly different picture evolves. In 2005, the New Jersey gubernatorial race was the most expensive at $39.42 per vote, followed by the 2003 Louisiana race at $32.48 per vote. Both races were for an open seat. The least expensive gubernatorial race per vote in the 2004–2007 election cycle was in the 2006 Arizona race when the candidates spent $2.49 per vote in 2007 dollars. Close behind the Arizona race was the 2006 race in South Dakota when the candidates spent only $3.97 per vote and also the 2006 race in Tennessee when the candidates spent only $4 per vote. These races were won by an incumbent seeking a second term.

In Figure A, by converting the actual dollars spent each year into the equivalent 2007 dollars, we can see the cost of these elections has increased over time. Since 1981, the costs of each four-year cycle of elections can be compared with the previous and subsequent cycle of elections.

In the 54 gubernatorial elections held from 1977 to 1980, total expenditures were $550 million in equivalent 2007 dollars. In the 52 elections held from 2004 to 2007—just over two and a half decades later—total expenditures were slightly more than $1.1 billion in 2007 dollars, an increase of 101 percent. Comparing the 1977–1980 election cycle expenditures to the 2001–2004 election cycle reveals a considerably greater increase (128 percent) as was reported in the last two editions of *The Book of the States*. The reason for this difference has to do with

Table C: Cost of Gubernatorial Campaigns, Most Recent Elections, 2004–2007

				Total campaign expenditures				
						Winner		
State	*Year*	*Winner*	*Point margin*	*All candidates (2007$)*	*Cost per vote (2007$)*	*Spent (2007$)*	*Percent of all expenditures*	*Vote percent*
Alabama	2006	R★	+15.8	$19,057,119	$15.24	$12,402,864	65.1	57.4
Alaska	2006	R★★	+7.4	5,211,390	21.87	1,364,641	26.2	48.3
Arizona	2006	D★	+27.2	3,812,538	2.49	1,658,332	43.5	62.6
Arkansas	2006	D#	+14.4	10,229,307	13.64	6,653,165	65.0	55.4
California	2006	R★	+16.9	132,606,809	15.28	47,165,436	35.6	55.9
Colorado	2006	D#	+16.8	7,992,782	5.13	4,391,539	54.9	57.0
Connecticut	2006	R★	+27.8	14,663,006	13.05	4,299,122	29.3	63.2
Delaware	2004	D★	+5.1	2,904,244	7.96	1,936,977	66.7	50.9
Florida	2006	R#	+7.1	43,111,786	8.93	20,435,625	47.4	52.2
Georgia	2006	R★	+19.7	29,875,586	14.08	13,307,665	44.5	57.9
Hawaii	2006	R★	+27.1	7,155,914	20.78	6,672,826	93.2	62.5
Idaho	2006	R#	+8.6	3,714,999	8.24	2,006,150	54.0	52.7
Illinois	2006	D★	+10.6	49,805,734	14.29	27,001,018	54.2	49.8
Indiana	2004	R★★★	+5.3	35,157,001	14.36	18,473,207	52.5	50.8
Iowa	2006	D#	+9.5	17,115,172	16.33	7,763,362	45.4	54.0
Kansas	2006	D★	+17.5	6,592,408	7.76	4,887,199	74.1	57.9
Kentucky	2007	D★★★	+17.4	33,676,869	31.91	9,418,836	28.0	58.7
Louisiana	2007	R#	+36.4	42,149,344	32.48	11,227,661	26.6	53.9
Maine	2006	D★	+7.9	5,126,069	9.30	1,240,526	24.2	38.1
Maryland	2006	D★★★	+6.5	29,742,547	16.63	14,467,478	48.6	52.7
Massachusetts	2006	D#	+20	43,487,885	19.38	9,130,132	21.0	55.0
Michigan	2006	D★	+14	54,281,847	14.28	11,513,932	21.2	56.3
Minnesota	2006	R★	+0.96	8,910,606	4.05	4,039,499	45.3	46.7
Mississippi	2007	R★	+15.8	17,976,455	24.16	12,952,035	72.0	57.9
Missouri	2004	R★★	+2.9	17,043,604	6.27	5,299,374	31.1	50.8
Montana	2004	D#	+4.4	4,150,139	9.30	1,895,665	45.7	50.4
Nebraska	2006	R★	+48.9	5,350,636	9.01	2,794,576	55.6	73.4
Nevada	2006	R#	+4	15,270,089	26.23	5,835,879	38.2	47.9
New Hampshire	2006	D★	+48.1	2,288,668	5.66	1,702,390	74.4	74.0
New Jersey	2005	D#	+10.5	90,272,548	39.42	47,333,191	52.4	53.5
New Mexico	2006	D★	+37.6	8,662,008	15.49	8,014,472	92.5	68.8
New York	2006	D#	+40.9	47,387,405	10.68	34,305,945	72.4	69.6
North Carolina	2004	D★	+12.7	19,954,458	5.72	9,031,351	45.3	55.6
North Dakota	2004	R★	+43.9	1,532,147	4.94	990,636	64.7	71.3
Ohio	2006	D#	+23.9	30,168,499	7.50	16,234,126	53.8	60.5
Oklahoma	2006	D★	+33	7,528,773	8.13	4,103,380	54.5	66.5
Oregon	2006	D★	+8	14,562,556	10.55	4,402,997	30.2	50.7
Pennsylvania	2006	D★	+20.8	42,131,096	10.30	31,465,509	74.7	60.4
Rhode Island	2006	R★	+2	4,592,752	11.87	2,351,598	51.2	51.0
South Carolina	2006	R★	+10.3	12,923,101	11.84	7,458,111	57.7	55.1
South Dakota	2006	R★	+25.6	1,331,669	3.97	304,055	22.8	61.7
Tennessee	2006	D★	+38.9	7,236,365	4.00	5,604,264	77.4	68.6
Texas	2006	R★	+9.2	35,506,572	8.07	23,439,111	66.0	39.0
Utah	2004	R★★	+16.4	6,913,606	7.52	3,596,371	52.0	57.7
Vermont	2006	R★	+15.2	1,795,893	6.84	1,155,724	64.4	56.3
Virginia	2005	D#	+5.7	49,850,389	25.13	21,970,325	44.1	51.7
Washington	2004	D#	+0.005	15,991,554	5.69	6,986,481	43.7	48.9
West Virginia	2004	D#	+29.5	12,681,979	17.04	3,886,629	30.6	63.5
Wisconsin	2006	D★	+7.4	17,088,822	7.90	9,502,630	55.6	52.7
Wyoming	2006	D★	+39.9	1,423,120	7.34	1,010,475	71.0	69.9

Source: Thad Beyle, *www.unc.edu/~beyle*.

Note: Using the 2007 CPI Index which was 2.073 of the 1982–84 Index = 1,000, the actual 2004 expenditures were based on a 1.889 value or .911 of the 2007$ index, the actual 2005 expenditures were based on a 1.953 index value or .942 of the 2007$ index, the 2006 expenditures were based on a 2.016 index value or .973 of the 2007$ index, and the 2007 expenditures were exact dollars spent in that election year. Then the actual expenditures of each state's governor's race were divided by the .9 value for that year to get the equivalent 2007$ value of those expenditures.

Key:
D — Democrat
I — Independent
R — Republican
— Open seat
★ — Incumbent ran and won.
★★ — Incumbent ran and lost in party primary.
★★★ — Incumbent ran and lost in general election.

Figure A: Gubernatorial Elections Expenditures (by millions)

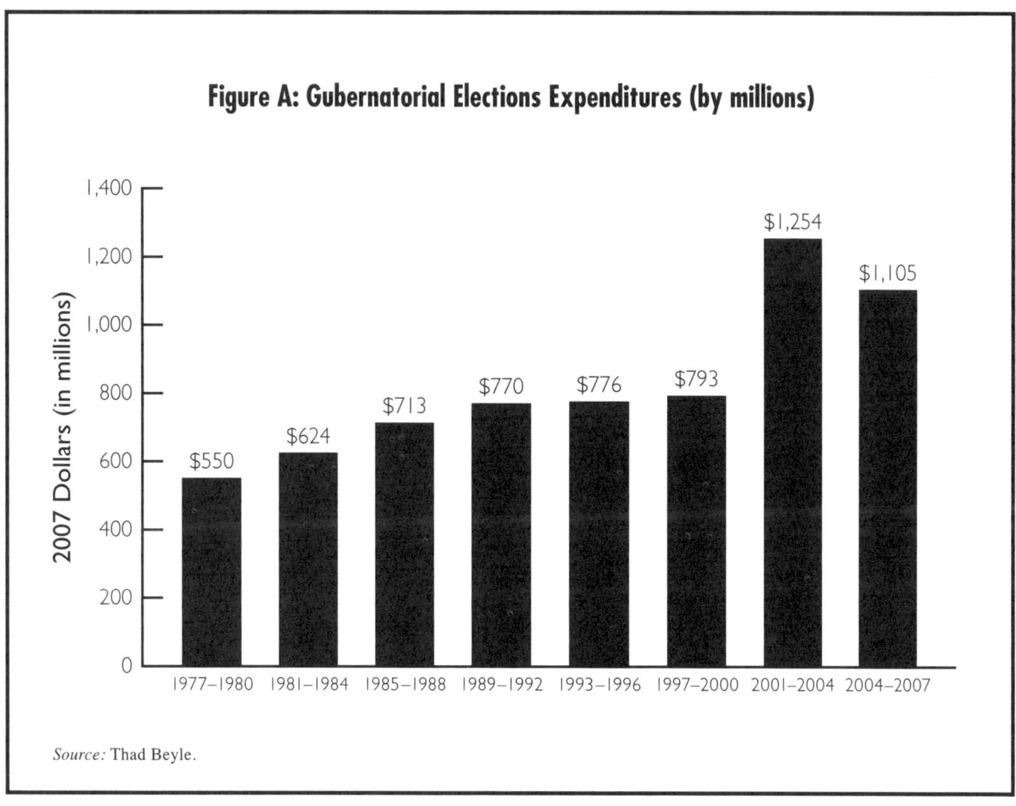

Source: Thad Beyle.

the 36 races in the 2002 elections and how they compared with the 36 races in the 2006 elections.

In 2002, there were 20 open-seat races compared to only nine in the 2006 elections. Open-seat races with no incumbent seeking another term generally attract more candidates who are willing to spend a lot of money to win the governorship as they usually have so few opportunities to win the office. Also, in the 2002 elections, four incumbent governors lost their re-election bids compared to only two incumbents who lost in 2006. In total, 24 new governors were elected in 2002 compared to only 11 in 2006.

The net of all this is that there was nearly a $222 million decline in the total expenditures between the 2002 and 2006 gubernatorial races. This reversed the general trend of increasingly expensive gubernatorial races over the 1977 to 2006 election period. But, the three 2007 races at $93.8 million moved up just over 19 percent over the three 2003 races—so that continuing growth in expenditures may still be in place. Now, forecasts indicate that when the 2010 races come around, there could be a lot of money spent in these races—as of now there will be 17 open-seat races, plus some additional open-seat races in which an incumbent decides not to seek re-election, and those races in which an incumbent governor is defeated. A caveat to this is the current condition of the economy and how that might affect the amount of money put into political races by both candidates and donors.

The rising costs of elections continue to reflect the new style of campaigning for governor, with the candidates developing their own personal party by using outside consultants, opinion polls, media ads and buys, and extensive fundraising efforts to pay for all this. This style reaches into almost every state now, and air-war campaigns now replace the older style of ground-war campaigns across the states.

Gubernatorial Forced Exits

California's 2003 gubernatorial recall and replacement votes highlighted the fact that some elected governors faced situations in which they could lose their office in ways other than being beaten by a challenger at the ballot box or becoming ill or dying. In 2004, two governors resigned from office, former Connecticut Gov. John Rowland, facing the threat of

Table D: Women Governors in the States

Governor	State	Year elected or succeeded to office	How woman became governor	Tenure of service	Previous offices held	Last elected position held before governorship
Phase I—From initial statehood to adoption of the 19th Amendment to U.S. Constitution (1920)						
No women elected or served as governor						
Phase II—Wives of former governors elected governor, 1924–1966						
Nellie Tayloe Ross (D)	Wyoming	1924	E	1/1925–1/1927	F	. . .
Miriam "Ma" Ferguson (D)	Texas	1924	E	1/1925–1/1927 1/1933–1/1935	F	. . .
Lurleen Wallace (D)	Alabama	1966	E	1/1967–5/1968	F	. . .
Phase III—Women who became governor on their own merit, 1970 to date						
Ella Grasso (D)	Connecticut	1974	E	1/1975–12/1980	SH, SOS, (a)	(a)
Dixy Lee Ray (D)	Washington	1976	E	1/1977–1/1981	(b)	. . .
Vesta M. Roy (R)	New Hampshire	1982	S (c)	12/1982–1/1983	(d)	(d)
Martha Layne Collins (D)	Kentucky	1983	E	12/1983–12/1987	(e), LG	LG
Madeleine M. Kunin (D)	Vermont	1984	E	1/1985–1/1991	SH, LG	LG
Kay A. Orr (R)	Nebraska	1986	E	1/1987–1/1991	T	T
Rose Mofford (D)	Arizona	1988	S (f)	4/1988–1/1991	SOS	SOS
Joan Finney (D)	Kansas	1990	E	1/1991–1/1995	T	T
Barbara Roberts (D)	Oregon	1990	E	1/1991–1/1995	(g), C, SH, SOS	SOS
Ann Richards (D)	Texas	1990	E	1/1991–1/1995	C, T	T
Christy Whitman (R)	New Jersey	1993	E	1/1994–1/2001	(h)	(h)
Jeanne Shaheen (D)	New Hampshire	1996	E	1/1997–1/2003	(d)	(d)
Jane Dee Hull (R)	Arizona	1997	S (i)	9/1997–1/2003	(j), SOS	SOS
Nancy P. Hollister (R)	Ohio	1998	S (k)	12/1998–1/1999	LG	LG
Ruth Ann Minner (D)	Delaware	2000	E	1/2001–1/2009	SH, SS, LG	LG
Judy Martz (R)	Montana	2000	E	1/2001–1/2005	LG	LG
Sila Calderón (Pop D)	Puerto Rico	2000	E	1/2001–1/2005	M	M
Jane Swift (R)	Massachusetts	2001	S (l)	4/2001–1/2003	SS, LG	LG
Janet Napolitano (D)	Arizona	2002	E	1/2003–1/2009	(m), AG	AG
Linda Lingle (R)	Hawaii	2002	E	12/2002–	C, M (n)	M
Kathleen Sebelius (D)	Kansas	2002	E	1/2003–4/2009	SH, (o)	(o)
Jennifer Granholm (D)	Michigan	2002	E	1/2003–	(p), AG	AG
Olene Walker (R)	Utah	2003	S (q)	11/2003–1/2005	SH, LG	LG
Kathleen Blanco (D)	Louisiana	2003	E	1/2004–1/2008	SH, LG	LG
M. Jodi Rell (R)	Connecticut	2004	S (r)	7/2004–	SH, LG	LG
Christine Gregoire (D)	Washington	2004	E	1/2005–	AG	AG
Sarah Palin (R)	Alaska	2006	E	1/2007–	M (s)	M
Beverly Perdue (D)	North Carolina	2008	E	1/2009–	SH, SS, LG	LG
Jan Brewer (R)	Arizona	2009	S (t)	1/2009–	C, SH, SS, SOS	SOS

Sources: National Governors Association Web site, *www.nga.org*, and individual state government Web sites.

Key:

S — Succeeded to office upon death, resignation or removal of the incumbent governor.

AG — Attorney general
C — City council or county commission
E — Elected governor
F — Former first lady
LG — Lieutenant governor
M — Mayor
SH — State House member
SOS — Secretary of state
SS — State Senate member
T — State treasurer

(a) Congresswoman.

(b) Ray served on the U.S. Atomic Energy Commission from 1972 to 1975 and was chair of the AEC from 1973 to 1975.

(c) Roy as state Senate president succeeded to office upon the death of Gov. Hugh Gallen.

(d) State Senate president.

(e) State Supreme Court clerk.

(f) Mofford as secretary of state became acting governor in February 1988 and governor in April 1988 upon the impeachment and removal of Gov. Evan Mecham.

(g) Local school board member.

(h) Whitman was a former state utilities official.

(i) Hull as secretary of state became acting governor when Gov. Fife Symington resigned. Elected to full term in 1998.

(j) Speaker of the state House.

(k) Hollister as lieutenant governor became governor when Gov. George Voinovich stepped down to serve in the U.S. Senate.

(l) Swift as lieutenant governor succeeded Gov. Paul Celluci who resigned after being appointed ambassador to Canada. Was the first governor to give birth while serving in office.

(m) U.S. attorney.

(n) Lingle was mayor of Maui for two terms, elected in 1990 and 1996.

(o) Insurance commissioner.

(p) Federal prosecutor.

(q) Walker as lieutenant governor succeeded to the governorship upon the resignation of Gov. Mike Leavitt in 2003.

(r) Rell as lieutenant governor succeeded to the governorship upon the resignation of Gov. John Rowland in 2004.

(s) Palin was a two-term Mayor of Wasilla, Alaska, and had unsuccessfully sought the lieutenant governor's office in 2002.

(t) Brewer as secretary of state succeeded to the governorship upon the resignation of Gov. Janet Napolitano in January 2009 after her confirmation as head of the U.S. Department of Homeland Security.

a potential impeachment move, and former New Jersey Gov. Jim McGreevey due to personal reasons.

From 2005 to 2007, such situations were rather quiet and no governor was driven out or recalled from office. Some governors faced difficult times in terms of things that may have happened while in office, as well as low job approval ratings in state-level polls, indicating that many residents were not happy with their governor's performance.

In early 2008, New York Gov. Eliot Spitzer, a Democrat, under siege after he was linked to a prostitution ring, ultimately resigned on March 12, midway through his term. Democratic Lt. Gov. David Paterson became New York's new governor, and was sworn into office March 17. Paterson became the second African-American governor serving in 2008, along with Democratic Gov. Deval Patrick of Massachusetts.

Later in 2008, word leaked that Democratic Gov. Rod Blagojevich of Illinois was under federal investigation for potential criminal actions committed while in office. He was arrested on criminal charges and then was released to return to work. This suddenly took on very high visibility when newly elected President Barack Obama resigned his U.S. Senate seat in preparation of becoming the 44th president. As governor, Blagojevich had the right and power to appoint Obama's replacement. But the governor used some questionable tactics, including allegedly putting the Senate seat up for bids.

The year closed with both an increase in the intensity of the federal investigation and action by the Illinois State Legislature to impeach the governor for his unethical, and probable criminal actions, in this nomination process. The Illinois House voted 114 to 1 to impeach the governor Jan. 9. The Senate conducted the conviction and removal trial, then voted 59 to zero after a four-day trial Jan. 30 to remove the governor—and then to have the new governor sworn in immediately.[5] Democratic Lt. Gov. Patrick Quinn was sworn in as governor the same day and Illinois state government began its recovery process. Blagojevich only appeared on the last day of the trial to plead his defense.

Gubernatorial Powers[6]

One way to view changes occurring in gubernatorial powers is to look at the "Index of Formal Powers of the Governorship." The index was first developed by Joseph Schlesinger in the 1960s,[7] which this author continued to update.[8] The index used here consists of six different indices of gubernatorial power as seen in 1960 and 2009. These indices include the number and importance of separately elected branch officials, the tenure potential of governors, the appointment powers of governors for administrative and board positions in the executive branch, the governor's budgetary power, the governor's veto power and the governor's party control in the legislature. Each of the individual indices is set in a five-point scale, with five being the most power and one being the least.

During nearly five decades from 1960 to 2009, the overall institutional powers of the nation's governors increased by 0.8 percent, according to the index. The greatest increase among the individual gubernatorial institutional powers was an 80 percent increase in their veto power as more governors gained an item veto. In 1996, North Carolina voters approved by a 3-to-1 margin a constitutional amendment finally giving their governor veto power.

The indices measuring the governor's tenure potential—or length of term and ability to seek an additional term or terms—showed a 28 percent increase in power, as it did vis-à-vis the number of separately elected executive branch officials. However, the governor's appointment power over specific functional area executive officials increased by only 7 percent.

In addition, the states continue to adhere to the concept of multiple executives in terms of the number of statewide elected officials. In 2006, there were 308 separately elected executive officials covering 12 major offices in the states.[9] Compare that to the 306 elected officials in 1972. Ten states also had multimember boards, commissions or councils with members selected by statewide or district election.

The gubernatorial budgetary power actually decreased by 22 percent. However, during this same time period, state legislatures were undergoing considerable reform, and gaining more power to work on the governor's proposed budget was one of the reforms sought. Hence, the increased legislative budgetary power more than balanced out any increases in gubernatorial budgetary power.

There has also been a 34 percent drop in the gubernatorial party control in the state legislatures over the period. Much of this can be attributed to the major partisan shifts occurring in the Southern states as the region moved from one-party dominance to a very competitive two-party system.[10] In 1960, 13 of the 14 governors were Democrats, and all 28 state legislative chambers were under Democratic control. In 2009, Republicans and Democrats each control seven governorships, and also split the control of the 28 houses of the state legislatures holding control of 14 each.

Three Republican Southern governors face a legislature completely controlled by Democrats,[11] while two Democratic governors face a legislature completely controlled by Republicans.[12] Two Democratic governors face a legislature with split partisan control.[13] Only three Democratic governors have legislative chambers controlled by their own party,[14] and only four Republican governors have legislative chambers controlled by their own party.[15]

Table E: Impeachments and Removals of Governors

Name, party and state	*Year*	*Process of impeachment and outcome*		
Charles Robinson (R-Kan.)	1862	Impeached	Acquitted	
Harrison Reed (R-Fla.)	1868	Impeached	Acquitted	
William Holden (R-N.C.)	1871	Impeached	Convicted	Removed
Powell Clayton (R-Ark.)	1871	Impeached	Acquitted	
David Butler (R-Neb.)	1871	Impeached	Convicted	Removed
Henry Warmouth (R-La.)	1872	Impeached		Term ended
Harrison Reed (R-Fla.)	1872	Impeached	Acquitted	
Adelbert Ames (R-Miss.)	1876	Impeached		Resigned
William P. Kellogg (R-La.)	1876	Impeached	Acquitted	
Wiliam Sulzer (D-N.Y.)	1913	Impeached	Convicted	Removed
James "Pa" Ferguson (D-Texas)	1917	Impeached	Convicted	Resigned
John C. Walton (D-Okla.)	1923	Impeached	Convicted	Removed
Henry S. Johnston (D-Okla.)	1928	Impeached	Acquitted	
Henry S. Johnston (D-Okla.)	1929	Impeached	Convicted	Removed
Huey P. Long (D-La.)	1929	Impeached	Acquitted	
Henry Horton (D-Tenn.)	1931	Impeached	Acquitted	
Richard Leche (D-La.)	1939	Threatened		Resigned
Evan Mecham (R-Ariz.)	1988	Impeached	Convicted	Removed
John Rowland (R-Conn.)	2004	Threatened		Resigned
Rod R. Blagojevich (D-Ill.)	2009	Impeached	Convicted	Removed

Other removals of incumbent governors		
John A. Quitman (D-Miss.)	1851	Resigned after federal criminal indictment.
Rufus Brown (R-Ga.)	1871	Resigned while under criminal investigation.
Lynn J. Frazier (R-N.D.)	1921	Recalled by voters during third term.
Warren T. McCray (R-Ind.)	1924	Resigned after federal criminal conviction.
William Langer (I-N.D.)	1934	Removed by North Dakota Supreme Court.
Thomas L. Moodie (D-N.D.)	1935	Removed by North Dakota Supreme Court.
J. Howard Pyle (R-Ariz.)	1955	Recall petition certified, but term ended before date set for recall election.
Marvin Mandel (D-Md.)	1977	Removed after federal criminal conviction.
Ray Blanton (D-Tenn.)	1979	Term shortened in bipartisan agreement (a).
Evan Mecham (R-Ariz.)	1987	Recall petition certified, but impeached, convicted and removed from office before the date set for the recall election.
H. Guy Hunt (R-Ala.)	1993	Removed after state criminal conviction.
Jim Guy Tucker Jr. (D-Ark.)	1996	Resigned after federal criminal conviction.
J. Fife Symington (R-Ariz.)	1997	Resigned after federal criminal conviction.
Gray Davis (D-Calif.)	2003	Recalled by voters during second term.
James McGreevey (D-N.J.)	2004	Resigned due to personal reasons.
Eliot Spitzer (D-N.Y.)	2008	Resigned after being linked to a prostitution ring.

Sources: Thad Beyle and The Council of State Governments, National Governors Association database, and Eric Kelderman, "Spitzer, 22nd disgraced gov to leave office," *www.stateline.org* (March 12, 2008).

Key:

(a) See Lamar Alexander, *Steps Along the War: A Governor's Scrapbook* (Nashville, TN: Thomas Nelson, 1986), 21–9 for a discussion of this unique transition between governors.

Notes

[1] The former governors winning the presidency over the past four decades were Jimmy Carter (D-Ga., 1971–1975) in 1976, Ronald Reagan (R-Calif., 1967–1975) in 1980 and 1984, Bill Clinton (D-Ark., 1979–1981 and 1983–1992) in 1992 and 1996, and George W. Bush (R-Texas, 1995–2001) in 2000 and 2004.

[2] New Jersey and Virginia.

[3] Kentucky, Louisiana and Mississippi.

[4] For more detail on these races since 1977, visit my Web site at *www.unc.edu/~beyle*.

[5] Since the 1960s, three other Illinois governors have ended up in prison after their terms were up: Democrat Otto

Kerner Jr. served 1961–1968 and was in prison 1974–1975; Democrat Dan Walker served 1973–1977 and was in prison 1988–1989; and Republican George Ryan served 1999–2003 and has been in prison since 2007.

[6]For more detail on this topic, check Thad Beyle and Margaret Ferguson, "Governors and the Executive Branch," in Virginia Gray and Russell L. Hanson, eds., *Politics in the American States: A Comparative Analysis* 9th ed. (Washington, D.C.: CQ Press, 2008), 192–228.

[7]Joseph A. Schlesinger, "The Politics of the Executive," *Politics in the American States*, 1st and 2nd ed., Herbert Jacob and Kenneth N. Vines, eds., (Boston: Little Brown, 1965 and 1971).

[8]Thad L. Beyle and Margaret Ferguson, *op. cit.* Earlier versions of this index by the author appeared in the 4th edition (1983), the 5th edition (1990), the 6th edition (1996), the 7th edition (1999), and the 8th edition (2003).

[9]Kendra Hovey and Harold Hovey, "D-12: Number of Statewide Elected Officials, 2007," *CQ's State Fact Finder*, 2007 (Washington, D.C.: CQ Press, 2007): 113.

[10]The following states are included in this definition of the South: Alabama, Arkansas, Florida, Georgia, Kentucky, Louisiana, Mississippi, North Carolina, Oklahoma, South Carolina, Tennessee, Texas, Virginia and West Virginia.

[11]They are Bob Riley in Alabama, Bobby Jindal in Louisiana and Haley Barber in Mississippi.

[12]They are Brad Henry in Oklahoma and Phil Bredesen in Tennessee.

[13]They are Steven Beshear in Kentucky and Tim Kaine in Virginia.

[14]They are Mike Beebe in Arkansas, Beverly Perdue in North Carolina and Joe Manchin in West Virginia.

[15]They are Charlie Crist in Florida, Sonny Perdue in Georgia, Mark Sanford in South Carolina and Rick Perry in Texas.

About the Author

Thad Beyle is a professor-emeritus of political science at the University of North Carolina at Chapel Hill. A Syracuse University A.B. and A.M., he received his Ph.D. at the University of Illinois. He spent a year in the North Carolina governor's office in the mid-1960s followed by two years with Terry Sanford's "A Study of American States" project at Duke University, and has worked with the National Governors Association in several capacities on gubernatorial transitions.

The Governors' Offices

By Barry L. Van Lare

Each state provides its governor with an office staff dedicated to supporting the governor and to assisting the governor in the leadership and management of state government.

Overview

As the state's chief executive officer, the governor is responsible for the leadership and management of the executive branch of government. While this responsibility is primarily carried out through political appointees the governor will name to head numerous executive departments and agencies, every governor also relies on a personal staff to oversee and coordinate these appointees, to assist in carrying out a number of additional functions providing logistical support to the governor, and to assist the governor in operational responsibilities assigned to the governor's office. Together the governors' offices in the 50 states employ nearly 3,200 staff members.

These offices play significant roles, and it is important to understand the tasks they perform and the way in which staff are assigned and organized to perform those tasks.

The Critical Tasks of the Governor's Office

While specifics will vary from state to state, most governors' offices will be responsible for all or most of the following tasks:

Manning State Government

A new governor must move quickly to fill critical appointments in state departments and agencies. In addition, the new governor will be faced with making appointments to a wide range of state boards and agencies of varying importance. The governor's office must find appointees who share the governor's priorities and have the management and political skills needed to implement those priorities and deliver other government services effectively and efficiently. Moreover, the governor's office must find candidates who can withstand the public scrutiny of the confirmation process and ensure that gubernatorial appointees conform to appropriate ethical standards. While these functions are particularly challenging at the beginning of a governor's term, they continue throughout the governor's administration as vacancies occur due to the expiration of terms or other personnel changes.

Developing Policies and Programs

While the vast majority of state programs and policies may proceed unchanged during a governor's tenure, every governor comes to office with a number of priority issues that have developed during the election campaign. The governor's office will need to develop specific policies and programs to address those priorities and to build a convincing case for their adoption. As with appointments, these tasks are often most intense during the early months of a governor's term, but will continue as initial policies are implemented and as new problems and opportunities arise.

Allocating Financial Resources

The governors also play a critical role in proposing the allocation of state resources through the executive budget. In a few states, the process of budget analysis and development is carried out by budget staff assigned directly to the governor's office. More commonly, the formal budget process is managed by a separate budget office reporting to the governor or to a department head appointed by the governor. However, governors often want to supplement the efforts of this specialized staff with political and policy input from their personal staff members.

Securing Public and Legislative Support

Appointments, budgets and policy initiatives generally all require legislative approval. As a result, one of the critical tasks of the governor's office is to establish a productive working relationship with the state legislature. In addition, the governor's office will be expected to take the lead in communicating the governor's priorities to key stakeholders and in mobilizing public support for their adoption.

Overseeing Government Operations

State government provides a wide variety of services to millions of residents every day. Ultimately the public will hold the governor responsible for how well these services are delivered. Individual governors attempt to oversee these activities in many different ways. In some cases, the governor will rely on management by exception, weighing in only when an issue arises. More often a governor will work with department and agency heads to define priorities and to maintain a general sense of agency performance. In other cases, the governor will create and manage a system of performance review that will monitor performance on an ongoing basis.

Constituent Services

Governors, like other elected officials, are the focal point for residents who encounter problems in their dealings with state government. These requests come to the governor by mail, e-mail, telephone and personal visits. Individual governors have responded to these demands in different ways. At the minimum, the governor's office will serve as a conduit seeing that government agencies are responsive to the issues. In other offices, the governor's staff serves as case managers working actively to evaluate and respond to problems.

Emergency Management

The governor is expected to play an important role in responding to emergencies in every state. While operational responsibility will generally reside in a designated emergency management agency, the governor will be held responsible for seeing that the necessary systems are in place, for ensuring effective interagency coordination and for maintaining critical communications with the public. In some states, the coordination of homeland security is assigned to a unit within the governor's office.

Communication

The governor also plays an important role in communicating his or her priorities and concerns to the public, as well as an equally important role in allowing citizen input into the policy process.

Organizing the Governor's Office

Historically governors have chosen from one of three organizational options. Many governors choose a hierarchical model with all staff reporting to the governor through a designated chief of staff. In other states, the governor prefers a decentralized model with several senior staff members and heads of functional areas reporting directly to him or her. In other states, the governor selects a hybrid model with the chief and a limited number of senior staff members reporting directly to the governor.

In most states, the governor's office is structured around some combination of the individual functions discussed below. In fewer states, the governor's offices include separate staff and/or offices with specific liaison and/or operational responsibilities. Examples include special commissions on crosscutting topics such as economic development or tax reform, the management of high priority initiatives such as homeland security and small offices addressing concerns of special populations such as children or minorities.

Functional Assignments in the Governor's Office

While there is no single model governing the functional units or assignments that will be included in the governor's office, most governors' offices, whether large or small, will include staff, either units or individuals charged with many or all of these functions.

Chief of Staff

The chief of staff is the most senior member of the governor's staff. While the specific functions assigned to the chief and his deputies or assistants may vary, those staff members usually serve in a variety of roles including leadership and management of the governor's staff, political and policy adviser, personal confidant and primary liaison with state departments and agencies.

Government Operations

As chief executive officer, the governor is responsible for how well these services are delivered. Most governors' offices include individuals or units that are charged with working with department and agency heads to see that services are delivered economically and efficiently, that the governor's priorities and programs are implemented, and that problems are anticipated and addressed.

In some states the oversight of government operations will rest primarily on the chief of staff. In other states this responsibility is distributed among a number of senior advisers, policy staff or agency liaisons. In other states the governor's office includes a director of state operations, a chief operating officer or performance management staff.

Appointments

The appointments staff is responsible for tracking the membership of often hundreds of state boards and commissions, identifying vacancies, recruiting and evaluating candidates, and recommending appointments to the governor. The appointments staff will often also assume responsibility for training or orienting new board and commission members and serving as a liaison with many boards and agencies to ensure they are responsive to the governor's priorities.

In some states this staff will assist in filling high-level vacancies in state departments and agencies. In other states, recruiting for these executive positions may rest with the governor's chief of staff or other members of the governor's senior staff.

Budgeting

Most states have created an office outside the governor's office to manage the development and execution of the state budget. (See Table A.) In 10 states, however, this budget staff is included in the governor's direct office. Even when the governor is supported by a separate budget agency, the chief of staff, the policy director, agency liaison and other senior staff may be called upon to participate in the development and review of recommendations prepared by that agency.

Table A: Location of State Budget Functions

Location	*Number of states*
In governor's office	10
Freestanding agency	10
In finance department	12
In management or administrative department	21

Source: National Association of State Budget Officers, "Budget Processes in the States," Summer 2008.

Legislative Relations

The staff members responsible for dealing with the state legislature may have a variety of titles, including legislative liaison, legislative counsel, legislative assistant, legislative coordinator, legislative secretary and deputy assistant for legislation. In a few states, the legislative liaison and counsel functions may be handled by the governor's counsel or legal adviser.

This staff will oversee the development of the governor's legislative program, coordinate lobbying activities of the administration and negotiate many issues with the legislature. The legislative staff will usually monitor the progress on legislation and in many cases will have a strong role in recommending whether to sign or veto legislation.

Legal Counsel

The legal counsel's primary responsibility is to protect the legal interests of the governor and the governor's office, as well as to interpret federal and state laws and regulations and determine the impact they may have on the governor's initiatives and priorities. The legal counsel may also be responsible for a variety of other tasks, such as making appointments to the state judiciary, advising on clemency for state prison inmates, serving as liaison with the state attorney general, coordinating the work of departmental legal counsel, reviewing proposed and enacted legislation, and overseeing the administration of ethics laws or regulations.

Scheduling

The governor's scheduling office is charged with creating and managing a process that will protect the governor's time and allow the governor the opportunity to set priorities while ensuring adequate time for personal and family needs. The scheduling office is also used strategically to schedule meetings, events and appearances that will promote the governor's programs and priorities. In many states the scheduling office is also responsible for advancing the governor's appearances and coordinating the preparation of briefing material for those appearances.

Correspondence and Constituent Services

The governor's correspondence staff is responsible for ensuring those who contact the governor receive a thoughtful and timely response and that their concerns are shared with the governor, the governor's staff, and appropriate departments and agencies. The correspondence staffs may also provide a number of other services, such as issuing proclamations or recognizing constituents for special events, such as milestone birthdays or graduations.

Constituent services activities can help make government more accessible and responsive. In some states the governor's staff serves primarily as a referral mechanism seeing that constituent service requests are referred to state agencies for necessary action. In other states the governor's constituent services staff will play an active case management role working to personally oversee state efforts to resolve the constituent's problems or issues.

Policy Development

Policy staffs in the governors' offices develop, analyze and recommend policies and programs to address governors' priorities. In some states the policy function may be assigned to one or more senior staff members, such as the chief of staff, legal counsel or legislative director, as an addition to their primary responsibility. In other cases the governor may have designated staff members with specific substantive expertise to be responsible for particular policy areas.

Table B: Size of Governors' Offices in 2009

Office size	*Number of states*
1–9	1
10–14	1
15–19	3
20–24	7
25–29	1
30–34	4
35–39	5
40–44	3
45–49	2
50–74	13
75–99	4
100+	6
Average	63

Source: Compiled using various editions of *The Book of the States*.

In other cases the governor may have named a policy director who is expected to work independently calling on department or agency staff when necessary.

Finally, several states have created an organizational unit within the governor's office with a central mission of developing policy and serving as liaison with department and agency heads around policy development. In some states this same policy unit may also be responsible for working with the governor's cabinet to provide oversight of government operations more generally.

Information Technology

Information technology plays a critical role in many tasks, such as scheduling, appointments, correspondence and constituent services. In many cases these functions are unique to a governor's office and are not supported well by off-the-shelf software or by existing systems serving traditional state agencies. In addition, a governor is expected to develop and maintain a Web site to provide information about his or her office and priorities.

Intergovernmental Relations

Many states have established Washington offices to maintain relationships and communication with their delegations and with the departments and agencies of the federal government. These offices monitor and evaluate legislative and regulatory proposals, advocate for federal legislation and coordinate efforts to secure grants and contracts for their states. In a number of states, these staff members are considered part of the governor's offices. In addition, some governors' offices have designated staff members to serve as liaisons to local government officials or to coordinate the interaction of department and agency heads with the federal government.

Staffing the Governor's Office

Current Staffing

According to state-reported figures, 3,142 positions were assigned to the offices of the 50 governors in 2008. The smallest office, Nebraska, had only nine staff members, while two of the largest, Florida and Texas, had more than 250 staff members. The governors' offices had 63 staff members on average. As shown in Table B, fewer than half of the governors had more than 49 staff members assigned to their offices, while 12 had fewer than 25 staff assigned.

Table C shows the staffing of the offices of the governors in the largest and smallest states. Not surprisingly, there is a fairly direct correlation between

Table C: Growth of Governors' Offices in Selected States, 1980–81 Through 2009

State by magnitude of state and local spending	*1980–81*	*2009*	*Change (%)*
Ten Largest			
California	82.6	185	124%
New York	180	180	0
Texas	266	266	0
Florida	10	293	2,830
Pennsylvania	70	68	-3
Illinois	6	130	2,067
Ohio	18	60	233
Michigan	60	85	42
New Jersey	60	126	110
North Carolina	57	74	30
Ten Smallest			
Maine	12	19	58
Rhode Island	7	46	557
Idaho	21	22	5
New Hampshire	19	23	21
Delaware	17	32	88
Montana	20	61	205
North Dakota	13	17	31
South Dakota	8	21.5	169
Vermont	12	14	17
Wyoming	6	22	267

Source: Compiled using various editions of *The Book of the States*.

the size of the state and local expenditures in the state and the size of the governor's staff, although there are some exceptions.

More recent data provided by the states suggests that a significant number of governors are moving to reduce the size of the offices below that initially provided. Of 38 states responding to the survey conducted by the National Governors Association in late 2008, 25 have already made reductions and or plan to do so in 2009.

Table D: Growth of Governors' Offices over Time, 1980–81 Through 2009

Year	*Total number of staff*
1980–81	1,564
1990–91	2,529
2000–01	3,010
2003	2,867
2006	3,016
2009	3,142

Source: Compiled using various editions of *The Book of the States*.

Historical Trends

As shown in Table D, the size of the staff assigned to governors' offices has doubled since 1980–81 when the reported staff totaled 1,562. While all but four states reported a larger staff in 2009 than in 1980, almost one-half of the total growth was experienced in four states, with Florida and Texas showing increases of more than 250 positions each and Illinois and California growing by in excess of 100 positions each.

Most of the growth in the number of staff members assigned to governor's offices came in the twenty years between 1980 and 2000 when the increase totaled almost 1,500. The size of governors' staffs has grown slowly since 2000, increasing by only 132; it appears likely these staffs will decrease at least somewhat during the current economic crisis.

About the Author

Barry L. Van Lare is an independent consultant and a senior adviser to the National Governors Association's Office of Management Consulting and Training that assists governors and their staffs in the leadership and management of state government and the organization and operation of the governor's office. Van Lare has more than 45 years of experience in managing federal, state and local agencies and in developing and implementing national health and human services programs.

Table 4.1
THE GOVERNORS, 2009

State or other jurisdiction	Name and party	Length of regular term in years	Date of first service	Present term ends	Number of previous terms	Maximum consecutive terms allowed by constitution	Joint election of governor and lieutenant governor (a)	Official who succeeds governor	Birthdate	Birthplace
Alabama	Bob Riley (R)	4	1/2003	1/2011	1	2	No	LG	10/3/1944	AL
Alaska	Sarah H. Palin (R)	4	12/2006	12/2010	. . .	2	Yes	LG	2/11/1964	ID
Arizona	Jan Brewer (R)	4	1/2009 (b)	1/2011	. . .	2	(c)	SS	9/26/1944	CA
Arkansas	Mike Beebe (D)	4	1/2007	1/2011	. . .	2	No	LG	12/28/1946	AR
California	Arnold Schwarzenegger (R)	4	11/2003 (d)	1/2011	1 (d)	2	No	LG	7/30/1947	Aus.
Colorado	Bill Ritter (D)	4	1/2007	1/2011	. . .	2	Yes	LG	9/6/1956	CO
Connecticut	M. Jodi Rell (R)	4	7/2004 (e)	1/2011	1 (e)	. . .	Yes	LG	6/16/1946	VA
Delaware	Jack Markell (D)	4	1/2009	1/2013	. . .	2	No	LG	11/26/1960	DE
Florida	Charlie Crist (R)	4	1/2007	1/2011	. . .	2	Yes	LG	7/24/1956	PA
Georgia	Sonny Perdue (R)	4	1/2003	1/2011	1	2	No	LG	12/20/1946	GA
Hawaii	Linda Lingle (R)	4	12/2002	12/2010	1	2	Yes	LG	6/4/1953	MO
Idaho	C.L. "Butch" Otter (R)	4	1/2007	1/2011	. . .	. . .	No	LG	5/3/1942	ID
Illinois	Patrick Quinn (D)	4	1/2009 (f)	1/2011	. . .	. . .	Yes	LG	12/16/1948	IL
Indiana	Mitch Daniels (R)	4	1/2005	1/2013	1	2 (g)	Yes	LG	4/7/1949	PA
Iowa	Chet Culver (D)	4	1/2007	1/2011	. . .	. . .	Yes	LG	1/25/1966	DC
Kansas	Mark Parkinson (D)	4	4/2009 (h)	1/2011	. . .	2	Yes	LG	6/25/1957	KS
Kentucky	Steven L. Beshear (D)	4	12/2007	12/2011	. . .	2	Yes	LG	9/21/1944	KY
Louisiana	Bobby Jindal (R)	4	1/2008	1/2012	. . .	2	No	LG	6/10/1971	LA
Maine	John E. Baldacci (D)	4	1/2003	1/2011	1	2	(c)	PS	1/30/1955	ME
Maryland	Martin O'Malley (D)	4	1/2007	1/2011	. . .	2	Yes	LG	1/18/1963	MD
Massachusetts	Deval L. Patrick (D)	4	1/2007	1/2011	. . .	. . .	Yes	LG	7/31/1956	IL
Michigan	Jennifer Granholm (D)	4	1/2003	1/2011	1	2	Yes	LG	2/5/1959	BC
Minnesota	Tim Pawlenty (R)	4	1/2003	1/2011	1	. . .	Yes	LG	11/27/1960	MN
Mississippi	Haley Barbour (R)	4	1/2004	1/2012	1	2	Yes	LG	10/22/1947	MS
Missouri	Jay Nixon (D)	4	1/2009	1/2013	. . .	2	No	LG	2/13/1956	MO
Montana	Brian Schweitzer (D)	4	1/2005	1/2013	1	2 (i)	Yes	LG	9/4/1955	MT
Nebraska	Dave Heineman (R)	4	1/2005 (j)	1/2011	1 (j)	2 (g)	Yes	LG	5/12/1948	NE
Nevada	James A. Gibbons (R)	4	1/2007	1/2011	. . .	2	No	LG	12/16/1944	NV
New Hampshire	John Lynch (D)	2	1/2005	1/2011	2	. . .	(c)	PS	11/25/1952	MA
New Jersey	Jon Corzine (D)	4	1/2006	1/2010	. . .	2	(k)	(k)	1/1/1947	IL
New Mexico	Bill Richardson (D)	4	1/2003	1/2011	1	2	Yes	LG	11/15/1947	CA
New York	David A. Paterson (D)	4	3/2008 (l)	1/2011	. . .	. . .	Yes	LG (l)	5/20/1954	NY
North Carolina	Beverly Perdue (D)	4	1/2009	1/2013	. . .	2	No	LG	1/14/1947	VA
North Dakota	John Hoeven (R)	4	12/2000	12/2012	2	. . .	Yes	LG	3/13/1957	ND
Ohio	Ted Strickland (D)	4	1/2007	1/2011	. . .	2 (g)	Yes	LG	8/4/1941	OH
Oklahoma	Brad Henry (D)	4	1/2003	1/2011	1	2	No	LG	6/10/1963	OK
Oregon	Ted Kulongoski (D)	4	1/2003	1/2011	1	2	(c)	SS	11/5/1940	MO
Pennsylvania	Edward G. Rendell (D)	4	1/2003	1/2011	1	2	Yes	LG	1/5/1944	NY
Rhode Island	Don Carcieri (R)	4	1/2003	1/2011	1	2	No	LG	12/16/1942	RI
South Carolina	Mark Sanford (R)	4	1/2003	1/2011	1	2	No	LG	5/28/1960	FL

See footnotes at end of table.

THE GOVERNORS, 2009—Continued

State or other jurisdiction	Name and party	Length of regular term in years	Date of first service	Present term ends	Number of previous terms	Maximum consecutive terms allowed by constitution	Joint election of governor and lieutenant governor (a)	Official who succeeds governor	Birthdate	Birthplace
South Dakota	Mike Rounds (R)	4	1/2003	1/2011	1	2	Yes	LG	10/24/1954	SD
Tennessee	Phil Bredesen (D)	4	1/2003	1/2011	1	2	No	SpS (m)	11/21/1943	NJ
Texas	Rick Perry (R)	4	12/2000 (n)	1/2011	2	. . .	No	LG	3/4/1950	TX
Utah	Jon M. Huntsman Jr. (R)	4	1/2005	1/2013	1	. . .	Yes	LG	3/26/1960	CA
Vermont	Jim Douglas (R)	2	1/2003	1/2011	3	. . .	No	LG	6/21/1951	MA
Virginia	Tim Kaine (D)	4	1/2006	1/2010	. . .	(o)	No	LG	2/26/1958	MN
Washington	Christine Gregoire (D)	4	1/2005	1/2013	1	. . .	No	LG	3/24/1957	WA
West Virginia	Joe Manchin III (D)	4	1/2005	1/2013	1	2	(c)	PS (m)	8/24/1947	WV
Wisconsin	Jim Doyle (D)	4	1/2003	1/2011	1	. . .	Yes	LG	11/23/1945	DC
Wyoming	Dave Freudenthal (D)	4	1/2003	1/2011	1	2	(c)	SS	10/12/1950	WY
American Samoa	Togiola Tulafono (D)	4	4/2003 (p)	1/2013	2	2	Yes	LG	2/28/1947	AS
Guam	Felix P. Camacho (R)	4	1/2003	1/2011	1	2	Yes	LG	10/30/1957	Japan
No. Mariana Islands	Benigno Fitial (C)	4	1/2006	1/2010	. . .	2 (q)	Yes	LG	11/27/1945	CNMI
Puerto Rico	Luis G. Fortuño (R) (NPP)	4	1/2009	1/2013	. . .	. . .	(c)	SS	10/31/1960	PR
U.S. Virgin Islands	John deJongh Jr. (D)	4	1/2007	1/2011	. . .	2 (g)	Yes	LG	11/13/1957	USVI

Source: The Council of State Governments, March 2009.

Key:

C — Covenant
D — Democrat
NPP — New Progressive Party
R — Republican
LG — Lieutenant Governor
SS — Secretary of State
PS — President of the Senate
SpS — Speaker of the Senate
. . . — Not applicable

(a) The following also choose candidates for governor and lieutenant governor through a joint nomination process: Florida, Kansas, Maryland, Minnesota, Montana, North Dakota, Ohio, Utah, American Samoa, Guam, No. Mariana Islands and U.S. Virgin Islands.

(b) Secretary of State Jan Brewer succeeded to the office of governor on January 21, 2009, upon Governor Napolitano's appointment as U.S. Secretary of Homeland Security.

(c) No lieutenant governor.

(d) Governor Schwarzenegger was sworn in on November 17, 2003 after winning the replacement election following the recall vote that removed Governor Gray Davis from office in the same election.

(e) Lieutenant Governor Rell was sworn in as governor on July 1, 2004 after Governor John Rowland resigned.

(f) Lieutenant Governor Patrick Quinn became governor on January 29, 2009 after Governor Blagojevich was removed from office.

(g) After two consecutive terms as governor, the candidate must wait four years before becoming eligible to run again.

(h) Lieutenant Governor Parkinson on April 28, 2009 assumed the office of governor when Governor Sebelius was appointed U.S. Secretary of Health and Human Services.

(i) Absolute limit of eight years of service out of every 16 years.

(j) Governor Heineman, as lieutenant governor, was sworn-in as Nebraska's governor on Friday, January 21, 2005 after Governor Johanns resigned on January 20, 2005 upon being confirmed as the United States Secretary of Agriculture.

(k) New Jersey will elect a lieutenant governor in 2009. The governor and lieutenant governor will be elected jointly. In the event of a permanent vacancy in the office before the inauguration date of the first lieutenant governor, the president of the senate, followed by the speaker of the assembly, would succeed the governor in the event of a permanent vacancy.

(l) Lieutenant Governor David A. Paterson was sworn in as governor on March 17, 2008 after Governor Eliot Spitzer resigned. The position of Lieutenant Governor will remain vacant until the general election in 2010. In the event Gov. Paterson cannot fulfill his duties, Senate Majority Leader Malcolm Smith would be next in the line of succession.

(m) Official bears the additional title of " lieutenant governor."

(n) Lt. Gov. Perry was sworn in on December 21, 2000 to complete President George W. Bush's term as governor of Texas.

(o) Governor cannot serve immediate successive terms, but may be elected to non-consecutive terms.

(p) Governor Tulafono, as lieutenant governor, became Governor in April 2003 after Governor Sunia's death.

(q) Absolute two-term limitation, but terms need not be consecutive.

Table 4.2
THE GOVERNORS: QUALIFICATIONS FOR OFFICE

State or other jurisdiction	Minimum age	State citizen (years)	U.S. citizen (years) (a)	State resident (years) (b)	Qualified voter (years)
Alabama	30	...	10	7	★
Alaska	30	★	7	7	★
Arizona	25	5	10	...	...
Arkansas	30	★	★	7	★
California	18	...	5	5	★
Colorado	30	...	★	2	...
Connecticut	30	(c)	★	★	(c)
Delaware	30	...	12	6	...
Florida	30	★	...	7	7
Georgia	30	...	15	6	...
Hawaii	30	...	5	5	★
Idaho	30	...	★	2	...
Illinois	25	3	★	3	★
Indiana	30	...	5	5	★
Iowa	30	2	2	2	★
Kansas	...	...	...	...	...
Kentucky	30	6	...	6	...
Louisiana	25	5	5	5	★
Maine	30	...	15	5	...
Maryland	30	...	(d)	5	5
Massachusetts	...	...	...	7	...
Michigan	30	...	★	★	4
Minnesota	25	...	★	1	★
Mississippi	30	★	20	5	★
Missouri	30	...	15	10	...
Montana	25	★	★	2	★
Nebraska	30	5	5	5	...
Nevada	25	2	2	2	★
New Hampshire	30	...	...	7	...
New Jersey	30	...	20	7	...
New Mexico	30	...	★	5	★
New York	30	...	★	5	...
North Carolina	30	...	5	2	★
North Dakota	30	...	★	5	★
Ohio	18	...	★	★	★
Oklahoma	31	...	10	10	10
Oregon	30	...	★	3	...
Pennsylvania	30	★	★	7	★
Rhode Island	18	30 days	30 days	30 days	30 days
South Carolina	30	5	5	5	...
South Dakota	18	★	★	★	★
Tennessee	30	7	★	...	...
Texas	30	...	★	5	...
Utah	30	5	3	5	★
Vermont	18	1	...	4	★
Virginia	30	★	★	★	5
Washington	18	...	★	★	★
West Virginia	30	5	★	1	★
Wisconsin	18	★	★	★	★
Wyoming	30	★	★	5	★
American Samoa	35	...	★	5	...
Guam	30	...	5	5	★
No. Mariana Islands	35	...	★	10	★
Puerto Rico	35	5	5	5	...
U.S. Virgin Islands	30	...	5	5	★

Source: The Council of State Governments' survey of governor's offices, December 2008.

Key:

★ — Formal provision; number of years not specified.

. . . — No formal provision.

(a) In some states you must be a U.S. citizen to be an elector, and must be an elector to run.

(b) In some states you must be a state resident to be an elector, and must be an elector to run.

(c) Must be an elector of the state, not a state citizen.

(d) *Crosse v. Board of Supervisors of Elections* 243 Md. 555, 221A.2d431 (1966)—opinion rendered indicated that U.S. citizenship was, by necessity, a requirement for office.

Table 4.3
THE GOVERNORS: COMPENSATION, STAFF, TRAVEL AND RESIDENCE

State or other jurisdiction	Salary	Governor's office staff (a)	Access to state transportation: Automobile	Access to state transportation: Airplane	Access to state transportation: Helicopter	Receives travel allowance	Reimbursed for travel expenses	Official residence
Alabama	$112,895	60	★	★	★	. . .	. . .	★
Alaska	125,000	71	★	★	. . .	. . .	★(b)	★
Arizona	95,000	39	★	★	. . .	. . .	★(b)	. . .
Arkansas	87,352	67	★	★	. . .	. . .	★	★
California	212,179 (c)	185	★	. . .	. . .	(b)	(d)	(e)
Colorado	90,000	50	★	★	. . .	★	★	★
Connecticut	150,000	37	★	. . .	. . .	. . .	. . .	(e)
Delaware	171,000	32	★	. . .	. . .	. . .	. . .	★
Florida	132,932	293 (f)	★	★	. . .	. . .	★(b)	★
Georgia	139,339	56 (f)	★	★	★	. . .	. . .	★
Hawaii	123,480	67	★	★	★	★	★	★
Idaho	108,727	22	★	★	. . .	★(b)	(d)	(e)
Illinois	177,500	130	★	★	★	★	(d)	★
Indiana	95,000	34	★	★	★	★(b)	★(b)	★
Iowa	130,000	32	★	. . .	. . .	. . .	★	★
Kansas	110,707	24	★	★	★	. . .	★	★
Kentucky	142,498	80	★	★	★	. . .	★(b)	★
Louisiana	130,000	93 (f)	★	★	★	. . .	★	★
Maine	70,000	19	★	. . .	. . .	★	★	★
Maryland	150,000	85 (f)	★	★	★	(b)	(b)	★
Massachusetts	140,535	70	★	. . .	★	★(b)	★(b)	. . .
Michigan	177,000 (c)	85	★	★	. . .	(b)	(b)	★
Minnesota	120,303	43	★	★	★	. . .	★	★
Mississippi	122,160	46	★	★	. . .	. . .	★	★
Missouri	133,821	38	★	★	. . .	(b)	(d)	★
Montana	100,121	61 (f)	★	★	★	★	★	★
Nebraska	105,000	9	★	★	. . .	★	★	★
Nevada	141,000	23 (f)	★	★	. . .	(b)	. . .	★
New Hampshire	113,834	23	★	. . .	. . .	(b)	(d)	★(e)
New Jersey	175,000 (c)	126	★	. . .	★	. . .	★(b)	★
New Mexico	110,000	39.3	★	★	★	. . .	. . .	★
New York	179,000	180	★	★	★	. . .	★	★
North Carolina	139,590	74	★	★	★	★	★	★
North Dakota	100,030	17	★	★	. . .	. . .	★	★
Ohio	144,269	60	★	★	★	(b)	(d)	★
Oklahoma	147,000	34	★	★	. . .	★(b)	★(b)	★
Oregon	93,600	65 (f)	★	. . .	. . .	★(b)	★(b)	★
Pennsylvania	174,914	68	★	★	. . .	. . .	★(b)	★
Rhode Island	117,817	46	★	. . .	★	. . .	★	. . .
South Carolina	106,078	22	★	★	. . .	★	. . .	★
South Dakota	115,331	21.5	★	★	. . .	. . .	★	★
Tennessee	164,292 (c)	36	★	★	★	(b)	(d)	★
Texas	150,000	266	★	★	★	. . .	★	★
Utah	109,900	16	★	★	★	. . .	★	★
Vermont	142,542	14	★	. . .	. . .	★	. . .	. . .
Virginia	175,000	44	★	★	★	. . .	★	★
Washington	166,891	36	★	★	. . .	(b)	(d)	★
West Virginia	95,000	56	★	★	★	(b)	(d)	★
Wisconsin	137,092	25	★	★	. . .	. . .	(d)	★
Wyoming	105,000	22	★	★	. . .	. . .	★(b)	★
American Samoa	50,000	23	★	. . .	. . .	(b)	. . .	★
Guam	90,000	42	★	. . .	. . .	$218/day	. . .	★
No. Mariana Islands	70,000	16	★	. . .	. . .	(b)	. . .	★
Puerto Rico	70,000	28	★	(g)	(g)	. . .	★	★
U.S. Virgin Islands	80,000	86	★	. . .	. . .	. . .	★	★

See footnotes at end of table.

THE GOVERNORS: COMPENSATION, STAFF, TRAVEL AND RESIDENCE—Continued

Source: The Council of State Governments' survey, December 2008.
Key:
★ — Yes
. . . — No
N.A. — Not available.

(a) Definitions of "governor's office staff" vary across the states—from general office support to staffing for various operations within the executive office.

(b) Travel expenses:

Alaska—$42/day per diem plus actual lodging expenses.

American Samoa—$105,000. Amount includes travel allowance for entire staff.

Arizona—Receives up to $38/day for meals based on location; receives per diem for lodging out-of-state; default $28/day for meals and $50/day lodging in-state.

California—$145,000 in-state; $36,000 out-of-state.

Florida—Reimbursed at same rate as other state officials: in-state, choice between $50 per diem or actual expenses; out-of-state, actual expenses.

Idaho—Travel allowance included in office budget.

Indiana—Statute allows $12,000 but due to budget cuts the amount has been reduced to $9,800 and reimbursed for actual expenses for travel/lodging.

Kentucky—Mileage at same rate as other state officials.

Maryland—Travel allowance included in office budget.

Massachusetts—As necessary.

Michigan—The governor is provided a $60,000 annual expense allowance, as determined by the State Officers Compensation Commission in 2000. "Expense allowance" is for normal, reimbursable personal expenses such as food, lodging, and travel costs incurred by an individual in carrying out the responsibilities of state office.

Missouri—Amount includes travel allowance for entire staff. Amount not available.

Nevada—Amount includes travel allowance for entire staff. The following figures include travel expenses for governor and staff: $45,750 in-state; $32,800 out-of-state.

New Hampshire—Travel allowance included in office budget.

New Jersey—Reimbursement may be provided for necessary expenses.

Northern Mariana Islands—Travel allowance included in office budget. Governor has a "contingency account" that can be used for travel expenses and expenses in other departments or other projects.

Ohio—Set administratively.

Oklahoma—Reimbursed for actual and necessary expenses.

Oregon—$1,000 a month for expenses, not specific to travel. Reimbursed for actual travel expenses.

Pennsylvania—Reimbursed for reasonable expenses.

Tennessee—Travel allowance included in office budget.

Washington—Travel allowance included in office budget.

West Virginia—Included in general expense account.

Wyoming—$99/day or actual.

(c) Governor's salary:

California—Governor Schwarzenegger waives his salary.

Michigan—Governor Granholm returns five percent of her salary to the general fund.

New Jersey—Governor Corzine only accepts $1.

Tennessee—Governor Bredesen returns his salary to the state. Tennessee statute mandates the governor and the chief justice of the Supreme Court receive the same salary, currently $160,000. However a state law exists which prohibits a sitting governor's salary from being increased or decreased during his term of office.

(d) Information not provided.

(e) Governor's residence:

California—Provided by Governor's Residence Foundation, a nonprofit organization which provides a residence for the governor of California. No rent is charged; maintenance and operational costs are provided by California Department of General Services.

Connecticut—Maintained by the Department of Public Works.

Idaho—J.R. and Esther Simplot donated their home to the state of Idaho in December 2004 for use as the future governor's residence. Efforts are underway to raise private monies for renovation.

New Hampshire—The current governor does not occupy the official residence.

(f) Governor's staff:

Florida—The governor's office budget includes the following staff for the Executive Office: 119 Drug Control, 5 Office of Tourism, 21 Trade and Economic Development, 43 System Design, 105 Office of Policy and Budget.

Georgia—Full-time employees—56, and 2 part-time employees.

Louisiana—Full-time employees—93, part-time (non-student)—21, students—25.

Maryland—Full-time employees—85, and 1 part-time employee.

Montana—Including 20 employees from the Office of Budget and Program Planning.

Nevada—For 2006 the number of authorized staff was 23; however, not all positions were filled as of September 10, 2006.

Oregon—Of this total, 45 are true governor's staff and 20 are on loan for agency staff.

(g) The governor's office pays for access to an airplane or helicopter with a corporate credit card and requests a refund of those expenses with the corresponding documentation to the Department of Treasury.

Table 4.4
THE GOVERNORS: POWERS

State or other jurisdiction	Budget making power		Item veto power					Authorization for reorganization through executive order (a)
	Full responsibility	Shares responsibility	Governor has item veto power on all bills	Governor has item veto power on appropriations only	Governor has no item veto power	Item veto— 2/3 legislators present or 3/5 elected to override	Item veto— majority legislators elected to override	
Alabama	★(b)	. . .	★	. . .	. . .	. . .	★	. . .
Alaska	★	. . .	. . .	★	. . .	★	. . .	★
Arizona	★(b)	. . .	. . .	★	. . .	★	(c)	. . .
Arkansas	. . .	★	. . .	★	. . .	. . .	★	★
California	★(b)	. . .	. . .	★	. . .	★	. . .	★(d)
Colorado	. . .	★	. . .	★	. . .	★	. . .	★
Connecticut	. . .	★	. . .	★	. . .	★	. . .	. . .
Delaware	★(b)	. . .	★	. . .	. . .	★	. . .	★
Florida	. . .	★	★	. . .	. . .	★	. . .	★
Georgia	★	. . .	. . .	★	. . .	(c)	. . .	★
Hawaii	. . .	★	★	. . .	. . .	★	. . .	★
Idaho	★	. . .	★	. . .	. . .	★	. . .	. . .
Illinois	. . .	★	★	. . .	. . .	★	. . .	★
Indiana	★	. . .	. . .	. . .	★	. . .	. . .	★
Iowa	. . .	★	. . .	★	. . .	★	. . .	★
Kansas	★	. . .	. . .	★	. . .	★	. . .	★
Kentucky	★(b)	. . .	★	. . .	. . .	★	. . .	★
Louisiana	. . .	★	. . .	★	. . .	. . .	★(e)	★(f)
Maine	. . .	★	. . .	★	. . .	. . .	★	★
Maryland	★	. . .	★	. . .	. . .	★	. . .	★
Massachusetts	★	. . .	★	. . .	. . .	. . .	★(e)	★(d)
Michigan	★(g)	. . .	. . .	★(h)	. . .	. . .	★(e)	★
Minnesota	. . .	★	. . .	★	. . .	. . .	★(e)	★(i)
Mississippi	. . .	★(j)	★	. . .	. . .	★	. . .	★
Missouri	★(b)	. . .	. . .	★	. . .	★	. . .	★
Montana	★	. . .	. . .	★	. . .	★	. . .	★(k)
Nebraska	. . .	★	. . .	★	. . .	★(l)	. . .	. . .
Nevada	★	. . .	. . .	. . .	★	. . .	. . .	. . .
New Hampshire	★(b)	. . .	. . .	. . .	★	. . .	. . .	. . .
New Jersey	★(b)	. . .	★	. . .	. . .	. . .	★(e)	. . .
New Mexico	★	. . .	. . .	★	. . .	★	. . .	. . .
New York	. . .	★	★	. . .	. . .	★	. . .	. . .
North Carolina	★	. . .	. . .	. . .	★	. . .	. . .	★
North Dakota	★	. . .	. . .	★	. . .	★	. . .	★
Ohio	★	. . .	. . .	★	. . .	★	. . .	. . .
Oklahoma	. . .	★	. . .	★	. . .	. . .	★(e)	. . .
Oregon	. . .	★	. . .	★	. . .	★	. . .	★
Pennsylvania	★	. . .	. . .	★	. . .	★	. . .	. . .
Rhode Island	. . .	★	. . .	. . .	★	. . .	. . .	. . .
South Carolina	. . .	★	. . .	★	. . .	★	. . .	. . .

See footnotes at end of table.

THE GOVERNORS: POWERS — Continued

State or other jurisdiction	Budget making power: Full responsibility	Budget making power: Shares responsibility	Item veto power: Governor has item veto power on all bills	Item veto power: Governor has item veto power on appropriations only	Item veto power: Governor has no item veto power	Item veto power: Item veto— 2/3 legislators present or 3/5 elected to override	Item veto power: Item veto— majority legislators elected to override	Authorization for reorganization through executive order (a)
South Dakota	★	. . .	. . .	★	. . .	★(m)	. . .	★
Tennessee	. . .	★	. . .	★	. . .	. . .	★	★
Texas	. . .	★	. . .	★	. . .	★	. . .	★
Utah	. . .	★	. . .	★	. . .	★	. . .	★
Vermont	★	. . .	. . .	. . .	★	. . .	. . .	★
Virginia	★	. . .	. . .	★	. . .	★(m)	. . .	★
Washington	★	. . .	★(n)	. . .	. . .	★	. . .	. . .
West Virginia	★	. . .	. . .	★	. . .	★	. . .	. . .
Wisconsin	★(b)	. . .	. . .	★(o)	. . .	★	. . .	. . .
Wyoming	. . .	★	★	. . .	. . .	★	. . .	. . .
American Samoa	. . .	★	. . .	. . .	. . .	. . .	. . .	★
Guam	★	. . .	★	. . .	. . .	★	. . .	★
No. Mariana Islands	. . .	★	. . .	★	. . .	★	. . .	★
Puerto Rico	. . .	★	. . .	★	. . .	★	. . .	★(p)
U.S. Virgin Islands	★	. . .	. . .	★	. . .	★	. . .	★

Source: The Council of State Governments' survey of governor's offices, December 2008.

Key:

★ — Yes; provision for.

. . . — No; not applicable.

(a) For additional information on executive orders, see Table 4.5.

(b) Full responsibility to propose; legislature adopts or revises and governor signs or vetoes.

(c) Two-thirds of members to which each house is entitled required to override veto.

(d) Authorization for reorganization provided for in state constitution.

(e) Two-thirds of elected legislators of each house to override.

(f) Only for agencies and offices within the Governor's Office.

(g) Governor has sole authority to propose annual budget. No money may be paid out of state treasury except in pursuance of appropriations made by law.

(h) Governor may veto any distinct item or items appropriating money in any appropriations bill.

(i) Statute provides for reorganization by the Commissioner of Administration with the approval of the governor.

(j) Governor has the responsibility of presenting a balanced budget. The budget is based on revenue estimated by the governor's office and the Legislative Budget Committee.

(k) The office of the governor shall continuously study and evaluate the organizational structure, management practices, and functions of the executive branch and of each agency. The governor shall, by executive order or other means within the authority granted to him, take action to improve the manageability of the executive branch.

(l) Three-fifths majority required to override line-item veto.

(m) Requires 2/3 of legislators present to override.

(n) Governor has veto power of selections for nonappropriations and item veto in appropriations.

(o) In Wisconsin, governor has "partial" veto over appropriation bills. The partial veto is broader than item veto.

(p) Only if it is not prohibited by law.

Table 4.5
GUBERNATORIAL EXECUTIVE ORDERS: AUTHORIZATION, PROVISIONS, PROCEDURES

		Provisions								Procedures		
State or other jurisdiction	Authorization for executive orders	Civil defense disasters, public emergencies	Energy emergencies and conservation	Other emergencies	Executive branch reorganization plans and agency creation	Create advisory, coordinating, study or investigative committees/ commissions	Respond to federal programs and requirements	State personnel administration	Other administration	Filing and publication procedures	Subject to administrative procedure act	Subject to legislative review
Alabama	S,I, Case Law	★	★	★	. . .	★	. . .	. . .	. . .	★	. . .	. . .
Alaska	C	. . .	. . .	. . .	★	. . .	. . .	. . .	. . .	★	. . .	★
Arizona	I	★(a)	★(a)	★(a)	. . .	★	. . .	. . .	. . .	★(b)	. . .	. . .
Arkansas	S,I, Common Law	★	★	★	★	★	. . .	. . .	. . .	. . .	. . .	. . .
California	I	★	★	★	★	★	★	★	★	. . .	. . .	. . .
Colorado	C	★	★	. . .	★	★	★	★	. . .	★	★	. . .
Connecticut	C,S	★	★	★	. . .	★	. . .	. . .	. . .	★	★	. . .
Delaware	C	★	★	★	★	★	★	★	. . .	★	. . .	. . .
Florida	C	★	★	★	★(c)	★	★	★	. . .	. . .	★(d)	. . .
Georgia	S,I (e)	★	★	★	★	★	★	★	. . .	★	. . .	. . .
Hawaii	C	★	★	★	★	★	★	★	. . .	★	★	★
Idaho	S	. . .	I	I	. . .	I	I	. . .	. . .	(b)(f)	. . .	. . .
Illinois	C,S	★	★	★	★	★	★	★	★	★	★	★
Indiana	C,S, Case Law	★	★	. . .	★(limited)	★	★	★	. . .	. . .	. . .	. . .
Iowa	(g)	★	★	★	★	★	★	★	(h)	★	★	★
Kansas	C,S	★	★	★	★	★	. . .	★	★	. . .	. . .	(i)
Kentucky	C,S	★	★	★(j)	★	★	★	★	★(k)(l)(m)	★(b)	★	★
Louisiana	C,S (n)	★	★	★	★	★	★	★	. . .	★	. . .	. . .
Maine	I	★	★	★	★	★	★	★	. . .	. . .	. . .	. . .
Maryland	C,S	★	★	★	★	★	★	★	★(o)	★	★	★(p)
Massachusetts	C,S	★	★	★	★	★	. . .	★	★	★	. . .	. . .
Michigan	C,S,I	★	★	★	★(v)	★	★	★	★	★(v)	. . .	. . .
Minnesota	S	★	★(x)	★	★	★	★	. . .	(u)	★(b)	★	★(p)
Mississippi	C,S	★	★	★	★	★	★	★	. . .	(y)	(y)	. . .
Missouri	C,S, Common Law	★	I	★	★	★	★	★	★	★(p)	. . .	★(p)(z)
Montana	S,I, Common Law	★	★	★	★	★	★	. . .	. . .	★	. . .	. . .
Nebraska	C,S	★	★	★	. . .	★	. . .	. . .	. . .	★	. . .	. . .
Nevada	S,I	★	. . .	I	. . .	★	. . .	. . .	I	. . .	. . .	. . .
New Hampshire	S	★	★(a)	★	. . .	★	★	. . .	★(l)	★	. . .	. . .
New Jersey	C,S,I	★	★	★	. . .	★	. . .	. . .	★(q)	. . .	. . .	. . .
New Mexico	C,S	★	★	★	★	★	. . .	★	. . .	★	. . .	. . .
New York	C,S	★	★	★	. . .	★	. . .	. . .	. . .	★	. . .	. . .
North Carolina	C,S	★	★	★	★	★	★	★	. . .	★	. . .	★
North Dakota	S,I	★	★	★	. . .	. . .	. . .	. . .	(m)(q)(r)(s)(t)(u)	. . .	. . .	. . .
Ohio	S,I (aa)	★	★	★	★	★	★	. . .	. . .	★	. . .	. . .
Oklahoma	C	★	★	★	(cc)	★	★	★	. . .	★	. . .	. . .
Oregon	I	★	★	★	. . .	★	★	★	. . .	. . .	. . .	. . .
Pennsylvania	C,S	★	. . .	★(o)(w)(bb)(dd)	. . .	★	★	. . .	★(dd)	★(b)(w)	. . .	. . .
Rhode Island	I, Case Law	★	★	★	★	★	★	★	. . .	★	. . .	. . .
South Carolina	S	★	★	★	. . .	★	. . .	. . .	★	★	. . .	. . .

See footnotes at end of table.

GUBERNATORIAL EXECUTIVE ORDERS: AUTHORIZATION, PROVISIONS, PROCEDURES — Continued

State or other jurisdiction	Authorization for executive orders	Provisions: Civil defense disasters, public emergencies	Provisions: Energy emergencies and conservation	Provisions: Other emergencies	Provisions: Executive branch reorganization plans and agency creation	Provisions: Create advisory, coordinating, study or investigative committees/ commissions	Provisions: Respond to federal programs and requirements	Provisions: State personnel administration	Provisions: Other administration	Procedures: Filing and publication procedures	Procedures: Subject to administrative procedure act	Procedures: Subject to legislative review
South Dakota	C	★	★	★	★	★	★	★	★	★	. . .	. . .
Tennessee	S	★	★	★	★	★	★	★	★	★(b)	. . .	. . .
Texas	I	★	★	★	★	★	★	★	. . .	. . .	. . .	. . .
Utah	S,I	★	★	★	★	★	★	★	. . .	. . .	. . .	. . .
Vermont	S,I	★	★	. . .	★(ee)	★	★	. . .	. . .	. . .	. . .	★(ff)
Virginia	S	★	★	★	★	★	★	★	. . .	. . .	★	. . .
Washington	S	★	. . .	. . .	. . .	. . .	. . .	. . .	. . .	. . .	. . .	. . .
West Virginia	C,S	★	★	. . .	. . .	★	★	. . .	. . .	. . .	. . .	. . .
Wisconsin	S	★	★	★	. . .	★	★	. . .	. . .	★	★	★
Wyoming	(gg)	. . .	. . .	. . .	. . .	. . .	. . .	. . .	. . .	. . .	. . .	. . .
American Samoa	C,S	★	★	★	★	★	★	★	★	★(hh)	★(hh)	. . .
Guam	C	★	★	. . .	(ii)	★	★	★	★	★	. . .	. . .
No. Mariana Islands	C	★	I	★	C	S,I	S	. . .	★	S	I	. . .
Puerto Rico	C,S,I, Case Law	★	★	★	★	★	★	★	★	(jj)	. . .	. . .
U.S. Virgin Islands	C	★	★	★	★	★	★	★	★	★	. . .	. . .

Source: The Council of State Governments' survey, December 2008.

Key:

C — Constitutional

S — Statutory

I — Implied

★ — Formal provision.

. . . — No formal provision.

(a) Broad interpretation of gubernatorial authority.

(b) Executive orders must be filed with secretary of state or other designated officer. In Idaho, must also be published in state general circulation newspaper.

(c) It could be debatable if the governor has the authority to create agencies by executive order; practically, a governor certainly would not do so without support from the legislature as they must approve funding.

(d) Under some circumstances the Cabinet must approve before an order becomes law. The Joint Administrative Procedure Committee must make sure agency rules have legislative authority to do so.

(e) Implied from Constitution.

(f) Some implied.

(g) Constitution, statute, implied, case law, common law.

(h) Executive clemency.

(i) Only for EROs. When an ERO is submitted, the legislature has 30 days to veto the ERO or it becomes law.

(j) To give immediate effect to state regulation in emergencies.

(k) To control administration of state contracts and procedures.

(l) To impound or freeze certain state matching funds.

(m) To reduce state expenditures in revenue shortfall.

(n) Inherent.

(o) To control procedures for dealing with public.

(p) Reorganization plans and agency creation.

(q) To administer and govern the armed forces of the state.

(r) To suspend certain officials and/or other civil actions.

(s) To designate game and wildlife areas or other public areas.

(t) Appointive powers.

(u) To assign duties to lieutenant governor, issue writ of special election.

(v) Executive reorganizations not effective if rejected by both houses of legislature within 60 days. Executive orders reducing appropriations not effective unless approved by appropriations committees of both houses of legislature.

(w) Filing.

(x) If an energy emergency is declared by the state's Executive Council or legislature.

(y) Governor is exempt from the Administrative Procedures Act and filing and administrative procedures Miss. Code Ann. § 25-43-102 (1972).

(z) Reorganization plans and agency creation and for meeting federal program requirements.

(aa) Executive authority implied except for emergencies which are established by statute.

(bb) For fire emergencies.

(cc) Limited authority in executive branch reorganization/agency creation.

(dd) To transfer funds in an emergency.

(ee) Subject to legislative approval.

(ff) Only if reorganization order filed with the legislature.

(gg) No specific authorization granted, general authority only.

(hh) If executive order fits definition of rule.

(ii) Can reorganize, but not create.

(jj) Executive orders are filed in the Department of State.

Table 4.6
STATE CABINET SYSTEMS

State or other jurisdiction	Authorization for cabinet system: State statute	State constitution	Governor created	Tradition in state	Criteria for membership: Appointed to specific office (a)	Elected to specified office (a)	Gubernatorial appointment regardless of office	Number of members in cabinet (including governor)	Frequency of cabinet meetings	Open cabinet meetings
Alabama	★	. . .	★	★	★	. . .	. . .	26	Quarterly	. . .
Alaska	. . .	. . .	★	. . .	★	. . .	. . .	19	Gov.'s discretion	★(b)
Arizona	. . .	. . .	★	. . .	★	. . .	★	38	Monthly	. . .
Arkansas	. . .	. . .	★	. . .	★	. . .	. . .	47	Monthly	. . .
California	★	. . .	★	. . .	★	. . .	★	11	Every two weeks	. . .
Colorado	★	. . .	★	. . .	. . .	. . .	★	21	Monthly	. . .
Connecticut	★	. . .	. . .	. . .	. . .	. . .	★	27	Gov.'s discretion	. . .
Delaware	★	. . .	. . .	. . .	★	. . .	★	19	Gov.'s discretion	. . .
Florida	. . .	★	. . .	. . .	. . .	★	. . .	4	Monthly	. . .
Georgia	(d)									
Hawaii	. . .	★	. . .	. . .	★	. . .	★	22	Monthly	. . .
Idaho	(d)							22	Gov.'s discretion	. . .
Illinois	★	. . .	. . .	. . .	. . .	. . .	★	18	N.A.	. . .
Indiana	. . .	. . .	★	. . .	. . .	. . .	★	16	Bi-monthly	. . .
Iowa	★	. . .	★	★	★	. . .	. . .	30	(c)	. . .
Kansas	★	. . .	. . .	. . .	. . .	. . .	★	14	Bi-weekly	. . .
Kentucky	★	. . .	★	. . .	★	. . .	★	10	Weekly	. . .
Louisiana	★	. . .	★	★	★	. . .	. . .	16	Monthly	. . .
Maine	. . .	. . .	. . .	★	. . .	. . .	★	16	Weekly	. . .
Maryland	★	. . .	. . .	. . .	★	. . .	. . .	25	Every other week	. . .
Massachusetts	★	. . .	. . .	. . .	★	. . .	. . .	10	Bi-weekly	. . .
Michigan	. . .	. . .	★	★	. . .	. . .	(e)	22	Bi-weekly and Gov.'s discretion	. . .
Minnesota	. . .	. . .	★	. . .	★	. . .	. . .	24	Regularly	. . .
Mississippi	(d)									
Missouri	. . .	★	. . .	★	★	. . .	. . .	17	Gov.'s discretion	. . .
Montana	★	★	. . .	. . .	★	. . .	. . .	22	Weekly	. . .
Nebraska	. . .	. . .	★	★	★	. . .	★	30	Monthly	. . .
Nevada	(d)							23	At call of the governor	. . .
New Hampshire	(d)									
New Jersey	★	★	. . .	. . .	★	. . .	. . .	24	Gov.'s discretion	. . .
New Mexico	★	. . .	. . .	★	★	. . .	. . .	25	Gov.'s discretion	. . .
New York	. . .	. . .	. . .	★	. . .	. . .	★	75	Gov.'s discretion	. . .
North Carolina (f)	★	★	★	. . .	. . .	. . .	★	10	Monthly	. . .
North Dakota	. . .	. . .	★	. . .	. . .	. . .	★	18	Monthly	★
Ohio	★	. . .	. . .	. . .	★	. . .	. . .	24	Gov.'s discretion	★
Oklahoma	★	. . .	. . .	. . .	. . .	. . .	★	10–15 (g)	Monthly	. . .
Oregon	(d)									
Pennsylvania	★	★	★	. . .	★(h)	. . .	★	28	Gov.'s discretion	★
Rhode Island	. . .	. . .	. . .	★	. . .	. . .	★	20	Bi-monthly	. . .
South Carolina	★	. . .	. . .	. . .	★(h)	. . .	. . .	15	Monthly	★
South Dakota	★	★	. . .	. . .	★	. . .	. . .	19	Monthly	. . .
Tennessee	★	. . .	. . .	. . .	★	. . .	. . .	28	Monthly	. . .
Texas	(d)									
Utah	★	. . .	★	. . .	★	. . .	. . .	21	Monthly, weekly during legislative session	. . .
Vermont	★	. . .	. . .	. . .	★	. . .	. . .	7	Gov.'s discretion	. . .
Virginia	★	. . .	. . .	. . .	. . .	. . .	★(i)	14	Weekly	. . .
Washington	. . .	. . .	★	. . .	★	. . .	. . .	28	Bi-weekly, weekly during legislative session	. . .
West Virginia	. . .	. . .	★	★	★	. . .	. . .	10	Weekly	. . .
Wisconsin	★	. . .	. . .	. . .	★	. . .	. . .	16	Gov.'s discretion	★
Wyoming	. . .	. . .	★	. . .	. . .	. . .	★	20	Monthly	. . .
American Samoa	★	★	. . .	. . .	★	. . .	★	16	Gov.'s discretion	★
Guam	. . .	. . .	★	. . .	★	. . .	. . .	55	Bi-monthly	. . .
No. Mariana Islands	. . .	★	. . .	. . .	★	. . .	. . .	16	Gov.'s discretion	★
Puerto Rico	★	★	. . .	. . .	. . .	. . .	★	10 (j)	Every 6 weeks	. . .
U.S. Virgin Islands	. . .	★	. . .	. . .	★	. . .	. . .	21	Monthly	★

See footnotes at end of table.

STATE CABINET SYSTEMS — Continued

Source: The Council of State Governments' survey, December 2008.

Key:

★ — Yes

. . . — No

N.A. — Not available.

(a) Individual is a member by virtue of election or appointment to a cabinet-level position.

(b) Except when in executive session.

(c) Every other month, and every month during session.

(d) No formal cabinet system. In Idaho, however, sub-cabinets have been formed, by executive order; the chairs report to the governor.

(e) Membership determined by governor. Some officers formally designated as cabinet members by executive order.

(f) Constitution provides for a Council of State made up of elective state administrative officials, which makes policy decisions for the state while the cabinet acts more in an advisory capacity.

(g) Maximum of 16.

(h) With the consent of the senate.

(i) Appointed by the governor and confirmed by each house.

(j) The Constitutional Cabinet has 10 members including the governor. There are other members of the Cabinet provided by statute.

Table 4.7
THE GOVERNORS: PROVISIONS AND PROCEDURES FOR TRANSITION

State or other jurisdiction	Legislation pertaining to gubernatorial transition	Appropriation available to gov-elect ($)	Provision for:					
			Gov-elect's participation in state budget for coming fiscal year	Gov-elect to hire staff to assist during transition	State personnel to be made available to assist gov-elect	Office space in buildings to be made available to gov-elect	Acquainting gov-elect staff with office procedures and routine office functions	Transfer of information (files, records, etc.)
Alabama	. . .	. . .	★	●	●	●	●	●
Alaska	●	★(a)	. . .	●	●	●	●	★
Arizona	. . .	. . .	★	. . .	●	●	●	●
Arkansas	●	10,000	. . .	. . .	. . .	. . .	. . .	. . .
California	★	450,000	★	★	★	★	●	●
Colorado	★	10,000	★	★	★	★	●	★
Connecticut	★	★	★	★	★	★	★	★
Delaware	★	15,000	●	★	●	●	●	●
Florida	★	2,500,000 (b)	●	★	●	★(b)	●	●
Georgia	★	50,000	●	★	★	★	●	★
Hawaii	★	50,000	★	★	●	★	●	●
Idaho	★	15,000	★	★	★	★	★	★
Illinois	. . .	. . .	. . .	★	. . .	★	★	★
Indiana	★	40,000	. . .	. . .	. . .	★	★	★
Iowa	●	100,000	★	●	●	●	●	★
Kansas	★	150,000 (c)	★	★	★	★	★	★
Kentucky	★	200,000	★	★	★	★	★	★
Louisiana	★	●65,000	★	★	. . .	★	. . .	●
Maine	●	5,000	★	●	●	●	●	●
Maryland	★	●	. . .	★	★	★	★	★
Massachusetts	●	●	●	. . .	●	●	●	★
Michigan	●	●	. . .	●	●	●	●	●
Minnesota	★	(d)	★	★	★	★	●	★
Mississippi	●	★(e)	★	★	★	★	★	★
Missouri	★	100,000	★	★	●	★	●	●(f)
Montana	★	★	★	★	★	★	★	●
Nebraska	★	★	★	★	★	★	★	★
Nevada	★	Reasonable amount	★	. . .	. . .	. . .	. . .	★(g)
New Hampshire	★	75,000	★	★	★	★	★	. . .
New Jersey	★	(h)	●	★	★	★	●	★
New Mexico	★	(i)	★	★	★	★	★	★
New York	. . .	. . .	. . .	. . .	★	★	★	★
North Carolina	★	★(j)	★	★	★	★	★	★
North Dakota	●	10,000	(k)	(l)	●	. . .	●	★
Ohio	★	Unspecified (m)	●	★	●	. . .	●	★
Oklahoma	●	●	★	●	●	★	●	●
Oregon	★	★	★	★	★	★	★	★
Pennsylvania	★	. . .	. . .	★	●	●	●	. . .
Rhode Island	★	500,000	. . .	★	★	★	●	●
South Carolina	. . .	●	●	●	●	●	●	●
South Dakota	★	. . .	. . .	. . .	. . .	. . .	. . .	. . .
Tennessee	★	★	●	★	★	★	●	●
Texas	●	●	●	●	●	●	●	●
Utah	★	★(n)	★	★	★	★	★	★
Vermont	. . .	★(o)	. . .	. . .	. . .	. . .	. . .	. . .
Virginia	★	★(p)	★	★	★	★	★	★
Washington	★	★	●	★	●	★	●	●
West Virginia	. . .	●	. . .	●	. . .	●	●	●
Wisconsin	★	Unspecified	★	★	★	★	★	★
Wyoming	●	. . .	●	●	●	●	●	●
American Samoa	. . .	Unspecified	★(q)	★	●	●	★	●
Guam	★	(r)	. . .	. . .	★	★	★	. . .
No. Mariana Islands	★	Unspecified	. . .	★	★	★	★	★
Puerto Rico	★	. . .	★	★	★	★	★	★
U.S. Virgin Islands	★	100,000	. . .	★	★	★	★	★

See footnotes at end of table.

THE GOVERNORS: PROVISIONS AND PROCEDURES FOR TRANSITION—Continued

Source: The Council of State Governments' survey, November 2008.

Key:

. . . — No provisions or procedures.

★ — Formal provisions or procedures.

• — No formal provisions, occurs informally.

N.A. — Not applicable.

(a) Varies.

(b) There is a budget for the governor-elect to use during transition. Very specific procedures include legislative review to access the funds. Some of these funds may be shared with Cabinet transitions: CFO and Commissioner of Agriculture. Transition information is available with no formal provisions. Budget allows for space, etc., but actual office space is determined by availability at the time.

(c) Transition funds are used by both the incoming and the outgoing administrations.

(d) 1.5% of amount appropriated for the fiscal year to the governor's office.

(e) Miss. Code Ann.§ 7-1-101 provides as follows: the governor's office of general services shall provide a governor-elect with office space and office equipment for the period between the election and inauguration. A special appropriation to the governor's office of general services is hereby authorized to defray the expenses of providing necessary staff employees and for the operation of the office of governor-elect during the period between the election and inauguration. The state fiscal management board shall make available to a governor-elect and his designated representatives information on the following: (a) all information and reports used in the preparation of the budget report; and (b) all information and reports on projected income and revenue estimates for the state.

(f) Activity is traditional and routine, although there is no specific statutory provision.

(g) As determined in budget.

(h) No specific amount—necessary services and facilities.

(i) Legislature required to make appropriation; no dollar amount stated in legislation.

(j) Governor receives $80,000 and lieutenant governor receives $10,000.

(k) Responsible for submitting budget for coming biennium.

(l) Governor usually hires several incoming key staff during transition.

(m) Determined in budget.

(n) Appropriated by legislature at the time of transition.

(o) Governor-elect entitled to 70% of governor's salary.

(p) Determined every four years.

(q) Can submit reprogramming or supplemental appropriation measure for current fiscal year.

(r) Appropriations given upon the request of governor-elect.

Table 4.8
IMPEACHMENT PROVISIONS IN THE STATES

State or other jurisdiction	Governor and other state executive and judicial officers subject to impeachment	Legislative body which holds power of impeachment	Vote required for impeachment	Legislative body which conducts impeachment trial	Chief justice presides at impeachment trial (a)	Vote required for conviction	Official who serves as acting governor if governor impeached (b)	Legislature may call special session for impeachment
Alabama	★	H	maj. mbrs.	S	★	majority of elected mbrs.	LG	★
Alaska	★	S	2/3 mbrs.	H	(c)	2/3 mbrs.	LG	★
Arizona	★(d)	H	maj. mbrs.	S	★(e)	2/3 mbrs.	SS	★
Arkansas	★	H	maj. mbrs.	S	★	2/3 mbrs.	LG	. . .
California	★	H	. . .	S	. . .	2/3 mbrs.	LG	. . .
Colorado	★	H	maj. mbrs.	S	★	2/3 mbrs.	LG	. . .
Connecticut	★	H	maj. mbrs.	S	★(f)	2/3 mbrs. must be present	LG	★
Delaware	★	H	2/3 mbrs.	S	★	2/3 mbrs.	LG	. . .
Florida	★	H	2/3 mbrs.	S	★(g)	2/3 mbrs. present (h)	LG (i)	★
Georgia	★	H	. . .	S	★(e)	2/3 mbrs.	. . .	★(j)
Hawaii	★	H	2/3 mbrs.	S	. . .	2/3 mbrs.	LG	★
Idaho	★	H	2/3 mbrs.	S	★	2/3 mbrs.	LG	. . .
Illinois	★	H	2/3 mbrs.	S	★	2/3 mbrs.	LG	★
Indiana	★(k)	H	2/3 mbrs.	S	. . .	2/3 mbrs.	LG	. . .
Iowa	★	H	maj. mbrs.	S	. . .	majority of elected mbrs.	LG	★
Kansas	★	H	(l)	S	. . .	2/3 mbrs.	LG	. . .
Kentucky	★	H	. . .	S	★	2/3 mbrs. present	LG	. . .
Louisiana	★	H	(m)	S	. . .	(m)	LG	★
Maine	★	H	. . .	S	. . .	2/3 mbrs. present	PS	. . .
Maryland	★	H	maj. mbrs.	S	. . .	2/3 mbrs.	LG	. . .
Massachusetts	★	H	maj. mbrs.	S	. . .	. . .	LG	★
Michigan	★	H	maj. mbrs.	S	★(n)	2/3 mbrs.	LG	. . .
Minnesota	★	H	maj. mbrs.	S	. . .	2/3 mbrs. present	LG	. . .
Mississippi	★	H	2/3 mbrs. present	S	★(o)	2/3 mbrs. present (p)	LG	(q)
Missouri	★	H	. . .	(r)	(r)	(r)	LG	. . .
Montana	★	H	2/3 mbrs.	S	★	2/3 mbrs.	LG	★
Nebraska	★	S (s)	maj. mbrs.	(t)	(t)	(t)	LG	. . .
Nevada	★(d)	H	maj. mbrs.	S	★	2/3 mbrs.	LG	. . .
New Hampshire	★	H	. . .	S	★	. . .	PS	. . .
New Jersey	★	H	maj. mbrs.	S	★	2/3 mbrs.	PS (u)	★
New Mexico	★	H	maj. mbrs.	S	★(n)	2/3 mbrs.	LG	★
New York	★	H	maj. mbrs.	S	★	2/3 mbrs. present	LG	★
North Carolina	★	H	2/3 maj. mbrs.	S	★	2/3 mbrs. present	LG	★
North Dakota	★(d)	H	maj. mbrs.	S	★	2/3 mbrs.	LG	. . .
Ohio	★	H	maj. mbrs.	S	. . .	2/3 mbrs. present	LG	. . .
Oklahoma	★	H	maj. mbrs.	S	★	2/3 mbrs. present	LG	★
Oregon	(v)							
Pennsylvania	★	H	. . .	S	. . .	2/3 maj. mbrs.	LG	★
Rhode Island	★	H	2/3 maj. mbrs.	S	★	2/3 maj. mbrs.	LG	★
South Carolina	★	H	2/3 mbrs.	S	★	2/3 mbrs.	LG	. . .

See footnotes at end of table.

IMPEACHMENT PROVISIONS IN THE STATES—Continued

State or other jurisdiction	Governor and other state executive and judicial officers subject to impeachment	Legislative body which holds power of impeachment	Vote required for impeachment	Legislative body which conducts impeachment trial	Chief justice presides at impeachment trial (a)	Vote required for conviction	Official who serves as acting governor if governor impeached (b)	Legislature may call special session for impeachment
South Dakota	★	H	maj. mbrs.	S	★	2/3 mbrs.	LG	★
Tennessee	★	H	maj. mbrs.	S	★	2/3 mbrs. (w)	PS	★
Texas	★	H	maj. mbrs.	S	. . .	2/3 mbrs. present	LG	. . .
Utah	★	H	2/3 mbrs.	S	★	2/3 mbrs.	LG	★
Vermont	★	H	2/3 mbrs.	S	. . .	2/3 mbrs.	LG	. . .
Virginia	★	H	maj. mbrs.	S	. . .	2/3 mbrs. present	LG	★
Washington	★(d)	H	maj. mbrs.	S	★	2/3 mbrs.	LG	★
West Virginia	★	H	. . .	S	★	2/3 mbrs.	PS	★
Wisconsin	★	H	maj. mbrs.	S	. . .	2/3 mbrs.	LG	. . .
Wyoming	★	H	maj. mbrs.	S	★	2/3 mbrs.	SS	★
Dist. of Columbia	(x)							
American Samoa	(y)	H	2/3 mbrs.	S	★	2/3 mbrs.	. . .	. . .
Guam	(x)							
No. Mariana Islands	★	H	2/3 mbrs.	S	. . .	2/3 mbrs.	LG	. . .
Puerto Rico	★	H	2/3 mbrs.	S	★	3/4 mbrs.	SS	★
U.S. Virgin Islands	(x)							

Source: The Council of State Governments' survey, December 2008.

Key:

★ — Yes; provision for.

. . . — Not specified, or no provision for.

H — House or Assembly (lower chamber)

S — Senate

LG — Lieutenant Governor

PS — President or Speaker of the Senate

SS — Secretary of State

(a) Presiding justice of state court of last resort. In many states, provision indicates that chief justice presides only on occasion of impeachment of governor.

(b) For provisions on official next in line of succession if governor is convicted and removed from office, refer to Chapter 4, "The Governors."

(c) An appointed Supreme Court justice presides.

(d) With exception of certain judicial officers. In Arizona and Washington—justices of courts not of record. In Nevada—justices of the peace. In North Dakota—county judges, justices of the peace, and police magistrates. In Oklahoma—all judicial officers not serving on the Supreme Court.

(e) Should the chief justice be on trial, or otherwise disqualified, the Senate shall elect a judge of the Supreme Court to preside.

(f) Only if governor is on trial.

(g) Except in a trial of the chief justice, in which case the governor shall preside.

(h) An officer impeached by the House of Representatives shall be disqualified from performing any official duties until acquitted by the Senate, and, unless impeached, the governor may by appointment fill the office until completion of the trial.

(i) Governor may appoint someone to serve until the impeachment procedures are final.

(j) Special sessions of the General Assembly shall be limited to a period of 40 days unless extended by 3/5 vote of each house and approved by the governor or unless at the expiration of such period an impeachment trial of some officer of state government is pending, in which event the House shall adjourn and the Senate shall remain in session until such trial is completed.

(k) Judges not included.

(l) No statute, simple majority is the assumption.

(m) Concurrence of 2/3 of the elected senators.

(n) Only if governor or lieutenant governor is on trial.

(o) When the governor is tried; if chief justice is unable to preside, the next longest serving justice shall preside.

(p) No person shall be convicted without concurrence of 2/3 of all senators present. Miss. Const. 1890 Art. IV § 52.

(q) It is implied but not addressed directly in Miss. Const. 1890 Art. IV §§ 49–53.

(r) All impeachments are tried before the state Supreme Court, except that the governor or a member of the Supreme Court is tried by a special commission of seven eminent jurists to be elected by the Senate. A vote of 5/7 of the court of special commission is necessary to convict.

(s) Unicameral legislature; members use the title "senator."

(t) Court of impeachment is composed of chief justice and Supreme Court. A vote of 2/3 present of the court is necessary to convict.

(u) Beginning in 2009, New Jersey will elect a lieutenant governor. Until the inauguration of the first lieutenant governor in 2010, the president of the senate would succeed the governor if necessary.

(v) No provision for impeachment. Public officers may be tried for incompetence, corruption, malfeasance, or delinquency in office in same manner as criminal offenses.

(w) Vote of 2/3 of members sworn to try the officer impeached.

(x) Removal of elected officials by recall procedure only.

(y) Governor, lieutenant governor.

Table 4.9
CONSTITUTIONAL AND STATUTORY PROVISIONS FOR NUMBER OF CONSECUTIVE TERMS OF ELECTED STATE OFFICIALS
(All terms are four years unless otherwise noted)

State or other jurisdiction	*Governor*	*Lt. Governor*	*Secretary of state*	*Attorney general*	*Treasurer*	*Auditor*	*Comptroller*	*Education*	*Agriculture*	*Labor*	*Insurance*
Alabama	2	2	2	2	2	. . .	. . .	. . .	2	. . .	. . .
Alaska	2	2	(a)	. . .	(b)	. . .	. . .	. . .	. . .	. . .	. . .
Arizona	2 (c)	(d)	2	2	2	. . .	. . .	2	. . .	. . .	. . .
Arkansas	2 (c)	2	2	2	2	. . .	. . .	. . .	. . .	. . .	. . .
California	2	2	2	2	2	. . .	2	2	. . .	. . .	. . .
Colorado	2	2	2	2	2	. . .	. . .	. . .	. . .	. . .	. . .
Connecticut	N	N	N	N	N	. . .	N	. . .	. . .	. . .	. . .
Delaware	2 (f) (c)	2	. . .	N	N	N	. . .	. . .	. . .	. . .	N
Florida	2	2	. . .	2	2 (g) (e)	. . .	2	N	N	. . .	(g) (e)
Georgia	2	N	N	N	. . .	. . .	. . .	N	N	N	N
Hawaii	2	2	(a)	. . .	. . .	. . .	. . .	. . .	. . .	. . .	. . .
Idaho	N	N	N	N	N	. . .	2	N	. . .	. . .	. . .
Illinois	N	N	N	N	N	. . .	N	. . .	. . .	. . .	. . .
Indiana	(h)	2	2	. . .	(f)	. . .	2 (g)	. . .	. . .	. . .	. . .
Iowa	N	N	N	N	N	N	. . .	. . .	. . .	. . .	. . .
Kansas	2	2	N	N	. . .	. . .	. . .	. . .	. . .	. . .	. . .
Kentucky	2	2	2	2	2	2	. . .	. . .	2	2	. . .
Louisiana	2 (h)	N	N	N	N	. . .	. . .	N	N	. . .	N
Maine	2	(i)	(j)	(j)	(j)	. . .	. . .	. . .	. . .	. . .	. . .
Maryland	2 (h)	2	. . .	N	. . .	. . .	N	. . .	. . .	. . .	. . .
Massachusetts	N	N	N	2	N	N	. . .	. . .	. . .	. . .	. . .
Michigan	2	2	2	2	. . .	. . .	. . .	. . .	. . .	. . .	. . .
Minnesota	N	N	N	N	(k)	N	. . .	. . .	. . .	. . .	(l)
Mississippi	2	2 (h)	N	N	N	N	. . .	. . .	. . .	. . .	. . .
Missouri	2	N	N	N	2 (c)	N	. . .	. . .	. . .	. . .	. . .
Montana	2 (m)	2 (m)	2 (m)	2 (m)	. . .	N	. . .	2 (m)	. . .	. . .	. . .
Nebraska	2 (h)	2 (h)	N	N	2 (h)	N	. . .	. . .	. . .	. . .	. . .
Nevada	2	2	2	2	2	. . .	2	. . .	. . .	. . .	. . .
New Hampshire	(t)	(i)	. . .	. . .	. . .	. . .	. . .	. . .	. . .	. . .	. . .
New Jersey	2	(i)	. . .	. . .	. . .	. . .	. . .	. . .	. . .	. . .	. . .
New Mexico	2	2 (h)	2 (h)	2 (h)	2 (h)	2 (h)	. . .	. . .	. . .	. . .	. . .
New York	N	N	. . .	N	. . .	N (p)	N	. . .	. . .	. . .	. . .
North Carolina	2	2	N	N	N	N	. . .	N	N	N	N
North Dakota	N	N	N (n)	N (n)	N	N	. . .	N	N (n)(o)	N (n)	N
Ohio	2 (z)	2	2	2	2	2	. . .	. . .	. . .	. . .	. . .
Oklahoma	2 (h)	N	. . .	N	N	N	. . .	2 (h)	. . .	2 (h)	N
Oregon	2 (f)	(q)	2 (f)	N	2 (f)	. . .	. . .	. . .	. . .	. . .	. . .
Pennsylvania	2	2	. . .	2	2 (r)	2 (h)	. . .	. . .	. . .	. . .	. . .
Rhode Island	2	2(h)	2 (h)	2 (h)	2 (h)	. . .	. . .	. . .	. . .	. . .	. . .
South Carolina	2 (h)	2	N	N	N	. . .	N	N	N	. . .	. . .
South Dakota	2	2 (h)	2 (h)	2 (h)	2 (h)	. . .	2	. . .	. . .	. . .	. . .
Tennessee	2 (h)	(i)	. . .	(s)	. . .	. . .	. . .	. . .	. . .	. . .	. . .
Texas	N	N	N	N	(p)	. . .	N	. . .	. . .	. . .	. . .
Utah	N	N	(a)	N	N	N	. . .	. . .	. . .	. . .	. . .
Vermont	(t)	(t)	(t)	(t)	(t)	(t)	. . .	. . .	. . .	. . .	. . .
Virginia	(v)	(u)	. . .	(u)	. . .	. . .	. . .	. . .	. . .	. . .	. . .
Washington	N	N	N	N	N	N	. . .	N	. . .	. . .	. . .
West Virginia	2	N (i)	N	N	N	. . .	N	. . .	N	. . .	. . .
Wisconsin	N	N	N	N	N	. . .	. . .	N	. . .	. . .	. . .
Wyoming	2 (m)	(q)	N	. . .	2	. . .	2	N	. . .	. . .	. . .
Dist. of Columbia	N (w)	2	. . .	. . .	. . .	. . .	. . .	. . .	. . .	. . .	. . .
American Samoa	2	2	(a)	. . .	. . .	. . .	(x)	. . .	. . .	. . .	. . .
Guam	2	2	(a)	. . .	. . .	. . .	(y)	. . .	. . .	. . .	. . .
No. Mariana Islands	2 (f)	2	. . .	. . .	. . .	2	(x)	. . .	. . .	. . .	(l)
Puerto Rico	(h)	(d)	. . .	. . .	. . .	1	. . .	. . .	. . .	. . .	. . .
U.S. Virgin Islands	2 (h)	2	(p)	. . .	(d)	. . .	(d)	. . .	. . .	. . .	(a)

See footnotes at end of table.

CONSTITUTIONAL AND STATUTORY PROVISIONS FOR NUMBER OF CONSECUTIVE TERMS OF ELECTED STATE OFFICIALS—Continued
(All terms are four years unless otherwise noted)

Source: The Council of State Governments, November 2008.

Note: All terms last four years unless otherwise noted. Footnotes specify if a position's functions are performed by an appointed official under a different title.

Key:

N — No provision specifying number of terms allowed.

. . . — Position is appointed or elected by governmental entity (not chosen by the electorate).

(a) Lieutenant Governor performs this function.

(b) Deputy Commissioner of Department of Revenue performs function.

(c) Absolute two-term limitation, but not necessarily consecutive.

(d) Finance Administrator performs function.

(e) Chief Financial Officer performs this function as of January 2003.

(f) Eligible for eight out of any period of twelve years.

(g) State auditor performs this function.

(h) After two consecutive terms, must wait four years and/or one full term before being eligible again.

(i) President or Speaker of the Senate is next in line of succession to the governorship. In Tennessee and West Virginia, Speaker of the Senate has the statutory title "Lieutenant Governor".

(j) Serves 2 year term and is eligible to serve 4 terms.

(k) Office of the State Treasurer was abolished on the first Monday in January 2003.

(l) Commerce administrator performs this function.

(m) Eligible for eight out of sixteen years.

(n) The terms of the office of the elected officials are four years, except that in 2004 the agricultural commissioner, attorney general, secretary of state and the tax commissioner are elected to a term of two years.

(o) Constitution provides for a secretary of agriculture and labor. However, the legislature was given constitutional authority to provide for (and has provided for) a department of labor distinct from agriculture, and a commissioner of labor distinct from the commissioner of agriculture.

(p) Comptroller performs this function.

(q) Secretary of State is next in line to the governorship.

(r) Treasurer must wait four years before being eligible for the office of auditor general.

(s) Term is for eight years and official is appointed by judges of the State Supreme Court.

(t) Serves two-year term, no provision specifying the number of terms allowed.

(u) Provision specifying individual may hold office for an unlimited number of terms.

(v) Cannot serve consecutive terms, but after 4 year respite can seek re-election.

(w) Mayor.

(x) State treasurer performs this function.

(y) General services administrator performs function.

(z) After two consecutive terms as Governor, the candidate must wait four years before becoming eligible to run again.

Table 4.10
SELECTED STATE ADMINISTRATIVE OFFICIALS: METHODS OF SELECTION

State or other jurisdiction	*Governor*	*Lieutenant governor*	*Secretary of state*	*Attorney general*	*Treasurer*	*Adjutant general*	*Administration*	*Agriculture*	*Auditor*	*Banking*
Alabama*	CE	CE	CE	CE	CE	GS	G	SE	CE	GS
Alaska	CE	CE	(a-1)	GB	AG	GB	GB	AG	L	AG
Arizona	CE	(a-2)	CE	CE	CE	GS	GS	GS	L	GS
Arkansas	CE	CE	CE	CE	CE	G	G	G	CE	GS
California	CE	CE	CE	CE	CE	GS	. . .	G	GB	GS
Colorado	CE	CE	CE	CE	CE	GS	GS	GS	L	CS
Connecticut	CE	CE	CE	CE	CE	GE	GE	GE	L	GE
Delaware	CE	CE	GS	CE	CE	GS	(c)	GS	CE	GS
Florida	CE	CE	GS	CE	(b)	G	GS	CE	L	(b)
Georgia	CE	CE	CE	CE	G	G	G	CE	(d)	G
Hawaii	CE	CE	. . .	GS	GS	GS	(e)	GS	CL	AG
Idaho	CE	CE	CE	CE	CE	GS	GS	GS	. . .	GS
Illinois	CE	CE	CE	CE	CE	GS	GS	GS	SL	B
Indiana	CE	CE	CE	SE	CE	G	G	LG	CE	G
Iowa	CE	CE	CE	CE	CE	GS	GS	CE	CE	AGS
Kansas	CE	CE	CE	CE	CE	GS	GS	GS	N.A.	GS
Kentucky	CE	CE	CE	CE	CE	G	(f)	CE	CE	G
Louisiana	CE	CE	CE	CE	CE	GS	GS	CE	G	GLS
Maine	CE	(g)	CL	CL	CL	GLS	GLS	GLS	L	GLS
Maryland	CE	CE	GS	CE	CL	G	GS	GS	. . .	AG
Massachusetts	CE	CE	CE	CE	CE	G	G	CG	CE	G
Michigan*	CE	CE	CE	CE	GS	GS	GS	B	CL	GS
Minnesota	CE	CE	CE	CE	(a-24)	GS	GS	GS	CE	A
Mississippi	CE	CE	CE	CE	CE	GE	GS	SE	CE	GS
Missouri	CE	CE	CE	CE	CE	G	GS	GS	CE	. . .
Montana	CE	CE	CE	CE	(a-6)	GS	GS	G	CE	A
Nebraska	CE	CE	CE	CE	CE	GS	GS	GS	CE	GS
Nevada	CE	CE	CE	CE	CE	G	G	BG	. . .	A
New Hampshire	CE	(g)	CL	GC	CL	GC	GC	GC	. . .	GC
New Jersey	CE	(g)	GS	GS	GS	GS	. . .	BG	(h)	GS
New Mexico	CE	CE	CE	CE	CE	G	(a-26)	B	CE	G
New York	CE	CE	GS	CE	A	G	. . .	GS	(a-14)	GS
North Carolina	CE	CE	CE	CE	CE	A	G	CE	CE	G
North Dakota	CE	CE	CE	CE	CE	G	. . .	CE	CE	GS
Ohio	CE	CE	CE	CE	CE	G	GS	GS	CE	A
Oklahoma	CE	CE	GS	CE	CE	GS	GS	GS	CE	GS
Oregon	CE	(a-2)	CE	SE	CE	G	GS	GS	SS	. . .
Pennsylvania	CE	CE	GS	CE	CE	GS	G	GS	CE	GS
Rhode Island	SE	SE	CE	SE	SE	GS	GS	GS	LS	GS
South Carolina	CE	CE	CE	CE	CE	CE	B	CE	B	A
South Dakota	CE	CE	CE	CE	CE	GS	GS	GS	L	A
Tennessee	CE	(g)	CL	CT	CL	G	G	G	(a-14)	G
Texas	CE	CE	G	CE	(a-14)	G	A	SE	L	B
Utah	CE	CE	(a-1)	CE	CE	GS	GS	GS	CE	GS
Vermont	CE	CE	CE	SE	CE	CL	GS	GS	CE	GS
Virginia	CE	CE	GB	CE	GB	GB	GB	GB	SL	B
Washington	CE	CE	CE	CE	CE	GS	GS	GS	CE	GS
West Virginia	CE	(g)	CE	CE	CE	GS	GS	CE	CE	GS
Wisconsin	CE	CE	CE	CE	CE	G	GS	GS	LS	A
Wyoming	CE	(a-2)	CE	G	CE	G	GS	GS	CE	A
American Samoa*	CE	CE	(a-1)	GB	GB	N.A.	GB	GB	N.A.	N.A.
Guam*	CE	CE	. . .	CE	CS	GS	GS	GS	CE	GS
No. Mariana Islands*	CE	CE	. . .	GS	CS	. . .	G	. . .	GB	C
U.S. Virgin Islands*	SE	SE	(a-1)	GS	GS	GS	GS	GS	GS	LG

Source: The Council of State Governments' survey of state personnel agencies, March 2009.

Note: Alabama and Michigan responded for the 2008 edition; American Samoa, Guam, No Mariana Islands, U.S. Virgin Islands responded for the 2007 edition.

Key:

N.A. — Not available.

. . . — No specific chief administrative official or agency in charge of function.

CE — Constitutional, elected by public.

CL — Constitutional, elected by legislature.

SE — Statutory, elected by public.

SL — Statutory, elected by legislature.

L — Selected by legislature or one of its organs.

CT — Constitutional, elected by state court of last resort.

CP — Competitve process.

Appointed by:	*Approved by:*
G — Governor	
GS — Governor	Senate (in Nebraska, unicameral legislature)
GB — Governor	Both houses
GE — Governor	Either house
GC — Governor	Council
GD — Governor	Departmental board
GLS — Governor	Appropriate legislative committee & Senate
GOC — Governor & Council or cabinet	
LG — Lieutenant Governor	
LGS — Lieutenant Governor	Senate
AT — Attorney General	
SS — Secretary of State	
C — Cabinet Secretary	
CG — Cabinet Secretary	Governor

SELECTED STATE ADMINISTRATIVE OFFICIALS: METHODS OF SELECTION—Continued

State or other jurisdiction	*Budget*	*Civil rights*	*Commerce*	*Community affairs*	*Comptroller*	*Consumer affairs*	*Corrections*	*Economic development*	*Education*	*Election administration*
Alabama*	CS	. . .	G	G	CS	CS	G	(a-13)	B	CS
Alaska	G	GB	GB	(a-12)	AG	(a-12)	GB	(a-12)	GD	AG
Arizona	L	AT	GS	AT	A	AT	GS	(a-12)	CE	(a-2)
Arkansas	A	. . .	GS	N.A.	G	A	B	GS	BG	(i)
California	(a-24)	. . .	. . .	GS	CE	G	GS	. . .	CE	G
Colorado	G	A	G	A	A	AT	GS	G	AB	CS
Connecticut	CS	GE	GE	GE	CE	GE	GE	GE	BG	CS
Delaware	GS	CG	(a-2)	. . .	CG	AT	GS	GS	GS	GS
Florida	G	AB	G	GS	CE (b)	A	GS	G	GS	A
Georgia	G	G	BG	BG	CE	G	GD	N.A.	CE	A
Hawaii	GS	B	GS	. . .	GS	A	GS	GS	B	B
Idaho	GS	B	GS	. . .	CE	(a-3)	B	GS	CE	CE
Illinois	G	GS	GS	(a-12)	CE	(a-3)	GS	(a-12)	B	B
Indiana	G	G	G	G	(a-8)	N.A.	G	G	CE	(j)
Iowa	AGS	AGS	AGS	AGS	. . .	AGS	AGS	AGS	AGS	AGS
Kansas	G	B	GS	A	C	AT	GS	C	B	(k)
Kentucky	G	B	G	G	CG	AT	G	GC	B	B
Louisiana	A	B	GS	G	GS	AG	GS	GS	BG	A
Maine	C	B	(a-17)	(a-17)	C	GLS	GLS	GLS	GLS	SS
Maryland	GS	G	GS	. . .	CE	A	AGS	GS	B	B
Massachusetts	CG	G	G	G	G	G	CG	G	B	CE
Michigan*	GS	GS	GS	. . .	CS	. . .	GS	. . .	B	(l)
Minnesota	(a-24)	GS	GS	(a-17)	(a-24)	A	GS	GS	GS	(a-2)
Mississippi	GS	. . .	SE	A	(a-6)	A	GS	GS	BS	A (m)
Missouri	AGS	AGS	GS	A	A	CE	GS	GS	BG	SS
Montana	G	CP	GS	CP	CP	CP	GS	G	CE	SS
Nebraska	A	B	GS	A	A	(a-3)	GS	GS	B	A
Nevada	(a-5)	G	G	. . .	CE	A	G	GD	B	(n)
New Hampshire	GC	CS	GC	G	AGC	AGC	GC	AGC	B	CL
New Jersey	GS	A	(a-17)	GS	GS	A	GS	G	GS	A
New Mexico	G	G	(a-17)	G	ALS	G	GS	GS	B	G
New York	G	GS	GS	(a-2)	CE	GS	GS	GS	B	B
North Carolina	G	A	G	A	G	(i)	G	A	CE	G
North Dakota	A	G	G	. . .	A	AT	G	N.A.	CE	SS
Ohio	GS	B	GS	A	GS	A	GS	GS	B	(a-2)
Oklahoma	A	B	GS	(i)	A	B	B	GS	CE	L
Oregon	A	A	GS	G	A	GS	GS	GS	SE	A
Pennsylvania	G	B	GS	AG	G	AT	GS	GS	GS	C
Rhode Island	AG	B	GS	. . .	A	(a-3)	GS	GS	B	B
South Carolina	A	B	GS	N.A.	CE	B	GS	(a-12)	CE	B
South Dakota	(a-24)	N.A.	(a-44)	(a-48)	(a-40)	N.A.	GS	(a-48)	GS	SS
Tennessee	A	G	G	G	SL	A	G	G	G	A
Texas	G	B	G	G	CE	(a-3)	B	G	B	(o)
Utah	G	A	GS	GS	AG	GS	GS	A	B	A
Vermont	CG	AT	GS	CG	CG	AT	CG	CG	BG	CE
Virginia	GB	G	GB	GB	GB	A	GB	B	GB	GB
Washington	GS	B	GS	GS	GS	CE	GS	GS	CE	A
West Virginia	CS	GS	GS	B	(a-8)	AT	GS	(a-13)	B	(a-2)
Wisconsin	A	A	GS	. . .	A	A	GS	CS	CE	B
Wyoming	A	A	G	G	(a-8)	G	GS	(a-12)	CE	A
American Samoa*	GB	N.A.	GB	(a-12)	(a-4)	(a-3)	A	(a-12)	GB	G
Guam*	GS	GS	GS	. . .	CS	CS	GS	B	GS	GS
No. Mariana Islands*	G	A	GS	GS	C	GS	C	C	B	B
U.S. Virgin Islands*	GS	GS	GS	GS	(a-24)	GS	GS	GS	GS	B

A — Agency head
AB — Agency head Board
AG — Agency head Governor
AGC — Agency head Governor & Council
AGS — Agency head Senate
ALS — Agency head Appropriate legislative committee
ASH — Agency head Senate president & House speaker
B — Board or commission
BG — Board Governor
BGS — Board Governor & Senate
BS — Board or commission Senate
BA — Board or commission Agency head
CS — Civil Service
LS — Legislative Committee Senate
(a) Chief administrative official or agency in charge of function:
(a-1) Lieutenant governor.
(a-2) Secretary of state.
(a-3) Attorney general.
(a-4) Treasurer.
(a-5) Adjutant general.
(a-6) Administration.
(a-7) Agriculture.
(a-8) Auditor.
(a-9) Banking.
(a-10) Budget.
(a-11) Civil rights.
(a-12) Commerce.
(a-13) Community affairs.
(a-14) Comptroller.
(a-15) Consumer affairs.
(a-16) Corrections.
(a-17) Economic development.
(a-18) Education (chief state school officer).

SELECTED STATE ADMINISTRATIVE OFFICIALS: METHODS OF SELECTION—Continued

State or other jurisdiction	Emergency management	Employment services	Energy	Environmental protection	Finance	Fish & wildlife	General services	Health	Higher education	Highways
Alabama*	G	CS	CS	B	G	CS	CS	B	B	G
Alaska	AG	AG	B	GB	AG	GB	. . .	AG	B	GB
Arizona	G	A	. . .	GS	(a-14)	B	A	GS	B	A
Arkansas	GS	G	A	BG/BS	G	(i)	A	BG	BG	(a-49)
California	GS	GS	G	GS	G	G	GS	GS (p)	B (q)	(a-49)
Colorado	A	A	G	A	A	A	A	GS	GS	GS
Connecticut	GE	A	A	GE	GE	CS (r)	GE	GE	BG	(a-49)
Delaware	CG	CG	A	(a-35)	GS	CG	CG	CG	B	(a-49)
Florida	GS	GS	A	GS	CE (b)	GS	GS	GS	B	GOC
Georgia	G	A	G	B	G	A	A	A	B	(a-49)
Hawaii	A	CS	CS	CS	(s)	CS	(a-14)	GS	B	CS
Idaho	A	GS	A	GS	GS	B	. . .	GS	B	(a-49)
Illinois	GS	GS	(a-12)	GS	(a-10)	(a-35)	(a-6)	GS	B	(a-49)
Indiana	G	G	LG	G	(a-10)	A	(a-6)	G	G	(a-49)
Iowa	AGS	AGS	. . .	A	A	A	A	AGS	. . .	A
Kansas	(t)	GS	B	C	. . .	CS	GS	C	B	(a-49)
Kentucky	AG	AG	AG	G	G	G	(a-6)	CG	B	CG
Louisiana	GS	A	CS	GS	GS	GS	GS	GS	B	GS
Maine	C	C	(a-38)	GLS	(a-6)	GLS	C	C	N.A.	(a-49)
Maryland	AG	A	G	GS	GS	. . .	GS	GS	G	AG
Massachusetts	G	CG	CG	CG	G	CG	G	CG	B	G
Michigan*	CS	CS	. . .	GS	(a-10)	(u)	. . .	GS	CS	(a-49)
Minnesota	GS	A	A	GS	(a-24)	A	(a-6)	GS	B	GS
Mississippi	GS	GS	A	GS	(a-6)	GS	. . .	BS	BS	(a-49)
Missouri	A	A	. . .	A	AGS	(v)	A	GS	B	(a-49)
Montana	CP	CP	CP	GS	CP	GS	CP	(a-45)	CP	(a-49)
Nebraska	A	A	A	GS	(w)	(x)	A	GS	B	(a-49)
Nevada	A	A	G	A	(a-14)	GD	. . .	(y)	B	(a-49)
New Hampshire	G	GC	G	GC	(a-6)	BGC	GC	AGC	B	(a-49)
New Jersey	GS	A	A	GS	A	B	(z)	GS	B	A
New Mexico	G	(a-32)	GS	GS	GS	G	GS	GS	B	(a-49)
New York	G	(a-32)	B	GS	(a-14)	GS	G	GS	(a-18)	(a-49)
North Carolina	G	G	A	G	G	G	G	G	B	A
North Dakota	A	G	A	A	A	G	G	G	B	(a-49)
Ohio	AG	GS	A	GS	A (aa)	A	A	GS	B	GS
Oklahoma	GS	B	GS	B	GS	B	GS	B	B	B
Oregon	AG	GS	G	B	(a-4)	B	(a-6)	A	B	A
Pennsylvania	G	AG	AG	GS	G	B	GS	GS	AG	AG
Rhode Island	(a-5)	GS	GS	GS	(a-44)	(a-23)	GS	GS	B	GS
South Carolina	A	B	A	B	B	B	A	GS	B	B
South Dakota	A	(a-37)	(a-48)	(a-35)	GS	GS	(a-6)	GS	B	(a-47)
Tennessee	A	G	A	G	G	B	G	G	B	(a-49)
Texas	A	B	. . .	B	(a-14)	B	B	BG	B	(a-49)
Utah	A	GS	A	GS	AG	A	A	GS	B	(a-49)
Vermont	CG	GS	GS	CG	CG	CG	CG	CG	. . .	(a-49)
Virginia	GB	GB	A	GB	GB	B	GB	GB	B	GB
Washington	A	GS	GS	GS	GS	B	GS	GS	N.A.	B
West Virginia	GS	GS	GS	(a-22)	(a-6)	CS	C	GS	B (q)	GS
Wisconsin	A	GS	A	A	A	A	(a-6)	A	N.A.	A
Wyoming	G	GS	A	GS	(a-8)	CS	A	GS	B	(a-49)
American Samoa*	G	A	GB	GB	(a-4)	GB	G	GB	(a-18)	(a-49)
Guam*	GS	GS	G	GS	GS	GS	CS	GS	B	GS
No. Mariana Islands*	G	C	C	G	GS	C	GS	GS	B	C
U.S. Virgin Islands*	GS	GS	GS	GS	GS	GS	GS	GS	GS	GS

(a-19) Election administration
(a-20) Emergency management
(a-21) Employment Services
(a-22) Energy.
(a-23) Environmental protection.
(a-24) Finance.
(a-25) Fish and wildlife
(a-26) General services.
(a-27) Health
(a-28) Higher education
(a-29) Highways.
(a-30) Information systems
(a-31) Insurance
(a-32) Labor.
(a-33) Licensing
(a-34) Mental Health
(a-35) Natural resources.
(a-36) Parks and recreation.
(a-37) Personnel.
(a-38) Planning
(a-39) Post audit.
(a-40) Pre-audit.
(a-41) Public library development
(a-42) Public utility regulation.
(a-43) Purchasing.
(a-44) Revenue.
(a-45) Social services.
(a-46) Solid waste management
(a-47) State police
(a-48) Tourism.
(a-49) Transportation.
(a-50) Welfare.

(b) Effective Jan. 1, 2003 the positions of Commissioner & Treasurer, Banking, Comptroller, Finance, Insurance, Post audit, and Pre-audit merged into one Chief Financial Officer.

(c) Department abolished July 1, 2005; responsibilities transferred to office of

SELECTED STATE ADMINISTRATIVE OFFICIALS: METHODS OF SELECTION—Continued

State or other jurisdiction	*Information systems*	*Insurance*	*Labor*	*Licensing*	*Mental health & retardation*	*Natural resources*	*Parks & recreation*	*Personnel*	*Planning*	*Post audit*
Alabama*	G	G	G	. . .	G	G	CS	B	(a-13)	LS
Alaska	AG	AG	GB	AG	AG	GB	AG	AG	. . .	B
Arizona	A	GS	B	. . .	G	GS	B	A	(a-10)	. . .
Arkansas	GS	GS	GS	. . .	A	A	GS	A	. . .	L
California	G	CE	AG	G	(bb)	GS	GS	GS	. . .	. . .
Colorado	G	BA	GS	A	A	GS	A	A	G	(a-8)
Connecticut	GE	GE	GE	CS	GE(cc)	CS	CS	GE	A	(a-8)
Delaware	GS	CE	GS	CG	CG (dd)	GS	CG	CG	CG	(a-8)
Florida	A	CE (b)	GS	A	A (ee)	GS	A	A	GS	CE (b)
Georgia	GD	CE	CE	A	A	B	A	GS	G	(d)
Hawaii	CS	AG	GS	CS	(ff)	GS	CS	GS	CS	CS
Idaho	GS	GS	GS	GS	. . .	B	B	GS	. . .	(a-14)
Illinois	(a-6)	(a-9)	GS	GS	(a-45)	GS	(a-35)	(a-6)	. . .	(a-8)
Indiana	G	G	G	G	A	G	A	G	. . .	G
Iowa	A	AGS	AGS	A	A	AGS	A	A	. . .	. . .
Kansas	C	SE	GS	B	(gg)	GS	CS	C	. . .	L
Kentucky	G	G	G	. . .	CG	G	CG	G	G	CE
Louisiana	A	CE	GS	. . .	GS	GS	LGS	B	CS	CL
Maine	C	GLS	GLS	C	(a-45)	GLS	(a-35)	C	G	. . .
Maryland	A	GS	GS	A	A (hh)	GS	A	A	GS	N.A.
Massachusetts	C	G	G	G	CG (ii)	CG	CG	CG	G	CE
Michigan*	GS	GS	(a-12)	CS	CS	GS	CS	CS	. . .	CL
Minnesota	GS	A	GS	A	GS (jj)	GS	A	(a-24)	N.A	(a-8)
Mississippi	BS	SE	. . .	. . .	B	GS	GS	B	A	(a-8)
Missouri	A	GS	GS	A	A	GS	A	G	AGS	(a-8)
Montana	A	CE	GS	CP	CP	GS	CP	CP	G	L
Nebraska	A	GS	GS	A	A	GS	B	A	GS	(a-8)
Nevada	G	A	A	. . .	(kk)	G	A	G	. . .	. . .
New Hampshire	GC	GC	GC	GC	AGC	GC	AGC	AGC	. . .	(a-14)
New Jersey	A	GS	GS	...	A (ll)	A	A	GS	A	. . .
New Mexico	G	G	GS	G	G	GS	G	G	. . .	(a-8)
New York	G	GS	GS	(mm)	(nn)	(a-23)	GS	GS	(a-17)	(a-14)
North Carolina	G	CE	CE	. . .	A	G	A	G	N.A.	(a-8)
North Dakota	G	CE	G	. . .	A	. . .	G	A	. . .	A
Ohio	G	GS	A	. . .	(oo)	GS	A	A	LG	CE
Oklahoma	A	CE	CE	. . .	B	(a-48)	(a-48)	GS	. . .	. . .
Oregon	A	GS	SE	GS	A	GOC	B	A	. . .	SS
Pennsylvania	G	GS	GS	G	AG	GS	A	G	G	(a-8)
Rhode Island	AG	A	GS	CS	GS	GS	GS	A	A	N.A.
South Carolina	A	GS	GS	GS	B (pp)	B	GS	A	AB	B
South Dakota	GS	A	GS	. . .	GS	GS	A	GS	. . .	(a-8)
Tennessee	A	G	G	A	G	G	A	G	A	(a-14)
Texas	B	G	B	B	B	B	B	A	G	L
Utah	GS	GS	GS	AG	AB	GS	AG	GS	G	(a-8)
Vermont	CG	GS	GS	SS	CG	GS	CG	CG	. . .	CE (a-8)
Virginia	B	B	GB	GB	GB	GB	GB	GB	(a-10)	(a-8)
Washington	GS	CE	GS	GS	GS	CE	B	GS	GS	N.A.
West Virginia	C	GS	GS	. . .	GS	GS	GS	C	(a-17)	LS
Wisconsin	A	GS	GS	GS	A	GS	A	GS	. . .	(a-8)
Wyoming	G	G	A	A	A	G	GS	A	G	(a-8)
American Samoa*	(a-49)	G	N.A.	N.A.	(a-45)	AG	GB	A	(a-12)	G
Guam*	GS	GS	GS	GS	GS	GS	GS	GS	GS	CE
No. Mariana Islands*	C	CS	C	B	C	GS	C	GS	G	GS
U.S. Virgin Islands*	G	SE	GS	GS	GS	GS	GS	GS	G	L

Management and Budget, General Services and Department of State.

(d) Appointed by the House and approved by the Senate.

(e) Responsibilities shared between Director of Budget and Finance, (GS): Director of Human Resource Development, (GS) and the Comptroller, (GS).

(f) Vacant due to reorganization.

(g) In Maine, New Hampshire, New Jersey, Tennessee and West Virginia, the Presidents (or Speakers) of the Senate are next in line of succession to the Governorship. In Tennessee and West Virginia, the Speaker of the Senate bears the statutory title of Lieutenant Governor. The office will be filled in New Jersey beginning with the Nov. 2009 General election.

(h)The auditor is a Constitutional office, but is appointed by the Senate and General Assembly in joint meeting as mandated in the New Jersey Constitution.

(i) Method not specified.

(j) Responsibilities shared between Co-Directors in Election Commission (G); appointed by the Governor, subject to approval by the Chairs of the State Republican/Democratic parties.

(k) Responsibilities shared between Secretary of the State (CE); and Deputy Assistant Secretary of State (SS).

(l) Responsibilities shared between Secretary of State (CE); and Director, Bureau of Elections (CS).

(m) Responsibilities shared between the Assistant Secretary of State (A) and the Senior Counsel for Elections (A).

(n) Responsibilities shared between Secretary of State (CE); Deputy Secretary of State for Elections, Office of Secretary of State (SS); and Chief Deputy Secretary of State, same office (A).

(o) Responsibilities shared between Secretary of State (G); and Division Director of Elections, Elections Division, Secretary of State (A).

(p) Responsibilities shared betwee Director of Health Care Services and Director of Public Health, both (GS).

(q) Responsibilities shared between Chancellor of California Community Colleges (B) and California Postseconddary Education Commission (B).

(r) Responsibilities shared between Director of Wildlife, Director of Inland Fisheries and Director of Marine Fisheries (CS).

(s) Responsibilities shared between Director of Budget and Finance (GS) and the Comptroller (GS).

SELECTED STATE ADMINISTRATIVE OFFICIALS: METHODS OF SELECTION — Continued

State or other jurisdiction	Pre-audit	Public library development	Public utility regulation	Purchasing	Revenue	Social services	Solid waste mgmt.	State police	Tourism	Transportation	Welfare
Alabama*	(a-14)	B	SE	CS	G	B	CS	G	G	(a-29)	(a-45)
Alaska	. . .	AG	GB	AG	GB	GB	AG	AG	AG	GB	AG
Arizona	(a-14)	B	B	A	GS	GS	A	GS	GS	GS	GS
Arkansas	N.A.	B	A	A	A	GS	N.A.	G	GS	BS	(a-45)
California	(a-14)	. . .	GS	(a-26)	BS	GS	G	GS	. . .	GS	AG
Colorado	(a-14)	BA	CS	CS	GS	GS	CS	A	CS	GS	CS
Connecticut	(a-14)	CS	GB	CS	GE	GE	CS	GE	GE	GE	GE
Delaware	(a-8)	CG	CG	(a-26)	CG	GS (qq)	B	CG	CG	GS	CG
Florida	CE(b)	A	L	A	GOC	GS	A	A	G	GS	A
Georgia	(d)	AB	CE	A	G	GD	A	B	A	B	A
Hawaii	CS	B	GS	GS	GS	GS	CS	. . .	B	GS	CS
Idaho	(a-14)	B	GS	GS	GS	GS	. . .	GS	A	B	A
Illinois	(a-14)	SS	GS	(a-6)	GS	GS	GS	GS	(a-12)	GS	GS
Indiana	CE	G	G	A	G	G	A	G	LG	G	G
Iowa	A	AGS	AGS	A	AGS	AGS	A	AGS	A	AGS	(a-45)
Kansas	CS	GS	B	C	GS	GS	C	GS	C	GS	C
Kentucky	G	G	G	G	G	G	AG	G	G	G	(a-45)
Louisiana	CS	BGS	BS	CS	GS	GS	GS	GS	LGS	GS	GS
Maine	(a-14)	B	G	CS	C	GLS	CS	C/GLS	(a-17)	GLS	(a-45)
Maryland	A	A	GS	A	A	GS	A	GS	A	GS	(a-45)
Massachusetts	CE	B	G	CG	CG	CG	CG	CG	CG	G	CG
Michigan*	. . .	CL	GS	CS	CS	GS	CS	GS	. . .	GS	(a-45)
Minnesota	(a-8)	N.A.	G (rr)	A	GS	GS	GS	A	A	GS	GS (jj)
Mississippi	(a-8)	B	GS	A	GS	GS	A	GS	A	B	GS
Missouri	A	B	GS	A	GS	GS	A	GS	A	B	A
Montana	L	CP	CE	CP	GS	GS	GS	CP	CP	GS	(a-45)
Nebraska	A	B	B	A	GS	GS	A	GS	A	(a-29)	GS
Nevada	. . .	(ss)	G	A	G	G	. . .	G	GD	B	(tt)
New Hampshire	(a-14)	AGC	GC	CS	GC	GC	AGC	AGC	AGC	GC	AGC
New Jersey	. . .	. . .	GS	GS	A	GS	A	GS	A	GS	A
New Mexico	N.A.	G	G	G	GS	G	(i)	GS	GS	GS	GS
New York	(a-14)	(a-18)	GS	(a-26)	GS	GS	(a-23)	G	(a-17)	GS	(a-45)
North Carolina	(a-8)	A	G	A	G	A	A	G	A	G	A
North Dakota	. . .	. . .	CE	A	CE	G	A	G	G	G	G
Ohio	GS	B	BG	A	GS	(uu)	A	GS	LG	A	GS
Oklahoma	(a-14)	B	(vv)	A	GS	GS	A	A	B	B	GS
Oregon	(a-10)	B	GS	A	GS	GS	B	GS	A	GS	GS
Pennsylvania	(a-4)	G	GS	A	GS	AG	A	GS	G	GS	GS
Rhode Island	(a-14)	A	GS	A	GS	GS	(ww)	GS	N.A.	GS	GS
South Carolina	(a-14)	B	B	A	GS	GS	A	GS	GS	B	GS
South Dakota	CE	A	CE	A	GS	GS	A	A	GS	GS	(a-45)
Tennessee	A	A	SE	A	G	G	A	G	G	G	G
Texas	(a-14)	A	B	B	(a-14)	(i)	A	B	A	B	BG
Utah	AG	A	A	A	BS	GS	A	A	A	GS	GS
Vermont	(a-24)	CG	BG	CG	CG	GS	CG	GS	CG	GS	CG
Virginia	(a-14)	B	(xx)	A	GB	GB	(a-23)	GB	G	GB	(a-45)
Washington	CE	A	GS	A	GS	GS	GS	GS	N.A.	B	GS
West Virginia	(a-8)	B	GS	CS	GS	C	B	GS	GS	(a-29)	GS
Wisconsin	A	A	GS	A	GS	A	A	A	GS	GS	A
Wyoming	(a-8)	A	G	A	G	GS	A	A	A	(a-29)	(a-45)
American Samoa*	(a-4)	(a-18)	N.A.	A	(a-4)	GB	GB	GB	(a-12)	(a-29)	N.A.
Guam*	CE	(i)	N.A.	CS	GS	GS	GS	GS	CS	GS	GS
No. Mariana Islands*	G	B	B	C	C	C	A	GS	GB	CS	A
U.S. Virgin Islands* ..GS	GS	G	GS	GS	G	GS	GS	GS	GS	GS	

(t) Responsibilities shared between Adjutant General (GS) and Deputy Director (CS)

(u) Responsibilities shared between Director (GS), Chief of Fisheries (CS) and Chief of Wildlife (CS).

(v) Responsibilities shared between Administrator, Division of Fisheries, Department of Conservation; Administrator, Division of Wildlife, same department (AB).

(w) Responsibilities shared between State Tax Commissioner, Department of Revenue (GS); Administrator, Budget Division (A) and the Auditor of Public Accounts (CE).

(x) Responsibilities shared between Director, Game and Parks Commission (B), Division Administrator, Wildlife Division, Game & Parks Commission (A) and Assistant Director of Fish and Wildlife (A).

(y) Responsibilities shared between Director of Health and Human Services (G) and Division Administrator, Health (AG).

(z) Responsibilities shared between Director, Division of Purchasing, Dept. of Treasury (GS), and Director, Division of Property and Management, Dept. of the Treasury (A).

(aa) Responsibilities shared between Assistant Director, Office of Budget and Management (A) and Deputy Director same office (A).

(bb) Responsibilities shared between Director of Mental Health (GS) and Director of Developmental Disabilities (GS).

(cc) Responsibilities shared between Commissioner of Mental Health (GE) and Commissioner of Retardation (GE).

(dd) Responsibilities shared between Director, Division of Substance Abuse and Mental Health Department of Health and Social Services (CG); and Director, Division of Developmental Disabilities Services, same department (CG).

(ee) Responsibilities shared between Director, Mental Health, Dept. of Children and Families (A) and Director, Substance Abuse, Dept of Children and Families (A).

(ff) Responsibilities shared between Deputy Director of Mental Health (G) and Deputy Director of Retardation (G).

SELECTED STATE ADMINISTRATIVE OFFICIALS: METHODS OF SELECTION—Continued

(gg) Responsibilities shared between Director of Mental Health (C) and Director of Community Support (C).

(hh) Responsibilities shared between Executive Director, Mental Hygiene Administration (A); and Director, Developmental Disabilities Administration, Department of Health and Mental Hygiene (A).

(ii) Responsibilities shared between Commissioner, Department of Mental Retardation (CG); and Commissioner, Department of Mental Health, Executive Office of Human Services (CG).

(jj) Human/Social Services, Mental Health and Retardation and Welfare are under the Commissioner of Human Services (GS).

(kk) Responsibilities shared between Director of Health and Human Services (G) and Division Administrator,MHDS (G).

(ll) Responsibilities shared between Director, Division of Mental Health Services, Dept of Human Services (A) and Director, Division of Developmental Disabilities, Dept. of Human Services (A).

(mm) Responsibilities shared between Secretary of State (GS) and Commissioner of State Education Department (B).

(nn) Responsibilities shared between Commissioner, Office of Mental Health, and Commissioner, Office of Mental Retardation and Developmental Disabilities, both (GS).

(oo) Responsibilities shared between Director, Dept. of Mental Retardation and Developmental Disabilities (GS) and Director, Department of Mental Health (GS).

(pp) Responsibilities shared between Director of Disabilities and Special Needs (B) and Director of Mental Health (B).

(qq) Responsibilities shared between Secretary of Health and Social Services (GS) ; and Secretary , Department of Services of Children, Youth and their Families (GS).

(rr) Responsibilities shared between the five Public Utility Commissioners (G).

(ss) Responsibilities shared between Director, Dept. of Cultural Affairs (G) and Division Administrator of Library and Archives (A).

(tt) Responsibilities shared between Director of Health and Human Services (G) and Division Administrator,Welfare and Support Services (AG).

(uu) Responsibilities shared between Director, OH Dept. of Job and Family Services (GS), Superintendent of Dept. of Education (B), Executive Director of Rehabilitation Commission (B), Director of Dept. of Aging (GS).

(vv) Responsibilities shared between General Administrator Public Utility Division, Corporation Commission (B); and 3 Commissioners, Corporation Commission (CE).

(ww) Solid waste is managed by the Rhode Island Resource Recovery Corporation (RIRRC). Although not a department of the state government, RIRRC is a public corporation and a component of the State of Rhode Island for financial reporting purposes. To be financially self-sufficient, the agency earns revenue through the sale of recyclable products, methane gas royalties and fees for it services.

(xx) No single position. Functions are shared between Communication, Energy Regulation and Utility and Railroad Safety, all (B).

Table 4.11
SELECTED STATE ADMINISTRATIVE OFFICIALS: ANNUAL SALARIES BY REGION

State or other jurisdiction	*Governor*	*Lieutenant governor*	*Secretary of state*	*Attorney general*	*Treasurer*	*Adjutant general*	*Administration*	*Agriculture*	*Auditor*	*Banking*
Eastern Region										
Connecticut	$150,000	$110,000	$110,000	$110,000	$110,000	$162,617	$138,624	$120,200	(c)	$128,935
Delaware	171,000	76,250	123,850	140,950	110,050	118,250	. . .	115,550	105,350	108,150
Maine	70,000	(d)	83,844	92,248	83,844	102,689	102,689	102,689	89,460	96,553
Massachusetts	140,535	124,920	130,916	133,644	130,916	151,347	150,000	120,000	130,916	123,204
New Hampshire	113,834	(d)	104,364	110,114	104,364	104,364	116,170	93,812	. . .	104,364
New Jersey	175,000 (e)	(d)	141,000	141,000	141,000	141,000	. . .	141,000	N.A.	130,625
New York	179,000	151,500	120,800	151,500	127,000	120,800	. . .	120,800	151,500	127,000
Pennsylvania	174,914	146,926	125,939	145,529	145,529	125,939	142,847	125,939	145,529	125,939
Rhode Island (f)	117,817	99,214	99,214	105,416	99,214	94,769	143,011	(a-23)	183,021	(a-17)
Vermont (g)	142,542*	60,507*	90,376*	108,202*	90,376*	87,090	115,606	109,387	63,232 (h)	96,054
Regional average	143,464	109,902	113,030	123,860	114,229	120,887	129,850	117,953	132,347	114,242
Midwestern Region										
Illinois	177,500	135,700	156,600	156,600	130,800	115,700	142,400	133,300	139,800	135,100
Indiana	95,000	79,192	68,772	100,000	68,772	129,293	105,386	110,000	68,772	104,562
Iowa	130,000	103,212	103,212	123,669	103,212	N.A.	144,200	103,212	103,212	108,338
Kansas	110,707	31,313	86,003	98,901	82,563	106,394	114,199	108,004	. . .	94,095
Michigan**	177,000	123,900	124,900	124,900	174,204	139,118	129,842	129,842	148,135	112,199
Minnesota	120,303	78,197	90,227	114,288	(a-24)	157,268	108,388	108,388	102,257	94,795
Nebraska	105,000	75,000	85,000	95,000	85,000	92,699	93,359	99,395	85,000	97,856
North Dakota	100,030	77,655	79,572	87,351	75,146	152,064	. . .	81,743	79,571	89,232
Ohio	144,269	142,501	109,554	109,554	109,554	108,930	125,008	111,072	109,554	100,984
South Dakota	115,331	17,699 (i)	78,363	97,928	78,363	103,000	103,000	103,000	98,345	99,740
Wisconsin	137,092	72,394	65,079	133,033	65,079	115,502	136,944	123,248	121,973	103,325
Regional average	128,385	85,160	95,207	112,839	98,280	121,997	120,273	110,109	105,662	103,657
Southern Region										
Alabama**	112,895	61,714	79,580	161,794	79,580	87,936	112,892	79,026	79,580	152,058
Arkansas	87,352	42,219	54,594	72,794	54,594	101,826	134,860	101,266	54,594	120,591
Florida	132,932	127,399	120,000	131,604	131,604	157,252	120,000	131,604	135,000	(a-4)
Georgia	139,339	91,609	123,636	137,791	130,927	157,251	147,420	121,556	152,160	133,204
Kentucky	142,498	105,840	105,840	105,840	105,840	138,075	(j)	105,840	105,840	120,000
Louisiana	130,000	115,000	115,000	115,000	115,000	180,294	204,402	115,000	132,620	115,024
Maryland	150,000	125,000	87,500	125,000	125,000	130,560	138,374	130,050	. . .	117,751
Mississippi	122,160	60,000	90,000	108,960	90,000	124,443	124,000	90,000	90,000	133,721
Missouri	133,821	86,484	107,746	116,437	107,746	90,112	123,967	120,000	107,746	. . .
North Carolina	139,590	123,198	123,198	123,198	123,198	103,657	120,363	123,198	123,198	123,198
Oklahoma	147,000	114,713	94,500	132,850	114,713	157,251	90,451	87,005	114,713	137,239
South Carolina	106,078	46,545	92,007	92,007	92,007	92,007	173,380	92,007	N.A.	101,101
Tennessee	164,292 (k)	57,027 (d)	180,000	159,288	180,000	135,000	180,000	135,000	180,000	135,000
Texas	150,000	7,200 (l)	125,880	150,000	(a-14)	139,140	N.A.	137,500	198,000	136,191
Virginia	175,000	36,321	152,793	150,000	146,943	131,903	152,793	137,280	159,907	142,425
West Virginia	95,000	(d)	70,000	85,000	75,000	92,500	95,000	75,000	75,000	75,000
Regional average	132,997	80,018	107,642	122,973	113,885	126,200	136,993	111,333	122,026	124,940
Western Region										
Alaska	125,000	100,000	(a-1)	122,640	119,868	127,236	122,640	96,516	107,604	107,616
Arizona	95,000	(a-2)	70,000	90,000	70,000	134,000	154,654	102,260	128,785	110,650
California	212,179 (m)	159,134	159,134	184,301	169,743	209,866	. . .	175,000	175,000	150,112
Colorado	90,000	68,500	68,500	80,000	68,500	146,040	146,040	146,040	145,147	N.A.
Hawaii	123,480	120,444	. . .	120,444	114708	200,129	(n)	108,960	114,708	100,248
Idaho	108,727	28,655	88,374	98,105	88,374	136,427	(o)	106,620	. . .	102,731
Montana	100,121	79,007	79,129	89,602	(a-6)	100,959	96,967	96,972	79,137	97,576
Nevada	141,000	60,000	87,982	133,000	97,000	117,030	115,847	107,465	. . .	97,901
New Mexico	110,000	85,000	85,000	95,000	85,000	166,910	111,767	150,524	85,000	95,965
Oregon	93,600	(a-2)	72,000	77,200	72,000	160,884	150,252	130,044	N.A.	. . .
Utah	109,900	104,405	(a-1)	104,405	104,405	101,999	113,671	101,999	104,405	113,671
Washington	166,891	93,948	116,950	151,718	116,950	146,940	120,587	122,478	116,950	120,579
Wyoming	105,000	(a-2)	92,000	137,150	92,000	113,914	137,280	103,443	92,000	96,156
Regional Average	121,608	81,776	93,623	114,120	99,655	143,256	115,208	119,102	114,874	108,473
Regional Average without California	114,060	75,330	87,667	108,272	93,814	137,706	115,208	114,443	108,193	104,309
Guam**	90,000	85,000	. . .	90,000	49,026	N.A.	88,915	60,850	100,000	74,096
No. Mariana Islands**	70,000	65,000	. . .	80,000	40,800 (b)	. . .	54,000	40,800 (b)	80,000	40,800 (b)
U.S. Virgin Islands**	80,000	75,000	(a-1)	76,500	76,500	85,000	76,500	76,500	76,500	75,000

Sources: The Council of State Governments' survey of state personnel agencies, March 2009.

Note: The data for Alabama and Michigan are from 2008. The data for Guam, Northern Mariana Islands and U.S. Virgin Islands are from 2007.

Key:

N.A. — Not available.

. . . — No specific chief administrative official or agency in charge of function.

(a) Chief administrative official or agency in charge of function:

(a-1) Lieutenant governor.

(a-2) Secretary of state.

(a-3) Attorney general.

SELECTED STATE ADMINISTRATIVE OFFICIALS: ANNUAL SALARIES BY REGION—Continued

State or other jurisdiction	Budget	Civil rights	Commerce	Community affairs	Comptroller	Consumer affairs	Corrections	Economic development	Education	Election administration
Eastern Region										
Connecticut	$168,049	$118,450	$144,283	$163,910	$110,000	$127,307	$167,496	$144,283	$180,353	$132,804
Delaware	143,050	72,150	(a-2)	. . .	143,050	106,994	143,050	123,850	155,450	78,750
Maine	90,355	69,409	(a-17)	(a-17)	90,355	96,553	102,689	102,689	102,689	83,574
Massachusetts	130,592	113,850	150,000	140,000	154,669	135,000	143,986	150,000	154,500	130,916
New Hampshire	104,364	79,774	112,861	. . .	104,364	86,229	116,170	86,131	112,861	(a-2)
New Jersey	133,507	108,000 (p)	(a-17)	141,000	141,000	136,000	141,000	186,600	141,000	115,000
New York	178,000	109,800	120,800	120,800	151,500	101,600	136,000	120,800	170,165	(q)
Pennsylvania	148,011	120,744	132,934	115,345	N.A.	112,548	139,931	129,313	139,931	76,010
Rhode Island (f)	152,540	71,421	(a-17)	N.A.	109,748	(a-3)	142,610	101,598	155,843	93,742
Vermont (g)	(a-24)	87,901	104,499	66,581	(a-24)	87,901	98,550	95,950	113,402	(a-2)
Regional average	133,814	95,150	128,011	121,475	121,595	109,555	133,148	124,121	142,619	93,054
Midwestern Region										
Illinois	137,832	111,892	142,400	(a-12)	135,700	(a-3)	150,300	(a-12)	189,996	124,848
Indiana	134,244	88,000	(a-17)	115,267	(a-8)	70,000	101,000	150,000	82,734	N.A.
Iowa	144,813	97,460	108,338	93,829	. . .	128,877	142,105	145,811	148,526	97,454
Kansas	(a-6)	76,476	105,888	69,000	97,375	85,000	124,611	101,592	170,775	(r)
Michigan**	135,252	129,842	135,000	. . .	116,591	. . .	135,252	. . .	168,300	(s)
Minnesota	(a-24)	108,388	108,388	(a-17)	(a-24)	107,135	108,388	108,388	108,388	(a-2)
Nebraska	125,187	71,024	106,090	64,260	109,175	(a-3)	117,909	106,090	166,000	76,000
North Dakota	99,204	70,800	132,756	. . .	99,204	86,232	94,284	99,648	90,588	36,840
Ohio	126,402	96,408	115,690	98,342	126,401	99,486	119,454	142,500	194,501	109,554
South Dakota	(a-24)	N.A.	(a-44)	(a-48)	(a-40)	63,654	113,455	(a-48)	110,000	56,650
Wisconsin	122,973	96,543	121,000	. . .	114,385	85,782	123,628	99,447	109,587	101,000
Regional average	126,197	94,683	121,441	103,273	105,435	97,777	120,944	123,057	139,945	86,107
Southern Region										
Alabama**	171,271	. . .	159,500	87,936	136,990	77,573	119,543	(a-13)	191,270	56,938
Arkansas	111,414	. . .	(a-17)	N.A.	96,071	110,064	129,134	121,065	217,025	79,997
Florida	138,600	93,000	120,000	120,000	(a-4)	96,660	128,750	120,000	275,000	95,000
Georgia	124,000	105,202	123,600	146,795	N.A.	114,280	121,013	156,817	123,269	85,000
Kentucky	N.A.	115,500	136,500	112,350	104,060	85,215	92,400	136,500	175,000	118,794
Louisiana	180,000	82,347	320,000	85,000	204,402	88,400	136,719	320,000	341,171	109,803
Maryland	166,082	110,699	166,082	. . .	125,000	109,946	92,640 (b)	166,082	195,000	109,372
Mississippi	(a-6)	. . .	90,000	130,000	(a-6)	82,000	132,761	176,500	307,125	(t)
Missouri	102,000	67,078	120,000	93,787	95,285	(a-3)	120,000	120,000	154,512	77,256
North Carolina	(a-24)	76,298	120,363	95,374	153,319	N.A.	120,363	101,702	123,198	117,397
Oklahoma	74,000	64,386	112,500	N.A.	90,000	61,337	132,309	112,500	124,373	97,815
South Carolina	124,331	91,947	152,000	N.A.	92,007	101,295	144,746	(a-12)	92,007	84,375
Tennessee	106,620	84,996	180,000	(a-17)	180,000	69,780	150,000	180,000	180,000	115,008
Texas	142,800	83,933	. . .	129,250	150,000	106,399	181,500	. . .	180,000	(u)
Virginia	150,000	73,090	152,793	118,414	133,972	89,233	147,321	220,000	167,111	104,000
West Virginia	97,416	55,000	95,000	95,000	(a-8)	N.A.	80,000	(a-13)	175,000	(a-2)
Regional average	131,036	84,883	144,627	116,159	126,114	93,473	126,825	151,007	188,816	96,767
Western Region										
Alaska	121,716	129,372	122,640	(a-12)	107,616	(a-12)	122,640	(a-12)	122,640	96,516
Arizona	N.A.	127,685	100,000	128,525	112,455	128,525	125,000	100,000	85,000	(a-2)
California	(a-24)	. . .	. . .	142,964	169,743	175,000	225,000	. . .	184,301	132,396
Colorado	156,468	124,572	. . .	137,280	126,540	124,728	146,040	146,040	223,860	N.A.
Hawaii	114,708	97,776	114,708	. . .	114,708	97,644	108,960	108,960	150,000	94,795
Idaho	115,918	63,294	87,568	. . .	88,374	98,015	123,676	87,568	88,374	88,374
Montana	99,999	68,617	96,984	77,272	81,129	65,005	98,426	99,999	99,274	68,950
Nevada	(a-6)	87,773	115,847	. . .	97,000	97,901	108,850	117,030	113,295	(v)
New Mexico	122,880	86,890	136,000	N.A.	111,767	80,642	114,025	136,000	177,407	85,000
Oregon	127,884	100,380	143,340	136,320	127,884	143,340	158,712	143,340	72,000	127,884
Utah	141,232	84,355	110,643	110,643	123,317	110,643	116,803	133,757	198,193	79,887
Washington	163,056	108,000	141,549	141,549	163,056	(a-3)	147,000	141,549	121,618	101,496
Wyoming	109,200	69,253	147,145	147,145	(a-8)	147,145	130,114	(a-12)	92,000	94,359
Regional average	130,326	95,664	119,675	127,149	116,584	118,688	132,711	123,669	132,920	94,738
Regional average without California	126,264	95,664	119,675	125,172	112,154	113,688	125,021	123,669	128,638	91,315
Guam**	88,915	88,915	75,208	. . .	75,576	51,662	67,150	74,096	125,000	61,939
No. Mariana Islands**	54,000	49,000	52,000	52,000	40,800 (b)	52,000	40,800 (b)	45,000	80,000	53,000
U.S. Virgin Islands**	76,500	60,000	76,500	(w)	76,500	76,500	76,500	85,000	76,500	76,500

(a-4) Treasurer.
(a-5) Adjutant general
(a-6) Administration.
(a-7) Agriculture
(a-8) Auditor
(a-9) Banking
(a-10) Budget.
(a-11) Civil rights
(a-12) Commerce.
(a-13) Community affairs.
(a-14) Comptroller.
(a-15) Consumer affairs.
(a-16) Corrections
(a-17) Economic development.

SELECTED STATE ADMINISTRATIVE OFFICIALS: ANNUAL SALARIES BY REGION—Continued

State or other jurisdiction	Emergency management	Employment services	Energy	Environmental protection	Finance	Fish & widlife	General services	Health	Higher education	Highways
Eastern Region										
Connecticut	$135,062	$132,613	$121,146	$139,052	$163,910	(x)	$138,624	$162,617	$184,244	$169,745
Delaware	80,050	83,202	55,790	(a-35)	143,050	95,650	83,350	165,000	95,960	(a-49)
Maine	72,800	82,846	(a-38)	102,689	(a-6)	98,737	90,355	145,620	N.A.	(a-49)
Massachusetts	124,659	150,000	120,000	130,000	150,000	123,000	118,671	138,216	197,122	125,658
New Hampshire	104,364	104,364	79,774	112,861	(a-10)	98,691	(a-6)	98,691	72,852	(a-49)
New Jersey	132,300	124,020	N.A.	141,000	127,200	105,783	(y)	141,000	135,620	126,000
New York	140,864	127,000	120,800	136,000	151,500	136,000	136,000	136,000	170,165	136,000
Pennsylvania	121,428	122,446	106,015	139,931	148,011	118,084	132,934	139,931	121,917	129,311
Rhode Island (f)	(a-5)	124,729	105,881	130,152	(a-44)	(a-23)	(a-6)	134,975	167,095	(a-49)
Vermont (g)	79,186	93,870	96,283	81,494	89,669	79,290	89,357	115,606	. . .	(a-49)
Regional average	108,548	114,509	99,560	123,703	131,039	111,090	114,974	137,766	143,122	128,513
Midwestern Region										
Illinois	129,000	142,400	(a-12)	133,300	(a-10)	(a-35)	(a-6)	150,300	191,100	(a-49)
Indiana	101,500	104,559	83,212	115,006	(a-10)	79,878	(a-6)	(z)	162,245	(a-49)
Iowa	108,084	145,811	. . .	117,728	117,728	117,728	102,294	127,987	. . .	150,405
Kansas	(aa)	(a-32)	65,063	105,019	. . .	73,330	(a-6)	88,953	193,000	(a-49)
Michigan**	119,802	110,531	. . .	140,452	(a-10)	(bb)	. . .	135,252	103,655	(a-49)
Minnesota	108,388	104,358	108,388	108,388	108,388	108,367	(a-6)	108,388	360,000	108,388
Nebraska	82,156	93,804	84,999	111,093	(cc)	(dd)	97,849	138,894	160,865	(a-49)
North Dakota	81,984	88,692	96,240	88,152	99,204	97,344	120,924	155,124	200,000	(a-49)
Ohio	100,901	141,981	81,266	125,008	(ee)	98,155	105,123	154,378	186,701	120,016
South Dakota	73,181	(a-37)	(a-48)	(a-35)	139,668	115,607	(a-6)	116,531	323,502	(a-47)
Wisconsin	99,445	104,287	97,501	130,623	122,973	130,623	136,944	123,233	414,593	(a-47)
Regional average	99,422	113,807	99,307	117,391	121,733	106,252	113,651	129,904	229,566	122,807
Southern Region										
Alabama**	74,159	71,962	94,459	139,320	87,936	109,642	87,658	225,021	179,664	87,936
Arkansas	84,364	127,546	96,735	112,869	(a-6)	115,019	114,796	190,633	136,615	(a-49)
Florida	116,220	115,500	115,000	123,295	(a-4)	129,430	120,000	120,000	216,686	124,381
Georgia	122,003	88,455	116,452	133,508	130,308	107,732	N.A.	157,526	558,378	(a-49)
Kentucky	75,000	N.A.	N.A.	N.A.	136,500	131,704	N.A.	153,797	400,000	125,000
Louisiana	165,000	106,631	114,296	137,197	(a-6)	123,614	(a-6)	236,000	377,000	(a-49)
Maryland	127,500	115,000	130,050	123,850	166,082	. . .	(a-6)	166,082	154,194	159,858
Mississippi	107,868	135,315	137,996	120,386	(a-6)	120,636	. . .	230,000	341,250	(a-49)
Missouri	N.A,	103,860	. . .	95,108	N.A.	(ff)	95,288	113,891	155,004	(a-49)
North Carolina	97,284	120,363	92,647	113,410	153,000	105,000	120,363	171,486	477,148	154,388
Oklahoma	75,705	93,190	90,000 (gg)	99,922	108,045	123,033	90,451	N.A.	387,650	(a-49)
South Carolina	97,292	134,227	103,451	151,942	(a-6)	121,380	120,154	144,746	154,840	143,000
Tennessee	90,576	135,000	103,260	135,000	180,000	135,000	135,000	153,540	183,792	(a-49)
Texas	139,974	140,000	. . .	140,004	(a-14)	130,000	126,500	183,750	180,000	(a-49)
Virginia	114,650	124,741	88,000	150,218	152,793	124,740	141,231	191,906	234,000	189,280
West Virginia	65,000	75,000	95,000	(a-22)	(a-6)	77,772	78,492	95,000	(hh)	92,500
Regional average	103,506	112,453	105,950	125,495	141,861	116,317	120,978	168,892	267,224	145,825
Western Region										
Alaska	107,616	107,616	84,000	122,640	115,836	122,640	. . .	122,640	300,000	115,257
Arizona	90,685	110,002	. . .	N.A.	(a-14)	160,000	116,725	116,788	184,000	121,025
California	142,964	150,112	132,396	175,000	175,000	150,112	150,112	(ii)	(jj)	(a-49)
Colorado	131,208	124,500	126,000	138,000	126,540	144,876	130,404	146,040	146,040	135,840
Hawaii	94,795	83,040 (b)	83,040 (b)	83,040 (b)	(kk)	83,040 (b)	(a-14)	114,708	392,400	90,792 (b)
Idaho	111,571	111,945	101,982	112,340	102,731	129,043	. . .	141,710	110,011	(a-49)
Montana	N.A.	89,094	97,089	96,967	81,129	96,963	80,498	(a-45)	211,201	(a-49)
Nevada	86,757	127,721	99,397	112,275	(a-14)	117,030	. . .	(ll)	23,660 (mm)	(a-49)
New Mexico	124,684	123,648	136,000	118,273	153,600	95,000	117,767	188,159	169,343	N.A.
Oregon	95,628	150,252	123,660	130,044	(a-4)	136,320	(a-6)	178,668	219,504	127,884
Utah	69,760	130,187	126,700	116,803	123,317	116,803	107,678	195,562	130,187	(a-49)
Washington	126,204	141,549	147,000	147,000	163,056	116,208	(a-6)	141,549	N.A.	(a-49)
Wyoming	86,742	123,089	73,042	115,273	(a-8)	132,749	105,814	198,843	124,803	125,417
Regional average	105,718	120, 981	110,859	122,305	117,644	123,137	119,455	149,703	182,832	126,881
Regional average without California	102,332	118,554	108,901	117,514	112,864	120,889	116,048	146,053	182,832	124,769
Guam**	68,152	73,020	55,303	60,850	88,915	60,850	54,475	74,096	174,787	88,915
No. Mariana Islands**	45,000	40,800 (b)	45,000	58,000	54,000	40,800 (b)	54,000	80,000	80,000	40,800 (b)
U.S. Virgin Islands**	71,250	76,500	69,350	76,500	76,500	76,500	76,500	76,500	76,500	65,000

(a-18) Education (chief state school officer).
(a-19) Election administration
(a-20) Emergency administration
(a-21) Employment Services
(a-22) Energy.
(a-23) Environmental protection.
(a-24) Finance.
(a-25) Fish and wildlife
(a-26) General services.
(a-27) Health
(a-28) Higher education
(a-29) Highways.
(a-30) Information systems
(a-31) Insurance

SELECTED STATE ADMINISTRATIVE OFFICIALS: ANNUAL SALARIES BY REGION — Continued

State or other jurisdiction	Information systems	Insurance	Labor	Licensing	Mental health & retardation	Natural resources	Parks & recreation	Personnel	Planning	Post audit
Eastern Region										
Connecticut	$158,446	$143,222	$132,613	$104,954	(nn)	$138,123	$138,123	$138,624	$121,146	(a-8)
Delaware	155,450	105,350	115,530	94,850	(oo)	123,850	96,350	108,850	92,363	(a-8)
Maine	96,553	96,553	102,689	98,737	(a-45)	102,689	(a-35)	90,355	90,355	N.A.
Massachusetts	135,000	127,326	125,000	107,332	(pp)	150,000	135,000	133,000	150,000	130,916
New Hampshire	106,496	104,364	104,364	104,364	104,364	112,861	90,605	88,933	...	(a-14)
New Jersey	130,380	132,263	141,000	...	(qq)	123,600	104,831 (p)	141,000	95,697	...
New York	169,214	127,000	127,000	(rr)	(ss)	136,000	127,000	120,800	120,800	151,500
Pennsylvania	130,015	125,939	139,931	111,316	122,211	132,934	115,521	126,066	143,062	(a-8)
Rhode Island (f)	126,541	106,996	(a-21)	(tt)	127,678	(a-23)	(a-23)	131,846	101,499	N.A.
Vermont (g)	85,883	96,054	93,870	75,005	99,008	104,499	81,494	82,659	...	63,232 (h)
Regional average	129,398	116,507	120,673	105,255	127,182	112,177	112,177	116,213	114,365	127,237
Midwestern Region										
Illinois	(a-6)	(a-9)	124,100	(a-9)	(a-45)	133,300	(a-35)	(a-6)	...	(a-8)
Indiana	110,909	99,320	99,180	96,393	105,386	105,000	79,878	111,657	...	98,717
Iowa	154,270	104,533	112,069	89,710	150,405	106,090	102,294	117,728	...	...
Kansas	112,883	86,003	107,990	58,938	(uu)	111,490	73,320	92,319	...	115,296
Michigan**	146,017	112,199	135,000	116,591	122,198	135,252	109,315	146,143	...	148,135
Minnesota	122,400	97,217	108,388	78,571	(a-45)	108,388	108,367	(a-24)	N.A.	(a-8)
Nebraska	121,852	107,120	111,394	96,025	116,698	104,499	120,600	96,240	93,359	(a-8)
North Dakota	109,992	79,571	70,800	...	86,364	...	81,306	83,616	...	87,000
Ohio	105,123	128,564	87,547	(vv)	(ww)	128,003	100,589	98,342	128,357	(a-8)
South Dakota	137,060	83,015	113,448	N.A	105,583	116,531	82,995	107,468	N.A.	(a-8)
Wisconsin	118,104	117,980	106,031	111,121	109,534	130,623	91,279	104,287	...	(a-8)
Regional average	125,546	104,602	106,904	97,806	112,835	117,918	98,477	109,872	110,858	110,608
Southern Region										
Alabama**	158,858	87,936	87,936	...	140,383	87,936	94,459	147,458	(a-13)	212,293
Arkansas	122,351	113,365	111,658	...	104,768	96,743	105,883	96,071	...	140,345
Florida	120,000	(a-4)	115,500	107,171	(xx)	123,295	109,279	100,000	120,000	(a-4)
Georgia	122,850	120,394	121,570	100,000	128,164	141,103	111,420	152,250	124,000	(a-8)
Kentucky	100,000	94,500	136,500	...	N.A.	94,500	115,500	136,500	136,500	105,840
Louisiana	167,000	115,000	137,000	...	236,000	129,210	115,627	111,592	92,227	N.A.
Maryland	166,082	156,060	143,270	100,851	(yy)	123,850	115,000	117,416	124,848	N.A.
Mississippi	160,047	90,000	...	...	164,357	120,386	120,636	105,850	96,303	(a-8)
Missouri	110,000	103,860	120,000	N.A.	113,878	N.A.	95,108	95,288	102,000	(a-8)
North Carolina	153,227	123,198	123,198	...	129,011	120,363	106,974	120,363	N.A.	(a-8)
Oklahoma	101,500	126,713	105,053	...	133,455	86,310	86,310	80,955	...	...
South Carolina	137,500	112,407	116,797	116,797	(zz)	121,380	112,504	116,984	N.A.	94,730
Tennessee	150,000	135,000	135,000	92,832	135,000	135,000	83,628	135,000	N.A.	(a-14)
Texas	175,000	163,800	140,000	123,750	163,200	140,004	130,000	N.A.	142,800	198,000
Virginia	189,280	142,425	125,759	127,124	189,280	152,793	128,004	137,955	(a-10)	(a-8)
West Virginia	109,999	92,500	70,000	...	95,000	75,000	78,636	70,000	(a-13)	81,400
Regional average	140,231	119,298	119,283	107,143	144,008	118,187	106,811	114,912	118,368	136,709
Western Region										
Alaska	107,616	111,648	122,640	96,516	71,208	127,236	100,116	107,616	...	107,604
Arizona	117,903	115,650	126,069	...	94,183	132,000	142,812	117,702	N.A.	...
California	142,965	169,743	175,000	150,112	(aaa)	175,000	150,112	150,112	...	...
Colorado	132,000	110,388	146,200	126,516	114,948	146,040	144,876	128,484	156,468	(a-8)
Hawaii	83,040 (b)	100,248	108,960	112,596 (b)	(bbb)	108,960	83,040 (b)	108,960	88,128 (b)	83,040 (b)
Idaho	(o)	97,323	111,945	74,609	...	112,798	100,360	90,417	...	(a-14)
Montana	111,623	79,134	96,967	88,016	90,521	96,967	N.A.	85,118	99,999	111,001
Nevada	123,783	117,030	88,799	...	(ccc)	127,721	107,465	97,474	...	...
New Mexico	109,999	112,640	123,648	112,640	N.A.	136,000	98,363	107,519	...	85,000
Oregon	128,040	143,340	72,000	N.A.	134,484	122,004	136,320	110,556	...	N.A.
Utah	130,187	107,678	101,999	96,612	101,999	126,700	110,643	126,700	(a-10)	(a-8)
Washington	141,549	116,950	139,320	120,579	163,056	121,618	120,579	141,549	(a-24)	N.A.
Wyoming	187,200	97,660	85,037	69,400	74,880	43,842	97,003	105,600	100,000	(a-8)
Regional average	126,325	113,802	115,839	104,760	111,806	121,751	115,974	113,677	124,814	104,939
Regional average without California	124,813	109,141	109,923	99,720	106,487	117,314	112,871	110,641	124,814	104,939
Guam**	88,915	74,096	73,020	74,096	67,150	60,850	60,850	88,915	75,208	100,000
No. Mariana Islands**	45,000	40,800 (b)	45,000	45,360	40,800 (b)	52,000	40,800 (b)	60,000	45,000	80,000
U.S. Virgin Islands**	71,250	75,000	76,500	76,500	70,000	76,500	76,500	76,500	76,500	55,000

(a-32) Labor.
(a-33) Licensing
(a-34) Mental Health
(a-35) Natural resources.
(a-36) Parks and recreation.
(a-37) Personnel.
(a-38) Planning
(a-39) Post audit.
(a-40) Pre-audit.
(a-41) Public library development
(a-42) Public utility regulation.
(a-43) Purchasing.
(a-44) Revenue.
(a-45) Social services.

SELECTED STATE ADMINISTRATIVE OFFICIALS: ANNUAL SALARIES BY REGION—Continued

State or other jurisdiction	Pre-audit	Public library development	Public utility regulation	Purchasing	Revenue	Social services	Solid waste management	State police	Tourism	Transportation	Welfare
Eastern Region											
Connecticut	(a-14)	$113,525	$163,154	$124,537	$167,496	$159,137	$127,707	$155,953	$118,450	$169,745	$159,137
Delaware	(a-8)	81,350	93,250	(a-26)	120,950	(ddd)	155,000	151,350	90,000	133,950	111,650
Maine	(a-14)	87,172	117,104	74,297	96,553	114,670	74,297	92,830	(a-17)	102,689	(a-45)
Massachusetts	130,916	104,020	(eee)	118,671	142,939	136,619	130,000	157,469	108,248	150,000	137,000
New Hampshire	(a-14)	90,606	110,036	72,852	116,170	120,095	98,691	104,364	90,606	116,170	90,606
New Jersey	. . .	. . .	141,000	117,500	124,765	(fff)	N.A.	132,300	96,616	141,000	127,200
New York	151,500	170,165	127,000	136,000	127,000	136,000	136,000	121,860	120,800	136,000	136,000
Pennsylvania	(a-4)	115,795	135,434	120,001	132,934	N.A.	105,820	132,934	115,345	139,931	139,931
Rhode Island (f)	(a-14)	111,418	110,045	128,399	130,000	121,353	(ggg)	148,937	N.A.	(a-29)	(a-45)
Vermont (g)	(a-24)	83,990	116,688	89,357	89,253	121,763	81,494	106,912	79,227	115,606	100,714
Regional average	115,270	106,449	122,968	106,496	124,806	131,843	113,626	130,491	102,442	133,509	123,826
Midwestern Region											
Illinois	(a-14)	93,804	110,772	(a-6)	142,400	134,000	N.A.	132,600	(a-12)	150,300	142,400
Indiana	68,772	93,620	109,262	91,507	115,006	130,520	92,712	130,682	85,401	118,356	(a-45)
Iowa	97,968	128,123	119,029	102,294	148,526	152,006	102,294	125,186	102,294	147,909	(a-45)
Kansas	76,960	98,704	91,416	83,640	107,990	112,743	76,960	107,990	82,961	107,990	76,150
Michigan**	. . .	127,296	113,612	N.A.	116,591	130,050	122,198	129,842	. . .	140,000	(a-45)
Minnesota	(a-8)	N.A.	(hhh)	104,358	108,388	(a-34)	108,388	108,388	108,388	108,388	(a-34)
Nebraska	109,175	90,332	118,387	97,849	135,508	N.A.	65,168	103,798	57,805	119,883	N.A.
North Dakota	. . .	. . .	81,743	62,400	86,360	124,656	72,924	81,120	90,312	116,268	124,656
Ohio	126,401	N.A.	109,595	105,123	126,401	(iii)	89,794	128,544	87,984	98,300	141,980
South Dakota	78,363	70,298	91,390	63,194	110,303	116,531	83,843	92,855	134,698	103,000	(a-45)
Wisconsin	(a-8)	109,981	113,502	95,426	121,144	121,200	106,887	106,722	108,501	126,412	92,000
Regional average	101,952	103,118	104,338	94,819	119,874	124,822	92,117	113,430	100,074	121,528	111,742
Southern Region											
Alabama**	(a-14)	104,094	96,609	127,181	136,990	160,479	107,009	87,936	87,936	(a-29)	(a-45)
Arkansas	N.A.	95,076	109,835	96,071	120,048	139,549	N.A.	102,937	82,422	149,058	(a-45)
Florida	(a-4)	95,545	132,464	97,531	120,000	120,640	95,000	133,875	120,000	120,000	113,300
Georgia	(a-8)	N.A.	116,452	141,625	159,786	171,600	105,088	132,863	138,545	175,000	134,000
Kentucky	136,500	100,150	N.A.	85,000	120,428	110,250	78,950	110,250	110,250	136,500	(a-45)
Louisiana	122,595	100,922	110,000	102,814	124,446	129,995	102,000	134,351	130,000	170,000	105,000
Maryland	123,708	115,000	150,000	98,783	120,026	159,000	114,167	166,082	114,444	166,082	(a-27)
Mississippi	(a-8)	108,000	141,505	79,633	108,185	130,000	78,008	122,179	91,662	144,354	130,000
Missouri	95,285	84,072	88,267	95,288	120,000	120,000	N.A.	107,184	77,250	158,244	N.A.
North Carolina	(a-8)	106,787	123,936	101,517	120,363	117,193	110,105	117,406	101,702	120,363	89,882
Oklahoma	(a-14)	77,805	(jjj)	78,296	111,933	162,750	98,793	101,030	86,310	117,705	162,750
South Carolina	(a-14)	N.A.	160,272	109,323	130,063	144,746	151,942	145,000	112,504	146,000	144,746
Tennessee	105,588	115,008	150,000	70,296	150,000	150,000	86,880	135,000	135,000	150,000	150,000
Texas	(a-14)	95,000	115,500	111,188	(a-14)	168,000	N.A.	157,500	N.A.	192,500	200,000
Virginia	(a-14)	132,890	(kkk)	128,447	136,806	143,450	150,218	145,787	150,000	152,793	143,450
West Virginia	(a-8)	72,000	85,000	98,928	92,500	81,204	75,984	85,000	70,000	92,500	95,000
Regional average	117,240	100,168	121,616	101,370	126,348	138,054	104,165	124,024	107,202	142,440	135,827
Western Region											
Alaska	. . .	96,516	93,144	124,692	127,236	127,640	111,648	122,640	73,524	122,640	107,616
Arizona	(a-14)	142,812	120,124	103,464	139,971	139,050	96,510	139,549	120,627	N.A	139,050
California	(a-14)	. . .	138,528	(a-26)	150,112	165,000	126,588	186,336	. . .	150,112	175,000
Colorado	(a-14)	112,548	114,948	114,948	146,040	146,040	114,948	139,560	84,084	146,040	N.A.
Hawaii	83,040 (b)	105,000	94,795	89,812	114,708	108,960	79,104 (b)	. . .	N.A.	114,708	. . .
Idaho	(a-14)	93,808	92,167	(o)	85,447	141,710	. . .	112,008	63,400	142,937	104,400
Montana	111,001	83,224	82,169	80,498	96,967	96,967	96,967	87,588	82,682	96,968	96,967
Nevada	. . .	(lll)	112,275	88,799	115,847	115,847	(a-23)	115,847	117,030	115,847	(ll)
New Mexico	79,200	73,728	90,000	94,769	140,000	140,005	76,841	124,684	135,000	N.A.	148,481
Oregon	(a-10)	N.A.	143,136	100,380	150,252	158,004	N.A.	150,252	N.A.	157,680	158,004
Utah	(a-24)	110,643	99,264	107,678	116,677	130,187	116,803	116,803	103,794	137,432	130,187
Washington	(a-4)	97,536	120,579	98,736	141,549	163,056	147,000	137,160	N.A.	163,056	(a-45)
Wyoming	(a-8)	93,978	115,711	82,800	111,977	112,638	104,021	107,811	111,266	(a-29)	(a-45)
Regional average	111,897	101,055	108,988	103,057	125,906	134,939	107,519	128,353	99,045	133,894	131,582
Regional average without California	110,432	101,055	106,526	98,780	123,889	131,675	105,612	123,082	99,045	132,273	127,240
Guam**	100,000	55,303	N.A.	54,475	74,096	74,096	88,915	74,096	55,303	88,915	74,096
No. Mariana Islands**	54,000	45,000	80,000	40,800 (b)	45,000	40,800 (b)	54,000	54,000	70,000	40,800 (b)	52,000
U.S. Virgin Islands**	76,500	53,350	54,500	76,500	76,500	76,500	76,500	76,500	76,500	65,000	76,500

(a-46) Solid waste management
(a-47) State police
(a-48) Tourism.
(a-49) Transportation.
(a-50) Welfare.
(b) Salary ranges, top figure in ranges follow: Alabama: Employment Services, $109,642. Hawaii: Employment Services, $118,212; Energy, $118,212, Environmental Protection, $118,212; Fish and Wildlife, $118,212; Highways, $129,180; Information Systems, $118,212; Licensing, $112,596;Parks and Recreation,$118,212; Planning,$125,436; Post-Audit, $118,212; Pre-Audit, $118,212; Solid Waste Management, $112,596. Maryland: Corrections, $123,708. Northern Mariana Islands: $49,266 top of range applies to the

SELECTED STATE ADMINISTRATIVE OFFICIALS: ANNUAL SALARIES BY REGION—Continued

following positions: Treasurer, Banking, Comptroller, Corrections, , Employment Services, Fish and Wildlife, Highways, Insurance, Mental Health and Retardation, Parks and Recreation, Purchasing, Social/Human Services, Transportation.

(c) Responsibilities shared between Kevin P. Johnston, $189,770 and Robert G. Jaekle, $189,770.

(d) In Maine, New Hampshire, New Jersey, Tennessee and West Virginia, the presidents (or speakers) of the Senate are next in line of succession to the governorship. In Tennessee and West Virginia, the speaker of the Senate bears the statutory title of lieutenant governor.

(e) Governor Corzine accepts $1 in salary.

(f) A number of the employees receive a stipend for their length of service to the State (known as a longevity parymen). This amount can vary significantly among employees and, depending on state turnover, can show dramatic changes in actual salaries from year-to-year.

(g) As part of a budget rescission the Governor imposed a five percent pay cut for all non-elected Executive Branch exempt employees making over $60,000 per annum; All of the salaries represented in this table were affected. The officials who voluntarily took the five percent reduction are marked with an *.

(h) State Auditor Thomas Salmon is on a military leave of absence. The salary reduction is at the request of the official during activation to duty, 33.5 percent pay reduction.

(i) Annual salary for duties as presiding officer of the Senate.

(j) Position is vacant due to reorganization.

(k) Governor Bredesen returns his salary to the state.

(l) Lieutenant Governor Dewhurst receives additional pay when serving as acting governor.

(m) Governor Schwarzenegger waives his salary.

(n) There is no one single agency for Administration. The functions are divided amongst the Director of Budget and Finance, $114,708; Director of Human Resources Development, $108,960; and the Comptroller,$114,708.

(o) Does not draw a salary.

(p) Acting salary.

(q) The statutory salary for each of the four members of the Board of Elections is $25,000, including the two co-chairs, Douglas A. Kellner and James A. Walsh.

(r) Responsibilities shared between Secretary of State, $86,003 and Deputy Secretary of State, $78,770.

(s) Responsibilities shared between Secretary of State, $124,900 and Bureau Director, $110,531.

(t) Responsibilities shared between Assistant Secretary of State, $84,000 and Senior Counsel for Elections, $83,000.

(u) Responsibilities shared between Secretary of State, $125,880; and Division Director, $112,151.

(v) Responsibilities shared between Secretary of State, $87,982; Deputy Secretary of State for Elections, $97,474 and Chief Deputy Secretary of State, $106,150.

(w) Responsibilities for St. Thomas, $74,400; St. Croix, $76,500; St. John, $74,400.

(x) Responsibilities shared between Director of Wildlife, $127,707, Director of Inland Fisheries, $127,707 and Director of Marine Fisheries, $121,133.

(y) Responsibilities shared between Ating Director, Division of Purchasing, Dept. of the Treasury, $117,500 and Director, Division of Property Management, and Construction, Dept. of the Treasury, $120,000.

(z) Contractual.

(aa) Responsibilities shared between Adjutant General, $106,394 and deputy director, $72,000.

(bb) Responsibilities shared between Director, Dept. of Natural Resources, $135,200 and Chief, Fish, $110,531 and Chief, Wildlife, $99,606.

(cc) Responsibilities shared between, Auditor of Public Accounts-$85,000; Director ofAdministration-$125,187 and State Tax Commissioner-$135,508.

(dd) Responsibilities shared between Game & Parks Director-$120,600; Fish & Wildlife Asst Dir. -$92,887; Wildlife Division Administrator-$84,500.

(ee) Responsibilities shared between Assistant Director of Budget, Payroll and Revenue Estimating, $99,757 and Deputy Director of Accounting, $113,859.

(ff) Responsibilities shared between Administrator, Division of Fisheries, Department of Conservation, $92,688; Administration, Division of Wildlife, same department, $87,408.

(gg) Salary from position with Interstate Oil Compact Commission.

(hh) Responsibilities shared between Community and Technical, $131,222 and Higher Education Policy Commission, $147,500.

(ii) Responsibilities shared between Director of Health Care Services, $165,000 and Director Department of Public Health $222,000.

(jj) Responsibilities shared between Chancellor of California Community Colleges, $198,504 and California Post Secondary Education Commission $168,300.

(kk) Responsibilities shared between Director of Budget and Finance, $109,248 and Comptroller, $109,248.

(ll) Responsibilities shared between Director, Health and Human Services, $115,847 and Division Administrator, $106,150.

(mm) The Chancellor elected to receive a lower wage than authorized.

(nn) Responsibilities shared between Commissioner Thomas Kirk, Mental Health: $189,773 and Commissioner Peter O'Meara, Retardation: $167,496.

(oo) Responsibilities shared between Director, Division of Substance Abuse and Mental Health, Department of Health and Social Services, $137,250 and Director, Division of Developmental Disabilities Service, same department, $111,550.

(pp) Responsibilities shared between Commissioners Barbara Leadholm, $136,000 and Elin M. Howe, $135,000.

(qq) Responsibilities shared between Director, Division of Mental Health Services, Dept. of Human Services, $127,673 and Director, Division of Developmental Disabilities, Dept. of Human Services, $131,040.

(rr) Responsibilities shared between Commissioner, State Education Department, $170,165; Secretary of State, Department of State, $120,800.

(ss) Responsibilities shared between Commissioner of Office of Mental Retardation and Developmental Disabilities, $136,000 and Commissioner of Office of Mental Health, $136,000.

(tt) Varies by department.

(uu) Responsibilities shared between Director of Mental Health, $79,097 and Director of Community Support, $74,064.

(vv) Numerous licensing boards, no central agency.

(ww) Responsibilities shared between Director of Dept. of Mental Retardation and Developmental Disabilities, $126,089 and Director, Dept. of Mental Health, $126,006.

(xx) Responsibilities shared between, Director of Mental Health, Department of Children and Familes, $105,594; and Director, Substance Abuse, same department, $105,575.

(yy) Responsibilities shared between Executive director of Mental Hygiene Administration,$211,632 and Director of Developmental Disabilities Administration,$120,870.

(zz) Responsibilities shared between Director for Disabilities and Special Needs, vacant and Director of Mental Health, $155,787.

(aaa) Responsibilities shared between Director of Mental Health, $165,000 and Director of Developmental Services, $165,000.

(bbb) Responsibilities shared between Deputy Director of Mental Health, $105,528 and Deputy Director of Retardation, $105,528.

(ccc) Responsibilities shared between Director, Health and Human Services, $115,847 and Division Administrator, $112,275

(ddd) Function split between two cabinet positions: Secretary, Dept. of Health and Social Services : $143,050 (if incumbent holds a medical license, amount is increased by $12,000; if board-certified physician, a supplement of $3,000 is added) and Secretary, Dept. of Svcs. for Children, Youth and their Families, $128,850.

(eee) Responsibilities shared by Chairman Paull Hibbard $115,360 and Commissioner Sharon Gillett $116,575

(fff) Responsibilities shared between Commissioner, Department of Human Services, $141,000 and Commissioner, Department of Children and Families, $141,000.

(ggg) Solid waste is managed by the Rhode Island Resource Recovery Corporation (RIRRC). Although not a department of the stte government, RIRRC is a public corporation and a component of the State of Rhode Island for financial reporting purposes. To be financially self-sufficient, the agency earns revenue through the sale of recyclable products, methane gas royalties and fees for it services.

(hhh) Responsibilities shared between five commissioner's with salaries of $89,011 for each.

(iii) Responsibilities shared between Director, Dept. of Job and Family Services, $141,980; Superintendent of Dept. of Education, $194,500; Executive Director of Rehabilitation Services Commission, $120,328 and Director of Dept. of Aging, $105,684.

(jjj) Responsibilities shared between three Commissioners, $114,713, $114,713 and $111,250 and General Administrator, $96,000.

(kkk) Function split between three agencies: Communications—$142,425; Energy Regulation—$139,762; Utility and Railroad Safety—$123,498.

(lll) Responsibilities shared between Director, Department of Cultural Affairs, $ $106,150 and Division Administrator, Library and Archives, $97,474.

Executive Branch Successors and the Line of Succession

By Julia Nienaber Hurst

Crises demand leadership. The time to address an orderly succession of executive branch power is before a crisis occurs. This decade offers states examples of questions and legal challenges which may arise if state constitutional language or statute on executive branch succession is incomplete, unclear or in conflict with other state statutes. The governor's office may be vacated before the official completion of a term due to death, resignation, incapacitation, impeachment or recall. State law should define a clear and sufficiently deep line of gubernatorial succession. State leaders should consider establishing a specific process to declare a governor incapacitated, either temporarily or permanently. States may also review to ensure statute surrounding impeachment and recall provisions are not in conflict with Constitutional and other statutory language on succession.

Executive Branch Succession

This decade provides many examples of needs states have to revisit their succession laws and continuity of government planning. When executive branch succession is not thoroughly addressed in law, problems can ensue. The issues may include predominant control of two branches by one person, lack of checks and balances, a question of one state senator with two votes in the senate, that the governor is not a statewide elected official, or related legal challenges.

Generally, every state should address which officials constitute the line of gubernatorial succession, in what order they form the line, how deep the line is, and under what circumstances a person succeeds, with specificity. Gubernatorial succession begins when the office is vacated prior to completion of a person's official term. The office may be vacated as a result of death, resignation, incapacitation, impeachment or recall. A leader may be incapacitated due to location, physical ailment, unconscious state (anesthetized or in a coma), or the inability to effectively function. State law should also specify if incapacitation may be temporary, how incapacitation is determined, and when and how a succession due to incapacitation is enacted.

Once a line of succession has activated, state law should also be clear as to whether successors become "acting" officials or whether they assume the title and office. Lawmakers are well advised to carefully consider whether resulting vacancies should be filled, and if so, how. And, depending on which officials step into executive roles and under what circumstances, law should specify whether the succeeding official retains any part or power of their previous position.

Line of Succession

While not every state addresses gubernatorial succession the same way, there are some tenets which arguably should be consistent across states and other tenets which must be clearly addressed, even if not uniformly. Each state should establish, before it is needed, a clear line of succession of sufficient depth. This year, New Jersey voters will elect the state's first lieutenant governor, and when they do, 43 states will have a lieutenant governor first in line of gubernatorial succession. Arizona, Oregon and Wyoming designate the Secretary of State first in line while four states rely on the Senate President as first in line. These include Maine, New Hampshire, Tennessee and West Virginia.

In the states without a lieutenant governor, several legislatures have debated the merits of creating the office. The governor and lieutenant governor successor line most closely model the federal line of executive succession of president and vice president. According to one Arizona newspaper, in today's mobile society, voters who have recently moved may not realize they are voting for a gubernatorial successor if that successor does not hold the title of lieutenant governor. Others point out the succession of a senate president may allow a person who was not elected statewide to hold the office of governor, and the person may end up with significant powers over two branches of state government, such as the case in New Jersey this decade.

Death or Resignation

In November 2004, New Jersey Gov. Jim McGreevey resigned. It was the second time in less than four years a New Jersey governor had left office early. *State Legislatures* magazine noted that both resulting Acting Governors Richard Codey and Donald DiFrancesco, became governor assuming those powers while retaining their senate seat and all powers of the senate presidency. Both men gaveled in each senate session and often led session voting while simultaneously acting as governor. State executive succession law should be specific as to the role and powers of an official who has succeeded.

Other states have the senate president third in line of succession. In that role, the official may become acting lieutenant governor when a vacancy occurs in that office. These situations may create additional questions of clarity. In March 2008, New York Lt. Gov. David Paterson succeeded to governor after former Gov. Eliot Spitzer resigned. From March 2008 to January 2009, New York had four different lieutenant or acting lieutenant governors. Paterson succeeded to governor, the next senate president resigned his senate seat, the following senate president was voted out when the majority changed in the November election, and a new senate president was seated in January. Some note this method of succession has led to instability in the second position of gubernatorial succession.

Likewise in New York, when the office of lieutenant governor is vacant, the senate president pro tem retains his or her senate seat, the senate presidency, and also assumes all duties and powers of the lieutenant governor. Since a lieutenant governor may cast tie-breaking votes in the senate in New York, there is a question of whether or not a senate president pro tem acting as lieutenant governor could potentially cast two votes on a question—one as a senator and a second as lieutenant governor in the event of a tie. Legal experts differ. Some say it is clear one official may only vote once. Others argue the lieutenant governor votes only on procedural matters in the event of a tie, not on legislation, so the acting lieutenant governor could vote on procedural ties. Since the voting issue has yet to occur, no definitive precedent has been set. However, states may learn from this circumstance in determining the order of the line of gubernatorial succession and in determining the best ways to fill resulting vacancies and power transfers.

The 2001 attacks on the United States showed the need for states to plan gubernatorial succession and continuity of government for a deeper line of succession. Some states convened commissions to study and report on succession and government continuity. In 2004, both Indiana and Virginia voters passed constitutional amendments clarifying and deepening lines of gubernatorial succession, some as deep as 14 officials.

In November 2008, the Pennsylvania lieutenant governor died while in office. Like New York, the state has the senate president pro tem retain his senate seat and leadership power while also assuming the role and power of acting lieutenant governor. Senate President Pro Tem Joe Scarnati, a Republican, is now first in line of succession to the sitting Democratic governor bringing to light another consideration in succession planning, the potential for cross party succession.

Gubernatorial resignation may occur for a variety of personal or professional reasons and may occur with or without notice. As a result of the 2008 presidential election, several governors announced the intent to resign their seats to take positions in Washington, D.C. One issue states may address is the availability of transition planning funds for the successor. The unusual issue of a postponed succession also arose in 2009. New Mexico Gov. Bill Richardson withdrew his name from consideration for a Cabinet post after gubernatorial transition planning had begun.

Incapacitation

A governor may become permanently or temporarily incapacitated through location, physical affliction, or the inability to effectively function.

Location Incapacitation

In 1979 in the Petition of the Commission on the Governorship of California (*Brown vs. Curb*), the state supreme court ruled the lieutenant governor becomes acting governor each time the governor is out of state, a position other states also hold. One basis of the ruling was that a leader must ideally be physically present to address issues of immediate concern and emergency. These may be natural disaster, mass violence, or other crises. Other states, though, adopted the opinion that modern communication devices make location irrelevant in regard to governance. But new issues have arisen since 2003. The Iraq war has provided examples of governors who have yielded authority while in dark communication zones or while in the war zone generally. In determining whether location can "incapacitate" a governor, state leaders should consider physical presence, availability of immediate and reliable communication, and the safety of the governor wherever he or she may be.

Physical Incapacitation

Physical incapacitation of a governor may range from sedation or questionable lucidity to anesthetized unconsciousness or coma. In 2006, Kentucky Gov. Ernie Fletcher was hospitalized. News reports indicated he would continue to govern with assistance from designees of his Cabinet and leadership team, none of which was the lieutenant governor. Some public debate ensued. In subsequent hospitalizations, the governor prepared formal transfers of power to the lieutenant governor, which may or may not have been activated based on the seriousness of the diagnosis and treatment.

Former Indiana Gov. Frank O' Bannon unexpectedly suffered a stroke Sept. 8, 2003, and reportedly remained unconscious. Indiana law spells out how gubernatorial incapacitation is determined. The house speaker and senate president must file a letter with the Supreme Court suggesting the governor is incapacitated. The Supreme Court must meet within 48 hours to rule on the question. On Sept. 10, 2003, such a letter was filed and the court declared the governor incapacitated making the lieutenant governor acting governor. The governor died Sept. 13, 2003. Senate President Pro Tem Bob Garton was quoted saying, "If anyone has ever questioned the importance of the office of lieutenant governor, that question has now been answered."

Functional Incapacitation

In December 2008, Illinois Gov. Rod Blagojevich was arrested on federal corruption charges involving the office of governor. Unlike Indiana, Illinois lacked a specific statutory process for declaring a governor incapacitated. In that vacuum, the attorney general filed an incapacitation motion with the Supreme Court which would have granted temporary incapacitation pending the federal trial. However, the court rejected the effort. Nearly one month to the day after his arrest, the legislature voted to impeach him. Some papers opined the state should consider adopting a clear, statutory process for declaring incapacitation.

Temporary Incapacitation

At least one Tennessee body made a similar declaration in 2008. In January 2008, a Tennessee state task force recommended the state adopt a process by which a governor could temporarily transfer his or her duties due to temporary incapacitation. In 2006, Tennessee Gov. Phil Bredesen was seriously ill for three weeks from a tick-borne illness doctors were unable to specifically diagnose. The state learned it lacked such provision through the incident.

Recall or Impeachment

Recall and impeachment are processes citizens or legislators may follow to forcibly remove a governor from office before his or her term has officially ended. Most states have provisions in law for one or both processes. Typically a recall involves a petition process which results in a vote of the people to remove a person from office. An impeachment is a vote of the legislature typically to have hearings and a vote on the removal of an official. A recall this decade showed that a state's line of gubernatorial succession provisions and the state's statute governing a recall can be in conflict.

In 2003, a petition in California was certified to hold a recall election on Gov. Gray Davis. A question was raised whether a recall would elevate the lieutenant governor to the vacant position or whether voters would get to choose a new governor from among a slate. In *Frankel vs. Shelley*, the California Supreme Court ruled since the state's recall statute indicated voters should elect a successor, if appropriate, simultaneous to the recall vote, the Constitutional provisions regarding a lieutenant governor succeeding did not apply because the office would never be vacant. The simultaneous recall and gubernatorial replacement election took place Oct. 7, 2003. In reviewing succession law, state leaders may review recall and impeachment statutes for congruity with gubernatorial succession lines and planning.

Acting

Acting Governor

State law should be clear about whether, and under what circumstances, a gubernatorial successor is stepping into the governor role permanently or temporarily. In Utah, language which indicated a lieutenant governor would be "acting as governor" opened the question of whether that meant the person was "Acting Governor" or was "Governor" acting in that role. In 2003, former Utah Gov. Michael Leavitt announced he would join the president's Cabinet. Preparations began for the succession of Lt. Gov. Olene Walker. At the governor's request, the Utah Attorney General released opinion 03-001 Aug. 18, 2003, regarding this question. It found the state's Constitutional language that upon a vacancy in the office of governor the powers and duties of the Governor "shall devolve" to the Lieutenant Governor indicated permanent succession. The Attorney General noted the intent of the constitutional language was to model Presidential succession.

Filling Vacancies

Some states have no provisions for filling a vacancy in the office of lieutenant governor. As noted above, this can result in lines of succession which yield top officials of opposite parties, one official who arguably has two votes in the legislature, or one official who maintains significant powers across two branches of government. New Mexico is among the states to address that issue this decade. The state passed a law in 2008 which allows a governor to fill a vacancy in the office of lieutenant governor.

About the Author

Julia Nienaber Hurst is executive director of the National Lieutenant Governors Association (*www.nlga.us*). Hurst's nearly 20 years of state government experience include time as chief operating officer of The Council of State Governments, four sessions as a legislative chief of staff, and time as a multistate lobbyist.

Table 4.12
THE LIEUTENANT GOVERNORS, 2009

State or other jurisdiction	Name and party	Method of selection	Length of regular term in years	Date of first service	Present term ends	Number of previous terms	Joint election of governor and lieutenant governor (a)
Alabama	Jim Folsom Jr. (D) (b)	CE	4	1/1986 (b)	1/2011	1	No
Alaska	Sean R. Parnell (R)	CE	4	12/2006	12/2010	. . .	Yes
Arizona	(c)						
Arkansas	Bill Halter (D)	CE	4	1/2007	1/2011	. . .	No
California	John Garamendi (D)	CE	4	1/2007	1/2011	. . .	No
Colorado	Barbara O'Brien (D)	CE	4	1/2007	1/2011	. . .	Yes
Connecticut	Michael Fedele (R)	CE	4	1/2007	1/2011	. . .	Yes
Delaware	Matthew Denn (D)	CE	4	1/2009	1/2013	. . .	No
Florida	Jeff Kottkamp (R)	CE	4	1/2007	1/2011	. . .	Yes
Georgia	Casey Cagle (R)	CE	4	1/2007	1/2011	. . .	No
Hawaii	James Aiona (R)	CE	4	12/2002	12/2010	1	Yes
Idaho	Brad Little (R)	CE	4	1/2009 (d)	1/2011	. . .	No
Illinois	Vacant (D) (e)	CE	4	. . .	1/2011(e)	. . .	Yes
Indiana	Becky Skillman (R)	CE	4	1/2005	1/2013	1	Yes
Iowa	Patty Judge (D)	CE	4	1/2007	1/2011	. . .	Yes
Kansas	Vacant (f)	CE	4	1/2007	1/2011	. . .	Yes
Kentucky	Daniel Mongiardo (D)	CE	4	1/2007	1/2011	. . .	Yes
Louisiana	Mitch Landrieu (D)	CE	4	1/2004	1/2012	1	No
Maine	(c)						
Maryland	Anthony Brown (D)	CE	4	1/2007	1/2011	. . .	Yes
Massachusetts	Tim Murray (D)	CE	4	1/2007	1/2011	. . .	Yes
Michigan	John D. Cherry (D)	CE	4	1/2003	1/2011	1	Yes
Minnesota	Carol Molnau (R)	CE	4	1/2003	1/2011	1	Yes
Mississippi	Phil Bryant (R)	CE	4	1/2008	1/2012	. . .	Yes
Missouri	Peter Kinder (R)	CE	4	1/2005	1/2013	1	No
Montana	John Bohlinger (R)	CE	4	1/2005	1/2013	1	Yes
Nebraska	Rick Sheehy (R)	CE	4	1/2005 (g)	1/2011	(g)	Yes
Nevada	Brian Krolicki (R)	CE	4	1/2007	1/2011	. . .	No
New Hampshire	(c)						
New Jersey	Beginning with the November 3, 2009 general election this office will be filled (h)						
New Mexico	Diane Denish (D)	CE	4	1/2003	1/2011	1	Yes
New York	Vacant (i)	CE	4	1/2007	1/2011	. . .	Yes
North Carolina	Walter Dalton (D)	CE	4	1/2009	1/2013	. . .	No
North Dakota	Jack Dalrymple (R)	CE	4	12/2000	12/2012	1	Yes
Ohio	Lee Fisher (D)	SE	4	1/2007	1/2011	. . .	Yes
Oklahoma	Jari Askins (D)	CE	4	1/2007	1/2011	. . .	No
Oregon	(c)						
Pennsylvania	Joseph B. Scarnati (R) (j)	CE	4	11/2008 (j)	1/2011	. . .	Yes
Rhode Island	Elizabeth H. Roberts (D)	SE	4	1/2007	1/2011	. . .	No
South Carolina	R. André Bauer (R)	CE	4	1/2003	1/2011	1	No
South Dakota	Dennis Daugaard (R)	CE	4	1/2003	1/2011	1	Yes
Tennessee	Ron Ramsey (R)	(k)	2	1/2007	1/2011	. . .	No
Texas	David Dewhurst (R)	CE	4	1/2003	1/2011	1	No
Utah	Gary Herbert (R)	CE	4	1/2005	1/2013	1	Yes
Vermont	Brian Dubie (R)	CE	2	1/2003	1/2011	3	No
Virginia	William T. Bolling (R)	CE	4	1/2006	1/2010	. . .	No
Washington	Brad Owen (D)	CE	4	1/1997	1/2013	2	No
West Virginia	Earl Ray Tomblin (D)	(l)	2	1/1995	1/2011	7	No
Wisconsin	Barbara Lawton (D)	CE	4	1/2003	1/2011	1	Yes
Wyoming	(c)						
American Samoa	Ipulasi Aitofele Sunia (D)	CE	4	4/2003 (m)	1/2009	1 (m)	Yes
Guam	Michael W. Cruz (R)	CE	4	1/2007	1/2011	. . .	Yes
No. Mariana Islands	Timothy Villagomez (D) (n)	CE	4	1/2006	1/2010	. . .	Yes
Puerto Rico	(c)						
U.S. Virgin Islands	Greg Francis (D)	SE	4	1/2007	1/2011	. . .	Yes

See footnotes at end of table.

THE LIEUTENANT GOVERNORS, 2009—Continued

Source: The Council of State Governments, March 2009.

Key:

CE — Constitutional, elected by public.

SE — Statutory, elected by public.

. . . — Not applicable.

(a) The following also choose candidates for governor and lieutenant governor through a joint nomination process: Florida, Kansas, Maryland, Minnesota, Montana, North Dakota, Ohio, Utah, American Samoa, Guam, No. Mariana Islands, and U.S. Virgin Islands. For additional information see The National Lieutenant Governors Association website at http://www.nlga.us.

(b) Previously served as Lieutenant Governor from 1986 to 1993. He assumed the office of governor when Guy Hunt was removed in 1993 and served until 1995 when Fob James was sworn in. He was elected to the office of lieutenant governor for another term in November 2006.

(c) No lieutenant governor.

(d) Brad Little was appointed by Governor Otter and confirmed by the state senate after Lieutenant Governor Ritsch won the U.S. Senate seat.

(e) Lisa Madigan, the Illinois Attorney General, is next in the line of sucession to the governor's office. Lieutenant Governor Patrick Quinn became governor upon the removal from office of Gov. Blagojevich in January 2009.

(f) Lieutenant Governor Parkinson assumed the office of governor when Governor Sebelius was appointed U.S. Secretary of Health and Human Services. Per K.S.A. Chapter 75-127, "Whenever the lieutenant governor is provided by law to be a member or officer or both, of any board, commission, council or other statutory body, and the office of lieutenant governor is vacant, the president of the senate shall be such member or officer, unless some other provision of law provides to the contrary.

(g) Lt. Governor Sheehy was appointed to the position of Lieutenant Governor January 24, 2005, by Governor Heineman.

(h) New Jersey will elect a lieutenant governor in 2009. The governor and lieutenant governor will be elected jointly. In the event of a permanent vacancy in the office before the inauguration date of the first lieutenant governor, the president of the senate, followed by the speaker of the assembly, would succeed the governor.

(i) Lieutenant Governor David A. Paterson was sworn in as governor on March 17, 2008 after Governor Eliot Spitzer resigned. The position of Lieutenant Governor will remain vacant until the general election in 2010. In the event Gov. Paterson cannot fulfill his duties, Senate Majority Leader Malcolm Smith would be next in the line of succession.

(j) Lieutenant Governor Catherine Baker Knoll died November 12, 2008 and Joseph Scarnati, Senate president pro tempore, assumed the role of Acting Lt. Governor.

(k) In Tennessee, the President of the Senate and the Lieutenant Governor are one in the same. The legislature provided in statute the title of Lieutenant Governor upon the Senate President. The Senate President serves 2 year terms, elected by the Senate on the first day of the first session of each two year legislative term.

(l) In West Virginia, the President of the Senate and the Lieutenant Governor are one in the same. The legislature provided in statute the title of Lieutenant Governor upon the Senate President. The Senate President serves 2 year terms, elected by the Senate on the first day of the first session of each two year legislative term.

(m) Lt. Governor Sunia was appointed to the position of Lieutenant Governor in April 2003 by Governor Togiola Tulafono.

(n) Covenant Party.

Table 4.13
LIEUTENANT GOVERNORS: QUALIFICATIONS AND TERMS

State or other jurisdiction	Minimum age	State citizen (years)	U.S. citizen (years) (a)	State resident (years) (b)	Qualified voter (years)	Length of term (years)	Maximum consecutive terms allowed
Alabama	30	7	10	7	. . .	4	2
Alaska	30	★	7	7	★	4	2
Arizona	(c)						
Arkansas	30	7	★	7	. . .	4	2
California	18	★	★	5	★	4	2
Colorado	30	. . .	★	2	. . .	4	2
Connecticut	30	. . .	. . .	★	★	4	. . .
Delaware	30	★	12	6	★	4	2
Florida	30	★	★	7	★	4	2
Georgia	30	★	15	6	★	4	. . .
Hawaii	30	5	★	5	★	4	2
Idaho	30	. . .	★	2	. . .	4	. . .
Illinois	25	. . .	★	3	. . .	4	. . .
Indiana	30	★	★	★	★	4	2
Iowa	30	. . .	2	2	. . .	4	. . .
Kansas	. . .	. . .	. . .	. . .	. . .	4	2
Kentucky	30	6	★	★	★	4	2
Louisiana	25	5	5	5	. . .	4	. . .
Maine	(c)						
Maryland	30	★	★	★	★	4	2
Massachusetts	. . .	★	★	★	★	4	. . .
Michigan	30	★	★	4	4	4	2 (d)
Minnesota	25	. . .	★	1	. . .	4	. . .
Mississippi	30	. . .	20	5	★	4	2
Missouri	30	10	15	10	. . .	4	. . .
Montana	25	2	★	2	. . .	4	2 (e)
Nebraska	30	5	★	5	★	4	2
Nevada	25	2	★	2	★	4	2
New Hampshire	(c)						
New Jersey	Beginning with the November 3, 2009 general election, this office will be filled.						
New Mexico	30	★	★	5	★	4	2
New York	30	★	★	5	★	4	. . .
North Carolina	30	. . .	5	2	. . .	4	2
North Dakota	30	5	. . .	. . .	. . .	4	. . .
Ohio	18	. . .	★	★	★	4	2
Oklahoma	31	10	★	★	★	4	. . .
Oregon	(c)						
Pennsylvania	30	★	★	7	★	4	2
Rhode Island	18	★	★	★	★	4	2
South Carolina	30	5	5	5	★	4	2
South Dakota	21	2	★	2	★	4	2
Tennessee (f)	30	★	★	3	1	2	. . .
Texas	30	. . .	★	5	. . .	4	. . .
Utah	30	★	★	★	★	4	. . .
Vermont	18	4	★	4	★	2	. . .
Virginia	30	. . .	★	5	5	4	. . .
Washington	18	★	★	★	★	4	. . .
West Virginia (g)	25	1	1	1	★	2	. . .
Wisconsin	18	★	★	★	★	4	. . .
Wyoming	(c)						
American Samoa	35	(h)	★	5	★	4	2
Guam	30	. . .	5	5	★	4	2
No. Mariana Islands	35	★	★	★	★	4	2
Puerto Rico	(c)						
U.S. Virgin Islands	30	. . .	5	5	5	4	2

Source: The Council of State Government's survey, December 2008.

Note: This table includes constitutional and statutory qualifications.

Key:

★ — Formal provision; number of years not specified.

. . . — No formal provision.

(a) In some states you must be a U.S. citizen to be an elector, and must be an elector to run.

(b) In some states you must be a state resident to be an elector, and must be an elector to run.

(c) No lieutenant governor.

(d) In 1993 a constitutional limit of two lifetime terms in the office was enacted.

(e) Eligible for eight out of 16 years.

(f) In Tennessee, the speaker of the Senate, elected from Senate membership, has statutory title of "lieutenant governor."

(g) In West Virginia, the president of the Senate and the lieutenant governor are one in the same. The legislature provided in statute the title of lieutenant governor upon the Senate president. The Senate president serves two-year terms, elected by the Senate on the first day of the first session of each two-year legislative term.

(h) Must be a U.S. national.

Table 4.14
LIEUTENANT GOVERNORS: POWERS AND DUTIES

State or other jurisdiction	*Presides over Senate*	*Appoints committees*	*Breaks roll-call ties*	*Assigns bills*	*Authority for governor to assign duties*	*Member of governor's cabinet or advisory body*	*Serves as acting governor when governor out of state*	*Other duties (a)*
Alabama	★	★	★	★	. . .	. . .	★(b)	. . .
Alaska	. . .	. . .	. . .	. . .	★	★	. . .	(c)
Arizona	(d)							
Arkansas	★	. . .	★	. . .	. . .	. . .	★	. . .
California	★	. . .	★	. . .	★	. . .	★	(e)
Colorado	. . .	. . .	. . .	. . .	★	★	★	(f)
Connecticut	★	. . .	★	. . .	★	. . .	★	. . .
Delaware	★	. . .	★	. . .	. . .	. . .	★	(g)
Florida	. . .	. . .	. . .	. . .	★	. . .	★	. . .
Georgia	★	★	. . .	★	. . .	. . .	. . .	(h)
Hawaii	. . .	. . .	. . .	. . .	★	. . .	★	(i)
Idaho	★	. . .	★	★	★	. . .	★	. . .
Illinois	. . .	. . .	. . .	. . .	★	★	. . .	. . .
Indiana	★	. . .	★	. . .	. . .	. . .	★	. . .
Iowa	. . .	(j)	. . .	. . .	★	(k)	(l)	. . .
Kansas	. . .	. . .	. . .	. . .	. . .	★	. . .	. . .
Kentucky	. . .	. . .	. . .	. . .	★	. . .	(m)	(m)
Louisiana	. . .	. . .	. . .	. . .	★	★	★	. . .
Maine	(n)							
Maryland	. . .	. . .	. . .	. . .	. . .	★	★	. . .
Massachusetts	. . .	★	. . .	. . .	★	★	★	(o)
Michigan	★	. . .	★	. . .	★	★	★(p)	(q)
Minnesota	. . .	. . .	. . .	. . .	★	. . .	★	(r)
Mississippi	★	★	★	★	. . .	. . .	★	(s)
Missouri	★	. . .	★	. . .	★	. . .	★	(t)
Montana	. . .	. . .	. . .	. . .	★	★	★	. . .
Nebraska	★(u)	. . .	. . .	. . .	. . .	. . .	★	. . .
Nevada	★	. . .	★(v)	. . .	. . .	. . .	★	. . .
New Hampshire	(n)							
New Jersey	(n)							
New Mexico	★	. . .	★	. . .	. . .	★	★	. . .
New York	★	. . .	★(w)	. . .	★	★	★	. . .
North Carolina	★	. . .	★	. . .	★	★	★	. . .
North Dakota	★	. . .	. . .	. . .	. . .	★	★	. . .
Ohio	. . .	. . .	. . .	. . .	★	★	. . .	. . .
Oklahoma	★(x)	. . .	★	. . .	. . .	. . .	★	(y)
Oregon	(d)							
Pennsylvania	★	. . .	★	. . .	. . .	. . .	. . .	. . .
Rhode Island	. . .	. . .	. . .	. . .	. . .	. . .	. . .	(z)
South Carolina	★	★	★	★	. . .	★	★	(aa)
South Dakota	★	. . .	★	. . .	★	. . .	. . .	(bb)
Tennessee	★	★	★	★	. . .	. . .	. . .	. . .
Texas	★	★	★	★	. . .	. . .	★	. . .
Utah	. . .	. . .	. . .	. . .	. . .	★	. . .	(cc)
Vermont	★	★(dd)	★	★(ee)	. . .	. . .	★	. . .
Virginia	★	. . .	★	. . .	. . .	. . .	. . .	. . .
Washington	★	★	★	. . .	. . .	. . .	★	. . .
West Virginia	★	★	. . .	★	. . .	. . .	. . .	(ff)
Wisconsin	. . .	. . .	. . .	. . .	★	. . .	. . .	. . .
Wyoming	(d)							
American Samoa	. . .	. . .	. . .	. . .	. . .	. . .	★	. . .
Guam	(u)	. . .	. . .	. . .	★	★	★	. . .
No. Mariana Islands	. . .	. . .	. . .	. . .	. . .	★	★	(gg)
Puerto Rico	(d)							
U.S. Virgin Islands	. . .	. . .	. . .	. . .	★(k)	★	★	. . .

See footnotes at end of table.

LIEUTENANT GOVERNORS: POWERS AND DUTIES — Continued

Sources: The Council of State Governments' survey, December 2008 and state constitutions and statutes. For additional information on the powers and duties, visit the National Lieutenant Governors Association Web site at *http://www.nlga.us*.

Key:

★ — Provision for responsibility.

. . . — No provision for responsibility.

(a) Lieutenant governors may obtain duties through gubernatorial appointment, statute, the Constitution, direct democracy action, or personal intiative. Hence, an exhaustive list of duties is not maintained, but this chart provides examples which are not all inclusive.

(b) The lieutenant governor performs the duties of the governor in the event of the governor's death, impeachment, disability, or absence from the state for more than 20 days.

(c) The lieutenant governor bears these additional responsibilities: Alaska Historical Commission Chair; Alaska Workforce Investment Board; supervise the Division of Elections: supervise the certification process for citizen ballot initiatives and referenda; provide constituent care and communications; lend support to governor's legislative and administrative initiatives; review, sign and file regulations; publish the Alaska Administrative Code and the Online Public Notice System; commission notaries public; regulate use of State Seal; co-chair Alaska Criminal Justice Working Group; member of Clemency Advisory Committee; represent Alaska in the Aerospace States Association (ASA), the National Association of Secretaries of State and the National Lieutenant Governors Association; Arctic Winter Games; Experimental Program to Stimulate Competitive Research (EPSCoR), Chair; Project GRAD.

(d) No lieutenant governor; secretary of state is next in line of succession to governorship.

(e) Lieutenant governor also sits on the UC Board of Regents and the CSU Board of Trustees, serves as the chair of the Commission for Economic Development, chair of the State Lands Commission, member of the Ocean Protection Council, and as a member of the California Emergency Council.

(f) Additional responsibilities include: Chair of the Colorado Commission of Indian Affairs (by statute); member of the Homeland Security and All-Hazards Senior Advisory Committee (Cabinet duty).

(g) Serves as President of the Board of Pardons.

(h) The lieutenant governor, by statute, is responsible for board, commission and committee appointments. In addition, the lieutenant governor appoints conference committees, rules on germaneness, and must sign all acts of the General Assembly.

(i) Serves as Secretary of State.

(j) Appoints all standing committees. Iowa—appoints some special committees.

(k) Presides over Cabinet meetings in absence of governor.

(l) Only in emergency situations.

(m) The Kentucky Constitution specifically gives the lieutenant governor the power to act as governor, in the event he/she is unable to fulfill the duties of office. In addition to the duties set forth by the Kentucky Constitution, state law also gives the lieutenant governor the responsibility to act as chair, or serve as a member, on various boards and commissions. Some of these include: the State Property and Buildings Commission, Kentucky Turnpike Authority, Kentucky Council on Agriculture, Board of the Kentucky Housing Corporation and the Appalachian Development Council. The governor also has the power to give the lieutenant governor other specific job duties.

(n) No lieutenant governor; Senate president or speaker is next in line of succession to governorship.

(o) The lieutenant governor is a member of, and presides over, the Governor's Council, an elected body of eight members which approves all judicial nominations.

(p) As defined in the state constitution, the lieutenant governor performs gubernatorial functions in the governor's absence. In the event of a vacancy in the office of governor, the lieutenant governor is first in line to succeed to the position.

(q) The lieutenant governor serves as a member of the State Administrative Board; and represents the governor and the state at selected local, state, and national meetings. In addition, the governor may delegate additional responsibilities.

(r) Serves as the Chair of the Capitol Area Architectural and Planning Board Committee.

(s) The lieutenant governor also appoints chairs of standing committees, appoints conferees to committees and is a member of the Legislative Budget Committee, chair of this committee every other year.

(t) Other duties of the lieutenant governor include: Official Senior Advocate for State of Missouri and Advisor to Department of Elementary and Secondary Education on early childhood education and Parents-as-Teachers program. The lieutenant governor also serves on the following boards and commissions: Board of Fund Commissioners; Board of Public Buildings; Governor's Advisory Council for Veterans (chair); Missouri Community Service Commission; Missouri Development Finance Board; Missouri Housing Development Commission; Missouri Rural Economic Development Council; Missouri Senior Rx Program (chair); Missouri Tourism Commission (vice-chair); Personal Independence Commission (co-chair); Second State Capitol Commission; Statewide Safety Steering Committee; Veteran's Benefits Awareness Task Force (chair); Special Health, Psychological, and Social Needs of Minority Older Individuals Commission; Mental Health Task Force (chair); Missouri Energy Task Force.

(u) Unicameral legislative body. In Guam, that body elects own presiding officer.

(v) Except on final passage of bills and joint resolutions.

(w) With respect to procedural matters, not legislation.

(x) May preside over the Senate when desired.

(y) Lieutenant governor also serves on 10 boards and commissions including Tourism and School Land Commission.

(z) Serves as Chair of a number of Advisory Councils including issues related to Emergency Management, Long Term Care and Small Business. Each year submits a legislative package to the General Assembly.

(aa) The lieutenant governor heads the State Office on Aging; appoints members and chairs the South Carolina Affordable Housing Commission.

(bb) The lieutenant governor also serves as the Chair of the Workers' Compensation Advisory Commission and as a member of the Constitutional Revision Commission.

(cc) The lieutenant governor serves as Secretary of State (Constitution); Chair of the Lieutenant Governor's Commission on Volunteers (statutory); Chair of the Lieutenant Governor's Commission on Civic and Character Education (statutory); Chair of the Utah Capitol Preservation Board (statutory); Chair (Governor's Cabinet). Direct Cabinet oversight of following departments: 1. Utah Department of Public Safety and Homeland Security, 2. Utah Department of Transportation, 3. Utah Division of Water Rights, 4. Utah Division of Rural Affairs.

(dd) Appoints committees with the president pro tem and one senator on Committee on Committees.

(ee) Committee on Committees assigns bills.

(ff) In West Virginia, the president of the Senate and the lieutenant governor are one in the same. The legislature provided in statute the title of lieutenant governor upon the Senate president. The Senate president serves two-year terms, elected by the Senate on the first day of the first session of each two-year legislative term.

(gg) The lieutenant governor is charged with overseeing administrative functions.

States Worry About Impacts of Congressional Push to Federalize Corporate Disclosure Laws

By Kay Stimson

Secretaries of state and other officials are concerned about a push by Congress to federalize corporate disclosure laws. Those interviewed for this article say federal intervention is unwarranted, and they worry about the impacts of such a move on cash-strapped state budgets, as well as on small businesses. Meanwhile, several states that have been singled out for problems related to shell companies have amended their laws to help address real or perceived loopholes. Other states are working with national organizations to produce legislative language for states on this issue.

As states grapple with severe budget shortfalls and a grim financial outlook for the foreseeable future, secretaries of state and other state officials are concerned Congress could intervene in matters of state commerce and inadvertently hurt small business through efforts to address perceived gaps in domestic corporate disclosure practices.

At issue is whether states should be compelled to obtain—and verify—beneficial ownership information for the corporations formed under their laws, and the process by which law enforcement authorities and other interested parties can access such information.

U.S. Sen. Carl Levin, D-Mich., chairman of the Permanent Subcommittee on Investigations, has been pursuing the issue since 2000 and is once again pushing for legislation designed to help detect and prosecute abuses in the corporate formation process. His bill, the Incorporation Transparency and Law Enforcement Act, would restrict the level of corporate ownership privacy that states can allow and require them to collect, store and provide ownership information to law enforcement upon receipt of a subpoena or summons.

"This could make state business laws irrelevant and bring about a fundamental shift in the way we do business in the U.S.," said North Carolina Secretary of State Elaine Marshall, co-chair of the National Association of Secretaries of State (NASS) Company Formation Task Force, a bipartisan panel of state officials that has studied the company formation process and developed a series of specific recommendations to help states address the federal government's concerns.[1] "It will send a message that our government intends to make it more difficult to form a business entity in this country."

Proponents of the tighter regulations—who include officials from the U.S. Department of Treasury, Internal Revenue Service, U.S. Department of Justice and U.S. Department of Homeland Security—say they are necessary to help eliminate legal shelter for "shell companies"—business entities with no real operations, no employees and no physical assets—that may be involved with illegal activities such as tax evasion, money laundering or financial support for terrorism.

State officials opposing such broad federal intervention say current congressional proposals go too far and place unreasonable burdens on states and businesses, while adding that states themselves are better positioned to address any shortcomings in their corporate formation and reporting laws.

"I would do anything to help law enforcement, even up to asking our legislature to change what information we collect from companies, but it doesn't have to be done by the federal government," said Kansas Secretary of State Ron Thornburgh, co-chair of the NASS Company Formation Task Force.

Anonymity in Corporate Law

For the estimated 2 million corporations and limited liability companies—or LLCs—currently being formed within the U.S. each year, the process is generally a simple, inexpensive and potentially private matter. It is the level of anonymity many states accord to new corporations that has drawn the greatest share of criticism, particularly in the post-9/11 world.

Unlike publicly held companies, private corporations are not required to reveal ownership information. Most states require companies to list the names of their officers in their corporation reports, but at least a half dozen allow the use of nominee officers,[2] who may be registered agents or other paid representatives handling the entity's paperwork and shielding the identities of true owners.

This process can be challenging for law enforcement authorities when the anonymity and privacy provided by laws of incorporation, combined with a large volume of case law, provide legal shelter for companies (or owners) that may be involved with criminal activities or other misconduct. A 2005 multi-agency federal government report singled out Delaware, Nevada and Wyoming for allowing levels of corporate confidentiality that approached what is available offshore.[3] National publications have also called attention to the thriving mini-industry in these states, where promoters often try to capitalize on the ease and privacy with which corporations can be formed.[4]

But how widespread is the problem? Secretaries of state, who handle corporate registrations in 41 states and Puerto Rico,[5] say although there is no hard and fast data, corporate abuse is not widespread or common enough to justify federal intervention.

"It would be burning down the haystack to find a needle," said North Carolina's Marshall, who points out that the vast majority of corporations are operating legally, generating new jobs, fueling economic expansion, and providing registration and reporting fee revenues.[6]

Officials involved in business filing matters point out there are good reasons that state statutes and case law have allowed for confidentiality in the process—the protection of trade secrets and high-profile investors are two of the most common examples cited. They are also concerned about the potential erosion of privacy and property rights that have historically been granted to business owners in the U.S., particularly to small business owners.

"We've always assumed the U.S. government has a role in the process when it comes to large corporations with securities activities, but why should small, privately-held businesses be held to disclosure requirements about their ownership matters involving familial relationships, marriages, divorces and trust information?" asked Richard Geisenberger, Delaware's assistant secretary of state and the director of its division of corporations. "Once you put that information into a state database and require it to be stored, there's no reason to believe it wouldn't be accessible to the public."

States Taking Action

Spurred by federal efforts to fight money laundering and other corporate abuses among shell companies, several states that have come under criticism for a lack of transparency in their statutes have already taken the initiative to enact changes that close real or perceived loopholes in their laws of incorporation.

Wyoming is no longer the place where anyone can "smile and file," according to Secretary of State Max Maxfield. Citing a case where overseas employees of a Turkish airline were discovered to be illegally funneling money through a Wyoming-based shell corporation, Maxfield said he realized that he needed to work with the state legislature to make the process more transparent. A 2008 law now requires businesses to register a local company representative who must serve as the entity's primary contact with the law enforcement community.

"For the longest time, our leaders were using our company formation laws as an economic development tool to bring corporations to the state," said Maxfield. "But over time, we realized that a problem had evolved and we needed to do a better job of finding a balance between being business-friendly and protecting against fraud." He added that his office can now impose stricter penalties and quickly dissolve companies for failing to comply with state law. The Wyoming Secretary of State's office is also tracking the number and types of requests it receives from law enforcement agencies related to corporate fraud.

Meanwhile, in an effort to help thwart criminals, a new Nevada law permits law enforcement investigators to request ownership records from corporations and LLCs. If the company fails to respond, the secretary of state can dissolve the corporation.[7]

In business-friendly Delaware, where chartering out-of-state companies is big business, the state has attempted to shore up its laws by retooling its requirements for registered agents.

Other states have worked together to provide input on uniform state legislation currently being drafted by the American Bar Association and the Uniform Law Commission, a collection of lawyers from across the U.S. who research, draft and promote the enactment of uniform laws in the states. The final language from these groups is likely to address the key recommendations of the NASS Company Formation Task Force, including a call to require corporate entities to file a report that includes the name and address of a person in the U.S. who has access to the list of owners of record for the corporation; that person would also serve as the official contact for law enforcement inquiries on such matters.

Secretaries of state and state business services division chiefs serving on the NASS Company Formation Task Force are hopeful that the resulting legislation, developed with state input, will keep the burden of tracking beneficial company ownership information where it belongs—with the private sector, including registered agents and financial institutions. At the same time, it would enable states to better assist federal government and law enforcement officials who need to track down company owners whenever necessary. State officials argue this is the better solution to address concerns about shell companies during a recession that is hitting states hard.

"In the current economic climate, states are not prepared to foot the bill for additional employees and technology costs they would incur in order to achieve the requirements in the current congressional proposals," said Leslie Reynolds, executive director of the National Association of Secretaries of State.

Added Delaware's Geisenberger, "The reality is, criminals will simply find new ways to hide their assets and evade the law, but people who play by the rules—and the states that are responsible for assisting them with the corporate registration and filings process—will bear the brunt of any new federal regulations."

Notes

[1]National Association of Secretaries of State (NASS), *NASS Company Formation Task Force Report & Recommendations*, (July 2007), available at *http://nass.org/index.php?option=com_content&task=view&id=113&Itemid=312*.

[2]National Association of Secretaries of State (NASS), *NASS State Business Entity Law Survey*, (March 2008), available at *http://nass.org/index.php?option=com_content&task=view&id=113&Itemid=312*.

[3]U.S. Department of Treasury, et al., *Money Laundering Threat Assessment,* (December 2005), available at *http://www.treas.gov/press/releases/reports/js3077_01112005_MLTA.pdf*.

[4]Kevin McCoy, "Corporate Owners Hide Assets, Identities," *USA Today*, May 23, 2007, 1A.

[5]Council of State Governments, *The Book of the States 2008*, Volume 40, 226.

[6]According to annual reports provided by the International Association of Commercial Administrators (IACA), more than 18 million corporations currently exist in the U.S., with states such as Delaware, Florida, and Nevada collecting large revenues from corporate filing and reporting fees. Available at *http://www.iaca.org/node/80*.

[7]John G. Edwards, "Transparency Bill Draws Mixed Reactions," *Las Vegas Review-Journal*, May 3, 2008, B1, available at *http://www.lvrj.com/business/18544189.html*.

About the Author

Kay Stimson is director of communications and special projects for the National Association of Secretaries of State in Washington, D.C. A former television news reporter who covered the state legislatures in Maryland and South Carolina, she frequently writes about state and federal policy issues for lawmakers.

Table 4.15
THE SECRETARIES OF STATE, 2009

State or other jurisdiction	Name and party	Method of selection	Length of regular term in years	Date of first service	Present term ends	Number of previous terms	Maximum consecutive terms allowed by constitution
Alabama	Beth Chapman (R)	E	4	1/2007	1/2011	. . .	2
Alaska	(a)						
Arizona	Ken Bennett (R)	E(b)	4	1/2009 (b)	1/2011	. . .	2
Arkansas	Charlie Daniels (D)	E	4	12/2002	12/2010	1	2
California	Debra Bowen (D)	E	4	1/2007	1/2011	. . .	2
Colorado	Bernie Buescher (D)	E (c)	4	12/2008 (c)	1/2011	. . .	2
Connecticut	Susan Bysiewicz (D)	E	4	1/1999	1/2011	2	. . .
Delaware	Jeffrey Bullock (D)	A (d)	. . .	1/2009	. . .	. . .	. . .
Florida	Kurt Browning (R)	A	. . .	12/2006	. . .	. . .	. . .
Georgia	Karen Handel (R)	E	4	1/2007	1/2011	. . .	. . .
Hawaii	(a)						
Idaho	Ben Ysursa (R)	E	4	1/2003	1/2011	1	. . .
Illinois	Jesse White (D)	E	4	1/1999	1/2011	2	. . .
Indiana	Todd Rokita (R)	E	4	1/2003	1/2011	1	2
Iowa	Michael A. Mauro (D)	E	4	12/2006	12/2010	. . .	. . .
Kansas	Ron Thornburgh (R)	E	4	1/1995	1/2011	3	. . .
Kentucky	Trey Grayson (R)	E	4	12/2003	12/2011	1	2
Louisiana	Jay Dardenne (R)	E	4	11/2006	1//2012(e)	. . .	. . .
Maine	Matthew Dunlap (D)	L	2	1/2005	1/2011	2	4 (f)
Maryland	John P. McDonough (D)	A	. . .	6/2008	. . .	. . .	. . .
Massachusetts	William Francis Galvin (D)	E	4	1/1995	1/2011	3	. . .
Michigan	Terri Lynn Land (R)	E	4	1/2003	1/2011	1	2
Minnesota	Mark Ritchie (DFL)	E	4	1/2007	1/2011	. . .	. . .
Mississippi	C. Delbert Hosemann, Jr.(R)	E	4	1/2008	1/2012	. . .	. . .
Missouri	Robin Carnahan (D)	E	4	1/2005	1/2013	1	. . .
Montana	Linda McCulloch (D)	E	4	1/2009	1/2013	. . .	(g)
Nebraska	John Gale (R)	E	4	12/2000 (h)	1/2011	(h)	. . .
Nevada	Ross Miller (D)	E	4	1/2007	1/2011	. . .	2
New Hampshire	William Gardner (D)	L	2	12/1976	12/2010	16	. . .
New Jersey	Nina Mitchell Wells (D)	A	. . .	1/2006	1/2010	. . .	. . .
New Mexico	Mary E. Herrera (D)	E	4	1/2006	12/2010	. . .	2
New York	Lorraine Cortes-Vazquez (D)	A	. . .	3/2007	. . .	. . .	. . .
North Carolina	Elaine Marshall (D)	E	4	1/1997	1/2013	2	. . .
North Dakota	Alvin A. Jaeger (R)	E	4 (i)	1/1993	12/2010	4	. . .
Ohio	Jennifer Brunner (D)	E	4	1/2007	1/2011	. . .	2
Oklahoma	M. Susan Savage (D)	A	4	1/2003	1/2011	1	. . .
Oregon	Kate Brown (D)	E	4	1/2009	1/2013	. . .	2
Pennsylvania	Pedro A. Cortes (D)	A	. . .	5/2003	. . .	. . .	. . .
Rhode Island	Ralph Mollis (D)	E	4	1/2007	1/2011	. . .	2
South Carolina	Mark Hammond (R)	E	4	1/2003	1/2011	1	. . .
South Dakota	Chris Nelson (R)	E	4	1/2003	1/2011	1	2
Tennessee	Tre Hargett (R)	L	4	1/2009	1/2013	. . .	. . .
Texas	Esperanza Andrade	A	. . .	7/2008	. . .	. . .	. . .
Utah	(a)						
Vermont	Deb Markowitz (D)	E	2	1/1999	1/2013	5	. . .
Virginia	Katherine K. Hanley (D)	A	. . .	3/2006	. . .	. . .	. . .
Washington	Sam Reed (R)	E	4	1/2001	1/2013	2	. . .
West Virginia	Natalie Tennant (D)	E	4	1/2009	1/2013	. . .	. . .
Wisconsin	Douglas LaFollette (D)	E	4	1/1999	1/2011	2	. . .
Wyoming	Max Maxfield (R)	E	4	1/2007	1/2011	. . .	. . .
American Samoa	(a)						
Guam	(a)						
No. Mariana Islands	(a)						
Puerto Rico	Kenneth McClintock (NPP)	A	. . .	1/2009	. . .	. . .	. . .
U.S. Virgin Islands	(a)						

See footnotes at end of table.

THE SECRETARIES OF STATE, 2009—Continued

Sources: The Council of State Governments' survey March 2009.

Key:

E — Elected by voters

A — Appointed by governor.

L — Elected by legislature.

. . . — No provision for.

(a) No secretary of state; lieutenant govenor performs functions of this office. See Tables 4.12 through 4.14.

(b) Ken Bennett was appointed by Governor Brewer in January 2009 to fill her term after she was sworn in as governor; replacing Janet Napolitano who became the U.S. Secretary of Homeland Security.

(c) Bernie Buescher was appointed by Governor Ritter in December 2008 to fill the term fo Mike Coffman who won the Nov. 2008 race for Congress.

(d) Appointed by the governor and confirmed by the Senate.

(e) Dardenne was elected in a special election Sept. 20, 2006 after the death of W. Fox McKeithen in July 2005, First Deputy Secretary Al Ater assumed the duties of Secretary of State until the special election could be held. Dardenne was first elected to a full term in the 2007 general election.

(f) Statutory term limit of 4 consecutive 2-year terms.

(g) Eligible for eight out of 16 years.

(h) Secretary Gale was appointed by Gov. Mike Johanns in December 2000 upon the resignation of Scott Moore. He was elected to full four-year terms in November 2002 and again in 2006.

(i) Because of a constitutional change approved by voters in 2000, the term for the secretary elected in 2004 was for two years. It reverted to a four

Table 4.16
SECRETARIES OF STATE: QUALIFICATIONS FOR OFFICE

State or other jurisdiction	*Minimum age*	*U.S. citizen (years) (a)*	*State resident (years) (b)*	*Qualified voter (years)*	*Method of selection to office*
Alabama	25	7	5	★	E
Alaska			(c)		
Arizona	25	10	5	. . .	E
Arkansas	18	★	★	★	E
California	18	★	★	★	E
Colorado	25	★	2	. . .	E
Connecticut	18	★	★	★	E
Delaware	. . .	. . .	. . .	. . .	A
Florida			(d)		A
Georgia	25	10	4	★	E
Hawaii			(c)		
Idaho	25	★	2	★	E
Illinois	25	★	3	. . .	E
Indiana	. . .	. . .	★	. . .	E
Iowa	18	★	. . .	. . .	E
Kansas	. . .	★	★	★	E
Kentucky	30	★	★	★	E
Louisiana	25	5	5	★	E
Maine	. . .	. . .	. . .	. . .	(e)
Maryland	. . .	. . .	. . .	. . .	A
Massachusetts	18	★	5	★	E
Michigan	18	★	★	★	E
Minnesota	25	★	1	★	E
Mississippi	25	★	5	★	E
Missouri	. . .	★	★	2	E
Montana	25	★	2	★	E
Nebraska	. . .	★	★	★	E
Nevada	25	2	2	. . .	E
New Hampshire	18	★	★	★	(e)
New Jersey	18	★	★	★	A
New Mexico	30	★	5	★	E
New York	18	★	★	. . .	A
North Carolina	21	★	★	★	E
North Dakota	25	★	5	5	E
Ohio	18	. . .	★	★	E
Oklahoma	31	★	★	10	A
Oregon	18	. . .	★	★	E
Pennsylvania	. . .	. . .	. . .	. . .	A
Rhode Island	18	★	30 days	★	E
South Carolina	. . .	★	★	★	E
South Dakota	. . .	. . .	. . .	. . .	E
Tennessee	. . .	. . .	. . .	. . .	(e)
Texas	18	★	. . .	. . .	A
Utah			(c)		
Vermont	18	★	★	★	E
Virginia	. . .	. . .	. . .	. . .	A
Washington	18	★	★	★	E
West Virginia	. . .	★	★	★	E
Wisconsin	18	★	★	★	E
Wyoming	25	★	1	★	E
American Samoa			(c)		
Guam			(c)		
No. Mariana Islands			(c)		
Puerto Rico	. . .	5	5	. . .	A
U.S. Virgin Islands			(c)		

Source: The Council of State Governments' survey of secretaries of state, December 2008.

Key:

★ — Formal provision; number of years not specified.

. . . — No formal provision.

A — Appointed by governor.

E — Elected by voters.

(a) In some states you must be a U.S. citizen to be an elector, and must be an elector to run.

(b) In some states you must be a state resident to be an elector, and must be an elector to run.

(c) No secretary of state.

(d) As of January 1, 2003, the office of secretary of state shall be an appointed position (appointed by the governor). It will no longer be a Cabinet position, but an agency head and the Department of State shall be an agency under the governor's office.

(e) Chosen by joint ballot of state senators and representatives. In Maine and New Hampshire, every two years. In Tennessee, every four years.

Table 4.17
SECRETARIES OF STATE: ELECTION AND REGISTRATION DUTIES

State or other jurisdiction	Election								Registration				
	Chief election officer	*Determines ballot eligibility of political parties*	*Receives initiative and/or referendum petition*	*Files certificate of nomination or election*	*Supplies election ballots or materials to local officials*	*Files candidates' expense papers*	*Files other campaign reports*	*Conducts voter education programs*	*Registers charitable organizations*	*Registers corporations (a)*	*Processes and/or commissions notaries public*	*Registers securities*	*Registers trade names/marks*
Alabama	★	★	...	★	★	★	★	★	★	★	★	...	★
Alaska (b)	★	★	★	★	★	...	...	★	...	...	★	...	...
Arizona	★	★	★	★	...	★	★	★	★	...	★	...	★
Arkansas	★	★	★	★	...	★	★	★	...	★	★	...	★
California	★(c)	★	★	★	★	★	★	★	★(d)	★	★	...	★
Colorado	★	★	★	★	...	★	★	★	★	★	★	...	★
Connecticut	★	★	...	★	★	★	★	★	★	★	★	...	★
Delaware	...	...	...	(e)	...	...	(f)	...	★(g)	★	★	...	★
Florida	★	★	★	★	...	★	★	...	...	★	...	...	★
Georgia	★	★	...	★	★	★	★	★	★	★	...	★	★
Hawaii (b)	...	...	...	...	...	...	...	...	...	...	...	...	...
Idaho	★	★	★	★	★	★	★	★	...	★	★	...	★
Illinois	...	...	★	(h)	...	...	...	...	...	★	★	★	★
Indiana	★	★	...	★	★	★	★	★	★	★	★	★	★
Iowa	★	★	...	★	★	...	...	★	...	★	★	...	★
Kansas	★	★	...	★	★	★	...	★	★	★	★	...	★
Kentucky	★	★	...	★	...	...	...	★	...	★	★	...	★
Louisiana	★	...	...	★	★	...	...	★	★	★	★	...	★
Maine	★	★	★	★	★	...	...	★	...	★	★	...	★
Maryland	...	★	★	★	...	...	...	...	★	★	★	...	★
Massachusetts	★	★	★	★	★	(f)	(f)	★	...	★	★	★	★
Michigan	★	★	★	★	...	★	★	★	...	...	★	...	...
Minnesota	★	★	...	★	★	...	...	★	...	★	★	...	★
Mississippi	★	★	★	★	★	★	★	★	★	★	★	★	★
Missouri	★	★	★	★	...	...	...	★	★	★	★	★	★
Montana	★	★	★	★	★	...	...	★	★	★	★	...	★
Nebraska	★	★	★	★	★	...	...	★	...	★	★	...	★
Nevada	★	★	★	★	★	★	★	★	...	★	★	★	★
New Hampshire	★	★	...	★	★	★	★	...	★	★	★	★	★
New Jersey	★	★	★	★	★	★	★	★	...	★	★	...	★
New Mexico	★	★	...	★	★	★	★	★	...	...	★	...	★
New York	...	...	...	...	...	...	...	...	...	★	★	...	★
North Carolina (i)	...	...	...	...	...	...	...	...	★	★	★	★	★
North Dakota	★	★	★	★	★	★	★	★	★	★	★	...	★
Ohio	★	★	★	...	★	★	...	★	...	★	★	...	★
Oklahoma	...	...	★	★(j)	...	...	...	...	★	★(j)	★	...	★
Oregon	★	★	★	★	★	★	★	★	...	★	★	★	★
Pennsylvania	★	★	...	★	...	...	★	★	★	★	★	...	★
Rhode Island	★	★	...	★	★	...	...	★	...	★	★	...	★
South Carolina	...	...	...	...	...	...	...	...	★	★(k)	★	...	★
South Dakota	★	★	★	★	...	★	★	★	...	★	★	...	★
Tennessee (l)	...	★	...	★	★	...	...	★	★	★	★	...	★
Texas	★	★	...	★	★	...	...	★	★	★	★	...	★
Utah (b)	★	★	★	★	★	★	★	★	...	...	...	...	...
Vermont	★	...	...	★	★	★	...	★	★	★	★	...	★
Virginia	...	...	...	...	...	...	...	...	...	...	...	...	...
Washington	★	★	★	★	...	...	...	★	★	★	...	★	★
West Virginia	★	★	...	★	...	★	★	★	★	★	★	...	★
Wisconsin	...	...	...	...	...	...	...	...	...	...	★	...	★
Wyoming	★	★	★	★	(m)	★	★	★	★	★	★	★	★
American Samoa (b)	...	...	...	★	...	★	★	★	★	★	★	...	...
Guam (b)	...	...	...	...	...	...	...	...	...	...	...	...	...
Puerto Rico	...	...	...	...	...	...	...	...	★	★	★	★	★
U.S. Virgin Islands (b)	...	...	...	...	...	...	...	...	★	★(n)	★	...	★

See footnotes at end of table.

SECRETARIES OF STATE: ELECTION AND REGISTRATION DUTIES — Continued

Source: The Council of State Governments' survey of secretaries of state, December 2008.

Key:

★ — Responsible for activity.

. . . — Not responsible for activity.

(a) Unless otherwise indicated, office registers domestic, foreign and nonprofit corporations.

(b) No secretary of state. Duties indicated are performed by lieutenant governor. In Hawaii, election-related responsibilities have been transferred to an independent Chief Election Officer.

(c) Other election duties include: tallying votes from all 58 counties, testing and certifying voting systems, maintaining statewide voter registration database, publishing Voter Information Guide/State Ballot Pamphlet.

(d) This office does not register charitable trusts, but does register charitable organizations as nonprofit corporations; also limited partnerships, limited liability corporations, and domestic partners.

(e) Files certificates of election for publication purposes only; does not file certificates of nomination.

(f) Federal candidates only.

(g) Incorporated organizations only.

(h) Office issues document, but does not receive it.

(i) Other election duties: administers the Electoral College. Other registration duties: registers state legislative and executive branch lobbyists, and maintains secure online registry of advance health care directives.

(j) Certifies U.S. Congressional election results to Washington, D.C. Also registers limited partnerships, limited liability companies and limited liability partnerships.

(k) Also registers the Cable Franchise Authority.

(l) Appoints the Coordinator of Elections who performs the election duties indicated.

(m) Materials not ballots.

(n) Both domestic and foreign profit; but only domestic nonprofit.

Table 4.18
SECRETARIES OF STATE: CUSTODIAL, PUBLICATION AND LEGISLATIVE DUTIES

	Custodial				Publication					Legislative			
State or other jurisdiction	Archives state records and regulations	Files state agency rules and regulations	Administers uniform commercial code provisions	Files other corporate documents	State manual or directory	Session laws	State constitution	Statutes	Administrative rules and regulations	Opens legislative sessions (a)	Enrolls or engrosses bills	Retains copies of bills	Registers lobbyists
Alabama	...	...	★	★	...	★	★	★	...	...	★	★	...
Alaska (b)	...	★	...	...	...	...	★	...	★	★	...	★	...
Arizona	★	★	★	...	...	...	★	...	★	...	...	★	★
Arkansas	★	★	★	★	...	★	...	...	★	...	...	★	★
California	★	...	★	★	★	...	...	...	...	...	(c)	...	★
Colorado	...	★	★	★	...	...	★	...	★	...	...	★	★
Connecticut	★(d)	★	★	★	★	...	...	...	...	S	...	★	★
Delaware	★	★	★	★	...	...	...	...	★	...	...	...	...
Florida	★	★	...	★	...	★	★	★	★	...	...	...	...
Georgia	★	★	...	...	★	...	★	...	★	...	...	...	...
Hawaii (b)	...	★	...	...	...	★	...	★	★	...	...	★	...
Idaho	...	...	★	...	★	★	★	...	...	...	...	★	★
Illinois	★	★	★	★	★	★	★	...	★	H	...	★	★
Indiana	★	★	★	★	...	...	...	...	...	...	...	★	...
Iowa	★	...	★	★	...	★	★	...	...	...	★	★	...
Kansas	...	★	★	★	★	...	...	★	★	...	...	...	★
Kentucky	★	...	★	★	...	...	...	...	...	...	★	★	...
Louisiana	★	...	★	★	★	...	...	★	★	...	★	★	(e)
Maine	★	★	★	★	...	...	★	...	★	...	...	...	...
Maryland	...	...	...	...	...	...	...	...	(f)	...	...	★	...
Massachusetts	★	★	★	★	★	★	★	★	★	...	...	★	★
Michigan	★	★	★	...	...	★	★	★	★	...	...	...	★
Minnesota	★	★	★	★	★	...	...	...	...	H	...	...	...
Mississippi	...	★	★	★	★	★	★	...	★	H	...	★	★
Missouri	★(g)	★	★	★	★	...	★	...	★	H	★	★	...
Montana	★	★	★	★	...	...	★	...	★	H	★	★	...
Nebraska	★	★	★	★	...	...	...	...	★	...	...	★	...
Nevada	★	★	★	★	...	...	...	...	...	...	...	★	...
New Hampshire	★	...	★	★	★	...	★	...	...	...	★	★	★
New Jersey	★	...	...	...	...	...	★	...	...	...	...	★	...
New Mexico	...	★	★	...	★	★	★	...	★	H	★	★	★
New York	...	★	★	...	★	...	★	...	★	...	...	...	...
North Carolina	★	★	★	...	★	...	★	...	...	...	...	...	★
North Dakota	...	...	★	★	...	...	...	...	...	...	...	★	★
Ohio	...	★	★	★	★	★	★	...	...	...	★	★	...
Oklahoma (h)	...	★	...	★	...	...	...	...	★	...	...	★	...
Oregon	★	★	★	★	★	...	★	...	★	...	...	★	...
Pennsylvania	...	...	★	★	...	...	...	...	...	...	★	★	...
Rhode Island (i)	★	★	★	★	★	...	★	...	★	...	...	★	★
South Carolina	...	...	★	★	...	...	...	...	...	...	...	★	...
South Dakota	★	★	★	★	★	★	...	★	★	★	★	★	★
Tennessee (j)	★	★	★	★	★	★	...	...	★	...	...	...	...
Texas	★	★	★	★	...	★	...	...	★	...	...	★	...
Utah (b)	...	...	...	...	...	...	...	...	...	...	...	★	★
Vermont	★	★	★	★	★	★	★	...	★	H	...	★	★
Virginia	...	...	...	...	★	...	...	...	...	...	...	...	★
Washington	★	...	...	★	★	...	...	...	...	...	...	★	...
West Virginia	★	★	★	★	...	...	...	...	★	...	...	★	...
Wisconsin	...	...	...	...	...	...	...	...	...	...	...	...	...
Wyoming	★	★	★	★	★	...	★	...	...	H	...	★	★
American Samoa (b)	...	★	...	★	...	★	★	★	★	...	...	...	...
Guam (b)	...	...	...	...	...	...	...	...	...	...	...	...	...
Puerto Rico	...	★	★	★	...	★	★	★	★	...	...	...	...
U.S. Virgin Islands (b)	...	★	★	★	...	...	...	★	...	...	★	★	...

See footnotes at end of table.

SECRETARIES OF STATE: CUSTODIAL, PUBLICATION AND LEGISLATIVE DUTIES — Continued

Source: The Council of State Governments' survey of secretaries of state, December 2008.

Key:

★ — Responsible for activity.

. . . — Not responsible for activity.

(a) In this column only: ★ — Both houses; H — House; S — Senate.

(b) No secretary of state. Duties indicated are performed by the lieutenant governor.

(c) Office does not enroll or engross bills but does chapter them.

(d) The secretary of state is keeper of public records, but the state archives is a department of the Connecticut State Library.

(e) Only registers political pollsters.

(f) Code of Maryland regulations.

(g) Also responsible for the State Library.

(h) Other custodial duties include: Effective Financing Statements identifying farm products that are subject to a security interest, UCC and mortgage documents pertaining to transmitting utilities and also railroads and files open meeting notices.

(i) Additional duties include administering oaths of office to general officers and legislators.

(j) Additional duties include the Tennessee State Library and Archives, administrative law judges, charitable gaming regulation, service of process/summons, sports agent registration and temporary liens.

Attorneys General: Role and Issues

As the chief legal officers of the states, commonwealths and territories of the United States, attorneys general serve as counselors to state government agencies and legislatures, and as representatives of the public interest. In many areas traditionally considered the exclusive responsibility of the federal government, attorneys general now share enforcement authority and enjoy cooperative working relationships with their federal counterparts, particularly in the areas of antitrust, bankruptcy, consumer protection, criminal law, cybercrime and the environment.

The Role of Attorneys General

They keep intrusive and unwanted telemarketers away. They protect consumers against fraud and abuse. They ensure a fair marketplace. They fight crime. They defend criminal convictions on appeal. These are among the myriad of legal activities in which attorneys general are involved. The following highlights some of their primary issue areas:

Antitrust

State attorneys general have worked together for more than a century to halt anticompetitive practices that raise prices, stifle innovation and hurt consumers. The first meeting of a group of state attorneys general took place in 1907 to discuss ways to protect consumers from the monopoly power wielded by Standard Oil. And today, state attorneys general are still working together to prevent anticompetitive behavior in a variety of markets, including pharmaceuticals, technology, food and health care.

State antitrust laws predate the major federal antitrust statutes, the Sherman and Clayton acts, and state attorneys general have long pursued anticompetitive activities, such as price fixing and bid rigging, within their own states. In the mid-1980s, state attorneys general became concerned by what they perceived as a void in federal antitrust enforcement. They began working closely together on antitrust cases that they were able to bring together in a single federal court. Since then, the attorneys general have developed sophisticated litigation strategies and policy positions, and are now viewed as an equal partner with the federal antitrust enforcement agencies, the Federal Trade Commission and the U.S. Department of Justice Antitrust Division.

The strength of multistate antitrust enforcement is the result of several factors. Attorneys general can enforce federal antitrust laws on behalf of the state—for example, when the state is the purchaser and the seller is fixing prices—and can recover damages. The attorney general can also get equitable relief to prevent injury to the general economy of the state. Finally, state attorneys general also have authority to bring *parens patriae* actions—lawsuits filed on behalf of residents of the state but not corporations—for violations of the Sherman Act. Attorneys general can thus file a single case together in a single federal court. There is a large body of federal court decisions interpreting federal antitrust law and making it relatively consistent across jurisdictions. Most multistate litigation is handled through the National Association of Attorneys General (NAAG) Multi-state Antitrust Task Force. The task force is comprised of the antitrust staff—assistant attorneys general—from all states.

The attorneys general have typically focused their attention on items that are important to the health and welfare of residents in their states. For example, 18 states and the District of Columbia filed a multistate action in March 2008 against two pharmaceutical companies alleging they manipulated the patent and generic drug approval processes to block a cheaper, generic version of the prescription drug TriCor, which is used to reduce high levels of triglycerides and cholesterol. The case, *Florida vs. Abbott Laboratories*, was still pending at press time.

In another area important to consumers, attorneys general have reached settlements with insurance companies and brokers over claims they rigged bids and fixed prices in the commercial general insurance market. The conspiracy included a "pay-to-play" scheme in which certain companies paid contingent commissions to insurance brokers, who then steered policy holders to the paying companies. These commissions were not revealed to the policy holders, including public entities, who paid higher premiums for insurance coverage.

State attorneys general can also sue to prevent anticompetitive mergers under section 7 of the Clayton Act. Again, attorneys general focus on mergers that will have an effect on important products for consumers. For example, a group of states reached a settlement with two school bus companies that planned to merge. The companies sold school bus routes and depots in several states in order to preserve competition for school districts seeking school bus services. Another recent example is the joint federal-state challenge to the merger of two large beef processors, which would have made the company the largest beef processor in the United States and would have allowed the company to reduce the price paid to ranchers for cattle while raising the price of beef to consumers.

The attorneys general establish their policy positions through the NAAG Antitrust Committee, comprised of attorneys general, and other policy statements, including the NAAG Horizontal Merger Guidelines and the NAAG Vertical Restraints Guidelines. The Horizontal Merger Guidelines are designed to provide guidance to the business community on the enforcement intentions of the attorneys general; they were last revised in 1993. The Vertical Restraints Guidelines were last revised in 1995. Recent legal developments have made them out-of-date, and a staff group is beginning the revision process.

Appellate Advocacy

Attorneys general frequently appear on behalf of their states, state agencies and state officers in the U.S. Supreme Court and other appellate courts. Indeed, in the U.S. Supreme Court, only the U.S. Solicitor General's office appears more often than the attorneys general. The issues the attorneys general address in appellate courts run the gamut from defending criminal convictions to enforcing environmental laws to defending state statutes against First Amendment challenges.

One noteworthy trend in attorney general appellate advocacy is the growth of the solicitor general position. More than 35 attorney general offices now have a designated attorney—usually called the solicitor general—who oversees the office's appellate work in civil cases. The solicitor general ensures that the office's work product is of the highest quality and helps ensure the office is taking consistent positions in its many appeals.

Attorneys general are also assisted in their appellate advocacy by the NAAG Supreme Court Project, which is dedicated to helping states present cases effectively before the U.S. Supreme Court. The project does this by organizing moot courts for virtually every state attorney who argues in the court; by editing 40 to 50 briefs filed by states in the Supreme Court each year, including merits briefs, amicus briefs, cert petitions, and briefs in opposition; by facilitating communication among states on amicus briefs; and by holding annual training programs.

Criminal Law Enforcement

In most jurisdictions, the attorney general's prosecutorial role is limited and focused on complex crimes such as public corruption, environmental crime and Medicaid fraud. In many jurisdictions, the attorney general assists the locally-elected prosecutors upon request but otherwise does not assume primary responsibility for criminal matters. In Delaware, Rhode Island and Alaska, however, the attorney general serves as the sole prosecutorial authority. Still other jurisdictions, such as in Connecticut, have the attorney general almost completely removed from the criminal process. Most attorneys general handle their jurisdiction's criminal appellate responsibilities.

While most attorneys general are limited in their prosecutorial authority, attorneys general use their offices to advance criminal justice initiatives within their own jurisdiction and nationwide. For example, many states have passed statutes restricting access to precursor chemicals used in the manufacturing of methamphetamine, based on a statute originally developed in Oklahoma in 2004. Oklahoma Attorney General W.A. Drew Edmondson traveled extensively to speak about his state's efforts and many attorneys general similarly championed measures within their own respective jurisdictions. Other examples include initiatives related to sex offenders, cybercrime, gang violence and identity theft.

Attorneys general also advocate for adequate state and local law enforcement assistance funding. In March 2008, all 56 attorneys general from around the nation and its affiliated territories signed a letter urging Congress to restore funding for the Byrne Justice Assistance Grant Program, which was cut by 67 percent in fiscal year 2008.

NAAG's Criminal Law Project supports the work of attorneys general related to criminal justice concerns, including its active Criminal Law Committee, and works to facilitate communication among the offices of attorneys general and their staff. The project monitors legislative and regulatory developments related to criminal justice matters and stays abreast of legal developments in the field. The project helps to coordinate and share NAAG information with related associations, federal agencies and coalitions working in the area of criminal justice.

Cybercrime

Attorneys general offices became heavily vested in prosecuting cases involving technology-facilitated crimes when the U.S. Office of Juvenile Justice and Delinquency Prevention (OJJDP), under the authority of the 1998 Justice Appropriations Act, P.L. 105-

119, created the Internet Crimes Against Children (ICAC) program. This program provided funding to help state and local law enforcement agencies develop an effective response to online child pornography and online child exploitation. Today, 14 of the 59 ICAC task forces are housed in an attorney general's office. Most recently, legislation authorizing the creation of additional ICAC task forces was passed, and undoubtedly more attorneys general offices will seek to establish a task force.

Most states have enacted laws that criminalize online child solicitation and pornography, often with enhanced penalties for repeat offenders. Many states have also enacted criminal statutes for computer intrusions, often with enhanced penalties for hacking of a government computer. Computer crimes such as Internet fraud, Internet auction fraud and computer-facilitated identity theft are often addressed through state consumer protection laws.

The NAAG Cybercrime Project assists attorneys general by training their prosecutors and civil enforcement attorneys in handling cases involving technology-facilitated crimes. To date, 700 of these attorneys have attended project trainings. In addition, the project publishes a bi-monthly e-newsletter which keeps attorneys general abreast of new developments, case law and legislation in the computer crime area. Most recently, the project has assumed responsibility for providing training on best practices in electronic discovery.

Energy and Environment

State attorneys general have been at the forefront of environmental law developments in the last 30 years. As national legislation protecting the environment was enacted, many states followed suit with parallel state statutes. Attorneys general made use of the new laws and built on existing common law to reduce pollution of the air, land and water. One area specific to state enforcement is environmental protection at federal facilities, and attorneys general have been diligent in working to safeguard the health and safety of their states' residents by pushing the federal government to meet the same standards that private industry must follow. As energy concerns have come to the attention of policymakers at the state and federal level, the work of attorneys general has come to reflect the intertwined questions of balancing environmental protection and energy reliability. NAAG's Energy and Environment Project assists the attorneys general in activities to influence national and regional legal strategies on energy and environmental matters and provides assistance that allows the offices of the attorneys general to function at a higher level of efficiency and knowledge.

Legislative

Frequently, attorneys general across the country are asked by Congress, the media, business organizations and constituents for their views on bills pending in Congress that affect the powers and duties of attorneys general. Often, such legislation seeks to pre-empt state law in the areas of consumer protection, environment, antitrust, bankruptcy, securities, criminal law and many other areas within the jurisdiction of attorneys general. NAAG's Legislative Project serves as the initial point of contact for information requests from attorney general offices, members of Congress/staff, and other interested associations and individuals about attorney general view on federal legislation. NAAG has requested that the Obama administration and the 111th Congress resist federal pre-emption of state laws, particularly in the enforcement of state banking and mortgage foreclosure laws.

Medicaid Fraud

The state Medicaid Fraud Control Units were created more than 30 years ago by the Medicare-Medicaid Anti-Fraud and Abuse Amendments of 1977 (P.L. 95-142). The units are 75 percent federally funded and are annually certified by the secretary of the U.S. Department of Health and Human Services. This responsibility has been delegated to the department's Office of Inspector General, which also has administrative oversight for the units. The jurisdiction of the fraud units is limited to investigating and prosecuting Medicaid provider fraud and to reviewing complaints of resident abuse and neglect in nursing homes. However, in 1999, Congress passed the Ticket to Work and Work Incentives Improvement Act that granted the Medicaid Fraud Control Units authority to investigate and prosecute fraud in other federally funded health care programs, if the case is primarily related to Medicaid, with the approval of the inspector general of the relevant federal agency. This law also authorizes the Medicaid Fraud Control Units, on an optional basis, to investigate and prosecute resident abuse or neglect in non-Medicaid board and care facilities.

Medicaid Fraud Control Units are located in the office of 43 state attorneys general. Connecticut, the District of Columbia, Georgia, Illinois, Iowa, Tennessee and West Virginia have units that are located in other departments of state government. A unit is intended to operate using a strike force concept of investigators, auditors and attorneys working together full-time to develop Medicaid fraud investigations and prosecutions. The unit staff must include attorneys experienced in the investigation and prosecution of civil fraud or criminal cases, auditors capable of reviewing financial records, and investigators with substantial experience in commercial or financial investigations. A unit director, generally an assistant attorney general, manages the unit, although some units are managed by an investigator.

The National Association of Medicaid Fraud Control Units was founded in 1978 to provide a forum for a nationwide sharing of information concerning the problems of Medicaid fraud, to improve the quality of Medicaid fraud investigations and prosecutions by conducting training programs, to provide technical assistance to association members, and to provide the public with information about the Medicaid Fraud Control Units program (*www.namfcu.net*). All 50 units are members of the association. The association is headquartered in Washington, D.C. at the NAAG offices and is staffed by a counsel, an association administrator and a part-time association assistant.

Conclusion

Nearly every aspect of citizen life is affected in some way by the work of attorneys general. Although states are experiencing increased caseloads and diminished resources, stemming from decreased state funding, the state attorneys general will continue to serve and protect citizens, and preserve the rule of law.

About the National Association of Attorneys General

The **National Association of Attorneys General** was founded in 1907 to help attorneys general fulfill the responsibilities of their office and to assist in the delivery of high quality legal services to the states and territorial jurisdictions.

The association fosters interstate cooperation on legal and law enforcement issues, conducts policy research and analysis of issues, and facilitates communication between the states' chief legal officers and all levels of government. The association's members are the attorneys general of the 50 states and the District of Columbia and the chief legal officers of the commonwealths of Puerto Rico (secretary of justice) and the Northern Mariana Islands, and the territories of American Samoa, Guam and the U.S.Virgin Islands.

This article was submitted by **Marjorie Tharp**, director of communications for the National Association of Attorneys General, *www.naag.org*.

Table 4.19
THE ATTORNEYS GENERAL, 2009

State or other jurisdiction	Name and party	Method of selection	Length of regular term in years	Date of first service	Present term ends	Number of previous terms	Maximum consecutive terms allowed
Alabama	Troy King (R)	E	4	3/2004 (a)	1/2011	(a)	2
Alaska	Rick Svobodny (Acting) (R)	A	. . .	2/2009 (b)	. . .	0	. . .
Arizona	Terry Goddard (D)	E	4	1/2003	1/2011	1	2
Arkansas	Dustin McDaniel (D)	E	4	1/2007	1/2011	0	2
California	Edmund Gerald Brown Jr. (D)	E	4	1/2007	1/2011	0	2
Colorado	John W. Suthers (R)	E	4	1/2005(c)	1/2011	(c)	2
Connecticut	Richard Blumenthal (D)	E	4	1/1991	1/2011	4	★
Delaware	Joseph R. Biden III (D)	E	4	1/2007	1/2011	0	★
Florida	Bill McCollum (R)	E	4	1/2007	1/2011	0	2
Georgia	Thurbert E. Baker (D)	E	4	6/1997(d)	1/2011	2 (d)	★
Hawaii	Mark J. Bennett (R)	A	4 (e)	1/2003	12/2010	1	. . .
Idaho	Lawrence Wasden (R)	E	4	1/2003	1/2011	1	★
Illinois	Lisa Madigan (D)	E	4	1/2003	1/2011	1	★
Indiana	Greg Zoeller (R)	E	4	1/2009	1/2013	0	★
Iowa	Tom Miller (D)	E	4	1/1979 (f)	1/2011	6 (f)	★
Kansas	Stephen Six (D)	E	4	1/2008	1/2012	0	★
Kentucky	Jack Conway (D)	E	4	12/2007	1/2011	0	2
Louisiana	James D. Caldwell (D)	E	4	1/2008	1/2012	0	★
Maine	Janet T. Mills (D)	L (g)	2	1/2009	1/2011	0	4
Maryland	Douglas F. Gansler (D)	E	4	1/2007	1/2011	0	★
Massachusetts	Martha Coakley (D)	E	4	1/2007	1/2011	0	2
Michigan	Mike Cox (R)	E	4	1/2003	1/2011	1	2
Minnesota	Lori Swanson (D)	E	4	1/2007	1/2011	0	★
Mississippi	Jim Hood (D)	E	4	1/2004	1/2012	1	★
Missouri	Chris Koster (D)	E	4	1/2009	1/2013	0	★
Montana	Steve Bullock (D)	E	4	1/2009	1/2013	0	2
Nebraska	Jon Bruning (R)	E	4	1/2003	1/2011	1	★
Nevada	Catherine Cortez Masto (D)	E	4	1/2007	1/2011	0	2
New Hampshire	Kelly Ayotte (R)	A	4	7/2004	3/2009	0	. . .
New Jersey	Anne Milgram (D)	A	4	6/2007	. . .	0	. . .
New Mexico	Gary King (D)	E	4	1/2007	1/2011	0	2 (h)
New York	Andrew Cuomo (D)	E	4	1/2007	1/2011	0	★
North Carolina	Roy Cooper (D)	E	4	1/2001	1/2013	2	★
North Dakota	Wayne Stenehjem (R)	E	4 (i)	1/2001	12/2010	2 (i)	★
Ohio	Richard Cordray (D)	E	4	1/2009 (j)	1/2011	0	2
Oklahoma	W. A. Drew Edmondson (D)	E	4	1/1995	1/2011	3	★
Oregon	John R. Kroger (D)	E	4	1/2009	1/2013	0	★
Pennsylvania	Tom Corbett (R)	E	4	1/2005	1/2013	1	2
Rhode Island	Patrick Lynch (D)	E	4	1/2003	1/2011	1	2
South Carolina	Henry McMaster (R)	E	4	1/2003	1/2011	1	★
South Dakota	Larry Long (R)	E	4	1/2003	1/2011	1	2 (h)
Tennessee	Robert E. Cooper Jr. (D)	(k)	8	10/2006	8/2014	0	. . .
Texas	Greg Abbott (R)	E	4	1/2003	1/2011	1	★
Utah	Mark Shurtleff (R)	E	4	1/2001	1/2013	2	★
Vermont	William H. Sorrell (D)	E	2	5/1997 (l)	1/2011	5 (l)	★
Virginia	Bill Mims (R)	E (m)	4	2/2009	1/2010	0	(n)
Washington	Rob McKenna (R)	E	4	1/2005	1/2013	1	★
West Virginia	Darrell Vivian McGraw Jr. (D)	E	4	1/1993	1/2013	4	★
Wisconsin	J. B. Van Hollen (R)	E	4	1/2007	1/2011	0	★
Wyoming	Bruce A. Salzburg (D)	A (o)	. . .	8/2007	. . .	0	. . .
Dist. of Columbia	Peter Nickles (D)	A	. . .	1/2008	. . .	0	. . .
American Samoa	Fepulea'i Afa Ripley Jr.	A	4	1/2007	. . .	0	. . .
Guam	Alicia G. Limtiaco	E	4	1/2006	1/2010	0	. . .
No. Mariana Islands	Gregory Baka (Acting)	A	4	1/2009	. . .	0	. . .
Puerto Rico	Antonio Sagardía	A	4	1/2009	. . .	0	. . .
U.S. Virgin Islands	Vincent Frazer	A	4	1/2007	1/2011	0	. . .

See footnotes at end of table.

THE ATTORNEYS GENERAL, 2009—Continued

Sources: The Council of State Governments' survey of attorneys general, March 2009.

Key:

★ — No provision specifying number of terms allowed.

. . . — No formal provision, position is appointed or elected by governmental entity (not chosen by the electorate).

A — Appointed by the governor.

E — Elected by the voters.

L — Elected by the legislature.

N.A.— Not available.

(a) Appointed to fill unexpired term in March 2004 and elected to a full term in November 2006.

(b) Talis J. Colberg resigned Feb. 17, 2009. Deputy Attorney General Svobodny is serving as Acting AG until a new appointment is made.

(c) Appointed to fill unexpired term in January 2005 and elected to a full term in November 2006.

(d) Appointed to fill unexpired term in June 1997. He was elected in 1998 to his first full term.

(e) Term runs concurrently with the Governor.

(f) Attorney General Miller was elected in 1978, 1982, 1986, 1994, 1998, 2002 and in 2006.

(g) Chosen biennially by joint ballot of state senators and representatives.

(h) After two consecutive terms , must wait four years and/or one full term before being eligible again.

(i) The term of the office of the elected official is four years, except that in 2004 the attorney general was elected for a term of two years.

(j) Marc Dann (D) resigned May 14, 2008 as attorney general and Nancy Rogers was appointed acting attorney general until the office was filled in the November 2008 general election. Treasurer Richard Cordray won the office and will serve the remainder of the term.

(k) Appointed by judges of state Supreme Court.

(l) Appointed to fill unexpired term in May 1997. He was elected in 1998 to his first full term.

(m) Robert F. McDonnell stepped down Feb 20, 2009 to run for governor. The General Assembly elected Bill Mims to fill the remainder of the term.

(n) Provision specifying individual may hold office for an unlimited number of terms.

(o) Must be confirmed by the Senate.

Table 4.20
ATTORNEYS GENERAL: QUALIFICATIONS FOR OFFICE

State or other jurisdiction	Minimum age	U.S. citizen (years) (a)	State resident (years) (b)	Qualified voter (years)	Licensed attorney (years)	Membership in the state bar (years)	Method of selection to office
Alabama	25	7	5	★	. . .	. . .	E
Alaska	18	★	. . .	. . .	★	★	A
Arizona	25	10	5	★	5	. . .	E
Arkansas	. . .	. . .	★	★	. . .	. . .	E
California	18	★	★	★	★	5	E
Colorado	27	★	2	★	★	. . .	E
Connecticut	18	★	★	★	10	10	E
Delaware	. . .	. . .	. . .	. . .	. . .	. . .	E
Florida	30	★	7	★	★	5	E
Georgia	25	10	4	★	7	7	E
Hawaii	. . .	1	1	. . .	★	(d)	A
Idaho	30	★	2	. . .	★	★	E
Illinois	25	★	3	★	★	★	E
Indiana	. . .	2	2	★	5	. . .	E
Iowa	18	★	★	. . .	. . .	. . .	E
Kansas	. . .	. . .	. . .	. . .	. . .	. . .	E
Kentucky	30	. . .	2 (e)	. . .	8	2	E
Louisiana	25	★	5	★	★	★	E
Maine	. . .	. . .	. . .	. . .	★	★	(f)
Maryland	. . .	★(g)	★	★	★	10	E
Massachusetts	18	. . .	5	★	. . .	★	E
Michigan	18	★	★	. . .	★	★	E
Minnesota	21	★	30 days	★	. . .	. . .	E
Mississippi	26	★	5	★	5	★	E
Missouri	. . .	★	1	. . .	. . .	. . .	E
Montana	25	★	2	. . .	5	★	E
Nebraska	. . .	. . .	★	. . .	. . .	. . .	E
Nevada	25	★	2	★	. . .	. . .	E
New Hampshire	. . .	★	★	. . .	★	★	A (h)
New Jersey	18	. . .	★	. . .	. . .	. . .	A
New Mexico	30	★	5	★	★	. . .	E
New York	30	★	5	. . .	(i)	. . .	E
North Carolina	21	★	★	★	★	(i)	E
North Dakota	25	★	5	★	★	★	E
Ohio	18	★	★	★	. . .	. . .	E
Oklahoma	31	★	★	10	. . .	. . .	E
Oregon	18	★	★	★	. . .	. . .	E
Pennsylvania	30	★	. . .	. . .	★	. . .	E
Rhode Island	18	. . .	. . .	. . .	★	★	E
South Carolina	. . .	★	30 days	★	. . .	. . .	E
South Dakota	18	★	★	★	(i)	(i)	E
Tennessee	. . .	. . .	. . .	. . .	. . .	. . .	(j)
Texas	. . .	. . .	★	. . .	(i)	(i)	E
Utah	25	★	5 (e)	★	★	★	E
Vermont	18	★	★	★	. . .	. . .	E
Virginia	30	★	1 (k)	★	. . .	5 (k)	E
Washington	18	★	★	★	★	★	E
West Virginia	25	. . .	5	★	. . .	. . .	E
Wisconsin	. . .	★	★	. . .	. . .	. . .	E
Wyoming	. . .	★	★	★	4	4	A (l)
Dist. of Columbia	. . .	. . .	★	. . .	★	★	A
American Samoa	. . .	. . .	(c)	. . .	(i)	(i)	A
Guam	. . .	. . .	. . .	. . .	. . .	. . .	A
No. Mariana Islands	. . .	. . .	3	. . .	5	. . .	A
Puerto Rico	. . .	★	. . .	. . .	★	★	A
U.S. Virgin Islands	. . .	. . .	★	★	★	★	A

Sources: The Council of State Governments' survey of attorneys general, November 2008 and state constitutions and statutes, January 2009.

Key:

★ — Formal provision; number of years not specified.

. . . — No formal provision.

A — Appointed by governor.

E — Elected by voters.

(a) In some states you must be a U.S. citizen to be an elector, and must be an elector to run.

(b) In some states you must be a state resident to be an elector, and must be an elector to run.

(c) No statute specifically requires this, but the State Bar Act can be interpreted as making this a qualification.

(d) No period specified; all licensed attorneys are members of the state bar.

(e) State citizenship requirement.

(f) Chosen biennially by joint ballot of state senators and representatives.

(g) *Crosse v. Board of Supervisors of Elections* 243 Md. 555, 221A.2d431 (1966)—opinion rendered indicated that U.S. citizenship was, by necessity, a requirement for office.

(h) Appointed by the governor and confirmed by the governor and the Executive Council.

(i) Implied.

(j) Appointed by state Supreme Court.

(k) Same as qualifications of a judge of a court of record.

(l) Must be confirmed by the Senate.

Table 4.21
ATTORNEYS GENERAL: PROSECUTORIAL AND ADVISORY DUTIES

State or other jurisdiction	Authority in local prosecutions: Authority to initiate local prosecutions	May intervene in local prosecutions	May assist local prosecutor	May supersede local prosecutor	Issues advisory opinions (a): To state executive officials	To legislators	To local prosecutors	On the constitutionality of bills or ordinances	Reviews legislation (b): Prior to passage	Before signing
Alabama	A	A,D	A,D	A	★	★	★	. . .	★	. . .
Alaska	(c)	(c)	(c)	(c)	★	★	. . .	★	★	★
Arizona	A	A	A,B	A,F	★	★	★	★	(u)	(u)
Arkansas	. . .	. . .	D	. . .	★	★	★	★	. . .	. . .
California	A,B,D,E	A,B,D,E	A,B,C,D,E	A,B,D,E,G	★	★	★	★	(v)	(v)
Colorado	A,F	B	D,F	B	★	★	★	★	★	★
Connecticut	. . .	. . .	. . .	. . .	★	(d)	. . .	★	(e)	(e)
Delaware	A (f)	(f)	(f)	(f)	★	★	. . .	★	★(g)	★(g)
Florida	F	. . .	D	. . .	★	★	★	. . .	. . .	. . .
Georgia	B,D,F,G	. . .	A,D	. . .	★	★	★	. . .	. . .	. . .
Hawaii	A,B,C,D,E	A,B,C,D,E	A,B,C,D,E	A,B,C,D,E	★	★	. . .	★(h)	★	★
Idaho	B,D,F	. . .	D	. . .	★	★	★	★	★	★
Illinois	D,F	D,G	D	G	★	★	★	. . .	(i)	(i)
Indiana	F	. . .	D	. . .	★	★	★	★	. . .	. . .
Iowa	D,F	D,F	D,F	D,E,F	★	★	★	. . .	(j)	(j)
Kansas	A,B,C,D,F	A,D	D	A,F	★	★	★	★	. . .	. . .
Kentucky	D,F,G	B,D,G	D	B	★	★	★	★	. . .	. . .
Louisiana	D,E,G	D,E,G	D,E,G	E,G	★	★	★	. . .	★	★
Maine	A	A	A	A	★	★	. . .	. . .	. . .	. . .
Maryland	B,F	D	D	. . .	★	★	★	★	★	★
Massachusetts	A	A	A,D	A	★	★(k)	★	★	(l)	(l)
Michigan	A	A	A	A	★	★	★	★	. . .	. . .
Minnesota	B,F	B,D,G	A,B,D,G	B	★	★(k)	★	. . .	. . .	(l)
Mississippi	A,D,F	D,F	A,D,F	D,F	★	★	★	. . .	. . .	. . .
Missouri	B,F,G	F	B,F	G	★	★	★	. . .	(l)	(l)
Montana	D	E	E	E	★	★(m)	★	. . .	. . .	. . .
Nebraska	A	. . .	. . .	. . .	★	★	★	★	. . .	. . .
Nevada	D,F,G	D	. . .	. . .	★	. . .	★	★	. . .	. . .
New Hampshire	A,E,F	A,E,F	A,D,E,F	A,E,F	★	★	★	. . .	(n)	(n)
New Jersey	A,B,C,D	A,B,C,D	A,B,C,D	A,B,C,D	★	★	★	★	★	★
New Mexico	B,D,E,F	D,E,F	A,B,D,E,F	D,E,F,G	★	★	★	★	★	★
New York	B,F	B,D,F	D	B	★	★(k)	★	★	★	★
North Carolina	. . .	D	D	. . .	★	★	★	★	★	. . .
North Dakota	A,D,E,F,G	A,D,E,G	A,B,D,E,F,G	A,D,E,G	★	★	★	★	. . .	. . .
Ohio	F	D	D	F	★	(m)	★	. . .	. . .	. . .
Oklahoma	A,B,C,D,E,F,G	A,B,C,D,E,F,G	A,B,C,D,E,F,G	A,B,C,D,E,F,G	★	★	★	★	★	★
Oregon	B,D,F	B,D	B,D	. . .	★	★	★	. . .	. . .	★
Pennsylvania	A,D,F	D,F	D,F	. . .	★	. . .	. . .	. . .	. . .	. . .
Rhode Island	A	A	A	A	★	★	. . .	. . .	. . .	. . .
South Carolina	A,D,E,F (p)	A,B,C,D,E,F	A,D	A,E	★	(q)	★	★	★(r)	★(l)
South Dakota	A,B,D,E,F (p)	D,G (b)	A,B,D,E	D,F	★	★	★	. . .	★	. . .
Tennessee	D,F,G	D,G	D	. . .	★	★	★	★	. . .	. . .
Texas	. . .	. . .	. . .	. . .	. . .	. . .	. . .	. . .	. . .	. . .
Utah	A,B,D,E,F,G	E,G	D,E	E	★	★(q)	★	★	★(l)	★(l)
Vermont	A	A	A	G	★	★	★	★	★	★
Virginia	B,F	B,D,F	B,D,F	B	★	★	★	★	★	★
Washington	B,D,G	B,D,G	B,D,G	B,D,G	★	★	★	. . .	(o)	(o)
West Virginia	. . .	. . .	. . .	. . .	★	★	★	★	. . .	. . .
Wisconsin	B,C,D,F	B,C,D	D	B	★	★	★	★	(e)	(e)
Wyoming	B,D,F	B,D	B,D	G	★	★	★	★(h)	★	★
Dist. of Columbia	F	D	D	F	★	★	(s)	★	★	★
American Samoa	A (t)	(t)	(t)	(t)	★	. . .	(t)	(e)	(l)	(l)
Guam	A	A	A	A	★	★	★	★	(l)	B
No. Mariana Islands	A (t)	(t)	(t)	(t)	★	★	. . .	★	. . .	. . .
Puerto Rico	A	(t)	(t)	(t)	★	★	. . .	. . .	★	★
U.S. Virgin Islands	A (t)	(t)	(t)	(t)	★	. . .	. . .	★	★	★

See footnotes at end of table.

ATTORNEYS GENERAL: PROSECUTORIAL AND ADVISORY DUTIES—Continued

Source: The Council of State Governments' survey of attorneys general, November 2008.

Key:

A — On own initiative.

B — On request of governor.

C — On request of legislature.

D — On request of local prosecutor.

E — When in state's interest.

F — Under certain statutes for specific crimes.

G — On authorization of court or other body.

★ — Has authority in area.

. . . — Does not have authority in area.

(a) Also issues advisory opinions to: Alabama—designated heads of state departments, agencies, boards, and commissions; local public officials; and political subdivisions. Hawaii—judges/judiciary as requested. Kansas—to counsel for local units of government. Montana—county and city attorneys, city commissioners. Wisconsin—corporation counsel.

(b) Also reviews legislation: Alabama—when requested by the governor. Alaska—after passage. Arizona—at the request of the legislature. Kansas—upon request of legislator, no formal authority.

(c) The attorney general functions as the local prosecutor.

(d) To legislative leadership.

(e) Informally reviews bills or does so upon request.

(f) The attorney general prosecutes all criminal offenses in Delaware.

(g) Also at the request of agency or legislature.

(h) Bills, not ordinances.

(i) Reviews and tracks legislation that relates to the office of attorney general and the office mission.

(j) No requirements for review.

(k) To legislature as a whole, not individual legislators.

(l) Only when requested by governor or legislature.

(m) To either house of legislature, not individual legislators.

(n) Provides information when requested by the legislature. Testifies for or against bills on the attorney general's own initiative.

(o) May review legislation at request of clients or legislature.

(p) Certain statutes provide for concurrent jurisdiction with local prosecutors.

(q) Only when requested by legislature.

(r) Has concurrent jurisdiction with state's attorneys.

(s) The office of attorney general prosecutes local crimes to an extent. The office's Legal Counsel Division may issue legal advice to the office's prosecutorial arm. Otherwise, the office does not usually advise the OUSA, the district's other local prosecutor.

(t) The attorney general functions as the local prosecutor.

(u) Reviews enacted legislation only when there is a compelling need.

(v) May review legislation at any time but does not have a de jure role in approval of bills as to form or constitutionality; California has a separate Legislative Counsel to advise the legislature on bills.

Table 4.22
ATTORNEYS GENERAL: CONSUMER PROTECTION ACTIVITIES, SUBPOENA POWERS AND ANTITRUST DUTIES

State or other jurisdiction	*May commence civil proceedings*	*May commence criminal proceedings*	*Represents the state before regulatory agencies (a)*	*Administers consumer protection programs*	*Handles consumer complaints*	*Subpoena powers (b)*	*Antitrust duties*
Alabama	★	★	★	★	★	•	A,B,C
Alaska	★	★	★	★	★	★	A,B,C,D
Arizona	★	. . .	. . .	★	★	★	A,B,C,D
Arkansas	★	. . .	★	★	★	•	A,B
California	★	★	★	★	★	★	A,B,C,D
Colorado	★	★	★	★	★	•	A,C,D
Connecticut	★	(c)	★	★	★	•	A,B,D
Delaware	★	★	★	★	★	★	A,B,D
Florida	★	. . .	. . .	★	★	★	A,B,D
Georgia	★	★	★	. . .	. . .	•	. . .
Hawaii	★	★	★	. . .	★	★	A,B,C,D
Idaho	★	. . .	★	★	★	★	A,B,D
Illinois	★	. . .	★	★	★	•	A,B,C
Indiana	★	. . .	★	★	★	★	A,B
Iowa	★	★	★	★	★	★	B,C
Kansas	★	★	★	★	★	★	B,C,D
Kentucky	★	★	★	★	★	★	A,B,C,D
Louisiana	★	★	★	★	★	★	A,B,C
Maine	★	★	★	★	★	★	A,B,C
Maryland	★	★(d)	. . .	★	★	★	B,C,D
Massachusetts	★	★	★	★	★	★	A,B,C,D
Michigan	★	★	★	★	★	★	A,B,C,D
Minnesota	★	. . .	★	★	★	•	A,B,C
Mississippi	★	★	. . .	★	★	★	A,B,C,D
Missouri	★	★	★	★	★	★	A,B,C,D
Montana	★	★	. . .	★	★	. . .	A,B
Nebraska	★	★	★	★	★	. . .	A,B,C,D
Nevada	★	★	★	★	★	•	A,B,C,D
New Hampshire	★	★	★	★	★	★	A,B,C,D
New Jersey	★	★	★	★	★	★	A,B,C,D
New Mexico	★	★	★	★	★	★	A,B,C (f)
New York	★	★	★	★	★	★	A,B,C,D
North Carolina	★	★(e)	★	★	★	★	A,B,C,D
North Dakota	★	. . .	★	★	★	★	A,B,D
Ohio	★	★	★	★	★	★	A,B,C,D
Oklahoma	★	★	★	★	★	★	A,B,C,D
Oregon	★	★(e)	★	★	★	•	A,B,C
Pennsylvania	★	★	★	★	★	★	A,B
Rhode Island	★	★	. . .	★	★	★	A,B,C
South Carolina	★(a)	★(g)	★	. . .	★(h)	•	A,B,C,D
South Dakota	★	★	★	★	★	★	A,B,C
Tennessee	★	(d)(e)	(e)	. . .	. . .	★	B,C,D
Texas	★	★	★	★	★	•	A,B,C,D
Utah	★(i)	★	★(i)	. . .	★(j)	•	A (k),B,C,D (k)
Vermont	★	★	★	★	★	★	A,B,C
Virginia	★	(e)	★	★(j)	★(j)	•	A,B,C,D
Washington	★	. . .	★	★	★	★	A,B,D
West Virginia	★	. . .	★	★	★	★	A,B,D
Wisconsin	★	★	★	★	★	•	A,B,C (f)
Wyoming	★	. . .	★	★	★	•	A,B
Dist. of Columbia	★	★(l)	★	★	★	★	A,B,C,D
American Samoa	★	★	★	★	★	. . .	. . .
Guam	★	★	★	★	★	•	A,B,C,D
No. Mariana Islands	★	★	★	★	★	★	A,B
Puerto Rico	★	★	. . .	. . .	. . .	★	A,B,C,D
U.S. Virgin Islands	★	★	★	★	★	•	A

See footnotes at end of table.

ATTORNEYS GENERAL: CONSUMER PROTECTION ACTIVITIES, SUBPOENA POWERS AND ANTITRUST DUTIES — Continued

Source: The Council of State Governments' survey of attorneys general, November 2008.

Key:

A — Has parens patriae authority to commence suits on behalf of consumers in state antitrust damage actions in state courts.

B — May initiate damage actions on behalf of state in state courts.

C — May commence criminal proceedings.

D — May represent cities, counties and other governmental entities in recovering civil damages under federal or state law.

★ — Has authority in area.

. . . — Does not have authority in area.

(a) May represent state on behalf of: the "people" of the state; an agency of the state; or the state before a federal regulatory agency.

(b) In this column only: ★ — broad powers and • — limited powers.

(c) In certain cases only.

(d) May commence criminal proceedings with local district attorney.

(e) To a limited extent.

(f) May represent other governmental entities in recovering civil damages under federal or state law.

(g) When permitted to intervene.

(h) On a limited basis because the state has a separate consumer affairs department.

(i) Attorney general has exclusive authority.

(j) Attorney general handles legal matters only with no administrative handling of complaints.

(k) Opinion only, since there are no controlling precedents.

(l) In antitrust, not criminal proceedings.

Table 4.23
ATTORNEYS GENERAL: DUTIES TO ADMINISTRATIVE AGENCIES AND OTHER RESPONSIBILITIES

			Duties to administrative agencies							
					Conducts litigation:					
State or other jurisdiction	Serves as counsel for state	Appears for state in criminal appeals	Issues official advice	Interprets statutes or regulations	On behalf of agency	Against agency	Prepares or reviews legal documents	Represents the public before the agency	Involved in rule-making	Reviews rules for legality
Alabama	A,B,C (a)	★(a)	★	★	★	★	(b)	(b)	★	★
Alaska	A,B,C	★	★	★	★	★	★	★	★	★
Arizona	A,B,C	★	★	★	★	★	★	. . .	★	★
Arkansas	A,B,C	★	★	★	★	★	★	★	. . .	. . .
California	A,B,C	★	★	★	★	. . .	★	. . .	★	★
Colorado	A,B,C	★	★	★	★	★	★	★	★	★
Connecticut	A,B,C	(b)	★	★	★	★	★	★	★	★
Delaware (f)	A,B,C	★	★	★	★	★(g)	★	★	★	★
Florida	A,B,C	★	★	★	★	. . .	★	. . .	. . .	. . .
Georgia	A,B,C	★	★	★	★	. . .	★	. . .	. . .	★
Hawaii	A,B,C	★	★	★	★	★	★	★	★	★
Idaho	A,B,C	★(a)	★	★	★	★	★	★	★	★
Illinois	A,B,C	★	. . .	★	★	. . .	★	. . .	. . .	. . .
Indiana	A,B,C	★	★	★	★	. . .	★	. . .	★	★
Iowa	A,B,C	★	★	★	★	★	★	★	★	★
Kansas	A,B,C	★	★	★	★	★	★	. . .	★	★
Kentucky	A,B,C	★	★	★	★	. . .	. . .	★	. . .	. . .
Louisiana	A,B,C	. . .	★	★	★	. . .	★	★	★	★
Maine	A,B,C	★	★	★	★	. . .	★	. . .	. . .	★
Maryland	A,B,C	★	★	★	★	(b)	★	★	★	★
Massachusetts	A,B,C	(b)(c)(d)	★	★	★	★	★	★	★	★
Michigan	A,B,C	★	★	★	★	★	★	★	★	★
Minnesota	A,B,C	(c)(d)	★	★	(a)	★	★	★	★	★
Mississippi	A,B,C	. . .	★	★	★	. . .	★	. . .	. . .	. . .
Missouri	A,B,C	★	★	★	★	. . .	★	★	★	. . .
Montana (h)	A,B	. . .	★	★	★	. . .	★	. . .	. . .	. . .
Nebraska	A,B,C	★	★	★	★	★	★	. . .	★	★
Nevada	A,B,C	★	★	★	★	. . .	★	. . .	★	★
New Hampshire	A,B,C	★	★	★	★	. . .	★	★	★	. . .
New Jersey	A,B,C	★	★	★	★	. . .	★	. . .	★	★
New Mexico	A,B,C	★	★	★	★	★	★	★	★	★
New York	A,B,C	(b)	. . .	★	★	(b)	★	(b)	. . .	. . .
North Carolina	A,B,C	★	★	★	★	★	★	(b)	★	★
North Dakota	A,B,C	★	★	★	★	★	★	. . .	★	★
Ohio	A,B,C	★	★	. . .	★	. . .	★	. . .	. . .	. . .
Oklahoma	A,B,C	★	★	★	★	★	★	★	★	★
Oregon	A,B	★	★	★	★	. . .	★	. . .	★	★
Pennsylvania	A,B	. . .	. . .	. . .	★	. . .	★	. . .	. . .	★
Rhode Island	A,B,C	★	★	★	★	★	★	. . .	. . .	. . .
South Carolina	A,B,C	★(d)	(a)	★	★	(b)	★	. . .	★	★
South Dakota	A,B,C	★	★	★	★	★	★	. . .	. . .	. . .
Tennessee	A,B,C	★	★	★	★	. . .	★	(e)	(e)	★
Texas	A,B,C	★(i)	★	★	★	★	★	★	★	. . .
Utah	A,B,C	★(a)	★	★	★	★	★	(b)	★	★
Vermont	A,B,C	★	★	★	★	★	★	★	★	★
Virginia	A,B,C	★	★	★	★	★	★	★	★	★
Washington	A,B,C	★(k)	★	★	★	★	★	★	★	★
West Virginia	A,B,C	★	★	★	★	★	★	. . .	. . .	. . .
Wisconsin	A,B,C	★	★	★	★	(b)	(b)	(b)	(b)	(b)
Wyoming	A,B,C	★	★	★	★	★	★	. . .	★	★
Dist. of Columbia	A,B	★(j)	★	★	★	. . .	★	. . .	★	★
American Samoa	A,B,C	★(a)	★	★	★	. . .	★	. . .	★	★
Guam	A,B,C	★	★	★	(d)	★	★	(b)	★	★
No. Mariana Islands	A,B,C	★	★	★	★	★	★	. . .	★	★
Puerto Rico	A,B,C	★	★	★	★	. . .	★	. . .	★	★
U.S. Virgin Islands	A,B	★	★	★	★	★	★	★	. . .	★

See footnotes at end of table.

ATTORNEYS GENERAL: DUTIES TO ADMINISTRATIVE AGENCIES AND OTHER RESPONSIBILITIES — Continued

Source: The Council of State Governments' survey of attorneys general, November 2008.

Key:

A — Defend state law when challenged on federal constitutional grounds.

B — Conduct litigation on behalf of state in federal and other states' courts.

C — Prosecute actions against another state in U.S. Supreme Court.

★ — Has authority in area.

. . . — Does not have authority in area.

(a) Attorney general has exclusive jurisdiction.

(b) In certain cases only.

(c) When assisting local prosecutor in the appeal.

(d) Can appear on own discretion.

(e) Consumer Advocate Division represents the public in utility rate-making hearings and rule-making proceedings.

(f) Except as otherwise provided by statute, the attorney general represents all state agencies and officials.

(g) Rarely.

(h) Most state agencies are represented by agency counsel who do not answer to the attorney general. The attorney general does provide representation for agencies in conflict situations and where the agency requires additional or specialized assistance.

(i) Primarily federal habeas corpus appeals only.

(j) However, OUSA handles felony cases and most major misdemeanors.

(k) Limited to federal death penalty habeas corpus.

The Role of Treasurers in the States

By Kevin Johnson

State treasurers are responsible for providing independent oversight of public funds. They manage resources to meet state financial obligations and professionally invest money that is not immediately needed. Treasurers have numerous additional duties, including pension fund governance, administration of unclaimed property and college savings programs, and issuance of state debt. In these and other areas, they serve as guardians of the public purse.

Legal Authority

State treasurers are elected constitutional officers in most states. The laws of 37 states call for the popular election of a treasurer; in four states, legislatures make the selection. In the remaining states and the District of Columbia, the governor or another executive official appoints the treasurer. These officials serve at the pleasure of the appointing authority, while elected treasurers serve a fixed term.

Core Duties: Cash Management and Investment

State constitutions and statutes give treasurers a wide variety of duties. All treasurers have responsibility for cash management—the daily assessment of how much the state needs to meet its immediate obligations. This critical task ensures that the various parts of government have funds available to purchase goods, pay salaries and undertake routine financial transactions. States can also capitalize by investing funds that are not needed on a given day.

Most treasurers are responsible for short-term investments. By identifying how much idle cash the state has and investing it in short-term vehicles, state treasuries earn interest income that adds an important source of revenue for public programs.

Three priorities govern short-term investing: safety, liquidity and yield. The first of these is the most important principle: Public funds are only placed in instruments that protect the principal of the investment. In other words, state treasurers ensure taxpayer resources are protected and do not lose value. The second priority, liquidity, means cash will be available when the state needs it to pay expenses. This may be in a few days or months, and treasury offices must keep track of spending patterns and know how long funds can be invested before they are needed. The third priority, which comes into play only after safety and liquidity are achieved, is finding the best yield available at the time the funds are invested.

Treasurers manage cash and make short-term investments by developing in-house expertise and contracting for services with banks and other financial firms. Many treasurers are responsible for evaluating and purchasing banking services for their states. Technology has dramatically changed the way treasuries have offered these services in recent years. For instance, states now issue and receive far fewer paper checks than in the past and instead utilize a variety of electronic payment options. These new techniques have improved the efficiency of many tasks, such as paying employee salaries, providing child support and unemployment benefits, and processing fees paid to state agencies. They also allow treasuries to reduce instances of fraud and human error.

Pension and Trust Investment

In addition to general operating budgets, states also manage long-term funds such as retirement systems and trusts. These funds are collectively among the largest institutional investors in the world; in 2008, state and local government retirement programs held nearly $3 trillion in assets.[1] Treasurers are involved in the governance of public pension plans in 38 states and the District of Columbia, most commonly as members of boards of trustees that oversee the plans. Seventeen treasury offices are responsible for the daily management of pension investments. Treasurers also manage state rainy day funds, lottery, tobacco settlement, land trust and other special funds in a number of states.

The performance of retirement and other funds depends on effective governance, and treasurers who serve as managers and trustees of these funds act on behalf of the beneficiaries to ensure that resources will be available to meet obligations in the future. Recently, many treasurers have advocated for improvements in the way state retirement investments are made. They are actively engaged in corporate governance issues for the companies that states invest in through stocks and corporate debt based on the idea that well-managed companies will produce better long-term value. Some treasurers are also working to include geopolitical and environmental considerations into the analysis of investment options for pension funds.

Debt Management

States borrow money for many reasons, including large-scale capital projects like road construction. Forty treasurers are involved in the issuance or maintenance of public debt. Tax-exempt bonds are an important funding tool for states, cities and other entities like universities and water districts. They allow governments to borrow at low rates because the purchasers of the bonds do not have to pay income taxes on the earnings. Tax-exempt bonds allow governments to use more of the funds they borrow for public projects and pay less interest than with other types of debt.

State bonds are notable for the high level of security they offer to investors. When a state sells a general obligation bond, it signals to the public that the state's resources will be available in the future to pay the promised interest and principal. The exact interest rate a state must pay on its bonds depends on market conditions and the state's credit rating. State treasurers play a key role in promoting sound financial practices so their states can maintain good credit ratings and thus the ability to borrow money at relatively low interest rates. In doing so, they help states build projects and offer services in a cost-effective manner.

The downturn in the U.S. economy and financial markets during 2008 had significant implications for state borrowing. General investor unease led many states to delay bond offerings and interrupted financing for a variety of projects. Treasurers and other officials sought alternative avenues for borrowing to keep many initiatives on track.

In the recent past, institutional investors were the major purchasers of municipal bonds, but after major events such as bank failures in the autumn of 2008, they retreated from the market. Earlier in the year, institutional investors bought 65 percent of municipal bonds, but by October they purchased only 22 percent.[2] This dramatic shift in the marketplace left states and localities without a major conventional source of financing. Treasurers and other officials in some states helped fill this gap by promoting bonds directly to individuals. The success of so-called retail bond sales prevented some state projects from being cancelled. As the economic downturn continues to affect states in 2009, the availability of capital in the bond market will continue to be a significant consideration in the implementation of new capital projects.

Unclaimed Property

Treasurers administer unclaimed property programs in 33 states and the District of Columbia. Every state has laws governing assets held by a firm but belonging to another party. When the firm loses contact with the original owner of the asset, the asset becomes unclaimed property after a certain amount of time dictated by statute. The firm must then turn the property over to the state, which safeguards it until the owner can be found. Common types of unclaimed property include checking accounts, utility deposits, certain insurance policies, shares of stock and safe deposit box contents. In 2006, states held approximately $33 billion in unclaimed property.[3]

Unclaimed property programs are one of the nation's oldest consumer protection initiatives. State treasurers actively promote the programs in order to encourage more people to search the rolls of owners. Each state maintains a web site that citizens can use to search for assets that might belong to them; a portal to all the states' sites is at *www.unclaimed.org*. States also use print advertising and public events to raise awareness of their unclaimed property programs.

College Savings Programs

Another function commonly housed in the state treasurer's office is administration of state-sponsored college savings and prepaid tuition programs. Forty-nine states and the District of Columbia offer such programs, and 28 are run by treasurers' offices. The programs are also known as 529 plans, named after the section of the Internal Revenue Code that governs them. They offer individuals and families the ability to save for higher education in tax-advantaged accounts. Investment earnings in the plans are exempt from federal income taxes as well as income taxes in some states.

Congress made the federal exemption a permanent part of the tax code in 2006, signifying its support of the states' efforts to encourage greater savings for college. There are two types of 529 plans. Savings programs allow participants to deposit funds and choose from several investment options. The funds and earnings can be withdrawn to pay for higher education expenses for designated beneficiaries. Prepaid tuition programs allow participants to buy tuition credits at current prices and use them in the future. States actively promote the plans and citizens have opened more than 11 million accounts.[4] 529 programs are an important tool to make higher education affordable to all citizens.

One emerging priority for many states is helping low- and moderate-income households take advantage of the programs. Most plans set low account opening and deposit requirements—often less than $100. Some also sponsor scholarship programs for eligible participants. State treasurers and other officials who administer the plans recognize that enrolling more families in the plans helps them save for college and demonstrate to their children that higher education is a goal they can and should attain.

Financial Literacy

Many treasurers have taken an interest in promoting personal financial education in their states. They recognize that high levels of household debt and inadequate money management skills lead to significant problems for many households. Many Americans are failing to save for the future as well. In the third quarter of 2008, the U.S. personal saving rate was just above 1 percent.[5]

Treasurers across the country employ a variety of tools to improve financial literacy. Many work with local schools and nonprofit organizations to incorporate basic skills into existing curriculum. Some treasurers also organize conferences for adults; seminars targeted to women have been successful in several states. Treasurers also devote sections of their Web sites to financial literacy. Over the past five years, 35 treasurers have offered some type of personal finance program to the public.

Notes

[1] U.S. Census Bureau, *http://ftp2.census.gov/govs/qpr/table1.txt*.

[2] Monika Conley, presentation to the National Association of State Treasurers, Dec. 9, 2008.

[3] Data provided by the National Association of Unclaimed Property Administrators.

[4] Data provided by the College Savings Plans Network.

[5] Bureau of Economic Analysis, *http://www.bea.gov/briefrm/saving.htm*.

About the Author

Kevin Johnson is communications director with the National Association of State Treasurers.

Table 4.24
THE TREASURERS, 2009

State or other jurisdiction	Name and party	Method of selection	Length of regular term in years	Date of first service	Present term ends	Maximum consecutive terms allowed by constitution
Alabama	Kay Ivey (R)	E	4	1/2003	1/2011	2
Alaska (a)	Jerry Burnett	A	Governor's Discretion	1/2009	. . .	. . .
Arizona	Dean Martin (R)	E	4	1/2007	1/2011	2
Arkansas	Martha Shoffner (D)	E	4	1/2007	1/2011	2
California	Bill Lockyer (D)	E	4	1/2007	1/2011	2
Colorado	Cary Kennedy (D)	E	4	1/2007	1/2011	2
Connecticut	Denise L. Nappier (D)	E	4	1/1999	1/2011	★
Delaware	Velda Jones-Potter (D)	E	4	1/2009	1/2011	★
Florida (b)	Adelaide "Alex" Sink (D)	E	4	1/2007	1/2011	2
Georgia	W. Daniel Ebersole	A	Pleasure of the Board	11/1997	. . .	. . .
Hawaii (c)	Georgina Kawamura	A	Governor's Discretion	12/2002	. . .	. . .
Idaho	Ron G. Crane (R)	E	4	1/1999	1/2011	★
Illinois	Alexi Giannoulias (D)	E	4	1/2007	1/2011	★
Indiana	Richard Mourdock (R)	E	4	2/2007	2/2011	(d)
Iowa	Michael L. Fitzgerald (D)	E	4	1/1983	1/2011	★
Kansas	Dennis McKinney	E	4	1/2009	1/2011	★
Kentucky	Todd Hollenbach (D)	E	4	12/2007	12/2011	2
Louisiana	John Kennedy (D)	E	4	1/2000	1/2012	★
Maine	David G. Lemoine (D)	L	2	1/2005	1/2011	4
Maryland	Nancy K. Kopp (D)	L	4	2/2002	1/2011	★
Massachusetts	Timothy Cahill (D)	E	4	1/2003	1/2011	★
Michigan	Robert J. Kleine	A	Governor's Discretion	5/2006	. . .	. . .
Minnesota (e)	Tom Hanson	A	Governor's Discretion	12/2006	. . .	. . .
Mississippi	Tate Reeves (R)	E	4	1/2004	1/2012	★
Missouri	Clint Zweifel (D)	E	4	1/2009	1/2013	2
Montana	Janet Kelly	A	Governor's Discretion	1/2005	. . .	. . .
Nebraska	Shane Osborn (R)	E	4	1/2007	1/2011	2
Nevada	Kate Marshall (D)	E	4	1/2007	1/2011	2
New Hampshire	Catherine Provencher	L	2	1/2007	12/2010	★
New Jersey	R. David Rousseau	A	Governor's Discretion	4/2008	. . .	. . .
New Mexico	James B. Lewis (D)	E	4	1/2007	1/2011	2
New York	Aida Brewer	A	Governor's Discretion	2/2002	. . .	. . .
North Carolina	Jane Cowell (D)	E	4	1/2009	1/2013	★
North Dakota	Kelly L. Schmidt (R)	E	4	1/2005	1/2013	★
Ohio	Kevin L. Boyce	E	4	1/2009 (f)	1/2011	2
Oklahoma	Scott Meacham (D)	E	4	6/2005	1/2011	★
Oregon	Ben Westlund (D)	E	4	1/2009	1/2013	2
Pennsylvania	Robert McCord (D)	E	4	1/2009	1/2013	2
Rhode Island	Frank T. Caprio (D)	E	4	1/2007	1/2011	2
South Carolina	Converse Chellis (R)	E	4	8/2007 (g)	1/2011	★
South Dakota	Vernon L. Larson (R)	E	4	1/2003	1/2011	2
Tennessee	David H. Lillard Jr.	L	2	1/2009	1/2011	. . .
Texas (h)	Susan Combs (R)	E	4	1/2007	1/2011	★
Utah	Richard K. Ellis (R)	E	4	1/2009	1/2013	★
Vermont	Jeb Spaulding (D)	E	2	1/2003	1/2011	★
Virginia	Manju Ganeriwala	A	Governor's Discretion	1/2009	. . .	. . .
Washington	James L. McIntire (D)	E	4	1/2009	1/2013	★
West Virginia	John D. Perdue (D)	E	4	1/1997	1/2013	★
Wisconsin	Dawn Marie Sass (D)	E	4	1/2007	1/2011	★
Wyoming	Joseph B. Meyer (R)	E	4	1/2007	1/2011	2
American Samoa	Magalei Logovii	A	4	1/2009	. . .	. . .
Dist. of Columbia	Lasana Mack	A	Pleasure of CFO	8/2005	N.A.	. . .
Guam	Yasela Pereira	CS	. . .	10/1996	. . .	. . .
No. Mariana Islands	Antoinette S. Calvo	A	4	N.A.	N.A.	. . .
Puerto Rico	Juan Carlos Puig	A	4	1/2009	N.A.	. . .
U.S. Virgin Islands	Laurel Payne	A	4	2007	N.A.	. . .

Source: National Association of State Treasurers, November 2008, and The Council of State Governments, February 2009.

Key:

★ — No provision specifying number of terms allowed.

. . . — No formal provision; position is appointed or elected by governmental entity (not chosen by the electorate).

A — Appointed by the governor. (In the District of Columbia, the Treasurer is appointed by the Chief Financial Officer. In Georgia, position is appointed by the State Depository Board.)

E — Elected by the voters.

L — Elected by the legislature.

CS — Civil Service.

N.A. — Not available.

(a) The Deputy Commissioner of Department of Revenue performs this function.

(b) The official title of the office of state treasurer is Chief Financial Officer.

(c) The Director of Finance performs this function.

(d) Eligible for eight out of any period of 12 years.

(e) The Commissioner of Finance performs this function.

(f) Kevin Boyce was appointed by Governor Strickland to fill the Treasurer position after Richard Cordray was elected in November 2008 to fill the Attorney General seat vacated by Marc Dann's resignation in May 2008.

(g) Representative Converse Chellis was elected treasurer on August 3, 2007, by the legislature after Governor Sanford suspended Thomas Ravenel from the office.

(h) The Comptroller of Public Accounts performs this function.

Table 4.25
TREASURERS: QUALIFICATIONS FOR OFFICE

State or other jurisdiction	Minimum age	U.S. citizen (years)	State resident (years)	Qualified voter (years)
Alabama	25	7	5	. . .
Alaska	. . .	. . .	★	. . .
Arizona	25	10	5	. . .
Arkansas	21	★	★	. . .
California	18	★	★	★
Colorado	25	★	★	★
Connecticut	. . .	★	★	★
Delaware	18	★	★	★
Florida	30	★	7	★
Georgia	. . .	. . .	. . .	. . .
Hawaii	. . .	★	5	. . .
Idaho	25	★	2	. . .
Illinois	25	★	★	. . .
Indiana	. . .	★	★	★
Iowa	18	. . .	. . .	. . .
Kansas	. . .	. . .	. . .	. . .
Kentucky	30	★	6	★
Louisiana	25	5	(a)	★
Maine	. . .	★	★	. . .
Maryland	. . .	. . .	. . .	. . .
Massachusetts	. . .	. . .	★	. . .
Michigan	. . .	. . .	. . .	. . .
Minnesota	. . .	. . .	. . .	. . .
Mississippi	25	★	5	★
Missouri	. . .	★	5	★
Montana	. . .	. . .	. . .	. . .
Nebraska	19	★	★	★
Nevada	25	★	★	★
New Hampshire	. . .	. . .	. . .	. . .
New Jersey	. . .	. . .	★	. . .
New Mexico	30	★	★	★
New York	. . .	★	★	N.A.
North Carolina	21	★	1	★
North Dakota	25	★	5	★
Ohio	18	★	★	★
Oklahoma	31	★	(b)	(c)
Oregon	18	. . .	★	. . .
Pennsylvania	. . .	. . .	. . .	. . .
Rhode Island	18	★	★	★
South Carolina	. . .	★	★	★
South Dakota	. . .	. . .	. . .	. . .
Tennessee	. . .	. . .	. . .	. . .
Texas	18	★	★	. . .
Utah	25	★	5	★
Vermont	. . .	★	2	. . .
Virginia	. . .	. . .	. . .	. . .
Washington	18	★	. . .	★
West Virginia	18	5	5	★
Wisconsin	18	★	★	★
Wyoming	25	★	1	★
Dist. of Columbia	. . .	. . .	. . .	. . .

Source: National Association of State Treasurers, March 2008.

Key:

★ — Formal provision; number of years not specified.

. . . — No formal provision.

N.A. — Not applicable.

(a) Five years immediately preceding the date of qualification for office.

(b) For at least 10 years immediately preceding.

(c) Must be able to vote for at least 10 years immediately preceding election.

Table 4.26
RESPONSIBILITIES OF THE TREASURER'S OFFICE

State or other jurisdiction	*Cash management*	*Investment of retirement funds*	*Investment of trust funds*	*Deferred compensation*	*Management of bonded debt*	*Bond issuance*	*Debt service*	*Arbitrage rebate*	*Banking services*	*Unclaimed property*	*Archives for disbursement of documents*	*College savings*	*Collateral programs*	*Local government investment pool*	*Other*
Alabama	★	. . .	. . .	. . .	★	. . .	★	. . .	★	★	. . .	★	★	. . .	. . .
Alaska	★	★	★	. . .	★	★	★	★	★	★	. . .	. . .	. . .	. . .	(a)
Arizona	★	. . .	★	. . .	. . .	. . .	. . .	★	★	. . .	. . .	. . .	. . .	★	. . .
Arkansas	★	. . .	★	. . .	. . .	. . .	. . .	. . .	★	. . .	. . .	. . .	. . .	★	. . .
California	★	. . .	★	. . .	★	★	★	★	★	. . .	. . .	. . .	★	★	. . .
Colorado	★	. . .	. . .	. . .	. . .	★	. . .	. . .	★	★	. . .	. . .	. . .	. . .	. . .
Connecticut	★	★	★	. . .	★	★	★	★	★	★	. . .	★	. . .	★	(b)
Delaware	★	. . .	. . .	★	. . .	★	★	★	★	. . .	. . .	★	★	★	(c)
Florida	★	. . .	★	★	. . .	. . .	. . .	. . .	★	★	. . .	. . .	★	. . .	(d)
Georgia	★	. . .	. . .	. . .	. . .	. . .	★	. . .	★	. . .	. . .	★	★	★	. . .
Hawaii	★	★	. . .	. . .	★	★	★	★	★	★	. . .	★	★	. . .	. . .
Idaho	★	. . .	. . .	. . .	. . .	. . .	. . .	. . .	★	. . .	. . .	★	. . .	★	. . .
Illinois	★	. . .	★	. . .	. . .	. . .	★	★	★	★	. . .	★	. . .	★	. . .
Indiana	★	. . .	★	. . .	★	. . .	. . .	. . .	★	. . .	★	★	. . .	★	. . .
Iowa	★	★	. . .	. . .	★	★	★	★	★	★	. . .	★	★	. . .	. . .
Kansas	★	. . .	. . .	. . .	. . .	. . .	. . .	. . .	★	★	. . .	★	. . .	. . .	(e)
Kentucky	★	. . .	. . .	. . .	. . .	. . .	. . .	. . .	★	★	★	. . .	. . .	. . .	. . .
Louisiana	★	. . .	★	. . .	★	★	★	★	★	★	. . .	. . .	★	. . .	(f)
Maine	★	. . .	★	. . .	★	★	★	★	★	★	. . .	★	. . .	. . .	(g)
Maryland	★	. . .	. . .	. . .	★	★	★	★	★	. . .	. . .	. . .	★	★	. . .
Massachusetts	★	★	★	★	★	★	★	★	★	★	. . .	. . .	. . .	★	(h)
Michigan	★	★	★	. . .	★	★	★	★	★	★	. . .	★	. . .	. . .	. . .
Minnesota	★	. . .	. . .	. . .	★	★	★	★	★	. . .	. . .	. . .	★	. . .	. . .
Mississippi	★	★	★	. . .	★	★	★	★	★	★	. . .	★	★	. . .	. . .
Missouri	★	. . .	★	. . .	. . .	. . .	. . .	★	★	★	. . .	★	. . .	. . .	(i)
Montana	★	. . .	. . .	. . .	★	★	★	★	★	. . .	. . .	. . .	. . .	. . .	. . .
Nebraska	★	. . .	. . .	. . .	. . .	. . .	. . .	. . .	★	★	. . .	★	. . .	. . .	(j)
Nevada	★	. . .	★	. . .	★	★	★	. . .	★	★	. . .	★	★	★	. . .
New Hampshire	★	. . .	★	. . .	★	★	★	★	★	★	. . .	★	. . .	. . .	. . .
New Jersey	★	★	. . .	★	★	★	★	. . .	★	★	. . .	. . .	. . .	★	. . .
New Mexico	★	. . .	. . .	. . .	★	. . .	. . .	. . .	★	. . .	★	. . .	. . .	★	. . .
New York	★	. . .	. . .	. . .	. . .	. . .	★	. . .	★	★	. . .	. . .	★	. . .	(k)
North Carolina	★	★	★	. . .	★	★	★	★	★	★	. . .	★	. . .	★	. . .
North Dakota	★	. . .	★	. . .	. . .	. . .	. . .	. . .	. . .	. . .	. . .	. . .	. . .	. . .	. . .
Ohio	★	. . .	★	. . .	★	★	★	. . .	★	. . .	. . .	. . .	. . .	★	. . .
Oklahoma	★	. . .	★	. . .	. . .	. . .	★	. . .	★	★	. . .	★	★	. . .	. . .
Oregon	★	★	★	★	★	★	★	★	★	. . .	. . .	★	★	★	(l)
Pennsylvania	★	★	★	. . .	. . .	★	★	★	★	★	. . .	★	. . .	★	. . .
Rhode Island	★	★	. . .	. . .	. . .	. . .	★	★	. . .	★	★	. . .	. . .	. . .	. . .
South Carolina	★	★	★	★	★	★	★	★	★	★	. . .	★	★	★	. . .
South Dakota	★	★	★	. . .	. . .	. . .	. . .	. . .	★	★	. . .	. . .	★	. . .	(m)
Tennessee	★	★	. . .	★	. . .	. . .	. . .	. . .	★	★	. . .	★	★	★	. . .
Texas	★	. . .	★	. . .	. . .	★	. . .	. . .	★	★	. . .	★	★	★	(n)
Utah	★	. . .	★	. . .	★	★	★	★	★	★	. . .	. . .	. . .	★	. . .
Vermont	★	★	★	★	★	★	★	★	★	★	. . .	. . .	. . .	. . .	. . .
Virginia	★	. . .	★	. . .	★	★	★	★	★	★	. . .	. . .	★	★	(o)
Washington	★	. . .	★	. . .	★	★	★	★	★	. . .	. . .	. . .	. . .	★	. . .
West Virginia	★	. . .	. . .	. . .	. . .	. . .	★	. . .	★	★	. . .	★	★	. . .	. . .
Wisconsin	. . .	. . .	. . .	. . .	. . .	. . .	. . .	. . .	. . .	★	. . .	★	. . .	★	. . .
Wyoming	★	. . .	★	. . .	★	★	★	★	★	★	. . .	★	★	★	. . .
Dist. of Columbia	★	★	★	★	★	★	★	★	★	★	. . .	★	★	. . .	. . .

Source: National Association of State Treasurers, March 2008.
Key:
★ — Responsible for activity.
. . . — Not responsible for activity.
(a) Revenue collection including oil and gas royalties and corporate income taxes; child support enforcement; permanent fund dividend eligibility.
(b) Second Injury Fund.
(c) General Fund account reconcilement; disbursements.
(d) State Accounting Disbursement, Fire Marshall, Insurance and Banking Consumer Services, Insurance Rehabilitation and Liquidation, Risk Management, Workers' Compensation, Insurance Fraud, Insurance Agent and Agency Services.
(e) Municipal bond servicing.
(f) Social Security for Section 218 Agreements.
(g) Municipal Revenue Sharing.
(h) Massachusetts Municipal Depository Trust Funds for Cities and Towns.
(i) Investment of all state funds.
(j) Nebraska Child Support Payment Center.
(k) Linked Deposit Program.
(l) Legislation pending to move Unclaimed Property program to Treasurer's office.
(m) Treasurer is a member of the trust and retirement investment programs.
(n) Tax Administration/Collection.
(o) Risk Management.

Table 4.27
STATE INVESTMENT BOARD MEMBERSHIP

State or other jurisdiction	Name of board	Board membership: Governor	Lt. Governor	Treasurer	Auditor	Comptroller	Attorney General	Secretary of State	Secretary/Director of Finance	Gubernatorial Appointments	Other
Alabama	No Board	...	...	...	...	...	...	...	...	...	...
Alaska	No Board	...	...	...	...	...	...	...	...	...	(a)
Arizona	Arizona State Board of Investment	...	...	★	...	...	...	...	...	...	(b)
Arkansas	Board of Finance	★	...	★	★	...	...	...	★	1	(c)
California	Pooled Money Investment Board	...	...	★	...	★	...	...	★	...	...
Colorado	Investment Advisory Board	...	...	★	...	...	...	...	...	...	(d)
Connecticut	No Board	...	...	...	...	...	...	...	...	...	...
Delaware	Cash Management Policy Board	...	...	★	...	★	...	★	...	5	(e)
Florida	No Board	...	...	...	...	...	...	...	...	...	...
Georgia	State Depository Board	★	...	★	★	...	...	...	...	...	(f)
Hawaii	No Board	...	...	...	...	...	...	...	...	...	...
Idaho	No Board	...	...	...	...	...	...	...	...	...	...
Illinois	No Board	...	...	...	...	...	...	...	...	...	(g)
Indiana	No Board	...	...	...	...	...	...	...	...	...	(h)
Iowa	Treasurer's Investment Committee	...	...	★	...	...	...	...	...	...	(g)
Kansas	Pooled Money Investment Board	...	...	★	...	...	...	...	...	4	...
Kentucky	Kentucky State Investment Commission	★	...	★	...	...	...	...	★	2	...
Louisiana	No Board	...	...	...	...	...	...	...	...	...	...
Maine	Trust Committee	...	...	★	...	...	★	...	★	...	(h)
Maryland	No Board	...	...	...	...	...	...	...	...	...	(h)
Massachusetts	Investment Advisory Council	...	...	★	...	...	...	...	...	2	(i)
Michigan	No Board	...	...	★	...	...	...	...	...	...	(a)
Minnesota	Minnesota State Board of Investment	★	...	...	★	...	★	★	...	...	...
Mississippi	No Board	...	...	...	...	...	...	...	...	...	...
Missouri	No Board	...	...	...	...	...	...	...	...	...	...
Montana	Montana Board of Investments	...	...	...	...	...	...	...	...	9	...
Nebraska	Nebraska Investment Council	...	...	★	...	...	...	...	...	5	(j)
Nevada	Board of Finance	★	...	★	...	★	...	...	...	2	...
New Hampshire	No Board	...	...	...	...	...	...	...	...	...	...
New Jersey	State Investment Council	...	...	★	...	...	...	...	...	6	(k)
New Mexico	Board of Finance	★	★	...	...	...	...	...	★	4 to 5	...
New York	No Board	...	...	...	...	...	...	...	...	...	(h)
North Carolina	No Board	...	...	...	...	...	...	...	...	...	(a)
North Dakota	State Investment Board	...	★	★	...	...	...	...	...	...	(l)
Ohio	No Board	...	...	...	...	...	...	...	...	...	...
Oklahoma	Cash Management and Investment Oversight Commission	...	...	...	...	...	...	...	★	1	(m)
Oregon	Oregon Investment Council	...	...	★	...	...	...	...	...	...	(j)
Pennsylvania	No Board	...	...	...	...	...	...	...	...	...	...
Rhode Island	State Investment Commission	...	...	★	...	...	...	...	...	3	...
South Carolina	No Board	...	...	...	...	...	...	...	...	...	...
South Dakota	South Dakota Investment Council	...	...	★	...	...	...	...	...	...	(n)
Tennessee	State Pooled Investment Fund	★	...	★	...	★	...	★	★	...	...
Texas	No Board	...	...	...	...	...	...	...	...	...	...
Utah	No Board	...	...	...	...	...	...	...	...	...	...
Vermont	No Board	...	...	...	...	...	...	...	...	...	(a)
Virginia	Commonwealth of Virginia Treasury Board	...	...	★	...	★	...	...	...	4	(o)
Washington	Office of the State Treasurer	...	...	★	...	...	...	...	...	...	...
West Virginia	West Virginia Investment Management Board	★	...	★	★	...	...	...	...	10	...
Wisconsin	State of Wisconsin Investment Board	...	...	...	...	...	...	...	...	5	...
Wyoming	Wyoming State Loan and Investment Board	★	...	★	★	...	...	★	...	...	(h)
Dist. of Columbia	No Board	...	...	...	...	...	...	...	...	...	(h)

See footnotes at end of table.

STATE INVESTMENT BOARD MEMBERSHIP — Continued

Source: National Association of State Treasurers, March 2008.

Key:

★ — Yes

. . . — No

(a) Treasurer/Commissioner is sole fiduciary.

(b) Director of the Department of Administration, State Banking Superintendent. Two individuals appointed by Treasurer.

(c) Bank Commissioner.

(d) Deputy Treasurer and a representative from the Land Board, Department of Labor. Three investment officers and nine public investment professionals from private sector.

(e) Secretary of Administration.

(f) Insurance Commissioner, Transportation Commissioner, Banking and Finance Commissioner, Revenue Commissioner.

(g) Deputy Treasurers and Chief Investment Officer.

(h) Commissioner of Education.

(i) Two Treasury appointees. Executive Director of both state and teacher's retirement system.

(j) Public Employees Retirement System Director.

(k) Five representatives of Pension Fund Boards.

(l) Commissioner of University and School Lands. Director of Workers' Compensation. Commissioner of Insurance.

(m) Senate appoint. President Pro Tempore appoint.

(n) Commissioners of School and Public Lands. State Retirement Director and five others appointed by state legislature.

(o) Tax Commissioner.

Accountability and Transparency: Finding the Correct Balance

By Thomas H. McTavish

In an age when information on just about anything is available with the click of a mouse, it is not surprising that governments are using technology to share financial data in the name of accountability and transparency. Accountability and transparency are essential components of what most would consider to be good government. But it also raises some questions. For instance, just because information can be made available, is it by default valuable or meaningful? Is data timeliness or accuracy more important? Can information shared by our governments for the sake of fiscal responsibility put us at risk? Transparency projects being implemented by the federal government and by states around the country are providing some answers to those questions.

As public and private financial systems and transactions have grown more and more complex over the past decade, the calls for increased accountability and transparency have also grown. This call is due, at least in part, to the monumental frauds enabled by complicated financial systems that can, in skilled hands, be manipulated for personal gain. The call may also be due to a culture in which information is readily accessible through countless databases, search engines, video clips and sound bytes.

Politicians and special interest groups, as well as the media and general public, are increasingly looking for accountability and transparency in government at all levels. Accountability is the state of being liable or the willingness to accept responsibility. At its most basic level, transparency simply means to make clear or visible. The principles upon which the United States government was formed included both accountability and transparency.

Fiscal transparency is of key importance if governments, at least in the United States, are truly to represent and serve citizens. That will require a certain amount of access to and disclosure of fiscal information. The International Monetary Fund defines fiscal transparency this way:

> Openness toward the public at large about government structure and functions, fiscal policy intentions, public sector accounts and projections. It involves ready access to reliable, comprehensive, timely, understandable and internationally comparable information on government activities so that the electorate and financial markets can accurately assess the government's financial position and the true costs and benefits of government activities, including their present and future economic and social implications.[1]

We expect clear rules and processes to be established, systems to be agreed upon and then implemented, oversight of the systems to be ensured and, finally, an accounting of what has occurred to be provided. As citizens, we also have responsibilities in this process—our task is to closely scrutinize our governments' fiscal activities and seek to ensure their continued integrity and progress.

A Push for More

Efforts to make government more accountable and transparent have paid off. Then-President George W. Bush signed the Federal Funding Accountability and Transparency Act into law on Sept. 26, 2006.[2] The law requires the development of a free and searchable database to provide information about federal grants and contract awards. The Web site *www.usaspending.gov*, which went live in December 2007, provides expenditure data on most federal awards and contracts of more than $25,000; ultimately, the site will be required to provide deeper levels of data all the way down to the sub-recipient award level.[3] But an effort to strengthen the law by the bill's original sponsors—Sens. Tom Coburn, Tom Carper and John McCain, along with President Barack Obama when he was still in the Senate—failed to pass. The proposed legislation, the Strengthening Transparency and Accountability in Federal Spending Act of 2008, would have greatly expanded the list of required elements to be reported on the Web site. Although that effort failed, the push for even more accountability and transparency in government spending is likely to surface again during the upcoming year, as fiscal accountability and transparency in government has been a focus for President Obama.

In addition to managing the transparency Web site, the U.S. Office of Management and Budget is also undertaking several other disclosure efforts. The agency's Office of Federal Financial Management is working to compile a database of all real property owned by the federal government, the Federal Real Property Database. The Office of Management and Budget also manages a searchable database of federal earmarks at *http://earmarks.omb.gov*.

The push for additional accountability and transparency has also reached state and local levels. Prior to the Federal Funding Accountability and Transparency Act, most states already had some sort of online disclosure system, most often related specifically to contracts, grants or employee salary data. Since the transparency act was enacted, officials in many states have followed the federal government in passing legislation to require more robust transparency initiatives. Virginia's Commonwealth Datapoint system was the first to provide detailed expenditure data. The system predated the federal act when it went live in November 2005. By mid-2007, states including Kansas, Minnesota, Oklahoma, Texas and Hawaii had signed into law initiatives mandating the creation of Web sites detailing state expenditure data. In several states, governors set forth this type of disclosure through executive order. Even some local governments are on board and are working to implement various types of disclosure databases.[4]

Logistics: Do the Benefits Outweigh the Costs?

A number of states have increased accountability and transparency in government and are sharing fiscal data with the public. As of July 2008, 14 states had passed transparency legislation and four states had issued executive orders mandating some sort of transparency initiative. Executive efforts toward increasing transparency are underway in seven other states, and local governments in at least seven states are embarking on their own initiatives. Additionally, many states have ongoing transparency legislation or efforts that were stalled in 2008.[5]

While many agree the pursuit of increased fiscal accountability and transparency in government is desirable, there are problems with implementing it. Opponents of some state initiatives contend that searchable databases of fiscal information are too costly to develop and maintain and that the costs may outweigh the benefits of the efforts, especially during years when states are facing huge budget shortfalls resulting from the economic downturn. Some even question the impetus for the databases, and states are debating whether additional transparency is needed as well as who will use the information. Some question whether the efforts are being undertaken in the spirit of public disclosure or whether the data will simply be used by private entities to gain a competitive advantage in gaining government contracts.

For those states that decide the effort to develop a transparency Web site is worthwhile, they must decide how to implement the site, who will manage and maintain the site, how the site will be funded, what data will be included and how private information will be protected.

The federal government's major transparency initiatives are spearheaded through the Office of Management and Budget. At the state level, and to some degree at the local level, however, there is little consistency to the logistics of the projects being either proposed or implemented. The mandate falls to the state comptroller in several states, to the state auditor or state treasurer in others, and to still other offices in the remaining states with initiatives. Transparency Web sites developed by states so far feature a potpourri of data including one or more of the following elements: grants, contracts, salaries, tax credits, expenditures, vendor data, geographic data and demographic data. Some states report expenditure data down to the voucher level, whereas most states only report expenditures above a certain dollar amount. Some sites contain years of data, while others contain considerably less. Some of the data is reported in real time, other data are static. The one area in which there is some consistency for states is funding: Most state auditors, comptrollers and treasurers tasked with implementing these transparency initiatives have had do so without additional funding.

Data Timeliness, Accuracy and Meaning

Timeliness of fiscal reports from governments has long been an issue. Is it more important to see timely information or more important to have audited data? In many cases, by the time audited reports are issued for public consumption, public interest has waned and the window of opportunity for any practical application of the information has passed. States have struggled for years to find a way to finish their comprehensive annual financial reports in a timely manner. For some states, issuing the financial reports within six months after the year-end close is a challenge.[6] To address the lag, several years ago many called for voluntary interim financial reporting by states, but that concept brought with it other complications, including the risk of issuing unaudited financial information. Some states decided the risk of liability for decisions based on unaudited data that could prove to be inaccurate was too great and chose not to issue voluntary interim financial information.

Other states lacked the resources to do ongoing interim reporting, and some questioned the demand for the interim reports.

The timeliness of transparency for expenditure data is often better. In most cases, information provided through state transparency initiatives is timely and, in many states, the data is real-time, being updated daily. Even the data that is more static in nature is certainly timelier than a state's six-month or older comprehensive annual financial report.

But should accuracy be sacrificed for timeliness? Data used in state comprehensive annual financial reports are carefully reviewed and audited prior to publication and distribution, but data linked to state transparency Web sites is typically unaudited, and its accuracy is by no means guaranteed. That could lead to liability problems for the state if inaccurate data on the transparency Web sites adversely affects the outcome of important decisions.

In addition to discussions about timeliness and accuracy, another question that arises is whether the raw data featured on state transparency sites has any real meaning for most citizens. Some would argue that without context or at least some assurance of reasonable accuracy, a piece of data is not worth all that much. States will have that information as they can analyze usage information, including who is accessing information on the site and how the information is being used.

Data Security

Increased automation and reliance on technology carry with them inherent risks—for individuals, for the private sector and ultimately for governments as well. Vast electronic stores of data open new challenges for protection from hackers and e-fraudsters, and data held by governmental entities is no exception.

In the past few decades, states have moved into the digital arena to meet the needs and expectations of a tech-savvy public. In fact, the transparency databases posted on Web sites around the country would not have been possible without a move by governments to embrace technology and its full potential. With that move came a huge responsibility and, now more than ever, state governments must be thorough and diligent in fulfilling the public trust of data protection.

Privacy: Is It Too Much to Expect?

Privacy is among the primary concerns about transparency databases. Officials need to decide the amount of information about a financial transaction by a government that can be shared. They also must consider whether providing the name of a person who received a payment from the state amounts to transparency or an infringement of the recipient's privacy.

Certain personal information, such as Social Security numbers and health care information, is protected by law. But other types of information made available through searches on transparency Web sites can lead to problems as well. In at least two instances, individuals were assaulted by former spouses who used one state's transparency site to find contact information. These are isolated incidents, but carried to an extreme, the ramifications are clear.

States are attempting to scrub data to remove protected and sensitive information, but issues of privacy likely will continue to be discussed as state transparency Web sites become more prevalent and more widely promoted and utilized.

Federal and State Initiatives: Putting the Puzzle Together

All these issues leave government officials with an accountability and transparency puzzle that needs to be pieced together. Though the federal government is moving forward with the requirements of the Federal Funding Accountability and Transparency Act, much work remains to accomplish the intent of the legislation. Further development of the transparency Web site is underway, including efforts to determine how information will be made available for federal awards down to the sub-recipient level. The pilot project to test how sub-recipient information is to be gathered and entered into the database did not begin until August 2008. The Office of Management and Budget is expected to request an 18-month delay in implementing the sub-recipient portion of the site—a delay the statute allows—in order to examine the results of the pilot and make any necessary adjustments.

Some states and local governments are also moving forward with their own transparency projects. Each project is different and includes different data sets managed and developed by different parties within each state. These efforts may someday work in concert to provide a comprehensive, easily understandable view of the fiscal integrity of state and federal governments. The federal transparency pilot database will at some point enter a phase that will look at how the state sites can interface with the federal database to ease state compliance with federal requirements. Even though the original Federal Funding Accountability and Transparency Act legislation has yet to be successfully implemented, legislation that surfaced last year to strengthen the requirements is likely to resurface, potentially requiring even more data about federal contracts and grants to be reported. This could place a tremendous burden upon states and local governments, and it would be necessary for them to find a way to report the required information.

Notes

[1] George Kopits and Jon Craig, *Transparency in Government Operations*, IMF Occasional Paper No. 158 (Washington: International Monetary Fund, 1998), 1.

[2] "President Bush Signs Federal Funding Accountability and Transparency Act," *www.whitehouse.gov*, September 26, 2006.

[3] *www.usaspending.gov*.

[4] *www.atr.org/state/projects/govtransparency.html*.

[5] *www.atr.org/state/projects/govtransparency.html*.

[6] "Time to Complete the States' CAFRs, Fiscal Years 2003, 2004, 2005, 2006, and 2007," a report by the National Association of State Comptrollers, *www.nasact.org/techupdates/downloads/CAFR_FY_03-07.pdf*.

About the Author

Thomas H. McTavish, CPA, is president of the National Association of State Auditors, Comptrollers and Treasurers. He has served as Michigan's auditor general since 1989. He is a retired captain, U.S. Naval Reserve. He is a graduate of The Pennsylvania State University. In addition to being a member of NASACT, he is also a member of various professional organizations, including the National State Auditors Association, of which he is a past president.

Table 4.28
THE STATE AUDITORS, 2009

State or other jurisdiction	State agency	Agency head	Title	Legal basis for office	Method of selection	Term of office	U.S. citizen	State resident	Maximum consecutive terms allowed
Alabama	Office of the Examiner of Public Accounts	Ronald L. Jones	Chief Examiner	S	LC	7 yrs.	★	. . .	None
Alaska	Office of the Legislative Auditor	Pat Davidson	Legislative Auditor	C, S	L	(a)	. . .	. . .	None
Arizona	Office of the Auditor General	Debra K. Davenport	Auditor General	S	LC	5 yrs.	. . .	. . .	None
Arkansas	Division of Legislative Audit	Roger A. Norman	Legislative Auditor	S	LC	Indefinite	. . .	. . .	N.A.
California	Bureau of State Audits	Elaine Howle	State Auditor	S	G	4 yrs.	★	. . .	None
Colorado	Office of the State Auditor	Sally Symanski	Colorado State Auditor	C,S	L	5 yrs.	★	★	None
Connecticut	Office of the Auditors of Public Accounts	Kevin P. Johnston, Robert G. Jaekle	State Auditors	C	L	4 yrs.	. . .	. . .	None
Delaware	Office of the Auditor of Accounts	R.Thomas Wagner, Jr.	Auditor of Accounts	C	E	4 yrs.	★	★	None
Florida	Office of the Auditor General	David Martin	Auditor General	C, S	L	(a)	. . .	. . .	None
Georgia	Department of Audits and Accounts	Russell W. Hinton	State Auditor	S	L	Indefinite	. . .	. . .	N.A.
Hawaii	Office of the Auditor	Marion M. Higa	State Auditor	C, S	L	8 yrs.	. . .	★	None
Idaho	Legislative Services Office—Legislative Audits	Don Berg	Division Manager	S	LC	Indefinite	. . .	. . .	None
Illinois	Office of the Auditor General	William G. Holland	Auditor General	C, S	L	10 yrs.	. . .	. . .	None
Indiana	State Board of Accounts	Bruce Hartman	State Examiner	S	G	4 yrs.	. . .	. . .	None
Iowa	Office of the Auditor of State	David A. Vaudt	Auditor of State	C, S	E	4 yrs.	★	★	None
Kansas	Legislative Division of Post Audit	Barbara J. Hinton	Legislative Post Auditor	S	LC	(b)	. . .	. . .	None
Kentucky	Office of the Auditor of Public Accounts	Crit Luallen	Auditor of Public Accounts	C, S	E	4 yrs.	★	★	2
Louisiana	Office of the Legislative Auditor	Steve J. Theriot	Legislative Auditor	C, S	L	Indefinite	. . .	. . .	N.A.
Maine	Department of Audit	Neria Douglass	State Auditor	S	L	4	★	★	2
Maryland	Office of Legislative Audits	Bruce A. Myers	Legislative Auditor	S	ED	Indefinite	. . .	. . .	None
Massachusetts	Office of the Auditor of the Commonwealth	A. Joseph DeNucci	Auditor of the Commonwealth	C, S	E	4 yrs.	★	★	None
Michigan	Office of the Auditor General	Thomas H. McTavish	Auditor General	C	L	8 yrs.	. . .	★	None
Minnesota	Office of the Legislative Auditor	James R. Nobles	Legislative Auditor	S	LC	6 yrs.	. . .	. . .	None
	Office of the State Auditor	Rebecca Otto	State Auditor	C	E	4 yrs.	★	★	None
Mississippi	Office of the State Auditor	Stacey E. Pickering	State Auditor	C, S	E	4 yrs.	★	★	None
Missouri	Office of the State Auditor	Susan Montee	State Auditor	C, S	E	4 yrs.	★	★	None
Montana	Legislative Audit Division	Tori Hunthausen	Legislative Auditor	C, S	LC	2 yrs.	. . .	. . .	None
Nebraska	Office of the Auditor of Public Accounts	Mike Foley	Auditor of Public Accounts	C, S	E	4 yrs.	★	★	None
Nevada	Legislative Council Bureau, Audit Division	Paul Townsend	Legislative Auditor	S	LC	Indefinite	. . .	. . .	N.A.
New Hampshire	Legislative Budget Office	Jeffry Pattison	Legislative Budget Assistant	S	LC	2 yrs.	. . .	. . .	None
New Jersey	Office of the State Auditor	Richard L. Fair	State Auditor	C, S	L	5 yr. term and until successor is appointed	. . .	. . .	N.A.
	Office of the State Comptroller	Matthew Boxer	State Comptroller						
New Mexico	Office of the State Auditor	Hector Balderas	State Auditor	C	E	4 yrs.	★	★	2
New York	Office of the State Comptroller, State Audit Bureau	Thomas P. DiNapoli	State Comptroller	C, S	E	4 yrs.	★	★	None

See footnotes at end of table.

THE STATE AUDITORS, 2009—Continued

State or other jurisdiction	State agency	Agency head	Title	Legal basis for office	Method of selection	Term of office	U.S. citizen	State resident	Maximum consecutive terms allowed
North Carolina	Office of the State Auditor	Beth Wood	State Auditor	C, S	E	4 yrs.	★	★	None
North Dakota	Office of the State Auditor	Robert R. Peterson	State Auditor	C, S	E	4 yrs.	★	★	None
Ohio	Office of the Auditor of State	Mary Taylor	Auditor of State	C	E	4 yrs.	★	★	2
Oklahoma	Office of the State Auditor and Inspector	Steve Burrage	State Auditor and Inspector	C, S	E	4 yrs.	★	★	None
Oregon	Secretary of State, Audits Division	Charles Hibner	Director	C	SS	(c)	. . .	. . .	N.A.
Pennsylvania	Department of the Auditor General	Jack Wagner	Auditor General	C	E	4 yrs.	. . .	. . .	2
	Legislative Finance and Budget Cmte.	Philip R. Durgin	Executive Director	S	LC	(b)	. . .	. . .	None
Rhode Island	Office of the Auditor General	Ernest A. Almonte	Auditor General	S	LC	(b)	. . .	. . .	None
South Carolina	Legislative Audit Council	George L. Schroeder	Director	S	LC	4 yrs.	. . .	. . .	None
	Office of the State Auditor	Richard Gilbert	State Auditor	S	SB	Indefinite	. . .	. . .	N.A.
South Dakota	Department of Legislative Audit	Martin L. Guindon	Auditor General	S	L	8 yrs.	. . .	. . .	None
Tennessee	Comptroller of the Treasury, Dept. of Audit	Justin Wilson	Comptroller of the Treasury	C, S	L	2 yrs.	. . .	. . .	None
Texas	Office of the State Auditor	John Keel	State Auditor	S	LC	(b)	★	★	None
Utah	Office of the State Auditor	Auston G. Johnson	State Auditor	C, S	E	4 yrs.	★	★	None
Vermont	Office of the State Auditor	Thomas M. Salmon	State Auditor	C, S	E	2 yrs.	★	★	None
Virginia	Office of the Auditor of Public Accounts	Walter J. Kucharski	Auditor of Public Accounts	C, S	L	4 yrs.	. . .	. . .	None
Washington	Office of the State Auditor	Brian Sonntag	State Auditor	C, S	E	4 yrs.	★	★	None
West Virginia	Office of the Legislative Auditor	Aaron Allred	Legislative Auditor	. . .	. . .				
Wisconsin	Legislative Audit Bureau	Janice Mueller	State Auditor	C, S	LC	(b)	. . .	. . .	None
Wyoming	Department of Audit	Michael Geesey	Director	S	GC	6 yrs.	. . .	. . .	None
Dist. Of Columbia	Office of the D.C. Auditor	Deborah Kay Nichols	District of Columbia Auditor						
Guam	Office of the Public Auditor	Doris Flores Brooks	Public Auditor	S	E	4 yrs.	★	★	None
No. Mariana Islands	Office of the Public Auditor	Michael S. Sablan	Public Auditor	C,S,	GL	6 yrs.	N.A.	N.A.	2
Puerto Rico	Office of the Comptroller of Puerto Rico	Manuel Diaz Saldaña	Comptroller of Puerto Rico	C	GL	10 yrs.	★	★	1

Sources: *Auditing in the States: A Summary*, 2006 and 2008 editions, The National Association of State Auditors, Comptrollers and Treasurers and state constitutions and statutes January 2009.

Key:

★ — Provision for.

. . . — No provision for

E — Elected by the public.

L — Appointed by the legislature.

G — Appointed by the governor.

SS — Appointed by the secretary of state.

LC — selected by legislative committee, commission or council.

ED — appointed by the executive director of legislative services

GC — Appointed by governor, secretary of state and treasurer.

GL — Appointed by the governor and confirmed by both chambers of the legislature

SB — Appointed by state budget and control board.

C — Constitutional

S — Statutory

N.A. — Not applicable.

(a) Serves at the pleasure of the legislature

(b) Serves at the pleasure of a legislative committee.

(c) Serves at the pleasure of the secretary of state.

Table 4.29
STATE AUDITORS: SCOPE OF AGENCY AUTHORITY

State or other jurisdiction	Authority to audit all state agencies	Authority to audit local governments	Authority to obtain information	Authority to issue subpoenas	Authority to specify accounting principles for local governments	Investigations: Agency investigates fraud, waste, abuse, and/or illegal acts	Investigations: Agency operates a hotline
Alabama	★	★	★	★	★(a)	★	. . .
Alaska	★	. . .	★	★	. . .	★	. . .
Arizona	★	★	★	. . .	★(b)	★	. . .
Arkansas	★	★	★	★	. . .	★	. . .
California	★	★	★	★	. . .	★	★
Colorado	★	★	★	★	★	★	. . .
Connecticut	★	. . .	★	. . .	. . .	★	★
Delaware	★	★	★	★	. . .	★	★
Florida	(c)	★	★	. . .	. . .	★	. . .
Georgia	★	★	★	★	★	★	. . .
Hawaii	(c)	★	★	★	. . .	★	. . .
Idaho	★	. . .	★	★	. . .	★	. . .
Illinois	★	★	★	★	. . .	★	. . .
Indiana	★	★	★	★	★	★	. . .
Iowa	★	★	★	★	. . .	★	. . .
Kansas	★	★	★	. . .	. . .	. . .	. . .
Kentucky	★	★	★	★	. . .	★	★
Louisiana	★	★	★	★(d)	. . .	★	. . .
Maine	★	. . .	★	(e)	. . .	★	. . .
Maryland	(c)	★(f)	★	★	. . .	★	★
Massachusetts	★	★	★	. . .	. . .	★	★
Michigan	★	. . .	★	★	. . .	★	. . .
Minnesota							
Legislative Auditor	★	. . .	★	★	. . .	★	. . .
State Auditor	(g)	★	★	★	★	★	. . .
Mississippi	★	★	★	. . .	★	★	★
Missouri	★	★(h)	★	★	. . .	★	★
Montana	★	. . .	★	. . .	. . .	★	★
Nebraska	★	★	N.A.	. . .	★(i)	★	★
Nevada	★	★	★	. . .	. . .	★	. . .
New Hampshire	★	. . .	★	. . .	. . .	. . .	. . .
New Jersey	★	★	★	. . .	. . .	★	. . .
New Mexico	(j)	★	★	. . .	. . .	★	. . .
New York	★	★	★	★	★	★	★
North Carolina	★	. . .	★	★	. . .	★	★
North Dakota	(k)	★	★	. . .	★	★	. . .
Ohio	★	★	★	★	★	★	★
Oklahoma	★	★	★	★	. . .	★	. . .
Oregon	★	. . .	★	★	★	★	★
Pennsylvania							
Auditor General	(l)	★	★	★	. . .	★	★
Rhode Island	★	. . .	★	★	★	★	. . .
South Carolina							
Legislative Audit Council	★	. . .	★	. . .	. . .	★	. . .
State Auditor	(m)	. . .	★	. . .	. . .	★	. . .
South Dakota	★	★	★	★	★	★	. . .
Tennessee	★	★	★	★	★	★	★
Texas	★	★	★	★	★(n)	★	★
Utah							
State Auditor	(o)	. . .	★	★	★	★	★
Vermont	★	★	★	★	★(p)	★	. . .
Virginia	★	. . .	★	. . .	★	★	. . .
Washington	★	★	★	★	★	★	. . .
West Virginia	N.A.	N.A.	N.A.	N.A.	N.A.	N.A.	N.A.
Wisconsin	★	. . .	★	★	. . .	★	. . .
Wyoming	★	★	★	★	. . .	★	. . .
Guam	. . .	★	★	★	★	★	★
No. Mariana Islands	★	N.A.	★	★	★	★	N.A.
Puerto Rico	★	★	★	★	★	★	★

See footnotes at end of table.

STATE AUDITORS: SCOPE OF AGENCY AUTHORITY — Continued

Source: *Auditing in the States*, 2006 Edition, The National Association of State Auditors, Comptrollers and Treasurers. Local government information updated December 2008.

Key:

★ — Provision for responsibility.

. . . — No provision for responsibility.

N.A. — Not available.

(a) Municipalities not covered.

(b) Except for cities and towns, and certain special taxing districts.

(c) The legislature or legislative branch is excluded from audit authority.

(d) Only through oversight council.

(e) Municipalities only.

(f) Local school systems.

(g) State agencies are audited by the Office of Legislative Auditor.

(h) Has audit authority for counties that do not elect a county auditor and other political subdivisions upon petition by the voters of those subdivisions.

(i) Only counties.

(j) The Gaming Commission, Mortgage Finance Authority, State Lottery Commission, Student Loan Guarantee Corporation are excluded from audit authority.

(k) The Bank of North Dakota, State Fair Association, and a few others are excluded from audit authority.

(l)The legislative and judicial branches are excluded from audit authority.

(m) State Ports Authority, State Public Service Authority, Research Authority are excluded from audit authority.

(n) Comptroller prescribes guidelines but the State Auditor's Office has responsibility to review and comment.

(o) State Retirement and Worker's Compensation Fund are excluded from audit authority.

(p) Required for county sheriff's departments and at the request of town governments.

Table 4.30
STATE AUDITORS: TYPES OF AUDITS

State or other jurisdiction	Financial statement	Single audit	Attestation engagements	Compliance only	Economy and efficiency	Program	Sunset	Performance measures	IT	Accounting and review services	Other audits
Alabama	★	★	. . .	. . .	. . .	. . .	. . .	. . .	. . .	. . .	. . .
Alaska	★	★	★	★	★	★	★	★	★	. . .	. . .
Arizona	★	★	. . .	. . .	★	★	★	. . .	★	. . .	(a)
Arkansas	★	★	. . .	. . .	. . .	★	. . .	. . .	★	. . .	(b)
California	★	★	. . .	★	★	★	. . .	★	★	. . .	(c)
Colorado	★	★	. . .	. . .	. . .	★	. . .	★	★	. . .	. . .
Connecticut	★	★	. . .	★	★	★	. . .	★	★	. . .	(d)
Delaware	★	★	★	★	★	★	. . .	★	★	★	. . .
Florida	★	★	★	★	★	. . .	★	. . .	★	. . .	. . .
Georgia	★	★	★	★	★	★	★	. . .	★	★	(e)
Hawaii	. . .	. . .	. . .	. . .	★	★	★	★	★	. . .	(f)
Idaho	★	★	. . .	★	★	. . .	. . .	. . .	★	. . .	(g)
Illinois	★	★	★	★	★	★	★	. . .	★	. . .	(d)
Indiana	★	★	★	★	. . .	. . .	. . .	. . .	★	. . .	. . .
Iowa	★	★	★	. . .	★	★	. . .	. . .	★	. . .	. . .
Kansas	★	★	. . .	★	★	★	. . .	. . .	★	. . .	. . .
Kentucky	★	★	★	★	★	★	. . .	★	★	★	. . .
Louisiana	★	★	★	★	★	★	★	★	★	. . .	. . .
Maine	★	★	★	. . .	. . .	★	. . .	. . .	. . .	. . .	. . .
Maryland	. . .	. . .	. . .	★	★	★	. . .	★	★	. . .	(h)
Massachusetts	★	★	★	★	★	★	★	★	★	★	(i)
Michigan	★	★	★	. . .	★	★	. . .	★	★	. . .	. . .
Minnesota											
Legislative Auditor	★	★	. . .	. . .	. . .	★	. . .	. . .	★	. . .	(j)
State Auditor	★	★	. . .	. . .	. . .	. . .	. . .	. . .	. . .	. . .	(d)
Mississippi	★	★	. . .	★	. . .	. . .	. . .	. . .	. . .	. . .	(k)
Missouri	★	★	. . .	★	★	★	. . .	. . .	★	. . .	. . .
Montana	★	★	★	★	★	★	. . .	★	★	. . .	. . .
Nebraska	★	★	★	★	. . .	★	. . .	. . .	★	★	. . .
Nevada	. . .	. . .	. . .	★	★	★	. . .	★	★	. . .	. . .
New Hampshire	★	. . .	. . .	. . .	★	. . .	. . .	★	. . .	. . .	. . .
New Jersey	★	★	. . .	★	★	. . .	. . .	. . .	★	. . .	. . .
New Mexico	★	★	. . .	. . .	. . .	. . .	. . .	. . .	★	. . .	. . .
New York	★	. . .	★	★	★	★	. . .	★	★	. . .	(l)
North Carolina	★	★	. . .	. . .	★	★	. . .	. . .	★	. . .	(m)
North Dakota	★	★	. . .	. . .	★	. . .	. . .	. . .	★	. . .	. . .
Ohio	★	★	★	★	★	. . .	. . .	★	★	★	. . .

See footnotes at end of table.

STATE AUDITORS: TYPES OF AUDITS — Continued

State or other jurisdiction	Financial statement	Single audit	Attestation engagements	Compliance only	Economy and efficiency	Program	Sunset	Performance measures	IT	Accounting and review services	Other audits
Oklahoma	★	★	★	. . .	★	★	. . .	. . .	★	. . .	. . .
Oregon	★	★	★	★	★	★	. . .	. . .	★	★	(n)
Pennsylvania											
Auditor General	★	★	★	★	★	★	. . .	★	★	. . .	(o)
Legislative Budget and Finance Cmte.	. . .	. . .	. . .	. . .	★	★	. . .	. . .	. . .	. . .	. . .
Rhode Island	★	★	★	★	. . .	. . .	. . .	. . .	★	. . .	. . .
South Carolina											
Legislative Audit Council	. . .	. . .	. . .	. . .	★	★	. . .	. . .	. . .	. . .	. . .
State Auditor	★	★	★	. . .	. . .	. . .	. . .	. . .	. . .	. . .	. . .
South Dakota	★	★	★	. . .	. . .	. . .	. . .	. . .	. . .	★	. . .
Tennessee	★	★	★	★	★	★	★	★	★	. . .	(p)
Texas	★	★	★	★	★	★	. . .	★	★	. . .	(q)
Utah											
Legislative Auditor	. . .	. . .	. . .	. . .	★	★	★	★	. . .	. . .	. . .
State Auditor	★	★	★	. . .	★	. . .	. . .	. . .	. . .	. . .	(r)
Vermont	★	★	★	★	★	★	. . .	★	★	★	. . .
Virginia	★	★	★	. . .	. . .	. . .	. . .	★	★	. . .	. . .
Washington	★	★	★	★	. . .	★	. . .	★	★	. . .	. . .
West Virginia	N.A.	N.A.	N.A.	N.A.	N.A.	N.A.	N.A.	N.A.	N.A.	N.A.	N.A.
Wisconsin	★	★	. . .	★	★	★	. . .	. . .	. . .	. . .	. . .
Wyoming	. . .	. . .	. . .	★	. . .	. . .	. . .	★	. . .	. . .	. . .
Guam	. . .	★	. . .	. . .	★	★	. . .	. . .	. . .	. . .	(c)
No. Mariana Islands	★	★	★	. . .	★	★	. . .	. . .	. . .	★	. . .
Puerto Rico	. . .	. . .	. . .	★	★	. . .	. . .	. . .	★	. . .	. . .

Sources: *Auditing in the States: A Summary*, 2006 edition. The National Association of State Auditors, Comptrollers and Treasurers and state constitutions and statutes. Updated January 2008.

Note: Government audits are divided into two types, financial and performance audits. Financial audits include financial statement audits and financial related audits. Performance audits include economy and efficiency audits and program audits. In addition, government auditors perform a number of other audit-related functions that do not fall into one of these categories. State audit agencies must make certain that audit coverage is broad enough to fulfill the needs of potential audit report users.

Key:

★ — Provision for responsibility.

. . . — No provision for responsibility.

N.A.— Not available.

(a) Fraud, special audits, studies, and program evaluations.

(b) Internal control and compliance reviews.

(c) Investigations.

(d) Agreed upon procedures.

(e) Financial related audits, desk reviews.

(f) Mandatory health insurance analyses, financial-related audits.

(g) Federal grant audits.

(h) Special requests and follow-up reviews.

(i) Referrals.

(j) Investigation.

(k) Performance reviews.

(l) Internal control reviews: studies.

(m) Fraud and abuse investigations, internal control audits.

(n) Investigations (reviews).

(o) Informational reports, including referrals or investigation of fraud.

(p) Special investigations.

(q) Special investigative audits, classification audits, internal controls review, training and other educational services.

(r) Special projects, consulting, feasibility studies.

Table 4.31
THE STATE COMPTROLLERS, 2009

State	Agency or office	Name	Title	Legal basis for office	Method of selection	Approval or confirmation, if necessary	Date of first service	Present term ends	Consecutive time in office	Length of term	Elected comptroller's maximum consecutive terms	Civil service or merit system employee
Alabama	Office of the State Comptroller	Robert L. Childree	State Comptroller	S	(c)	AG	5/1987	(b)	21 yrs.	(b)	. . .	★
Alaska	Division of Finance	Kim J. Garnero	Director of Finance	S	(d)	AG	8/1999	(a)	8 yrs.	(a)	. . .	. . .
Arizona	Financial Services Division	D. Clark Partridge	State Comptroller	S	(d)	AG	4/2002	. . .	5 yrs.	. . .	. . .	. . .
Arkansas	Dept. of Finance and Administration	Richard A. Weiss	Director	S	G	. . .	5/2002	(a)	5.5 yrs.	(a)	. . .	. . .
California	Office of the State Controller	John Chiang (D)	State Controller	C	E	. . .	1/2007	1/2011	2 yrs.	4 yrs.	2 terms	. . .
Colorado	Office of the State Controller	David J. McDermott	State Controller	S	(d)	. . .	7/2008	(b)	0.5 yr.	(b)	. . .	★
Connecticut	Office of the Comptroller	Nancy Wyman (D)	Comptroller	C	E	. . .	1/1995	1/2011	13 yrs.	4 yrs.	unlimited	. . .
Delaware	Dept. of Finance	Gary M. Pfeiffer	Secretary of Finance	C,S	G	AS	2/2009	(a)	1 mo.	(a)	. . .	. . .
Florida	Dept. of Financial Services	Alex Sink (D)	Chief Financial Officer	C	E	. . .	1/2007	1/2011	2 yrs.	4 yrs.	2 terms	. . .
Georgia (l)	State Accounting Office	Greg S. Griffin	State Accounting Officer	S	G	. . .	8/2008	(a)	0.5 yr.	(a)	. . .	. . .
Hawaii	Dept. of Accounting and General Services	Russ K. Satio	State Comptroller	S	G	AS	12/2002	12/2010	7 yrs.	(a)	. . .	. . .
Idaho	Office of State Controller	Donna Jones (R)	State Controller	C,S	E	. . .	1/2007	1/2011	2 yrs.	4 yrs.	2 terms	★
Illinois	Office of the State Comptroller	Daniel W. Hynes (D)	State Comptroller	C	E	. . .	11/1999	1/2011	9 yrs.	4 yrs.	unlimited	. . .
Indiana	Office of the Auditor of State	Tim Berry (R)	Auditor of State	C	E	. . .	1/2007	1/2011	2 yrs.	4 yrs.	2 terms	. . .
Iowa	State Accounting Enterprise	Calvin McKelvogue	Chief Operating Officer	S	G	AS	5/2004	N.A.	4 yrs.	(a)	. . .	. . .
Kansas	Division of Accounts and Reports	Kent Olson	Director	S	(d)	. . .	6/2007	(b)	1.5 yr.	(b)	. . .	★
Kentucky	Office of the Controller	Edgar C. Ross	Controller	S	(f)	AG	6/1975	N.A.	33 yrs.	(i)	. . .	. . .
Louisiana	Division of Administration	Afranie Adomako	Director	S	G	. . .	4/2008	. . .	1 yr.	. . .	. . .	Exempt
Maine	Office of the State Controller	Edward Karass	State Controller	S	(f)	AG	3/2003	(i)	6 yrs.	(i)	. . .	. . .
Maryland	Office of the Comptroller of the Treasury	Peter Franchot (D)	State Comptroller	C,S	E	. . .	1/2007	1/2011	2 yrs.	4 yrs.	unlimited	. . .
Massachusetts	Office of the Comptroller	Martin J. Benison	State Comptroller	S	G	. . .	1/1999	(j)	9 yrs.	(j)	unlimited	. . .
Michigan	Office of Financial Management	Michael J. Moody	Director	S	SBD	SBD	8/2002	8/2008	5 yrs.	(k)	. . .	★
Minnesota	Department of Finance	Tom J. Hanson	Commissioner	S	G	AS	12/2006	1/2011	2 yrs.	(a)	. . .	. . .
Mississippi	Department of Finance and Administration	Kevin Upchurch	Executive Director	S	G	AS	1/2009	N.A.	1 mo.	(a)	. . .	. . .
Missouri	Division of Accounting	Mark A. Kaiser	Director of Accounting	C,S	(d)	. . .	1/2009	(g)	1 mo.	(g)	. . .	. . .
Montana	State Accounting Division	Paul Christofferson	Administrator	S	(m)	. . .	6/2004	(b)	4 yrs.	(b)	. . .	★
Nebraska	Accounting Division	Paul Carlson	State Accounting Administrator	S	(d)	. . .	11/2000	(g)	7 yrs.	(g)	. . .	. . .
Nevada	Office of the State Controller	Kim Wallin (D)	State Controller	C	E	. . .	1/2007	1/2011	2 yrs.	4 yrs.	2 terms	. . .
New Hampshire	Division of Accounting Services	Steven Smith	Acting Comptroller	S	G	. . .	N.A.	N.A.	N.A.	4 yrs.	. . .	. . .
New Jersey	Office of Management and Budget	Charlene M. Holzbaur	Director	S	G	AS	12/1999	(b)	9 yrs.	(b)	. . .	. . .
New Mexico	Department of Finance and Administration, Financial Control Division	Anthony I. Armijo	State Controller and Director	S	G	. . .	1/1991	N.A.	17 yrs.	(a)	. . .	★
New York	Office of the State Comptroller	Thomas P. DiNapoli	State Comptroller	C,S	E	. . .	1/2007	12/2010	2 yrs.	4 yrs.	unlimited	. . .
North Carolina	Office of the State Controller	David McCoy	State Controller	S	G	GA	8/2008	7/2013	0.5 yr.	7 yrs.	. . .	. . .
North Dakota	Office of Management and Budget	Pam Sharp	Director	S	G	. . .	1/2003	(a)	5 yrs.	(a)	. . .	. . .
Ohio	Office of Budget and Management	J. Pari Sabety	Director	S	G	AS	1/2007	(a)	2 yrs.	(a)	. . .	. . .

See footnotes at end of table.

THE STATE COMPTROLLERS, 2009—Continued

State	Agency or office	Name	Title	Legal basis for office	Method of selection	Approval or confirmation, if necessary	Date of first service	Present term ends	Consecutive time in office	Length of term	Elected comptroller's maximum consecutive terms	Civil service or merit system employee
Oklahoma	Office of State Finance	Brenda Bolander	State Comptroller	S	(e)	. . .	10/2001	(b)	7 yrs.	(h)	. . .	. . .
Oregon	State Controller's Division	John J. Radford	State Controller	S	(d)	AG	11/1989	(b)	18 yrs.	(g)	. . .	. . .
Pennsylvania	Comptroller Operations	Anna Maria Kiehl	Chief Accounting Officer	S	G	. . .	12/2007	(b)	2 yrs.	(a)	. . .	. . .
Rhode Island	Office of Accounts and Control	Lawrence C. Franklin Jr.	State Controller	S	CS	. . .	8/1986	N.A.	21 yrs.	(b)	. . .	★
South Carolina	Office of the Comptroller General	Richard Eckstrom (R)	Comptroller General	C,S	E	. . .	1/2003	1/2011	5 yrs.	4 yrs.	unlimited	. . .
South Dakota	Office of the State Auditor	Richard L. Sattgast (R)	State Auditor	C	E	. . .	1/2003	1/2011	5 yrs.	4 yrs.	2 terms	. . .
Tennessee	Division of Accounts	Jan I. Sylvis	Chief of Accounts	C,S	(f)	. . .	12/1995	N.A.	12 yrs	(b)	. . .	. . .
Texas	Office of the Comptroller of Public Accounts	Susan Combs (R)	Comptroller of Public Accounts	C,S	E	. . .	1/2007	1/2011	2 yrs.	4 yrs.	unlimited	. . .
Utah	Division of Finance	John Reidhead	Director	S	(d)	AG	9/2005	N.A.	3 yrs.	(g)	. . .	★
Vermont	Department of Finance and Management	James Reardon	Commissioner	S	G	AS	2/2005	N.A.	3 yrs.	(a)	. . .	. . .
Virginia	Department of Accounts	David A. Von Moll	State Comptroller	S	G	GA	11/2001	N.A.	7 yrs.	(a)	. . .	★
Washington	Office of Financial Management	Sadie Rodriguez-Hawkins	Senior Assistant Director	N.A.	N.A.	N.A.	N.A.	N.A.	N.A.	N.A.	N.A.	N.A.
West Virginia	Office of the State Auditor	Glen B. Gainier III (D)	State Auditor	C,S	E	. . .	1/1993	1/2012	15 yrs.	4 yrs.	unlimited	. . .
	Finance Division, Office of the State Comptroller	Ross Taylor	State Comptroller and Finance Director	S	(d)	AG	10/2005	N.A.	3 yrs	(g)	. . .	. . .
Wisconsin	State Controller's Office	Steve Censky	State Controller	S	CS	. . .	9/2007	N.A.	1.5 yrs	(b)	. . .	★
Wyoming	Office of the State Auditor	Rita Meyer (R)	State Auditor	C,S	E	. . .	1/2007	1/2011	2 yrs.	4 yrs.	2 terms	. . .

Sources: *Comptrollers: Technical Activities and Functions*, 2006 and 2008 editions, National Association of State Auditors, Comptrollers and Treasurers. Updated March 2009.

Key:

. . . — No provision for.
C — Constitutional
S — Statutory
E — Elected by the public.
G — Appointed by the Governor.
CS — Civil Service.
AG — Approved by the governor.
AS — Approved/confirmed by the Senate.
SBD — Approved by State Budget Director.
GA — Confirmed by the General Assembly.
SDB — Confirmed by State Depository Board.
(a) Serves at the pleasure of the governor.
(b) Indefinite.
(c) Appointed by the Director of the Dept. of Finance (merit system position).
(d) Appointed by the head of the department of administration or administrative services.
(e) Appointed by the head of finance. department or agency.
(f) Appointed by the head of financial and administrative services.
(g) Serves at the pleasure of the head of the department of administration or administrative services.
(h) Serves at the pleasure of the head of the finance department or agency.
(i) Serves at the pleasure of the head of the financial and administrative services.
(j) Appointed by the governor for a term coterminous with the governor.
(k) Two-year renewable contractual term; classified executive service.
(l) As of July 1, 2005, the responsibility for accounting and financial reporting in Georgia was transferred to the newly-created State Accounting Office.
(m) Classified position.

Table 4.32
STATE COMPTROLLERS: QUALIFICATIONS FOR OFFICE

State	Minimum age	U.S. citizen (years)	State resident (years) (b)	Education years or degree	Professional experience and years	Professional certification and years	Other qualifications	No specific qualifications for office
Alabama	★	★	★	★, B.S.	★, 6 yrs.	. . .	. . .	. . .
Alaska	. . .	. . .	. . .	. . .	. . .	. . .	. . .	★
Arizona	. . .	★, 1 yr.	★, 1 yr.	★, B.S.	★, 7-10 yrs.	★(a)	. . .	. . .
Arkansas	30	. . .	. . .	. . .	★	. . .	. . .	. . .
California	★	. . .	. . .	. . .	. . .	. . .	(b)	. . .
Colorado	. . .	. . .	★	★(i)	★ 6,yrs.	★, CPA	. . .	. . .
Connecticut	. . .	. . .	★	. . .	. . .	. . .	. . .	. . .
Delaware	. . .	. . .	. . .	. . .	. . .	. . .	. . .	★
Florida	★	. . .	★, 7 yrs.	. . .	. . .	. . .	. . .	. . .
Georgia	. . .	. . .	. . .	. . .	. . .	. . .	. . .	★
Hawaii	. . .	. . .	. . .	. . .	. . .	. . .	. . .	★
Idaho	★	★(j)	★, 2 yrs.	. . .	. . .	. . .	. . .	. . .
Illinois	25	★	★, 3 yrs.	. . .	. . .	. . .	. . .	. . .
Indiana	. . .	. . .	★(j)	. . .	. . .	. . .	. . .	. . .
Iowa	. . .	. . .	. . .	. . .	. . .	. . .	. . .	★
Kansas	. . .	. . .	. . .	. . .	. . .	. . .	. . .	★
Kentucky	. . .	. . .	. . .	. . .	. . .	. . .	(c)	★
Louisiana	. . .	. . .	. . .	. . .	. . .	. . .	. . .	★
Maine	. . .	. . .	. . .	. . .	. . .	. . .	(d)	★
Maryland	18	★	★	. . .	. . .	. . .	. . .	. . .
Massachusetts	. . .	. . .	. . .	★(k)	★, 7 yrs.	. . .	. . .	. . .
Michigan	. . .	. . .	. . .	★(l)	★, 5 yrs.	(l)	(l)	. . .
Minnesota	. . .	. . .	. . .	. . .	. . .	. . .	. . .	★
Mississippi	. . .	. . .	. . .	★(k)	★, 10 yrs.	★, CPA	(e)	. . .
Missouri	. . .	. . .	. . .	. . .	. . .	. . .	. . .	★
Montana	. . .	. . .	. . .	★(p)	★, 5 yrs.	★, CPA	. . .	★
Nebraska	. . .	. . .	. . .	★(m)	★(n)	★, CPA	. . .	. . .
Nevada	25	★	★	. . .	. . .	. . .	. . .	. . .
New Hampshire	. . .	. . .	. . .	. . .	. . .	. . .	(f)	★
New Jersey	. . .	. . .	. . .	. . .	. . .	. . .	. . .	★
New Mexico	30	★	5	N.A.	N.A.	N.A.	N.A.	N.A.
New York	★	★	★, 5 yrs.	. . .	. . .	. . .	. . .	. . .
North Carolina	. . .	. . .	. . .	★	★	. . .	(g)	. . .
North Dakota	. . .	. . .	. . .	. . .	. . .	. . .	. . .	★
Ohio	. . .	. . .	. . .	. . .	. . .	. . .	. . .	. . .
Oklahoma	. . .	★	★	★(q)	★, 5 yrs.	. . .	. . .	★
Oregon	. . .	. . .	. . .	. . .	. . .	. . .	. . .	★
Pennsylvania	. . .	. . .	. . .	. . .	. . .	. . .	. . .	★
Rhode Island	. . .	★	★	★(h)	★, 5 yrs.	★, CPA	. . .	. . .
South Carolina	18	★	★	. . .	. . .	. . .	. . .	. . .
South Dakota	★	★	★, 1 yr.	. . .	. . .	. . .	. . .	. . .
Tennessee	. . .	. . .	. . .	★	★, 7 yrs.	★, CPA	. . .	. . .
Texas	18	★(j)	★, 1 yr.	. . .	. . .	. . .	. . .	. . .
Utah	. . .	. . .	. . .	★	★, 6 yrs.	★, CPA	. . .	. . .
Vermont	. . .	. . .	. . .	. . .	. . .	. . .	. . .	★
Virginia	. . .	. . .	. . .	. . .	. . .	. . .	. . .	★
Washington	★	★, Whole life	★	★(o)	★	★, J.D.	. . .	. . .
West Virginia-								
Office of State Auditor	. . .	★	★	. . .	. . .	. . .	. . .	. . .
Division of Finance, Office of State Comptroller	. . .	★	★	★, B.S.B.A.	★, 7 yrs.	. . .	. . .	. . .
Wisconsin	. . .	. . .	. . .	★(p)	. . .	★, CPA	. . .	. . .
Wyoming	★	★	★	. . .	. . .	. . .	. . .	. . .

Sources: *Comptrollers: Technical Activities and Functions*, 2006 Edition, The National Association of State Auditors, Comptrollers and Treasurers. Updated January 2008.

Key:

★ — Formal provision.

. . . — No formal provision.

N.A. — Not applicable.

(a) Any of those mentioned or CFE, CPM, etc

(b) 18 yrs. At time of election or appointment and a citizen of the state.

(c) The Kentucky Revised Statutes state that "The state controller shall be a person qualified by education and experience for the position and held in high esteem in the accounting community."

(d) There are no educational or professional mandates, yet the appointed official is generally qualified by a combination of experience and education.

(e) At least 5 yrs. experience in high level management.

(f) Education and relevant experience.

(g) Qualified by education and experience for the position.

(h) Master's degree in accounting, finance or business management or public administration.

(i) 5 yrs. or college degree.

(j) Years not specified.

(k) Master's degree.

(l) Bachelor's degree no professional certification required, but CPA certification is considered desirable. Financial management experience, knowledge of GAAP and good communication skills are other qualifications.

(m) 4 yrs. with major in accounting.

(n) 3 yrs. directing the work of others.

(o) 7 yrs. and law degree.

(p) Bachelor's degree in accounting.

(q) Bachelor's degree.

Table 4.33
STATE COMPTROLLERS: DUTIES AND RESPONSIBILITIES

State	Comprehensive annual financial report (CAFR)	Disbursement of state funds	Payroll processing	Pre-auditing of payments	Post-audit	Operation of statewide financial management system	Management of state travel policies
Alabama	★	★	★	★	. . .	★	★
Alaska	★	★	★	. . .	. . .	★	★
Arizona	★	★	★	★	★	★	★
Arkansas	★	★	★	★	. . .	. . .	. . .
California	★	★	★	★	★	★	. . .
Colorado	★	★	★	★	★	★	. . .
Connecticut	★	. . .	★	. . .	★	. . .	. . .
Delaware	★	★	★	★	★	★	★
Florida	★	★	★	★	★	★	★
Georgia	★	★	★	. . .	. . .	★	★
Hawaii	★	★	★	★	★	★	★
Idaho	★	★	★	. . .	. . .	★	. . .
Illinois	★	★	★	★	★	★	. . .
Indiana	★	★	★	★	. . .	★	. . .
Iowa	★	★	★	★	★	★	★
Kansas	★	★	★	★	★	★	★
Kentucky	★	★	. . .	★	. . .	★	★
Louisiana	★	★	★	★	★	★	. . .
Maine	★	★	★	★	★	★	★
Maryland	★	★	★	★	★	★	. . .
Massachusetts	★	★	★	★	★	★	. . .
Michigan	★	. . .	★	. . .	. . .	★	. . .
Minnesota	★	★	★	. . .	. . .	★	. . .
Mississippi	★	★	★	★	. . .	★	★
Missouri	★	★	★	. . .	. . .	★	★
Montana	★	★	. . .	. . .	. . .	★	★
Nebraska	★	★	★	★	. . .	★	★
Nevada	★	★	★	. . .	. . .	★	. . .
New Hampshire	★	. . .	★	★	. . .	★	. . .
New Jersey	★	★	★	. . .	★	★	★
New Mexico	★	★	★	★	★	★	★
New York	★	★	★	★	★	. . .	★
North Carolina	★	★	★	★	★	★	. . .
North Dakota	★	★	★	. . .	. . .	★	★
Ohio	★	★	. . .	★	. . .	★	★
Oklahoma	★	★	★	. . .	. . .	★	★
Oregon	★	. . .	★	. . .	. . .	★	★
Pennsylvania	★	★	★	★	★	★	★
Rhode Island	★	★	★	★	. . .	★	★
South Carolina	★	★	★	★	. . .	★	★
South Dakota	★	★	★	★	. . .	. . .	. . .
Tennessee	★	★	★	★	★	★	★
Texas	★	★	★	. . .	★	★	. . .
Utah	★	★	★	. . .	★	★	★
Vermont	★	★	. . .	. . .	★	★	★
Virginia	★	★	★	★	★	★	★
Washington	★	. . .	. . .	. . .	. . .	★	★
West Virginia							
Office of State Auditor	. . .	★	★	★	. . .	. . .	. . .
Division of Finance, Office of State Comptroller	★	. . .	. . .	★	. . .	★	★
Wisconsin	★	★	★	. . .	★	★	★
Wyoming	★	. . .	★	★	★	★	★

Sources: *Comptrollers: Technical Activities and Functions*, 2006 Edition, The National Association of State Auditors, Comptrollers and Treasurers 2006. Updated January 2008.

Key:

★ — Formal provision.

. . . — No formal provision.

Chapter Five

STATE JUDICIAL BRANCH

Decimated Budgets, Judges as Conveners, and Bloody Judicial Elections: The State Courts in 2008

By David Rottman

Budget crises associated with the general economic downturn overshadowed other issues confronting the state courts. Judicial branches developed objective measures of their efficiency, accessibility, and fairness to demonstrate their accountability for how public funds are spent. Courts also helped lead interbranch efforts to confront problems like mortgage foreclosures and child abuse and neglect.

State judiciaries, like the other branches of government, scrambled to adjust to declining state revenues while maintaining their core functions. Budgetary woes in some states created flashpoints between the judiciary and other branches. Hard times also accelerated a positive trend toward creative partnerships among the branches to address problems in policy areas related to the administration of justice. The unique capacity of judges to serve as conveners for such efforts became a sought after commodity. Another round of judicial elections and a new U. S. Supreme Court case highlighted the continuation of heavily politicized, interest group-laden races for an office charged with administering fair and impartial justice.

State Court Budgets

"Our budgets are being decimated, even as we know that in times of economic stress, people turn in even greater numbers to their state courts for relief," was one chief justice's summary of 2008.[1] At least 20 states cut judicial budgets during the year.[2] As 2008 progressed, the practical consequences of such cutbacks on the public became clear. New Hampshire halted all civil and criminal trials for a month to save the expense of giving per diem payments to jurors. The costs, however, are merely deferred as trials are only rescheduled, not dismissed.[3] Florida's courts experienced two rounds of budget cuts that forced the firing of hundreds of clerks and legal staff amid warnings that additional budget cuts could virtually suspend processing civil cases.[4] Vermont's chief justice proposed closing seven county courts and laying off employees to help ease the budget crisis his court system faced.[5]

The negative effects associated with court budget cutbacks are not limited to citizens and businesses who need access to the courts. There is evidence that the harmful effects are felt throughout the legal process statewide. A study in Florida quantified the costs incurred because of increased delays in processing civil cases. Longer delays impose additional costs on businesses seeking to resolve issues quickly without using the courts and create lost opportunities for businesses and individuals as they await the outcome of their cases. The study estimates the cost to the state of Florida's backlogs is $17.4 billion per year.[6]

Draconian budget cuts imposed on other parts of the justice system also hindered the fair and timely disposition of criminal civil cases. Notably, in many states the budgets of both public defenders and prosecutors were severely cut. Late in 2008, public defenders' offices in at least seven states were refusing to take on new cases—or filed lawsuits to limit their numbers—because they were unable to provide adequate legal representation. In a Florida court, the caseload per public defender grew from 1,380 cases to 2,225 cases over a three-year period.[7] The Constitution guarantees the right to counsel in most serious cases and the state must provide legal representation through its indigent defense system if a defendant is unable to afford it. Prosecutors' offices were similarly affected, requiring cuts that included "treating drug-related felony crimes as misdemeanors, dismantling specialty units to prosecute domestic violence and child abuse, and placing prosecutors and staff on unpaid leave to save money."[8]

Judicial branch budgets have distinctive features that explain why cuts, particularly across the board, can have such a severe impact on court activities. First, between 80 percent and 90 percent of the judiciary budget is dedicated to the salaries of judges and court employees.[9] Judges cannot be removed from office or have their salaries reduced to cut costs, so the burden of cuts falls on the court staff that judges and the public depend upon to process cases.[10] "Thus, where a 5 percent across-the-board reduction in an executive department's budget may be absorbed through operational restructuring or pro-rata staff reductions, a similar cut to the judiciary's budget can result in significant staff reductions."[11]

Second, the Constitution imposes rigid limits on where the burden of cuts in the judicial budget will fall. The guarantee of a speedy trial in criminal cases means the brunt of deep cuts in the court budget will be at the expense of the adjudication of civil and family cases, which must be placed on the back burner to give criminal cases priority. Yet recessions tend to increase the number of civil cases involving mortgage foreclosure, eviction and divorce. The burden on the courts and the parties to civil/criminal cases is further magnified because often litigants cannot afford an attorney and represent themselves. Self-represented litigants draw disproportionately on court staff's time, and require more, not fewer clerks, to process their cases fairly and expeditiously.[12]

Budget cutbacks imposed on the courts are a common source of friction between the judiciary and the legislature. To place this in context, state expenditure on their respective judiciaries accounts for 1 percent to 3 percent of the total budgets.[13] The exact proportion within this range varies from state to state depending primarily on the extent to which trial courts are locally funded and whether the courts are responsible for providing adult and juvenile probation, an executive branch function in most states.

Clashes over the judicial budget are relatively recent. In many ways, they emerged as an unintended consequence of a court reform program. As reformers forged state judiciaries into statewide systems with central leadership, the budgets for state trial courts previously set by individual counties and cities became centralized in the state budget. This rendered the setting of the judicial budget into a single high stakes process. State funding, a desired outcome, made the judiciary budget vulnerable to cuts introduced as payback for an appellate court decision that displeased the state legislature.[14] The stakes are heightened because historically the trend has been that cuts in court programs are rarely fully restored to full funding after a budget crisis is over.[15]

Friction between the branches is enhanced because the judiciary lacks a formal role in the budget process of most states. There is also a tendency to downplay or ignore the distinctive status of the judiciary as a separate branch of government. Judicial leaders often find themselves treated like the heads of executive branch agencies.[16] Such treatment increases the potential for conflict.

In response, some states have developed mechanisms that improve the flow of information between the branches to ensure a strong case for the judicial budget. More direct efforts to reduce potential conflict include negotiating processes through which state court leaders can work with legislators and state executives to gain more control over their own budgets. Thus, instead of requesting increased appropriations, some court systems reached a compromise to allocate a larger proportion of state funding to general funds rather than allotments to specific programs. This allows the courts, who are in the best position to prioritize, to direct internally the use of state funding.[17] California is a good example. Most of its $3.8 billion annual budget is allocated to general court operations. The California system has the additional benefit of giving the courts the ability to decide on where the court-created revenue streams such as civil assessment fees and civil filing fees are used.

State court systems have also recognized the importance of demonstrating accountability for how their budgets are spent. During 2008, state courts emphasized programs that allow them to demonstrate they are being run efficiently. A growing number of state courts are providing better information about their performance to the public and the legislature for their state.[18] The courts in Massachusetts, for example, initiated a comprehensive effort to utilize caseflow management measures to improve the performance in a variety of areas, including clearance rate, time to disposition, age of pending cases and trial date certainty.[19] The state courts in Massachusetts took the additional step of setting statewide goals for its measures and publishing the results for all to see.[20]

When recessions hit, states may seek to improve their revenue stream by increasing filing fees and fines. This will not necessarily provide relief for the state courts in every case, however, as many states funnel the proceeds of such increases into programs unrelated to the administration of justice or directly into general revenue. One consequence of imposing higher court costs is a diminished access to justice for the public: "When legislatures and the courts themselves turn to fee-based structures to replace general funding obligations, the image of courts as a cornerstone of democratic government is substantially eroded."[21]

Building Interbranch Relations

During difficult economic times, clashes between the branches tend to multiply beyond the immediate flashpoint of the budget. Looking for some hints of blue in a stormy sky, economic crises can also serve as spurs for positive change, allowing for reforms that may have met more resistance in better financial times.

One positive development is a trend toward cooperative ventures between the judiciary and other branches to address problems related to the administration of justice. Recognition of this trend came at a May 2008 national conference on "The Role of State Court Leaders in Support Public Policy Affecting the Administration of Justice." More than 60 state supreme court chief justices and state court administrators met to discuss what role they should play in supporting and reforming public policy that affects the administration of justice.

The conference highlighted a number of examples of how the branches are working together to address critical economic and social problems. Three states—Arizona, Indiana and Ohio—provide examples that reflect the diversity of the problems addressed and the methods being used.

In 2005, Arizona courts confronted a puzzling trend. Despite increasingly severe penalties for offenses involving driving under the influence, the number of such offenses was increasing each year. The state's chief justice established a DUI Case Processing Committee, whose recommendations led to an interbranch effort involving new legislation, action by local governments, and an annual DUI summit attended by representatives from all three branches. The summits examined the effectiveness of alternative DUI sanctions, leading to a recommended pilot program in 11 courts. The results of the pilot were sufficiently promising for the supreme court to take the program statewide in July of 2008.[22]

The Indiana "Summit on Children—Partners Planning for Permanency" in December 2007 brought together more than 300 judges and their staff, legislators, mental health professionals, foster parents, educators and government caseworkers. The Indiana Supreme Court's Court Improvement Program sponsored the summit as a forum to generate change in how by the justice and foster care systems at the state and local levels helped abused and neglected children.[23] Most participants came as members of teams led by their county's juvenile court judges. Indiana's Supreme Court chief justice set the stage for discussion and action and the director of the Department of Child Service framed the issues and objectives. The summit was structured to provide time for an exchange of ideas, while also allowing the county teams to start planning the implementation of changes in their own communities.[24]

In Ohio, the governor established the Foreclosure Legal Assistance Group of Ohio—called FLAG-Ohio—consisting of representatives from the judicial and executive branches, to recommend remedial action to ease the foreclosure crisis that, among many other consequences, brought 83,000 cases filed in the state's courts.[25] The group's work culminated in the creation of the "Save the Dream Program: Ohio's Foreclosure Prevention Effort," announced at a December 2007 joint news conference held by the governor, chief justice, attorney general and director of commerce outlining the new program. The judiciary's contribution included a Foreclosure Mediation Program Model, the first of its kind in the nation, and a letter sent by the chief justice to all registered attorneys in the state requesting they volunteer their services to provide no cost legal assistance to those affected by foreclosure. More than 1,200 attorneys answered that call in 2008.[26]

The 2008 Role of the State Court Leaders Conference generated a number of ground rules that such programs should follow. First, the participants dealt at length with how judges and other court leaders should participate in public policy issues. The Code of Judicial Conduct is a fundamental limiting factor shaping the judicial role in policy issues. Judges are uniquely constrained in how they interact with litigants and others potentially influenced by the outcomes of court cases, and on what they can do and say regarding controversial matters. Basically, judges can be collaborators but not partners, conveners but not issue advocates. In a formulation that gained consensus, "Public policy for today's purposes relates to the effect or intentions of state court administrative actions—practices, priorities, rules—that impact the public beyond the substantive adjudicative actions that we all take."[27] Such actions are necessarily limited to public policy that affects the administration of justice.

Clear boundaries need to be respected. There was consensus that court leaders cannot become involved in such questions as the distribution of state spending between highways and parks, even though there is substantive law relevant to those areas. Because court leaders can be collaborators in policy ventures, but never partners, a participating justice or judge at times will need to leave the room during these public policy discussions.

The conference also identified ways in which court leaders can make a unique contribution to interbranch collaborations. Participants offered examples of what was termed the most underutilized resource in public policy at both the state and local levels: the convening power of a judge. Typically, court leaders have worked as part of a broad coalition consisting of the other branches and key groups associated with the policy issue at hand. Judicial leaders are qualified to be the convener who brings together the diverse interests relevant to responding to a particular problem area be it substance abuse, domestic violence, or the mortgage foreclosure crisis. Here the prestige of the judiciary and the courts is critical, as is the widespread perception of the judiciary as non-partisan.

Information in the possession of the courts is another contribution judicial leaders bring to the table. One chief justice noted, it is the "repeat low-level offenders, often drug-addicted, in our state courts who corrode their own lives and vitality of our neighborhoods."[28] Such information can be the spur toward working collaboratively with the rest of state government and community groups to forge better options: "So as we study our court dockets we can simply watch the numbers rise. Or we can ask: Are we using our resources as effectively as possible? Can repeated court interventions perhaps help to stop the downward spiral of these lives? Are we simply counting cases, or can we make each case count?"[29]

The importance of a chief justice maintaining high visibility in the community was also asserted. In this view, a chief justice needs to devote adequate time to attend meetings of various groups concerned with policies affecting the administration of justice to demonstrate the chiefs' accessibility. Demonstrating interest in issues makes other groups more willing to work with the judiciary.

Questions were raised at the conference but not fully answered: What is the proactive role of the court in pointing out problems? If the judiciary is to be proactive, which responsibilities lie with the trial bench and which with the supreme court and state court administrator? How should the judiciary decide on priorities for becoming involved in public policy issues? Although the policy issues may be similar across the states, the tools required by court leaders to address these issues will vary significantly by state.

The dialogue on how the branches can work together to achieve public policy goals will be taken up in May 2009. That's when 300 representatives of the three branches of state government will continue the discussion of how such joint efforts can be expanded and strengthened at a summit on "Justice is the Business of Government: The Importance of Fair and Impartial State Courts." The goal is to agree on concrete recommendations that can both reduce tensions between the branches and make inroads into some of the most intractable economic and social problems confronting the states.

There are existing models for how the branches can work together more smoothly and productively. Judicial councils composed of legislators, judges and administrators in some states make recommendations to the legislature. Other programs include having legislators "ride-along" (sit in during court proceedings) and holding "meet-and-greet" events where legislators and judges can discuss issues of mutual interest and learn about each other's work.[30]

Judicial Elections in 2008

Judicial elections in 2008 confirmed their transformation into "high dollar free-for-alls marked by dueling campaign salvos by organized interest groups, often located outside the state of the election."[31] Thirty-nine elections for state supreme court seats went before the electorate in 2008. In the 26 seats filled by partisan or non-partisan elections, twenty incumbents sought re-election. Thirteen justices did not draw an opponent. Six of the 20 incumbents were defeated, including the chief justices of Michigan, Mississippi and West Virginia (in a party primary). All 20 justices running against their own record in retention elections were retained by the voters.

The contested races featured negative, even scurrilous, television advertising, partisanship and under the radar clashes between powerful economic interests. Nearly $20 million was spent on television advertising in supreme court races, an increase of 24 percent from 2006. Most of the ads were paid for by interest group or political parties rather than by the candidates. At this point, Minnesota and North Dakota are the only states using contestable elections not to have television advertising in their judicial races.

The 2008 election outcomes, however, broke with a post-2000 trend in which candidates backed by the business community fared relatively well. The propriety of interest group support became a core issue influencing the outcome of judicial elections.

The impact of national political developments on judicial races affected the outcome of some trial court races. This was particularly notable in partisan election states that use straight-ticket levers. In Houston, Texas, (Harris County) 22 of 26 incumbent Republican circuit court judges on the ballot were swept from office.[32] President Obama's coattails and demographic changes in a once Republican stronghold leveraged the switch.

The judicial election scene in 2008 was enlivened by some rare ballot victories by opponents of contestable judicial elections. Two decades have passed since a state switched from contestable elections, partisan or non-partisan, to the Missouri Plan favored by reformers. The victories occurred at the local level.

Voters in Arkansas, Kansas, and Missouri either rejected bids to further politicize their elections or took the affirmative step to end contestable elections.

The judicial election that received the most national coverage in 2008 actually took place four years before in West Virginia. That election gained notoriety when it led to a case now before the U.S. Supreme Court.[33] *Caperton v. Massey* originated in an election challenge to an incumbent West Virginia Supreme Court justice. The specific issue was whether a judge having benefited from $3 million of support should sit in judgment on a case in which his benefactor was a party.

Conclusion

As 2008 progressed, the state courts confronted budgets often inadequate to maintaining even their core adjudicative functions. Courthouses were closed and jury trials halted to cut costs. With criminal cases necessarily given priority, the access to justice for civil litigants and others with business in the courthouse was limited. Budget cuts to the judiciary fall disproportionately on staff.

Good news was in short supply. A promising trend amidst the gloom is the development of innovative interbranch efforts that tackle problems of great concern to the public. It is clear that a top priority for state judiciaries is to nurture relations with the other branches consistent with the distinctive, non-political role courts are expected to play.

Judicial elections continue to be conducted in a manner that many observers find problematic for a non-political branch of government. In 2009, attention is focused on the U. S. Supreme Court's decision in *Caperton v. Massey*, which may resolve the question of when campaign contributions that helped elect a judge can be so substantial as to require that judge to step aside from hearing a case in which the contributor is a party. There were some stirrings of a renewed drive to move away from contestable elections, but also a flurry of legislation introduced that would move in the opposite direction. Past experience suggests there is little prospect of change in the methods states now use to select their judges. 2009 may test the continued applicability of that experience.

Notes

[1]President of the Conference of Chief Justices to the American Bar Association House of Delegates, by Chief Justice Margaret H. Marshall (Massachusetts), February 16, 2009 (transcript on file with author).

[2]Bob Drogin, "Even jury hiring is frozen," *Los Angeles Times*, December 22, 2008 (available at *http://www.latimes.com/news/nationworld/nation/la-na-courts22-2008dec22,0,387609.story*).

[3]Ibid.

[4]Ibid.

[5]Ibid.

[6]The Washington Economics Group, Inc., *The Economic Impacts of Delays in Civil trials in Florida's Courts Due to Under-Funding of Court System* (prepared for the Florida Bar Association, January 12, 2009) (available at *http://www.floridabar.org/TFB/TFBResources.nsf/Attachments/1C1C563F8CAFFC2C8525753E005573FF/$FILE/WashingtonGroup.pdf?OpenElement*). The report estimates $10.1 billion in direct economic impacts annually, with an additional $7.3 billion in indirect costs.

[7]*The New York Times* editorial board, "Hard Times and the Right to Counsel," *New York Times*, November 21, 2008 (available at *http://www.nytimes.com/2008/11/21/opinion/21fri2.html*).

[8]Donna Leinwand, "Budget cuts hamper abilities of prosecutors across U.S.", *USA Today*, November, 21, 2008 (available at *http://www.usatoday.com/news/nation/2008-11-20-prosecutors_n.htm*).

[9]Carol Flango, Chuck Campbell, and Neal Kauder, "State Courts and Budget Challenges," *Future Trends in State Courts 2006* (Williamsburg, VA: National Center for State Courts, 2006) (available at *http://contentdm.ncsconline.org/cgi-bin/showfile.exe?CISOROOT=/financial&CISOPTR=126*).

[10]The Associated Press, "Poor economy hits courts, hurts programs for poor," *International Herald Tribune*, January 24, 2009 (available at *http://www.iht.com/articles/ap/2009/01/24/america/NA-US-Meltdown-Justice-In-Peril.php*).

[11]Michael L. Buenger, "The Challenges of Funding State Courts in Tough Fiscal Times," *Court Review* 41, 2 (Summer, 2004), p. 16 (available at *http://digitalcommons.unl.edu/cgi/viewcontent.cgi?article=1070&context=ajacourtreview*).

[12]John Greacen, "Legal information versus legal advice: developments during the last five years," *Judicature* 84, 2, 2001.

[13]David Rottman and Shauna Strickland, *State Court Organization 2004* (U.S. Department of Justice, Bureau of Justice Statistics, Washington DC: USGPO, 2006), Table 16 (available at *http://www.ojp.usdoj.gov/bjs/pub/pdf/sco04.pdf*).

[14]The incomplete process of unifying the courts at the state level through simplifying their structure, centralizing their management, and switching to state funding with a centralized state budget is described in David Rottman, "The Court Reform Agenda: A Progress Report from 2007" *The Book of the States* 40, 2008 (available at *http://www.csg.org/pubs/Documents/TableofContents.pdf*). It should be noted here that most states continue to fund their courts out of a combination of local and state funding, as well as from revenue generated from fees and fines. State funding currently provides for all judicial salaries in 44 states and court reporter services in 33 states for courts of general jurisdiction (the main trial court hearing felonies and high-stakes civil cases).

[15]Carol Flango, Chuck Campbell, and Neal Kauder, p. 14.

[16]True, courts possess "inherent powers" to mandate funding at an "appropriate level" defined in most states as what is "reasonably necessary." Court leaders understand that inherent power in the context of a dispute over funding levels is "a weapon of last resort." Buenger, 2004, p. 18.

[17]Carol Flango, Chuck Campbell, and Neal Kauder.

[18]Kleiman and Schauffler, "Measuring Court Performance: Access and Fairness in the State Courts," in this volume.

[19]Richard Schauffler, "Judicial accountability in the US state courts: Measuring court performance," *Utrecht Law Review*, Volume 3, Issue 1 (June 2007), page 122 (available at *http://www.utrechtlawreview.org/publish/articles/000040/article.pdf*).

[20]Ibid.

[21]Buenger, 2004, p. 19.

[22]Report of the DUI Case Processing Committee, Re-engineering DUI Case Processing in Arizona, November 2005 at iv (available at *http://www.supreme.state.az.us/media/archive/2006/optDUI_Report_10405.pdf*).

[23]The Federal Court Improvement Program is administered by the Children's Bureau of the US Department of Health and Human Services, which provides funding to state supreme courts. It was established in 1993 to "assist State courts in performing their role in the continuum of care provided for families and children at risk. This program offers support for the implementation of alternatives and improvements as well as support for the expansion of successful court systems." (available at *http://www.federal-grantswire.com/state-court-improvement-program.html*).

[24]Nancy Gettinger, "Indiana Summit on Children Meets in Indianapolis" *Indiana Courttimes*, Issue 17.1, Jan/Feb 2008, p. 5 (available at *http://issuu.com/incourts/docs/news17-1*).

[25]"Save the Dream," the Task Force's report, is available at *www.com.ohio.gov*/SavetheDream/ and the details of the Foreclosure Mediation Program at *www.sconet.state.oh.us/dispute_resolution/foreclosure/foreclosureMediation.pdf*.

[26]David Rottman (Reporter), *The Role of State Court Leaders in Supporting Public Policy that Affects the Administration of Justice: Highlights and Themes from a Conference* (National Center for State Courts for the Pew Center on the States, 2009).

[27]Quote from Indiana Chief Justice Randall Shepard, as reported in Ibid.

[28]New York Chief Judge Judith S. Kaye, "Interview," *Judges' Journal*, Winter 2009.

[29]Ibid.

[30]Carol Flango, Chuck Campbell, and Neal Kauder.

[31]Conference of Chief Justices, Brief of the Conference of Chief Justices as Amicus Curiae in Support of Neither Party in Supreme Court of the United States, *Caperton v. Massey*, p. 8 (available at *http://brennan.3cdn.net/d6274e472669a87b58_dqm6ii1z9.pdf*).

[32]Nathan Koppel, "Obama's Coattails Stretch to Texas Trial Courts," *Wall Street Journal Law Blog*, November 5, 2008 (available at *http://blogs.wsj.com/law/2008/11/05/obamas-coattails-stretch-to-texas-trial-courts/?referer=sphere_related_content*).

[33]While approximately ten thousand petitions seeking review are filed annually with the U.S. Supreme Court, in recent years approximately 100 petitions are accepted ("granted cert") for full review by the Court. Supreme Court of the United States, *The Justices' Caseload*, (available at *http://www.supremecourtus.gov/about/justicecaseload.pdf*).

About the Author

David Rottman is principal court research consultant at the National Center for State Courts (NCSC). His current research concerns judicial selection, public opinion on the courts, the evolution of court structures, and problem-solving courts. Rottman also is the NCSC coordinator of the Election Law Program established jointly by the NCSC and the William & Mary School of Law. He is the author of books on community courts, social inequity, and modern Ireland. Rottman has a Ph.D. in sociology from the University of Illinois at Urbana, and previously worked at the Economic and Social Institute in Dublin, Ireland.

Measuring Court Performance: Access and Fairness in State Courts

By Matthew Kleiman and Richard Schauffler

State courts are improving public service by adopting the CourTools Access and Fairness survey to gather the views of court users. Key issues of access to court services and fairness in court proceedings are highlighted.

Introduction

Government agencies and institutions have placed a primacy on evaluating the views and perspectives of their customers. This renewed focus on customer satisfaction emphasizes the need for the public sector to deliver quality goods and services to those who use them and the taxpayers who pay for them. Collecting, reporting and responding to the views of customers helps ensure that public agencies meet the dual goals of transparency and accountability.

Information collected from customers can be utilized to assess whether different categories of customers (e.g., men, women, young, old, etc.) have equal access to those goods and services. Where that is not the case, this data can help identify and eliminate perceived barriers to effective service. Not only that, but assessing the customer helps to determine the effect policy reforms and program initiatives have on the end users of goods and services. Assessments can determine if the program had the intended result. This is especially true in the provision of legal information through self-help centers, Web sites and weekly drop-in workshops—in determining which of these services work and for whom is each most effective.

Unlike some public sector organizations, courts are not fundamentally in the business of satisfying customers with a discrete and concrete service, such as renewing a driver's license. What courts are designed to do is to resolve disputes in a timely, fair and independent manner. Judges, not unlike doctors, must get to the matter at hand quickly and spend enough time to determine an appropriate and individualized response to each particular case.

State courts nationwide handle over 100 million incoming cases a year, half of which are traffic cases.[1] State courts provide the forum in which residents of a jurisdiction can resolve legal problems and disputes ranging from the most simple actions (such as making a name change, paying a traffic ticket) to the most complex (such as defending themselves in a felony trial, dissolving a marriage and terminating parental rights). Judicial officers and court staff serve as unbiased, neutral arbiters of disputes while ensuring impartial access, due process and fair and consistent decisions. A positive image of the court "rests upon the perception of the courts as meeting constitutional obligations to protect rights, ensuring that litigants have adequate legal representation, that judges are honest, fair and well-trained, and court staff are respectful."[2] However, public opinion surveys have suggested that the public perceives courts as being "too costly, too slow, unfair in the treatment of racial and ethnic minorities, out of touch with the public, and negatively influenced by political considerations."[3] Sadly, these results were replicated across 33 state-specific surveys and six national surveys, and even in states with robust court reform programs, opinion did not change in response to the reforms.[4] But public opinion is shaped by many factors, is difficult for courts to change, and is an expensive thing to measure. As David Rottman notes, rather than attempting to influence public trust and confidence directly, courts are better off examining issues of access and procedural justice; soliciting the views of those who use the court rather than the broader public provides a practical strategy for improving court services.

What Are State Courts Doing?

State courts around the country have recently embraced a different approach to assess how court users (e.g., litigants, attorneys, witnesses, jurors and others) assess court performance. This approach focuses on two fundamental values associated with the resolution of disputes: access to justice and procedural fairness. Rather than implement reforms and hope the public notices (an unsuccessful and costly strategy), state courts are increasingly turning to a simple but effective approach to measuring the satisfaction of court users.

Before turning to the specifics of these programs, it is important to note several distinguishing characteristics of the interaction between court users and the courts. First, for matters other than a simple traffic ticket, a plurality of those entering a courthouse are doing it for the first time. During that visit to the courthouse (or the court's Web site), these people are trying to understand an enormous amount of information about their case: Where will it be heard? When will it be heard? Can they represent themselves in court? How do they get an interpreter? Who must attend? What papers must be filed with the court? What will it cost? How long will it take? Court cases represent complex events that are highly infrequent in the lives of most people, a combination that puts a premium on issues related to access, among them the availability of plain English forms and instructions, meaningful assistance from self-help centers, clear signage and helpful front counter staff.

Second, for those who turn to the courts to resolve disputes, the expectation is not that they will win, but that the process will be fair and understandable. In popular parlance, they expect to have their day in court, a chance to tell their side of the story and have a judicial officer consider what they have said in making a final judgment in the case. This places the emphasis on procedural fairness.[5]

The critical importance of procedural fairness means that courts must pay attention not only to the outcomes in cases, but to the process that produces these outcomes. Doing so is not motivated by a desire to be popular, but rather by the knowledge that court decisions that are arrived at by processes perceived to be fair are more likely to be complied with by the litigants, whether they win or lose.

Third, an increasing number of litigants appear in court without attorneys and represent themselves in court. This is true not only for small claims and traffic cases, but also for landlord-tenant cases, probate cases and domestic relations cases (e.g., divorce, custody, child support, visitation). The proportion of self-represented litigants in these case types is an estimated 50 percent to 80 percent of the litigants. Self representation is making itself felt in criminal and civil cases as well. Guiding the self-represented litigant through their case (without giving legal advice on their particular case) is a challenge for state courts everywhere, with major implications for how the court operates and for the perceptions of the court in terms of access and fairness.

For all of these reasons, state courts are turning to a straightforward survey of court users that measures their views of access to justice and procedural fairness. The new wave of court reform is based not on general public opinion, but on the experiences and views of those who use the courts.

Access and Fairness Survey

In the past three years, courts around the country have begun to administer Access and Fairness surveys, utilizing the *CourTools* Measure 1 version.[6] To date, assessments have been conducted statewide in Minnesota and Utah and in select courts in Arizona, California, Colorado, Illinois, Maryland, Massachusetts and Ohio. Courts that implement the survey are asking all of those who come to the courthouse on a typical day to fill out a brief self-administered survey as they exit the court. Individuals surveyed include litigants and their families and friends, victims and witnesses, attorneys, law enforcement officers, representatives of social service agencies, and individuals doing records searches or having other business at the clerk's office, among others. Because the intent is to assess the views of the court's customers, judges and court staff are excluded. The survey is available in English, Spanish, and Vietnamese and is administered on a periodic basis (e.g., annually).

The survey itself consists of 15 substantive statements, divided into two parts. The first 10 items focus on the issue of access, while the last five items focus on fairness and are answered only by those who saw a judicial officer during their visit to court that day. Each of the 15 statements has five possible responses ranging from strongly disagree (1) to strongly agree (5). The closer the average score is to 5, the more positive is the public's opinion of the court.

In addition, respondents are asked to provide some basic background information that allows for an assessment of differential treatment or the ability to access court services. Respondents are asked what they did in court that day (e.g., search court records, file papers, jury duty, attend a hearing or trial, make a payment); how often they are typically in this courthouse; the type of case that brought the respondent to the courthouse (e.g., traffic, criminal, civil, divorce, small claims, juvenile); what gender they are; and how they identify themselves (e.g., American Indian or Alaska Native, Asian, Black or African-American, Hispanic or Latino, Native Hawaiian or Other Pacific Islander, White, Mixed Race, Other).

Access

The state constitutions of 12 states contain an identical statement on the purposes of state courts: "All courts shall be open; every person for injury done to his goods, lands, or person shall have remedy by due process of law; and right and justice shall be administered without self denial or delay."[7] These guiding principles of access to justice imply that court services should be available and open to all. Courts have a fundamental responsibility to minimize geographic, architectural, language, procedural and economic barriers to the court's services. Individuals who come to a court—regardless of their socioeconomic status, race or ethnicity, level of experience with legal proceedings, type of legal representation, proficiency in English and their abilities and disabilities—must be offered and receive equal access to justice. There are many nuances to the idea of access: physical access (e.g., ramps along with stairs); language access (for non-native English speakers, and plain English forms for everyone that overcome complicated legalese); informational access (what does a litigant need to do, and how do they get it done), to name but a few. The survey probes some of the most critical of those, relying on 10 statements:

- Finding the courthouse was easy.
- The forms I needed were clear and easy to understand.
- I felt safe in the courthouse.
- The court makes reasonable efforts to remove physical and language barriers to service.
- I was able to get my court business done in a reasonable amount of time.
- Court staff paid attention to my needs.
- I was treated with courtesy and respect.
- I easily found the courtroom or office I needed.
- The court's Web site was useful.
- The court's hours of operation made it easy for me to do my business.

What Are Courts Learning about Access?

The access portion of the survey points out a fact with major implications for state courts: the biggest share of those visiting the courts is doing so for the first time. Those using the courts are likely to be lost, confused, and frustrated if the courts do not pay attention to structuring their world to make it accessible. Many courts are discovering that their access issues begin with poor signage. This includes signage on roadways as well as signage inside court facilities. Far too many court users end up in the wrong place, and as a result of being lost, often arrive at the wrong time.

Once in the right place, court users consistently point out that they are not able to get their business done in a reasonable amount of time. Courts that have explored this issue discover a variety of reasons for this, including insufficient staffing of front counters at peak periods, inefficient processes that require more than one stop to complete a transaction, the time required to explain the legal process to each court user, and more. Courts also are learning that the public finds it less than optimal to be summoned to a process only to wait for a long time before it is their turn (e.g., jury voir dire, or traffic court). Those using the court refer to these kinds of events as a "cattle call," noting that the herd is first rounded up only to wait for the action to begin.

Many courts find that the public does not think that the court's hours of operation are convenient. Since the courts are generally open only during the business day, those working during those daytime hours must rush in before work, on their lunch hour, or immediately after work, along with dozens others just like themselves. Courts have started to reevaluate on the basis of these findings, and are experimenting with night court, Saturday sessions, mobile court services, and other flexible approaches.

Finally, another general finding is that those coming to the courthouse are often unaware of the court's Web site or were not able to use it to complete their business. Many states and individual courts have invested heavily in their Web sites, but have not marketed these sites well to the public or partnered with other public institutions to promote awareness of and access to these online services (through computers in public libraries, for example). As a result, the frustrated person standing in line for traffic court complaining about how long it takes might have been able to pay their ticket online, reschedule their hearing, obtain the forms they need, or attend online traffic school, and as a result might never have needed to come to the courthouse at all.

Fairness

Trial courts have the responsibility to provide "due process and individual justice in each case, treat similar litigants equally, and ensure that their actions and consequences thereof, are consistent with established law."[8]

Fairness is a complex, multidimensional concept that is difficult to measure, yet it lies at the heart of what courts are supposed to embody in their actions. A solution to this challenge is provided by research on what is referred to as "procedural fairness." This approach focuses on key dimensions of the process by which cases are heard and decided, focusing primarily on the time when litigants appear before a judicial officer. The research demonstrates repeatedly when key expectations of fairness held by litigants are met, litigants are more likely to comply with court orders and view the court system and the law favorably.

The surprising and even counterintuitive finding of this research is that litigants do not base their views and behavior on whether they won or lost their case. While no one is happy when they do not prevail, their more important views of the law and the courts, and moreover, their compliance with court orders, is not negatively affected if the process by which a decision is reached is perceived as fair.

What is a fair process? Research suggest that it is a process in which 1) parties in a case get to tell their side of the story; 2) the judicial officer is neutral, listens to both sides; 3) parties in a case are treated with courtesy and respect, and in a non-discriminatory fashion; and 4) parties understand the decision made and the reasons for it.[9]

Consistent with this approach, the *CourTools* Measure 1 Access and Fairness survey contains the following five items, designed to be completed by all those who appeared before a judicial officer on the day of the survey, rating the items from strongly disagree to strongly agree on a five-point scale:

- The way my case was handled was fair.
- The judge listened to my side of the story before he or she made a decision.
- The judge had the information necessary to make good decisions about my case.
- I was treated the same as everyone else.
- As I leave the court, I know what to do next about my case.

What Are Courts Learning about Fairness?

The results on the fairness survey items are generally more positive than observers or even court practitioners might predict. Most courts find that the results indicate that courts are perceived as operating in a fair manner, and that this positive rating does not vary in a systematic and significant way when analyzed by race/ethnicity, gender, case type, court size, or other background variable, including whether the respondent won or lost their case (an item some jurisdictions have asked).

Overall, state courts that have conducted the survey are doing an excellent job in providing fair decisions. It could be argued that the courts that have undertaken this survey represent the best courts; where individual courts have done this on their own, that might be the case. Nonetheless, that does not diminish the significance of the results for those courts—being fair is neither easy nor automatic. In states with a statewide approach (e.g., Massachusetts, Utah) all courts are being measured, and the positive results are all the more impressive.

Of course, within specific jurisdictions, state courts are discovering and exploring the meaning of some important differences. In some jurisdictions, there are important differences between responses from whites and non-whites, for example. Differences also appear in certain case types within a jurisdiction, which suggests that individual judges are behaving differently in those jurisdictions. Sometimes this is a matter of inexperience (a new judge, or a judge new to an assignment to a division (e.g., juvenile)), and sometimes it might be attributable to ways of doing court business that need to be changed. In these cases, courts are developing training plans for the court generally as well as for specific judges. For example, when the court learns that one division's ratings on the item "As I leave the court, I know what to do next about my case" are significantly lower than other divisions, observation can be conducted to determine what is driving the lack of clear communication in those courtrooms, and peer training can be designed by the judges.

Conclusion

The significance of the state courts' willingness to undertake this form of public evaluation can be understood when placed in the context of the dynamics of this branch of state government. While the public can and does vote to change decision makers in the executive and legislative branches, that mechanism is—by constitutional design—far less dynamic in the judicial branch. The judicial branch has largely been insulated from political influence in this way, for the purpose of minimizing undue influence over decision making. This makes it all the more important that the judiciary find other ways to give the public a role in evaluating the work of the state courts.

For this reason the courts have historically made use of public trust and confidence surveys to gauge public opinion on the work of the courts. These public opinion surveys are complex in design and deployment, difficult to interpret, and expensive to undertake. By design, the Access and Fairness survey is straightforward and inexpensive, designed to produce actionable information for state court managers and judges. This practical approach is being adopted by an increasing number of states and courts, providing the basis for court improvement. In the face of mounting fiscal pressures and budget reductions and service cutbacks, state courts are also using this information to document current court performance, establishing a baseline against which actual or anticipated reductions in court services brought on by the economic recession can be compared in the years ahead.

Notes

[1] Robert C. LaFountain et al., *Examining the Work of State Courts, 2007: A National Perspective from the Court Statistics Project*, (Williamsburg, Va.: National Center for State Courts, 2008), 11.

[2] David B. Rottman, "Public Perceptions of the State Courts: A Primer," *The Court Manager*, Vol. 15, No. 3, (2000), 9.

[3] Ibid.

[4] David B. Rottman, "Procedural Fairness as a Court Reform Agenda," *Court Review*, Vol. 44, Issue 1-2, (2007–2008), 32.

[5] For an excellent exploration of this topic, including the extensive research by Tom R. Tyler and others, see the special Issue on Procedural Fairness of *Court Review*, Vol. 44, Issue 1-2, (2007–2008).

[6] Brian J. Ostrom et al., *CourTools*, (Williamsburg, Va.: National Center for State Courts, 2005). See Measure 1 Access and Fairness, available for download at *www.courtools.org*. Some jurisdictions have implemented slightly modified versions of the original *CourTools* survey.

[7] See the state constitutions of Connecticut, Delaware, Indiana, Kentucky, Louisiana, Nebraska, North Dakota, Pennsylvania, Texas, Tennessee, Utah and Wyoming. Even in the old days, cutting and pasting of well-formulated language was practiced in the development of the law, albeit by hand and not with a computer.

[8] National Center for State Courts, *Trial Court Performance Standards with Commentary*, (Williamsburg, Va.: National Center for State Courts, 1990), 12.

[9] Tom R. Tyler, "Procedural Justice and the Courts," *Court Review*, Vol. 44, No. 1-2, (2007–2008), 26–31.

About the Authors

Matthew Kleiman is a senior court research associate with the National Center for State Courts (NCSC). His work has focused on the development and implementation of: a set of court specific performance measures (*CourTools*); a framework to understand court culture; and statewide workload assessment models for judicial officers, court staff, prosecutors, and public defenders. He has a Ph.D. in political science from Michigan State University.

Richard Schauffler is the director of Research Services at the National Center for State Courts, where he heads the Court Statistics Project. He also works on the *CourTools* initiative, developing and assisting states and courts to implement performance measures. He holds a B.S. degree from the School of Criminology, University of California at Berkeley, and an M.A. in sociology from Johns Hopkins University.

State Judicial Diversity

By Barbara L. Graham

This article investigates the nature and extent to which state courts are racially and ethnically diverse. Judicial diversity is examined for African-Americans, Hispanics, Asian-Pacific Islanders and Native Americans. The findings indicate that only modest increases in judicial diversity have occurred in the states' major appellate and trial courts since 2008. Minority judges are more likely to obtain seats on state courts through gubernatorial appointment, especially in states that formally use elections to select judges. This research underscores the complexity of state judicial selection and the role governors play in increasing racial and ethnic judicial diversity.

Introduction

In 1973, the American Judicature Society reported that African-American judges made up about 1.3 percent of the nation's state court judges. By 1986, African-American judges on state courts increased to 3.5 percent. Hispanic and Asian-American representation on the major state courts was negligible during the 1970s and early 1980s. By 2001, however, racial and ethnic minorities were becoming more visible on the states' major courts but progress was exceedingly slow. Calls for greater racial and ethnic representation on state courts are consistent with the assumption that state judiciaries should reflect the racial and ethnic diversity of America and that the courts are open to all.

Diversity can be defined in many ways, but this study focuses specifically on racial and ethnic groups that have a history of exclusion and discrimination in the political process and have been historically underrepresented in our nation's political and legal institutions.[1] Judicial diversity is explicitly measured in the context of the African-American, Hispanic, Asian-Pacific Islander and Native American presence on the major state trial and appellate courts.[2]

This study is based on data collected by the author on minority judges presiding on general jurisdiction state courts as of December 2008.[3] The judges were identified and included in the analysis from a variety of sources, including *The Directory of Minority Judges of the United States*, lists provided by state court administrators, state court directories and state court Web sites. Additional data were collected on methods of state judicial selection, name and type of court, dates of judicial selection, method of appointment or election, names of appointing governors and their partisan identification, and census region.

Racial and Ethnic Diversity of State Courts

This study identified 1,295 minority judges sitting on the states' 10,999 major trial and appellate courts.[4] According to the figures on state court diversity by state and type of court as shown in Table 1, 11.8 percent of the state judiciaries are members of racial and ethnic groups. Five states lacked minority representation on their major courts: Montana, New Hampshire, South Dakota, Vermont and Wyoming. The states with the highest levels of minority representation include Hawaii (57 percent), New Mexico (29.3 percent), Maryland (19 percent), Louisiana (18.5 percent) and New York (18.2 percent). Minorities make up 17.7 percent of the Texas judiciary, and California, the state with the largest judicial system, has 17.4 percent minority representation. Racial and ethnic diversity on state courts has increased approximately 2 percent since 2001.

African-Americans constitute the largest proportion of minorities on state courts, 6.5 percent, and Hispanics follow with 3.4 percent state court representation. Asian-Pacific Islander judges make up only 1.4 percent and the Native American presence on state courts is negligible (less than 1 percent). The data show that minorities have made the best gains on state intermediate appellate courts since 2001 (13 percent), and their representation on state supreme courts is 11.5 percent and the trial courts, 11.7 percent is strikingly similar. Most minority judges preside over courts in the census regions of the West (34 percent), followed by the South (32 percent), Northeast (18.5 percent) and the Midwest (14.9 percent). A breakdown of the data by gender shows that 61 percent of minority judges are male and 37 percent are female.

Judicial Selection and State Judicial Diversity

State judicial selection is inextricably linked to state judicial diversity. In order to understand the racial and ethnic composition of state courts, the analysis must begin with how judges are selected in the 50 states. Unlike the federal system, which uses a single method to select judges—presidential appointment with Senate confirmation, states use a variety of methods to select state court judges. Not only do judicial selection methods vary among the states, they can also vary within a state. In addition, not all states have adopted a unified, three-tier hierarchical model for their state court systems. State judicial selection is complex, nuanced and is influenced by a state's political culture; therefore, we would expect that selection methods are likely to influence the degree to which minorities are represented on the state bench.

States select their judges by three methods: elections, appointment or some combination of both. Thirty-two states use either partisan or nonpartisan elections to initially select all or some of their judges. But with the exception of Illinois and Louisiana, which use elections, and South Carolina, which uses legislative appointment, governors are given the authority to make interim appointments to the bench to fill vacancies when they arise. The governors of 47 states make judicial appointments, with or without a commission's input, or with or without some form of legislative or executive approval. This could mean that in addition to electoral politics, the appointment politics of the governor play an important role in understanding the extent to which members of racial and ethnic groups will obtain seats on state courts.

Under the formal methods of judicial selection, 74 percent of the minority judges studied in this research occupied seats on state courts where partisan or nonpartisan election is the state's primary way of selecting judges. By comparison, only 23.9 percent of minority judges obtained their seats through selection systems that formally use gubernatorial appointment, with or without a commission, or some other form of approval. A completely different picture emerges when the data were analyzed to determine whether those minority judges in states that use elections initially obtained their seats through elections or gubernatorial appointment. The data show that 90.2 percent of the minority judges were initially selected to the bench by some form of gubernatorial appointment and only 4.4 percent were initially elected to the state bench. This finding is consistent with previous research that demonstrates minority judges are more likely to initially obtain their state court seats by appointment, even in states that use elections. A breakdown of these appointments by political party reveals that Democratic governors initially appointed 55.1 percent of the minority judges to their current position, while Republican governors appointed 43.2 percent.

Implications and Trends for State Court Diversity

More attention must be paid to the role of governors in state judicial selection, especially when considering efforts to increase diversity on state courts. The November 2008 elections did not produce a major shift in the partisan control of governorships; therefore, there is little reason to expect that the impact of the election on state judicial diversity will be significant. One exception may be in Missouri, where the governorship shifted to a Democrat. In Missouri, the governor appoints judges under the gubernatorial appointment with commission system (also known as the merit system or the Missouri plan). It is expected that Gov. Jay Nixon will be attentive to calls for a more diverse Missouri judicial system given his support from African-American voters. In addition, Gov. David Paterson, New York's first African-American governor, has already made two minority appointments to New York's intermediate appellate court in addition to former Gov. Eliot Spitzer's five appointments to the appellate bench. Paterson has voiced criticism about the lack of diversity among candidates from the New York Commission on Judicial Nomination submitted to the governor.[5] In contrast, Gov. Deval Patrick, the first African-American governor of Massachusetts, was recently criticized for his lack of minority appointments to the state bench during his two years in office.[6] Former Democratic Gov. Gray Davis of California made judicial diversity a prime objective during his one term in office by appointing 105 minorities to the bench. In contrast, Gov. Arnold Schwarzenegger has appointed 50 minorities to the California state bench since 2003.[7]

Conclusion

The way judges should be selected in the states continues to be a controversial issue for a number of reasons. An important component of that debate is which system is likely to produce greater racial and ethnic diversity on state courts. Although that question is beyond the scope of this article, the research does reveal that minority judges are more likely to gain seats through gubernatorial appointment in systems that use elections; not merit systems (gubernatorial appointment with commission). Most of the African-American judges (38.5 percent) presided over courts in the South whereas a majority of Hispanic judges (44.2 percent) were located in the West. Most Southern states use judicial elections and Republican governors dominate the South. It is unlikely that we will see significant increases in judicial diversity in the South without major changes in judicial elections, such as the use of judicial subdistricts for electing judges.[8] In conclusion, despite the prominence and controversy surrounding judicial elections, greater attention must be paid to the reality of the appointive character of state judicial selection and the considerable influence governors yield in shaping the diversity of state courts.

Notes

[1] Women as a group also have a long history of exclusion from the legal profession and judgeships; however, gender diversity is not addressed in this research because of data collection limitations.

[2] The racial and ethnic categories used in this study are based on self identification. A small number of judges identified themselves as biracial or used other ethnic categories. These judges are placed in the "Other" category. See the figures in Table A.

[3] Limited jurisdiction judges are excluded from this study. Table A includes the names of the courts used in this study. See the National Center for State Courts' *State Court Organization, 2004*, for a complete description of state court systems.

[4] The reader should keep in mind that these figures are approximate as of December 2008. In addition, some states have incomplete data or the race and/or ethnicity of the judge was not made available. In these instances, the judges were excluded from the analysis.

[5] See Jeremy W. Peters, "Paterson Criticizes Panel for Its Judicial Selection." *New York Times*, December 4, 2008, *http://www.nytimes.com/2008/12/04/nyregion/04judge.html*.

[6] See Matt Viser, "Governor Picks Fewer Minorities for Bench." *The Boston Globe*, December 5, 2008, *http://www.boston.com/news/local/massachusetts/articles/2008/12/05/governor_picks_fewer_minorities_for_bench/*.

[7] See Raul Hernandez, "Governor, Legal Groups Working to Get More Minority Judges Seated." *Ventura County Star*, May 11, 2008, *http://www.venturacountystar.com/news/2008/may/11/courting-ethnic-diversity-on-bench/*. The California figures are based on the judges identified in this study.

[8] See the Brennan Center's 2008 Report on *Improving Judicial Diversity* for a discussion of barriers to judicial diversity at the state level and potential remedies.

References

Graham, Barbara L. 1990. "Do Judicial Selection Systems Matter? A Study of Black Representation on State Courts." *American Politics Quarterly*, Vol. 18: 316–336.

Graham, Barbara L. 2004. "Toward an Understanding of Judicial Diversity in American Courts." *Michigan Journal of Race & Law*, Vol. 10: 153–93.

Holmes, Lisa M. and Jolly A. Emrey. 2006. "Court Diversification: Staffing the State Courts of Last Resort Through Interim Appointments." *The Justice System Journal*, Vol. 27: 1–11.

Judicial Division, Standing Committee on Minorities in the Judiciary. 2008. *The Directory of Minority Judges of the United States, 4th ed*. Chicago: American Bar Association.

Martin, Elaine and Barry Pyle. 2002. "Gender and Racial Diversification of State Supreme Courts." *Women and Politics*, Vol. 24: 35–52.

Rottman, David B. and Shauna M. Strickland. 2006. *State Court Organization, 2004*. U.S. Department of Justice, Bureau of Justice Statistics, Washington, D.C. An electronic version of this report may be found on the Internet at *http://www.ojp.usdoj.gov/bjs/*.

Torres-Spelliscy, Ciara, Monique Chase and Emma Greenman. 2008. "Improving Judicial Diversity." New York University School of Law: Brennan Center for Justice. An electronic version of this report may be found on the Internet at *http://www.brennancenter.org/content/resource/diversity_report*.

About the Author

Barbara L. Graham is associate professor of political science and director of graduate studies at the University of Missouri-St. Louis. Her research interests include the politics of representation in state and federal courts and judicial policymaking. She has published articles in *American Politics Quarterly*, *Judicature* and the *Michigan Journal of Race & Law*.

Table A
STATE COURT DIVERSITY

State (a)	Type of court	Number of judgeships	African-American		Hispanic		Asian-Pacific Islander		Native American		Other (b)	
			Number	Percent	Number	Percent	Number	Percent	Number	Percent	Number	Percent
Total Judgeships Nationwide		10,999	...	6.5%	...	3.4%	...	1.4%	...	0.2%	...	0.3%
Total Minority Judges........		1,295	714	55.0%	375	29.0%	156	12.1%	18	1.4%	32	2.5%
Alabama, 6.1%	Supreme Court	9	...	...	...	...	...	...	...	...	...	...
	Court of Civil Appeals	5	...	...	...	...	...	...	...	...	...	...
	Court of Criminal Appeals	5	...	...	...	...	...	...	...	...	...	...
	Circuit Court	144	10	6.9%	...	...	...	...	...	...	...	...
	Total Number of Seats	163	10	6.1%	...	...	...	...	...	...	...	...
Alaska, 2%	Supreme Court	5	...	...	...	...	...	...	...	...	...	...
	Court of Appeals	3	...	...	...	...	...	...	...	...	...	...
	Superior Court	40	...	...	...	...	1	2.5%	...	...	...	...
	Total Number of Seats	48	...	...	...	...	1	2.0%	...	...	...	...
Arizona, 14.2%	Supreme Court	5	...	...	...	...	...	...	...	...	...	...
	Court of Appeals	22	1	4.5%	3	13.6%	...	...	...	...	...	...
	Circuit Court	162	3	1.8%	15	9.2%	5	3.0%	...	...	...	...
	Total Number of Seats	189	4	2.1%	18	9.5%	5	2.6%	...	...	...	...
Arkansas, 9.4%	Arkansas	7	...	...	...	...	...	...	...	...	...	...
	Court of Appeals	12	1	8.3%	...	...	...	...	...	...	...	...
	Circuit Court	120	12	10.0%	...	...	...	...	...	...	...	...
	Total Number of Seats	139	13	9.4%	...	...	...	...	...	...	...	...
California, 17.4%	Supreme Court	7	...	...	1	14.2%	2	29.0%	...	...	...	...
	Court of Appeals	105	3	2.9%	4	3.8%	4	3.8%	1	0.9%	...	...
	Superior Courts	1,598	91	5.6%	97	60.0%	78	3.8%	4	0.3%	12	0.8%
	Total Number of Seats	1,710	94	5.5%	102	6.0%	84	4.9%	5	0.3%	12	0.7%
Colorado, 11.1%	Supreme Court	7	...	...	...	...	...	...	...	...	...	...
	Court of Appeals	19	...	...	2	10.5%	...	...	...	...	...	...
	District Court	144	6	4.1%	11	7.6%	...	...	...	...	...	...
	Total Number of Seats	170	6	3.5%	13	7.6%	...	...	...	...	...	...
Connecticut, 14.7%	Supreme Court	7	1	14.2%	...	...	...	...	...	...	...	...
	Appellate Court	10	2	20.0%	...	...	...	...	...	...	...	...
	Superior Court	180	15	8.3%	7	3.8%	2	1.1%	...	...	2	1.1%
	Total Number of Seats	197	18	9.1%	7	3.6%	2	1.0%	...	...	2	1.0%
Delaware, 6.9%	Supreme Court	5	...	...	...	...	...	...	...	...	...	...
	Court of Chancery	5	...	...	...	...	...	...	...	...	...	...
	Superior Court	19	2	11.0%	...	...	...	...	...	...	...	...
	Total Number of Seats	29	2	6.9%	...	...	...	...	...	...	...	...
Florida, 13.6%	Supreme Court	7	1	14.2%	...	...	...	...	...	...	...	...
	District Courts of Appeals	62	5	8.0%	6	9.7%	...	...	...	...	...	...
	Circuit Court	599	29	4.8%	42	7.0%	1	0.1%	1	0.1%	6	1.0%
	Total Number of Seats	668	35	5.2%	48	7.2%	1	0.2%	1	0.2%	6	0.8%

See footnotes at end of table.

STATE COURT DIVERSITY — Continued

State (a)	Type of court	Number of judgeships	African-American		Hispanic		Asian-Pacific Islander		Native American		Other (b)	
			Number	Percent	Number	Percent	Number	Percent	Number	Percent	Number	Percent
Georgia, 12%	Supreme Court	7	3	42.8%	...	...	...	...	...	...	...	...
	Court of Appeals	12	3	25.0%	...	...	...	...	...	...	...	...
	Superior Court	198	20	10.1%	...	...	...	...	...	...	...	...
	Total Number of Seats	217	26	12.0%	...	...	...	...	...	...	...	...
Hawaii, 57%	Supreme Court	5	...	...	...	...	3	60.0%	...	...	...	...
	Intermediate Court of Appeals	6	...	...	...	...	2	33.3%	...	...	1	16.6%
	Circuit Court and District Family	47	...	...	...	...	28	40.5%	...	...	5	10.6%
	Total Number of Seats	58	...	...	...	...	33	57.0%	...	...	6	10.3%
Idaho, 2.0%	Supreme Court	5	...	...	...	...	...	...	...	...	...	...
	Court of Appeals	3	...	...	1	33.3%	...	...	...	...	...	...
	District Court	42	...	...	...	...	...	...	...	...	...	...
	Total Number of Seats	50	...	...	1	2.0%	...	...	...	...	...	...
Illinois, 11%	Supreme Court	7	1	14.3%	...	...	...	...	...	...	...	...
	Appellate Court	54	4	7.4%	1	1.9%	...	...	...	...	...	...
	Circuit Court	514	45	8.8%	11	2.1%	1	0.2%	...	...	...	...
	Total Number of Seats	575	50	8.7%	12	2.1%	1	0.2%	...	...	...	...
Indiana, 5%	Supreme Court	5	1	20.0%	...	...	...	...	...	...	...	...
	Court of Appeals	15	1	6.7%	...	...	...	...	...	...	...	...
	Circuit and Superior Court	302	10	3.3%	4	1.3%	...	...	...	...	...	...
	Total Number of Seats	322	12	3.7%	4	1.3%	...	...	...	...	...	...
Iowa, 3.8%	Supreme Court	7	...	...	...	...	...	...	...	...	...	...
	Court of Appeals	9	...	...	...	...	1	11.1%	...	...	...	...
	District Court	116	4	3.4%	...	...	...	...	...	...	...	...
	Total Number of Seats	132	4	3.0%	...	...	1	0.8%	...	...	...	...
Kansas, 2.3%	Supreme Court	7	...	...	...	...	...	...	...	...	...	...
	Court of Appeals	13	1	7.7%	...	...	...	...	...	...	...	...
	District Court	244	4	1.6%	1	0.4%	...	...	...	...	...	...
	Total Number of Seats	264	5	2.0%	1	0.3%	...	...	...	...	...	...
Kentucky, 1.1%	Supreme Court	7	...	...	...	...	...	...	...	...	...	...
	Court of Appeals	14	1	7.1%	...	...	...	...	...	...	...	...
	Circuit Court	163	1	0.6%	...	...	...	...	...	...	...	...
	Total Number of Seats	184	2	1.1%	...	...	...	...	...	...	...	...
Louisiana, 18.5%	Supreme Court	7	1	14.3%	...	...	...	...	...	...	...	...
	Court of Appeals	53	10	18.9%	...	...	...	...	...	...	...	...
	District Court	231	43	18.6%	...	...	...	...	...	...	...	...
	Total Number of Seats	291	54	18.5%	...	...	...	...	...	...	...	...
Maine, 1.6%	Supreme Judicial Court	7	...	...	...	...	...	...	...	...	...	...
	Superior Court	17	...	...	...	...	...	...	...	...	...	...
	District Court	36	1	2.7%	...	...	...	...	...	...	...	...
	Total Number of Seats	60	1	1.6%	...	...	...	...	...	...	...	...

See footnotes at end of table.

STATE COURT DIVERSITY — Continued

State (a)	Type of court	Number of judgeships	African-American		Hispanic		Asian-Pacific Islander		Native American		Other (b)	
			Number	Percent	Number	Percent	Number	Percent	Number	Percent	Number	Percent
Maryland, 19%	Court of Appeals	7	2	28.6%	...	...	...	...	...	...	...	...
	Court of Special Appeals	13	2	15.4%	...	...	...	...	...	...	...	...
	Circuit Court	153	28	18.3%	1	0.6%	...	...	...	...	...	...
	Total Number of Seats	173	32	18.5%	1	0.5%	...	...	...	...	...	...
Massachusetts, 9.6%	Supreme Judicial Court	7	1	14.3%	...	...	...	...	...	...	...	...
	Appeals Court	25	1	4.0%	...	...	...	...	...	...	...	...
	Superior Court	82	7	8.5%	...	...	2	2.4%	...	...	...	...
	Total Number of Seats	114	9	7.9%	...	...	2	1.7%	...	...	...	...
Michigan, 12.9%	Supreme Court	7	1	14.3%	...	...	...	...	...	...	...	...
	Court of Appeals	28	2	7.1%	...	...	...	...	...	...	...	...
	Circuit Court	221	26	11.8%	4	1.8%	...	...	...	...	...	...
	Total Number of Seats	256	29	11.3%	4	1.6%	...	...	...	...	...	...
Minnesota, 6.2%	Supreme Court	7	1	14.3%	...	...	...	...	...	...	...	...
	Court of Appeals	19	4	21.0%	...	...	...	...	...	...	...	...
	District Court	289	7	2.4%	1	0.3%	3	1.0%	3	1.0%	1	0.3%
	Total Number of Seats	315	12	3.8%	1	0.3%	3	0.9%	3	0.9%	1	0.3%
Mississippi, 15.7%	Supreme Court	9	1	11.1%	...	...	...	...	...	...	...	...
	Court of Appeals	10	2	20.0%	...	...	...	...	...	...	...	...
	Circuit Court	51	8	15.6%	...	...	...	...	...	...	...	...
	Total Number of Seats	70	11	15.7%	...	...	...	...	...	...	...	...
Missouri, 8.3%	Supreme Court	7	...	...	...	...	...	...	...	...	...	...
	Court of Appeals	32	5	15.6%	...	...	1	3.1%	...	...	...	...
	Circuit Court	141	6	4.3%	3	2.1%	...	...	...	...	...	...
	Total Number of Seats	180	11	6.1%	3	1.7%	1	0.5%	...	...	...	...
Montana, 0	Supreme Court	7	...	...	...	...	...	...	...	...	...	...
	District Court	43	...	...	...	...	...	...	...	...	...	...
	Total Number of Seats	50	...	...	...	...	...	...	...	...	...	...
Nebraska, 1.4%	Supreme Court	7	...	...	...	...	...	...	...	...	...	...
	Court of Appeals	6	...	...	...	...	...	...	...	...	...	...
	District Court	55	1	1.8%	...	...	...	...	...	...	...	...
	Total Number of Seats	68	1	1.4%	...	...	...	...	...	...	...	...
Nevada, 4.2%	Supreme Court	7	1	14.3%	...	...	...	...	...	...	...	...
	District Court	64	...	...	1	1.6%	1	1.6%	...	...	...	...
	Total Number of Seats	71	1	1.4%	1	1.4%	1	1.4%	...	...	...	...
New Hampshire, 0	Supreme Court	5	...	...	...	...	...	...	...	...	...	...
	Superior Court	20	...	...	...	...	...	...	...	...	...	...
	Total Number of Seats	25	...	...	...	...	...	...	...	...	...	...
New Jersey, 15.7%	Supreme Court	7	1	14.3%	1	14.3%	...	...	...	...	...	...
	Appellate Division	35	2	5.7%	3	8.6%	...	...	...	...	...	...
	Superior Court	370	39	10.5%	18	4.9%	1	0.2%	...	...	...	...
	Total Number of Seats	412	42	10.2%	22	5.3%	1	0.2%	...	...	...	...

See footnotes at end of table.

STATE COURT DIVERSITY — Continued

State (a)	Type of court	Number of judgeships	African-American		Hispanic		Asian-Pacific Islander		Native American		Other (b)	
			Number	Percent	Number	Percent	Number	Percent	Number	Percent	Number	Percent
New Mexico, 29.3%	Supreme Court	5	. . .	. . .	3	60.0%	. . .	. . .	. . .	. . .	. . .	. . .
	Court of Appeals	10	. . .	. . .	5	50.0%	. . .	. . .	. . .	. . .	. . .	. . .
	District Court	84	3	3.6%	17	20.2%	. . .	. . .	. . .	. . .	1	1.2%
	Total Number of Seats	99	3	3.0%	25	25.3%	. . .	. . .	. . .	. . .	1	1.0%
New York, 18.2%	Court of Appeals	7	1	14.3%	1	14.3%	. . .	. . .	. . .	. . .	. . .	. . .
	Appellate Division	60	5	8.3%	4	6.6%	2	3.3%	. . .	. . .	. . .	. . .
	Supreme Court and County Court	455	56	12.3%	23	5.1%	3	0.7%	. . .	. . .	. . .	. . .
	Total Number of Seats	522	62	11.9%	28	5.4%	5	0.9%	. . .	. . .	. . .	. . .
North Carolina, 17.4%	Supreme Court	7	1	14.3%	. . .	. . .	. . .	. . .	. . .	. . .	. . .	. . .
	Court of Appeals	15	2	13.3%	. . .	. . .	. . .	. . .	. . .	. . .	. . .	. . .
	Superior Court	109	18	16.5%	1	0.9%	. . .	. . .	1	0.9%	. . .	. . .
	Total Number of Seats	131	21	16.0%	1	0.7%	. . .	. . .	1	0.7%	. . .	. . .
North Dakota, 2%	Supreme Court	5	. . .	. . .	. . .	. . .	. . .	. . .	. . .	. . .	. . .	. . .
	Court of Appeals	3	. . .	. . .	. . .	. . .	. . .	. . .	. . .	. . .	. . .	. . .
	District Court	42	. . .	. . .	. . .	. . .	. . .	. . .	1	2.4%	. . .	. . .
	Total Number of Seats	50	. . .	. . .	. . .	. . .	. . .	. . .	1	2.0%	. . .	. . .
Ohio, 4.5%	Supreme Court	7	. . .	. . .	. . .	. . .	. . .	. . .	. . .	. . .	. . .	. . .
	Court of Appeals	68	3	4.4%	. . .	. . .	. . .	. . .	. . .	. . .	. . .	. . .
	Court of Common Pleas	391	16	4.0%	1	0.3%	1	0.3%	. . .	. . .	. . .	. . .
	Total Number of Seats	466	19	4.1%	1	0.2%	1	0.2%	. . .	. . .	. . .	. . .
Oklahoma, 9.9%	Supreme Court	9	2	22.2%	. . .	. . .	. . .	. . .	. . .	. . .	. . .	. . .
	Court of Criminal Appeals	5	. . .	. . .	. . .	. . .	. . .	. . .	. . .	. . .	. . .	. . .
	Court of Civil Appeals	12	3	25.0%	. . .	. . .	. . .	. . .	1	8.3%	. . .	. . .
	District Court	75	3	4.0%	. . .	. . .	. . .	. . .	1	1.3%	. . .	. . .
	Total Number of Seats	101	8	7.9%	. . .	. . .	. . .	. . .	2	2.0%	. . .	. . .
Oregon, 4.2%	Supreme Court	7	. . .	. . .	1	14.3%	. . .	. . .	. . .	. . .	. . .	. . .
	Court of Appeals	10	. . .	. . .	1	10.0%	. . .	. . .	. . .	. . .	. . .	. . .
	Circuit Court	173	2	1.2%	2	1.2%	2	1.2%	. . .	. . .	. . .	. . .
	Total Number of Seats	190	2	1.1%	4	2.1%	2	1.0%	. . .	. . .	. . .	. . .
Pennsylvania, 7.9%	Supreme Court	7	1	14.3%	. . .	. . .	. . .	. . .	. . .	. . .	. . .	. . .
	Superior Court	15	. . .	. . .	. . .	. . .	. . .	. . .	. . .	. . .	. . .	. . .
	Commonwealth Court	9	1	11.1%	. . .	. . .	. . .	. . .	. . .	. . .	. . .	. . .
	Court of Common Pleas	434	32	7.4%	2	0.5%	1	0.2%	. . .	. . .	. . .	. . .
	Total Number of Seats	465	34	7.3%	2	0.4%	1	0.2%	. . .	. . .	. . .	. . .
Rhode Island, 7.4%	Supreme Court	5	. . .	. . .	. . .	. . .	. . .	. . .	. . .	. . .	. . .	. . .
	Superior Court	22	2	9.0%	. . .	. . .	. . .	. . .	. . .	. . .	. . .	. . .
	Total Number of Seats	27	2	7.4%	. . .	. . .	. . .	. . .	. . .	. . .	. . .	. . .
South Carolina, 8.5%	Supreme Court	5	1	20.0%	. . .	. . .	. . .	. . .	. . .	. . .	. . .	. . .
	Court of Appeals	9	1	11.1%	. . .	. . .	. . .	. . .	. . .	. . .	. . .	. . .
	Circuit Court	68	5	7.4%	. . .	. . .	. . .	. . .	. . .	. . .	. . .	. . .
	Total Number of Seats	82	7	8.5%	. . .	. . .	. . .	. . .	. . .	. . .	. . .	. . .

See footnotes at end of table.

STATE COURT DIVERSITY—Continued

State (a)	Type of court	Number of judgeships	African-American		Hispanic		Asian-Pacific Islander		Native American		Other (b)	
			Number	Percent	Number	Percent	Number	Percent	Number	Percent	Number	Percent
South Dakota, 0	Supreme Court	5	. . .	. . .	. . .	. . .	. . .	. . .	. . .	. . .	. . .	. . .
	Circuit Court	38	. . .	. . .	. . .	. . .	. . .	. . .	. . .	. . .	. . .	. . .
	Total Number of Seats	43	. . .	. . .	. . .	. . .	. . .	. . .	. . .	. . .	. . .	. . .
Tennessee, 7.6%	Supreme Court	5	. . .	. . .	. . .	. . .	. . .	. . .	. . .	. . .	. . .	. . .
	Court of Appeals	12	2	16.6%	. . .	. . .	. . .	. . .	. . .	. . .	. . .	. . .
	Court of Criminal Appeals	12	. . .	. . .	. . .	. . .	. . .	. . .	. . .	. . .	. . .	. . .
	Circuit, Chancery and Criminal	154	12	7.8%	. . .	. . .	. . .	. . .	. . .	. . .	. . .	. . .
	Total Number of Seats	183	14	7.6%	. . .	. . .	. . .	. . .	. . .	. . .	. . .	. . .
Texas, 17.7%	Supreme Court	9	2	22.2%	1	11.1%	. . .	. . .	. . .	. . .	. . .	. . .
	Court of Criminal Appeals	9	. . .	. . .	. . .	. . .	. . .	. . .	. . .	. . .	. . .	. . .
	Court of Appeals	80	2	2.5%	10	12.5%	. . .	. . .	1	1.3%	. . .	. . .
	District Court	445	14	3.2%	58	13.0%	2	0.4%	2	0.4%	4	0.8%
	Total Number of Seats	543	18	3.3%	69	12.7%	2	0.4%	3	0.6%	4	0.7%
Utah, 7.2%	Supreme Court	5	. . .	. . .	. . .	. . .	. . .	. . .	. . .	. . .	. . .	. . .
	Court of Appeals	7	. . .	. . .	. . .	. . .	. . .	. . .	. . .	. . .	. . .	. . .
	District Court	71	1	1.4%	1	1.4%	3	4.2%	1	1.4%	. . .	. . .
	Total Number of Seats	83	1	1.2%	1	1.2%	3	3.6%	1	1.2%	. . .	. . .
Vermont, 0	Supreme Court	5	. . .	. . .	. . .	. . .	. . .	. . .	. . .	. . .	. . .	. . .
	Superior Court	12	. . .	. . .	. . .	. . .	. . .	. . .	. . .	. . .	. . .	. . .
	District Court	17	. . .	. . .	. . .	. . .	. . .	. . .	. . .	. . .	. . .	. . .
	Total Number of Seats	34	. . .	. . .	. . .	. . .	. . .	. . .	. . .	. . .	. . .	. . .
Virginia, 12.6%	Supreme Court	7	2	28.6%	. . .	. . .	. . .	. . .	. . .	. . .	. . .	. . .
	Court of Appeals	11	3	27.3%	. . .	. . .	. . .	. . .	. . .	. . .	. . .	. . .
	Circuit Court	157	17	10.8%	. . .	. . .	. . .	. . .	. . .	. . .	. . .	. . .
	Total Number of Seats	175	22	12.6%	. . .	. . .	. . .	. . .	. . .	. . .	. . .	. . .
Washington, 7.8%	Supreme Court	9	. . .	. . .	. . .	. . .	. . .	. . .	. . .	. . .	. . .	. . .
	Court of Appeals	22	1	4.5%	. . .	. . .	1	4.5%	. . .	. . .	. . .	. . .
	Superior Court	186	9	4.8%	2	1.1%	4	2.1%	. . .	. . .	. . .	. . .
	Total Number of Seats	217	10	4.6%	2	0.9%	5	2.3%	. . .	. . .	. . .	. . .
West Virginia, 2.8%	Supreme Court of Appeals	5	. . .	. . .	. . .	. . .	. . .	. . .	. . .	. . .	. . .	. . .
	Circuit Court	66	2	3.0%	. . .	. . .	. . .	. . .	. . .	. . .	. . .	. . .
	Total Number of Seats	71	2	2.8%	. . .	. . .	. . .	. . .	. . .	. . .	. . .	. . .
Wisconsin, 4.8%	Supreme Court	7	. . .	. . .	. . .	. . .	. . .	. . .	. . .	. . .	. . .	. . .
	Court of Appeals	16	. . .	. . .	. . .	. . .	. . .	. . .	. . .	. . .	. . .	. . .
	Circuit Court	246	8	3.2%	4	1.6%	1	0.4%	. . .	. . .	. . .	. . .
	Total Number of Seats	269	8	3.0%	4	1.5%	1	0.3%	. . .	. . .	. . .	. . .
Wyoming, 0	Supreme Court	5	. . .	. . .	. . .	. . .	. . .	. . .	. . .	. . .	. . .	. . .
	District Court	21	. . .	. . .	. . .	. . .	. . .	. . .	. . .	. . .	. . .	. . .
	Total Number of Seats	26	. . .	. . .	. . .	. . .	. . .	. . .	. . .	. . .	. . .	. . .

Source: Barbara Graham, unpublished dataset on racial and ethnic diversity of state courts of general jurisdiction, 2008.

Key:

. . . — None

(a) Percentage following state is total percentage of minority judges in state.

(b) Other category includes biracial, multiracial and nonwhite.

Judicial Elections in 2008

By David Rottman

Thirty nine states elect some or all of their judges. In 2008, the trend continued toward costly and negative campaigns dominated by the efforts of interest groups rather than the candidates themselves. Local elections in three states gave comfort to proponents of non-contestable races but prospects for state level changes remain unclear.

Judicial elections in 2008 confirmed their transformation into "high dollar free-for-alls marked by dueling campaign salvos by organized interest groups, often located outside the state of the election."[1] Thirty-nine elections were held in 2008 for supreme court judgeships. In the 26 seats filled by partisan or nonpartisan elections, 20 incumbents sought re-election. Thirteen other justices did not draw an opponent. Six of the 20 incumbent justices were defeated, including the chief justices of Michigan, Mississippi (along with two of his colleagues) and West Virginia (in a party primary). The defeat of that many chief justices last happened in 1986.[2] All 20 justices running in retention elections were retained by the voters.[3]

Elections Costly and Nasty

The contested races featured negative, even scurrilous, television advertising, partisanship and under-the-radar clashes between powerful economic interests. Nearly $20 million was spent on television advertising in supreme court races, an increase of 24 percent over 2006. Most of the ads were paid for by interest groups or political parties rather than by the candidates. At this point, Minnesota and North Dakota are the only states using contestable elections that have not seen television advertising in judicial races. Television advertising, of course, has the potential to inform voters. In practice, its most notable impact is to force judicial candidates to raise large sums of money from groups likely to be involved in litigation or to represent litigants. As in past elections, television advertising, particularly when run by interest groups, tends to be highly negative in tone and dubious in accuracy.

The 2008 outcomes, however, broke with a recent trend in which candidates backed by the business community fared relatively well. Another novel feature was the extent to which the support interest groups provided to candidates, either directly via contributions or indirectly through independent expenditures, became a core issue influencing the outcome of judicial elections. One group observed, "While expensive advertising helped candidates get their message out, it came with a cost."[4] Their opponents were able to turn the sources of the funding for the ads to their own advantage. Supreme court candidates in Alabama, West Virginia and other states ran television ads declaring they "can't be bought" and proclaiming that they would restore integrity to the state's judiciary.

The Landscape of Judicial Elections

States use 16 distinct systems to select judges. Only one state—Rhode Island—follows the federal example of lifetime appointments. With some loss of detail, the states can be placed into four basic categories of selection methods out of which each state has devised its own selection system. Today, 89 percent of general jurisdiction trial and appellate judges face an election of some kind to get or retain office. To retain their office as an appellate judge, 11 percent face re-appointment, 43 percent face retention elections, 20 percent face nonpartisan elections, and 26 percent face partisan elections. The comparable percentages for trial judges are 10 percent by re-appointment, 19 percent by retention, 44 percent by nonpartisan election, and 27 percent by partisan election.

Appointment is by either the governor or (in South Carolina and Virginia by the legislature), with their choice often restricted to the names submitted by a non-partisan nominating commission. The "Missouri Plan" combines gubernatorial appointments followed thereafter by retention elections. Retention elections occur after a judge has served a fixed period of time on the bench, with voters asked to vote "yes" or "no" on whether a judge should continue in office. Nonpartisan elections are between candidates whose party labels are not on the ballot.[5] Partisan elections feature judicial candidates who run in party primaries and are listed on the ballot as a candidate of a specific political party.[6] Recent years have narrowed the differences between methods of selection. Politics and big money are pervasive in all four methods, though far less so in retention elections.

The Defeat of Three Chief Justices

The stories behind the defeats of incumbent chief justices capture the changing face of judicial elections in the 21st century. In Michigan, where Supreme Court candidates are chosen at party conventions and run as partisans although no party label is on the ballot, the incumbent chief justice, a Republican, lost his bid for re-election in a landslide few had predicted. Partisanship and opposing economic interests added venom to the race, particularly a long-running feud between the incumbent and the state's Democratic Party, which ran television ads attacking the incumbent long before an opposing candidate emerged. Ads attacked the incumbent by using a look-alike actor to show the incumbent nodding off during a case that involved the deaths of six Detroit youths, and described him as the "good soldier" of business groups. Ads run by or on behalf of the incumbent included claims that the challenger, a trial judge, was a "terrorist sympathizer" who wanted the job to allow her to spend more winter vacation time in Florida, and as having made "dangerous rulings" that set a "sexual predator" free.[7] In the race, the candidates spent a combined $2.5 million and interest groups spent $3.8 million. The sources of the funds underlying the interest group efforts are unknown because there is no required disclosure of who contributed funding.

The defeat ended conservatives' nine-year lock on the Michigan Supreme Court. [8] The chief justice lost the election by a large margin, with a Libertarian candidate attracting more than 400,000 votes. To an unknowable degree, the presidential contest affected the outcome—but the presidential contest was closer than this one. Both political parties were very active: "The Sunday before the election, Obama's foot soldiers papered thousands of Michigan precincts with door-hangers featuring photos of Hathaway [the challenger] and popular Democratic Sen. Carl Levin beneath a larger one of Obama and running mate Joe Biden."[9]

In Mississippi, a nonpartisan election state, three of the four justices up for re-election were defeated, one by a huge margin—his opponent garnered 67 percent of the votes. The real campaign, one commentator explained, was a power struggle between plaintiffs and defendants: "The pro-business lobby wants to maintain high invulnerability to lawsuits, while attorneys want to be able to take a chunk out of them."[10] Claims were made that the Mississippi Supreme Court in recent years had reversed 88 percent of all jury verdicts in favor of plaintiffs.[11] The 2008 elections reversed a trend started in 2002 in which candidates supported by the state's chamber of commerce and various other in-state and out-of-state pro-business groups had triumphed. The successful challengers ran television ads alleging that outside interests were seeking to change the state in a manner that would fit their ambitions and not the state's needs.

In West Virginia, the incumbent chief justice was defeated in his party's four-candidate primary. The incumbent raised the most campaign money but was doomed by photographs showing him on vacation in Monaco with the CEO of a coal company with cases pending before the court. The state's chamber of commerce and medical association purchased television and radio ads supporting the incumbent chief. A labor group ran ads that featured photographs of the incumbent arm in arm with the CEO who had cases pending before the court. Parodying TV's"Lifestyles of the Rich and Famous," the announcer began: "Blue skies, sandy beaches, cocktails on the Riviera, a vacation to remember for this coal baron. He met up with a West Virginia Supreme Court Justice. ..."[12] as photographs were displayed of the two arm-in-arm on a balcony raising glasses in a toast. The state's chamber of commerce and medical association purchased television and radio ads supporting the incumbent chief.

Other Judicial Races

Other states featuring nasty and noisy supreme court races include Alabama and Wisconsin. Alabama, with an open supreme court seat, had the most costly election of the year. Nearly $4 million was spent by the two candidates, while an out-of-state group spent more than $800,000 on television ads backing a candidate.[13]

The imbalance between candidate and interest group expenditures was still more pronounced in Wisconsin's Supreme Court race. An incumbent justice was challenged with interest groups lining up both on the side of the challenger as well as the incumbent. The overwhelming majority of spending on the race was by interest groups mounting their own campaigns. The incumbent justice was narrowly defeated.[14]

The impact of national political developments on judicial races also affected the outcome of trial court races. This was particularly notable in partisan election states that use straight-ticket levers. In Houston (Harris County), Texas, 22 of 26 incumbent Republican circuit court judges on the ballot were swept from office.[15] President Obama's coattails and demographic changes in a once Republican stronghold leveraged the switch. Judicial candidates in Texas are included under "straight-ticket" ballots that cast a vote for all of a party's candidates. Obama's popularity gave Democratic judicial candidates the benefit of 47,000 more straight-ticket votes than their Republican opponents received. Demographic trends in the county over recent years have increased the proportion of the electorate likely to support the Democratic Party.

Efforts to Change the Method of Judicial Elections

The judicial election scene in 2008 was enlivened by some rare ballot victories by opponents of contestable judicial elections. Two decades have passed since a state switched from contestable elections, partisan or nonpartisan, to the Missouri Plan traditionally favored by reformers. The victories occurred at the local level. Voters in Arkansas, Kansas and Missouri either rejected bids to return to contestable elections or took the affirmative step to end contestable elections. All these localities tended to be conservative and, arguably, tough targets for reformers interested in limiting the voters' role in selecting judges.[16]

In Arkansas, the change enacted was modest. Voters in two counties approved by large margins the creation of judicial nominating commissions to submit potential candidates for filling a vacancy when a judge dies or retires. The commissions will consist of five members, two selected by the county commission, two by the local bar association and one by the state's chief justice. When a vacancy occurs, the commission will forward three names for the governor to consider and the person appointed then serves until the next scheduled judicial election.[17] The adoption of nominating commissions is significant. Even in states with partisan elections, one-half of their judges first join the bench through an appointment to fill a vacancy.[18]

In Kansas, 59 percent of voters in affluent Johnson County—a suburb of Kansas City, Missouri just over the river—rejected a proposed return to partisan judicial elections, opting instead to keep their system of appointments followed by retention elections. The Kansas Constitution allows each of the state's 31 judicial districts to decide whether it will select its trial judges by partisan election or by appointments followed by retention elections.

The national spotlight shined brightest on Greene County, Mo., (the Springfield area) where 52 percent of voters approved a change from partisan elections to appointments vetted by a nominating commission followed by retention elections thereafter. Both sides mounted an intense campaign. Springfield voters were Missouri's largest advocates for retaining the status quo. Former Attorney General John Ashcroft and current Republican Gov. Matt Blunt, both native sons, taped ads opposing the change. As noted, this was the first national affirmative move in more than two decades and the first in Missouri in 35 years. The Springfield area was the largest jurisdiction in population size using partisan elections. Whether this change is a harbinger of things to come in Missouri or elsewhere is impossible to determine.[19]

No changes in statewide methods of judicial selection were recorded in 2008. Nonetheless, there was legislative activity pointing to such a change in many states. A scorecard of this activity would probably show more efforts have been made toward contestable elections than to accomplish the reverse move.

The Caperton Case

The judicial election receiving the most national coverage in 2008 actually took place four years before in West Virginia. That election gained notoriety when it led to a case, now pending, in the U.S. Supreme Court.[20] That case, *Caperton v. Massey*, originated in an election challenge to an incumbent West Virginia Supreme Court justice. The CEO of Massey Energy, a major coal mining concern, contributed $1,000 to aid the challenger, the maximum allowed under the state's law, but spent $3 million of his own money to run television ads attacking the incumbent. As the campaign proceeded, a case was winding its way to the West Virginia Supreme Court, in which Massey Energy sought to overturn a $50 million jury award in a case of fraud that forced another mining firm out of business. The challenger narrowly won and several years later voted with the majority to overturn the jury verdict and the resulting damages award.[21]

The U.S. Supreme Court agreed to hear claims from the losing party that the challenger, now a justice, should have disqualified himself from participating in the case. The specific issue was whether a judge that benefited from such a large sum of campaign support should sit in judgment on a case in which his benefactor was a party. Oral arguments in the case were held March 3 with a decision expected in June 2009. That decision may answer the question of whether campaign contributions that helped elect a judge can be so substantial as to require a judge to step aside from hearing a case in which the contributor is a party.

Conclusion

The 2008 judicial elections featured some "nasty, noisey, and costly" races for supreme court seats. Nationally, however, there was no evident acceleration of trends toward judicial elections that are indistinguishable from those held for political office in the executive and legislative branches of state government. Few judicial candidates chose to campaign by staking out positions on hot-button economic or social issues. Much of what was problematic about judicial races could be attributed to the spending and actions of interest groups, not by candidates themselves.

There were some stirrings in local races of a renewed drive to move away from contestable judicial elections, but also a flurry of legislation introduced that would move states in the opposite direction. Past experience suggests there is little prospect of change anytime soon in the methods states now use to select their judges. In 2009, attention will be focused on the U. S. Supreme Court's decision in Caperton v.Massey, which may resolve the question of when campaign contributions that helped elect a judge can be so substantial as to require that judge to step aside from hearing a case in which the contributor is a party. The media coverage of that case will ensure that judicial elections will remain very much in the news.

Notes

[1]Conference of Chief Justices, Brief of the Conference of Chief Justices as Amicus Curiae in Support of Neither Party in Supreme Court of the United States, Caperton v. Massey, p. 8.

[2]The three chief justices were Bird of California, Celebrezze of Ohio, and Billings of North Carolina.

[3]Charles Hall (ed.), *The New Politics of Judicial Elections*, Justice at Stake Campaign, 2009.

[4]Justice at Stake Campaign, "2008 Supreme Court Elections: More Money, More Nastiness," Press Release, November 5, 2009.

[5]However, in Ohio (all judges), Michigan (only for supreme court contests), Arizona (trial judges), and Maryland (trial judges) candidates are chosen in party primaries and backed by their party.

[6]Lee Epstein, Jack Knight and Olga Shvetsova, "Selecting Selection Systems," in S. Burbank and B. Friedman (eds.), *Judicial Independence at the Crossroads: An Interdisciplinary Approach*, (Sage Publications, 2002), 194.

[7]These television advertisements have been archived by the Brennan Center for Justice's "Buying Time-2008" Project and can be viewed at: *www.brennancenter.org/content/resource/buying_time_2008_michigan*.

[8]"Supreme Court chief justice upset," *The Oakland Press*, November 5, 2008.

[9]Brian Dickerson, "How Dems took out a chief justice," *Freep.com* (a subsidiary of the Detroit Free Press), November 7, 2008.

[10]Adam Lynch, "Court Showdown: Chamber v. Plaintiffs," *Jackson Free Press*, October 29, 2008.

[11]Ibid.

[12]Ian Urbina, "West Virginia's Top Judge Loses his Re-Election Bid," *New York Times*, May 15, 2008

[13]Eric Velasco, "Alabama high court race again garners most expensive price tag in U.S.," *Birmingham News*, January 31, 2009.

[14]Patrick Marley and Stacy Forester, "Gableman victorious: Challenger beats Butler in high court race; 1st such ouster since '67," *Milwaukee-Wisconsin Journal Sentinel*, April 2, 2008.

[15]Nathan Koppel, "Obama's Coattails Stretch to Texas Trial Courts," *Wall Street Journal*, November 5, 2008.

[16]All of the counties mentioned voted for John McCain by significant margins.

[17]Tom Smith, "Amendment would establish judicial selection committee," *Times Daily*, October 26. 2008.

[18]Lisa Holmes and Jolly Emery, "Court diversification: staffing the states courts of last resort through interim appointments," *Justice System Journal*, Vol. 27, No. 1, 2006.

[19]Chris Blank, "Missouri judge selection fight picks up in Springfield," *News Tribune*, October 29, 2008.

[20]While thousands of petitions seeking review are filed annually with the U.S. Supreme Court, in recent years only 70 to 80 petitions are accepted ("granted cert") for full review by the Court.

[21]Robert Barnes, "Case may define when a judge must recuse himself: W.Va. Justice ruled for a man who spent millions to elect him," *The Washington Post*, March 2, 2009, A01.

About the Author

David Rottman is principal court research consultant at the National Center for State Courts (NCSC). His current research concerns judicial selection, public opinion on the courts, the evolution of court structures, and problem-solving courts. Rottman also is the NCSC coordinator of the Election Law Program established jointly by the NCSC and the William & Mary School of Law. He is the author of books on community courts, social inequality, and modern Ireland. Rottman has a Ph.D. in sociology from the University of Illinois at Urbana, and previously worked at the Economic and Social Institute in Dublin, Ireland.

Table 5.1
STATE COURTS OF LAST RESORT

State or other jurisdiction	Name of court	Justices chosen (a)		No. of judges (b)	Term (in years) (c)	Chief justice	
		At large	By district			Method of selection	Term of office for chief justice
Alabama	S.C.	★		9	6	Non-partisan popular election	6 years
Alaska	S.C.	★		5	10	By court	3 years
Arizona	S.C.	★		5	6	By court	5 years
Arkansas	S.C.	★		7	8	Non-partisan popular election	8 years
California	S.C.	★		7	12	Appointed by governor	12 years
Colorado	S.C.	★		7	10	By court	Indefinite
Connecticut	S.C.	★		7	8	Gubernatorial appointment from judicial nominating commission with consent of legislature	8 years
Delaware	S.C.	★		5	12	Appointed by governor	12 years
Florida	S.C.	(d)		7	6	By court	2 years
Georgia	S.C.	★		7	6	By court	2 years
Hawaii	S.C.	★		5	10	Gubernatorial appointment from judicial nominating commission with consent of legislature	10 years
Idaho	S.C.	★		5	6	By court	4 years
Illinois	S.C.		★	7	10	By court	3 years
Indiana	S.C.	★		5	10 (e)	Judicial nominating commission appointment	5 years
Iowa	S.C.	★		7	8	By court	8 years
Kansas	S.C.	★		7	6	Rotation by seniority	Indefinite
Kentucky	S.C.		★	7	8	By court	4 years
Louisiana	S.C.		★	7	10	By seniority of service	Duration of service
Maine	S.J.C.	★		7	7	Appointed by governor	7 years
Maryland	C.A.		★	7	10	Appointed by governor	Indefinite
Massachusetts	S.J.C.	★		7	To age 70	Appointed by governor (f)	To age 70
Michigan	S.C.	★		7	8	By court	2 years
Minnesota	S.C.	★		7	6	Gubernatorial appointment	6 years
Mississippi	S.C.		★	9	8	By seniority of service	Duration of service
Missouri	S.C.	★		7	12	By court	2 years
Montana	S.C.	★		7	8	Non-partisan popular election	8 years
Nebraska	S.C.	★(g)	★(g)	7	6 (h)	Appointed by governor from judicial nominating commission	Duration of service
Nevada	S.C.	★		7	6	Rotation	2 years (i)
New Hampshire	S.C.	★		5	5	Seniority	5 years
New Jersey	S.C.	★		7	7 (j)	Gubernatorial appointment with consent of the legislature	Duration of service
New Mexico	S.C.	★		5	8	By court	2 years
New York	C.A.	★		7	14	Appointed by governor from judicial nomination commission	14 years
North Carolina	S.C.	★		7	8	Non-partisan popular election	8 years
North Dakota	S.C.	★		5	10	By Supreme and district court judges	5 years (k)
Ohio	S.C.	★		7	6	Popular election (l)	6 years
Oklahoma	S.C.		★	9	6	By court	Duration of service
	C.C.A.		★	5	6	By court	5 years
Oregon	S.C.	★		7	6	By court	6 years
Pennsylvania	S.C.	★		7	10	Seniority	Duration of term
Rhode Island	S.C.	★		5	Life	Appointed by governor from judicial nominating commission	Life
South Carolina	S.C.	★		5	10	Legislative appointment	10 years

See footnotes at end of table.

STATE COURTS OF LAST RESORT—Continued

State or other jurisdiction	Name of court	Justices chosen (a)		No. of judges (b)	Term (in years) (c)	Chief justice	
		At large	By district			Method of selection	Term of office for chief justice
South Dakota	S.C.	★(m)	★(m)	5	8	By court	4 years
Tennessee	S.C.	★		5	8	By court	4 years
Texas	S.C.	★		9	6	Partisan election	6 years
	C.C.A.	★		9	6	Partisan election	6 years (n)
Utah	S.C.	★		5	10 (o)	By court	4 years
Vermont	S.C.	★		5	6	Appointed by governor from judicial nomination commission, with consent of the legislature	6 years
Virginia	S.C.	★		7	12	Seniority	4 years
Washington	S.C.	★		9	6	By court	4 years
West Virginia	S.C.A.	★		5	12	Seniority	1 year
Wisconsin	S.C.	★		7	10	Seniority	Until declined
Wyoming	S.C.	★		5	8	By court	4 years
Dist. of Columbia	C.A.	★		9	15	Judicial nominating commission appointment	4 years
Puerto Rico	S.C.	★		7	To age 70	Gubernatorial appointment with consent of the legislature	To age 70

Sources: State Court Organization, 2004, U.S. Department of Justice Statistics, National Center for State Courts, February 2009.

Key:

S.C. — Supreme Court
S.C.A. — Supreme Court of Appeals
S.J.C. — Supreme Judicial Court
C.A. — Court of Appeals
C.C.A. — Court of Criminal Appeals
H.C. — High Court

(a) See Chapter 5 table entitled, "Selection and Retention of Appellate Court Judges," for details.

(b) Number includes chief justice.

(c) The initial term may be shorter. See Chapter 5 table entitled, "Selection and Retention of Appellate Court Judges," for details.

(d) Regional (5), Statewide (2), Regional based on District of Appeal.

(e) Initial term is two years; retention 10 years.

(f) Chief justice, in the appellate courts, is a separate judicial office from that of an associate justice. Chief justices are appointed, until age 70, by the governor with the advice and consent of the Executive (Governor's) Council.

(g) Chief justice chosen statewide; associate judges chosen by district.

(h) More than three years for first election and every six years thereafter.

(i) The term may be split between eligible justices.

(j) Followed by tenure. All judges are subject to gubernatorial reappointment and consent by the Senate after an initial seven-year term; thereafter, they may serve until mandatory retirement at age 70.

(k) Or expiration of term, whichever is first.

(l) Party affiliation is not included on the ballot in the general election, but candidates are chosen through partisan primary nominations.

(m) Initially chosen by district; retention determined statewide.

(n) Presiding judge of Court of Criminal Appeals.

(o) The initial term of appointment is until the next general election immediately following the third year from the time of the initial appointment.

Table 5.2
STATE INTERMEDIATE APPELLATE COURTS AND GENERAL TRIAL COURTS: NUMBER OF JUDGES AND TERMS

State or other jurisdiction	Intermediate appellate court			General trial court		
	Name of court	No. of judges	Term (years)	Name of court	No. of judges	Term (years)
Alabama	Court of Criminal Appeals	5	6	Circuit Court	144	6
	Court of Civil Appeals	5	6			
Alaska	Court of Appeals	3	8	Superior Court	34	6 (a)
Arizona	Court of Appeals	22	6	Superior Court	166	4
Arkansas	Court of Appeals	12	8	Chancery/Probate Court and Circuit Court	120	6
California	Courts of Appeal	88	12	Superior Court	1,548	6
Colorado	Court of Appeals	19	8	District Court	153	6 (b)
Connecticut	Appellate Court	10	8	Superior Court	180	8
Delaware	. . .	. . .	. . .	Superior Court	19	12
				Court of Chancery	5	12
Florida	District Courts of Appeals	62	6	Circuit Court	599	6
Georgia	Court of Appeals	12	6	Superior Court	188	4
Hawaii	Intermediate Court of Appeals	6	10	Circuit Court	33	10
Idaho	Court of Appeals	3	6	District Court	42	4
Illinois	Appellate Court	53	10	Circuit Court	494	6
Indiana	Court of Appeals	15	12 (c)	Superior Court, Probate Court and Circuit Court	203	6
Iowa	Court of Appeals	9	6	District Court	337 (d)	6 (e)
Kansas	Court of Appeals	12	4	District Court	243 (f)	4
Kentucky	Court of Appeals	14	8	Circuit Court	95	8
Louisiana	Courts of Appeal	53 (g)	10	District Court	242	6
Maine	. . .	. . .	. . .	Superior Court	17	7
Maryland	Court of Special Appeals	13	10	Circuit Court	153	15
Massachusetts	Appeals Court	28 (h)	To age 70	Superior Court	73	To age 70
Michigan	Court of Appeals	28	6	Circuit Court	221	6
Minnesota	Court of Appeals	16	6	District Court	276	6
Mississippi	Court of Appeals	10	8	Circuit Court	51	4
Missouri	Court of Appeals	32	12	Circuit Court	334 (i)	6 (j)
Montana	. . .	. . .	. . .	District Court	39 (k)	6
Nebraska	Court of Appeals	6	3 (l)	District Court	55	6(m)
Nevada	. . .	. . .	. . .	District Court	64	6
New Hampshire	. . .	. . .	. . .	Superior Court	26	To age 70
New Jersey	Appellate Division of Superior Court	35	7 (n)	Superior Court	408	7 (o)
New Mexico	Court of Appeals	10	8	District Court	88	6
New York	Appellate Division of Supreme Court	57	5 (p)	Supreme Court	498	14
	Appellate Terms of Supreme Court	(q)		County Court	129	10
North Carolina	Court of Appeals	15	8	Superior Court	105 (r)	8 (s)
North Dakota	Temporary Court of Appeals	3 (hh)	1 (ii)	District Court	42	6
Ohio	Courts of Appeal	68	6	Court of Common Pleas	391	6

See footnotes at end of table.

STATE INTERMEDIATE APPELLATE COURTS AND GENERAL TRIAL COURTS: NUMBER OF JUDGES AND TERMS — Continued

State or other jurisdiction	Intermediate appellate court			General trial court		
	Name of court	No. of judges	Term (years)	Name of court	No. of judges	Term (years)
Oklahoma	Court of Appeals	10	6	District Court	241 (t)	4 (u)
Oregon	Court of Appeals	10	6	Circuit Court	173	6
				Tax Court	4	6
Pennsylvania	Superior Court	23 (v)	10	Court of Common Pleas	493 (x)	10
	Commonwealth Court	9 (w)	10			
Rhode Island	. . .	. . .	Life	Superior Court	27 (y)	Life
South Carolina	Court of Appeals	10 (z)	6	Circuit Court	46 (aa)	6
South Dakota	. . .	. . .	. . .	Circuit Court	38	8
Tennessee	Court of Appeals	12	8	Chancery Court	34	8
	Court of Criminal Appeals	12	8	Circuit Court	85	8
				Criminal Court	33	8
				Probate Court	2	8
Texas	Courts of Appeal	80	6	District Court	439	4
Utah	Court of Appeals	7	6 (bb)	District Court	71	6 (cc)
Vermont	. . .	. . .	. . .	Superior Court and District Court	32 (dd)	6
Virginia	Court of Appeals	11	8	Circuit Court	157	8
Washington	Courts of Appeal	22 (ee)	6	Superior Court	176	4
West Virginia	. . .	. . .	. . .	Circuit Court	66	8
Wisconsin	Court of Appeals	16	6	Circuit Court	240	6
Wyoming	. . .	. . .	. . .	District Court	21	6
Dist. of Columbia	. . .	. . .	. . .	Superior Court	59	15
Puerto Rico	Circuit Court of Appeals	39	16	Court of First Instance	328 (ff)	12 (gg)

Sources: State Court Organization, 2004, U.S. Department of Justice Statistics, update from the National Center for State Courts, February 2009.

Key:

. . . — Court does not exist in jurisdiction or not applicable.

(a) The initial term for Superior Court judges is three years.

(b) The initial term for District Court, Denver Probate Court, Denver Juvenile Court and County Court judges is two years.

(c) Two years initial; 10 years retention.

(d) The number of District Court judges includes associate judges and magistrates.

(e) The initial term for District judges is at least one year. Associate judges serve a term of four years with an initial term of at least one year, and magistrate judges serve a term of four years.

(f) The number of District Court judges includes magistrates.

(g) The Courts of Appeal have 55 authorized judicial positions.

(h) The Appeals Court has 25 authorized judicial positions. The judges of the Appeals Court are assisted by the services on recall of several retired judges.

(i) The number of Circuit Court judges includes associate judges.

(j) Associate Circuit judges serve a term of four years.

(k) There are actually 43 District Court judges. Three of those judges serve the Water Court and are included in the data for that court.

(l) More than three years for first election and retention is every six years thereafter.

(m) The initial term is for three years but not more than five years.

(n) Followed by tenure. All judges are subject to gubernatorial reappointment and consent by the Senate after an initial seven-year term; thereafter, they may serve until mandatory retirement at age 70.

(o) After an initial seven-year term, the reapportionment term for Superior and Tax Court judges is open-ended until mandatory retirement age at age 70.

(p) Or duration.

(q) Appellate Terms of the Supreme Court have been established within the First and Second Departments of the Appellate Division. Data for the Appellate Terms are not included in the information presented here.

(r) The number of Superior Court judges includes special judges.

(s) Special judges serve a term of four years.

(t) The number of District Court judges includes associate judges and special judges.

(u) District and associate judges serve four-year terms; special judges serve at pleasure.

(v) The Superior Court has 15 authorized judicial positions. The judges of the Superior Court are assisted by senior judges specially appointed by the Supreme Court.

(w) The judges of the Commonwealth Court are assisted by senior judges specially appointed by the Supreme Court. Also, senior Common Pleas Court judges occasionally serve on the Commonwealth Court.

(x) These numbers include both active and senior judges.

(y) The number of judges includes magistrates.

(z) The Court of Appeals has nine authorized judicial positions. The judges of the Court of Appeals are assisted by a retired Court of Appeals judge now on special appointment to the court.

(aa) Four to five judges are currently working as active retired judges.

(bb) The initial term of appointment is until the next general election immediately following the third year from the time of the initial appointment.

(cc) The initial term of appointment is until the next general election immediately following the third year from the time of the initial appointment.

(dd) Plus five magistrates for Family Court.

(ee) The Courts of Appeal have 23 authorized judicial positions.

(ff) The number of Court of First Instance judges includes Municipal Division judges.

(gg) Municipal judges serve a term of eight years.

(hh) The Supreme Court may provide for the assignment of active or retired District Court judges, retired justices of the Supreme Court, and lawyers, to serve on three-judge panels.

(ii) Assignments are for a specified time, not to exceed one year or the completion of one or more cases on the docket of the Supreme Court.

Table 5.3
QUALIFICATIONS OF JUDGES OF STATE APPELLATE COURTS AND GENERAL TRIAL COURTS

State or other jurisdiction	Residency requirement: State A	Residency requirement: State T	Residency requirement: Local A	Residency requirement: Local T	Minimum age A	Minimum age T	Legal credentials A	Legal credentials T
Alabama	1 yr.	1 yr.	. . .	1 yr.	. . .	. . .	Licensed attorney	Licensed attorney
Alaska	5 yrs.	5 yrs.	. . .	. . .	. . .	. . .	8 years practice	5 years practice
Arizona	10 yrs. (a)	5 yrs.	(b)	1 yr.	(e)	30	(c)	(d)
Arkansas	2 yrs.	2 yrs.	(b)	. . .	30	28	8 years practice	6 years licensed in state
California	. . .	. . .	. . .	. . .	. . .	. . .	10 years state bar	10 years state bar
Colorado	★	★	. . .	★	. . .	. . .	5 years state bar	5 years state bar
Connecticut	★	★	. . .	. . .	. . .	. . .	Licensed attorney	Member of the bar
Delaware	★	★	. . .	★	. . .	. . .	"Learned in law"	"Learned in law"
Florida	★(f)	★	★(f)	★(g)	. . .	. . .	10 years state bar	5 years state bar
Georgia	★	3 yrs.	. . .	. . .	. . .	30	7 years state bar	7 years state bar
Hawaii	★	★	. . .	. . .	. . .	. . .	10 years state bar	10 years state bar
Idaho	2 yrs.	1 yr.	. . .	. . .	30	. . .	10 years state bar	10 years state bar
Illinois	★	★	★	★	. . .	. . .	Licensed attorney	. . .
Indiana	★	1 yr.	. . .	★	. . .	. . .	10 years state bar (h)	. . .
Iowa	★	★	. . .	★	. . .	. . .	Licensed attorney	Admitted to state bar
Kansas	. . .	. . .	. . .	. . .	30	. . .	10 years active and continuous practice (i)	5 years state bar
Kentucky	2 yrs.	2 yrs.	2 yrs.	2 yrs.	. . .	. . .	8 years state bar and licensed attorney	8 years state bar
Louisiana	2 yrs.	2 yrs.	2 yrs.	2 yrs.	. . .	. . .	5 years state bar	5 years state bar
Maine	. . .	. . .	. . .	. . .	. . .	. . .	"Learned in law"	"Learned in law"
Maryland	5 yrs.	5 yrs.	6 mos.	6 mos.	30	30	State bar member	State bar member
Massachusetts	. . .	. . .	. . .	. . .	. . .	. . .	. . .	. . .
Michigan	★	★	. . .	. . .	. . .	. . .	State bar member and 5 years practice	State bar member
Minnesota	. . .	. . .	. . .	. . .	. . .	. . .	Licensed attorney	Licensed attorney
Mississippi	5 yrs.	5 yrs.	★(j)	. . .	30	26	5 years state bar	5 years practice
Missouri	9 yrs. (k)	3 yrs. (k)	. . .	★(k)	30	30	State bar member	State bar member
Montana	2 yrs.	2 yrs.	. . .	. . .	. . .	. . .	5 years state bar	5 years state bar
Nebraska	3 yrs.	★	★	★	30	30	5 years practice	5 years practice
Nevada	2 yrs.	2 yrs.	. . .	. . .	25	25	State bar member (l)	2 years state bar member and 10 years practice
New Hampshire	. . .	. . .	. . .	. . .	. . .	. . .	. . .	. . .
New Jersey	. . .	(m)	. . .	(m)	. . .	. . .	Admitted to practice in state for at least 10 years	10 years practice of law
New Mexico	3 yrs.	3 yrs.	. . .	★	35	35	10 years practice and/or current state judge	6 years active practice
New York	★	★	. . .	. . .	. . .	18	10 years state bar	10 years state bar
North Carolina	. . .	★	. . .	(n)	. . .	. . .	State bar member	State bar member
North Dakota	★	★	. . .	★	. . .	. . .	License to practice law	State bar member
Ohio	★	★	. . .	★	. . .	. . .	6 years practice	6 years practice
Oklahoma	★	(o)	1 yr.	★	30	. . .	5 years state bar	(p)
Oregon	3 yrs.	3 yrs.	. . .	1 yr.	. . .	. . .	State bar member	State bar member
Pennsylvania	1 yr.	★	. . .	1 yr.	. . .	. . .	State bar member	State bar member
Rhode Island	. . .	. . .	. . .	. . .	21	. . .	License to practice law	State bar member
South Carolina	5 yrs.	5 yrs.	. . .	(q)	32	32	8 years state bar	8 years state bar
South Dakota	★	★	★	★	. . .	. . .	State bar member	State bar member
Tennessee	5 yrs.	5 yrs.	★(r)	1 yr.	35	30	Qualified to practice law	Qualified to practice law
Texas	★	. . .	. . .	2 yrs.	35	25	(s)	(t)
Utah	5 yrs.	3 yrs.	. . .	★	30	25	Admitted to practice law	Admitted to practice law
Vermont	. . .	. . .	. . .	. . .	. . .	. . .	5 years state bar	5 years state bar
Virginia	. . .	★	. . .	★	. . .	. . .	5 years state bar	5 years state bar
Washington	1 yr.	1 yr.	1 yr.	1 yr.	. . .	. . .	State bar member	State bar member
West Virginia	5 yrs.	★	. . .	★	30	30	10 years state bar	5 years state bar
Wisconsin	10 days	10 days	10 days	10 days	. . .	. . .	5 years state bar	5 years state bar
Wyoming	3 yrs.	2 yrs.	. . .	. . .	30	28	9 years state bar	. . .
Dist. of Columbia	★	★	90 days	90 days	. . .	. . .	5 years state bar	5 years state bar (u)
Puerto Rico	5 yrs.	. . .	. . .	. . .	. . .	. . .	10 years state bar	7 years state bar

See footnotes at end of table.

QUALIFICATIONS OF JUDGES OF STATE APPELLATE COURTS AND GENERAL TRIAL COURTS — Continued

Sources: State Court Organization, 2004, U.S. Department of Justice Statistics, update from the National Center for State Courts, February 2009.

Key:

A — Judges of courts of last resort and intermediate appellate courts.

T — Judges of general trial courts.

★ — Provision; length of time not specified.

. . . — No specific provision.

N.A. — Not applicable.

(a) For court of appeals, five years.

(b) No local residency requirement stated for Supreme Court. Local residency required for Court of Appeals.

(c) Supreme Court—ten years state bar; Court of Appeals—five years state bar.

(d) Admitted to the practice of law in Arizona for five years.

(e) Court of Appeals minimum age is 30.

(f) The candidate must be a resident of the district at the time of the original appointment.

(g) Circuit Court judge must reside within the territorial jurisdiction of the court.

(h) In the Supreme Court and the Court of Appeals, five years service as a general jurisdiction judge may be substituted.

(i) Relevant legal experience, such as being a member of a law faculty or sitting as a judge, may qualify under the 10-year requirement.

(j) Must reside within the district.

(k) At the appellate level must have been a state voter for nine years. At the general trial court level must have been a state voter for three years and resident of the circuit for one year.

(l) Minimum of two years state bar member and at least 15 years of legal practice.

(m) For Superior Court: out of a total of 441 authorized judgeships there are 283 restricted Superior Court judgeships that require residence within the particular county of assignment at time of appointment and reappointment; there are 158 unrestricted judgeships for which assignment of county is made by the chief justice.

(n) Resident judges of the Superior Court are required to have local residency, but special judges are not.

(o) District and associate judges must be state residents for six months if elected, and associate judges must be county residents.

(p) District Court: judges must be a state bar member for four years or a judge of a court of record. Associate judges must be a state bar member for two years or a judge of a court of record.

(q) Circuit judges must be county electors and residents of the circuit.

(r) Supreme Court: one justice from each of three divisions and two seats at large; no more than two may be from any grand division. Court of Appeals and Court of Criminal Appeals: must reside in the grand division served.

(s) Ten years practicing law or a lawyer and judge of a court of record at least 10 years.

(t) District Court: judges must have been a practicing lawyer or a judge of a court in this state, or both combined, for four years.

(u) Superior Court: judge must also be an active member of the unified District of Columbia bar and have been engaged, during the five years immediately preceding the judicial nomination, in the active practice of law as an attorney in the District, been on the faculty of a law school in the District, or been employed by either the United States or District of Columbia government.

Table 5.4
COMPENSATION OF JUDGES OF APPELLATE COURTS AND GENERAL TRIAL COURTS

State or other jurisdiction	Appellate courts: Court of last resort	Chief Justice salaries	Associate Justice salaries	Intermediate appellate court	Chief/Presiding salaries	Judges salaries	General trial courts	Salary
Eastern Region								
Connecticut	Supreme Court	$176,000	$162,520	Appellate Court	$160,722	$152,637	Superior courts	$146,780
Delaware	Supreme Court	194,750	185,050	. . .	. . .	. . .	Superior courts	168,850
Maine	Supreme Judicial Court	138,294	119,594	. . .	. . .	. . .	Superior courts	112,145
Massachusetts	Supreme Judicial Court	151,239	145,984	Appellate Court	140,358	135,087	Superior courts	129,694
New Hampshire	Supreme Court	143,580	139,258	. . .	. . .	. . .	Superior courts	130,620
New Jersey	Supreme Court	183,182	176,488	Appellate division of	167,023	167,023	Superior courts	157,000
New York	Court of Appeals	156,000	151,200	Appellate divisions of	148,000	144,000	Supreme courts	136,700
Pennsylvania	Supreme Court	186,649	181,371	Superior Court	176,409	171,131	Courts of common pleas	157,441
Rhode Island	Supreme Court	167,644	152,403	. . .	. . .	. . .	Superior courts	137,212
Vermont	Supreme Court	135,421	129,245	. . .	. . .	. . .	Superior/District/Family	122,867
Regional average		163,276	154,311		158,502	153,976		139,931
Midwestern Region								
Illinois	Supreme Court	196,322	196,322	Court of Appeals	184,775	184,775	Circuit courts	169,555
Indiana	Supreme Court	151,328	151,328	Court of Appeals	147,103	147,103	Circuit courts	125,647
Iowa	Supreme Court	170,850	163,200	Court of Appeals	153,000	147,900	District courts	137,700
Kansas	Supreme Court	139,310	135,905	Court of Appeals	134,750	131,518	District courts	120,037
Michigan	Supreme Court	164,610	164,610	Court of Appeals	151,441	151,441	Circuit courts	139,919
Minnesota	Supreme Court	160,579	145,981	Court of Appeals	144,429	137,552	District courts	129,124
Nebraska	Supreme Court	135,881	135,881	Court of Appeals	129,087	129,087	District courts	125,690
North Dakota	Supreme Court	121,513	118,121	. . .	. . .	. . .	District courts	108,236
Ohio	Supreme Court	150,850	141,600	Court of Appeals	132,000	132,000	Courts of common pleas	121,350
South Dakota	Supreme Court	120,173	118,173	. . .	. . .	. . .	Circuit courts	110,377
Wisconsin	Supreme Court	148,165	140,165	Court of Appeals	132,230	132,230	Circuit courts	124,746
Regional Average		150,871	146,481		145,424	143,734		128,398
Southern Region								
Alabama	Supreme Court	(a)	(b)	Court of Criminal Appeals	(c)	(d)	Circuit courts	(e)
Arkansas	Supreme Court	151,049	139,821	Court of Appeals	137,669	135,515	Chancery courts	131,206
Florida	Supreme Court	161,200	161,200	District Court of Appeals	153,140	153,140	Circuit courts	145,080
Georgia	Supreme Court	167,210	167,210	Court of Appeals	166,186	166,186	Superior courts	120,252
Kentucky	Supreme Court	139,164	134,160	Court of Appeals	131,760	128,760	Circuit courts	123,384
Louisiana	Supreme Court	143,815	136,967	Court of Appeals	136,704	130,194	District courts	124,085
Maryland	Court of Appeals	181,352	162,352	Court of Special Appeals	149,552	149,552	Circuit courts	140,352
Mississippi	Supreme Court	115,390	112,530	Court of Appeals	108,130	105,050	Chancery courts	104,170
Missouri	Supreme Court	139,534	137,034	Court of Appeals	128,207	128,207	Circuit courts	120,484
North Carolina	Supreme Court	140,932	137,249	Court of Appeals	135,061	131,531	Superior courts	124,382
Oklahoma	Supreme Court	147,000	137,655	Court of Appeals	142,485	132,825	District courts	124,373
South Carolina	Supreme Court	144,029	137,171	Court of Appeals	135,799	133,741	Circuit courts	130,312
Tennessee	Supreme Court	164,292	159,288	Court of Appeals	156,480	153,984	Chancery courts	148,668
Texas	Supreme Court	152,500	150,000	Court of Appeals	(e)	(f)	District courts	(g)
Virginia	Supreme Court (h)	178,043	166,999	Court of Appeals (i)	161,650	158,650	Circuit courts	155,033
West Virginia	Supreme Court	121,000	121,000	. . .	. . .	. . .	Circuit courts	116,000
Regional averages		149,767	144,042		141,756	139,026		129,127

See footnotes at end of table.

COMPENSATION OF JUDGES OF APPELLATE COURTS AND GENERAL TRIAL COURTS—Continued

State or other jurisdiction	Appellate courts: Court of last resort	Chief Justice salaries	Associate Justice salaries	Intermediate appellate court	Chief/Presiding salaries	Judges salaries	General trial courts	Salary
Western Region								
Alaska	Supreme Court	180,048	179,520	Court of Appeals	169,608	169,608	Superior courts	(j)
Arizona	Supreme Court	145,294	142,341	Court of Appeals	139,388	139,388	Superior courts	135,824
California	Supreme Court	228,856	218,237	Court of Appeals		204,599	Superior court	178,789
Colorado	Supreme Court	142,708	139,660	Court of Appeals	137,201	134,128	District courts	128,598
Hawaii	Supreme Court	164,976	159,072	Intermediate Court	153,192	147,288	Circuit courts	143,292
Idaho	Supreme Court	121,006	119,506	Court of Appeals	118,506	118,506	District courts	112,043
Montana	Supreme Court	107,404	106,185	. . .	. . .	. . .	District courts	99,234
Nevada	Supreme Court	(k)	(k)	. . .	. . .	. . .	District courts	(l)
New Mexico	Supreme Court	125,691	123,691	Court of Appeals	119,406	117,506	District courts	111,631
Oregon	Supreme Court	128,556	125,688	Court of Appeals	125,688	122,820	Circuit courts	114,468
Utah	Supreme Court	147,350	145,350	Court of Appeals	140,750	138,750	District courts	132,150
Washington	Supreme Court	155,557	155,557	Court of Appeals	148,080	148,080	Superior courts	140,979
Wyoming	Supreme Court	126,500	126,500	. . .	. . .	. . .	District courts	120,400
Regional averages		147,829	145,109		107,769	105,923		126,769
Regional averages w/o California		135,000	133,167		135,959	140,600		128,681
Dist. of Columbia	Court of Appeals	180,000	179,500	. . .	. . .	. . .	Superior courts	169,300
American Samoa	High Court	125,000	119,000	. . .	. . .	. . .	District courts	97,000
Guam	Supreme Court	(m)	(n)	. . .	. . .	. . .	Superior courts	(o)
No. Mariana Islands	Commonwealth Supreme Court	130,000	126,000	. . .	. . .	. . .	Superior courts	120,000
Puerto Rico	Supreme Court	125,000	120,000	Appellate Court	105,000	105,000	Superior courts	90,000
U.S. Virgin Islands	Territorial Court	162,000	152,000	. . .	. . .	. . .	. . .	. . .

Source: National Center for State Courts, July 2008.

Note: Compensation is shown rounded to the nearest thousand, and is reported according to most recent legislation, even though laws may not yet have taken effect. There are other non-salary forms of judicial compensation that can be a significant part of a judge's compensation package. It should be noted that many of these can be important to judges or attorneys who might be interested in becoming judges or justices. These include retirement, disability, and death benefits, expense accounts, vacation, holiday, and sick leave and various forms of insurance coverage.

(a) Salary range is between $156,946–$196,183.
(b) Salary range is between $155,946–$194,933.
(c) Salary range is between $155,446–$193,683.
(d) Salary range is between $151,527–$189,409.
(e) Salary range is between $140,000–$147,500.
(f) Salary range is between $137,500–$145,000.
(g) Salary range is between $125,000–$140,000.
(h) Plus $13,500 in lieu of travel, lodging, and other expenses.
(i) Plus $6,500 in lieu of travel, lodging, and other expenses.
(j) Salary range is between $165,996–$172,992.
(k) Salary range is between $140,000–$171,000.
(l) Salary range is between $130,000–$159,000.
(m) Salary range is between $128,000–$165,000.
(n) Salary range is between $126,000–$163,000.
(o) Salary range is between $104,000–$132,000.

Table 5.5
SELECTED DATA ON COURT ADMINISTRATIVE OFFICES

State or other jurisdiction	*Title*	*Established*	*Appointed by (a)*	*Salary*
Alabama	Administrative Director of Courts	1971	CJ (b)	(g)
Alaska	Administrative Director	1959	CJ (b)	177,520
Arizona	Administrative Director of Courts	1960	SC	(h)
Arkansas	Director, Administrative Office of the Courts	1965	CJ (c)	104,558
California	Administrative Director of the Courts	1960	JC	(i)
Colorado	State Court Administrator	1959	SC	137,201
Connecticut	Chief Court Administrator (d)	1965	CJ	168,783
Delaware	Director, Administrative Office of the Courts	1971	CJ	126,550
Florida	State Courts Administrator	1972	SC	134,879
Georgia	Director, Administrative Office of the Courts	1973	JC	140,949
Hawaii	Administrative Director of the Courts	1959	CJ (b)	116,416
Idaho	Administrative Director of the Courts	1967	SC	118,506
Illinois	Administrative Director of the Courts	1959	SC	184,775
Indiana	Executive Director, Division of State Court Administration	1975	CJ	112,886
Iowa	Court Administrator	1971	SC	145,000
Kansas	Judicial Administrator	1965	CJ	120,037
Kentucky	Administrative Director of the Courts	1976	CJ	123,384
Louisiana	Judicial Administrator	1954	SC	130,194
Maine	Court Administrator	1975	CJ	112,145
Maryland	State Court Administrator	1955	CJ (b)	142,287
Massachusetts	Chief Justice for Administration & Management	1978	SC	140,358
Michigan	State Court Administrator	1952	SC	(j)
Minnesota	State Court Administrator	1963	SC	(k)
Mississippi	Court Administrator	1974	SC	76,500
Missouri	State Courts Administrator	1970	SC	118,450
Montana	State Court Administrator	1975	SC	96,990
Nebraska	State Court Administrator	1972	CJ	113,550
Nevada	Director, Office of Court Administration	1971	SC	123,783
New Hampshire	Director of the Administrative Office of the Court	1980	SC	111,678
New Jersey	Administrative Director of the Courts	1948	CJ	167,023
New Mexico	Director, Administrative Office of the Courts	1959	SC	120,752
New York	Chief Administrator of the Courts	1978	CJ	147,600
North Carolina	Director, Administrative Office of the Courts	1965	CJ	126,738
North Dakota	Court Administrator (h)	1971	CJ	96,528
Ohio	Administrative Director of the Courts	1955	SC	(l)
Oklahoma	Administrative Director of the Courts	1967	SC	130,410
Oregon	Court Administrator	1971	SC	(m)
Pennsylvania	Court Administrator	1968	SC	171,131
Rhode Island	State Court Administrator	1969	CJ	(n)
South Carolina	Director of Court Administration	1973	CJ	122,231
South Dakota	State Court Administrator	1974	SC	105,020
Tennessee	Director	1963	SC	147,000
Texas	Administrative Director of the Courts (i)	1977	SC	110,770
Utah	Court Administrator	1973	SC	132,150
Vermont	Court Administrator	1967	SC	122,867
Virginia	Executive Secretary to the Supreme Court	1952	SC	165,149
Washington	Administrator for the Courts	1957	SC (e)	144,480
West Virginia	Administrative Director of the Supreme Court of Appeals	1975	SC	114,000
Wisconsin	Director of State Courts	1978	SC	132,230
Wyoming	Court Coordinator	1974	SC	114,234
Dist. of Columbia	Executive Officer, Courts of D.C.	1971	(f)	169,300
American Samoa	Administrator/Comptroller	N.A	N.A.	46,000 (o)
Guam	Administrative Director of Superior Court	N.A.	CJ	120,000 (p)
No. Mariana Islands	Director of Courts			70,000
Puerto Rico	Administrative Director of the Courts	1952	CJ	111,000
U.S. Virgin Islands	Court/Administrative Clerk	N.A.	N.A.	121,600

Source: National Center for State Courts, July 2008.

Note: Compensation shown is rounded to the nearest thousand, and is reported according to most recent legislation, even though laws may not yet have taken effect. Other information from State Court Administrator Web sites.

Key:

SC — State court of last resort.

CJ — Chief justice or chief judge of court of last resort.

JC — Judicial council.

N.A. — Not available

(a) Term of office for all court administrators is at pleasure of appointing authority.

(b) With approval of Supreme Court.

(c) With approval of Judicial Council.

(d) Administrator is an associate judge of the Supreme Court.

(e) Appointed from list of five submitted by governor.

(f) Joint Committee on Judicial Administration.

(g) Salary range is between $100,197 and $152,618.

(h) Salary range is between $109,000 and $179,000.

(i) Salary range is between $192,000 and $211,000.

(j) Salary range is between $109,704 and $148,123.

(k) Salary range is between $97,322 and $150,816.

(l) Salary range is between $125,000 and $145,000.

(m) Salary range is between $96,672 and 149,892.

(n) Salary range is between $114,140 and $126,541.

(o) Plus $1,170/yr. increment.

(p) After supplements: $149,000.

Table 5.6
SELECTION AND RETENTION OF APPELLATE COURT JUDGES

State or other jurisdiction	Name of court	Type of court	Method of selection: Unexpired term	Method of selection: Full term	Method of retention	Geographic basis for selection
Alabama	Supreme Court	SC	GU	PE	PE	SW
	Court of Civil Appeals	IA	GU	PE	PE	SW
	Court of Criminal Appeals	IA	GU	PE	PE	SW
Alaska	Supreme Court	SC	GN	GN	RE (a)	SW
	Court of Appeals	IA	GN	GN	RE (a)	SW
Arizona	Supreme Court	SC	GN	GN	RE	SW
	Court of Appeals	IA	GN	GN	RE	DS
Arkansas	Supreme Court	SC	GU	NP	NP	SW
	Court of Appeals	IA	GU	NP	NP	DS
California	Supreme Court	SC	GU	GU	RE	SW
	Courts of Appeal	IA	GU	GU	RE	DS
Colorado	Supreme Court	SC	GN	GN	RE	SW
	Court of Appeals	IA	GN	GN	RE	SW
Connecticut	Supreme Court	SC	GNL	GNL	GNL	SW
	Appellate Court	IA	GNL	GNL	GNL	SW
Delaware	Supreme Court	SC	GNL	GNL	GNL	SW
Florida	Supreme Court	SC	GN	GN	RE	DS and SW (b)
	District Courts of Appeal	IA	GN	GN	RE	DS
Georgia	Supreme Court	SC	GN	NP	NP	SW
	Court of Appeals	IA	GN	NP	NP	SW
Hawaii	Supreme Court	SC	GNL	GNL	JN	SW
	Intermediate Court of Appeals	IA	GNL	GNL	JN	SW
Idaho	Supreme Court	SC	GN	NP	NP	SW
	Court of Appeals	IA	GN	NP	NP	SW
Illinois	Supreme Court	SC	CS	PE	RE	DS
	Appellate Court	IA	SC	PE	RE	DS
Indiana	Supreme Court	SC	GN	GN	RE	SW
	Court of Appeals	IA	GN	GN	RE	DS
	Tax Court	IA	GN	GN	RE	SW
Iowa	Supreme Court	SC	GN	GN	RE	SW
	Court of Appeals	IA	GN	GN	RE	SW
Kansas	Supreme Court	SC	GN	GN	RE	SW
	Court of Appeals	IA	GN	GN	RE	SW
Kentucky	Supreme Court	SC	GN	NP	NP	DS
	Court of Appeals	IA	GN	NP	NP	DS
Louisiana	Supreme Court	SC	CS (c)	PE (d)	PE (d)	DS
	Courts of Appeal	IA	SC (c)	PE (d)	PE (d)	DS
Maine	Supreme Judicial Court	SC	GL	GL	GL	SW
Maryland	Court of Appeals	SC	GNL	GNL	RE	DS
	Court of Special Appeals	IA	GNL	GNL	RE	DS
Massachusetts	Supreme Judicial Court	SC	(e)	GNE (f)	(g)	SW
	Appeals Court	IA	(e)	GNE (f)	(g)	SW
Michigan	Supreme Court	SC	GU	NP (h)	NP (h)	SW
	Court of Appeals	IA	GU	NP (h)	NP (h)	DS
Minnesota	Supreme Court	SC	GU	NP	NP	SW
	Court of Appeals	IA	GU	NP	NP	SW
Mississippi	Supreme Court	SC	GU	NP	NP	DS
	Court of Appeals	IA	GU	NP	NP	DS
Missouri	Supreme Court	SC	GN	GN	RE	SW
	Court of Appeals	IA	GN	GN	RE	DS
Montana	Supreme Court	SC	GNL	NP	NP (i)	SW
Nebraska	Supreme Court	SC	GN	GN	RE	SW and DS (j)
	Court of Appeals	IA	GN	GN	RE	DS
Nevada	Supreme Court	SC	GN	NP	NP	SW

See footnotes at end of table.

SELECTION AND RETENTION OF APPELLATE COURT JUDGES—Continued

State or other jurisdiction	Name of court	Type of court	Method of selection: Unexpired term	Method of selection: Full term	Method of retention	Geographic basis for selection
New Hampshire	Supreme Court	SC	GE	GE	(k)	SW
New Jersey	Supreme Court	SC	GL	GL	GL	SW
	Superior Court, Appellate Div.	IA	GL	GL (l)	GL (l)	SW
New Mexico	Supreme Court	SC	GN	PE	RE	SW
	Court of Appeals	IA	GN	PE	RE	SW
New York	Court of Appeals	SC	GNL	GNL	GNL	SW
	Supreme Court, Appellate Div.	IA	GN	GN	GN	SW (m)
North Carolina	Supreme Court	SC	GU	NP	NP	SW
	Court of Appeals	IA	GU	NP	NP	SW
North Dakota	Supreme Court	SC	GN (n)	NP	NP	SW
	Temporary Court of Appeals	IA	(w)	SC (x)	(w)	SW
Ohio	Supreme Court	SC	GU	PE (o)	PE (o)	SW
	Courts of Appeals	IA	GU	PE (o)	PE (o)	DS
Oklahoma	Supreme Court	SC	GN	GN	RE	DS
	Court of Criminal Appeals	SC	GN	GN	RE	DS
	Court of Civil Appeals	IA	GN	GN	RE	DS
Oregon	Supreme Court	SC	GU	NP	NP	SW
	Court of Appeals	IA	GU	NP	NP	SW
Pennsylvania	Supreme Court	SC	GL	PE	RE	SW
	Superior Court	IA	GL	PE	RE	SW
	Commonwealth Court	IA	GL	PE	RE	SW
Rhode Island	Supreme Court	SC	GN	GN	(p)	SW
South Carolina	Supreme Court	SC	LA	LA	LA	SW
	Court of Appeals	IA	LA	LA	LA	SW
South Dakota	Supreme Court	SC	GN	GN	RE	DS and SW (q)
Tennessee	Supreme Court	SC	GN	GN	RE	SW
	Court of Appeals	SC	GN	GN	RE	SW
	Court of Criminal Appeals	IA	GN	GN	RE	SW
Texas	Supreme Court	SC	GU	PE	PE	SW
	Court of Criminal Appeals	SC	GU	PE	PE	SW
	Courts of Appeals	IA	GU	PE	PE	DS
Utah	Supreme Court	SC	GNL	GNL	RE	SW
	Court of Appeals	IA	GNL	GNL	RE	SW
Vermont	Supreme Court	SC	GNL	GNL	LA	SW
Virginia	Supreme Court	SC	GU (r)	LA	LA	SW
	Court of Appeals	IA	GU (r)	LA	LA	SW
Washington	Supreme Court	SC	GU	NP	NP	SW
	Courts of Appeals	IA	GU	NP	NP	DS
West Virginia	Supreme Court of Appeals	SC	GU (s)	PE	PE	SW
Wisconsin	Supreme Court	SC	GN	NP	NP	SW
	Court of Appeals	IA	GN	NP	NP	DS
Wyoming	Supreme Court	SC	GN	GN	RE	SW
Dist. of Columbia	Court of Appeals	SC	(t)	(t)	(t)	SW (u)
Puerto Rico	Supreme Court	SC	GL	GL	(v)	SW
	Court of Appeals	IA	GL	GL	GL	SW

See footnotes at end of table.

SELECTION AND RETENTION OF APPELLATE COURT JUDGES — Continued

Source: Bureau of Justice Statistics, *State Court Organization, 2004* NCJ 212351, update from the National Center for State Courts, February 2009.

Key:

SC — Court of last resort
IA — Intermediate appellate court
N/S — Not stated
N.A. — Not applicable
AP — At pleasure
CS — Court selection
DS — District
DU — Duration of service
GE — Gubernatorial appointment with approval of elected executive council
GL — Gubernatorial appointment with consent of the legislature
GN — Gubernatorial appointment from judicial nominating commission
GNE — Gubernatorial appointment from judicial nominating commission with approval of elected executive council
GNL — Gubernatorial appointment from judicial nominating commission with consent of the legislature
GU — Gubernatorial appointment
ID — Indefinite
JN — Judicial nominating commission appoints
LA — Legislative appointment
NP — Nonpartisan election
PE — Partisan election
RE — Retention election
SC — Court of last resort appoints
SCJ — Chief justice/judge of the court of last resort appoints
SN — Seniority
SW — Statewide

(a) A judge must run for a retention election at the next election, immediately following the third year from the time of initial appointment.

(b) Five justices are selected by region (based on the District Courts of Appeal) and two justices are selected statewide.

(c) The person selected by the Supreme Court is prohibited from running for that judgeship; an election is held within one year to serve the remainder of the term.

(d) Louisiana uses a blanket primary, in which all candidates appear with party labels on the primary ballot. The two top vote getters compete in the general election.

(e) There are no expired judicial terms. A judicial term expires upon the death, resignation, retirement, or removal of an incumbent.

(f) The Executive (Governor's) Council is made up of nine people elected by geographical area and presided over by the lieutenant governor.

(g) There is no retention process. Judges serve during good behavior to age 70.

(h) Candidates may be nominated by political parties and are elected on a nonpartisan ballot.

(i) If the justice/judge is unopposed, a retention election is held.

(j) Chief justices are selected statewide while associate justices are selected by district.

(k) There is no retention process. Judges serve during good behavior to age 70.

(l) All Superior Court judges, including Appellate Division judges, are subject to gubernatorial reappointment and consent by the Senate after an initial seven-year term. Among all the judges, the chief justice designates the judges of the Appellate Division.

(m) The presiding judge of each Appellate Division must be a resident of the department.

(n) The governor may appoint from a list of names or call a special election at his discretion.

(o) Party affiliation is not included on the ballot in the general election, but candidates are chosen through partisan primary nominations.

(p) There is no retention process. Judges serve during good behavior for a life tenure.

(q) Initial selection is by district, but retention selection is statewide.

(r) Gubernatorial appointment is for interim appointments.

(s) Appointment is effective only until the next election year; the appointee may run for election to any remaining portion of the unexpired term.

(t) Initial appointment is made by the President of the United States and confirmed by the Senate. Six months prior to the expiration of the term of office, the judge's performance is reviewed by the tenure commission. Those found "well qualified" are automatically reappointed. If a judge is found to be "qualified," the president may nominate the judge for an additional term (subject to Senate confirmation). If the president does not wish to reappoint the judge, the District of Columbia Nomination Commission compiles a new list of candidates.

(u) The geographic basis of selection is the District of Columbia.

(v) There is no retention process. Judges serve during good behavior to age 70.

(w) The Supreme Court may provide for the assignment of active or retired District Court judges, retired justices of the Supreme Court, and lawyers, to serve on three-judge panels.

(x) There is neither a retention process nor unexpired terms. Assignments are for a specified time, not to exceed one year or the completion of one or more cases on the docket of the Supreme Court.

Table 5.7
SELECTION AND RETENTION OF TRIAL COURT JUDGES

State or other jurisdiction	Name of Court	Types of court	Method of selection: Unexpired term	Method of selection: Full term	Method of retention	Geographic basis for selection
Alabama	Circuit	GJ	GU (a)	PE	PE	Circuit
	District	LJ	GU (a)	PE	PE	County
	Municipal	LJ	MU	MU	RA	Municipality
	Probate	LJ	GU	PE	PE	County
Alaska	Superior	GJ	GN	GN	RE (b)	State (c)
	District	LG	GN	GN	RE (d)	District
	Magistrate's Division	N.A.	PJ	PJ	PJ	District
Arizona	Superior	GJ	GN or VA (e)	GN or NP (f)	NP or RE (f)	County
	Justice of the Peace	LJ	CO	PE	PE	Precinct
	Municipal	LJ	CC (g)	CC (g)	CC (g)	Municipality
Arkansas	Circuit	GJ	GU (h)	NP	NP	Circuit
	District	LJ	GU	NP	NP	District
	City	LJ	LD	LD	LD	City
California	Superior	GJ	GU	NP	NP (i)	County
Colorado	District	GJ	GN	GN	RE	District
	Denver Probate	GJ	GN	GN	RE	District
	Denver Juvenile	GJ	GN	GN	RE	District
	Water	GJ	SC (j)	SC (j)	RE	District
	County	LJ	GN	GN (k)	RE	County
	Municipal	LJ	MU	MU	RA	Municipality
Connecticut	Superior	GJ	GNL	GNL	GNL	State
	Probate	LJ	PE	PE	PE	District
Delaware	Superior	GJ	GNL	GNL	GNL	State
	Chancery	LJ	GNL	GNL	GNL	State
	Justice of the Peace	LJ	GNL (l)	GNL (l)	GU	County
	Family	LJ	GNL	GNL	GNL	County
	Common Pleas	LJ	GNL	GNL	GNL	County
	Alderman's	LJ	LD	CC	LD	Town
Florida	Circuit	GJ	GN	NP	NP	Circuit
	County	LJ	GN	NP	NP	County
Georgia	Superior	GJ	GN	NP	NP	Circuit
	Juvenile	LJ	CS (m)	CS (m)	CS (m)	County/Circuit
	Civil	LJ	GU	PE	PE	County
	State	LJ	GU	NP	NP	County
	Probate	LJ	GU	PE (n)	PE (n)	County
	Magistrate	LJ	LD	LD (o)	LD (o)	County
	Municipal/of Columbus	LJ	MA	Elected	Elected	Municipality
	County Recorder's	LJ	LD	LD	LD	County
	Municipal/City of Atlanta	LJ	MU	MU	LD	Municipality
Hawaii	Circuit	GJ	GNL	GNL	JN	State
	District	LJ	SCJ (p)	SCJ (p)	JN	Circuit
Idaho	District	GJ	GN	NP	NP	District
	Magistrate's Division	LJ	JN (q)	JN (q)	RE	County
Illinois	Circuit	GJ	SC	PE	RE	Circuit/County (r)
	Associate Division	N.A.	SC	PE	RE	Circuit/County (r)
Indiana	Superior	GJ	GU	PE (s)	PE (s)	County
	Circuit	GJ	GU	PE (t)	PE (t)	County
	Probate	GJ	GU	PE	PE	County
	County	LJ	GU	PE	PE	County
	City	LJ	GU	PE	PE	Municipality
	Town	LJ	GU	PE	PE	Municipality
	Small Claims/Marion County	LJ	GU	PE	PE	Township
Iowa	District	GJ	GN (u)	GN (u)	RE (u)	District
Kansas	District	GJ	GN and PE(v)	GN and PE (v)	RE and PE (v)	District
	Municipal	LJ	MU	MU	MU	City
Kentucky	Circuit	GJ	GN	NP	NP	Circuit
	District	LJ	GN	NP	NP	District
Louisiana	District	GJ	SC (w)	PE	PE	District
	Juvenile & Family	GJ	SC (w)	PE	PE	District
	Justice of the Peace	LJ	SC (w)	PE(x)	PE	Ward
	Mayor's	LJ	MA	LD	LD	City
	City & Parish	LJ	SC (w)	PE	PE	Ward

See footnotes at end of table.

SELECTION AND RETENTION OF TRIAL COURT JUDGES—Continued

State or other jurisdiction	Name of Court	Types of court	Method of selection: Unexpired term	Method of selection: Full term	Method of retention	Geographic basis for selection
Maine	Superior	GJ	GL	GL	GL	State
	District	GJ	GL	GL	GL	State and District (y)
	Probate	LJ	GU	PE	PE	County
Maryland	Circuit	GJ	GNL	GNL	NP	County
	District	LJ	GNL	GNL	RA	District
	Orphan's	LJ	GU	PE (z)	PE (z)	County
Massachusetts	Superior	GJ	(aa)	GNE (bb)	(cc)	State
	District	LJ	(aa)	GNE (bb)	(cc)	State
	Probate & Family	LJ	(aa)	GNE (bb)	(cc)	State
	Juvenile	LJ	(aa)	GNE (bb)	(cc)	State
	Housing	LJ	(aa)	GNE (bb)	(cc)	State
	Boston Municipal	LJ	(aa)	GNE (bb)	(cc)	State
	Land	LJ	(aa)	GNE (bb)	(cc)	State
Michigan	Circuit	GJ	GU	NP	NP	Circuit
	Claims	GJ	GU	NP	NP	Circuit
	District	LJ	GU	NP	NP	District
	Probate	LJ	GU	NP	NP	District and Circuit
	Municipal	LJ	LD	NP	NP	City
Minnesota	District	GJ	GN	NP	NP	District
Mississippi	Circuit	GJ	GU	NP	NP	District
	Chancery	LJ	GU	NP	NP	District
	County	LJ	GU	NP	NP	County
	Municipal	LJ	LD	LD	LD	Municipality
	Justice	LJ	LD	PE	PE	District in County
Missouri	Circuit	GJ	GU and GN (dd)	PE and GN (ee)	PE and RE (ff)	Circuit/County (gg)
	Municipal	LJ	LD	LD	LD	City
Montana	District	GJ	GN	NP	NP	District
	Workers' Compensation	GJ	GN	GN	RA	State
	Water	GJ	SCJ (hh)	SCJ (hh)	SCJ (ii)	State
	Justice of the Peace	LJ	CO	NP	NP	County
	Municipal	LJ	MU	NP	NP	City
	City	LJ	CC	NP	NP	City
Nebraska	District	GJ	GN	GN	RE	District
	Separate Juvenile	LJ	GN	GN	RE	District
	County	LJ	GN	GN	RE	District
	Workers' Compensation	LJ	GN	GN	RE	District
Nevada	District	GJ	GN	NP	NP	District
	Justice	LJ	CO	NP	NP	Township
	Municipal	LJ	CC	NP	NP	City
New Hampshire	Superior	GJ	GE	GE	(jj)	State
	District	LJ	GE	GE	(jj)	District
	Probate	LJ	GE	GE	(jj)	County
New Jersey	Superior	GJ	GL	GL	GL	County
	Tax	LJ	GL	GL	GL	State
	Municipal	LJ	MA or MU (kk)	MA or MU (kk)	MU	Municipality
New Mexico	District	GJ	GN	PE	RE	District
	Magistrate	LJ	GU	PE	PE	County
	Metropolitan/Bernalillo County	LJ	GN	PE	RE	County
	Municipal	LJ	MU	PE	PE	City
	Probate	LJ	CO	PE	PE	County
New York	Supreme	GJ	GL	PE	PE	District
	County	GJ	GL	PE	PE	County
	Claims	GJ	GNL	GNL	GU	State
	Surrogates'	LJ	GNL	PE	PE	County
	Family	LJ	GNL and MU (ll)	PE and MU (ll)	PE and MU (ll)	County and NYC
	District	LJ	(mm)	PE	PE	District
	City	LJ	Elected	Elected	LD	City
	NYC Civil	LJ	MA (nn)	PE	PE	City
	NYC Criminal	LJ	MA	MA	MA	City
	Town & Village Justice	LJ	LD	LD	LD	Town or Village
North Carolina	Superior	GJ	GU	NP	NP	District
	District	LJ	GU	NP	NP	District

See footnotes at end of table.

SELECTION AND RETENTION OF TRIAL COURT JUDGES—Continued

State or other jurisdiction	Name of Court	Types of court	Method of selection: Unexpired term	Method of selection: Full term	Method of retention	Geographic basis for selection
North Dakota	District	GJ	GN	NP	NP	District
	Municipal	LJ	MA	NP	NP	City
Ohio	Common Pleas	GJ	GU	PE (oo)	PE (oo)	County
	Municipal	LJ	GU	PE (oo)	PE (oo)	County/City
	County	LJ	GU	PE (oo)	PE (oo)	County
	Claims	LJ	SCJ	SCJ	SCJ	N.A.
	Mayor's	LJ	Elected	PE	PE	City/Village
Oklahoma	District	GJ	GN (pp)	NP (pp)	NP (pp)	District
	Municipal Not of Record	LJ	MM	MM	MM	Municipality
	Municipal of Record	LJ	MU	MU	MU	Municipality
	Workers' Compensation	LJ	GN	GN	GN	State
	Tax Review	LJ	SCJ	SCJ	SCJ	District
Oregon	Circuit	GJ	GU	NP	NP	District
	Tax	GJ	GU	NP	NP	State
	County	LJ	CO	NP	NP	County
	Justice	LJ	GU	NP	NP	County
	Municipal	LJ	CC	CC/Elected	CC/Elected	(qq)
Pennsylvania	Common Pleas	GJ	GL	PE	RE	District
	Philadelphia Municipal	LJ	GL	PE	RE	City/County
	Magisterial District Judges	LJ	GL	PE	PE	District
	Philadelphia Traffic	LJ	GL	PE	RE	City/County
Rhode Island	Superior	GJ	GN	GN	(rr)	State
	Workers' Compensation	LJ	GN	GN	(rr)	State
	District	LJ	GN	GN	(rr)	State
	Family	LJ	GN	GN	(rr)	State
	Probate	LJ	CC	CC or MA	RA	Town
	Municipal	LJ	CC	CC or MA	CC or MA	Town
	Traffic Tribunal	LJ	GN	GN	(rr)	State
South Carolina	Circuit	GJ	LA and GN (ss)(tt)	LA and GN (tt)	LA and GL (tt)	Circuit and State (tt)
	Family	LJ	LA	LA	LA	Circuit
	Magistrate	LJ	GL	GL	GL	County
	Probate	LJ	GU	PE	PE	County
	Municipal	LJ	CC	CC	CC	District
South Dakota	Circuit	GJ	GN	NP	NP	Circuit
	Magistrate	LJ	PJS	PJS	PJS	Circuit
Tennessee	Circuit	GJ	GU	PE (uu)	PE	District
	Chancery	GJ	GU	PE (uu)	PE	District
	Criminal	GJ	GU	PE (uu)	PE	District
	Probate	GJ	(vv)	PE (uu)	PE	District
	Juvenile	LJ	(vv)	PE (uu)	PE	County
	Municipal	LJ	LD	LD (uu)	LD	Municipality
	General Sessions	LJ	MU	PE (uu)	PE	County
Texas	District	GJ	GL	PE	PE	District
	Constitutional County	LJ	CO	PE	PE	County
	Probate	LJ	CO	PE	PE	County
	County at Law	LJ	CO	PE	PE	County
	Justice of the Peace	LJ	CO	PE	PE	Precinct
	Municipal	LJ	CC	LD	LD	Municipality
Utah	District	GJ	(ww)	GNL	RE	District
	Justice	LJ	MM (xx)	MM (xx)	RE and RA (yy)	County/Municipality
	Juvenile	LJ	(ww)	GNL	RE	District
Vermont	Superior	GJ	GNL	GNL	LA	State
	District	GJ	GNL	GNL	LA	State
	Family	GJ	(zz)	(zz)	(zz)	(zz)
	Probate	LJ	GU	PE	PE	District
	Environmental	LJ	GNL	GNL	LA	State
	Judicial Bureau	LJ	PJ	PJ	AP	State
Virginia	Circuit	GJ	GU	LA	LA	Circuit
	District	LJ	CS (aaa)	LA	LA	District
Washington	Superior	GJ	GU	NP	NP	County
	District	LJ	CO	NP	NP	District
	Municipal	LJ	CC	MA/CC	MA/CC (bbb)	Municipality

See footnotes at end of table.

SELECTION AND RETENTION OF TRIAL COURT JUDGES — Continued

State or other jurisdiction	Name of Court	Types of court	Method of selection: Unexpired term	Method of selection: Full term	Method of retention	Geographic basis for selection
West Virginia	Circuit	GJ	GU	PE	PE	Circuit
	Magistrate	LJ	PJ	PE	PE	County
	Municipal	LJ	LD	LD	LD	Municipality
	Family	LJ	GU	PE	PE	Circuit
Wisconsin	Circuit	GJ	GU	NP	NP	District
	Municipal	LJ	MU (ccc)	NP	NP	Municipality
Wyoming	District	GJ	GN	GN	RE	District
	Circuit	LJ	GN	GN	RE	Circuit
	Municipal	LJ	MA	MA	LD	Municipality
Dist. of Columbia	Superior	GJ	(ddd)	(ddd)	(ddd)	State (eee)
Puerto Rico	First Instance	GJ	GL	GL	GL	State

Source: Bureau of Justice Statistics, State Court Organization, 2004 NCJ 212351, Update from the National Center for State Courts, February 2009.

Key:

GJ — General jurisdiction court
LJ — Limited jurisdiction court
N/S — Not stated
N.A. — Not applicable
AP — At pleasure
CA — Court administrator appointment
CC — City or town council/commission appointment
CO — County board/commission appointment
CS — Court selection
DU — Duration of service
GE — Gubernatorial appointment with approval of elected executive council
GL — Gubernatorial appointment with consent of the legislature
GN — Gubernatorial appointment from judicial nominating commission
GNE — Gubernatorial appointment from judicial nominating commission with approval of elected executive council
GNL — Gubernatorial appointment from judicial nominating commission with consent of the legislature
GU — Gubernatorial appointment
JN — Judicial nominating commission appoints
LA — Legislative appointment
LD — Locally determined
MA — Mayoral appointment
MC — Mayoral appointment with consent of city council
MM — Mayoral appointment with consent of governing municipal body
MU — Governing municipal body appointment
NP — Non-partisan election
PE — Partisan election
PJ — Presiding judge of the general jurisdiction court appoints
PJS — Presiding judge of the general jurisdiction court appoints with approval of the court of last resort
RA — Reappointment
RE — Retention election
SC — Court of last resort appoints
SCJ — Chief justice/judge of the court of last resort appoints

(a) The counties of Baldwin, Jefferson, Madison, Mobile, and Tuscaloosa use gubernatorial appointment from the recommendations of the Judicial Nominating Commission.

(b) A judge must run for retention at the next election immediately following the third year from the time of the initial appointment.

(c) Judges are selected on a statewide basis, but run for retention on a district-wide basis.

(d) Judges must run for retention at the first general election held more than one year after appointment.

(e) Maricopa and Pima counties use the gubernatorial appointment from the Judicial Nominating Commission process. The method for submitting names for the other 13 counties varies.

(f) Maricopa and Pima counties use the gubernatorial appointment from the Judicial Nominating Commission process. The other 13 counties hold non-partisan elections.

(g) Municipal court judges are usually appointed by the city or town council except in Yuma, where judges are elected.

(h) The office can be held until December 31 following the next general election and then the judge must run in a non-partisan election for the remainder of the term.

(i) If unopposed for reelection, incumbent's name does not appear on the ballot unless a petition was filed not less than 83 days before the election date indicating that a write-in campaign will be conducted for the office. An unopposed incumbent is not declared elected until the election date. This is for the general election; different timing may apply for the primary election (see Elec. Code §8203).

(j) Judges are chosen by the Supreme Court from among District Court judges.

(k) The mayor appoints Denver County Court judges.

(l) The Magistrate Screening Commission recommends candidates.

(m) Juvenile Court judges are appointed by Superior Court judges in all but one county, in which juvenile judges are elected. Associate judges (formerly referees) must be a member of the state bar or law school graduates. They serve at the pleasure of the judge(s).

(n) Probate judges are selected in non-partisan elections in 66 of 159 counties.

(o) Magistrate judges are selected in nonpartisan elections in 41 of 159 counties.

(p) Selection occurs by means of Chief Justice appointment from the Judicial Nominating Commission with consent of the Senate.

(q) The Magistrate Commission consists of the administrative judge, three mayors and two electors appointed by the governor, and two attorneys (nominated by the district bar and appointed by the state bar). There is one commission in each district.

(r) There exists a unit less than county in Cook County.

(s) Non-partisan elections are used in the Superior Courts in Allen and Vanderburgh counties. Nominating commissions are used in St. Joseph County and in some courts in Lake County. In those courts that use the nominating commission process for selection; retention elections are used as the method of retention.

(t) Non-partisan elections are used in the Circuit Courts in Vanderburgh County.

(u) This applies to district judges only. Associate judges are selected by the district judges and retention is by a retention election. Magistrates are selected and retained by appointment from the County Judicial Magistrate Nominating Commission. The County Judicial Magistrate Nominating Commission consists of three members appointed by the county board and two elected by the county bar, presided over by a District Court judge.

(v) Seventeen districts use gubernatorial appointment from the Judicial Nominating Commission for selection and retention elections for retention. Fourteen districts use partisan elections for selection and retention.

(w) Depending on the amount of time remaining, selection may be by election following a Supreme Court appointment.

(x) Louisiana uses a blanket primary in which all candidates appear with party labels on the primary ballot. The top two vote getters compete in the general election.

(y) At least one judge who is a resident of the county in which the district lies must be appointed from each of the 13 districts.

(z) Two exceptions are Hartford and Montgomery counties where Circuit Court judges are assigned.

(aa) There are no expired judicial terms. A judicial term expires upon the death, resignation, retirement, or removal of an incumbent.

(bb) The Executive (Governor's) Council is made up of eight people elected by geographical area and presided over by the lieutenant governor.

(cc) There is no retention process. Judges serve during good behavior to age 70.

SELECTION AND RETENTION OF TRIAL COURT JUDGES—Continued

(dd) Gubernatorial appointment occurs in 40 partisan circuits; gubernatorial appointment from Judicial Nominating Commission takes place in five non-partisan circuits.

(ee) Partisan elections occur in 40 circuits; gubernatorial appointment from the Judicial Nominating Commission with a non-partisan election takes place in five circuits.

(ff) Partisan elections take place in 40 circuits; retention elections occur in five metropolitan circuits.

(gg) Associate circuit judges are selected on a county basis.

(hh) Selection occurs through Chief Justice appointment from Judicial Nominating Commission.

(ii) Other judges are designated by the District Court judges.

(jj) There is no retention process. Judges serve during good behavior to age 70.

(kk) In multi-municipality, joint, or countywide municipal courts, selection is by gubernatorial appointment with consent of the senate.

(ll) Mayoral appointment occurs in New York City.

(mm) The appointment is made by the County Chief Executive Officer with confirmation by District Board of Supervisors.

(nn) Housing judges are appointed by the Chief Administrator of the courts.

(oo) Party affiliation is not included on the ballot in the general election, but candidates are chosen through partisan primary nominations.

(pp) This applies to district and associate judges; special judges are selected by the district judges.

(qq) The geographic basis for selection is the municipality for those judges that are elected. Judges that are either appointed or are under contract may be from other cities.

(rr) There is no retention process. Judges serve during good behavior for a life tenure.

(ss) The governor may appoint a candidate if the unexpired term is less than one year.

(tt) In addition to Circuit Court judges, the Circuit Court has masters-in-equity whose jurisdiction is in matters referred to them in the Circuit Court. Masters-in-equity are selected by gubernatorial appointment from the Judicial Merit Selection Commission, retained by gubernatorial appointment with the consent of the senate, and the geographic basis for selection is the state.

(uu) Each county legislative body has the discretion to require elections to be non-partisan.

(vv) The selection method used to fill an unexpired term is established by a special legislative act.

(ww) There are no expired terms; each new judge begins a new term.

(xx) Appointment is by the local government executive with confirmation by the local government legislative body (may be either county or municipal government).

(yy) County judges are retained by retention election; municipal judges are reappointed by the city executive.

(zz) Superior and District Court judges serve as Family Court judges.

(aaa) Circuit Court judges appoint.

(bbb) Full-time municipal judges must stand for non-partisan election.

(ccc) A permanent vacancy in the office of municipal judge may be filled by temporary appointment of the municipal governing body or jointly by the governing bodies of all municipalities served by the judge.

(ddd) The Judicial Nomination Commission nominates for Presidential appointment and Senate confirmation. Not less than six months prior to the expiration of the term of office, the judge's performance is reviewed by the Commission on Judicial Disabilities and Tenure. A judge found "well qualified" is automatically reappointed for a new term of 15 years; a judge found "qualified" may be renominated by the President (and subject to Senate confirmation). A judge found "unqualified" is ineligible for reappointment or if the President does not wish to reappoint a judge, the Nomination Commission compiles a new list of candidates.

(eee) The geographic basis for selection is the District of Columbia.

Table 5.8
JUDICIAL DISCIPLINE: INVESTIGATING AND ADJUDICATING BODIES

State or other jurisdiction	Investigating body	Adjudicating body	Appeals from adjudication are filed with:	Final disciplining body	Point at which reprimands are made public
Alabama	Judicial Inquiry Committee	Court of the Judiciary	Supreme Court	Court of the Judiciary	Filing of the complaint with the Court of the Judiciary
Alaska	Committee on Judicial Conduct	Supreme Court	N.A.	Supreme Court	Filing of recommendation with Supreme Court
Arizona	Commission on Judicial Conduct	Commission on Judicial Conduct	Discretionary with Supreme Court	Supreme Court	Commission on Judicial Conduct determines if there is probable cause to bring formal charges.
Arkansas	Judicial Discipline and Disability Committees	Commission	Supreme Court	Supreme Court	At disposition of case
California	Commission on Judicial Performance	Commission on Judicial Performance	Supreme Court has discretionary review	Commission on Judicial Performance	Upon commission determination (a)
Colorado	Committee on Judicial Discipline	Commission on Judicial Discipline	No appeal	Supreme Court	Adjudication
Connecticut	Judicial Review Council	Judicial Review Council; Supreme Court	Supreme Court	Supreme Court	Public censure is issued at between 10 and 30 days after notice to the judge, provided that if the judge appeals, there is an automatic stay of disclosure.
	Council on Probate Judicial Conduct	Council on Probate Judicial Conduct	Supreme Court	Supreme Court	
Delaware	Preliminary Committee of the Court on the Judiciary Investigatory Committee of the Court on the Judiciary	Court on the Judiciary	No appeal	Court on the Judiciary	Upon issuance of opinion and imposition of sanction
Florida	Judicial Qualifications Commission	Judicial Qualifications Commission (b)	No appeal	Supreme Court (c)	Filing of formal charges by Committee with Supreme Court Clerk
Georgia	Judicial Qualifications Commission	Supreme Court	No appeal	Supreme Court	Formal Hearing
Hawaii	Commission on Judicial Conduct	Commission on Judicial Conduct	No appeal	Supreme Court	Imposition of public discipline by Supreme Court
Idaho	Judicial Council	Supreme Court	Supreme Court	Supreme Court	Filing with Supreme Court
Illinois	Judicial Inquiry Board	Courts Commission	No appeal	Courts Commission	Filing of complaint by Judicial Inquiry Board to Courts Commission
Indiana	Judicial Qualifications Committee	Supreme Court	N.A.	Supreme Court	Institution of Formal Proceedings
Iowa	Judicial Qualifications Commission	Judicial Qualifications Commission	Supreme Court	Supreme Court	Application by the commission to the Supreme Court
Kansas	Commission on Judicial Qualifications	Supreme Court	Supreme Court	Supreme Court	Reprimand is published by Supreme Court if approved by Supreme Court.
Kentucky	Judicial Conduct Committee	Judicial Conduct Committee	Supreme Court	Judicial Conduct Committee	Application of judge under investigation
Louisiana	Judiciary Commission	Supreme Court	No appeal	Supreme Court	Filing of formal complaint by commission with Supreme Court
Maine	Committee on Judicial Responsibility and Disability	Supreme Judicial Court	No appeal	Supreme Judicial Court	Filing of report to Supreme Judicial Court
Maryland	Commission on Judicial Disabilities	Court of Appeals	N.A.	Court of Appeals	Filing of record by Committee to Court of Appeals

See footnotes at end of table.

JUDICIAL DISCIPLINE: INVESTIGATING AND ADJUDICATING BODIES — Continued

State or other jurisdiction	Investigating body	Adjudicating body	Appeals from adjudication are filed with:	Final disciplining body	Point at which reprimands are made public
Massachusetts	Commission on Judicial Conduct	Supreme Judicial Court	N.A.	Supreme Judicial Court	After final of formal charges with the Supreme Judicial Court
Michigan	Judicial Tenure Commission	Supreme Court	Supreme Court	Supreme Court	Filing of formal complaint by commission with Supreme Court
Minnesota	Board of Judicial Standards	Supreme Court	No appeal	Supreme Court	Filing of formal charges by Committee with Supreme Court
Mississippi	Commission on Judicial Performance	Supreme Court	N.A.	Supreme Court	Recommendation of Commission to Supreme Court
Missouri	Commission on Retirement, Removal and Discipline	Commission on Retirement, Removal and Discipline	Supreme Court	Supreme Court	Filing of recommendation by Committee to Supreme Court
Montana	Judicial Standards Commission	Supreme Court	No appeal	Supreme Court	Filing of record by Committee with Supreme Court
Nebraska	Commission on Judicial Qualification	Supreme Court	No appeal	Supreme Court	Commission may issue a public reprimand
Nevada	Commission on Judicial Discipline	Commission on Judicial Discipline	Supreme Court	Commission on Judicial Discipline	Upon filing of report by Committee and service upon judge
New Hampshire	Supreme Court Committee on Judicial Conduct		Supreme Court	Supreme Court	On issuance of reprimand (d)
New Jersey	Advisory Committee on Judicial Conduct	Supreme Court	N.A.	Supreme Court	Filing of formal complaint
New Mexico	Judicial Standards Commission	Supreme Court	N.A.	Supreme Court	Filing of record by Commission with Supreme Court
New York	Commission on Judicial Conduct	Commission on Judicial Conduct	Court of Appeals	Commission on Judicial Conduct and Court of Appeals	Completion of service of record on respondent
North Carolina	Judicial Standards Commission	Supreme Court	No appeals	Supreme Court	Upon recommendation of Commission to Supreme Court
North Dakota	Commission on Judicial Conduct	Supreme Court	N.A.	Supreme Court	At formal hearing
Ohio	Board of Commissioners on Grievance and Discipline (e)	Board of Commissioners on Grievance and Discipline	Supreme Court	Supreme Court	Adjudication
Oklahoma	Court on the Judiciary Trial Division Council Council on Judicial Complaints	Court on the Judiciary Trial Division; Council on Judicial Complaints	Court on the Judiciary Division; no appeal from Council on Judicial Complaints	Court on the Judiciary Appellate Division	Filing with clerk of the Appellate Court
Oregon	Commission of Judicial Fitness and Disability (f)	Supreme Court	No appeal	Supreme Court	(g)
Pennsylvania	Judicial Conduct Board	Court of Judicial Discipline	Supreme Court	Supreme Court	Once a final decision has been made
Rhode Island	Commission on Judicial Tenure and Discipline	Supreme Court	No appeals	Supreme Court	When Supreme Court affirms a recommendation for reprimand or removal
South Carolina	Commissioners on Judicial Conduct	Supreme Court	N.A.	Supreme Court	Adjudication
South Dakota	Judicial Qualifications Commission	Supreme Court	No appeals	Supreme Court	Filing with the Supreme Court

See footnotes at end of table.

JUDICIAL DISCIPLINE: INVESTIGATING AND ADJUDICATING BODIES — Continued

State or other jurisdiction	Investigating body	Adjudicating body	Appeals from adjudication are filed with:	Final disciplining body	Point at which reprimands are made public
Tennessee	Court of the Judiciary	Court of the Judiciary	Supreme Court, then General Assembly	Supreme Court or General Assembly	Filing of complaint in Appellate Court Clerk's office
Texas	State Commission on Judicial Conduct	Supreme Court, Commission on Judicial Conduct, or review tribunal consisting of Justices of Courts of Appeals	Supreme Court	Supreme Court, Commission on Judicial Conduct, or review tribunal consisting of Justices of the Courts of Appeals	Convening of formal hearing by the Commission on Judicial Conduct
Utah	Judicial Conduct Commission	Judicial Conduct Commission	Supreme Court	Supreme Court	10 days after filing appeal
Vermont	Judicial Conduct Board	Supreme Court	Supreme Court	Supreme Court	Filing of formal charges by Board with Supreme Court
Virginia	Judicial Inquiry and Review Commission	Supreme Court	Supreme Court	Supreme Court	Filing of formal complaint by Committee with Supreme Court
Washington	Commission on Judicial Conduct	Supreme Court	No appeal	Committee on Judicial Conduct or Supreme Court	Beginning of fact finding hearing by Committee
West Virginia	Judicial Investigation Committee and Judicial Hearing Board	Judicial Hearing Board (JHB)	JHB recommends to SCA (i)	Supreme Court of Appeals (h)	Upon decision by Supreme Court of Appeals
Wisconsin	Judicial Commission	Supreme Court (i)	No appeal	Supreme Court	Filing of petitioner formal complaint by Judicial Commission w/Supreme Court
Wyoming	Commission on Judicial Conduct and Ethics	Supreme Court	N.A.	Supreme Court	Filing with Supreme Court
Dist. of Columbia	Commission on Judicial Disabilities and Tenure	Commission on Judicial Disabilities and Tenure	Federal judge panel: 3 appointments by Chief Justice of Supreme Court	Commission on Judicial. Disabilities and Tenure	Filing of order with D.C. Court of Appeals (j)
Puerto Rico	Disciplinary and Removal from office for health reasons	Supreme Court	N.A.	Supreme Court	Filing of formal complaint to the Discipline Commission

Source: Bureau of Justice Statistics, State Court Organization, 2004 NCJ 212351, update from the National Center for State Courts, February 2009.

Key:

N.A. — Not applicable

(a) In cases involving more serious misconduct, the commission may issue a public admonishment or public censure. The nature and impact of the misconduct generally determine the level of discipline. Both public admonishments and public censures are notices sent to the judge describing the improper conduct and stating the findings made by the commission. These notices are also made available to the press and the general public.

(b) The Judicial Qualifications Commission investigates and makes recommendations to the Supreme Court for discipline or removal.

(c) The Supreme Court power of removal is alternative and cumulative to the power of impeachment and suspension by the Governor and Senate.

(d) The Supreme Court Committee on Judicial Conduct may admonish, reprimand or order conditions, and the Supreme Court may impose formal discipline.

(e) Initial review is carried out by a panel of three commissioners.

(f) Technically, the Commission of Judicial Fitness and Disability does not adjudicate disciplinary matters. It hears the evidence and makes recommendations to the Supreme Court, which must review the records, or any stipulation for discipline and can hear additional evidence. Technically, then, there is no appeal. The Supreme Court orders any discipline, including any stipulated sanction.

(g) In Oregon, the allegations become public when the Commission issues a notice of public hearing, generally 14 days in advance of the hearing (although it can be less in the public interest). The actual complaint is not made public then, but the notice includes the general nature of the allegations. In a disciplinary case (but not a disability case), the Commission hearing, the evidence received there, and the Commission's decisions and recommendations are public. The Supreme Court decision is public when the Court files its opinion. There is no reprimand or other sanction until the Supreme Court decision.

(h) The final disciplining body is the same for both the Commission and Judicial Hearing Board.

(i) The Judicial Conduct and Disability Panel, through an ad hoc three-judge panel (two must be Court of Appeals judges, one can be a retired, reserve judge or Court of Appeals judge appointed as a hearing examiner) makes a report to the Supreme Court.

(j) This only applies in cases of removal or involuntary retirement wherein the Chief Justice appoints a three-member federal judge panel to review commission's order of removal.

Chapter Six

ELECTIONS

Wants vs. Needs: States Have Fulfilled Election Reform *Needs* but Congress Still has *Wants*

By Doug Lewis

Election reform has been a consistent issue for states and Congress since the 2000 general election. After Congress created the Help America Vote Act of 2002, state legislators and Congress have offered thousands of pieces of legislation to cure the perceived problems in elections.

Although most of the legislation offered would not have fixed any issues related to the presidential election in Florida, the 2000 election is the reason offered for continuing election reform. Clearly some of the legislation was aimed at rehabilitating the election infrastructure and providing an infusion of cash and mandates to bring states more into the official power structure of elections and to give them tools to bring local governments into compliance with a state plan for elections.

Elections have gone exceedingly well in recent years. The 2004 election was, at that point, the largest election in 40 years and it still was successful in terms of election administration. With more than 130 million voters going to the polls in 2008—more than in any previous election in history—election administration was again successful.

Dr. Charles Stewart of MIT reported preliminary findings of polling research conducted by a group of academicians from Caltech, MIT and Utah and reported in December 2008.[1] According to the preliminary report, the overall experience of voters on Election Day was positive:

- 92 percent said it was very easy to find their polling place.
- The average voter waited 13 minutes to vote—most of the time was waiting to check in.
- 83 percent said their polling place was run "very well."
- 70 percent said the performance of the poll workers was "excellent."
- 75 percent said they were "very confident" that their vote was counted as cast.
- 2 percent said they encountered voting equipment problems.
- 2 percent said they encountered a registration problem when they went to vote.
- 95 percent of all voters have a driver's license.
- 99 percent of all voters have at least one form of government identification.

Although there has been a consistent record of election successes since 2002, states shouldn't count on the notion that Congress is finished with election reform. Clearly, there appears to be few real needs to propel lawmakers to impose additional mandates for the states. While a perceived need existed after the 2000 election—and both political parties agreed that some legislation would be passed—it took nearly two years for the parties to reach an agreement. And because the two parties were close to parity in the House, and even closer in the Senate, any election reform would require a bipartisan effort. That resulted in the enactment of the Help America Vote Act.

The Help America Vote Act—commonly known as HAVA—is a model of how state and federal cooperation can work to fashion desired objectives. Perhaps for the first time, at least related to elections and other federal and state programs, HAVA created a synergistic relationship whereby the federal government established minimum standards (to avoid the concept of mandates) and appropriated money to achieve desired results. While the original legislation authorized up to $3.89 billion, actual appropriations came to $3.1 billion.

HAVA is unique for federal legislation, especially dealing with elections, because while the law did contain mandates for the states, it actually directed the states to find their own answers to achieve the mandates. Congress actually engaged the states as trusted partners to find solutions that meet voters' needs, and then appropriated money for the states to meet the mandates.

But unlike any previous federal programs, the appropriations became "no year money." That means states did not have to spend—or lose—the funds in any given federal fiscal year. As a result, the states have been able to maintain funds in accounts that give them the flexibility to continue to spend on election infrastructure improvements. The cost of elections has grown as states strive to comply with HAVA. Additionally, while states received money to build statewide voter databases, they will foot the bill to upgrade and maintain those databases. HAVA funded the purchase of voting equipment but left state and local governments with the ongoing costs of programming, maintenance and storage—all of which are considerably higher than pre-HAVA costs.

The legislation was immensely different from other state-federal programs because Congress established goals and objectives, but allowed the states to devise their own methods for meeting those mandates. And, unlike most federal legislation, the states—not a federal agency—would evaluate whether those methods were appropriate or effective. The U.S. Department of Justice does take enforcement action when it believes states are not conforming to relevant federal law, but HAVA's language gives states great latitude in determining the appropriate methods to achieve the mandates.

Opponents of the way the money was appropriated, including some in Congress, indicate states have had too much autonomy in spending the available federal money. They point to the July 2008 U.S. Election Assistance Commission report, which indicated states reported HAVA fund expenditures of nearly $2 billion and more than $1.2 billion in unspent funds. The balance includes $230,563,031 in interest earned on HAVA funds deposited in the State Election Fund accounts. This amount does not include state matching funds.

In general, HAVA funds may be used for the following activities:

- Improving, acquiring, leasing, modifying or replacing voting systems and technology, as well as methods for casting and counting votes.
- Developing and implementing a computerized statewide voter registration list.
- Implementing provisional voting.
- Providing voter information at the polling place.
- Establishing identification requirements for first-time voters who register to vote by mail.
- Improving the administration of elections for federal office.

Congressional action on HAVA and the National Voter Registration Act may have created more of an appetite for continuing legislation on election reform. The normal rationale is that more uniformity is necessary so national elections are the same throughout the nation.

But there is disagreement. Tim Storey, senior fellow at the National Conference of State Legislatures in Denver, has said national uniformity "is not a useful way to conduct elections. Congress likes to allege that it is ideal, but making decisions at the state level is best. HAVA gave much more responsibility to the states and they have responded. In fact, states have been ahead of Congress in passing election legislation."

Susan Frederick of NCSL's Washington office echoed that sentiment: "There is no crisis which would be the basis for Congressional action. As to uniformity, what fits a state with a small agrarian population spread out over hundreds of miles is different than what works for a densely populated urban state."

According to NCSL statistics on election legislation, states introduced more than 2,100 bills on elections and voter registration in 2007. Those figures exclude campaign finance legislation. States enacted 245 laws affecting voter registration, primary elections, absentee balloting, election administration or voting equipment. Similarly, in 2008 states introduced 1,907 election bills and enacted 171 laws affecting elections in 2008 and the future.

"At some point Congress needs to realize that states conduct far more elections than the federal government," Frederick said. "Why would we continue to try to change elections to fit the limited number of elections for federal office when there are so many more in state and local governments?"[2]

Leslie Reynolds, executive director of the National Association of Secretaries of State, said states have met their obligations. "One of the most important outcomes of the states' work in adopting election administration improvements is the number of innovative practices that have emerged," she said. "Virtually every recent voting innovation—including early voting, expedited military and overseas ballot delivery and return methods, mail balloting and vote centers—have all come from the states, not the federal government. It is the states that are responding directly with solutions that can be shared and adapted according to the unique history, laws and cultures of other states."

"Congress, advocates and many times the media all push for uniformity, as if that is a magic answer," Reynolds said. "But the reality is that practical applications mean significant differences in how to implement the concept with very different circumstances in 50 states and the District of Columbia."

Close senate elections in 2008 raised questions about the need for Congressional action and more uniformity in elections. But John Lindback, president of the National Association of State Election Directors, said the answers lie with the states. "The real strength of American elections has been the states' leadership on changes to make elections responsive to voters needs. Under HAVA, states got changes implemented within fairly short time periods to better serve their voters," he said. "Had that been under the federal government every state would have had to try to implement a one-size fits all concept—and the voters would have suffered for it."

Advocacy groups and some Congressional representatives have criticized the fact that states still had in excess of $1 billion of the original HAVA funds left. "Just because there is money in the bank does not mean that money is not allocated," Lindback said. "We have more needs left to fully implement the mandates of HAVA than we have money left, and we are making sure that the money is spent in the way it will best serve the voters in the coming years."

And Reynolds pointed out that the federal government required states to buy new voting equipment. "And how much of that equipment has since been replaced? States have been more cautious and looked at the long-term costs of the mandates and they have tried to spend responsibly rather than blowing all the money in a couple of years," she said.

Storey said states should not be criticized for not spending all their allocated money. "Thank the heavens that we have some money dedicated to elections left because the lean years are here for the foreseeable future as far as state budgets are concerned in all other areas."

Frederick said states are facing more pressing matters. "Logic should dictate that the financial crisis facing both the nation and the states means that further changes to the elections process is of low priority. But the reality is that when it comes to election legislation, Congress has almost always been driven by wants, not needs."

Who will win the battle of wants versus needs? States can make a significant case that they have responded successfully and the proof is in a series of well run elections that clearly has voters' confidence.

Notes

[1] Survey was to gauge the quality of the voting experience and included 200 respondents from each state conducted over the Internet or 10,000 respondents total. The survey was supplemented by 2,000 respondents contacted by phone in 10 states. Research team: Dr. Charles Stewart III, MIT; Michael Alvarez, Caltech; Stephen Ansolabehere, MIT; Adam Berinsky, MIT; Thad Hall, Utah; Gabriel Lenz, MIT. *2008 Survey of the Performance of American Elections*.

[2] According to a study by the U.S. Census Bureau there are 87,525 separate governmental units in the U.S. (Compendium of Public Employment: 2002 Census of Governments), issued September 2004 and accessed 1-14-2009. And, according to information from the Election Center in Houston, Texas, there are more than 511,000 state and local elected offices compared to the 535 seats for Congress plus a president/vice president ticket at the national level.

About the Author

Doug Lewis, a certified elections/registration administrator (CERA), is executive director of The Election Center, a nonpartisan, nonprofit organization representing the nation's election officials. He has been called on by Congress, federal agencies, state legislatures, and national and worldwide news media for solutions to voting issues.

Table 6.1
STATE EXECUTIVE BRANCH OFFICIALS TO BE ELECTED: 2009–2013

State or other jurisdiction	*2009*	*2010*	*2011*	*2012*	*2013*
Alabama	. . .	G,LG,AG,AR,A,SS,T	. . .	. . .	. . .
Alaska	. . .	G,LG	. . .	. . .	. . .
Arizona	. . .	G,AG,SS,SP,T (a)	. . .	. . .	. . .
Arkansas	. . .	G,LG,AG,A,SS,T (b)	. . .	. . .	. . .
California	. . .	G,LG,AG,C,CI,SS,SP,T (c)	. . .	. . .	. . .
Colorado	. . .	G,LG,AG,SS,T	. . .	. . .	. . .
Connecticut	. . .	G,LG,AG,C,SS,T	. . .	. . .	. . .
Delaware	. . .	AG,A,T	. . .	G,LG,CI	. . .
Florida	. . .	G,LG,AG,AR,CFO	. . .	. . .	. . .
Georgia	. . .	G,LG,AG,AR,C,SS,SP (d)	. . .	. . .	. . .
Hawaii	. . .	G,LG	. . .	. . .	. . .
Idaho	. . .	G,LG,AG,C,SS,SP,T	. . .	. . .	. . .
Illinois	. . .	G,LG,AG,C,SS,T	. . .	. . .	. . .
Indiana	. . .	A,SS,T	. . .	G,LG,AG,SP	. . .
Iowa	. . .	G,LG,AG,AR,A,SS,T	. . .	. . .	. . .
Kansas	. . .	G,LG,AG,CI,SS,T	. . .	. . .	. . .
Kentucky	. . .	. . .	G,LG,AG,AR,A,SS,T	. . .	. . .
Louisiana	. . .	. . .	G,LG,AG,AR,CI,SS,T	. . .	. . .
Maine (e)	. . .	G	. . .	. . .	. . .
Maryland	. . .	G,LG,AG,C	. . .	. . .	. . .
Massachusetts	. . .	G,LG,AG,A,SS,T	. . .	. . .	. . .
Michigan	. . .	G,LG,AG,SS (f)	. . .	(f)	. . .
Minnesota	. . .	G,LG,AG,A,SS	. . .	. . .	. . .
Mississippi	. . .	. . .	G,LG,AG,AR,A,CI,SS,T	. . .	. . .
Missouri	. . .	A	. . .	G,LG,AG,SS,T	. . .
Montana	. . .	. . .	. . .	G,LG,AG,A,SS,SP	. . .
Nebraska	. . .	G,LG,AG,A,SS,T	. . .	. . .	. . .
Nevada	. . .	G,LG,AG,C,SS,T	. . .	. . .	. . .
New Hampshire	. . .	G	. . .	G	. . .
New Jersey	G,LG	. . .	. . .	. . .	G,LG
New Mexico	. . .	G,LG,AG,A,SS,T (g)	. . .	. . .	. . .
New York	. . .	G,LG,AG,C	. . .	. . .	. . .
North Carolina	. . .	. . .	. . .	G,LG,AG,AR,A,CI,SS,SP,T (h)	. . .
North Dakota	. . .	AG,AR,SS (i)(j)	. . .	G,LG,A,CI,SP,T (i)	. . .
Ohio	. . .	G,LG,AG,A,SS,T	. . .	. . .	. . .
Oklahoma	. . .	G,LG,AG,A,CI,SP,T (k)	. . .	(k)	. . .
Oregon	. . .	G,SP (l)	. . .	AG,SS,T	. . .
Pennsylvania	. . .	G,LG	. . .	AG,A,T	. . .
Rhode Island	. . .	G,LG,AG,SS,T	. . .	. . .	. . .
South Carolina	. . .	G,LG,AG,AR,C,SS,SP,T (m)	. . .	. . .	. . .

See footnotes at end of table.

STATE EXECUTIVE BRANCH OFFICIALS TO BE ELECTED: 2009–2013—Continued

State or other jurisdiction	2009	2010	2011	2012	2013
South Dakota	. . .	G,LG,AG,A,SS,SP,T (n)	. . .	(n)	. . .
Tennessee	. . .	G	. . .	. . .	. . .
Texas	. . .	G,LG,AG,AR,C (o)	. . .	(o)	. . .
Utah	. . .	. . .	. . .	G,LG,AG,A,T	. . .
Vermont	. . .	G,LG,AG,A,SS,T	. . .	G,LG,AG,A,SS,T	. . .
Virginia	G,LG,AG	. . .	. . .	. . .	G,LG,AG
Washington	. . .	. . .	. . .	G,LG,AG,A,CI,SS,SP,T (p)	. . .
West Virginia	. . .	. . .	. . .	G,AG,AR,A,SS,T	. . .
Wisconsin	SP	G,LG,AG,SS,T	. . .	. . .	SP
Wyoming	. . .	G,A,SS,SP,T	. . .	. . .	. . .
American Samoa	. . .	. . .	. . .	G,LG	. . .
Guam	. . .	G,LG,AG,A	. . .	. . .	. . .
No. Mariana Islands	G,LG	. . .	. . .	. . .	G,LG
Puerto Rico	. . .	. . .	. . .	G	. . .
U.S. Virgin Islands	. . .	G,LG	. . .	. . .	. . .
Totals for year					
Governor	3	38	3	13	3
Lieutenant Governor	3	32	3	10	3
Attorney General	1	31	3	10	1
Agriculture	0	7	3	2	0
Auditor	0	16	2	8	0
Chief Financial Officer	0	1	0	0	0
Comptroller	0	10	0	0	0
Comm. of Insurance	0	3	2	4	0
Secretary of State	0	26	3	7	0
Supt. of Public Inst. or Comm. of Education	1	9	0	5	1
Treasurer	0	24	3	9	0

Sources: The Council of State Governments' survey and state election administration offices and Web sites, October 2008.

Note: This table shows the executive branch officials up for election in a given year. Footnotes indicate other offices (e.g., commissioners of labor, public service, etc.) also up for election in a given year. The data contained in this table reflect information available at press time.

Key:

. . . — No regularly scheduled elections of state executive officials.
G — Governor
LG — Lieutenant Governor
AG — Attorney General
AR — Agriculture
A — Auditor
C — Comptroller/Controller
CFO — Chief Financial Officer
CI — Commissioner of Insurance
SS — Secretary of State
SP — Superintendent of Public Instruction or Commissioner of Education
T — Treasurer

(a) Corporation commissioners (5)—4-year terms, 2012–2016—3 seats, 2010—2 seats. State Mine Inspector—4-year term, 2010 election.

(b) Commissioner of State Lands.

(c) Five (5) Board of Equalization members are elected to serve 4-year concurrent terms that will expire January 2011.

(d) Commissioner of Labor—4-year term, 2010 and 2014.

(e) In Maine the legislature elects constitutional officers (AG,SS,T) in even-numbered years for 2-year terms; the Auditor was elected by the legislature in 2008 and will serve a 4-year term.

(f) Michigan State University trustees (8)—8-year terms, 2010—2, 2012—2, 2014—2, 2016—2; University of Michigan regents (8)—8-year terms, 2010—2, 2012—2, 2014—2, 2016—2. Wayne State University governors (8)—8-year terms, 2010—2, 2012—2, 2014—2, 2016—2; State Board of Education (8)—8-year terms, 2010—2, 2012—2, 2014—2, 2016—2.

(g) Commissioner of Public Lands—4-year term, 2010.

(h) Commissioner of Labor elected in 2010.

(i) There are three Public Service Commissioners. One is up for election every two years. (3)—6-year terms, 2010—1, 2012—1, 2014—1.

(j) Tax Commissioner.

(k) Corporation Commissioners (3)—6-year terms, 2010—1, 2012—1, 2014—1; Commissioner of Labor—2010, 4-year term.

(l) Commissioner of the Bureau of Labor and Industries.

(m) Adjutant General—4-year term.

(n) The title is Commissioner of School and Public Lands; Public Utility Commissioners (3)—6-year terms, 2010—1, 2012—1, 2014—1.

(o) Commissioner of General Land Office—4-year term, 2010; Railroad Commissioners (3)—6-year terms, 2010—1, 2012—1, 2014—1.

(p) Commissioner of Public Lands.

Table 6.2
STATE LEGISLATURE MEMBERS TO BE ELECTED: 2009–2013

State or other jurisdiction	Total legislators		2009		2010		2011		2012		2013	
	Senate	House/Assembly	Senate	House/Assembly	Senate	House/Assembly	Senate	House/Assembly	Senate	House/Assembly	Senate	House/Assembly
Alabama	35	105	. . .	. . .	35	105	. . .	. . .	. . .	. . .	. . .	. . .
Alaska	20	40	. . .	. . .	10	40	. . .	. . .	10	40	. . .	. . .
Arizona	30	60	. . .	. . .	30	60	. . .	. . .	30	60	. . .	. . .
Arkansas	35	100	. . .	. . .	17	100	. . .	. . .	18	100	. . .	. . .
California	40	80	. . .	. . .	20	80	. . .	. . .	20	80	. . .	. . .
Colorado	35	65	. . .	. . .	18	65	. . .	. . .	17	65	. . .	. . .
Connecticut	36	151	. . .	. . .	36	151	. . .	. . .	36	151	. . .	. . .
Delaware	21	41	. . .	. . .	. . .	. . .	. . .	. . .	11	41	. . .	. . .
Florida	40	120	. . .	. . .	20	120	. . .	. . .	20	120	. . .	. . .
Georgia	56	180	. . .	. . .	56	180	. . .	. . .	56	180	. . .	. . .
Hawaii	25	51	. . .	. . .	13	51	. . .	. . .	12	51	. . .	. . .
Idaho	35	70	. . .	. . .	35	70	. . .	. . .	35	70	. . .	. . .
Illinois	59 (a)	118	. . .	. . .	20	118	. . .	. . .	39	118	. . .	. . .
Indiana	50	100	. . .	. . .	25	100	. . .	. . .	25	100	. . .	. . .
Iowa	50	100	. . .	. . .	25 (c)	100	. . .	. . .	25 (b)	100	. . .	. . .
Kansas	40	125	. . .	. . .	. . .	125	. . .	. . .	40	125	. . .	. . .
Kentucky	38	100	. . .	. . .	19	100	. . .	. . .	19	100	. . .	. . .
Louisiana	39	105	. . .	. . .	. . .	. . .	39	105	. . .	. . .	. . .	. . .
Maine	35	151	. . .	. . .	35	151	. . .	. . .	35	151	. . .	. . .
Maryland	47	141	. . .	. . .	47	141	. . .	. . .	. . .	. . .	. . .	. . .
Massachusetts	40	160	. . .	. . .	40	160	. . .	. . .	40	160	. . .	. . .
Michigan	38	110	. . .	. . .	38	110	. . .	. . .	. . .	110	. . .	. . .
Minnesota	67	134	. . .	. . .	67	134	. . .	. . .	. . .	134	. . .	. . .
Mississippi	52	122	. . .	. . .	. . .	. . .	52	122	. . .	. . .	. . .	. . .
Missouri	34	163	. . .	. . .	17	163	. . .	. . .	17	163	. . .	. . .
Montana	50	100	. . .	. . .	25	100	. . .	. . .	25	100	. . .	. . .
Nebraska	49	U	. . .	. . .	24	U	. . .	. . .	25	U	. . .	. . .
Nevada	21	42	. . .	. . .	11	42	. . .	. . .	10	42	. . .	. . .
New Hampshire	24	400	. . .	. . .	24	400	. . .	. . .	24	400	. . .	. . .
New Jersey	40	80	. . .	80	. . .	. . .	40	80	. . .	. . .	. . .	80
New Mexico	42	70	. . .	. . .	. . .	70	. . .	. . .	42	70	. . .	. . .
New York	62	150	. . .	. . .	62	150	. . .	. . .	62	150	. . .	. . .
North Carolina	50	120	. . .	. . .	50	120	. . .	. . .	50	120	. . .	. . .
North Dakota	47	94	. . .	. . .	24 (c)	47 (c)	. . .	. . .	23 (b)	47 (c)	. . .	. . .
Ohio	33	99	. . .	. . .	17	99	. . .	. . .	16	99	. . .	. . .
Oklahoma	48	101	. . .	. . .	24	101	. . .	. . .	24	101	. . .	. . .
Oregon	30	60	. . .	. . .	15	60	. . .	. . .	15	60	. . .	. . .
Pennsylvania	50	203	. . .	. . .	25 (b)	203	. . .	. . .	25 (c)	203	. . .	. . .
Rhode Island	38	75	. . .	. . .	38	75	. . .	. . .	38	75	. . .	. . .
South Carolina	46	124	. . .	. . .	. . .	124	. . .	. . .	46	124	. . .	. . .

See footnotes at end of table.

STATE LEGISLATURE MEMBERS TO BE ELECTED: 2009–2013—Continued

State or other jurisdiction	Total legislators		2009		2010		2011		2012		2013	
	Senate	House/Assembly	Senate	House/Assembly	Senate	House/Assembly	Senate	House/Assembly	Senate	House/Assembly	Senate	House/Assembly
South Dakota	35	70	. . .	. . .	35	70	. . .	. . .	35	70	. . .	. . .
Tennessee	33	99	. . .	. . .	17	99	. . .	. . .	16	99	. . .	. . .
Texas	31	150	. . .	. . .	16	150	. . .	. . .	15	150	. . .	. . .
Utah	29	75	. . .	. . .	14	75	. . .	. . .	15	75	. . .	. . .
Vermont	30	150	. . .	. . .	30	150	. . .	. . .	30	150	. . .	. . .
Virginia	40	100	. . .	100	. . .	. . .	40	100	. . .	. . .	. . .	100
Washington	49	98	. . .	. . .	24	98	. . .	. . .	25	98	. . .	. . .
West Virginia	34	100	. . .	. . .	17	100	. . .	. . .	17	100	. . .	. . .
Wisconsin	33	99	. . .	. . .	17	99	. . .	. . .	16	99	. . .	. . .
Wyoming	30	60	. . .	. . .	15	60	. . .	. . .	15	60	. . .	. . .
Dist. of Columbia	13	U	. . .	. . .	7	. . .	. . .	. . .	6	U	. . .	. . .
American Samoa	18	20	. . .	. . .	(d)	20	. . .	. . .	(d)	20	. . .	. . .
Guam	15	U	. . .	. . .	15	. . .	. . .	. . .	15	. . .	. . .	. . .
No. Mariana Islands	9	18	6	18	. . .	. . .	3	18	. . .	. . .	6	18
Puerto Rico (e)	28	51	. . .	. . .	. . .	. . .	. . .	. . .	28	51	. . .	. . .
U.S. Virgin Islands	15	U	. . .	. . .	15	U	. . .	. . .	15	U	. . .	. . .
State Totals	1,971	5,411	0	180	1,148	4,792	171	407	1,113	4,711	0	180
Totals	2,068	5,502	6	198	1,185	4,936	174	425	1,177	4,782	6	198

Source: The Council of State Governments' survey, October 2008.

Note: This table shows the number of legislative seats up for election in a given year. As a result of redistricting, states may adjust some elections. The data contained in this table reflect information available at press time. See the Chapter 3 table entitled, "The Legislators: Numbers, Terms, and Party Affiliations," for specific information on legislative terms.

Key:

. . . — No regularly scheduled elections.

U — Unicameral legislature

(a) The Illinois Senate operates on a ten-year election cycle. All 59 senators are elected in each year ending in "2" (following the redistricting based upon the decennial census). Senate districts are then divided into three groups. One group of senators is elected for terms of four years, four years and two years; two years, four years and four years; four years, two years and four years.

(b) Even-numbered Senate districts.

(c) Odd-numbered Senate districts.

(d) In American Samoa, Senators are not elected by popular vote. They are selected by county councils of chiefs.

(e) If in the general election more than two-thirds of the members of either house are elected from one party or from a single ticket, as both are defined by law, the numbers shall be increased in accordance with Article III Section 7 of the Puerto Rico Constitution.

Table 6.3
METHODS OF NOMINATING CANDIDATES FOR STATE OFFICES

State or other jurisdiction	*Methods of nominating candidates*
Alabama	Primary election; however, the state executive committee or other governing body of any political party may choose instead to hold a state convention for the purpose of nominating candidates. Submitting a petition to run as an independent or third-party candidate or an independent nominating procedure.
Alaska	Primary election. Petition for no-party candidates.
Arizona	Candidates who are members of a recognized party are nominated by an open primary election. Candidates who are not members of a recognized political party may file petitions to appear on the general election ballot. A write-in option is also available.
Arkansas	Primary election, convention and petition.
California	Primary election or independent nomination procedure.
Colorado	Primary election, convention or by petition.
Connecticut	Convention/primary election. Major political parties hold state conventions (convening not earlier than the 68th day and closing not later than the 50th day before the date of the primary) for the purpose of endorsing candidates. If no one challenges the endorsed candidate, no primary election is held. However, if anyone (who received at least 15 percent of the delegate vote on any roll call at the convention) challenges the endorsed candidate, a primary election is held to determine the party nominee for the general election.
Delaware	Primary election for Democrats and primary election and convention for Republicans.
Florida	Primary election. Minor parties may nominate their candidate in any manner they deem proper.
Georgia	Primary election.
Hawaii	Primary election.
Idaho	Primary election and convention. New political parties hold a convention to nominate candidates to be placed on a general election ballot.
Illinois	Primary election. The primary election nominates established party candidates. New political parties and independent candidates go directly to the general election file based on a petition process.
Indiana	Primary election, convention and petition. The governor is chosen by a primary. All other state officers are chosen at a state convention, unless the candidate is an independent. Any party that obtains between 2 percent and 8 percent of the vote for secretary of state may hold a convention to select a candidate.
Iowa	Primary election, convention and petition.
Kansas	Candidates for the two major parties are nominated by primary election. Candidates for minor parties are nominated for the general election at state party conventions. Independent candidates are nominated for the general election by petition.
Kentucky	Primary election. A slate of candidates for governor and lieutenant governor that receives the highest number of its party's votes but which number is less than 40 percent of the votes cast for all slates of candidates of that party, shall be required to participate in a runoff primary with the slate of candidates of the same party receiving the second highest number of votes.
Louisiana	Candidates may qualify for any office they wish, regardless of party affiliation, by completing the qualifying document and paying the appropriate qualifying fee; or a candidate may file a nominating petition.
Maine	Primary election or non-party petition.
Maryland	Primary election, convention and petition. Unaffiliated candidates or candidates affiliated with non-recognized political parties may run for elective office by collecting the requisite number of signatures on a petition. The required number equals 1 percent of the number of registered voters eligible to vote for office. Only recognized non-principal political parties may nominate their candidates by a convention in accordance with their bylaws. (At this time, Maryland has four non-principal parties: Libertarian, Green, Constitution and Populist.)
Massachusetts	Primary election.
Michigan	Governor, State House, State Senate use primary election. Lieutenant governor runs as the running mate to gubernatorial candidate, not separately, and is selected through the convention process. Secretary of state and attorney general candidates are chosen at convention. Nominees for State Board of Education, University of Michigan regents, Michigan State University trustees and Wayne State University governors are nominated by convention. Minor parties nominate candidates to all partisan offices by convention.
Minnesota	Primary election. Candidates for minor parties or independent candidates are by petition. They must have the signatures of 2,000 people who will be eligible to vote in the next general election.
Mississippi	Primary election, petition (for independent candidates), independent nominating procedures (third-party candidates).
Missouri	Primary election.
Montana	Primary election and independent nominating procedure.
Nebraska	Primary election.
Nevada	Primary election. Independent candidates are nominated by petition for the general election. Minor parties nominated by petition or by party.
New Hampshire	Primary election. Minor parties by petition.
New Jersey	Primary election. Independent candidates are nominated by petition for the general election.

See footnotes at end of table.

METHODS OF NOMINATING CANDIDATES FOR STATE OFFICES — Continued

State or other jurisdiction	Methods of nominating candidates
New Mexico	Statewide candidates petition to go to convention and are nominated in a primary election. District and legislative candidates petition for primary ballot access.
New York	Primary election/petition.
North Carolina	Primary election. Newly recognized parties just granted access submit their first nominees by convention. All established parties use primaries.
North Dakota	Convention/primary election. Political parties hold state conventions for the purpose of endorsing candidates. Endorsed candidates are automatically placed on the primary election ballot, but other candidates may also petition their name on the ballot.
Ohio	Primary election, petition and by declaration of intent to be a write-in candidate.
Oklahoma	Primary election.
Oregon	Primary election. Minor parties hold conventions.
Pennsylvania	Primary election, and petition. Nomination petitions filed by major party candidates to access primary ballot. Nomination papers filed by minor party and independent candidates to access November ballot.
Rhode Island	Primary election.
South Carolina	Primary election for Republicans and Democrats; party conventions held for minor parties. Candidates can have name on ballot via petition.
South Dakota	Convention, petition and independent nominating procedure.
Tennessee	Primary election/petition.
Texas	Primary election/convention. Minor parties without ballot access nominate candidates for the general election after qualifying for ballot access by petition.
Utah	Convention, primary election and petition.
Vermont	Primary election. Major parties by primary, minor parties by convention, independents by petition.
Virginia	Primary election, convention and petition.
Washington	Primary election.
West Virginia	Primary election, convention, petition and independent nominating procedure.
Wisconsin	Primary election/petition. Candidates must file nomination papers (petitions) containing the minimum number of signatures required by law. Candidates appear on the primary ballot for the party they represent. The candidate receiving the most votes in each party primary goes on to the November election.
Wyoming	Primary election.
Dist. of Columbia	Primary election. Independent and minor party candidates file by nominating petition.
American Samoa	Individual files petition for candidacy with the chief election officer. Petition must be signed by statutorily mandated number of qualified voters.
Guam	Individual files petition for candidacy with the chief election officer. Petition must be signed by statutorily mandated number of qualified voters.
No. Mariana Islands	Candidates are all nominated by petition. Candidates seeking the endorsement of recognized political parties must also include in their submitted petition a document signed by the recognized political party's chairperson/president and secretary attesting to such nomination. Recognized political parties may, or may not, depending on their bylaws and party rules, conduct primaries separate from any state election agency participation.
Puerto Rico	Primary election and convention.
U.S. Virgin Islands	Primary election.

Source: The Council of State Governments' survey of state election administration offices, January 2007, and state Web sites, October 2008.

Note: The nominating methods described here are for state offices; procedures may vary for local candidates. Also, independent candidates may have to petition for nomination.

Table 6.4
ELECTION DATES FOR NATIONAL AND STATE ELECTIONS
(Formulas and dates of state elections)

State or other jurisdiction	Type of primary	National (a)			State (b)		
		Primary	Runoff	General	Primary	Runoff	General
Alabama	O	Feb., 1st T	. . .	Nov.,★	June, 1st T	July, 1st T after 2nd M (even yrs.)	Nov.,★
		Feb. 7, 2012	. . .	Nov. 6, 2012	June 1, 2010	July 13, 2010	Nov. 2, 2010
Alaska	C	Aug., 4th T	. . .	Nov.,★	Aug., 4th T	. . .	Nov.,★
		Aug. 28, 2012	. . .	Nov. 6, 2012	Aug. 24, 2010	. . .	Nov. 2, 2010
Arizona	C	Feb., 1st T	. . .	Nov.,★	8th T Prior	. . .	Nov.,★
		Feb. 7, 2012	. . .	Nov. 6, 2012	Aug. 31, 2010	. . .	Nov. 2, 2010
Arkansas	O	Feb., 1st T	. . .	Nov.,★	T 3 wks. prior to runoff	June, 2nd T	Nov.,★
		Feb. 7, 2012	. . .	Nov. 6, 2012	May 18, 2010	June 8, 2010	Nov. 2, 2010
California	SO	Feb., 1st T	. . .	Nov.,★	June ★	. . .	Nov.,★
		Feb. 7, 2012	. . .	Nov. 6, 2012	June 8, 2010	. . .	Nov. 2, 2010
Colorado	C	Caucus	. . .	Nov., ★	Aug., 2nd T	. . .	Nov.,★
		Feb. 7, 2012	. . .	Nov. 6, 2012	Aug. 10, 2010	. . .	Nov. 2, 2010
Connecticut	C	Feb., 1st T	. . .	Nov.,★	Aug. 2nd T	. . .	Nov.,★
		Feb. 7, 2012	. . .	Nov. 6, 2012	Aug. 10, 2010	. . .	Nov. 2, 2010
Delaware	C	Feb., 1st T	. . .	Nov.,★	Sept., 1st S after 1st M	. . .	Nov.,★
		Feb. 7, 2012	. . .	Nov. 6, 2012	Sept. 14, 2010	. . .	Nov. 2, 2010
Florida	C	(d)	. . .	Nov., ★	9th T prior to General	. . .	Nov.,★
		Jan. 31, 2012	. . .	Nov. 6, 2012	August 24, 2010	. . .	Nov. 2, 2010
Georgia	O	Feb., 1st T	. . .	Nov., ★	(d)	. . .	Nov.,★
		Feb. 7, 2012	. . .	Nov. 6, 2012	July 20, 2010	Aug. 10, 2010	Nov. 2, 2010
Hawaii	O	Caucus	. . .	Nov.,★	Sept., 2nd Last S	. . .	Nov.,★
		(c)	. . .	Nov. 6, 2012	Sept. 18, 2010	. . .	Nov. 2, 2010
Idaho	O	May, 4th T	. . .	Nov.,★	May, 4th T	. . .	Nov.,★
		May 22, 2012	. . .	Nov. 6, 2012	May 25, 2010	. . .	Nov. 2, 2010
Illinois	O	Feb., 1st T	. . .	Nov.,★	Feb., 1st T	. . .	Nov.,★
		Feb. 7, 2012	. . .	Nov. 6, 2012	Feb. 9, 2010	. . .	Nov. 2, 2010
Indiana	O	May,★	. . .	Nov.,★	May,★	. . .	Nov.,★
		May 1, 2010	. . .	Nov. 6, 2012	May 5, 2010	. . .	Nov. 2, 2010
Iowa	C	Caucus (e)	. . .	Nov., ★	June, ★	. . .	Nov.,★
		Jan. 16, 2012	. . .	Nov. 6, 2012	June 1, 2010	. . .	Nov. 2, 2010
Kansas	C	Feb., 1st T	. . .	Nov., ★	Aug. 1st T	. . .	Nov.,★
		Feb. 7, 2012	. . .	Nov. 6, 2012	Aug. 3, 2010	. . .	Nov. 2, 2010
Kentucky	C	May, 1st T after 3rd M	. . .	Nov.,★	May, 1st T after 3rd M	35 days AP	Nov.,★
		May 22, 2012	. . .	Nov. 6, 2012	May 18, 2010	June 22, 2010	Nov. 2, 2010
Louisiana	O (f)	(d)	. . .	Nov.,★	(f)	(f)	(f)
		Feb. 11, 2012	. . .	Nov. 6, 2012	Aug. 28 and Oct. 2	None scheduled	Nov. 2, 2010
Maine	C	Caucus	. . .	Nov.,★	June, 2nd T	. . .	Nov.,★
		(c)	. . .	Nov. 6, 2012	June 8, 2010	. . .	Nov. 2, 2010
Maryland	C	Feb., 2nd T	. . .	Nov.,★	2nd T after 1st M in Sept.	. . .	Nov.,★
		Feb. 14, 2012	. . .	Nov. 6, 2012	Sept. 14, 2010	. . .	Nov. 2, 2010
Massachusetts	SO	(d)	. . .	Nov.,★	7th T Prior	. . .	Nov.,★
		Mar. 6, 2012	. . .	Nov. 6, 2012	Sept. 14, 2010	. . .	Nov. 2, 2010
Michigan	O	(d)	. . .	Nov., ★	Aug., ★	. . .	Nov.,★
		Feb. 28, 2012	. . .	Nov. 6, 2012	Aug. 3, 2010	. . .	Nov. 2, 2010
Minnesota	O	(g)	. . .	Nov.,★	(g)	. . .	Nov.,★
		Mar. 6, 2012	. . .	Nov. 6, 2012	Sept. 14, 2010	. . .	Nov. 2, 2010
Mississippi	O	Mar., 2nd T (g)	3 wks. after 1st Primary	Nov.,★	(d)	3rd T AP	Nov.,★
		Mar. 13, 2012	Apr. 3, 2012	Nov. 6, 2012	August 2, 2011	August 23, 2011	Nov. 8, 2011
Missouri	O	Feb., ★	. . .	Nov.,★	Aug., ★	. . .	Nov.,★
		Feb. 7, 2012	. . .	Nov. 6, 2012	Aug. 3, 2010	. . .	Nov. 2, 2010
Montana	O	June, ★	. . .	Nov.,★	June, ★	. . .	Nov.,★
		June 5, 2012	. . .	Nov. 6, 2012	June 8, 2010	. . .	Nov. 2, 2010
Nebraska	C	May, 1st T after 2nd M	. . .	Nov.,★	May, 1st T after 2nd M	. . .	Nov.,★
		May 15, 2012		Nov. 6, 2012	May 11, 2010		Nov. 2, 2010
Nevada	C	Caucus	. . .	Nov.,★	3rd T Aug.	. . .	Nov.,★
		Jan. 28, 2012		Nov. 6, 2012	Aug. 17, 2010		Nov. 2, 2010
New Hampshire	SO	Set by SS	. . .	Nov., ★	(d)	. . .	Nov.,★
		Jan. 24, 2012		Nov. 6, 2012	Sept. 14, 2010		Nov. 2, 2010

See footnotes at end of table.

ELECTION DATES FOR NATIONAL AND STATE ELECTIONS
(Formulas and dates of state elections)

State or other jurisdiction	Type of primary	National (a)			State (b)		
		Primary	Runoff	General	Primary	Runoff	General
New Jersey	SO	Feb., ★ Feb. 7, 2012	. . .	Nov.,★ Nov. 6, 2012	June, ★ June 2, 2009	. . .	Nov.,★ Nov. 3, 2009
New Mexico	C	Feb., ★ Feb. 7, 2012	. . .	Nov.,★ Nov. 6, 2012	June, 1st T June 1, 2010	. . . . . .	Nov.,★ Nov. 2, 2010
New York	C	Feb., ★ Feb. 7, 2012	. . .	Nov.,★ Nov. 6, 2012	Sept.,★ Sept. 7, 2010	. . .	Nov.,★ Nov. 2, 2010
North Carolina	C (h)	May, ★ May 8, 2012	7 wks. AP June 26, 2012	Nov.,★ Nov. 6, 2012	May, ★ May 4, 2010	7 wks. AP June 22, 2010	Nov.,★ Nov. 2, 2010
North Dakota	O	(i) Caucus—Feb. 7, 2012	. . .	Nov.,★ Nov. 6, 2012	June, 2nd T June 8, 2010	. . . . . .	Nov.,★ Nov. 2, 2010
Ohio	SO	Mar.,★ Mar. 6, 2012	. . .	Nov.,★ Nov. 6, 2012	Mar.,★ Mar. 2, 2010	. . .	Nov.,★ Nov. 2, 2010
Oklahoma	C	Feb., ★ Feb. 7, 2012	. . .	Nov., ★ Nov. 6, 2012	July, last T July 27, 2010	Aug., 4th T Aug. 24, 2010	Nov.,★ Nov. 2, 2010
Oregon	C	May, 3rd T May 15, 2012	. . .	Nov., ★ Nov. 6, 2012	May, 3rd T May 18, 2010	. . .	Nov.,★ Nov. 2, 2010
Pennsylvania	C	Apr., 4th T Apr. 24, 2012	. . .	Nov.,★ Nov. 6, 2012	Apr., 4th T Apr. 27, 2010	. . . . . .	Nov.,★ Nov. 2, 2010
Rhode Island	O	(d) (c)	. . .	Nov.,★ Nov. 6, 2012	Sept., 2nd T after 1st M Sept. 14, 2010	. . . . . .	Nov.,★ Nov. 2, 2010
South Carolina	O	(d) (c)	. . . . . .	Nov.,★ Nov. 6, 2012	June, 2nd T June 8, 2010	2nd T AP June 22, 2010	Nov.,★ Nov. 2, 2010
South Dakota	C	June, ★ June 5, 2012	2nd T AP June 19, 2012	Nov.,★ Nov. 6, 2012	June, ★ June 1, 2010	2nd T AP June 15, 2010	Nov.,★ Nov. 2, 2010
Tennessee	O	Feb., ★ Feb. 7, 2012	. . . . . .	Nov., ★ Nov. 6, 2012	Aug., 1st TH Aug. 5, 2010	. . . . . .	Nov.,★ Nov. 2, 2010
Texas	O	Mar., 1st T Mar. 6, 2012	. . . . . .	Nov., ★ Nov. 6, 2012	Mar., 1st T Mar. 2, 2010	Apr., 2nd T Apr. 13, 2010	Nov.,★ Nov. 2, 2010
Utah	C	Feb., ★ Feb. 7, 2012	. . .	Nov., ★ Nov. 6, 2012	June, 4th T June 22, 2010	. . . . . .	Nov.,★ Nov. 2, 2010
Vermont	O	Mar., 1st T Mar. 6, 2012	. . .	Nov.,★ Nov. 6, 2012	Sept., 2nd T Sept. 14, 2010	. . . . . .	Nov.,★ Nov. 2, 2010
Virginia	O	Feb., 2nd T Feb. 14, 2012	. . .	Nov.,★ Nov. 6, 2012	June, 2nd T June 9, 2009	. . . . . .	Nov.,★ Nov. 3, 2009
Washington	PC	(d) (c)	. . .	Nov.,★ Nov. 6, 2012	Aug., 3rd T Aug. 17, 2010	. . . . . .	Nov.,★ Nov. 2, 2010
West Virginia	C	May, 2nd T May 8, 2012	. . .	Nov.,★ Nov. 6, 2012	May, 2nd T May 11, 2010	. . . . . .	Nov.,★ Nov. 2, 2010
Wisconsin	O	(d) Feb. 21, 2012	. . .	Nov.,★ Nov. 6, 2012	Sept., 2nd T Sept. 14, 2010	. . . . . .	Nov.,★ Nov. 2, 2010
Wyoming	C	Caucus (c)	. . .	Nov.,★ Nov. 6, 2012	Aug., 1st T after 3rd M Aug. 17, 2010	. . . . . .	Nov.,★ Nov. 2, 2010
Dist. of Columbia	C	(d) (c)	. . . . . .	Nov.,★ Nov. 6, 2012	(d) Sept. 14, 2010	. . . . . .	Nov.,★ Nov. 2, 2010
American Samoa	N.A.	(j) Nov. 6, 2012	14 days after general	Nov., ★ Nov. 16, 2010	(j) Nov. 2, 2010	14 days after general	Nov.,★
Puerto Rico	N.A.	. . . (c)	. . .	. . . Nov. 6, 2012	(d) (c)	. . . . . .	Nov.,★ Nov. 2, 2010
U.S. Virgin Islands	N.A.	. . . (c)	. . . . . .	. . . Nov. 6, 2012	Sept., 2nd S Sept. 11, 2010	14 day AP Sept. 25, 2010	Nov.,★ Nov. 2, 2010

See footnotes at end of table.

ELECTION DATES FOR NATIONAL AND STATE ELECTIONS
(Formulas and dates of state elections)

Sources: The Council of State Governments, March 2009.

Note: This table describes the basic formulas for determining when national and state will be held. For specific information on a particular state, the reader is advised to contact the state election administration office. All dates provided are based on the state election formula and dates are subject to change.

Key:

★ — First Tuesday after first Monday.
. . . — No provision.
M —Monday.
T — Tuesday.
TH — Thursday.
S — Saturday.
Nat. — Same date as national elections.
State — Same date as state elections.
Prior — Prior to general election.
AP — After primary.
V — Varies.

Key: Column 1:
C — Closed primary
O — Open primary
PC — Private-choice primary
SC — Semi-closed primary
SO — Semi-open primary

(a) National refers to presidential elections.

(b) State refers to election in which a state executive official or U.S. senator is to be elected. See Table 6.2, State Officials to be Elected.

(c) Date not available at press time.

(d) Formula not available at press time.

(e) Iowa does not have a presidential primary. The Iowa Caucuses mark the beginning of the presidential candidate selection process by choosing delegates to the next level of political party conventions.

(f) Louisiana has an open primary which requires all candidates, regardless of party affiliation, to appear on a single ballot. If a candidate receives over 50 percent of the vote in the primary, that candidate is elected to the office. If no candidate receives a majority vote, then a single election is held between the two candidates receiving the most votes. For national elections, the first vote is held on the first Saturday in October of even-numbered years with the general election held on the first Tuesday after the first Monday in November. For state elections, the election is held on the second to last Saturday in October with the runoff being held on the fourth Saturday after first election. Local elections vary depending on the location and the year.

(g) Parties must notify the Secretary of State's Office in writing prior to Dec. 1st the year preceding the date of the election of their intentions to hold a preference primary election.

(h) Unaffiliated voters, by state statute and with permission of a party, may vote in a party primary. Currently both the Democratic and Republican parties allow this.

(i) On one designated day, following presidential nominating contests in the states of Iowa and New Hampshire and prior to the first Wednesday in March in every presidential election year, every political party entitled to a separate column may conduct a presidential preference caucus. Before August 15 of the odd-numbered year immediately preceding the presidential election year, the secretary of state shall designate the day after consulting with and taking recommendations from the two political parties casting the greatest vote for president of the United States at the most recent general elections when the office of president appeared on the ballot.

(j) American Samoa does not conduct primary elections (In addition, elections are conducted for territory-wide offices. There are no local elections).

Table 6.5
POLLING HOURS: GENERAL ELECTIONS

State or other jurisdiction	Polls open	Polls close	Notes on hours (a)
Alabama	7 a.m.	7 p.m.	
Alaska	7 a.m.	8 p.m.	
Arizona	6 a.m.	7 p.m.	
Arkansas	7:30 a.m.	7:30 p.m.	
California	7 a.m.	8 p.m.	
Colorado	7 a.m.	7 p.m.	
Connecticut	6 a.m.	8 p.m.	
Delaware	7 a.m.	8 p.m.	
Florida	7 a.m.	7 p.m.	
Georgia	7 a.m.	7 p.m.	
Hawaii	7 a.m.	6 p.m.	
Idaho	8 a.m.	8 p.m.	Clerk has the option of opening all polls at 7 a.m. Idaho is in two time zones—MST and PST.
Illinois	6 a.m.	7 p.m.	
Indiana	6 a.m.	6 p.m.	
Iowa	7 a.m.	9 p.m.	Hours for school and city elections: polls open at 7 a.m. or noon (depending upon choice of county auditor, with legal limitations on opening the polls at noon). Polls close at 8 p.m.
Kansas	7 a.m.	7 p.m.	Counties may choose to open polls as early as 6 a.m. and close as late as 8 p.m. Several western counties are on Mountain time.
Kentucky	6 a.m.	6 p.m.	
Louisiana	6 a.m.	8 p.m.	
Maine	Between 6 and 10 a.m.	9 p.m.	Applicable opening time depends on variables related to the size of the precinct.
Maryland	7 a.m.	8 p.m.	Anyone in line at 8 p.m. will be allowed to vote.
Massachusetts	7 a.m.	8 p.m.	
Michigan	7 a.m.	8 p.m.	
Minnesota	7 a.m.	8 p.m.	Towns outside of theTwin Cities metro area with less than 500 inhabitants may have a later time for the polls to open as long as it is not later than 10 a.m.
Mississippi	7 a.m.	7 p.m.	
Missouri	6 a.m.	7 p.m.	Those individuals in line at 7 p.m. will be allowed to vote.
Montana	7 a.m.	8 p.m.	Polling places with fewer than 200 registered electors must be open from noon until 8 p.m. or until all registered electors in any precinct have voted.
Nebraska	7 a.m MST/8 a.m. CST	7 p.m. MST/8 p.m. CST	
Nevada	7 a.m.	7 p.m.	
New Hampshire	No later than 11 a.m.	No earlier than 7 p.m.	Polling hours vary from town to town. The hours of 11 a.m. to 7 p.m. are by statute.
New Jersey	6 a.m.	8 p.m.	
New Mexico	7 a.m.	7 p.m.	
New York	6 a.m.	9 p.m.	
North Carolina	6:30 a.m.	7:30 p.m.	
North Dakota	Between 7 and 9 a.m.	Between 7 and 9 p.m.	Counties must have polls open by 9 a.m., but can choose to open as early as 7 a.m. Polls must remain open until 7 p.m., but can be open as late as 9 p.m. The majority of polls in the state are open from 8 a.m. to 7 p.m. in their respective time zones (CST and MST).
Ohio	6:30 a.m.	7:30 p.m.	
Oklahoma	7 a.m.	7 p.m.	
Oregon	7 a.m.	8 p.m.	Oregon's polls (County Clerk's office and dropsites) are open from 7 a.m. to 8 p.m.
Pennsylvania	7 a.m.	8 p.m.	
Rhode Island	6 a.m.	9 p.m.	
South Carolina	7 a.m.	7 p.m.	
South Dakota	7 a.m.	7 p.m.	Local time.
Tennessee	7 a.m.	7 p.m. CST/8 p.m. EST	Poll hours are set by each county election commission. Polling places shall be open a minimum of 10 hours but no more than 13 hours. All polling locations in the Eastern time zone shall close at 8 p.m. and those in the Central time zone shall close at 7 p.m.
Texas	7 a.m.	7 p.m.	
Utah	7 a.m.	8 p.m.	
Vermont	Between 5 and 10 a.m.	7 p.m.	The opening time for polls is set by local boards of civil authority.

See footnotes at end of table.

POLLING HOURS: GENERAL ELECTIONS — Continued

State or other jurisdiction	Polls open	Polls close	Notes on hours (a)
Virginia	6 a.m.	7 p.m.	
Washington	7 a.m.	8 p.m.	
West Virginia	6:30 a.m.	7:30 p.m.	
Wisconsin	Between 7 and 9 a.m.	8 p.m.	In cities with a population of 10,000 or more, the polls must open at 7:00 a.m. In cities, towns and villages with populations of 10,000, the polls may open anytime between 7:00 a.m. and 9:00 a.m.
Wyoming	7 a.m.	7 p.m.	
Dist. of Columbia	7 a.m.	8 p.m.	
American Samoa	6 a.m.	6 p.m.	Election proclamation issued by Chief Election Officer contains a statement of time and place for each territorial election.
Guam	7 a.m.	8 p.m.	
No. Mariana Islands	7 a.m.	7 p.m.	Elections are held on six separate islands. At the close of the polls, ballots are flown to Saipan where they are tabulated at election headquarters.
Puerto Rico	8 a.m.	3 p.m.	
U.S. Virgin Islands	7 a.m.	7 p.m.	

Sources: The Council of State Governments' survey, January 2007 and state election Web sites, October 2008.

Note: Hours for primary, municipal and special elections may differ from those noted.

(a) In all states, voters standing in line when the polls close are allowed to vote; however, provisions for handling those voters vary across jurisdictions.

Table 6.6
VOTER REGISTRATION INFORMATION

State or other jurisdiction	Closing date for registration before general election (days)	Absentee voting: Persons eligible for absentee voting (a)	Absentee voting: Cut-off for receiving absentee ballots	Absentee voting: Absentee votes signed by witness or notary	Residency requirements	Registration in other places	Provision for felons: Voting rights revoked	Provision for felons: Method/process or provision for restoration	Mental competency
Alabama	10	B,D,O,P,T	5 p.m. day before election	N or 2W	S, 1 day	★	★	★	★
Alaska	30	No excuse required	10 days prior to Election Day	N or 1W	S, D, 30	★	★	★	★
Arizona	29	No excuse required	7 p.m. Election Day	. . .	S, C, 29	★	★	★	★
Arkansas	30	No excuse required	7:30 p.m. Election Day	. . .	C, 30	★	★	★	★
California	15	No excuse required	8 p.m. Election Day	. . .	S	. . .	★	★	★
Colorado	29	No excuse required	7 p.m. Election Day	. . .	S, P, 30	★	★	★	. . .
Connecticut	(b)	A	8 p.m. Election Day	. . .	S, T	★	★	★	. . .
Delaware	20	A	12 p.m. day before election	N or W	S	★	★	★	★
Florida	29	No excuse required	7 p.m. Election Day	. . .	S, C, 29	. . .	★	★	★
Georgia	(d)	No excuse required	Close of polls	W (e)	S, C	. . .	★	★	★
Hawaii	30	No excuse required	6 p.m. Election Day	. . .	S	★	★	★(f)	★
Idaho	25	No excuse required	8 p.m. Election Day	. . .	S, C, 30	. . .	★	★	. . .
Illinois	28 (g)	A	Close of polls on Election Day (h)	. . .	S, P, 30	★	★	★	. . .
Indiana	29	A	Close of polls	. . .	S, P, 30	. . .	★	★	. . .
Iowa	Election Day (o)	No excuse required	Postmarked by day before election (i)	. . .	S (j)	★	★	★	★
Kansas	15	No excuse required	Close of polls	. . .	S	★	★	★	★
Kentucky	29	A	Close of polls	. . .	S, C, 28	★	★	★	★
Louisiana	30	A	Election Day	N and 2W	S, 30 (k)	★	★	★	★
Maine	Election Day	No excuse required	8 p.m. Election Day	N or W	S, M	★	. . .	. . .	★
Maryland	21	No excuse required	Friday after election	. . .	S, 21 (l)	★	★	★	★
Massachusetts	20	B,D,O,P,R,T	10 days after election	. . .	S	. . .	★	★	★
Michigan	30	B,C,D,O,R,T	(m)	. . .	S, M, 30	★	★(n)	★	. . .
Minnesota	Election Day (o)	B,D,O,P,R,T	Election Day	N or 1W	S, 20	. . .	★	★	★
Mississippi	30	A	5 p.m. day before election	W	S, C, 30	★	★	. . .	★
Missouri	28	A	Close of polls	N	S	. . .	★	★	★
Montana	30	No excuse required	Close of polls	. . .	S, C, 30	★	★	★	★
Nebraska	(u)	No excuse required	10 a.m. 2 days after election	W	S	★	★	★	★
Nevada	(v)	No excuse required	Close of polls	. . .	S, C, 30; P, 10 (r)	★	★	★	★
New Hampshire	Election Day (o)	B, D, E, O, R, S, T	(s)	. . .	S	★	★	★	. . .
New Jersey	21	No excuse required	8 p.m. Election Day	W or N	S, C, 30	★	★	★	. . .
New Mexico	28	No excuse required	7 p.m. Election Day	. . .	S	. . .	★	★	★
New York	25	A	Postmarked day before election (e)	W	S, C, 30	★	★	★	★
North Carolina	25	No excuse required	5 p.m. day before election	2W	S, C, 30	★	★	★	. . .
North Dakota	(t)	No excuse required	2 days after election	N or W	S,P, 30	(t)	★	★	. . .
Ohio	30	No excuse required	Close of polls (u)	. . .	S, 30	★	★	★	★
Oklahoma	25	No excuse required	7 p.m. Election Day	N or W	S	. . .	★	★	★
Oregon	21	No excuse required	8 p.m. Election Day	. . .	S, 20	★	★	★	★
Pennsylvania	30	B,C,D, O, P, R, S, T	5 p.m. Friday before election	. . .	S, D, 30	★	★	★	. . .
Rhode Island	30	B,D,O,R,S	21 days	N or 2W	S,30	★	. . .	. . .	★
South Carolina	30	A	7 p.m. Election Day	N or 1W	S,C,P, 30	★	★	★	★

See footnotes at end of table.

VOTER REGISTRATION INFORMATION—Continued

State or other jurisdiction	Closing date for registration before general election (days)	Absentee voting: Persons eligible for absentee voting (a)	Absentee voting: Cut-off for receiving absentee ballots	Absentee voting: Absentee votes signed by witness or notary	Residency requirements	Registration in other places	Provision for felons: Voting rights revoked	Provision for felons: Method/process or provision for restoration	Mental competency
South Dakota	15	No excuse required (v)	Close of polls	(w)	(x)	★	★	★	★
Tennessee	30	A	Close of polls	W (e)	S	★	★	★	★
Texas	30	A	Before close of polls	(y)	S, C	. . .	★	★	★
Utah	(dd)	No excuse required	Noon on day of canvass	. . .	S, 30	★	★	★	★
Vermont	6 (z)	No excuse required	7 p.m. Election Day	. . .	S, C	. . .	. . .	. . .	. . .
Virginia	29	A	Close of polls	1W	S	★	★	★	★
Washington	(ee)	No excuse required (aa)	(cc)	2W	S, 30	★	★	★	★
West Virginia	21	A	6 days prior to election	. . .	(cc)	★	★	. . .	★
Wisconsin	Election Day (o)	No excuse required	Close of polls	W	S, 10	. . .	★	★	★
Wyoming	Election Day (o)	No excuse required	7 p.m. Election Day	. . .	S, P	. . .	★	★	★
Dist. of Columbia	30	A	10 days after election	. . .	D, 30	★	★	★	★
American Samoa	30	A	1:30 p.m. Election Day	. . .	S, 30	N.A.	N.A.	N.A.	N.A.
Guam	10	A	N.A.	N.A.	N.A.	N.A.	N.A.	N.A.	N.A.
No. Mariana Islands	50	B, D, E, O, R, S,T	14 days after election	N (ff)	(gg)	★	★	N.A.	★
Puerto Rico	40 or 60	A	30 or 45 days after election	N.A.	S (hh)	. . .	. . .	N.A.	★
U.S. Virgin Islands	30	A	14 days before election	Affidavit	(ii)	★	★	★	★

Sources: The Council of State Governments survey of state election Web sites, March 2009.

Key:

★ – Column 6: State provision prohibiting registration or claiming the right to vote in another state or jurisdiction. Columns 7, 8 and 9: State provision regarding criminal status or mental competency.

. . . – No state provision.

N.A. – Information not available.

Column 4: N — Notary, W — Witness. Numbers indicated the number of signatures required.

Column 5: S – State, C – County, D – District, M – Municipality, P – Precinct, T – Town. Numbers represent the number of days before an election for which one must be a resident.

Note: Previous editions of this chart contained a column for "Automatic cancellation of registration for failure to vote for ___ years". However, the National Voter Registration Act requires a confirmation notice prior to any cancellation and thus effectively bans any automatic cancellation of voter registration. In addition, all states and territories except Puerto Rico and the U.S. Virgin Islands allow mail-in registration.

(a) In this column: A — All of these; B – Absent on business; C – Senior citizen; D – Disabled persons; E – Not absent, but prevented by employment from registering; M/O – No absentee registration except military and oversees citizens as required by federal law; O – Out of state; P – Out of precinct (or municipality in PA); R – Absent for religious reasons; S – Students; T – Temporarily out of jurisdiction, or no excuse required.

(b) For primary, must be postmarked five days before election or registration may be completed in person by noon on the last business day before election. For general, must be postmarked 14 days before election or registration may be completed in person by the seventh day before election.

(c) Must be a permanent state resident.

(d) The 5th Monday before a general primary, general election, or presidential preference primary; the 5th day after the date of the call for all other special primaries and special elections.

(e) The request deadline is 6 days before the election, to be mailed the next day, the receipt deadline is before canvass with election day postmark, the day after the election with no post mark, and before canvas for military and oversees regardless of post mark.

(f) Upon parole, pardon, or probation, felons are required to re-register to coter to restore lost voting rights.

(g) Closing date for registration before general election is 28 days before. Illinois now has grace period registration which allows for registration of voters and change of address during a period from close of registration for a primary or election and until 14th day before the primary or election, If a voter who registers during this time period wishes to vote at that first election occurring after grace period, he/she must do so by grace period voting (at the discretion of the election authority a grace period registrant may vote by mail).

(h) Except that mailed abentee ballots which are postmarked prior to election may be received up to the 14th day after election day.

(i) An absentee ballot must be returned before the polls are closed on election day; or if the ballot is mailed, the envelope must be postmarked before election day.Timely postmarked ballots are considerd on time if the ballot is received befor noon on Monday following the election day. However, if the canvass of votes for the election is required by law to be held earlier, the ballot must be received by the time set for the canvass of votes. The canvass of votes for the school election and some city election will be held on Thursday or Friday after the election.

(j) Iowa does not have a residency length of time requirement, it does require that a person be a resident when registering to vote. One must be registered at least 10 days before a primary and general elctions; 11 days before all others.

(k) A voter must be registered to vote 30 days before an election, and must be a resident in order to register.

(l) State election law does not apply to Municipal elections. Therefore each municipality may have a separate requirement.

(m) If a voter wishes to have a ballot mailed, clerk must receive written request by 2 p.m. on the Saturday prior to the election. Voters can obtain an absentee ballot in person anytime through 4 p.m on the day prior to the election. If the voter qualifies for an emergency ballot, request can be submitted through 4 p.m. on the date of the election.

(n) Only while confined, automatic restoration after release.

(o) Iowa– Delivered by 5 p.m. 10 days before the election, if it is a state primary or general election; 11 days before all others or election-day registration at precincts. Minnesota — delivered 21 days before an election or election-day registration at polling precincts. New Hampshire– Received by city or town clerk 10 days before election or election-day registration at precincts. Wisconsin– Twenty days before the election, or completed in

VOTER REGISTRATION INFORMATION—Continued

the local voter registration officeb by 5:00 p.m. one day before election, or election-day registration at polling precincts. Wyoming– delivered 30 days before or election-day registration at polling precincts.

(p) Received by the 2nd Friday before election or postmarked by the 3rd Friday before the election.

(q) By 9 p.m. on the 5th Saturday preceding any primary or general election.

(r) Must have continuously resided in the state and county at least 30 days and in precinct at least 10 days before election. Must claim no other place as legal residence.

(s) In person: day before election. By mail: day of election.

(t) No voter registration.

(u) Voted ballots on in-country electors must be received by close of polls; voted ballots returned from outside the United States must be received within 10 days of election day.

(v) No excuse required. In South Dakota must submit the application for absentee ballot to the person in charge of the election.

(w) Absentee ballot applications (not absentee ballots) are required to be notarized or submitted with a copy of the voter's photo identification.

(x) Municipality: at least thirty days during the year preceding the election. Town: thirty consecutive days each year.

(y) If unable to sign.

(z) Must be received by 5:00 p.m. on the Wednesday preceding the day of the election.

(aa) There is a late registration date, 15 days prior, for in person new registrations and the voter must vote an absentee ballot.

(bb) 15 days following a primary; 21 days following a general election.

(cc) A voter must be a resident for 30 days prior to the election. West Virginia poll books for each election require that the voters acknowledge that their address is current and that they have been at that location for thirty days prior to the election.

(dd) Must be postmarked 30 days before an election if mailed. May register in person the 15th day before an election, but you will only be eligible to vote on elections.

(ee) Thirty days before the election if mailed or 15 days before the election if delivered in-person to the local voter registration office.

(ff) Notary public or commissioned officer authorized to administer oath for Armed Services personnel.

(gg) State/territory: one hundred twenty days, district, municipality, precinct: fifty days.

(hh) According to Electoral Law the voter must have a permanent residence in Puerto Rico to be a qualified elector.

(ii) 90 days residency requirement, 30 days for district.

Table 6.7
VOTING STATISTICS FOR GUBERNATORIAL ELECTIONS BY REGION

State or other jurisdiction	Date of last election	Primary election				Total votes	General election								Total votes
		Republican	Democrat	Independent	Other		Republican	Percent	Democrat	Percent	Independent	Percent	Other	Percent	
Eastern Region															
Connecticut	2006	(b)					710,048	63.2	398,220	35.4	0	0.0	15,198	1.4	1,123,466
Delaware	2008	28,972	73,961	0	0	102,933	126,662	32.0	266,861	67.5	0	0.0	1,681	0.5	395,204
Maine	2006	68,574	54,422	0	0	120,996	166,425	30.2	209,927	38.1	118,715	21.5	55,798	10.1	550,865
Massachusetts	2006	71,430	912,348	0	0	983,778	784,342	35.0	1,234,984	55.0	154,628	7.0	69,881	3.1	2,243,835
New Hampshire	2008	53,120	49,124	0	0	102,444	188,555	27.6	479,042	70.2	14,987	2.2	326	0.05	682,910
New Jersey	2005	302,521	235,778	0	0	538,299	985,271	43.0	1,224,551	53.5	0	0.0	80,277	3.5	2,290,099
New York	2006	138,263	624,684	0	0	762,947	1,105,681	23.5	2,740,864	58.3	190,661(c)	4	660,661	14	4,697,867
Pennsylvania	2006	572,375(d)	644,444 (d)	0	0	1,216,819	1,622,135	39.6	2,470,517	60.4	0	0.0	0	0	4,092,652
Rhode Island	2006	63,148	88,688	0	0	151,836	197,306	51.0	189,503	48.9	0	0.0	0	0.0	387,870
Vermont	2008	11,798	18,851	0	135	30,784	170,492	53.4	69,534	21.7	0	0	79,059	24.7	319,085
Regional total		1,310,201	2,057,856	0	135	4,010,836	6,056,917	36.1	9,284,003	55.3	478,991	2.9	962,881	5.9	16,783,853
Midwestern Region															
Illinois	2006	699,786	931,779	0	0	1,631,565	1,368,682	38.2	1,736,219	48.4	0	0.0	381,770	10.6	3,586,292
Indiana	2008	350,390	1,151,951	0	0	1,502,341	1,563,885	57.8	1,082,463	40.0	28	0.0	57,376	2.1	2,703,752
Iowa	2006	73,903 (d)	148,000	0	0	221,903	467,425	44.1	569,021	53.7	0	0.0	22,618	2.1	1,059,064
Kansas	2006	194,295	76,046 (d)	0	0	382,003	343,586	40.4	491,993	57.9	0	0.0	14,121	1.7	849,700
Michigan	2006	581,404	531,322	0	119	1,112,845	1,608,086	42.3	2,142,513	56.3	0	0.0	50,657	1.3	3,801,256
Minnesota	2006	166,112	316,470	11,689	0	514,373	1,028,568	46.4	1,007,460	45.4	141,735	6.4	25,174	1.1	2,217,719
Nebraska	2006	271,487	73,592	0	128	345,207	435,507	73.3	145,115	24.5	0	0.0	12,735	2.1	593,357
North Dakota	2008	50,226	38,784	0	18	89,028	235,009	74.4	74,279	23.5	6,404	2.0	0	0.0	315,692
Ohio	2006	812,388	783,044	0	0	1,816,916	1,470,708	35.2	2,428,013	58.0	112,742	2.7	0	0.0	4,184,072
South Dakota	2006	(d)	36,389	0	0	92,763	206,990	61.7	121,226	36.1	0	0.0	7,292	2.2	335,508
Wisconsin	2006	234,020	320,782	0	1,812	556,614	979,427	45.3	1,139,115	52.7	0	0.0	43,158	2.0	2,161,700
Regional total		3,434,011	4,408,159	11,689	2,077	8,265,558	9,707,873	44.5	10,937,417	50.2	260,909	1.2	614,901	2.8	21,808,112
Southern Region															
Alabama	2006	460,019	466,537	0	0	925,467	718,327	57.4	519,827	41.5	0	0.0	12,247	1.0	1,250,401
Arkansas	2006	No primary in 2006 due to only one candidate per party					314,630	40.7	430,090	55.5	15,739	2.0	13,093	1.7	773,552
Florida	2006	985,986	857,814	0	0	1,843,800	2,519,845	52.2	2,178,289	45.1	92,595	1.9	38,541	0.8	4,829,270
Georgia	2006	419,254	482,117	0	0	901,371	1,229,724	57.9	811,049	38.2	0	0.0	81,412	3.8	2,122,185
Kentucky	2007	202,339	348,238	0	0	458,341	435,773	41.3	619,552	58.7	0	0.0	0	0.0	1,055,325
Louisiana (a)	2007	699,275	397,755	200,810	0	1,297,840	699,275 (a)	54.0	397,755	30.6	200,810	15.4	0	0.0	1,297,840
Maryland	2006	213,744	524,671	0	0	738,415	825,464	46.2	942,279	52.7	0	0.0	20,573	1.1	1,717,068
Mississippi	2007	197,647	446,722	0	0	644,369	430,807	57.9	313,232	42.1	0	0.0	0	0.0	744,039
Missouri	2008	395,885	358,016	0	1,729	755,630	1,136,364	39.5	1,680,611	58.4	0	0.0	60,803	2.1	2,877,778
North Carolina	2008	504,973	1,494,998	0	0	1,999,971	2,001,168	46.9	2,146,189	50.3	0	0.0	121,584	2.9	4,268,941
Oklahoma	2006	182,136	264,467	0	0	446,603	310,327	66.5	616,135	33.5	0	0.0	0	0.0	926,462
South Carolina	2006	247,281	138,343	0	0	395,905	601,868	55.1	489,076	44.8	0	0.0	1,008	0.1	1,091,952
Tennessee	2006	534,824	539,018	0	809	1,074,651	540,853	29.7	1,247,491	68.6	30,205	1.6	0	0.0	1,818,549
Texas	2006	655,919	508,602	0	0	1,164,521	1,716,792	39.0	1,310,337	29.8	1,344,525	30.5	27,462	0.7	4,399,116
Virginia	2005	175,170	(b)	(b)	(b)	175,170	912,327	46.0	1,025,942	52.0	43,953	2.0	1,556	0.1	1,983,778
West Virginia	2008	81,019	354,849	0	0	435,868	181,612	25.7	492,697	69.8	31,486	0.0	0	0.0	705,795
Regional total		5,955,471	7,182,147	200,810	2,538	13,257,922	14,575,156	45.7	15,220,551	47.7	1,759,313	5.5	378,279	1.2	31,862,051

See footnotes at end of table.

VOTING STATISTICS FOR GUBERNATORIAL ELECTIONS BY REGION—Continued

State or other jurisdiction	Date of last election	Primary election				Total votes	General election								Total votes
		Republican	Democrat	Independent	Other		Republican	Percent	Democrat	Percent	Independent	Percent	Other	Percent	
Western Region															
Alaska	2006	101,695	97,238	22443	2,944	160,874	114,697	48.1	97,238	40.8	22,443	7.9	2,944	1.2	238,307
Arizona	2006	333,604	246,876	0	4,046	584,526	543,528	35.4	959,830	62.6	0	0.0	30,287	2.0	1,533,645
California	2006	1,809,189	2,360,529	27,195	49,693	4,246,606	4,850,157	55.9	3,376,732	39.0	61,901	0.7	390,258	4.4	8,679,048
Colorado	2006	193,804 (d)	142,586 (d)	0	0	336,390	625,886	40.2	888,096	57.0	0	0.0	44,405	2.8	1,558,387
Hawaii	2006	32,107	179,227	0	642	211,976	215,313	61.7	121,717	34.9	0	0.0	11,721	3.4	348,751
Idaho	2006	137,175	30,443	0	0	184,456	276,029	52.7	198,845	44.1	0	0.0	14,550	3.2	489,424
Montana	2008	81,526	175,043	0	0	204,993	158,268	32.5	318,670	65.5	0	0.0	9,796	2.0	486,734
Nevada	2006	140,515	119,046	0	0	259,561	279,003	47.9	255,684	43.9	0	0.0	47,471	8.2	582,158
New Mexico	2006	53,974	107,520	0	0	160,575	174,364	31.2	384,806	68.8	0	0.0	0	0.0	559,170
Oregon	2006	300,554	319,177	0	0	619,731	533,650	38.1	579,060	41.3	248,655	17.7	37,925	2.7	1,399,650
Utah	2008	(b)					700,565	77.9	175,031	19.5	0	0.0	23,449	2.6	906,706
Washington	2008	695,116	712,952	10,884	23,505	1,442,457	1,404,124	46.8	1,598,738	53.2	0	0.0	0	0.0	3,002,862
Wyoming	2006	69,401	29,612	0	0	99,013	58,100	29.9	135,516	69.8	0	0.0	276	0.1	193,892
Regional total		3,948,660	4,520,249	60,522	80,830	8,511,158	9,933,684	49.7	9,089,963	45.4	332,999	1.6	613,082	3.0	19,978,734
Regional total without California		2,139,471	2,159,720	33,327	31,137	4,264,552	5,083,527	44.9	5,713,231	50.5	271,098	2.4	222,824	2.0	11,299,686
American Samoa (e)	2008	N.A	N.A	N.A	N.A	N.A	0	0.0	6,590	56.5	5,084	43.6	0	0.0	11,674
U.S. Virgin Islands	2006	2,803	31,615	1,740	0	36,158	2,838	6.2	32,308	59.2	1,778	30.8	16,093	3.7	53,017

Sources: The Council of State Governments' survey of election administration offices, February 2007 and state elections web sites, February 2008 and 2009.

Key:

N.A. — Not applicable

(a) Louisiana has an open primary which requires all candidates, regardless of party affiliation, to appear on a single ballot. If a candidate receives over 50 percent of the vote in the primary, he is elected to the office. If no candidate receives a majority vote, then a single election is held between the two candidates receiving the most votes. In the October 20, 2007 primary election Bobby Jindahl (R) received 54 percent of the vote, the five Democrats received 30.6 percent of the vote and the other candidates received the remaining 15.6 percent of the vote. No run-off election was required.

(b) Candidate nominated by convention.

(c) Governor Eliot Spitzer was also the Independence Party candidate.

(d) Candidate ran unopposed.

(e) The results displayed in the table are from the Nov. 18, 2008 run-off election.

Table 6.8
VOTER TURNOUT FOR PRESIDENTIAL ELECTIONS BY REGION: 2000, 2004 AND 2008
(In thousands)

State or other jurisdiction	2008			2004			2000		
	Voting age population (a)	Number registered	Number voting (b)	Voting age population (a)	Number registered	Number voting (b)	Voting age population (a)	Number registered	Number voting (b)
U.S. Total	227,719	189,391	128,628	208,247	170,937	122,501	205,410	156,420	105,587
Eastern Region									
Connecticut	2,682	2,210	1,645	2,574	1,823	1,579	2,499	1,874	1,460
Delaware	659	602	391	594	554	376	582	505	328
Maine	1,037	1,000	731	1,042	957	741	968	882	652
Massachusetts	5,016	4,220	3,103	4,931	3,973	2,927	4,749	4,009	2,734
New Hampshire	1,017	864	708	991	856	684	911	857	569
New Jersey	6,622	5,379	3,868	6,669	5,009	3,612	6,245	4,711	3,187
New York	14,884	12,031	7,675	14,206	11,837	7,448	13,805	11,263	6,960
Pennsylvania	9,646	8,730	5,995	9,404	8,367	5,770	9,155	7,782	4,912
Rhode Island	824	701	470	803	709	437	753	655	409
Vermont	489	454	325	490	445	312	460	427	294
Regional total	42,876	36,191	24,911	41,704	34,530	23,886	40,127	32,965	21,505
Midwestern Region									
Illinois	9,653	7,790	5,578	9,519	7,499	5,274	8,983	7,129	4,742
Indiana	4,758	4,515	2,751	4,420	4,163	2,468	4,448	4,001	2,180
Iowa	2,276	2,076	1,537	2,212	2,107	1,522	2,165	1,841	1,314
Kansas	2,079	1,750	1,751	2,038	1,694	1,188	1,983	1,624	1,072
Michigan	7,624	7,471	5,044	7,541	7,164	4,839	7,358	6,861	4,233
Minnesota	3,937	3,200	2,910	3,823	2,977	2,828	3,547	3,265	2,439
Nebraska	1,328	1,157	801	1,257	1,160	778	1,234	1.085	697
North Dakota	496	(d)	317	487	(d)	316	477	(c)	288
Ohio	8,715	8,163	5,698	8,604	7,973	5,426	8,433	7,538	4,702
South Dakota	599	508	382	573	502	395	543	471	316
Wisconsin	4,280	3,405 (d)	2,983	4,119	2,957 (d)	2,997	3,930	(d)	2,599
Regional total	45,745	40,035	24,174	44,593	38,196	28,031	43,101	33,815	24,582
Southern Region									
Alabama	3,504	2,841	2,100	3,252	2,597	1,883	3,333	2,529	1,666
Arkansas	2,134	1,686	1,087	1,951	1,686	1,055	1,929	1,556	922
Florida	14,207	11,248	8,358	12,539	10,301	7,610	11,774	8,753	5,963
Georgia	7,013	5,266	3,924	6,080	4,249	3,285	5,893	3,860	2,583
Kentucky	3,237	2,907	1,827	3,012	2,819	1,796	2,993	2,557	1,544
Louisiana	3,213	2,945	1,961	3,249	2,923	1,957	3,255	2,730	1,766
Maryland	4,259	3,429	2,632	3,922	3,070	2,396	3,925	2,715	2,024
Mississippi	2,150	1,873	1,290	2,014	1,865	1,140	2,047	1,740	994
Missouri	4,453	4,181	2,925	4,297	4,194	2,731	4,105	3,861	2,360
North Carolina	6,843	6,226	4,311	6,453	5,527	3,501	5,797	5,122	2,915
Oklahoma	2,717	2,184	1,463	2,515	2,143	1,464	2,531	2,234	1,234
South Carolina	3,347	2,554	1,921	3,214	2,315	1,618	2,977	2,157	1,386
Tennessee	4,685	3,978	2,600	4,284	3,532	2,437	4,221	3,181	2,076
Texas	17,281	13,575	8,077	16,071	13,098	7,411	14,479	12,365	6,408
Virginia	5,885	5,044	3,724	5,194	4,528	3,195	5,263	3,770	2,790
West Virginia	1,424	1,212	713	1,406	1,169	744	1,416	1,068	648
Regional total	86,352	71,149	48,923	79,453	66,016	44,223	75,938	60,198	37,279
Western Region									
Alaska	501	496	326	460	472	313	436	474	286
Arizona	4,668	2,987	2,321	3,800	2,643	2,038	3,625	2,173	1,532
California	27,169	23,209	13,214	22,075	16,557	12,589	21,461	15,707	11,142
Colorado	3,668	3,209	2,401	3,246	2,890	2,130	3,067	2,274	1,741
Hawaii	997	691	454	873	647	429	909	637	368
Idaho	1,091	862	655	996	798	613	921	728	502
Montana	738	668	490	680	596	450	668	698	411
Nevada	1,905	1,208	968	1,580	1,094	830	1,390	898	609
New Mexico	1,469	1,193	830	1,318	1,105	756	1,263	973	599
Oregon	2,884	2,154	1,828	2,665	2,120	1,837	2,530	1,944	1,534
Utah	1,828	1,433	905	1,522	1,278	928	1,465	1,123	771
Washington	4,932	3,630	3,037	4,596	3,508	2,883	4,368	3,336	2,487
Wyoming	397	276	255	370	246	244	358	220	214
Regional total	52,247	42,016	30,620	44,181	33,954	26,040	42,461	31,185	22,196
Regional total without California	25,078	18,807	17,406	22,106	17,397	13,451	21,000	15,478	11,054
Dist. of Columbia	474,572	427	267	435	384	228	411	354	202

Sources: U.S. Congress, Clerk of the House, Statistics of the Presidential and Congressional Election, 2004, U.S. Census Bureau, Current Population Survey, December 2008. The Council of State Governments survey of election officials, January 2009. 2000 data provided by the Federal Election Commission.

Key:
(a) Estimated population, 18 years old and over. Includes armed forces in each state, aliens and institutional population.
(b) Number voting is number of ballots cast in presidential race.
(c) Information not available.
(d) No statewide registration required. Excluded from totals for persons registered.

2008 Ballot Propositions

By John G. Matsusaka

Voters approved 58 percent of the 174 ballot propositions considered in 37 states in 2008. The number of measures as well as the approval rate was down modestly from recent years. No ideological trend appeared—both liberal and conservative measures were approved. The highest profile issue was a ban on gay marriage in California. Nationwide, voters approved more than $13 billion in state bonds despite the ongoing financial crisis.

In 2008, beyond the glare of the presidential campaign and the economic meltdown, voters decided hundreds of ballot propositions, approving numerous laws that will have an immediate and material impact on the lives of Americans across the country. Altogether, 174 statewide ballot propositions and an untold—but much larger—number of local ballot propositions went before the voters in 2008. As usual, the state measures received the most attention, with California's Proposition 8, through which voters banned same-sex marriage, leading the way. Voters surged toward the Democratic Party in federal elections, but there was no apparent ideological drift in ballot propositions. Voters decided on an issue-by-issue basis in response to state-specific conditions, providing victories and defeats for both liberal and conservative measures.

Overview

The 174 state-level ballot propositions in 2008 (see Table A) included 153 propositions that were decided Nov. 4, as well as 21 propositions that appeared on primary and special election ballots before November. The number of November propositions was down somewhat from the 162 in 2004, the last presidential election year. One of the more interesting patterns in 2008 was the relative dearth of tax and spending measures, usually a staple issue for ballot propositions. Social issues took their place, with a set of highly contentious measures appearing across the country.

The propositions considered by voters reached the ballot in several ways. The most common method was action by legislators; 53 percent of the propositions were placed on the ballot by the legislature. Voters approved 73 percent of these legislative measures. Citizen petitions, the second most common method for reaching the ballot, were responsible for 43 percent of the measures. There were 68 citizen-qualified initiatives that proposed new laws, and six citizen-qualified referendums that proposed to repeal existing laws. Voters approved 38 percent of the initiatives and repealed only one of the laws challenged by referendum.

Historically, voters have been more reluctant to approve initiatives than legislative measures. The initiative approval rate in 2008 was slightly below the historical average of 41 percent. In addition to legislative measures, initiatives and referendums, five measures were placed on the ballot by special commission and three were required by state constitutions. Three of the commission-sponsored measures were approved, but none of the constitutionally mandated measures gained approval.

Initiative Trends

In some states where the initiative process is available, ballot propositions have become a veritable fourth branch of government. The initiative process was promoted by the Progressive movement at the turn of the 19th century and the goal was to provide a means for ordinary citizens to counteract what they saw as excessive influence by special interest groups on the legislature. The initiative process allows ordinary citizens to propose new laws without approval of the legislature. South Dakota in 1898 was the first state to adopt the process, followed by Utah in 1900 and Oregon in 1902. By 1918, 19 states had adopted the process. Since then, about one state every 20 years has adopted the process, bringing the total number of states that allow initiatives to 24. Figure A shows the current initiative states and the year they adopted the process.[1] Cities also began to adopt the process during the Progressive movement, beginning with San Francisco and Vallejo in California in 1898. Eighty-two percent of the country's 1,500 largest cities now provide the initiative process.[2] All told, more than 80 percent of Americans live in either a city or a state with the initiative process.

Initiatives were intended to be used when the legislature failed to represent the interests of the people, and the number of initiatives on the ballot

Table A
State-by-State Totals for 2008

State	Initiatives	Referendums	Legislative measures	Other	Notable issues
Alabama	. . .	. . .	6 (5)	. . .	Rainy day fund for education
Alaska*	4 (0)	. . .	1 (1)	. . .	Public funding of campaigns, aerial hunting
Arizona	6 (1)	. . .	1 (1)	1 (0)	Same-sex marriage, universal health care, payday lending
Arkansas	2 (2)	. . .	3 (3)	. . .	Water bonds, unwed foster parents
California*	15 (6)	4 (4)	2 (2)	. . .	Same-sex marriage, eminent domain, bonds
Colorado	10 (2)	. . .	4 (2)	. . .	Racial preferences/affirmative action, union dues
Connecticut	. . .	. . .	1 (1)	1 (0)	Constitutional convention, voting age
Florida*	1 (1)	. . .	2 (1)	4 (3)	Same-sex marriage, property tax exemptions
Georgia	. . .	. . .	3 (2)	. . .	Forest land protection
Hawaii	. . .	. . .	1 (0)	1 (0)	Constitutional convention, age of governor
Illinois	. . .	. . .	. . .	1 (0)	Constitutional convention
Iowa	. . .	. . .	1 (1)	. . .	. . .
Louisiana	. . .	. . .	7 (3)	. . .	Term limits for boards and commissions
Maine*	1 (0)	1 (0)	2 (2)	. . .	Sales tax increase, casino, bonds
Maryland	. . .	. . .	2 (2)	. . .	Video lottery
Massachusetts	3 (2)	. . .	. . .	. . .	Income tax repeal, dog racing, marijuana legalization
Michigan	2 (2)	. . .	. . .	. . .	Medical marijuana, stem cell research
Minnesota	. . .	. . .	1 (1)	. . .	Sales tax for clean water, parks, and arts
Missouri	3 (3)	. . .	2 (2)	. . .	Renewable energy, English as official language
Montana	1 (1)	. . .	2 (1)	. . .	Health care for uninsured children, property tax
Nebraska*	1 (1)	. . .	2 (1)	. . .	Racial preferences/affirmative action
Nevada	1 (1)	. . .	3 (1)	. . .	Eminent domain, sales tax
New Jersey	. . .	. . .	2 (1)	. . .	Voter approval for bonds
New Mexico	. . .	. . .	9 (7)	. . .	Bonds
New York	. . .	. . .	1 (1)	. . .	Veterans in civil service exams
North Dakota*	3 (2)	. . .	2 (0)	. .	Corporate and personal income tax reduction
Ohio	1 (0)	1 (1)	3 (3)	. . .	Park bonds, casino, payday lending interest rates
Oklahoma	. . .	. . .	4 (4)	. . .	Right to hunt, wine sales, property tax exemptions
Oregon*	8 (0)	. . .	7 (7)	. . .	Bilingual education, crime victims, open primary
Pennsylvania	. . .	. . .	1 (1)	. . .	Bonds for sewers
Rhode Island	. . .	. . .	2 (2)	. . .	Bonds for roads, bonds for open spaces
South Carolina	. . .	. . .	3 (1)	. . .	Age of consent, public pension funds
South Dakota	3 (0)	. . .	4 (1)	. . .	Abortion ban, term limits repeal
Utah	. . .	. . .	5 (4)	. . .	Governor succession, legislature sessions
Washington	3 (2)	. . .	. . .	. . .	Physician-assisted suicide, carpool lanes
Wisconsin*	. . .	. . .	1 (1)	. . .	Governor's partial veto
Wyoming	. . .	. . .	2 (1)	. . .	Initiative petition requirements
Total	68 (26)	6 (5)	92 (67)	8 (3)	

Source: Initiative & Referendum Institute (*www.iandrinstitute.org*).

Note: The table reports the total number of propositions during 2008, including primary and special elections as well as the November general election. The number of measures that were approved is reported in parentheses. A referendum in which the original law is retained is considered to have been "approved." "Other" includes measures placed on the ballot by state commission (AZ, FL) and constitutionally required votes on whether to call a constitutional convention (CT, HI, IL).

* Includes results from pre-November elections.

suggests the degree to which groups feel disenfranchised. Figure B shows the number of initiatives by decade since they first appeared in Oregon in 1904. Initiatives were used extensively in the second, third and fourth decades of the 20th century. Much of that activity arose from tensions between the new urban majorities in many states and the rural interests that controlled the legislature.[3] The initiative process fell out of use in the middle decades of the century, with only 54 measures in the 1960s.

Beginning in the 1970s, initiative use picked up again. The triggering event was California's property tax-cutting Proposition 13 in 1978 that set off a national tax revolt. At first it was not clear if the burst of initiatives would be a passing fad, but with the initiative use growing in each subsequent decade, it seems that something more fundamental is transpiring. The total number of initiatives for the first decade of the 21st century stands at 371, but it is likely that more initiatives will appear in 2009, mak-

Figure A
States with Initiatives in 2008 (adoption year in parentheses)

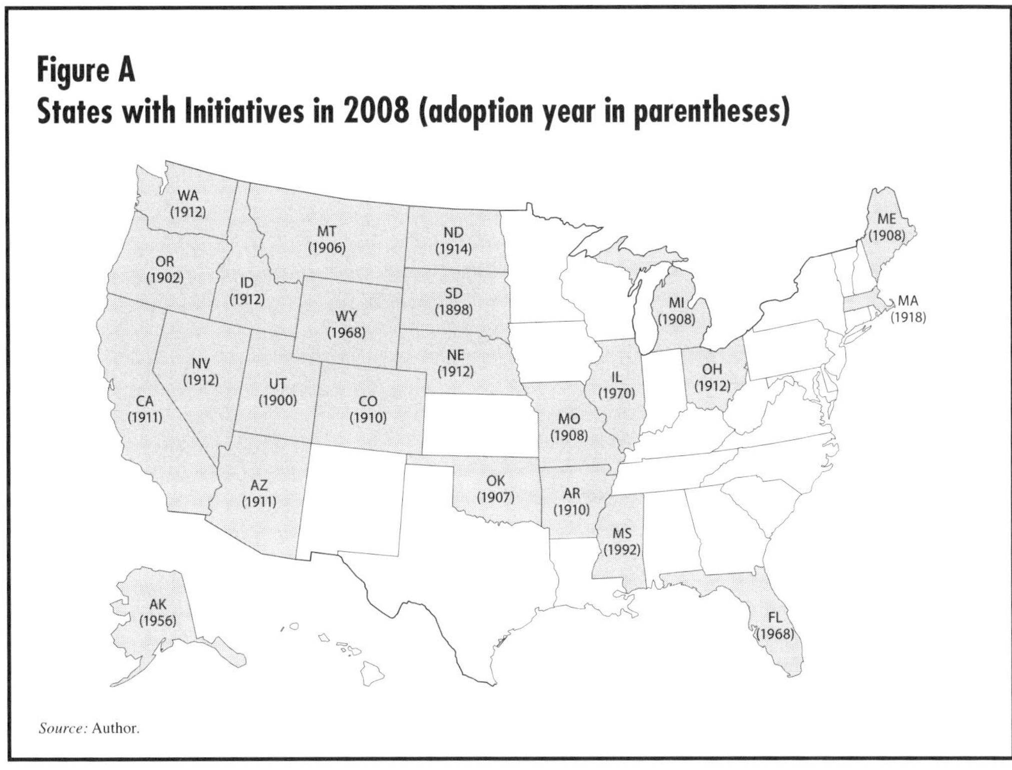

Source: Author.

ing the total for this decade comparable to the 1990s. For the first time in four decades, then, initiative use may not increase from the previous decade.

Whether this represents a plateau, a breather before renewed acceleration or the end of a wave is unclear. However, direct democracy continues to spread around the world, with countries including Taiwan, New Zealand and many of the post-Soviet states adopting the initiative and referendum process. The underlying cause for the long-run growth of direct democracy may be dissatisfaction with elected officials, but innovation in information technologies that allow ordinary citizens access to unprecedented amounts of information also seems to have created a hunger for greater participation. The implication is that direct democracy is likely to continue to play a central role in state government for the foreseeable future, although the level of activity has reached something of an equilibrium.

Key Issues and Trends

Marriage

The highest profile issue in 2008 was marriage, with propositions to ban same-sex marriage on the ballot in Arizona, California and Florida. California's Proposition 8 was the focus of extensive national media coverage. Proponents and opponents together raised more than $85 million—$45 million from the opposition and $40 million from supporters. Approximately 80 percent of the contributions to both campaigns came from within California, but the opposition relied more on out-of-state contributors. The opposition had more big contributors compared to the supporters, which received many more small contributions from individuals. Only a handful of initiatives involving wealthy industries such as gaming, tobacco and oil have broken the $100 million barrier—the amount spent on Proposition 8 is the most ever for a social issue.[4]

The issue of gay marriage entered the national debate in 1993 when the Hawaii Supreme Court ruled in *Baehr v. Lewin* that a refusal to grant same-sex marriage licenses was sex discrimination under the state constitution. State legislators responded by placing a constitutional amendment on the ballot in 1998 authorizing the legislature to define marriage solely as between one man and one woman. That measure was approved with 68 percent of voters in favor. At about the same time, fearing similar judicial developments in their states, conservative activists

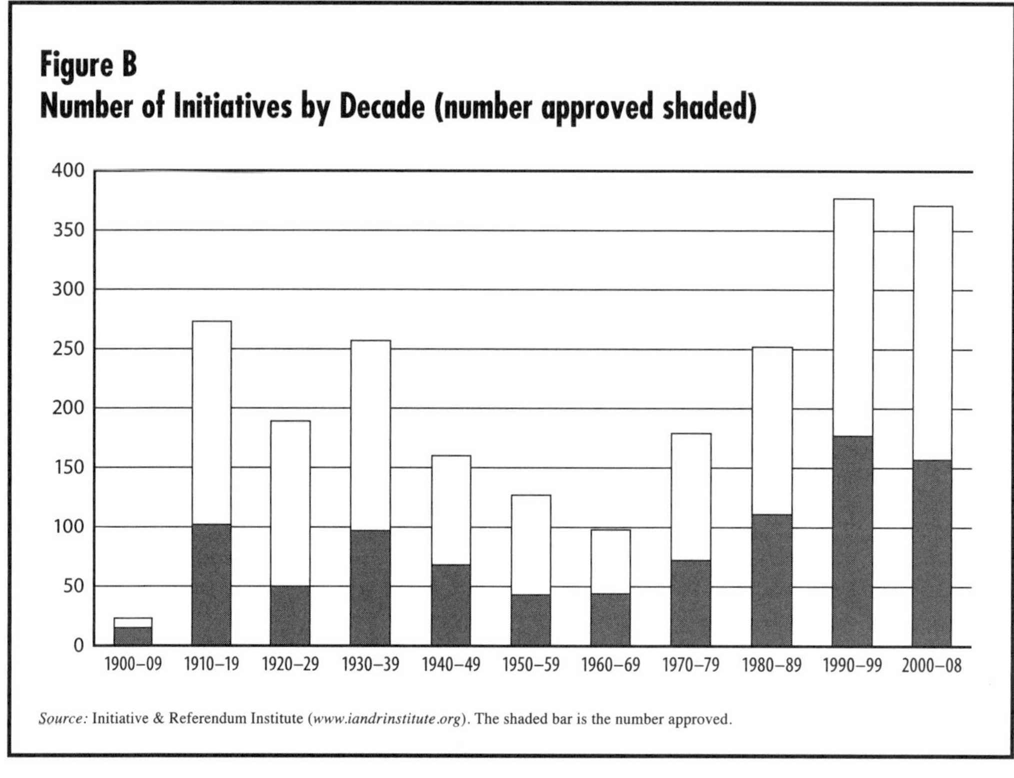

Figure B
Number of Initiatives by Decade (number approved shaded)

Source: Initiative & Referendum Institute (*www.iandrinstitute.org*). The shaded bar is the number approved.

placed "defense of marriage" measures on the ballot in Alaska (1998), California (2000), Nebraska (2000) and Nevada (2000); all were approved.

In May 2004, the Massachusetts Supreme Judicial Court ruled in *Goodridge v. Department of Public Health* that gay marriage was allowed under the state constitution. This ruling set off a pitched battle across the nation as marriage traditionalists in 24 states qualified constitutional amendments prohibiting gay marriage for the ballot. Two-thirds of these amendments were proposed and placed on the ballot by state legislatures, and one-third were proposed and qualified by citizen groups using the initiative process. All passed, usually by large margins, except for Proposition 107 in Arizona, which narrowly failed. See Table B for a list of all state same-sex marriage propositions.

California's Proposition 8 proposed to amend the state constitution to define marriage as only between one man and one woman. Voters approved a similar measure, Proposition 22, in 2000, but it was a statutory rather than a constitutional initiative, and thus vulnerable to being overruled on constitutional grounds. That is exactly what happened in May 2008, when the California Supreme Court ruled (*In Re Marriage Cases*) that the state constitution contained a right to gay marriage, and invalidated Proposition 22.

Throughout the fall, California voters seemed poised to reject Proposition 8, with virtually every opinion survey from August to October showing a large margin against it. However, 52 percent of voters approved the proposition. Analysts are still sifting through exit polls and other data to understand what happened. At least part of the story was a surge in turnout by African-American voters who overwhelmingly supported the ban, but this can account for only part of the discrepancy between the pre-election surveys and the final outcome.

Arizona's marriage amendment was approved with 56 percent in favor, and Florida's amendment received 62 percent in favor, surpassing the 60 percent threshold required for approval in that state.

Where this leaves the movement for same-sex marriage is unclear. Opponents of Proposition 8 have challenged the measure before the California Supreme Court, arguing that it was a constitutional revision, not a constitutional amendment, and thus could not be approved by initiative. It remains to be seen whether this technical argument will gain trac-

Table B
Complete List of Same-Sex Marriage Propositions

State	Year	Measure	Vote	Source
Alaska	1998	Ballot Measure 2	68-32	Legislature
Hawaii	1998	Amendment 2	69-31	Legislature
California	2000	Proposition 22	61-39	Initiative
Nebraska	2000	Initiative 416	70-30	Initiative
Nevada	2000	Question 2	70-30	Initiative
Nevada	2002	Question 2	67-33	Initiative
Arkansas	2004	Amendment 3	75-25	Initiative
Georgia	2004	Amendment 1	77-23	Legislature
Kentucky	2004	Amendment 1	75-25	Legislature
Louisiana	2004	Amendment 1	78-22	Legislature
Michigan	2004	Proposal 04-2	59-41	Initiative
Mississippi	2004	Amendment 1	86-14	Legislature
Missouri	2004	Amendment 2	71-29	Legislature
Montana	2004	CI-96	67-33	Initiative
North Dakota	2004	Amendment 1	68-32	Initiative
Ohio	2004	Issue 1	62-38	Initiative
Oklahoma	2004	Question 711	76-24	Legislature
Oregon	2004	Measure 36	57-43	Initiative
Utah	2004	Amendment 3	66-34	Legislature
Kansas	2005	Amendment	70-30	Legislature
Texas	2005	Proposition 2	76-24	Legislature
Alabama	2006	Amendment	81-19	Legislature
Arizona	2006	Proposition 107	48-52	Initiative
Colorado	2006	Amendment 43	55-45	Initiative
Idaho	2006	HJR 2	63-37	Legislature
South Carolina	2006	Amendment 1	78-22	Legislature
South Dakota	2006	Amendment C	52-48	Legislature
Tennessee	2006	Amendment 1	81-19	Legislature
Virginia	2006	Ballot Question 1	57-43	Legislature
Wisconsin	2006	NA	59-41	Legislature
Arizona	2008	Proposition 102	56-44	Legislature
California	2008	Proposition 8	52-48	Initiative
Florida	2008	Amendment 2	62-38	Initiative

Source: Initiative & Referendum Institute (*www.iandrinstitute.org*).

tion. Regardless of how the court rules, voters have chosen to ban gay marriage in 32 of 33 propositions, an almost unbroken firewall. This shows that the electorate overall is not supportive of gay marriage. On the other hand, the California vote in 2008 was much closer than in 2000, and younger voters appear to be less opposed to gay marriage than older voters, suggesting that time and demographic trends may lead to victories for gay marriage supporters down the line.

Abortion

Abortion is one the most polarizing issues in American politics, but the legal fundamentals have been settled since the Supreme Court's *Roe v. Wade* decision in 1974. With the replacement of liberal with conservative justices, some observers believe a majority of the court may be prepared to reverse *Roe v. Wade*. In order to give the court an opportunity to rule on this issue, pro-life activists in Colorado and South Dakota placed measures banning abortion on the ballot. Colorado's Amendment 48 did not mention abortion, but rather defined a "person" as a human being from the point of fertilization, which would have made abortion equivalent to murder. This amendment, which contained no exceptions for rape or the health of the mother, was far too extreme for Colorado voters—73 percent of them voted against it.

The more interesting contest was in South Dakota. In 2006, the state's legislature passed a law banning abortion that was challenged by a referendum. After a heated campaign that attracted interest from pro-choice and pro-life groups across the nation, voters repealed the law by a vote of 56 percent to 44 percent. The omission of an exception for rape and the health of the mother contributed to the repeal. Pro-life activists responded to that defeat by qualifying an initiative for the November ballot that would have banned abortion, but this time provided exceptions for rape and the health of the mother. Given the generally conservative reputation of the South Dakota electorate, the prospects for Initiated Measure 11 appeared to be reasonable, but voters rejected it 55 percent to 45 percent, almost the same margin as before. Although voters continue to express a discomfort with abortion, the majority does not seem to have an appetite for reversing *Roe v. Wade*.

Civil Rights/Affirmative Action

Race was a subtext of the presidential campaign, but was front and center in Colorado and Nebraska, where voters faced propositions that simply stated: "The state shall not discriminate against or grant preferential treatment to any group or individual on the basis of race, sex, color, ethnicity, or national origin in the operation of public employment, public contracting, or public education." In effect, these measures proposed to ban many affirmative action programs and require outreach to be based on economic circumstances, residence or other such indicators. Identical measures were approved in California (1996, 55 percent to 45 percent), Washington (1998, 58 percent to 42 percent), and Michigan (2006, 58 percent to 42 percent). In all three campaigns, the initiatives were opposed by leaders of both political parties, and by prominent business and social leaders, yet were passed by large margins. Nebraska voters approved Initiated Measure 424 with 58 percent in favor, but Colorado voters delivered the first defeat to this movement, turning down Amendment 46 in a close election with 51 percent opposed and 49 percent in favor of the change.

Bonds

With the economy souring, in part because of unsustainable borrowing that led to a collapse of credit markets, voters might have been expected to hold the line on government borrowing. But voters approved 15 of 16 statewide bond measures (Alaska, Arkansas, California, Maine, New Mexico, Ohio, Pennsylvania and Rhode Island) authorizing more than $13.5 billion in all. California voters were the most surprising. The state is in the midst of a serious fiscal crisis, with an estimated structural deficit in excess of $10 billion, and voters had approved $43 billion in borrowing in 2006. Yet voters authorized three more bond issues in 2008 worth $11.83 billion: $9.95 billion for high speed trains, $980 million for children's hospitals and $900 million for aid to veterans.

California's appetite for borrowing extended to the local level as well, where voters approved a variety of bond issues including $7 billion for Los Angeles Unified School District and $2.1 billion for San Diego Unified School District. The only state-level bond measure to fail was California's Proposition 10 that would have authorized $5 billion borrowing for alternative fuel vehicles. The clear implication from these results is that voters are not averse to having their governments take on additional debt as a way to continue funding for services they consider important.

Energy

With soaring gas prices in the months leading up the election as a backdrop, voters faced several propositions that proposed to increase use of renewable fuels. Two measures proposed to require electric utilities to generate a fraction of their power from renewable energy sources, following in the footsteps of Colorado's successful Amendment 37 in 2004. Missouri voters approved Proposition C that requires 2 percent of electricity to be generated from renewable sources initially, rising to 15 percent by 2021. California voters previously approved minimum requirements, but rejected Proposition 7 that would have extended the rule to publicly owned utilities and required all utilities to generate 20 percent of their energy from renewable fuel sources by 2010, rising to 40 percent in 2020 and 50 percent by 2025. The solar power industry and most of the prominent environmental organizations opposed the proposal on the grounds that the measure was poorly written and could have ended up reducing use of renewable energy sources. California voters also rejected Proposition 10, which would have authorized $5 billion in borrowing for alternative fuel vehicles and renewable energy. Voters seem amenable to requiring greater use of alternative fuels, but not without limit.

Animals

Animal rights have emerged as an active political arena over the last decade, but voter opinion seems mixed. In 2008, animal rights groups promoted Proposition 2 in California, a constitutional amendment that required minimum living space for farm animals, including calves, egg-laying hens and pregnant pigs. Similar measures were approved by Florida voters in 2002 and Arizona voters in 2006, in both cases by large margins. Florida's "pregnant pigs" measure has

Table C
COMPLETE LIST OF STATEWIDE BALLOT PROPOSITIONS IN 2008

State	Type	Description	Result
Alabama			
Amendment 1	L/CA	Reestablishes Education Trust Rainy Day Fund.	Approved 57-43
Amendment 2	L/CA	Shelby County judges	Approved 60-40
Amendment 3	L/CA	Madison City school tax	Approved 50.5-49.5
Amendment 4	L/CA	Blount County annexations	Approved 57-43
Amendment 5	L/CA	Russel County court costs	Failed 45-55
Amendment 6	L/CA	Tuskegee City utility board	Approved 58-42
Alaska			
Measure 1 (Aug. 26)	I/ST	Authorizes lotteries and casino games.	Failed 39-61
Measure 2 (Aug. 26)	I/ST	Limits aerial hunting of wolves and bears.	Failed 45-55
Measure 3 (Aug. 26)	I/ST	Establishes system for public funding of campaigns.	Failed 36-64
Measure 4 (Aug. 26)	I/ST	Bans toxic discharges by new metallic mining operations.	Failed 44-56
Bond Proposition A	L/ST	$315.05 million bonds for transportation projects.	Approved 63-37
Arizona			
Prop. 100	I/CA	Prohibits state and local governments from new taxes on property sales.	Approved 77-23
Prop. 101	I/CA	Prohibits state from mandating a universal health care program.	Failed 49.8-50.2
Prop. 102	L/CA	Defines marriage as solely between one man and one woman.	Approved 56-44
Prop. 105	I/CA	Requires approval by majority of registered voters for new taxes, fees, or spending.	Failed 34-66
Prop. 200	I/ST	Allows payday loan industry to exist after 2010.	Failed 40-60
Prop. 201	I/ST	Requires new home sellers to provide 10-year warranty.	Failed 22-78
Prop. 202	I/ST	Reduces employer responsibility for identifying illegal immigrants.	Failed 41-59
Prop. 300	Z/ST	Increases salaries for elected state officers to at least $30,000.	Failed 36-64
Arkansas			
Amendment 1	L/CA	Removes constitutional language referring to voting by "idiot or insane" person.	Approved 73-27
Amendment 2	L/CA	Allows legislative sessions in even-numbered years.	Approved 69-31
Amendment 3	I/CA	Authorizes state lottery with money dedicated to educaion.	Approved 63-37
Proposed Initiative Act 1	I/ST	Prohibits unwed couples from being foster parents.	Approved 57-43
Referred Question 1	L/ST	$300 million bonds for water projects.	Approved 66-34
California			
Prop. 91 (Feb. 5)	I/CA+ST	Prohibits diversion of transportation funds.	Failed 42-58
Prop. 92 (Feb. 5)	I/CA+ST	Guarantees community colleges 10.46% of Prop 98 funds and caps tuition at $15/unit.	Failed 43-57
Prop. 93 (Feb. 5)	I/CA	Increases legislative term limits.	Failed 46-54
Prop. 94 (Feb. 5)	R/ST	Gaming compact with Pechanga Band of Luiseno Mission Indians	Approved 56-44
Prop. 95 (Feb. 5)	R/ST	Gaming compact with Morongo Band of Mission Indians	Approved 56-44
Prop. 96 (Feb. 5)	R/ST	Gaming compact with Sycuan Band of Kumeyaay Nation	Approved 55-45
Prop. 97 (Feb. 5)	R/ST	Gaming compact with Agua Caliente Band of Cahuilla Indians	Approved 55-45
Prop. 98 (June 3)	I/CA	Restricts use of eminent domain, defines "just compensation," prohibits rent control.	Failed 38-62
Prop. 99 (June 3)	I/CA	Restricts use of eminent domain to seize residences.	Approved 62-38
Prop. 1A	L/ST	$9.95 billion for high speed train systems	Approved 53-47
Prop. 2	I/ST	Requires minimum space for farm animals including calves, egg-laying hens, and pregnant pigs.	Approved 63-37
Prop. 3	I/ST	$980 million bonds for children's hospitals; designates 20% to University of California.	Approved 55-45
Prop. 4	I/CA	Requires parental notification and 48-hour waiting period for abortion by minor.	Failed 48-52
Prop. 5	I/ST	Reduces penalties for nonviolent drug offenses.	Failed 41-59
Prop. 6	I/ST	Increases spending and penalties on gang crimes.	Failed 31-69
Prop. 7	I/ST	Requires all utilities to generate 20% of their power from renewable energy by 2010.	Failed 36-64
Prop. 8	I/CA	Defines marriage as solely between one man and one woman.	Approved 52-48
Prop. 9	I/CA+ST	Requires notification of victim and opportunity for input during criminal process.	Approved 54-46
Prop. 10	I/ST	$5 billion bonds for alternative fuel vehicles and renewable energy.	Failed 41-59
Prop. 11	I/CA+ST	Establishes nonpartisan redistricting commission.	Approved 51-49
Prop. 12	L/ST	$900 million bonds for farm and home aid for California veterans.	Approved 64-36
Colorado			
Amendment 46	I/CA	Prohibits government racial preferences/affirmative action.	Failed 49-51
Amendment 47	I/CA	Prohibits employer from requiring union membership and payment of union dues.	Failed 44-56
Amendment 48	I/CA	Defines a "person" to be any human being from the moment of fertilization.	Failed 27-73
Amendment 49	I/CA	Prohibits the deduction of union dues from public employee paychecks.	Failed 39-61
Amendment 50	I/CA	Allows local control over casino hours, adjusts distribution of gaming funds.	Approved 59-41
Amendment 51	I/CA	Increases sales tax to provide long-term services to people with developmental disabilities.	Failed 38-62
Amendment 52	I/CA	Dedicates portion of severance tax revenue to highway transportation projects.	Failed 36-64
Amendment 54	I/CA	Prohibits labor unions from contributing to political campaigns.	Approved 51-49
Amendment 58	I/CA	Increases oil and gas severance tax to 5% of gross income.	Failed 42-58
Amendment 59	I/CA	Requires excess revenue currently rebated to taxpayers to be spent on education.	Failed 46-54
Referendum L	L/CA	Lowers age requirement for either house of state legislature from 25 to 21 years.	Failed 47-53
Referendum M	L/CA	Eliminates obsolete constitutional provisions regarding land value increase.	Approved 62-38
Referendum N	L/CA	Eliminates obsolete constitutional provisions regarding intoxicating liquor.	Approved 69-31
Referendum O	L/CA	Changes initiative signature requirements.	Failed 47-53

See footnotes at end of table.

COMPLETE LIST OF STATEWIDE BALLOT PROPOSITIONS IN 2008—Continued

State	Type	Description	Result
Connecticut			
CA Question 1	X	Calls for a constitutional convention.	Failed 40-60
CA Question 2	L/CA	Lowers voting age in primary elections to 17 for certain people.	Approved 64-36
Florida			
Amendment 1 (Jan. 29)	L/CA	Allows home owners to keep assessment cap when selling property, increases exemption.	Approved 64-36
Amendment 1	L/CA	Deletes provisions that allow legislature to prohibit ownership of property by aliens.	Failed 48-52
Amendment 2	I/CA	Defines marriage as solely between one man and one woman.	Approved 62-38
Amendment 3	Z/CA	Property tax exemption for wind resistance and renewable energy devices.	Approved 61-39
Amendment 4	Z/CA	Property tax exemption for conservation property.	Approved 69-31
Amendment 6	Z/CA	Requires assessment of waterfront property to be based on use.	Approved 71-29
Amendment 8	Z/CA	Allows sales taxes for community colleges to be levied with voter approval.	Failed 44-56
Georgia			
Amendment 1	L/CA	Lowers taxes for landowners preserving forest land.	Approved 68-32
Amendment 2	L/CA	Authorizes local tax allocation bonds for redevelopment purposes.	Approved 52-48
Amendment 3	L/CA	Allows creation of infrastructure development districts	Failed 48-52
Hawaii			
Constitutional Amendment	L/CA	Reduces minimum age from 30 to 25 years for governor and lt. governor.	Failed 18-82
Constitutional Question	X	Calls for a constitutional convention.	Failed 35-65
Illinois			
Question	X	Calls for a constitutional convention.	Failed 33-67
Iowa			
CA Question	L/CA	Replaces constitutional language on "idiot or insane" persons.	Approved 82-18
Louisiana			
Amendment 1	L/CA	Establishes three-term limits on certain public boards and commissions.	Approved 69-31
Amendment 2	L/CA	Requires proclamation in advance for extraordinary legislative sessions.	Approved 60-40
Amendment 3	L/CA	Requires temporary successor for legislators ordered to active military duty.	Approved 62-38
Amendment 4	L/CA	Increases local government share of revenue from severance taxes.	Failed 45-55
Amendment 5	L/CA	Allows transfer of special assessment to replacement property.	Failed 49.9-50.1
Amendment 6	L/CA	Removes certain restrictions on the disposition of blighted property.	Failed 49-51
Amendment 7	L/CA	Authorizes public employee non-pension retirement funds to invest in equities.	Failed 44-56
Maine			
Question 1 (June 10)	I/ST	$29.725 million bond issue for roads, bridges, dams, landfills, and other public facilities.	Approved 58-42
Question 1	R/ST	Sales tax for state universal health care program.	Failed 35-65
Question 2	I/ST	Allows a certain Maine company to operate a casino in Oxford County.	Failed 46-54
Question 3	I/ST	$3.4 million in bonds for drinking water and water treatment	Approved 50.3-49.7
Maryland			
Question 1	L/CA	Allows absentee voting up to two weeks before an election.	Approved 72-38
Question 2	L/CA	Allows 15,000 video lottery terminals in five locations throughout the state.	Approved 59-41
Massachusetts			
Question 1	I/ST	Repeals the state income tax.	Failed 31-69
Question 2	I/ST	Decriminalizes the possession of marijuana.	Approved 65-35
Question 3	I/ST	Eliminates commercial dog racing by 2010.	Approved 56-44
Michigan			
Proposal 08-1	I/ST	Allows medical use of marijuana.	Approved 63-37
Proposal 08-2	I/CA	Removes some restrictions on embyronic stem cell research.	Approved 53-47
Minnesota			
Constitutional Amendment	L/CA	Increases sales tax for water and other projects.	Approved 59-41
Missouri			
Amendment 1	L/CA	Establishes English as the language of all governmental meetings.	Approved 86-14
Amendment 4	L/CA	Alters operation of state grant and loan program for storm water control.	Approved 58-42
Prop. A	I/ST	Increases gaming tax to 21%, dedicates revenue to schools, eliminates $500 buy-in limit.	Approved 56-44
Prop. B	I/ST	Creates program to recruit and train home care workers, allows workers to unionize.	Approved 75-25
Prop. C	I/ST	Requires utility companies to generate 2% of electricity from renewable fuels, 15% by 2021.	Approved 66-34
Montana			
C-44	L/CA	Allows up to 25% of certain public funds to be invested in stocks.	Failed 26-74
I-155	I/ST	Dedicates a share of state funds to health care for uninsured children.	Approved 70-30
LR-118	L/ST	Continues for 10 years a $6 million levy for Montana university system.	Approved 57-43
Nebraska			
Amendment 1 (May 13)	L/CA	Allows cities to invest public endowment funds in more than savings accounts and bonds.	Approved 58-42
Amendment 1	L/CA	Removes requirement that cities use only general tax revenue for economic development.	Failed 46-54
Measure 424	I/CA	Prohibits government racial preferences/affirmative action.	Approved 58-42

See footnotes at end of table.

COMPLETE LIST OF STATEWIDE BALLOT PROPOSITIONS IN 2008—Continued

State	Type	Description	Result
Nevada			
Question 1	L/CA	Removes requirement that person must reside in state for 6 months to vote.	Failed 47-53
Question 2	I/CA	Restricts use of eminent domain for private purposes.	Approved 61-39
Question 3	L/CA	Requires legislature to make certain findings before allowing sales and use taxes.	Approved 60-40
Question 4	L/ST	Authorizes legislature to amend/repeal sales taxes without voter approval.	Failed 27-73
New Jersey			
Public Question 1	L/CA	Requires voter approval for bonds issued through any state agency.	Approved 58-42
Public Question 2	L/CA	Allows local governments to appoint judges to regional municipal courts.	Failed 45-5
New Mexico			
Bond Question A	L/ST	$14.725 million bonds for senior citizen facilities improvements	Approved 59-41
Bond Question B	L/ST	$11.019 million bonds for library acquisitions	Approved 52-48
Bond Question C	L/ST	$57.925 million bonds for health facility improvements	Approved 65-35
Bond Question D	L/ST	$140.133 million bonds for higher ed and special schools capital improvements	Approved 58-42
Amendment 1	L/CA	Allows midterm salary increases for county officials.	Approved 53-47
Amendment 2	L/CA	Increases the size of certain school boards to 9 members and conducts elections by mail.	Failed 27-73
Amendment 3	L/CA	Requires confirmation of Cabinet secretaries at beginning of each term of a governor.	Approved 72-28
Amendment 4	L/CA	Allows school elections to be held at same time as nonpartisan elections.	Failed 74-26*
Amendment 5	L/CA	Authorizes governor with consent of Senate to fill vacancy in office of lt governor.	Approved 69-31
New York			
Prop. 1	L/CA	Allows disabled veterans extra points on state and local civil service exams.	Approved 78-22
North Dakota			
Constitutional Measure 1 (June 10)	L/CA	Allows legislators to be appointed to office even if office salary was recently increased.	Failed 42-58
Constitutional Measure 1	L/CA	Creates Oil Tax Trust Fund.	Failed 36-64
Statutory Measure 2	I/ST	Lowers corporate income tax rate by 15 percent, personal income tax rate by 50 percent.	Failed 30-70
Statutory Measure 3	I/ST	Dedicates more money from tobacco settlement to tobacco prevention.	Approved 54-46
Statutory Measure 4	I/ST	Allows governor to appoint director of Workplace Safety and Insurance.	Approved 67-33
Ohio			
Issue 1	L/CA	Extends the deadline for qualifying a ballot issue from 90 to 125 days before election.	Approved 69-31
Issue 2	L/CA	$400 million bonds for land conservation, parks, and redevelopment.	Approved 69-31
Issue 3	L/CA	Protects rights of property owners in the areas of the Great Lakes Water Compact.	Approved 72-28
Issue 5	R/ST	Caps payday lending interest rates.	Approved 64-36
Issue 6	I/CA	Allows a privately owned $600 million resort casino in southwest Ohio.	Failed 38-62
Oklahoma			
State Question 735	L/CA	Provides property tax exemption for disabled veterans.	Approved 85-15
State Question 741	L/CA	Requires a person claiming a property tax exemption to file an application.	Approved 68-32
State Question 742	L/CA	Establishes a right to hunt, trap, fish, and take game and fish.	Approved 80-20
State Question 743	L/CA	Allows smaller winemakers to sell directly to retail package stores and restaurants.	Approved 79-21
Oregon			
Measure 51 (May 20)	L/CA	Empowers crime victims to seek remedies for violations of Section 42 constitutional rights.	Approved 75-25
Measure 52 (May 20)	L/CA	Empowers crime victims to seek remedies for violations of Section 43 constitutional rights.	Approved 75-25
Measure 53 (May 20)	L/CA	Allows forfeiture of property for crimes that are substantially similar to crime of conviction.	Approved 50.03-49.97
Measure 54	L/CA	Allows citizens younger than 21 to vote in school board elections.	Approved 73-27
Measure 55	L/CA	Changes effective date of redistricting plans.	Approved 77-23
Measure 56	L/CA	Requires property tax elections to be decided by majority of voters in the election.	Approved 57-43
Measure 57	L/ST	Increases sentences for drug trafficking and other crimes.	Approved 61-39
Measure 58	I/ST	Restricts a student from having more than two years of bilingual education.	Failed 44-56
Measure 59	I/ST	Makes federal income taxes fully deductible on state return.	Failed 36-64
Measure 60	I/ST	Requires teacher compensation to be based on classroom performance.	Failed 39-61
Measure 61	I/ST	Establishes mandatory sentences for drug dealers, identity thieves, burglars, and car thieves.	Failed 49-51
Measure 62	I/CA	Dedicates 15% of lottery profit for crime prevention, investigation, and prosecution.	Failed 39-61
Measure 63	I/ST	Eliminates requirement of a building permit for projects that cost less than $35,000.	Failed 46-54
Measure 64	I/ST	Prohibit political use of public employee union dues.	Failed 49-51
Measure 65	I/ST	Establishes "top two" open primary system.	Failed 34-66
Pennsylvania			
Bond Referendum	L/ST	$400 million bonds for sewers	Approved 62-38
Rhode Island			
Question 1	L/ST	$87.215 million bonds for highways, roads, bridges, buses	Approved 77-23
Question 2	L/ST	$2.5 million bonds for conservation of open spaces and recreation areas	Approved 68-32
South Carolina			
Amendment 1	L/CA	Adjusts age of consent for umarried women.	Approved 52-48
Amendment 2	L/CA	Allows stock investments for public pension funds for state employees and teachers.	Failed 42-58
Amendment 3	L/CA	Alllows stock investments for public pension funds for local government employees.	Failed 44-56

See footnotes at end of table.

COMPLETE LIST OF STATEWIDE BALLOT PROPOSITIONS IN 2008—Continued

State	Type	Description	Result
South Dakota			
Amendment G	L/CA	Repeals current limit on legislator's travel reimbursements.	Failed 41-59
Amendment H	L/CA	Removes constitutional restrictions on issue of stocks and bonds.	Failed 31-69
Amendment I	L/CA	Limits legislative sessions to 40 days each year.	Approved 52-48
Amendment J	L/CA	Repeals term limits for legislators.	Failed 24-76
Initiated Measure 10	I/ST	Prohibits government workers from using their salaries for campaigning or lobbying.	Failed 35-65
Initiated Measure 11	I/ST	Prohibits abortion except in case of rape, health of mother.	Failed 45-55
Initiated Measure 9	I/ST	Prohibits short sales of stock.	Failed 43-57
Utah			
Amendment A	L/CA	Establishes succession procedures for governor and lt. governor.	Approved 76-24
Amendment B	L/CA	Regulates state trust fund.	Approved 66-34
Amendment C	L/CA	Changes beginning of annual general sessions of legislature.	Approved 71-29
Amendment D	L/CA	Requires legislature to redistrict no later than next legislative session after Census count.	Approved 78-22
Amendment E	L/CA	Allows state to invest in stocks and bonds.	Failed 43-57
Washington			
I-1000	I/ST	Allows physician-assisted suicide.	Approved 58-42
I-1029	I/ST	Requires certification and training for long-term workers caring for elderly and disabled.	Approved 73-37
I-985	I/ST	Opens carpool lanes to all drivers outside of rush hours.	Failed 40-60
Wisconsin			
Question 1 (Apr. 1)	L/CA	Limits governor's partial veto power.	Approved 71-29
Wyoming			
Amendment A	L/CA	Changes the language of the oath of office for all state and county officials.	Approved 82-18
Amendment B	L/CA	Changes initiative petition distribution requirement.	Failed 54-46**

Source: Initiative & Referendum Institute.

Note: Unless another date is given, a proposition appeared on the November 4 ballot. For referendums, "approved" means that the challenged law was upheld by the voters; "failed" means it was repealed.

Key:

CA — Constitutional amendment

I — Initiative

L — Legislative measure

R — Referendum

ST — Statute

X — Vote on whether to call constitutional convention, required by constitution

Z — Commission

*Proposition failed to satisfy supermajority requirement of 3/4 affirmative statewide, and 2/3 affirmative in each county.

**Proposition received majority of votes cast but failed to satisfy quorum requirement.

been ridiculed as an example of a frivolous constitutional amendment, but voters continue to embrace this agenda. Proposition 2 was more ambitious than its predecessors in including chickens. The opposition campaign argued that the measure would drive up the cost of eggs and lead to importation of unregulated eggs from other states and Mexico, but voters overwhelmingly approved the measure 63 percent to 37 percent. In Massachusetts, voters approved Question 3, which banned commercial dog racing in the state by 2010, requiring closure of two tracks. In Alaska, voters rejected Ballot Measure 2 that would have banned aerial hunting of bears, wolves and wolverines. In Oklahoma voters approved State Question 742 that established a state constitutional right to hunt and fish.

Notes

[1] For detailed information on initiative adoption and provisions see the appendixes of John G. Matsusaka, *For the Many or the Few: The Initiative, Public Policy, and American Democracy* (University of Chicago Press, 2004) and M. Dane Waters, *Initiative and Referendum Almanac* (Carolina Academic Press, 2003).

[2] For data on the initiative status of the 1,500 largest cities in the country, see the Initiative & Referendum Institute's *Legal Landscape Database*, available at *www.iandrinstitute.org*.

[3] See Chapter 7 in Matsusaka, *For the Many or the Few* (2004).

[4] These numbers are calculated from information reported on the California Secretary of State's Web site, and are conservative estimates of the total amounts. To avoid potential double counting, this total includes $13.6 million in contributions from the "No on 8—Equality California" campaign to "No on 8—Equality for All" campaign, but does not separately include contributions to "No on 8—Equality California."

About the Author

John G. Matsusaka is a professor in the Marshall School of Business, Gould School of Law, and Department of Political Science, and president of the Initiative & Referendum Institute, all at the University of Southern California. He is the author of *For the Many or the Few: The Initiative, Public Policy, and American Democracy* (University of Chicago Press, 2004).

Chapter Seven

STATE FINANCE

State Budgets in 2008 and 2009: Mired by the Ongoing National Recession and Sharp Revenue Declines, States are Forced to Make Difficult Budgetary Decisions

By Brian Sigritz

Fiscal conditions in the states began to decline in fiscal 2008. State spending and revenues grew at a lower rate than the prior year and balances were well-below their near record levels of fiscal 2007. While fiscal 2008 saw somewhat moderate declines, the fiscal situation in the states has deteriorated much more sharply in fiscal 2009. State spending is projected to be negative for the first time since 1983, balance levels are being reduced as states use reserves to address shortfalls, and recent data shows state revenues declining by 4 percent. As a result, states are likely to face a difficult budgetary environment in fiscal 2010 and beyond.

Introduction

After three straight years of strong revenue growth, near record-high balance levels and few budget cuts, state fiscal conditions began to deteriorate in fiscal 2008. Whereas fiscal 2007 saw general fund spending growth of 9.4 percent, the highest level since 1985, fiscal 2008 saw spending growth decline to 5.3 percent, below the historical average of 6.3 percent. Fiscal years 2005–2007 were marked by states using increased revenues and budget surpluses to bolster spending on programs that experienced significant budget cuts during the fiscal downturn of the early 2000s. This began to change in fiscal 2008 as some states, most notably those significantly impacted by the housing market collapse, saw a sharp decline in revenue, and other states adjusted their revenue forecasts downward in anticipation of the economic slowdown.

While fiscal 2008 marked a turning point for states, fiscal 2009 has seen states hampered by the ongoing national recession and rapidly declining revenues forcing them to make painful budget cuts, use rainy day funds, and examine tax and fee increases. Spending is projected to decline by 0.1 percent in fiscal 2009.[1] This would mark the first decline in actual dollars spent since 1983. The number of states making midyear budget cuts has also rapidly increased. As of December 2008, 22 states had made midyear cuts to their fiscal 2009 budget, compared to 13 states that made cuts in fiscal 2008 and three states that made cuts in fiscal 2007. More than two-thirds of states likely will have made cuts to their midyear budgets by the end of fiscal 2009. Furthermore, states are very concerned about fiscal 2010 and beyond, as it typically takes states several years to fully recover after a national recession ends. With the most recent economic data showing fourth-quarter 2008 Gross Domestic Product declining by 6.2 percent[2], and January unemployment rates reaching double-digits in several states[3], negative state fiscal conditions are likely to persist for several years.

The Current State Fiscal Condition

Revenues in Fiscal 2008

After several years of strong revenue collections, the rate of state revenue growth declined in fiscal 2008. Revenue collections from all sources[4] were higher than budgeted amounts in 25 states, were on target in five states, and were lower than anticipated in 20 states. By comparison, in fiscal 2007, 38 states exceeded projections, four states met projections, and only eight states had lower than projected revenue collections.[5] As recently as fiscal 2005 and fiscal 2006 all states either met or surpassed their budgeted estimates for revenue collections.

Combined revenue collections of sales, personal income and corporate income grew 2.2 percent in fiscal 2008 from fiscal 2007 levels. While still positive, the growth rate was considerably less than fiscal 2007 when collections grew 6 percent. Individually, sales tax collections grew 0.8 percent, personal income tax collections grew 4.8 percent, and corporate income tax collections declined 4.5 percent. In actual dollar terms, sales tax revenues increased by $1.6 billion and personal income tax revenues by $12.7 billion, while corporate income tax collections declined by $2.4 billion.[6]

Revenues in Fiscal 2009

While revenue growth was weak but positive for most states in fiscal 2008, revenue growth is now expected to turn negative for the majority of states in fiscal 2009. The latest information from the Nelson A. Rockefeller Institute of Government illustrates this point. According to preliminary figures from the second quarter of fiscal 2009, a majority of states that have reported data are experiencing a decline in both sales and personal income tax collections. Overall, states are experiencing a 4 percent decline in revenue.[7]

Economic conditions have declined much more sharply in fiscal 2009 than states expected. When states passed their fiscal 2009 budgets, they projected revenues from sales, personal income and corporate income taxes would be 2.9 percent higher than those collected in fiscal 2008. It should be noted that most states passed their fiscal 2009 budgets in the spring of 2008, well before the financial sector meltdown in the fall of 2008. As a result of the economic collapse, few states are meeting revenue projections. Through the first few months of fiscal 2009, only eight states have exceeded their revenue projections, 15 states are on target with their projections, and 25 states are below projections.[8] The number of states with revenue collections below projections is expected to grow considerably by end of fiscal 2009. The sharp decline in revenue has led to budget shortfalls in all regions of the country. As of December 2008, 31 states were experiencing a fiscal 2009 budget gap. Perhaps not surprisingly, this total is also expected to increase significantly by the time the fiscal year ends.

Tax and Fee Changes in Fiscal 2009

Overall, states enacted a net tax and fee increase of $1.5 billion in fiscal 2009. While collectively states enacted a net tax and fee increase, individually more states adopted net tax and fee decreases than increases, with 20 states adopting net decreases and 14 adopting net increases. Most states enacted tax and fee changes for fiscal 2009 in the spring of 2008, before the collapse of the financial sector. It is highly unlikely that states will enact net tax and fee decreases in fiscal 2010 due to declining state revenues and the continued weakening of the national economy. Instead, many states are more likely to consider measures such as increasing tobacco and motor fuel taxes as a partial solution to their current revenue shortfalls.

Corporate income taxes comprised the largest enacted revenue increase nationwide for fiscal 2009, totaling $1.36 billion. The largest enacted increase was in California, where the state suspended net operating loss credits and limited business credits, resulting in a revenue increase of $1.69 billion. The largest enacted decrease was in Ohio, where the state reduced the corporate franchise tax by 20 percent, which resulted in a decrease of $350 million. Along with the enacted increase in corporate income taxes, fees ($805.2 million), sales taxes ($676.8 million), cigarette/tobacco taxes ($270.6 million), motor fuel taxes ($67.7 million), and alcohol taxes ($7.5 million) also experienced net increases in fiscal 2009.

The largest enacted tax and fee decrease for fiscal 2009 was seen in other taxes, totaling $1.34 billion. Those taxes include personal property taxes, provider taxes, and levies on hotels and rental cars. Changes in Indiana's tax structure compromised the largest percentage of the overall decrease in other taxes as the state instituted a property tax reduction for local units, resulting in a decrease of $1.17 billion. In addition to reductions in other taxes, states also enacted a net decrease in personal income taxes ($321.7 million).[9]

State Spending in 2008

General funds serve as the primary source for financing a state's operations. General funds typically receive revenue from broad-based state taxes such as sales taxes and personal income taxes. In fiscal 2008, state general fund expenditures were $689.4 billion (preliminary actual), a 5.3 percent increase over fiscal 2007. That fiscal 2008 increase was slightly lower than the 31-year historical average of 6.3 percent. Fiscal 2008 marked the first year since fiscal 2003 that state general fund expenditures grew at a lower rate than the prior year. In fiscal 2007, general fund expenditures grew at 9.4 percent, the highest level since fiscal 1985. Spending growth slowed in fiscal 2008 as states began to be impacted by the economic slowdown. Several states most severely impacted by the housing market decline—such as Arizona, Florida and Nevada—enacted negative growth budgets. Overall, six states reported negative expenditure growth in fiscal 2008, 35 states reported growth that was positive but less than 10 percent, and nine states had growth rates of 10 percent or higher.[10] By comparison, 18 states reported general fund expenditure growth rates of 10 percent or higher for fiscal 2007.[11]

According to estimated fiscal 2008 numbers from the National Association of State Budget Officers' *State Expenditure Report*, general funds accounted for 44.3 percent of total state expenditures. Federal funds accounted for 27.1 percent of total expenditures, bonds accounted for 2.7 percent, and other state funds were 25.9 percent.[12] General fund spending has decreased substantially as a percentage of total state expenditures since NASBO first began compiling the *State Expenditure Report* in 1987. For example, in fiscal 1988 general fund spending accounted for 56.7 percent of total state expenditures, while in fiscal 2008 general fund spending decreased to 44.3 percent of total spending. This can partly be attributed to the increased use of bonds and other state funds, which includes money restricted by law for specific governmental functions or activities.

Elementary and secondary education remained the largest category of general fund expenditures in fiscal 2008, accounting for 34.5 percent of general fund expenditures. Medicaid represented 16.9 percent, and higher education accounted for 11.5 percent. Combined, Medicaid and education comprised nearly 63 percent of total state general fund spending. Other categories of general fund spending included corrections at 6.9 percent, public assistance at 1.8 percent, transportation at 0.8 percent, and all other spending[14] at 27.6 percent.

While elementary and secondary education remains by far the largest category of general fund expenditures, K–12 and Medicaid represent nearly the same level of total state expenditures. In fiscal 2008, elementary and secondary education is estimated to account for 20.9 percent of total state expenditures, with Medicaid close behind at 20.7 percent. Fiscal 2008 marks the first time since fiscal 2003 that elementary and secondary education represented a larger component of total state spending than Medicaid. Because Medicaid is a long-term health care program for low-income individuals, however, that spending is expected to increase sharply as more people feel the impact of the recession. Other categories of total state spending for fiscal 2008 include higher education at 10.3 percent, transportation at 8.1 percent, corrections at 3.4 percent, public assistance at 1.6 percent, and all other spending at 35.1 percent.[15]

State Spending in 2009

According to appropriated budgets, general fund expenditure growth is expected to decrease by 0.1 percent in fiscal 2009.[16] This will mark the first year since fiscal 1983 that nominal spending growth has been negative. Fiscal 2009's negative growth rate shows the rapid decline of state finances. As recently as fiscal 2007 states experienced spending growth of 9.4 percent, while fiscal 2008 saw growth at 5.3 percent. Not surprisingly, the number of states enacting negative growth budgets greatly increased in fiscal 2009. Eighteen states reported negative growth budgets, while another 23 states enacted budgets with either no spending growth or up to 4.9 percent.[17]

Additionally, the final figures for fiscal 2009 will likely show spending growth to be even less than -0.1 percent. In January 2009, the National Governors Association and NASBO asked states to submit estimated budget shortfall figures for fiscal 2009 and fiscal 2010 in order to gauge current fiscal conditions. The survey results determined that states face a cumulative $77 billion shortfall in fiscal 2009, and are potentially facing a $99 billion shortfall in fiscal 2010. These massive shortfall amounts will lead to even further spending reductions in fiscal 2009.

Budget Cuts

More states were forced to make midyear budget cuts in fiscal 2008 as the nation entered into a recession and state revenues began to decline. Thirteen states made midyear cuts in fiscal 2008, for a total $3.6 billion. By comparison, only three states made midyear budget cuts in fiscal 2007. The number of states cutting their budgets midyear has increased even more in fiscal 2009 as states' economic outlook continues to erode. As of December 2008, 22 states had made cuts to their enacted fiscal 2009 budgets for a total of $12.1 billion, and another five states are planning to do so.[18] More than two-thirds of states are expected to have to cut their budgets by the end of fiscal 2009. It should also be noted that even if the recession ends in fiscal 2010, many states will likely be forced to make midyear budget cuts for several years to come since states typically lag the economy as a whole in recovering from an economic downturn. Evidence of this can be seen in the fact that 37 states made midyear budget cuts in fiscal 2003, well after the 2001 recession ended.

Balances

Total balances include both ending balances as well as the amounts in states' budget stabilization funds; they reflect the funds states may use to respond to unforeseen circumstances after budget obligations have been met. Forty-eight states have either a budget stabilization fund or a rainy day fund, with about three-fifths of the states having limits on the size of these funds.[19]

Balances, like spending growth, declined in fiscal 2008 and are expected to decline even more in fiscal 2009. In fiscal 2008, balances were $50.8 billion or 7.4 percent of expenditures, considerably less than fiscal 2007 when balances were $65.9 billion, or 10.1 percent of expenditures. According to governors' enacted budgets, balances are projected to be 7.0 percent of expenditures, or $48.0 billion, in fiscal 2009. That amount, however, is likely to decline as a number of states have used rainy day funds and balances to partially address their current year budget shortfalls. Over the last 31 years, balances have averaged 5.7 percent of general fund expenditures.[20]

Looking Ahead

Negative fiscal conditions are expected to persist in the states for the remainder of fiscal 2009 and throughout fiscal 2010. Even if the national recession ended today, states will likely face several years of negative or low revenue growth. Typically, state tax revenues remain weak for several years after a recession. For example, it took state revenues at least five years to fully recover after the last two recessions.[21] Increased demands in areas such as health care and education, along with declining revenues, will continue to force states to use rainy day funds and balances, examine tax and fee increases, and make painful reductions in spending. Additionally, using history as a guide, a number of states will likely be forced to make midyear budget cuts in fiscal 2010, and perhaps in fiscal 2011. Thirty-seven states made midyear budget cuts in fiscal 2003, well after the 2001 recession ended. All these factors combined have led credit rating agencies to rate states' outlook as negative.[22]

While the immediate outlook for states may be negative, there are several factors that may help states weather the economic downturn. First, states did a good job building their rainy day funds and reserves during the preceding period of strong revenue growth. For example, in fiscal 2006 total balances reached $69.0 billion or 11.5 percent of expenditures, a record level. States may now tap these reserves to address their shortfalls. Second, states have been aggressive over the past five years in pursuing cost containment measures to help slow spending increases. One area where this has been readily evident is in Medicaid. According to the Kaiser Commission on Medicaid and the Uninsured, every state instituted cost-containment measures during this period. Finally, states will benefit from the passage of the American Recovery and Reinvestment Act, which will provide approximately $200 billion for states over the next couple of years in areas such as Medicaid, education and infrastructure. These federal funds will help states address current and ongoing budget shortfalls. That being said, the Recovery Act funds alone are unlikely to solve states' budget gaps. States will continue to have to make painful decisions to close budget deficits, and should begin to plan for the eventual end of the stimulus funding.

Notes

[1]National Association of State Budget Officers, The Fiscal Survey of States, (December 2008), 5.

[2]Bureau of Economic Analysis, *Gross Domestic Product: Fourth Quarter 2008*, (February 2009).

[3]Bureau of Labor Statistics, *January 2009 Regional and State Employment and Unemployment Summary*, (March 2009).

[4]"All Sources" includes revenues from sales, personal income, corporate income, gaming taxes, and all other taxes and fees.

[5]*The Fiscal Survey of States*, (December 2008), 15.

[6]*The Fiscal Survey of States*, (December 2008), 48–49.

[7]Nelson A. Rockefeller Institute of Government, State Revenue Report, (January 2009), 1.

[8]*The Fiscal Survey of States*, (December 2008), 18.

[9]*The Fiscal Survey of States*, (December 2008), 18–19.

[10]*The Fiscal Survey of States*, (December 2008), 7.

[11]*The Fiscal Survey of States*, (December 2007), 2.

[12]National Association of State Budget Officers, *2007 State Expenditure Report*, (Fall 2008), 6.

[13]National Association of State Budget Officers, *1988 State Expenditure Report*, 11.

[14]"All Other" spending in states includes the State Children's Health Insurance Program (SCHIP), institutional and community care for the mentally ill and developmentally disabled, public health programs, employer contributions to pensions and health benefits, economic development, environmental projects, state police, parks and recreation, housing, and general aid to local governments.

[15]*2007 State Expenditure Report*, (Fall 2008), 8.

[16]See note 1 above.

[17]See note 8 above.

[18]*The Fiscal Survey of States*, (December 2008), 1–4.

[19]National Association of State Budget Officers, *Budget Processes in the States*, (Summer 2008), 67–69.

[20]*The Fiscal Survey of States*, (December 2008), 24.

[21]Nelson A. Rockefeller Institute of Government, *Fiscal Features: What will Happen to State Budgets When the Money Runs Out?*, (February 2009), 2.

[22]Moody's Public Finance, *Outlook Remains Negative for U.S. States*, (February 2009), 1.

About the Author

Brian Sigritz is a staff associate at the National Association of State Budget Officers. He received his M.P.A. from the George Washington University and his B.A. from St. Bonaventure University. Prior to working at NASBO, Sigritz worked for the Ohio Senate and the Ohio House of Representatives.

Table 7.1
FISCAL 2007 STATE GENERAL FUND, ACTUAL, BY REGION
(In millions of dollars)

State	*Beginning balance*	*Revenues*	*Adjustments*	*Total resources*	*Expenditures*	*Adjustments*	*Ending balance*	*Budget stabilization fund*
U.S. totals	$51,673	$654,744	. . .	$710,264	$655,037	. . .	$46,805	$29,894
Eastern Region								
Connecticut (a)	0	15,784	-80	15,704	15,434	0	269	1,382
Delaware*	691	3,290	0	3,981	3,390	0	591	175
Maine (b)	15	3,020	26	3,060	3,024	0	36	116
Massachusetts (c)	1,053	29,169	0	30,222	28,923	0	1,299	2,335
New Hampshire (d)	26	1,422	0	1,488	1,366	20	62	89
New Jersey* (e)	1,779	31,202	0	32,981	30,284	111	2,586	485
New York* (f)	3,257	51,379	0	54,636	51,591	0	3,045	1,031
Pennsylvania (g)	514	26,399	93	27,006	26,319	156	531	713
Rhode Island (h)	56	3,212	-46	3,221	3,218	0	4	79
Vermont (i)	0	1,151	56	1,207	1,160	47	0	55
Regional totals	7,391	166,028	. . .	173,506	164,709	334	8,423	6,460
Midwestern Region								
Illinois* (j)	591	26,393	2,246	29,230	25,615	2,973	642	276
Indiana (k)	815	12,704	0	13,519	12,247	331	941	344
Iowa (l)	0	5,646	0	5,646	5,385	185	76	535
Kansas	734	5,809	0	6,543	5,608	0	935	0
Michigan (m)	3	8,280	963	9,245	8,986	0	259	2
Minnesota* (n)	1,813	16,379	0	18,192	15,947	0	2,245	1,145
Nebraska (o)	566	3,404	-253	3,716	3,125	0	591	504
North Dakota (p)	185	1,224	0	1,409	1,012	101	296	200
Ohio	632	25,778	0	26,410	25,148	1,047	216	1,012
South Dakota (q)	0	1,080	12	1,092	1,091	1	0	133
Wisconsin (r)	49	12,618	494	13,161	13,105	-11	66	0
Regional totals	5,388	119,315	. . .	128,163	117,269	. . .	6,267	4,151
Southern Region								
Alabama (s)	950	7,477	20	8,477	7,972	-40	515	677
Arkansas	0	4,059	0	4,059	4,059	0	0	0
Florida	4,990	26,660	0	31,650	28,216	0	3,434	1,237
Georgia* (t)	1,958	19,896	98	21,952	19,167	0	2,786	1,545
Kentucky (u)	681	8,682	292	9,655	8,787	289	579	232
Louisiana (v)	827	9,681	45	10,553	9,465	0	1,088	683
Maryland (w)	1,362	12,940	157	14,459	14,174	0	285	1,432
Mississippi (x)	35	4,790	0	4,825	4,372	0	435	54
Missouri (y)	695	7,921	0	8,616	7,864	0	752	268
North Carolina (z)	749	19,460	222	20,432	18,662	548	1,221	787
Oklahoma (aa)	134	6,547	-89	6,592	6,256	140	196	572
South Carolina*	988	6,659	0	7,646	6,565	0	1,081	168
Tennessee (bb)	745	10,737	-166	11,317	9,776	535	1,007	543
Texas (cc)	7,073	39,263	88	46,423	36,119	1,689	8,615	405
Virginia	1,804	16,455	0	18,260	17,934	0	326	1,190
West Virginia (dd)	469	3,753	0	4,222	3,701	89	432	515
Regional totals	23,460	204,980	. . .	229,138	203,089	. . .	22,752	10,308
Western Region								
Alaska (ee)	0	4,912	592	5,505	5,505	0	0	3,015
Arizona (ff)	1,023	9,958	-2	10,579	10,201	0	378	677
California	9,898	95,415	0	105,313	101,413	0	3,900	3,015
Colorado* (gg)	252	7,540	-229	7,563	7,047	0	516	267
Hawaii	732	5,142	0	5,874	5,381	0	493	62
Idaho (hh)	302	2,813	-283	2,831	2,577	0	255	122
Montana (ii)	409	1,838	0	2,247	1,697	0	550	0
Nevada (jj)	351	3,379	0	3,730	3,592	0	138	268
New Mexico* (kk)	798	5,828	193	6,819	5,957	211	651	651
Oregon (ll)	653	6,430	0	7,083	5,646	0	1,437	0
Utah (mm)	308	5,308	-383	5,233	4,992	0	242	313
Washington (nn)	699	14,443	-218	14,924	14,144	0	781	293
Wyoming (oo)	10	1,818	0	1,828	1,823	0	5	295
Regional totals	15,435	164,824	. . .	179,529	169,975	. . .	9,346	8,978
Regional totals without California	5,537	69,409	. . .	74,216	68,562	. . .	5,446	5,963

See footnotes at end of table.

FISCAL 2007 STATE GENERAL FUND, ACTUAL, BY REGION—Continued
(In millions of dollars)

Source:National Association of State Budget Officers, *The Fiscal Survey of the States* (December 2008).

Note: For all states, unless otherwise noted, transfers into budget stabilization funds are counted as expenditures, and transfers from budget stabilization funds are counted as revenues.

Key:

* In these states, the ending balance includes the balance in the budget stabilization fund.

NA — Indicates data are not available.

. . .— Not applicable

(a) $80 million in fiscal year 2007 revenue was transferred for use in fiscal year 2009.

(b) Adjustments reflect year end adjustments to fund balance.

(c) Includes budgeted fund balances.

(d) $20.0 million transfer to rainy day fund.

(e) Includes General Fund and Property Tax Relief Fund—Budget vs. Generally Accepted Accounting Principles (GAAP) Adjustment. In keeping with past practice, and to ensure consistency in survey results over time, the figures in this table exclude New Jersey's Casino Revenue Fund, Casino Control Fund and Gubernatorial Elections Fund.

(f) The ending balance includes $1.7 billion from prior-year reserves, $1 billion in Rainy Day Reserve funds, $278 million in a Community Projects Fund, and $21 million in a reserve for litigation risks.

(g) Revenue adjustment includes $8.1 million adjustment to the beginning balance and $84.5 million in prior year lapses. Expenditure adjustment reflects current year lapses of $20.9 million and a transfer of $177 million (25 percent of the ending balance) to the Rainy Day Fund.

(h) Opening balance includes a free surplus of $38.3 million and re-approprations from the prior year of $17.4 million. Adjustments to revenues represent (net) transfers to the Budget Stabilization (Rainy Day) Fund, including a transfer-in of $65.4 million and an appropriation of $19.4 million out of the fund.

(i) Revenue adjustments include $25.7 million in direct applications and transfers-in, a $8.3 million increase in property transfer tax revenue estimate, and $21.8 million from the General Fund Surplus Reserve. Expenditure adjustments include $10 million to the Transportation Fund, $13.7 to the Education Fund, $0.2 million reserved for the fiscal 2006 bond issuance premium, -$8.5 million from Federal Funds—Medicare Part D refund, $6.3 million to Internal Service Funds, $5.0 million to miscellaneous other funds, $3.4 million to the Budget Stabilization Reserve, $8.5 million to the Human Services Caseload Reserve, and $21.1 million to the General Fund Surplus Reserve.

(j) Revenue adjustments include $2,246.0 million in transfers to General Funds. Expenditure adjustments include $2,973.0 million in transfers out, $429.0 million for Pension Obligation Bond Debt Service, and $14.0 million in interest for Short-term Borrowing.

(k) Expenditure adjustments: Local Option Income Tax Distributions Reversal of Payment Delay, Property Tax Replacement Fund adjust for abstracts.

(l) Expenditure adjustments include $131.9 million appropriated from the ending balance of the General Fund to the Property Tax Credit Fund to pay for property tax credits in fiscal year 2008. $53.5 million of the ending balance was credited to the Senior Living Trust Fund.

(m) FY 2007 revenue adjustments include the impact of federal and state law changes ($38.0 million); revenue sharing law changes ($540.8 million); tobacco securitization proceeds ($207.2 million) and other revenue adjustments ($176.5 million).

(n) Ending balance includes budget reserve of $653 million, Cash Flow Account of $350 million and Tax Relief Account of $109.7 million and reserve for appropriations carried forward of $32.6 million.

(o) Revenue adjustments are transfers between the General Fund and other funds. Per Nebraska law, includes a transfer of $259.9 million to the Cash Reserve Fund (Rainy Day Fund) of the amount the prior year's net General Fund receipts exceeded the official forecast.

(p) Transfer to budget stablilization fund to reach 2007–09 cap of $200.0 million.

(q) Adjustments in Revenues: $6.55 million was from one-time receipts, $4.9 million was transferred from the Property Tax Reduction Fund to cover the budget shortfall, and $0.3 million was obligated cash carried forward from FY2006 Adjustments in Expenditures: $0.3 million was transferred to the Budget Reserve Fund from the prior year's obligated cash, and $0.2 million was obligated cash to the Budget Reserve Fund.

(r) Revenue adjustments include Indian Gaming ($22.1 m) and other revenue ($317.3); Expenditure adjustments include transfers to MA ($25.4), designation for continuing balances ($6.8), and unreserved designated balance (-$43.2).

(s) Revenue adjustments include release of Prior Year Debt Service Reserve and Tobacco Settlement transfers. Expenditure adjustments include reversions and reserve for General Obligation Debt Service payment.

(t) Adjustment of data due to return of agency surplus. Final totals include funds from Lottery and Tobacco sales.

(u) Revenue includes $107.8 million in Tobacco Settlement funds. Adjustment for Revenues includes $177.3 million that represents appropriation balances carried over from the prior fiscal year, and $114.3 million from fund transfers into the General Fund. Adjustment to Expenditures represents appropriation balances forwarded to the next fiscal year.

(v) Act 640 of 2006 transferred $3.0M from Incentive Fund and $3.0M from Mineral Resources Operating Funds; Bond Premium Dedication $14.3; FY2006 carry-forward $23.0; IEB carryforward of $1.3M; Act 27 of 2006 reappropriations of $0.6M; Carryforward of FY2006 $23.0M

(w) Adjustments reflect a $2.9 million reimbursement from the reserve for Heritage Tax Credits and $154.2 million from the local income tax reserve.

(x) Prior Year's Ending Balance adjusted to 50 percent of actual ending balance; remaining 50 percent transferred to the Rainy Day Fund.

(y) Revenues are net of refunds. Refunds for FY 2007 totaled $1,208.8 million. Revenues include $204.3 million transferred to the General Revenue Fund.

(z) $222 million R&R appropriation from FY 2005-06 year-end balance, $145 million increase to Repair & Renovation Reserve and $181.2 million increase to Rainy Day Reserve from FY 2006–07 year-end balance and $6.2 million usage of available credit balance.

(aa) Revenue adjustments include the Rainy Day Fund deposit of $76m and the Cash flow difference of $13m. Adjustments to expenditures are spillover appropriations.

(bb) Revenue Adjustments include a $100 million transfer from debt service fund unexpended appropriations, -$218.2 million transfer to rainy day fund, and -$47.9 million was reserved for dedicated revenue appropriations. Expenditure adjustments included $48.7 million transfer to Transportation Equity Fund, $103.5 million transfer to capital outlay projects fund, $163.7 million transfer to TennCare reserve, $50.3 million transfer to CoverTN - Health Safety Net reserves, $48.5 million transfer to systems development projects, and $120 million transfer to dedicated revenue appropriations.

(cc) FY 2007 information is from the Comptroller's Revenue Estimate. 2008 actual revenues are from the CPA's monthly revenue collections report. The revenue adjustment is the increase in dedicated account balances. The expenditure adjustment is a transfer to the Rainy Day Fund.

(dd) Fiscal Year 2007 beginning balance includes $266.4 million in re-appropriations, un-appropriated surplus balance of $177.6 million, and FY 2006 13th month expenditures of $25 million. Revenue adjustments are from prior year redeposit. Expenditure adjustment represents the amount transferred to the Rainy Day Fund.

(ee) Revenues adjustments include: 592.4 Re-appropriations and Carry Forward.

(ff) Adjustments to FY07 revenues include School Facilities Board adjustment transfer, payments to lawsuit, and excess interest transfer from the rainy day fund.

(gg) Revenue adjustments include General Fund (GF) diversion (which are not counted as expenditures) to fund the State's transportation needs. The difference between the rainy day fund balance and the ending GF balance is allocated to capital construction and transportation purposes in the following fiscal year. Pursuant to NASBO's definitions, Colorado's GF statutory reserve equal to 4.0 percent of appropriations represents a rainy day fund.

(hh) Revenue adjustments include the following: $4.6 million for deficiency warrants; $21.3 million from the Revolving Development Loan; $25 million to Public Schools Facilities; $10 million to the Public Education Stabilization Fund; $21 million to the Permanent Building Fund; $99.2 additional funding for Permanent Building Fund; $5.1 to the Capitol Commission Endowment; $23.8 to the Economic Recovery Reserve Fund; $100 million to the Public Education Stabilization fund; $12.9 to the Budget Stabilization Fund; and $3.2 to the Disaster Emergency Fund.

(ii) Adjustments include expenditures, revenues and direct to fund balance net impact.

(jj) Includes adjustments to expenditures not accounted for in the spring survey.

(kk) All adjustments are transfers between reserve accounts, except for $18.1 million transferred out from Tobacco Settlement Permanent Fund, a reserve account to the Tobacco Settlement Program Fund, a non-reserve account.

(ll) Oregon budgets on a biennial basis. The constitution requires the state to be balanced at the end of each biennium.

(mm) Revenue adjustments include: $460.1m reserve from prior fiscal year, $7.4m lapsing from agencies, $1.3m from various restricted accounts, $1.4m Industrial Assistance Fund reserve from previous fiscal year, $3.0m Tourism Marketing Performance Fund, $0.4m transfer from Justice Court Technology Fund, ($22.1)m transfer to Disaster Recovery Fund, ($45.4)m transfer to Rainy Day Fund, ($1.5) m reserved for the Industrial Assistance Fund for the following fiscal year, and $(787.2)m reserved for the following fiscal year. Included with General Fund is Education Fund (income tax revenue) which in Utah is restricted by the Utah State Constitution for the sole use of public and higher education.

(nn) ($218.1) million is a net of transfers between other accounts and the General Fund, and other miscellaneous adjustments.

(oo) WY budgets on a biennial basis. To arrive at annual figures certain assumptions and estimates were required.

Table 7.2
FISCAL 2008 STATE GENERAL FUND, PRELIMINARY ACTUAL, BY REGION
(In millions of dollars)

State	Beginning balance	Revenues	Adjustments	Resources	Expenditures	Adjustments	Ending balance	Budget stabilization fund
U.S. totals	$44,153	$676,777	. . .	$728,901	$689,478	. . .	$28,245	$32,860
Eastern Region								
Connecticut (a)	0	16,403	0	16,403	16,319	0	83	1,382
Delaware*	591	3,357	0	3,948	3,422	0	526	183
Maine (b)	36	3,041	54	3,131	3,129	0	1	130
Massachusetts (c)	566	31,524	0	32,090	31,273	0	817	2,247
New Hampshire	62	1,484	0	1,546	1,528	0	17	89
New Jersey* (d)	2,586	32,019	0	34,605	32,822	685	1,098	698
New York* (e)	3,045	53,094	0	56,139	53,385	0	2,754	1,206
Pennsylvania (f)	531	26,878	142	27,551	27,182	-214	583	742
Rhode Island (g)	4	3,428	-35	3,397	3,395	0	2	103
Vermont (h)	0	1,200	31	1,230	1,201	30	0	58
Regional totals	7,421	172,428	. . .	180,040	173,656	. . .	5,881	6,838
Midwestern Region								
Illinois* (i)	642	27,759	1,900	30,301	26,958	3,202	141	276
Indiana (j)	941	13,051	152	14,145	12,730	364	1,050	363
Iowa (k)	0	6,084	0	6,084	5,888	148	48	592
Kansas	935	5,736	0	6,671	6,139	0	532	0
Michigan (l)	259	8,121	1,749	10,129	9,989	0	140	2
Minnesota* (m)	2,245	16,282	0	18,527	17,210	0	1,317	1,003
Nebraska (n)	591	3,501	-260	3,832	3,248	0	584	546
North Dakota	296	1,361	0	1,657	1,204	0	453	200
Ohio	808	26,659	0	27,285	26,477	0	808	1,012
South Dakota (o)	0	1,444	32	1,177	1,176	0	0	107
Wisconsin (p)	66	13,043	568	13,678	13,526	21	131	0
Regional totals	6,783	123,041	. . .	133,486	124,545	. . .	5,204	4,101
Southern Region								
Alabama (q)	515	7,803	476	8,793	8,595	16	182	248
Arkansas	0	4,353	0	4,353	4,353	0	0	0
Florida	3,434	24,759	0	28,193	27,866	0	326	1,345
Georgia* (r)	2,786	19,790	141	21,717	20,500	0	2,217	949
Kentucky (s)	579	8,779	457	9,816	9,450	280	86	215
Louisiana (t)	1,015	10,181	130	11,327	9,633	828	866	776
Maryland (u)	285	13,546	1,096	14,962	14,439	0	487	685
Mississippi (v)	226	4,933	0	5,159	5,083	0	76	364
Missouri (w)	752	8,157	0	8,909	8,074	0	835	279
North Carolina (x)	1,221	19,824	145	21,190	20,376	215	599	787
Oklahoma (y)	196	6,575	-35	6,737	6,447	0	290	597
South Carolina*	1,081	6,392	0	7,473	7,149	0	324	95
Tennessee (z)	1,007	10,826	164	11,997	11,361	299	338	750
Texas (aa)	6,987	38,148	61	45,197	41,347	1,052	2,797	1,222
Virginia	326	17,250	0	17,576	17,263	0	313	1,015
West Virginia (bb)	432	3,928	0	4,361	3,757	53	550	581
Regional totals	20,842	205,244	. . .	227,760	215,693	. . .	10,286	9,908
Western Region								
Alaska (cc)	0	9,454	270	9,723	5,463	4,261	0	6,128
Arizona (dd)	390	8,790	859	10,038	10,037	0	1	147
California (ee)	3,900	103,027	249	107,176	103,333	-155	3,998	3,113
Colorado* (ff)	267	7,743	-244	7,766	7,441	0	325	284
Hawaii	493	5,245	0	5,738	5,407	0	331	74
Idaho (gg)	255	2,862	-126	2,991	2,814	0	177	141
Montana (hh)	550	1,956	0	2,506	2,068	-1	438	0
Nevada	138	3,605	0	3,743	3,434	0	309	73
New Mexico* (ii)	651	6,092	72	6,814	6,007	94	713	713
Oregon (jj)	1,437	5,868	-319	6,986	7,223	0	-237	330
Utah (kk)	242	5,294	408	5,943	5,943	0	0	414
Washington (ll)	781	14,610	18	15,408	14,601	0	807	303
Wyoming (mm)	5	1,818	0	1,823	1,813	0	10	296
Regional totals	9,109	176,364	. . .	186,655	178,584	. . .	6,872	12,016
Regional totals without California	5,209	73,337	. . .	79,479	75,251	. . .	2,874	8,903

See footnotes at end of table.

FISCAL 2008 STATE GENERAL FUND, PRELIMINARY ACTUAL, BY REGION — Continued
(In millions of dollars)

Source: National Association of State Budget Officers, *The Fiscal Survey of the States* (December 2008).

Note: For all states unless otherwise noted, transfers into budget stabilization funds are counted as expenditures and transfers from budget stabilization funds are counted as revenue.

Key:

* In these states, the ending balance includes the balance in the budget stabilization fund.

NA — Indicates data are not available.

. . . — Not applicable

(a) The fiscal year 2008 surplus of $83.4 million was transferred for use in fiscal year 2009.

(b) Revenue and Expenditure adjustments reflect legislatively authorized transfers.

(c) Includes budgeted fund balances.

(d) Includes General Fund and Property Tax Relief Fund—Transfers to Other Funds. In keeping with past practice, and to ensure consistency in survey results over time, the figures in this table exclude New Jersey's Casino Revenue Fund, Casino Control Fund and Gubernatorial Elections Fund.

(e) The ending balance includes $1.2 billion in rainy day reserve funds, $1.1 billion reserved for labor settlements and other risks, $340 million in a community projects fund, $122 million reserved for debt reduction and $21 million in a reserve for litigation risks.

(f) Revenue adjustment reflects $142.1 million in prior year lapses. Expenditure adjustment reflects current year lapses of $213.9 million. The year-end transfer to the Rainy Day Fund (25 percent of the ending balance) was suspended for FY 2008.

(g) Opening balance includes a free surplus of $0 and re-appropriations of $3.6 million from the prior year. Adjustments to revenues represent (net) transfers to the Budget Stabilization (Rainy Day) Fund, including a transfer-in of $68.6 million and an appropriation to be requested of $33.6 million out of the fund. Note that for FY 2008, the state's preliminary closing report shows a deficit of $33.6 million—it is assumed that the General Assembly will approve an appropriation from the Budget Stabilization Fund to accommodate this shortfall.

(h) Revenue adjustments include $16.6 million in direct appropriations and transfers-in, a $3.2 million increase in the property transfer tax revenue estimate, and $10.9 million from the General Fund Surplus Reserve. Expenditure adjustments include -$4.7 million to the Education Fund, a $0.8 million reserved, bond issuance premium, a $0.3 million refund in federal funds from Medicare Part D, $3.5 million to the Catamount Fund, $0.5 million to the Internal Service Funds, $7.5 million to miscellaneous other funds, $2.6 million to the Budget Stabilization Reserve, and $19.0 million to the General Fund Surplus Reserve.

(i) Revenue adjustments include $1,900.0 million in transfers to General Funds. Expenditure adjustments include $3,202.0 million in transfers out, $467.0 million for Pension Obligation Bond Debt Service and $11.0 million in interest for Short-term Borrowing.

(j) Revenue Adjustments: Property Tax Reform (HEA 1001-2008) Revenues Expenditure Adjustments: Local Option Income Tax Distributions, Reversal of Payment Delay, PTRF Adjust for Abstracts, Property Tax Reform (HEA 1001-2008) Appropriations.

(k) Expenditure adjustments include $99.8 million appropriated from the ending balance of the general fund to the Property Tax Credit fund to pay for property tax credits in FY09. $48.3 million of the ending balance is credited to the Senior Living Trust Fund.

(l) FY 2008 revenue adjustments include the impact of federal and state law changes ($1,043.2 million, including $722.4 from income tax rate increase and $274.0 million from Michigan Business Tax surcharge); revenue sharing law changes ($577.5 million); property sale proceeds ($22.9 million); deposits from state restricted revenues ($87.1 million); and pending revenue options ($18.0 million).

(m) Ending balance includes budget reserve of $653 million, Cash Flow Account of $350 million.

(n) Revenue adjustments are transfers between the General Fund and other funds. Per Nebraska law, includes a transfer of $191.4 million to the Cash Reserve Fund (Rainy Day Fund) of the amount the prior year's net General Fund receipts exceeded the official forecast. The Revenue adjustment also includes a $105 million transfer from the General Fund to the Property Tax Credit Cash Fund.

(o) Adjustments in Revenues: $6.5 million was from one-time receipts, $25.7 million was transferred from the Property Tax Reduction Fund to cover the budget shortfall, and $0.2 million was obligated cash carried forward from FY2007 Adjustments in Expenditures: $0.2 million was transferred to the Budget Reserve Fund from the prior year's obligated cash, and $0.2 million was obligated cash to the Budget Reserve Fund.

(p) Revenue adjustments include departmental revenue ($307.5 m), Indian gaming ($17.9), and transfer to general fund ($242.9). Expenditure adjustment include designation for continuing balances ($27.4) and beginning unreserved designated balance (-$6.8).

(q) Revenue adjustments include release of prior year Debt Service Reserve, Public School and College Authority repayment for Enterprise School, and a transfer from the Proration Prevention Account. Expenditure adjustments include supplemental appropriations and re-appropriation of reverted general funds.

(r) Rainy day balance excludes $187.2 million which will be included in the governor's amended revenue estimate for mid-year adjustment in education funding as provided by statute (up to 1 percent of prior year's revenue). Adjustments to revenue are due to return of agency surplus. Final totals include funds from Lottery and Tobacco sales.

(s) Revenue includes $115.1 million in Tobacco Settlement funds. Adjustment for Revenues includes $288.6 million that represents appropriation balances carried over from the prior fiscal year, and $168.4 million from fund transfers into the General Fund. Adjustment to Expenditures represents appropriation balances forwarded to the next fiscal year.

(t) Revenues—Act 208 of 2007 Transfers $3M from Incentive Fund and $9.9M from Higher Education Initatives Fund; FY 2006-2007 carry-forward of mid-year budget adjustments into FY 2007-2008 of $114.7M; Carry-forward of Interim Emergency Board (IEB) prior years appropriations $1.5M; "Re-Appropriation" of capital outlay per Act 28 of 2007 from various prior years $1.2M. Expenses—FY 2007-2008 IEB carry-forward balances $3.3M; FY 2007-2008 carry-forward of mid-year budget adjustments $91.2M; Capital Outlay carry-forward $733.7M.

(u) Adjustments reflect a $11.7 million reimbursement from the reserve for Heritage Tax Credits, $6 million reimbursement from the reserve for Biotechnology Tax Credits, and transfers of $1,078 million from the State Reserve Fund. FY 2008 expenditures are final.

(v) Prior Year's Ending Balance adjusted to 50 percent of actual ending balance less 750,000 to aid municipalities; remaining 50 percent transferred to the Rainy Day Fund. $82.5 million transferred to the Rainy Day Fund from the Hurricane Relief Fund.

(w) Revenues are net of refunds. Refunds for FY 2008 totaled $2,258.4 million. Revenues include $153.1 million transferred to the General Revenue Fund.

(x) $145 million Repair and Renovation Reserve increase to appropriation and $145 million R&R expenditure plus $69.8 increase to R&R for FY 2008-09.

(y) Revenue adjustments include the Rainy Day Fund deposit of $25m and the Cash flow difference of $9.6m. No spillover money was appropriated.

(z) Revenue adjustments include $106 million transfer from debt service fund unexpended appropriations, $265.5 million transfer from statutory and other reserves, -$207.1 million transfer to Rainy Day Fund. Expenditure adjustments include $264.1 million transfer to capital outlay projects fund, $15.1 million transfer to Highway Fund, and $19.7 million for dedicated revenue appropriations.

(aa) FY 2008 information is from the Comptroller's Revenue Estimate. The revenue adjustment is the increase in dedicated account balances. The expenditure adjustment is a transfer to the Rainy Day Fund.

(bb) Fiscal Year 2008 beginning balance includes $287.1 million in re-appropriations, un-appropriated Surplus Balance of $106.8 million, and FY 2007 13th month expenditures of $38.2 million. Expenditures include regular, surplus and re-appropriated and $37.9 million of 31 day prior year expenditures. Revenue adjustments are from prior year re-deposited. Expenditure adjustment represents the amount transferred to the Rainy Day Fund.

(cc) Revenue adjustments include: 250.0 Oil & Gas Tax Credits and 19.9 Re-appropriations and Carry Forward. Expenditure Adjustments are deposits to the Constitutional Budget Reserve, the Statutory Budget Reserve, the Community Revenue Sharing Fund, the Marine Highway Stabilization Fund and a Public Education Fund Adjustment.

(dd) Adjustments to FY08 revenues include agency fund transfers, transfer from the rainy day fund, and reclassification of negative administrative adjustments as revenues.

(ee) The revenue and expenditure adjustments are adjustments to the FY 2007 beginning fund balance.

(ff) Revenue adjustments include General Fund (GF) diversions (which are not counted as expenditures) to fund the state's transportation needs. The difference between the rainy day fund balance and the ending GF balance is allocated to capital construction and transportation purposes in the following fiscal year. Pursuant to NASBO's definitions, Colorado's GF statutory reserve equal to 4.0 percent of appropriations represents a rainy day fund.

(gg) Revenue adjustments include the following: $209,000 in from Agric. Crop Residue Burning; $19 million to Budget Stabilization fund; $351,500 Public School Perm. Endowment; $1.5 million to Environmental Quality; $638,000 Aquifer Study; $690,000 Biofuel infrastructure; $60 million Economic Recovery Fund; $10 million Opportunity Scholarship Fund; $2 million Disaster Emergency Account; $10 million Water Board Revolving Fund.

(hh) The high level of fund balance is considered a type of rainy day fund. It will be used to cushion shortfalls in revenue or unexpected expenditures such as forest fires. $386 million of the FY 2008 expenditures were one time expenditures and will not continue.

(ii) All adjustments are transfers between reserve accounts, except for $22.4 million transferred out from Tobacco Settlement Permanent Fund, a reserve account

FISCAL 2008 STATE GENERAL FUND, PRELIMINARY ACTUAL, BY REGION — Continued
(In millions of dollars)

to the Tobacco Settlement Program Fund, a non-reserve account.

(jj) Revenues are after $1.1 billion "kicker" refunds were returned to taxpayers. Revenue adjustment is the transfer of revenues to the new Rainy Day Fund.

(kk) Revenue adjustments include $787.3m reserve from prior fiscal year, $1.5m Industrial Assistance Fund reserve from previous fiscal year, $6.0m Tourism Marketing Performance Fund, ($4.4)m set-aside for the Economic Development Tax Incentive Fund (EDTIF), ($100.5)m transfer to Rainy Day Fund, ($5.9)m for legislation impacting state revenue, and $(276.5)m reserved for the following fiscal year. Included with General Fund is Education Fund (income tax revenue) which in Utah is restricted by the Utah State Constitution for the sole use of public and higher education.

(ll) $17.9 million is a net of transfers between other accounts and the General Fund.

(mm) WY budgets on a biennial basis. To arrive at annual figures certain assumptions and estimates were required.

Table 7.3
FISCAL 2009 STATE GENERAL FUND, APPROPRIATED, BY REGION
(In millions of dollars)

State	*Beginning balance*	*Revenues*	*Adjustments*	*Resources*	*Expenditures*	*Adjustments*	*Ending balance*	*Budget stabilization fund*
U.S. totals	$26,577	$684,005	. . .	$718,550	$689,098	. . .	$21,283	$34,176
Eastern Region								
Connecticut	0	17,073	0	17,073	17,083	0	-10	1,382
Delaware* (a)	526	3,451	0	3,977	3,553	0	424	187
Maine (b)	1	3,096	13	3,110	3,092	16	1	130
Massachusetts* (c)	248	32,339	0	32,587	32,141	0	446	1,942
New Hampshire	17	1,544	0	1,561	1,566	0	5	89
New Jersey* (d)	1,098	31,878	0	32,976	32,373	3	600	483
New York* (e)	2,754	55,638	0	58,392	56,361	0	2,031	1,206
Pennsylvania (f)	583	27,689	0	28,272	28,264	2	6	762
Rhode Island (g)	2	3,347	-74	3,275	3,312	0	-37	114
Vermont (h)	0	1,155	62	1,217	1,211	6	0	60
Regional totals	5,229	177,210	. . .	182,440	178,956	. . .	3,466	6,355
Midwestern Region								
Illinois* (i)	141	27,892	2,599	30,592	26,714	3,667	141	276
Indiana (j)	1,050	13,245	1,128	15,423	13,220	1,232	970	376
Iowa (k)	0	6,189	14	6,203	6,118	37	48	620
Kansas	532	5,993	0	6,525	6,404	0	121	0
Michigan (l)	140	8,102	1,442	9,684	9,682	0	2	2
Minnesota* (m)	1,317	16,575	0	17,892	17,383	0	509	503
Nebraska (n)	584	3,532	-182	3,943	3,482	248	204	574
North Dakota (o)	453	1,260	0	1,713	1,258	0	455	200
Ohio* (p)	808	27,218	0	28,026	27,889	0	137	948
South Dakota (q)	0	1,208	12	1,220	1,220	0	0	95
Wisconsin (r)	130	13,287	561	13,978	14,118	-297	156	0
Regional totals	5,155	124,401	. . .	135,379	127,488	. . .	2,743	3,594
Southern Region								
Alabama (s)	182	7,887	331	8,399	8,385	0	14	46
Arkansas	0	4,411	0	4,411	4,411	0	0	0
Florida	326	23,981	0	24,307	25,775	0	-1,468	1,354
Georgia* (t)	2,217	21,411	0	23,628	21,411	0	2,217	949
Kentucky (u)	63	9,006	535	9,604	9,331	234	40	215
Louisiana (v)	0	9,703	0	9,703	9,700	0	2	776
Maryland (w)	487	14,089	177	14,753	14,677	0	74	737
Mississippi (x)	40	5,110	0	5,150	5,150	0	0	364
Missouri (y)	835	8,384	0	9,219	8,859	0	360	281
North Carolina (z)	599	20,850	70	21,519	21,356	70	93	787
Oklahoma	290	6,563	0	6,853	6,266	0	587	NA
South Carolina*	324	6,749	0	7,073	6,832	0	242	108
Tennessee (aa)	338	11,080	0	11,418	11,349	69	0	750
Texas	2,797	38,045	61	40,903	30,966	957	8,980	3,032
Virginia	313	16,722	0	17,035	16,970	0	65	1,078
West Virginia (bb)	550	3,903	0	4,453	4,414	18	21	600
Regional totals	9,361	207,894	. . .	218,428	205,852	. . .	11,227	11,077
Western Region								
Alaska (cc)	0	7,123	400	7,523	5,980	1,544	0	8,981
Arizona (dd)	1	9,334	645	9,980	9,906	0	74	130
California	3,998	101,991	0	105,990	103,401	0	2,589	1,703
Colorado* (ee)	284	8,076	-228	8,131	7,830	0	302	302
Hawaii	331	5,230	0	5,561	5,500	0	61	63
Idaho (ff)	177	2,942	-108	3,011	2,959	0	52	141
Montana (gg)	438	1,875	0	2,314	1,974	0	340	0
Nevada (hh)	309	3,391	0	3,700	3,815	0	-115	1
New Mexico* (ii)	713	5,881	268	6,862	6,164	292	407	407
Oregon (jj)	-237	6,987	0	6,750	6,726	0	24	341
Utah (kk)	0	5,314	285	5,599	5,574	0	25	414
Washington (ll)	807	14,520	-3	15,324	15,237	0	87	442
Wyoming (mm)	10	1,738	0	1,748	1,748	0	0	229
Regional totals	6,831	174,402	. . .	182,223	176,814	. . .	3,846	13,154
Regional totals without California	2,833	72,411	. . .	76,233	73,413	. . .	1,257	11,451

See footnotes at end of table.

FISCAL 2009 STATE GENERAL FUND, APPROPRIATED, BY REGION — Continued
(In millions of dollars)

Source: National Association of State Budget Officers, *The Fiscal Survey of the States* (December 2008).

Note: For all states, unless otherwise noted, transfers into budget stabilization funds are counted as expenditures, and transfers from budget stabilization funds are counted as revenues.

Key:

* In these states, the ending balance includes the balance in the budget stabilization fund.

NA — Indicates data are not available.

. . . — Not applicable.

(a) The FY 2009 revenue figures reported reflect June 2008 estimates of the Delaware Economic and Financial Advisory Council (DEFAC) as adjusted by legislative changes. As per the September 15 DEFAC meeting, the FY 2009 revenue estimate was reduced by $38.9 million. An interim meeting of the DEFAC revenue subcommittee held November 17 further reduced the FY 2009 revenue estimate by an additional $151.7 million, however this estimate has not been adopted by the full council. The full council will meet again to provide official updates to the forecast on December 15, 2008.

(b) Revenue & Expenditure adjustments reflect legislatively authorized transfers.

(c) Includes Budgeted fund balances - it is important to note that the Secretary for Administration and Finance more than likely will revise, on or about October 15th, the consensus tax revenue figure that the Commonwealth's FY09 budget was based upon. The Governor would then be able to enact emergency spending reductions. This obviously impacts both our revenue and spending projections included in this survey, which reflect the current consensus tax revenue number and the signed GAA.

(d) Includes General Fund and Property Tax Relief Fund—Transfers to Other Funds. In keeping with past practice, and to ensure consistency in survey results over time, the figures in this table exclude New Jersey's Casino Revenue Fund, Casino Control Fund and Gubernatorial Elections Fund.

(e) The ending balance includes $1.2 billion in rainy day reserve funds, $445 million reserved for labor settlements and other risks, $237 million in a community projects fund, $122 million reserved for debt reduction and $21 million in a reserve for litigation risks.

(f) Expenditure adjustment reflects a transfer of $1.9 million (25 percent of the ending balance) to the Rainy Day Fund.

(g) Opening balance includes a free surplus of $0 and re-appropriations of $1.7 million from the prior year. Total expenditures include the presumed appropriation of $33.6 million to restore the Budget Stabilization Fund.

(h) Revenue adjustments include, $2.6 million in revenue changes, $1.2 million funding change—General Fund to Special Fund, $ 6.0 million in streamline sales tax and other tax credits, -$0.3 million in Vermont Economic Development Authority (VEDA) debt forgiveness, $29.3 million in direct applications and transfers in, -$0.3 in other bills, a $4.6 million increase in property transfer tax revenue estimate, and $18.8 from the General Fund Surplus Reserve. Expenditure adjustments include -â$1.0 million from the Human Services Caseload Reserve, -$0.7 million from tobacco settlement funds, $0.7 million to the education Fund, $1.8 million to the Catamount Fund, $0.4 million to Internal Service Funds, $2.4 million to miscellaneous other funds, $1.8 million to the Budget Stabilization Reserve, and $0.6 million to the General Fund Surplus Reserve.

(i) Revenue adjustments include $1,984.0 million in transfers to General Funds and $575 million from the sale of the State's 10th Riverboat license. Expenditure adjustments include $3,667 million in transfers out and $470.0 million for Pension Obligation Bond Debt Service.

(j) Revenue adjustments: Property Tax Reform (HEA 1001-2008) Revenues Expenditure Adjustments: Reversal of Payment Delay, Property Tax Replacement Fund (PTRF) Adjust for Abstracts, Property Tax Reform (HEA 1001-2008) Appropriations.

(k) Revenue adjustments include improved collection of court fines and other small legislative adjustments. Expenditure adjustments include $36.8 million of the ending balance is credited to the Senior Living Trust Fund.

(l) FY 2009 revenue adjustments include the impact of federal and state law changes ($782.5 million); revenue sharing law changes ($550.6 million); property sale proceeds ($6.5 million); deposits from state restricted revenues ($96.0 million); and pending revenue option ($6.0 million).

(m) Ending balance includes budget reserve of $153 million and cash flow account of $350 million.

(n) Revenue adjustments are transfers between the General Fund and other funds. Per Nebraska law, includes a transfer of $117 million to the Cash Reserve Fund (Rainy Day Fund) of the amount the prior year's net General Fund receipts exceeded the official forecast. The Revenue adjustment also includes a $115 million transfer from the General Fund to the Property Tax Credit Cash Fund. Expenditure adjustments are re-appropriations ($243.2 million) of the unexpended balance of appropriations from the first fiscal year of the biennium and a small amount ($5 million) reserved for supplemental/deficit appropriations.

(o) Adjustments—Current law requires that the end of the biennium balance shall be transferred to the budget stabilization fund until the fund reaches 10 percent of current appropriations. The current balance is $200.0 million. Appropriations won't be known until after the 2009 legislative session. A transfer of $+100-115 million is possible.

(p) In FY 2009, the General Revenue Fund is slated to receive $63.3 million from the Budget Stabilization Fund in order to support additional Medicaid costs.

(q) Adjustments in Revenues: $11.9 million is the estimated that will be needed from Property Tax Reserves to balance the budget in FY 2009.

(r) Revenue adjustments include Indian Gaming ($46.3 m) and departmental revenue ($514.2); Expenditure adjustments include departmental lapses (-$429.3) and Compensation Reserves (132.6).

(s) Revenue adjustments include proposed transfer from the Business Privilege Tax Escrow account, Corporate Add Back Statute (Act-2008-543), Middle Class Tax Relief (Act 2008-543), and Small Business Health Insurance (Act 2008-559), and estimated transfer from Educational Trust Fund (ETF) Rainy Day Account. FY 2009 revenues are preliminary unofficial revised estimates.

(t) Final totals include funds from Lottery and Tobacco sales.

(u) Revenue includes $119.7 million in Tobacco Settlement funds. Adjustment for Revenues includes $233.5 million that represents appropriation balances carried over from the prior fiscal year, and $301.7 million from fund transfers into the General Fund. Adjustment to Expenditures represents appropriation balances forwarded to the next fiscal year.

(v) Revenue Estimating Conference of 05/09/2008; The final state revenue receipts used in the calculation of the Budget Stabilization Fund maximum balance for FY 2008/09 will not be available until after publication of the State's Comprehensive Annual Financial Report (CAFR) report for the Fiscal Year Ended June 30, 2008. This report will not be available until December 2008. Therefore, the fund balance is held fixed at the FY 2007/08 level.

(w) Adjustments reflect a $18.1 million reimbursement from the reserve for Heritage Tax Credits, $6 million reimbursement from the reserve for Biotechnology Tax Credits, a transfer of $125 million from the State Reserve Fund, and a transfer of $25 million from the Central Collection Unit fund balance. Expenditures reflect reduction totaling $297.2 million approved in October 2008.

(x) Prior Year's Ending Balance adjusted to provide $35.8 million transfer to the Rainy Day Fund and $750,000 to aid municipalities.

(y) Revenues are net of refunds. Estimated refunds for FY 2009 total $1,356 million. Estimated revenues include $154.1 million transferred to the General Revenue Fund.

(z) $69.8 increase to FY 2008-09 Repair & Renovation Reserve appropriation from year-end balance and anticipated expenditure of this R&R reserve.

(aa) Expenditure adjustments include $52.2 million transfer to capital outlay projects and $16.7 million transfer to dedicated revenue appropriations.

(bb) Fiscal Year 2009 Beginning balance includes $409.6 million in re-appropriations, un-appropriated surplus balance of $35.3 million, and FY 2008 13th month expenditures of $105.5 million. Expenditures include regular, surplus and re-appropriated and $105.5 million of 31 day prior year expenditures. Total expenditures for fiscal year 2009 assume all appropriations will be expended (no re-appropriations to carry forward). However, historically amounts will remain and be re-appropriated to the next fiscal year. Ending Balance is the amount that is available for appropriation (From FY 09 revenue estimate and from surplus {previous year} general revenue).

(cc) Revenue Adjustments include: 400.0 Oil & Gas Tax Credits. Expenditure Adjustments are deposits a $1,348.3 deposit to the Constitutional Budget Reserve, a $175.3 deposit to the Public Education Fund and a $20.0 short term loan.

(dd) Adjustments to the FY 2009 revenues include agency fund transfers, rainy day fund transfer, and proceeds from FY08 lease-purchase financing.

(ee) Revenue adjustments include General Fund (GF) diversion (which are not counted as expenditures) to fund the State's transportation needs. Pursuant to NASBO's definitions, Colorado's GF statutory reserve equal to 4.0 percent of appropriations represents a rainy day fund.

(ff) Revenue adjustments include the following: $5.6 million to the Permanent Building Fund; $20 million Aquifer study; $1 million Community Health Center Grant; $10 million Opportunity Scholarship Fund; $1.8 million Water Resource Board Revolving Fund; and other misc. adjustments due to legislation.

(gg) $163 million of the FY 2009 appropriations are one time and will not continue.

(hh) Negative ending balance will require further budget reductions.

(ii) All adjustments are transfers between reserve accounts, except for $23.6 million transferred out from Tobacco Settlement Permanent Fund, a reserve account to the Tobacco Settlement Program Fund, a nonreserve account.

(jj) Oregon budgets on a biennial basis. The constitution requires the state to be balanced at the end of each biennium.

(kk) Revenue adjustments include $276.5m held in reserve from prior fiscal year, $3.0m transfer from non-lapsing balances, $6.6m for legislation impacting state revenue, ($15.5)m set-aside for Economic Development Tax Incentive Fund, $9.0m Tourism Marketing Performance Fund, and $5.2 from various restricted accounts. Included with General Fund is Education Fund (income tax revenue) which in Utah is restricted by the Utah State Constitution for the sole use of public and higher education.

(ll) 2.6 million is a net of transfers between other accounts and the General Fund, including the transfer to the Rainy Day Fund.

(mm) Budgets on a biennial basis. To arrive at annual figures certain assumptions and estimates were required.

Table 7.4
FISCAL 2008 STATE TAX COLLECTIONS COMPARED WITH PROJECTIONS USED IN ADOPTING FISCAL 2008 BUDGETS, BY REGION
(In millions of dollars)

	Sales tax		*Personal income tax*		*Corporate income tax*		
State	*Original estimate*	*Current estimate*	*Original estimate*	*Current estimate*	*Original estimate*	*Current estimate*	*Revenue collection (a)*
U.S. totals (b)	$218,166	$214,528	$270,699	$276,413	$51,434	$50,152	. . .
Eastern Region							
Connecticut	3,599	3,582	7,194	7,513	870	734	H
Delaware	NA	NA	1,055	1,007	156	179	L
Maine	1,029	1,035	1,400	1,444	182	185	H
Massachusetts	4,215	4,087	11,605	12,485	1,519	1,512	H
New Hampshire	NA	NA	NA	NA	301	317	L
New Jersey	8,900	8,944	12,379	12,600	2,753	3,066	T
New York	10,495	10,592	36,820	36,564	6,679	6,018	L
Pennsylvania	8,529	8,497	10,750	10,908	2,578	2,418	H
Rhode Island	853	845	1,069	1,074	157	151	L
Vermont	239	226	577	622	55	75	H
Regional totals	37,559	37,808	82,849	84,217	15,250	14,655	. . .
Midwestern Region							
Illinois	7,293	7,215	9,832	10,320	1,904	1,860	H
Indiana	5,578	5,534	4,681	4,838	924	910	H
Iowa	2,023	2,000	3,150	3,360	421	484	H
Kansas	1,984	1,958	2,974	2,897	420	432	L
Michigan (c)	6,661	6,649	7,052	7,174	2,642	2,377	L
Minnesota	4,616	4,577	7,551	7,784	1,141	1,028	H
Nebraska	1,293	1,322	1,630	1,726	241	233	H
North Dakota	492	555	243	307	78	141	H
Ohio	7,681	7,614	9,147	9,115	833	754	L
South Dakota	642	645	NA	NA	NA	NA	L
Wisconsin	4,210	4,268	6,660	6,714	810	838	H
Regional totals	42,483	42,337	52,920	54,235	6,772	9,057	. . .
Southern Region							
Alabama	2,223	2,067	3,110	2,971	647	501	L
Arkansas	2,120	2,111	2,193	2,345	298	318	H
Florida	20,367	18,429	NA	NA	2,704	2,217	L
Georgia	6,031	5,798	9,288	8,830	1,007	942	L
Kentucky	2,890	2,878	3,235	3,483	868	435	L
Louisiana	3,143	3,156	2,569	3,169	521	706	H
Maryland	3,623	3,675	7,041	6,940	598	552	L
Mississippi	2,044	1,947	1,497	1,542	475	501	L
Missouri	2,002	1,931	5,145	5,210	422	459	H
North Carolina	5,049	4,982	10,895	10,902	1,095	1,112	H
Oklahoma	1,599	1,612	2,162	2,239	452	279	H
South Carolina	2,600	2,463	2,927	2,864	285	269	L
Tennessee (d)	7,093	6,857	263	292	1,821	1,650	L
Texas	20,355	21,512	NA	NA	NA	NA	H
Virginia	3,315	3,096	10,189	10,171	780	699	T
West Virginia	1,073	1,037	1,504	1,614	374	400	H
Regional totals	85,528	83,551	62,108	62,572	12,347	11,040	. . .
Western Region							
Alaska	NA	NA	NA	NA	565	758	H
Arizona	4,526	4,354	3,545	3,407	867	785	L
California (e)	27,787	26,613	52,243	54,289	10,171	11,690	H
Colorado	2,297	2,318	4,957	4,974	452	508	T
Hawaii	2,701	2,620	1,631	1,545	138	86	L
Idaho	1,197	1,143	1,255	1,430	213	190	H
Montana	15	16	803	867	161	160	H
Nevada	1,065	966	NA	NA	NA	NA	L
New Mexico	2,392	2,306	1,127	1,198	401	404	T
Oregon (f)	NA	NA	4,808	4,973	489	441	T
Utah	1,885	1,795	2,572	2,709	422	382	L
Washington	8,056	8,216	NA	NA	NA	NA	H
Wyoming	405	486	NA	NA	NA	NA	H
Regional totals	52,326	50,833	72,941	75,365	13,879	15,404	. . .
Regional totals without California	24,539	24,220	20,698	21,076	3,408	3,714	

See footnotes at end of table.

FISCAL 2008 STATE TAX COLLECTIONS COMPARED WITH PROJECTIONS USED IN ADOPTING FISCAL 2008 BUDGETS, BY REGION—Continued
(In millions of dollars)

Source: National Association of State Budget Officers, *The Fiscal Survey of the States* (December 2008).

Note: Unless otherwise noted, original estimates reflect the figures used when the fiscal 2008 budget was adopted, and current estimates reflect preliminary actual tax collections.

Key:

H — Revenues higher than estimates.

L — Revenues lower than estimates.

T — Revenues on target.

NA — Indicates data are not available because, in most cases, these states do not have that type of tax.

(a) Refers to whether actual fiscal 2008 collections of Sales, Personal income and Corporate taxes were higher than, lower than, or on target eith original estimates.

(b) Totals include only those sates with data for both original and current estimates for fiscal 2008.

(c) The original fiscal 2008 budget has been modified and is based on the May 2008 consensus estimates and is net of all enacted tax changes. Tax estimates represent total tax collections. Sales tax collections are for the Michigan sales tax only and do not include collections from Michigan use tax. Michigan does not have a Corporate Income tax; estimates are for the Michigan Business Tax that replaced Michigan's Single Business Tax effective December 2007. The final fiscal 2008 revenue figures will be available when the State of Michigan Comprehensive Annual Financial report is published in December 2008.

(d) Corporate Income Tax includes excise tax and franchise tax. Sales tax, personal income tax and corporate excise tax are shared with local governments.

(e) As compared to the forecast in the 2008-09 May Revision. It is too early in our 2008-09 FY to judge revenues.

(f) Fiscal Year 2008 Personal Income Tax is shown after $1.08 billion "kicker" refunds were returned to taxpayers.

Table 7.5
COMPARISON OF TAX COLLECTIONS IN FISCAL 2007, FISCAL 2008, AND ENACTED FISCAL 2009, BY REGION
(In millions of dollars)

State	*Sales tax*			*Personal income tax*			*Corporate income tax*		
	Fiscal 2007	*Fiscal 2008*	*Fiscal 2009*	*Fiscal 2007*	*Fiscal 2008*	*Fiscal 2009*	*Fiscal 2007*	*Fiscal 2008*	*Fiscal 2009*
U.S. totals (a)	$212,920	$214,528	$220,605	$263,834	$276,413	$284,780	$52,516	$50,152	$51,141
Eastern Region									
Connecticut	3,496	3,582	3,748	6,750	7,513	7,676	891	734	792
Delaware	N.A.	N.A.	N.A.	1,008	1,007	1,038	140	179	92
Maine	1,021	1,035	1,062	1,354	1,444	1,398	184	185	197
Massachusetts	4,068	4,087	4,286	11,400	12,485	12,762	1,588	1,512	1,705
New Hampshire	N.A.	N.A.	N.A.	N.A.	N.A.	N.A.	287	317	320
New Jersey	8,610	8,944	9,136	11,727	12,600	12,700	3,208	3,066	2,898
New York	10,050	10,592	10,914	34,580	36,564	38,149	6,468	6,018	6,559
Pennsylvania	8,591	8,497	8,731	10,262	10,908	11,489	2,493	2,418	2,321
Rhode Island	873	845	863	1,065	1,074	1,124	148	151	161
Vermont	223	226	229	581	622	588	73	75	59
Regional totals	36,932	37,808	37,979	78,727	84,217	86,924	15,480	14,655	15,104
Midwestern Region									
Illinois	7,136	7,215	7,332	9,408	10,320	10,432	1,750	1,860	1,937
Indiana	5,379	5,534	5,827	4,616	4,838	4,934	987	910	947
Iowa	1,910	2,000	2,055	3,086	3,360	3,502	425	484	424
Kansas	2,052	1,958	1,994	2,709	2,897	3,071	442	432	325
Michigan (b)	6,552	6,649	6,645	6,442	7,174	7,010	1,816	2,377	2,661
Minnesota	4,506	4,577	4,601	7,231	7,784	7,767	1,171	1,028	969
Nebraska	1,304	1,322	1,359	1,651	1,726	1,750	213	233	215
North Dakota (c)	511	555	649	315	307	308	121	141	112
Ohio	7,425	7,614	7,984	8,885	9,115	9,201	1,077	754	522
South Dakota	603	645	676	N.A.	N.A.	N.A.	N.A.	N.A.	N.A.
Wisconsin	4,159	4,268	4,479	6,574	6,714	7,106	890	838	860
Regional totals	41,537	42,337	36,956	50,918	54,235	55,081	8,892	9,057	8,972
Southern Region									
Alabama	2,087	22,067	2,196	2,938	2,971	3,245	455	501	481
Arkansas	2,188	2,111	2,185	2,169	2,345	2,295	338	318	306
Florida	19,435	18,429	19,093	N.A.	N.A.	N.A.	2,444	2,217	2,223
Georgia	5,916	5,798	6,301	8,821	8,830	9,896	1,019	942	1,023
Kentucky	2,818	2,878	2,978	3,042	3,483	3,473	988	435	513
Louisiana (d)	3,156	3,156	3,189	3,257	3,169	2,873	1,052	706	707
Maryland (e)	3,420	3,675	4,034	6,679	6,940	7,445	590	552	673
Mississippi	1,931	1,947	2,019	1,475	1,542	1,617	485	501	528
Missouri	1,955	1,931	1,937	4,918	5,210	5,448	458	459	471
North Carolina	4,996	4,982	5,374	10,508	10,902	11,386	1,451	1,112	1,192
Oklahoma	1,531	1,612	1,695	2,338	2,239	2,155	435	279	274
South Carolina	2,631	2,463	2,699	2,882	2,864	2,970	262	269	249
Tennessee (f)	6,815	6,857	7,019	248	292	262	1,766	1,650	1,664
Texas	20,183	21,152	20,809	N.A.	N.A.	N.A.	N.A.	N.A.	N.A.
Virginia	3,049	3,096	3,226	9,788	10,171	10,777	880	899	706
West Virginia	1,035	1,037	1,096	1,414	1,614	1,585	368	400	315
Regional totals	83,146	103,191	85,850	60,477	62,572	65,436	12,991	11,240	11,325
Western Region									
Alaska	N.A.	N.A.	N.A.	N.A.	N.A.	N.A.	771	758	810
Arizona	4,458	4,354	4,644	3,736	3,407	3,615	986	785	841
California	27,445	26,613	26,813	51,971	54,289	54,380	11,158	11,690	11,926
Colorado (g)	2,210	2,318	2,416	4,871	4,974	5,167	498	508	505
Hawaii	2,558	2,620	2,698	1,560	1,545	1,633	82	86	93
Idaho	1,077	1,143	1,223	1,400	1,430	1,385	190	190	185
Montana	16	16	16	827	867	851	178	160	167
Nevada	1,000	966	1,140	N.A.	N.A.	N.A.	N.A.	N.A.	N.A.
New Mexico (h)	2,315	2,306	2,460	1,180	1,198	1,174	460	405	451
Oregon (i)	NA	NA	NA	5,597	4,973	6,375	406	441	432
Utah	1,858	1,795	1,821	2,573	2,709	2,769	425	382	330
Washington	7,892	8,216	8,508	N.A.	N.A.	N.A.	N.A.	N.A.	N.A.
Wyoming	479	486	485	N.A.	N.A.	N.A.	N.A.	N.A.	N.A.
Regional totals	51,308	50,833	52,224	73,715	76,847	77,349	15,154	15,505	15,740
Regional totals without California	23,863	24,220	25,411	21,744	22,558	22,969	3,996	3,815	3,814

See footnotes at end of table.

COMPARISON OF TAX COLLECTIONS IN FISCAL 2007, FISCAL 2008, AND ENACTED FISCAL 2009, BY REGION—Continued
(In millions of dollars)

Source: National Association of State Budget Officers, The Fiscal Survey of the States (December 2008).

Note: Unless otherwise noted, fiscal 2007 figures reflect preliminary actual tax collections, 2008 figures reflect preliminary actual tax collections estimates, and fiscal 2009 figures reflect the estimates used in enacted budgets.

Key:

N.A. — Indicates data are not available because, in most cases, these states do not have that type of tax.

(a) Totals include only those states with data for all years.

(b) The fiscal 2009 enacted budget is based on the May 2008 consensus estimates and is net of all enacted tax changes. Tax estimates represent total tax collections. Sales tax collections are for the Michigan sales tax only and do not include collections from Michigan use tax. Michigan does not have a Corporate Income tax; estimates are for the Michigan Business Tax that replaced Michigan's Single Business Tax effective December 2007. Updated fiscal 2009 revenue figures will be released at the next regularly scheduled consensus revenue conference in January 2009.

(c) Based on July 2008 estimates.

(d) Revenue figures are based on 2008 estimates not preliminary actual figures.

(e) Sales tax rate increased from 5 to 6 percent effective January 2008. Personal income tax was restructured and a 6.25 percent bracket on net taxable income over $1 million was established effective tax year 2008. Corporate income tax rate increased from 7 to 8.25 percent effective tax year 2008.

(f) Corporate Income Tax includes excise tax and franchise tax. Sales tax, personal income tax and corporate excise tax are shared with local governments.

(g) Adopted FY 2008 totals come from Legislative Council Staff (LCS) March 2007 forecast. Adopted FY 2009 totals come from LCS March 2008 forecast.

(h) Current FY 2009 revenue estimates compared with those used when the budget was enacted indicate weakness in sales tax and corporate income tax collections and State Treasurer's Office investments. Further shortfalls may be caused by weakness in oil and gas revenues.

(i) Fiscal Year 2008 Personal Income Tax is shown after $1.08 billion "kicker" refunds were returned to taxpayers.

Table 7.6
TOTAL STATE EXPENDITURES: CAPITAL INCLUSIVE, BY REGION
(In millions of dollars)

State	Actual fiscal 2006					Actual fiscal 2007					Estimated fiscal 2008				
	General fund	Federal funds	Other state funds	Bonds	Total	General fund	Federal funds	Other state funds	Bonds	Total	General fund	Federal funds	Other state funds	Bonds	Total
U.S. total	$600,072	$368,668	$344,550	$29,828	$1,343,118	$652,272	$380,699	$366,051	$39,049	$1,438,071	$688,595	$421,624	$403,624	$43,210	$1,555,690
Eastern Regon															
Connecticut (a)	$14,502	$1,189	$3,182	$1,609	$20,482	$15,294	$1,540	$3,876	$2,088	$22,798	$16,340	$1,684	$3,495	$1,926	$23,445
Delaware	3,193	1,029	3,121	222	7,565	3,390	1,174	3,160	224	7,948	3,281	1,169	3,411	210	8,071
Maine	2,824	2,361	1,845	70	7,100	3,024	2,190	1,912	70	7,196	3,110	2,501	1,769	138	7,518
Massachusetts	25,601	2,466	9,430	1,682	39,179	27,586	2,557	9,853	1,780	41,776	27,278	2,388	10,175	1,349	41,190
New Hampshire	1,346	1,415	1,620	90	4,471	1,391	1,409	1,682	58	4,540	1,480	1,420	1,690	75	4,665
New Jersey (b)	28,033	8,420	4,791	1,060	42,304	30,284	8,751	4,991	1,367	45,393	32,638	9,609	5,258	1,584	49,089
New York (c)	46,495	34,618	21,373	1,855	104,341	51,591	35,453	23,476	2,244	112,764	53,385	34,680	26,122	1,869	116,056
Pennsylvania	24,665	17,305	11,262	680	53,912	26,298	17,820	11,906	898	56,992	27,206	18,474	13,446	737	59,863
Rhode Island	3,073	1,981	1,453	133	6,640	3,218	1,864	1,468	182	6,732	3,370	2,040	1,615	274	7,299
Vermont	1,136	1,214	2,553	43	4,946	1,200	1,250	2,661	37	5,148	1,229	1,281	2,662	49	5,221
Regional totals	150,868	71,998	60,630	7,444	290,940	163,276	74,008	64,985	8,948	311,287	169,317	75,246	69,643	8,211	322,417
Midwestern Region															
Illinois	19,470	10,685	12,373	894	43,422	20,846	11,398	13,372	599	46,215	22,165	12,091	13,198	369	47,823
Indiana	11,911	6,683	2,844	192	21,630	12,247	7,107	3,406	37	22,797	12,730	7,818	3,380	161	24,089
Iowa	4,989	3,922	5,680	78	14,669	5,363	3,959	5,678	69	15,069	5,859	4,467	5,953	86	16,635
Kansas	5,139	3,265	2,821	208	11,433	5,608	3,131	2,985	245	11,969	6,112	3,582	3,122	281	13,097
Michigan (d)	9,248	11,499	20,353	447	41,729	9,186	11,853	20,906	625	42,570	9,898	14,040	19,726	175	43,839
Minnesota	16,117	5,628	3,518	494	25,757	16,517	5,965	3,911	709	27,102	17,864	6,394	3,981	695	28,934
Nebraska (e)	2,915	2,303	2,755	0	7,973	3,126	2,366	2,670	0	8,162	3,491	2,804	3,279	0	9,574
North Dakota	966	1,263	1,017	49	3,295	1,012	1,239	1,050	68	3,369	1,202	1,180	1,158	62	3,602
Ohio	24,866	8,616	18,536	1,430	53,448	23,766	9,181	18,807	1,414	53,168	24,623	8,832	20,653	753	54,861
South Dakota	1,006	1,177	776	20	2,979	1,058	1,200	791	10	3,059	1,147	1,367	866	18	3,398
Wisconsin	12,386	7,166	13,930	0	33,482	13,106	7,246	13,904	0	34,256	13,446	7,536	15,109	0	36,091
Regional totals	109,013	62,207	84,603	3,812	259,817	111,835	64,645	87,480	3,776	267,736	118,537	70,111	90,425	2,600	281,943
Southern Region															
Alabama (f)	12,859	10,344	10,240	232	33,675	14,807	10,399	10,935	278	36,419	16,535	12,377	13,948	563	43,423
Arkansas	3,783	4,602	6,859	59	15,303	4,026	4,594	7,439	54	16,113	4,346	6,219	8,413	210	19,188
Florida	25,904	18,750	15,274	1,651	61,579	27,680	13,849	16,282	3,301	66,112	28,063	19,615	19,371	3,311	70,630
Georgia	15,632	9,775	8,191	923	34,521	16,880	13,664	8,831	999	37,374	18,565	10,012	9,071	1,031	38,679
Kentucky	8,333	6,767	5,392	0	20,492	8,781	7,051	6,448	0	22,280	9,444	7,690	8,436	0	25,570
Louisiana	7,750	8,166	6,891	189	22,996	9,327	11,151	8,820	175	29,473	9,713	19,836	10,623	281	40,453
Maryland	12,356	6,214	7,618	680	26,868	14,204	6,368	8,184	713	29,469	14,462	6,673	8,832	841	30,808
Mississippi	3,654	5,828	3,285	245	13,012	3,900	7,424	3,551	427	15,302	4,163	8,598	3,768	198	16,727
Missouri (g)	7,126	5,539	6,641	383	19,689	7,800	5,333	7,034	863	21,030	8,449	6,361	7,725	445	22,980
North Carolina	17,196	10,163	7,237	370	34,966	18,622	11,069	9,136	803	39,670	20,376	17,316	9,353	200	47,245
Oklahoma	5,322	5,336	5,441	277	16,376	5,949	5,690	7,363	325	19,327	7,000	5,593	7,667	628	20,888
South Carolina (h)	5,640	6,521	5,680	119	17,960	6,565	6,680	6,633	111	19,989	7,406	7,345	6,527	0	21,278
Tennessee (i)	9,421	9,137	4,563	257	23,378	10,182	9,211	4,906	461	24,760	12,196	9,637	5,166	296	27,295
Texas	34,866	24,710	10,384	3,410	73,370	39,002	24,485	11,665	5,871	81,023	43,595	26,330	15,994	3,731	89,650
Virginia	14,512	5,960	10,557	893	31,922	16,546	6,244	10,946	1,097	34,833	16,523	6,336	11,606	848	35,313
West Virginia	3,559	3,277	13,354	213	20,403	3,714	3,263	11,342	223	18,542	3,857	3,489	11,297	277	18,920
Regional totals	187,913	141,089	127,607	9,901	466,510	207,985	148,475	139,515	15,701	511,716	224,693	173,427	157,347	12,860	569,047

See footnotes at end of table.

TOTAL STATE EXPENDITURES: CAPITAL INCLUSIVE, BY REGION—Continued
(In millions of dollars)

State	Actual fiscal 2006					Actual fiscal 2007					Estimated fiscal 2008				
	General fund	Federal funds	Other state funds	Bonds	Total	General fund	Federal funds	Other state funds	Bonds	Total	General fund	Federal funds	Other state funds	Bonds	Total
Western Region															
Alaska	3,145	2,856	3,336	304	9,641	4,335	3,002	3,910	299	11,546	5,080	2,862	4,536	26	12,504
Arizona	8,676	8,289	7,933	478	25,376	10,478	9,207	7,220	536	27,441	10,059	10,083	8,107	388	28,637
California	91,592	53,569	22,716	5,304	173,181	101,413	52,935	22,554	6,001	182,903	103,542	58,669	28,719	12,767	203,697
Colorado (j)	6,291	3,571	5,771	0	15,633	6,815	3,776	6,121	0	16,712	7,240	3,987	6,766	0	17,993
Hawaii	4,679	1,539	2,854	403	9,475	5,381	1,645	3,153	474	10,653	5,360	1,947	4,508	844	12,659
Idaho	2,217	1,811	993	9	5,030	2,589	1,804	1,054	9	5,456	2,844	2,138	1,438	9	6,429
Montana (k)	1,558	1,528	1,384	0	4,470	1,657	1,544	1,502	0	4,703	1,972	1,768	1,905	0	5,645
Nevada	2,891	1,745	2,707	230	2,573	2,903	1,861	3,079	354	8,197	3,195	1,503	2,635	409	7,742
New Mexico (l)	5,415	4,098	2,894	490	12,897	5,966	4,226	3,428	844	14,464	6,016	4,558	2,964	673	14,241
Oregon	6,085	4,504	9,424	209	20,222	5,646	4,419	9,983	246	20,294	7,223	5,087	10,888	198	23,396
Utah	4,223	2,401	2,275	5	8,904	4,711	2,369	2,794	111	9,985	5,784	2,471	3,223	1,100	12,578
Washington	13,623	6,097	6,880	1,239	27,839	14,144	6,326	7,723	1,750	29,943	14,601	6,799	8,720	2,225	32,345
Wyoming	1,883	1,366	2,361	0	5,610	3,098	457	1,550	0	5,105	3,132	475	1,350	0	4,957
Regional totals	152,278	93,374	71,528	8,671	320,851	169,136	93,571	74,071	10,624	347,402	176,048	102,347	85,759	18,639	382,823
Regional totals without California	60,686	39,805	48,812	3,367	147,670	67,723	40,636	51,517	4,623	164,449	72,506	43,678	57,040	5,872	179,126

Source: National Association of State Budget Officers, *State Expenditure Report 2007* (December 2008).

Note: State funds refers to general funds plus other state fund spending. State spending from bonds is excluded. Total funds refers to funding from all sources-general fund, federal funds, other state funds and bonds.

Key:

(a) Total expenditures are equivalent to final annual appropriations for FY 2005–06 and FY 2006–07. The FY 2007–08 total expenditures is the appropriation as of the end of the 2008 legislative session (May 2008). This is essentially the most recent estimate of FY 2007–08 expenditures. "Other State Funds" includes Cash Funds and Cash Funds Exempt.

(b) Totals include pension, post retirement medical, debt service on pension bonds, payroll taxes, and health benefits expenditures which total $1.35 billion in State General Fund in fiscal 2007 and $1.48 billion in fiscal 2008 spread across Education, Corrections, Transportation and All Other.

(c) New York budgets most employer contributions to employees' benefits and pensions centrally. The portion of employer contributions to employees' benefits not distributed to an expenditure category has been included in the All Other Expenditures category.

(d) Fiscal 2007 expenditures are artificially low and fiscal 2008 estimated spending is artificially high, distorting year-to-year comparisons. Partial fiscal 2007 payments to higher education institutions are deferred to fiscal 2008, and fiscal 2007 use of restricted revenue is replaced with General Fund revenue in fiscal 2008. Adjusting for these one-time actions results in nominal expenditure changes of 1.8% (Total Funds) and 2.2% (General Fund) from fiscal 2007.

(e) Fiscal 2007–08 amounts shown are equal to appropriations for the year. It is assumed that some level of appropriations will not be expended.

(f) Amounts shown in fiscal years 2005–06 and 2006–07 are based on the actual expenditures during these years, regardless of the year appropriated. Fiscal 2007–08 amounts shown are equal to appropriations for the year, except for bond proceeds, which are estimated. It is assumed that some level of appropriations will not be expended this fiscal year.

(g) Total expenditures exclude refunds. Fiscal 2006 expenditures exclude refunds of $1,186 million, including $1,129 million general revenue. Fiscal 2007 expenditures exclude refunds of $1,258 million, including $1,208 million general revenue. Fiscal 2008 estimates exclude refunds of $1,348 million, including $1,300 million general revenue. Other funds include federal reimbursements received by the Department of Highways and Transportation and the Department of Conservation which have constitutionally created funds. Federal and other funds for FY 2008 represent appropriations available to state agencies. These appropriations establish ceilings on what agencies may spend. The appropriations are often established at higher levels to provide agencies with appropriation authority in the event that revenues are available for various programs. Final expenditures will be lower.

(h) Estimated capital expenditures are no longer collected. Therefore, no capital expenditure data is included for estimated fiscal 2008.

(i) Tennessee collects personal income tax on income from dividends on stocks and interest on certain bonds. Tax revenue estimates do not include federal funds and other departmental revenues. However, federal funds and other departmental revenues are included in the budget as funding sources for the general fund, along with state tax revenues.

(j) Total expenditures are equivalent to final annual appropriations for FY 2005–06 and FY 2006–07. The FY 2007–08 total expenditures is the appropriation as of the end of the 2008 legislative session (May 2008). This is essentially the most recent estimate of FY 2007–08 expenditures. "Other State Funds" includes Cash Funds and Cash Funds Exempt.

(k) Fiscal 2006 expenditures include a one-time-only general fund transfer to state retirement programs of $125 million. Other one-time-only general fund appropriations for fiscal 2006 total approximately $43 million. Fiscal 2007 expenditures include a one-time-only general fund transfer to state retirement programs of $50 million and over $100 million in other one-time-only general fund expenditures. Fiscal 2008 appropriations include over $400 million in one-time-only general fund revenue to address one-time-only expenditures. Other funds shown in fiscal 2008 include increased distributions of revenue to local governments from Oil and Gas taxes as well as one-time-only investments in infrastructure. Principal and interest payments on bonds are included in Total Expenditures. Capital expenditures are not reported separately but are included in Total Expenditures.

(l) Source of fiscal 2006 and fiscal 2007 federal funds numbers is the combined annual financial report (governmental funds and proprietary funds) for the state of New Mexico; excludes community colleges. Source of fiscal 2006 and fiscal 2007 other state funds numbers is the combined annual financial report (governmental and proprietary funds) for the state of New Mexico, less GF revenue, federal revenue and two trust funds; excludes community colleges. Source of the fiscal 2008 other state funds numbers is the state agency budget requests; excludes community colleges. Source of the fiscal 2006 and fiscal 2007 bond funds is the combined annual financial report (governmental and proprietary funds); excludes community colleges. New Mexico is unable to accurately break out capital outlay by revenue source from total expenditures for federal funds and other state funds.

Table 7.7
ELEMENTARY AND SECONDARY EDUCATION EXPENDITURES, BY STATE AND REGION
(In millions of dollars)

	Actual fiscal 2006					Actual fiscal 2007					Estimated fiscal 2008				
State	General fund	Federal funds	Other state funds	Bonds	Total	General fund	Federal funds	Other state funds	Bonds	Total	General fund	Federal funds	Other state funds	Bonds	Total
U.S. totals	$206,613	$44,553	$27,987	$5,335	$284,488	$224,819	$45,235	$30,700	$4,404	$305,208	$237,399	$47,016	$35,995	$4,624	$325,034
Eastern Region															
Connecticut	2,233	414	4	741	3,392	2,312	416	4	672	3,404	2,558	422	4	726	3,710
Delaware	1,016	142	461	207	1,826	1,088	136	486	205	1,915	1,050	140	475	205	1,870
Maine	1,044	182	2	14	1,242	1,170	185	4	0	1,359	1,221	182	2	2	1,407
Massachusetts	4,142	840	479	0	5,461	4,414	828	549	0	5,791	4,675	749	607	0	6,031
New Hampshire	0	159	844	3	1,006	0	166	844	10	1,020	0	161	899	8	1,068
New Jersey	9,438	811	29	0	10,278	10,347	334	17	0	11,198	11,053	799	18	0	11,870
New York	14,992	3,687	2,390	5	21,074	16,282	3,655	2,735	45	22,717	17,946	3,404	2,910	17	24,277
Pennsylvania	8,132	1,904	15	0	10,051	8,804	1,945	18	0	10,767	9,375	2,016	12	0	11,403
Rhode Island	834	180	4	3	1,021	888	174	5	7	1,074	906	189	9	11	1,115
Vermont	22	111	1,127	7	1,267	38	120	1,191	2	1,351	46	117	1,236	10	1,409
Regional totals	41,853	8,430	5,355	980	56,618	45,343	8,459	5,853	941	60,596	48,830	8,179	6,172	979	64,160
Midwestern Region															
Illinois	6,730	1,952	40	193	8,915	7,360	1,873	30	33	9,296	8,190	2,124	29	30	10,373
Indiana	4,558	781	17	0	5,356	4,638	826	18	0	5,482	4,801	870	36	0	5,707
Iowa	2,191	378	0	0	2,569	2,329	385	12	0	2,726	2,521	395	18	0	2,934
Kansas	2,594	381	107	0	3,082	2,830	386	99	0	3,315	3,079	401	97	0	3,557
Michigan (a)	82	1,464	11,279	0	12,825	43	1,483	11,573	0	13,099	45	1,580	11,400	0	13,025
Minnesota	6,871	590	36	7	7,504	6,478	641	40	14	7,173	6,842	650	39	22	7,553
Nebraska	894	250	29	0	1,173	938	263	39	0	1,240	1,000	293	42	0	1,335
North Dakota	322	125	37	0	484	332	127	36	0	495	367	127	38	0	532
Ohio	6,861	1,620	1,060	578	10,119	7,159	1,660	1,909	596	11,324	6,933	1,647	2,251	56	10,887
South Dakota	399	147	3	0	489	341	153	3	0	497	370	152	5	0	527
Wisconsin	5,669	660	68	0	6,397	5,812	671	70	0	6,553	5,974	688	85	0	6,747
Regional totals	37,171	8,348	12,676	778	58,913	38,260	8,468	13,829	643	61,200	40,122	8,927	14,040	108	63,177
Southern Region															
Alabama (b)	3,513	838	155	0	4,506	4,061	797	150	0	5,008	4,502	1,159	159	0	5,820
Arkansas	1,701	464	743	0	2,908	1,771	472	811	0	3,054	1,912	694	1,265	0	3,871
Florida	9,467	2,413	464	0	12,344	9,967	2,491	584	0	13,042	9,957	2,598	641	0	13,196
Georgia	6,602	1,594	0	134	8,330	7,380	1,559	0	442	9,381	7,995	1,500	0	454	9,949
Kentucky	3,595	677	14	0	4,286	3,769	697	19	0	4,485	4,078	727	23	0	4,828
Louisiana	2,600	970	332	0	3,902	2,754	1,216	635	0	4,605	3,371	1,016	516	0	4,903
Maryland	4,129	867	10	0	5,006	4,644	867	10	0	5,521	5,325	945	11	0	6,281
Mississippi	1,837	776	336	7	2,956	1,975	715	355	7	3,052	2,213	647	356	7	3,223
Missouri	2,566	852	1,334	0	4,752	2,793	832	1,334	0	4,959	2,849	956	1,433	0	5,238
North Carolina	6,867	1,143	177	0	8,187	7,377	1,161	191	0	8,729	7,977	1,450	36	0	9,463
Oklahoma	2,175	563	642	0	3,380	2,369	566	691	0	3,626	2,820	600	369	1	3,790
South Carolina	2,046	684	735	0	3,465	2,189	682	765	0	3,636	2,460	690	722	0	3,872
Tennessee	3,136	834	37	0	4,007	3,379	839	61	0	4,279	3,816	906	50	0	4,772
Texas	13,107	4,013	1,772	39	18,931	16,502	4,061	1,613	0	22,176	16,597	4,183	5,332	68	26,180
Virginia	5,030	570	130	0	5,730	5,686	827	121	0	6,634	5,367	826	618	0	6,811
West Virginia	1,684	337	44	72	2,137	1,704	338	40	84	2,166	1,715	346	43	88	2,192
Regional totals	70,055	17,595	6,955	252	97,827	78,320	18,120	7,380	533	101,717	82,954	19,243	11,574	618	114,389

See footnotes at end of table.

ELEMENTARY AND SECONDARY EDUCATION EXPENDITURES, BY STATE AND REGION—Continued
(In millions of dollars)

	Actual fiscal 2006					Actual fiscal 2007					Estimated fiscal 2008				
State	General fund	Federal funds	Other state funds	Bonds	Total	General fund	Federal funds	Other state funds	Bonds	Total	General fund	Federal funds	Other state funds	Bonds	Total
Western Region															
Alaska	879	193	102	0	1,174	990	184	118	0	1,292	1,013	213	116	0	1,342
Arizona (c)	3,380	865	696	0	4,941	4,267	885	515	0	5,667	4,063	892	806	0	5,761
California	34,321	5,819	-133	3,132	43,139	37,026	5,838	-10	2,217	45,017	38,189	6,052	331	2,832	47,404
Colorado	2,719	460	484	0	3,663	2,882	523	456	0	3,861	3,023	497	437	0	3,957
Hawaii	1,844	210	177	137	2,368	2,028	241	199	0	2,468	2,150	269	77	0	2,496
Idaho	1,019	186	50	0	1,255	1,316	195	60	0	1,571	1,392	242	71	0	1,705
Montana	539	145	74	0	758	630	144	56	0	830	688	154	64	0	906
Nevada	824	200	161	0	1,185	988	218	173	0	1,379	1,120	157	94	0	1,371
New Mexico	2,290	415	47	0	2,752	2,380	384	6	0	2,770	2,517	530	19	0	3,066
Oregon	2,525	529	266	0	3,320	2,610	509	361	0	3,480	2,902	516	404	0	3,822
Utah (d)	1,873	372	50	0	2,295	2,111	372	32	0	2,515	2,519	376	63	0	2,958
Washington	5,373	682	566	56	6,677	5,656	672	679	70	7,077	5,905	696	934	87	7,622
Wyoming	8	104	491	0	603	12	73	993	0	1,078	12	73	793	0	878
Regional totals	57,594	10,180	3,031	3,325	74,130	62,896	10,241	3,638	2,287	79,005	65,493	10,667	4,209	2,919	83,288
Regional totals without California	23,273	4,361	3,164	193	30,991	25,870	4,403	3,648	70	33,988	27,304	4,615	3,878	87	35,884

Source: National Association of State Budget Officers, *State Expenditure Report 2007* (December 2008).

Key:

(a) Figures reflect K-12 education, the Michigan Department of Education, adult education and pre-school. Employer contributions to current employees' pensions and health benefits are reported for Department of Education employees but excluded for employees of K-12 schools. General fund revenue support has declined from fiscal 2006 as support from other revenue sources in the State School Aid Fund have grown, especially property tax revenue as taxable values have increased.

(b) Federal funds received directly by local school systems are not reported at the state budget level.

(c) Deferred $272 million of Fiscal 2008 school aid payments to Fiscal 2009.

(d) Included with General Fund is Education Fund (income tax revenue) which in Utah is restricted by the Utah state constitution for the sole use of public and higher education. Public Education in Utah is organized to include the Utah State Office of Rehabilitation (USOR). The numbers reflected in this report for Public Education include USOR. The USOR amounts are as follows: for fiscal 2006, $20 million in General Fund and Education Fund, $33 million in federal funds, and $1 million in other state funds; for fiscal 2007, $21 million in General Fund and Education Fund, $34 million in federal funds, and $1 million in other state funds; for fiscal 2008, $23 million in General Fund and Education Fund, $35 million in federal funds, and $1 million in other state funds.

Table 7.8
MEDICAID EXPENDITURES BY STATE AND REGION
(In millions of dollars)

State	Actual fiscal 2006				Actual fiscal 2007				Estimated fiscal 2008			
	General fund	Federal funds	Other state funds	Total	General fund	Federal funds	Other state funds	Total	General fund	Federal funds	Other state funds	Total
U.S. totals	$104,590	$157,982	$25,069	$287,641	$110,228	$167,930	$26,966	$305,124	$116,572	$177,619	$27,836	$322,027
Eastern Region												
Connecticut (a)	3,141	0	780	3,921	3,152	0	775	3,927	3,519	0	785	4,304
Delaware	459	464	0	923	486	490	0	976	509	550	0	1,059
Maine	677	1,429	166	2,272	660	1,342	169	2,171	666	1,548	187	2,401
Massachusetts	6,889	0	28	6,917	7,551	0	0	7,551	8,248	0	0	8,248
New Hampshire	409	553	153	1,115	440	580	157	1,177	468	615	167	1,250
New Jersey	4,274	4,519	185	8,978	4,380	4,554	129	9,063	4,422	4,341	136	8,899
New York (b)	8,291	18,687	3,231	30,209	9,017	19,867	3,504	32,388	8,568	19,102	3,370	31,040
Pennsylvania	6,111	9,106	2,005	17,222	6,418	9,441	1,634	17,493	6,533	9,915	1,648	18,096
Rhode Island	775	917	0	1,692	796	848	0	1,644	890	930	0	1,820
Vermont	168	529	193	890	197	556	188	941	193	581	178	952
Regional totals	31,194	36,204	6,741	74,139	33,097	37,678	6,556	77,331	34,016	37,582	6,471	78,069
Midwestern Region												
Illinois	3,778	5,479	2,135	11,392	4,235	5,977	2,336	12,548	4,449	6,623	2,886	13,958
Indiana	1,400	3,034	388	4,822	1,461	3,117	415	4,993	1,537	3,335	380	5,252
Iowa	599	1,538	521	2,658	665	1,470	490	2,625	617	1,575	539	2,731
Kansas	763	1,331	72	2,166	835	1,310	86	2,231	889	1,397	93	2,379
Michigan (c)	2,219	4,698	1,480	8,397	2,326	5,227	1,682	9,235	2,373	5,930	1,840	10,143
Minnesota	2,704	2,833	0	5,537	2,965	3,060	0	6,025	3,173	3,296	0	6,469
Nebraska	579	855	18	1,452	619	889	20	1,528	719	977	23	1,719
North Dakota	162	342	5	509	165	326	4	495	191	362	4	557
Ohio	9,991	1,987	1,461	13,439	9,251	2,355	1,150	12,756	10,272	2,480	1,338	14,090
South Dakota	209	431	0	640	219	420	0	639	254	463	0	717
Wisconsin	1,380	2,693	421	4,494	1,788	2,835	147	4,770	1,699	2,932	290	4,921
Regional totals	23,784	25,221	6,501	55,506	24,529	26,986	6,330	57,845	26,173	29,370	7,393	62,936
Southern Region												
Alabama (d)	506	2,999	726	4,231	491	3,107	898	4,496	563	2,972	790	4,325
Arkansas	560	2,307	277	3,144	652	2,297	255	3,204	647	2,567	359	3,573
Florida (e)	4,167	8,135	1,543	13,845	4,549	8,291	1,500	14,340	4,942	8,327	1,644	14,913
Georgia	2,040	3,692	416	6,148	2,211	4,472	730	7,413	2,051	4,747	937	7,735
Kentucky	967	3,126	397	4,490	982	3,107	442	4,531	1,133	3,313	391	4,837
Louisiana	791	3,716	240	4,747	752	4,018	413	5,183	895	4,643	468	6,006
Maryland (f)	2,479	2,609	103	5,191	2,559	2,775	115	5,449	2,546	2,787	220	5,533
Mississippi	315	2,577	422	3,314	315	2,577	422	3,314	51	2,689	418	3,158
Missouri (g)	1,328	4,024	1,526	6,878	1,106	4,002	2,360	7,468	1,285	4,376	1,972	7,633
North Carolina	2,508	5,466	865	8,839	2,650	6,152	1,692	10,494	2,915	6,395	1,684	10,994
Oklahoma	827	1,952	210	2,989	869	2,143	309	3,321	1,292	2,124	300	3,716
South Carolina	721	2,695	488	3,904	754	3,062	659	4,475	834	3,410	681	4,925
Tennessee (h)	2,058	4,458	400	6,916	2,259	4,567	267	7,093	2,696	4,648	267	7,611
Texas (i)	6,216	10,782	856	17,854	6,589	12,373	1,634	20,596	7,485	13,270	1,432	22,187
Virginia	2,393	2,378	2	4,773	2,586	2,456	0	5,042	2,743	2,603	0	5,346
West Virginia	315	1,542	258	2,115	409	1,547	201	2,157	401	1,726	242	2,369
Regional totals	28,191	62,458	8,729	99,378	29,733	66,946	11,897	108,576	32,479	70,597	11,805	114,861

See footnotes at end of table.

MEDICAID EXPENDITURES BY STATE AND REGION—Continued
(In millions of dollars)

State	Actual fiscal 2006				Actual fiscal 2007				Estimated fiscal 2008			
	General fund	Federal funds	Other state funds	Total	General fund	Federal funds	Other state funds	Total	General fund	Federal funds	Other state funds	Total
Western Region												
Alaska	349	670	47	1,066	374	656	27	1,057	434	750	28	1,212
Arizona	1,373	4,180	545	6,098	1,523	4,436	549	6,508	1,272	4,947	567	6,786
California	12,180	17,311	1,683	31,174	13,403	19,418	643	33,464	14,071	21,865	703	36,639
Colorado (j)	1,262	1,297	60	2,619	1,226	1,296	93	2,615	1,286	1,375	85	2,746
Hawaii	390	582	3	975	440	616	6	1,062	479	672	10	1,161
Idaho	308	709	79	1,096	321	713	85	1,119	349	771	88	1,208
Montana	162	522	35	719	158	510	51	719	162	565	60	787
Nevada	387	673	103	1,163	437	700	106	1,243	450	637	80	1,167
New Mexico	703	1,810	51	2,564	764	1,941	44	2,749	833	2,090	48	2,971
Oregon	914	1,941	307	3,162	901	1,924	395	3,220	1,052	2,013	303	3,368
Utah	301	1,028	185	1,514	318	984	184	1,486	328	1,080	195	1,603
Washington	2,956	3,103	0	6,059	2,791	2,887	0	5,678	2,941	3,048	0	5,989
Wyoming	136	273	0	409	213	239	0	452	247	257	0	504
Regional totals	21,421	34,099	3,098	58,618	22,869	36,320	2,183	61,372	23,904	40,070	2,167	66,141
Regional totals without California	9,241	16,788	1,415	27,444	9,466	16,902	1,540	27,908	9,833	18,205	1,464	29,502

Source: National Association of State Budget Officers, *State Expenditure Report 2007* (December 2008).

Note: States were asked to report Medicaid expenditures as follows: General funds: all general funds appropriated to the Medicaid agency and any other agency which are used for direct Medicaid matching purposes under Title XIX. Other state funds: other funds and revenue sources used as Medicaid match, such as local funds and provider taxes, fees, donations, assessments (as defined by the Health Care Finance Administration). Federal Funds: all federal matching funds provided pursuant to Title XIX.As noted above, "the figures reported as Other State Funds reflect the amounts reported as provider taxes, fees, donations, assessments and local funds by states. State Medicaid agencies report these amounts to the Health Care Financing Administration (HCFA) on form 37, as defined by the Medicaid Voluntary Contribution and Provider-specific Tax Amendments of 1991 (P.L. 102-234). However, some state budget offices are unable to align their financial reporting to separate these costs for the NASBO State Expenditure Report. Thus, this report does not capture 100 percent of state provider taxes, fees, donations, assessments and local funds. Small dollar amounts, when rounded, cause an aberration in the percentage increase. In these instances, the actual dollar amounts should be consulted to determine the exact percentage increase. The states were asked to separately detail the amount of provider taxes, fees, donations, assessments and local funds reported as Other State Funds.

Key:

(a) Medicaid Appropriation is "gross funded"—Federal funds are deposited directly to the State Treasury. Connecticut's FMAP is currently at 50 percent of Medicaid benefit costs. Excludes state portion of Qualified Medicare Beneficiaries and School Based Child Health as those expenditures are netted out of federal Medicaid reimbursement.

(b) State Medicaid spending does not include local government shares.

(c) Other state funds include local funds of $103.0 million, and provider taxes of $674.0 million for fiscal 2006; local funds of $102.0 million and provider taxes of $856.0 million for fiscal 2007; and local funds of $62.0 million and provider taxes of $1,008.0 million for fiscal 2008. Public health and community and institutional care for mentally and developmentally disabled persons are partially reported in the Medicaid totals.

(d) Fiscal 2006 through fiscal 2008 Other State Funds includes provider taxes in the amounts of $58 million, $58 million, and $59 million, respectively.

(e) For fiscal 2005-06, Other State Funds include provider assessments of $391 million, cigarette taxes of $115 million, tobacco settlement funds of $83 million, state drug rebates of $346 million, other non-general funds transferred as matching funds of $34 million, state fraud recoupments of $18 million, and local county funds of $556 million. For fiscal 2006-07, Other State Funds include provider assessments of $362 million, cigarette taxes of $113 million, tobacco settlement funds of $83 million, state drug rebates of $156 million, other non-general funds transferred as matching of $53 million, state fraud recoupments of $18 million, and local county funds of $716 million. For fiscal 2007-08, Other State Funds include provider assessments of $416 million, cigarette taxes of $112 million, tobacco settlement funds of $83 million, state drug rebates of $156 million, other non-general funds transferred as matching of $47 million, state fraud recoupments of $18 million, and local county funds of $813 million.

(f) Medicaid funds are estimates for each fiscal year; some expenditures may have been recorded in other fiscal years than are shown here.

(g) Medicaid and SCHIP data are from the CMS 64 Report used for federal reporting of Medicaid expenditures. The split between the General Revenue Fund and Other Funds is an estimate. While state-only Medicaid program expenditures are tracked, local and administrative expenditures are estimated based on CMS 64 data. Other Funds include estimated local funds of $404 million for fiscal 2006, $1,002 million for fiscal 2007, and $601 million for fiscal 2008.

(h) Regarding premium revenue: fiscal 2006 totals $71 million, fiscal 2007 totals $64 million, and fiscal 2008 totals $64 million. Regarding Certified Public Expenditures—Local fund from Hospitals: fiscal 2006 totals $251 million, fiscal 2007 totals $416 million, and fiscal 2008 totals $265 million. Regarding Nursing Home Tax: fiscal 2006 totals $85 million, fiscal 2007 totals $85 million, and fiscal 2008 totals $85 million. Regarding the ICF/MR 6 percent Gross Receipts Tax: fiscal 2006 totals $16 million, fiscal 2007 totals $16 million, and fiscal 2008 totals $15 million. Regarding Intergovernmental Transfers: fiscal 2006 totals $0 million, fiscal 2007 totals $0 million, and fiscal 2008 totals $0 million.

(i) For fiscal 2006, Medicaid amounts were revised to coincide with the finalized FY 2006 CMS 64 report for statewide expenditures.

(j) "Medicaid Spending" includes all Title XIX expenditures—Medical Services Premiums (the actual cost of providing medical services to clients), Medicaid Mental Health services, and Medicaid services provided by the Department of Human Services. Any Medicaid community or institutional mental health funding is included in the Medicaid expenditures.

Table 7.9
ALLOWABLE INVESTMENTS

State or other jurisdiction	CDs within state	CDs nationally	State and local government obligations	U.S. Treasury obligations	U.S. agency obligations	Other time deposits	Bankers' acceptances	Commercial paper	Corporate notes/bonds	Mortgage backed securities	Mutual/ Money Market funds	Eurodollars—CDs or TDs	Derivatives	Real estate	Repurchase agreements	Venture capital/ Private equity	Corporate stocks (foreign)	Corporate stocks (domestic)	Other
Alabama	★	...	...	★	★	...	...	...	...	★	...	...	...	...	★	...	...	...	...
Alaska	...	...	...	...	...	...	...	...	...	...	...	...	...	...	...	...	...	...	...
Arizona	★	★	★	★	★	★	★	★	★	★	★	...	...	...	★	...	...	★	...
Arkansas	★	...	★	★	★	★	★	★	★	★	★	...	...	...	★	...	...	★	...
California	★	★	★	★	★	★	★	★	★	★	...	...	...	...	★	...	...	...	(a)
Colorado	★	...	★	★	★	...	★	★	★	...	...	...	...	...	★	...	...	★	(b)
Connecticut	★	★	...	★	★	★	★	★	★	...	★	...	...	...	★	...	...	...	...
Delaware	★	★	★	★	★	★	★	★	★	★	★	...	...	...	★	...	...	...	...
Florida	★	...	★	★	★	★	★	★	★	★	★	★	★	...	★	...	...	...	(c)
Georgia	★	...	...	★	★	...	★	★	★	★	...	...	...	...	★	...	...	...	(c)
Hawaii	★	★	★	★	★	...	★	★	...	★	★	...	...	...	★	...	...	...	...
Idaho	★	...	★	★	★	...	★	★	★	★	★	...	★	...	★	...	...	...	...
Illinois	★	...	...	★	★	...	...	★	...	...	★	...	...	...	★	★	...	...	...
Indiana	★	...	★	★	★	...	...	...	...	...	★	...	...	...	★	...	...	...	...
Iowa	★	...	★	★	★	★	★	★	★	★	★	...	...	...	★	...	...	...	...
Kansas	★	...	...	★	★	...	...	★	...	...	...	...	...	...	★	...	...	...	...
Kentucky	★	★	★	★	★	★	★	★	...	★	★	...	★	...	★	...	...	...	(d)
Louisiana	★	...	★	★	★	...	...	★	★	★	★	...	...	...	★	...	...	...	...
Maine	★	★	★	...	...	...	★	★	★	★	★	...	...	...	★	...	...	...	...
Maryland	★	...	★	★	★	★	★	★	...	...	★	...	...	...	★	...	...	★	...
Massachusetts	★	★	★	★	★	...	★	★	...	...	...	...	...	...	★	...	...	...	(e)
Michigan	★	★	★	★	★	★	★	★	★	...	★	...	...	...	★	...	...	★	(f)
Minnesota	...	...	...	★	★	...	★	★	★	★	...	...	...	...	...	...	★	★	...
Mississippi	★	...	★	★	★	★	...	★	★	★	★	...	...	...	★	...	★	★	...
Missouri	...	...	...	★	★	...	★	★	...	★	...	...	...	...	★	...	...	...	(g)
Montana	★	★	★	★	★	★	...	...	...	...	...	...	...	...	★	...	...	...	...
Nebraska	★	★	★	★	★	★	★	★	★	★	★	★	★	★	★	...	★	★	...
Nevada	★	★	...	★	★	★	★	★	★	★	★	...	...	...	★	...	...	...	...
New Hampshire	★	...	★	★	★	...	★	★	★	★	★	...	...	...	★	...	...	★	...
New Jersey	★	★	...	★	★	...	★	★	★	★	★	...	...	★	★	...	★	★	...
New Mexico	★	...	★	★	★	★	...	★	★	★	★	...	...	...	★	...	...	...	...
New York	★	...	★	★	★	★	★	★	...	★	...	...	...	...	★	...	...	...	...
North Carolina	★	...	★	★	★	★	★	★	★	★	★	...	...	...	★	...	...	...	...
North Dakota	★	★	...	★	★	★	★	★	★	★	★	★	★	★	★	...	★	★	...
Ohio	★	...	★	★	...	★	★	★	...	★	...	...	...	...	★	...	...	...	...

See footnotes at end of table.

ALLOWABLE INVESTMENTS — Continued

State or other jurisdiction	CDs within state	CDs nationally	State and local government obligations	U.S. Treasury obligations	U.S. agency obligations	Other time deposits	Bankers' acceptances	Commercial paper	Corporate notes/bonds	Mortgage backed securities	Mutual/ Money Market funds	Eurodollars—CDs or TDs	Derivatives	Real estate	Repurchase agreements	Venture capital/ Private equity	Corporate stocks (foreign)	Corporate stocks (domestic)	Other
Oklahoma	★	★	★	★	★	. . .	★	★	. . .	. . .	★	. . .	. . .	. . .	★	. . .	. . .	. . .	. . .
Oregon	★	. . .	★	★	★	★	★	★	★	★	. . .	. . .	★	. . .	★	. . .	. . .	. . .	(h)
Pennsylvania	★	★	★	★	★	★	★	★	★	★	★	. . .	. . .	. . .	★	. . .	. . .	. . .	. . .
Rhode Island	★	★	. . .	★	★	★	. . .	★	★	. . .	. . .	. . .	. . .	★	★	★	. . .	. . .	. . .
South Carolina	★	. . .	★	★	★	. . .	. . .	★	★	★	. . .	. . .	. . .	. . .	★	. . .	. . .	. . .	. . .
South Dakota	★	★	★	★	★	★	★	★	★	★	. . .	. . .	★	★	★	. . .	★	★	. . .
Tennessee	★	. . .	. . .	★	★	. . .	★	★	. . .	. . .	. . .	. . .	. . .	. . .	★	. . .	. . .	. . .	. . .
Texas	. . .	. . .	. . .	★	★	★	★	★	★	★	★	. . .	★	★	★	★	★	★	(i)
Utah	★	★	★	★	★	. . .	★	★	★	★	★	. . .	. . .	. . .	★	. . .	. . .	★	. . .
Vermont	★	★	★	★	★	★	★	★	. . .	★	★	. . .	. . .	. . .	★	. . .	. . .	. . .	(j)
Virginia	★	★	★	★	★	. . .	★	★	★	★	★	. . .	. . .	. . .	★	. . .	. . .	. . .	. . .
Washington	★	. . .	★	★	★	. . .	★	★	. . .	. . .	. . .	. . .	. . .	. . .	★	. . .	. . .	. . .	. . .
West Virginia	★	★	★	★	★	. . .	. . .	★	★	★	★	. . .	★	. . .	★	. . .	★	★	(k)
Wisconsin	★	★	★	★	. . .	. . .	. . .	. . .	. . .	. . .	. . .	. . .	. . .	. . .	. . .	. . .	★	★	. . .
Wyoming	★	★	★	★	★	★	★	★	★	★	★	★	★	★	★	★	★	★	. . .
Dist. of Columbia	★	★	★	★	★	. . .	★	★	★	★	★	. . .	. . .	. . .	★	. . .	. . .	. . .	. . .

Source: National Association of State Treasurers, March 2008.

Key:

★ — Yes, allowed

. . . — No, not allowed

(a) Small Business Administration guaranteed loans.

(b) Asset backed securities.

(c) Convertible Bonds.

(d) Collateralized Mortgage Obligation's & Other Mortgages; Assets Banking.

(e) Massachusetts Municipal Depository Trust; Chapter 29 Section 38A.

(f) Emergency loans to municipalities within the state.

(g) Time deposits within state.

(h) Reverse repurchase agreements.

(i) Private Equity.

(j) For certain non pension trust funds identified by statute, equities and corporate bonds/notes are permitted investments.

(k) Economic Development Loans.

Table 7.10
CASH FLOW MANAGEMENT: FORECASTING AND DISTRIBUTION OF DEMAND DEPOSITS

State or other jurisdiction	Forecasting			Distribution of demand deposits			
				Used as depositories		Number of	
	Development of cash flow forecasting method	Float analysis in collection and disbursement processes	Automated system for cash flow forecasting	Banks	Savings and loans	Banks in state	Savings and loans in state
Alabama	. . .	. . .	. . .	171	0	175	. . .
Alaska	In-house	. . .	★	4	0	3	0
Arizona	In-house	★	. . .	7	0	61	4
Arkansas	In-house	★	★	6	0	152	7
California	In-house	★	★	7	0	268	33
Colorado	In-house	. . .	★	3	0	. . .	. . .
Connecticut	In-house	★	★	9	. . .	91	8
Delaware	In-house	★	. . .	4	0	36	14
Florida	In-house	. . .	★	5	0	254	29
Georgia	In-house	★	. . .	(a)	0	340+	0
Hawaii	In-house	. . .	★	7	0	7	0
Idaho	In-house	★	. . .	11	0	30	5
Illinois	In-house	★	★	9	0	5	0
Indiana	In-house	★	. . .	232	37	300	55
Iowa	In-house	★	. . .	80	0	. . .	. . .
Kansas	In-house	. . .	. . .	2	0	354	16
Kentucky	In-house	★	★	(b)	(c)	. . .	. . .
Louisiana	In-house	★	. . .	15	0	120	9
Maine	In-house	★	. . .	14	0	. . .	. . .
Maryland	In-house	★	. . .	12	. . .	62	. . .
Massachusetts	In-house	★	. . .	19	0	270	. . .
Michigan	In-house	★	. . .	61	0	139	5
Minnesota	In-house	★	. . .	200	0	463	22
Mississippi	In-house	★	★	106	0	106	9
Missouri	In-house	★	. . .	80	2	300	6
Montana	In-house	★	. . .	62	. . .	267	. . .
Nebraska	In-house	★	. . .	46	0	332	16
Nevada	In-house	★	. . .	3	0	41	1
New Hampshire	In-house	★	. . .	5	. . .	42	. . .
New Jersey	In-house	★	. . .	45	4	110	74
New Mexico	In-house	★	. . .	44	6	48	9
New York	In-house	★	. . .	100+	NA	. . .	. . .
North Carolina	In-house	★	★	87	9	93	16
North Dakota	In-house	★	. . .	(d)	0	1	0
Ohio	In-house	. . .	. . .	137	. . .	. . .	. . .
Oklahoma	In-house	★	★	190	2	325	20
Oregon	In-house	. . .	. . .	20	0	55	4
Pennsylvania	Outsourced	★	★	96	15	96	15
Rhode Island	In-house	. . .	★	5	0	17	. . .
South Carolina	In-house	★	. . .	30	. . .	. . .	. . .
South Dakota	In-house	★	. . .	106	1	103	5
Tennessee	In-house	★	★	50	. . .	. . .	. . .
Texas	In-house	★	. . .	363	8	661	20
Utah	In-house	★	. . .	13	. . .	38	4
Vermont	In-house	★	. . .	13	0	24	1
Virginia	In-house	★	★	60	0	150	8
Washington	In-house	★	★	46	2	86	16
West Virginia	In-house	★	. . .	51	0	68	6
Wisconsin	In-house	★	. . .	70	8	273	37
Wyoming	In-house	★	. . .	1	. . .	47	3
Dist. of Columbia	In-house	★	★	10	4	21	6

Source: National Association of State Treasurers, March 2008.
Key:
★ — Yes
. . . — No
(a) 7 primary plus 100's of others.
(b) 1 Primary Depository.
(c) 0–100 + Interest + Local Receipt Accounts.
(d) 1 State owned bank.

Table 7.11
UTILIZATION OF CASH MANAGEMENT

State or other jurisdiction	Collection services	Lock boxes	Wire transfers	Federal reserve wire transfer	Bank wire transfer	Depository transfer checks	Zero balance accounts	Bank drafts	Controlled disbursement programs	Information systems	Account reconciliation services	Data transfer services	Business services	Automated clearinghouse
Alabama	NU	B	B	B	I, B	B	B	I, B	NU	I	I	I, B	NU	I, B
Alaska	B	B	I	NU	B	I	B	I	I	I	NU	NU	NU	B
Arizona	NU	B	I, B	NU	B	NU	B	NU	NU	I, B	I	I, B	B	I, B
Arkansas	NU	NU	B	B	B	NU	B	NU	NU	I	I	I	NU	B
California	I	B	I	I	I	I	I	NU	NU	I	I, B	B	I, B	B
Colorado	NU	B	B	B	B	B	B	B	B	B	B	B	NU	B
Connecticut	I, B	B	I, B	I, B	I, B	NU	B	B	B	I, B	I, B	I, B	NU	I, B
Delaware	B	B	I, B	I, B	B	NU	B	NU	B	I, B	I	I, B	NU	I, B
Florida	NU	I, B	B	B	B	NU	NU	NU	NU	NU	I	NU	NU	B
Georgia	NU	B	I	NU	I	NU	NU	NU	I	NU	NU	NU	NU	I
Hawaii	NU	B	I	NU	B	NU	B	NU	NU	B	I, B	NU	B	I, B
Idaho	NU	NU	I	I	I	NU	I	NU	NU	NU	NU	NU	NU	B
Illinois	NU	B	I	Used	I	NU	B	NU	NU	I, B	NU	B	NU	I
Indiana	I	B	I	I	I	I	B	NU	NU	NU	I	NU	NU	I
Iowa	B	B	I	I	I	NU	B	I	I	I	I	NU	NU	I
Kansas	NU	B	B	B	B	NU	B	NU	NU	I	I	B	NU	I, B
Kentucky	B	NU	B	B	B	NU	B	NU	B	I	I	B	NU	B
Louisiana	I	Used	Used	Used	Used	Used	Used	NU	Used	Used	Used	Used	NU	Used
Maine	B	NU	I, B	NU	NU	NU	B	NU	NU	NU	I, B	I, B	NU	I, B
Maryland	NU	B	I	B	NU	NU	B	NU	B	I, B	I, B	I, B	NU	I, B
Massachusetts	Used	B	I, B	I, B	I, B	NU	B	NU	Used	I, B	I, B	I, B	NU	I, B
Michigan	NU	B	I, B	B	B	NU	B	NU	NU	NU	I, B	NU	NU	B
Minnesota	NU	NU	I	I	I	NU	B	NU	NU	I	I	NU	NU	I
Mississippi	NU	B	B	B	B	I	NU	NU	NU	NU	NU	NU	NU	B
Missouri	I	I, B	I, B	I	I	NU	B	NU	NU	I, B	I, B	I, B	NU	I, B
Montana	NU	NU	I, B	NU	NU	NU	NU	NU	NU	I	NU	NU	NU	I, B
Nebraska	I, B	B	B	B	B	NU	I, B	NU	NU	I, B	I	I	NU	B
Nevada	I	B	I	I	I	NU	I	NU	I	B	I, B	I, B	NU	I
New Hampshire	NU	NU	B	NU	NU	NU	B	NU	B	I, B	I, B	NU	NU	I, B
New Jersey	B	B	I	I	I	NU	B	NU	B	B	I	I	NU	I
New Mexico	B	B	B	B	B	B	B	I	I	I, B	I	NU	NU	B
New York	NU	B	I, B	I, B	NU	NU	B	NU	B	I	I, B	I	NU	I, B
North Carolina	I	B	I	I	I	NU	B	I	I, B	I	I	I, B	NU	I, B
North Dakota	NU	NU	B	B	B	NU	B	NU	I	NU	I	NU	NU	B
Ohio	I	B	I, B	I, B	I, B	NU	I	NU	NU	B	I	I, B	NU	I, B

See footnotes at end of table.

UTILIZATION OF CASH MANAGEMENT — Continued

State or other jurisdiction	Collection services	Lock boxes	Wire transfers	Federal reserve wire transfer	Bank wire transfer	Depository transfer checks	Zero balance accounts	Bank drafts	Controlled disbursement programs	Information systems	Account reconciliation services	Data transfer services	Business services	Automated clearinghouse
Oklahoma	NU	B	B	NU	Used	I	B	NU	NU	NU	NU	NU	NU	B
Oregon	B	B	I	I	I	NU	I	I	B	I	I, B	I, B	NU	I
Pennsylvania	B	B	I, B	I, B	I, B	NU	B	NU	I, B	I, B	I, B	I, B	NU	I, B
Rhode Island	B	B	I, B	B	I, B	I, B	I, B	NU	B	I, B	I, B	NU	NU	I, B
South Carolina	NU	B	I, B	I, B	I, B	I	I, B	I	NU	I	I	I	NU	B
South Dakota	I	I	B	B	B	B	B	NU	I	NU	I	NU	NU	B
Tennessee	I	I	I, B	I, B	NU	NU	B	I	NU	I	I	I	NU	B
Texas	NU	I, B	I	I	I	NU	B	I	I	I	I	I	NU	I, B
Utah	NU	B	NU	B	NU	NU	B	NU	NU	I	NU	NU	NU	I
Vermont	I, B	B	I, B	B	B	B	B	NU	I, B	I, B	I, B	I	I, B	I, B
Virginia	NU	B	I	I	I	NU	B	NU	B	B	I	I	NU	B
Washington	NU	B	B	B	B	NU	B	NU	NU	I	NU	I	NU	I, B
West Virginia	NU	I	NU	NU	B	NU	NU	NU	NU	I	I	NU	NU	I
Wisconsin	I, B	B	B	B	B	B	B	B	B	I, B	B	Used	NU	Used
Wyoming	NU	NU	Used	I	I	I	B	NU	B	I, B	I, B	I	NU	I
Dist. of Columbia	I	B	I	I	I	NU	B	NU	B	I	I, B	I	NU	IB

Source: National Association of State Treasurers, March 2008.

Key:

B — Performed by bank

I — Performed in-house

NU — Not utilized

Table 7.12
BOND AUTHORIZATION

State or other jurisdiction	Central agency overseeing debt issuance	Party which holds issuance authority: General obligation bonds	Revenue bonds	Taxable bonds	Taxable debt	Short-term debt	Authority to issue foreign currency denominated debt
Alabama	No Central Agency	R, L, C	L, C	. . .	. . .	. . .	. . .
Alaska	Alaska State Bond Committee	R, L, G, C	L, G, C	L,G,C	L, G, C	C	No
Arizona	State does not issue debt	. . .	. . .	. . .	. . .	. . .	. . .
Arkansas	Development Finance Authority	R, L, G, B	L, G, B	B	B	B	Yes
California	California State Treasurer's Office	R (a)	B	. . .	. . .	(RANS)	No
Colorado	No Central Agency	. . .	. . .	. . .	. . .	. . .	No
Connecticut	Debt Management Division, Office of the Treasurer	L, C, TR	L, G, C, TR	L, C, TR	L, C, TR	L, G, C, TR	No
Delaware	Department of Finance	L	L	. . .	. . .	L	No
Florida	Division of Bond Finance	L, B	L, B	L, B	L, B	L, B	Yes
Georgia	Georgia State Financing and Investment Commission	L, C	L, C	L, C	L, C	L, C	No
Hawaii	Department of Budget and Finance	L	L	L	L	L	No
Idaho	No Central Agency	. . .	. . .	. . .	. . .	B	No
Illinois	. . .	L, G	L, G, B	. . .	. . .	R, L, G	No
Indiana	Public Finance Officer	(b)	(b)	(b)	(b)	(b)	. . .
Iowa	Treasury	R, L, G	L, G, B	L, G, B	. . .	G, TR	No
Kansas	Kansas Development Finance Authority	. . .	R, B	. . .	R, B	R, B	Yes
Kentucky	Office of Financial Management	R	R	R	R	R	Yes (c)
Louisiana	State Bond Commission	L, C	L, C	L, C	C	L, C	No
Maine	Office of the State Treasurer	R, L, G, TR	L, G	. . .	R, L, G, TR	TR, Other	No
Maryland	General Obligation Debt - State Treasurer	L, B	L	L, B	. . .	B, TR	No
Massachusetts	Financial Advisory Board	L, G	L, G	L, G	L, G	L, G	No
Michigan	State Administrative Board	R, L, B, TR	L, B, TR	L, B, TR	L, B, TR	L, B, TR	No
Minnesota	Department of Finance (d)	L	L	L	L	L	No
Mississippi	State Treasury/OFA—Bond Advisory Division	L, C	L, C	L, C	L, C	L, C	No
Missouri	Office of Administration	R, L, B	L, B	. . .	. . .	. . .	No
Montana	No Central Agency	L, B, TR	L, B, TR	. . .	L, B, TR	B, TR	No
Nebraska	State does not issue debt	. . .	. . .	. . .	. . .	. . .	. . .
Nevada	No Central Agency	L, B	L, B	L, B	L, B	L, B	No
New Hampshire	Treasury	L	. . .	. . .	. . .	. . .	No
New Jersey	Treasury, Office of Public Finance	R, L	L, G, B	R	. . .	. . .	No
New Mexico	State Board of Finance	. . .	. . .	. . .	. . .	L, B, TR	No
New York	(e)	R, L, G Comptroller issues (d)	L, G (f)	L, G (f)	L, G (f)	L, G (f)	No
North Carolina	State and Local Government Finance Division, Dept. of State Treasurer	R, L	L	L	L	L	No
North Dakota	No Central Agency	. . .	. . .	. . .	. . .	. . .	. . .
Ohio	Office of Budget and Management	. . .	. . .	. . .	. . .	. . .	No

See footnotes at end of table.

BOND AUTHORIZATION—Continued

State or other jurisdiction	Central agency overseeing debt issuance	Party which holds issuance authority: General obligation bonds	Revenue bonds	Taxable bonds	Taxable debt	Short-term debt	Authority to issue foreign currency denominated debt
Oklahoma	State Bond Advisor's Office	R	L, B, C	B, C	B, C	B, C	No
Oregon	Oregon State Treasury Debt Management Division	L, G, TR	L, G, TR	. . .	L, G, TR	L, G, TR	No
Pennsylvania	Office of Budget	R, L	L, B, C	Not authorized	Not authorized	L	No
Rhode Island	Budget Office & Treasury	R, G	. . .	. . .	. . .	L	No
South Carolina	State Budget and Control Board	R, L, G, B, TR	L, G, B, C, TR	L, B, TR	L, B, TR	L, B, TR	No
South Dakota	State does not issue debt	. . .	. . .	. . .	. . .	. . .	. . .
Tennessee	Comptroller's Office—Division of Bond Finance	L, C	. . .	C	C	C	No
Texas	Texas Bond Review Board	R, L, B, C	L, B, C	L, B, C	L, B, C	L, B, C	No
Utah	Treasurer	L	L		L	TR	Yes (g)
Vermont	Office of the State Treasurer	L	L	L	. . .	TR	No
Virginia	Department of the Treasury	R, L, G	L, G, B, TR	. . .	. . .	. . .	No
Washington	Division of Debt Management	R, L	R, L	R, L	R, L	R, L	No
West Virginia	No Central Agency	R, L, G, TR, AG	L, B, C	L, G, B, C	L, G, B, C	L, G	No
Wisconsin	Capital Finance Office, Wisconsin Department of Administration	L	L	C	C	C	. . .
Wyoming	No Central Agency	Not authorized	L, C	L, C	Not authorized	L, G, C, TR	No
Dist. of Columbia	Office of the Chief Financial Officer	L, TR, A, (h)	L, (h)	. . .	. . .	L, TR, (h)	No

Source: National Association of State Treasurers, March 2008.

Key:

A — Auditor
AG — Auditor General
B — Board
C — Commission
G — Governor
L — Legislation
R — Referendum
TR — Treasurer
. . . — Not applicable

(a) Committee.

(b) Indiana by statute cannot issue debt, so quasi-agencies are set up to do so.

(c) Requires legislative approval. Previously issued debt in Yen.

(d) Only for general obligation debt or for reporting purposes.

(e) No, the Office of the State Comptroller approves terms and conditions for certain negotiated bond deals of public authorities and local governments and issues State General Obligation bonds and LGAC bonds. Various state public authorities issue state-supported debt.

(f) Taxable debt may be issued for general obligation as well as revenue bonds. If general obligation, referendum is needed.

(g) Requires entering into a foreign exchange agreement with a AA or higher rated institution when bonds are issued to hedge the currency risk.

(h) Mayor.

Table 7.13
RESERVE FUNDS

State or other jurisdiction	Official title	Start year	Administrator	Limit on fund's size	Deposit requirements	Withdrawal rules	Replenishment requirement
Alabama	Education Trust Fund Rainy Day Account	2000	Board	$225,000,000	. . .	Proration	5 Years
Alaska	Constitutional Budget Reserve Fund	. . .	. . .	. . .	. . .	. . .	. . .
Arizona	Budget Stabilization Fund	1994	Treasurer	No	. . .	Supermajority vote of legislature.	No
Arkansas	None	. . .	. . .	. . .	. . .	. . .	. . .
California	None	. . .	. . .	. . .	. . .	. . .	. . .
Colorado	None	. . .	. . .	. . .	. . .	. . .	. . .
Connecticut	Budget Reserve Fund	1991	Treasurer	10% of current year's budget.	Statutory; No requirement/Deposit made at will of legislature.	Revenue below forecast/budget controlled by state constitution and statute.	Inappropriate surplus goes to fund first.
Delaware	Reserve Cash Intermediate Account	. . .	Investment Manager	No	No requirement/Deposits made at will of legislature.	Cash Management Policy Board guidelines	No
Florida	Budget Stabilization Fund	1994	Treasurer	10% of previous fiscal year net revenue	Constitutional	Constitution and legislation set guidelines.	5 Years
Georgia	Revenue Shortfall Reserve/ Midyear Adjustment Reserve	1976	State Auditor	5% of net revenue collections	Statutory	Revenue below forecast/budget.	No
Hawaii	Emergency Budget and Reserve Fund	1999	Treasurer	No	Statutory	2/3 majority vote in each chamber of state legislature.	No
Idaho	Budget Stabilization Fund	1984	Dept. of Administration	No	Statutory	Limit on amount withdrawn in a given year.	No
Illinois	Budget Stabilization Fund	2000	Secretary/Director of Revenue	. . .	. . .	. . .	End of Fiscal Year
Indiana	Indiana Rainy Day Fund	. . .	Treasurer	No	Deposits made when economic growth exceeds specified levels.	Revenue below forecast/budget	No
Iowa	The Cash Reserve Fund and the Economic Emergency Fund	1992	Dept. of Management	(a)	Statutory	(b)	No
Kansas	None	. . .	. . .	. . .	. . .	. . .	. . .
Kentucky	Budget Reserve Trust Fund	1995	Office of Financial Management (Finance Cabinet)	No	NA	NA	NA
Louisiana	Budget Stabilization Fund	1998	Treasurer	Balance can not exceed 4% of state total revenue receipts for the previous year.	Constitutional	Revenue below budget. Supermajority vote of legislature. Limit on withdrawals.	No
Maine	Budget Stabilization Fund	. . .	Controller	. . .	Statutory	. . .	. . .

See footnotes at end of table.

RESERVE FUNDS — Continued

State or other jurisdiction	Official title	Start year	Administrator	Limit on fund's size	Deposit requirements	Withdrawal rules	Replenishment requirement
Maryland	State Reserve Fund—Revenue Stabilization Account	1986	Dept. of Budget and Management	No	Statutory	None	. . .
Massachusetts	Commonwealth Stabilization Fund	1986	Treasurer	15% of budgeted revenues.	Statutory	Vote of legislature.	No
Michigan	Budget Stabilization Fund	1985	Dept. of Management and Budget	No	Statutory	Revenue below forecast/budget. formula in statute.	Depends on revenue growth.
Minnesota	None	. . .	. . .	. . .	. . .	. . .	No
Mississippi	Working Cash Stabilization Reserve Fund	. . .	Treasurer	. . .	Statutory	Statutory	. . .
Missouri	Budget Reserve Fund	1986	Office of Administration	7 1/2% of general revenue collections of previous fiscal year.	Constitutional	(c)	. . .
Montana	None	. . .	. . .	. . .	. . .	. . .	. . .
Nebraska	Cash reserve fund	1983	Treasurer	No	Statutory	(d)	No
Nevada	The Fund to Stabilize the Operation of State Government	1991	Controller	Must not exceed total appropriation of state.	Statutory; No requirement/ Deposits made at will of legislature.	(e)	Yearly, if revenue is sufficient.
New Hampshire	Revenue Stabilization Fund	1980s	Treasurer	10% of prior year's revenues.	Contingent upon financial performance.	No, funds may be used for any reason.	No
New Jersey	Surplus Revenue Fund	. . .	. . .	. . .	. . .	. . .	. . .
New Mexico	Emergency Fund	. . .	Treasurer	(f)	No requirement/Deposits made at will of legislature.	Emergencies as ruled such by Board of Finance.	. . .
New York	Rainy Day Fund	Mid 1990s	Comptroller	. . .	Statutory	Revenue below forecast/budget.	. . .
North Carolina	Rainy Day Fund	. . .	. . .	No	. . .	No, funds may be used for any reason.	No
North Dakota	Budget Stabilization Fund	1987	State Investment Board	(g)	Statutory	Revenue below forecast/budget.	End of each biennium.
Ohio	Budget Stabilization Fund	. . .	. . .	. . .	. . .	. . .	. . .
Oklahoma	Rainy Day Fund	. . .	Secretary/Director of Revenue	. . .	Statutory	Limit on amount withdrawn in a given year	. . .
Oregon	Education Stability Fund	2002	(h)	5% of general fund revenues of prior biennium	Statutory; Constitutional	(i)	No
Oregon	Rainy Day Fund	2007	Treasurer	7.5% of the amount of general fund revenues collected during prior biennium	Statutory	Supermajority vote of legislature; revenue below forecast/budget	No
Pennsylvania	Budget Stabilization Reserve Fund	(j)	Secretary of Budget and Administration	(k)	Statutory	Supermajority vote of legislature.	(l)
Rhode Island	Budget Reserve and Cash Stabilization Account	. . .	. . .	. . .	. . .	. . .	. . .

See footnotes at end of table.

RESERVE FUNDS—Continued

State or other jurisdiction	Official title	Start year	Administrator	Limit on fund's size	Deposit requirements	Withdrawal rules	Replenishment requirement
South Carolina	General Reserve Fund	. . .	Treasurer	3% prior year revenues.	Statutory	To avoid year end deficit	3 Years
South Dakota	Budget Reserve Fund	. . .	. . .	. . .	. . .	. . .	. . .
Tennessee	Rainy Day Fund	. . .	Commissioner of Finance and Administration	. . .	. . .	. . .	. . .
Texas	Economic Stabilization Fund	1989	Treasurer	(m)	Statutory	(n)	No
Utah	Budget Reserve Fund	1996	Treasurer	(o)	No requirement/Deposits made at will of legislature	Majority vote of legislature.	(p)
Vermont	(q)	1987	Commissioner of Finance and Management	(r)	Statutory	(s)	(t)
Virginia	Revenue Stabilization Fund	1993	(u)	(v)	Statutory	(w)	No
Washington	Emergency Reserve Fund	1993	Treasurer; Office of Financial Management	No	Statutory	Supermajority vote of legislature.	No
West Virginia	Revenue Shortfall Reserve Fund	1995	Budget	Aggregate amount—not to exceed 5% of total revenue fund.	Statutory	(x)	90 days for fiscal borrowing.
Wisconsin	Budget Reserve Fund	1992	Dept. of Administration	No	No requirement/Deposits made at will of legislature.	No, funds may be used for any reason.	No
Wyoming	Budget Reserve Account	1984	State Auditor's Office	No	Statutory	Supermajority vote of legislature.	No
Dist. of Columbia	Emergency and Contingency Reserve Fund	2001	Treasurer	6% of local funds.	Statutory	Mayor and CFO declares.	By the end of the next fiscal year.

Source: National Association of State Treasurers, March 2008.

Key:

(a) CRF: 7.5% of general fund's estimated revenue. EEF: 5% of general fund's estimated revenue.

(b) Non-recurring emergencies. 3/5 majority required if balance of Cash Reserve Fund is below 3% of general fund revenues.

(c) 100% for cash flow loans within fiscal year, must be repaid by May 15. Can appropriate 50% upon 2/3 approval of legislature to be repaid in 3 equal annual installments.

(d) Upon certification of DAS director that current cash balance of the general fund is inadequate to meet current obligations.

(e) Revenue below forecast/budget. Simple majority vote of legislature and governor if fiscal emergency exists.

(f) Zeros out at end of year.

(g) No activity since 1991.

(h) Treasurer controlled by state constitution and statute.

(i) Revenue below forecast/budget or emergency declared by the governor; supermajority vote of legislature. Funds to be used for education.

(j) July 2002–2003 replaced Tax Stabilization Reserve Fund.

(k) No, if the fund balance equals or exceeds 6% of the general fund revenues for the fiscal year in which the surplus occurs then the transfer is reduced to 10%.

(l) 25% of general funds fiscal year ending surplus.

(m) Amount not to exceed 10 % of General Revenue income during the previous biennium.

(n) Revenue below forecast/budget; supermajority vote of legislature.

(o) 6% of the total of appropriations for the general fund and uniform school fund.

(p) No set time. Fund reserves one half of any year-end surplus.

(q) Various Budget Stabilization Reserves (not a separate fund, but a reserve in the general fund, transportation fund, and education fund).

(r) Generally 5% of the prior year appropriation for the fund (general, transportation, education).

(s) Certification of an undesignated fund deficit by the Commissioner of Finance and Management.

(t) Up to statutory levels in the next fiscal year or subsequent years as needed to reach the required level.

(u) The General Assembly appropriates funds pursuant to Article X, Section 8 of the Constitution of Virginia.

(v) 10% of average annual tax revenues derived from taxes on income and retail sales.

(w) Revenue below forecast/budget; limit on amount withdrawn in a given year.

(x) Funds may be borrowed as defined in code, or withdrawn for emergency or fiscal needs by act of legislature.

Table 7.14
AGENCIES ADMINISTERING MAJOR STATE TAXES

State or other jurisdiction	Income	Sales	Gasoline	Motor vehicle
Alabama	Dept. of Revenue	Dept. of Revenue	Dept. of Revenue	Dept. of Revenue
Alaska	Dept. of Revenue	. . .	Dept. of Revenue	Dept. of Public Safety
Arizona	Dept. of Revenue	Dept. of Revenue	Dept. of Transportation	Dept. of Transportation
Arkansas	Dept. of Fin. & Admin.	Dept. of Fin. & Admin.	Dept. of Fin. & Admin.	Dept. of Fin. & Admin.
California	Franchise Tax Bd.	Bd. of Equalization	Bd. of Equalization	Dept. of Motor Vehicles
Colorado	Dept. of Revenue	Dept. of Revenue	Dept. of Revenue	Dept. of Revenue
Connecticut	Dept. of Revenue Serv.	Dept. of Revenue Serv.	Dept. of Revenue Serv.	Dept. of Motor Vehicles
Delaware	Div. of Revenue	. . .	Dept. of Transportation	Dept. of Public Safety
Florida	Dept. of Revenue	Dept. of Revenue	Dept. of Revenue	Dept. of Highway Safety and Motor Vehicles
Georgia	Dept. of Revenue	Dept. of Revenue	Dept. of Revenue	Dept. of Revenue
Hawaii	Dept. of Taxation	Dept. of Taxation	Dept. of Taxation	County Treasurer
Idaho	Tax Commission	Tax Commission	Tax Commission	Dept. of Transportation
Illinois	Dept. of Revenue	Dept. of Revenue	Dept. of Revenue	Secretary of State
Indiana	Dept. of Revenue	Dept. of Revenue	Dept. of Revenue	Bur. of Motor Vehicles
Iowa	Dept. of Revenue	Dept. of Revenue	Dept. of Revenue	Local
Kansas	Dept. of Revenue	Dept. of Revenue	Dept. of Revenue	Local (a)
Kentucky	Dept. of Revenue	Dept. of Revenue	Dept. of Revenue	Transportation Cabinet
Louisiana	Dept. of Revenue	Dept. of Revenue	Dept. of Revenue	Dept. of Public Safety
Maine	Revenue Services	Revenue Services	Revenue Services	Secretary of State
Maryland	Comptroller	Comptroller	Comptroller	Dept. of Transportation
Massachusetts	Dept. of Revenue	Dept. of Revenue	Dept. of Revenue	Registry of Motor Vehicles
Michigan	Dept. of Treasury	Dept. of Treasury	Dept. of Treasury	Secretary of State
Minnesota	Dept. of Revenue	Dept. of Revenue	Dept. of Revenue	Dept. of Public Safety
Mississippi	Tax Commission	Tax Commission	Tax Commission	Tax Commission
Missouri	Dept. of Revenue	Dept. of Revenue	Dept. of Revenue	Dept. of Revenue
Montana	Dept. of Revenue	. . .	Dept. of Transportation	Local
Nebraska	Dept. of Revenue	Dept. of Revenue	Dept. of Revenue	Dept. of Motor Vehicles
Nevada	. . .	Dept. of Taxation	Dept. of Motor Vehicles	Dept. of Motor Vehicles
New Hampshire	Dept. of Revenue Admin.	. . .	Dept. of Safety	Dept. of Safety
New Jersey	Dept. of Treasury	Dept. of Treasury	Dept. of Treasury	Dept. of Law & Public Safety
New Mexico	Tax. & Revenue Dept.	Tax. & Revenue Dept.	Tax. & Revenue Dept.	Tax. & Revenue Dept.
New York	Dept. of Tax. & Finance	Dept. of Tax. & Finance	Dept. of Tax. & Finance	Dept. of Motor Vehicles
North Carolina	Dept. of Revenue	Dept. of Revenue	Dept. of Revenue	Dept. of Transportation
North Dakota	Tax Commissioner	Tax Commissioner	Tax Commissioner	Dept. of Transportation
Ohio	Dept. of Taxation	Dept. of Taxation	Dept. of Taxation	Bur. of Motor Vehicles
Oklahoma	Tax Commission	Tax Commission	Tax Commission	Tax Commission
Oregon	Dept. of Revenue	. . .	Dept. of Transportation	Dept. of Transportation
Pennsylvania	Dept. of Revenue	Dept. of Revenue	Dept. of Revenue	Dept. of Transportation
Rhode Island	Dept. of Administration	Dept. of Administration	Dept. of Administration	Dept. of Administration
South Carolina	Dept. of Revenue	Dept. of Revenue	Dept. of Revenue	Dept. of Public Safety
South Dakota	. . .	Dept. of Revenue & Reg.	Dept. of Revenue & Reg.	Dept. of Revenue & Reg.
Tennessee	Dept. of Revenue	Dept. of Revenue	Dept. of Revenue	Dept. of Safety
Texas	. . .	Comptroller	Comptroller	Dept. of Transportation
Utah	Tax Commission	Tax Commission	Tax Commission	Tax Commission
Vermont	Dept. of Taxes	Dept. of Taxes	Commr. of Motor Vehicles	Commr. of Motor Vehicles
Virginia	Dept. of Taxation	Dept. of Taxation	Dept. of Motor Vehicles	Dept. of Motor Vehicles
Washington	. . .	Dept. of Revenue	Dept. of Licensing	Dept. of Licensing
West Virginia	Dept. of Revenue	Dept. of Revenue	Dept. of Revenue	Div. of Motor Vehicles
Wisconsin	Dept. of Revenue	Dept. of Revenue	Dept. of Revenue	Dept. of Transportation
Wyoming	. . .	Dept. of Revenue	Dept. of Revenue	Dept. of Transportation
Dist. of Columbia	Office of Tax & Rev.	Office of Tax & Rev.	Office of Tax & Rev.	Office of Tax & Rev.

See footnotes at end of table.

AGENCIES ADMINISTERING MAJOR STATE TAXES — Continued

State or other jurisdiction	Tobacco	Death	Alcoholic beverage	Number of agencies administering taxes
Alabama	Dept. of Revenue	Dept. of Revenue	Alcoh. Bev. Control Bd.	2
Alaska	Dept. of Revenue	Dept. of Revenue	Dept. of Revenue	2
Arizona	Dept. of Revenue	Dept. of Revenue	Dept. of Revenue	2
Arkansas	Dept. of Fin. & Admin.	Dept. of Fin. & Admin.	Dept. of Fin. & Admin.	1
California	Bd. of Equalization	Controller	Bd. of Equalization	4
Colorado	Dept. of Revenue	Dept. of Revenue	Dept. of Revenue	1
Connecticut	Dept. of Revenue Serv.	Dept. of Revenue Serv.	Dept. of Revenue Serv.	2
Delaware	Div. of Revenue	Div. of Revenue	Dept. of Public Safety	3
Florida	Department of Business and Professional Regulation	Dept. of Revenue	Department of Business and Professional Regulation	3
Georgia	Dept. of Revenue	Dept. of Revenue	Dept. of Revenue	1
Hawaii	Dept. of Taxation	Dept. of Taxation	Dept. of Taxation	2
Idaho	Tax Commission	Tax Commission	Tax Commission	2
Illinois	Dept. of Revenue	Attorney General	Dept. of Revenue	3
Indiana	Dept. of Revenue	Dept. of Revenue	Dept. of Revenue	2
Iowa	Dept. of Revenue	Dept. of Revenue	Dept. of Revenue	2
Kansas	Dept. of Revenue	Dept. of Revenue	Dept. of Revenue	2
Kentucky	Dept. of Revenue	Dept. of Revenue	Dept. of Revenue	2
Louisiana	Dept. of Revenue	Dept. of Revenue	Dept. of Revenue	2
Maine	Revenue Services	Revenue Services	Bureau of Liquor Enf.	3
Maryland	Comptroller	Local	Comptroller	3
Massachusetts	Dept. of Revenue	Dept. of Revenue	Dept. of Revenue	2
Michigan	Dept. of Treasury	Dept. of Treasury	Liquor Control Comm.	3
Minnesota	Dept. of Revenue	Dept. of Revenue	Dept. of Revenue	2
Mississippi	Tax Commission	Tax Commission	Tax Commission	1
Missouri	Dept. of Revenue	Dept. of Revenue	Dept. of Revenue	1
Montana	Dept. of Revenue	Dept. of Revenue	Dept. of Revenue	3
Nebraska	Dept. of Revenue	Dept. of Revenue	Liquor Control Comm.	3
Nevada	Dept. of Taxation	Dept. of Taxation	Dept. of Taxation	2
New Hampshire	Dept. of Revenue Admin.	Dept. of Revenue Admin.	Liquor Comm.	3
New Jersey	Dept. of Treasury	Dept. of Treasury	Dept. of Treasury	2
New Mexico	Tax. & Revenue Dept.	Tax. & Revenue Dept.	Tax. & Revenue Dept.	1
New York	Dept. of Tax. & Finance	Dept. of Tax. & Finance	Dept. of Tax & Finance	2
North Carolina	Dept. of Revenue	Dept. of Revenue	Dept. of Revenue	2
North Dakota	Tax Commissioner	Tax Commissioner	Treasurer	3
Ohio	Dept. of Taxation	Dept. of Taxation	State Treasurer	3
Oklahoma	Tax Commission	Tax Commission	Tax Commission	1
Oregon	Dept. of Revenue	Dept. of Revenue	Liquor Control Comm.	3
Pennsylvania	Dept. of Revenue	Dept. of Revenue	Dept. of Revenue	2
Rhode Island	Dept. of Administration	Dept. of Administration	Dept. of Administration	1
South Carolina	Dept. of Revenue	Dept. of Revenue	Dept. of Revenue	2
South Dakota	Dept. of Revenue & Reg.	Dept. of Revenue & Reg.	Dept. of Revenue & Reg.	1
Tennessee	Dept. of Revenue	Dept. of Revenue	Dept. of Revenue	2
Texas	Comptroller	Comptroller	Comptroller	2
Utah	Tax Commission	Tax Commission	Tax Commission	1
Vermont	Dept. of Taxes	Dept. of Taxes	Dept. of Taxes	2
Virginia	Dept. of Taxation	Dept. of Taxation	Alcoh. Bev. Control	3
Washington	Dept. of Revenue	Dept. of Revenue	Liquor Control Board	3
West Virginia	Dept. of Revenue	Dept. of Revenue	Dept. of Revenue	2
Wisconsin	Dept. of Revenue	Dept. of Revenue	Dept. of Revenue	2
Wyoming	Dept. of Revenue	Dept. of Revenue	Dept. of Revenue	2
Dist. of Columbia	Office of Tax & Rev.	Office of Tax & Rev.	Office of Tax & Rev.	1

Source: The Federation of Tax Administrators, January 2006, with updates by The Council of State Governments, March 2009.

Key:

. . . — Not applicable

(a) Joint state and local administration. State level functions are performed by the Department of Revenue in Kansas.

Table 7.15
STATE TAX AMNESTY PROGRAMS
1982—2009

State or other jurisdiction	Amnesty period	Legislative authorization	Major taxes covered	Accounts receivable included	Collections ($millions) (a)	Installment arrangements permitted (b)
Alabama	1/20/84–4/1/84	No (c)	All	No	3.2	No
	2/1/09–5/15/09	No (c)	All	N.A.	N.A.	No
Arizona	11/22/82–1/20/83	No (c)	All	No	6.0	Yes
	1/1/02–2/28/02	Yes	Individual income	No	N.A.	No
	9/1/03–10/31/03	Yes	All (t)	N.A.	73.0	Yes
	5/1/09–6/1/09	Yes	Individual income	N.A.	N.A.	No
Arkansas	9/1/87–11/30/87	Yes	All	No	1.7	Yes
	7/1/04–12/31/04	Yes	All	N.A.	N.A.	No
California	12/10/84–3/15/85	Yes	Individual income	Yes	154.0	Yes
		Yes	Sales	No	43.0	Yes
	2/1/05–3/31/05	Yes	Income, Franchise, Sales	N.A.	N.A.	Yes
Colorado	9/16/85–11/15/85	Yes	All	No	6.4	Yes
	6/1/03–6/30/03	N.A.	All	N.A.	18.4	Yes
Connecticut	9/1/90–11/30/90	Yes	All	Yes	54.0	Yes
	9/1/95–11/30/95	Yes	All	Yes	46.2	Yes
	9/1/02–12/2/02	N.A.	All	N.A.	109.0	N.A.
	5/1/09–6/25/09	Yes	All (v)	N.A.	N.A.	N.A.
Florida	1/1/87–6/30/87	Yes	Intangibles	No	13.0	No
	1/1/88–6/30/88	Yes (d)	All	No	8.4 (d)	No
	7/1/03–10/31/03	Yes	All	N.A.	80.0	N.A.
Georgia	10/1/92–12/5/92	Yes	All	Yes	51.3	No
Idaho	5/20/83–8/30/83	No (c)	Individual income	No	0.3	No
Illinois	10/1/84–11/30/84	Yes	All (u)	Yes	160.5	No
	10/1/03–11/17/03	Yes	All	N.A.	532.0	N.A.
Indiana	9/15/05–11/15/05	N.A.	All	N.A.	255.0	Yes
Iowa	9/2/86–10/31/86	Yes	All	Yes	35.1	N.A.
	9/4/07–10/31/07	Yes	All	Yes	N.A.	N.A.
Kansas	7/1/84–9/30/84	Yes	All	No	0.6	No
	10/1/03–11/30/03	Yes	All	Yes	53.7	N.A.
Kentucky	9/15/88–9/30/88	Yes (c)	All	No	100.0	No
	8/1/02-9/30/02	Yes (c)	All	No	100.0	No
Louisiana	10/1/85–12/31/85	Yes	All	No	1.2	Yes (f)
	10/1/87–12/15/87	Yes	All	No	0.3	Yes (f)
	10/1/98-12/31/98	Yes	All	No (q)	1.3	No
	9/1/01-10/30/01	Yes	All	Yes	192.9	No
Maine	11/1/90–12/31/90	Yes	All	Yes	29.0	Yes
	9/1/03–11/30/03	Yes	All	N.A.	37.6	N.A.
Maryland	9/1/87–11/2/87	Yes	All	Yes	34.6 (g)	No
	9/1/01–10/31/01	Yes	All	Yes	39.2	No
Massachusetts	10/17/83–1/17/84	Yes	All	Yes	86.5	Yes (h)
	10/1/02–11/30/02	Yes	All	Yes	96.1	Yes
	1/1/03–2/28/03	Yes	All	Yes	11.2	N.A.
	1/1/09–6/30/09	Yes	All	N.A.	N.A.	N.A.
Michigan	5/12/86–6/30/86	Yes	All	Yes	109.8	No
	5/15/02–6/30/02	Yes	All	Yes	N.A.	N.A.
Minnesota	8/1/84–10/31/84	Yes	All	Yes	12.1	No
Mississippi	9/1/86–11/30/86	Yes	All	No	1.0	No
	9/1/04–12/31/04	Yes	All	No	7.9	No
Missouri	9/1/83–10/31/83	No (c)	All	No	0.9	No
	8/1/02–10/31/02	Yes	All	Yes	76.4	N.A.
	8/1/03–10/31/03	Yes	All	Yes	20.0	N.A.
Nebraska	8/1/04–10/31/04	Yes	All	No	7.5	No
Nevada	2/1/02–6/30/02	N.A.	All	N.A.	7.3	N.A.
	7/1/08–10/28/08	No	Sales, business, license	Yes	40.5	No
New Hampshire	12/1/97–2/17/98	Yes	All	Yes	13.5	No
	12/1/01–2/15/02	Yes	All	Yes	13.5	N.A.

See footnotes at end of table.

STATE TAX AMNESTY PROGRAMS — Continued
1982 — 2009

State or other jurisdiction	Amnesty period	Legislative authorization	Major taxes covered	Accounts receivable included	Collections ($millions) (a)	Installment arrangements permitted (b)
New Jersey	9/10/87–12/8/87	Yes	All	Yes	186.5	Yes
	3/15/96–6/1/96	Yes	All	Yes	359.0	No
	4/15/02–6/10/02	Yes	All	Yes	276.9	N.A.
	5/4/09–6/15/09	No	All	N.A.	N.A.	No
New Mexico	8/15/85–11/13/85	Yes	All (i)	No	13.6	Yes
	8/16/99–11/12/99	Yes	All	Yes	45.0	Yes
New York	11/1/85–1/31/86	Yes	All (j)	Yes	401.3	Yes
	11/1/96–1/31/97	Yes	All	Yes	253.4	Yes (o)
	11/18/02–1/31/03	Yes	All	Yes	582.7	Yes (s)
	10/1/05–3/1/06	N.A.	Income, corporate	N.A.	349.0	N.A.
North Carolina	9/1/89–12/1/89	Yes	All (k)	Yes	37.6	N.A.
North Dakota	9/1/83–11/30/83	No (c)	All	No	0.2	Yes
	10/1/03–1/31/04	Yes	N.A.	N.A.	6.9	N.A.
Ohio	10/15/01–1/15/02	Yes	All	No	48.5	No
	1/1/06–2/15/06	Yes	All	No	63.0	No
Oklahoma	7/1/84–12/31/84	Yes	Income, Sales	Yes	13.9	No (l)
	8/15/02–11/15/02	N.A.	All (r)	Yes	N.A.	N.A.
	9/15/08–11/14/08	Yes	All	Yes	115.0	Yes
Pennsylvania	10/13/95–1/10/96	Yes	All	Yes	N.A.	No
Rhode Island	10/15/86–1/12/87	Yes	All	No	0.7	Yes
	4/15/96–6/28/96	Yes	All	Yes	7.9	Yes
	7/15/06–9/30/06	N.A.	All	Yes	6.5	Yes
South Carolina	9/1/85–11/30/85	Yes	All	Yes	7.1	Yes
	10/15/02–12/2/02	Yes	All	Yes	66.2	N.A.
South Dakota	4/1/99–5/15/99	Yes	All	Yes	0.5	N.A.
Texas	2/1/84–2/29/84	No (c)	All (m)	No	0.5	No
	3/11/04–3/31/04	No (c)	All (m)	No	N.A.	No
	6/15/07–8/15/07	No (c)	All (m)	No	N.A.	No
Vermont	5/15/90–6/25/90	Yes	All	Yes	1.0 (e)	No
Virginia	2/1/90–3/31/90	Yes	All	Yes	32.2	No
	9/2/03–11/3/03	Yes	All	Yes	98.3	N.A.
West Virginia	10/1/86–12/31/86	Yes	All	Yes	15.9	Yes
	9/1/04–10/31/04	Yes	All	N.A.	10.4	Yes
Wisconsin	9/15/85–11/22/85	Yes	All	Yes (n)	27.3	Yes
	6/15/98–8/14/98	Yes	All	Yes	30.9	N.A.
Dist. of Columbia	7/1/87–9/30/87	Yes	All	Yes	24.3	Yes
	7/10/95–8/31/95	Yes	All (p)	Yes	19.5	Yes (p)
No. Mariana Islands	9/30/05–3/30/06	Yes	All	N.A.	N.A.	N.A.

Source: The Federation of Tax Administrators, July 2007. With an update by The Council of State Governmnents March 2009.

Key:

N.A. — Not available.

(a) Where applicable, figure indicates local portions of certain taxes collected under the state tax amnesty program.

(b) "No" indicates requirement of full payment by the expiration of the amnesty period. "Yes" indicates allowance of full payment after the expiration of the amnesty period.

(c) Authority for amnesty derived from pre-existing statutory powers permitting the waiver of tax penalties.

(d) Does not include intangibles tax and drug taxes. Gross collections totaled $22.1 million, with $13.7 million in penalties withdrawn.

(e) Preliminary figure.

(f) Amnesty taxpayers were billed for the interest owed, with payment due within 30 days of notification.

(g) Figure includes $1.1 million for the separate program conducted by the Department of Natural Resources for the boat excise tax.

(h) The amnesty statute was construed to extend the amnesty to those who applied to the department before the end of the amnesty period, and permitted them to file overdue returns and pay back taxes and interest at a later date.

(i) The severance taxes, including the six oil and gas severance taxes, the resources excise tax, the corporate franchise tax, and the special fuels tax were not subject to amnesty.

(j) Availability of amnesty for the corporation tax, the oil company taxes, the transporation and transmissions companies tax, the gross receipts oil tax and the unincorporated business tax restricted to entities with 500 or fewer employees in the United States on the date of application. In addition, a taxpayer principally engaged in aviation, or a utility subject to the supervision of the State Department of Public Service was also ineligible.

(k) Local taxes and real property taxes were not included.

(l) Full payment of tax liability required before the end of the amnesty period to avoid civil penalties.

(m) Texas does not impose a corporate or individual income tax. In practical effect, the amnesty was limited to the sales tax and other excises.

(n) Waiver terms varied depending upon the date the tax liability was assessed.

(o) Installment arrangements were permitted if applicant demonstrated that payment would present a severe financial hardship.

(p) Does not include real property taxes. All interest was waived on tax payments made before July 31, 1995. After this date, only 50% of the interest was waived.

(q) Exception for individuals who owed $500 or less.

(r) Except for property and motor fuel taxes.

(s) Multiple payments could be made so long as the required balance was paid in full no later than March 15, 2003.

(t) All taxes except property, estate and unclaimed property.

(u) Does not include the motor fuel use tax.

(v) Does not include motor carrier road taxes.

Table 7.16
STATE EXCISE TAX RATES
(As of January 1, 2009)

State or other jurisdiction	General sales and gross receipts tax (percent)	Cigarettes (cents per pack of 20)	Distilled spirits ($ per gallon)*	Motor fuel excise tax rates (cents per gallon) (a)		
				Gasoline	Diesel	Gasohol
Alabama	4.0	42.5 (b)	(c)	16.0	19.0	16.0
Alaska	. . .	200	12.80 (d)	8.0	8.0	8.0
Arizona	5.6	200	3.00	18.0	26.0	18.0
Arkansas	6	115	2.50 (d)	21.5	22.5	21.5
California	8.25 (e)(f)	87	3.30 (d)	18.0 (g)	18.0 (g)	18.0 (g)
Colorado	2.9	84	2.28	22.0	20.5	22.0
Connecticut	6.0	200	4.50 (d)	25.0	43.4	25.0
Delaware	. . .	115	5.46 (d)	23.0	22.0	23.0
Florida	6.0	33.9	6.50 (h)	16.1 (g)	29.8 (g)	16.1 (g)
Georgia	4.0	37	3.79 (d)	7.5 (g)	7.5 (g)	7.5 (g)
Hawaii	4.0	200	5.98	17.0 (g)	17.0	17.0
Idaho	6.0	57	(c)	25.0	25.0	22.5
Illinois	6.25	98 (b)	4.50 (d)	19.0 (g)	21.5 (g)	19.0 (g)
Indiana	7.0	99.5	2.68 (d)	18.0 (g)	16.0 (g)	18.0 (g)
Iowa	6.0	136	(c)	21.0	22.5	19.0
Kansas	5.3	79	2.50 (d)	24.0	26.0	24.0
Kentucky	6.0	60	1.92 (d)(h)	21.0 (g)	18.0 (g)	21.0 (g)
Louisiana	4.0	36	2.50 (d)	20.0	20.0	20.0
Maine	5.0	200	(c)	28.4	29.6	18.7
Maryland	6.0	200	1.50	23.5	24.25	23.5
Massachusetts	5.0	251	4.05 (h)(d)	21 .0	21.0	21.0
Michigan	6.0	200	(c)	19.0 (g)	15.0 (g)	19.0 (g)
Minnesota	6.875 (j)	123 (i)	5.03 (d)	25.0	25.0	17.8
Mississippi	7.0	18	(c)	18.4 (g)	18.4 (g)	18.4 (g)
Missouri	4.225	17 (b)	2.00	17.0 (g)	17.0 (g)	17.0 (g)
Montana	. . .	170	(c)	27.75	27.75	27.75
Nebraska	5.5	64	3.75	26.4 (g)	26.4 (g)	26.4 (g)
Nevada	6.5	80	3.60 (d)	23.0 (g)	27.0 (g)	23.0 (g)
New Hampshire	. . .	133	(c)	18.0 (g)	18.0 (g)	18.0 (g)
New Jersey	7.0	257.5	4.40	14.5 (g)	17.5 (g)	14.5 (g)
New Mexico	5.0	91	6.06	18.8 (g)	21.0 (g)	18.8 (g)
New York	4.0	275 (b)	6.44 (d)	41.0 (g)	39.0 (g)	41.0 (g)
North Carolina	4.5	35	(c)(h)	29.9 (g)	29.9 (g)	29.9 (g)
North Dakota	5.0	44	2.50 (d)	23.0	23.0	23.0
Ohio	5.5	125	(c)	28.0 (g)	28.0 (g)	28.0 (g)
Oklahoma	4.5	103	5.56 (d)	16.0 (g)	13.0 (g)	16.0 (g)
Oregon	. . .	118	(c)	24.0	24.0	24.0
Pennsylvania	6.0	135	(c)	31.2 (g)	38.1 (g)	31.2 (g)
Rhode Island	7.0	246	3.75	30.0 (g)	30.0 (g)	30.0 (g)
South Carolina	6.0	7	2.72 (d)	16.0	16.0	16.0
South Dakota	4.0	153	3.93(d)	22.0 (g)	22.0 (g)	20.0 g
Tennessee	7.0	62 (b)	4.40 (d)	20.0 (g)	17.0(g)	14.0 (g)
Texas	6.25	141	2.40 (d)	20.0	20.0	20.0
Utah	4.7	69.5	(c)	24.5	24.5	24.5
Vermont	6.0	199	(c)(d)	20.0 (g)	26.0 (g)	20.0 (g)
Virginia	5.0 (f)	30 (b)	(c)	17.5	17.5	17.5
Washington	6.5	202.5	(c)(h)	37.5	37.5	37.5
West Virginia	6.0	55	(c)	32.2 (g)	32.2 (g)	32.2 (g)
Wisconsin	5.0	177	3.25	30.9 (g)	30.9 (g)	30.9 (g)
Wyoming	4.0	60	(c)	14.0 (g)	14.0 (g)	14.0 (g)
Dist. of Columbia	5.75	200	1.50 (d)	20.0	20.0	20.0

See footnotes at end of table.

STATE EXCISE TAX RATES—Continued (As of January 1, 2009)

Source: Compiled by The Federation of Tax Administrators from various sources, January 2008 with updates by The Council of State Governments March 2009 from state government Web sites and Center for Disease Control Web site.

Key:

. . . — Tax is not applicable.

(a) The tax rates listed are fuel excise taxes collected by distributor/supplier/retailers in each state. Additional taxes may apply to motor carriers. Carrier taxes are coordinated by the International Fuel Tax Association.

(b) Counties and cities may impose an additional tax on a pack of cigarettes in Alabama 1¢ to 6¢; Illinois, 10¢ to 15¢; Missouri, 4¢ to 7¢; New York City $1.50; Tennessee 1¢; and Virginia 2¢ to 15¢.

(c) In 18 states, the government directly controls the sales of distilled spirits. Revenue in these states is generated from various taxes, fees and net liquor profits.

(d) Other taxes in addition to excise taxes for the following states: Alaska, under 21 percent—$2.50/gallon; Arkansas, under 5 percent—$0.50/gallon, under 21 percent—$1.00/gallon, $0.20/case and 3 percent off—14 percent on-premise retail taxes; California, over 50 percent—$6.60/gallon; Connecticut, under 7 percent—$2.05/gallon; Delaware, under 25 percent—$3.64/gallon, Florida under 17.259% -$2.25/gallon, over 55.780%-$9.53/gallon and 6.67 cents ounce; Georgia, $0.83/gallon local tax; Illinois, under 20 percent—$0.73/gallon, $1.845/gallon in Chicago and $2.00/gallon in Cook County; Indiana, under 15 percent—$0.47/gallon; Kansas, 8 percent off- and 10 percent on-premise retail tax; Kentucky, under 6 percent—$0.25/gallon, $0.05/case and 11 percent wholesale tax; Louisiana, under 6 percent—$0.32/gallon; Massachusetts, under 15 percent—$1.10/gallon, over 50 percent alcohol—$4.05/proof gallon, 0.57 percent on private club sales; Minnesota, $0.01/bottle (except miniatures) and 9 percent sales tax; Nevada, under 14 percent—$0.70/gallon and under 21 percent—$1.30/gallon; New York, no more than 24 percent—$2.54/gallon, $1.00/gallon New York City; North Dakota, 7 percent state sales tax; Oklahoma, 13.5 percent on-premise; South Carolina, $5.36/case and 9 percent surtax; South Dakota, under 14 percent—$0.93/gallon, 2 percent wholesale tax; Tennessee, $0.15/case and 15 percent on-premise, under 7 percent—$1.21/gallon; Texas, 14 percent on-premise and $0.05/drink on airline sales; Vermont, 10% on-premise sales tax and District of Columbia, 8 percent off- and 10 percent on-premise sales tax.

(e) Tax rate may be adjusted annually according to a formula based on balances in the unappropriated general fund and the school foundation fund.

(f) Includes statewide local tax; in California and Virginia, 1.0 percent.

(g) Other taxes and fees; California—sales tax applicable; Florida—sales tax added to excise; Georgia—sales tax added to excise; Hawaii—sales tax applicable; Illinois- sales tax applicable, environmental fee and leaking underground storage tax (LUST); Indiana—sales tax applicable; Kentucky—environmental fee; Michigan—sales tax applicable; Mississippi—environmental fee; Missouri—inspection fee; Nebraska—petroleum fee; Nevada—Inspection fee; New Hampshire—oil discharge cleanup fee; New Jersey—petroleum fee; New Mexico—petroleum loading fee; New York—sales tax applicable and petroleum tax; North Carolina—inspection tax; Ohio—plus 3 cents commercial; Oklahoma—environmental fee; Pennsylvania—oil franchise tax; Rhode Island—leaking underground storage tank tax (LUST); Tennessee—petroleum tax and environmental fee; Vermont—petroleum cleanup fee;Washington—$0.5 percent privilege tax; West Virginia—sales tax added to excise; Wisconsin—petroleum inspection fee; Wyoming—license tax.

(h) Sales tax is applied to on-premise sales only.

(i) Plus an additional 27.4 cent sales tax is added to the wholesale price of a tax stamp (total $1.504).

(x) On July 1, 2009 the new rate of 6.875 percent will go into effect.

Table 7.17
FOOD AND DRUG SALES TAX EXEMPTIONS
(As of January 1, 2009)

State or other jurisdiction	Tax rate (percentage)	Exemptions		
		Food (a)	Prescription drugs	Nonprescription drugs
Alabama	4.0	. . .	★	. . .
Alaska	0.0	N.A.	N.A.	N.A.
Arizona	5.6	★	★	. . .
Arkansas	6.0	3% (b)	★	. . .
California (c)	8.25 (d)	★	★	. . .
Colorado	2.9	★	★	. . .
Connecticut	6.0	★	★	★
Delaware	0.0	N.A.	N.A.	N.A.
Florida	6.0	★	★	★
Georgia	4.0	★(b)	★	. . .
Hawaii	4.0	. . .	★	. . .
Idaho	6.0	. . .	★	. . .
Illinois	6.25	1%	1%	1%
Indiana	7.0	★	★	. . .
Iowa	6.0	★	★	. . .
Kansas	5.3	. . .	★	. . .
Kentucky	6.0	★	★	. . .
Louisiana	4.0	★(b)	★	. . .
Maine	5.0	★	★	. . .
Maryland	6.0	★	★	★
Massachusetts	5.0	★	★	. . .
Michigan	6.0	★	★	. . .
Minnesota	6.875 (e)	★	★	★
Mississippi	7.0	. . .	★	. . .
Missouri	4.225	1.23%	★	. . .
Montana	0.0	N.A.	N.A.	N.A.
Nebraska	5.5	★	★	. . .
Nevada	6.5	★	★	. . .
New Hampshire	0.0	N.A.	N.A.	N.A.
New Jersey	7.0	★	★	★
New Mexico	5.0	★	★	. . .
New York	4.0	★	★	★
North Carolina	4.5	★(b)	★	. . .
North Dakota	5.0	★	★	. . .
Ohio	5.5	★	★	. . .
Oklahoma	4.5	. . .	★	. . .
Oregon	0.0	N.A.	N.A.	N.A.
Pennsylvania	6.0	★	★	★
Rhode Island	7.0	★	★	★
South Carolina	6.0	★	★	. . .
South Dakota	4.0	. . .	★	. . .
Tennessee	7.0	5.50%	★	. . .
Texas	6.25	★	★	★
Utah	4.7	1.75 (b)	★	. . .
Vermont	6.0	★	★	★
Virginia	5.0 (d)	2.5% (d)	★	★
Washington	6.5	★	★	. . .
West Virginia	6.0	3% (b)	★	. . .
Wisconsin	5.0	★	★	. . .
Wyoming	4.0	★	★	. . .
Dist. of Columbia	5.75	★	★	★

Source: The Federation of Tax Administrators, January 2008; with updates by The Council of State Governments, March 2009.

Key:

★ — Yes, exempt from tax.

. . . — Subject to general sales tax,

N.A. — Not applicable.

(a) Some states tax food, but allow a rebate or income tax credit to compensate poor households. They are: Hawaii, Idaho, Kansas, Oklahoma, South Dakota and Wyoming.

(b) Food sales are subject to local sales tax.

(c) The tax rate may be adjusted annually according to a formula based on balances in the unappropriated general fund and the school foundation fund.

(d) Includes statewide local tax of 1.0 percent in California and 1.0 percent in Virginia.

(e) On July 1, 2009 the new rate of 6.875 percent will go into effect.

Table 7.18
STATE INDIVIDUAL INCOME TAX RATES, 2009
Local Rates Excluded (as of January 1, 2009, except where noted)

State or other jurisdiction	Federal deductibility	Marginal rates and tax brackets for single filers (a)	Standard deduction		Personal exemptions (b)	
			Single	Joint	Single	Dependents
Alabama (x)	Yes	2% > $0 4% > $500 5% > $3K (s)	$2,000	$4,000	$1,500	$300
Alaska	No	None	n.a.	n.a.	n.a.	n.a.
Arizona	No	2.59% >$0 2.88% > $10K 3.36% > $25K 4.24% > $50K 4.54% > $150K (s)	$4,521 (n)	$9,042 (n)	$2,100	$2,100
Arkansas (x)	No	1% > $0 2.5% > $3,700 3.5% > $7,400 4.5% > $11,100 6% > $18,600 7% > $31,000 (i), (n), (s)	$2,000	$4,000	$23 (c)	$23 (c)
California	No	1% > $0 2% > $7,168 4% > $16,994 6% > $26,821 8% > $37,233 9.3% > $47,055 10.3% > $1,000,000 (n), (s)	$3,692 (n)	$7,384 (n)	$99 (c)(n)	$309 (c)(n)
Colorado	No	4.63% of federal taxable income	n.a.	n.a.	n.a.	n.a.
Connecticut	No	3.0% > $0 5.0% > $10,000 (s)	n.a.	n.a.	$13,000 (d)	$0
Delaware (x)	No	2.2% > $2,000 3.9% > $5,000 4.8% > $10,000 5.2% > $20,000 5.55% > $25,000 5.95% > $60,000 (s)	$3,250	$6,500	$110 (c)	$110 (c)
Florida	No	none	n.a.	n.a.	n.a.	n.a.
Georgia	No	1% > $0 2% > $750 3% > $2,250 4% > $3,750 5% > $5,250 6% > $7,000 (s)	$2,300	$3,000	$2,700	$3,000
Hawaii	No	1.4% > $0 3.2% > $2,400 5.5% > $4,800 6.4% > $9,600 6.8% > $14,400 7.2% > $19,200 7.6% > $24,000 7.9% > $36,000 8.25% > $48,000 (s)	$2,000	$4,000	$1,040	$1,040
Idaho	No	1.6% > $0 3.6% > $1,237 4.1% > $2,474 5.1% > $3,710 6.1% > $4,987 7.1% > $6,184 7.4% > $9,276 7.8% > $24,736 (n) (s)	$5,450 (o)	$10,900 (o)	$3,500 (o) (e)	$3,500 (o) (e)

See footnotes at end of table.

STATE INDIVIDUAL INCOME TAX RATES, 2009—Continued
Local Rates Excluded (as of January 1, 2009, except where noted)

State or other jurisdiction	Federal deductibility	Marginal rates and tax brackets for single filers (a)	Standard deduction		Personal exemptions (b)	
			Single	Joint	Single	Dependents
Illinois	No	3% of federal adjusted gross income with modification	n.a.	n.a.	$2,000	$2,000
Indiana (x)	No	3.4% of federal adjusted gross income with modification	n.a.	n.a.	$1,000	$2,500 (g)
Iowa (x)	Yes	0.36% > $0 0.72% > $1,407 2.43% > $2,814 4.5% > $5,628 6.12% > $12,663 6.48% > $21,105 6.8% > $28,140 7.92% > $42,210 8.98% > $63,315 (n), (s)	$1,780 (n)	$4,390 (n)	$40 (c)	$40 (c)
Kansas	No	3.5% > $0 6.25% > $15,000 6.45% > $30,000 (s)	$5,450	$10,900	$2,250	$2,250
Kentucky (x)	No	2% > $0 3% > $3,000 4% > $4,000 5% > $5,000 5.8% > $8,000 6% > $75,000 (s)	$2,100 (n)	$2,100 (n)	$20 (c)	$20 (c)
Louisiana	Yes	2% > $0 4% > $12,500 6% > $50,000 (s)	n.a.	n.a.	$4,500 (j)	$1,000
Maine	No	2% > $0 4.5% > $4,850 7% > $9,700 8.5% > $19,450 (n) (s)	$5,450 (n)	$9,100 (n)	$2,850	$2,850
Maryland (x)	No	2% > $0 3% > $1,000 4% > $2,000 4.75% > $3,000 5% > $150,000 5.25% > $300,000 5.5% > $500,000 6.25% > $1,000,000 (s)	$2,000 (k)	$4,000 (k)	$3,200	$3,200
Massachusetts	No	5.3% and 12% (w)	n.a.	n.a.	$4,400	$1,000
Michigan (x)	No	4.35% of federal adjusted gross income with modification	n.a.	n.a.	$3,500 (o)	$3,500 (o) (q)
Minnesota	No	5.35% > $0 7.05% > $22,730 7.85% >$74,650 (n), (s)	$5,450 (o)	$10,900 (o)	$3,500 (o)	$3,500 (o)
Mississippi	No	3% > $0 4% > $5,000 5% > $10,000 (s)	$2,300	$4,600	$6,000	$1,500
Missouri (x)	Yes (p)	1.5% > $0 2% > $1,000 2.5% > $2,000 3% > $3,000 3.5% > $4,000 4% > $5,000 4.5% > $6,000 5% > $7,000 5.5% > $8,000 6% > $9,000 (s)	$5,450 (o)	$10,900 (o)	$2,100	$1,200

STATE INDIVIDUAL INCOME TAX RATES, 2009—Continued
Local Rates Excluded (as of January 1, 2009, except where noted)

State or other jurisdiction	Federal deductibility	Marginal rates and tax brackets for single filers (a)	Standard deduction		Personal exemptions (b)	
			Single	Joint	Single	Dependents
Montana	Yes (r)	1% > $0 2% > $2,600 3% > $4,600 4% > $7,000 5% > $9,500 6% > $12,200 6.9% > $15,600 (n), (s)	$4,010 (n)	$8,020 (n)	$2,140 (n)	$2,140 (n)
Nebraska	No	2.56% > $0 3.57% > $2,400 5.12% > $17,500 6.84% > $27,000 (s)	$5,450 (n)	$10,900 (n)	$106 (c)	$106 (c)
Nevada	No	none	n.a.	n.a.	n.a.	n.a.
New Hampshire	No	5% > $0 (f)	$2,400	$4,800	n.a.	n.a.
New Jersey (x)	No	1.4% > $0 1.75% > $20,000 3.5% > $35,000 5.525% > $40,000 6.37% > $75,000 8.97% > $500,000 (s)	n.a.	n.a.	$1,000	$1,500
New Mexico	No	1.7% > $0 3.2% > $5,500 4.7% > $11,000 4.9% > $16,000 (s)	$5,450 (o)	$10,900 (o)	$3,500 (o)	$3,500 (o)
New York (x)	No	4% > $0 4.5% > $8,000 5.25% > $11,000 5.9% > $13,000 6.85% > $20,000 (s)	$7,500	$15,000	n.a.	$1,000
North Carolina	No	6% > $0 7% > $12,750 7.75% > $60,000 (s)	$3,000	$6,000	(l)	(l)
North Dakota	No	2.1% > $0 3.92% > $32,550 4.34% > $78,850 5.04% > $164,550 5.54% > $357,700 (n), (s)	$5,450 (o)	$10,900 (o)	$3,500 (o)	$3,500 (o)
Ohio (x)	No	0.587% > $0 1.174% > $5,000 2.348% > $10,000 2.935% > $15,000 3.521% > $20,000 4.109% > $40,000 4.695% > $80,000 5.451% > $100,000 5.925% > $200,000 (s)	n.a.	n.a.	$1,450 (e) (n)	$1,450 (e) (n)
Oklahoma	No	0.5% > $0 1% > $1,000 2% > $2,500 3% > $3,750 4% > $4,900 5% > $7,200 5.5% > $8,700 (s)	$4,250	$8,500	$1,000	$1,000

See footnotes at end of table.

STATE INDIVIDUAL INCOME TAX RATES, 2009—Continued
Local Rates Excluded (as of January 1, 2009, except where noted)

State or other jurisdiction	Federal deductibility	Marginal rates and tax brackets for single filers (a)	Standard deduction		Personal exemptions (b)	
			Single	Joint	Single	Dependents
Oregon (x)	Yes (t)	5% > $0 7% > $3,050 9% > $7,600 (n) (s)	$1,865 (n)	$3,735 (n)	$169 (c)(n)	$169 (c)(n)
Pennsylvania (x)	No	3.07% > $0	n.a.	n.a.	n.a.	n.a.
Rhode Island	No	3.75% > $0 7% > $32,550 7.75%> $78,850 9% > $164,550 9.9% >$357,700 (n) (s) (u)	$5,450 (o)	$9,100	$3,500 (o)	$3,500 (o)
South Carolina	No	0% > $0 3% > $2,630 4% > $5,260 5% > $7,890 6% > $10,520 7% > $13,150 (n), (s)	$5,450 (o)	$10,900 (o)	$3,500 (o)	$3,500 (o)
South Dakota	No	none	n.a.	n.a.	n.a.	n.a.
Tennessee	No	6% > $0 (f)	n.a.	n.a.	$1,250	n.a.
Texas	No	none	n.a.	n.a.	n.a.	n.a.
Utah	No	5% > $0	(v)	(v)	$2,625 (m)	$2,625 (m)
Vermont	No	3.6% > $0 7.2% > $32,550 8.5% > $78,850 9% > $164,550 9.5% > $357,700 (n), (s)	$5,450 (o)	$10,900 (o)	$3,500 (o)	$3,500 (o)
Virginia	No	2% > $0 3% > $3,000 5% > $5,000 5.75% > $17,000 (s)	$3,000	$6,000	$930	$930
Washington	No	none	n.a.	n.a.	n.a.	n.a.
West Virginia	No	3% > $0 4% > $10,000 4.5% > $25,000 6% > $40,000 6.5% > $60,000 (s)	n.a.	n.a.	$2,000	$2,000
Wisconsin	No	4.60% > $0 6.15% > $9,700 6.50% > $19,400 6.75% > $145,460 (n), (s)	$8,960 (h)	$16,140 (h)	$700	$700
Wyoming	No	none	n.a.	n.a.	n.a.	n.a.
Dist. of Columbia	No	4% > $0 6% > $10,000 8.5% > $40,000 (s)	$4,200	$4,200	$1,750	$1,750

See footnotes at end of table.

STATE INDIVIDUAL INCOME TAX RATES, 2009—Continued
Local Rates Excluded (as of January 1, 2009, except where noted)

Source: Tax Foundation, based on state tax forms and instructions, January 2009. For the current year and past years back to 2000, see *www.taxfoundation.org/taxdata/show/228.html*. For additonal information contact the Tax Foundation at *www.taxfoundation.org* or at (202) 464-6200.

Key:

n.a. – Not applicable

(a) Applies to single taxpayers and married people filing separately. Some states increase bracket widths for joint filers. See note(s)

(b) Married joint filers generally receive double the single exemption.

(c) Tax credit.

(d) Maximum equals $13,500. Value decreases as income increases. There is a $1,000 reduction in the exemption for every $1,000 of CT AGI over $27,000.

(e) Taxpayers receive a $20 tax credit per exemption in addition to the normal exemption amount. Called the grocery credit in Idaho.

(f) Applies to interest and dividend income only.

(g) $2,500 exemption is for each dependent child. If the dependent is not the taxpayer's child the exemption is $1,000.

(h) Deduction phases out to zero for single filers at $87,500 and joint filers at $99,736.

(i) Rates apply to regular tax table. A special tax table is available for low income taxpayers that reduces their tax payments.

(j) Standard deduction and personal exemptions are combined: $4,500 for single and married filing separately; $9,000 married filing jointly and head of household.

(k) The standard deduction is 15 percent of income with a minimum of $1,500 and a cap of $2,000 for single filers, married-filing-separately filers and dependent filers earning more than $13,333. The standard deduction is capped at $4,000 for married filing jointly filers, head of households filers and qualifying widowers earning more than $26,667.

(l) Federal taxable income (AGI less all deductions and exemptions) is the starting point for determining North Carolina taxable income. Filers must make an adjustment on the North Carolina return for the difference in the NC and federal personal exemption. For tax year 2008 single filers with income less than $60,000 ($100,000 for married filing jointly) must add $1,000 to their taxable income. If the filer's income is over the applicable threshold $1,500 must be added to their taxable income.

(m) Three-quarters of the federal exemption.

(n) Values adjusted for inflation each year.

(o) Deduction or exemption tied to federal tax system. Federal deductions and exemptions are indexed for inflation.

(p) Federal tax deduction limited to $5,000 or $10,000.

(q) Additional $600 exemption per dependent under 18 years old.

(r) Available only if itemizing deductions.

(s) Some states effectively double the bracket widths for joint filers (AL, AZ, CT, HI, ID, KS, LA, ME, NE, NY, OR). CA doubles all bracket widths except the $1,000,000 bracket. Some states increase, but don't double, all or some bracket widths for joint filers (GA, MN, NM, NC, ND, OK, RI, VT, WI). Some states do not adjust their brackets for joint filers (AR, DE, IA, KY, MS, MO, MT, OH, SC, VA, WV, DC). Of these states, some permit married couples to file separately to avoid a marriage penalty, and some allow joint filers to make an adjustment to reduce their tax after it is calculated. MD decreases some of its bracket widths and increases others. NJ adds a 2.45% rate and doubles some bracket widths.

(t) Deduction limited to no more than $5,000.

(u) Taxpayers calculate tax under a flat tax system and pay the lesser of the liability. The flat tax applies to all types of income with no exemptions or deductions and treats capital income as wages. The flat tax rates are 7.5 percent for 2007; 7 percent for 2008; 6.5 percent for 2009; 6 percent for 2010; and 5.5 percent for 2011 and beyond.

(v) The standard deduction is taken in the form of a nonrefundable credit of 6% of the federal standard or itemized deduction amount, excluding the deduction for state or local income tax. This credit phases out at 1.3 cents per dollar above $12,000 of AGI ($24,000 for married couples). For 2008 the federal standard deduction is $5,450 for single filers and $10,900 for joint filers.

(w) Taxpayers have the choice of paying an optional higher rate of 5.85%. The 12% rate applies to short-term capital gains, long- and short-term capital gains on collectibles and pre-1996 installment sales classified as capital gain income for Massachusetts purposes.

(x) Local rates are excluded; 14 states have county or city level income taxes. In each of these states the average rate for all counties and cities, weighted by total personal income within each jurisdiction, is: 0.19% in Ala.; 0.06% in Ark.; 0.16% in Del.; 1.16% in Ind.; 0.3% in Iowa; 0.76% in Ky.; 2.98% in Md.; 0.44% in Mich.; 0.12% in Mo.; 0.09% in N.J.; 1.7% in N.Y.; 1.82% in Ohio; 0.36% in Ore.; and 1.25% in Pa.

Table 7.19
RANGE OF STATE CORPORATE INCOME TAX RATES as of January 1, 2009

State	Tax rates and brackets	Special rates or notes
Alabama	6.5%	Federal deductibility
Alaska	1.0% > $0 2.0 > 10K 3.0 > 20K 4.0 > 30K 5.0 > 40K 6.0 > 50K 7.0 > 60K 8.0 > 70K 9.0 > 80K 9.4 > 90K	4.5% alternative tax rate on capital gains. Alternative minimum tax equal to 18% of federal alternative minimum tax.
Arizona	6.968%	Minimum tax is $50.
Arkansas	1.0% > $0 2.0 > 3K 3.0 > 6K 5.0 > 11K 6.0 > 25K 6.5 > 100K	
California	8.84%	Minimum tax is $800. 10.84% on financial institutions. The tax rate on S-Corporations is 1.5% (3.5% for financial S-Corporations). A 6.65% AMT is also imposed.
Colorado	4.63%	
Connecticut	7.5%	Pay higher of income tax or tax on capital (3.1 mills per dollar, with a minimum of $250 and a maximum of $1,000,000).
Delaware	8.7%	Banking tax: 8.7% on first $20 million, 6.7% for next $5 million, 4.7% for next $5 million, 2.7% for next $620 million, and 1.7% for amounts greater than $650 million. A franchise tax is due on the greater of the tax calculated on authorized shares or gross assets ($35 minimum, $165,000 maximum).
Florida	5.5%	Taxpayers who owe federal AMT must pay higher of FL corporate income tax or 3.3% alternative minimum rate.
Georgia	6.0%	Financial institutions: 0.25% of Georgia gross receipts.
Hawaii	4.4% > $0 5.4 > 25K 6.4 > 100K	Banks and financial institutions are taxed at 7.92%. An alternative tax rate on capital gains is imposed at a rate of 4%.
Idaho	7.6%	Minimum tax $20.
Illinois	7.3%	Includes 2.5% income replacement tax. S-Corporations pay only a 1.5% replacement tax.
Indiana	8.5%	
Iowa	6.0% > $0 8.0 > 25K 10.0 > 100K 12.0 > 250K	50% federal deductibility. 7.2% alternative minimum tax. Financial institutions are subject to a 5% franchise tax.
Kansas	4.0% > $0 7.1 > 50K	The top rate is a result of a 3.1% surtax on income over $50,000. Corporate franchise tax of 0.09375% in 2008; 0.0625% in 2009; and 0.03125% in 2010 on total net worth for entities of $1,000,000 or more. Banking privilege tax is 2.25% of total net income plus 2.125% surtax on taxable income over $25,000.
Kentucky	4.0% > $0 5.0 > 50K 6.0 > 100K	Corporations must also pay the limited liability entity tax, which is the lesser of 0.095% of gross receipts or 0.75% of gross profits. The tax phases in between $3 million and $6 million of gross receipts or profits. Minimum tax $175.
Louisiana	4.0% > $0 5.0 > 25K 6.0 > 50K 7.0 > 100K 8.0 > 200K	Federal deductibility. Corporation franchise tax: $1.50 for each $1000 up to $300,000 of capital employed in LA; and $3 for each $1000 over $300,000 ($10 minimum).
Maine	3.5% > $0 7.93 > 25K 8.33 > 75K 8.93 > 250K	An AMT is imposed at 5.4%. Banks and financial institutions choose to pay either 1% of income plus 0.008% of assets, or 0.039% of assets only.
Maryland	8.25%	
Massachusetts	9.5%	There is an additional tax of $2.60 per $1,000 on taxable tangible property (or net worth allocable to the state, for intangible property corporations); minimum tax of $456. 10.5% on financial institutions.
Michigan	4.95%	There is an additional modified gross receipts tax (sales minus purchases from other firms) at a rate of 0.8%. The income and gross receipts taxes are subject to a 21.99% surtax on the calculated liability, with the maximum surtax being $6 million. Banks pay a tax on net worth at a rate of 0.235%.

See footnotes at end of table.

RANGE OF STATE CORPORATE INCOME TAX RATES—Continued
as of January 1, 2009

State	Tax rates and brackets	Special rates or notes
Minnesota	9.8%	5.8% alternative minimum tax rate. A minimum tax ranging from $0 to $5000 is levied based on Minnesota property, payroll and sales.
Mississippi	3.0% > $0 4.0 > 5K 5.0 >10K	Franchise tax of $2.50 per $1,000 of taxable capital, with a minimum tax of $25
Missouri	6.25%	Additional franchise tax at 0.0333% of taxable capital. Financial institutions pay a 7% net income tax. 50% of federal tax deductible.
Montana	6.75%	7% for corporations filing under a water's edge election. Minimum tax is $50.
Nebraska	5.58% > $0 7.81 > 100K	Financial institutions: lesser of 0.047% of average deposits or 3.81% of net income before taxes and extraordinary items.
Nevada	None	
New Hampshire	8.5%	NH has two corporate taxes: the business profits tax (BPT) and the business enterprise tax (BET). The BPT rate is 8.5% of income for corporations with gross receipts over $50K. The BET rate is 0.75% on the enterprise value tax base (total compensation paid out, including dividends and interest). The BET is assessed on corporations with gross receipts over $150K or an enterprise value tax base over $75K.
New Jersey	6.5% > $0 7.5 > 50K 9.0 > 100K	Companies with income greater than $100K pay 9% on all income; companies with income greater than $50K but less than $100K pay 7.5% on all income, and companies with income under $50K pay 6.5%. The minimum tax is $500. An alternative minimum assessment based on gross receipts or profits applies if greater than corporate franchise tax. 4% surtax applied to tax liability for 2008. Banking and financial institutions are subject to the income tax.
New Mexico	4.8% > $0 6.4 > 500K 7.6 > 1,000,000	
New York	7.1%	Businesses pay greatest of regular income tax, 1.5% AMT, 0.178% of capital base, or a fixed dollar minimum tax between $100 and $1500. There is an additional 0.09% tax on subsidiary capital. Some banking corporations are subject to a tax of 7.5% of entire net income, or an alternative tax on net income or assets. A surcharge of 17% of the computed tax is imposed on business activity within the Metropolitan Commuter Transportation District.
North Carolina	6.9%	The franchise tax rate is $1.50 per $1,000 and is applied to the greatest of three different tax bases, with a minimum of $35.
North Dakota	2.6% > $0 4.1 > 3K 5.6 > 8K 6.4 > 20K 6.5 > 30K	7% for financial institutions, with a minimum of $50. Corporations making a water's-edge election must pay an additional 3.5% tax.
Ohio	5.1% > $0 8.5 > 50K	A value added-style tax on gross receipts, the commercial activity tax (CAT), was instituted in 2005. It will be phased in through 2010 while the corporate franchise tax (Ohio's income tax) is phased out. From April 2008 through March 2009, the CAT rate is 0.208%. Beginning April 1, 2009 the CAT rate is fully phased in and equals 0.26%. For tax year 2009 companies owe 20% of Corporate Franchise Tax liability. For tax year 2010 and thereafter the corporate franchise tax is fully phased out.
Oklahoma	6.0%	Additional franchise tax of $1.25 for each $1,000 of capital invested or used in Oklahoma.
Oregon	6.6%	Minimum tax $10. Financial institutions are subject to the income tax.
Pennsylvania	9.99%	Imposes a capital stock and foreign franchise tax of 0.189% on taxable income over $125K. Bank and trust company shares tax is 1.25%.
Rhode Island	9.0%	Greater of 9% of net income apportioned to Rhode Island or a franchise tax on authorized capital stock at the rate of $2.50 for each $10,000.00 or fractional part thereof (minimum of $500).
South Carolina	5.0%	4.5% for banks; 6% for savings and loans.
South Dakota	None	Banks pay 6% on net income. Minimum tax is $200 per location.
Tennessee	6.5%	Franchise tax of 0.25% of the greater of net worth or real and tangible property (minimum $100).
Texas	None	Texas has a 1% franchise tax which is a gross receipts tax paid by most taxable entities. Qualified entities with $10 million or less in total revenue pay 0.575%. Qualifying retailers and wholesalers pay 0.5%. Taxable entities with total revenue of $300,000 or less will owe no tax. Taxable entities with tax due of less than $1,000 will owe no tax.
Utah	5.0%	Minimum tax $100.
Vermont	6.0% > $0 7.0 > 10k 8.5 > 25k	Minimum tax $250.
Virginia	6.0%	Bank franchise tax is 1.0% of net capital.

See footnotes at end of table.

RANGE OF STATE CORPORATE INCOME TAX RATES—Continued as of January 1, 2009

State	Tax rates and brackets	Special rates or notes
Washington	None	Washington has no income tax but has a gross receipts tax called the business & occupation (B&O) tax which is levied at various rates. The major rates are 0.471% for retail sales, 0.484% for wholesale and manufacturing, and 1.5% for service and other activities.
West Virginia	8.5%	Business franchise tax of 0.55% of taxable capital (minimum of $50).
Wisconsin	7.9%	
Wyoming	None	
Dist. of Columbia	9.975%	Minimum tax is $100. DC's ballpark fee is levied on gross receipts over $5 million at varying rates.

Source: Tax Foundation, based on state tax forms and instructions, January 2009. For the current year and past years back to 2000, see *www.taxfoundation.org/taxdata/show/230.html*.

Table 7.20
STATE GOVERNMENT TAX REVENUE, BY TYPE OF TAX: 2007
(In thousands of dollars)

State	Total taxes	Sales and gross receipts	Licenses	Individual income	Corporation net income	Severance	Property taxes	Death and gift	Documentary and stock transfer	Other
United States	$749,785,186	$345,363,685	$46,799,430	$266,355,603	$52,977,642	$10,728,931	$12,160,656	$4,901,473	$10,256,669	$241,097
Alabama	8,868,314	4,390,386	477,462	3,019,510	505,886	144,306	273,501	671	56,592	0
Alaska	3,442,930	219,776	127,226	0	813,762	2,216,253	65,780	133	0	0
Arizona	12,396,587	7,338,904	402,597	3,196,156	986,170	43,560	429,200	0	0	0
Arkansas	7,391,778	3,854,708	298,309	2,168,441	362,983	21,579	633,016	0	42,433	10,309
California	114,736,981	40,433,533	7,501,648	53,318,287	11,157,898	15,175	2,304,092	6,348	0	0
Colorado	9,205,912	3,450,208	343,346	4,795,423	479,445	136,888	0	602	0	0
Connecticut	12,847,554	4,963,682	362,255	6,335,078	824,915	0	0	178,380	183,244	0
Delaware	2,905,905	459,209	1,006,434	1,025,416	302,222	0	0	893	110,935	796
Florida	35,738,291	27,535,367	1,875,317	0	2,442,516	45,870	40,518	43,397	3,755,306	0
Georgia	18,170,913	7,744,262	497,388	8,799,415	1,017,187	0	78,958	1,403	0	32,300
Hawaii	5,093,842	3,227,965	156,238	1,560,306	100,847	0	0	162	48,324	0
Idaho	3,536,574	1,668,798	264,108	1,406,462	188,229	6,649	0	177	0	2,151
Illinois	30,578,017	14,310,390	2,440,961	10,469,797	2,936,360	354	60,397	260,123	99,635	0
Indiana	14,008,033	7,752,229	496,368	4,615,605	987,111	1,003	5,427	150,290	0	0
Iowa	6,469,752	2,767,626	615,343	2,666,601	325,077	0	0	77,750	17,355	0
Kansas	6,893,359	3,057,029	302,685	2,744,934	527,427	132,281	73,383	55,620	0	0
Kentucky	9,895,207	4,590,295	459,329	3,041,535	988,065	275,313	493,623	43,578	3,469	0
Louisiana	10,863,502	5,373,662	568,849	3,214,163	752,773	904,164	38,757	11,134	0	0
Maine	3,581,680	1,690,705	227,273	1,358,301	183,852	0	37,241	54,820	29,488	0
Maryland	15,094,183	5,811,886	722,214	6,679,168	782,030	0	595,373	224,322	214,347	64,843
Massachusetts	20,666,972	5,995,840	675,925	11,399,649	2,106,898	0	3,382	249,597	235,681	0
Michigan	23,848,753	11,602,093	1,375,194	6,442,678	1,786,213	81,874	2,322,506	712	237,483	0
Minnesota	17,780,164	7,302,090	973,363	7,230,854	1,183,816	34,591	674,559	107,599	261,562	11,730
Mississippi	6,394,513	4,098,390	395,529	1,401,809	369,205	81,814	47,621	145	0	0
Missouri	10,704,834	4,814,498	630,431	4,834,820	390,657	58	26,397	0	7,945	28
Montana	2,319,992	530,159	308,304	832,916	178,707	264,740	201,825	755	0	2,586
Nebraska	4,071,032	1,952,603	207,013	1,650,895	213,027	2,499	2,395	27,366	15,234	0
Nevada	6,304,753	5,126,064	801,560	0	0	62,178	184,467	759	129,725	0
New Hampshire	2,175,057	734,894	209,662	107,452	595,789	0	385,268	377	141,605	10
New Jersey	29,106,788	11,942,242	1,512,520	11,539,894	2,876,591	0	3,796	586,589	645,156	0
New Mexico	5,205,322	2,483,021	237,561	1,149,805	425,087	843,900	57,097	0	0	8,851
New York	63,161,582	19,505,685	1,327,930	34,579,992	5,416,105	0	0	1,053,384	1,278,486	0
North Carolina	22,612,798	8,866,005	1,338,413	10,588,951	1,565,544	1,898	0	177,543	74,444	0
North Dakota	1,782,990	808,706	127,842	316,894	136,424	391,337	1,787	0	0	0
Ohio	24,810,567	11,223,322	2,139,072	10,031,665	1,302,582	7,558	34,259	72,109	0	0
Oklahoma	8,267,606	2,939,995	952,971	2,774,851	561,375	942,148	0	66,650	17,218	12,398
Oregon	7,742,862	782,874	832,937	5,595,831	405,857	12,513	21,791	79,649	11,410	0
Pennsylvania	30,837,657	14,482,543	2,847,005	9,812,726	2,286,527	0	64,467	736,610	583,427	24,352
Rhode Island	2,766,046	1,356,587	94,012	1,085,600	179,168	0	1,479	35,962	13,144	94
South Carolina	8,688,935	4,577,312	471,080	3,239,468	311,902	0	9,361	1,560	78,252	0

See footnotes at end of table.

STATE GOVERNMENT TAX REVENUE, BY TYPE OF TAX: 2007
(In thousands of dollars)—Continued

State	Total taxes	Sales and gross receipts	Licenses	Individual income	Corporation net income	Severance	Property taxes	Death and gift	Documentary and stock transfer	Other
South Dakota	1,257,084	1,018,603	156,488	0	76,665	4,700	0	506	122	0
Tennessee	11,370,768	8,355,174	1,259,679	249,145	1,120,422	1,604	0	111,191	239,872	33,681
Texas	40,314,714	31,811,384	5,735,796	0	0	2,762,940	0	4,594	0	0
Utah	5,889,423	2,625,037	202,454	2,561,001	398,894	101,539	0	498	0	0
Vermont	2,558,806	844,977	116,683	581,189	83,362	0	889,022	17,806	19,855	5,912
Virginia	18,571,160	6,000,415	673,592	10,238,776	879,575	2,006	20,676	152,864	582,309	20,947
Washington	17,692,767	13,851,911	882,114	0	0	48,727	1,688,530	182,853	1,038,632	0
West Virginia	4,654,213	2,227,596	182,098	1,360,511	539,136	328,320	4,104	199	12,249	0
Wisconsin	14,482,624	6,037,081	860,536	6,333,633	923,359	4,960	120,103	121,113	71,730	10,109
Wyoming	2,025,090	825,964	126,316	0	0	803,632	266,498	2,680	0	0

Source: U.S. Department of Commerce, U.S. Census Bureau, Governments Division, March 2009. 2007 Survey of State Government Finances. Data users who create their own estimates using data from this report should cite the U.S. Census Bureau as the source of the original data only. The data in this table are based on information from public records and contain no confidential data. Although the data in this table come from a census of governmental units and are not subject to sampling error, the census results do contain nonsampling error. Additional information on nonsampling error, response rates, and definitions may be found at *http://www.census.gov/govs/www/surveymethodology07.html*.

Table 7.21
STATE GOVERNMENT SALES AND GROSS RECEIPTS TAX REVENUE: 2007
(In thousands of dollars)

State	Total	General sales or gross receipts	Selective sales taxes								
			Total	Motor fuels	Insurance premiums	Public utilities	Tobacco products	Alcoholic beverages	Amusements	Pari-mutuels	Other
United States	$345,363,685	$235,867,056	$109,496,629	$36,523,953	$15,345,345	$10,986,363	$15,262,111	$5,156,536	$5,929,715	$296,258	$19,996,348
Alabama	4,390,386	2,278,027	2,112,359	567,791	276,814	744,890	150,779	158,886	103	2,968	210,128
Alaska	219,776	0	219,776	39,303	55,402	4,096	70,458	35,044	2,446	0	13,027
Arizona	7,338,904	5,683,866	1,655,038	768,914	440,696	23,074	358,113	63,190	619	432	0
Arkansas	3,854,708	2,904,401	950,307	462,056	138,612	0	148,317	46,755	2,655	5,417	146,495
California	40,433,533	32,669,175	7,764,358	3,432,527	2,178,336	600,518	1,078,536	333,789	0	37,527	103,125
Colorado	3,450,208	2,218,951	1,231,257	661,832	182,111	9,750	227,662	34,394	112,536	2,972	0
Connecticut	4,963,682	3,030,353	1,933,329	439,673	233,942	172,989	253,774	40,411	465,737	8,650	318,153
Delaware	459,209	0	459,209	117,484	110,167	47,665	88,085	14,802	0	147	80,859
Florida	27,535,367	21,748,908	5,786,459	2,305,859	785,875	1,043,515	454,017	653,721	0	28,098	515,374
Georgia	7,744,262	5,915,521	1,828,741	1,082,874	343,000	0	242,799	160,068	0	0	0
Hawaii	3,227,965	2,557,644	670,321	89,729	99,079	124,017	85,779	46,034	0	0	225,683
Idaho	1,668,798	1,277,533	391,265	231,894	85,622	2,260	55,320	7,416	0	1,931	6,822
Illinois	14,310,390	7,817,291	6,493,099	1,453,706	308,637	1,833,624	638,846	155,680	821,860	8,515	1,272,231
Indiana	7,752,229	5,423,501	2,328,728	880,874	190,811	12,167	360,530	39,704	830,330	4,572	9,740
Iowa	2,767,626	1,786,668	980,958	447,484	105,223	0	135,207	14,237	276,132	2,675	0
Kansas	3,057,029	2,242,025	815,004	431,394	129,841	892	120,587	101,260	535	2,760	27,735
Kentucky	4,590,295	2,817,636	1,772,659	570,540	148,247	52,584	177,527	102,201	190	5,833	715,537
Louisiana	5,373,662	3,481,242	1,892,420	616,636	402,298	18,635	103,296	53,881	610,163	55,506	32,005
Maine	1,690,705	1,054,812	635,893	231,484	85,026	24,442	158,953	20,283	20,468	3,488	91,749
Maryland	5,811,886	3,447,828	2,364,058	753,988	385,026	132,789	277,755	28,682	7,540	2,019	776,259
Massachusetts	5,995,840	4,075,549	1,920,291	676,119	397,280	0	438,074	71,728	3,805	3,859	329,426
Michigan	11,602,093	7,983,098	3,618,995	1,034,462	223,754	20,829	1,131,712	136,483	159,363	9,168	903,224
Minnesota	7,302,090	4,470,596	2,831,494	644,172	318,179	50	448,380	72,315	49,137	1,520	1,297,741
Mississippi	4,098,390	3,155,622	942,768	448,826	191,973	9,611	55,631	41,977	185,847	0	8,903
Missouri	4,814,498	3,272,919	1,541,579	736,652	294,947	0	108,876	31,324	339,579	0	30,201
Montana	530,159	0	530,159	210,693	63,060	40,674	91,470	25,669	60,179	136	38,278
Nebraska	1,952,603	1,484,170	468,433	320,509	36,625	2,887	71,526	25,828	5,869	233	4,956
Nevada	5,126,064	3,212,848	1,913,216	328,433	259,329	11,193	137,649	39,862	1,089,065	0	47,685
New Hampshire	734,894	0	734,894	129,182	87,346	73,494	138,511	12,519	191	3,148	290,503
New Jersey	11,942,242	8,345,601	3,596,641	565,154	444,535	982,202	785,130	101,721	460,222	0	257,677
New Mexico	2,483,021	1,843,613	639,408	244,617	104,215	15,988	46,082	30,014	60,588	395	137,509
New York	19,505,685	10,879,888	8,625,797	516,224	1,172,298	773,876	981,861	194,222	671	28,087	4,958,558
North Carolina	8,866,005	5,202,423	3,663,582	1,608,984	487,119	372,028	241,314	246,163	15,882	0	692,092
North Dakota	808,706	484,341	324,365	138,813	30,168	35,475	24,236	6,447	8,927	255	80,044
Ohio	11,223,322	7,781,270	3,442,052	1,719,809	449,767	172,114	996,572	91,674	0	12,116	0
Oklahoma	2,939,995	1,964,098	975,897	396,991	197,026	29,969	231,428	79,694	11,096	1,834	27,859
Oregon	782,874	0	782,874	416,964	56,167	22,071	271,101	13,889	90	2,592	0
Pennsylvania	14,482,543	8,661,711	5,820,832	2,142,989	693,984	1,299,169	1,018,438	264,665	255,074	24,737	121,776
Rhode Island	1,356,587	875,619	480,968	131,696	56,581	102,119	119,867	11,356	0	2,902	56,447
South Carolina	4,577,312	3,233,632	1,343,680	533,285	123,003	39,985	31,672	147,401	38,095	0	430,239

See footnotes at end of table.

STATE GOVERNMENT SALES AND GROSS RECEIPTS TAX REVENUE: 2007—Continued
(In thousands of dollars)

State	Total	General sales or gross receipts	Selective sales taxes								
			Total	Motor fuels	Insurance premiums	Public utilities	Tobacco products	Alcoholic beverages	Amusements	Pari-mutuels	Other
South Dakota	1,018,603	711,321	307,282	123,484	58,981	1,384	46,665	13,414	7,765	303	55,286
Tennessee	8,355,174	6,763,657	1,591,517	859,743	374,502	7,813	135,802	112,035	0	0	101,622
Texas	31,811,384	20,434,675	11,376,709	3,075,308	1,292,460	995,056	1,330,589	735,650	26,390	10,919	3,910,337
Utah	2,625,037	1,953,643	671,394	382,381	123,665	30,231	62,473	35,872	0	0	36,772
Vermont	844,977	334,413	510,564	87,370	55,131	10,310	64,300	19,204	0	0	274,249
Virginia	6,000,415	3,539,061	2,461,354	918,849	384,894	139,705	172,077	167,754	130	0	677,945
Washington	13,851,911	10,861,327	2,990,584	1,128,798	391,949	444,134	444,688	253,225	76	1,994	325,720
West Virginia	2,227,596	1,129,531	1,098,065	349,167	111,176	152,529	111,392	9,012	0	17,352	347,437
Wisconsin	6,037,081	4,158,611	1,878,470	996,200	156,765	350,583	313,645	52,205	360	1,018	7,694
Wyoming	825,964	698,437	127,527	72,037	23,701	2,977	24,610	2,776	0	180	1,246

Source: U.S. Department of Commerce, U.S. Census Bureau, Governments Division, March 2009. 2007 Survey of State Government Finances. Data users who create their own estimates using data from this report should cite the U.S. Census Bureau as the source of the original data only. The data in this table are based on information from public records and contain no confidential data. Although the data in this table come from a census of governmental units and are not subject to sampling error, the census results do contain nonsampling error. Additional information on nonsampling error, response rates, and definitions may be found at *http://www.census.gov/govs/www/surveymethodology07.html*.

Table 7.22
STATE GOVERNMENT LICENSE TAX REVENUE: 2007
(In thousands of dollars)

State	Total license tax revenue	Motor vehicle license revenue	Occupation and business license, NEC	Corporation license	Motor vehicle operator's license	Hunting and fishing license	Public utility license	Alcoholic beverage license	Amusement license	Other license taxes
United States	$46,799,430	$19,269,162	$13,376,489	$8,307,892	$2,131,455	$1,413,091	$481,537	$441,698	$623,176	$754,930
Alabama	477,462	204,831	124,694	98,831	16,163	16,903	12,477	3,563	0	0
Alaska	127,226	59,848	29,845	1,405	0	27,002	324	1,777	0	7,025
Arizona	402,597	213,008	98,885	11,221	27,013	30,549	0	9,986	26	11,909
Arkansas	298,309	131,292	92,376	22,810	14,967	20,496	7,914	1,822	445	6,187
California	7,501,648	2,621,956	4,345,609	64,014	227,996	90,360	86,646	48,881	12,241	3,945
Colorado	343,346	204,994	35,221	8,887	10,427	76,146	0	6,097	831	743
Connecticut	362,255	203,399	87,471	17,800	38,026	3,863	0	6,385	40	5,271
Delaware	1,006,434	34,783	240,730	624,210	2,665	1,049	6,987	977	450	94,583
Florida	1,875,317	1,176,282	239,006	196,157	172,643	14,750	33,519	36,846	5,048	1,066
Georgia	497,388	235,722	133,000	61,100	43,572	22,500	0	1,483	0	11
Hawaii	156,238	108,314	29,519	1,478	446	440	14,580	0	0	1,461
Idaho	264,108	125,306	56,481	2,448	6,599	33,889	34,068	1,600	359	3,358
Illinois	2,440,961	1,473,073	645,145	201,405	67,797	36,032	0	11,387	1,306	4,816
Indiana	496,368	182,932	39,189	7,111	228,873	18,466	0	10,848	4,896	4,053
Iowa	615,343	401,265	91,931	35,742	6,864	27,076	11,543	10,499	22,053	8,370
Kansas	302,685	169,653	25,309	56,152	19,718	20,877	5,237	2,603	215	2,921
Kentucky	459,329	209,881	110,597	76,602	17,442	24,911	10,110	5,345	284	4,157
Louisiana	568,849	110,997	95,046	315,296	11,870	28,312	4,174	0	0	3,154
Maine	227,273	88,093	92,414	6,639	10,637	17,119	0	3,739	704	7,928
Maryland	722,214	459,907	146,027	73,779	25,559	13,708	0	1,089	26	2,119
Massachusetts	675,925	300,426	162,032	25,418	82,302	5,437	0	3,118	447	96,745
Michigan	1,375,194	909,353	152,040	20,314	51,430	49,981	21,884	13,461	0	156,731
Minnesota	973,363	512,656	297,385	6,763	48,450	59,512	0	1,602	1,052	45,943
Mississippi	395,529	124,836	79,679	125,580	31,192	14,709	0	2,777	5,866	10,890
Missouri	630,431	253,464	165,609	76,570	16,992	30,697	20,191	4,199	49	62,660
Montana	308,304	150,082	85,425	3,023	8,560	47,076	14	1,665	4,988	7,471
Nebraska	207,013	91,150	63,250	7,081	8,945	15,270	0	282	0	21,035
Nevada	801,560	170,142	433,814	72,119	15,639	9,114	0	0	95,256	5,476
New Hampshire	209,662	85,806	84,118	4,425	13,225	8,782	6,867	3,266	322	2,851
New Jersey	1,512,520	463,133	587,255	319,622	40,273	12,527	22	15,336	71,536	2,816
New Mexico	237,561	182,821	26,537	2,586	5,076	18,400	876	870	324	71
New York	1,327,930	817,299	149,476	71,518	157,241	40,763	19,016	58,173	67	14,377
North Carolina	1,338,413	614,000	162,303	399,207	126,775	17,419	0	14,371	0	4,338
North Dakota	127,842	57,635	50,997	0	4,008	14,626	4	280	292	0
Ohio	2,139,072	736,563	837,042	401,591	82,476	36,541	5,335	34,301	0	5,223
Oklahoma	952,971	608,318	202,577	49,999	13,650	20,286	29	4,843	52,207	1,062
Oregon	832,937	460,186	275,423	11,355	32,002	39,890	1,991	2,836	2,768	6,486
Pennsylvania	2,847,005	818,588	723,015	776,886	58,400	67,636	56,405	16,183	313,973	15,919
Rhode Island	94,012	52,539	32,887	4,189	565	1,781	0	149	948	954
South Carolina	471,080	171,778	141,521	67,065	52,183	17,156	0	8,629	1,494	11,254

See footnotes at end of table.

STATE GOVERNMENT LICENSE TAX REVENUE: 2007—Continued
(In thousands of dollars)

State	Total license tax revenue	Motor vehicle license revenue	Occupation and business license, NEC	Corporation license	Motor vehicle operator's license	Hunting and fishing license	Public utility license	Alcoholic beverage license	Amusement license	Other license taxes
South Dakota	156,488	45,417	75,011	3,101	2,478	26,437	964	315	92	2,673
Tennessee	1,259,679	271,080	259,037	635,002	44,811	34,108	6,799	1,066	309	7,467
Texas	5,735,796	1,433,781	763,108	3,215,219	116,929	91,384	17,481	51,375	7,945	38,574
Utah	202,454	105,710	36,588	5,038	22,054	26,111	0	1,842	0	5,111
Vermont	116,683	71,131	27,326	4,693	5,412	5,775	0	375	0	1,971
Virginia	673,592	367,848	160,516	57,257	45,733	26,402	0	11,157	116	4,563
Washington	882,114	459,158	220,024	24,022	61,148	32,214	16,869	11,099	13,574	44,006
West Virginia	182,098	87,715	42,282	8,691	957	16,701	13,956	11,560	15	221
Wisconsin	860,536	365,968	302,866	16,957	31,269	71,017	65,255	1,641	612	4,951
Wyoming	126,316	65,043	18,851	9,514	2,003	30,891	0	0	0	14

Source: U.S. Department of Commerce, Bureau of the Census, January 2009. 2007 Survey of State Government Finances. Data users who create their own estimates using data from this report should cite the U.S. Census Bureau as the source of the original data only. The data in this table are based on information from public records and contain no confidential data. Although the data in this table come from a census of governmental units and are not subject to sampling error, the census results do contain nonsampling error. Additional information on nonsampling error, response rates, and definitions may be found at *http://www.census.gov/govs/www/surveymethodology07.html*.

Table 7.23
PER CAPITA PERSONAL INCOME, PERSONAL INCOME, AND POPULATION, BY STATE AND REGION, 2007–2008

State or other jurisdiction	Per capita personal income (dollars)								Personal income (millions of dollars)				Population (thousands of persons)			
			Rank in the U.S.		Percent of the U.S.		Percent change	Rank of percent change			Percent change	Rank of percent change			Percent change	Rank of percent change
	2007r	2008p	2007r	2008p	2007r	2008p	2007–08	2007–08	2007r	2008p	2007–08	2007–08	2007r	2008p	2007–08	2007–08
United States	$38,615	$39,751	—	—	100	100	2.9	—	$11,634,332	$12,086,534	3.9	—	301,290	304,290	0.9	—
Alabama	32,419	33,643	42	41	84	85	3.8	14	149,991	158,840	4.6	13	4,627	4,662	0.8	27
Alaska	40,042	43,321	16	7	104	109	8.2	2	27,273	29,731	9.0	2	681	686	0.8	28
Arizona	32,833	32,953	41	42	85	83	0.4	50	208,603	214,203	2.7	47	6,353	6,500	2.3	2
Arkansas	30,177	31,266	47	47	78	79	3.6	19	85,418	89,277	4.5	15	2,831	2,855	0.9	22
California	41,805	42,696	7	11	108	107	2.1	42	1,520,755	1,569,370	3.2	38	36,378	36,757	1.0	17
Colorado	41,192	442,377	11	13	107	107	2.9	30	199,483	209,321	4.9	10	4,843	4,939	2.0	5
Connecticut	54,981	56,248	1	1	142	142	2.3	41	191,877	196,939	2.6	48	3,490	3,501	0.3	40
Delaware	40,112	40,852	114	16	104	103	1.8	44	34,575	35,667	3.2	40	862	873	1.3	13
Florida	38,417	39,070	20	21	99	98	1.7	45	699,176	716,089	2.4	49	18,200	18,328	0.7	30
Georgia	33,499	33,975	37	40	87	85	1.4	47	319,018	329,071	3.2	41	9,523	9,686	1.7	9
Hawaii	39,242	40,490	18	17	102	102	3.2	26	50,125	52,159	4.1	25	1,277	1,288	0.8	24
Idaho	31,804	32,133	43	43	82	81	1.0	49	47,583	48,965	2.9	45	1,496	1,524	1.8	6
Illinois	41,012	42,397	13	12	106	107	3.4	23	526,006	546,985	4.0	30	12,826	12,902	0.6	34
Indiana	33,215	34,103	40	39	86	86	2.7	37	210,448	217,487	3.3	37	6,336	6,377	0.6	31
Iowa	34,916	36,680	31	29	90	92	5.1	5	104,168	110,135	5.7	6	2,983	3,003	0.6	32
Kansas	36,525	37,978	23	24	95	96	4.0	12	101,444	106,421	4.9	11	2,777	2,802	0.9	21
Kentucky	30,824	31,826	45	46	80	80	3.3	25	130,581	135,873	4.1	26	4,236	4,269	0.8	26
Louisiana	35,100	36,271	29	30	91	91	3.3	24	153,504	159,983	4.2	21	4,373	4,411	0.9	23
Maine	33,991	35,381	34	33	88	89	4.1	9	44,711	46,578	4.2	22	1,315	1,316	0.1	47
Maryland	46,471	48,091	5	5	120	121	3.5	22	261,115	270,924	3.8	34	5,619	5,634	0.3	43
Massachusetts	48,995	50,735	3	3	127	128	3.6	21	316,896	329,673	4.0	27	6,468	6,498	0.5	38
Michigan	34,423	35,299	33	34	89	89	2.5	38	345,940	353,113	2.1	50	10,050	10,003	-0.5	50
Minnesota	41,105	42,772	12	10	106	108	4.1	10	213,022	223,288	4.8	12	5,182	5,220	0.7	29
Mississippi	28,541	29,569	50	50	74	74	3.6	20	83,368	86,891	4.2	20	2,921	2,939	0.6	33
Missouri	33,964	35,228	35	35	88	89	3.7	17	199,655	208,255	4.3	14	1,769	1,783	0.8	36
Montana	33,225	34,256	39	38	86	86	3.1	27	31,783	33,140	4.3	18	957	967	1.1	14
Nebraska	36,372	37,730	24	25	94	95	3.7	15	64,360	67,288	4.5	14	1,769	1,783	0.8	25
Nevada	39,853	40,353	16	18	103	102	1.3	48	101,799	104,924	3.1	44	2,554	2,600	1.8	8
New Hampshire	41,639	42,830	9	9	108	108	2.9	32	54,640	56,356	3.1	42	1,312	1,051	-0.2	49
New Jersey	49,551	50,919	2	2	128	128	2.8	33	428,425	442,116	3.2	39	8,653	8,683	0.3	39
New Mexico	30,706	32,091	46	44	80	81	4.5	8	60,318	63,680	5.6	8	1,964	1,984	1.0	18
New York	46,364	48,076	6	6	120	121	3.7	18	900,819	937,010	4.0	29	19,429	19,490	0.3	41
North Carolina	33,735	34,439	36	36	87	87	2.1	43	305,022	317,613	4.1	23	9,042	9,222	2.0	4
North Dakota	36,082	39,321	26	20	93	99	9.0	1	23,017	25,224	9.6	1	638	641	0.6	36
Ohio	34,648	35,511	32	32	89	89	3.0	28	395,614	407,874	3.1	43	11,478	11,486	0.1	48
Oklahoma	34,997	36,899	30	28	91	93	5.4	4	126,273	134,400	6.4	4	3,608	3,642	0.9	19
Oregon	35,143	35,956	28	31	91	90	2.3	40	131,278	136,277	3.8	33	3,736	3,790	1.5	12
Pennsylvania	38,793	40,265	19	19	100	101	3.8	13	481,806	501,225	4.0	28	12,420	12,448	0.2	45
Rhode Island	39,829	41,008	17	15	103	103	3.0	29	41,946	43,091	2.7	46	1,053	1,051	-0.2	49
South Carolina	31,103	31,848	44	45	81	80	2.5	39	137,066	142,836	4.3	19	4,405	4,480	1.7	10

See footnotes at end of table.

PER CAPITA PERSONAL INCOME, PERSONAL INCOME, AND POPULATION, BY STATE AND REGION, 2007–2008—Continued

State or other jurisdiction	Per capita personal income (dollars)								Personal income (millions of dollars)				Population (thousands of persons)			
			Rank in the U.S.		Percent of the U.S.											
	2007r	2008p	2007r	2008p	2007r	2008p	Percent change 2007–08	Rank of percent change 2007–08	2007r	2008p	Percent change 2007–08	Rank of percent change 2007–08	2007r	2008p	Percent change 2007–08	Rank of percent change 2007–08
South Dakota	35,760	37,375	27	26	93	94	4.5	7	28,454	30,057	5.6	7	796	804	1.1	16
Tennessee	33,395	34,330	38	37	86	86	2.8	34	205,350	213,359	3.9	31	6,149	6,215	1.1	15
Texas	37,083	38,575	22	23	96	97	4.0	11	884,191	938,406	6.1	5	23,843	24,327	2.0	3
Utah	29,831	30,291	48	49	77	76	1.5	46	79,618	82,890	4.1	24	2,669	2,736	2.5	1
Vermont	37,483	38,880	21	22	97	98	3.7	16	23,267	24,155	3.8	32	621	621	0.1	46
Virginia	41,727	42,876	8	8	108	108	2.8	36	321,245	333,110	3.7	35	7,699	7,769	0.9	20
Washington	41,203	42,356	10	14	107	107	2.8	35	265,738	277,397	4.4	16	6,450	6,549	1.5	11
West Virginia	29,385	30,831	49	48	76	76	4.9	6	53,181	55,941	5.2	9	1,810	1,814	0.2	44
Wisconsin	36,272	37,314	25	27	94	94	2.9	31	203,084	209,999	3.4	36	5,599	5,628	0.5	37
Wyoming	47,047	49,719	4	4	122	125	5.7	3	24,618	26,484	7.6	3	523	533	1.8	7
Dist. of Columbia	62,484	64,991	—	—	162	163	4.0	—	36,732	38,464	4.7	—	588	592	0.7	—

Source: U.S. Bureau of Economic Analysis and Bureau of the Census, released March 24, 2009.
Key:
r — revised
p — preliminary

The Impact of Permitted Gambling on States

By William R. Eadington

For the past four decades, states have turned to legalization of various forms of gambling to generate tax revenues or to stimulate economic or tourism development. Legal gaming industries generated more than $92 billion in gaming revenues in 2007, with about two-thirds of that coming from commercial or tribal casinos. By 2009, lotteries had become nearly ubiquitous in the United States, and casinos are within a few hours drive of virtually every American. Internet gambling, however, is presently prohibited by federal law, and certain forms of gambling, such as sports wagering, are generally prohibited outside Nevada.

The 2007–2009 recession and the financial crisis of 2008 have negatively affected both gaming and tax revenues, as well as the survivability of major private sector gaming companies. Other public policies, such as smoking bans, have also had adverse impacts on gaming revenues in many jurisdictions, and ongoing concerns over the social costs associated with problem and pathological gambling have slowed legalization and liberalization efforts in many states. Nonetheless, the financial difficulties that prevail in 2009 will likely push efforts to expand permitted gambling to the forefront in many jurisdictions.

Gambling in America

In 2007, commercial and government-owned gaming and wagering enterprises in the United States generated gross revenues of more than $92 billion, representing the total amount of money spent on gaming by customers, or alternatively the total net losses of all players to legal gaming operators. This represented approximately 0.8 percent of aggregate personal income in the United States for that year. In comparison, in 1982, when Americans spent about $10.2 billion on legal gambling activities, gambling losses were less than 0.4 percent of aggregate personal income. In the past three decades, commercial gaming has been a significant growth industry, one of the largest created primarily by legislative actions, ballot initiatives or court interpretations that have extended legal gambling's franchise both geographically and in terms of what products and services its purveyors can legally offer to the public.

Casino gaming makes up the largest sector of legal gaming offerings in the United States, constituting roughly two-thirds of total gaming revenues, nearly $60 billion in 2007. Of this amount, more than three-quarters is generated by slot machines and other electronic gaming devices, the most popular instrument for gambling in America. The American commercial casino industry is composed of private sector casinos, both land-based and riverboat, as well as racetrack casinos, each legal in more than a dozen states (with some overlap). Furthermore, about 230 distinct tribes operated more than 425 government-owned Indian casinos in 28 states in 2007.[1] Tribal casinos generated more than 40 percent of all gaming revenues for casinos in 2007. Traditional lottery games—Lotto, scratch tickets and numbers games—authorized in 42 states and the District of Columbia generated total sales of about $40 billion in 2008, and retained gross revenues of about $21 billion after payment of prizes. Gaming devices located outside casinos, including video lottery terminals (in states such as Oregon and South Dakota) and video poker (in Montana, New Mexico and Louisiana) added another $5 billion in gaming revenues. Other sectors of legal gambling—such as horse racing, dog racing, legal bookmaking, charitable gambling, bingo and card rooms—together account for well under 10 percent of all the gaming revenues generated in the United States. Table A summarizes the revenues by sector for American gaming in 2006 and 2007.[2]

State Revenues from Gambling

In terms of contributions to the various states, legal gambling industries paid taxes or otherwise contributed approximately $25 billion to state governments in 2007. The largest share came from lotteries (excluding video lottery terminals at racetrack casinos) at about $15 billion.[3] Lotteries have characteristics of natural monopolies and are explicitly authorized for the purpose of generating revenues for state governments. Casinos, which typically have been authorized more for economic or tourism development than for their fiscal contribution capabilities, or as a means to save the racing industry from economic disintegration, paid approximately $7.5 billion in taxes in 2007. Since tribal casinos are

Table A
Gross Gaming Revenues by Sector, 2007

	2006 ($millions)	2007 ($millions)	Dollar change ($)	Percent change (%)
Pari-Mutuels				
Horse Totals	$3,235.3	$3,180.9	$(54.4)	-1.70%
Greyhound Total	322.6	298.3	(24.3)	-7.50
Jai Alai Total	21.6	20.8	(0.8)	-3.70
Total Pari-Mutuels	**3,579.5**	**3,500.0**	**(79.5)**	**-2.20**
Lotteries				
Video Lotteries	3,592.8	3,726.3	133.5	3.70
Traditional Games	21,038.6	21,053.7	15.1	0.10
Total Lotteries	**24,631.4**	**24,780.0**	**148.6**	**0.60**
Casinos				
Nevada/NJ Slot Machines	12,109.7	11,915.3	(194.4)	-1.60
Nevada/NJ Table Games	5,408.6	5,854.5	445.9	8.20
Deepwater Cruise Ships	324.7	333.4	8.7	2.70
Cruises-to-nowhere	495.5	528.7	33.2	6.70
Riverboats	11,739.0	11,777.1	38.1	0.30
Other Land-Based Casinos	2,175.3	2,209.0	33.7	1.50
Other Commercial Gambling	84.6	84.0	(0.6)	0.70
Non-Casino Devices	1,775.2	1,704.8	(70.4)	-4.00
Total Casinos	**34,112.6**	**34,406.9**	**294.3**	**0.90**
Legal Bookmaking				
Sports Books	191.5	168.4	(23.1)	-12.10
Horse Books	(0.5)	0.4	0.9	-180.40
Total Bookmaking	**191.0**	**168.8**	**(22.2)**	**-11.60**
Card Rooms	**1,103.5**	**1,180.3**	**76.8**	**7.00**
Charitable Bingo	**783.8**	**770.0**	**13.8**	**-1.80**
Charitable Games	**1,452.9**	**1,450.0**	**2.9**	**-0.20**
Indian Reservations				
Class II	2,883.7	3,171.4	287.6	10.00
Class III	22,192.1	22,844.7	652.7	2.90
Total Indian Reservations	**25,075.8**	**26,016.1**	**940.3**	**3.70**
Grand Total	**90,930.5**	**92,272.1**	**1,341.6**	**1.50**

Source: Christiansen Capital Advisors, LLC.

government owned, states do not have the ability to tax them. In a number of states, including Arizona, California, Connecticut, Michigan, New Mexico and Wisconsin, however, tribes share their revenues with the states in exchange for something of "significant economic value," typically in the form of some degree of exclusivity with respect to offering gambling services in that jurisdiction. For example, the two tribal casinos in Connecticut—Foxwood's and Mohegan Sun—contributed more than $400 million to the state in fiscal year 2008 as part of the compact agreements entered into between the tribes and the state in the 1990s. Table B summarizes the tax contribution of casinos and race track casinos to states.[4]

Legal and Illegal Gambling

The dimensions of illegal gambling in America remain difficult to determine, though it is clear that certain segments of the market are likely substantial. "Amusement with prize" gaming machines or other types of gaming devices can be found in many parts of the country, typically in bars and taverns or service clubs, and are often used for gambling purposes. In some states, governors have cited their presence as a reason to legalize gaming devices outside casinos, a direction that has had only limited acceptance to date within the United States. Sports betting in America is illegal in all states except Nevada, but the ongoing popularity of collegiate and professional sports, especially football and basketball, suggests a vibrant illegal market for such wagering continues. The passage of the Unlawful Internet Gambling Enforcement Act of 2006 (Public Law 109-347) clarified the legal status of Internet gaming companies and companies that facilitate financial transfers involving Internet gambling. Despite the new law, however, Internet gambling within the United States is still estimated as a $5.7 billion activity.[5]

Over most of its history, legalization of casino gaming by states has generally been encouraged by

Table B
Taxes Paid by Commercial Casinos and Racetrack Casinos, 2007

2007 Commercial Casino Tax Revenues (in millions)	
Colorado	$115.4
Illinois	833.9
Indiana	842.0
Iowa	314.8
Louisiana	559.2
Michigan	365.6
Mississippi	350.4
Missouri	417.3
Nevada	1,034.0
New Jersey	474.7
South Dakota	14.9
Total	**$5,322.2 billion**

2007 Racetrack Casino Tax Revenues (in millions)	
Delaware	$216.6
Florida	101.2
Iowa	109.9
Louisiana	68.2
Maine	20.6
New Mexico	63.6
New York	449.9
Oklahoma	10.2
Pennsylvania*	461.1
Rhode Island	283.6
West Virginia	439.9
Total	**$2,224.8 billion**

Source: American Gaming Association, State regulatory body reports.
*Includes one resort casino without racing.

harsh economic circumstances. Nevada's legislature authorized casinos as an economic measure during the Great Depression in 1931. New Jersey voters authorized casinos for Atlantic City in 1976 as a means to save the dying seaside resort. Riverboat and mining town casino jurisdictions were legalized in eight states by initiative processes or legislative action between 1989 to 1993 in response to the slumping and recession of the national economy, declining local or regional economic conditions, or cross-border competition for gaming customers. Michigan voters authorized three casinos in Detroit in 1996, motivated both by the promise of urban renewal that casinos might bring and cross-border competition from a Canadian casino in the neighboring city of Windsor. In recent years, there have been more and more casinos or "hybrid casinos"—either racetrack casinos or slots-only casinos—authorized with the intent of either contributing to state coffers as in Pennsylvania, saving the horse racing industry as in Iowa, Delaware, Pennsylvania and Maine, keeping gaming spending within state borders rather than losing it to neighboring states as in Pennsylvania and Maryland, or contributing to economic and tourist development objectives as in Kansas.

Legalization of lotteries, on the other hand, has been driven by a combination of desire for state revenues and cross-border competition. The bulk of legalization by states occurred in the 1970s and 1980s, but in the past two decades, a number of states, mainly in the South, have authorized lotteries. As of 2009, only seven sparsely populated states have not legalized the lottery.

States have become increasingly aware of the economic rents that can be captured through legalization of casinos and casino-style gaming, and have developed strategies that better allow them to capture economic rents either through high tax rates or competitive bidding processes in the allocation of exclusive casino licenses. The negative economic conditions that have emerged in the U.S. and global economies since 2007, however, have led to some disappointing results of legalization implementation, as the experiences in Kansas in 2008 and Maryland in early 2009 attest.

The primary constraint to further legalization of gambling is typically related to concerns over social costs resulting from the unintended negative consequences associated with problem and pathological gambling that might be incurred with more liberal permitted gaming. Estimates of problem and pathological gambling typically range from 1 percent to 5 percent of the adult population, though there is still only limited research available regarding causality, correlations with legal status of gambling, and the mitigation effects of possible safeguards such as wagering limits, prohibition of credit or bans on advertising.[6] Furthermore, opponents of legal gambling have been relatively effective in keeping problem gambling as the primary argument against further legalization or liberalization, even if their true motives are religious or aesthetic.[7]

Current Economic Conditions and the Gaming Industries

The effects of the economic recession that began in December 2007 on the gaming industries and on state tax revenues they generate have become increasingly pronounced. Between 2006 and 2007, gross gaming revenues grew only 1.5 percent, from $90.9 billion to $92.3 billion. Among the largest gaming jurisdictions, Nevada gaming revenues increased only 1.8 percent between 2006 and 2007, and then declined 9.7 percent between 2007 and 2008. Atlantic City experienced gaming revenue declines of 5.7 percent between 2006 and 2007, and an additional 7.6 percent between 2007 and 2008. Tribal gaming facilities in the United States, which had grown more rapidly than any other gaming sector since the early 1990s, slowed to only 3.7 percent growth in revenues from 2006 to 2007, with strong indications that the sector as a whole experienced negative growth between 2007 and 2008.

The other significant result of the 2007–2009 recession on the gaming sector has been the near-collapse of many of the major casino companies in the United States. Like the financial sector and the automobile industry, gaming companies rapidly found themselves in desperate economic straits, but without much likelihood of government sponsored bailouts. Between October 2007 and February 2009, the market values of the major publicly traded American casino companies—MGM, Las Vegas Sands, Wynn and Boyd—had lost between 85 percent and 98 percent of their market value, with concerns that some or most may ultimately be forced into bankruptcy. All these companies encountered severe difficulties due to debt that had been incurred as a result of expansion projects started under more promising circumstances. For example, in 2005 MGM undertook the largest private sector development project in U.S. history with the roughly $10 billion CityCenter project in Las Vegas, scheduled to open in late 2009. Las Vegas Sands, owner of the Venetian, was developing a $12 billion multi-casino hotel project in Macau when the credit crisis and slowdown in business intervened. Other major casino companies, Harrah's and Station Casinos, had similar over-leveraging and debt burden problems that arose from private equity buyouts completed in 2007 and 2008.

Smoking Bans and Casinos, and Lottery Privatization

Partial and complete smoking bans have also adversely affected casino gaming revenues in recent years. As part of a much broader public policy trend, smoking bans have been applied to casinos in a number of jurisdictions over the past decade, and it is likely such bans will continue to proliferate. The impacts of smoking bans on casino revenues have been consistent and dramatic, often bringing about declines in the range of 10 percent to 20 percent over the first two years following adoption.[8] Because of the mounting evidence of negative health effects associated with secondhand smoke, as well as potential liability issues related to workers who are exposed to tobacco smoke in the workplace, the pressure to extend smoking bans to all casinos is likely to continue.

Finally, it is worth noting the attempts of some states to capitalize future income streams from their lotteries by privatizing lotteries and selling them to private sector entities. Such privatization has been successful in Greece, which sold its lottery to OPAP, SA, and in Australia, which sold to TabCorp, with the result of generating immediate payoffs for governments in search of revenue, and providing a vehicle for private sector growth and development. One U.S. study suggested that states considering privatization in 2007—including Texas, Illinois, Indiana and New Jersey—could expect between $3 billion and $13 billion from selling their lotteries, based on the experience of the Greek company OPAP, SA.[9] Of course, this was before the financial markets collapsed in 2008. Whether such endeavors would be attractive in a post-financial crisis environment is difficult to project.

In summary, the challenging fiscal and economic conditions that prevail in the aftermath of the financial collapse of 2008 and the related recession will likely once again focus the attention of many states on the potential financial benefits that might be derived by further legalization or liberalization of gambling within their borders or over the Internet. Unlike earlier situations, however, the incremental revenues that states might realize by further legalization of gambling may be limited because of the current availability of popular gambling, especially casino-style gaming. Exceptions might be found among the major states that still prohibit casinos, such as Massachusetts, Ohio and Texas.

Notes

[1] Alan Meister, *Indian Gaming Industry Report, 2008–2009*, Casino City Press, (2008).

[2] Table A can be found in Eugene Martin Christiansen, "The 2007 Gross Annual Wager of the United States," *Insight: The Journal of the North American Gambling Industry*, Vol. 6, No. 10, (2009).

[3] Lucy Dadayan, Nino Giguashvili, and Robert B. Ward, "From a Bonanza to a Blue Chip? Gambling Revenue to the States," Rockefeller Institute, (June 2008).

[4] American Gaming Association Web page and state gaming regulatory body Web pages.

[5] Christiansen, op. cit., 7.

[6] See, for example, Blaszczynski, A., Ladouceur, R., Nower, L., and Shaffer, H.J., "Informed choice and gambling: Principles for consumer protection," *Journal of Gambling Business and Economics*, 2(1), (2008) 103–18.

[7] See, for example, William R. Eadington (2004), "Comment on 'The costs of addicted gamblers: Should the states initiate mega-lawsuits similar to the tobacco cases?'" in *Managerial and Decision Economics*, Vol. 25, (2004) 191–96.

[8] Richard Thalheimer and Mukhtar M. Ali, "The Demand for Casino Gaming with Special Reference to the Effect of a Smoking Ban," *Economic Inquiry*, 46(2), (2008) 273–82; and Michael R. Pakko, "Smoke-free law did affect revenue from gaming in Delaware," Working Paper 2005-028B, Federal Reserve Bank of St. Louis, (2005).

[9] Eugene Martin Christiansen, "What Are Lotteries Worth?," *Insight: The Journal of the North American Gambling Industry*, Vol. 5, No. 2 (2007); and "How Well Do Privatized Lotteries Perform?," *Insight: The Journal of the North American Gambling Industry*, Vol. 5, No. 10, (2007).

About the Author

William R. Eadington is professor of economics and director of the Institute for the Study of Gambling and Commercial Gaming at the University of Nevada, Reno. He is an internationally recognized authority on the legalization and regulation of commercial gambling, and has written extensively on issues relating to the economic and social impacts of gaming since the 1970s.

Table 7.24
SUMMARY OF FINANCIAL AGGREGATES, BY STATE: 2007
(In millions of dollars)

	Revenue				Expenditure					
State	Total	General	Utilities and liquor store	Insurance trust	Total	General	Utilities and liquor store	Insurance trust	Total debt outstanding at end of fiscal year	Total cash and security holdings at end of fiscal year
United States	$1,992,826	$1,450,636	$22,529	$519,661	$1,634,801	$1,423,311	$29,031	$182,459	$937,799	$3,917,961
Alabama	27,536	21,287	236	6,013	23,193	20,674	199	2,319	7,059	43,865
Alaska	12,478	10,336	17	2,124	9,192	8,291	76	825	6,553	59,081
Arizona	29,876	24,182	28	5,666	28,333	25,474	31	2,828	9,546	51,214
Arkansas	18,176	14,161	0	4,015	14,949	13,762	0	1,187	4,509	27,390
California	299,949	189,544	5,920	104,484	233,578	198,541	5,640	29,397	114,702	579,171
Colorado	26,881	18,481	0	8,400	21,244	17,981	28	3,235	14,906	64,491
Connecticut	25,492	20,382	27	5,082	22,115	19,010	318	2,787	23,836	45,219
Delaware	7,433	6,313	12	1,108	6,751	6,229	89	433	5,243	13,994
Florida	95,045	66,006	18	29,022	72,773	65,738	86	6,949	36,332	202,274
Georgia	45,067	36,314	0	8,753	41,843	37,749	42	4,053	11,370	77,655
Hawaii	11,176	9,073	0	2,103	9,848	8,970	0	878	5,959	19,552
Idaho	9,095	6,409	106	2,580	6,895	6,146	80	670	2,813	17,415
Illinois	71,255	52,377	0	18,878	59,302	51,037	0	8,265	54,535	136,240
Indiana	32,429	27,338	0	5,092	28,810	26,522	37	2,250	19,180	63,338
Iowa	19,053	14,120	180	4,753	15,462	13,843	123	1,496	6,727	35,280
Kansas	14,999	12,004	0	2,995	13,183	11,982	0	1,202	5,671	22,064
Kentucky	25,425	20,058	0	5,367	23,680	20,863	0	2,817	10,857	44,731
Louisiana	33,286	27,411	5	5,870	27,856	25,016	4	2,835	14,252	59,460
Maine	9,434	7,428	0	2,006	7,936	7,263	0	672	5,327	20,428
Maryland	34,848	27,374	116	7,358	31,611	28,266	552	2,792	19,017	63,003
Massachusetts	49,426	38,709	172	10,545	44,048	39,432	248	4,369	67,939	98,390
Michigan	63,071	48,785	743	13,543	54,745	48,040	604	6,101	33,657	111,745
Minnesota	38,745	28,476	0	10,269	31,880	28,163	104	3,613	8,867	64,495
Mississippi	22,399	17,397	235	4,766	18,629	16,899	191	1,539	5,858	34,702
Missouri	32,728	23,099	0	9,630	25,319	22,441	0	2,877	18,716	74,552
Montana	7,129	5,192	64	1,874	5,554	4,896	56	602	4,650	16,435
Nebraska	9,986	8,380	0	1,606	7,830	7,431	0	399	2,197	14,350
Nevada	14,184	9,734	75	4,375	10,755	9,459	77	1,220	4,141	27,766
New Hampshire	7,172	5,472	439	1,261	6,226	5,382	388	456	7,690	13,194
New Jersey	65,495	49,747	774	14,975	56,076	44,921	2,060	9,096	51,385	111,844
New Mexico	16,782	12,672	0	4,110	14,907	13,641	16	1,250	7,323	47,611
New York	178,908	130,399	7,655	40,854	151,339	124,834	12,389	14,115	110,085	347,377
North Carolina	51,841	42,340	0	9,501	44,009	39,736	151	4,122	19,246	95,292
North Dakota	4,786	3,942	0	844	3,778	3,441	0	336	1,792	11,135
Ohio	86,430	52,148	688	33,594	66,207	53,953	431	11,824	26,065	199,957
Oklahoma	22,330	17,234	476	4,619	18,104	15,846	428	1,830	8,667	38,543
Oregon	30,587	17,011	376	13,200	20,606	16,703	202	3,700	11,303	79,486
Pennsylvania	83,385	59,386	1,349	22,649	68,293	58,496	1,332	8,465	37,125	142,731
Rhode Island	8,418	6,279	32	2,107	7,071	5,909	125	1,037	8,419	16,967
South Carolina	27,531	20,942	1,401	5,187	24,825	20,887	1,627	2,311	14,981	42,943
South Dakota	4,920	3,293	0	1,627	3,572	3,263	0	308	3,232	12,948
Tennessee	29,470	24,812	0	4,658	24,993	23,330	6	1,657	4,142	38,495
Texas	114,728	88,863	0	25,865	90,624	80,768	0	9,856	23,909	297,038
Utah	15,864	12,463	194	3,207	12,774	11,611	141	1,022	5,927	31,346
Vermont	5,437	4,786	41	611	4,994	4,687	66	241	3,052	7,243
Virginia	47,156	35,145	502	11,508	36,774	33,652	470	2,652	19,684	79,118
Washington	47,030	31,214	504	15,313	37,116	31,980	479	4,657	21,059	85,562
West Virginia	11,945	10,648	70	1,227	9,767	9,290	71	406	5,628	12,480
Wisconsin	40,164	26,648	0	13,516	30,896	26,801	6	4,089	21,461	99,560
Wyoming	5,845	4,820	74	951	4,536	4,062	59	415	1,205	18,793

Source: U.S. Department of Commerce, U.S. Census Bureau, March 2009. 2007 Survey of State Government Finances. Data users who create their own estimates using data from this report should cite the U.S. Census Bureau as the source of the original data only. The data in this table are based on information from public records and contain no confidential data. Although the data in this table come from a census of governmental units and are not subject to sampling error, the census results do contain nonsampling error. Additional information on nonsampling error, response rates, and definitions may be found at *http://www.census.gov/govs/www/surveymethodology07.html*.

Note: Detail may not add to total due to rounding. Data presented are statistical in nature and do not represent an accounting statement. Therefore, a difference between an individual government's total revenue and expenditure does not necessarily indicate a budget surplus or deficit.

Table 7.25
NATIONAL TOTALS OF STATE GOVERNMENT FINANCES FOR SELECTED YEARS: 2003–2007

Item	*2007*	*2006*	*2005*	*2004*	*2003*
Revenue total	**$1,992,826,296**	**$1,773,012,744**	**$1,637,820,897**	**$1,586,718,729**	**$1,295,658,820**
General revenue	1,450,636,262	1,385,181,235	1,282,347,838	1,194,055,987	1,112,349,024
Taxes	749,785,186	710,606,931	408,456,380	590,413,778	548,990,867
Intergovernmental revenue	430,202,361	419,143,477	408,456,380	394,613,110	361,617,049
From Federal Government	409,751,859	397,597,199	386,034,095	374,693,902	343,307,800
Public welfare	233,432,273	222,915,684	221,932,568	214,528,312	196,954,235
Education	73,399,424	73,493,091	68216590	64,913,198	56,361,735
Highways	35,186,919	33,535,989	32,735,017	29,606,251	29,481,357
Employment security administration	3,854,284	4,733,548	4,630,281	4,876,406	5,026,880
Other	63,878,959	62,918,887	58,519,639	59,124,638	55,483,593
From local government	20,450,502	21,546,278	22,422,285	19,919,208	18,309,249
Charges and miscellaneous revenue	270,648,715	255,430,827	225,780,200	209,029,099	201,741,108
Liquor stores revenue	5,799,273	5,429,820	5,212,064	4,865,703	4,517,992
Utility revenue	16,729,965	15,816,052	14,627,471	12,954,913	12,517,945
Insurance trust revenue	519,660,796	366,585,637	335,633,524	374,842,126	166,273,859
Employee retirement	456,789,127	300,350,329	269,763,309	308,949,942	110,838,528
Unemployment compensation	34,063,242	36,863,504	35,242,919	38,229,928	35,190,504
Worker compensation	19,412,978	21,514,198	23,018,659	21,757,876	16,122,680
Other	9,395,449	7,857,606	7,608,637	5,904,380	4,122,147
Expenditure and debt redemption	**1,732,595,151**	**1,647,861,131**	**1,551,947,283**	**1,497,114,170**	**1,426,714,871**
Debt redemption	97,793,975	96,285,125	81,484,825	90,938,903	67,666,492
Expenditure total	1,634,801,176	1,551,576,006	1,470,462,458	1,406,175,267	1,359,048,379
General expenditure	1,423,311,388	1,347,150,647	91,532,787	1,209,435,776	1,163,968,202
Education	514,923,754	481,877,471	455,104,018	429,340,569	411,093,625
Intergovernmental expenditure	298,883,069	279,403,028	263,155,197	248,356,196	240,408,489
State institutions of higher education	180,483,441	170,053,080	152,556,732	152,783,448	145,941,224
Other education	334,440,313	311,824,391	276,158,620	276,557,121	265,152,401
Public welfare	393,142,174	376,762,874	368,806,663	339,408,778	314,406,504
Intergovernmental expenditure	56,945,447	53,891,394	51,512,090	47,440,301	49,301,258
Cash assistance, categorical program	6,406,925	9,833,025	10343253	9,924,609	9,487,944
Cash assistance, other	4,100,539	2,660,348	2,474,923	2,358,980	1,993,148
Other public welfare	382,634,710	364,269,501	331,289,629	279,851,755	302,925,412
Highways	103,166,635	99,518,879	90,273,738	86,165,985	85,726,099
Intergovernmental expenditure	14,844,331	15,230,034	14,486,020	13,972,060	13,271,218
Regular state highway facilities	95,809,797	92,641,261	83,854,936	78,751,658	78,142,687
State toll highways/facilities	7,356,838	6,877,618	6,418,802	7,414,327	7,583,412
Health and hospitals	106,098,820	95,920,791	92,060,367	90,600,268	88,615,522
Hospitals	48,284,647	44,799,566	43,103,003	40,349,143	38,394,884
Health	57,814,173	51,121,225	48,957,364	50,251,125	50,220,638
Natural resources	21,981,075	20,034,067	18,360,179	18,651,542	18,576,793
Corrections	46,490,177	42,720,103	40,689,366	39,313,812	39,187,839
Financial administration	22,449,589	21,666,571	22,811,548	21,386,771	20,805,632
Employment security administration	3,964,905	4,608,709	4,377,732	4,673,666	5,258,083
Police protection	12,875,855	12,232,958	11,362,668	9,471,421	11,144,395
Interest on general debt	40,812,038	37,808,472	34,362,180	32,953,170	31,294,763
Veterans' services	1,030,506	953,623	1,349,107	1,503,741	1,016,563
Utility expenditure	24,367,151	24,904,119	22,785,073	21,676,258	22,404,931
Insurance trust expenditure	182,458,527	175,182,982	167,974,677	171,139,160	168,978,731
Employee retirement	135,759,777	127,492,686	118,332,771	111,375,680	103,048,619
Unemployment compensation	28,854,007	28,008,860	29,776,222	43,173,792	51,410,604
Other	17,844,743	19,681,436	19,865,684	16,589,688	14,519,508
Total expenditure by character and object	**1,634,801,176**	**1,551,576,006**	**1,470,462,458**	**1,406,175,267**	**1,359,048,379**
Direct expenditure	1,177,424,507	1,122,651,290	1,066,995,248	1,016,469,065	976,851,809
Current operation	810,498,421	774,651,394	738,068,643	691,651,637	656,989,385
Capital outlay	110,302,205	101,452,960	94,550,657	90,950,079	91,942,748
Construction	90,728,130	83,857,561	72,609,708	73,372,464	72,374,446
Other capital outlay	19,574,075	17,595,399	21,940,949	17,577,615	19,568,302
Assistance and subsidies	31,362,708	31,644,069	30,307,592	28,104,471	25,900,969
Interest on debt	42,802,646	39,719,885	36,093,679	34,623,718	33,039,976
Insurance benefits and repayments	182,458,527	175,182,982	167,974,677	171,139,160	168,978,731
Intergovernmental expenditure	457,376,669	428,924,716	403,467,210	389,706,202	382,196,570
Cash and security holdings at end of fiscal year	**3,917,961,292**	**3,436,442,021**	**3,144,241,774**	**2,930,126,017**	**2,594,215,994**
Insurance trust	91,745,190	2,491,498,005	2,305,723,853	2,142,907,100	1,859,116,896
Unemployment fund balance	39,795,912	35,053,864	27,595,746	23,794,035	28,795,978
Debt offsets	422,501,416	386,862,630	349,347,741	328,219,839	315,588,433

Source: U.S. Department of Commerce, U.S. Census Bureau, Governments Division, March 2009. 2007 Survey of State Government Finances. Data users who create their own estimates using data from this report should cite the U.S. Census Bureau as the source of the original data only. The data in this table are based on information from public records and contain no confidential data. Although the data in this table come from a census of governmental units and are not subject to sampling error, the census results do contain nonsampling error. Additional information on nonsampling error, response rates, and definitions may be found at *http://www.census.gov/govs/www/surveymethodology07.html*.

Table 7.26
STATE GENERAL REVENUE, BY SOURCE AND BY STATE: 2007

		Taxes									
			Sales and gross receipts			Licenses					Charges and
State	Total general revenue (a)	Total	Total (b)	General	Motor fuels	Total (b)	Motor vehicle	Individual income	Corporation net income	Intergovernmental revenue	miscellaneous general revenue
United States	$1,450,636,262	$749,785,186	$345,363,685	$235,867,056	$36,523,953	$46,799,430	$19,269,162	$266,355,603	$52,977,642	$430,202,361	$270,648,715
Alabama	21,287,228	8,868,314	4,390,386	2,278,027	567,791	477,462	204,831	3,019,510	505,886	7,732,269	4,686,645
Alaska	10,336,331	3,442,930	219,776	0	39,303	127,226	59,848	0	813,762	2,288,253	4,605,148
Arizona	24,181,785	12,396,587	7,338,904	5,683,866	768,914	402,597	213,008	3,196,156	986,170	8,122,068	3,663,130
Arkansas	14,161,006	7,391,778	3,854,708	2,904,401	462,056	298,309	131,292	2,168,441	362,983	4,286,094	2,483,134
California	189,543,916	114,736,981	40,433,533	32,669,175	3,432,527	7,501,648	2,621,956	53,318,287	11,157,898	49,889,749	24,917,186
Colorado	18,481,180	9,205,912	3,450,208	2,218,951	661,832	343,346	204,994	4,795,423	479,445	4,732,975	4,542,293
Connecticut	20,382,270	12,847,554	4,963,582	3,030,353	439,673	362,255	203,399	6,335,078	824,915	4,167,175	3,367,541
Delaware	6,312,846	2,905,905	459,209	0	117,484	1,006,434	34,783	1,025,416	302,222	1,241,741	2,165,200
Florida	66,005,588	35,738,291	27,535,367	21,748,908	2,305,859	1,875,317	1,176,282	0	2,442,516	19,239,807	11,027,490
Georgia	36,313,631	18,170,913	7,744,262	5,915,521	1,082,874	497,388	235,722	8,799,415	1,017,187	13,005,370	5,137,348
Hawaii	9,073,319	5,093,842	3,227,965	2,557,644	89,729	156,238	108,314	1,560,306	100,847	2,063,945	1,915,532
Idaho	6,409,015	3,536,574	1,668,798	1,277,533	231,894	264,108	125,306	1,406,462	188,229	1,842,758	1,029,683
Illinois	52,377,362	30,578,017	14,310,390	7,817,291	1,453,706	2,440,961	1,473,073	10,469,797	2,936,360	14,234,520	7,565,025
Indiana	27,337,514	14,008,033	7,752,229	5,423,501	880,874	496,368	182,932	4,615,605	987,111	7,941,998	5,387,483
Iowa	14,119,773	6,469,752	2,767,626	1,786,668	447,484	615,343	401,265	2,666,601	325,077	4,378,744	3,271,277
Kansas	12,003,844	6,893,359	3,057,029	2,242,025	431,394	302,685	169,653	2,744,934	527,427	3,156,389	1,954,096
Kentucky	20,058,096	9,895,207	4,590,295	2,817,636	570,540	459,329	209,881	3,041,535	988,065	6,338,156	3,824,733
Louisiana	27,411,283	10,863,502	5,373,662	3,481,242	616,636	568,849	110,997	3,214,163	752,773	12,417,474	4,130,307
Maine	7,428,346	3,581,680	1,690,705	1,054,812	231,484	227,273	88,093	1,358,301	183,852	2,393,954	1,452,712
Maryland	27,374,133	15,094,183	5,811,886	3,447,828	753,988	722,214	459,907	6,679,168	782,030	7,199,413	5,080,537
Massachusetts	38,708,809	20,666,972	5,995,840	4,075,549	676,119	675,925	300,426	11,399,649	2,106,898	9,617,501	8,424,336
Michigan	48,784,813	23,848,753	11,602,093	7,983,098	1,034,462	1,375,194	909,353	6,442,678	1,786,213	13,083,153	11,852,907
Minnesota	28,476,103	17,780,164	7,302,090	4,470,596	644,172	973,363	512,656	7,230,854	1,183,816	6,680,661	4,015,278
Mississippi	17,397,398	6,394,513	4,098,390	3,155,622	448,825	395,529	124,836	1,401,809	369,205	9,103,302	1,899,583
Missouri	23,098,517	10,704,834	4,814,498	3,272,919	736,652	630,431	253,464	4,834,820	390,657	8,005,044	4,388,639
Montana	5,191,640	2,319,992	530,159	0	210,693	308,304	150,082	832,916	178,707	1,813,956	1,057,692
Nebraska	8,380,410	4,071,032	1,952,603	1,484,170	320,509	207,013	91,150	1,650,895	213,027	2,532,557	1,776,821
Nevada	9,733,699	6,304,753	5,126,064	3,212,848	328,433	801,560	170,142	0	0	2,091,256	1,337,690
New Hampshire	5,471,722	2,175,057	734,894	0	129,182	209,662	85,806	107,452	595,789	1,775,088	1,521,577
New Jersey	49,746,594	29,106,788	11,942,242	8,345,601	565,154	1,512,520	463,133	11,539,894	2,876,591	11,462,648	9,177,158
New Mexico	12,672,012	5,205,322	2,483,021	1,843,613	244,617	237,561	182,821	1,149,805	425,087	4,219,834	3,246,856
New York	130,399,016	63,161,582	19,505,685	10,879,888	516,224	1,327,930	817,299	34,579,992	5,416,105	47,324,109	19,913,325
North Carolina	42,340,472	22,612,798	8,866,005	5,202,423	1,608,934	1,338,413	614,000	10,588,951	1,565,544	13,231,264	6,496,410
North Dakota	3,942,336	1,782,990	808,706	484,341	138,813	127,842	57,635	316,894	136,424	1,227,870	931,476
Ohio	52,147,780	24,810,567	11,223,322	7,781,270	1,719,809	2,139,072	736,563	10,031,665	1,302,582	16,691,614	10,645,599
Oklahoma	17,234,417	8,267,606	2,939,995	1,964,098	396,991	952,971	608,318	2,774,851	561,375	5,406,356	3,560,455
Oregon	17,010,752	7,742,862	782,874	0	416,964	832,937	460,186	5,595,831	405,857	4,653,941	4,613,949
Pennsylvania	59,386,391	30,837,657	14,482,543	8,661,711	2,142,989	2,847,005	818,588	9,812,726	2,286,527	16,323,614	12,225,120
Rhode Island	6,279,168	2,766,046	1,356,587	875,619	131,696	94,012	52,539	1,085,600	179,168	2,036,752	1,426,370
South Carolina	20,942,385	8,688,935	4,577,312	3,233,632	533,285	471,080	171,778	3,239,468	311,902	7,097,636	5,155,814

See footnotes at end of table.

STATE GENERAL REVENUE, BY SOURCE AND BY STATE: 2007—Continued

State	Total general revenue (a)	Taxes: Total	Sales and gross receipts: Total (b)	Sales and gross receipts: General	Sales and gross receipts: Motor fuels	Licenses: Total (b)	Licenses: Motor vehicle	Individual income	Corporation net income	Intergovernmental revenue	Charges and miscellaneous general revenue
South Dakota	3,293,293	1,257,084	1,018,603	711,321	123,484	156,488	45,417	0	76,665	1,276,075	760,134
Tennessee	24,811,808	11,370,768	8,355,174	6,763,657	859,743	1,259,679	271,080	249,145	1,120,422	8,341,938	5,099,102
Texas	88,863,456	40,314,714	31,811,384	20,434,675	3,075,308	5,735,796	1,433,781	0	0	28,277,613	20,271,129
Utah	12,463,416	5,889,423	2,625,037	1,953,643	382,381	202,454	105,710	2,561,001	398,894	3,076,320	3,497,673
Vermont	4,785,531	2,558,806	844,977	334,413	87,370	116,683	71,131	581,189	83,362	1,379,970	846,755
Virginia	35,145,300	18,571,160	6,000,415	3,539,061	918,849	673,592	367,848	10,238,776	879,575	6,883,654	9,690,486
Washington	31,213,802	17,692,767	13,851,911	10,861,327	1,128,798	882,114	459,158	0	0	7,892,810	5,628,225
West Virginia	10,648,164	4,654,213	2,227,596	1,129,531	349,167	182,098	87,715	1,360,511	539,136	3,256,627	2,737,324
Wisconsin	26,648,132	14,482,624	6,037,081	4,158,611	996,200	860,536	365,968	6,333,633	923,359	6,769,288	5,396,220
Wyoming	4,820,460	2,025,090	825,964	698,437	72,037	126,316	65,043	0	0	1,947,258	848,112

Source: U.S. Department of Commerce, U.S. Census Bureau, Governments Division, March 2009. 2007 Survey of State Government Finances. Data users who create their own estimates using data from this report should cite the U.S. Census Bureau as the source of the original data only. The data in this table are based on information from public records and contain no confidential data. Although the data in this table come from a census of governmental units and are not subject to sampling error, the census results do contain nonsampling error. Additional information on nonsampling error, response rates, and definitions may be found at *http://www.census.gov/govs/www/surveymethodology07.html*.

Note: Detail may not add to total due to rounding.

(a) Total general revenue equals total taxes plus intergovernmental revenue plus charges and miscellaneous revenue.

(b) Total includes other taxes not shown separately in this table.

Table 7.27
STATE EXPENDITURE, BY CHARACTER AND OBJECT AND BY STATE: 2007 (In thousands of dollars)

State	Intergovernmental expenditures	Direct expenditures									
				Capital outlay							
		Total	Current operation	Total	Construction	Other	Assistance and subsidies	Interest on debt	Insurance benefits and repayments	Exhibit: Total salaries and wages
United States	$457,376,669	$1,177,424,507	$810,498,421	$110,302,205	$90,728,130	$19,574,075	$31,362,708	$42,802,646	$182,458,527	$215,876,248
Alabama	6,088,940	17,103,567	12,220,463	1,871,280	1,538,186	333,094	409,178	283,593	2,319,053	3,795,023
Alaska	1,365,793	7,825,951	5,530,107	959,289	771,734	187,555	182,754	328,541	825,260	1,449,862
Arizona	9,860,543	18,472,298	13,380,387	1,313,852	1,019,907	293,945	480,745	469,133	2,828,181	3,152,977
Arkansas	4,300,048	10,648,518	8,128,452	919,377	825,385	93,992	239,278	174,807	1,186,604	1,749,690
California	92,415,603	141,162,418	94,215,741	8,857,338	7,294,511	1,562,827	2,907,776	5,784,317	29,397,246	25,414,823
Colorado	6,000,582	15,243,400	10,005,070	1,069,262	935,882	133,380	210,204	723,526	3,235,338	3,255,396
Connecticut	3,831,974	18,283,216	12,311,151	1,653,862	1,429,520	224,342	388,033	1,142,993	2,787,177	4,088,537
Delaware	1,194,559	5,556,893	4,184,189	577,139	419,705	157,484	111,453	250,588	433,474	2,162,325
Florida	19,680,891	53,092,159	36,361,614	6,732,934	5,334,817	1,398,167	1,888,470	1,159,925	6,949,166	8,268,077
Georgia	10,515,856	31,327,496	20,390,323	5,501,850	5,280,029	221,821	830,496	552,214	4,052,613	4,292,075
Hawaii	138,054	9,710,156	7,634,781	639,902	486,121	153,781	98,982	458,350	878,141	2,372,147
Idaho	1,931,829	4,963,490	3,485,759	561,201	475,669	85,532	116,064	130,573	669,893	983,367
Illinois	14,259,666	45,042,555	29,686,739	3,695,239	3,277,612	417,627	1,118,125	2,277,114	8,265,338	8,099,483
Indiana	8,178,674	20,650,912	14,914,519	1,906,332	1,599,232	307,100	694,551	865,678	2,249,832	3,695,037
Iowa	3,892,136	11,569,630	7,977,492	1,292,035	1,064,333	227,702	464,646	339,556	1,495,901	2,137,369
Kansas	3,869,984	9,313,452	6,582,271	1,058,528	917,594	140,934	171,658	299,060	1,201,935	2,965,227
Kentucky	4,469,153	19,211,266	13,304,538	1,916,163	1,619,760	296,403	698,908	474,495	2,817,162	3,532,348
Louisiana	6,262,247	21,593,684	15,396,317	1,947,983	1,627,361	320,622	561,968	852,184	2,835,232	3,807,032
Maine	1,276,381	6,659,292	5,141,624	362,318	284,851	77,467	244,921	238,030	672,399	741,360
Maryland	7,568,283	24,042,265	17,171,780	2,104,467	1,364,629	739,838	1,091,802	881,751	2,792,465	4,512,655
Massachusetts	9,364,680	34,683,744	23,753,330	2,447,945	2,181,880	266,065	662,936	3,450,712	4,368,821	4,782,098
Michigan	19,423,935	35,221,420	24,902,318	1,971,018	1,509,506	461,512	1,150,139	1,196,808	6,101,137	5,594,998
Minnesota	10,686,237	21,194,241	14,855,123	1,449,984	1,119,606	330,378	784,705	491,432	3,612,997	4,619,074
Mississippi	5,086,220	13,542,419	10,093,179	1,500,204	1,303,439	196,765	183,551	226,874	1,538,611	2,063,464
Missouri	5,626,071	19,692,615	13,641,255	1,689,175	1,433,841	255,334	435,697	1,049,234	2,877,254	3,470,202
Montana	1,175,674	4,378,570	2,865,098	622,143	576,103	46,040	99,584	189,635	602,110	830,166
Nebraska	1,793,817	6,335,767	4,687,774	696,360	620,772	75,588	166,229	86,687	398,717	1,978,616
Nevada	3,826,539	6,928,787	4,391,712	965,809	871,632	94,177	157,558	193,670	1,220,038	1,553,557
New Hampshire	1,408,445	4,817,676	3,466,957	405,815	314,436	91,379	123,974	364,436	456,494	897,160
New Jersey	10,667,575	45,408,590	29,361,123	4,073,545	3,321,185	752,360	942,007	1,936,088	9,095,827	8,784,646
New Mexico	4,144,807	10,762,253	7,922,191	1,015,784	875,118	141,666	237,591	335,295	1,250,392	2,049,143
New York	50,525,675	100,813,316	70,215,442	10,269,777	7,505,947	2,763,830	1,427,044	4,785,608	14,115,445	16,094,566
North Carolina	12,646,039	31,363,254	23,101,400	3,215,202	2,462,334	752,868	317,556	606,787	4,122,309	7,549,959
North Dakota	741,535	3,035,988	2,083,147	414,737	384,270	30,467	60,205	141,551	336,348	757,505
Ohio	17,755,241	48,451,897	29,490,697	3,819,803	3,416,572	403,231	1,922,679	1,395,173	11,823,545	7,502,351

See footnotes at end of table.

STATE EXPENDITURE, BY CHARACTER AND OBJECT AND BY STATE: 2007 (In thousands of dollars)—Continued

State	Intergovernmental expenditures	Direct expenditures								Exhibit: Total salaries and wages
				Capital outlay						
		Total	Current operation	Total	Construction	Other	Assistance and subsidies	Interest on debt	Insurance benefits and repayments	
Oklahoma	4,067,276	14,036,992	10,042,003	1,380,559	1,025,407	355,152	288,671	496,214	1,829,545	2,939,901
Oregon	5,047,346	15,558,251	9,657,585	1,305,315	1,030,600	274,715	386,890	508,642	3,699,819	3,608,556
Pennsylvania	15,189,027	53,103,719	36,045,335	5,035,059	4,469,754	565,305	1,785,701	1,772,811	8,464,813	7,856,097
Rhode Island	1,009,313	6,062,083	4,131,213	390,998	337,164	53,834	125,455	377,458	1,036,959	1,083,955
South Carolina	4,870,680	19,953,948	14,216,031	1,829,973	1,354,058	475,915	861,432	735,705	2,310,807	3,360,557
South Dakota	652,117	2,919,624	1,959,292	469,307	423,074	46,233	61,159	121,534	308,332	789,124
Tennessee	6,161,614	18,831,014	14,091,929	1,727,797	1,617,971	109,826	1,147,708	206,511	1,657,069	3,653,960
Texas	21,915,924	68,707,824	47,432,209	8,631,940	6,853,604	1,778,336	1,743,694	1,043,989	9,855,992	13,203,180
Utah	2,601,367	10,172,829	7,361,819	1,140,723	914,719	226,004	373,507	274,292	1,022,488	2,289,095
Vermont	1,415,922	3,577,938	2,761,752	294,121	260,520	33,601	121,286	159,856	240,923	703,493
Virginia	10,438,607	26,335,435	19,362,185	2,315,170	1,718,385	596,785	1,184,514	821,973	2,651,593	5,795,140
Washington	8,644,100	28,472,077	18,849,406	3,044,145	2,396,930	647,215	980,953	940,373	4,657,200	5,775,895
West Virginia	2,074,429	7,692,543	6,005,588	943,538	813,973	129,565	161,837	175,633	405,947	1,380,391
Wisconsin	9,744,914	21,151,049	13,689,876	1,891,883	1,676,741	215,142	508,765	971,438	4,089,087	3,860,864
Wyoming	1,570,347	2,966,026	2,038,135	402,925	371,751	31,174	49,669	59,799	415,498	573,725

Source: U.S. Department of Commerce, U.S. Census Bureau, Governments Division, March 2009. 2007 Survey of State Government Finances. Data users who create their own estimates using data from this report should cite the U.S. Census Bureau as the source of the original data only. The data in this table are based on information from public records and contain no confidential data. Although the data in this table come from a census of governmental units and are not subject to sampling error, the census results do contain nonsampling error. Additional information on nonsampling error, response rates, and definitions may be found at *http://www.census.gov/govs/www/surveymethodology07.html*.

Note: Detail may not add to total due to rounding.

Table 7.28
STATE GENERAL EXPENDITURE, BY FUNCTION AND BY STATE: 2007 (In thousands of dollars)

State	Total general expenditures (a)	Education	Public welfare	Highways	Hospitals	Natural Resources	Health	Corrections	Financial administration	Employment security administration	Police
United States	$1,423,311,388	$514,923,754	$393,142,174	$103,166,635	$48,284,647	$21,981,075	$57,814,173	$46,490,177	$22,449,589	$3,964,905	$12,875,855
Alabama	20,674,219	9,350,536	4,768,598	1,358,627	1,622,375	277,607	643,313	514,385	210,766	79,285	167,962
Alaska	8,290,628	1,985,407	1,478,593	1,203,249	31,850	273,914	242,726	237,144	211,973	31,231	78,978
Arizona	25,473,702	9,160,086	7,249,710	1,968,139	70,490	336,109	1,450,493	946,922	367,210	44,486	252,728
Arkansas	13,761,962	6,023,402	3,624,917	897,313	742,881	221,573	238,276	331,717	337,220	50,975	70,632
California	198,541,221	72,804,824	56,305,480	9,122,677	6,245,491	4,864,214	11,494,714	8,093,209	3,739,039	342,246	1,450,630
Colorado	17,980,929	7,646,922	4,271,325	1,085,183	394,763	272,789	758,113	895,827	463,390	54,138	114,975
Connecticut	19,009,516	5,339,202	5,136,934	742,087	1,297,077	103,206	839,811	668,179	390,387	81,597	205,351
Delaware	6,229,345	2,140,583	1,324,814	408,068	63,217	112,614	374,705	265,937	242,711	13,792	104,878
Florida	65,738,088	22,249,987	17,340,927	6,855,857	697,587	2,215,080	3,305,874	2,542,387	1,238,939	72,940	462,320
Georgia	37,748,738	15,580,870	9,685,127	5,009,405	730,547	463,217	1,150,842	1,465,496	416,294	99,221	267,801
Hawaii	8,969,744	3,239,562	1,494,003	306,179	454,935	142,296	611,503	197,273	112,467	51,367	15,661
Idaho	6,145,614	2,506,932	1,485,151	632,101	43,860	189,751	139,552	210,533	156,658	34,547	47,038
Illinois	51,036,882	15,353,554	15,565,800	4,695,631	953,052	300,115	2,255,034	1,209,228	591,413	108,298	452,122
Indiana	26,522,496	10,317,966	6,823,359	1,689,200	247,022	288,238	587,329	632,737	299,329	110,679	229,609
Iowa	13,842,578	5,353,934	3,612,004	1,445,447	1,021,701	255,776	229,321	259,104	189,022	35,051	94,776
Kansas	11,981,501	5,329,513	2,970,898	1,240,990	296,477	200,618	179,841	317,649	162,339	22,647	108,582
Kentucky	20,863,257	7,963,410	5,827,463	2,138,616	1,007,977	361,199	577,490	471,523	262,813	52,103	191,395
Louisiana	25,016,388	7,708,209	4,518,292	1,656,383	843,838	483,495	588,283	651,468	287,211	58,296	316,352
Maine	7,263,274	1,977,451	2,442,219	497,630	54,830	176,617	476,005	130,051	128,479	11,294	71,324
Maryland	28,266,243	9,705,518	6,847,770	2,396,270	494,736	519,805	1,890,053	1,376,322	545,922	50,734	419,201
Massachusetts	39,431,782	10,657,235	12,195,223	1,735,159	512,551	336,316	960,808	1,209,443	550,058	55,084	567,989
Michigan	48,040,183	21,420,912	12,690,079	2,808,637	2,055,355	299,768	1,090,937	1,801,658	487,094	185,330	311,262
Minnesota	28,163,216	11,654,016	8,415,365	1,861,145	327,807	482,422	599,726	535,237	239,962	73,418	327,884
Mississippi	16,899,143	5,116,749	4,175,865	1,494,109	860,626	277,718	354,827	326,751	83,209	22,693	115,294
Missouri	22,441,427	7,964,401	5,804,854	2,172,262	1,210,980	339,545	1,077,855	669,121	203,665	18,992	198,852
Montana	4,896,244	1,688,003	837,857	599,237	42,590	234,061	289,725	146,574	213,151	14,343	40,448
Nebraska	7,430,867	2,661,012	2,024,945	557,579	225,283	186,188	426,557	212,598	93,388	40,360	80,482
Nevada	9,458,516	3,924,517	1,641,032	810,196	240,770	140,048	263,325	294,380	110,119	41,696	96,649
New Hampshire	5,381,944	1,942,448	1,445,654	438,894	56,244	63,123	143,143	110,297	79,698	28,030	49,463
New Jersey	44,920,677	14,863,769	11,895,707	2,615,630	1,957,266	537,755	1,311,145	1,489,950	702,533	156,364	525,964
New Mexico	13,640,543	4,844,691	3,115,453	996,883	734,720	213,460	447,156	341,179	180,233	18,133	168,929
New York	124,834,333	37,086,748	46,614,760	4,250,420	4,599,507	499,438	6,747,721	3,126,699	2,103,010	304,363	906,359
North Carolina	39,735,713	16,547,989	10,972,023	2,998,418	1,371,677	593,500	1,536,226	1,271,328	344,027	160,514	593,039
North Dakota	3,441,175	1,245,407	706,358	446,733	15,044	152,590	63,730	54,283	72,433	7,498	23,737
Ohio	53,953,051	19,699,442	16,352,684	3,479,916	1,958,958	381,157	2,537,498	1,335,897	1,283,558	262,288	221,605

See footnotes at end of table.

STATE GENERAL EXPENDITURE, BY FUNCTION AND BY STATE: 2007 (In thousands of dollars)—Continued

State	Total general expenditures (a)	Education	Public welfare	Highways	Hospitals	Natural Resources	Health	Corrections	Financial administration	Employment security administration	Police
Oklahoma	15,846,257	6,438,290	4,432,291	1,285,952	167,555	204,439	704,210	586,836	217,405	43,000	145,801
Oregon	16,703,334	6,076,628	3,854,060	1,524,387	1,002,426	392,433	415,065	697,622	549,492	43,217	228,593
Pennsylvania	58,496,337	18,257,623	19,146,526	5,983,144	2,523,454	622,515	1,779,089	1,720,374	954,451	185,002	719,268
Rhode Island	5,909,356	1,660,195	2,079,486	263,915	93,996	43,561	162,119	178,364	158,186	34,038	60,470
South Carolina	20,887,140	7,462,708	5,404,269	1,125,851	1,309,736	259,490	970,251	470,894	745,175	59,974	196,501
South Dakota	3,263,409	1,005,279	759,061	521,948	55,287	122,972	116,675	103,166	84,737	19,324	29,632
Tennessee	23,329,875	7,860,649	8,067,623	1,913,472	393,670	282,659	1,207,745	769,362	296,002	124,539	140,725
Texas	80,767,756	34,408,665	20,646,360	8,133,944	3,288,025	941,465	2,232,519	3,302,304	584,846	178,934	611,716
Utah	11,610,881	5,230,850	2,113,615	829,412	767,175	176,761	344,488	310,334	261,527	17,865	116,946
Vermont	4,686,834	2,153,209	1,202,700	332,316	18,162	70,337	149,948	114,748	50,642	17,169	77,135
Virginia	33,652,244	13,185,813	6,982,641	2,633,577	2,541,320	225,791	944,144	1,425,372	460,107	152,406	661,221
Washington	31,979,762	13,027,431	6,982,213	2,764,159	1,598,218	799,327	1,709,620	1,090,342	382,762	154,634	311,756
West Virginia	9,289,844	3,572,629	2,405,778	972,049	88,713	178,911	307,646	233,639	265,538	21,305	61,691
Wisconsin	26,801,374	10,176,419	6,393,090	1,859,187	951,128	595,231	661,206	1,027,163	266,347	88,812	125,814
Wyoming	4,061,846	1,352,159	610,218	409,052	1,697	269,861	225,791	117,171	72,652	30,653	38,315

Source: U.S. Department of Commerce, U.S. Census Bureau, Governments Division, March 2009. 2007 Survey of State Government Finances. Data users who create their own estimates using data from this report should cite the U.S. Census Bureau as the source of the original data only. The data in this table are based on information from public records and contain no confidential data. Although the data in this table come from a census of governmental units and are not subject to sampling error, the census results do contain nonsampling error. Additional information on nonsampling error, response rates, and definitions may be found at *http://www.census.gov/govs/www/surveymethodology07.html.*

Note: Detail may not add to total due to rounding.

Key:

(a) Does not represent sum of state figures because total includes miscellaneous expenditures not shown.

Table 7.29
STATE DEBT OUTSTANDING AT END OF FISCAL YEAR, BY STATE: 2007
(In thousands of dollars, per capita in dollars)

State	Total	Long-term total	Short-term	Net long-term total (a)
United States	$937,799,233	$930,400,925	$7,398,308	$507,899,509
Alabama	7,059,343	7,027,968	31,375	5,053,681
Alaska	6,553,080	6,433,354	119,726	2,064,896
Arizona	9,546,428	9,505,723	40,705	5,692,824
Arkansas	4,508,511	4,499,668	8,843	1,965,614
California	114,701,797	114,696,797	5,000	83,399,547
Colorado	14,905,758	14,540,286	365,472	2,806,445
Connecticut	23,836,187	23,822,905	13,282	12,677,820
Delaware	5,242,613	5,242,613	0	2,541,687
Florida	36,331,829	36,292,049	39,780	32,446,550
Georgia	11,370,040	11,325,040	45,000	8,832,823
Hawaii	5,959,064	5,959,064	0	4,904,054
Idaho	2,812,655	2,804,156	8,499	387,882
Illinois	54,535,159	54,523,542	11,617	26,049,778
Indiana	19,180,194	19,149,361	30,833	2,900,958
Iowa	6,727,065	6,727,065	0	1,687,450
Kansas	5,671,144	5,635,261	35,883	3,606,991
Kentucky	10,857,128	10,854,027	3,101	4,553,596
Louisiana	14,251,968	14,242,932	9,036	7,040,413
Maine	5,326,692	5,323,202	3,490	984,713
Maryland	19,017,465	18,647,277	370,188	7,617,516
Massachusetts	67,938,742	67,891,312	47,430	34,061,688
Michigan	33,657,214	33,490,564	166,650	15,065,067
Minnesota	8,866,611	8,661,096	205,515	4,223,398
Mississippi	5,858,340	5,786,890	71,450	4,351,483
Missouri	18,715,821	18,691,235	24,586	4,209,609
Montana	4,649,819	4,647,532	2,287	975,985
Nebraska	2,196,880	2,195,675	1,205	320,425
Nevada	4,140,910	4,140,910	0	3,026,155
New Hampshire	7,690,409	7,683,244	7,165	1,822,404
New Jersey	51,384,806	51,355,354	29,452	31,855,414
New Mexico	7,323,101	7,251,094	72,007	3,004,411
New York	110,084,829	109,707,411	377,418	67,659,537
North Carolina	19,245,613	18,973,199	272,414	10,770,268
North Dakota	1,792,485	1,791,884	601	710,620
Ohio	26,065,238	25,874,819	190,419	16,060,457
Oklahoma	8,667,100	8,658,963	8,137	4,715,556
Oregon	11,303,477	11,303,477	0	8,142,365
Pennsylvania	37,125,118	34,182,180	2,942,938	14,313,010
Rhode Island	8,418,744	8,414,425	4,319	3,318,022
South Carolina	14,981,290	14,781,718	199,572	12,608,841
South Dakota	3,232,457	3,230,049	2,408	559,183
Tennessee	4,141,541	3,815,796	325,745	1,908,711
Texas	23,909,021	22,825,263	1,083,758	12,439,007
Utah	5,926,589	5,897,242	29,347	1,853,404
Vermont	3,052,469	2,979,168	73,301	760,514
Virginia	19,683,529	19,565,175	118,354	7,982,390
Washington	21,058,558	21,058,558	0	12,982,130
West Virginia	5,628,065	5,628,065	0	2,275,780
Wisconsin	21,461,270	21,461,270	0	8,619,611
Wyoming	1,205,067	1,205,067	0	88,826

Source: U.S. Department of Commerce, U.S. Census Bureau, Governments Division, March 2009. 2007 Survey of State Government Finances. Data users who create their own estimates using data from this report should cite the U.S. Census Bureau as the source of the original data only. The data in this table are based on information from public records and contain no confidential data. Although the data in this table come from a census of governmental units and are not subject to sampling error, the census results do contain nonsampling error. Additional information on nonsampling error, response rates, and definitions may be found at *http://www.census.gov/govs/www/surveymethodology07.html*.

Note: Detail may not add to total due to rounding.

Key:

(a) Long-term debt outstanding minus long-term debt offsets.

Table 7.30
NUMBER AND MEMBERSHIP OF STATE AND LOCAL GOVERNMENT EMPLOYEE-RETIREMENT SYSTEMS BY STATE: FISCAL YEAR 2006–07

State and type of government	Number of systems	Membership: Total	Membership: Active members	Membership: Inactive members	Total beneficiaries receiving periodic benefit payments
United States	2,547	18,583,270	14,422,883	4,160,387	7,463,567
State	218	16,768,128	12,800,553	3,967,575	6,353,414
Local	2,329	1,815,142	1,622,330	192,812	1,110,153
County	158	558,381	483,444	74,937	266,080
Municipality	1,660	1,095,976	993,601	102,375	751,835
Township	394	40,842	37,098	3,744	22,471
Special District	106	49,643	46,102	3,541	26,597
School District	11	70,300	62,085	8,215	43,170
Alabama	11	267,414	239,708	27,706	106,983
Alaska	5	53,344	45,301	8,043	42,928
Arizona	6	482,799	269,873	212,926	105,396
Arkansas	36	158,054	132,279	25,775	52,383
California	59	2,265,816	1,760,512	505,304	1,014,149
Colorado	60	359,720	217,518	142,202	97,780
Connecticut	61	148,072	135,312	12,760	88,613
Delaware	6	45,672	44,287	1,385	23,656
Florida	162	731,311	646,127	85,184	296,032
Georgia	31	590,260	386,287	203,973	144,343
Hawaii	1	70,805	65,251	5,554	33,118
Idaho	4	75,535	65,857	9,678	29,745
Illinois	370	951,332	628,060	323,272	379,988
Indiana	71	278,895	229,461	49,434	106,713
Iowa	9	232,804	170,162	62,642	89,384
Kansas	7	184,271	146,411	37,860	67,924
Kentucky	21	320,238	225,461	94,777	119,667
Louisiana	34	293,955	219,142	74,813	141,381
Maine	1	59,912	52,060	7,852	33,586
Maryland	13	292,394	237,124	55,270	140,707
Massachusetts	100	375,611	314,309	61,302	181,665
Michigan	138	448,984	416,292	32,692	293,370
Minnesota	89	509,719	296,449	213,270	155,456
Mississippi	4	286,856	163,617	123,239	73,708
Missouri	62	325,278	272,372	52,906	136,030
Montana	9	72,384	51,644	20,740	30,088
Nebraska	13	85,275	62,557	22,718	22,158
Nevada	2	114,759	103,755	11,004	35,748
New Hampshire	4	57,169	52,363	4,806	21,903
New Jersey	10	532,455	468,966	63,489	230,399
New Mexico	5	152,364	119,182	33,182	52,784
New York	10	1,323,517	1,183,660	139,857	750,709
North Carolina	8	582,236	497,672	84,564	194,783
North Dakota	12	34,388	29,746	4,642	13,240
Ohio	6	1,178,884	695,321	483,563	373,484
Oklahoma	12	178,655	158,049	20,606	85,224
Oregon	2	218,720	166,161	52,559	106,061
Pennsylvania	903	571,606	486,779	84,827	333,873
Rhode Island	13	47,669	40,729	6,940	27,995
South Carolina	6	371,627	209,571	162,056	108,013
South Dakota	4	52,403	38,348	14,055	19,261
Tennessee	14	272,143	243,252	28,891	119,585
Texas	48	1,504,044	1,296,009	208,035	443,937
Utah	6	129,983	99,589	30,394	38,796
Vermont	5	33,701	26,018	7,683	11,264
Virginia	14	426,063	387,230	38,833	160,034
Washington	24	303,191	260,713	42,478	130,269
West Virginia	41	51,013	37,526	13,487	22,159
Wisconsin	3	425,392	280,115	145,277	155,227
Wyoming	6	42,006	36,922	5,084	18,788
Dist. of Columbia	6	12,572	11,774	798	3,080

Source: U.S. Department of Commerce, U.S. Census Bureau, Governments Division, March 2009. 2007 Census of Governments, Survey of Public Employee-Retirement Systems. Data users who create their own estimates using data from this report should cite the U.S. Census Bureau as the source of the original data only. The data in this table are based on information from public records and contain no confidential data. Although the data in this table come from a census of state governments and are not subject to sampling error, the census results do contain nonsampling error. Additional information on nonsampling error, response rates, and definitions may be found at *http://www.census.gov/govs/www/retire07.html*. Created: December 9, 2008; Last Revised: December 9, 2008.

Table 7.31
FINANCES OF STATE-ADMINISTERED EMPLOYEE RETIREMENT SYSTEMS, BY STATE: FISCAL YEAR 2007
(In thousands of dollars)

	Receipts during fiscal year						Payments during fiscal year			
			Government contributions							
State and type of government	*Total receipts*	*Employee contributions*	*Total*	*From state governments*	*From local governments*	*Earnings on investments*	*Total payments*	*Benefits*	*Withdrawals*	*Other*
United States	$486,784,479	$29,086,809	$56,445,347	$29,995,352	$26,449,995	$401,252,323	$148,356,597	$131,201,708	$4,558,069	$12,596,820
Alabama	6,458,577	486,902	830,756	694,589	136,167	5,140,919	2,137,511	2,038,886	69,618	29,007
Alaska	2,060,509	109,783	318,220	116,391	201,829	1,632,506	749,590	711,756	11,698	26,136
Arizona	4,923,196	904,127	850,035	174,957	675,078	3,169,034	2,308,107	2,111,213	103,381	93,513
Arkansas	3,939,639	132,162	577,137	212,227	364,910	3,230,340	1,087,262	896,204	8,592	182,466
California	94,885,102	5,610,882	9,863,495	3,917,436	5,946,059	79,410,725	19,334,880	18,385,789	378,629	570,462
Colorado	7,411,563	532,092	723,686	240,532	483,154	6,155,785	2,988,797	2,354,816	161,478	472,503
Connecticut	5,569,129	315,451	1,133,937	1,088,407	45,530	4,119,741	2,439,778	2,224,321	0	215,457
Delaware	1,146,452	42,856	142,110	133,381	8,729	961,486	360,379	331,966	3,164	25,249
Florida	24,530,537	25,891	3,037,686	671,356	2,366,330	21,466,960	5,453,502	4,127,516	1,099,147	226,839
Georgia	8,962,428	581,526	1,247,764	965,680	282,084	7,133,138	3,471,017	3,308,662	65,069	97,286
Hawaii	2,292,138	144,659	465,494	358,431	107,063	1,681,985	811,454	761,005	3,498	46,951
Idaho	2,270,166	159,886	259,822	85,964	173,858	1,850,458	493,312	439,263	0	54,049
Illinois	17,875,637	1,610,402	2,115,774	1,397,083	718,691	14,149,461	6,860,084	6,396,933	156,362	306,789
Indiana	5,527,409	315,343	1,165,545	1,006,853	158,692	4,046,521	1,752,415	1,449,118	64,674	238,623
Iowa	4,492,461	246,883	411,131	84,038	327,093	3,834,447	1,351,103	1,129,878	39,242	181,983
Kansas	2,963,637	250,546	398,818	278,688	120,130	2,314,273	1,055,544	970,272	46,129	39,143
Kentucky	5,439,528	572,943	737,694	515,034	222,660	4,128,891	2,488,935	2,312,017	40,063	136,855
Louisiana	6,746,643	629,501	1,502,933	1,238,148	264,785	4,614,209	2,768,653	2,491,663	126,547	150,443
Maine	2,200,122	155,061	323,377	323,377	0	1,721,684	757,036	541,388	21,939	193,709
Maryland	7,193,361	319,274	854,654	764,265	90,389	6,019,433	2,098,360	1,984,830	16,021	97,509
Massachusetts	9,888,656	1,133,683	1,153,070	1,020,623	132,447	7,601,903	3,034,786	2,866,093	15,878	152,815
Michigan	12,201,577	440,194	1,330,752	238,687	1,092,065	10,430,631	5,002,698	4,193,899	40,180	768,619
Minnesota	9,444,171	618,962	684,568	152,217	532,351	8,140,641	3,161,692	2,815,950	50,774	294,968
Mississippi	4,848,360	394,444	634,645	230,449	404,196	3,819,271	1,761,079	1,347,473	72,617	340,989
Missouri	9,477,815	598,814	1,133,128	462,961	670,167	7,745,873	2,779,269	2,365,241	59,549	354,479
Montana	1,587,212	140,258	168,016	70,063	97,953	1,278,938	440,737	392,283	21,167	27,287
Nebraska	1,508,931	128,952	156,427	45,709	110,718	1,223,552	349,225	278,988	35,908	34,329
Nevada	4,138,965	128,892	1,046,813	161,845	884,968	2,963,260	955,889	929,778	17,456	8,655
New Hampshire	1,233,035	272,987	121,612	47,459	74,153	838,436	450,928	347,678	34,080	69,170
New Jersey	14,687,129	1,450,135	2,232,900	2,185,677	47,223	11,004,094	6,723,265	6,564,256	119,814	39,195
New Mexico	4,316,742	374,134	526,642	345,718	180,924	3,415,966	1,173,513	1,073,828	62,205	37,480
New York	37,775,006	434,147	3,956,820	2,194,217	1,762,603	33,384,039	11,940,504	10,043,573	65,953	1,830,978
North Carolina	8,960,870	1,038,072	627,283	386,143	241,140	7,295,515	3,573,434	3,294,081	141,168	138,185
North Dakota	696,347	43,245	65,477	16,181	49,296	587,625	198,798	160,208	8,500	30,090
Ohio	31,119,514	2,586,331	3,631,942	1,849,829	1,782,113	24,901,241	9,064,880	8,425,686	413,459	225,735
Oklahoma	4,549,294	398,877	935,569	520,375	415,194	3,214,848	1,599,985	1,392,554	71,431	136,000
Oregon	11,789,523	13,681	598,399	116,529	481,870	11,177,443	3,240,778	2,574,589	41,223	624,966
Pennsylvania	20,429,540	1,189,428	877,398	545,979	331,419	18,362,714	6,925,014	6,041,151	44,630	839,233
Rhode Island	1,937,552	176,598	333,177	214,917	118,260	1,427,777	757,932	647,678	10,557	99,697
South Carolina	5,060,348	578,019	769,167	271,856	497,311	3,713,162	1,848,672	1,704,010	89,825	54,837
South Dakota	1,627,209	86,933	85,362	28,941	56,421	1,454,914	288,410	256,250	28,777	3,383
Tennessee	4,842,330	232,746	794,428	562,729	231,699	3,815,156	1,296,996	1,230,431	36,344	30,221
Texas	25,587,831	2,774,172	3,088,374	1,860,559	1,227,815	19,725,285	10,349,260	8,128,708	475,849	1,744,703
Utah	3,144,839	44,518	533,860	533,860	0	2,566,461	784,603	709,799	5,228	69,576
Vermont	630,194	49,110	85,174	85,174	0	495,910	185,142	155,075	3,704	26,363
Virginia	11,499,472	29,489	1,804,558	470,845	1,333,713	9,665,425	2,571,811	2,219,350	89,716	262,745
Washington	12,062,079	427,768	638,385	637,881	504	10,995,926	2,742,364	2,342,467	39,200	360,697
West Virginia	818,920	52,239	121,183	87,179	34,004	645,498	230,854	217,540	9,217	4,097
Wisconsin	13,168,419	22,209	1,265,338	368,020	897,318	11,880,872	3,875,102	3,264,200	25,100	585,802
Wyoming	864,365	81,602	84,812	15,893	68,919	697,951	281,258	251,395	13,309	16,554

Source: U.S. Department of Commerce, U.S. Census Bureau, Governments Division, March 2009. 2007 Census of Governments, Survey of Public Employee-Retirement Systems. Data users who create their own estimates using data from this report should cite the U.S. Census Bureau as the source of the original data only. The data in this table are based on information from public records and contain no confidential data. Although the data in this table come from a census of state governments and are not subject to sampling error, the census results do contain nonsampling error. Additional information on nonsampling error, response rates, and definitions may be found at *http://www.census.gov/govs/www/retire07.html*. Created: December 9, 2008; Last Revised: December 9, 2008.

Table 7.32
NATIONAL SUMMARY OF FINANCES OF STATE-ADMINISTERED EMPLOYEE RETIREMENT SYSTEMS: SELECTED YEARS, 2003–2007

	Amount (in millions of dollars)				*Percentage distribution*			
	2006–07	*2005–06*	*2004–05*	*2003–04*	*2006–07*	*2005–06*	*2004–05*	*2003–04*
Total Receipts	**580,451,170**	**392,754,067**	**351,454,866**	**407,335,732**	**100.00**	**100.00**	**100.00**	**100.00**
Employee contributions	34,054,270	32,688,995	31,324,625	30,785,801	5.87	8.32	8.91	7.56
Government contributions	72,913,582	64,421,776	59,197,693	60,995,984	12.56	16.40	16.84	14.97
From State Government	30,608,843	26,364,650	24,050,633	31,159,060	5.27	6.71	6.84	7.65
From Local Government	42,304,739	38,057,126	35,147,060	29,836,924	7.29	9.69	10.00	7.32
Earnings on investments	473,483,318	295,643,296	260,932,548	315,553,947	81.57	75.27	74.24	77.47
Total Payments	**182,972,467**	**166,325,971**	**155,325,508**	**145,449,071**	**100.00**	**100.00**	**100.00**	**100.00**
Benefits paid	162,715,716	152,071,780	141,341,189	133,106,842	88.93	91.43	91.00	91.51
Withdrawals	5,233,579	4,107,721	3,777,732	4,430,593	2.86	2.47	2.43	3.05
Other payments	15,023,172	10,146,470	10,206,587	7,911,636	8.21	6.10	6.57	5.44
Total cash and investment holdings at end of fiscal year	**3,377,382,371**	**2,912,494,412**	**2,657,525,869**	**2,495,352,487**	**100.00**	**100.00**	**100.00**	**100.00**
Cash and short-term investments	118,027,997	92,891,182	89,741,655	84,811,257	3.49	3.19	3.38	3.40
Total Securities	2,911,338,315	2,564,247,428	2,355,561,132	2,213,581,060	86.20	88.04	88.64	88.71
Government securities	264,970,849	244,881,577	231,482,987	223,412,871	7.85	8.41	8.71	8.95
Federal government	263,034,370	242,996,381	229,937,493	215,159,724	7.79	8.34	8.65	8.62
United States Treasury	160,245,054	148,981,749	169,551,462	134,943,113	4.74	5.12	6.38	5.41
Federal agency	102,789,316	94,014,632	60,386,031	80,216,611	3.04	3.23	2.27	3.21
State and local government	1,936,479	1,885,196	1,545,494	8,253,147	0.06	0.06	0.06	0.33
Nongovernment securities	**2,646,367,466**	**2,319,365,851**	**2,124,078,145**	**1,990,168,189**	**78.36**	**79.64**	**79.93**	**79.75**
Corporate bonds	448,533,332	411,366,986	390,101,290	421,340,923	13.28	14.12	14.68	16.89
Corporate stocks	1,231,684,279	1,126,012,368	1,033,302,329	930,524,635	36.47	38.66	38.88	37.29
Mortgages	13,080,308	13,254,459	11,674,518	17,754,616	0.39	0.46	0.44	0.71
Funds held in trust	79,665,260	91,171,541	79,922,026	52,227,528	2.36	3.13	3.01	2.09
Foreign and international	518,304,128	437,928,142	375,064,878	311,642,945	15.35	15.04	14.11	12.49
Other nongovernmental	355,100,159	239,632,355	234,013,104	256,677,542	10.51	8.23	8.81	10.29
Other investments	**348,016,059**	**255,355,802**	**212,223,082**	**196,960,170**	**10.30**	**8.77**	**7.99**	**7.89**
Real property	99,158,659	66,783,925	41,978,140	43,715,769	2.94	2.29	1.58	1.75
Miscellaneous investments	248,857,400	188,571,877	170,244,942	153,244,401	7.37	6.47	6.41	6.14

Source: U.S. Department of Commerce, U.S. Census Bureau, Governments Division, March 2009. 2007 Census of Governments, Survey of Public Employee-Retirement Systems. Data users who create their own estimates using data from this report should cite the U.S. Census Bureau as the source of the original data only. The data in this table are based on information from public records and contain no confidential data. Although the data in this table come from a census of state governments and are not subject to sampling error, the census results do contain nonsampling error. Additional information on nonsampling error, response rates, and definitions may be found at *http://www.census.gov/govs/www/retire07.html*. Created: December 9, 2008; Last Revised: December 9, 2008.

Chapter Eight

STATE MANAGEMENT, ADMINISTRATION AND DEMOGRAPHICS

The National Performance Management Advisory Commission, An Oregon Perspective

By Sen. Richard Devlin and Michael J. Mucha

Performance management is more important than ever during tough times as officials strive to deliver better results with reduced resources. To help governments implement effective performance management systems, the National Performance Management Advisory Commission is developing a national framework for performance management.

Few qualities are more important for public sector organizations than having the public's confidence. Governments are entrusted with public funds and are responsible for carrying out vital services at all levels—federal, state and local. Performance measurement is essential to demonstrate and communicate the effectiveness of these services to stakeholders. In this capacity, performance measurement acts as a tool for objectively assessing output efficiency and outcome effectiveness.

Oregon has a long history of focusing on performance. In 1989, Oregon became the first state to articulate a 20-year strategic vision—Oregon Shines. Updated in 1997, Oregon Shines II recognizes how economic, social and environmental factors are interrelated and sets three high-level goals for the state:

- Quality jobs for all Oregonians;
- Engaged, caring and safe communities; and
- Healthy and sustainable environment.

Linked to these high-level goals are more than 90 Oregon Benchmarks—societal-level performance metrics that provide data on the current condition of the economy, education, civic engagement, social support, public safety, community development and the environment.

In 2001, the Oregon legislature set a statutory requirement that all state agencies develop performance measures and that they be linked to Oregon Benchmarks. State agencies are expected to report performance results during budget development and publish annual performance reports on their agency Web sites. A recent study published in the *Journal of Government Financial Management* concluded that "quality performance reporting is limited to a few departments scattered across the states, and only one state (Oregon) has consistently good reports in the four state departments reviewed."[1] But like many state and local governments, Oregon has learned over time that tracking and reporting performance measurement data by itself ignores the great opportunity government has to use performance management to improve services.

Performance management implies an organized approach to determining priorities, setting outcome goals and actively using performance data to allocate resources, manage programs and services, and evaluate results. Performance management goes beyond simply reporting on operations to creating a culture focused on improving services and meeting stakeholder expectations.

Oregon state government is working to transform its performance reporting system into a performance management system. This requires the use of metric-based information to drive the assessment of performance so the link between actions and results can be identified allowing successful programs to continue and less successful programs to be improved. To accomplish this task, the executive and legislative branch budget offices are working with agencies to increase the value of performance measurement and management for budgeting and agency management. Not all performance measures are appropriate for all situations. For example, some measures may help answer the question "Are we doing things right?" Those measures can be used to increase an agency's efficiency at delivering services. Other measures may be used to answer the question "Are we doing the right work?" Those can lead to improvements in aligning services to the agency's core mission and reducing or eliminating services that do not result in valued outcomes. Recognizing the many potential uses of performance measurement information has helped entice state government agencies to take ownership of performance data and a greater interest in pursuing performance management to improve rather than just to report.

These experiences are not unique to Oregon. Most states are now addressing the issue of how to improve efficiency and effectiveness of services through performance management. To address common challenges, representatives of 11 leading public interest associations[2] created the National Performance Management Advisory Commission to develop common language and provide a conceptual framework for public sector performance management. The framework is intended to assist governments in designing new performance measurement and management systems and offer practical strategies for successfully implementing and sustaining performance management efforts. Members of the commission have been working to establish an overall framework for performance management that:

- Creates a list of value-based principles that apply to all applications of performance management;
- Defines public sector performance management using a common language that allows the more rapid advancement of the field;
- Identifies performance measurement and management best practices and highlights specific examples within government where these practices are used; and
- Emphasizes the value of evidence-based and data-driven decision-making in effectively delivering government services.

The framework being developed by the commission will reflect the issues and challenges associated with committing to develop, implement and sustain performance management systems from a broad range of perspectives, including elected and appointed officials and program and operational managers. To be effective, the framework must be flexible and adaptable to the unique and diverse environments found throughout state and local governments. Similarly, all successful applications of performance management share a few essential components, such as the development of a shared vision, commitment from all stakeholders and strong leadership.

Shared Vision

Defining a shared vision is a complex process of working to align key stakeholders and getting them focused on achieving desired future results. This can often be a challenging task in government. The motivation to take on this effort often requires a catalyst. For example, one Oregon legislator took the initiative to request that the Oregon Judicial Department lead an effort to engage the courts, human services and nonprofit service providers to develop shared outcome measures related to child welfare. This collective group agreed to focus on the shared objective of ensuring children in foster care have permanency in their living situations as quickly as possible. To measure this, the group used an indicator that combined two composite numbers:

- timeliness and permanency of reunification of children discharged from foster care, and
- timeliness of foster-care-related adoptions.

As a result of this effort, several government agencies and nonprofit service providers now look more closely at how their individual performance contributes to this higher level outcome and what they might do separately or jointly to improve performance results.

Commitment

Agreeing to a shared vision sets the direction for change; however, sustaining change over time requires commitment because it can take many years of focused improvements before sufficient organizational processes and behaviors take root and lead to shifts in an organization's culture. Commitment from top-level executives is essential, but not the complete solution. It is not enough for state legislators to promote performance management by setting the expectations that state agencies focus on measuring performance outcomes; they also must be willing to buy into and invest in the business practices and data resources required to do the job. State agencies cannot just pay lip service to performance reporting and meet minimum requirements; agencies also need to focus more on measurable results and embrace tools and changes that improve business process efficiency. And, since state agencies funnel billions of dollars to local entities, performance management practices need to engage on-the-ground service providers to focus their efforts on attaining results and not just delivering services.

Oregon's successful performance measurement system can largely be attributed to sustained commitment. Over the last 20 years, leadership has vacillated somewhat between the governor's office, the legislature and key agency leaders; however, commitment to performance measurement remains strong. This commitment has enabled Oregon to become a leader in performance reporting. But it will take more time for its performance management processes to reach this standard.

Leadership

A final factor in successful application of performance management is effective leadership. Leaders drive efforts to achieve a shared vision and garner commitment. One of the most challenging dynamics governments face is the revolving door of elected officials, which often results in agency leadership adjustments. Changes in leadership often can bring changes to priorities and commitments, but the system of managing resources to achieve those priorities should be sustained. A rigorous performance management system can be adapted to new desired outcomes as its focus is largely about ensuring effective processes for collecting, tracking, analyzing and evaluating performance.

To the extent that performance management can be institutionalized, its chance of surviving leadership changes increases. For example, the 2008 Oregon legislature passed Senate Bill 1099, which forms a committee on performance excellence with participants from private industry, government and unions. The committee's role is to help promote performance management and continuous improvement in state government and to make recommendations to the legislature on actions and potential investments that will enhance state government performance. This committee is comprised of representatives from the legislative, executive and judicial branches of government. This structural design sends a strong message that responsibility for performance management is shared across all branches of state government.

Conclusion

Governments throughout the country are facing trying economic times and some may believe this is the wrong time to focus on performance management. Performance management will never have all the answers and, burdened by the task at hand, there will be pressure to abandon the tenets of performance management to deliver more expedient solutions. During times of economic downturn, governments are forced to make tough decisions about what to fund and what to cut, while at the same time constituents are demanding more and more from government. It is precisely during these times that an effective performance management system becomes an asset. Thus, the National Performance Management Advisory Commission's work could not have come at a more critical time. Meeting the challenge for most governments will require more than simply improving efficiency to make funds go further. It will require a framework that assists governments to design appropriate performance management systems that allow effective communication of expectations to all stakeholders, create linkages between planning documents and results, and encourage a process for making decisions based on data to improve services and most effectively deliver results.

Notes

[1] Ken A. Smith, Rita Hartung Cheng, Ola M. Smith and Ottalee Schiffel, "Performance Reporting by State Agencies: Bridging the Gap between Current Practice and GASB Suggested Criteria," *Journal of Government Financial Management*, Vol. 57, No. 2, 42–47, Summer 2008. *http://ssrn.com/abstract=1081443*.

[2] Sponsor organizations making up the commission include: Association of School Business Officials International (ASBO); National Association of State Budget Officers (NASBO); The Council of State Governments (CSG); Government Finance Officers Association (GFOA); International City/County Management Association (ICMA); National Association of Counties (NACo); National Association of State Auditors, Comptrollers, and Treasurers (NASACT); National Center for State Courts (NCSC); National Conference of State Legislatures (NCSL); National League of Cities (NLC); and U.S. Conference of Mayors (USCM).

About the Authors

Sen. Richard Devlin is the Senate majority leader in Oregon. He has served in the Oregon legislature since 1996. Devlin also serves on the National Performance Management Advisory Commission and is the immediate past chair of the National Conference of State Legislatures' Budget and Revenue Committee.

Michael J. Mucha is a senior consultant/analyst focusing on performance management research and technology consulting for the Government Finance Officers Association. He also coordinates work for the National Performance Management Advisory Commission.

Both authors also appreciate the assistance in the development of this article by **Dawn Farr**, legislative analyst for the Oregon Legislative Fiscal Office.

GMAP: Government Management Accountability and Performance in Action

By Larisa Benson and Christopher Stanley

Since its implementation in 2005, Washington's Government Management Accountability and Performance (GMAP) program has become an invaluable tool to Washington Gov. Chris Gregoire in measuring and improving the performance of state agencies.

In these difficult economic times, citizens demand change and a government that is better and faster than ever at providing the services they need. The focus of the Government Management Accountability and Performance program—better known as GMAP—has been just that. By measuring results and delivering practical, useful tools and solutions, the program is driving accountability and helping make Washington state government better.

Washington's Strong Foundation in Open Government

Over the past 35 years, Washington state has been a model for open government. The Open Public Meetings Act of 1975 and Television Washington transformed the operation of government at both the state and local levels by providing increased access to public policy discussions and action. More recent programs such as Priorities of Government and GMAP, as well as increased public engagement, dramatically increased the practice of performance-based budgeting and managing for results that Washington residents depend on.

In January 2005, Gov. Chris Gregoire created GMAP, which was modeled after Baltimore's *CitiStat*, New York's *CompStat* and Virginia Performs. Like the others, GMAP's mission is to improve government performance.

In June 2005, the first live, open-to-the-public GMAP accountability discussion centered on how the state protects Washington's most vulnerable children and adults.

Shining the Management Spotlight on Important Issues

Gregoire, her leadership team and state agency leaders review performance reports in regular public forums to evaluate progress toward meeting performance objectives. They engage in candid conversations about what is and is not working, and who will take specific actions to improve results. Adam Wilson, a local newspaper reporter, said, "you can actually watch the governor direct government."[1]

How Does GMAP Work?

GMAP is a multidisciplinary approach to performance improvement in the public sector. GMAP provides the support, services and tools agencies need to determine whether government programs provide value to residents and are effectively implemented.

The Centerpiece of GMAP

GMAP performance reports are regular, open-to-the-public meetings with the governor, her executive management team and agency directors. During the meetings, the governor reviews the past quarter's progress toward achieving results that align with her priorities. More than 30 state agencies participate in performance reports to the governor. In addition, Gregoire's 2005 executive order creating GMAP requires all state agencies to engage in similar management conversations at the agency level.

The GMAP approach is to make critical decisions on the spot, remove bureaucratic obstacles and redirect resources as necessary to achieve goals. The tenor of the dialogue is forthright and challenging. Ideally, the governor and her management team base decisions on the best available performance information coupled with the expertise of agency leaders and staff.

How are GMAP Reports Organized and Prepared?

GMAP reports focus on one of six priority policy areas: Health Care, Public Safety, Transportation, Vulnerable Children and Adults, Economic Vitality, and Government Efficiency. This approach has several advantages for state government. It emphasizes how the agencies are jointly responsible for the state's performance in high priority areas in which residents expect results and accountability. It helps break down communication barriers between agencies because they are jointly responsible for creating and participating in performance reports. Combining the work of several agencies by policy area also makes the reports more accessible and easier to understand for the state's residents. The average resident cares more about the results achieved in cleaning up the Puget Sound than about the division of responsibility between the Puget Sound Action Team, the Department of Ecology, the Department of Health and a host of other agencies and offices.

Each priority area has a measurement team that consists of the lead GMAP analyst, the governor's budget and policy analysts, and program staff from each agency. Each team meets to prepare and analyze the data in the report. The reports are used by the governor and leadership team as a guide for management discussions. Performance reports have three essential ingredients:

- A chart or table showing data for each performance measure,
- Analysis of the data written by the agency and the GMAP analyst, and
- An action plan to improve performance. Action plans detail *who* will do *what* by *when*.

Performance Reporting 'Live' with the Governor

The governor and her management team meet with agency directors to review the reports. They ask specific questions, ask for more information to better understand agency performance (like breaking down information into regions to understand gaps in performance on a regional level), suggest new solutions to issues, and direct agency leaders on the next steps to achieve results. Follow-up is central to these reports. After each report, GMAP sends agency directors a follow-up memo capturing action items so agencies can report back on progress before the next report.

Although other states and local governments have developed performance measurement systems, GMAP is unique because:

1. It produces high-level results that cut across multiple agencies.
2. GMAP reports include policy and management measures. Policy measures relate to high-level objectives, such as preventing child abuse. Management measures, such as overtime, are tracked across agencies.
3. Performance reports are reviewed live with agency directors and these meetings are open to the public.
4. GMAP initiated a widespread, lasting effort to change the culture of state government. Although every agency doesn't participate in performance reports with the governor, every agency is required to have an internal GMAP program. And GMAP staff provides technical assistance, tools and training on performance measures, data analysis, setting targets and communicating with data.
5. One of GMAP's most important innovations is an annual citizen engagement tour to validate that Washington is focused on the results that are most important to the state's residents and the performance measures used are meaningful to them.

Bob Behn, chairman of the leadership strategies program at Harvard University's Kennedy School of Government, said, "There are 48 states that aren't having this conversation. It's remarkably more efficient than doing nothing at all."[2]

Working with Agencies to Improve Performance

These reports also provide opportunities for GMAP to provide services and technical assistance to agencies to improve performance. Several activities fall under this umbrella, including performance audit coordination and assistance, research on best practices and new measures, process improvement consulting, observation and review of agency internal performance reports, quality assessment coordination and assistance, and training and education to build technical expertise in agencies.

Previous performance efforts in Washington state addressed only one aspect of performance management, such as customer service or budgeting. Improvement in just one area does not necessarily lead to better government. GMAP's innovation is merging these powerful management tools into a comprehensive framework that state agencies use to achieve results. The seven elements of this management framework are:

1. Plan strategically.
2. Prioritize the allocation of resources.
3. Manage people by connecting individual progress to organizational goals.
4. Analyze data and monitor progress.
5. Respond with decisions and action.
6. Improve business processes.
7. Communicate results and listen to customers and citizens.

Figure A: Data View Dashboard

1. Safety

Measure	Target	Actual	Status	Agency	Notes
1.1 Number of fatalities on state routes and interstates	0	211	●	WTSC	Compared to 252 fatalities as of November 24, 2007; 2008 data are preliminary and thus subject to change as further information becomes available. Target zero by 2030 on all roads.
1.2 Number of serious injuries on state routes and interstates		470	●	WSDOT, WSP, WTSC, DOL	Data reflects Jan.–June 2008. Serious injuries on state highways and interstates have decreased by 13% between 2002–2007.

2. Preservation

Measure	Target	Actual	Status	Agency	Notes
2.1 Percent of state highway pavement in fair or better condition	90%	93%	●	WSDOT	Data reflected through 2007. WSDOT maintains over 18,000 lane miles of state highway pavements, 100% of which is inspected annually.
2.2 Percent of state bridges in fair or better condition	97%	97%	●	WSDOT	Data reflected through 2007. WSDOT manages over 3,140 vehicular bridge structures, which at a minimum, are inspected every two years.
2.3 Percent of targets met for state highway maintenance levels		53%	◆	WSDOT	During 2007, 17 of the 32 Maintenance Accountability Process activity targets were achieved. Rising highway inventories and increased costs of doing business pose challenges for the Maintenance Program.

3. Mobility

Measure	Target	Actual	Status	Agency	Notes
3.1 Percent reduction in travel times before and after mobility improvements				WSDOT	In response to a Governor's request, WSDOT is collecting comprehensive data on travel time results, though this information is not yet available on a statewide basis. A sample of 21 projects studied to date shows a 10% reduction in travel time.
3.2 Average time to clear incidents longer than 90 minutes on key highway segments	155 min.	154 min.	●	WSP	This data is the annualized average for the three quarters of 2008 to date and is just below the GMAP target of 155 minutes. YTD the goal is being met.
3.3 Number of commute trips taken while driving alone	42,000 trips	26,037 trips	●	WSDOT	Data as of Sept. 2007. Measure includes two state trip reduction programs focused on reducing drive alone trips: the Commute Trip Reduction and the Growth and Transportation Efficiency Center programs. Establish GTEC target by 2009.

4. Environment

Measure	Target	Actual	Status	Agency	Notes
4.1 Cumulative number of WSDOT fish passage barrier improvements constructed		218		WSDOT	Data includes all barriers removed 1991–2007. 218 completed projects have created a potential 467 miles of fish habitat.

5. Stewardship

Measure	Target	Actual	Status	Agency	Notes
5.1 Percent of capital projects completed on time and within budget	90%	78%	◆	WSDOT	As a whole, WSDOT has successfully delivered 167 Nickel and TPA projects on target with the $1.8 billion legislative budget (program). Data reflects individual projects completed through Sept. 2008.

Source: http://performance.wa.gov/Transportation, as of December 2008.

Key: ●—Good, within expected parameters. ◆—Problem, probably needs attention.

Getting Results that Washington Residents Can Count On

GMAP produces concrete results. Among them:

- A decrease in the percent of children who are re-abused. Social workers now respond to reports of suspected child abuse within 24 hours 95 percent of the time, up from 65 percent in 2004. As a result, repeat instances of child abuse have declined by more than 25 percent.
- A decrease in traffic fatalities. The state's highways are safer than they've ever been in state history, despite more people driving on the roads. In 2007, fatalities per vehicle mile travelled hit an all-time low of 1 per 100 million.
- A savings of more than $46 million through consolidated purchasing of common prescription drugs for state-sponsored health care programs.

The use of data, performance measures and sound management tools is changing how Washington governs, and that change is being noticed. In 2007, GMAP was awarded one of eight annual Innovations Awards from The Council of State Governments. More recently, GMAP was the first recipient of CSG's Governance Transformation Award. Earlier this year, the citizen engagement aspect was also named as a Top 50 program by Harvard's Kennedy School.

What Comes Next?

As both the national and state economic situations darken, the accountability and performance work that Washington state is doing has never been more important. Through the data-based performance reports, agency and state leaders can easily see which programs are performing at or above par and which are not. Although GMAP has done quite a bit so far, there are many challenges and new opportunities that lie ahead.

Building New Technology to Evaluate Performance

When GMAP was launched, performance reports were completed in PowerPoint. Each slide was individually crafted by agencies without a consistent look and feel. Rather than navigating through the report by referring to a particular measure, the operative phrase was "what slide is that?" Today, GMAP is using a new Web-based reporting tool known as DataView. Not only does this tool include a dashboard that gives the governor and her leadership team a quick snapshot of agency performance, but it also improves performance reports in several ways:

- It is easier to read and navigate through various layers of information;
- The connection between strategic goals and day-to-day operations is clearer;
- Deeper analysis is still available to help tell the story behind the numbers; and
- There is a more consistent look and feel, standardized for all agencies.

Emerging Trends and Issues in Accountability and Transparency

Demands for increased accountability and transparency are not unique to Washington state. Other state governments have implemented similar initiatives, such as Virginia Performs and Maryland's StateStat program. We borrowed generously from their experience and expertise in developing our program. Launching an accountability or transparency initiative isn't easy; there are several challenges that will likely arise:

- Concerns about calling attention publicly to the problems state government faces.
- Resistance to the possibility that the state's work can't be measured.
- Lack of measurement expertise and analytic capacity in state agencies, and,
- Lack of technological capability to collect, store, retrieve, and analyze data.

In Washington state, we're putting more performance information than ever online for residents to access. The Transportation Improvement Board has a real-time dashboard, the Office of Financial Management posts the strategic plans of every state agency, and the Department of Social and Health Services has a Web page dedicated to its own *internal* GMAP forums. Agency Web sites are more customer-focused and service-oriented, and by using "plain talk" principles, we're translating official documents into simple language that everyone can understand clearly.

In the words of the late Dr. Keon Chi of CSG, "GMAP represents a mix of good management tools that are being successfully implemented across Washington state government. Many states are watching GMAP and the results it has achieved in critical areas such as jobs and child safety and are working to implement similar programs in their own states."[3]

Notes

[1] Jonathan Walters, "VISUAL EFFECTS: Using graphics to present performance data can help make the case for policy or budget changes," *Governing* magazine, (October 2007).

[2] Adam Wilson, "Government Accountability: Gregoire, Rossi Debate Plan's Merits," *The Olympian*, (October 29, 2008).

[3] Office of Gov. Chris Gregoire, "Innovations in Washington State Government Yield Results Citizens Can Count On," *Washington State Governor's Office*, (November 15, 2007).

About the Authors

Larisa Benson was the director of Government Management Accountability and Performance (GMAP) from 2005 to early 2009. Benson is currently the deputy for the statewide performance reviews with the Washington State Auditor's Office. She has previously served as faculty at the Evans School at the University of Washington, where she was the director of the Executive M.P.A. program and taught courses in performance, financial management and executive leadership. She also worked as a senior budget analyst for the city of Seattle and a negotiator for the Seattle School District.

Christopher Stanley is the governor's office program assistant for Government Management Accountability and Performance (GMAP) performance reports and DataView —a Web-based tool used to manage agency performance. Stanley previously served at the Washington state Department of Transportation in the Environmental Services Office and was the clerk for the Washington Senate Ways and Means Committee.

States Anticipate Talent Shortage

By Leslie Scott

Most states collect and analyze data on their government work force. With the baby boomer population reaching retirement age and 27 percent of the state work force across the country eligible to retire within the next five years, assessing the shrinking work force will continue as a critical exercise.

Employees are state government's greatest asset. Having systems and structures in place to ensure state government employees can effectively do their work in an environment that enables them to make the most of their knowledge, skills and abilities is critical to the success of state government.

State government human resources professionals manage these structures and systems that include a variety of components such as work force planning, technology and measures to evaluate human resources programs and initiatives.

Work Force Planning

Effective work force planning ensures the right people are in the right jobs at the right time. Human resources management professionals in state government have worked diligently in recent years to develop work force plans to make sure successful recruitment, retention and career progression processes are in place for talented employees.

Members of the National Association of State Personnel Executives—NASPE—have identified work force planning as a priority in state government human resource management . Approaches to work force planning vary from state to state, but all aim for the same goal—making state government an employer of choice, not an employer of last resort. Most plans involve completing a detailed analysis of the work force, developing aggressive recruitment and retention strategies, allowing more flexibility in hiring and implementing innovative pay practices within the confines of public sector employment.

Assessing the Work Force and Future Needs

Most states collect and analyze data on their government work force. Human resource professionals review a number of categories, from basic demographic information such as race and gender to more detailed information on turnover rates and retirement eligibility. With the baby boomer population reaching retirement age and 27 percent of the state work force across the country eligible to retire within the next five years, assessing the shrinking work force will continue as a critical exercise.

By identifying occupations and job classes in state government that have higher than average turnover rates, human resources professionals can assist agencies in identifying and correcting the issues that may be causing exceptional turnover. In addition, in examining retirement eligibility, human resources professionals can help agencies plan for their future work force needs by identifying potential positions that may be significantly affected by retiring employees.

Furthermore, with the continued implementation of new technology and the changing roles of state government, human resources professionals work with state agencies to assess the types of positions needed in the future and the current positions that may not be as necessary in years to come.

Recruitment

After states identify work force needs, they need to look at recruiting talented, committed employees.

Louisiana has made strides in its recruiting efforts with the program, *Recruiting Tomorrow's Leaders Today*. The program includes videos broadcast on the state Web site and local television stations showing successful younger workers in state government discussing the opportunities they've had as state employees. These are opportunities they may not have gotten elsewhere. In addition, the program utilizes another strategy—marketing the value of a career in public service.

Oklahoma offers paid internships for graduate students that typically lead to permanent employment opportunities with the state after graduation. Not only do the internships benefit the graduate students, but the program also benefits the state as it can hire new graduates already trained and experienced in state government.

Most states are also giving additional attention to positions that are often deemed "hard to fill and retain," such as nurses, corrections officers and engineers. Some states, such as South Carolina, offer bonuses to employees who refer a successful candidate for "hard-to fill" health care positions. Wyoming has recruited for corrections officers outside the state in areas of the country with high unemployment rates.

Michigan's Department of Transportation utilizes a comprehensive recruitment program for graduates of the state universities' engineering programs. By using open houses and special recruiting events that include on-the-spot interviews—and offering co-ops—the effort was successful in attracting recent engineering graduates to state government, when they could likely find a job in the private sector at a higher salary.

State human resources professionals also are aware that some potential applicants may not know how to apply for a job in state government, so they have focused on making the application process simpler. In addition, some states are working to reduce the time it takes to fill a position to avoid losing qualified applicants to the private sector. Some states are even able to make job offers for "hard-to-fill" positions to interviewees on the spot.

Most recently, a number of states have implemented online recruitment and applicant tracking systems that allow for quick posting of open positions, online applications and even online testing, if required by the state. States utilizing the latest online application and applicant tracking technologies indicate they have seen an increase in number of applicants for positions.

Training and Development

Training and development is also a component of work force plans. Not only is training vital for any organization to keep its employees current, it also allows employees to acquire new skills and information that will assist them in career progression opportunities—a key selling point for state government as an employer.

Training initiatives within state government can include anything from technical training to supervisory training; they can also include classroom training, mentoring and job rotation. Under some of these training initiatives, states also are focusing on leadership development and executive leadership programs.

For example, a number of states offer Certified Public Manager programs and many have developed leadership and executive leadership programs. The primary purpose of these programs is to develop staff and create a pipeline of qualified candidates for managerial positions as they are vacated by retiring baby boomers. The Certified Public Manager programs also seek to develop the decision-making skills of the state's managers.

Another example is a significant portion of Maine's work force planning effort—the Maine Management Service Program. This program is a multi-phased initiative for 700 managers, excluded from collective bargaining, in Maine state government who are in policymaking positions. The program focuses on the core competencies of leadership. Like Maine, Georgia runs the Georgia Leadership Institute, which offers six levels of manager training from pre-supervisory all the way through executive leadership.

Human Resources Information Technology

Technology continues to play a key role in state human resources management and is expected to take a greater role as states begin to utilize online application systems for state jobs and learning management systems for training and development administration.

States utilize human resource information systems that are sometimes independent systems that may be commercial or developed in-house. Some of these systems are part of larger statewide systems called Enterprise Resource Planning Systems, which typically include budgeting and financial components, along with procurement.

Whether states use an independent human resources information system or one that's part of an Enterprise Resource Planning System, they can use these systems to track and analyze work force data. The systems are an essential tool states utilize in managing state human resources, particularly as the need for this data increases with work force planning and other accountability efforts in the states.

According to NASPE's 2009 Survey, 10 states were in the process of getting a new Enterprise Resource Planning System. Two states were formulating the business case, three were seeking funding for the effort, three were in the design or blueprinting phase of the project, and two were preparing to implement the systems.

Online application and tracking systems have taken off in a big way. According to the NASPE 2008 HR Technology survey, at least 29 states have online application and tracking systems. States indicate these systems are attracting higher quality applicants and are allowing them to fill open positions more quickly.

Other automated human resources functions include training/learning management, performance evaluation, leave request and approval, time and attendance, computerized testing, competency management and online position descriptions. Training and learning management and time attendance are the most frequently used functions.

Human Resources Operation Structure

The organizational structure states use to provide human resources services can be quite different. Some states, such as Alaska, have their human resources operations and functions centralized in one management office. Other states, such as Texas, have a completely decentralized model where each state agency conducts its own human resource management work with no guidance from a central state agency. Minnesota and Idaho also are investigating a primarily decentralized model. Most states fall somewhere in the middle with a hybrid model in which much of the policy setting, as well as some operational work, is done in the central human resources office; line agencies maintain their own human resources staffs who conduct most of the day-to-day human resource management support for respective agency employees.

The trend with the hybrid model is that the central human resources offices are playing a more strategic and less transactional role, focusing on policy setting and consulting while pushing as much day-to-day operational work and oversight to the human resources staffs in the line agencies.

Some states have implemented shared services models, where a number of routine human resources transactions and services are performed for some or all state agencies in one center. This model is more efficient, particularly for smaller agencies that may not have the funding, manpower or expertise to efficiently conduct this type of work. More states are expected to move to this model during tougher economic times.

Strategic Human Resources Measures

As with other state government administrators, human resources professionals are continually asked to demonstrate value and effectiveness.

Because little was available in the area of public sector human resources management measures, NASPE's HR Metrics Task Force created a Metrics Toolkit that includes 22 strategic measures and formulas for state human resources operations to utilize, including Quality of Hire, Job Offers Accepted Rate, Voluntary Turnover of Key Performers in Key Jobs, Diversity Turnover, Salary Competitiveness of Market Rate and Training Impact on Performance.

While states at this point aren't using all 22 measures, they've typically identified a handful they deem most important. These will typically serve as a benchmark.

In addition, in states such Virginia, work force management is a factor used in evaluation of agency heads by the governor. The central human resources departments, along with the agency human resources staff, work closely with the agency heads to identify any areas of concern and to correct them as quickly as possible. They also develop long-term agency work force plans.

Alternative Work Schedules

Much was made of Utah's pilot effort in August 2008 to implement mandatory four-day work weeks for most state government employees. On Monday through Thursday of each week, state government offices are open for 10 hours and are closed on Fridays. Implemented at a time of $4 plus per gallon gasoline and an increased focus on "green" issues, the state hoped to reduced commuting time for employees, thus saving on gas, as well as its own energy costs, by having state government-owned buildings shut down for three days (Friday-Sunday) instead of two.

While energy savings is a big focus of the program, it was also a program developed to allow employees a better work-life balance, by having an extra day to spend with friends and family.

While Utah was certainly a pioneer in implementing a mandatory four-day work week, most states do offer some type of alternative work schedule for their employees, but it's not mandatory. These alternative work schedules may be the "4/10s" like Utah, "9/9s" (nine, nine-hour days, with the 10th day off), or allowing employees to set their own work schedule, such as coming in early and leaving earlier in the afternoon. Other options may include offering telecommuting.

Human resources directors encourage agency managers and supervisors to allow employees to utilize alternative work schedules and telecommuting if at all possible. These options can be used as rewards and incentives. In addition, it's something a younger work force, which states want and need to attract, may expect.

Challenges Ahead

The current economic conditions have caused states to look at a number of options, many of which may exacerbate current problems. Many states have implemented or are considering furloughs, hiring freezes, salary cuts, reductions in force (layoffs), early retirement incentives and buyouts. State government human resources professionals encourage agencies to keep their work force planning goals in mind when implementing these personnel actions. Most state systems reward seniority in many instances, but it's also important to consider special skill sets that are currently needed and those that will be needed in the future.

States will be challenged in the years ahead with baby boomer retirements, an aging work force and a multigenerational work force. But with strategic planning, increased use of technology, organizational efficiencies and demonstrated accountability, states will be up to the task to handle these challenges.

About the Author

Leslie Scott is the association director for the National Association of State Personnel Executives. Before joining NASPE, she worked with a number of state government associations, including the National Association for Government Training and Development and the National Association of State Procurement Officials. She holds a bachelor's degree in corporate and organizational communication from Western Kentucky University.

Table 8.1
SUMMARY OF STATE GOVERNMENT EMPLOYMENT: 1953–2007

Year (October)	*Employment (in thousands)*						*Monthly payrolls (in millions of dollars)*			*Average monthly earnings of full-time employees*		
	Total, full-time and part-time			*Full-time equivalent*								
	All	*Education*	*Other*	*All*	*Education*	*Other*	*All*	*Education*	*Other*	*All*	*Education*	*Other*
1953	1,082	294	788	966	211	755	$278.6	$73.5	$205.1	$289	$320	$278
1954	1,149	310	839	1,024	222	802	300.7	78.9	221.8	294	325	283
1955	1,199	333	866	1,081	244	837	325.9	88.5	237.4	302	334	290
1956	1,268	353	915	1,136	250	886	366.5	108.8	257.7	321	358	309
1957 (April)	1,300	375	925	1,153	257	896	372.5	106.1	266.4	320	355	309
1958	1,408	406	1,002	1,259	284	975	446.5	123.4	323.1	355	416	333
1959	1,454	443	1,011	1,302	318	984	485.4	136.0	349.4	373	427	352
1960	1,527	474	1,053	1,353	332	1,021	524.1	167.7	356.4	386	439	365
1961	1,625	518	1,107	1,435	367	1,068	586.2	192.4	393.8	409	482	383
1962	1,680	555	1,126	1,478	389	1,088	634.6	201.8	432.8	429	518	397
1963	1,775	602	1,173	1,558	422	1,136	696.4	230.1	466.3	447	545	410
1964	1,873	656	1,217	1,639	460	1,179	761.1	257.5	503.6	464	560	427
1965	2,028	739	1,289	1,751	508	1,243	849.2	290.1	559.1	484	571	450
1966	2,211	866	1,344	1,864	575	1,289	975.2	353.0	622.2	522	614	483
1967	2,335	940	1,395	1,946	620	1,326	1,105.5	406.3	699.3	567	666	526
1968	2,495	1,037	1,458	2,085	694	1,391	1,256.7	477.1	779.6	602	687	544
1969	2,614	1,112	1,501	2,179	746	1,433	1,430.5	554.5	876.1	655	743	597
1970	2,755	1,182	1,573	2,302	803	1,499	1,612.2	630.3	981.9	700	797	605
1971	2,832	1,223	1,609	2,384	841	1,544	1,741.7	681.5	1,060.2	731	826	686
1972	2,957	1,267	1,690	2,487	867	1,619	1,936.6	746.9	1,189.7	778	871	734
1973	3,013	1,280	1,733	2,547	887	1,660	2,158.2	822.2	1,336.0	843	952	805
1974	3,155	1,357	1,798	2,653	929	1,725	2,409.5	932.7	1,476.9	906	1,023	855
1975	3,271	1,400	1,870	2,744	952	1,792	2,652.7	1,021.7	1,631.1	964	1,080	909
1976	3,343	1,434	1,910	2,799	973	1,827	2,893.7	1,111.5	1,782.1	1,031	1,163	975
1977	3,491	1,484	2,007	2,903	1,005	1,898	3,194.6	1,234.4	1,960.1	1,096	1,237	1,031
1978	3,539	1,508	2,032	2,966	1,016	1,950	3,483.0	1,332.9	2,150.2	1,167	1,311	1,102
1979	3,699	1,577	2,122	3,072	1,046	2,026	3,869.3	1,451.4	2,417.9	1,257	1,399	1,193
1980	3,753	1,599	2,154	3,106	1,063	2,044	4,284.7	1,608.0	2,676.6	1,373	1,523	1,305
1981	3,726	1,603	2,123	3,087	1,063	2,024	4,667.5	1,768.0	2,899.5	1,507	1,671	1,432
1982	3,747	1,616	2,131	3,083	1,051	2,032	5,027.7	1,874.0	3,153.7	1,625	1,789	1,551
1983	3,816	1,666	2,150	3,116	1,072	2,044	5,345.5	1,989.0	3,357.0	1,711	1,850	1,640
1984	3,898	1,708	2,190	3,177	1,091	2,086	5,814.9	2,178.0	3,637.0	1,825	1,991	1,740
1985	3,984	1,764	2,220	2,990	945	2,046	6,328.6	2,433.7	3,884.9	1,935	2,155	1,834
1986	4,068	1,800	2,267	3,437	1,256	2,181	6,801.4	2,583.4	4,226.9	2,052	2,263	1,956
1987	4,115	1,804	2,310	3,491	1,264	2,227	7,297.8	2,758.3	4,539.5	2,161	2,396	2,056
1988	4,236	1,854	2,381	3,606	1,309	2,297	7,842.3	2,928.6	4,913.7	2,260	2,490	2,158
1989	4,365	1,925	2,440	3,709	1,360	2,349	8,443.1	3,175.0	5,268.1	2,372	2,627	2,259
1990	4,503	1,984	2,519	3,840	1,418	2,432	9,083.0	3,426.0	5,657.0	2,472	2,732	2,359
1991	4,521	1,999	2,522	3,829	1,375	2,454	9,437.0	3,550.0	5,887.0	2,479	2,530	2,433
1992	4,595	2,050	2,545	3,856	1,384	2,472	9,828.0	3,774.0	6,054.0	2,562	2,607	2,521
1993	4,673	2,112	2,562	3,891	1,436	2,455	10,288.2	3,999.3	6,288.9	2,722	3,034	2,578
1994	4694	2115	2579	3,917	1,442	2,475	10,666.3	4,176.8	6,489.3	2,776	3,073	2,640
1995	4,719	2,120	2,598	3,971	1,469	2,502	10,926.5	4,173.3	6,753.2	2,854	3,138	2,725
1996	(a)	(a)	(a)	(a)	(a)	(a)	(a)	(a)	(a)	(a)	(a)	(a)
1997 (March)	4,733	2,114	2,619	3,987	1,484	2,503	11,413.1	4,372.0	7,041.1	2,968	3,251	2,838
1998 (March)	4,758	2,173	2,585	3,985	1,511	2,474	11,845.2	4,632.1	7,213.1	3,088	3,382	2,947
1999 (March)	4,818	2,229	2,588	4,034	1,541	2,493	12,564.1	4,957.0	7,607.7	3,236	3,544	3,087
2000 (March)	4,877	2,259	2,618	4,083	1,563	2,520	13,279.1	5,255.3	8,023.8	3,374	3,692	3,219
2001 (March)	4,985	2,329	2,656	4,173	1,615	2,559	14,136.3	5,620.7	8,515.6	3,521	3,842	3,362
2002 (March)	5,072	2,414	2,658	4,223	1,659	2,564	14,837.8	5,996.6	8,841.2	3,657	4,007	3,479
2003 (March)	5,043	2,413	2,630	4,191	1,656	2,534	15,116.4	6,154.4	8,962.0	3,751	4,115	3,566
2004 (March)	5,041	2,432	2,609	4,188	1,673	2,515	15,477.5	6,411.8	9,065.7	3,845	4,256	3,631
2005 (March)	5,078	2,459	2,620	4,209	1,684	2,525	16,061.6	6,668.9	9,392.6	3,966	4,390	3,745
2006 (March)	5,128	2,493	2,635	4,251	1,708	2,542	16,769.4	6,960.9	9,808.6	4,098	4,505	3,883
2007 (March)	5,200	2,538	2,663	4,307	1,740	2,566	17,788.7	7,418.9	10,369.9	4,276	4,670	4,063

Source: U.S. Department of Commerce, U.S. Census Bureau, March 2009. 2007 Census of Government Employment. For information on nonsampling error and definitions, see *http://www.census.gov/govs/www/apesstl07.html.* Data users who create their own estimates from these tables should cite the U.S. Census Bureau as the source of the original data only.

Note: Detail may not add to totals due to rounding.

Key:

. . . — Not applicable.

(a) Due to a change in the reference period, from October to March, the October 1996 Annual Survey of Government Employment and Payroll was not concluded. This change in collection period was effective beginning with the March 1997 survey.

Table 8.2
EMPLOYMENT AND PAYROLLS OF STATE AND LOCAL GOVERNMENTS BY FUNCTION: MARCH 2007

Functions	All employees, full-time and part-time (in thousands)			March payrolls (in millions of dollars)			Average March earnings of full-time employees
	Total	State government	Local government	Total	State government	Local government	
All functions	19,386	5,200	14,186	$64,156,490	$17,788,745	$46,367,745	$4,030
Education:							
Higher education	2,940	2,375	565	8,228,499	6,820,621	1,407,878	4,698
Instructional personnel only	1,045	768	277	3,820,842	3,063,472	757,370	6,361
Elementary/Secondary schools	7,875	64	7,812	24,493,925	229,078	24,264,847	3,722
Instructional personnel only	5,310	46	5,265	19,218,110	191,308	19,026,802	4,181
Libraries	189	1	188	392,286	1,790	390,496	3,350
Other Education	99	99	0	369,194	369,194	0	4,087
Selected functions:							
Streets and Highways	558	241	316	2,054,398	958,970	1,095,428	3,844
Public Welfare	543	240	303	1,800,578	812,720	987,858	3,516
Hospitals	1,078	444	634	3,984,522	1,666,480	2,318,042	4,039
Police protection	997	109	889	4,404,193	512,653	3,891,540	4,812
Police Officers	715	68	647	3,550,171	367,683	3,182,488	5,174
Fire protection	417	0	417	1,748,644	0	1,748,644	5,352
Firefighters only	383	0	383	1,629,120	0	1,629,120	5,423
Natural Resources	204	159	45	702,741	561,998	140,743	3,957
Correction	743	475	268	2,810,039	1,808,401	1,001,639	3,858
Social Insurance	82	81	0	312,531	310,299	2,232	3,966
Financial Admin.	432	177	254	1,580,316	692,228	888,088	4,028
Judicial and Legal	448	178	271	1,897,645	823,435	1,074,210	4,520
Other Government Admin.	424	62	362	1,130,760	236,315	894,445	4,131
Utilities	514	39	476	2,237,002	203,817	2,033,185	4,585
State Liquor stores	9	9	0	22,302	22,302	0	3,080
Other and unallocable	1,835	448	1,386	5,986,913	1,758,444	4,228,468	3,929

Source: U.S. Department of Commerce, U.S. Census Bureau, March 2009. 2007 Census of Government Employment. For information on nonsampling error and definitions, see *http://www.census.gov/govs/www/apesstl07.html*.

Data users who create their own estimates from these tables should cite the U.S. Census Bureau as the source of the original data only.

Table 8.3
STATE AND LOCAL GOVERNMENT EMPLOYMENT, BY STATE: MARCH 2007

State or other jurisdiction	All employees (full-time and part-time)			Full-time equivalent employment		
	Total	State	Local	Total	State	Local
United States	19,385,969	5,200,347	14,185,622	16,453,570	4,306,623	12,146,947
Alabama	320,500	106,494	214,006	284,680	88,617	196,063
Alaska	61,483	29,197	32,286	52,173	25,653	26,520
Arizona	352,500	85,197	267,303	300,564	68,224	232,340
Arkansas	187,503	67,681	119,822	165,666	59,386	106,280
California	2,228,966	479,594	1,749,372	1,835,452	387,168	1,448,284
Colorado	320,836	89,361	231,475	262,424	67,784	194,640
Connecticut	225,827	75,194	150,633	187,545	61,823	125,722
Delaware	59,606	31,223	28,383	51,612	26,148	25,464
Florida	1,023,033	216,390	806,643	890,834	188,772	702,062
Georgia	584,924	153,234	431,690	519,684	126,420	393,264
Hawaii	85,631	70,409	15,222	71,503	57,210	14,293
Idaho	101,128	28,413	72,715	80,585	22,190	58,395
Illinois	789,388	152,021	637,367	645,306	125,015	520,291
Indiana	405,039	113,574	291,465	339,787	89,558	250,229
Iowa	228,477	65,744	162,733	182,356	53,427	128,929
Kansas	234,006	56,311	177,695	187,953	45,098	142,855
Kentucky	284,815	98,665	186,150	246,837	80,307	166,530
Louisiana	296,612	99,296	197,316	264,622	84,593	180,029
Maine	96,816	28,900	67,916	76,382	22,870	53,512
Maryland	337,253	95,475	241,778	300,723	90,333	210,390
Massachusetts	392,184	116,026	276,158	334,715	96,109	238,606
Michigan	624,535	182,654	441,881	493,466	144,807	348,659
Minnesota	355,662	94,788	260,874	280,783	78,266	202,517
Mississippi	213,410	64,354	149,056	189,188	55,824	133,364
Missouri	384,840	105,664	279,176	327,622	89,532	238,090
Montana	72,290	26,337	45,953	55,982	20,017	35,965
Nebraska	139,462	37,995	101,467	113,600	32,465	81,135
Nevada	132,118	35,619	96,499	110,317	28,506	81,811
New Hampshire	88,105	25,241	62,864	72,175	19,588	52,587
New Jersey	590,055	177,973	412,082	513,111	155,685	357,426
New Mexico	149,717	59,842	89,875	133,660	52,255	81,405
New York	1,391,699	285,062	1,106,637	1,232,744	253,354	979,390
North Carolina	629,279	166,591	462,688	542,180	142,985	399,195
North Dakota	62,445	24,228	38,217	41,431	17,918	23,513
Ohio	739,727	189,679	550,048	613,581	143,206	470,375
Oklahoma	249,907	86,213	163,694	215,723	69,961	145,762
Oregon	237,147	73,386	163,761	190,197	59,619	130,578
Pennsylvania	694,350	191,548	502,802	594,225	160,177	434,048
Rhode Island	62,157	24,918	37,239	53,798	20,435	33,363
South Carolina	285,416	87,402	198,014	254,272	76,213	178,059
South Dakota	58,721	16,748	41,973	43,421	13,897	29,524
Tennessee	366,049	101,799	264,250	324,520	84,875	239,645
Texas	1,492,766	334,378	1,158,388	1,344,442	290,451	1,053,991
Utah	174,230	66,001	108,229	132,073	51,001	81,072
Vermont	48,185	16,347	31,838	39,792	14,759	25,033
Virginia	517,305	155,445	361,860	441,928	124,536	317,392
Washington	415,557	152,737	262,820	340,052	119,970	220,082
West Virginia	116,184	45,513	70,671	101,073	38,060	63,013
Wisconsin	372,090	98,587	273,503	281,645	68,714	212,931
Wyoming	57,164	14,899	42,265	48,050	12,842	35,208
Dist. of Columbia	48,870	0	48,870	47,116	0	47,116

Source: U.S. Department of Commerce, U.S. Census Bureau, March 2009. 2007 Census of Government Employment. For information on nonsampling error and definitions, see *http://www.census.gov/govs/www/apesstl07.html*. Data users who create their own estimates from these tables should cite the U.S. Census Bureau as the source of the original data only.

Note: Statistics for local governments are estimates subject to sampling variation. Detail may not add to totals due to rounding.

Table 8.4
STATE AND LOCAL GOVERNMENT PAYROLLS AND AVERAGE EARNINGS OF FULL-TIME EMPLOYEES, BY STATE: MARCH 2007

State or other jurisdiction	Amount of payroll (in thousands of dollars)			Percentage of March payroll		Average earnings of full-time state and local government employees (dollars)		
	Total	State government	Local governments	State government	Local government	All	Education employees	Other
United States	$59,170,995	$16,146,025	$43,024,970	27	73	$4,030	$3,910	$4,159
Alabama	857,097	298,097	559,000	35	65	3,246	3,266	3,226
Alaska	212,917	107,947	104,970	51	49	4,504	4,235	4,732
Arizona	1,084,364	230,539	853,825	21	79	4,059	3,662	4,496
Arkansas	458,593	179,747	278,846	39	61	2,963	3,045	2,854
California	8,569,119	1,901,011	6,668,107	22	78	5,454	5,214	5,656
Colorado	920,899	249,407	671,492	27	73	4,059	3,819	4,313
Connecticut	788,852	275,698	513,155	35	65	4,750	4,590	4,968
Delaware	181,932	93,905	88,027	52	48	3,996	4,442	3,677
Florida	3,080,989	639,747	2,441,241	21	79	3,787	3,521	4,003
Georgia	1,602,864	401,415	1,201,449	25	75	3,338	3,446	3,200
Hawaii	266,385	204,193	62,193	77	23	4,084	3,941	4,210
Idaho	234,207	73,179	161,028	31	69	3,320	3,051	3,612
Illinois	2,401,350	506,505	1,894,845	21	79	4,210	3,998	4,467
Indiana	1,027,363	288,120	739,243	28	72	3,432	3,532	3,299
Iowa	573,791	205,436	368,355	36	64	3,765	3,564	4,026
Kansas	549,995	148,002	401,993	27	73	3,292	3,264	3,327
Kentucky	695,218	261,315	433,903	38	62	3,047	2,925	3,238
Louisiana	772,474	284,240	488,233	37	63	3,138	3,056	3,216
Maine	228,657	79,508	149,150	35	65	3,403	3,207	3,683
Maryland	1,217,595	363,910	853,685	30	70	4,526	4,654	4,389
Massachusetts	1,342,956	402,542	940,414	30	70	4,487	4,293	4,701
Michigan	1,776,982	554,353	1,222,629	31	69	4,317	4,421	4,173
Minnesota	995,420	311,542	683,878	31	69	4,255	4,156	4,375
Mississippi	510,542	165,623	344,919	32	68	2,899	2,858	2,946
Missouri	939,182	255,697	683,485	27	73	3,173	3,155	3,193
Montana	158,260	64,606	93,654	41	59	3,318	3,289	3,348
Nebraska	351,650	95,654	255,996	27	73	3,510	3,349	3,681
Nevada	460,276	117,986	342,290	26	74	4,671	4,053	5,183
New Hampshire	226,077	65,140	160,937	29	71	3,658	3,522	3,857
New Jersey	2,385,455	770,878	1,614,577	32	68	5,054	5,179	4,913
New Mexico	384,902	161,949	222,954	42	58	3,182	3,097	3,277
New York	5,359,301	1,161,865	4,197,436	22	78	4,773	4,684	4,843
North Carolina	1,673,320	474,145	1,199,175	28	72	3,424	3,371	3,483
North Dakota	119,256	49,766	69,490	42	58	3,482	3,716	3,220
Ohio	2,099,888	531,297	1,568,591	25	75	3,903	3,892	3,915
Oklahoma	615,573	223,552	392,021	36	64	3,081	2,960	3,235
Oregon	649,293	213,316	435,977	33	67	4,031	3,817	4,218
Pennsylvania	2,101,017	585,472	1,515,545	28	72	3,953	4,106	3,778
Rhode Island	226,750	88,756	137,993	39	61	4,592	4,718	4,466
South Carolina	750,378	237,491	512,887	32	68	3,160	3,201	3,115
South Dakota	119,526	42,991	76,535	36	64	3,104	3,053	3,170
Tennessee	986,691	269,220	717,471	27	73	3,272	3,209	3,332
Texas	4,255,196	1,004,129	3,251,067	24	76	3,400	3,317	3,517
Utah	406,207	166,886	239,320	41	59	3,726	3,774	3,672
Vermont	130,290	57,368	72,922	44	56	3,698	3,503	4,018
Virginia	1,498,831	431,961	1,066,870	29	71	3,786	3,737	3,849
Washington	1,301,487	443,041	858,447	34	66	4,647	4,617	4,667
West Virginia	283,340	110,953	172,387	39	61	3,035	3,286	2,726
Wisconsin	959,195	253,259	705,936	26	74	4,048	4,062	4,028
Wyoming	149,702	42,669	107,033	29	71	3,602	3,706	3,514
Dist. of Columbia	229,393	0	229,393	0	100	5,174	4,443	5,379

Source: U.S. Department of Commerce, U.S. Census Bureau, March 2009. 2007 Census of Government Employment. For information on nonsampling error and definitions, see *http://www.census.gov/govs/www/apesstl07.html*. Data users who create their own estimates from these tables should cite the U.S. Census Bureau as the source of the original data only.

Note: Statistics for local governments are estimates subject to sampling variation. Detail may not add to totals due to rounding.

Table 8.5
STATE GOVERNMENT EMPLOYMENT (FULL-TIME EQUIVALENT) FOR SELECTED FUNCTIONS, BY STATE: MARCH 2007

		Selected functions									
		Education									
State	*All functions*	*Higher education (a)*	*Other education (b)*	*Highways*	*Public welfare*	*Hospitals*	*Corrections*	*Police protection*	*Natural resources*	*Financial and other governmental administration*	*Judicial and legal administration*
United States	4,306,623	1,596,652	143,570	236,758	235,305	417,113	470,464	106,595	145,114	229,066	173,021
Alabama	88,617	37,864	3,218	4,572	4,530	11,717	4,975	1,560	2,227	3,236	3,553
Alaska	25,653	5,256	3,401	3,065	1,809	229	1,791	403	2,394	1,805	1,362
Arizona	68,224	28,273	3,380	2,733	5,939	708	8,954	2,002	2,985	4,267	2,379
Arkansas	59,386	23,277	1,476	3,540	3,698	5,718	5,112	1,193	1,944	2,677	1,482
California	387,168	143,157	4,197	20,816	3,745	39,829	55,710	13,283	14,022	26,046	4,710
Colorado	67,784	35,953	1,339	3,124	2,114	5,273	6,833	1,181	1,462	2,615	3,884
Connecticut	61,823	17,915	2,857	3,028	2,460	9,427	7,556	2,102	863	4,269	4,776
Delaware	26,148	7,692	358	1,568	1,648	1,910	2,857	1,021	521	1,173	1,706
Florida	188,772	56,564	3,381	7,343	9,358	3,761	29,084	4,441	9,876	9,192	20,685
Georgia	126,420	51,243	3,249	5,918	9,169	7,124	19,819	2,036	4,432	5,536	3,629
Hawaii	57,210	8,884	26,718	845	941	4,309	2,362	0	1,145	1,475	2,413
Idaho	22,190	7,961	509	1,593	1,659	798	1,892	487	2,076	1,609	459
Illinois	125,015	54,003	2,089	6,392	9,792	10,486	12,064	3,953	3,562	7,864	2,594
Indiana	89,558	54,783	1,195	4,365	4,550	2,554	7,340	1,882	2,773	3,592	1,333
Iowa	53,427	25,215	1,120	2,423	3,050	7,359	3,213	964	1,925	1,746	2,361
Kansas	45,098	19,918	677	3,452	2,464	3,162	3,596	1,149	846	2,639	2,138
Kentucky	80,307	33,000	2,726	4,575	6,679	4,897	4,128	2,390	3,965	3,908	5,355
Louisiana	84,593	27,353	4,718	4,910	5,182	13,873	7,189	1,727	4,521	4,759	1,484
Maine	22,870	7,074	324	2,431	3,184	637	1,302	536	1,140	1,935	760
Maryland	90,333	26,321	2,253	4,702	6,828	4,931	12,169	2,394	1,780	5,072	4,952
Massachusetts	96,109	30,217	1,180	3,656	6,895	7,553	5,968	6,388	1,431	5,794	9,931
Michigan	144,807	70,493	2,348	2,974	10,196	17,873	17,014	2,730	4,553	6,082	1,541
Minnesota	78,266	36,190	3,760	4,424	2,980	5,186	4,112	976	3,055	3,700	3,440
Mississippi	55,824	19,080	1,546	3,233	2,449	12,151	3,547	1,235	3,226	1,630	677
Missouri	89,532	28,482	1,736	6,583	7,888	11,621	12,435	2,338	2,549	4,305	3,481
Montana	20,017	7,033	364	2,174	1,630	599	1,189	420	1,489	1,615	670
Nebraska	32,465	12,388	552	2,161	2,599	4,068	2,877	776	2,173	1,082	748
Nevada	28,506	10,569	133	1,749	1,594	1,384	3,786	796	986	2,792	647
New Hampshire	19,588	6,626	320	1,828	1,511	768	1,358	448	406	1,307	944
New Jersey	155,685	31,318	22,761	7,230	9,323	18,529	10,170	4,592	2,421	7,982	14,462
New Mexico	52,255	19,165	1,207	2,571	1,938	10,407	3,971	690	1,128	2,249	3,070
New York	253,354	50,865	4,641	12,792	6,472	45,376	34,368	6,423	3,537	17,199	20,425
North Carolina	142,985	53,912	3,011	11,144	2,092	17,430	21,441	3,797	4,266	5,107	6,609
North Dakota	17,918	7,956	285	1,093	472	963	700	190	1,670	964	531
Ohio	143,206	69,256	2,629	7,221	2,980	15,469	16,725	2,711	2,968	9,129	2,748
Oklahoma	69,961	29,111	1,983	2,972	6,636	2,797	5,758	1,887	1,946	2,602	2,780
Oregon	59,619	19,708	752	3,742	6,685	5,386	5,094	1,285	2,694	5,391	3,110
Pennsylvania	160,177	56,679	4,477	13,379	12,045	11,850	17,336	6,419	6,278	11,460	3,006
Rhode Island	20,435	5,617	1,105	775	1,612	1,108	1,737	310	498	1,620	1,228
South Carolina	76,213	28,575	2,654	4,779	4,327	7,515	7,809	2,054	2,111	4,106	701
South Dakota	13,897	5,183	405	997	1,080	953	890	298	862	766	588
Tennessee	84,875	32,840	2,131	4,382	8,212	7,607	7,159	2,014	4,040	4,431	2,363
Texas	290,451	110,581	4,878	16,024	23,272	33,998	45,075	4,210	10,460	12,207	5,530
Utah	51,001	23,432	1,164	1,636	3,062	6,951	3,257	809	1,279	2,917	1,598
Vermont	14,759	4,728	604	1,073	1,316	219	1,203	636	635	1,318	635
Virginia	124,536	51,955	2,977	8,968	2,449	15,046	14,500	3,157	2,890	4,976	3,643
Washington	119,970	53,025	2,086	7,490	9,414	9,859	8,854	2,131	5,318	4,366	1,949
West Virginia	38,060	12,384	1,389	4,978	3,256	1,614	3,301	1,007	2,340	2,206	1,404
Wisconsin	68,714	33,997	1,075	1,502	1,385	3,360	9,864	885	2,472	3,602	2,028
Wyoming	12,842	3,581	232	1,833	736	771	1,020	279	974	746	519

Source: U.S. Department of Commerce, U.S. Census Bureau, March 2009. 2007 Census of Government Employment. For information on nonsampling error and definitions, see *http://www.census.gov/govs/www/apesstl07.html*. Data users who create their own estimates from these tables should cite the U.S. Census Bureau as the source of the original data only.

Key:
(a) Includes instructional and other personnel.
(b) Includes instructional and other personnel in elementary and secondary schools.

Table 8.6
STATE GOVERNMENT PAYROLLS FOR SELECTED FUNCTIONS, BY STATE: MARCH 2007
(In thousands of dollars)

		Selected functions									
		Education									
State	All functions	Higher education (a)	Other education (b)	Highways	Public welfare	Hospitals	Corrections	Police protection	Natural resources	Financial and other governmental administration	Judicial and legal administration
United States	$17,788,745	$6,820,621	$598,272	$958,970	$812,720	$1,666,480	$1,808,401	$512,653	$561,998	$928,543	$823,435
Alabama	324,869	152,293	11,205	14,000	13,176	42,441	14,188	6,070	7,956	12,028	14,940
Alaska	114,168	24,323	12,576	14,799	6,659	1,046	8,013	2,115	10,400	8,143	6,682
Arizona	259,357	119,673	11,105	9,886	17,066	2,485	29,647	9,090	12,633	14,940	10,129
Arkansas	191,039	81,621	4,622	11,466	10,057	18,179	13,166	3,828	5,610	8,465	4,644
California	2,118,773	752,252	19,531	137,971	16,710	231,778	343,367	72,486	69,796	116,665	27,521
Colorado	301,751	164,780	5,589	13,753	9,157	19,654	27,627	5,741	7,163	11,634	18,004
Connecticut	308,094	87,941	14,767	14,855	11,058	50,613	37,339	11,163	4,215	20,303	22,389
Delaware	105,524	34,083	1,910	5,166	5,675	6,320	11,640	5,860	1,862	4,234	7,624
Florida	691,312	251,236	11,162	29,320	28,048	11,350	88,425	16,715	31,181	34,226	83,165
Georgia	441,675	212,194	12,917	17,674	25,351	18,803	51,983	7,190	13,543	20,479	17,001
Hawaii	224,849	41,176	96,443	3,645	3,434	17,527	10,633	0	4,861	5,561	10,495
Idaho	83,182	29,586	2,006	5,365	5,318	2,310	6,818	1,803	8,080	6,392	3,380
Illinois	556,184	210,031	10,106	38,620	44,607	47,682	56,211	21,909	13,516	37,009	19,720
Indiana	317,085	203,582	4,145	13,163	13,137	7,483	21,225	6,802	8,624	13,105	8,234
Iowa	239,303	109,255	5,098	10,454	12,194	38,644	13,597	4,812	8,429	7,450	11,182
Kansas	163,014	81,169	2,497	10,943	7,062	9,077	10,529	4,621	3,020	8,651	7,996
Kentucky	282,497	127,204	10,587	14,800	19,999	17,691	11,066	8,903	11,727	15,740	17,627
Louisiana	300,929	107,589	17,067	11,170	16,672	45,517	23,902	7,982	15,985	17,404	5,522
Maine	87,022	27,410	1,159	8,885	10,717	2,480	5,225	2,550	4,519	7,005	3,382
Maryland	391,121	124,534	10,132	19,391	25,205	18,156	48,619	11,178	7,568	22,324	24,653
Massachusetts	450,309	138,287	6,043	18,738	32,179	29,980	27,024	33,076	7,215	26,602	48,405
Michigan	627,824	309,858	9,261	13,851	44,718	64,948	77,692	11,144	19,654	27,925	10,158
Minnesota	352,923	170,273	17,560	19,762	10,515	20,554	16,468	4,316	13,059	15,988	16,528
Mississippi	176,865	67,596	4,626	8,675	5,786	34,549	11,505	3,958	8,897	5,696	3,622
Missouri	277,544	102,890	5,176	22,794	19,424	32,564	30,489	9,041	7,573	13,890	9,665
Montana	72,476	27,178	1,275	8,503	5,250	1,850	3,837	1,489	5,202	5,137	2,696
Nebraska	105,466	41,240	2,108	6,954	7,139	12,587	8,568	3,052	6,274	3,656	3,262
Nevada	128,939	47,976	647	7,633	6,051	6,374	17,398	4,454	4,479	11,690	4,014
New Hampshire	74,983	28,529	1,162	6,412	4,931	2,665	5,363	2,061	1,546	4,839	3,582
New Jersey	811,663	181,751	127,888	35,201	42,809	77,712	55,469	29,419	12,649	36,134	75,365
New Mexico	179,110	61,105	4,337	8,291	5,509	37,343	13,445	3,539	4,507	8,504	11,558
New York	1,225,581	228,934	20,925	58,179	27,963	198,641	161,510	47,254	17,063	74,555	122,002
North Carolina	520,115	209,228	11,576	35,713	8,112	60,657	64,510	15,322	14,295	19,066	28,052
North Dakota	58,489	26,712	927	3,640	1,373	2,653	1,982	700	4,714	3,530	2,090
Ohio	597,896	276,966	12,092	30,596	14,734	65,512	65,782	12,696	10,848	12,175	14,191
Oklahoma	243,246	106,555	6,820	9,218	19,257	8,270	18,553	8,066	6,151	9,313	11,761
Oregon	238,803	83,360	2,901	15,773	23,282	22,648	19,106	5,460	9,925	20,096	12,250
Pennsylvania	656,086	257,034	18,813	46,139	43,918	38,688	66,677	32,607	27,043	43,325	15,749
Rhode Island	94,855	24,144	4,753	3,415	7,822	4,518	8,660	1,891	2,460	7,483	6,264
South Carolina	252,164	106,714	9,278	13,834	11,609	17,356	21,434	7,215	6,487	13,599	3,262
South Dakota	46,524	19,240	1,266	3,146	3,008	2,638	2,386	1,095	2,737	2,701	2,225
Tennessee	290,746	119,916	7,200	12,718	25,381	23,650	19,852	7,203	14,225	16,977	11,429
Texas	1,099,482	480,822	18,530	55,142	66,180	144,230	117,153	15,807	42,958	45,557	26,296
Utah	193,191	96,073	4,046	6,097	9,707	24,412	10,398	3,027	4,464	11,830	6,260
Vermont	60,864	19,678	2,525	4,678	5,226	748	4,659	3,204	2,809	4,878	2,790
Virginia	486,559	219,718	12,600	36,403	9,363	53,293	42,569	13,572	12,020	19,190	16,034
Washington	503,731	219,851	8,575	34,783	34,466	48,651	33,194	12,362	22,040	18,146	9,564
West Virginia	119,944	47,111	4,780	14,002	7,761	3,780	7,374	3,572	7,327	6,469	5,424
Wisconsin	295,616	147,431	5,015	7,096	5,442	13,612	38,987	3,914	9,384	14,844	12,383
Wyoming	45,002	12,517	940	6,257	2,503	2,161	3,138	1,318	3,305	2,991	2,262

Source: U.S. Department of Commerce, U.S. Census Bureau, March 2009. 2007 Census of Government Employment. For information on nonsampling error and definitions, see *http://www.census.gov/govs/www/apesstl07.html*. Data users who create their own estimates from these tables should cite the U.S. Census Bureau as the source of the original data only.

Key:

(a) Includes instructional and other personnel.

Demographic Trends for State Policymakers

By Ron Crouch

The U.S. is undergoing a major demographic revolution that will have major public policy implications across regions and states and within regions and states. Our population is aging, we are becoming more diverse, dramatic migration patterns are occurring and social indicators reveal major challenges ahead.

Emerging Demographic Trends and Policy Issues for States

As we approach the second decade of the 21st century, states are confronted with serious challenges as well as potential opportunities. It's not just the United States. The world is experiencing a longevity revolution and an aging population that will change all the current rules. Growing diversity in the U.S. must be viewed as an asset to be nurtured, along with investments in education, training and economic well-being. The U.S. is becoming more uneven across regions and states as well as across economic classes as the economy creates more losers and fewer winners. The role of "government as a necessary good" needs to be better understood and communicated to the citizenry.

The Aging of the World and the U.S.

The world's population is projected to grow from 6.7 billion people to 9.4 billion people in 2050, according to the International Data Base, U.S. Census Bureau. The projected 50 percent increase in the world's population will put a strain on global resources, especially if other countries approach the consumption levels of the U.S. However, the mistaken thinking is that world population growth is entirely due to fertility, when the reality is that two-thirds of world population growth is due to increased longevity of the current population. A number of demographers predict that world total fertility rates will fall below the replacement rate of 2.1 children by 2050 resulting in a declining world population of children and youth after 2050. These trends are much more dramatic in the developed countries with a number of countries already having more deaths than births and experiencing population decline.

New Age Cohort Realities for the U.S.

As a developed nation, the U.S. is experiencing these demographic trends. Census Bureau state population projections for 2000 to 2010 indicate 88.4 percent of the population growth in the U.S. will be in the mature adult population—69.3 percent in the group ages 45 to 64, and 19.1 percent for those over 65, Table A details age cohort changes by region and by state between 2000 and 2010.

Census Bureau population projections for the future from 2010 to 2020, however, indicate 63.3 percent of population growth in the U.S. will be in the mature adult population—9.8 percent in ages 45 to 64, and 53.5 percent for those over 65. Table B details age cohort changes by region and by state for 2010 to 2020.

The U.S. already has a 2005 total fertility rate of 2.05, meaning an average of 2.05 children would be born to a woman over her lifetime. But that's below replacement rate, according to the 2007 National Vital Statistics Report. In 2005, 36 of the 50 states had a fertility rate below the replacement rate including all states East of the Mississippi River except for Georgia with a total fertility rate of 2.14. Those numbers mean basically that these states would all be experiencing population decline without domestic in-migration or foreign immigration.

Additional data tables including region and state data mentioned but not included in this overview article can be found at the Kentucky State Data Center homepage, *http://ksdc.louisville.edu*, under presentations in the world and U.S. trends handout. There are additional handouts for selected states and sub-state regions.

The growth of the U.S. population from 2000 to 2010 was primarily due to the baby boomers, ages 45 to 64, with a much smaller growth in the U.S. population in the group of people over age 65. There was a baby bust between 1930 and 1945 so the younger old, between age 65 and age 80, is growing much more slowly than the mature adult baby boomers.

All that to say that the real aging of the U.S. is just beginning. From 2010 to 2020 the majority of the total population growth, 53.5 percent, in the U.S. will be people over age 65. Census population projections for the Northeast from 2010 to 2020 are that all growth will be those over age 65. This will also

Table A
PROJECTIONS: POPULATION CHANGE BY AGE: 2000–2010

State or other jurisdiction	2000–2010 Change									
	<18		18–24		25–44		45–64		65+	
	Number	Percent	Number	Percent	Number	Percent	Number	Percent	Number	Percent
United States	2,137,699	3.0%	3,337,182	12.3%	-2,272,902	-2.7%	19,059,736	30.8%	5,251,960	15.0%
Northeast	-538,186	-4.1	606,677	12.8	-1,430,075	-8.8	3,019,105	24.8	533,280	7.2
Connecticut	-27,680	-3.3	56,511	20.8	-103,297	-10.0	200,953	25.5	45,438	9.7
Maine	-32,006	-10.6	9,612	9.3	-21,861	-5.9	97,590	30.9	28,876	15.7
Massachusetts	-16,211	-1.1	90,856	15.7	-220,092	-11.1	397,388	28.0	48,403	5.6
New Hampshire	-5,398	-1.7	19,291	18.7	-9,548	-2.5	114,576	39.0	30,853	20.9
New Jersey	666	0.0	102,069	15.1	-150,867	-5.7	533,564	27.9	118,449	10.6
New York	-269,231	-5.7	209,159	11.8	-578,869	-9.9	902,853	21.3	203,303	8.3
Pennsylvania	-174,626	-6.0	96,970	8.9	-314,951	-9.0	658,970	23.2	37,070	1.9
Rhode Island	1,451	-0.6	12,834	12.0	-19,927	-6.4	69,019	29.9	4,956	3.3
Vermont	-15,151	-10.3	9,375	16.6	-10,663	-6.0	44,192	29.3	15,932	20.6
Midwest	-410,161	-2.5	271,992	4.4	-1,041,685	-5.5	3,559,812	25.0	618,699	7.5
Illinois	-48,545	-1.5	58,874	4.9	-223,190	-5.9	609,624	22.9	100,838	6.7
Indiana	21,789	1.4	5,675	0.9	-83,921	-4.7	309,652	23.0	58,459	7.8
Iowa	-22,582	-3.1	-22,458	-7.5	-34,623	-4.3	149,572	23.0	13,674	3.1
Kansas	-13,997	-2.0	215	0.1	-40,760	-5.3	152,508	26.6	19,086	5.4
Michigan	-108,709	-4.2	81,133	8.7	-151,475	-5.1	553,817	24.8	115,473	9.5
Minnesota	3,069	0.2	65,027	13.8	-5,849	-0.4	362,747	33.9	76,163	12.8
Missouri	-16,298	-1.1	37,157	6.9	-88,014	-5.4	327,756	26.2	66,266	8.8
Nebraska	-3,986	-0.9	-4,983	-2.9	-37,352	-7.7	92,937	25.3	11,118	4.8
North Dakota	-18,885	-11.7	-4,202	-5.7	-20,396	-11.7	35,276	25.4	2,630	2.8
Ohio	-143,908	-5.0	37,402	3.5	-295,811	-8.9	546,134	21.2	79,224	5.3
South Dakota	-8,497	-4.2	-5,026	-6.5	-10,462	-5.1	49,212	30.8	6,328	5.9
Wisconsin	-49,612	-3.6	23,178	4.5	-49,832	-3.2	370,577	31.1	69,440	9.9
South	2,199,349	8.6	1,244,379	12.7	-89,224	-0.3	7,582,207	34.2	2,410,083	19.4
Alabama	-31,238	-2.8	-17,278	-3.9	-106,245	-8.2	234,900	23.1	69,091	11.9
Arkansas	22,287	3.3	-1,328	-0.5	-15,815	-2.1	158,362	26.1	38,133	10.2
Delaware	7,621	3.9	5,198	6.9	-8,457	-3.6	73,134	41.7	23,246	22.9
Dist. of Columbia	-928	-0.8	-7,024	-9.7	-18,476	-9.8	-6,984	-5.6	-8,862	-12.7
Florida	439,783	12.1	348,857	26.2	66,608	1.5	1,802,965	49.7	611,100	21.8
Georgia	333,152	15.4	138,143	16.5	95,682	3.6	640,101	36.8	195,549	24.9
Kentucky	7,489	0.8	-1,350	-0.3	-71,194	-5.9	235,725	25.4	52,678	10.4
Louisiana	-48,297	-4.0	-9,965	-2.1	-92,336	-7.1	228,890	23.7	65,411	12.7
Maryland	50,122	3.7	154,169	34.2	-57,321	-3.4	342,834	28.0	118,680	19.8
Mississippi	-15,737	-2.0	-28,882	-9.3	-37,547	-4.7	173,418	28.5	35,502	10.3
North Carolina	304,791	15.5	155,504	19.3	7,864	0.3	636,235	35.2	192,116	19.8
Oklahoma	2,713	0.3	-7,718	-2.2	-60,734	-6.2	167,585	21.8	39,016	8.6
South Carolina	26,708	2.6	32,029	7.9	-47,272	-4.0	302,900	32.8	120,327	24.8
Tennessee	80,394	5.7	48,661	8.9	-66,462	-3.9	353,264	26.8	125,712	17.9
Texas	898,649	15.3	305,579	13.9	428,143	6.6	1,649,846	39.2	514,851	24.8
Virginia	141,922	8.2	155,398	22.9	-75,480	-3.4	507,864	31.1	202,026	25.5
West Virginia	-20,082	-5.0	-25,614	-14.9	-30,182	-6.0	81,168	17.8	15,507	5.6
West	886,697	5.2	1,214,134	19.2	288,082	1.5	4,898,612	36.6	1,689,898	24.4
Alaska	-6,734	-3.5	24,518	42.8	-15,673	-7.7	44,217	31.7	20,849	58.4
Arizona	321,517	23.5	142,614	27.7	180,920	12.0	607,527	56.8	254,171	38.1
California	247,149	2.7	771,813	22.9	-65,425	-0.6	2,444,899	35.2	797,050	22.2
Colorado	87,788	8.0	56,880	13.2	-25,339	-18.0	309,618	32.5	101,346	24.4
Hawaii	20,496	6.9	26,526	23.1	-26,999	-7.5	78,650	28.3	30,464	19.0
Idaho	31,207	8.5	-1,327	-1.0	54,565	15.1	103,393	37.2	35,500	24.3
Montana	-17,750	-7.7	-2,523	-2.9	-4,235	-1.7	66,899	30.4	24,012	19.9
Nevada	153,286	30.0	62,287	34.7	90,378	14.4	275,631	60.0	110,692	50.6
New Mexico	-29,169	-5.7	14,663	8.3	-38,996	-7.6	147,939	36.6	66,742	31.4
Oregon	16,640	2.0	23,445	7.2	63,260	6.3	210,101	25.9	56,151	12.8
Utah	100,287	14.0	-9,349	-2.9	86,418	13.8	139,912	36.8	44,576	23.4
Washington	-25,420	-1.7	108,995	19.5	-3,769	-0.2	434,656	32.4	133,380	20.1
Wyoming	-12,600	-9.8	-4,408	-8.8	-7,023	-5.1	35,170	29.6	14,965	25.9

Source: U.S. Census Bureau, Population Division, Interim State Population Projections, 2005.

be true for many individual Northeast region states. In the Western region, 42 percent of total population growth will be those over age 65, the smallest of the four regions, but still significant.

All regions and states are aging. The U.S. median age is projected to increase from age 35.3 in 2000 to age 38 in 2020—ranging from age 36.8 to age 39.6 in the Northeast, from age 35.6 to age 38.3 in the Midwest, from age 35.3 to age 38 in the South and from age 33.8 to age 36.5 in the West.

The good news is that people are living longer. The bad news is that people are living longer. This can be seen using the quarters of life analogy, where the first quarter is ages 0 to 24, the second quarter is ages 25 to 49, the third quarter is ages 50 to 74 and the fourth quarter is ages 75 to 100. A growing percentage of people are living into their fourth quarter and a few may even go into overtime—over age 100. What does it mean for people to start work late in their first quarter of life and retire before halftime?

As longevity becomes the driving force of demographic changes over the next few decades, states will need to reconsider the retirement age for employees. In addition, states may need to develop retirement strategies that allow phased retirement that require employees to work longer but reduce their work hours in the third quarter of life. There will also be implications for state Medicaid programs where the cost per aging recipient is much greater than young recipients. States will also need to cope with long-term care cost since Medicaid currently pays for the majority of long-term care in the U.S. Another problem for Medicaid is this: As the baby boomers start turning age 65 in 2011, those with limited or no Social Security and Medicare coverage, will automatically qualify for Medicaid and Supplemental Security Income.

The Younger Work Force

The difference between perception and reality is that reality changes. Many times our incorrect perceptions rather than reality drive public policy. Many states are concerned about their younger adult work force, ages 25 to 44, leaving. The reality is that the younger adult population in 42 states is projected to decline between 2000 and 2010; however, the major reason is not that they are leaving but that they were never there in the first place. The baby boom cohort of 1946 to 1964 is the largest population cohort in the U.S. They keep getting 10 years older every decade. It has also grown due to immigration of foreign born residents in the same age cohort.

Age cohorts are considered over time, not across time. If you want to know how many 25- to 34-year-olds you should have, you do not compare those ages 25 to 34 across time, for example, 1990 compared to 2000. You look at the 1990 population ages 15 to 24 and compare it over time with the 2000 population ages 25 to 34 when those same people are 10 years older. Several years ago, a report said Michigan had lost 212,000 younger adults, ages 25 to 34, and public policies were being developed to encourage them to return to Michigan. If you actually looked at the ages 15 to 24 cohort in 1990 compared to those ages 25 to 34 in 2000 in Michigan, you do find a loss of 40,000 but you will have a hard time bringing back the other 172,000 that were never there in the first place. The largest age cohort, those born between 1955 and 1964—the younger baby boomers—just got 10 years older and turned ages 35 to 44 in 2000.

These are questions states should consider: What does it mean for most states that their younger adult work force, ages 25 to 44, is projected to decline? Is it important to retain the mature work force for a longer period? How do states handle transfer of knowledge across work force age cohorts?

Diversity as an Opportunity for the U.S., Regions and States

The Census Bureau projects that the population in the U.S. in 2042 will have no majority population. All groups—American Indian and Alaska Native, Asian, Black, Hispanic, Native Hawaiian and Other Pacific Islander, Non-Hispanic White, and Two or More Races—will be minority populations. This will be the case in 2024 for the child and youth population as the younger the age cohort the more diverse they are. In 2000, 69.1 percent of the U.S. population was Non-Hispanic White, 12.5 percent was Hispanic, 12.3 percent was Black, and 3.6 percent was Asian. When broken down by age in 2000 for those over age 85, Non-Hispanic Whites made up 86.7 percent of the U.S. population but dropped to 58.4 percent for those under age 5. A number of states, primarily in the Southwest, already have no majority populations.

Between the 1990 and 2000 Census, the Asian and Pacific Islander population in the United Sates grew by 52.2 percent; the Black population grew by 16.2 percent; the Hispanic population grew by 57.9 percent; and the Non-Hispanic White population grew by 3.4 percent. These trends varied dramatically by state. Immigration has been a major factor for Asian and Hispanic growth. As the Hispanic population increases, however, the native born Hispanic population is becoming the major driver of Hispanic population growth. Hispanic women now account

Table B
PROJECTIONS: POPULATION CHANGE BY AGE: 2010–2020

State or other jurisdiction	2010–2020 Change									
	<18		18–24		25–44		45–64		65+	
	Number	Percent	Number	Percent	Number	Percent	Number	Percent	Number	Percent
United States	5,868,295	7.9%	-1,142,135	-3.7%	5,114,111	6.2%	2,640,516	3.3%	14,388,178	35.8%
Northeast	72,548	0.6	-623,171	-11.6	267,648	1.8	-359,512	-2.4	1,992,745	25.2
Connecticut	2,337	0.3	-29,514	-9.0	30,545	3.3	-32,128	-3.2	126,920	24.6
Maine	-797	-0.3	-23,590	-20.8	11,723	3.4	-17,517	-4.2	81,712	38.5
Massachusetts	9,314	0.6	-52,708	-7.9	6,111	0.3	-7,864	-0.4	251,252	27.7
New Hampshire	25,700	8.4	-13,685	-11.2	45,552	12.3	-1,409	-0.3	83,033	46.4
New Jersey	50,140	2.4	-45,786	-5.9	50,394	2.0	67,697	2.8	320,959	26.1
New York	-45,836	-1.0	-268,781	-13.6	13,477	0.3	-163,977	-3.2	598,365	22.6
Pennsylvania	23,485	0.9	-161,175	-13.5	75,416	2.4	-181,742	-5.2	446,883	22.8
Rhode Island	4,738	1.9	-15,466	-12.9	15,741	5.4	-8,049	-2.7	40,614	25.8
Vermont	3,467	2.6	-12,466	-18.9	18,689	11.3	-14,523	-7.4	43,007	46.0
Midwest	285,506	1.8	-481,304	-7.4	277,577	1.5	-440,111	-2.5	2,422,074	27.3
Illinois	58,864	1.8	-84,885	-6.7	-2,818	-0.1	-39,236	-1.2	387,901	24.2
Indiana	38,803	2.4	-2,682	-0.4	18,415	1.1	-28,084	-1.7	208,417	25.7
Iowa	-13,687	-1.9	-20,642	-7.5	-17,959	-2.3	-43,776	-5.5	106,653	23.7
Kansas	14,903	2.1	-17,148	-6.2	12,900	1.8	-30,163	-4.1	104,604	27.9
Michigan	-7,794	-0.3	-100,048	-9.9	46,591	1.7	-48,424	-1.7	376,985	28.2
Minnesota	126,261	9.8	-32,096	-6.0	130,039	8.7	16,408	1.1	239,521	35.7
Missouri	49,178	3.5	-35,183	-6.1	67,616	4.4	-29,233	-1.9	225,426	27.4
Nebraska	12,356	2.8	-8,739	-5.2	-9,797	-2.2	-25,820	-5.6	65,681	27.0
North Dakota	-4,335	-3.1	-11,632	-16.9	-336	-0.2	-18,123	-10.4	27,915	28.7
Ohio	-40,915	-1.5	-102,770	-9.4	-15,565	-0.5	-164,356	-5.3	391,483	24.7
South Dakota	3,060	-1.6	-7,683	-10.6	-2,412	-1.2	-11,364	-5.4	33,939	29.7
Wisconsin	48,812	3.7	-57,796	-10.6	50,903	3.3	-17,940	-1.1	253,549	32.8
South	3,292,253	11.9	224,611	2.0	2,227,891	7.4	2,244,477	7.6	5,997,973	40.4
Alabama	-5,845	-0.5	-14,566	-3.4	-34,353	-2.9	-6,369	-0.5	193,718	29.9
Arkansas	35,110	5.0	5,328	2.0	4,749	0.6	21,117	2.8	118,876	28.8
Delaware	13,115	6.5	-5,138	-6.4	2,219	1.0	17,522	7.0	51,149	40.9
Dist. of Columbia	-918	-0.8	-16,872	25.7	-13,020	-7.6	-18,934	-16.0	499	0.8
Florida	801,488	19.6	37,899	2.3	688,879	14.9	938,408	17.3	1,688,160	49.4
Georgia	334,877	13.4	74,630	7.6	141,810	5.2	274,257	11.5	429,099	43.7
Kentucky	4,969	0.5	-5,037	-1.3	-10,677	-0.9	-2,211	-0.2	172,270	30.9
Louisiana	1,274	0.1	-40,108	-8.6	13,572	1.1	-49,385	-4.1	181,128	31.1
Maryland	179,767	12.8	-41,815	-6.9	215,540	13.4	-5,009	-0.3	244,173	34.0
Mississippi	-22,396	-2.9	-14,623	-5.2	-28,823	-3.7	19,077	2.4	120,165	31.7
North Carolina	356,565	15.7	97,125	10.1	167,577	6.7	284,785	11.6	457,414	39.4
Oklahoma	38,970	4.4	-6,478	-1.9	9,064	1.0	-27,800	-3.0	130,418	26.3
South Carolina	49,035	4.7	-10,625	-2.4	27,715	2.4	49,158	4.0	260,590	43.0
Tennessee	128,297	8.7	21,162	3.5	54,018	3.3	54,301	3.2	292,040	35.2
Texas	1,182,859	17.4	153,748	6.1	819,426	11.9	661,544	11.3	1,168,431	45.2
Virginia	219,727	11.7	4,178	0.5	206,284	9.5	66,740	3.1	410,221	41.3
West Virginia	-24,641	-6.4	-14,197	-9.7	-36,089	-7.7	-32,724	-6.1	79,622	27.2
West	2,217,988	12.4	-262,271	-3.5	2,340,995	11.8	1,195,662	6.5	3,975,386	46.2
Alaska	34,643	18.8	-11,639	-14.2	38,006	20.2	-20,538	-11.2	39,840	70.5
Arizona	439,916	26.1	81,110	12.4	307,412	18.2	392,017	23.4	598,612	64.9
California	917,130	9.7	-346,025	-8.4	1,254,676	11.8	507,410	5.4	1,806,418	41.1
Colorado	138,884	11.7	7,079	1.5	66,091	4.8	1,775	0.1	233,484	45.1
Hawaii	22,874	7.2	-16,560	-11.7	19,371	5.8	-27,448	-7.7	73,462	38.4
Idaho	48,183	12.0	4,706	3.4	53,185	12.8	29,945	7.9	88,023	48.5
Montana	5,738	2.7	-13,362	-16.1	11,901	4.9	-16,962	-5.9	66,822	46.1
Nevada	191,676	28.8	43,514	18.0	109,121	15.2	215,942	29.4	201,499	61.1
New Mexico	9,310	1.9	-36,171	-18.8	4,084	0.9	-13,830	-2.5	140,723	50.4
Oregon	117,336	13.6	3,702	1.1	121,374	11.4	16,447	1.6	210,538	42.6
Utah	101,134	12.3	49,645	16.1	62,565	8.8	75,440	14.5	106,297	45.3
Washington	194,925	13.1	-20,307	-3.0	292,749	16.2	50,135	2.8	372,671	46.8
Wyoming	-3,761	-3.2	-7,963	-17.5	460	0.3	-14,671	-9.5	36,997	50.9

Source: U.S. Census Bureau, Population Division, Interim State Population Projections, 2005.

for one-fourth of all births in the U.S., and Hispanic women have the only fertility rate, 2.7, above the replacement rate in the U.S. The fertility rate for Asian women is 1.7, for Black women, 2.0, and for Non-Hispanic White women, 1.8—all below the replacement rate. Although the Asian population is growing at a rate nearly as fast as the Hispanic population, albeit from a smaller base, the fertility rate for Asian women is below replacement so all Asian growth is due to immigration.

Non-Hispanic White Population Growing

Only two developed countries in the world today are experiencing population growth: the U.S. and Canada. That's mainly because the two countries are "settler" nations that allow significant immigration. The 15 countries of the European Union are 30 percent below replacement. As mentioned earlier, world population is growing significantly because of longevity, not fertility. Most countries around the world are approaching a fertility rate of replacement level only or below the replacement level. This is certainly true of North America, Central America and South America. Mexico's population of children and youth is projected to be moving downward as the fertility rate falls below the replacement level.

Many states in the coming decade will experience significant declines in their Non-Hispanic White population and only increases in diversity and immigration will allow them to have stable population numbers. Growth in and of itself may be viewed as a problem, but an aging population will need a younger population to support it. Some states already have an inverted pyramid shaped population where older age cohorts are larger than younger population cohorts and will face a population decline over time. In Kansas, for instance, all population growth is due to Hispanic immigration or children born to Hispanic women. Most states now have inverted Non-Hispanic White populations.

Consider this: Los Angeles County with a 2007 population of 9,878,554 has a population greater than 42 states. In the 2007 American Community Survey Census, 58.4 percent of the population over age 85 in Los Angeles County is Non-Hispanic White and 19.3 percent Hispanic, but only 17.1 percent of the child population under age 5 is Non-Hispanic White while 63.2 percent is Hispanic. The 2007 per capita income for Non-Hispanic Whites in Los Angeles County is $42,332; for Hispanics, it's $13,890. In Los Angeles County, 42.5 percent of Non-Hispanic Whites over age 25 have a college degree, compared to 8.7 percent of Hispanics in that same age group. This data is evidence that all states need to ensure equal educational funding across all public school districts.

Will the U.S. have a battle between an aging Non-Hispanic White population concerned about retirement, health care, and taxes and a growing minority population interested in education, training, jobs and affordable housing? Bureau of Economic Analysis transfer payment data shows that welfare and food stamps are small state expenditures compared to the retirement and health care cost of an aging population. So how do states educate their populations about economic realities?

Beyond race and Hispanic origin, 36.9 percent of children are now born to unmarried mothers, from a high of 50.8 percent in New Mexico to a low of 17.7 percent in Utah. These percentages are up significantly and continuing to grow from the single digits of the 1970s. The major predictor of an unmarried mother is a poorly educated woman in her 20s. Only 13 percent of unmarried births are to teens under age 18, and 60 percent are to women in their 20s. New Census data indicates that one-half of all births now in the U.S. to women in their 20s are unmarried births. New 2005–2007 Census American Community Survey data indicates that the number of children in poverty is increasing, and as county population size goes down, child poverty goes up. Smaller more rural counties have higher poverty rates and greater growth in child poverty than larger more urban counties.

Regional Demographic Realities and the Issue of Migration/Immigration

Census Bureau projections indicate movement of the population from the Northeast and Midwest to the South and West. Table C shows population estimates for the regions and states, which indicate between 2000 and 2008 the Northeast had internal/domestic outmigration of 2,447,750 people and the Midwest had internal/domestic outmigration of 1,607,600 people, while the South had 89 percent of internal/domestic in-migration of 3,609,854 people with 11 percent of internal/domestic in-migration of 445,496 being in the West. The growth in the West is primarily due to international immigration of 2,685,286 people.

Without international immigration, many states, particularly in the Northeast, would have experienced declining populations between 2000 and 2008. The other factor in growth or decline is natural increase/decrease. But those shifts may require a national dialogue to determine, for instance, what has created the

Table C
CUMULATIVE ESTIMATES OF THE COMPONENTS OF POPULATION CHANGE FOR THE UNITED STATES AND STATES: APRIL 1,2000 TO JULY 1, 2008

		Natural increases			Net migration		
Geographic area	*Total population change (a)*	*Total*	*Births*	*Deaths*	*Total*	*Net international migration*	*Net internal migration*
United States	22,635,122	14,124,166	34,126,003	20,001,837	8,114,516	8,114,516	N.A.
Northeast	1,329,982	1,687,413	5,606,717	3,919,304	-687,008	1,760,742	-2,447,750
Connecticut	95,648	108,503	349,142	240,639	5,127	102,954	-97,827
Maine	41,534	12,652	115,128	102,476	34,624	5,371	29,253
Massachusetts	148,854	199,512	654,936	455,424	-84,830	212,930	-297,760
New Hampshire	80,024	39,684	121,931	82,247	46,235	14,241	31,994
New Jersey	268,301	343,965	933,185	589,220	-53,930	384,687	-438,617
New York	513,481	803,680	2,072,765	1,269,085	-698,895	876,969	-1,575,864
Pennsylvania	167,227	143,390	1,202,038	1,058,648	77,383	133,564	-56,181
Rhode Island	2,469	24,100	103,887	79,787	-16,268	24,945	-41,213
Vermont	12,444	11,927	53,705	41,778	3,546	5,081	-1,535
Midwest	2,166,241	2,677,922	7,390,395	4,712,473	-536,305	1,071,295	-1,607,600
Illinois	481,903	644,967	1,505,709	860,742	-159,182	425,893	-585,075
Indiana	296,270	264,562	721,567	457,005	53,231	70,998	-17,767
Iowa	76,174	96,250	322,292	226,042	-13,010	36,665	-49,675
Kansas	113,318	130,828	330,717	199,889	-21,213	46,742	-67,955
Michigan	64,930	366,566	1,076,193	709,627	-315,621	157,174	-472,795
Minnesota	300,901	270,607	581,309	310,702	48,311	90,111	-41,800
Missouri	314,927	199,168	647,107	447,939	90,674	52,563	38,111
Nebraska	72,166	90,323	214,642	124,319	-11,435	27,560	-38,995
North Dakota	-714	20,460	67,788	47,328	-17,787	3,323	-21,110
Ohio	132,750	353,444	1,245,352	891,908	-249,542	96,251	-345,793
South Dakota	49,357	36,903	93,397	56,494	9,694	4,592	5,102
Wisconsin	264,259	203,844	584,322	380,478	49,575	59,423	-9,848
South	11,482,701	5,148,467	12,684,109	7,535,642	6,207,047	2,597,193	3,609,854
Alabama	214,545	121,054	502,457	381,403	104,991	31,180	73,811
Arkansas	182,004	93,223	321,462	228,239	96,503	27,399	69,104
Delaware	89,497	36,658	94,756	58,098	56,652	14,270	42,382
Dist. of Columbia	19,780	19,284	65,262	45,978	-19,173	26,071	-45,244
Florida	2,345,527	405,457	1,807,546	1,402,089	1,973,423	694,850	1,278,573
Georgia	1,498,932	605,129	1,152,539	547,410	785,691	243,788	541,903
Kentucky	226,961	130,645	461,118	330,473	105,235	31,392	73,843
Louisiana	-58,172	185,540	529,099	343,559	-302,162	23,233	-325,395
Maryland	337,081	256,285	618,156	361,871	51,063	137,096	-86,033
Mississippi	93,952	126,304	359,230	232,926	-17,028	10,717	-27,745
North Carolina	1,175,914	412,906	1,015,065	602,159	783,382	192,099	591,283
Oklahoma	191,721	139,048	429,240	290,192	63,268	42,897	20,371
South Carolina	467,991	157,981	474,308	316,327	317,782	41,786	275,996
Tennessee	525,618	198,506	666,266	467,760	306,693	61,962	244,731
Texas	3,475,163	1,884,947	3,165,880	1,280,933	1,563,694	851,909	711,785
Virginia	690,064	376,015	850,119	474,104	321,605	162,200	159,405
West Virginia	6,123	-515	171,606	172,121	15,428	4,344	11,084
West	7,656,198	4,610,364	8,444,782	3,834,418	3,130,782	2,685,286	445,496
Alaska	59,362	60,994	86,062	25,068	-5,469	4,418	-9,887
Arizona	1,369,573	418,871	777,821	358,950	934,622	216,347	718,275
California	2,885,016	2,549,081	4,498,700	1,949,619	446,991	1,825,697	-1,378,706
Colorado	637,441	333,902	572,317	238,415	311,974	142,990	168,984
Hawaii	76,660	76,747	149,871	73,124	5,035	31,317	-26,282
Idaho	229,861	101,210	185,668	84,458	131,362	17,780	113,582
Montana	65,250	27,986	96,154	68,168	38,505	2,178	36,327
Nevada	601,910	145,812	291,976	146,164	463,706	85,475	378,231
New Mexico	165,315	114,583	235,551	120,968	59,499	34,375	25,124
Oregon	368,623	135,914	386,610	250,696	251,213	92,394	158,819
Utah	503,220	315,269	424,054	108,785	110,952	63,855	47,097
Washington	655,081	306,025	682,387	376,362	365,045	166,335	198,710
Wyoming	38,886	23,970	57,611	33,641	17,347	2,125	15,222

Source: Population Division, U.S. Census Bureau, (NST-EST2008-04), Table 4, Release Date: December 22, 2008.

Note: The April 1, 2000 Population Estimates base reflects changes to the Census 2000 population from the Count Question Resolution program and geographic program revisions.

Key:

N.A. — Not applicable.

(a) Total population change includes residual—see "State and County Terms & Definitions."

internal/domestic migration to the South. Air conditioning may have helped to open up the lower South by providing more livable conditions in the heat of summer, but there could be other factors at play. One may be the economics of lower wages and nonunion environments attracting companies to the region.

Inside the Numbers in the States

The U.S. and the world are going through a major transformation. Recently, the world's population became 50 percent urban/50 percent rural, and forecasts are for this trend to accelerate to 70 percent urban by 2050. The U.S. is seeing major shifts within states as well as between states. An analysis of county data in Nebraska, for example, indicated that only two of the state's counties experienced nearly all the state's growth, according to the 2007 Census population estimates. New York has 62 counties, but 47 have internal/domestic population outmigration. Kansas has 105 counties and 84 are losing population. Alabama has 67 counties and 43 have internal/domestic population outmigration. Within states, large numbers of counties have a natural decrease where the number of deaths exceeds the number of births. In this regard, states face some difficult questions with no easy answers. For instance: Do states need to stabilize rural counties? Do states need to put their resources into their growth counties and cities?

About the Author

Ron Crouch is director of the Kentucky State Data Center located at the University of Louisville. His background is in analyzing data and developing information in ways that enhance understanding and utilization. He is a graduate of the University of Louisville with a major in sociology, holds a master's degree in sociology from U of L, a master's in Social Work from U of L, and an M.B.A. from Bellarmine University in Louisville. He did doctoral work in sociology at the University of Kentucky.

Chapter Nine

SELECTED STATE POLICIES AND PROGRAMS

A New Direction in Washington and Making Smarter Investments in Tough Economic Times

By Beverly Bell

Economic uncertainty in January 2008 evolved into a full-blown recession by the year's end, impacting everything in its wake, from state budgets to mortgages and from college endowments to car loans. American consumers dealt with rising food costs, plummeting home values and jobs cuts while riding a rollercoaster of fluctuating gas prices. The downturn has meant the loss of sales, income and property taxes, which could have serious ramifications for important state government functions such as emergency management and homeland security. Complicating the fiscal challenges is the first transition of the U.S. Department of Homeland Security to a new administration. This has led to a debate over the continued placement of the Federal Emergency Management Agency within Homeland Security. Yet even as that discussion ensues, the most destructive hurricane to hit U.S. soil since 2005—Ike—and the November 2008 terrorist attacks in Mumbai, India, serve as reminders that an all-hazards approach to emergency preparedness and experienced leadership are the real answers to threats, whether they are natural or man-made.

Introduction

The United States once again learned of nature's destructive force when Texas was hit in September 2008 by Hurricane Ike, a Category 2 storm that resulted in dozens of deaths, millions of homes without power and an estimated $30 billion in damages. This was preceded by hurricanes Gustav and Dolly, which struck Louisiana and Texas, and Tropical Storm Faye, which caused extensive flooding in Florida.

There were other natural disasters, including an earthquake in Oregon, tornadoes in Virginia and Alabama, wildfires in California, relentless snowfalls in the Northeast and record-breaking flooding throughout Iowa, Missouri, Illinois and other areas of the Midwest.

A different storm hit as the Dow Jones Industrial Average lost approximately 34 percent of its value in 2008 and the country fell into a recession. It's estimated that 44 states are facing budget shortfalls in either 2009 and/or 2010.[1] The repercussions for state emergency management and homeland security are very serious for two main reasons. First, these agencies could be confronted with budget cuts. Secondly, most receive federal grants that require a state match. The Emergency Management Performance Grant program, for example, is a core state emergency management funding mechanism. As the only source of federal money directed to state and local governments for planning, training, exercises and personnel for all-hazards emergency preparedness, it requires a 50-50 match. If states aren't able to provide the match, they will lose critical dollars. Investments made thus far in terrorism-preparedness programs, response equipment, planning efforts and training could be jeopardized without adequate money to sustain them.

With a new president, questions persist as to the direction of the U.S. Department of Homeland Security and the Federal Emergency Management Agency. In the last months of the previous administration, there appeared to be a push to create and secure legacy systems within the Department of Homeland Security and FEMA. The more important issue for states is being engaged in the strategy and development of such systems from the beginning. This makes for better use and allocation of public money. It also helps ensure that new programs are practical, realistic and have state and local buy-in.

Emergency Management and Homeland Security Structures

When a disaster strikes, emergency management becomes one of the most important functions of state government. It is the central coordination point for all resources and assistance provided during disasters and emergencies, including acts of terrorism. It also has the overarching responsibility of saving lives, protecting property and helping residents recover once a disaster has occurred. Typically, emergency management comes to the forefront once an event has taken place. In reality, much of the critical work comes before—in the form of disaster drills and exercises, hazard mitigation programs, public warning tests and preparedness education.

Emergency management includes four main parts, referred to as the Four Pillars:

- Mitigation—activities that reduce or eliminate the degree of risk to human life and property
- Preparedness—pre-disaster activities to develop and maintain a capability to respond rapidly and effectively to emergencies and disasters.
- Response—activities to assess and contain the immediate effects of disasters, provide life support to victims and deliver emergency services.
- Recovery—activities to restore damaged facilities and equipment, and support the economic and social revitalization of affected areas to their pre-emergency status.

On the state level, these four elements encompass many different aspects, from planning and implementation to training and exercising. A state emergency manager will interact with all sectors of the population, including other state agencies, elected officials, local jurisdictions, all public safety personnel, the private sector and the general public.

Emergency Management Organizations/ Budgets/Staff

There is no one organizational structure for a state emergency management agency—most states design it based on their specific needs. In 13 states,[2] the emergency management agency is located within the department of public safety; in 18 states it is located within the military department under the auspices of the adjutant general; and in 12 states, it is within the governor's office. It should be noted that in seven of the 10 states with the most disaster declarations since 1953, the emergency management director reports directly to the governor.[3]

Regardless of agencies' organizational structure for daily operations, emergency management ranks high among governors' priorities. In 28 states, the emergency management director is appointed by the governor. The position is appointed by the adjutant general in 11 states and by the secretary of public safety in eight states.

The 2009 fiscal year state operating budgets for these agencies range from a low of $50,000 in Guam to a high of more than $46 million in California for a total of $294.3 million. This represents a nominal increase of less than four percent from the previous year's total budget, which was $284.3 million. In fact, only 23 responding states saw their emergency management budgets grow, while 20 states have fewer financial resources. Current budgets average $5,886,944 with a median of $3.4 million. In comparison, fiscal year 2008 operating budgets averaged $5,363,214 with a median of $3 million.

Despite state budgets inching up only slightly, total staffing increased by more than 11 percent. State emergency management full-time equivalents stand at 5,217, up from 4,688 the previous year. It should be noted that the current number represents several states that combine their emergency management/homeland security personnel.

The state emergency management agency continues to benefit from knowledgeable leadership. Thirty directors have 12 years or more experience in the field. Compared to last year when 35 directors had been in the director position specifically for three years or less, only 27 directors have that level of experience. As their tenure extends, directors face an increased likelihood of experiencing a presidential-declared disaster. Last year, 15 directors had not had such a declaration. The number has now fallen to nine.

Of course, like many state government positions, emergency management directors are politically appointed and their length of service is affected by newly elected governors or shifting political landscapes. The aging U.S. work force and retirements have also affected the field.

Homeland Security Structures and Funding

State homeland security offices continue to evolve. This is apparent from the wide range of structures and responsibilities under which state homeland security offices operate. In some cases, state homeland security directors manage grants and budgets; in other cases, they have very limited roles. The inconsistent approach is a clear indication that the relationship between homeland security and emergency management is still being defined.

All states have a designated homeland security point of contact and this position has become a critical component of a governor's staff. It has the enormous job of preparing residents, businesses and governments for the next emergency or large-scale disaster.

Who takes on this responsibility varies from state to state. Sixteen states have established a unique position of homeland security adviser. In nine states, either the emergency management director or a combined emergency management/homeland security director is the primary point of contact. Eight states

Table A: State Emergency Management: Agency Structure, Budget and Staffing

State or other jurisdiction	Position appointed	Appointed/ selected by	Organizational structure	Agency operating budget FY 2009	Full-time employee positions
Alabama	★	G	Governor's Office	$3,600,000	100
Alaska	★	G	Adjutant General/Military Affairs	3,180,300	62 (c)
Arizona	★	ADJ	Adjutant General/Military Affairs	1,433,000	62
Arkansas	★	G	Governor's Office	2,593,474	82
California	★	G	Governor's Office	46,278,000	526
Colorado	★	ED	Department of Local Affairs	600,000	25
Connecticut	. . .	HSEMC	Governor's Office	4,000,000	85 (c)
Delaware			(a)		
Florida	★	G	Governor's Office	15,382,543	138
Georgia	★	G	Governor's Office	3,213,000	97
Hawaii	★	ADJ	Adjutant General/Military Affairs	1,500,000	105
Idaho	★	ADJ	Adjutant General/Military Affairs	1,490,000	66
Illinois	★	G	Governor's Office	34,016,300	259
Indiana	★	G	Department of Homeland Security	15,000,000	275 (b)
Iowa	★	G	Adjutant General/Military Affairs	2,271,581	54
Kansas	★	G	Adjutant General/Military Affairs	1,421,712	33
Kentucky	★	ADJ	Adjutant General/Military Affairs	2,400,000	60
Louisiana	★	G	Governor's Office	12,084,833	394
Maine	★	G	Adjutant General/Military Affairs	1,232,000	24
Maryland	★	ADJ	Adjutant General/Military Affairs	2,500,000	69
Massachusetts	★	G	Public Safety	4,000,000	94
Michigan	★	G	State Police	3,155,600	85
Minnesota	★	PSS	Public Safety	5,268,620	65.25 (c)
Mississippi	★	G	Governor's Office	6,000,000	243
Missouri	★	G	Public Safety	2,700,000	73.5
Montana	. . .	ADJ	Adjutant General/Military Affairs	831,544	23
Nebraska	★	ADJ	Adjutant General/Military Affairs	1,558,020	36
Nevada	★	PSS	Public Safety	705,000	29
New Hampshire	★	G	Public Safety	4,500,000	48
New Jersey	★	G	State Police	6,000,000	359
New Mexico	★	G	Independent Cabinet Agency	3,740,000	90
New York	★	G	Governor's Office	12,500,000	119
North Carolina	★	G	Public Safety	6,992,532	178
North Dakota	★	ADJ	Adjutant General/Military Affairs	4,400,000	56
Ohio	★	PSS	Public Safety	5,591,534	91
Oklahoma	★	G	Governor's Office	1,200,000	32
Oregon	★	ADJ	Adjutant General/Military Affairs	2,721,165	44
Pennsylvania	★	G	Governor's Office	6,753,000	168
Rhode Island	★	ADJ	Adjutant General/Military Affairs	725,000	35
South Carolina	★	ADJ	Adjutant General/Military Affairs	2,200,000	73
South Dakota	★	PSS	Public Safety	653,464	19
Tennessee	★	G	Adjutant General/Military Affairs	3,600,000	102
Texas	. . .	PSS	Public Safety	18,500,000	178
Utah	★	PSS	Public Safety	1,014,300	59
Vermont	★	PSS	Public Safety	1,913,000	22
Virginia	★	G	Public Safety	9,777,688	138
Washington	★	G	Adjutant General/Military Affairs	4,300,000	98
West Virginia	★	G	Public Safety	6,200,000	54
Wisconsin	★	G	Adjutant General/Military Affairs	7,500,000	46
Wyoming			(a)		
Dist. of Columbia	★	M	Stand-Alone/Cabinet Agency	4,700,000	50
Guam	. . .	G	Department of Homeland Security	50,000	12

Source: The National Emergency Management Association, January 2009.

Key:
★ — Yes
. . . — No
G — Governor
ADJ — Adjutant General
ED — Executive Director, Dept. of Local Affairs
M — Mayor
HSEMC — Homeland Security/Emergency Management Commissioner
PSS — Public Safety Secretary/Commissioner/Director
(a) Not a member of NEMA, and therefore is not represented in the survey data.
(b) Includes homeland security, emergency management and other positions.
(c) Includes both homeland security and emergency management positions.

have the adjutant general serving in this capacity. Eight public safety secretaries/commissioners are in this role.

Many states are also modifying the structure of their homeland security office, moving the day-to-day operations from their actual homeland security department. Only four states house the daily functions in a homeland security agency or office, a drop from nine last year. The biggest shift has been toward emergency management where 12 states now oversee daily operations, up from six. Ten states run it out of the governor's office while seven have it in the adjutant general/military affairs department. Eleven states keep the homeland security function in their public safety department. Six states have other structures in place.

Funding for these state homeland security offices is changing as well. In 2008, 36 states received 60 percent or more of the homeland security funding from federal money. This compares to 39 in 2007 and 46 in 2006. Of the 36 states, 18 operate with 100 percent federal funding, which is the same as last year and down from 22 in 2006. The change reflects a steady decline in various federal homeland security grants, and the decision by state legislatures to commit to these programs by investing more state dollars. Only two states—Georgia and Maryland—rely totally on state appropriations for their homeland security funding.

This money helps support one of the most important components of homeland security—people. The number of state personnel dedicated to homeland security is 1,620, down from the previous year's total of 1,811.

Taking Advantage of Opportunities in a Recession

Despite the country's financial challenges, opportunities do exist for state emergency management and homeland security. Infrastructure investment is a priority for the new administration in Washington. Infrastructure typically includes dams and bridges. In addition to the tragic loss of life, these types of infrastructure failures can destroy housing, businesses and farming operations. They can interrupt commerce for extended periods and make transportation nearly impossible. Shoring up existing facilities—and when warranted, building new ones—can avoid these types of incidents or at least, mitigate future disasters.

Transportation is also a part of infrastructure. Road improvements can help facilitate better traffic flow during mass evacuations for disasters and emergencies. In addition, making better use of existing mass transit and augmenting it could reduce global warming, which some suggest is contributing to the ever rising number of disasters. This increase is documented by Federal Emergency Management Agency data, which shows that federal disaster declarations have been going up since 1980. In that decade, there was an average of 23.7 declarations per year. The number rose to 46 per year in the 1990s, nearly double the amount in the previous decade. From 2000 through 2008, there have been more than 55 per year.

Another opportunity lies in the stagnant new home construction. Officials can consider strengthening building code requirements and providing sufficient enforcement. The lull also allows communities to re-evaluate the wisdom of building residential housing in areas highly susceptible to repeated natural disasters such as hurricanes, wildfires and mudslides. Repetitive events that devastate these at-risk locations result in higher insurance claims, lost jobs, millions of cubic yards in debris clean-up, increased housing costs and, most importantly, fatalities. All these losses can be greatly reduced if government and business leaders can focus on the long-term good rather than short-term financial gains.

Sticking with What Works

Mitigation

Investment in mitigation—those activities that reduce or eliminate the degree of risk to human life and property—has proven time after time that it pays off. A 2005 report published by the Multihazard Mitigation Council found that every $1 of federal funds spent on mitigation grants from the Federal Emergency Management Agency leads to an average of $3.65 in avoided post-disaster relief costs and increased federal tax revenues.[4]

Despite these findings, state mitigation spending has seen a decline for a decade. The initial drop could have been attributed to a 2003 fiscal year reduction in the funding formula when Congress cut state hazard mitigation funds from 15 percent to 7.5 percent of disaster costs. Reform legislation a few years later eliminated the 7.5 percent restriction, but the cap had already done its damage. It forced states to reduce the amount they spent on critically needed mitigation programs, suspend buy-out assistance programs for flooded communities, eliminate projects altogether and redistribute money that previously had been targeted to mitigation.

Beyond the savings of nearly $4 in post-disaster spending for every $1 in mitigation, this money

Table B: Homeland Security Structures

State or other jurisdiction	State homeland security advisor: Designated homeland security advisor	State homeland security advisor: Operates under authority of	Homeland security organizations: Day-to-day operations under	Homeland security organizations: Full-time employee positions
Alabama	Homeland Security Advisor/Director	SS	Homeland Security Department	14
Alaska	Homeland Security Advisor/Director	SS	Adjutant General/Military Affairs	62 (c)
Arizona	Homeland Security Advisor/Director	SS	Homeland Security Department	15
Arkansas	Emergency Management Director	GA	Emergency Management	6
California	Homeland Security Advisor/Director	EAO	Governor's Office	82
Colorado	Homeland Security Advisor/Director	EAO	Governor's Office	12
Connecticut	Commissioner of HS/EM	SS	Governor's Office	85 (c)
Delaware	(a)			
Florida	Florida Dept. of Law Enforcement	SS	Florida Dept. of Law Enforcement	73
Georgia	Emergency Management Director	EAO	Emergency Management	13
Hawaii	Adj. General/Director of Civil Defense	GA	Emergency Management	8
Idaho	Adjutant General	EAO	Adjutant General/Military Affairs	10
Illinois	Emergency Management Director	GA	Emergency Management	4.5
Indiana	Homeland Security Advisor/Director	SS	Homeland Security Department	275 (b)
Iowa	Lieutenant Governor	GA	Adjutant General/Military Affairs	13
Kansas	Adjutant General	SS	Adjutant General/Military Affairs	2
Kentucky	Homeland Security Advisor/Director	GA	Governor's Office	22
Louisiana	Homeland Security/ Emergency Management Director	SS	Governor's Office	10
Maine	Adjutant General	GA	Emergency Management	4
Maryland	Special Assistant to Governor	EAO	Governor's Office	2
Massachusetts	Public Safety Secretary/Commissioner	EAO	Public Safety	12
Michigan	Special Assistant to Governor	EAO	State Police	15
Minnesota	Public Safety Secretary/Commissioner	EAO	Emergency Management/Homeland Security	62.25 (c)
Mississippi	Homeland Security Advisor/Director	EAO	Public Safety	18
Missouri	Public Safety Secretary/Commissioner	EAO	Public Safety	25
Montana	Adjutant General	GA	Emergency Management	3
Nebraska	Lieutenant Governor	SS	Emergency Management	8
Nevada	Homeland Security Advisor/Director	GA	Governor's Office	3
New Hampshire	Homeland Security/ Emergency Management Director	SS	Public Safety	1
New Jersey	Special Assistant to Governor	EAO	Attorney General	135
New Mexico	Homeland Security/ Emergency Management Director	SS	Emergency Management/Homeland Security	90
New York	Public Safety Secretary/Commissioner	GA	Homeland Security Department	184
North Carolina	Public Safety Secretary/Commissioner	GA	Emergency Management	11
North Dakota	Homeland Security Advisor/Director	EAO	Adjutant General/Military Affairs	6
Ohio	Public Safety Secretary/Commissioner	GA	Public Safety	23
Oklahoma	Homeland Security Advisor/Director	SS	Public Safety	19
Oregon	Adjutant General	GA	Emergency Management	n/a
Pennsylvania	Emergency Management Director	EAO	Emergency Management	6
Rhode Island	Adjutant General	GA	Emergency Management	3
South Carolina	State Police Superintendent/Director/ Commander	SS	State Police	10
South Dakota	Homeland Security Advisor/Director	GA	Public Safety	3
Tennessee	Homeland Security Advisor/Director	EAO	Public Safety	28
Texas	Homeland Security Advisor/Director	EAO	Governor's Office	6
Utah	Homeland Security Advisor/Director	SS	Public Safety	110
Vermont	Public Safety Secretary/Commissioner	EAO	Public Safety	8
Virginia	Special Assistant to Governor	SS	Governor's Office	8
Washington	Adjutant General	EAO	Adjutant General/Military Affairs	26
West Virginia	Public Safety Secretary/Commissioner	GA	Public Safety	11
Wisconsin	Adjutant General	EAO	Adjutant General/Military Affairs	0
Wyoming	(a)			
Dist. of Columbia	Homeland Security/ Emergency Management Director	SS	Emergency Management	47
Guam	Homeland Security Advisor/Director	EAO	Governor's Office	23

Source: The National Emergency Management Association, January 2009.

Key:

GA — Governor's Verbal Authority

EAO — Executive/Administrative Order

SS — State Statute

(a) Not a member of NEMA, and therefore is not represented in the survey data.

(b) Includes homeland security, emergency management and other positions.

(c) Includes homeland security and emergency management positions.

could be redirected to other projects. At a time when financial resources are being stretched to their limits, mitigation investment is a proven approach in making dollars work harder and smarter.

Mutual Aid

Mutual aid agreements, which allow support across lines of jurisdictions when a disaster occurs, continue to show why they're so important. The Emergency Management Assistance Compact played a crucial role in the aftermath of hurricanes Katrina and Rita. The state-to-state agreement deployed nearly 66,000 people from 48 states, at a cost of more than $830 million. This represented the largest deployment of mutual aid assistance in United States History.

Now, states are moving to the next level of mutual aid, developing intrastate agreements, which are geared toward a local jurisdiction, such as a city or county, rather than a state. Forty-five states now either have intrastate agreements in place or have proposed compacts. This is a 67 percent increase from 2003 when there were only 27 such states. In tough economic times and diminishing budgets, it's impossible for a city to purchase everything that might be required for a disaster or emergency. Shared equipment and personnel available through mutual aid can bridge the gap between demand and supply.

In addition, there is growing interest in international mutual aid. Twelve states have agreements with bordering countries. Since disasters don't respect political boundaries, these agreements are essential for prompt response and recovery efforts.

Persistent Worries

In a recent survey[5] of states on natural and human-related emergencies, several common concerns were cited. These included interoperability, effective large-scale evacuations, mass sheltering in the event of a major disaster, the public's responsibility for preparedness and sustaining current programs and personnel.

Achieving interoperability—the ability of various emergency responders to talk to each other through both voice and data systems—is not easily solved. The proliferation of systems, the cost, the difficulty in defining common communication standards—all these factors contribute to the slow progress toward true interoperability.

Personal preparedness responsibility lags as citizens rely too heavily on government to rescue them when a disaster strikes. States believe that adequate public resources must be in place to manage a disaster, but individuals have to take a larger, more proactive role in protecting themselves, their families and their property. The challenges of evacuations, sheltering and adequate, sustained funding continue to confront all states. The financial burden takes the shape of not only greater restrictions on federal grants, but also shifting more of the grant management and administration costs back to the states.

Beyond these problems are other related issues, such as the proper role of the military in disaster response. States are adamant about governors retaining control of their National Guard troops, yet there are increasing discussions about armed forces assuming more authority in a disaster. Another question involves the next generation of qualified emergency managers and the loss of institutional knowledge as current state directors retire or move into the private sector.

Notes

[1] Center on Budget and Policy Priorities, December 2008.

[2] This data is based on an annual NEMA survey of state emergency management directors. There were a total of 50 responses which included 48 states, the District of Columbia and Guam. The term "state" throughout the text refers to all respondents.

[3] *Declared Disasters by Year or State*; Federal Emergency Management Agency.

[4] *Natural Hazard Mitigation Saves: An Independent Study to Assess the Future Savings from Mitigation Activities*, Multihazard Mitigation Council, 2005.

[5] *Innovative Programs in Funding State Homeland Security Needs*, Southern Legislative Conference, November 2008.

About the Author

Beverly Bell is the senior policy analyst for the National Emergency Management Association, an affiliate of The Council of State Governments. In her position, she coordinates and conducts research, interacts with the states on changing federal policy, and acts as an information clearinghouse for emergency management and homeland security issues.

Early College High Schools: A Promising Approach for Underserved Youth

By Jennifer Dounay Zinth

Early college high schools provide low-income, minority and other at-risk youth the opportunity to earn a high school diploma and as much as two years' postsecondary credit within five years of high school entry. While many programs are still relatively new, emerging research suggests that students in early college programs perform better than their peers, as measured by attendance rates, enrollment in college-track mathematics courses, state assessment scores and other indicators. A small but growing number of states have enacted state-level policies to provide the unique funding mechanisms and supports that maximize student success in early college high schools.

For numerous reasons, the role of high schools—and, by extension, transitions to postsecondary—has proved to be one of the key education policy issues of this decade. Emerging from this focus on improving high school graduation and college entry rates is the concept of early college high schools, a relatively new but promising policy approach to integrating high school and the first years of postsecondary education to improve student outcomes, particularly among traditionally underserved students.

Early college high schools are not to be confused with similar longstanding efforts, such as dual/concurrent programs and middle college high schools. Dual/concurrent enrollment programs were first adopted by states in the 1980s and 1990s to expand access to and set state policy parameters for what the most gifted high school students had already been doing for decades—taking college-level courses before high school graduation. Dual/concurrent programs are typically geared toward middle- to high-achieving students, and allow students to pick and choose college courses that are taken either at the college campus, at the high school, or, more recently, online.

State policies typically reflect that dual/concurrent enrollment programs are designed to serve a somewhat select student population. In 20 states, students must be high school juniors or seniors; in 25 states, dual/concurrent enrollment students must meet eligibility criteria set by the postsecondary institution—for example, scores on placement exams. In many states, students must demonstrate academic aptitude with a minimum grade point average, completion of certain high school courses, scores on high school assessments, a written recommendation from a high school staff member, or a combination thereof before entering the program. But those criteria often blocked participation in dual/concurrent enrollment programs by students with college potential who were not well-served by their local schools or whose academic achievement reflects their disengagement from the traditional high school structure.[1]

By contrast, middle college high schools, or middle colleges, were first created in the 1970s as programs to serve students with academic and social challenges. As Janet Lieberman, the creator of the middle college concept, describes in a 2004 publication, a middle college is a small high school with a maximum enrollment of 450 students located on a college campus, with strong student support programs offering peer and group counseling on a daily basis. Absent are the 50-minute class period, the class bell and other traditional hallmarks of the high school experience; students are treated as college students and interact with both high school and postsecondary faculty.[2]

The strong high school completion and postsecondary continuation rates of middle college students—and the fact that some 11th and 12th grade middle college students had already completed high school graduation requirements and were academically and emotionally prepared to enroll in postsecondary courses—encouraged program leaders to seek and obtain a grant to develop a new "early college" concept. Lieberman notes that, unlike the middle college model, the early college approach stresses the importance of deeper collaboration between high school and postsecondary partners, and offers an articulated high school/college curriculum such that, five years after entering a program in ninth grade, students may earn a high school diploma along with technical certification, an associate's degree or enough credits to enter a four-year postsecondary institution as a junior. But similar to middle colleges, the target student population is traditionally underserved youth, schools are small and programs offer strong academic and other supports to help prepare students for college-level academic and social expectations.[3]

More than 160 early college high schools have opened since the beginning of this decade, largely through partnerships between individual high schools or districts and community colleges or four-year institutions. These programs have seen impressive results to date, documented by the American Institutes for Research and SRI International. True to the aim of early college high schools, students in early colleges were more likely than their peers in the local school district to be at-risk, either minority (67 percent vs. 61 percent, on average) or low-income (60 percent vs. 58 percent, on average), according to recent research from the two organizations.[4] Forty-four percent of the students in a spring 2007 survey were the first generation in their family to attend college.[5] Yet the average daily attendance rate at early colleges in the 2005–2006 school year was 94 percent, one percentile higher than the national average for elementary and secondary education. The AIR/SRI data on early colleges also backs up earlier research that taking mathematics courses correlates with higher high school graduation rates, college entry and completion. From the 2003–2004 school year to the 2006–2007 school year, 96 percent of ninth grade early college students in the nine schools with ninth grade transcript data were enrolled in Algebra I or higher, as opposed to 84 percent in the national sample. Thirty-eight percent of early college ninth graders were enrolled in geometry, while just 20 percent of the national sample was enrolled in the course.[6]

The AIR/SRI findings also indicate students in early college high schools are outperforming their peers in local school districts on state proficiency assessments. In the 2006–2007 school year, an average 82 percent of early college students scored proficient or above on their state's English language arts/reading assessment, as opposed to 72 percent of students in the local school district; for mathematics, an average 68 percent of students in early colleges scored proficient or above, compared to 59 percent in the local school district. And while few early college high schools have been in operation long enough to produce a cohort of high school graduates, the average estimated on-time graduation rate during the 2006–2007 school year for these longer established schools in the AIR/SRI study was 70 percent, exceeding the estimated on-time graduation rates for the states and districts in which these schools were located, as well as national on-time graduation rate estimates.[7]

Many early college high schools are established through local partnerships between a high school or district and a two- or four-year postsecondary partner, and are governed by dual/concurrent enrollment, charter school or other types of state-level policies. But these policies may not meet the needs of early college programs. Early college staff in select states told AIR/SRI researchers in interviews that state policies, in addition to local district/institution agreements, can contribute to the success of early college programs in providing the right supports (financial and otherwise) for early colleges.

In recent years, a small but growing number of states have enacted legislation and state board rules to address the unique structure and needs of early college high schools. These state programs go by various names—"Fast College Fast Jobs" in Colorado, "Cooperative Innovative High Schools" in North Carolina and Tennessee, although the program is commonly known as "Learn and Earn" in North Carolina, while Michigan uses early college and middle college interchangeably. All make clear that these are five-year high school programs geared toward traditionally underserved students, allowing youth to concurrently earn a high school diploma and up to two years of postsecondary credit.

In 2008, the Education Commission of the States completed a 50-state evaluation of legislation and state board rules to identify policies specific to these five-year high school programs. Six states—Colorado, Michigan, North Carolina, Pennsylvania, Tennessee and Texas—all have policies distinct from dual/concurrent, charter school or other types of policies designed to govern early college high schools. Some states, like Indiana, have policies that reference early college high schools but set limited policies to govern such programs. Other states, such as Ohio, have established a network of early college high schools but do not appear to have legislation or rules specifically designed to govern these programs.

An Education Commission of the States analysis of these policies revealed a potential set of model state policies to support early college high schools. These policies tend to fall into six general categories:

- Access and support for students and families;
- Program quality;
- Finance and facilities;
- Alignment of high school/postsecondary for optimal success;
- Program accountability and evaluation; and
- A catch-all "Other" category. A description of policies grouped into these categories and sample state legislation and rules follows.

Access and Support

Various state policy components ensure early college programs cast a broad net for potential students and provide students and families the supports they may need to maximize student success. Because students may enroll in early college programs in ninth grade, getting the word out to parents and students in the middle grades is essential. Legislation in North Carolina and Tennessee requires early colleges to develop methods to identify potential students in the middle grades. Colorado and Texas address underserved families' potential lack-of-connectedness in the school community by requiring school districts to notify *all* students and parents—those in target high schools in Colorado—of the availability of early college programs.

Parents who did not attend college are typically less equipped to support their child through the college entry experience. States have taken different approaches to confront this reality. Michigan requires an individualized education plan for every student in a state grant-supported health sciences early college. Texas requires early colleges to provide academic mentoring. North Carolina and Tennessee specify that "consistent counseling, advising and parent conferencing" must be provided, while Colorado directs early college offerings to include regularly scheduled counseling and other appropriate support services throughout the five years of the program.

State policies also stress the importance of parental involvement in general. Tennessee and North Carolina programs must emphasize parental involvement; in these two states, applications for K–12 and postsecondary partners to develop early colleges must indicate the process the program will use to ensure parental involvement.

Instructional and Curricula Quality with Strategic Vision

A model state policy recognizes preparing underserved youth for postsecondary instruction—and providing postsecondary content to this unique student population—requires special pedagogical approaches. Again, state policies target this issue in different ways. Early college programs in North Carolina and Tennessee must "encourage the use of different and innovative teaching methods" and offer "flexible, customized" instruction. Program applications must indicate the qualifications instructors must meet. Postsecondary partners in Texas early colleges must select staff who either are faculty members or meet equivalent expectations. Those teaching postsecondary-level courses in early colleges must be supervised and evaluated in the same manner as regular postsecondary faculty.

Model state early college policies also ensure quality of curricula. North Carolina and Tennessee pre-collegiate course offerings must be aligned to state academic standards. Texas and Pennsylvania note that postsecondary-level courses offered by early colleges must be the same as those provided to traditional postsecondary students. Michigan programs receiving state health sciences grants must incorporate language arts, math and science instruction into health sciences courses.

States should also seek to ensure that postsecondary-level coursework prepares students for jobs in high-demand, high-wage positions. Michigan programs emphasize health sciences and must provide students the opportunity to participate in clinical rotations. North Carolina and Tennessee early colleges may be co-sponsored by a private business or organization or the county board of commissioners, and must lead to advanced learning or careers in teaching, engineering or health sciences. Where applicable, programs must prepare students to pass employer tests.

Finance and Facilities

State policies should recognize that fully funding K–12 and postsecondary institutions in early college partnerships is not double-dipping. Rather, early colleges should be seen as a smart investment: They (ideally) reduce or eliminate the need for remediation when graduates enter postsecondary education; they reduce K–12 and postsecondary staff salary demands and maximize facility use, because most students have simultaneously earned high school and college credit; and they increase state coffers when early college and college graduates pay more taxes and are not dependent upon public aid. Alternatively, state policies that do not grant districts and postsecondary institutions the same levels of funding for early college students and traditional high school or postsecondary students may disincentivize districts and institutions from entering into early college partnerships. Education Commission of the States analysis found four states—Colorado, Michigan, Tennessee and Texas—fund traditional high school/postsecondary students and early college students equally. Likewise, given that low-income students, a target population of early colleges, will be less able to pay tuition costs, state policy should provide that early college students do not pay tuition or fees.

Nontraditional funding streams may defray early college program expenses. North Carolina and Tennessee, for example, allow programs that partner with a private business/organization or the county board of commissioners to accept funds from a county board of commissioners that is not a founding program partner, and are in fact encouraged to seek funding from sources beyond local, state and federal appropriations.

Alignment of High School/Postsecondary for Optimal Success

Early colleges do not achieve their potential when postsecondary credit awarded by the postsecondary partner is not recognized by an institution to which the student transfers after completing the early college program. Two states—Colorado and North Carolina—have developed articulation agreements to ensure all public two- and four-year postsecondary institutions in the state grant credit for students who have achieved a "C" or higher in early college courses.

Some state policies also provide financial supports to minimize the college debt early college graduates incur when transferring into a postsecondary institution as a junior. North Carolina's EARN grant program provides awards up to $4,000 a year for two years to North Carolina residents who are U.S. citizens and who meet family income and other qualifications. Students don't have to participate in a Learn and Earn early college program to qualify, but Learn and Earn graduates who have earned two years of college through an early college program may graduate from a four-year institution in the state with little or no debt.

Program Accountability and Evaluation

Most states with early college policies require programs to meet accountability criteria and/or undergo program evaluation. Accountability approaches include requiring programs to meet accountability criteria jointly established by state-level K–12 and postsecondary administering agencies (North Carolina and Tennessee); requiring programs to apply for re-approval on an annual basis (Texas); and requiring programs to submit to an explicit evaluation process (North Carolina, Pennsylvania, Tennessee and Texas). Legislation in North Carolina and Tennessee sets forth the indicators to measure early college programs' success, including high school completion rates, certification/two-year degree completion rates, admission to four-year institutions, postgraduation employment in study-related fields, and employer satisfaction with program graduates. Tennessee legislation also directs the state-level consortium overseeing early college programs to establish best practices and lessons learned from successful programs.

"Other" State Policy Components

Policymakers seeking to develop effective state policies to support early college high school offerings may also wish to consider developing online early college curricula. Through a 2007 legislative appropriation, North Carolina has developed "Learn and Earn Online," which provides participating high schools across the state access to early college courses in a variety of subjects. As of fall 2008, 325 North Carolina high schools offered access to Learn and Earn Online, with more high schools expected to join in spring 2009.

Early colleges can also benefit when state policy identifies a state-level entity responsible for providing technical assistance to district and postsecondary partners as they develop and implement early college programs. Tennessee legislation, for example, identifies the consortium overseeing early college programs—in practice, the Tennessee P-16 Council—as the entity to provide technical assistance to districts and postsecondary institutions, and specifies that one avenue for assistance must be replicating or adapting a successful program designed elsewhere.

Admittedly, research makes clear that not every early college program attains the same high rates of student success. Yet early colleges do appear to be a promising approach to increasing achievement, graduation rates and college coursetaking among low-income, minority and first-generation college students. As the Education Commission of the States analysis makes clear, state policy can play a crucial role in ensuring access, setting rigorous expectations for curriculum and instruction, providing incentive funding to K–12 and postsecondary partners, and establishing accountability and evaluation systems to maximize the success of students in early college high school programs.

Notes

[1] Jennifer Dounay, Education Commission of the States, Dual Enrollment database, last updated December 4, 2008, *http://www.ecs.org/html/educationissues/HighSchool/highschooldb1_intro.asp?topic=de*.

[2] Janet E. Lieberman, *The Early College High School Concept: Requisites for Success, Prepared for Jobs for the Future*, (June 2004), *http://www.earlycolleges.org/Downloads/ECHSConcept.pdf*.

[3] Ibid.

[4] *2003–2007 Early College High School Initiative Evaluation: Emerging Patterns and Relationships*, American Institutes for Research and SRI International for the Bill

and Melinda Gates Foundation, May 2008, *http://www.gatesfoundation.org/learning/Documents/ECHSI_Evaluation_2003-07.pdf.*

[5] Jamie Shkolnik and Joel Knudson, PowerPoint presentation, *Credit Where Credit Is Due: An Examination of College Course-Taking at Early College High Schools*, paper presented at AERA New York City, March 24, 2008.

[6] *2003–2007 Early College High School Initiative Evaluation: Emerging Patterns and Relationships.*

[7] Ibid.

About the Author

Jennifer Dounay Zinth is a senior policy analyst with the Education Commission of the States (ECS). Since 2005, she has led the ECS High School Policy Center, which provides state policy information, analysis and research findings on a number of issues related to high schools, transitions to postsecondary, and P-16/P-20 alignment.

Table 9.1
NUMBER AND TYPES OF PUBLIC ELEMENTARY AND SECONDARY SCHOOLS, BY STATE OR JURISDICTION: SCHOOL YEAR 2006–07

State or other jurisdiction	Total number of schools	Type of school: Regular	Special education	Vocational education	Alternative education	Charter	Magnet	Title I (a)	Title I schoolwide
Reporting states (b)	97,793	88,589	1,956	1,240	6,638	4,132	N.R.	58,021	37,269
Alabama	1,583	1,395	31	69	88	n/a	34	869	778
Alaska	503	452	1	1	49	23	13	279	121
Arizona	2,061	1,857	9	118	77	468	n/a	1,168	700
Arkansas	1,114	1,080	0	24	10	19	38	830	664
California	10,038	8,741	127	0	1,170	693	n/a	7,357	6,082
Colorado	1,736	1,639	8	5	84	135	21	607	367
Connecticut	1,114	1,022	37	17	38	16	40	462	134
Delaware	234	178	18	6	32	17	17	204	119
Florida	3,952	3,281	130	46	495	366	296	2,398	2,155
Georgia	2,463	2,163	90	0	210	55	61	1,191	985
Hawaii	286	282	3	0	1	28	n/a	193	170
Idaho	726	614	10	11	91	30	n/a	495	198
Illinois	4,392	4,063	116	50	163	34	343	3,017	1,260
Indiana	1,969	1,878	41	28	22	37	25	797	200
Iowa	1,509	1,427	10	0	72	8	n/a	943	199
Kansas	1,423	1,415	8	0	0	27	30	1,009	684
Kentucky	1,534	1,241	10	126	157	n/a	43	1,075	966
Louisiana	1,447	1,259	43	7	138	42	77	1,229	1,184
Maine	671	642	2	27	0	n/a	1	548	311
Maryland	1,445	1,312	45	24	64	23	79	370	317
Massachusetts	1,879	1,845	4	30	0	59	n/a	1,043	472
Michigan	4,133	3,536	238	56	303	279	420	2,250	1,043
Minnesota	2,655	1,641	300	12	712	155	63	921	264
Mississippi	1,062	909	0	89	64	1	17	689	689
Missouri	2,384	2,259	14	61	50	18	11	1,132	381
Montana	831	825	2	0	4	n/a	n/a	673	356
Nebraska	1,166	1,135	31	0	0	n/a	N.A.	495	210
Nevada	590	548	0	1	41	22	18	n/a	n/a
New Hampshire	482	482	0	0	0	9	n/a	233	35
New Jersey	2,470	2,339	77	54	0	53	N.A.	1,328	346
New Mexico	838	808	4	0	26	60	3	846	434
New York	4,708	4,412	153	30	113	93	196	3,224	1,517
North Carolina	2,470	2,344	30	9	87	93	121	1,127	939
North Dakota	534	497	31	6	0	n/a	n/a	388	74
Ohio	3,972	3,849	40	75	8	305	n/a	2,769	1,695
Oklahoma	1,794	1,785	4	0	5	16	n/a	1,189	953
Oregon	1,284	1,242	2	0	40	70	6	600	350
Pennsylvania	3,286	3,199	2	85	0	119	53	2,303	611
Rhode Island	336	304	3	12	17	11	N.A.	236	114
South Carolina	1,175	1,153	0	13	9	29	34	498	498
South Dakota	736	720	3	0	13	n/a	n/a	343	157
Tennessee	1,709	1,645	14	22	28	12	31	1,258	1,183
Texas	8,630	7,234	0	0	1,396	400	n/a	5,451	5,127
Utah	1,001	817	58	8	118	54	18	243	219
Vermont	330	314	0	15	1	n/a	n/a	215	130
Virginia	2,202	1,867	58	51	226	3	148	739	341
Washington	2,305	1,898	115	13	279	n/a	N.A.	1,251	557
West Virginia	766	701	7	31	27	n/a	n/a	379	357
Wisconsin	2,237	2,150	8	3	76	188	5	1,100	377
Wyoming	383	355	5	0	23	3	n/a	188	74
Dist. of Columbia	235	205	14	1	11	59	4	181	172
DoDDS:									
DoDs Overseas (c)	140	140	0	0	0	n/a	n/a	n/a	n/a
DDESS:									
DoDs Domestic (c)	68	68	0	0	0	n/a	n/a	n/a	n/a
Bureau of Indian Ed.	186	186	0	0	0	n/a	n/a	179	179
American Samoa	31	29	1	1	0	n/a	n/a	n/a	n/a
Guam	36	36	0	0	0	n/a	n/a	n/a	n/a
No. Mariana Islands	30	29	0	0	1	n/a	n/a	n/a	n/a
Puerto Rico	1,515	1,456	25	26	8	n/a	N.A.	1,496	1,389
U.S. Virgin Islands	34	32	0	1	1	n/a	n/a	34	0

See footnotes at end of table.

NUMBER AND TYPES OF PUBLIC ELEMENTARY AND SECONDARY SCHOOLS, BY STATE OR JURISDICTION: SCHOOL YEAR 2006–07—Continued

Source: U.S. Department of Education, National Center for Education Statistics, Common Core of Data (CCD), "Public Elementary/Secondary School Universe Survey," 2006–07, Version 1a.

Note: Every school is assigned a school type. A school may also be included under the Charter, Magnet, and/or Title I statuses, which are independent of one another and of school type.

Key:

N.A. — Not available.

n/a — Not applicable. Some states do not have charter school authorization and some states do not designate magnet schools.

N.R. — Reporting standards not met. Information about whether or not a school was a magnet school was missing for 18.2 percent of schools in the 50 states and District of Columbia.

(a) Number of Title I eligible schools includes those with and without schoolwide Title I programs.

(b) Data were missing in one or more states for the number of students and the number of students enrolled in vocational education, magnet, Title I, or Title I schoolwide program schools. A reporting states total is shown if data for any item in the table were missing for some, but not more than 15 percent, of all schools in the Untied States. If data for an item were unavailable for more than 15 percent of schools in the Untied States, the total for that item is shown as "reporting standards not met."

(c) DoDDS and DDESS are the Department of Defense dependents schools (overseas) and the Department of Defense dependents schools (domestic), respectively.

Table 9.2
TOTAL STUDENT MEMBERSHIP, STUDENT/TEACHER RATIO, AND NUMBER OF STAFF FOR PUBLIC SCHOOLS: SCHOOL YEAR 2006–07

State or other jurisdiction	Total number of students (a)	Type of school: Regular	Type of school: Special education	Type of school: Vocational education	Type of school: Alernative education	Charter	Magnet	Title I (b)	Title I schoolwide
Reporting states (c)	49,065,594	48,175,384	177,872	196,127	516,211	1,157,359	N.R.	27,927,097	18,715,682
Alabama	743,469	740,076	1,636	64	1,693	n/a	18,256	410,484	358,613
Alaska	132,608	119,975	55	n/a	12,578	4,643	4,162	43,523	24,842
Arizona	476,132	1,046,200	644	5,374	12,864	93,881	n/a	627,190	416,079
Arkansas	476,132	474,469	n/a	320	1,343	4,300	23,030	325,539	250,342
California	6,274,813	6,096,664	27,381	n/a	150,768	231,004	n/a	4,689,896	3,860,856
Colorado	793,269	778,639	611	765	13,254	52,332	7,601	208,140	138,075
Connecticut	574,516	557,702	3,714	10,012	3,088	3,577	16,225	214,765	65,880
Delaware	122,254	113,270	1,608	6,183	1,193	7,576	12,306	122,254	58,156
Florida	2,671,513	2,613,679	11,430	2,580	40,851	99,474	345,169	1,711,343	1,418,890
Georgia	1,629,157	1,622,293	1,274	n/a	5,590	23,612	57,169	751,855	607,361
Hawaii	180,720	18,450	99	n/a	171	6,350	n/a	111,505	92,734
Idaho	267,447	262,440	105	0	4,902	9,543	n/a	179,857	76,751
Illinois	2,118,276	2,101,340	5,670	0	11,266	20,948	235,462	1,472,981	689,496
Indiana	1,044,486	1,041,579	476	n/a	2,431	9,028	12,389	335,376	82,107
Iowa	481,688	476,271	1,018	n/a	4,399	699	n/a	274,069	68,669
Kansas	459,879	459,702	177	n/a	n/a	2,287	12,721	313,413	68,669
Kentucky	n/a	638,623	656	n/a	7,355	n/a	39,179	525,321	457,874
Louisiana	675,716	653,678	1,416	n/a	20,622	17,532	45,955	590,661	556,838
Maine	n/a	193,950	36	n/a	n/a	n/a	125	151,497	73,261
Maryland	851,640	833,077	5,354	8,318	4,891	5,071	71,390	159,386	134,946
Massachusetts	968,661	941,469	0	27,192	n/a	23,500	n/a	487,277	209,611
Michigan	1,713,777	1,655,548	22,324	2,416	33,489	98,462	192,801	934,872	426,713
Minnesota	840,565	808,665	13,179	1	18,720	23,701	29,276	322,513	82,547
Mississippi	495,026	495,026	n/a	0	0	363	4,313	338,379	338,379
Missouri	920,353	916,646	440	1,894	1,373	6,116	7,146	378,966	125,640
Montana	144,418	144,258	62	n/a	98	n/a	n/a	114,895	51,563
Nebraska	287,580	286,748	832	n/a	n/a	n/a	N.A.	102,305	50,168
Nevada	423,184	417,771	n/a	1,795	3,618	5,879	24,462	n/a	n/a
New Hampshire	203,551	203,551	n/a	n/a	n/a	324	n/a	78,300	10,308
New Jersey	1,387,123	1,354,386	9,286	23,451	n/a	15,800	N.A.	700,054	192,222
New Mexico	326,676	322,315	804	n/a	3,557	9,744	171	199,478	151,858
New York	2,808,117	2,711,921	45,822	39,171	11,203	26,273	121,007	1,783,397	924,874
North Carolina	1,444,215	1,433,856	2,360	141	7,858	28,453	87,690	546,717	440,125
North Dakota	96,670	96,670	n/a	n/a	n/a	n/a	n/a	52,062	11,730
Ohio	1,832,100	1,827,278	3,717	1,039	66	75,692	n/a	1,184,670	679,216
Oklahoma	639,009	637,643	241	n/a	1,125	4,649	n/a	392,013	300,738
Oregon	555,013	549,726	129	n/a	5,158	9,390	1,401	217,807	132,851
Pennsylvania	1,846,420	1,788,859	n/a	57,561	n/a	57,976	27,843	1,208,569	349,441
Rhode Island	149,925	145,494	180	1,783	2,468	2,812	N.A.	122,374	52,249
South Carolina	703,119	703,119	n/a	n/a	n/a	5,112	26,804	242,418	242,418
South Dakota	121,158	121,158	n/a	n/a	n/a	n/a	n/a	54,912	22,770
Tennessee	978,368	971,988	1,455	3,352	1,573	2,262	16,857	66,830	616,429
Texas	4,597,733	4,521,527	n/a	n/a	76,206	102,585	n/a	2,969,493	2,792,184
Utah	523,594	513,283	4,421	185	5,705	19,098	5,403	102,349	92,802
Vermont	93,217	93,198	n/a	n/a	19	n/a	n/a	51,966	30,952
Virginia	1,220,365	1,217,947	273	0	2,145	236	142,406	322,313	146,771
Washington	1,026,774	988,598	4,086	298	33,792	n/a	N.A.	531,775	227,234
West Virginia	281,074	280,080	248	14	732	n/a	n/a	104,736	97,941
Wisconsin	876,588	871,751	92	384	4,361	29,639	1,839	396,965	144,299
Wyoming	85,193	83,884	68	n/a	1,241	242	n/a	37,725	15,649
Dist. of Columbia	72,743	66,944	1,520	1,834	2,445	15,194	1,709	59,912	55,884
DoDDS:									
DoDs Overseas (d)	60,891	60,891	0	0	0	n/a	n/a	n/a	n/a
DDESS:									
DoDs Domestic (d)	26,631	26,631	0	0	0	n/a	n/a	n/a	n/a
Bureau of Indian Education	n/a	n/a	0	0	0	n/a	n/a	n/a	n/a
American Samoa	16,427	16,191	49	187	0	n/a	n/a	n/a	n/a
Guam	n/a	n/a	0	0	0	n/a	n/a	n/a	n/a
No. Mariana Islands	11,605	11,666	0	0	29	n/a	n/a	n/a	n/a
Puerto Rico	544,138	526,125	1,991	16,022	0	n/a	N.A.	542,720	496,640
U.S. Virgin Islands	n/a	16,251	0	n/a	63	n/a	n/a	16,314	0.0

See footnotes at end of table.

TOTAL STUDENT MEMBERSHIP, STUDENT/TEACHER RATIO, AND NUMBER OF STAFF FOR PUBLIC SCHOOLS: SCHOOL YEAR 2006–07—Continued

Source: U.S. Department of Education, National Center for Education Statistics, Common Core of Data (CCD), "Public Elementary/Secondary School Universe Survey," 2006–07, Version 1a.

Key:

N.A. — Not available.

n/a — Not applicable. Some states do not have charter school authorization and some states do not designate magnet schools.

N.R. — Reporting standards not met. Information about whether or not a school was a magnet school was missing for 18.2 percent of schools in the 50 states and District of Columbia.

(a) Individual state total number of students are included only if the state reports data for regular, special education, vocational education, and alternative school types.

(b) Number of Title I eligible schools includes those with or without schoolwide Title I programs.

(b) Data were missing in one or more states for the number of students and the number of vocational education, magnet, Title I, or Title I schoolwide program schools. A reporting states total is shown if data for any item in the table were missing for some, but not more than 15 percent, of all schools in the Untied States. If data for an item were unavailable for more than 15 percent of schools in the Untied States, the total for that item is shown as "reporting standards not met."

(c) DoDDS and DDESS are the Department of Defense dependents schools (overseas) and the Department of Defense dependents schools (domestic), respectively.

Table 9.3
PUBLIC SCHOOL GRADUATION RATE: SCHOOL YEAR 2004–05

State or other jurisdiction	Averaged freshman graduation rate (a)	High school completers		
		Total (b)	Regular diplomas	Other high school completers (b)
United States (c)	74.7	2,853,262	2,799,250	54,012
Alabama	65.9	39,990	37,453	2,537
Alaska	64.1	7,236	6,909	327
Arizona	84.7	59,498	59,498	N.A.
Arkansas	75.7	26,698	26,621	77
California	74.6	355,217	355,217	n/a
Colorado	76.7	45,058	44,532	526
Connecticut	80.9	35,560	35,515	45
Delaware	73.1	7,102	6,934	168
Florida	64.6	141,868	133,318	8,550
Georgia	61.7	79,128	70,834	8,294
Hawaii	75.1	11,014	10,813	201
Idaho	81.0	15,877	15,768	109
Illinois	79.4	123,615	123,615	n/a
Indiana	73.2	57,021	55,444	1,577
Iowa	86.6	33,641	33,547	94
Kansas	79.2	30,355	30,355	n/a
Kentucky	75.9	38,782	38,399	383
Louisiana	63.9	37,785	36,009	1,776
Maine	78.6	13,407	13,077	330
Maryland	79.3	54,750	54,170	580
Massachusetts	78.7	60,653	59,665	988
Michigan	73.0	101,835	101,582	253
Minnesota	85.9	58,391	58,391	n/a
Mississippi	63.3	25,180	23,523	1,657
Missouri	80.6	57,841	57,841	n/a
Montana	81.5	10,335	10,335	n/a
Nebraska	87.8	20,089	19,940	149
Nevada	55.8	18,236	15,740	2,496
New Hampshire (d)	80.1	13,847	13,775	72
New Jersey	85.1	86,502	86,502	n/a
New Mexico	65.4	17,837	17,353	484
New York	65.3	158,880	153,203	5,677
North Carolina	72.6	76,663	75,010	1,653
North Dakota	86.3	7,555	7,555	n/a
Ohio	80.2	116,702	116,702	n/a
Oklahoma	76.9	36,227	36,227	n/a
Oregon	74.2	36,868	32,602	4,266
Pennsylvania	82.5	124,758	124,758	n/a
Rhode Island	78.4	9,903	9,881	22
South Carolina	60.1	36,192	33,439	2,753
South Dakota	82.3	8,585	8,585	n/a
Tennessee	68.5	51,165	47,967	3,198
Texas	74.0	239,717	239,717	n/a
Utah	84.4	30,399	30,253	146
Vermont	86.5	7,179	7,152	27
Virginia	79.6	76,860	73,667	3,193
Washington	75.0	61,213	61,094	119
West Virginia	77.3	17,137	17,137	n/a
Wisconsin	86.7	64,160	63,229	931
Wyoming	76.7	5,653	5,616	37
Dist. of Columbia	68.8	3,098	2,781	317
DoDDS: DoDs Overseas (e)	N.A.	N.A.	N.A.	n/a
DDESS: DoDs Domestic (e)	N.A.	N.A.	N.A.	n/a
Bureau of Indian Education	N.A.	N.A.	N.A.	n/a
American Samoa	77.9	888	879	9
Guam	N.A.	1,179	1,179	n/a
No. Marianas Islands	75.4	614	614	N.A.
Puerto Rico	61.7	30,371	29,071	1,300
U.S. Virgin Islands	N.A.	940	940	n/a

See footnotes at end of table.

PUBLIC SCHOOL GRADUATION RATE: SCHOOL YEAR 2004–05—Continued

Source: U.S. Department of Education, National Center for Education Statistics, Common Core of Data (CCD), "State Nonfiscal Survey of Public Elementary/Secondary Education," 2000–01, Version 1b; 2001–02, Version 1b; 2002–03, Version 1b; and 2005–06, Version 1a.

Key:

N.A. — Not available.

n/a — Not applicable.

(a) Averaged freshman graduation rate (AFGR) is an estimate of the percentage of an entering freshman class graduating in 4 years. For 2004–05, it equals the total number of diploma recipients in 2004–05 divided by the average membership of the 8th-grade class in 2000–01, the 9th-grade class in 2001–02, and the 10th-grade class in 2002–03.

(b) Includes individuals who receive diplomas, certificates of attendance, or some other credential in lieu of diplomas.

(c) Total other high school completers were missing for 2 percent of states in the 50 states and the District of Columbia. U.S. totals include the 50 states and the District of Columbia.

(d) New Hampshire included home schooled students in reported membership in 2000-01. This could inflate the denominator for the AFGR slightly.

(e) DoDDS and DDESS are the Department of Defense dependents schools (overseas) and the Department of Defense dependents schools (domestic), respectively.

Table 9.4
TOTAL REVENUES, PERCENTAGE DISTRIBUTION, AND REVENUES PER PUPIL FOR PUBLIC ELEMENTARY AND SECONDARY SCHOOLS, BY SOURCE AND STATE OR JURISDICITION: FISCAL YEAR 2006

State or other jurisdiction	Revenues (in thousands of dollars)				Percentage distribution		
	Total	Local (a)	State	Federal	Local (a)	State	Federal
United States (b)	$520,643,954	$230,939,051	$242,151,076	$47,553,827	44.4	46.5	9.1
Alabama	6,345,033	2,040,115	3,547,078	758,840	32.5	55.9	12.0
Alaska	1,712,601	416,227	1,005,181	291,193	24.3	58.7	17.0
Arizona	8,833,520	3,520,951	4,272,320	1,040,249	39.9	48.4	11.8
Arkansas	4,282,506	1,364,486	2,432,920	485,100	31.9	56.8	11.3
California	63,785,872	19,048,880	37,847,078	6,889,913	29.9	59.3	10.8
Colorado	7,269,475	3,648,933	3,089,571	530,970	50.2	42.5	7.3
Connecticut	8,711,814	4,942,541	33,351,644	417,629	56.7	38.5	4.8
Delaware	1,533,399	436,604	969,854	126,940	28.5	63.2	8.3
Florida	24,816,807	12,518,858	9,795,679	2,502,270	50.4	39.5	10.1
Georgia	16,117,459	7,474,154	7,155,591	1,487,715	46.4	44.4	9.2
Hawaii (c)	2,703,718	48,403	2,431,735	223,580	1.8	89.9	8.3
Idaho	1,909,489	629,337	1,073,734	206,418	33.0	56.2	10.8
Illinois	22,344,947	13,858,385	6,619,663	1,866,900	62.0	29.6	8.4
Indiana	11,211,313	4,935,499	5,504,585	771,230	44.0	49.1	6.9
Iowa	4,734,934	2,169,503	2,158,230	407,201	45.8	45.6	8.6
Kansas	4,934,817	1,798,263	2,692,219	444,335	36.4	54.6	9.0
Kentucky	5,909,930	1,835,133	3,383,793	691,004	31.1	57.3	11.7
Louisiana	6,760,714	2,576,922	2,933,287	1,250,505	38.1	43.4	18.5
Maine	2,372,152	1,133,513	1,004,899	233,741	47.8	42.4	9.9
Maryland	10,680,716	5,828,189	4,189,323	663,204	54.6	39.2	6.2
Massachusetts	13,850,962	6,571,045	6,570,612	772,305	47.4	47.0	5.6
Michigan	18,978,793	6,158,717	11,259,666	1,560,410	32.5	59.3	8.2
Minnesota	9,191,384	2,052,372	6,543,838	595,175	22.3	71.2	6.5
Mississippi	4,132,345	1,166,890	2,108,727	856,727	28.2	51.0	20.7
Missouri	8,908,447	5,131,324	2,982,806	794,318	57.6	33.5	8.9
Montana	1,372,561	546,073	633,923	192,565	39.8	46.2	14.0
Nebraska	2,972,026	1,728,024	946,683	297,318	58.1	31.9	10.0
Nevada	3,696,968	2,474,464	958,743	263,761	66.9	25.9	7.1
New Hampshire	2,363,964	1,307,123	926,256	130,585	55.3	39.2	5.5
New Jersey	22,799,624	12,155,282	9,642,530	1,001,813	53.3	42.3	4.4
New Mexico	3,148,752	451,153	2,241,203	456,396	14.3	71.2	14.5
New York	46,776,452	23,533,105	19,859,481	3,383,866	50.3	42.5	7.2
North Carolina	11,137,110	2,971,285	6,966,133	1,199,692	26.7	62.5	10.8
North Dakota	958,109	459,781	347,093	151,235	48.0	36.2	15.8
Ohio	21,106,426	10,285,836	9,217,115	1,603,474	48.7	43.7	7.6
Oklahoma	4,859,546	1,618,449	2,591,377	649,719	33.3	53.3	13.4
Oregon	5,427,586	2,160,833	2,737,046	529,706	39.8	50.4	9.8
Pennsylvania	22,683,987	12,815,649	8,028,829	11,839,508	56.5	35.4	8.1
Rhode Island	2,047,019	1,049,791	840,435	156,794	51.3	41.1	7.7
South Carolina	6,706,259	2,990,559	3,033,281	682,419	44.6	45.2	10.2
South Dakota	1,094,021	551,962	361,531	180,528	50.5	33.0	16.5
Tennessee	7,307,380	3,385,282	3,105,334	816,764	46.3	42.5	11.2
Texas	39,691,436	21,496,767	13,421,855	4,772,813	54.2	33.8	12.0
Utah	3,441,688	1,214,036	1,897,355	330,297	35.3	55.1	9.6
Vermont	1,348,836	92,275	1,154,694	101,868	6.8	85.6	7.6
Virginia	12,922,017	6,942,601	5,112,423	866,993	53.7	39.6	6.7
Washington	9,759,939	2,948,407	5,933,610	877,922	30.2	60.8	9.0
West Virginia	2,910,905	821,067	1,739,376	350,462	28.2	59.8	12.0
Wisconsin	9,726,952	4,053,773	5,086,692	586,486	41.7	52.3	6.0
Wyoming	1,149,155	525,837	507,043	116,274	45.8	44.1	10.1
Dist. of Columbia (c)	1,201,091	1,054,392	n.a.	146,698	87.8	n.a.	12.2
American Samoa	86,082	89	15,856	70,136	0.1	18.4	81.5
Guam	207,709	154,679	n.a.	53,030	75.0	n.a.	26.0
No. Marianas Islands	66,905	322	37,210	29,372	0.5	55.6	43.9
Puerto Rico	2,917,236	133	1,984,178	932,924	0	68.0	32.0
U.S. Virgin Islands	193,291	152,997	n.a.	40,924	79.2	n.a.	20.8

Source: U.S. Department of Education, National Center for Education Statistics, Common Core of Data (CCD), "National Public Education Financial Survey (NPEFS)," fiscal year 2006, Version 1a.

Note: Detail may not sum to totals because of rounding.

Key:

N.A. — Not available.

n.a.— Not applicable.

(a) Local revenues include intermediate revenues.

(b) U.S. totals include the 50 states and the District of Columbia.

(c) Both the District of Columbia and Hawaii have only one school district each; therefore, neither is comparable to other states. Local revenues in Hawaii consist almost entirely of student fees and charges for services, such as food services, summer school, and student activities.

Table 9.5
TOTAL EXPENDITURES FOR PUBLIC ELEMENTARY AND SECONDARY SCHOOLS: FISCAL YEAR 2006

	Expenditures (in thousands of dollars)					
State or other jurisdiction	Total	Current for elementary/ secondary education (a)	Facilities acquisitions and construction	Replacement equipment	Other programs (b)	Interest on debt
United States (c)	$528,734,539 (d)(e)	$449,594,924 (d)	$51,201,787	$6,173,512 (d)(e)	$7,417,761(d)(e)	$ 14,346,556(d)
Alabama	6,607,382	5,699,076	604,657	64,084	112,922	126,642
Alaska	1,812,119	1,529,645	221,691	15,268	7,673	37,842
Arizona	8,529,997 (e)	7,130,341	849,085	281,300(e)	49,015(e)	220,257
Arkansas	4,424,593	3,808,011	416,664	79,202	24,995	95,721
California	65,854,208	53,436,103	9,741,869	235,834(d)	1,043,342	1,397,060
Colorado	7,781,436	6,368,289	881,673	147,091	63,862	320,522
Connecticut	8,892,083 (e)	7,517,025	1,001,825	86,612(d)(e)	140,272(e)	146,349
Delaware	1,684,615	1,405,465	224,117	8,760 (d)	16,160(d)	30,113
Florida	26,827,338	20,897,327	4,617,106	237,340	468,287	607,278
Georgia	15,875,012	13,739,263	1,754,496	175,499	36,210	169,544
Hawaii (f)	2,026,154	1,805,521	37,514	38,451	59,457	85,211
Idaho	1,928,348	1,694,827	161,131	30,567	4,519	37,303
Illinois	21,954,250	19,244,908	1,547,282	465,806	152,670	543,585
Indiana	10,713,543 (d)	9,241,986	815,910	156,105	63,064	436,478 (d)
Iowa	4,735,943	4,039,389	505,627	91,206	31,684	68,036
Kansas	4,506,242	4,039,417	159,941	167,017	4,485	135,381
Kentucky	6,095,728	5,213,620	552,605	121,942	80,655	126,907
Louisiana	6,188,015	5,554,278	355,390	104,766	68,602	104,980
Maine	2,299,359	2,119,408	79,713	30,154	24,121	45,963
Maryland	10,518,434	9,381,613	899,322	94,294	24,322	118,882
Massachusetts	13,757,817	12,210,581	1,170,963	29,399	59,408	287,467
Michigan	19,878,934	16,681,981	1,771,377	221,848	351,300	852,428
Minnesota	9,531,590	7,686,638	949,970	135,479	359,612	399,891
Mississippi	3,983,753	3,550,261	127,561	113,931(d)	32,942	69,059
Missouri	8,783,995	7,592,485	560,596	198,588	168,899	263,426
Montana	1,376,246	1,254,360	80,846	20,648	7,208	13,185
Nebraska	2,974,472	2,672,629	173,466	67,950 (d)	5,125 (d)	55,274
Nevada	3,940,869	2,959,728	677,668	75,854	17,141	210,478
New Hampshire	2,396,313	2,139,113	174,616	26,978	6,343	49,263
New Jersey	23,353,204	20,869,993	1,831,918	100,623(d)	205,034(d)	345,636
New Mexico	3,171,892	2,729,707	351,990	23,554	28,615	38,026
New York	46,269,766	41,149,457	1,824,655	369,212	1,678,175	1,248,257
North Carolina	12,133,667	10,476,056	1,152,944	87,487	49,326	367,854
North Dakota	968,112	857,774	66,992	25,976	6,262	11,108
Ohio	20,902,539	17,829,599	1,802,947	362,928	429,510	477,556
Oklahoma	4,852,418	4,406,002	317,416	72,510	13,487	43,003
Oregon	5,337,287	4,773,751	278,009	41,223	18,486	225,819
Pennsylvania	23,026,118	19,631,006	1,783,079	253,050	531,743	827,241
Rhode Island	2,046,113	1,934,429	17,985	12,531	49,253	31,941
South Carolina	6,990,040	5,696,629	902,499	78,624	70,282	242,006
South Dakota	1,058,470	948,671	50,743	35,528	3,138	20,390
Tennessee	7,439,050 (d)	6,681,456 (d)	437,803	114,467	53,328	151,996
Texas	42,152,918	33,851,773	5,781,724	388,727	303,929	1,826,766
Utah	3,457,129	2,778,236	451,752	60,064	86,803	80,274
Vermont	1,314,627	1,237,442	39,039	19,909	4,145	14,091
Virginia	13,185,745	11,470,735	1,025,388	273,364	67,595	348,663
Washington	10,051,241(d)	8,239,716 (d)	1,335,392	92,662	47,349	336,123
West Virginia	2,749,151	2,651,491	18,275	31,811(d)	36,574	11,000
Wisconsin	10,131,019	8,745,195	379,541	132,007	233,505	640,770
Wyoming	1,140,656	965,350	131,701	36,512	3,583	3,512
Dist. of Columbia (f)	1,214,589	1,057,166	105,335	38,770 (d)	13,318	0
American Samoa	67,460	58,539	3,571	958	4,392	0
Guam	214,020	210,119	0	3,293	0	607
No. Marianas Islands	59,817	57,694	1,328	288	507	0
Puerto Rico	3,282,288	3,082,295	22,622	67,472	96,459	13,440
U.S. Virgin Islands	161,374	146,872	11,650	1,095	1,757	0

See footnotes at end of table.

TOTAL EXPENDITURES FOR PUBLIC ELEMENTARY AND SECONDARY SCHOOLS: FISCAL YEAR 2006 —Continued

Source: U.S. Department of Education, National Center for Education Statistics, Common Core of Data (CCD), "National Public Education Financial Survey (NPEFS)," fiscal year 2006, Version 1a.

Note: Detail may not sum to totals because of rounding.

Key:

N.A.— Not available.

(a) Includes instruction, instruction-related, support services, and other elementary/secondary current expenditures, but excludes expenditures on capital outlay, other programs, and interest on long-term debt.

(b) Includes expenditures for community services, adult education, community colleges, private schools, and other programs that are not part of public elementary and secondary education.

(c) U.S. totals include the 50 states and the District of Columbia.

(d) Value affected by redistribution of reported values to correct for missing data itemsand/or to distribute state direct support expenditures.

(e) Value contains imputation for missing data.

(f) Both the District of Columbia and Hawaii have only one school district each; therefore, neither is comparable to other states.

Table 9.6
CURRENT EXPENDITURES AND PERCENTAGE DISTRIBUTION FOR PUBLIC ELEMENTARY AND SECONDARY SCHOOLS, BY FUNCTION AND STATE OR JURISDICTION: FISCAL YEAR 2006

State or other jurisdiction	Current expenditures (in thousands of dollars) (a)					Percentage distribution			
	Total (a)	Instruction and instruction related (b)	Student support (c)	Admin.	Ops.	Instruction and instruction related (a)	Student support	Admin.	Ops.
United States (d)	$449,594,924 (e)	$296,104,516 (e)	$23,356,971 (e)	$48,663,020	$81,470,417 (e)	65.9	5.2	10.8	18.1
Alabama	5,699,076	3,613,356,971	293,235	620,053	1,172,346	63.4	5.1	10.9	20.6
Alaska	1,529,645	957,744	96,524	170,363	305,013	62.6	6.3	11.1	19.9
Arizona	7,130,341	4,586,419 (e)	400,463 (e)	753,420 (e)	1,390,040 (e)	64.3	5.6	10.6	19.5
Arkansas	3,808,011	2,534,474 (e)	174,344 (e)	410,107 (e)	689,087 (e)	66.6	4.6	10.8	18.1
California	53,436,103	35,850,215 (e)	2,458,675 (e)	6,403,792 (e)	8,723,420 (e)	67.1	4.6	12.0	16.3
Colorado	6,368,289	3,907,295	289,312	127,383	1,054,299	61.4	4.4	17.7	16.6
Connecticut	7,517,025	5,003,775 (e)	452,267 (e)	739,244 (e)	1,321,739 (e)	66.6	6.0	9.8	17.6
Delaware	1,405,465	866,591	67,087	185,253	286,534	61.7	4.8	13.2	20.4
Florida	20,897,327	13,764,969 (e)	984,592 (e)	1,943,735 (e)	4,204,030 (e)	65.9	4.7	9.3	20.1
Georgia	13,739,263	9,348,593 (e)	654,685 (e)	1,448,155 (e)	2,287,331 (e)	68.0	4.8	10.5	16.7
Hawaii (f)	1,805,521	1,143,214	216,531	185,222	260,554	63.3	12.0	10.3	14.4
Idaho	1,694,827	1,117,513 (e)	94,777 (e)	166,178 (e)	316,359 (e)	65.9	5.6	9.8	18.7
Illinois	19,244,908	12,223,957 (e)	1,218,203 (e)	2,295,142 (e)	3,507,606 (e)	63.5	6.3	11.9	18.2
Indiana	9,241,986	5,843,838 (e)	407,131 (e)	1,076,875 (e)	1,914,142 (e)	63.2	4.4	11.7	20.7
Iowa	4,039,389	2,605,837	239,001	481,318	713,223	64.5	5.9	11.9	17.7
Kansas	4,039,417	2,605,113	227,655	467,277	739,373	64.5	5.6	11.6	18.3
Kentucky	5,213,620	3,392,033	214,671	519,407	1,087,509	65.1	4.1	10.0	20.9
Louisiana	5,554,278	3,516,871 (e)	226,554 (e)	565,732 (e)	1,243,121 (e)	63.3	4.1	10.2	22.4
Maine	2,119,408	1,467,136 (e)	78,432 (e)	194,004 (e)	379,837	69.2	3.7	9.2	17.9
Maryland	9,381,613	6,250,392 (e)	391,342 (e)	985,038 (e)	1,754,841	66.6	4.2	10.5	18.7
Massachusetts	12,210,613	8,530,548 (e)	670,672 (e)	1,050,219 (e)	1,959,142 (e)	69.9	5.5	8.6	16.0
Michigan	16,681,981	10,269,636	1,210,229	2,124,960	3,077,156	61.6	7.3	12.7	18.4
Minnesota	7,686,638	5,034,226 (e)	205,659 (e)	806,166 (e)	1,370,587 (e)	69.0	2.7	10.5	17.8
Mississippi	3,550,261	2,267,086 (e)	160,537 (e)	368,694 (e)	753,944 (e)	63.9	4.5	10.4	21.2
Missouri	7,592,485	497,406	357,737	797,335	1,490,008	65.2	4.7	10.5	19.6
Montana	1,254,360	807,561	67,429	137,969	241,400	64.4	5.4	11.0	19.2
Nebraska	2,672,629	1,783,853	111,972	289,967	486,836	66.7	4.2	10.8	18.2
Nevada	2,959,728	1,890,821	111,762	447,929	509,216	63.9	3.8	15.1	17.2
New Hampshire	2,139,113	1,446,317	146,729	207,774	338,292	67.6	6.9	9.7	15.8
New Jersey	20,869,993	13,016,486	1,882,174	2,027,580	3,943,753	62.4	9.0	9.7	18.9
New Mexico	2,729,707	1,662,234	263,342	300,906	503,225	60.9	9.6	11.0	18.4
New York	41,149,457	29,622,407 (e)	1,317,736 (e)	3,453,769 (e)	6,755,545 (e)	72.0	3.2	8.4	16.4
North Carolina	10,476,457	6,899,740	568,446	1,166,570	1,841,300	65.9	5.4	11.1	17.6
North Dakota	857,774	546,554	34,285	97,632	179,304	63.7	4.0	11.4	20.9
Ohio	17,829,599	11,360,796	1,066,791	2,328,375	3,073,637	63.7	6.0	13.1	17.2
Oklahoma	4,406,002	2,673,852	285,058	495,383	951,709	60.7	6.5	11.2	21.6
Oregon	4,773,751	2,992,083	337,295	659,225	785,148	62.7	7.1	13.8	16.4
Pennsylvania	19,631,429	12,803,055	952,558	2,150,984	3,724,409	65.2	4.9	11.0	19.0
Rhode Island	1,934,429	1,257,095 (e)	230,464 (e)	163,631 (e)	283,239 (e)	65.0	11.9	8.5	14.6
South Carolina	5,696,629	3,699,189	391,163	566,770	1,039,507	64.9	6.9	9.9	18.2
South Dakota	948,671	590,657	52,232	116,229	189,554	62.3	5.5	12.3	20.0
Tennessee	6,681,456 (e)	4,668,182 (e)	227,033	608,069	1,178,172	69.9	3.4	9.1	17.6
Texas	33,851,773	21,998,997 (e)	1,643,051 (e)	3,596,031 (e)	6,613,695 (e)	65.0	4.9	10.6	19.5
Utah	2,778,236	1,885,924	102,818	260,881	528,613	67.9	3.7	9.4	19.0
Vermont	1,237,442	833,389	91,604	139,560	172,889	67.3	7.4	11.3	14.0
Virginia	11,470,735	7,761,049	548,473	1,015,378	2,145,836	67.7	4.8	8.9	18.7
Washington	8,239,716 (e)	5,262,132 (e)	524,785	949,096	1,503,703	63.9	6.4	11.5	18.2
West Virginia	2,651,491	1,690,818 (e)	94,580 (e)	252,323 (e)	613,770 (e)	63.8	3.6	9.5	23.1
Wisconsin	8,745,195	5,782,750	399,759	1,105,744	1,456,943	66.1	4.6	12.6	16.7
Wyoming	965,350	624,347	56,760	109,246	174,996	64.7	5.9	11.3	18.1
Dist. of Columbia (f)	1,057,166	625,904	66,358	130,926	233,979	59.2	6.3	12.4	22.1
American Samoa	58,539	36,784	2,328	4,261	15,166	62.8	4.0	7.3	25.9
Guam	210,119	125,846 (e)	22,951	22,555	38,767	60	11	11	19
No. Marianas Islands	57,694	47,079(e)	1,064(e)	2,658(e)	6,893(e)	81.6	1.8	4.6	12.0
Puerto Rico	3,082,295	2,190,152	153,625	104,333	634,185	71.1	5.0	3.4	20.6
U.S. Virgin Islands	146,872	99,432	8,922	18,622	19,896	67.7	6.1	12.7	13.5

See footnotes at end of table.

CURRENT EXPENDITURES AND PERCENTAGE DISTRIBUTION FOR PUBLIC ELEMENTARY AND SECONDARY SCHOOLS, BY FUNCTION AND STATE OR JURISDICTION: FISCAL YEAR 2006 — Continued

Source: U.S. Department of Education, National Center for Education Statistics, Common Core of Data (CCD), "National Public Education Financial Survey (NPEFS)," fiscal year 2006, Version 1a.

Note: Detail may not sum to totals because of rounding.

Key:

N.A. — Not available.

(a) Include instruction, instruction-related, support services, and other elementary/secondary current expenditures, but exclude expenditures on capital outlay, other programs, and interest on long-term debt.

(b) Include current expenditures for classroom instruction(including teachers and teaching assistants), libraries, in-service teacher training, curriculum development, student assessment and instruction technology.

(c) Include attendance and social work, guidance, health, psychological services, speech pathology, audiology, and other student support services.

(d) U.S. totals include the 50 states and the District of Columbia.

(e) Value affected by redistribution of reported expenditure values to correct for missing data items, and/or to distribute stte direct support expenditures.

(f) Both the District of Columbia and Hawaii have only one school district each; therefore, neither is comparable to other states.

Table 9.7
CURRENT INSTRUCTION AND INSTRUCTION-RELATED EXPENDITURES FOR PUBLIC ELEMENTARY AND SECONDARY EDUCATION, BY OBJECT AND STATE OR JURISDICTION: FISCAL YEAR 2006

	Current instruction and instruction-related expenditures (in thousands of dollars)(a)						
State or other jurisdiction	*Total*	*Salaries*	*Employee benefits*	*Purchased services*	*Tuition to out-of-state and private schools*	*Supplies*	*Other*
United States (b)	$296,104,516 (c)	$199,910,397 (c)	$62,930,989 (c)	$13,046,741 (c)	$4,168,859 (c)	$14,652,214 (c)	$1,395,317 (c)
Alabama	3,613,442	2,335,209	837,940	125,267	2,900	296,752	15,374
Alaska	957,744	594,296	239,391	63,076	0	51,753	9,228
Arizona	4,586,418 (c)	3,551,676 (c)	663,018 (c)	173,724 (c)	6,053	164,494 (c)	27,454 (c)
Arkansas	2,534,474 (c)	1,733,179 (c)	443,175 (c)	100,560 (c)	8,078	229,213 (c)	20,269 (c)
California	35,850,215 (c)	23,763,975 (c)	7,556,588 (c)	1,895,694 (c)	693,885	1,934,524 (c)	5,550 (c)
Colorado	3,907,295	2,756,003	616,493	131,448	49,377	288,309	65,665
Connecticut	5,003,775 (c)	3,244,338 (c)	1,156,015 (c)	171,881	284,136	137,808 (c)	9,596 (c)
Delaware	866,591	550,805	236,452	20,147	6,777	42,972	9,439
Florida	13,764,969 (c)	8,931,468 (c)	2,459,697 (c)	1,533,867 (c)	666	725,330 (c)	113,940 (c)
Georgia	9,348,593 (c)	6,554,537 (c)	1,0928,885 (c)	247,041 (c)	4,983	558,444 (c)	54,702 (c)
Hawaii (d)	1,143,214	732,009	259,508	59,130	4,553	63,733	24,282
Idaho	1,117,513 (c)	765,320 (c)	245,399 (c)	45,768 (c)	606	59,680(c)	740 (c)
Illinois	12,223,957 (c)	8,688,110 (c)	2,301,040 (c)	507,091 (c)	220,610	489,250 (c)	17,856 (c)
Indiana	5,843,838 (c)	3,662,501 (c)	1,812,142 (c)	114,689 (c)	21	219,417 (c)	35,067 (c)
Iowa	2,605,837	1,846,871	554,720	66,982	19,795	114,110	3,358
Kansas	2,605,113	1,903,592	428,991	90,910	1,861	162,435	17,324
Kentucky	3,392,033	2,392,563	757,620	75,150	232	143,045	23,423
Louisiana	3,516,871 (c)	2,365,097 (c)	849,524 (c)	63,122 (c)	958	214,971 (c)	23,199 (c)
Maine	1,467,136 (c)	934,941	339,724 (c)	63,131	74,580	46,758	8,003
Maryland	6,250,392 (c)	4,155,790	1,449,597 (c)	168,672	237,608	237,319	11,407
Massachusetts	8,530,548 (c)	5,309,789	2,151,900 (c)	63,642	737,354	240,712	27,152
Michigan	10,269,636	6,404,262	2,933,838	567,430	0	336,026	28,080
Minnesota	5,304,226 (c)	3,687,553 (c)	1,086,298 (c)	251,240 (c)	51,405	211,713	16,017
Mississippi	2,267,086 (c)	1,584,772 (c)	446,853 (c)	74,921 (c)	4,331	145,066 (c)	11,144 (c)
Missouri	4,947,406	3,472,261	831,214	197,598 (c)	9,572	407,763	28,998 (c)
Montana	807,561	530,596	148,095	56,750	536	68,465	3,118
Nebraska	1,783,853	1,220,922	400,275	66,042	15,083	65,934	15,598
Nevada	1,890,821	1,201,311	409,337	51,548	879	145,388	82,358
New Hampshire	1,446,317	917,966	319,150	46,098	112,072	47,261	3,141
New Jersey	13,016,486	8,457,085	3,007,868	395,976	549,944	478,811	126,802
New Mexico	1,662,234	1,116,388	327,089	86,334	0	124,255	8,168
New York	29,622,407 (c)	19,461,937 (c)	7,517,909 (c)	1,453,853 (c)	251,214	933,469 (c)	4,024 (c)
North Carolina	6,899,740	5,064,850	1,169,200	216,223	0	442,156	7,311
North Dakota	546,554	387,719	106,123	20,014	1,914	27,127	3,656
Ohio	11,360,796	7,534,970	2,465,451	606,165	137,904	463,610	152,698
Oklahoma	2,673,852	1,891,332	487,010	57,653	0	224,147	13,711
Oregon	2,992,083	1,812,015	821,684	141,192	21,691	179,936	15,565
Pennsylvania	12,803,055	8,328,823	2,814,801	865,830	222,164	549,197	22,240
Rhode Island	1,257,095 (c)	828,442 (c)	305,471 (c)	24,938 (c)	68,901	26,893 (c)	2,451 (c)
South Carolina	3,669,189	2,594,045	707,475	156,533	440	211,640	29,056
South Dakota	590,657	395,215	108,250	30,202	6,203	49,230	1,556
Tennessee	4,668,182 (c)	3,210,744	856,532	129,090	260 (c)	453,461	18,095
Texas	21,998,997 (c)	16,666,996 (c)	2,629,856 (c)	927,639 (c)	53,356	1,507,959 (c)	213,191 (c)
Utah	1,885,924	1,233,293	501,726	44,229	344	101,220	5,112
Vermont	833,924	522,449	175,337	50,965	56,114	26,181	2,344
Virginia	7,761,049	547,481	1,632,588	234,277	5,368	408,426	4,909
Washington	5,262,132 (c)	3,703,581	1,016,678	266,519	9,630	228,263	37,462
West Virginia	1,690,818 (c)	1,023,870 (c)	525,323 (c)	44,421 (c)	708	96,217 (c)	279 (c)
Wisconsin	5,782,750	3,621,765	1,701,343	119,438	92,407	233,812	13,986
Wyoming	624,347	405,556	143,457	32,684	684	40,747	1,220
Dist. of Columbia(d)	625,904 (c)	382,399 (c)	46,639 (c)	49,950 (c)	140,103	6,812 (c)	0 (c)
American Samoa	36,784	21,342	4,126	6,556	0	3,009	1,751
Guam	125,846 (c)	92,958	22,977	2,140	0	7,424 (c)	347
No. Mariana Islands	47,079 (c)	32,431 (c)	8,755 (c)	4,330 (c)	0	1,538 (c)	26 (c)
Puerto Rico	2,190,152	1,763,778	266,163	17,850	0	84,223	58,138
U.S. Virgin Islands	99,432	77,115	20,498	225	0	1,544	49

See footnotes at end of table.

CURRENT INSTRUCTION AND INSTRUCTION-RELATED EXPENDITURES FOR PUBLIC ELEMENTARY AND SECONDARY EDUCATION, BY OBJECT AND STATE OR JURISDICTION: FISCAL YEAR 2006—Continued

Source: U.S. Department of Education, National Center for Education Statistics, Common Core of Data (CCD), "National Public Education Financial Survey (NPEFS)," fiscal year 2006, Version 1a.

Note: Detail may not sum to totals due to rounding.

Key:

N.A.— Not available.

(a) Include salaries and benefits for teachers, teaching assistants, librarians and library aides, in-service teacher trainers, curriculum development, student assessment, technology, and supplies and purchased services related to these activities.

(b) U.S. totals include the 50 states and the District of Columbia.

(c) Value affected by redistribution of reported values to correct for missing data items, and/or to distribute state direct support expenditures.

(d) Both the District of Columbia and Hawaii have only one school district each; therefore, neither is comparable to other states.

Table 9.8
AVERAGE UNDERGRADUATE TUITION AND FEES AND ROOM AND BOARD RATES IN INSTITUTIONS OF HIGHER EDUCATION, BY CONTROL OF INSTITUTION AND STATE: 2005–2006 AND 2006–2007

State or other jurisdiction	Public 4-year						Private 4-year						Public 2-year tuition only (in-state)	
	2005–2006		2006–2007 (a)				2005–2006		2006–2007 (a)					
	Total	Tuition (in-state)	Total	Tuition (in-state)	Room	Board	Total	Tuition	Total	Tuition	Room	Board	2005–2006	2006–2007
United States	$12,108	$5,351	$12,805	$5,685	$3,872	$3,248	$27,317	$19,292	$28,896	$20,492	$4,613	$3,792	$1,935	$2,017
Eastern Region														
Connecticut	14,658	6,709	15,457	7,151	4,426	3,880	36,026	26,183	38,036	27,702	5,698	4,635	2,536	2,672
Delaware	14,326	7,074	15,201	7,471	4,567	3,217	18,176	10,819	18,965	11,609	3,915	3,441	2,240	2,364
Maine	12,568	6,027	12,865	6,557	3,555	2,753	29,550	21,508	30,983	22,631	4,262	4,091	3,039	3,058
Massachusetts	14,651	7,290	15,199	7,629	4,433	3,136	37,282	27,335	39,500	29,002	5,881	4,616	2,925	2,983
New Hampshire	15,479	8,458	16,582	9,003	4,704	2,875	31,154	22,534	33,143	24,098	5,261	3,783	5,720	5,614
New Jersey	17,708	8,649	18,721	9,333	5,969	3,418	31,335	22,114	33,228	23,473	5,294	4,461	2,712	2,910
New York	13,275	4,987	13,683	5,022	5,175	3,486	32,478	22,900	34,297	24,396	5,822	4,079	3,181	3,287
Pennsylvania	15,464	8,710	16,263	9,092	4,035	3,137	31,963	23,450	33,953	25,094	4,876	3,984	2,976	3,093
Rhode Island	14,315	6,316	14,999	6,698	4,527	3,774	33,101	24,140	35,844	25,444	6,145	4,255	2,470	2,686
Vermont	16,571	9,279	17,280	9,783	4,786	2,711	29,072	21,273	30,978	22,679	4,441	3,857	4,012	4,204
Regional average	14,902	7,350	15,625	7,774	4,618	3,239	31,014	22,226	32,893	23,613	5,160	4,120	3,181	3,287
Midwestern Region														
Illinois	13,976	7,158	15,373	8,038	3,786	3,550	27,875	19,406	29,041	20,181	5,018	3,843	2,104	2,252
Indiana	12,388	5,892	13,413	6,284	3,712	3,147	27,582	20,851	29,295	22,060	3,660	3,574	2,589	2,731
Iowa	12,329	5,619	12,578	6,019	3,245	3,314	23,444	17,513	24,685	18,462	2,897	3,325	3,032	3,139
Kansas	9,980	4,560	10,696	4,966	2,789	2,941	20,741	15,044	21,856	16,016	2,637	3,204	1,938	1,942
Michigan	13,693	6,938	14,519	7,504	3,665	3,349	19,732	13,303	20,776	13,988	3,482	3,306	2,076	2,103
Minnesota	12,777	6,912	13,719	7,392	3,321	3,006	27,314	20,519	28,863	21,697	3,673	3,493	4,085	4,395
Nebraska	11,826	4,880	11,138	5,181	3,182	2,776	21,017	15,234	22,420	16,366	3,085	3,017	1,899	1,991
North Dakota	9,829	5,038	10,626	5,471	2,155	3,000	13,533	9,376	14,330	9,898	1,946	2,486	3,084	3,462
Ohio	16,032	8,457	16,919	9,010	4,498	3,411	26,906	19,901	28,502	21,127	3,766	3,609	3,127	3,248
South Dakota	9,493	4,908	10,018	5,077	2,241	2,700	18,930	13,686	19,552	14,214	2,571	2,767	3,154	3,495
Wisconsin	10,560	5,672	11,235	6,048	3,137	2,051	25,656	19,083	27,231	20,252	3,536	3,443	2,965	23,163
Regional average	12,080	6,003	12,749	6,454	3,248	3,022	22,975	16,720	24,233	17,660	3,297	3,279	2,732	4,720
Southern Region														
Alabama	9,625	4,578	10,699	4,712	2,913	3,074	18,520	12,426	19,483	13,144	3,186	3,154	2,764	2,795
Arkansas	9,192	4,643	9,779	4,937	2,714	2,127	18,122	12,691	19,244	13,396	2,769	3,079	1,780	1,890
Florida	10,141	2,941	10,455	3,050	4,234	3,171	24,985	17,503	26,641	18,443	4,637	3,561	1,844	1,979
Georgia	10,062	3,632	10,399	3,851	4,090	2,458	26,081	18,120	27,448	19,246	4,711	3,491	1,645	1,724
Kentucky	10,663	5,136	11,885	5,821	3,226	2,838	20,674	13,764	21,044	14,739	3,249	3,055	2,404	2,633
Louisiana	8,506	3,679	9,077	3,778	2,929	2,371	17,207	11,264	18,693	11,923	3,765	3,005	1,469	1,493
Maryland	14,793	7,045	15,253	7,106	4,596	3,551	32,617	23,934	34,388	25,503	5,330	3,555	2,833	2,945
Mississippi	9,461	4,177	10,040	4,457	2,991	2,591	17,112	11,839	17,791	12,300	2,803	2,688	1,660	1,709
Missouri	11,861	5,831	12,588	6,320	3,750	2,517	22,441	15,718	23,525	16,539	3,634	3,351	2,247	2,284
North Carolina	9,675	3,631	10,467	4,038	3,570	2,859	26,411	19,166	27,735	20,410	3,828	3,498	1,295	1,300
Oklahoma	9,404	3,806	9,825	4,176	2,937	2,712	20,113	14,033	21,480	15,161	3,045	3,273	2,111	22,263
South Carolina	13,145	7,337	14,205	7,914	3,819	2,472	22,170	16,165	23,566	17,219	3,106	3,240	2,932	3,100
Tennessee	9,956	4,765	10,528	5,009	2,973	2,546	23,039	16,552	24,517	17,576	3,768	3,173	2,395	2,474
Texas	10,973	4,666	11,827	5,144	3,522	3,191	23,440	16,809	25,295	18,285	3,702	3,309	1,273	1,370
Virginia	12,279	5,912	13,134	6,447	3,636	3,051	23,823	17,185	25,024	18,143	3,496	3,386	2,049	2,362
West Virginia	9,992	3,816	10,552	4,063	3,313	3,175	20,002	13,856	20,995	14,570	3,087	3,338	2,509	2,676
Regional average	10,608	4,725	11,295	5,051	3,451	2,794	22,297	15,689	23,554	16,662	3,632	3,260	2,076	3,437

See footnotes at end of table.

AVERAGE UNDERGRADUATE TUITION AND FEES AND ROOM AND BOARD RATES IN INSTITUTIONS OF HIGHER EDUCATION, BY CONTROL OF INSTITUTION AND STATE: 2005–2006 AND 2006–2007—Continued

State or other jurisdiction	Public 4-year						Private 4-year						Public 2-year tuition only (in-state)	
	2005–2006		2006–2007 (a)				2005–2006		2006–2007 (a)					
	Total	Tuition (in-state)	Total	Tuition (in-state)	Room	Board	Total	Tuition	Total	Tuition	Room	Board	2005–2006	2006–2007
Western Region														
Alaska	10,620	4,054	11,364	4,422	4,081	2,861	21,651	14,891	23,465	16,134	3,281	4,049	2,353	2,756
Arizona	11,480	4,426	11,978	4,669	4,122	3,188	18,734	11,397	20,248	12,484	4,237	3,527	1,344	1,456
California	13,685	4,408	14,358	4,452	5,032	4,874	31,266	21,691	33,108	23,175	5,581	4,352	718	674
Colorado	11,569	4,465	12,060	4,634	3,633	3,793	27,779	18,493	29,427	19,336	5,682	4,409	1,991	2,037
Hawaii	9,042	3,226	11,050	3,930	3,498	3,622	19,437	10,344	20,236	10,738	4,156	5,342	1,226	1,395
Idaho	8,982	3,919	9,529	4,155	2,471	2,903	11,614	5,490	12,014	5,813	2,518	3,683	1,891	2,005
Montana	10,613	4,952	11,292	5,378	2,697	3,217	18,093	12,937	20,057	13,935	2,586	2,537	2,721	2,814
Nevada	10,856	2,671	11,604	2,844	5,026	3,734	20,591	12,622	23,011	13,522	4,592	4,867	1,635	1,695
New Mexico	9,579	3,701	9,963	3,943	3,302	2,718	20,306	13,256	22,078	14,640	3,747	3,691	1,179	1,245
Oregon	12,720	5,348	13,198	5,598	3,765	3,835	27,945	20,844	29,603	22,031	3,835	3,737	2,635	2,834
Utah	8,745	3,445	9,044	3,757	2,128	3,159	11,275	5,249	11,415	5,550	2,918	2,947	2,224	2,339
Washington	12,384	5,250	13,150	5,636	3,589	3,925	27,280	20,110	29,107	21,504	4,065	3,538	2,554	2,671
Wyoming	8,946	2,874	9,627	2,951	2,978	3,698	. . .	9,450	. . .	10,500	. . .	. . .	1,772	1,817
Regional average	10,709	4,057	11,401	4,336	3,563	3,502	21,314	13,598	22,814	14,566	3,933	3,890	1,865	1,980
Regional average without California	10,461	4,028	11,155	4,326	3,441	3,388	20,410	12,924	21,878	13,849	3,783	3,848	1,960	2,089
Dist. of Columbia	. . .	2,070	. . .	2,670	. . .	. . .	32,556	22,748	34,282	23,971	6,560	3,751	. . .	. . .

Source: U.S. Department of Education, National Center for Education Statistics, 2005-06 and 2006-07 Integrated Postsecondary Education Data System (IPEDS), Fall 2005, Fall 2006, Spring 2006. (This table was prepared July 2007.)

Note: Data are for the entire academic year and are average charges. Tuition and fees were weighted by the number of full-time equivalent undergraduates, but are not adjusted to reflect student residency. Room and board are based on full-time students. Degree-granting institutions grant associate's or higher degrees and participate in Title IV federal financial aid programs. Some data have been revised from previously published figures. Detail may not sum to totals because of rounding.

Key:

. . . — Not applicable

(a) Peliminary data based on fall 2005 enrollment.

(b) Tuition includes required fees.

Table 9.9
DEGREE GRANTING INSTITUTIONS AND BRANCHES, BY TYPE AND CONTROL OF INSTITUTION, 2006–2007

			Public 4-year							Private 4-year					
State or other jurisdiction	Total	All public institutions	Total	Doctoral (a)	Master's (b)	Baccalaureate (c)	Other (d)	Public 2-year	All private institutions	Total	Doctoral (a)	Master's (b)	Baccalaureate (c)	Other (d)	Private 2-year
United States (e)	4,314	1,688	643	165	275	104	99	1,045	2,626	1,986	93	364	532	997	640
Eastern Region															
Connecticut	45	22	10	1	7	1	1	12	23	20	4	5	4	7	3
Delaware	10	5	2	1	1	0	0	3	5	4	1	0	1	2	1
Maine	30	15	8	1	1	5	1	7	15	12	0	3	5	4	3
Massachusetts	122	31	15	3	7	1	4	16	91	83	9	15	21	38	8
New Hampshire	28	12	5	1	2	2	0	7	16	14	2	1	5	6	2
New Jersey	59	33	14	3	8	2	1	19	26	25	3	6	6	10	1
New York	307	78	43	6	20	7	10	35	229	179	16	33	34	96	50
Pennsylvania	263	65	44	4	17	20	3	21	198	108	6	28	34	40	90
Rhode Island	14	3	2	1	1	0	0	1	11	10	1	4	1	4	1
Vermont	25	6	5	1	2	1	1	1	19	17	0	6	7	4	2
Regional total	903	270	148	66	39	21	122	633	472	42	101	118	211	161	
Midwestern Region															
Illinois	175	60	12	5	7	0	0	48	115	100	6	16	19	59	15
Indiana	105	29	15	5	6	3	1	14	76	53	1	8	20	24	23
Iowa	65	19	3	2	1	0	0	16	46	44	0	4	22	18	2
Kansas	59	34	9	3	4	0	2	25	25	22	0	7	10	5	3
Michigan	105	45	15	7	8	0	0	30	60	56	1	9	16	30	4
Minnesota	109	42	11	1	7	3	0	31	67	60	3	6	12	39	7
Nebraska	42	15	7	1	5	0	1	8	27	23	0	5	8	10	4
North Dakota	22	14	7	2	1	3	1	7	8	7	0	1	1	5	1
Ohio	205	61	29	10	1	6	12	32	144	78	3	15	25	35	66
South Dakota	24	12	7	2	1	2	2	5	12	11	0	2	5	4	1
Wisconsin	70	31	13	2	11	0	0	18	39	36	1	8	10	17	3
Regional total	981	362	128	40	52	17	19	234	619	490	15	81	148	246	129
Southern Region															
Alabama	65	39	14	6	7	1	0	25	26	23	0	4	9	10	3
Arkansas	49	33	11	2	5	2	2	22	16	14	0	1	8	5	2
Florida	174	40	18	6	4	1	7	22	134	101	4	20	26	51	33
Georgia	134	74	22	3	13	1	5	52	60	47	2	5	15	25	13
Kentucky	71	24	8	2	6	0	0	16	47	33	0	4	16	13	14
Louisiana	86	55	17	4	9	0	4	38	31	13	1	4	3	5	18
Maryland	58	29	13	3	9	1	0	16	29	25	1	5	6	13	4
Mississippi	41	26	9	4	3	1	1	17	15	11	0	2	5	4	4
Missouri	129	33	13	4	6	2	1	20	96	72	2	11	15	44	24
North Carolina	130	75	16	4	8	3	1	59	55	51	2	7	25	17	4
Oklahoma	57	29	16	2	7	3	4	13	28	22	1	5	5	11	6
South Carolina	65	33	13	3	5	3	2	20	32	27	0	3	15	9	5
Tennessee	99	22	9	5	4	0	0	13	77	57	1	11	16	29	20
Texas	214	109	45	12	20	2	11	64	105	65	4	14	20	27	40
Virginia	110	39	15	6	6	3	0	24	71	55	0	8	18	29	16
West Virginia	42	22	12	1	1	9	1	10	20	10	0	2	7	1	10
Regional total	1,524	682	251	67	113	32	39	431	842	626	18	106	209	293	216

See footnotes at end of table.

DEGREE GRANTING INSTITUTIONS AND BRANCHES, BY TYPE AND CONTROL OF INSTITUTION, 2006–2007—Continued

State or other jurisdiction	Total	All public institutions	Public 4-year: Total	Public 4-year: Doctoral (c)	Public 4-year: Master's (b)	Public 4-year: Baccalaureate (c)	Public 4-year: Other (d)	Public 2-year	All private institutions	Private 4-year: Total	Private 4-year: Doctoral (a)	Private 4-year: Master's (b)	Private 4-year: Baccalaureate (c)	Private 4-year: Other (d)	Private 2-year
Western Region															
Alaska	8	5	3	1	2	0	0	2	3	3	0	1	1	1	0
Arizona	77	27	6	3	1	1	1	21	50	35	0	6	1	28	15
California	412	147	35	10	21	2	2	112	265	196	11	30	26	129	69
Colorado	80	27	12	4	3	4	1	15	53	35	1	6	3	25	18
Hawaii	23	10	4	1	0	2	1	6	13	9	0	3	1	5	4
Idaho	14	7	4	2	1	1	0	3	7	6	0	1	1	4	1
Montana	23	18	6	2	2	1	1	12	5	4	0	1	2	1	1
Nevada	23	7	5	2	0	1	2	2	16	8	0	1	2	5	8
New Mexico	42	28	8	3	3	0	2	20	14	13	0	4	4	5	1
Oregon	61	26	9	3	3	1	2	17	35	31	0	6	10	15	4
Utah	34	14	7	2	2	2	1	7	20	12	1	2	1	8	8
Washington	79	43	9	2	5	1	1	34	36	32	0	11	4	17	4
Wyoming	10	8	1	1	0	0	0	7	2	1	0	0	0	1	1
Regional total	886	367	109	36	43	16	14	258	519	385	13	72	56	244	134
Regional total without California	474	220	74	26	22	14	12	146	254	189	2	42	30	115	65
Dist. of Columbia	15	2	2	0	1	0	1	0	13	13	5	4	1	3	0
U.S. Service Schools	5	5	5	0	0	0	5	0	. . .	. . .	. . .	. . .	. . .	. . .	. . .
American Samoa	1	1	0	0	0	0	0	1	0	0	0	0	0	0	0
Fed. States of Micronesia	1	1	0	0	0	0	0	1	0	0	0	0	0	0	0
Guam	3	2	1	0	1	0	0	1	1	1	0	0	0	1	0
Marshall Islands	1	1	0	0	0	0	0	1	0	0	0	0	0	0	0
Northern Marianas	1	1	1	0	0	0	1	0	0	0	0	0	0	0	0
Palau	1	1	0	0	0	0	0	1	0	0	0	0	0	0	0
Puerto Rico	75	17	14	1	1	7	5	3	58	44	0	7	19	18	14
Virgin Islands	1	1	1	0	1	0	0	0	0	0	0	0	0	0	0

Source: U.S. Department of Education, National Center for Education Statistics, 2006-07 Integrated Postsecondary Education Data System (IPEDS), Fall 2006. (This table was prepared July 2007.)

Note: Degree-granting institutions grant associate's or higher degrees and participate in Title IV federal financial aid programs. New institutions that do not have sufficient data to report by detailed level are included under "other 4-year" or 2-year, depending on the level reported by the institution.

Key:

. . .— Not applicable.

(a) Doctoral, extensive institutions are committed to graduate education through the doctorate, and award 50 or more doctor's degrees per year across at least 15 disciplines. Doctoral, intensive institutions are committed to education through the doctorate and award at least 10 doctor's degrees per year across 3 or more disciplines or at least 20 doctor's degrees overall.

(b) Master's institutions offer a full range of baccalaureate programs and are committed to education through the master's degree. They award at least 20 master's degrees per year.

(c) Baccalaureate institutions primarily emphasize undergraduate education.

(d) Other specialized 4-year institutions award degrees primarily in single fields of study, such as medicine, business, fine arts, theology and engineering. Includes some institutions which have 4-year programs, but have not reported sufficient data to identify program category. Also, includes institutions classified as 4-year under the IPEDS system, which had been classified as 2-year in the Carnegie classification system because they primarily award associate's degrees.

(e) U.S. totals include the District of Columbia and U.S. Service Schools.

State Safety Net Programs

By Sheila R. Zedlewski

States bear enormous responsibility for administering the nation's safety net programs. They are the first responders when unemployed workers apply for unemployment benefits, food assistance and welfare. The American Recovery and Reinvestment Act of 2009 expanded some safety net support, temporarily filling in some of the benefit gaps.

Safety Net Programs' Response to the Economic Downturn

States administer three key safety net programs designed to shore up income during an economic downturn: Unemployment Insurance, Supplemental Nutrition Assistance (known as SNAP, formerly called food stamps), and Temporary Assistance to Needy Families (called TANF). Unemployment insurance provides temporary benefits to eligible workers who are unemployed through no fault of their own. SNAP provides eligible low-income, low-asset families an electronic benefit card to purchase groceries. TANF provides cash and job search assistance to parents of dependent children with very low incomes and limited resources.

Other aspects of states' safety nets provide essential non-cash services to low-income families. States administer the Medicaid and the State Children's Health Insurance Program (commonly known as SCHIP) that insures more than 50 million people. They staff employment offices that help workers find jobs and sometimes train for new positions. They also help many low-income working families pay for child care. Many states also administer a General Assistance Program that provides cash benefits or vouchers that primarily help adults without children get by in an emergency.[1] All of the services together form a complex system with diverse eligibility rules and administrative structures.[2]

Much attention has focused on the three main income supports in the safety net during this recession. As families lose employment, states struggle to determine benefit eligibility fairly and efficiently and maintain program integrity. The discussion below describes how the primary income support programs have performed during the first year of this severe economic downturn.

Unemployment Insurance

Over the past two decades only about four in 10 unemployed workers received unemployment benefits, and only about two in 10 low-income (income below 200 percent of the federal poverty line) unemployed workers received benefits.[3] Eligibility for unemployment insurance requires workers to have sufficient wages and work hours in the 12-month period before being unemployed. Traditionally the eligibility period excludes the three months immediately before unemployment, although 19 states have recently adopted rules that allow consideration of higher earnings in the most recent three month period.

Workers file claims of eligibility usually through telephone or Internet contact with the state unemployment office. Former employers must verify that the unemployment spell was due to a layoff and not the fault of the worker. Workers that qualify must file weekly or biweekly claims and show evidence of active job search in order to continue benefits.

Most states limit the maximum length of unemployment insurance benefits to 26 weeks. In periods of high unemployment such as the 2008 recession, the federal government typically provides additional weeks of unemployment insurance coverage. During 2008, Congress enacted a 13-week extension in June and a 7-week extension in November (with 13 more weeks for workers in high-unemployment states). These extensions pushed the total weeks of unemployment insurance up to 46 weeks and 59 weeks for workers in high unemployment states.

Workers qualified for $295 per week on average in 2008 (about 70 percent of the federal poverty line for a family of four).[4] The amount is based on prior weekly earnings in covered work subject to a cap that varies by state. Regular unemployment insurance benefits are financed through an employer tax on wages that goes into a trust fund held by the U.S. Treasury. When trust fund balances get low, states must borrow from the federal government to continue paying benefits. While the cost of extended benefits typically is shared equally by states and the federal government, the emergency extended benefits are financed entirely by the federal government.

As the unemployment rate has risen, states have struggled to keep up with claims. Initial unemployment insurance claims across the U.S. increased by

42.3 percent in the 2008 fiscal year (Table A). Claims increased by more than 80 percent in 7 states (Alabama, Arizona, Hawaii, Louisiana, South Dakota, Texas and Utah). Many states saw their unemployment rates climb by 3 to nearly 5 percentage points during 2008.[5] Federal guidelines require timely processing of claims and appeals. This can be a challenging responsibility especially since more than one quarter of applicants has their rights to benefits challenged by former employers.[6]

While unemployment insurance plays an important role in providing safety net protection, it fails to cover the majority of unemployed workers. Many workers do not qualify because they do not meet the base period eligibility requirements due to part-time or short-tenured jobs. Some no longer qualify because their unemployment spells outlasted the period of benefit eligibility. Others do not qualify because they left their job for personal reasons such as the lack of child care, domestic violence or illness or they were fired due to misconduct or unexcused absences from work. Recent legislative proposals would provide incentive payments to states for adopting alternative base periods, compensation to otherwise eligible workers seeking part-time work and to those who leave jobs due to domestic violence, disability or illness of a family member.[7] These ideas are included in the recovery legislation as discussed below.

Supplemental Nutrition Assistance (SNAP/food stamps)[8]

Households with incomes near the poverty line and limited assets can qualify for SNAP. In 2008 the maximum SNAP benefit was an estimated $540 per month for a family of four (30 percent of the federal poverty threshold), providing a significant boost to family income. Over the last several years, many states have modernized their programs by taking advantage of new provisions that allow households to complete their initial eligibility assessment electronically, exclude the value of a vehicle in determining eligibility, and simplify the recertification process.[9] Many states also have reached out to families to explain the program and encourage participation. As a result, SNAP/food stamp participation rates (the number of enrolled households relative to the estimated number of eligible households) have increased from 54 percent to 67 percent between 2002 and 2006.[10]

SNAP caseloads also have increased as the economy deteriorated and more families qualified for new or higher benefits. At the end of the 2008 fiscal year, 12.7 million households received SNAP, an 8 percent increase since the 2007 fiscal year (Table A). Enrollment trends varied across the states. For example, Arizona, Florida, Louisiana and Nevada saw caseloads increase at double the national rate.

The federal government pays for all SNAP benefits and one-half the cost of administering the program. Several studies show that SNAP benefits stimulate states' economies, generating about $1.7 in economic activity for each $1 in benefits.[11]

States will have a difficult time keeping up with the demand for SNAP benefits as the recession continues. SNAP benefits are an entitlement for U.S. citizens and many legal immigrants except that benefits for able-bodied adults without dependents are time limited unless they live in high unemployment states awarded waivers from this provision. Caseloads likely will continue to grow as the recession continues. Some families will remain with low incomes and benefit eligibility for longer periods of time, more families will become eligible for benefits as they lose their jobs, and more may choose to participate as they see few other alternatives. Administrative systems will be challenged to process new applications, review recertifications and maintain the integrity of the program.

Temporary Assistance for Needy Families (TANF)

Reforms to welfare enacted in the mid-1990s have significantly curtailed the role that TANF has played in this recession so far. Reforms eliminated the individual entitlement to welfare and require states to meet strict work-participation rates for their caseloads. Despite the significant increase in unemployment, TANF caseloads declined by 3.4 percent between 2007 and 2008 (Table A). Individual state experiences varied. For example, TANF caseloads declined by 20 percent or more in Colorado, Illinois and Oklahoma and increased in 11 states (California, Delaware, Florida, Hawaii, Maryland, Massachusetts, Nevada, Ohio, Oregon, Washington and Wisconsin).

The variation in state caseload experience reflects diversity in state economies as well as state TANF policies. Some of the states with caseload increases experienced substantial increases in unemployment. (For example, unemployment rose by more than 3 percentage points in California, Florida and Nevada, three of the states with caseload increases.) However, the unemployment rate in Massachusetts, the state with the largest caseload increase, rose by just 2.6 percentage points. TANF policies that can also affect caseload trends include time limits, sanction and diversion policies. All else equal, states without time limits will see more upward pressure on caseloads when families find it more difficult to leave the rolls for employment.

It is likely that TANF caseloads will increase overall in 2009 or later if the recession deepens, and more families lose jobs and remain unemployed for an extended period of time. While the maximum TANF benefit for a family of three averaged only around $430 per month in 2008 (30 percent of the federal poverty threshold), many families affected by the recession will have no other source of cash income. (As noted earlier, only one in five low-income unemployed families qualified for unemployment insurance benefits in 2006.) Increased caseloads likely will strain state TANF programs. The program is funded through a fixed block grant from the federal government and maintenance of effort money from the state. TANF has a $2 billion contingency fund that states can tap into when unemployment is high, but the fund requires states to pay for one-half the cost of additional benefits. When state budgets are strained, it can be difficult if not impossible to meet this requirement.

States will face some difficult choices in their TANF programs. TANF rules designed to increase work such as earned income disregards and diversion policies that require up-front job search before enrollment are unlikely to bear fruit when unemployment is rising. Most parents that turn to welfare for assistance have multiple barriers to work such as mental and physical health disabilities, limited work experience and limited educations.[12] These individuals have a difficult time finding work when the economy is strong and likely will find a tougher road ahead. States may need to shift a larger share of TANF resources to cash assistance and away from social services for low-income families.

The American Recovery and Reinvestment Act of 2009 Increases Supports

The 2009 economic stimulus package enacted some significant expansions of these safety net programs. The expansions took effect in February 2009 and will phase out by the end of 2010. The expansions increase the administrative burden on state programs at least in the short term. Some of the benefit expansions are accompanied by additional administrative funds for the states.

This package extended the unemployment insurance emergency benefit program through Dec. 31, 2009. The emergency program, enacted in 2008 and discussed above, provides up to 33 weeks of extended unemployment benefits to workers exhausting their regular benefits. The bill also increases weekly unemployment benefits by $25 through 2009. The recovery legislation also offers one-time grants to encourage states to enact reforms that would increase unemployment insurance coverage among low-wage, part time and other jobless workers. As discussed earlier, such provisions would increase the share of unemployed workers that could qualify for benefits. The provisions would need to be financed in the longer run, presumably through an increase in the employer wage tax. The legislation includes $500 million to help states to offset the cost of administrating program expansions.

The ARRA provides a one-time increase in SNAP benefits of about 13.6 percent, and the increase phases out over two years. It also suspends time limits on eligibility for jobless adults without dependents through the 2010 fiscal year. The legislation also includes about $290 million for increases in states' administrative costs. These funds will be distributed based on relative caseload size and increases over the prior 12 months.

The economic recovery legislation also creates a temporary TANF Emergency Contingency Fund through the 2010 fiscal year capped at $5 billion.[13] The additional funds will go to states with increased costs for basic assistance, expanded subsidized employment programs, and short-term, non-recurrent aid to families. States with increased costs in these areas (relative to 2007 and 2008) will receive federal funding to cover 80 percent of the increase in expenditures. States must pay the other 20 percent by increasing their own spending or by cutting TANF-related funding from other areas such as child care. Also, recovery legislation prevents states' work participation rates from increasing during the recession.

Conclusions and Implications

States' safety nets will be challenged as the recession continues. State caseworkers will be delivering benefits to more families and for longer periods of time. States will need to finance some of the increased costs using their own funds. State economies, however, benefit when unemployed families have enough money to pay for the basics. Unemployed workers that qualify for unemployment insurance have a better chance to get by, especially if they enroll in SNAP to augment their unemployment benefit. Unemployed workers that do not qualify for unemployment insurance face a much more difficult challenge. Some will be eligible for TANF cash assistance but benefits are much lower than unemployment insurance.

The economic recovery legislation will help states

Table A: Trends in State Safety Net Caseloads

State or other jurisdiction	*Unemployment insurance—first payments* Oct. 2008	Percent change from Oct. 2007	*SNAP households (a)* FY2008	Percent change from FY2007	*TANF families (b)* FY2008	Percent change from FY2007
U.S. Totals	821,240	42.3%	12,728,248	8.0%	1,702,810	-3.4%
Alabama	12,815	80.9	231,740	4.9	17,736	-3.9
Alaska	1,992	-41.0	21,976	3.1	3,058	-5.8
Arizona	11,943	83.8	258,517	16.3	36,249	0.0
Arkansas	12,224	56.1	157,871	-0.1	8,513	-1.0
California	119,823	45.2	914,161	10.5	486,066	3.0
Colorado	8,315	60.0	109,405	2.3	8,816	-19.7
Connecticut	11,713	51.7	120,573	6.5	19,091	-8.7
Delaware	2,479	38.8	32,512	11.7	4,372	6.2
Florida	53,291	57.8	745,847	18.8	48,702	1.8
Georgia	30,452	61.9	417,427	7.8	22,158	-10.9
Hawaii	3,915	98.8	48,824	7.6	6,452	1.6
Idaho	4,570	59.5	40,835	13.5	1,492	-7.8
Illinois	31,947	13.9	595,832	4.7	19,846	-34.7
Indiana	18,354	14.8	267,802	5.5	41,047	-1.1
Iowa	7,220	36.1	116,899	8.1	19,059	-5.0
Kansas	5,887	34.5	85,784	3.5	12,496	-15.3
Kentucky	11,778	19.8	283,752	6.4	29,144	-3.1
Louisiana	10,350	83.4	324,887	22.1	10,465	-4.8
Maine	2,412	34.4	86,459	5.7	12,311	-2.1
Maryland	12,066	44.4	167,174	13.6	19,994	2.3
Massachusetts	18,397	35.6	266,430	11.1	56,621	25.6
Michigan	36,231	29.3	590,930	6.3	66,554	-9.1
Minnesota	9,505	33.5	140,423	6.6	23,057	-13.1
Mississippi	5,736	39.1	188,498	5.4	11,268	-2.9
Missouri	12,372	20.3	314,012	4.2	37,607	-5.0
Montana	2,115	49.2	35,494	1.9	3,122	-2.2
Nebraska	2,661	28.0	52,082	0.5	7,548	-1.2
Nevada	11,402	64.2	67,380	18.2	7,194	7.3
New Hampshire	2,469	50.2	31,244	8.3	4,463	-13.4
New Jersey	29,554	28.5	210,867	6.1	33,468	-4.6
New Mexico	3,113	41.6	95,769	4.0	12,983	-7.8
New York	42,399	29.1	1,036,676	8.9	153,817	-3.8
North Carolina	29,865	59.4	419,127	7.2	24,124	-6.8
North Dakota	424	28.9	21,825	7.0	2,023	-3.1
Ohio	24,537	31.6	526,800	6.9	80,796	3.1
Oklahoma	4,432	46.1	176,483	0.1	8,198	-55.9
Oregon	15,963	39.6	243,257	7.4	20,536	10.5
Pennsylvania	41,490	34.3	558,939	5.4	52,102	-18.5
Rhode Island	2,915	18.0	41,548	13.4	8,310	-1.3
South Carolina	14,147	44.5	255,702	9.6	14,933	-3.8
South Dakota	516	86.3	26,189	5.8	2,848	-1.1
Tennessee	15,594	51.9	410,458	5.9	53,831	-13.6
Texas	49,260	95.5	994,786	5.0	53,536	-14.5
Utah	3,665	82.5	53,715	5.8	5,025	-4.1
Vermont	1,648	50.5	27,642	6.1	3,620	-18.8
Virginia	12,228	51.0	5,036	5.8	31,141	-1.7
Washington	18,955	53.3	292,515	7.3	52,759	2.6
West Virginia	2,704	10.0	124,183	3.4	8,681	-11.7
Wisconsin	20,084	24.3	180,792	11.5	17,656	1.6
Wyoming	972	49.5	9,564	0.7	266	-1.4
Dist. of Columbia	1,842	25.0	47,721	5.7	5,375	-13.0

Source: TANF caseload data are from the Department of Health and Human Services, DHHS (*http://www.acf.hhs.gov/programs/ofa/data-reports/caseload/caseload_current.htm*). SNAP caseload data are from Food and Nutrition Service (*http://www.fns.usda.gov/pd/snapmain.htm*). The Unemployment Insurance First Payments data are from Employpment and Training Administration (*http://workforcesecurity.doleta.gov/unemploy/finance.asp*).

Key:
(a) SNAP caseloads are the average monthly number of households participating in the Food Stamps/SNAP Program.
(b) TANF caseloads are the average monthly number of families receiving assistance under the TANF program and the State Separate Programs (SSP-MOE).

by extending unemployment insurance benefits, increasing SNAP, and offering additional TANF dollars. States still will need to help families find new jobs. Their employment service offices are likely to be stretched to their limits. Those states that benefit from new infrastructure investments in the recovery legislation should be able to direct some of the unemployed into the newly created jobs. However, many unemployed workers, especially those that turn to TANF assistance, will not have the skills required for these jobs. It will be important for states to offer education and training services to more unemployed adults, and the recovery legislation offers states more money to train dislocated workers for jobs in high growth and emerging industry sectors. In the most optimistic scenario, many low-wage workers that experience unemployment will emerge with new skills and good prospects for employment in the longer run.

Notes

[1]In 2006 (the latest data available), 25 states had General Assistance Programs that provided cash payments to disabled, elderly and unemployable individuals and 7 other states provided vouchers to pay for some basic needs. Some states also provide GA to families with children that do not qualify for other assistance; a handful provides assistance to able-bodied adults without children. See Sheila Zedlewski and Brendan Hill, Urban Institute unpublished memorandum dated December 21, 2006.

[2]Sheila Zedlewski, Gina Adams, Lisa Dubay and Genevieve Kenney provide a discussion of the organization of safety net programs, including their incentives and behavioral effects in "Is There a System Supporting Low-Income Working Families?" (Washington, D.C.: The Urban Institute, February 2006).

[3]See Margaret Simms and Daniel Kuehn, "Unemployment Insurance during a Recession," (Washington, D.C.: The Urban Institute, December 2008).

[4]The National Employment Law Center (NELP), "Responding to Recession: Strengthen State UI Programs (January 2009).

[5]"Regional and State Employment and Unemployment," Bureau of Labor Statistics, *www.bls.gov/news.release/laus.nr0.htm*.

[6]Commentary from Wayne Vroman, the Urban Institute in "More Employers Fighting Unemployment Benefits," *The Washington Post*, February 12, 2009.

[7]See Margaret Simms, "Weathering Job Loss," The New Safety Net (July 2008), Washington, D.C.: The Urban Institute for a summary of these provisions.

[8]The 2008 Farm Bill changed the name of the Food Stamp Program to the Supplemental Nutrition Assistance Program (SNAP) to reduce the stigma associated with the former program.

[9]See Kenneth Finegold, "Food Stamps, Federalism and Working Families," Perspectives on Low-Income Working Families," (Washington, D.C.: The Urban Institute, September 2008).

[10]See "Reaching Those in Need: State Food Stamp Participation Rates in 2006," Office of Research and Analysis, (Washington, D.C.: USDA, November 2008).

[11]See Mark Zandi, "The Economic Impact of the American Recovery and Reinvestment Act," Moody's Economy.com, January 21, 2009.

[12]Pamela Loprest and Sheila Zedlewski report that 80 percent of TANF parents had at least one barrier to work in 2002 in The Changing Role of Welfare in the Lives of Low-Income Families with Children, Assessing the New Federalism Occasional Paper Number 73, (Washington, D.C.: The Urban Institute, August 2006).

[13]While the appropriation is capped at $5 billion total for two years, the Congressional Budget Office (CBO) estimates that this amount is double what states will draw down. Sharon Parrott and Liz Schott provide an overview of the TANF provisions in the Economic Recovery Act in "Overview of the TANF Provisions in the Economic Recovery Act" (Washington, D.C.: Center on Budget and Policy Priorities, February 2009).

About the Author

Sheila Zedlewski is the director of the Income and Benefits Policy Center at the Urban Institute, a nonpartisan think tank in Washington, D.C. Her recent work focuses on improvements to safety net programs and poverty measurement. She has written extensively about the TANF program with a focus on families unable to move from welfare to work.

Table 9.10
HEALTH INSURANCE COVERAGE STATUS BY STATE FOR ALL PEOPLE, BY REGION: 2007
(In thousands)

State or other jurisdiction	Total	*Covered and not covered by health insurance during the year*			
		Covered	*Percent*	*Not covered*	*Percent*
United States	299,106	253,449	84.7	45,657	15.3
Eastern Region					
Connecticut	3,476	3,150	90.6	326	9.4
Delaware	863	3,150	90.6	326	9.4
Maine	1,313	1,197	91.2	115	8.8
Massachusetts	6,340	6,000	94.6	340	5.4
New Hampshire	1,314	1,177	89.5	137	10.5
New Jersey	8,556	7,208	84.2	1,348	15.8
New York	19,062	16,543	86.8	2,519	13.2
Pennsylvania	12,313	11,138	90.5	1,176	9.5
Rhode Island	1,044	931	89.2	113	10.8
Vermont	614	545	88.8	69	(a)
Regional total	54,895	51,039	88.3	6,469	11.7
Midwestern Region					
Illinois	12,688	10,988	86.6	1,700	13.4
Indiana	6,263	5,546	88.6	717	11.4
Iowa	2,970	2,695	90.7	275	9.3
Kansas	2,722	2,376	87.3	345	12.7
Michigan	9,927	8,776	88.4	1,151	11.6
Minnesota	5,190	4,758	91.7	433	8.3
Nebraska	1,753	1,522	86.8	232	13.2
North Dakota	615	553	90.0	61	(a)
Ohio	11,300	9,979	88.3	1,322	11.7
South Dakota	788	708	89.9	80	10.1
Wisconsin	5,473	5,023	91.8	451	8.2
Regional total	59,689	52,924	88.6	6,767	11.4
Southern Region					
Alabama	4,570	4,021	88.0	549	12.0
Arkansas	2,805	2,354	83.9	451	16.1
Florida	18,074	14,426	79.8	3,648	20.2
Georgia	9,493	7,831	82.5	1,662	17.5
Kentucky	4,207	3,637	86.4	570	13.6
Louisiana	4,197	3,421	81.5	776	18.5
Maryland	5,565	4,804	86.3	762	13.7
Mississippi	2,903	2,358	81.2	545	18.8
Missouri	5,791	5,062	87.4	729	12.6
North Carolina	9,183	7,673	83.6	1,510	16.4
Oklahoma	3,551	2,920	82.2	631	17.8
South Carolina	4,384	3,664	83.6	721	16.4
Tennessee	6,150	5,268	85.6	883	14.4
Texas	23,704	17,742	74.8	5,962	25.2
Virginia	7,684	6,548	85.2	1,135	14.8
West Virginia	1,795	1,541	85.9	254	14.1
Regional total	114,056	93,270	81.7	20,778	18.2
Western Region					
Alaska	675	552	81.8	123	18.2
Arizona	6,368	5,204	81.7	1,164	18.3
California	36,295	29,682	81.8	6,613	18.2
Colorado	4,877	4,077	83.6	801	16.4
Hawaii	1,267	1,172	92.5	96	7.5
Idaho	1,501	1,292	86.1	209	13.9
Montana	939	793	84.4	146	15.6
Nevada	2,568	2,126	82.8	441	17.2
New Mexico	1,946	1,509	77.5	437	22.5
Oregon	3,762	3,130	83.2	632	16.8
Utah	2,657	2,317	87.2	340	12.8
Washington	6,509	5,773	88.7	737	11.3
Wyoming	518	447	86.4	770	(a)
Regional total	69,882	58,074	83.1	12,509	17.9
Regional total without California	33,587	28,392	84.5	5,896	17.5
Dist. of Columbia	582	526	90.5	55	(a)

Source: U.S. Census Bureau, Current Population Survey, 2008 Annual Social and Economic Supplement. URL: *http://pubdb3.census.gov/macro/032008/health/h06_000.htm*. Revised August 2008. A joint effort between the Bureau of Labor Statistics and the Census Bureau.

Note: Unrelated individuals under 15 are included.

Key:

(a) Base less than 75,000.

Table 9.11
NUMBER AND PERCENT OF CHILDREN UNDER 19 YEARS OF AGE, AT OR BELOW 200 PERCENT OF POVERTY, BY HEALTH INSURANCE COVERAGE, STATE AND REGION: 2007
(In thousands)

State or other jurisdiction	Total children under 19 years, all income levels	At or below 200 percent of poverty		Health insurance coverage: With		Without	
		Number	Percent	Number	Percent	Number	Percent
United States	78,245	30,452	38.9	25,023	32	5,430	6.9
Eastern Region							
Connecticut	878	234	26.6	213	24.2	21	(a)
Delaware	219	71	(a)	60	(a)	11	(a)
Maine	297	99	33.3	92	31.0	7	(a)
Massachusetts	1,516	480	31.6	463	30.6	17	(a)
New Hampshire	316	54	(a)	46	(a)	8	(a)
New Jersey	2,204	614	27.9	441	20.0	173	7.9
New York	4,681	1,924	41.1	1,678	35.8	247	5.3
Pennsylvania	2,897	1,032	35.6	880	30.4	152	5.2
Rhode Island	250	88	35.2	74	(a)	14	(a)
Vermont	133	45	(a)	38	(a)	7	(a)
Regional total	13,391	4,641	34.6	3,985	29.7	657	4.9
Midwestern Region							
Illinois	3,366	1,205	35.8	1,066	31.7	138	4.1
Indiana	1,692	641	37.9	586	34.6	55	(a)
Iowa	743	218	29.3	196	26.4	21	(a)
Kansas	747	295	39.6	257	34.4	39	(a)
Michigan	2,555	959	37.5	871	34.1	88	3.5
Minnesota	1,320	386	29.2	335	25.4	50	(a)
Nebraska	472	143	30.2	116	24.5	27	(a)
North Dakota	155	56	(a)	46	(a)	10	(a)
Ohio	2,940	1,109	37.7	947	32.2	162	5.5
South Dakota	207	67	(a)	60	(a)	7	(a)
Wisconsin	1,391	428	30.8	393	28.3	35	(a)
Regional total	15,588	5,507	35.3	4,873	31.3	632	4.0
Southern Region							
Alabama	1,189	499	42.0	446	37.5	53	(a)
Arkansas	755	391	51.9	360	47.7	31	(a)
Florida	4,298	1,716	39.9	1,175	27.3	541	12.6
Georgia	2,638	1,089	41.3	874	33.1	216	8.2
Kentucky	1,067	470	44.1	404	37.9	66	(a)
Louisiana	1,156	497	43.0	407	35.2	89	7.7
Maryland	1,455	356	24.5	273	18.8	83	5.7
Mississippi	814	435	53.4	353	43.4	82	10.1
Missouri	1,504	630	41.9	534	35.5	96	6.4
North Carolina	2,358	1009	42.8	800	33.9	210	8.9
Oklahoma	982	443	45.1	378	38.5	65	(a)
South Carolina	1,130	491	43.5	379	33.5	112	10.0
Tennessee	1,542	704	45.6	629	40.8	75	(a)
Texas	7,008	3,271	46.7	2,308	32.9	963	13.7
Virginia	1,950	648	33.2	536	27.5	112	5.7
West Virginia	421	193	45.9	183	43.5	10	(a)
Regional total	30,267	12,842	42.4	10,039	33.2	2,804	9.2
Western Region							
Alaska	195	50	(a)	40	(a)	10	(a)
Arizona	1,785	814	45.6	641	35.9	173	9.7
California	9,902	4,153	41.9	3,454	34.9	700	7.1
Colorado	1,252	372	29.7	263	21	109	8.7
Hawaii	301	90	29.9	84	27.8	6	(a)
Idaho	440	169	38.4	141	32.1	28	(a)
Montana	231	97	42.1	82	35.6	15	(a)
Nevada	697	257	36.9	192	27.5	65	(a)
New Mexico	518	214	41.3	169	32.6	45	(a)
Oregon	913	335	36.7	277	30.3	58	(a)
Utah	877	300	34.2	243	27.7	57	(a)
Washington	1,637	508	31.0	449	27.4	59	(a)
Wyoming	134	43	(a)	36	(a)	7	(b
Regional total	18,882	7,402	39.2	6,071	32.1	1,332	7.1
Regional total without California	8,980	3,249	36.2	2,617	29.1	632	7.0
Dist. of Columbia	118	60	(a)	55	(a)	5	(a)

Source: U.S. Census Bureau, Current Population Survey, 2008 Annual Social and Economic Supplement. URL: *http://pubdb3.census.gov/macro/032008/health/h10_000.htm*. Revised August 2008. A joint effort between the Bureau of Labor Statistics and the Census Bureau.

Key:

(a) Base less than 75,000.

State Economic Development Efforts during Extreme Fiscal Stress

By Sujit M. CanagaRetna

As states prepared for their 2009 legislative sessions, policymakers faced a series of grave economic crises on multiple fronts not experienced in many decades. States face enormous budget shortfalls with the combined budget shortfall for the remaining six months of this year (fiscal year 2009) and the two upcoming fiscal years estimated to total between $350 billion and $370 billion, a chasm of truly staggering proportions. Nevertheless, in the midst of all this gloom and doom, there are a number of bright sparks on the state economic landscape that require emphasis. For instance, the depreciating U.S. dollar has enabled U.S. exports to flourish, the automobile industry in the South remains a solid engine of growth and a number of enterprising projects across the country offer the promise of high-tech, high-wage jobs.

As states prepared for their 2009 legislative sessions, policymakers faced a series of grave, multifaceted economic crises not experienced in many decades. The crux of the nation's economic woes may be traced to a crisis in the housing sector, which in turn, has metastasized to create a crisis in economic output with the vastly diminished production in the U.S. economy. The reduced economic output, with a record number of businesses declaring bankruptcy or reporting significantly lower revenue numbers, has resulted in a revenue crisis that has battered American consumers, corporations and every level of government. Dwindling output levels have also caused unemployment rates to soar to heights not experienced in three decades. The faltering revenue picture, in turn, has strangled credit availability, the lifeblood of the economy, choking off most economic growth opportunities for both consumers and businesses. Finally, this unholy alliance of events has acted in concert to almost asphyxiate consumer confidence and create a crisis in confidence, which in turn, resulted in the wild gyrations and huge losses in the nation's three major stock markets. For the 2008 calendar year, the Dow Jones industrial average lost 34 percent of its value, making 2008 the worst year for the index since 1931; the broader Standard & Poor's 500 stock index lost more than 38 percent; and the technology-laden Nasdaq composite index posted its worst year ever, with a nearly 41 percent drop.[1] Consequently, when the National Bureau of Economic Research declared in early December 2008 that the economy had sunk into a recession some 12 months before, in December 2007, it only confirmed what many Americans had already come to realize.[2]

Even before the September 2008 tumult on Wall Street precipitated the catastrophic collapse of the U.S. economy, states were already looking at a very depressed financial picture. In fact, the dawn of fiscal year 2008—July 1, 2007—signaled what the National Association of State Budget Officers called "a turning point for state finances with a significant increase in states seeing fiscal difficulties, in stark contrast to the preceding several years."[3] Consequently, when most states began their legislative sessions in January 2008, the ongoing national economic fissures had already started percolating across their economies. A few states were insulated from budget difficulties in the first half of 2008 because of their ability to take advantage of high energy and agricultural commodity prices and minimal exposure to declines in their housing stock. By the second half of the fiscal year, however, the weakening national economy had affected every state in the country. In fact, at least 29 states, including several of the nation's largest, were forced to bridge an estimated $48 billion in combined shortfalls in their budgets for the fiscal year 2009 that began July 1, 2008.[4] By late December 2008, at least 44 states faced or will face shortfalls in their budgets for this and/or the next two fiscal years (fiscal years 2010 and 2011).[5] Combined budget shortfalls for the remaining six months of the 2009 fiscal year and the two upcoming fiscal years are estimated to total between $350 billion and $370 billion, a chasm of truly monumental proportions for states, far exceeding the cumulative shortfalls experienced during the last recession, in 2001.

In a fiscal environment that portends to be the worst in decades—by December 2008, the duration

Table A
Record of U.S. Dollar vs. Euro: April 1998 to April 2008

Year	*Value of one Euro to one dollar*	*Percentage change in dollar*
April 8, 1998	1.0882	. . .
April 7, 1999	1.0835	0
April 7, 2000	0.959003	11
April 9, 2001	0.901404	6
April 8, 2002	0.874998	3
April 8, 2003	1.0684	-22
April 8, 2004	1.2088	-13
April 7, 2005	1.29231	-7
April 7, 2006	1.2109	6
April 9, 2007	1.3367	-10
April 8, 2008	1.5705	-17

Source: http://www.x-rates.com/cgi-bin/hloopup.cgi.

of the current recession had already surpassed the average length of all the post World War II recessions—what does the state economic development landscape look like? Even though states face intense fiscal stress and looming expenditure categories in such areas as education, health care, pensions, infrastructure, unemployment insurance, transportation and emergency management, there are economic development success stories with the potential to generate and sustain jobs and revenue. Despite the gloomy winds that have blown across the state economic landscape, there are a number of exciting new ventures that require highlighting.[6] It should also be mentioned that states have high expectations the $787 billion economic stimulus package approved by Congress[7] will not only mitigate some of the current and potential job losses in the states but will also upgrade the nation's infrastructure system and, most importantly, revitalize the economic prospects of so many moribund areas of the country. In addition, a number of states—including California, Florida, North Carolina, Ohio and Vermont—embarked on their own set of infrastructure projects as early as mid-2008, considerably ahead of the federal initiatives to set the stage for sustained economic growth.

A bright spot in the dour economic landscape of the past few years has been the nation's export sector. Not only did exports increase twice as fast as imports in 2007, narrowing the U.S. trade deficit for the first time since 1995, the increased level of trade kept the economy afloat. The impetus for the blossoming export sector has been the depreciating U.S. dollar; a depreciating dollar makes U.S. exports much more competitive against exports from other countries. On a year-to-year basis for the past seven years or so, the U.S. dollar has depreciated steadily, thus providing a sizable boost not only to American exports but also in attracting foreign direct investment into the country. Buying or investing in America becomes relatively less expensive compared to times when the dollar's value is rising. As evidenced in Table A, the dollar depreciated by 79 percent between 2002 and 2008 and by 53 percent between 2002 and 2007. Further illustration of the eroding value of the dollar: In April 2001, 90 U.S. cents were sufficient to purchase a single Euro; by April 2008, it took $1.57 to purchase a single Euro. (It should be noted that in the final half of 2008, the U.S. dollar did appreciate relative to the other major currencies.)

The depreciating dollar had a hugely positive impact on U.S. exports. (See Table B for export information for all 50 states, the District of Columbia, Puerto Rico and the Virgin Islands.) Between 2002 and 2007, U.S. exports soared by nearly 68 percent with the export record in 2006 registering an impressive 15 percent growth over the previous year, the highest level for the six-year review period. In 2007, total U.S. exports amounted to $1.2 trillion, with Texas' $168.2 billion and California's $134.2 billion leading the way. Texas' top three export markets in 2007 were Mexico, Canada and China; for California, the top export markets were Mexico, Canada and Japan. In 2007, Texas' top three export items were chemical manufactures, computers and electronic products, and machinery manufactures, while California's top three export products were computers and electronic products, machinery manufactures, and transportation equipment. From 2002 to 2007, eight states and the Virgin Islands secured triple-digit growth rates, with Nevada (385 percent) reaching the top spot. Forty-one other states experienced double-digit growth rates, while Hawaii recorded a single-digit growth rate. In 2007, 30 states, along with the Virgin Islands and Puerto Rico, secured double-digit growth rates with North Dakota (35 percent) secur-

Table B
U.S. Exports of All Merchandise to World (Ordered by Value in 2007)

State or other jurisdiction	2002	2003	Yearly change	2004	Yearly change
U.S. Total	$693,257,299,708	$723,743,176,992	4.40%	$817,935,848,814	13.01%
Texas	95,396,196,650	98,846,082,565	3.62	117,244,970,494	18.61
California	92,214,291,621	93,994,882,282	1.93	109,967,840,247	16.99
New York	36,976,801,261	39,180,708,413	5.96	44,400,728,905	13.32
Washington	34,626,548,518	34,172,826,419	-1.31	33,792,503,705	-1.11
Illinois	25,686,413,863	26,472,902,154	3.06	30,213,626,405	14.13
Florida	24,544,204,050	24,953,413,564	1.67	28,981,515,202	16.14
Michigan	33,775,231,735	32,941,108,751	-2.47	35,625,007,725	8.15
Ohio	27,723,272,950	29,764,417,806	7.36	31,208,205,664	4.85
New Jersey	17,001,514,036	16,817,673,499	-1.08	19,192,130,841	14.12
Louisiana	17,566,658,462	18,390,130,016	4.69	19,922,345,769	8.33
Pennsylvania	15,767,793,573	16,299,211,662	3.37	18,487,253,385	13.42
Indiana	14,923,048,754	16,402,279,302	9.91	19,109,378,037	16.50
Massachusetts	16,707,593,003	18,662,575,189	11.70	21,837,411,438	17.01
North Carolina	14,718,504,679	16,198,733,368	10.06	18,114,767,389	11.83
Georgia	14,412,699,643	16,286,235,334	13.00	19,632,738,011	20.55
Tennessee	11,621,338,991	12,611,793,044	8.52	16,122,874,281	27.84
Kentucky	10,606,719,719	10,733,781,152	1.20	12,991,976,559	21.04
Wisconsin	10,684,271,079	11,509,835,058	7.73	12,706,343,147	10.40
Arizona	11,871,004,413	13,323,391,617	12.23	13,422,913,020	0.75
Puerto Rico	9,732,152,738	11,913,947,353	22.42	13,161,777,599	10.47
Minnesota	10,402,161,848	11,265,660,034	8.30	12,677,805,391	12.53
Virginia	10,795,528,315	10,852,980,547	0.53	11,630,743,511	7.17
South Carolina	9,656,247,356	11,772,894,482	21.92	13,375,889,564	13.62
Oregon	10,086,397,279	10,357,198,654	2.68	11,171,751,146	7.86
Alabama	8,266,884,455	8,340,387,183	0.89	9,036,640,599	8.35
Connecticut	8,313,390,369	8,136,442,912	-2.13	8,559,237,269	5.20
Missouri	6,790,778,019	7,233,937,387	6.53	8,997,288,404	24.38
Kansas	4,988,409,666	4,553,333,594	-8.72	4,930,773,941	8.29
Iowa	4,754,600,372	5,236,296,462	10.13	6,393,941,204	22.11
Maryland	4,473,575,879	4,940,630,648	10.44	5,746,142,322	16.30
Utah	4,542,724,908	4,114,540,443	-9.43	4,718,349,700	14.68
Colorado	5,521,684,934	6,109,121,348	10.64	6,650,998,549	8.87
Nevada	1,176,998,664	2,032,599,448	72.69	2,906,689,276	43.00
Mississippi	3,058,007,811	2,558,258,802	-16.34	3,179,373,553	24.28
Arkansas	2,803,644,920	2,962,152,830	5.65	3,493,133,417	17.93
Idaho	1,966,982,060	2,095,799,109	6.55	2,914,603,665	39.07
Oklahoma	2,443,577,842	2,659,603,110	8.84	3,177,874,248	19.49
Nebraska	2,527,632,208	2,723,669,948	7.76	2,316,114,025	-14.96
Delaware	2,003,814,025	1,886,118,089	-5.87	2,053,422,775	8.87
West Virginia	2,237,153,729	2,379,808,458	6.38	3,261,683,269	37.06
Alaska	2,516,219,755	2,738,557,708	8.84	3,156,910,610	15.28
Vermont	2,520,954,929	2,626,921,728	4.20	3,283,134,669	24.98
New Hampshire	1,863,287,991	1,931,411,721	3.66	2,285,589,133	18.34
Maine	1,973,060,885	2,188,413,025	10.91	2,432,218,855	11.14
New Mexico	1,196,144,288	2,325,609,448	94.43	2,045,805,871	-12.03
North Dakota	859,383,042	854,071,596	-0.62	1,007,926,753	18.01
Rhode Island	1,121,004,971	1,177,475,183	5.04	1,286,323,872	9.24
South Dakota	596,785,049	672,268,365	12.65	825,510,470	22.79
Montana	385,734,573	361,416,280	-6.30	564,690,618	56.24
Dist. of Columbia	1,065,873,322	809,220,172	-24.08	1,164,327,394	43.88
Wyoming	553,360,838	581,636,145	5.11	680,239,445	16.95
Virgin Islands	257,770,249	252,719,412	-1.96	389,407,492	54.09
Hawaii	513,650,873	368,226,673	-28.31	404,773,734	9.93
Unallocated	34,467,614,546	35,167,867,500	2.03	35,080,226,247	-0.25

See footnotes at end of table.

U.S. Exports of All Merchandise to World (Ordered by Value in 2007)—Continued

State or other jurisdiction	2005	Yearly change	2006	Yearly change	2007	Yearly change	Change: 2002–07
U.S. Total	$904,379,818,171	10.57%	$1,037,142,972,794	14.68%	$1,162,708,293,437	12.11%	67.72%
Texas	128,761,036,151	9.82	150,888,054,964	17.18	168,164,440,482	11.45	76.28
California	116,818,585,165	6.23	127,746,135,340	9.35	134,151,760,591	5.01	45.48
New York	50,492,176,404	13.72	57,369,299,166	13.62	69,333,647,127	20.85	87.51
Washington	37,948,360,874	12.30	53,074,909,007	39.86	66,258,480,342	24.84	91.35
Illinois	35,868,406,183	18.72	42,084,595,133	17.33	48,730,156,421	15.79	89.71
Florida	33,377,054,012	15.17	38,544,528,174	15.45	44,831,678,558	16.31	82.66
Michigan	37,584,052,274	5.50	40,405,378,487	7.51	44,371,424,346	9.82	31.37
Ohio	34,800,926,215	11.51	37,832,693,465	8.71	42,381,591,441	12.02	52.87
New Jersey	21,080,304,895	9.84	27,001,734,586	28.09	30,462,503,875	12.82	79.18
Louisiana	19,231,807,078	-3.47	23,503,359,105	22.21	30,374,690,456	29.24	72.91
Pennsylvania	22,270,841,318	20.47	26,333,930,898	18.24	29,126,894,132	10.61	84.72
Indiana	21,475,917,893	12.38	22,619,712,238	5.33	25,877,845,066	14.40	73.41
Massachusetts	22,042,806,091	0.94	24,047,035,294	9.09	25,285,006,276	5.15	51.34
North Carolina	19,463,348,583	7.44	21,218,226,522	9.02	23,346,792,842	10.03	58.62
Georgia	20,576,630,980	4.81	20,073,302,703	-2.45	23,342,329,363	16.29	61.96
Tennessee	19,069,849,639	18.28	22,019,725,551	15.47	21,814,580,482	-0.93	87.71
Kentucky	14,899,031,549	14.68	17,232,213,488	15.66	19,616,269,672	13.83	84.94
Wisconsin	14,923,486,505	17.45	17,169,113,077	15.05	19,185,669,961	11.75	79.57
Arizona	14,949,570,212	11.37	18,287,397,929	22.33	19,185,647,072	4.91	61.62
Puerto Rico	13,264,030,883	0.78	15,195,567,625	14.56	18,062,965,035	18.87	85.60
Minnesota	14,704,521,649	15.99	16,309,306,307	10.91	17,993,363,745	10.33	72.98
Virginia	12,215,566,619	5.03	14,103,999,655	15.46	16,884,684,739	19.72	56.40
South Carolina	13,943,964,664	4.25	13,615,040,574	-2.36	16,560,187,099	21.63	71.50
Oregon	12,380,658,350	10.82	15,288,284,418	23.49	16,515,409,603	8.03	63.74
Alabama	10,795,768,491	19.47	13,877,619,708	28.55	14,421,058,275	3.92	74.44
Connecticut	9,687,291,825	13.18	12,238,324,203	26.33	13,719,049,174	12.10	65.02
Missouri	10,462,295,740	16.28	12,775,705,710	22.11	13,416,806,856	5.02	97.57
Kansas	6,720,074,709	36.29	8,625,552,641	28.36	10,246,052,895	18.79	105.40
Iowa	7,347,677,812	14.92	8,409,956,822	14.46	9,614,139,024	14.32	102.21
Maryland	7,119,176,536	23.89	7,597,859,751	6.72	8,945,517,915	17.74	99.96
Utah	6,055,863,467	28.35	6,798,091,878	12.26	7,811,528,625	14.91	71.96
Colorado	6,783,558,703	1.99	7,955,966,266	17.28	7,350,176,264	-7.61	33.11
Nevada	3,936,547,625	35.43	5,493,142,094	39.54	5,713,221,890	4.01	385.41
Mississippi	4,007,570,892	26.05	4,673,796,240	16.62	5,170,097,650	10.62	69.07
Arkansas	3,862,282,872	10.57	4,265,023,769	10.43	4,880,221,534	14.42	74.07
Idaho	3,260,238,703	11.86	3,720,921,696	14.13	4,703,845,021	26.42	139.14
Oklahoma	4,313,910,209	35.75	4,375,113,341	1.42	4,538,096,291	3.73	85.72
Nebraska	3,003,585,336	29.68	3,624,877,816	20.69	4,255,683,830	17.40	68.37
Delaware	2,525,053,719	22.97	3,889,465,182	54.03	3,986,213,450	2.49	98.93
West Virginia	3,146,577,373	-3.53	3,225,356,589	2.50	3,972,153,382	23.15	77.55
Alaska	3,591,882,156	13.78	4,044,411,482	12.60	3,894,618,472	-3.70	54.78
Vermont	4,239,666,866	29.13	3,816,784,423	-9.97	3,434,557,326	-10.01	36.24
New Hampshire	2,548,041,028	11.48	2,810,960,357	10.32	2,910,358,212	3.54	56.19
Maine	2,309,788,889	-5.03	2,626,614,497	13.72	2,742,370,193	4.41	38.99
New Mexico	2,540,264,473	24.17	2,891,558,567	13.83	2,583,288,298	-10.66	115.97
North Dakota	1,185,396,565	17.61	1,508,753,773	27.28	2,033,458,140	34.78	136.62
Rhode Island	1,268,589,058	-1.38	1,531,226,439	20.70	1,646,586,644	7.53	46.88
South Dakota	941,477,276	14.05	1,185,197,429	25.89	1,506,426,892	27.10	152.42
Montana	710,727,172	25.86	886,585,134	24.74	1,131,166,762	27.59	193.25
Dist. of Columbia	825,442,237	-29.11	1,039,868,119	25.98	1,082,955,531	4.14	1.60
Wyoming	669,077,957	-1.64	830,045,552	24.06	801,821,846	-3.40	44.90
Virgin Islands	538,572,361	38.31	623,694,057	15.81	796,884,193	27.77	209.15
Hawaii	1,028,167,397	154.01	705,743,752	-31.36	560,425,925	-20.59	9.11
Unallocated	36,812,316,538	4.94	39,131,211,801	6.30	42,981,494,201	9.84	24.70

Source: Office of Trade and Industry Information, Manufacturing and Services, International Trade Administration, U.S. Department of Commerce.

ing the highest rate. Of the remaining states, 13 (and the District of Columbia) had single-digit growth rates, and seven states saw negative growth rates.

Another flourishing economic development trend involves the auto industry in the South. The current state of America's automobile industry is a study in stark contrasts.[8] The Big Three U.S. automakers—General Motors, Chrysler and Ford, located primarily in the Midwest—have been hemorrhaging vast amounts of cash, battling a range of structural problems, teetering on bankruptcy and securing emergency loans for survival from the federal government. Meanwhile, a roster of foreign automakers located primarily in the South have been thriving financially and generating a panoply of positive economic benefits, locally and regionally. While the debilitating effects of the current national recession have adversely affected the auto industry in the South,[9] the region has attracted an impressive roster of foreign automakers in the last 25 years or so. Table C provides a breakdown of these foreign automakers and their locations.

Table C
Foreign Automakers with Assembly Operations in the South

State and city	*Foreign manufacturer*
Alabama	
Vance	Mercedes
Lincoln	Honda
Huntsville	Toyota
Montgomery	Hyundai
Georgia	
West Point	Kia
Kentucky	
Georgetown	Toyota
Mississippi	
Canton	Nissan
Blue Springs	Toyota
South Carolina	
Greer	BMW
Tennessee	
Smyrna	Nissan
Nashville	Nissan North American HQ
Chattanooga	Volkswagen
Texas	
San Antonio	Toyota
Virginia	
Dublin	Volvo
Herndon	Volkswagen North American HQ
West Virginia	
Buffalo	Toyota

Source: Compiled by author, 2009.

Researchers cite a number of factors as being instrumental in the decisions of these foreign automakers to locate in the South:

- the ability to construct new manufacturing facilities, incorporating all the latest technologies, more efficiently and effectively at a Southern location, as opposed to reconfiguring older assembly plants in the Midwest;
- the economies of scale created by the cluster effect with the growing number of automobile assembly plants and thousands of auto parts suppliers in close proximity;
- the low or nonexistent rates of unionization and the negligible level of interest among Southern autoworkers to unionize;
- the attractive incentive packages, including tax breaks, worker training programs, an abundant labor pool and the ability to train a work force that has not worked in the auto industry previously, offered by Southern states;
- the extremely cost-effective intermodal transportation network in the region, spanning railways, highways, airports and, most importantly, ports;
- other attributes, such as the weather, reduced cost-of-living, lower or no personal income taxes, free or inexpensive property to build assembly plants, along with other attractive quality of life attributes; and
- the cutting-edge work being conducted by two high-end research and development facilities—the Advanced Vehicle Research Center in Garysburg, N.C., and Clemson University's International Center for Automotive Research in Clemson, S.C.—confirms that the automotive industry in the South now extends way beyond assembly operations.

The economic impact of these foreign automakers on the Southern economies continues to grow. For instance, Alabama, which did not produce a single car until 1995, produced 800,000 vehicles in 2007, making it the fifth-largest auto-producing state in the country;[10] a study commissioned to commemorate Mercedes' 10th anniversary in Alabama documented that the automaker and its top suppliers were responsible for a $6.8 billion economic impact in 2006, as well as 41,830 jobs.[11] By 2006, Toyota's first and now largest North American facility had invested $5.4 billion and generated about 35,000 direct and indirect jobs in Kentucky since it opened the Georgetown facility in 1986.[12] On the national level, throughout 2007, Toyota invested more than $17 billion in 10 production facilities scattered across the U.S.[13] Volkswagen's decision in July 2008 to locate its first North American production facility in Chattanooga, Tenn., a $1 billion investment, remains the biggest single investment ever made in Tennessee by a company; the Volkswagen investment also drew the state's largest-ever incentive package—$577.4 million in assistance and tax breaks over the next 30 years from state and local governments. In turn, an economic forecast study estimates that this investment and incentives will spur more than $11.8 billion in personal income growth over the same period, an estimated $1.4 billion in total tax revenue from the plant and its offshoots, and 11,477 new jobs.[14] BMW has been credited with transforming South Carolina's upstate region, formerly the stronghold of the state's now fading textile industry, into a thriving high-tech bastion. A September 2008 study released by the University of South Carolina noted that over the past 16 years, BMW has evolved to occupy a distinctive position in the South Carolina economy, supporting 23,050 jobs and generating $1.2 billion yearly in wages and salaries in the state. In 2007, the total annual economic output associated with BMW's economic activities—sales of goods and services to BMW and its employees from in-state vendors—amounted to more than $8.8 billion in South Carolina.[15] These statistics clearly demonstrate the enormous economic importance of the automobile industry in the South.

In these dire fiscal times, the emergence of additional stirring economic development projects remains very encouraging. The following passages will highlight several of these, particularly in the area of alternative/clean energy sources:

- In Mississippi, plans are underway to begin operation by 2015 of a $2.2 billion clean-coal power plant in Kemper County near Meridian that will pump millions of dollars into the local economy, generate nearly 300 direct jobs, lower utility bills and minimize adverse environmental impacts.[16] The plant would create power by separating carbon dioxide emissions from coal, which would then be stored in depleted underground oil wells and sold to companies that would use it to produce oil. The plant will use lignite, a low-quality coal with higher moisture content and reduced burning capability compared to other varieties of coal.
- In Georgia, Suniva, the state's only solar power cell manufacturing plant, opened in December 2008 with financial incentives from the state and local governments.[17] The technology used by Suniva to create solar cells soaks up the sun's energy more efficiently and at a lower cost compared to other competing products. The cells made by Suniva are deployed in solar-powered products manufactured by other companies. Company officials indicate that they already have lined up $1 billion in sales agreements with overseas solar module manufacturers.
- In Tennessee, construction was slated to begin in early 2009 on a $1.2 billion plant expected to employ up to 800 people in the production of polycrystalline silicon, the basic element of solar-electric panels and computer chips.[18] The factory is scheduled to open in 2012 and will be built in Clarksville, just north of Nashville. Michigan-based Hemlock Semiconductor Corporation is the parent company for the factory, which could be expanded to a $2.5 billion investment with thousands more jobs.
- In Oklahoma, the state is touting its decades-long expertise and experience in aviation and aeronautical technology and providing incentives to attract wind manufacturing companies.[19] Oklahoma's ideal geographical landscape for wind energy has the potential to supply 9 percent of the country's electricity needs while the state's extensive aviation and aeronautical background remains critical in wind resource manufacturing elements such as tower production, turbine assembly and blade construction.
- A number of other states are also aggressively pursuing wind energy, both as an economic development and clean energy generation strategy. For instance, Gov. Brian Schweitzer in Montana cites a planned wind turbine plant in Butte that will employ as many as 600 workers, while Gov. Bill Ritter in Colorado touts a Danish-based company Vestas that will employ 2,500 people by 2010 at four turbine manufacturing locations in his state. Similarly, in Newton, Iowa, a wind-turbine plant seeking to employ 500 workers began operations in fall 2008 at a shuttered Maytag factory.[20]
- In Kannapolis, N.C., 30 miles northeast of Charlotte, the $1.5 billion N.C. Research Campus opened in October 2008.[21] The facility is at the site of the century-old Pillowtex textile factory that closed in 2003, and the 350-acre biotech hub is projected to generate 30,000 direct and indirect

jobs when fully operational. State incentives were part of the strategy in establishing the facility and several labs have already been opened.

- In Groton, Conn., the submarine builder Electric Boat announced an expansion in its work force of up to 200 engineers, 50 designers and 400 trade staffers to meet the demand for new Virginia class submarines from the U.S. Navy.[22] In addition, the company's 10,000-person work force continues to retain a number of maintenance and modernization contracts for the U.S. Navy.
- In Missouri and Kansas, two recent major economic development projects offer promise for thousands of 21st century high-tech, high-wage jobs. First, the University of Missouri is in the process of establishing a new 500-acre research park in Blue Springs that would expand ties with bioscience and alternative energy companies.[23] Then, in Kansas, the December 2008 decision[24] of the U.S. Department of Homeland Security to locate the National Bio and Agro-Defense Facility in Manhattan, Kans., in the vicinity of Kansas State University, remains a huge boost to the state.[25] The facility will be the nation's premier federal lab specializing in animal diseases and other food supply threats. The 500,000-square-foot, $563 million laboratory's construction is expected to generate 1,000 jobs while paying an estimated $25 million in annual salaries to about 326 employees. Kansas' impressive biosciences sector has been nurtured for some years now by state policymakers, including the initiative to pump nearly $580 million into expanded bioscience research, and was undoubtedly influential in this federal decision.
- Finally, in Charleston, S.C., the closure of the U.S. Navy base in 1996 was a serious economic blow to the city and the state.[26] But after a decade of decay, some 340 acres of the former base is now part of a 3,000-acre redevelopment effort that will see an injection of $3 billion over 20 years. This has resulted in a number of "green" and technology-focused, defense and security businesses moving to the former Navy shipyard. The newly developed area includes a number of the companies that work on a range of high-tech military projects and is near the U.S. Navy's engineering and research unit, the Space and Naval Warfare Systems Center Atlantic. Consequently, between 2000 and 2007, the number of people working in information technology grew by 52 percent in the Charleston area; nationally, it went up by only 9 percent. South Carolina also has the second-highest concentration of industrial engineers in the country, after Michigan. Despite South Carolina's record high unemployment rate for some years now, job growth in the Charleston area was 16.5 percent between 2000 and 2007.

In closing, as foreboding as the severity of the ongoing recession has been and will be on both the national and state economies, the resiliency of states to bounce back from these dismal times by both initiating and continuing a number of promising economic development efforts remains impressive. The role of the federal government in this process remains critical and the Obama administration's proposals regarding both direct assistance to the states and the massive infrastructure repair and modernization program will be vital in revitalizing state economies. This will allow an urgent redirection of the energies of our economy—beginning at the local and state levels—that will eventually generate broad-based, sustained economic growth in all sectors of the country.

Notes

[1]"In 2008, 6 Years of Market Gains Are Lost," *The New York Times*, January 1, 2009 and "Stocks Close Out Worst Year Since 1931," *USA Today*, January 3, 2009.

[2]*http://www.nber.org/cycles/dec2008.html*

[3]"Fiscal Survey of States: June 2008," National Association of State Budget Officers (NASBO) and the National Governors Association (NGA), *www.nasbo.org*.

[4]"29 States Faced Total Budget Shortfall of At Least $48 Billion in 2009," The Center on Budget and Policy Priorities (CBPP), August 5, 2008, *www.cbpp.org*.

[5]"State Budget Troubles Worsen," Center on Budget and Policy Priorities, December 23, 2008, *www.cbpp.org*.

[6]While the focus of this chapter will be on a sampling of major economic developments in the Southern states, references will also be made to projects in other parts of the country.

[7]"As Outlook Dims, Obama Expands Recovery Plans," *The New York Times*, December 21, 2008.

[8]The Council of State Governments' Southern office, the Southern Legislative Conference, continues to focus on the economic impact of the automobile industry in the South. In November 2003, the SLC released a report titled *The Drive to Move South: The Growing Role of the Automobile Industry in the Southern Legislative Conference Economies*. This 148-page report featured an in-depth review of the auto industry in the South. The SLC has also published articles further clarifying the growing importance of the automobile industry in the South in *Global Corporate Expansion*. Visit *http://www.slcatlanta.org/Publications/EconDev/Autos.html* to read the publications.

[9]Toyota's decision in late 2008 to postpone the opening of its latest North American plant in Blue Springs, Missis-

sippi, and the decision to shutter the Toyota plant in San Antonio that manufactures the Tundra for three months in fall 2008 are two examples of the negative effects of the economic recession affecting foreign automaker operations in the South.

[10] "Southern Comfort," *Newsweek*, December 22, 2008.

[11] *http://www.ado.alabama.gov/content/media/publications/DevelopingAlabama/DevAlabamaNov07.pdf*

[12] *http://www.toyotageorgetown.com/pdfs/2008infokit.pdf*

[13] See note 10.

[14] "Chattanooga: VW Incentives, Investment Records in State," *The Chattanooga [Tennessee] Times Free Press*, August 30, 2008.

[15] Douglas P. Woodward, Ph.D. and Paulo Guimarães, Ph.D., "BMW in South Carolina: The Economic Impact of a Leading Sustainable Enterprise," Moore School of Business at the University of South Carolina, September 2008.

[16] "Mississippi Power Working on Clean-Coal Plant," *The [Mississippi] Clarion-Ledger*, December 19, 2008.

[17] "Rain Can't Stop Solar Panel Factory Opening," *The Atlanta Journal Constitution*, December 11, 2008.

[18] "Clarksville Factory Heralds Green Future," *The Tennessean*, December 16, 2008.

[19] "Oklahoma is Wind Energy," Oklahoma Department of Commerce, *www.OKcommerce.gov/wind*.

[20] Tom Arrandale, "Banking on the Wind," *Governing*, December 2008, *www.governing.com*.

[21] "Murdock's Biotech Hub Taking Form," *The [North Carolina] News & Observer*, October 21, 2008.

[22] "Submarine Company Thriving, Looking to Hire," *www.wfsb.com*, December 9, 2008.

[23] "Bioscience Hub Sought at Blue Springs Site," *The Kansas City [Missouri] Star*, December 15, 2008.

[24] Pending approval by the Obama Administration.

[25] Ibid. and "Flora Loses Biolab to Kansas over Access to Partner Universities," *The [Mississippi] Clarion-Ledger*, December 9, 2008.

[26] "A Turn in the South," *The Economist*, December 30, 2008.

About the Author

Sujit M. CanagaRetna is senior fiscal analyst for The Council of State Governments' Southern office, The Southern Legislative Conference.

Energy Infrastructure in the States: Pathways to Reliability

By Doug Myers

Energy infrastructure is vital to the nation's economy and the citizens' way of life. It supplies the nation with the energy required to conduct its daily operations, from supplying needs for industrial manufacturing to heating homes, running computers and fueling cars. The country requires an efficient energy generation and delivery system to keep the economy functioning smoothly, yet the infrastructure is aging, stressed and underfunded. At the same time, demand for energy continues to grow. States play a vital role in regulating and stimulating the creation of infrastructure, as well as siting new energy infrastructure. State officials are therefore in a position to institute policies that mitigate the infrastructure deficit and ensure energy reliability.

Overview

The United States' energy infrastructure is comprised of generation and transmission facilities, as well the network of roads, pipelines and waterways that supply the generation facilities with fuel. The infrastructure includes power plants, transmission lines, natural gas pipelines and, to a lesser extent, liquefied natural gas terminals for electricity generation services. It also includes oil rigs, pipelines, refineries and storage facilities for the energy that fuels the nation's transportation system.

Across the board, the energy industry is facing severe challenges as demand for safe, reliable and clean energy continues to grow. The U.S. will need to spend an estimated $85 billion to upgrade the transmission system to a smart grid capable of handling the expected increase in capacity and less prone to blackouts.[1] The rise of state renewable portfolio standards—which 28 states now have—requiring a certain percentage of electricity to come from renewable energy, means new renewable sources will need to be connected to the grid, further increasing the load and making grid upgrades critical to maintain reliability.

The 150 active oil refineries in the states are running near capacity,[2] yet the most recent one built was in 1976. There are 104 nuclear power plants in the U.S.; the last one became operational in 1996. Seven liquefied natural gas terminals receive natural gas imports from around the globe. That small number is likely to be insufficient to balance questionable U.S. supplies and increasing use of natural gas-fired generation. And proposed coal-fired power plants are simultaneously facing challenges from policymakers, environmental groups and financiers because of their carbon footprint and potential liability problems. Those plants will likely face new legislation mandating carbon capture and sequestration readiness.

The demand for electricity is expected to grow 1.1 percent per year[3] and demand for total energy is also increasing. That, combined with an aging and insufficient infrastructure, will force states to find ways to improve the reliability and efficiency of the energy generation and delivery system if a constant and affordable supply is to continue.

Challenges

While some demand can be offset by energy efficiency and conservation, new generation will be required. Coal, which supplies approximately 50 percent of the nation's electricity, will become more expensive and alternative sources of energy, such as wind and solar, will become more common as regulations governing carbon dioxide—or CO_2—emissions take effect. From an infrastructure standpoint, additional renewable sources will require new transmission lines to connect to the grid and will increase the grid load.

Increasing generation capacity poses a myriad of source-specific challenges. For nuclear energy, concerns over the storage and disposal of radioactive waste, as well as overall safety and security, have hampered new generation from coming online. Nuclear is an emissions-free source of energy making it more appealing under looming carbon controls, but it has high capital costs and a history of budget overruns that gives supporters pause.

For coal-fired power plants, uncertainty surrounding carbon legislation has made investors leery about lending funds for new projects. In the past two years, developers have dropped plans for 77 plants.[4] That trend is likely to continue. And for renewable energy, reluctance to fund or initiate projects over high per-kilowatt-hour costs are only mitigated by the continuation of federal and state tax credits, which are intermittent at best. Discontinuation of those credits halts the startup of new projects and delays the evolution of the industry into a competitive business.

Aside from source-specific concerns, another key challenge to securing energy infrastructure is deciding where to locate that infrastructure. Concern over the environmental effects of energy generating facilities—in particular, coal and nuclear, as well as concerns over scenic impairments and property value impacts from renewable facilities such as wind turbines—has prevented many proposed projects from proceeding beyond conception. Many municipalities oppose siting of infrastructure, whether it is a new power plant or transmission lines, in their boundaries.

As for the nation's fuel infrastructure, several states are trying to lessen oil's dominance in transportation and are exploring alternatives such as cellulosic ethanol and coal-to-liquids. But those options also face infrastructure challenges, the most prevalent of which is the absence of delivery infrastructure. In the case of ethanol, the current gasoline pipeline infrastructure is not compatible with the needs of cellulose and a new one would need to be designed.[5]

Given the inadequacy of established energy infrastructure, and in the face of local opposition, states are in a quandary over how to meet rising demand for energy.

Implications

Unresolved infrastructure issues pose several long-term problems for states. Overloaded grids and a dearth of new generation and efficiency policies will result in both insufficient and unstable supplies. This affects not only the economy but also the health of citizens during times of blackouts, especially ones that are extended or that occur in extreme weather.

Instability and tight supply—whether it be from the unavailability of natural gas as seen after hurricanes Katrina and Rita or the tight conditions under which oil refineries operate (where demand has exceeded supply and operators' capabilities to expand output[6])—also mean price spikes when supply is disrupted and higher overall prices for the delivered cost of energy.

And not ensuring new, cleaner generation through policies that support, for example, renewable energy or clean coal also means a reliance on old, carbon-intensive sources of generation that will make it difficult to achieve the greenhouse gas reduction goals needed to mitigate climate change.

Policy Options

States may undertake several efforts to improve energy reliability. Below are five policy options viable for state policymakers to consider.

1) States should require utilities to institute efficiency measures. Because utilities profit by increasing sales of electricity, states should incentivize efficiency programs by decoupling profits from sales to ensure utilities are appropriately compensated. Efficiency will offset the need for some new generation and is a low-cost option.[7]

2) States should promote demand-side management and distributed generation. Programs such as advanced metering will allow customers to see the real-time rates of electricity and control their energy usage accordingly. And promoting distributed generation—electricity generation from a non-centralized source such as mini windmills and rooftop solar panels that supplement centralized power—through interconnection standards that ensure favorable rates of return will incentivize homeowners and businesses owners to adopt distributed generation.[8]

These programs, which are shaping up to be part of the nation's Smart Grid—an effort to digitize and network all components of the transmission system to improve efficiency—have the potential to save consumers and utilities tens of billions of dollars annually in energy expenditures and forfeited economic activity resulting from power outages by offsetting the need for peak generation, repairing outages rapidly and remotely, and allowing consumers to monitor and control power consumption through pricing signals.[9]

3) States should work collaboratively to identify potential routes for transmission lines. This will allow utilities and transmission companies to fast-track development of new transmission. States should also map out acceptable sites for new generation facilities. Buy-in will be much easier to achieve by taking into consideration citizen, environmental and business concerns ahead of time.[10]

4) States should diversify their electricity generation and liquid fuel sources. An over-reliance on one type of fuel, such as natural gas, can pose problems when supply is heavily curtailed. For example, as a result of hurricanes Katrina and Rita, which struck the Gulf Coast in 2005, 75 percent of processing capacity was shut down.[11] This may require taking a closer look at nuclear power, instituting renewable portfolio standards and exploring alternative fuels such as coal-to-liquids with carbon capture and sequestration.

5) States should stimulate investment through tax credits favorable to all the above. This will ensure investors find it profitable to undertake new infrastructure projects and will help ensure stable and reliable service.

Conclusion

State officials have the power to greatly enhance and secure our nation's energy infrastructure—and thereby its environmental and economic security—by adopting policies that encourage efficiency and investment, facilitate decision-making processes and promote diversity of supply. Though trade-offs will be necessary, a robust energy infrastructure system is within reach.

Notes

[1]Presentation by William L. Massey, Covington & Burling LLP, before The Council of State Governments' Annual Meeting, Oklahoma City, Okla., November 13, 2007.

[2]National Commission on Energy Policy, Siting Critical Energy Infrastructure: An Overview of Needs and Challenges, (June 2006), 15.

[3]Energy Information Administration, Annual Energy Outlook 2008, June 2008, 10.

[4]Source Watch: A Project of The Center for Media and Democracy, Coal Plants Cancelled in 2007, 2008, *http://www.sourcewatch.org/index.php?title=Coal_plants_cancelled_in_2007 and http://www.sourcewatch.org/index.php?title=Coal_plants_cancelled_in_2008* (accessed on April 2, 2009).

[5]US Government Accountability Office (GAO), GAO-07- Key Challenges Remain for Developing and Deploying Advanced Energy Technologies to Meet Future Energy Needs, (December 2006), 28.

[6]GAO, GAO-08-14- Energy Markets: Increasing Globalization of Petroleum Products Markets, Tightening Refining Demand and Supply Balance, and Other Trends Have Implications for U.S. Energy Supply, Prices, and Price Volatility, (December 2007), 35.

[7]Presentation by Richard Sedano, Regulatory Assistance Project, before The Council of State Governments' Annual Meeting, Oklahoma City, Okla., November 13, 2007.

[8]Ibid.

[9]EAC (Electricity Advisory Committee), Smart Grid: Enabler of the New Economy, A Report by The Electricity Advisory Committee, December 2008, chapter 2.

[10]National Commission on Energy Policy, 11.

[11]US DOE Office of Fossil Energy, Impact of the 2005 Hurricanes on the Natural Gas Industry in the Gulf of Mexico Region, (July 2006), 2.

About the Author

Doug Myers is an energy and environment policy analyst for The Council of State Governments.

Table A
PERCENTAGE OF ELECTRICITY GENERATED BY SOURCE AND BY STATE IN JULY 2007

State	Coal	Natural Gas	Nuclear	Renewables
U.S. totals	47%	25%	19%	8%
Alabama	51%	20%	24%	5%
Alaska	11%	70%	0%	19%
Arizona	32%	38%	24%	6%
Arkansas	44%	22%	22%	11%
California	1%	53%	16%	30%
Colorado	66%	30%	0%	4%
Connecticut	13%	34%	50%	2%
Delaware	63%	36%	0%	1%
Florida	33%	51%	15%	2%
Georgia	61%	14%	22%	4%
Hawaii	69%	0%	0%	31%
Idaho	0%	8%	0%	92%
Illinois	48%	5%	46%	0%
Indiana	94%	5%	0%	1%
Iowa	81%	6%	9%	3%
Kansas	69%	9%	19%	3%
Kentucky	97%	2%	0%	2%
Louisiana	25%	54%	17%	4%
Maine	2%	48%	0%	50%
Maryland	63%	7%	27%	3%
Massachusetts	21%	64%	12%	3%
Michigan	59%	12%	27%	2%
Minnesota	63%	6%	25%	6%
Mississippi	33%	47%	17%	3%
Missouri	79%	8%	10%	3%
Montana	56%	0%	0%	44%
Nebraska	64%	6%	30%	1%
Nevada	21%	70%	0%	9%
New Hampshire	13%	33%	44%	11%
New Jersey	15%	39%	45%	1%
New Mexico	79%	21%	0%	0%
New York	13%	41%	28%	18%
North Carolina	60%	6%	31%	4%
North Dakota	93%	0%	0%	7%
Ohio	84%	4%	12%	0%
Oklahoma	46%	50%	0%	4%
Oregon	8%	25%	0%	67%
Pennsylvania	54%	13%	33%	1%
Rhode Island	0%	99%	0%	1%
South Carolina	43%	7%	49%	2%
South Dakota	53%	10%	0%	37%
Tennessee	62%	1%	30%	7%
Texas	34%	55%	9%	3%
Utah	85%	15%	0%	0%
Vermont	0%	0%	92%	8%
Virginia	40%	23%	32%	5%
Washington	7%	5%	8%	81%
West Virginia	100%	0%	0%	0%
Wisconsin	68%	11%	19%	2%
Wyoming	98%	1%	0%	1%

Source: Energy Information Administration, Annual Energy Outlook 2008 with Projections to 2030.

Meeting the Water Challenges for Sustainable Prosperity

By Edgar Ruiz

Effective management of water resources is critical to the economic sustainability and security of the U.S. Increased population, intensified use and climate change will continue to affect scarce water supplies. Governments, at all levels, will need to adopt collaborative strategies as our actions, or inactions, will have major repercussions on our ability to maintain our global competitiveness.

Adequate management of water resources is key to the economic well-being, public health, environmental sustainability and security of the United States. Most of the day-to-day activities that keep our country going, some of which are taken for granted, require water. But population growth, intensified use among numerous sectors and climate change all pose enormous challenges to our country's water resources.

To meet these 21st century water challenges, federal, state and local governments, along with numerous stakeholders, will need to develop national and regional collaborative strategies. The decisions will be difficult and necessitate a strong political will and a shared vision by policymakers and stakeholders. The stakes are high and the results of our actions, or inactions, will have major repercussions on our ability to maintain our global competitiveness and be responsible stewards of our water resources.

Population Growth Puts Pressure on Already Scarce Water Supplies

The country's growing population, particularly in the West and the South, is putting even more pressure on the already scarce water supplies. The country's changing demographic makeup is transforming its national and regional landscape profoundly. One of the most significant demographic trends of the 20th century was the steady shift of the population west and south from other regions.[1]

The population of the West grew faster than the other three regions of the country in every decade of the 20th century.[2] From 1900 to 2000, California's increase alone accounted for nearly one-sixth of the total U.S. increase and was more than the combined increase of 27 states.[3] Five of the fastest-growing metropolitan areas in the U.S. between 1990 and 2000 were in the West—Las Vegas, Yuma, Ariz., Boise, Idaho, Phoenix and Provo, Utah.[4]

In the South, Texas, Florida and Georgia were among the fastest-growing states in the country, with Georgia being the fastest-growing state in the region. Between 2006 and 2007, 70 of the 100 fastest-growing counties were in the South.[5] More than one-third of these 100 fastest-growing counties were in either Georgia or Texas.[6]

Increased population from net immigration, domestic migration and increased birth rates has major impacts on the delivery of water services by state and local governments. The ability of states to grapple with the quickly changing demographic trends will play a major role in water public policy debates in state capitols in the coming years.

Intensified Water Use

As population growth has intensified in the United States so has water use for energy, irrigation, industrial and urban uses. From 1950 to 2000, water for electricity production represented the biggest change —it grew by 500 percent.[7] In particular, the thermoelectric power industry, which uses water to cool electricity-generating equipment, has been the category with the largest water withdrawals. A trend showing the increase, decline and then stabilization of water withdrawals for thermoelectric power from 1950 to 2000 occurred as net electricity generated increased 15-fold to 3,450 billion kilowatt-hours during the same period.[8]

Irrigation water use increased by about 50 percent in the same period, as it takes more water to grow food for our rising population.[9] The total number of acres irrigated in the United States steadily increased from 25,000 thousand acres in 1950 to 58,000 thousand acres in 1980. The estimated number of acres irrigated stayed relatively constant from 1980 to 1995, and then increased to 61,900 thousand acres during 2000.[10]

While surface water historically has been the primary source for irrigation, data show an increase in the use of groundwater for this purpose since 1950. During 1950, 77 percent of all irrigation withdrawals were surface water; most of that was used in the

Figure A
Palmer Drought Index, Long-term (Meteorological) Conditions: July 2008

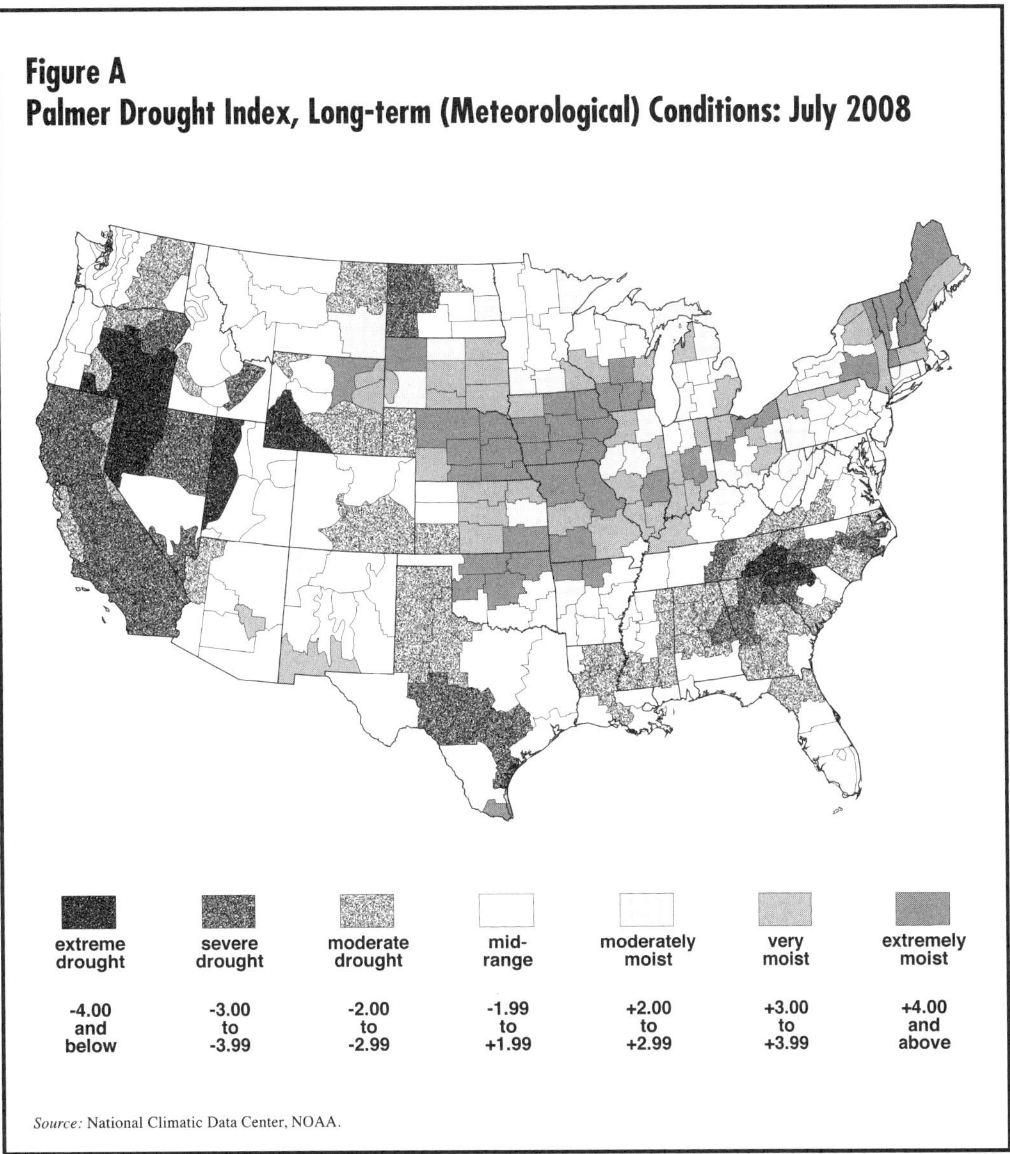

Source: National Climatic Data Center, NOAA.

western states. By 2000, surface-water withdrawals comprised only 58 percent of the total. Groundwater withdrawals for irrigation during 2000 were more than three times larger than during 1950.[11]

Likewise, the majority of the water for public supplies—63 percent—was withdrawn from surface sources. In 2000, about 242 million people depended on water from public suppliers.[12] Public supply withdrawals—water withdrawn by local county and city water departments to serve industries, restaurants and homes—more than tripled from 1950 to 2000, with an 8 percent increase between 1995 and 2000.[13] California, Texas, New York, Florida and Illinois accounted for 40 percent of total public-supply withdrawals and 38 percent of the total population served by public suppliers.[14]

Climate Change Impacts

Population growth isn't the only thing putting a strain on water resources. Recent warm climate trends have significantly affected annual precipitation and weather patterns across the country. Warming conditions have decimated snowfields far earlier than usual. These conditions have made weather patterns increasingly unpredictable. While lengthy droughts always have been a regular part of climate, particularly in the West, recent simulation models suggest that drought will continue to be a factor in the future.[15]

While in 2008 the U.S. experienced a national average temperature of 53 degrees Fahrenheit, which was the coolest in more than 10 years, the West, South and Northeast regions continue to experience anomalous warmth. The areas of the contiguous U.S. that experienced moderate to extreme drought expanded and contrasted several times during the year, starting at 27 percent of the country at the beginning of January, reaching a peak of about 31 percent in June, and declining to about 21 percent by the end of December.[16]

Conditions in the Southwestern U.S. were especially dry. While weeks without rain are not uncommon in the desert Southwest, serious problems can arise when the weeks turn into months. Because much of the region's drinking water comes from snowmelt, a dry winter can have serious implications in terms of how much water is available for the following summer season.[17] Moreover, low streams, reservoirs and stock ponds, as well as depleted soil moisture, ravage pastures, range land and cropland as the growing season progresses.

Changing climate conditions, particularly the length and severity of droughts, are having an impact on water supplies at a time of increased demands on regional water resources. The nation is also beginning to see changes in the magnitude, frequency and costs of extreme events like floods.[18]

Collaborative and Strategic Responses

These and other factors present critical challenges to government entities, water stakeholders and the general public across the country as we struggle to meet the water needs of the 21st century. While there has been much analysis and dialogue conducted regarding these challenges over the last few years, what is critically needed now is action and the implementation of immediate, mid-term and long-term national and regional strategies.

The lack of action, consensus and unwillingness to consider strategic planning and innovative solutions will result in greater conflict and inability to meet water needs. An example of this growing legal

Figure B
Trends in Water Use in the United States 1950–2000

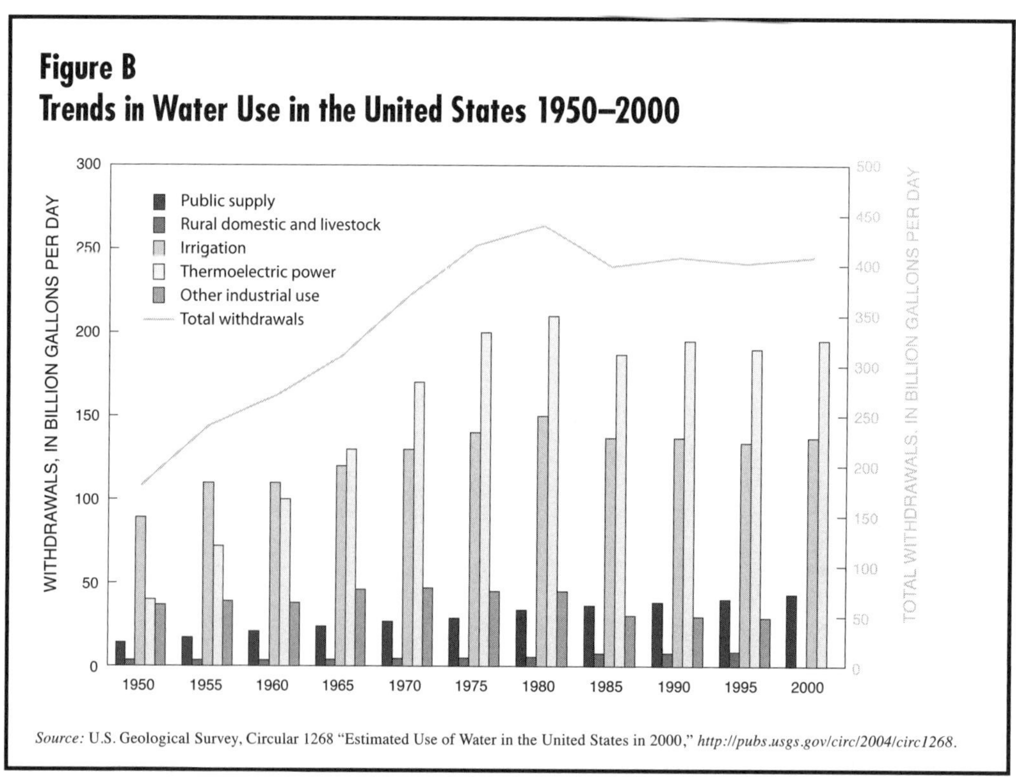

Source: U.S. Geological Survey, Circular 1268 "Estimated Use of Water in the United States in 2000," *http://pubs.usgs.gov/circ/2004/circ1268.*

and political tension is the ongoing debate over Colorado River water that serves upper basin states of Colorado, Wyoming, Utah and New Mexico, and lower basin states of Nevada, Arizona and California, as well as Mexico. Current levels in the river's two main reservoirs, Lake Powell and Lake Meade, are at historical lows.[19] Meeting the states' allocation demands may be impossible due to decreased water levels and as such, states may pursue legal actions, as opposed to collaborative approaches, which may delay or inhibit progress on sharing and meeting water needs.

The nation's limited and unevenly distributed freshwater resources are used inefficiently and ineffectively, in part because of the lack of a basic national water policy.[20] Such policy should be the goal of a new national, bipartisan Water Commission for the 21st Century, as proposed by current federal legislation, that can evaluate and recommend changes to national water policy, as well as encourage effective state and federal coordination and input from a variety of water management stakeholders. In effect, the aim of such a commission should be to translate a shared vision into actions.

In 2008, the National Governors Association released policy positions on water resource management, which included important principles for better managing our water resources. This included watershed management, water rights and allocations, groundwater management, funding of clean and safe drinking water programs, research and technical assistance, and flood plain management, among others. Similarly, the Western Governors Association, adopted broad recommendations as part of its "Water Needs and Strategies for Sustainable Future" report. The report was developed in consultations and meetings with numerous state and local water officials, as well as private sector water interests.

The enactment of land use and water planning strategies can also serve as effective tools in addressing long-term water needs. Historically, land use and water planning have occurred separately from one another in most parts of the United States where water is allocated by state agencies and local use planning is done by local officials.[21] This in turn has created a governance gap or disconnect between state-directed water supply planning and locally administered land use decisions processes.[22]

Several water stakeholders have commenced taking actions to bridge this disconnect and develop smart water management practices. In 2007, the Public Policy Research Institute at the University of Montana published a report, "Bridging the Governance Gap: Strategies to Integrate Water and Land Use Planning," which outlined a number of policy options, including water conscious land use planning, changes in state laws requiring consistency review with other land use and environmental laws and policies, watershed sensitive planning and realistic population projections, among others.

A number of western entities are responding to scarce water supplies in a variety of ways, including water transfers from rural to urban uses, regional water banks that store water and desalination projects. Water transfers are the most contentious of these alternative approaches because of the implications for the future of agriculture and rural land in the West, as well as to fish and wildlife in the region. In addition, the water supplies for other users can be affected when individuals or water entities, including water and irrigation districts, are allowed to obtain water from others within the same water basin without proper monitoring or control.

The potential impact of water transfers, however, can be mitigated if parties develop better mechanisms to deal with the needs of local water users and the environment. In California and other Western states, for example, local water districts put into place cooperative monitoring programs and rapid response programs aimed to address water-level issues as a result of water transfers. Data from monitoring programs and open communication with parties that might have been affected helped identify groundwater issues—as well as prompt actions such as halting pumping and deepening wells—before adverse impacts of transfers became serious.[23]

Other strategies include the enhancement of management strategies for conjunctive use of groundwater and surface water. Conjunctive water use management refers to planned efforts at the scheme and basin level to optimize productivity of crops, equity and environmental sustainability by simultaneously managing surface and groundwater resources.[24] Such efforts can be paramount, particularly in water scarce regions and in times of drought, because failure to integrate conjunctive water resources can result in groundwater overexploitation.[25]

These examples represent only a fraction of the potential policies and approaches to meet our country's water needs. As a new federal administration commences its work and states and water stakeholders continue to grapple with old and new water problems, however, the time is ripe to pursue robust and strategic efforts to better manage our water resources. Such efforts are desperately needed to meet current and future water needs.

Conclusion

Increased population growth, intensified water use and climate change impacts have and will continue to dramatically alter water supplies, water quality and water management practices across the United States. Population growth across the country may not be as fast-paced as the West and South; drought impacts may not be as prevalent as in the West and Southwest; and intensified water uses may not be the same across different sectors. But given the economic interdependence among all regions in the U.S., these impacts will cumulatively affect all of us.

As such, governments at all levels, along with a broad array of stakeholders and water interests, need to proactively pursue innovative solutions and collaborative approaches to better manage our nation's water resources. This needs to include developing a national water policy and providing states and local governments the financial and regulatory tools to implement national and regional recommendations.

The availability of an adequate and reliable water supply will dramatically affect the growth of our industries, our economic competitiveness and the sustainability of our environment. At no other time is regional and national leadership more critical on water issues than today.

Notes

[1]Demographic Trends in the 20th Century: Census 2000 Special Reports, U.S. Census Bureau, p. 1.

[2]Ibid.

[3]Demographic Trends in the 20th Century: Census 2000 Special Reports, U.S. Census Bureau, p. 24.

[4]"On the Move," by John Fetto, American Demographics, February 2003.

[5]U.S. Census Bureau News, Thursday, March 20, 2008.

[6]Ibid.

[7]Trends in Water Use: 1950–2000, U.S. Geological Survey Web page.

[8]Estimated Use of Water in the United States 2000: Trends, U.S. Geological Survey, Circular 1268.

[9]Trends in Water Use: 1950–2000, U.S. Geological Survey Web page.

[10]Estimated Use of Water in the United States 2000: Trends, U.S. Geological Survey, Circular 1268.

[11]Estimated Use of Water in the United States in 2000, U.S. Geological Survey, Revised Log.

[12]Ibid.

[13]Estimated Use of Water in the United States in 2000, U.S. Geological Survey, Circular 1268.

[14]Estimated Use of Water in the United States in 2000, U.S. Geological Survey, Revised Log.

[15]"Climate Change: a challenge looming for California," *San Diego Union Tribune*, August 15, 2004.

[16]Climate of 2008 Annual Review of U.S. Drought, NOAA, page 2 of 11.

[17]National Weather Service Forecast Office, Flagstaff, Arizona, Web site.

[18]Dr. Peter H. Gleick, "Water: Threats and Opportunities—Recommendations for the Next President," Pacific Institute, October 9, 2008.

[19]"Right move on West's water," *Denver Post* Editorial, December 31, 2004.

[20]Dr. Peter H. Gleick, "Water: Threats and Opportunities—Recommendations for the Next President," Pacific Institute, October 9, 2008.

[21]"Bridging the Governance Gap: Strategies to Integrate Water and Land Use Planning," Public Policy Research Institute, The University of Montana, 2007.

[22]Ibid.

[23]Gerald Jones, "Where is California Taking Water Transfers?," California Department of Water Resources, 2003.

[24]"Conjunctive Use of Groundwater and Surface Water," Agriculture and Rural Development, February 2006.

[25]Ibid.

About the Author

Edgar Ruiz is the deputy director of CSG's Western Regional Office. He holds a master's degree in public administration and a bachelor of arts degree in political science from San Diego State University.

"The Foundation for New Growth": Challenges for Transportation Officials

By John Horsley

Fiscal conditions in the states began to decline in fiscal 2008. State spending and revenues grew at a lower rate than the prior year and balances were well-below their near record levels of fiscal 2007. While fiscal 2008 saw somewhat moderate declines, the fiscal situation in the states has deteriorated much more sharply in fiscal 2009. State spending is projected to be negative for the first time since 1983, balance levels are being reduced as states use reserves to address shortfalls, and recent data shows state revenues declining by 4 percent. As a result, states are likely to face a difficult budgetary environment in fiscal 2010 and beyond.

A three-pronged financial crisis is engulfing transportation officials in every part of the country. That crisis involves the insolvency of the federal Highway Trust Fund, ever-escalating construction costs and the huger-than-before need for sustained and stable investment in transportation infrastructure to provide future generations with a modern, globally competitive system. This crisis will have long-term repercussions in the transportation industry.[1]

Spending from the Highway Trust Fund has exceeded the levels of revenue flowing into it. Congress provided a temporary patch to the Highway Trust Fund with a transfer of $8 million from the General Fund in September 2008. That was done to safeguard in the short-term those commitments made to the states under the current highway and transit authorization through October 2009. The fund, however, is still in danger of insolvency unless long-range action is taken in the near future. Congress, at minimum, will again need to provide interim financing through Oct. 1 just to sustain current funding levels. Otherwise, according to current revenue projections, the highway program will face a reduction of at least $20 billion for the 2010 fiscal year.[2]

Another problem facing the transportation industry is the skyrocketing costs of construction in recent years. From 2004 to 2008, construction prices for steel, concrete and machinery went through the roof. The costs for asphalt alone jumped a whopping 400 percent. Experts estimate that between 1993—when federal fuel taxes were last adjusted—through 2015, those costs will have increased by more than 80 percent.[3]

Those steadily mushrooming costs have dramatically reduced any purchasing power that once existed. To restore that purchasing power to what it was in 1993, federal highway funding must be increased from $43 billion this year to $75 billion by 2015. Federal transit funding would need to be increased from $10.3 billion this year to $18.5 billion in 2015.[4]

As if a depleted Highway Trust Fund or stratospheric construction costs were not enough, the industry must also contend with an unprecedented national economic collapse. Those ongoing financial woes have seriously affected innumerable individuals, institutions, industries and initiatives across the country. The need to preserve and upgrade existing transportation infrastructure, which is critical to large-scale and long-term mobility demands, has been especially hard-hit throughout the current financial slump.

A swift, strong and sweeping transportation infrastructure rebuilding program will play a pivotal role in creating urgently needed jobs and jump-starting the economy. President Barack Obama understands and embraces this need—both in the short-term to get our ailing country back on its feet and over the long haul to sustain a revitalized economy.

As the new President forcefully proclaimed in his historic inaugural address, "The state of the economy calls for action .... We will act, not only to create new jobs, but to lay the foundation for new growth. We will build the roads and bridges, the electric grids and digital lines that feed our commerce and bind us together."[5]

The American Association of State Highway and Transportation Officials, commonly called AASHTO, has consistently and strongly supported the President, his administration, Congress, and others in seeking to translate that stirring call for action into substantive accomplishments.

To signal to Congress and the Administration the scale of ready-to-go projects that the states could implement through an economic stimulus bill, AASHTO surveyed its members late last year on what was needed. The survey's findings were publicly announced in December 2008. Through that survey, we identified more than 5000 ready-to-go highway projects worth $64 billion that could be under contract within six months if included in an economic stimulus bill. The American Public Transportation Association (APTA), for its part, identified $12 billion in ready-to-go transit projects that could get underway within 90 days of economic stimulus funds being distributed by the Federal Transit Administration.[6]

We were therefore delighted when Congress and the Administration reached agreement on a wide-ranging and substantial economic recovery package. The American Recovery and Reinvestment Act (ARRA), which President Obama signed into law on Febraury 17, provides $48.1 billion for transportation projects. This includes $27.5 billion for highways and bridges, $8.4 billion for transit, $8.0 billion high-speed rail, $1.3 billion for Amtrak, another $1.3 billion for aviation, and $1.5 billion for a competitive grant program for major projects regardless of mode.[7]

This legislation is a huge step towards getting thousands of infrastructure projects underway rapidly and reliably, meeting urgent community needs, creating hundreds of thousands of family-wage jobs in the struggling construction industry, and fostering widespread economic recovery. After the bill signing on February 17, U.S. Secretary of Transportation Ray LaHood pledged to ensure that funds would be distributed to the states and others as quickly as possible. He also expressed the desire to hear the sounds of more shovels, hammers, and bulldozers in the upcoming months.[8]

The state departments of transportation, as key decisionmakers in how money and resources for those projects are ultimately put to use in the field, are more than up to that challenge. Missouri, to name but one example, wasted no time in putting its recovery dollars to work. Just seconds after Obama signed ARRA into law, the Missouri Highways and Transportation Commission voted to replace a crumbling 76-year-old, 1000-foot-long bridge over the Osage River. Other states, with similar determination and focus, have likewise been moving quickly to launch their recovery projects. Above all else, those states bring to their respective efforts a shared and solid record of historic achievements.[9]

In 1915, for example, state highway officials waged a daunting but ultimately victorious battle to modernize our roads and thereby get farmers out of the mud once and for all. The states came through again starting in 1956, when they built a web of superhighways that made it possible for us to drive from coast to coast without hitting a single stoplight. More than anything else, the Interstate Highway System brought our nation even closer together and unleashed far-reaching economic forces that have forever changed how we live, work and travel. Yet another milestone took place in 1991, when the landmark Intermodal Surface Transportation Efficiency Act—commonly known as ISTEA—enabled states to more effectively and seamlessly link highway, rail, air and marine modes of transportation.[10]

We have all benefited from those transportation visions brought to fruition. Now a new, even bolder vision is needed at this point in our history. This vision must build upon but also go well beyond what has already taken place, because the 21st century challenges we face are in many respects unprecedented. New dynamics, in other words, require new solutions.

First and foremost, that means setting aside the current laundry list of at least 100 different program objectives for highways and another 50 for transit. We need to better prepare for the future by identifying true program priorities and refocusing on objectives of genuine, lasting national interest. Meaningful reform, not business as usual, is critically needed.[11]

One leading objective involves preserving highways, transit and rail systems so they last for generations. Routine maintenance will no longer be enough for various structures already in place now for 40 to 50 years. Pavement foundations, to cite but one example, will need to be rebuilt on a widespread basis. Due to their own age and inevitable changes in specifications, many bridges will have to be rehabilitated and others replaced altogether. Major updates will also be due for a broad range of rail and transit facilities and vehicles. Overall, there will be plenty of need in the decades ahead to modernize our transportation network so that it better accommodates everything from heavier truck loads to faster design speeds.[12]

But all that will require major investment. A case in point involves the Interstate Highway System, which carries 24 percent of all traffic but is merely one percent of the nation's total system mileage. According to the U.S. Department of Transportation's 2004 *Conditions and Performance* report, an annual investment of $31 billion will be needed to preserve just that tiny fraction of the most heavily traveled highways in the United States. AASHTO has further calculated that, when adjusting the "constant dollar" estimate to "year of expenditure" dollars, it will actually take at least $49 billion annually to do what is necessary in 2015 and $72 billion per year by 2030. As shown by that example of a strategically significant but comparatively small segment of our transportation system, we face steep challenges when it comes to burgeoning costs and bare-minimum preservation requirements.[13]

We will also need to step up efforts to support our nation's global competitiveness, growth in productivity, economic development and national defense through an improved multi-modal freight system. More than ever before, our status as the world's economic superpower is under serious assault. Our competitors in China, India and Europe are investing heavily in upgrading transportation infrastructure and technologies for marketplaces across the globe.

This struggle for economic primacy is fierce and it is one that will continue to rage unabated in the decades ahead. China, for example, is expected to surpass the United States as the single largest economy in the world by 2030. So rather than resting on our laurels as the economic powerhouse of the 20th century, we will need to ensure that we have the transportation infrastructure and, in particular, the freight capacity to stay competitive throughout this century as well. A step toward accomplishing that goal entails fixing the 100 worst bottlenecks in the country by 2015 to guarantee that our nation—coupled with our NAFTA partners Canada and Mexico—can compete even more effectively with other large-scale trading blocs.[14]

The seismic shift toward our dependence on global trade and its ongoing implications for our future cannot be underrated. Since the dawn of the interstate highway era in 1956, the value of imports has jumped to an equivalent of about one-fourth of the nation's gross domestic product. We will need to meaningfully address current or prospective limitations within the transportation network to stay in the "just-in-time" world-trade competition.[15]

Those limitations can be readily seen in current trends. As one key example, the volume of international containers arriving at our nation's ports is projected to grow from 40 million in 2005 to 100 million by 2020. Rail freight, for its part, is expected to increase by 60 percent by 2040.[16]

This capacity crisis could have far-reaching negative implications for how the United States continues to fare economically. And it's why AASHTO president Allen D. Biehler of Pennsylvania has announced an initiative to address that crisis through development of a multi-modal freight strategic business plan.[17]

Those concerns about future capacity, in turn, led to consideration of another major objective that transportation officials must likewise remain focused on—safety. While we have already made considerable progress in improving transportation safety, a lot remains to be done to reduce the 40,000 fatalities and 3 million disabling injuries that still occur each year on the nation's highways. AASHTO is pushing Congress and others to work toward reducing those numbers by half in two decades.[18]

The need to work on this objective will become increasingly more urgent. One key reason involves the fastest-growing and largest segment of our population. One in eight people in the United States is 65 or older; by 2030, that number will be one in five.

Many in that group will continue to be active, contributing members of our society who appreciate and use our transportation network. Over time, however, more and more of them will also need to come to terms with the challenges of being elderly. Older people, for example, generally have slower reaction times when driving. They also do not see as well and are more vulnerable in crashes. Consequently, there will be an increased need to do what we can to keep them safe on the road. That will mean enhanced efforts to improve visibility of pavement markings and signage. There will also be a need for expanded licensing reviews. We also should be better prepared to offer those individuals no longer able to drive other appealing options for travel. Those options should include improved fixed-route and paratransit services.[19]

We also need to stay focused on another objective that concerns broad segments of our population—cutting down on congestion while also increasing connectivity for both urban and rural areas. That means not just holding onto and keeping up what has already been built, but also aggressively addressing ever-worsening capacity problems.

The numbers underscore these problems. The population is expected to jump from around 305 million today to 435 million by 2055. At least 80 percent of that growth is expected to occur in the nation's metropolitan areas; between 1955 and 2005, the number of people living in those regions did increase from 85 million to 225 million. This increase will further clog already heavily congested portions of the transportation network if nothing or little is done to increase capacity.[20]

Non-metropolitan areas will also continue to merit serious attention and assistance. Growth in those regions is projected to reach approximately 20 million people over the next three decades. Of the

20 states expected to grow fastest during that timeframe, several—including Alaska, Idaho, Montana, Nevada, New Mexico, Utah and Wyoming—are primarily rural.[21]

In light of these demographic patterns, it is incumbent on us to more fully connect rural America with the rest of the nation through state-of-the-art transportation systems. As an illustration of what might be required to accomplish this, the 2007 National Cooperative Highway Research Program study, *Future of the Interstate,* estimates that another 12,400 lane-miles would need to be added to rural parts of the National Highway System. Along with that, 40,000 lane-miles would need to be added to the existing 135,000 lane-miles of rural interstate routes; another 6,000 lane-miles would have to be added to current highway system routes that either exceed capacity or likely will in the future.[22]

We need to use advanced management techniques and technologies that better assure travel reliability and provide effective emergency response in disasters wherever and whenever possible. That means further harnessing and applying on a large scale those comparatively new and still-emerging tools and programs aimed at making travel safer and easier for all of us.

A case in point involves the dial-in 511 traveler information system. Now available in more than half the states, that service should be accessible in all 50 states by 2015. Many more people can then use the service to find the latest, most accurate reports on local surface transportation conditions.[23]

Other increasingly utilized technologies include recycling hot mix asphalt pavement to conserve resources and constructing perpetual pavements for long life. Concrete pavement technologies are likewise being improved, with unbounded overlays already in use as a rehabilitation option for composite—asphalt over concrete—pavements exhibiting significant deterioration.[24]

Another steadily growing trend involves design-build techniques that combine high-quality materials with incentives for contractors to finish transportation projects faster. An example of this contracting approach, and its potential application on an even wider scale, was the expedited rebuilding of the Escambia Bay Bridge on Interstate 10 near Pensacola, Fla. The estimated life for the new spans, which replaced those damaged by Hurricane Ivan, is 75 years.[25]

In addition, transportation officials must strive to enhance community quality of life and minimize impacts on the environment and global impact change. AASHTO president Bichler has made that issue one of his emphasis areas.

While the specific impact of climate change will likely vary from one part of the nation to another, a common denominator will be how it affects the planning, design, construction, operation and maintenance of transportation systems. Those impacts inevitably require major changes in how we retrofit existing infrastructure and design new infrastructure.[26]

As a part of that objective, AASHTO's member departments have adopted and will continue to pursue various environmentally sensitive actions. The association supports efforts to reduce greenhouse gas emissions to help meet global climate change goals. AASHTO supports better coordination of land use and transportation to reduce trips made by car and encourage greater travel via foot, bike and transit. We also champion the benefits of telecommuting. In addition, AASHTO supports doubling transit ridership over the next 20 years. State departments of transportation already invest $400 million annually in bike paths and other community enhancements.[27]

Highway construction is among America's biggest recyclers, remilling thousands of miles of asphalt pavement each year and reusing large quantities of slag and fly ash in concrete pavement. We want to see these recycling efforts broadened even further.[28]

All the above objectives for preservation and renewal, interstate commerce, safety, congestion reduction and connectivity for both urban and rural areas, system operations, and the environment unquestionably involve formidable challenges. But our nation is more than up to the task of handling those challenges and making a great transportation network even better.

AASHTO President Biehler, along with emphasizing sustainability and a multi-modal strategic freight plan, is also seeking to have those challenges addressed this year on Capitol Hill. "America needs a better transportation system," he has said. "The opportunity to create a dynamic and responsive system—accountable to the public and focused on the future—lies before us as Congress enacts new surface transportation authorization in 2009."[29]

In a similar assessment of future priorities and needs, the National Surface Transportation Policy and Revenue Study Commission asserted in its 2008 report, *Transportation for Tomorrow:* "We must take significant, decisive action now to create and sustain the pre-eminent transportation system in the world."[30]

We must all work together toward that end and help lay the foundation for new growth so that our fellow Americans will continue to have the transportation network they need and deserve in the decades ahead.

Notes

[1]The American Association of State Highway and Transportation Officials (AASHTO), *Creating America's Future Transportation System—2009* (Washington, D.C.: AASHTO, 2009), 6, 7.

[2]Ibid., 7; AASHTO, *How to Increase Transportation Revenue—2009* (Washington, D.C.: AASHTO, 2009), 2, 3; John Horsley, "Stimulus Funding and the Next Transportation Authorization Bill," Transportation Research Forum (Washington, D.C.), December 10, 2008.

[3]AASHTO, *Creating America's Future Transportation System—2009*, 7, 8; AASHTO, *How to Increase Transportation Revenue—2009*, 2, 3.

[4]AASHTO, *Creating America's Future Transportation System—2009*, 7, 8; AASHTO, *How to Increase Transportation Revenue—2009*, 2, 3.

[5]Barack Obama, Inaugural Address, January 20, 2009 (accessed 27 March 2009), available at *http://www.presidency.ucsb.edu/ws/index.php?pid=44&st=&st1*.

[6]"AASHTO, Other Groups Press Case for Transportation Spending in Stimulus Measure," *The AASHTO Journal* 108:48 (December 12, 2008), 1, 3.

[7]"Obama Signs Recovery Package into Law That Includes $48 Billion for Transportation Projects," *The AASHTO Journal* 109:7 (February 20, 2009), 1.

[8]Ibid., 2.

[9]Ibid., 2, 3.

[10]Horsley, "Stimulus Funding and the Next Transportation Authorization Bill."

[11]AASHTO, *Transportation Future*, 4.

[12]AASHTO, *A New Vision for the 21st Century* (Washington, D.C.: AASHTO, 2007), 10, 11, 35; AASHTO, *Bridging the Gap: Restoring and Rebuilding the Nation's Bridges* (Washington, D.C.: AASHTO, 2008) vi, vii.

[13]AASHTO, *A New Vision for the 21st Century*, 35, 37.

[14]Ibid., 49, 60.

[15]Ibid., 24, 25.

[16]AASHTO, *Creating America's Future Transportation System—2009*, 8; AASHTO, *2009AASHTO Emphasis Areas: Authorization, Sustainability, Strategic Freight Plan* (Washington, D.C.: AASHTO, 2008), 7.

[17]Ibid., 7, 8.

[18]AASHTO, *Creating America's Future Transportation System - 2009*, 14.

[19]AASHTO, *A New Vision for the 21st Century*, 40, 69; U.S. General Accountability Office (GAO), *Transportation-Disadvantaged Seniors*, 1, 6.

[20]AASHTO, *A New Vision for the 21st Century*, 39; AASHTO, *Rebuild Highways to Restore the American Dream—2009* (Washington, D.C.: AASHTO, 2008), 2.

[21]AASHTO, *A New Vision for the 21st Century*, 29.

[22]Ibid., 30.

[23]Ibid., 34.

[24]Ibid., 35, 37.

[25]Ibid., 35-37.

[26]AASHTO, *2009 AASHTO Emphasis Areas*, 6; Transportation Research Board, *Potential Impacts of Climate Change on U.S. Transportation* (Washington, D.C.: The National Academies, 2008).

[27]AASHTO, *Climate Change and Sustainability—2009* (Washington, D.C.: AASHTO, 2008) and Transportation: Invest in America, Bottom Line Report (Washington, DC: AASHTO, 2002), 16.

28Ibid.

[29]AASHTO, *2009 AASHTO Emphasis Areas*, 2.

[30]The National Surface Transportation Policy and Revenue Study Commission, *Transportation for Tomorrow* (Washington, D.C.: The National Surface Transportation Policy and Revenue Study Commission, 2007), 1.

About the Author

John Horsley is executive director of the American Association of State Highway and Transportation Officials in Washington, D.C. He previously served as county commissioner in Kitsap County, Washington, and as associate deputy secretary at the U.S. Department of Transportation. Mr. Horsley is a graduate of Harvard, and was a Peace Corps volunteer and congressional aide. He is also a past president of the National Association of Counties.

Table 9.12
TOTAL ROAD AND STREET MILEAGE, BY REGION: 2007
(Classified by jurisdiction)

State or other jurisdiction	Rural mileage: State highway agency	County	Town, township & municipal (a)	Other jurisdictions (b)	Federal agency (c)	Total rural roads	Urban mileage: State highway agency	County	Town, township & municipal (a)	Other jurisdictions (b)	Federal agency (c)	Total urban mileage	Total rural & urban mileage
Total	634,956	1,599,849	581,634	48,647	125,783	2,990,869	148,745	186,518	710,774	6,432	5,191	1,057,660	4,048,529
United States total	633,933	1,599,849	579,577	48,647	125,761	2,987,767	145,198	186,518	701,035	6,432	5,184	1,044,367	4,032,134
Eastern Region													
Connecticut	1,289	0	4,634	247	17	6,187	2,428	0	12,567	58	56	15,109	21,296
Delaware	3,063	0	100	31	84	3,278	2,246	0	669	5	44	2,964	6,242
Maine	7,527	0	11,975	136	167	19,805	992	0	1,970	21	4	2,987	22,792
Massachusetts	708	0	6,817	414	28	7,957	2,125	4	25,475	359	78	28,041	36,008
New Hampshire	3,218	0	7,612	41	146	11,017	772	0	4,046	3	0	4,821	15,838
New Jersey	455	1,986	3,849	585	422	7,297	1,872	4,456	24,605	421	100	31,454	38,751
New York	9,917	15,935	39,340	526	157	65,875	5,052	4,389	37,604	801	20	47,866	113,741
Pennsylvania	28,852	20	43,414	3,398	767	76,451	11,019	270	33,402	352	88	45,131	121,582
Rhode Island	317	0	945	0	10	1,272	788	0	4,423	3	25	5,239	6,511
Vermont	2,454	0	10,152	210	163	12,979	179	0	1,217	0	25	1,421	14,400
Regional total	57,800	17,941	128,838	5,588	1,961	212,128	27,473	9,119	145,978	2,023	440	185,033	397,161
Midwestern Region													
Illinois	10,960	14,170	72,448	404	224	98,206	5,098	2,181	33,345	303	26	40,953	139,159
Indiana (d)	9,358	60,439	3,524	0	0	73,321	1,830	5,711	14,610	0	0	22,151	95,472
Iowa	7,930	88,537	5,961	375	103	102,906	957	1,078	9,058	176	20	11,289	114,195
Kansas	9,620	111,687	5,188	178	939	127,612	749	703	11,146	60	0	12,658	140,270
Michigan	7,068	74,137	2,990	38	1,604	85,837	2,605	15,073	18,080	0	0	35,758	121,595
Minnesota (e)	10,728	42,902	61,809	1,014	2,858	119,311	1,153	1,985	15,213	10	21	18,382	137,693
Nebraska	9,548	60,196	17,009	263	161	87,177	407	625	5,190	0	0	6,222	93,399
North Dakota	7,167	10,067	66,145	23	1,543	84,945	217	0	1,680	0	0	1,897	86,842
Ohio	14,255	25,756	36,795	3,169	505	80,480	5,011	3,274	36,280	73	44	44,682	125,162
South Dakota	7,614	36,358	34,240	540	2,114	80,866	229	314	2,228	105	2	2,878	83,744
Wisconsin	9,738	19,205	62,764	12	839	92,558	2,031	1,498	18,562	57	0	22,148	114,706
Regional total	103,986	543,454	368,873	6,016	10,890	1,033,219	20,287	32,442	165,392	784	113	219,018	1,252,237
Southern Region													
Alabama	8,774	60,199	5,331	169	827	75,300	2,162	533	18,722	0	606	22,023	97,323
Arkansas	15,026	65,640	4,754	0	2,173	87,593	1,413	480	9,579	1	493	11,966	99,559
Florida	5,965	29,460	2,938	0	1,893	40,256	6,097	40,516	34,508	0	150	81,271	121,527
Georgia	13,928	62,261	3,505	87	1,315	81,096	3,986	22,063	11,053	39	541	37,682	118,778
Kentucky	25,121	37,751	2,199	255	783	66,109	2,426	1,635	8,224	47	148	12,480	78,589
Louisiana	13,200	28,433	2,474	3	618	44,728	3,481	4,053	8,719	14	9	16,276	61,004
Maryland	3,099	10,359	399	134	33	14,024	2,051	10,730	4,261	125	108	17,275	31,299
Mississippi	9,604	50,852	2,568	84	736	63,844	1,353	2,203	7,183	5	36	10,780	74,624
Missouri	30,803	69,254	5,033	0	1,324	106,414	2,882	3,516	16,311	0	0	22,709	129,123
North Carolina	62,733	0	4,834	748	2,991	71,306	16,555	0	16,189	0	361	33,105	104,411
Oklahoma	11,090	78,003	7,047	1,102	46	97,288	1,194	2,134	12,195	110	1	15,634	112,922
South Carolina	30,256	16,888	322	191	2,169	49,826	11,181	3,374	1,866	0	2	16,423	66,249
Tennessee	10,866	52,557	4,306	336	1,278	69,343	3,020	4,471	14,193	10	19	21,713	91,056

See footnotes at end of table.

TOTAL ROAD AND STREET MILEAGE, BY REGION: 2007—Continued
(Classified by jurisdiction)

State or other jurisdiction	Rural mileage: State highway agency	Rural mileage: County	Rural mileage: Town, township & municipal (a)	Rural mileage: Other jurisdictions (b)	Rural mileage: Federal agency (c)	Total rural roads	Urban mileage: State highway agency	Urban mileage: County	Urban mileage: Town, township & municipal (a)	Urban mileage: Other jurisdictions (b)	Urban mileage: Federal agency (c)	Total urban mileage	Total rural & urban mileage
Texas	68,357	139,180	13,289	3	831	221,660	11,618	6,334	66,086	156	0	84,194	305,854
Virginia	47,787	28	871	24	1,638	50,348	9,940	1,642	10,495	15	219	22,311	72,659
West Virginia	31,153	0	1,154	66	621	32,994	3,064	0	2,193	21	0	5,278	38,272
Regional total	387,762	700,865	61,024	3,202	19,276	1,172,129	82,423	103,684	241,777	543	2,693	421,120	1,603,249
Western Region													
Alaska	5,059	2,350	1,607	1,810	1,254	12,080	592	1,175	215	15	360	2,357	14,437
Arizona	5,814	15,378	3,178	240	13,066	37,676	971	2,808	18,617	188	333	22,917	60,593
California	10,830	52,066	3,996	3,017	13,536	83,445	4,439	13,026	69,574	50	620	87,709	171,154
Colorado	7,694	51,566	2,362	644	6,671	68,937	1,398	4,689	13,094	16	32	19,229	88,166
Hawaii	570	1,323	0	47	101	2,041	369	1,901	0	13	17	2,300	4,341
Idaho	4,636	15,347	28	14,873	7,926	42,810	323	152	2,700	2,420	11	5,606	48,416
Montana	10,486	44,290	1,209	286	13,949	70,220	299	5	2,678	0	0	2,982	73,202
Nevada	4,744	19,786	231	542	1,490	26,793	639	2,115	4,320	0	4	7,078	33,871
New Mexico	11,022	35,947	1,370	215	11,796	60,350	961	3,519	3,508	0	1	7,989	68,339
Oregon	6,684	30,320	1,661	545	7,765	46,975	852	2,885	8,949	82	14	12,782	59,757
Utah	4,778	21,356	2,346	0	4,193	32,673	1,053	2,420	7,885	0	192	11,550	44,223
Washington	5,732	33,701	2,170	10,729	8,549	60,881	1,312	6,156	14,825	64	194	22,551	83,432
Wyoming	6,336	14,159	684	893	3,338	25,410	417	422	1,523	211	69	2,642	28,052
Regional total	84,408	337,754	20,561	36,667	91,265	570,655	13,641	40,894	144,992	2,681	1,904	204,112	774,767
Regional total without California	73,555	285,523	16,846	30,824	80,098	486,846	9,186	28,247	78,314	3,009	1,227	119,983	606,829
Dist. of Columbia	0	0	0	0	0	0	1,392	0	0	19	89	1,500	1,500
Puerto Rico	1,027	0	2,057	0	22	3,106	3,542	0	9,613	0	7	13,162	16,268

Source: U.S. Department of Transportation, Federal Highway Administration, Highway Statistics, 2007, (October 2008).

Key:

. . .—Not applicable.

(a) Prior to 1999, municipal was included with other jurisdictions.

(b) Includes state park, state toll, other state agency, other local agency and other roadways not identified by ownership.

(c) Roadways in federal parks, forests, and reservations that are not part of the state and local highway systems.

(d) Excludes 788 miles of federal agency-owned roads.

(e) Excludes 437 miles of local government owned roads.

Table 9.13
APPORTIONMENT OF FEDERAL FUNDS ADMINISTERED BY THE FEDERAL HIGHWAY ADMINISTRATION BY REGION: FISCAL YEAR 2008 (In thousands of dollars)

State or other jurisdiction	*Interstate maintenance*	*National highway system*	*Surface transportation program*	*Bridge program*	*Congestion mitigation & air quality improvement*	*Appalachian development highway system*	*Recreation trails*
Total	6,210,374	7,674,597	8,110,299	5,160,899	2,143,941	470,000	79,160
United States Total	6,210,374	7,629,072	8,110,299	5,160,899	2,143,941	470,000	79,160
Eastern Region							
Connecticut	60,486	55,865	71,506	175,782	40,762	0	974
Delaware	6,453	53,090	36,191	14,618	9,847	0	854
Maine	26,483	29,399	32,148	31,738	8,618	0	1,146
Massachusetts	82,019	83,434	102,511	188,903	61,183	0	1,323
New Hampshire	21,976	41,622	36,824	27,253	9,982	0	1,025
New Jersey	123,118	181,739	182,464	206,434	101,490	0	1,296
New York	204,004	233,585	271,212	476,130	174,912	22,573	1,932
Pennsylvania	217,468	230,935	260,924	473,335	104,775	103,415	1,913
Rhode Island	10,581	42,681	30,839	64,315	8,858	0	851
Vermont	16,417	35,961	31,835	29,670	8,630	0	927
Regional average	76,901	98,831	105,645	168,818	52,906	12,599	1,224
Midwestern Region							
Illinois	263,866	201,036	290,499	151,938	96,037	0	2,101
Indiana	198,031	202,581	229,463	80,937	46,865	0	1,301
Iowa	71,917	105,342	101,558	67,042	9,386	0	1,344
Kansas	64,908	90,468	101,509	47,884	9,004	0	1,252
Michigan	170,759	214,798	268,973	123,622	73,738	0	2,281
Minnesota	107,632	130,560	166,075	36,878	29,589	0	1,715
Nebraska	45,983	79,311	68,670	26,351	9,443	0	1,114
North Dakota	32,118	89,082	43,460	11,770	9,605	0	954
Ohio	242,479	236,256	291,754	183,685	95,021	20,523	1,844
South Dakota	41,191	80,546	51,169	14,855	10,521	0	986
Wisconsin	115,211	197,257	191,606	32,008	25,712	0	1,700
Regional average	123,100	147,931	164,067	70,634	37,720	1,866	1,508
Southern Region							
Alabama	133,385	149,500	172,779	92,276	12,102	29,235	1,634
Arkansas	84,912	97,216	110,434	67,895	11,105	0	1,256
Florida	324,337	466,883	499,418	147,612	13,379	0	3,288
Georgia	292,198	267,496	339,199	89,563	61,529	17,918	2,008
Kentucky	117,212	135,253	127,593	71,047	12,317	68,567	1,315
Louisiana	79,211	90,508	108,864	189,715	9,626	0	1,635
Maryland	96,045	108,259	117,470	113,268	52,324	6,414	1,207
Mississippi	64,770	106,962	104,907	66,447	10,051	5,302	1,442
Missouri	158,333	176,415	192,987	143,396	21,371	0	1,532
North Carolina	175,784	207,390	236,306	143,432	49,228	38,236	1,781
Oklahoma	100,290	129,595	144,411	80,563	10,296	0	1,498
South Carolina	119,889	121,153	156,418	66,452	11,661	2,905	1,248
Tennessee	168,786	166,976	180,143	67,873	32,995	34,970	1,422
Texas	566,866	712,683	766,755	195,627	146,752	0	3,715
Virginia	184,563	181,390	219,183	116,080	53,050	33,435	1,431
West Virginia	54,904	55,651	60,126	63,572	11,225	86,508	1,125
Regional average	170,093	198,333	221,062	107,176	32,438	20,218	1,721
Western Region							
Alaska	60,686	71,976	61,394	27,244	18,285	0	1,183
Arizona	150,906	180,636	171,628	23,781	51,809	0	1,730
California	467,560	664,577	729,381	500,249	430,005	0	6,037
Colorado	95,766	128,204	120,340	37,092	33,255	0	1,421
Hawaii	9,874	50,423	34,912	25,045	9,464	0	887
Idaho	53,088	71,420	55,048	24,632	12,179	0	1,289
Montana	79,307	106,076	59,739	17,553	12,688	0	1,328
Nevada	57,277	64,076	59,499	13,558	24,493	0	1,106
New Mexico	83,415	100,368	71,643	15,916	10,901	0	1,336
Oregon	66,138	94,244	92,045	84,627	15,991	0	1,291
Utah	82,178	55,991	61,915	12,792	10,161	0	1,406
Washington	99,299	112,476	125,914	156,271	33,021	0	1,790
Wyoming	57,548	87,563	36,865	12,354	10,081	0	1,209
Regional average	104,849	137,541	129,256	73,163	51,718	0	1,693
Regional average without California	74,624	93,621	79,245	37,572	20,194	0	1,331
Dist. of Columbia	2,748	52,161	31,793	29,819	8,618	0	776
American Samoa	0	3,120	0	0	0	0	0
Guam	0	19,980	0	0	0	0	0
No. Mariana Islands	0	4,620	0	0	0	0	0
Puerto Rico (b)	0	0	0	0	0	0	0
U.S. Virgin Islands	0	17,805	0	0	0	0	0

Source: U.S. Department of Transportation, Federal Highway Administration, Highway Statistics, 2007(October 2008).

Note: Apportioned pursuant to the Safe, Accountable, Flexible, Efficient Transportation Act: A Legacy for Users (SAFETEA-LU). Does not include funds from the Mass Transit Account of the Highway Trust Fund.

(a) Does not include funds from the following programs: emergency relief,

APPORTIONMENT OF FEDERAL FUNDS ADMINISTERED BY THE FEDERAL HIGHWAY ADMINISTRATION BY REGION: FISCAL YEAR 2008 (In thousands of dollars)

State or other jurisdiction	*Metropolitan planning*	*Coordinated border infrastructure*	*Safe routes to school*	*Equity bonus (a)*	*Highway safety improvement program*	*Rail highway crossings program*	*Total (b)*
Total	299,209	1,354,037	220,000	190,000	147,000	2,692,857	34,752,372
United States	299,209	1,354,037	220,000	190,000	147,000	2,692,857	34,706,847
Eastern Region							
Connecticut	4,233	10,354	1,309	0	1,617	33,172	456,060
Delaware	1,496	6,018	1,100	0	1,000	6,502	137,169
Maine	1,496	5,267	1,187	11,592	1,000	0	150,074
Massachusetts	8,374	14,922	2,361	0	2,771	11,163	558,964
New Hampshire	1,496	6,100	1,100	301	1,000	8,084	156,763
New Jersey	11,523	24,549	3,589	0	4,088	75,586	915,877
New York	23,041	40,667	6,328	24,967	8,280	64,988	1,552,620
Pennsylvania	12,202	41,508	7,191	0	5,436	88,640	1,547,742
Rhode Island	1,496	5,267	1,100	0	1,000	0	166,987
Vermont	1,496	5,274	1,100	7,878	1,000	73	140,262
Regional average	6,685	15,993	2,637	4,474	2,719	28,821	578,252
Midwestern Region							
Illinois	14,471	46,197	10,055	0	6,049	91,908	1,174,157
Indiana	5,069	31,127	7,204	0	2,994	108,529	914,102
Iowa	1,657	17,308	4,948	0	1,340	12,539	394,380
Kansas	1,795	18,958	6,124	0	1,313	5,873	349,087
Michigan	9,776	42,620	7,769	26,583	4,812	72,013	1,017,743
Minnesota	4,030	27,547	5,914	3,778	2,324	44,408	560,450
Nebraska	1,496	11,958	3,705	0	1,000	8,689	257,721
North Dakota	1,496	8,269	3,473	9,110	1,000	8,214	218,550
Ohio	10,865	43,374	8,555	0	5,300	109,802	1,249,458
South Dakota	1,496	10,650	2,309	0	1,000	15,624	230,347
Wisconsin	4,224	33,009	5,361	0	2,500	78,769	687,358
Regional average	5,125	26,456	5,947	3,588	2,694	50,579	641,214
Southern Region							
Alabama	2,885	33,142	4,402	0	2,200	70,280	703,821
Arkansas	1,496	20,716	3,715	0	1,297	36,336	436,379
Florida	20,018	86,311	8,537	0	7,763	225,245	1,802,790
Georgia	7,445	56,709	8,181	0	4,487	156,856	1,303,590
Kentucky	2,328	21,597	3,568	0	1,885	40,963	603,645
Louisiana	3,768	19,349	4,159	0	2,106	21,500	530,442
Maryland	6,390	17,739	2,274	0	2,514	27,292	551,196
Mississippi	1,496	20,756	3,329	0	1,472	22,007	408,940
Missouri	4,593	36,302	6,034	0	2,646	67,025	810,635
North Carolina	5,589	36,755	6,172	0	4,051	88,818	993,541
Oklahoma	2,205	26,188	5,053	0	1,664	32,960	534,723
South Carolina	2,785	32,597	4,097	0	1,948	54,571	575,723
Tennessee	4,406	32,317	4,591	0	2,701	67,430	764,608
Texas	21,988	120,212	16,935	49,997	12,115	310,975	2,924,620
Virginia	7,004	34,671	4,459	0	3,371	83,640	922,277
West Virginia	1,496	11,927	1,985	0	1,000	24,715	374,234
Regional average	5,993	37,956	5,468	3,125	3,326	83,163	890,073
Western Region							
Alaska	1,496	11,174	1,100	1,273	1,000	55,948	312,759
Arizona	5,808	32,390	2,644	9,063	2,897	76,020	709,312
California	44,612	122,413	15,799	24,650	18,066	187,094	3,210,442
Colorado	4,775	20,180	3,131	0	2,120	26,792	473,074
Hawaii	1,496	5,783	1,100	0	1,000	4,984	144,968
Idaho	1,496	10,734	1,657	1,302	1,000	27,331	261,176
Montana	1,496	11,972	1,748	6,614	1,000	37,935	337,456
Nevada	2,491	10,479	1,100	0	1,153	20,868	256,100
New Mexico	1,496	14,569	1,565	1,567	1,000	25,725	329,502
Oregon	2,937	15,877	3,105	0	1,544	14,702	392,502
Utah	2,598	9,251	1,587	0	1,366	14,513	253,757
Washington	6,396	19,559	3,992	11,327	2,810	13,085	585,939
Wyoming	1,496	6,160	1,100	0	1,000	12,671	228,046
Regional average	6,046	22,349	3,048	4,292	2,766	39,821	576,541
Regional average without California	2,832	14,011	1,986	2,596	1,491	27,548	357,049
Dist. of Columbia	1,496	5,267	1,100	0	1,000	0	134,778
American Samoa	0	0	0	0	0	0	3,120
Guam	0	0	0	0	0	0	19,980
No. Mariana Islands	0	0	0	0	0	0	4,620
Puerto Rico (b)	0	0	0	0	0	0	0
U.S. Virgin Islands	0	0	0	0	0	0	17,805

federal lands highway programs, Commonwealth of Puerto Rico highway programs, high priority projects, Woodrow Wilson Bridge, National Byways, construction of ferry terminal facilities, and intelligent vehicle-system, among others. These funds are distributed from the Highway Trust Fund.

(b) Under SAFETEA-LU, Puerto Rico received a stand-alone authorization of $145,000,000 for FY 2008.

Table 9.14
TRENDS IN STATE PRISON POPULATION BY REGION, 2000, 2006, and 2007

State or other jurisdiction	*Total state prison population*			Average annual change 2000–2006	Percent change 2006–2007
	December 31, 2007	December 31, 2006	December 31, 2000		
United States (a)	1,532,817	1,504,660	1,331,278	2.1%	1.9%
Federal	179,204	173,533	125,044	5.6	3.3
State (a)	1,353,613	1,331,127	1,206,234	1.7	1.7
Eastern Region					
Connecticut (b)	14,397	13,746	13,155	0.7	4.7
Delaware (b)	4,201	4,195	3,937	1.1	0.1
Maine	2,093	1,997	1,635	3.4	4.8
Massachusetts	9,699	9,472	9,479	0.0	2.4
New Hampshire	2,930	2,737	2,257	3.3	7.1
New Jersey (c)	26,827	27,371	29,784	-1.4	-2.0
New York	62,177	62,974	70,199	-1.8	-1.3
Pennsylvania	45,446	43,998	36,844	3.0	3.3
Rhode Island (b)	2,481	2,149	1,966	1.5	15.4
Vermont (b)	1,617	1,634	1,313	3.7	-1.0
Regional total	171,868	170,273	170,569	-0.1	0.9
Midwestern Region					
Illinois	45,215	45,106	45,281	-0.1	0.2
Indiana	27,114	26,055	19,811	4.7	4.1
Iowa (c)(d)	8,732	8,838	7,955	1.8	-1.2
Kansas (c)	8,696	8,816	8,344	0.9	-1.4
Michigan	50,233	51,577	47,718	1.3	-2.6
Minnesota	9,468	9,108	6,238	6.5	4.0
Nebraska	4,329	4,204	3,816	1.6	3.0
North Dakota	1,416	1,363	994	5.4	3.9
Ohio (c)	50,731	49,166	45,833	1.2	3.2
South Dakota	3,306	3,350	2,613	4.2	-1.3
Wisconsin	22,307	22,618	20,336	1.8	-1.4
Regional total	231,547	230,201	208,939	1.6	0.5
Southern Region					
Alabama	28,605	27,526	26,034	0.9	3.9
Arkansas	14,310	13,713	11,851	2.5	4.4
Florida	98,219	92,874	71,318	4.5	5.8
Georgia (d)	54,232	52,781	44,141	3.0	2.7
Kentucky	21,823	19,514	14,919	4.6	11.8
Louisiana	37,341	36,376	35,207	0.5	2.7
Maryland	22,780	22,316	22,490	-0.1	2.1
Mississippi	21,502	19,219	19,239	0.0	11.9
Missouri	29,844	30,146	27,519	1.5	-1.0
North Carolina	33,016	32,219	27,043	3.0	2.5
Oklahoma	24,197	23,889	23,181	0.5	1.3
South Carolina	23,314	22,861	21,017	1.4	2.0
Tennessee	26,267	25,745	22,166	2.5	2.0
Texas	161,695	162,193	158,008	0.4	-0.3
Virginia	37,984	36,688	29,643	3.6	3.5
West Virginia	6,049	5,719	3,795	7.1	5.8
Regional total	641,178	623,779	557,571	1.7	2.8
Western Region					
Alaska (b)	3,072	3,116	2,128	6.6	-1.4
Arizona (d)	35,490	33,557	25,412	4.7	5.8
California	172,856	173,942	160,412	1.4	-0.6
Colorado (c)	22,841	22,481	16,833	4.9	1.6
Hawaii (b)	4,367	4,373	3,553	3.5	-0.1
Idaho	7,319	7,124	5,535	4.3	2.7
Montana	3,431	3,563	3,105	2.3	-3.7
Nevada	13,245	12,753	10,063	4.0	3.9
New Mexico	6,225	6,361	4,666	5.3	-2.1
Oregon (c)	13,918	13,667	10,553	4.4	1.8
Utah	6,415	6,340	5,541	2.3	1.2
Washington	17,757	17,483	14,666	3.0	1.6
Wyoming	2,084	2,114	1,680	3.9	-1.4
Regional total	309,020	306,874	264,147	2.5	0.6
Regional total without California	136,164	132,932	103,735	3.6	2.4

Source: U.S. Department of Justice, Bureau of Justice Statistics, *Prisoners in 2007*—NCJ 224200 (December 2, 2008)

Note: Sentenced prisoner is defined as a prisoner sentenced to more than one year.

Key:

(a) Totals estimated. Illinois did not provide data in 2006 and 2007. Maine and Nevada did not provide data in 2007.

(b) Prisons and jails form one integrated system. Data include total jail and prison populations.

(c) Includes some inmates sentenced to one year or less.

(d) Population based on custody counts.

Table 9.15
NUMBER OF SENTENCED PRISONERS ADMITTED AND RELEASED FROM STATE AND FEDERAL JURISDICTION, BY REGION: 2000, and 2006–2007

State or other jurisdiction	*Admissions (a)*					*Releases (a)*				
	2007	*2006*	*2000*	*Average annual change 2000–2006*	*Percent change 2006–2007*	*2007*	*2006*	*2000*	*Average annual change 2000–2006*	*Percent change 2006–2007*
United States	751,593	749,798	625,219	3.1%	0.2%	725,402	713,473	604,858	2.8%	1.7%
Federal	53,618	57,495	43,732	4.7	-7.0	48,411	47,920	35,259	5.2	1.0
State	697,975	692,303	581,487	2.9	1.0	676,991	665,553	569,599	2.6	1.7
Eastern Region										
Connecticut	6,982	6,904	6,185	1.8	1.0	6,056	6,019	5,918	0.3	0.6
Delaware	1,899	1,546	2,709	-8.9	23.0	1,905	1,470	2,260	-6.9	29.6
Maine (a)	640	609	751	-3.4	5.0	524	501	677	-4.9	4.6
Massachusetts	3,653	2,686	2,062	4.5	36.0	3,273	2,254	2,889	-4.1	45.2
New Hampshire	1,290	1,312	1,051	3.8	-2.0	1,179	1,187	1,044	2.2	-0.7
New Jersey	13,791	13,980	13,653	0.4	-1.0	14,358	13,986	15,362	-1.6	2.7
New York	26,291	25,710	27,601	-1.2	2.3	27,009	25,079	28,828	-2.3	7.7
Pennsylvania	17,666	17,106	11,777	6.4	3.0	16,340	15,648	11,759	4.9	4.4
Rhode Island	1,120	876	3,701	:	:	884	967	3,223	:	:
Vermont	2,362	2,340	984	:	:	2,345	2,329	946	:	:
Regional total	75,694	73,069	70,474	1.0	3.5	73,873	69,440	72,906	-0.8	6.4
Midwestern Region										
Illinois	/	/	29,344	:	:	/	/	28,876	:	:
Indiana	17,653	17,671	11,876	6.8	0.0	17,099	16,410	11,053	6.8	4.2
Iowa	5,706	6,565	4,656	5.9	-13.0	5,718	5,834	4,379	4.9	-2.0
Kansas	4,849	5,063	5,002	0.2	-4.0	4,966	5,318	5,231	0.3	-6.6
Michigan	13,330	14,643	12,169	3.1	-9.0	14,685	12,641	10,874	2.5	16.2
Minnesota	7,856	7,253	4,406	8.7	8.0	7,971	7,591	4,244	10.2	5.0
Nebraska	2,076	1,939	1,688	2.3	7.0	1,952	2,041	1,503	5.2	-4.4
North Dakota	1,028	1,101	605	10.5	-7.0	977	1,039	598	9.6	-6.0
Ohio	30,808	31,866	23,780	5.0	-3.0	29,236	28,552	24,793	2.4	2.4
South Dakota	3,227	2,429	1,400	9.6	33.0	3,259	3,137	1,327	15.4	3.9
Wisconsin	8,592	8,703	8,396	0.6	-1.0	8,903	8,749	8,158	1.2	1.8
Regional total	95,125	97,233	103,322	4.9	-2.2	94,766	91,312	101,036	5.2	3.8
Southern Region										
Alabama	10,708	10,039	6,296	8.1	7.0	11,079	11,283	7,136	7.9	-1.8
Arkansas	6,651	5,992	6,941	-2.4	11.0	6,045	5,668	6,308	-1.8	6.7
Florida (b)	33,552	36,295	35,683	0.3	-8.0	28,705	35,454	33,994	0.7	-19.0
Georgia	21,134	22,347	17,373	4.3	-5.0	19,119	17,468	14,797	2.8	9.5
Kentucky (a)	15,359	14,051	8,116	9.6	9.0	13,819	13,381	7,733	9.6	3.3
Louisiana	14,548	15,067	15,735	-0.7	-3.0	14,984	14,618	14,536	0.1	2.5
Maryland	10,716	10,295	10,327	-0.1	4.0	10,123	10,176	10,004	0.3	-0.5
Mississippi	9,749	9,918	5,796	9.4	-2.0	8,455	10,123	4,940	12.7	-16.5
Missouri	18,300	18,429	14,454	4.1	-1.0	19,323	20,092	13,346	7.1	-3.8
North Carolina	10,834	10,594	9,848	1.2	2.0	10,074	9,976	9,687	0.5	1.0
Oklahoma	8,795	8,508	7,426	2.3	3.0	8,486	7,867	6,628	2.9	7.9
South Carolina	9,912	9,597	8,460	2.1	3.0	9,461	9,208	8,676	1.0	2.7
Tennessee	14,535	13,655	13,675	0.0	6.0	15,537	15,298	13,893	1.6	1.6
Texas	72,525	71,927	58,197	3.6	1.0	73,023	70,413	59,776	2.8	3.7
Virginia	13,973	12,834	9,791	4.6	9.0	12,559	12,794	9,148	5.7	-1.8
West Virginia	3,333	2,830	1,577	10.2	18.0	2,969	2,391	1,261	11.3	24.2
Regional total	274,624	272,378	229,695	2.6	0.8	263,761	266,210	221,863	2.9	-0.9
Western Region										
Alaska	3,272	3,065	2,427	4.0	7.0	3,286	2,719	2,599	0.8	20.9
Arizona	14,046	13,954	9,560	6.5	1.0	12,560	12,209	9,100	5.0	2.9
California	139,608	138,523	129,640	1.1	1.0	135,920	133,905	129,621	0.5	1.5
Colorado	10,959	10,468	7,036	6.8	5.0	10,604	9,441	5,881	8.2	12.3
Hawaii	1,514	1,455	1,594	-1.5	4.0	1,518	1,500	1,379	1.4	1.2
Idaho	4,055	4,129	3,386	3.4	-2.0	3,850	3,808	2,697	5.9	1.1
Montana	2,055	2,304	1,202	11.5	-11.0	2,176	2,262	1,031	14.0	-3.8
Nevada (a)	6,375	6,108	4,929	3.6	4.0	4,904	4,700	4,374	1.2	4.3
New Mexico	4,146	4,337	3,161	5.4	-4.0	4,507	4,274	3,383	4.0	5.5
Oregon	5,331	5,484	4,059	5.1	-3.0	5,080	5,138	3,371	7.3	-1.1
Utah	3,466	3,532	3,270	1.3	-1.9	3,393	3,469	2,897	3.0	-2.2
Washington	16,478	15,540	7,094	14.0	6.0	16,488	15,363	6,764	14.7	7.3
Wyoming	746	837	638	4.6	-10.9	778	769	697	1.7	1.2
Regional total	212,051	209,736	177,996	2.8	1.0	205,064	199,557	173,794	2.3	2.8
Regional total without California	72,443	71,213	48,356	:	1.7	69,144	65,652	44,173	:	5.3

Source: U.S. Department of Justice, Bureau of Justice Statistics, *Prisoners in 2007*—NCJ 224280 (December 2, 2008).

Note: Totals exclude transfers, escapees, and AWOLs.

Key

: — Not calculated.

/ — Not reported.

(a) 2007 counts were estimated.

(b) A change in the reporting in 2004 excluded unsentenced prisoners and those sentenced to less than one year.

Table 9.16
STATE PRISON CAPACITIES, BY REGION, 2007

	Type of capacity measure			*Population as a percent of capacity: (a)*	
State	*Rated capacity*	*Operational capacity*	*Design capacity*	*Highest capacity*	*Lowest capacity*
Federal	122,461	...	...	136%	136%
Eastern Region					
Connecticut (b)	...	...	...	...	...
Delaware	7,103	6,757	5,319	100	134
Maine (c)	1,885	1,885	1,885	:	:
Massachusetts	...	...	7,875	141	141
New Hampshire	2,524	3,000	2,270	92	122
New Jersey	...	23,300	16,876	97	134
New York	60,242	61,390	57,768	102	109
Pennsylvania	41,692	41,692	41,692	107	107
Rhode Island	4,004	4,004	4,265	88	94
Vermont	1,732	1,732	1,371	94	119
Midwestern Region					
Illinois (c)	33,971	33,971	59,959	:	:
Indiana	...	24,989	...	94	94
Iowa	...	...	7,413	117	117
Kansas	9,317	...	...	94	94
Michigan	...	51,343	...	98	98
Minnesota	...	7,807	...	103	103
Nebraska	...	3,969	3,175	111	139
North Dakota	1,044	991	1,044	133	140
Ohio	38,320	...	...	125	125
South Dakota	...	3,487	...	93	93
Wisconsin (d)	...	17,383	...	131	131
Southern Region					
Alabama	...	25,686	13,728	97	181
Arkansas	12,961	13,610	12,863	98	103
Florida (e)	...	95,241	72,556	91	119
Georgia (f)	...	58,231	...	102	102
Kentucky	...	13,682	14,017	92	95
Louisiana (f)	20,461	20,641	...	114	115
Maryland	...	23,155	...	99	99
Mississippi (f)	...	22,725	22,725	77	77
Missouri	...	30,788	...	97	97
North Carolina (e)	33,359	38,512	...	99	115
Oklahoma (f)	24,845	24,845	24,845	96	96
South Carolina	...	23,918	...	99	99
Tennessee	20,258	19,804	...	70	71
Texas (d)	162,560	158,578	162,560	86	88
Virginia	32,765	...	...	96	96
West Virginia	4,135	5,015	4,135	98	119
Western Region					
Alaska	3,058	3,206	...	113	119
Arizona	29,119	39,690	34,474	75	103
California	...	165,409	82,936	101	201
Colorado	...	14,937	13,027	119	137
Hawaii	...	3,487	2,451	95	136
Idaho (f)	6,348	6,031	6,348	111	117
Montana (d)	...	2,441	...	119	119
Nevada (c)	11,061	10,811	8,326	:	:
New Mexico (f)	...	7,131	6,653	52	56
Oregon	...	13,188	13,188	101	101
Utah	...	6,650	6,886	75	78
Washington	13,777	15,502	15,502	109	123
Wyoming	1,511	1,436	1,428	86	91

Source: U.S. Department of Justice, Bureau of Justice Statistics, Prisoners in 2007—NCJ 224280 (December 2, 2008).

Key:

. . . — Not available.

:— Not calculated.

(a) Population counts are based on the number of inmates held in facilities operated by the jurisdiction. Excludes inmates held in local jails, in other states, or in private facilities.

(b) Connecticut no longer reports capacity because of a law passed in 1995.

(c) Capacity based on numbers reported in 2006.

(d) Excludes capacity of county facilities and inmates housed in them.

(e) Capacity definition differs from BJS definition, Florida—counts are not comparable to last year due to new methods of data collection by Florida correctional officials; North Carolina—capacity figures refer to standard operating capacity, based on single occupancy per cell and 50 square feet per inmate in multiple occupancy units.

(f) Includes capacity of private and contract facilities and inmates housed in them.

Table 9.17
ADULTS ON PROBATION BY REGION, 2007

State or other jurisdiction	Probation population				Percent change during 2007	Number on probation on 12/31/07 per 100,000 adult residents
		2007				
	1/1/07	Entries	Exits	12/31/07		
United States (a)	4,215,361	2,183,333	2,122,681	4,293,163	1.8%	1,873
Federal	24,465	11,815	12,830	23,450	-4.1	10
State (a)	4,190,896	2,171,518	2,109,851	4,269,713	1.9	1,863
Eastern Region						
Connecticut (b)	54,314	28,681	25,502	57,493	5.9	2,136
Delaware	16,958	15,334	15,596	16,696	-1.5	2,513
Maine	7,919	3,625	3,691	7,853	-0.8	754
Massachusetts (c)	172,383	94,000	90,964	175,419	1.8	3,484
New Hampshire (b)	4,590	3,080	3,020	4,650	1.3	454
New Jersey	133,158	40,223	46,991	126,390	-5.1	1,901
New York	122,359	36,952	39,348	119,963	-2.0	804
Pennsylvania (d)	172,184	2,534	2,180	176,987	2.8	1,829
Rhode Island (b)	26,017	5,747	5,627	26,137	0.5	3,167
Vermont (b)(c)	7,632	4,380	4,953	7,059	-7.5	1,436
Regional total	717,514	234,556	237,872	718,647	0.1	2,257
Midwestern Region						
Illinois (b)	141,000	59,734	57,944	142,790	1.3	1,471
Indiana (b)	128,655	96,049	98,142	126,562	-1.6	2,646
Iowa (b)	22,622	15,924	15,770	22,776	0.7	996
Kansas (c)	15,518	20,084	19,471	16,131	4.0	771
Michigan (b)(c)(d)	181,024	81,022	80,140	182,706	0.9	2,392
Minnesota	126,616	79,731	78,550	127,797	0.9	3,226
Nebraska	18,731	14,896	14,717	18,910	1.0	1,417
North Dakota	4,320	2,995	2,847	4,468	3.4	896
Ohio (b)(c)(d)	244,512	139,794	128,862	254,898	4.2	2,917
South Dakota (c)	5,661	3,698	3,489	5,870	3.7	972
Wisconsin	55,018	25,106	26,894	53,230	-3.2	1,237
Regional total	943,677	539,033	526,826	956,138	1.3	1,978
Southern Region (a)						
Alabama (e)	46,367	20,101	14,723	51,745	11.6	1,468
Arkansas	31,166	9,368	8,858	31,676	1.6	1,476
Florida (b)(c)(d)	272,242	236,182	233,891	274,079	0.7	1,917
Georgia (b)(f)	432,436	281,252	278,327	435,361	0.7	6,144
Kentucky (b)(c)	36,396	12,210	9,596	42,510	16.8	1,306
Louisiana	38,145	14,887	14,026	39,006	2.3	1,208
Maryland (b)(e)	94,100	36,786	32,416	98,470	4.6	2,301
Mississippi (c)	24,107	9,773	12,257	21,623	-10.3	1,001
Missouri	55,098	25,933	24,791	56,240	2.1	1,256
North Carolina (b)	110,419	66,432	65,405	111,446	0.9	1,612
Oklahoma (b)(g)	/	/	/	/	:	:
South Carolina	43,284	13,968	14,531	42,721	-1.3	1,264
Tennessee (c)	52,057	23,686	23,024	56,179	7.9	1,190
Texas	431,967	182,948	180,606	434,309	0.5	2,485
Virginia (b)	48,144	28,439	24,629	51,954	7.9	877
West Virginia (d)	7,668	1,657	1,452	7,890	2.9	553
Regional total	1,723,596	963,622	938,532	1,755,209	1.8	2,245
Western Region						
Alaska (c)	6,111	1,215	910	6,416	5.0	1,269
Arizona (b)	73,265	29,352	25,787	76,830	4.9	1,627
California (b)	346,495	195,554	188,080	353,969	2.2	1,295
Colorado (b)(c)(d)	63,032	47,993	33,351	77,635	23.2	2,094
Hawaii (b)	18,598	6,522	5,694	19,426	4.5	1,934
Idaho (b)(d)(h)	48,609	39,657	39,603	48,663	0.1	4,405
Montana (b)(c)	8,763	4,125	3,782	9,106	3.9	1,223
Nevada	13,208	7,549	7,296	13,461	1.9	697
New Mexico (b)(d)	17,878	3,484	3,042	20,774	16.2	1,400
Oregon	43,988	16,968	17,224	43,732	-0.6	1,504
Utah	10,417	5,542	5,130	10,829	4.0	584
Washington (b)(c)(d)(e)	116,487	66,041	67,152	118,885	2.1	2,390
Wyoming	5,225	2,516	2,383	5,358	2.5	1,334
Regional total	772,076	426,518	399,434	805,084	4.3	1,528
Regional total without California	425,581	230,964	211,354	451,115	5.9	1,778
Dist. of Columbia	6,670	5,004	5,189	6,485	-2.8	1,362

See footnotes at end of table.

ADULTS ON PROBATION BY REGION, 2007 — Continued

Source: U.S. Department of Justice, Bureau of Justice Statistics, *Probation and Parole in the United States*, 2007, Statistical Tables NCJ 224707 (December 9, 2008).

Note: Because of nonresponse or incomplete data, the probation population for some jurisdictions on December 31, 2007, does not equal the population on January 1, plus entries, minus exits. Rates were computed using the estimated adult resident population in each state on January 1, 2008.

Key:

/ — Not known.

: — Not calculated.

(a) Includes an estimated 26,000 probationers under supervision in Oklahoma on January 1 and December 31, 2007.

(b) Some or all detailed data are estimated.

(c) Excludes probationers in one of the following categories: absconder, warrant, supervised out of state, electronic monitoring, or intensive supervision.

(d) Data for entries and exits were estimated for non-reporting agencies.

(e) Due to a change in recordkeeping procedures, data are not comparable to previous reports.

(f) Counts include private agency cases and may overstate the number of persons under supervision.

(g) The state agency did not provide data. Two localities reported 1,363 probationers under supervision on January 1 and 2,150 probationers under supervision on December 31, 2007.

(h) Counts include estimates for misdemeanors based on entries.

Table 9.18
ADULTS ON PAROLE BY REGION, 2007

State or other jurisdiction	Parole population					Number on parole on 12/31/07 per 100,000 adult residents
	1/1/07	2007 Entries	2007 Exits	12/31/07	Percent change during 2007	
United States (a)(b)	799,058	505,965	482,180	824,365	3.2	360
Federal	88,993	43,077	39,397	92,673	4.1	40
State (a)(b)	710,065	462,888	442,783	731,692	3.0	319
Eastern Region						
Connecticut	2,567	2,319	2,709	2,177	-15.2	81
Delaware	544	366	375	535	-1.7	81
Maine	31	2	1	32	3.2	3
Massachusetts (c)	3,435	4,952	5,178	3,209	-6.6	64
New Hampshire	1,621	709	677	1,653	2.0	162
New Jersey	14,405	9,505	8,867	15,043	4.4	226
New York	53,001	25,467	24,799	53,669	1.3	360
Pennsylvania (d)	76,386	11,432	11,060	78,107	2.3	807
Rhode Island	332	515	385	462	39.2	56
Vermont (c)(e)	966	504	534	936	-3.1	190
Regional total	153,288	55,771	54,585	155,823	1.6	367
Midwestern Region (a)						
Illinois (c)	/	/	/	33,354	:	344
Indiana	8,205	9,217	7,060	10,362	26.3	217
Iowa	3,578	2,500	2,532	3,546	-0.9	155
Kansas (e)	4,886	5,278	5,322	4,842	-0.9	232
Michigan	18,486	13,173	10,528	21,131	14.3	277
Minnesota	4,445	5,715	5,416	4,744	6.7	120
Nebraska	797	1,015	1,012	800	0.4	60
North Dakota	372	784	814	342	-8.1	69
Ohio	17,603	10,007	10,035	17,575	-0.2	201
South Dakota	2,767	1,845	1,800	2,812	1.6	466
Wisconsin	16,767	7,457	7,238	16,986	1.3	395
Regional total	77,906	56,991	51,757	116,494	5.0	270
Southern Region (b)						
Alabama (c)(f)	7,508	2,464	2,182	7,790	3.8	221
Arkansas	18,057	9,082	7,751	19,388	7.4	904
Florida (c)	4,790	7,036	7,172	4,654	-2.8	33
Georgia	22,958	11,935	11,782	23,111	0.7	326
Kentucky	11,755	5,945	4,959	12,741	8.4	392
Louisiana	23,832	13,652	13,399	24,085	1.1	746
Maryland	14,351	7,122	7,617	13,856	-3.4	324
Mississippi	1,899	1,021	905	2,015	6.1	93
Missouri	18,815	14,114	13,080	19,849	5.5	443
North Carolina (c)	3,236	3,552	3,477	3,311	2.3	48
Oklahoma (c)	/	/	/	/	:	:
South Carolina	2,766	599	932	2,433	-12.0	72
Tennessee	9,570	4,568	3,474	10,496	9.7	222
Texas (c)	100,053	33,897	32,202	101,748	1.7	582
Virginia (f)	7,201	1,845	2,196	6,850	-4.9	116
West Virginia	1,523	1,437	1,130	1,830	20.2	128
Regional total	248,314	118,269	112,258	254,157	2.3	291
Western Region						
Alaska (f)	1,527	709	692	1,544	1.1	305
Arizona (c)	6,463	14,862	14,518	6,807	5.3	144
California (e)	118,592	178,161	174,076	123,764	4.4	453
Colorado	9,551	9,089	7,554	11,086	16.1	299
Hawaii	2,308	694	892	2,110	-8.6	210
Idaho	2,732	1,689	1,307	3,114	14	282
Montana	844	769	647	966	14.5	130
Nevada	3,824	3,653	3,824	3,653	-4.5	189
New Mexico (c)(e)(f)	3,517	2,013	2,003	3,527	0.3	238
Oregon	22,031	9,210	8,583	22,658	2.8	779
Utah	3,342	2,524	2,269	3,597	7.6	194
Washington	12,611	5,708	5,302	13,017	3.2	262
Wyoming	674	308	276	706	4.7	176
Regional total	188,016	229,389	221,943	196,549	4.5	373
Regional total without California	69,424	51,228	47,867	72,785	4.8	307
Dist. of Columbia	5,341	2,468	2,240	5,569	4.3	1,169

Source: U.S. Department of Justice, Bureau of Justice Statistics, Probation and Parole in the United States, 2007, Statistical Tables NCJ 224707 (December 9, 2008).

Note: Because of nonresponse or incomplete data, the parole population for some jurisdictions on December 31, 2007, does not equal the population on January 1, plus entries, minus exits. Rates were computed using the estimated adult resident population in each state on January 1, 2008.

Key:

/—Not known.

:—Not calculated.

(a) Includes an estimated 34,100 parolees under supervision in Illinois on January 1, 2007.

(b) Includes an estimated 3,100 parolees under supervision in Oklahoma on January 1 and December 31, 2007.

(c) Some or all data were estimated.

(d) Data for entries and exits were estimated for nonreporting county agencies. The December 31, 2007, population includes 25,475 parolees under state parole supervision. Reported entries are parolees who entered state parole supervision through a discretionary release from prison.

(e) Excludes parolees in one of the following categories: absconder, out of state, inactive, or only have financial conditions remaining.

(f) Due to a change in recordkeeping procedures, data are not comparable to previous reports.

Table 9.19
ADULTS LEAVING PAROLE BY TYPE OF EXIT, BY REGION, 2007

State or other jurisdiction	*Number of adults exiting parole, 2007*								
			Returned to prison or jail						
	Total reported exits	*Completion*	*Total*	*With new sentence*	*With revocation*	*Other*	*Other unsatisfactory (a)*	*Other (b)*	*Unknown*
United States	482,180	214,604	183,253	47,357	129,609	6,287	8,834	71,356	4,133
Federal	39,397	24,152	10,573	1,963	8,490	120	1,678	2,994	0
State	442,783	190,452	172,680	45,394	121,119	6,167	7,156	68,362	4,133
Eastern Region									
Connecticut (c)	2,709	849	1,463	0	0	1,463	0	198	199
Delaware	375	211	**	**	**	**	83	81	0
Maine	1	0	0	0	0	0	0	1	0
Massachusetts(c)	5,178	4,206	931	**	**	931	0	41	0
New Hampshire	677	94	569	569	0	0	0	13	1
New Jersey	8,867	6,052	2,757	274	2,483	0	0	58	0
New York	24,799	12,626	11,880	1,960	9,704	216	0	293	0
Pennsylvania	11,060	4,788	5,243	1,884	3,359	0	0	942	87
Rhode Island	385	273	111	23	88	0	0	1	0
Vermont (c)	534	307	171	64	83	24	0	56	0
Regional total	54,210	29,195	23,125	4,774	15,717	2,634	0	1,603	287
Midwestern Region									
Illinois (d)	/	/	/	/	/	/	/	/	/
Indiana	7,060	5,244	1,110	**	**	1,110	0	695	11
Iowa	2,532	1,731	774	**	774	0	0	27	0
Kansas	5,322	2,055	1,494	192	1,293	9	0	1,773	0
Michigan	10,528	6,273	4,095	1,994	2,101	0	0	160	0
Minnesota	5,416	2,692	2,286	222	2,064	0	0	438	0
Nebraska	1,012	730	278	33	245	0	0	4	0
North Dakota	814	639	168	32	136	0	0	7	0
Ohio	10,035	7,429	1,876	1,327	549	0	0	730	0
South Dakota	1,800	741	870	112	758	0	25	164	0
Wisconsin	7,238	3,310	3,821	741	3,080	0	29	78	0
Regional total	64,837	35,553	24,985	5,817	18,049	1,119	54	4,234	11
Southerb Region									
Alabama (c)	2,182	1,394	687	388	299	0	0	71	30
Arkansas	7,751	4,321	2,843	848	1,926	69	0	587	0
Florida	7,172	4,909	1,804	410	1,394	0	0	76	383
Georgia	11,782	7,225	4,491	17	3,514	960	0	66	0
Kentucky	4,959	1,316	3,101	535	2,566	0	0	542	0
Louisiana	13,399	7,205	2,688	1,406	1,036	246	3,268	238	0
Maryland	7,617	4,312	1,599	830	769	0	1,554	152	0
Mississippi	905	624	209	**	**	209	0	72	0
Missouri	13,080	4,709	8,213	1,164	7,049	0	~	158	0
North Carolina	3,477	2,862	198	93	105	0	23	200	194
Oklahoma (d)	/	/	/	/	/	/	/	/	/
South Carolina	932	697	209	37	172	0	0	26	0
Tennessee	3,474	1,759	1,606	697	909	0	0	109	0
Texas (c)	32,202	22,163	9,009	6,767	2,242	0	0	1,030	0
Virginia	2,196	1,076	0	0	0	**	**	1,120	0
West Virginia	1,130	686	416	10	406	0	0	28	0
Regional total	101,793	61,294	29,780	12,038	15,338	2,404	4,984	4,927	808
Western Region									
Alaska	692	**	**	**	**	**	**	**	692
Arizona (c)	14,518	11,003	2,934	206	2,728	0	0	577	4
California	174,076	40,456	81,431	19,829	61,602	0	0	52,189	0
Colorado	7,554	3,087	4,361	1,078	3,283	0	0	106	0
Hawaii	892	370	313	11	302	0	0	8	201
Idaho	1,307	503	501	112	389	0	289	14	0
Montana	647	336	195	12	183	0	0	116	0
Nevada	3,824	3,102	509	381	128	0	0	213	0
New Mexico	2,003	**	**	**	**	**	**	**	2,003
Oregon	8,583	4,696	2,823	806	2,012	5	770	167	127
Utah	2,269	533	1,648	323	1,320	5	1	87	0
Washington	5,302	158	0	~	~	0	1,058	4,086	0
Wyoming	276	166	75	7	68	0	0	35	0
Regional total	221,943	64,410	94,790	22,765	72,015	10	2,118	57,598	3,027
Regional total without California	47,867	23,954	13,359	2,936	10,413	10	2,118	5,409	3,027
District of Columbia	2,240	534	920	0	0	920	56	529	201

Source: U.S. Department of Justice, Bureau of Justice Statistics, Probation and Parole in the United States, 2007, Statistical Tables NCJ 224707 (December 9, 2008).

Key:

** – Not known.

/ – Not reported.

~ – Not applicable.

(a)Includes parolees released from parole supervision who failed to meet all conditions of supervision, including some with only financial conditions remaining whose case may have been turned over to a business office, and other types of unsatisfactory expirations of sentence.

(b) Includes 53,981 parolees who had absconded (including 47,281 in California), 4,975 who had died, 2,948 who had transferred to another jurisdiction, and 9,452 others.

(c) Some or all detailed data are estimated.

(d) No data provided. An estimated total of 36,000 adults exited parole supervision in Illinois (35,000) and Oklahoma (1,000) during 2007.

Table 9.20
CAPITAL PUNISHMENT (as of December 2007)

State or other jurisdiction	Capital offenses by state	Prisoners under sentence of death	Method of execution
Alabama	Intentional murder with 18 aggravating factors (Ala. Stat. Ann. 13A-5-40(a)(1)-(18)).	195	Electrocution or lethal injection
Alaska	. . .	. . .	. . .
Arizona	First-degree murder accompanied by at least 1 of 14 aggravating factors (A.R.S. § 13-703(F)).	124	Lethal gas or lethal injection (a)
Arkansas	Capital murder (Ark. Code Ann. 5-10-101) with a finding of at least 1 of 10 aggravating circumstances; treason.	37	Lethal injection or electrocution (b)
California	First-degree murder with special circumstances; train wrecking; treason; perjury causing execution.	660	Lethal gas or lethal injection
Colorado	First-degree murder with at least 1 of 17 aggravating factors; first-degree kidnapping resulting in death; treason.	2	Lethal injection
Connecticut	Capital felony with 8 forms of aggravated homicide (C.G.S. 53a-54b).	8	Lethal injection
Delaware	First-degree murder with at least 1 statutory aggravating circumstance.	18	Hanging or lethal injection (c)
Florida	First-degree murder; felony murder; capital drug trafficking; capital sexual battery.	397	Electrocution or lethal injection
Georgia	Murder; kidnapping with bodily injury or ransom when the victim dies; aircraft hijacking; treason.	107	Lethal injection
Hawaii	. . .	. . .	. . .
Idaho	First-degree murder with aggravating factors; aggravated kidnapping; perjury resulting in death.	20	Firing squad or lethal injection
Illinois	First-degree murder with 1 of 21 aggravating circumstances.	11	Lethal injection
Indiana	Murder with 16 aggravating circumstances (IC 35-50-2-9).	23	Lethal injection
Iowa	. . .	. . .	. . .
Kansas	Capital murder with 8 aggravating circumstances (KSA 21-3439, KSA 21-4625).	9	Lethal injection
Kentucky	Murder with aggravating factors; kidnapping with aggravating factors (KRS 32.025).	41	Electrocution or lethal injection (d)
Louisiana	First-degree murder; aggravated rape of victim under age 13; treason (La. R.S. 14:30, 14:42, and 14:113). Revision: Revised the definition of aggravated rape as a capital-eligible offense to include any offense involving victims under age 13. (2006 La. Sess. Law, Act 178), effective 8/15/2006.	88	Lethal injection
Maine	. . .	. . .	. . .
Maryland	First-degree murder, either premeditated or during the commission of a felony, provided that certain death eligibility requirements are satisfied.	8	Lethal injection
Massachusetts	. . .	. . .	. . .
Michigan	. . .	. . .	. . .
Minnesota	. . .	. . .	. . .
Mississippi	Capital murder (97-3-19(2) MCA); aircraft piracy (97-25-55(1) MCA).	66	Lethal injection
Missouri	First-degree murder (565.020 RSMO 2000).	51	Lethal injection or lethal gas
Montana	Capital murder with 1 of 9 aggravating circumstances (Mont. Code Ann. § 46-18-303); aggravated sexual intercourse without consent (Mont. Code Ann. § 45-5-503).	2	Lethal injection
Nebraska	First-degree murder with a finding of at least 1 statutorily-defined aggravating circumstance.	9	Electrocution
Nevada	First-degree murder with at least 1 of 15 aggravating circumstances (NRS 200.030, 200.033, 200.035).	80	Lethal injection
New Hampshire	Six categories of capital murder (RSA 630:1, RSA 630:5). Revision: Amended the capital statute to increase the minimum age of eligibility for a death sentence from 17 to 18 years at the time the offense was committed (N.H. Rev. Stat. Ann. 630:1,V), effective 1/1/2006.	0	Lethal injection or hanging (e)
New Jersey	On December 17, 2007 Governor Corzine signed legislation abolishing the death penalty in New Jersey. The death sentences of eight prisoners on death row were commuted to life without the eligibility of parole on Dec. 16, 2007.		

See footnotes at end of table.

CAPITAL PUNISHMENT—Continued

State or other jurisdiction	Capital offenses by state	Prisoners under sentence of death	Method of execution
New Mexico	First-degree murder with at least 1 of 7 statutorily-defined aggravating circumstances (Section 30-2-1 A, NMSA).	2	Lethal injection
New York	First-degree murder with 1 of 13 aggravating factors (NY Penal Law §125.27).	1	Lethal injection
North Carolina	First-degree murder (NCGS §14-17).	185	Lethal injection
North Dakota	. . .	. . .	. . .
Ohio	Aggravated murder with at least 1 of 10 aggravating circumstances (O.R.C. secs. 2903.01, 2929.02, and 2929.04).	191	Lethal injection
Oklahoma	First-degree murder in conjunction with a finding of at least 1 of 8 statutorily-defined aggravating circumstances; sex crimes against a child under 14 years of age. Revision: Added as a capital offense sex crimes against a child under 14 years of age when the offender has a previous conviction for a similar offense (Okla. Stat. Ann. 10 § 7115), effective 7/1/2006.	88	Electrocution, lethal injection or firing squad (f)
Oregon	Aggravated murder (ORS 163.095).	33	Lethal injection
Pennsylvania	First-degree murder with 18 aggravating circumstances.	226	Lethal injection
Rhode Island	. . .	. . .	. . .
South Carolina	Murder with 1 of 12 aggravating circumstances (§ 16-3-20(C)(a)); criminal sexual conduct with a minor with 1 of 9 aggravators (§ 16-3-655). Revision: Added as a capital offense second and subsequent offenses of first-degree criminal sexual conduct with a minor who is less than 11 years of age (§16-3-655). Lawmakers also added as an aggravating factor murder committed by a person deemed a sexually violent predator under South Carolina law (§16-3-20(C)(a)(12)). Both changes were effective 7/1/2006.	67	Electrocution or lethal injection
South Dakota	First-degree murder with 1 of 10 aggravating circumstances. Revision: Amended the definition of aggravated kidnapping to eliminate death as a possible sentence (SDCL 22-19-1), effective 7/1/2006.	4	Lethal injection
Tennessee	First-degree murder with 1 of 15 aggravating circumstances (Tenn. Code Ann. § 39-13-204).	107	Lethal injection or electrocution (g)
Texas	Criminal homicide with 1 of 9 aggravating circumstances (TX Penal Code 19.03).	393	Lethal injection
Utah	Aggravated murder (76-5-202, Utah Code Annotated).	9	Lethal injection or firing squad (h)
Vermont	. . .	. . .	. . .
Virginia	First-degree murder with 1 of 13 aggravating circumstances (VA Code § 18.2-31).	20	Electrocution or lethal injection
Washington	Aggravated first-degree murder.	9	Lethal injection or hanging
West Virginia	. . .	. . .	. . .
Wisconsin	. . .	. . .	. . .
Wyoming	First-degree murder.	2	Lethal injection or lethal gas (i)
Dist. of Columbia	. . .	. . .	. . .

Sources: U.S. Department of Justice, Bureau of Statistics, *Capital Punishment, 2006—Statistical Tables* (December 2007), "Capital Offenses by State 2007" National Prisoners Statistics Program (NPS-8).

Notes: The United States Supreme Court ruling in *Roper v. Simmons*, 543 U.S. 551 (2005) declared unconstitutional the imposition of the death penalty on persons under the age of 18.

The United States Supreme Court ruling in *Atkins v. Virginia*, 536 U.S. 304 (2002) declared unconstitutional the imposition of the death penalty on mentally handicapped persons.

Key:

. . . — No capital punishment statute.

(a) Arizona authorizes lethal injection for persons whose capital sentence was received after 11/15/92; for those sentenced before that date, the condemned may select lethal injection or lethal gas.

(b) Arkansas authorizes lethal injection for those whose capital offense occurred on or after 7/4/83; for those whose offense occurred before that date, the condemned may select lethal injection or electrocution.

(c) Delaware authorizes lethal injection for those whose capital offense occurred after 6/13/86; for those whose offense occurred before that date, the condemned may select lethal injection or hanging.

(d) Kentucky authorizes lethal injection for persons whose capital sentence was received on or after 3/31/98; for those sentenced before that date, the condemned may select lethal injection or electrocution.

(e) New Hampshire authorizes hanging only if lethal injection cannot be given.

(f) Oklahoma authorizes electrocution if lethal injection is ever held to be unconstitutional, and firing squad if both lethal injection and electrocution are held unconstitutional.

(g) Tennessee authorizes lethal injection for those whose capital offense occurred after 12/31/98; those whose offense occurred before that date may select electrocution by written waiver.

(h) Authorizes firing squad if lethal injection is held unconstitutional. Inmates who selected execution by firing squad prior to May 3, 2004, may still be entitled to execution by that method.

(i) Wyoming authorizes lethal gas if lethal injection is ever held to be unconstitutional.

Chapter Ten

STATE PAGES

Table 10.1
OFFICIAL NAMES OF STATES AND JURISDICTIONS, CAPITALS, ZIP CODES AND CENTRAL SWITCHBOARDS

State or other jurisdiction	Name of state capitol (a)	Capital	Zip code	Area code	Central switchboard
Alabama, State of	State House	Montgomery	36130	334	242-7000
Alaska, State of	State Capitol	Juneau	99801	907	465-4648
Arizona, State of	State Capitol	Phoenix	85007	602	926-4900
Arkansas, State of	State Capitol	Little Rock	72201	501	682-3000
California, State of	State Capitol	Sacramento	95814	916	322-9900
Colorado, State of	State Capitol	Denver	80203	303	866-5000
Connecticut, State of	State Capitol	Hartford	06106	860	240-0100
Delaware, State of	Legislative Hall	Dover	19903	302	744-4114
Florida, State of	The Capitol	Tallahassee	32399	850	488-4441
Georgia, State of	State Capitol	Atlanta	30334	404	656-2000
Hawaii, State of	State Capitol	Honolulu	96813	808	586-0221
Idaho, State of	State Capitol	Boise	83720	208	332-1000
Illinois, State of	State House	Springfield	62706	217	782-2000
Indiana, State of	State House	Indianapolis	46204	317	232-1000
Iowa, State of	State Capitol	Des Moines	50319	515	281-5011
Kansas, State of	Statehouse	Topeka	66612	785	296-0111
Kentucky, Commonwealth of	State Capitol	Frankfort	40601	502	564-8100
Louisiana, State of	State Capitol	Baton Rouge	70804	225	324-6600
Maine, State of	State House Station	Augusta	04333	207	287-6826
Maryland, State of	State House	Annapolis	21401	410	946-5400
Massachusetts, Commonwealth of	State House	Boston	02133	617	722-2000
Michigan, State of	State Capitol	Lansing	48909	517	373-0184
Minnesota, State of	State Capitol	St. Paul	55155	651	296-3962
Mississippi, State of	State Capitol	Jackson	39215	601	359-3770
Missouri, State of	State Capitol	Jefferson City	65101	573	751-2000
Montana, State of	State Capitol	Helena	59620	406	444-2511
Nebraska, State of	State Capitol	Lincoln	68509	402	471-2311
Nevada, State of	State Capitol	Carson City	89701	775	684-5670
New Hampshire, State of	State House	Concord	03301	603	271-1110
New Jersey, State of	State House	Trenton	08625	609	292-6000
New Mexico, State of	State Capitol	Santa Fe	87501	505	986-4600
New York, State of	State Capitol	Albany	12224	518	455-7545
North Carolina, State of	State Capitol	Raleigh	27601	919	733-4111
North Dakota, State of	State Capitol	Bismarck	58505	701	328-2000
Ohio, State of	Statehouse	Columbus	43215	614	466-2000
Oklahoma, State of	State Capitol	Oklahoma City	73105	405	521-2011
Oregon, State of	State Capitol	Salem	97301	503	986-1848
Pennsylvania, Commonwealth of	Main Capitol Building	Harrisburg	17120	717	787-2121
Rhode Island and Providence Plantations, State of	State House	Providence	02903	401	222-2653
South Carolina, State of	State House	Columbia	29211	803	896-0000
South Dakota, State of	State Capitol	Pierre	57501	605	773-3011
Tennessee, State of	State Capitol	Nashville	37243	615	741-2001
Texas, State of	State Capitol	Austin	78701	512	463-4630
Utah, State of	State Capitol	Salt Lake City	84114	801	538-3000
Vermont, State of	State House	Montpelier	05633	802	828-2231
Virginia, Commonwealth of	State Capitol	Richmond	23219	804	698-7410
Washington, State of	Legislative Building	Olympia	98504	360	786-7579
West Virginia, State of	State Capitol	Charleston	25305	304	558-3456
Wisconsin, State of	State Capitol	Madison	53702	608	266-0382
Wyoming, State of	State Capitol	Cheyenne	82002	307	777-7434
District of Columbia	District Building	. . .	20004	202	724-8000
American Samoa, Territory of	Maota Fono	Pago Pago	96799	684	633-4116
Guam, Territory of	Congress Building	Hagatna	96932	671	472-8931
No. Mariana Islands, Commonwealth of	Civic Center Building	Saipan	96950	670	664-2286
Puerto Rico, Commonwealth of	The Capitol	San Juan	00902	787	721-7000
U.S. Virgin Islands, Territory of St. Thomas	Government House	Charlotte Amalie,	00802	340	774-0001

(a) In some instances the name is not official.

Table 10.2
HISTORICAL DATA ON THE STATES

State or other jurisdiction	*Source of state lands*	*Date organized as territory*	*Date admitted to Union*	*Chronological order of admission to Union*
Alabama	Mississippi Territory, 1798 (a)	March 3, 1817	Dec. 14, 1819	22
Alaska	Purchased from Russia, 1867	Aug. 24, 1912	Jan. 3, 1959	49
Arizona	Ceded by Mexico, 1848 (b)	Feb. 24, 1863	Feb. 14, 1912	48
Arkansas	Louisiana Purchase, 1803	March 2, 1819	June 15, 1836	25
California	Ceded by Mexico, 1848	(c)	Sept. 9, 1850	31
Colorado	Louisiana Purchase, 1803 (d)	Feb. 28, 1861	Aug. 1, 1876	38
Connecticut	Fundamental Orders, Jan. 14, 1638; Royal charter, April 23, 1662	(e)	Jan. 9, 1788 (f)	5
Delaware	Swedish charter, 1638; English charter, 1638	(e)	Dec. 7, 1787 (f)	1
Florida	Ceded by Spain, 1819	March 30, 1822	March 3, 1845	27
Georgia	Charter, 1732, from George II to Trustees for Establishing the Colony of Georgia	(e)	Jan. 2, 1788 (f)	4
Hawaii	Annexed, 1898	June 14, 1900	Aug. 21, 1959	50
Idaho	Treaty with Britain, 1846	March 4, 1863	July 3, 1890	43
Illinois	Northwest Territory, 1787	Feb. 3, 1809	Dec. 3, 1818	21
Indiana	Northwest Territory, 1787	May 7, 1800	Dec. 11, 1816	19
Iowa	Louisiana Purchase, 1803	June 12, 1838	Dec. 28, 1846	29
Kansas	Louisiana Purchase, 1803 (d)	May 30, 1854	Jan. 29, 1861	34
Kentucky	Part of Virginia until admitted as state	(c)	June 1, 1792	15
Louisiana	Louisiana Purchase, 1803 (g)	March 26, 1804	April 30, 1812	18
Maine	Part of Massachusetts until admitted as state	(c)	March 15, 1820	23
Maryland	Charter, 1632, from Charles I to Calvert	(e)	April 28, 1788 (f)	7
Massachusetts	Charter to Massachusetts Bay Company, 1629	(e)	Feb. 6, 1788 (f)	6
Michigan	Northwest Territory, 1787	Jan. 11, 1805	Jan. 26, 1837	26
Minnesota	Northwest Territory, 1787 (h)	March 3, 1849	May 11, 1858	32
Mississippi	Mississippi Territory (i)	April 7, 1798	Dec. 10, 1817	20
Missouri	Louisiana Purchase, 1803	June 4, 1812	Aug. 10, 1821	24
Montana	Louisiana Purchase, 1803 (j)	May 26, 1864	Nov. 8, 1889	41
Nebraska	Louisiana Purchase, 1803	May 30, 1854	March 1, 1867	37
Nevada	Ceded by Mexico, 1848	March 2, 1861	Oct. 31, 1864	36
New Hampshire	Grants from Council for New England, 1622 and 1629; made Royal province, 1679	(e)	June 21, 1788 (f)	9
New Jersey	Dutch settlement, 1618; English charter, 1664	(e)	Dec. 18, 1787 (f)	3
New Mexico	Ceded by Mexico, 1848 (b)	Sept. 9, 1850	Jan. 6, 1912	47
New York	Dutch settlement, 1623; English control, 1664	(e)	July 26, 1788 (f)	11
North Carolina	Charter, 1663, from Charles II	(e)	Nov. 21, 1789 (f)	12
North Dakota	Louisiana Purchase, 1803 (k)	March 2, 1861	Nov. 2, 1889	39
Ohio	Northwest Territory, 1787	May 7, 1800	March 1, 1803	17
Oklahoma	Louisiana Purchase, 1803	May 2, 1890	Nov. 16, 1907	46
Oregon	Settlement and treaty with Britain, 1846	Aug. 14, 1848	Feb. 14, 1859	33
Pennsylvania	Grant from Charles II to William Penn, 1681	(e)	Dec. 12, 1787 (f)	2
Rhode Island	Charter, 1663, from Charles II	(e)	May 29, 1790 (f)	13
South Carolina	Charter, 1663, from Charles II	(e)	May 23, 1788 (f)	8
South Dakota	Louisiana Purchase, 1803	March 2, 1861	Nov. 2, 1889	40
Tennessee	Part of North Carolina until land ceded to U.S. in 1789	June 8, 1790 (l)	June 1, 1796	16
Texas	Republic of Texas, 1845	(c)	Dec. 29, 1845	28
Utah	Ceded by Mexico, 1848	Sept. 9, 1850	Jan. 4, 1896	45
Vermont	From lands of New Hampshire and New York	(c)	March 4, 1791	14
Virginia	Charter, 1609, from James I to London Company	(e)	June 25, 1788 (f)	10
Washington	Oregon Territory, 1848	March 2, 1853	Nov. 11, 1889	42
West Virginia	Part of Virginia until admitted as state	(c)	June 20, 1863	35
Wisconsin	Northwest Territory, 1787	April 20, 1836	May 29, 1848	30
Wyoming	Louisiana Purchase, 1803 (d)(j)	July 25, 1868	July 10, 1890	44
Dist. of Columbia	Maryland (m)	. . .	. . .	. . .
American Samoa	Became a territory, 1900			
Guam	Ceded by Spain, 1898	Aug. 1, 1950	. . .	. . .
No. Mariana Islands	. . .	March 24, 1976	. . .	. . .
Puerto Rico	Ceded by Spain, 1898	. . .	July 25, 1952 (n)	. . .
U.S. Virgin Islands	Purchased from Denmark, March 31, 1917			

See footnotes at end of table

HISTORICAL DATA ON THE STATES—Continued

Key:

(a) By the Treaty of Paris, 1783, England gave up claim to the 13 original Colonies, and to all land within an area extending along the present Canadian to the Lake of the Woods, down the Mississippi River to the 31st parallel, east to the Chattahoochee, down that river to the mouth of the Flint, border east to the source of the St. Mary's down that river to the ocean. The major part of Alabama was acquired by the Treaty of Paris, and the lower portion from Spain in 1813.

(b) Portion of land obtained by Gadsden Purchase, 1853.

(c) No territorial status before admission to Union.

(d) Portion of land ceded by Mexico, 1848.

(e) One of the original 13 Colonies.

(f) Date of ratification of U.S. Constitution.

(g) West Feliciana District (Baton Rouge) acquired from Spain, 1810; added to Louisiana, 1812.

(h) Portion of land obtained by Louisiana Purchase, 1803.

(i) See footnote (a). The lower portion of Mississippi also was acquired from Spain in 1813.

(j) Portion of land obtained from Oregon Territory, 1848.

(k) The northern portion of the Red River Valley was acquired by treaty with Great Britain in 1818.

(l) Date Southwest Territory (identical boundary as Tennessee's) was created.

(m) Area was originally 100 square miles, taken from Virginia and Maryland. Virginia's portion south of the Potomac was given back to that state in 1846. Site chosen in 1790, city incorporated 1802.

(n) On this date, Puerto Rico became a self-governing commonwealth by compact approved by the U.S. Congress and the voters of Puerto Rico as provided in U.S. Public Law 600 of 1950.

Table 10.3
STATE STATISTICS

State or other jurisdiction	Land area: In square miles	Land area: Rank in nation	Population (a): Size	Population (a): Rank in nation	Percentage change 2006 to 2007	Density per square mile	Rank in nation	Number of Representatives in Congress	Capital	Population (a)	Rank in state	Largest city	Population (a)
Alabama	50,744	28	4,627,851	23	0.82	91.2	27	7	Montgomery	204,086	2	Birmingham	229,800
Alaska	571,951	1	683,478	47	0.89	1.2	50	1	Juneau	30,690	2	Anchorage (b)	279,671
Arizona	113,635	6	6,338,755	16	2.81	55.8	33	8	Phoenix	1,552,259	1	Phoenix	1,552,259
Arkansas	52,068	27	2,834,797	32	0.91	54.4	34	4	Little Rock	187,452	1	Little Rock	187,452
California	155,959	3	36,553,215	1	0.84	234.4	11	53	Sacramento	460,242	7	Los Angeles	3,834,340
Colorado	103,718	8	4,861,515	22	2.00	46.9	37	7	Denver	588,349	1	Denver	588,349
Connecticut	4,845	48	3,502,309	29	0.19	722.9	4	5	Hartford	124,563	3	Bridgeport	136,695
Delaware	1,954	49	864,764	45	1.41	442.6	6	1	Dover	35,811	2	Wilmington	72,868
Florida	53,927	26	18,251,243	4	1.07	338.4	8	25	Tallahassee	168,979	8	Jacksonville	805,605
Georgia	57,906	21	9,544,750	9	2.17	164.8	18	13	Atlanta	519,145	1	Atlanta	519,145
Hawaii	6,423	47	1,283,388	42	0.37	199.8	13	2	Honolulu	375,571	1	Honolulu	375,571
Idaho	82,747	11	1,499,402	39	2.43	18.1	44	2	Boise	202,832	1	Boise	202,832
Illinois	55,584	24	12,852,548	5	0.59	231.2	12	19	Springfield	117,090	6	Chicago	2,836,658
Indiana	35,867	38	6,345,289	15	0.68	176.9	17	9	Indianapolis	795,458	1	Indianapolis	795,458
Iowa	55,869	23	2,988,046	30	0.52	53.5	35	5	Des Moines	196,998	1	Des Moines	196,998
Kansas	81,815	13	2,775,997	33	0.73	33.9	40	4	Topeka	122,642	4	Wichita	361,420
Kentucky	39,728	36	4,241,474	26	0.88	106.8	22	6	Frankfort	27,098	7	Louisville (c)	557,789
Louisiana	43,562	33	4,293,204	25	1.18	98.6	24	7	Baton Rouge	227,071	2	New Orleans	239,124
Maine	30,862	39	1,317,207	40	0.17	42.7	38	2	Augusta	18,367	9	Portland	62,825
Maryland	9,774	42	5,618,344	19	0.29	574.8	5	8	Annapolis	36,603	7	Baltimore	637,455
Massachusetts	7,840	45	6,449,755	14	0.24	822.7	3	10	Boston	599,351	1	Boston	599,351
Michigan	56,804	22	10,071,822	8	-0.30	177.3	16	15	Lansing	114,947	6	Detroit	916,952
Minnesota	79,610	14	5,197,621	21	0.83	65.3	31	8	St. Paul	277,251	2	Minneapolis	377,392
Mississippi	46,907	31	2,918,785	31	0.68	62.2	32	4	Jackson	175,710	1	Jackson	175,710
Missouri	68,886	18	5,878,415	18	0.70	85.3	28	9	Jefferson City	40,564	15	Kansas City	450,375
Montana	145,552	4	957,861	44	1.17	6.5	48	1	Helena	28,726	6	Billings	101,876
Nebraska	76,872	15	1,774,571	38	0.61	23.1	43	3	Lincoln	248,744	2	Omaha	424,482
Nevada	109,826	7	2,565,382	35	2.93	23.4	42	3	Carson City	54,939	6	Las Vegas	558,880
New Hampshire	8,968	44	1,315,828	41	0.31	146.7	20	2	Concord	42,392	3	Manchester	108,874
New Jersey	7,417	46	8,685,920	11	0.23	1,171.1	1	13	Trenton	82,804	9	Newark	280,135
New Mexico	121,356	5	1,969,915	36	1.42	16.2	45	3	Santa Fe	73,199	3	Albuquerque	518,271
New York	47,214	30	19,297,729	3	0.08	408.7	7	29	Albany	94,172	6	New York City	8,274,527
North Carolina	48,711	29	9,061,032	10	2.16	186.0	15	13	Raleigh	375,806	2	Charlotte	671,588
North Dakota	68,976	17	639,715	48	0.35	9.3	47	1	Bismarck	59,503	2	Fargo	92,660
Ohio	40,948	35	11,466,917	7	0.03	280.0	9	18	Columbus	747,755	1	Columbus	747,755
Oklahoma	68,667	19	3,617,316	28	1.11	52.7	36	5	Oklahoma City	547,274	1	Oklahoma City	547,274
Oregon	95,997	10	3,747,455	27	1.53	39.0	39	5	Salem	151,913	3	Portland	550,396
Pennsylvania	44,817	32	12,432,792	6	0.24	277.4	10	19	Harrisburg	47,196	13	Philadelphia	1,449,634
Rhode Island	1,045	50	1,057,832	43	-0.36	1,012.3	2	2	Providence	172,459	1	Providence	172,459
South Carolina	30,109	40	4,407,709	24	1.79	146.4	21	6	Columbia	124,818	1	Columbia	124,818

See footnotes at end of table.

STATE STATISTICS—Continued

State or other jurisdiction	Land area: In square miles	Land area: Rank in nation	Population (a): Size	Population (a): Rank in nation	Percentage change 2006 to 2007	Density per square mile	Rank in nation	Number of Representatives in Congress	Capital	Population (a)	Rank in state	Largest city	Population (a)
South Dakota	75,885	16	796,214	46	0.98	10.5	46	1	Pierre	14,032	7	Sioux Falls	151,505
Tennessee	41,217	34	6,156,719	17	1.35	149.4	19	9	Nashville (d)	590,807	2	Memphis	674,028
Texas	261,797	2	23,904,380	2	2.12	91.3	26	32	Austin	734,074	4	Houston	2,208,180
Utah	82,144	12	2,645,330	34	2.55	32.2	41	3	Salt Lake City	180,651	1	Salt Lake City	180,651
Vermont	9,250	43	621,254	49	0.08	67.2	30	1	Montpelier	7,806	13	Burlington	38,531
Virginia	39,594	37	7,712,091	12	0.94	194.8	14	11	Richmond	200,123	4	Virginia Beach	434,743
Washington	66,544	20	6,468,424	13	1.47	97.2	25	9	Olympia	44,925	18	Seattle	594,210
West Virginia	24,078	41	1,812,035	37	0.18	75.3	29	3	Charleston	50,478	1	Charleston	50,478
Wisconsin	54,310	25	5,601,640	20	0.52	103.1	23	8	Madison	228,775	2	Milwaukee	602,191
Wyoming	97,100	9	522,830	50	1.96	5.4	49	1	Cheyenne	55,641	1	Cheyenne	55,641
Dist. of Columbia	61	. . .	588,292	. . .	0.48	9,581.3	. . .	1 (e)	. . .	. . .	. . .	. . .	. . .
American Samoa	77	. . .	64,827	. . .	13.10	744.0	. . .	1 (e)	Pago Pago (g)	4,278	3	Tafuna (g)	8,409
Guam	210	. . .	175,877	. . .	13.60	737.2	. . .	1 (e)	Hagatna (g)	1,122	13	Tamuning (g)	10,833
No. Mariana Islands	179	. . .	86,616	. . .	25.10	386.7	. . .	1 (e)	Saipan (b)(g)	62,392	1	Saipan (b)(g)	62,392
Puerto Rico	3,425	. . .	3,942,375	. . .	0.40	1,146.8	. . .	1 (f)	San Juan	434,374	1	San Juan	434,374
U.S. Virgin Islands	134	. . .	109,840	. . .	1.13	810.5	. . .	1 (e)	Charlotte Amalie, St. Thomas	18,914	1	Charlotte Amalie, St. Thomas	18,914

Source: U.S. Census Bureau, October 2008.
Key:
. . . — Not applicable.
(a) 2007 Census Bureau estimate.
(b) Municipality.
(c) This city is part of a consolidated city-county government and is coextensive with Jefferson County.
(d) This city is part of a consolidated city-county government and is coextensive with Davidson County.
(e) Represented by one non-voting House Delegate.
(f) Represented by one non-voting House Resident Commissioner.
(g) 2000 Census figures.

Alabama

Nickname .... The Heart of Dixie
Motto .... Aldemus Jura Nostra Defendere (We Dare Defend Our Rights)
Flower .... Camellia
Bird .... Yellowhammer
Tree .... Southern (Longleaf) Pine
Song .... Alabama
Entered the Union .... December 14, 1819
Capital .... Montgomery

STATISTICS

Land Area (square miles) 50,744
Rank in Nation 28th
Population 4,627,851
Rank in Nation 23rd
Density per square mile 91.2
Capital City .... Montgomery
Population 204,086
Rank in State 2nd
Largest City .... Birmingham
Population 229,800
Number of Representatives in Congress 7
Number of Counties 67
Number of Municipal Governments 451
Number of 2009 Electoral Votes 9
Number of School Districts 128
Number of Special Districts 525

LEGISLATIVE BRANCH

Legislative Body .... Legislature

President of the Senate .... Jim Folsom Jr.
President Pro Tem of the Senate .... Rodger Smitherman
Secretary of the Senate .... McDowell Lee

Speaker of the House .... Seth Hammett
Speaker Pro Tem of the House .... Demetrius C. Newton
Clerk of the House .... Greg Pappas

2009 Regular Session .... Feb. 3-May 18
Number of Senatorial Districts 35
Number of Representative Districts 105

EXECUTIVE BRANCH

Governor .... Bob Riley
Lieutenant Governor .... Jim Folsom Jr.
Secretary of State .... Beth Chapman
Attorney General .... Troy King
Treasurer .... Kay Ivey
Auditor .... Samantha Shaw
Comptroller .... Robert Childree

Governor's Present Term 1/2003-1/2011
Number of Elected Officials in the Executive Branch 7
Number of Members in the Cabinet 26

JUDICIAL BRANCH

Highest Court .... Supreme Court
Supreme Court Chief Justice .... Sue Bell Cobb
Number of Supreme Court Judges 9
Number of Intermediate Appellate Court Judges 10
Number of U.S. Court Districts 3
U.S. Circuit Court .... 11th Circuit

STATE INTERNET ADDRESSES

Official State Website .... http://www.alabama.gov
Governor's Website .... http://www.governor.state.al.us
State Legislative Website .... http://www.legislature.state.al.us
State Judicial Website .... http://www.judicial.state.al.us

Alaska

Nickname .... The Last Frontier
Motto .... North to the Future
Flower .... Forget-Me-Not
Bird .... Willow Ptarmigan
Tree .... Sitka Spruce
Song .... Alaska's Flag
Entered the Union .... January 3, 1959
Capital .... Juneau

STATISTICS

Land Area (square miles) 571,951
Rank in Nation 1st
Population 683,478
Rank in Nation 47th
Density per square mile 1.2
Capital City .... Juneau
Population 30,690
Rank in State 2nd
Largest City .... Anchorage
Population 279,671
Number of Representatives in Congress 1
Number of Counties 12
Number of Municipal Governments 149
Number of 2009 Electoral Votes 3
Number of School Districts 0
Number of Special Districts 14

LEGISLATIVE BRANCH

Legislative Body .... Legislature

President of the Senate .... Gary Stevens
Secretary of the Senate .... Sean R. Parnell

Speaker of the House .... Mike Chenault
Chief Clerk of the House .... Suzanne Lowell

2009 Regular Session .... Jan. 20-April 19
Number of Senatorial Districts 20
Number of Representative Districts 40

EXECUTIVE BRANCH

Governor .... Sarah H. Palin
Lieutenant Governor .... Sean Parnell
Acting Attorney General .... Rick Svobodny
Treasurer .... Jerry Burnett
Auditor .... Pat Davidson
Comptroller .... Kim Garnero

Governor's Present Term 12/2006-12/2010
Number of Elected Officials in the Executive Branch 2
Number of Members in the Cabinet 18

JUDICIAL BRANCH

Highest Court .... Supreme Court
Supreme Court Chief Justice .... Dana Fabe
Number of Supreme Court Judges 5
Number of Intermediate Appellate Court Judges 3
Number of U.S. Court Districts 1
U.S. Circuit Court .... 9th Circuit

STATE INTERNET ADDRESSES

Official State Website .... http://www.alaska.gov
Governor's Website .... http://www.gov.state.ak.us
State Legislative Website .... http://www.legis.state.ak.us
State Judicial Website .... http://www.state.ak.us/courts

Arizona

Nickname....The Grand Canyon State
Motto....Ditat Deus (God Enriches)
Flower....Blossom of the Saguaro Cactus
Bird....Cactus Wren
Tree....Palo Verde
Songs....Arizona March Song and Arizona
Entered the Union....February 14, 1912
Capital....Phoenix

STATISTICS

Land Area (square miles)....113,635
Rank in Nation....6th
Population....6,338,755
Rank in Nation....16th
Density per square mile....55.8
Capital City....Phoenix
Population....1,552,259
Rank in State....1st
Largest City....Phoenix
Number Representatives in Congress....8
Number of Counties....15
Number of Municipal Governments....90
Number of 2009 Electoral Votes....10
Number of School Districts....231
Number of Special Districts....305

LEGISLATIVE BRANCH

Legislative Body....Legislature

President of the Senate....Robert Burns
President Pro Tem of the Senate....Thayer Verschoor
Secretary of the Senate....Kevin Bennett

Speaker of the House....Kirk Adams
Speaker Pro Tem of the House....Steven B. Yarbrough
Chief Clerk of the House....Norman L. Moore

2009 Regular Session....Jan. 12-April
Number of Senatorial Districts....30
Number of Representative Districts....30

EXECUTIVE BRANCH

Governor....Jan Brewer
Secretary of State....Ken Bennett
Attorney General....Terry Goddard
Treasurer....Dean Martin
Auditor....Debra K. Davenport
Comptroller....D. Clark Partridge

Governor's Present Term....1/2009-1/2011
Number of Elected Officials in the Executive Branch....11
Number of Members in the Cabinet....38

JUDICIAL BRANCH

Highest Court....Supreme Court
Supreme Court Chief Justice....Ruth V. McGregor
Number of Supreme Court Judges....5
Number of Intermediate Appellate Court Judges....22
Number of U.S. Court Districts....1
U.S. Circuit Court....9th Circuit

STATE INTERNET ADDRESSES

Official State Website....http://www.az.gov
Governor's Website....http://www.azgovernor.gov/
State Legislative Website....http://www.azleg.state.az.us
State Judicial Website....http://www.supreme.state.az.us

Arkansas

Nickname....The Natural State
Motto....Regnat Populus (The People Rule)
Flower....Apple Blossom
Bird....Mockingbird
Tree....Pine
Song....Arkansas
Entered the Union....June 15, 1836
Capital....Little Rock

STATISTICS

Land Area (square miles)....52,068
Rank in Nation....27th
Population....2,834,797
Rank in Nation....32nd
Density per square mile....54.4
Capital City....Little Rock
Population....187,452
Rank in State....1st
Largest City....Little Rock
Number of Representatives in Congress....4
Number of Counties....75
Number of Municipal Governments....499
Number of 2009 Electoral Votes....6
Number of School Districts....310
Number of Special Districts....704

LEGISLATIVE BRANCH

Legislative Body....General Assembly

President of the Senate....Lt. Gov. Bill Halter
President Pro Tem of the Senate....Bob Johnson
Secretary of the Senate....Charlie Daniels

Speaker of the House....Robbie Wills
Speaker Pro Tem of the House....Curren Everett
Chief Clerk of the House....Jo Renshaw

2009 Regular Session....Jan. 12 – Mar. 20
Number of Senatorial Districts....35
Number of Representative Districts....100

EXECUTIVE BRANCH

Governor....Mike Beebe
Lieutenant Governor....Bill Halter
Secretary of State....Charlie Daniels
Attorney General....Dustin McDaniel
Treasurer....Martha A. Shoffner
Auditor....Jim Wood
Comptroller....Richard Weiss

Governor's Present Term....1/2007-1/2011
Number of Elected Officials in the Executive Branch....7
Number of Members in the Cabinet....47

JUDICIAL BRANCH

Highest Court....Supreme Court
Supreme Court Chief Justice....Jim Hannah
Number of Supreme Court Judges....7
Number of Intermediate Appellate Court Judges....12
Number of U.S. Court Districts....2
U.S. Circuit Court....8th Circuit

STATE INTERNET ADDRESSES

Official State Website....http://www.state.ar.us
Governor's Website....http://www.governor.arkansas.gov/
State Legislative Website....http://www.arkleg.state.ar.us
State Judicial Website....http://courts.state.ar.us

California

Nickname....The Golden State
Motto....Eureka (I Have Found It)
Flower....Golden Poppy
Bird....California Valley Quail
Tree....California Redwood
Song....I Love You, California
Entered the Union....September 9, 1850
Capital....Sacramento

STATISTICS

Land Area (square miles)....155,959
Rank in Nation....3rd
Population....36,553215
Rank in Nation....1st
Density per square mile....234.4
Capital City....Sacramento
Population....460,242
Rank in State....7th
Largest City....Los Angeles
Population....3,834,340
Number of Representatives in Congress....53
Number of Counties....57
Number of Municipal Governments....475
Number of 2009 Electoral Votes....55
Number of School Districts....1,047
Number of Special Districts....2,830

LEGISLATIVE BRANCH

Legislative Body....Legislature

President of the Senate....Lt. Gov. John Garamendi
President Pro Tem of the Senate....Darrell Steinberg
Secretary of the Senate....Gregory Schmidt

Speaker of the Assembly....Karen Bass
Speaker Pro Tem of the Assembly....Lori Saldana
Chief Clerk of the Assembly....E. Dotson Wilson

2009 Regular Session....Dec. 1, 2008 – Sept. 12, 2009
Number of Senatorial Districts....40
Number of Representative Districts....80

EXECUTIVE BRANCH

Governor....Arnold Schwarzenegger
Lieutenant Governor....John Garamendi
Secretary of State....Debra Bowen
Attorney General....Edmund Gerald Brown
Treasurer....Bill Lockyer
Auditor....Elaine M. Howle
Controller....John Chiang

Governor's Present Term....11/2003-1/2011
Number of Elected Officials in the Executive Branch....8
Number of Members in the Cabinet....11

JUDICIAL BRANCH

Highest Court....Supreme Court
Supreme Court Chief Justice....Ronald M. George
Number of Supreme Court Judges....7
Number of Intermediate Appellate Court Judges....88
Number of U.S. Court Districts....4
U.S. Circuit Court....9th Circuit

STATE INTERNET ADDRESSES

Official State Website....http://www.ca.gov
Governor's Website....http://gov.ca.gov/
State Legislative Website....http://www.leginfo.ca.gov
State Judicial Website....http://www.courtinfo.ca.gov

Colorado

Nickname....The Centennial State
Motto....Nil Sine Numine
(Nothing Without Providence)
Flower....Columbine
Bird....Lark Bunting
Tree....Blue Spruce
Song....Where the Columbines Grow
Entered the Union....August 1, 1876
Capital....Denver

STATISTICS

Land Area (square miles)....103,718
Rank in Nation....8th
Population....4,861,515
Rank in Nation....22nd
Density per square mile....46.9
Capital City....Denver
Population....588,349
Rank in State....1st
Largest City....Denver
Number of Representatives in Congress....7
Number of Counties....62
Number of Municipal Governments....270
Number of 2009 Electoral Votes....9
Number of School Districts....182
Number of Special Districts....1,414

LEGISLATIVE BRANCH

Legislative Body....General Assembly

President of the Senate....Peter C. Groff
President Pro Tem of the Senate....Betty Boyd
Secretary of the Senate....Bernie Buescher

Speaker of the House....Terrance Carroll
Speaker Pro Tem of the House....Kathleen Curry
Chief Clerk of the House....Marilyn Eddins

2009 Regular Session....Jan. 7 – May 6
Number of Senatorial Districts....35
Number of Representative Districts....65

EXECUTIVE BRANCH

Governor....Bill Ritter
Lieutenant Governor....Barbara O'Brien
Secretary of State....Bernie Buescher
Attorney General....John W. Suthers
Treasurer....Cary Kennedy
Auditor....Sally Symanski
Controller....Leslie Shenefelt

Governor's Present Term....1/2007-1/2011
Number of Elected Officials in the Executive Branch....5
Number of Members in the Cabinet....21

JUDICIAL BRANCH

Highest Court....Supreme Court
Supreme Court Chief Justice....Mary Mullarkey
Number of Supreme Court Judges....7
Number of Intermediate Appellate Court Judges....16
Number of U.S. Court Districts....1
U.S. Circuit Court....10th Circuit

STATE INTERNET ADDRESSES

Official State Website....http://www.state.co.us
Governor's Website...http://www.state.co.us/gov_dir/governor_office.html
State Legislative Website....http://www.leg.state.co.us
State Judicial Website....http://www.courts.state.co.us

Connecticut

Nickname........The Constitution State
Motto........Qui Transtulit Sustinet
(He Who Transplanted Still Sustains)
Flower........Mountain Laurel
Bird........American Robin
Tree........White Oak
Song........Yankee Doodle
Entered the Union........January 9, 1788
Capital........Hartford

STATISTICS

Land Area (square miles)........4,845
Rank in Nation........48th
Population........3,502,309
Rank in Nation........29th
Density per square mile........722.9
Capital City........Hartford
Population........124,563
Rank in State........3rd
Largest City........Bridgeport
Population........136,695
Number of Representatives in Congress........5
Number of Counties........0
Number of Municipal Governments........30
Number of 2009 Electoral Votes........7
Number of School Districts........17
Number of Special Districts........384

LEGISLATIVE BRANCH

Legislative Body........General Assembly

President of the Senate........Michael C. Fedele
President Pro Tem of the Senate........Donald E. Williams
Clerk of the Senate........Thomas P. Sheridan

Speaker of the House........Christopher G. Donovan
Deputy Speakers
of the House........Emil Altobello, Demetrios Giannaros, Bob Godfrey, Marie Kirkley-Bey, Davis McCluskey, Linda Orange, Jim O'Rourke III
Clerk of the House........Garey E. Coleman

2009 Regular Session........Jan. 7 – Jun. 3
Number of Senatorial Districts........36
Number of Representative Districts........151

EXECUTIVE BRANCH

Governor........M. Jodi Rell
Lieutenant Governor........Michael Fedele
Secretary of State........Susan Bysiewicz
Attorney General........Richard Blumenthal
Treasurer........Denise L. Nappier
Auditor........Robert Jaekle and Kevin P. Johnston
Comptroller........Nancy Wyman

Governor's Present Term........7/2004-1/2011
Number of Elected Officials in the Executive Branch........6
Number of Members in the Cabinet........27

JUDICIAL BRANCH

Highest Court........Supreme Court
Supreme Court Chief Justice........Chase T. Rogers
Number of Supreme Court Judges........7
Number of Intermediate Appellate Court Judges........10
Number of U.S. Court Districts........1
U.S. Circuit Court........2nd Circuit

STATE INTERNET ADDRESSES

Official State Website........http://www. ct.us
Governor's Website........http://www.state.ct.us/governor
State Legislative Website........http://www.cga.ct.us
State Judicial Website........http://www.jud.state.ct.us

Delaware

Nickname........The First State
Motto........Liberty and Independence
Flower........Peach Blossom
Bird........Blue Hen Chicken
Tree........American Holly
Song........Our Delaware
Entered the Union........December 7, 1787
Capital........Dover

STATISTICS

Land Area (square miles)........1,954
Rank in Nation........49th
Population........864,764
Rank in Nation........45th
Density per square mile........442.6
Capital City........Dover
Population........35,811
Rank in State........2nd
Largest City........Wilmington
Population........72,868
Number of Representatives in Congress........1
Number of Counties........3
Number of Municipal Governments........57
Number of 2009 Electoral Votes........3
Number of School Districts........19
Number of Special Districts........260

LEGISLATIVE BRANCH

Legislative Body........General Assembly

President of the Senate........Matthew Denn
President Pro Tem of the Senate........Thurman Adams Jr.
Secretary of the Senate........Joseph Bullock

Speaker of the House........Robert F. Gilligan
Clerk of the House........Richard Puffer

2009 Regular Session........Jan. 13-June 30
Number of Senatorial Districts........21
Number of Representative Districts........41

EXECUTIVE BRANCH

Governor........Jack Markell
Lieutenant Governor........Matthew Denn
Secretary of State........Jeffrey Bullock
Attorney General........Joseph R. Biden III
Treasurer........Velda Jones-Potter
Auditor........R. Thomas Wagner
Comptroller........Gary M. Pfeiffer

Governor's Present Term........1/2001/2013
Number of Elected Officials in the Executive Branch........5
Number of Members in the Cabinet........19

JUDICIAL BRANCH

Highest Court........Supreme Court
Supreme Court Chief Justice........Myron T. Steele
Number of Supreme Court Judges........5
Number of Intermediate Appellate Court Judges........0
Number of U.S. Court Districts........1
U.S. Circuit Court........3rd Circuit

STATE INTERNET ADDRESSES

Official State Website........http://www.delaware.gov
Governor's Website........http://www.state.de.us/governor
State Legislative Website........http://legis.delaware.gov
State Judicial Website........http://courts.state.de.us

Florida

Nickname....The Sunshine State
Motto....In God We Trust
Flower....Orange Blossom
Bird....Mockingbird
Tree....Sabal Palmetto Palm
Song....The Swannee River (Old Folks at Home)
Entered the Union....March 3, 1845
Capital....Tallahassee

STATISTICS

Land Area (square miles)....53,927
Rank in Nation....26th
Population....18,251,243
Rank in Nation....4th
Density per square mile....338.4
Capital City....Tallahassee
Population....168,979
Rank in State....8th
Largest City....Jacksonville
Population....805,605
Number of Representatives in Congress....25
Number of Counties....66
Number of Municipal Governments....404
Number of 2009 Electoral Votes....27
Number of School Districts....95
Number of Special Districts....626

LEGISLATIVE BRANCH

Legislative Body....Legislature

President of the Senate....Jeffery Atwater
President Pro Tem of the Senate....Mike Fasano
Secretary of the Senate....Philip Twogood

Speaker of the House....Ray Sansom
Speaker Pro Tem of the House....Larry Cretul
Clerk of the House....Bob Ward

2009 Regular Session....March 3-May 1
Number of Senatorial Districts....40
Number of Representative Districts....120

EXECUTIVE BRANCH

Governor....Charlie Crist
Lieutenant Governor....Jeff Kottkamp
Secretary of State....Kurt Browning
Attorney General....Bill McCollum
Chief Financial Officer....Alex Sink
Auditor....David Martin

Governor's Present Term....1/2007-1/2011
Number of Elected Officials in the Executive Branch....5
Number of Members in the Cabinet....4

JUDICIAL BRANCH

Highest Court....Supreme Court
Supreme Court Chief Justice....Peggy A. Quince
Number of Supreme Court Judges....7
Number of Intermediate Appellate Court Judges....62
Number of U.S. Court Districts....3
U.S. Circuit Court....11th Circuit

STATE INTERNET ADDRESSES

Official State Website....http://www.myflorida.com
Governor's Website....http://www.flgov.com/
State Legislative Website....http://www.leg.state.fl.us
State Judicial Website....http://www.flcourts.org

Georgia

Nickname....The Empire State of the South
Motto....Wisdom, Justice and Moderation
Flower....Cherokee Rose
Bird....Brown Thrasher
Tree....Live Oak
Song....Georgia on My Mind
Entered the Union....January 2, 1788
Capital....Atlanta

STATISTICS

Land Area (square miles)....57,906
Rank in Nation....21st
Population....9,544,750
Rank in Nation....9th
Density per square mile....164.8
Capital City....Atlanta
Population....519,145
Rank in State....1st
Largest City....Atlanta
Number of Representatives in Congress....13
Number of Counties....156
Number of Municipal Governments....531
Number of 2009 Electoral Votes....15
Number of School Districts....180
Number of Special Districts....581

LEGISLATIVE BRANCH

Legislative Body....General Assembly

President of the Senate....Lt. Gov. Casey Cagle
President Pro Tem of the Senate....Tommie Williams
Secretary of the Senate....Bob Ewing

Speaker of the House....Glenn Richardson
Speaker Pro Tem of the House....Mark Burkhalter
Clerk of the House....Robert E. Rivers Jr.

2009 Regular Session....Jan. 12– March
Number of Senatorial Districts....56
Number of Representative Districts....180

EXECUTIVE BRANCH

Governor....Sonny Perdue
Lieutenant Governor....Casey Cagle
Secretary of State....Karen Handel
Attorney General....Thurbert E. Baker
Treasurer....W. Daniel Ebersole
Auditor....Russell W. Hinton

Governor's Present Term....1/2003-1/2011
Number of Elected Officials in the Executive Branch....13
Number of Members in the Cabinet....No formal cabinet system

JUDICIAL BRANCH

Highest Court....Supreme Court
Supreme Court Chief Justice....Leah Ward Sears
Number of Supreme Court Judges....7
Number of Intermediate Appellate Court Judges....12
Number of U.S. Court Districts....3
U.S. Circuit Court....11th Circuit

STATE INTERNET ADDRESSES

Official State Website....http://www.georgia.gov/
Governor's Website....http://gov.georgia.gov/
State Legislative Website....http://www.legis.state.ga.us
State Judicial Website....http://www.georgiacourts.org

Hawaii

Nickname....The Aloha State
Motto....Ua Mau Ke Ea O Ka Aina I Ka Pono
(The Life of the Land Is Perpetuated in Righteousness)
Flower....Native Yellow Hibiscus
Bird....Hawaiian Goose (Nene)
Tree....Kukue Tree (Candlenut)
Song....Hawaii Ponoi
Entered the Union....August 21, 1959
Capital....Honolulu

STATISTICS

Land Area (square miles)....6,423
Rank in Nation....47th
Population....1,283,388
Rank in Nation....42nd
Density per square mile....199.8
Capital City....Honolulu
Population....375,571
Rank in State....1st
Largest City....Honolulu
Number of Representatives in Congress....2
Number of Counties....3
Number of Municipal Governments....1
Number of 2009 Electoral Votes....4
Number of School Districts....0
Number of Special Districts....15

LEGISLATIVE BRANCH

Legislative Body....Legislature

President of the Senate....Colleen Hanabusa
Vice President of the Senate....Russell S. Kokubun
Chief Clerk of the Senate....Carol Taniguchi

Speaker of the House....Calvin K.Y. Say
Vice Speaker of the House....Michael Y. Magaoay
Chief Clerk of the House....Patricia A. Mau-Shimizu

2009 Regular Session....Jan. 21 - May 7
Number of Senatorial Districts....25
Number of Representative Districts....51

EXECUTIVE BRANCH

Governor....Linda Lingle
Lieutenant Governor....James "Duke" Aiona Jr.
Attorney General....Mark J. Bennett
Treasurer....Georgina Kawamura
Auditor....Marion M. Higa
Comptroller....Russ K. Saito

Governor's Present Term....12/2002-12/2010
Number of Elected Officials in the Executive Branch....2
Number of Members in the Cabinet....22

JUDICIAL BRANCH

Highest Court....Supreme Court
Supreme Court Chief Justice....Ronald T.Y. Moon
Number of Supreme Court Judges....5
Number of Intermediate Appellate Court Judges....6
Number of U.S. Court Districts....1
U.S. Circuit Court....9th Circuit

STATE INTERNET ADDRESSES

Official State Website....http://www.ehawaii.gov
Governor's Website....http://hawaii.gov/gov
State Legislative Website....http://www.capitol.hawaii.gov
State Judicial Website....http://www.courts.state.hi.us/

Idaho

Nickname....The Gem State
Motto....Esto Perpetua (Let It Be Perpetual)
Flower....Syringa
Bird....Mountain Bluebird
Tree....Western White Pine
Song....Here We Have Idaho
Entered the Union....July 3, 1890
Capital....Boise

STATISTICS

Land Area (square miles)....82,747
Rank in Nation....11th
Population....1,499,402
Rank in Nation....39th
Density per square mile....18.1
Capital City....Boise
Population....202,832
Rank in State....1st
Largest City....Boise
Number of Representatives in Congress....2
Number of Counties....44
Number of Municipal Governments....200
Number of 2009 Electoral Votes....4
Number of School Districts....116
Number of Special Districts....798

LEGISLATIVE BRANCH

Legislative Body....Legislature

President of the Senate....Lt. Gov. Brad Little
President Pro Tem of the Senate....Robert L. Geddes
Secretary of the Senate....Jeannine Wood

Speaker of the House....Lawerence Denney
Chief Clerk of the House....Bonnie Alexander

2009 Regular Session....Jan. 12 – April
Number of Senatorial Districts....35
Number of Representative Districts....35

EXECUTIVE BRANCH

Governor....C.L "Butch" Otter
Lieutenant Governor....Brad Little
Secretary of State....Ben Ysursa
Attorney General....Lawrence Wasden
Treasurer....Ron Crane
Controller....Donna Jones

Governor's Present Term....1/2007-1/2011
Number of Elected Officials in the Executive Branch....7
Number of Members in the Cabinet....22

JUDICIAL BRANCH

Highest Court....Supreme Court
Supreme Court Chief Justice....Daniel Eismann
Number of Supreme Court Judges....5
Number of Intermediate Appellate Court Judges....3
Number of U.S. Court Districts....1
U.S. Circuit Court....9th Circuit

STATE INTERNET ADDRESSES

Official State Website....http://www.state.id.us
Governor's Website....http://www2.state.id.us/gov
State Legislative Website....http://www2.state.id.us/legislat
State Judicial Website....http://www2.state.id.us/judicial

Illinois

Nickname.......The Prairie State
Motto.......State Sovereignty-National Union
Flower.......Native Violet
Bird.......Cardinal
Tree.......White Oak
Song.......Illinois
Entered the Union.......December 3, 1818
Capital.......Springfield

STATISTICS

Land Area (square miles).......55,584
Rank in Nation.......24th
Population.......12,852,548
Rank in Nation.......5th
Density per square mile.......231.2
Capital City.......Springfield
Population.......117,090
Rank in State.......6th
Largest City.......Chicago
Population.......2,836,658
Number of Representatives in Congress.......19
Number of Counties.......102
Number of Municipal Governments.......1,291
Number of 2009 Electoral Votes.......21
Number of School Districts.......934
Number of Special Districts.......3,145

LEGISLATIVE BRANCH

Legislative Body.......General Assembly

President of the Senate.......John J. Cullerton
Secretary of the Senate.......Debra Shipley

Speaker of the House.......Michael J. Madigan
House Chief Clerk.......Mark Mahoney

2009 Regular Session.......Jan. 14-Dec. 31
Number of Senatorial Districts.......59
Number of Representative Districts.......118

EXECUTIVE BRANCH

Governor.......Patrick Quinn
Lieutenant Governor.......Vacant
Secretary of State.......Jesse White
Attorney General.......Lisa Madigan
Treasurer.......Alexi Giannoulias
Auditor.......William G. Holland
Comptroller.......Daniel Hynes

Governor's Present Term.......1/2009-1/2011
Number of Elected Officials in the Executive Branch.......6
Number of Members in the Cabinet.......18

JUDICIAL BRANCH

Highest Court.......Supreme Court
Supreme Court Chief Justice.......Thomas Fitzgerald
Number of Supreme Court Judges.......7
Number of Intermediate Appellate Court Judges.......53
Number of U.S. Court Districts.......3
U.S. Circuit Court.......7th Circuit

STATE INTERNET ADDRESSES

Official State Website.......http://www.state.il.us
Governor's Website.......http://www.state.il.us/gov
State Legislative Website.......http://www.illinois.gov/government/gov_legislature.cfm
State Judicial Website http://www.illinois.gov/government/judiciary.cfm

Indiana

Nickname.......The Hoosier State
Motto.......Crossroads of America
Flower.......Peony
Bird.......Cardinal
Tree.......Tulip Poplar
Song.......On the Banks of the Wabash, Far Away
Entered the Union.......December 11, 1816
Capital.......Indianapolis

STATISTICS

Land Area (square miles).......35,867
Rank in Nation.......38th
Population.......6,345,289
Rank in Nation.......15th
Density per square mile.......176.9
Capital City.......Indianapolis
Population.......795,458
Rank in State.......1st
Largest City.......Indianapolis
Number of Representatives in Congress.......9
Number of Counties.......91
Number of Municipal Governments.......567
Number of 2009 Electoral Votes.......11
Number of School Districts.......294
Number of Special Districts.......1,125

LEGISLATIVE BRANCH

Legislative Body.......General Assembly

President of the Senate.......Lt. Gov. Becky Skillman
President Pro Tem of the Senate.......David C. Long
Secretary of the Senate.......Jennifer Mertzl

Speaker of the House.......B. Patrick Bauer
Speaker Pro Tem of the House.......Chet Dobis
Clerk of the House.......Clinton Mckay

2009 Regular Session.......Jan. 7 – April 29
Number of Senatorial Districts.......50
Number of Representative Districts.......100

EXECUTIVE BRANCH

Governor.......Mitch Daniels
Lieutenant Governor.......Becky Skillman
Secretary of State.......Todd Rokita
Attorney General.......Greg Zoeller
Treasurer.......Richard E. Mourdock
Auditor.......Tim Berry

Governor's Present Term.......1/2005-1/2013
Number of Elected Officials in the Executive Branch.......7
Number of Members in the Cabinet.......16

JUDICIAL BRANCH

Highest Court.......Supreme Court
Supreme Court Chief Justice.......Randall T. Shepard
Number of Supreme Court Judges.......5
Number of Intermediate Appellate Court Judges.......15
Number of U.S. Court Districts.......2
U.S. Circuit Court.......7th Circuit

STATE INTERNET ADDRESSES

Official State Website.......http://www.state.in.us
Governor's Website.......http://www.in.gov/gov
State Legislative Website.......http://www.in.gov/legislative
State Judicial Website.......http://www.in.gov/judiciary

Iowa

Nickname ..... The Hawkeye State
Motto ..... Our Liberties We Prize and Our Rights We Will Maintain
Flower ..... Wild Rose
Bird ..... Eastern Goldfinch
Tree ..... Oak
Song ..... The Song of Iowa
Entered the Union ..... December 28, 1846
Capital ..... Des Moines

STATISTICS

Land Area (square mile) 55,869
Rank in Nation 23rd
Population 2,988,046
Rank in Nation 30th
Density per square mile 53.5
Capital City ..... Des Moines
Population 196,998
Rank in State 1st
Largest City ..... Des Moines
Number of Representatives in Congress 5
Number of Counties 99
Number of Municipal Governments 948
Number of 2009 Electoral Votes 7
Number of School Districts 386
Number of Special Districts 542

LEGISLATIVE BRANCH

Legislative Body ..... General Assembly

President of the Senate ..... John P. Kibbie
President Pro Tem of the Senate ..... Jeff Danielson
Secretary of the Senate ..... Michael E. Marshall

Speaker of the House ..... Pat Murphy
Speaker Pro Tem of the House ..... Polly Bukta
Chief Clerk of the House ..... Mark Brandsgard

2009 Regular Session Jan.12-May 1
Number of Senatorial Districts 50
Number of Representative Districts 100

EXECUTIVE BRANCH

Governor ..... Chet Culver
Lieutenant Governor ..... Patty Judge
Secretary of State ..... Michael Mauro
Attorney General ..... Thomas Miller
Treasurer ..... Michael Fitzgerald
Auditor ..... David A. Vaudt
Chief Operating Officer ..... Calvin McKelvogue

Governor's Present Term 1/2007-1/2011
Number of Elected Officials in the Executive Branch 7
Number of Members in the Cabinet 30

JUDICIAL BRANCH

Highest Court ..... Supreme Court
Supreme Court Chief Justice ..... Marsha K. Ternus
Number of Supreme Court Judges 7
Number of Intermediate Appellate Court Judges 9
Number of U.S. Court Districts 2
U.S. Circuit Court ..... 8th Circuit

STATE INTERNET ADDRESSES

Official State Website ..... http://www.iowa.gov/
Governor's Website ..... http://www.governor.state.ia.us/
State Legislative Website ..... http://www.legis.state.ia.us
State Judicial Website ..... http://www.judicial.state.ia.us

Kansas

Nickname ..... The Sunflower State
Motto ..... Ad Astra per Aspera (To the Stars through Difficulties)
Flower ..... Wild Native Sunflower
Bird ..... Western Meadowlark
Tree ..... Cottonwood
Song ..... Home on the Range
Entered the Union ..... January 29, 1861
Capital ..... Topeka

STATISTICS

Land Area (square miles) 81,815
Rank in Nation 13th
Population 2,775,997
Rank in Nation 33rd
Density per square mile 33.9
Capital City ..... Topeka
Population 122,642
Rank in State 4th
Largest City ..... Wichita
Population 361,420
Number of Representatives in Congress 4
Number of Counties 104
Number of Municipal Governments 627
Number of 2009 Electoral Votes 6
Number of School Districts 324
Number of Special Districts 1,533

LEGISLATIVE BRANCH

Legislative Body ..... Legislature

President of the Senate ..... Stephen Morris
Secretary of the Senate ..... Pat Saville

Speaker of the House ..... Michael O'Neal
Speaker Pro Tem of the House ..... Arlen H. Siegfreid
Chief Clerk of the House ..... Susan W. Kannarr

2009 Regular Session ..... Jan. 12-April
Number of Senatorial Districts 40
Number of Representative Districts 125

EXECUTIVE BRANCH

Governor ..... Mark Parkinson
Lieutenant Governor ..... Vacant at press time
Secretary of State ..... Ron Thornburgh
Attorney General ..... Stephen Six
Treasurer ..... Dennis McKinney
Auditor ..... Barbara J. Hinton
Director, Division of Accounts & Reports ..... Kent Olson

Governor's Present Term 3/2009-1/2011
Number of Elected Officials in the Executive Branch 6
Number of Members in the Cabinet 14

JUDICIAL BRANCH

Highest Court ..... Supreme Court
Supreme Court Chief Justice ..... Robert E. Davis
Number of Supreme Court Judges 7
Number of Intermediate Appellate Court Judges 12
Number of U.S. Court Districts 1
U.S. Circuit Court ..... 10th Circuit

STATE INTERNET ADDRESSES

Official State Website ..... http://www.accesskansas.org
Governor's Website ..... http://www.ksgovernor.org
State Legislative Website ..... http://www.kslegislature.org
State Judicial Website ..... http://www.kscourts.org

Kentucky

Nickname....The Bluegrass State
Motto....United We Stand, Divided We Fall
Flower....Goldenrod
Bird....Cardinal
Tree....Tulip Poplar
Song....My Old Kentucky Home
Entered the Union....June 1, 1792
Capital....Frankfort

STATISTICS

Land Area (square miles)....39,728
Rank in Nation....36th
Population....4,241,474
Rank in Nation....26th
Density per square mile....106.8
Capital City....Frankfort
Population....27,098
Rank in State....7th
Largest City....Louisville
Population....557,789
Number of Representatives in Congress....6
Number of Counties....119
Number of Municipal Governments....424
Number of 2009 Electoral Votes....8
Number of School Districts....176
Number of Special Districts....720

LEGISLATIVE BRANCH

Legislative Body....General Assembly

President of the Senate....David L. Williams
President Pro Tem of the Senate....Katie Stine
Secretary of the Senate....Donna Holiday

Speaker of the House....Gregory Stumbo
Speaker Pro Tem of the House....Larry Clark
Chief Clerk of the House....Jean Burgin

2009 Regular Session....Jan. 6 – Mar. 30
Number of Senatorial Districts....38
Number of Representative Districts....100

EXECUTIVE BRANCH

Governor....Steve Beshear
Lieutenant Governor....Daniel Mongiardo
Secretary of State....Trey Grayson
Attorney General....Jack Conway
Treasurer....Todd Hollenbach
Auditor....Crit Luallen
Controller....Ed Ross

Governor's Present Term....12/2007-12/2011
Number of Elected Officials in the Executive Branch....7
Number of Members in the Cabinet....10

JUDICIAL BRANCH

Highest Court....Supreme Court
Supreme Court Chief Justice....John D. Minton
Number of Supreme Court Judges....7
Number of Intermediate Appellate Court Judges....14
Number of U.S. Court Districts....2
U.S. Circuit Court....6th Circuit

STATE INTERNET ADDRESSES

Official State Website....http://kentucky.gov
Governor's Website....http://governor.ky.gov/
Legislative Website....http://www.lrc.state.ky.us
Judicial Website....http://www.kycourts.net

Louisiana

Nickname....The Pelican State
Motto....Union, Justice and Confidence
Flower....Magnolia
Bird....Eastern Brown Pelican
Tree....Bald Cypress
Songs....Give Me Louisiana and You Are My Sunshine
Entered the Union....April 30, 1812
Capital....Baton Rouge

STATISTICS

Land Area (square miles)....43,562
Rank in Nation....33rd
Population....4,293,204
Rank in Nation....25th
Density per square mile....98.6
Capital City....Baton Rouge
Population....227,071
Rank in State....2nd
Largest City....New Orleans
Population....239,124
Number of Representatives in Congress....7
Number of Parishes....60
Number of Municipal Governments....302
Number of 2009 Electoral Votes....9
Number of School Districts....66
Number of Special Districts....45

LEGISLATIVE BRANCH

Legislative Body....Legislature

President of the Senate....Joel T. Chaisson II
President Pro Tem of the Senate....Sharon Weston Broome
Secretary of Senate....Glenn Koepp

Speaker of the House....Jim Tucker
Speaker Pro Tem of the House....Karen Carter Peterson
Clerk of the House and Chief of Staff....Alfred W. Speer

2009 Regular Session....Apr. 27 – Jun. 25
Number of Senatorial Districts....39
Number of Representative Districts....105

EXECUTIVE BRANCH

Governor....Bobby Jindal
Lieutenant Governor....Mitch Landrieu
Secretary of State....Jay Dardenne
Attorney General....James D. Caldwell
Treasurer....John Neely Kennedy

Governor's Present Term....1/2008-1/2012
Number of Elected Officials in the Executive Branch....8
Number of Members in the Cabinet....16

JUDICIAL BRANCH

Highest Court....Supreme Court
Supreme Court Chief Justice....Pascal F. Calogero Jr.
Number of Supreme Court Judges....7
Number of Intermediate Appellate Court Judges....53
Number of U.S. Court Districts....3
U.S. Circuit Court....5th Circuit

STATE INTERNET ADDRESSES

Official State Website....http://www.state.la.us
Governor's Website....http://www.gov.state.la.us
Legislative Website....http://www.legis.state.la.us
Judicial Website....http://www.state.la.us/gov_judicial.htm

Maine

Nickname....The Pine Tree State
Motto....Dirigo (I Direct or I Lead)
Flower....White Pine Cone and Tassel
Bird....Chickadee
Tree....White Pine
Song....State of Maine Song
Entered the Union....March 15, 1820
Capital....Augusta

STATISTICS

Land Area (square miles)....30,862
Rank in Nation....39th
Population....1,317,207
Rank in Nation....40th
Density per square mile....42.7
Capital City....Augusta
Population....18,367
Rank in State....9th
Largest City....Portland
Population....62,825
Number of Representatives in Congress....2
Number of Counties....16
Number of Municipal Governments....22
Number of 2009 Electoral Votes....4
Number of School Districts....99
Number of Special Districts....222

LEGISLATIVE BRANCH

Legislative Body....Legislature

President of the Senate....Elizabeth H. Mitchell
Secretary of the Senate....Joy J. O'Brien

Speaker of the House....Hannah M. Pingree
Clerk of the House....Millicent M. MacFarland

2009 Regular Session....Dec. 2, 2008 – June 17, 2009
Number of Senatorial Districts....35
Number of Representative Districts....151

EXECUTIVE BRANCH

Governor....John E. Baldacci
Secretary of State....Matthew Dunlap
Attorney General....Janet Mills
Treasurer....David G. Lemoine
Auditor....Neria R. Douglass
Controller....Edward Karass

Governor's Present Term....1/2003-1/2011
Number of Elected Officials in the Executive Branch....1
Number of Members in the Cabinet....21

JUDICIAL BRANCH

Highest Court....Supreme Judicial Court
Supreme Court Chief Justice....Leigh Ingalls Saufley
Number of Supreme Court Judges....7
Number of Intermediate Appellate Court Judges....0
Number of U.S. Court Districts....1
U.S. Circuit Court....1st Circuit

STATE INTERNET ADDRESSES

Official State Website....http://www.state.me.us
Governor's Website....http://www.maine.gov/governor/baldacci/index.shtml
Legislative Website....http://janus.state.me.us/legis
Judicial Website....http://www.courts.state.me.us

Maryland

Nicknames....The Old Line State and Free State
Motto....Fatti Maschii, Parole Femine (Manly Deeds, Womanly Words)
Flower....Black-eyed Susan
Bird....Baltimore Oriole
Tree....White Oak
Song....Maryland, My Maryland
Entered the Union....April 28, 1788
Capital....Annapolis

STATISTICS

Land Area (square miles)....9,774
Rank in Nation....42nd
Population....5,618,344
Rank in Nation....19th
Density per square mile....574.8
Capital City....Annapolis
Population....36,603
Rank in State....7th
Largest City....Baltimore
Population....637,455
Number of Representatives in Congress....8
Number of Counties....23
Number of Municipal Governments....157
Number of 2009 Electoral Votes....10
Number of School Districts....0
Number of Special Districts....85

LEGISLATIVE BRANCH

Legislative Body....General Assembly

President of the Senate....Thomas V. Mike Miller Jr.
President Pro Tem of the Senate....Nathaniel J. McFadden
Secretary of the Senate....William B.C. Addison Jr.

Speaker of the House....Michael Erin Busch
Speaker Pro Tem of the House....Adrienne A. Jones
Clerk of the House....Mary Monahan

2009 Regular Session....Jan. 14-April 13
Number of Senatorial Districts....47
Number of Representative Districts....47

EXECUTIVE BRANCH

Governor....Martin O'Malley
Lieutenant Governor....Anthony Brown
Secretary of State....John McDonough
Attorney General....Douglas Gansler
Treasurer....Nancy K. Kopp
Auditor....Bruce A. Myers
Comptroller....Peter Franchot

Governor's Present Term....1/2007-1/2011
Number of Elected Officials in the Executive Branch....4
Number of Members in the Cabinet....28

JUDICIAL BRANCH

Highest Court....Court of Appeals
Court of Appeals Chief Judge....Robert M. Bell
Number of Court of Appeals Judges....7
Number of Intermediate Appellate Court Judges....13
Number of U.S. Court Districts....1
U.S. Circuit Court....4th Circuit

STATE INTERNET ADDRESSES

Official State Website....http://www.marlyand.gov
Governor's Website....http://www.gov.state.md.us
Legislative Website....http://www.mlis.state.md.us
Judicial Website....http://www.courts.state.md.us/

Massachusetts

Nickname....The Bay State
Motto....Ense Petit Placidam Sub Libertate Quietem
(By the Sword We Seek Peace, but Peace Only under Liberty)
Flower....Mayflower
Bird....Chickadee
Tree....American Elm
Song....All Hail to Massachusetts
Entered the Union....February 6, 1788
Capital....Boston

STATISTICS

Land Area (square miles)....7,840
Rank in Nation....45th
Population....6,449,755
Rank in Nation....14th
Density per square mile....822.7
Capital City....Boston
Population....559,351
Rank in State....1st
Largest City....Boston
Number of Representatives in Congress....10
Number of Counties....5
Number of Municipal Governments....45
Number of 2009 Electoral Votes....12
Number of School Districts....82
Number of Special Districts....403

LEGISLATIVE BRANCH

Legislative Body....General Court

President of the Senate....Therese Murray
President Pro Tem of the Senate....Stanley C. Rosenberg
Clerk of the Senate....William F. Welch

Speaker of the House....Robert A. DeLeo
Speaker Pro Tempore....Thomas M. Petrolati
Clerk of the House....Steven T. James

2009 Regular Session....Jan. 7-Dec. 31
Number of Senatorial Districts....40
Number of Representative Districts....160

EXECUTIVE BRANCH

Governor....Deval Patrick
Lieutenant Governor....Tim Murray
Secretary of the Commonwealth....William F. Galvin
Attorney General....Martha Coakley
Treasurer & Receiver General....Timothy Cahill
Auditor....Joseph DeNucci
Comptroller....Martin J. Benison

Governor's Present Term....1/2007-1/2011
Number of Elected Officials in the Executive Branch....6
Number of Members in the Cabinet....10

JUDICIAL BRANCH

Highest Court....Supreme Judicial Court
Supreme Judicial Court Chief Justice....Margaret H. Marshall
Number of Supreme Judicial Court Judges....7
Number of Intermediate Appellate Court Judges....28
Number of U.S. Court Districts....1
U.S. Circuit Court....1st Circuit

STATE INTERNET ADDRESSES

Official State Website....http://www.mass.gov
Governor's Website....http://www.state.ma.us/gov
Legislative Website....http://www.state.ma.us/legis
Judicial Website....http://www.state.ma.us/courts

Michigan

Nickname....The Wolverine State
Motto....Si Quaeris Peninsulam Amoenam Circumspice
(If You Seek a Pleasant Peninsula, Look About You)
Flower....Apple Blossom
Bird....Robin
Tree....White Pine
Song....Michigan, My Michigan
Entered the Union....January 26, 1837
Capital....Lansing

STATISTICS

Land Area (square miles)....56,804
Rank in Nation....22nd
Population....10,071,822
Rank in Nation....8th
Density per square mile....177.3
Capital City....Lansing
Population....114,947
Rank in State....6th
Largest City....Detroit
Population....916,952
Number of Representatives in Congress....15
Number of Counties....83
Number of Municipal Governments....533
Number of 2009 Electoral Votes....17
Number of School Districts....580
Number of Special Districts....366

LEGISLATIVE BRANCH

Legislative Body....Legislature

President of the Senate....Lt. Gov. John Cherry
President Pro Tem of the Senate....Randy Richardville
Secretary of the Senate....Carol Morey Viventi

Speaker of the House....Andy Dillon
Speaker Pro Tem of the House....Pamela Byrnes
Clerk of the House....Rich Brown

2009 Regular Session....Jan. 14-Dec. 31
Number of Senatorial Districts....38
Number of Representative Districts....110

EXECUTIVE BRANCH

Governor....Jennifer Granholm
Lieutenant Governor....John Cherry
Secretary of State....Terri Lynn Land
Attorney General....Mike Cox
Treasurer....Robert J. Kleine
Auditor....Thomas McTavish
Director, Office of Financial Management....Michael J. Moody

Governor's Present Term....1/2003-1/2011
Number of Elected Officials in the Executive Branch....4
Number of Members in the Cabinet....24

JUDICIAL BRANCH

Highest Court....Supreme Court
Supreme Court Chief Justice....Marilyn Kelly
Number of Supreme Court Judges....7
Number of Intermediate Appellate Court Judges....28
Number of U.S. Court Districts....2
U.S. Circuit Court....6th Circuit

STATE INTERNET ADDRESSES

Official State Website....http://www.michigan.gov
Governor's Website....http://www.michigan.gov/gov
Legislative Website....http://www.michiganlegislature.org
Judicial Website....http://www.courts.michigan.gov

Minnesota

Nickname .... The North Star State
Motto .... L'Etoile du Nord (The North Star)
Flower .... Pink and White Lady-Slipper
Bird .... Common Loon
Tree .... Red Pine
Song .... Hail! Minnesota
Entered the Union .... May 11, 1858
Capital .... St. Paul

STATISTICS

Land Area (square miles) 79,610
Rank in Nation 14th
Population 5,197,621
Rank in Nation 21st
Density per square mile 65.3
Capital City .... St. Paul
Population 277,251
Rank in State 2nd
Largest City .... Minneapolis
Population 377,392
Number of Representatives in Congress 8
Number of Counties 87
Number of Municipal Governments 854
Number of 2009 Electoral Votes 10
Number of School Districts 345
Number of Special Districts 403

LEGISLATIVE BRANCH

Legislative Body .... Legislature

President of the Senate .... James Metzen
Secretary of the Senate for Legislation .... Peter Wattson
Secretary of the Senate for Administration .... JoAnne Zeff

Speaker of the House .... Margaret Anderson Kelliher
Chief Clerk of the House .... Al Mathiowetz

2009 Regular Session .... Jan. 6 – May 18
Number of Senatorial Districts 67
Number of Representative Districts 67

EXECUTIVE BRANCH

Governor .... Tim Pawlenty
Lieutenant Governor .... Carol Molnau
Secretary of State .... Mark Ritchie
Attorney General .... Lori Swanson
Commissioner of Finance .... Tom Hanson
Auditor .... Rebecca Otto

Governor's Present Term 1/2003-1/2011
Number of Elected Officials in the Executive Branch 5
Number of Members in the Cabinet 25

JUDICIAL BRANCH

Highest Court .... Supreme Court
Supreme Court Chief Justice .... Eric J. Magnuson
Number of Supreme Court Judges 7
Number of Intermediate Appellate Court Judges 16
Number of U.S. Court Districts 1
U.S. Circuit Court .... 8th Circuit

STATE INTERNET ADDRESSES

Official State Website .... http://www.state.mn.us
Governor's Website .... http://www.governor.state.mn.us
Legislative Website .... http://www.leg.state.mn.us
Judicial Website .... http://www.courts.state.mn.us/home/

Mississippi

Nickname .... The Magnolia State
Motto .... Virtute et Armis (By Valor and Arms)
Flower .... Magnolia
Bird .... Mockingbird
Tree .... Magnolia
Song .... Go, Mississippi
Entered the Union .... December 10, 1817
Capital .... Jackson

STATISTICS

Land Area (square miles) 46,907
Rank in Nation 31st
Population 2,918,785
Rank in Nation 31st
Density per square mile 62.2
Capital City .... Jackson
Population 175,710
Rank in State 1st
Largest City .... Jackson
Number of Representatives in Congress 4
Number of Counties 82
Number of Municipal Governments 296
Number of 2009 Electoral Votes 6
Number of School Districts 164
Number of Special Districts 458

LEGISLATIVE BRANCH

Legislative Body .... Legislature

President of the Senate .... Lt. Gov. Phil Bryant
President Pro Tem of the Senate .... Billy Hewes
Secretary of the Senate .... Tressa W. Guynes

Speaker of the House .... William J. McCoy
Speaker Pro Tem of the House .... J.P. Compretta
Clerk of the House .... Don Richardson

2009 Regular Session .... Jan. 6 – April 5
Number of Senatorial Districts 52
Number of Representative Districts 122

EXECUTIVE BRANCH

Governor .... Haley Barbour
Lieutenant Governor .... Phil Bryant
Secretary of State .... Delbert Hosemann
Attorney General .... Jim Hood
Treasurer .... Tate Reeves
Auditor .... Stacey Pickering

Governor's Present Term 1/2004-1/2012
Number of Elected Officials in the Executive Branch 8
Number of Members in the Cabinet .... No formal cabinet system

JUDICIAL BRANCH

Highest Court .... Supreme Court
Supreme Court Chief Justice .... William L. Waller Jr.
Number of Supreme Court Judges 9
Number of Intermediate Appellate Court Judges 10
Number of U.S. Court Districts 2
U.S. Circuit Court .... 5th Circuit

STATE INTERNET ADDRESSES

Official State Website .... http://www.ms.gov
Governor's Website .... http://www.governor.state.ms.us
Legislative Website .... http://billstatus.ls.state.ms.us/
Judicial Website .... http://www.mssc.state.ms.us

Missouri

Nickname........The Show Me State
Motto........Salus Populi Suprema Lex Esto
(The Welfare of the People Shall Be the Supreme Law)
Flower........White Hawthorn Blossom
Bird........Bluebird
Tree........Flowering Dogwood
Song........Missouri Waltz
Entered the Union........August 10, 1821
Capital........Jefferson City

STATISTICS

Land Area (square miles)........68,886
Rank in Nation........18th
Population........5,878,415
Rank in Nation........18th
Density per square mile........85.3
Capital City........Jefferson City
Population........40,564
Rank in State........15th
Largest City........Kansas City
Population........450,375
Number of Representatives in Congress........9
Number of Counties........114
Number of Municipal Governments........946
Number of 2009 Electoral Votes........11
Number of School Districts........536
Number of Special Districts........1,514

LEGISLATIVE BRANCH

Legislative Body........Legislative Assembly

President of the Senate........Lt. Gov. Peter Kinder
President Pro Tem of the Senate........Charlie Shields
Secretary of the Senate........Terry L. Spieler

Speaker of the House........Ron Richard
Speaker Pro Tem of the House........Bryan Pratt
Clerk of the House........D. Adam Crumbliss

2009 Regular Session........Jan. 7-May 30
Number of Senatorial Districts........34
Number of Representative Districts........163

EXECUTIVE BRANCH

Governor........Jay Nixon
Lieutenant Governor........Peter Kinder
Secretary of State........Robin Carnahan
Attorney General........Chris Koster
Treasurer........Clint Zweifel
Auditor........Susan Montee
Director, Division of Accounting........Mark A. Kaiser

Governor's Present Term........1/2009- 1/2013
Number of Elected Officials in the Executive Branch........6
Number of Members in the Cabinet........17

JUDICIAL BRANCH

Highest Court........Supreme Court
Supreme Court Chief Justice........Laura Denvir Stith
Number of Supreme Court Judges........7
Number of Intermediate Appellate Court Judges........32
Number of U.S. Court Districts........2
U.S. Circuit Court........8th Circuit

STATE INTERNET ADDRESSES

Official State Website........http://www.mo.gov/
Governor's Website........http://governor.mo.gov/
Legislative Website........http://www.moga.mo.gov/
Judicial Website........http://www.courts.mo.gov/

Montana

Nickname........The Treasure State
Motto........Oro y Plata (Gold and Silver)
Flower........Bitterroot
Bird........Western Meadowlark
Tree........Ponderosa Pine
Song........Montana
Entered the Union........November 8, 1889
Capital........Helena

STATISTICS

Land Area (square miles)........145,552
Rank in Nation........4th
Population........957,861
Rank in Nation........44th
Density per square mile........6.5
Capital City........Helena
Population........28,726
Rank in State........6th
Largest City........Billings
Population........101,876
Number of Representatives in Congress........1
Number of Counties........54
Number of Municipal Governments........129
Number of 2009 Electoral Votes........3
Number of School Districts........352
Number of Special Districts........592

LEGISLATIVE BRANCH

Legislative Body........Legislature

President of the Senate........Robert R. Story Jr.
President Pro Tem of the Senate........Daniel W. McGee
Secretary of the Senate........Marilyn Miller

Speaker of the House........Bob Bergen
Speaker Pro Tem of the House........Franke Wilmer
Chief Clerk of the House........Dave Hunter

2009 Regular Session........Jan. 5 – Apr. 28
Number of Senatorial Districts........50
Number of Representative Districts........100

EXECUTIVE BRANCH

Governor........Brian Schweitzer
Lieutenant Governor........John Bohlinger
Secretary of State........Linda McCulloch
Attorney General........Steve Bullock
Treasurer........Janet Kelly
Auditor........Monica J. Lindeen
Administrator, State Accounting........Paul Christofferson

Governor's Present Term........1/2005-1/2013
Number of Elected Officials in the Executive Branch........6
Number of Members in the Cabinet........22

JUDICIAL BRANCH

Highest Court........Supreme Court
Supreme Court Chief Justice........Mike McGrath
Number of Supreme Court Judges........7
Number of Intermediate Appellate Court Judges........0
Number of U.S. Court Districts........1
U.S. Circuit Court........9th Circuit

STATE INTERNET ADDRESSES

Official State Website........http://www.state.mt.us
Governor's Website........http;//www.discoveringmontana.com/gov2
Legislative Website........http://leg.mt.gov/css/default.asp
Judicial Website........www.montanacourts.org

Nebraska

Nickname....The Cornhusker State
Motto....Equality Before the Law
Flower....Goldenrod
Bird....Western Meadowlark
Tree....Western Cottonwood
Song....Beautiful Nebraska
Entered the Union....March 1, 1867
Capital....Lincoln

STATISTICS

Land Area (square miles)....76,872
Rank in Nation....15th
Population....1,774,571
Rank in Nation....38th
Density per square mile....23.1
Capital City....Lincoln
Population....248,744
Rank in State....2nd
Largest City....Omaha
Population....424,482
Number of Representatives in Congress....3
Number of Counties....93
Number of Municipal Governments....531
Number of 2009 Electoral Votes....5
Number of School Districts....575
Number of Special Districts....1,146

LEGISLATIVE BRANCH

Legislative Body....Unicameral Legislature

President of the Legislature....Lt. Gov. Rick Sheehy
Clerk of the Legislature....Patrick J. O'Donnell

2009 Regular Session....Jan.7 - June
Number of Legislative Districts....49

EXECUTIVE BRANCH

Governor....David Heineman
Lieutenant Governor....Rick Sheehy
Secretary of State....John Gale
Attorney General....Jon Bruning
Treasurer....Shane Osborn
Auditor....Mike Foley
State Accounting Administrator....Paul Carlson

Governor's Present Term....1/2005-1/2011
Number of Elected Officials in the Executive Branch....6
Number of Members in the Cabinet....29

JUDICIAL BRANCH

Highest Court....Supreme Court
Supreme Court Chief Justice....Michael G. Heavican
Number of Supreme Court Judges....7
Number of Intermediate Appellate Court Judges....6
Number of U.S. Court Districts....1
U.S. Circuit Court....8th Circuit

STATE INTERNET ADDRESSES

Official State Website....http://www.state.ne.us
Governor's Website....http://www.governor.nebraska.gov/
Legislative Website....http://nebraskalegislature.gov/
Judicial Website. http://www.supremecourt.ne.gov/supreme-court/index.shtml?sub1

Nevada

Nickname....The Silver State
Motto....All for Our Country
Flower....Sagebrush
Bird....Mountain Bluebird
Tree....Bristlecone Pine and Single-leaf Pinon
Song....Home Means Nevada
Entered the Union....October 31, 1864
Capital....Carson City

STATISTICS

Land Area (square miles)....109,826
Rank in Nation....7th
Population....2,565,382
Rank in Nation....35th
Density per square mile....23.4
Capital City....Carson City
Population....54,939
Rank in State....6th
Largest City....Las Vegas
Population....558,880
Number of Representatives in Congress....3
Number of Counties....16
Number of Municipal Governments....19
Number of 2009 Electoral Votes....5
Number of School Districts....17
Number of Special Districts....158

LEGISLATIVE BRANCH

Legislative Body....Legislature

President of the Senate....Lt. Gov. Brian K. Krolicki
President Pro Tem of the Senate....Michael A. Schneider
Secretary of the Senate....Claire Clift

Speaker of the Assembly....Barbara Buckley
Speaker Pro Tem of the Assembly....Bernie Anderson
Chief Clerk of the Assembly....Susan Furlong Reil

2009 Regular Session....Feb. 7- Jun. 8
Number of Senatorial Districts....21
Number of Representative Districts....42

EXECUTIVE BRANCH

Governor....James A. Gibbons
Lieutenant Governor....Brian Krolicki
Secretary of State....Ross Miller
Attorney General....Catherine Cortez Masto
Treasurer....Kate Marshall
Auditor....Paul V. Townsend
Controller....Kim Wallin

Governor's Present Term....1/2007-1/2011
Number of Elected Officials in the Executive Branch....6
Number of Members in the Cabinet....23

JUDICIAL BRANCH

Highest Court....Supreme Court
Supreme Court Chief Justice....James W. Hardesty
Number of Supreme Court Judges....7
Number of Intermediate Appellate Court Judges....0
Number of U.S. Court Districts....1
U.S. Circuit Court....9th Circuit

STATE INTERNET ADDRESSES

Official State Website....http://www.nv.gov
Governor's Website....http://www.gov.state.nv.us
Legislative Website....http://www.leg.state.nv.us
Judicial Website....http://silver.state.nv.us/elec_judicial.htm

New Hampshire

Nickname: The Granite State
Motto: Live Free or Die
Flower: Purple Lilac
Bird: Purple Finch
Tree: White Birch
Song: Old New Hampshire
Entered the Union: June 21, 1788
Capital: Concord

STATISTICS

Land Area (square miles): 8,968
Rank in Nation: 44th
Population: 1,315,828
Rank in Nation: 41st
Density per square mile: 146.7
Capital City: Concord
Population: 42,392
Rank in State: 3rd
Largest City: Manchester
Population: 108,874
Number of Representatives in Congress: 2
Number of Counties: 10
Number of Municipal Governments: 13
Number of 2009 Electoral Votes: 4
Number of School Districts: 167
Number of Special Districts: 148

LEGISLATIVE BRANCH

Legislative Body: General Court

President of the Senate: Sylvia B. Larsen
President Pro Tem of the Senate: Martha Fuller Clark
Clerk of the Senate: Tammy L. Wright

Speaker of the House: Terie N. Norelli
Clerk of the House: Karen O. Wadsworth

2009 Regular Session: Jan. 7-July 1
Number of Senatorial Districts: 24
Number of Representative Districts: 103

EXECUTIVE BRANCH

Governor: John Lynch
Secretary of State: William M. Gardner
Attorney General: Kelly Ayotte
Treasurer: Catherine Provencher
Auditor: Michael Buckley
Acting Comptroller: Steven Smith

Governor's Present Term: 1/2005-1/2011
Number of Elected Officials in the Executive Branch: 1
Number of Members in the Cabinet: No formal cabinet system

JUDICIAL BRANCH

Highest Court: Supreme Court
Supreme Court Chief Justice: John T. Broderick, Jr.
Number of Supreme Court Judges: 5
Number of Intermediate Appellate Court Judges: 0
Number of U.S. Court Districts: 1
U.S. Circuit Court: 1st Circuit

STATE INTERNET ADDRESSES

Official State Website: http://www.state.nh.us
Governor's Website: http://www.nh.gov/governor/
Legislative Website: http://www.gencourt.state.nh.us
Judicial Website: http://www.courts.state.nh.us/

New Jersey

Nickname: The Garden State
Motto: Liberty and Prosperity
Flower: Violet
Bird: Eastern Goldfinch
Tree: Red Oak
Song: I'm From New Jersey
Entered the Union: December 18, 1787
Capital: Trenton

STATISTICS

Land Area (square miles): 7,417
Rank in Nation: 46th
Population: 8,685,920
Rank in Nation: 11th
Density per square mile: 1,171.2
Capital City: Trenton
Population: 82,804
Rank in State: 9th
Largest City: Newark
Population: 280,135
Number of Representatives in Congress: 13
Number of Counties: 21
Number of Municipal Governments: 324
Number of 2009 Electoral Votes: 15
Number of School Districts: 549
Number of Special Districts: 276

LEGISLATIVE BRANCH

Legislative Body: Legislature

President of the Senate: Richard J. Codey
President Pro Tem of the Senate: Shirley K. Turner
Secretary of the Senate: Ellen M. Davenport

Speaker of the Assembly: Joseph J. Roberts Jr.
Speaker Pro Tem of the Assembly: Jerry Green
Clerk of the General Assembly: Dana M. Burley

2009 Regular Session: Jan. 13 – Dec. 31
Number of Senatorial Districts: 40
Number of Representative Districts: 40

EXECUTIVE BRANCH

Governor: Jon Corzine
Secretary of State: Nina Mitchell Wells
Attorney General: Anne Milgram
Treasurer: R. David Rousseau
Auditor: Richard L. Fair
Controller: Charlene Holzbaur

Governor's Present Term: 1/2006-1/2010
Number of Elected Officials in the Executive Branch: 1
Number of Members in the Cabinet: 24

JUDICIAL BRANCH

Highest Court: Supreme Court
Supreme Court Chief Justice: Stuart Rabner
Number of Supreme Court Judges: 7
Number of Intermediate Appellate Court Judges: 35
Number of U.S. Court Districts: 1
U.S. Circuit Court: 3rd Circuit

STATE INTERNET ADDRESSES

Official State Website: http://www.state.nj.us
Governor's Website: http://www.state.nj.us/governor
Legislative Website: http://www.njleg.state.nj.us
Judicial Website: http://www.judiciary.state.nj.us

New Mexico

Nickname .... The Land of Enchantment
Motto .... Crescit Eundo (It Grows As It Goes)
Flower .... Yucca (Our Lord's Candles)
Bird .... Chaparral Bird
Tree .... Pinon
Songs .... Asi es Nuevo Mexico and O, Fair New Mexico
Entered the Union .... January 6, 1912
Capital .... Santa Fe

STATISTICS

Land Area (square miles) 121,356
Rank in Nation 5th
Population 1,969,915
Rank in Nation 36th
Density per square mile 16.2
Capital City .... Santa Fe
Population 73,199
Rank in State 3rd
Largest City .... Albuquerque
Population 518,271
Number of Representatives in Congress 3
Number of Counties 33
Number of Municipal Governments 101
Number of 2009 Electoral Votes 5
Number of School Districts 96
Number of Special Districts 628

LEGISLATIVE BRANCH

Legislative Body .... Legislature

President of the Senate .... Lt. Gov. Diane Denish
President Pro Tem of the Senate .... Timothy Z. Jennings
Chief Clerk of the Senate .... Lenore Naranjo

Speaker of the House .... Ben Lujan
Chief Clerk of the House .... Stephen R. Arias

2009 Regular Session .... Jan. 20 – Mar. 21
Number of Senatorial Districts 42
Number of Representative Districts 70

EXECUTIVE BRANCH

Governor .... Bill Richardson
Lieutenant Governor .... Diane Denish
Secretary of State .... Mary Herrera
Attorney General .... Gary King
Treasurer .... James Lewis
Auditor .... Hector Balderas
Controller .... Anthony Armijo

Governor's Present Term 1/2003-1/2011
Number of Elected Officials in the Executive Branch 5
Number of Members in the Cabinet 25

JUDICIAL BRANCH

Highest Court .... Supreme Court
Supreme Court Chief Justice .... Edward L. Chavez
Number of Supreme Court Judges 5
Number of Intermediate Appellate Court Judges 10
Number of U.S. Court Districts 1
U.S. Circuit Court .... 10th Circuit

STATE INTERNET ADDRESSES

Official State Website .... http://www.state.nm.us
Governor's Website .... http://www.governor.state.nm.us
Legislative Website .... http://legis.state.nm.us
Judicial Website .... http://www.nmcourts.com

New York

Nickname .... The Empire State
Motto .... Excelsior (Ever Upward)
Flower .... Rose
Bird .... Bluebird
Tree .... Sugar Maple
Song .... I Love New York
Entered the Union .... July 26, 1788
Capital .... Albany

STATISTICS

Land Area (square miles) 47,214
Rank in Nation 30th
Population 19,297,729
Rank in Nation 3rd
Density per square mile 408.7
Capital City .... Albany
Population 94,172
Rank in State 6th
Largest City .... New York City
Population 8,274,527
Number of Representatives in Congress 29
Number of Counties 57
Number of Municipal Governments 616
Number of 2009 Electoral Votes 31
Number of School Districts 683
Number of Special Districts 1,135

LEGISLATIVE BRANCH

Legislative Body .... Legislature

Acting President of the Senate .... Malcolm A. Smith
President Pro Tem and Majority Leader of the Senate .... Malcolm A. Smith
Secretary of the Senate .... Angelo J. Aponte

Speaker of the Assembly .... Sheldon Silver
Speaker Pro Tem of the Assembly .... Aurelia Greene
Clerk of the Assembly .... Laurene R. Kretzler

2009 Regular Session .... Jan. 7 – Dec. 31.
Number of Senatorial Districts 62
Number of Representative Districts 150

EXECUTIVE BRANCH

Governor .... David A. Paterson
Lieutenant Governor .... Vacant
Secretary of State .... Lorraine Cortes-Vazquez
Attorney General .... Andrew Cuomo
Treasurer .... Aida Brewer
Comptroller .... Thomas P. DiNapoli

Governor's Present Term 3/2008-1/2011
Number of Elected Officials in the Executive Branch 4
Number of Members in the Cabinet 75

JUDICIAL BRANCH

Highest Court .... Court of Appeals
Court of Appeals Chief Justice .... Jonathan Lippman
Number of Court of Appeals Judges 7
Number of Intermediate Appellate Court Judges 57
Number of U.S. Court Districts 4
U.S. Circuit Court .... 2nd Circuit

STATE INTERNET ADDRESSES

Official State Website .... http://www.state.ny.us
Governor's Website .... http://www.state.ny.us/governor
Senate Website .... http://www.senate.state.ny.us
Assembly Website .... http://assembly.state.ny.us
Judicial Website .... http://www.courts.state.ny.us

North Carolina

Nickname .... The Tar Heel State and Old North State
Motto .... Esse Quam Videri
(To Be Rather Than to Seem)
Flower .... Dogwood
Bird .... Cardinal
Tree .... Long Leaf Pine
Song .... The Old North State
Entered the United States .... November 21, 1789
Capital .... Raleigh

STATISTICS

Land Area (square miles) 48,711
Rank in Nation 29th
Population 9,061,032
Rank in Nation 10th
Density per square mile 186.0
Capital City .... Raleigh
Population 375,806
Rank in State 2nd
Largest City .... Charlotte
Population 671,588
Number of Representatives in Congress 13
Number of Counties 100
Number of Municipal Governments 541
Number of 2009 Electoral Votes 15
Number of School Districts 117
Number of Special Districts 319

LEGISLATIVE BRANCH

Legislative Body .... General Assembly

President of the Senate .... Lt. Gov. Walter Dalton
President Pro Tem of the Senate .... Marc Basnight
Principal Clerk of the Senate .... Janet Pruitt

Speaker of the House .... Joe Hackney
Principal Clerk of the House .... Denise Weeks

2009 Regular Session .... Jan. 28 - July
Number of Senatorial Districts 50
Number of Representative Districts 120

EXECUTIVE BRANCH

Governor .... Beverly Perdue
Lieutenant Governor .... Walter Dalton
Secretary of State .... Elaine Marshall
Attorney General .... Roy A. Cooper III
Treasurer .... Jane Cowell
Auditor .... Beth Wood
Controller .... David McCoy

Governor's Present Term 1/2009- 1/2013
Number of Elected Officials in the Executive Branch 10
Number of Members in the Cabinet 10

JUDICIAL BRANCH

Highest Court .... Supreme Court
Supreme Court Chief Justice .... Sarah Parker
Number of Supreme Court Judges 7
Number of Intermediate Appellate Court Judges 15
Number of U.S. Court Districts 3
U.S. Circuit Court .... 4th Circuit

STATE INTERNET ADDRESSES

Official State Website .... http://www.ncgov.com
Governor's Website .... http://www.governor.state.nc.us
Legislative Website .... http://www.ncleg.net
Judicial Website .... http://www.nccourts.org

North Dakota

Nickname .... Peace Garden State
Motto .... Liberty and Union, Now and Forever,
One and Inseparable
Flower .... Wild Prairie Rose
Bird .... Western Meadowlark
Tree .... American Elm
Song .... North Dakota Hymn
Entered the Union .... November 2, 1889
Capital .... Bismarck

STATISTICS

Land Area (square miles) 68,976
Rank in Nation 17th
Population 639,715
Rank in Nation 48th
Density per square mile 9.3
Capital City .... Bismarck
Population 59,503
Rank in State 2nd
Largest City .... Fargo
Population 92,660
Number of Representatives in Congress 1
Number of Counties 53
Number of Municipal Governments 360
Number of 2009 Electoral Votes 3
Number of School Districts 226
Number of Special Districts 764

LEGISLATIVE BRANCH

Legislative Body .... Legislative Assembly

President of the Senate .... Lt. Gov. Jack Dalrymple
President Pro Tem of the Senate .... Tom Fischer
Secretary of the Senate .... Fran Gronberg

Speaker of the House .... David Monson
Clerk of the House .... Buell Reich

2009 Regular Session .... Jan. 6 – Apr. 30
Number of Senatorial Districts 47
Number of Representative Districts 47

EXECUTIVE BRANCH

Governor .... John Hoeven
Lieutenant Governor .... Jack Dalrymple
Secretary of State .... Alvin Jaeger
Attorney General .... Wayne Stenehjem
Treasurer .... Kelly Schmidt
Auditor .... Robert R. Peterson

Governor's Present Term 12/2000-12/2012
Number of Elected Officials in the Executive Branch 10
Number of Members in the Cabinet 18

JUDICIAL BRANCH

Highest Court .... Supreme Court
Supreme Court Chief Justice .... Jerry W. VandeWalle
Number of Supreme Court Judges 5
Number of Intermediate Appellate Court Judges 0
Number of U.S. Court Districts 1
U.S. Circuit Court .... 8th Circuit

STATE INTERNET ADDRESSES

Official State Website .... http://discovernd.com
Governor's Website .... http://www.governor.state.nd.us
Legislative Website .... http://www.legis.nd.gov/
Judicial Website .... http://www.court.state.nd.us

Ohio

Nickname .... The Buckeye State
Motto .... With God, All Things Are Possible
Flower .... Scarlet Carnation
Bird .... Cardinal
Tree .... Buckeye
Song .... Beautiful Ohio
Entered the Union .... March 1, 1803
Capital .... Columbus

STATISTICS

Land Area (square miles) 40,948
Rank in Nation 35th
Population 11,466,917
Rank in Nation 7th
Density per square mile 280.0
Capital City .... Columbus
Population 747,755
Rank in State 1st
Largest City .... Columbus
Number of Representatives in Congress 18
Number of Counties 88
Number of Municipal Governments 942
Number of 2009 Electoral Votes 20
Number of School Districts 667
Number of Special Districts 631

LEGISLATIVE BRANCH

Legislative Body .... General Assembly

President of the Senate .... Bill Harris
President Pro Tem of the Senate .... Tom Niehaus
Clerk of the Senate .... Vincent Keeran

Speaker of the House .... Armond Budish
Speaker Pro Tem of the House .... Matt Szollosi
Legislative Clerk of the House .... Tom Sherman

2009 Regular Session .... Jan. 5-Dec. 31
Number of Senatorial Districts 33
Number of Representative Districts 99

EXECUTIVE BRANCH

Governor .... Ted Strickland
Lieutenant Governor .... Lee Fisher
Secretary of State .... Jennifer Brunner
Attorney General .... Richard Cordray
Treasurer .... Kevin L. Boyce
Auditor .... Mary Taylor

Governor's Present Term 1/2007-1/2011
Number of Elected Officials in the Executive Branch 6
Number of Members in the Cabinet 24

JUDICIAL BRANCH

Highest Court .... Supreme Court
Supreme Court Chief Justice .... Thomas J. Moyer
Number of Supreme Court Judges 7
Number of Intermediate Appellate Court Judges 68
Number of U.S. Court Districts 2
U.S. Circuit Court .... 6th Circuit

STATE INTERNET ADDRESSES

Official State Website .... http://www.state.oh.us
Governor's Website .... http://governor.ohio.gov/
Legislative Website .... http://www.ohio.gov/ohio/GovState.stm#ohleg
Judicial Website .... http://www.sconet.state.oh.us

Oklahoma

Nickname .... The Sooner State
Motto .... Labor Omnia Vincit (Labor Conquers All Things)
Flower .... Mistletoe
Bird .... Scissor-tailed Flycatcher
Tree .... Redbud
Song .... Oklahoma
Entered the Union .... November 16, 1907
Capital .... Oklahoma City

STATISTICS

Land Area (square miles) 68,667
Rank in Nation 19th
Population 3,617,316
Rank in Nation 28th
Density per square mile 52.7
Capital City .... Oklahoma City
Population 547,274
Rank in State 1st
Largest City .... Oklahoma City
Number of Representatives in Congress 5
Number of Counties 77
Number of Municipal Governments 590
Number of 2009 Electoral Votes 7
Number of School Districts 571
Number of Special Districts 560

LEGISLATIVE BRANCH

Legislative Body .... Legislature

President of the Senate .... Lt. Gov. Jari Askins
President Pro Tem of the Senate .... Glenn Coffee
Secretary of the Senate .... Paul Ziriax

Speaker of the House .... Chris Benge
Speaker Pro Tem of the House .... Kris Steele
Chief Clerk/Administrator of the House .... Joel Kintsel

2009 Regular Session .... Feb. 2 - May 29
Number of Senatorial Districts 50
Number of Representative Districts 101

EXECUTIVE BRANCH

Governor .... Brad Henry
Lieutenant Governor .... Jari Askins
Secretary of State .... Susan Savage
Attorney General .... W. A. Drew Edmondson
Treasurer .... Scott Meacham
Auditor .... Steve Burrage
Comptroller .... Brenda Bolander

Governor's Present Term 1/2003-1/2011
Number of Elected Officials in the Executive Branch 8
Number of Members in the Cabinet 10-15

JUDICIAL BRANCH

Highest Court .... Supreme Court
Supreme Court Chief Justice .... James E. Edmondson
Number of Supreme Court Judges 9
Number of Intermediate Appellate Court Judges 10
Number of U.S. Court Districts 3
U.S. Circuit Court .... 10th Circuit

STATE INTERNET ADDRESSES

Official State Website .... http://www.state.ok.us
Governor's Website .... http://www.governor.state.ok.us/
Legislative Website .... http://www.lsb.state.ok.us
Judicial Website .... http://www.oscn.net

Oregon

Nickname	The Beaver State
Motto	She Flies with Her Own Wings
Flower	Oregon Grape
Bird	Western Meadowlark
Tree	Douglas Fir
Song	Oregon, My Oregon
Entered the Union	February 14, 1859
Capital	Salem

STATISTICS

Land Area (square miles)	95,997
Rank in Nation	10th
Population	3,747,455
Rank in Nation	27th
Density per square mile	39.0
Capital City	Salem
Population	151,913
Rank in State	3rd
Largest City	Portland
Population	550,396
Number of Representatives in Congress	5
Number of Counties	36
Number of Municipal Governments	240
Number of 2009 Electoral Votes	7
Number of School Districts	236
Number of Special Districts	927

LEGISLATIVE BRANCH

Legislative Body	Legislative Assembly
President of the Senate	Peter Courtney
President Pro Tem of the Senate	Rick Metsger
Secretary of the Senate	Judy M. Hall
Speaker of the House	Dave Hunt
Chief Clerk of the House	Arnie Robian
2009 Regular Session	Jan. 12 - June
Number of Senatorial Districts	30
Number of Representative Districts	60

EXECUTIVE BRANCH

Governor	Ted Kulongoski
Secretary of State	Kate Brown
Attorney General	John Kroger
Treasurer	Ben Westlund
Auditor	Charles Hibner
Controller	John Radford
Governor's Present Term	1/2003-1/2011
Number of Elected Officials in the Executive Branch	6
Number of Members in the Cabinet	No formal cabinet system

JUDICIAL BRANCH

Highest Court	Supreme Court
Supreme Court Chief Justice	Paul J. De Muniz
Number of Supreme Court Judges	7
Number of Intermediate Appellate Court Judges	10
Number of U.S. Court Districts	1
U.S. Circuit Court	9th Circuit

STATE INTERNET ADDRESSES

Official State Website	http://www.oregon.gov
Governor's Website	http://www.governor.state.or.us
Legislative Website	http://www.leg.state.or.us
Judicial Website	http://www.ojd.state.or.us

Pennsylvania

Nickname	The Keystone State
Motto	Virtue, Liberty and Independence
Animal	White-tailed Deer
Flower	Mountain Laurel
Tree	Hemlock
Song	Pennsylvania
Entered the Union	December 12, 1787
Capital	Harrisburg

STATISTICS

Land Area (square miles)	44,817
Rank in Nation	32nd
Population	12,432,792
Rank in Nation	6th
Density per square mile	277.4
Capital City	Harrisburg
Population	47,196
Rank in State	13th
Largest City	Philadelphia
Population	1,449,634
Number of Representatives in Congress	19
Number of Counties	66
Number of Municipal Governments	1,018
Number of 2009 Electoral Votes	21
Number of School Districts	516
Number of Special Districts	1,885

LEGISLATIVE BRANCH

Legislative Body	General Assembly
President of the Senate	Lt. Gov. Joseph Scarnati
President Pro Tem of the Senate	Joseph B. Scarnati
Secretary-Parliamentarian of the Senate	Mark R. Corrigan
Speaker of the House	Keith R. McCall
Chief Clerk of the House	Roger Nick
2009 Regular Session	Jan. 6 – Dec. 31
Number of Senatorial Districts	50
Number of Representative Districts	203

EXECUTIVE BRANCH

Governor	Ed Rendell
Lieutenant Governor	Joseph Scarnati
Secretary of State	Pedro A. Cortés
Attorney General	Tom Corbett
Treasurer	Robert McCord
Comptroller	Anna Marie Kiehl
Governor's Present Term	1/2003-1/2011
Number of Elected Officials in the Executive Branch	5
Number of Members in the Cabinet	28

JUDICIAL BRANCH

Highest Court	Supreme Court
Supreme Court Chief Justice	Ronald D. Castille
Number of Supreme Court Judges	7
Number of Intermediate Appellate Court Judges	23
Number of U.S. Court Districts	3
U.S. Circuit Court	3rd Circuit

STATE INTERNET ADDRESSES

Official State Website	http://www.state.pa.us
Governor's Website	http://www.governor.state.pa.us/
Legislative Website	http://www.legis.state.pa.us
Judicial Website	http://www.courts.state.pa.us

Rhode Island

Nicknames .... Little Rhody and Ocean State
Motto .... Hope
Flower .... Violet
Bird .... Rhode Island Red
Tree .... Red Maple
Song .... Rhode Island
Entered the Union .... May 29, 1790
Capital .... Providence

STATISTICS

Land Area (square mile) 1,045
Rank in Nation 50th
Population 1,057,832
Rank in Nation 43rd
Density per square mile 1,012.3
Capital City .... Providence
Population 172,459
Rank in State 1st
Largest City .... Providence
Number of Representatives in Congress 2
Number of Counties 5
Number of Municipal Governments 8
Number of 2009 Electoral Votes 4
Number of School Districts 38
Number of Special Districts 75

LEGISLATIVE BRANCH

Legislative Body .... General Assembly

President of the Senate .... M. Teresa Paiva-Weed
President Pro Tem of the Senate .... John F. McBurney III.
Secretary of the Senate .... Joseph Brady

Speaker of the House .... William J. Murphy
Speaker Pro Tem of the House .... Charlene Lima
Clerk of the House .... Frank McCabe

2009 Regular Session .... Jan. 6-June
Number of Senatorial Districts 38
Number of Representative Districts 75

EXECUTIVE BRANCH

Governor .... Donald L. Carcieri
Lieutenant Governor .... Elizabeth H. Roberts
Secretary of State .... Ralph Mollis
Attorney General .... Patrick Lynch
Treasurer .... Frank T. Caprio
Auditor .... Ernest A. Almonte
Controller .... Lawrence Franklin

Governor's Present Term 1/2003-1/2011
Number of Elected Officials in the Executive Branch 5
Number of Members in the Cabinet 20

JUDICIAL BRANCH

Highest Court .... Supreme Court
Supreme Court Chief Justice .... Maureen McKenna Goldberg
Number of Supreme Court Judges 5
Number of Intermediate Appellate Court Judges 0
Number of U.S. Court Districts 1
U.S. Circuit Court .... 1st Circuit

STATE INTERNET ADDRESSES

Official State Website .... http://www.state.ri.us
Governor's Website .... http://www.governor.state.ri.us
Legislative Website .... http://www.rilin.state.ri.us
Judicial Website .... http://www.courts.state.ri.us

South Carolina

Nickname .... The Palmetto State
Motto .... Animis Opibusque Parati (Prepared in Mind and Resources) and Dum Spiro Spero (While I breathe, I Hope)
Flower .... Yellow Jessamine
Bird .... Carolina Wren
Tree .... Palmetto
Songs .... Carolina and South Carolina on My Mind
Entered the Union .... May 23, 1788
Capital .... Columbia

STATISTICS

Land Area (square miles) 30,109
Rank in Nation 40th
Population 4,407,709
Rank in Nation 24th
Density per square mile 146.4
Capital City .... Columbia
Population 124,818
Rank in State 1st
Largest City .... Columbia
Number of Representatives in Congress 6
Number of Counties 46
Number of Municipal Governments 269
Number of 2009 Electoral Votes 8
Number of School Districts 85
Number of Special Districts 301

LEGISLATIVE BRANCH

Legislative Body .... General Assembly

President of the Senate .... Lt. Gov. R. Andre Bauer
President Pro Tem of the Senate .... Glenn F. McConnell
Clerk of the Senate .... Jeffrey S. Gossett

Speaker of the House .... Robert W. Harrell Jr.
Speaker Pro Tem of the House .... Harry F. Cato
Clerk of the House .... Charles F. Reid

2009 Regular Session .... Jan. 13-June 4
Number of Senatorial Districts 46
Number of Representative Districts 124

EXECUTIVE BRANCH

Governor .... Mark Sanford
Lieutenant Governor .... R. Andre Bauer
Secretary of State .... Mark Hammond
Attorney General .... Henry D. McMaster
Treasurer .... Converse A. Chellis III
Auditor .... Richard H. Gilbert Jr.
Comptroller .... Richard Eckstrom

Governor's Present Term 1/2003-1/2011
Number of Elected Officials in the Executive Branch 9
Number of Members in the Cabinet 15

JUDICIAL BRANCH

Highest Court .... Supreme Court
Supreme Court Chief Justice .... Jean Hoefer Toal
Number of Supreme Court Judges 5
Number of Intermediate Appellate Court Judges 10
Number of U.S. Court Districts 1
U.S. Circuit Court .... 4th Circuit

STATE INTERNET ADDRESSES

Official State Website .... http://www.sc.gov/
Governor's Website .... http://www.scgovernor.com
Legislative Website .... http://www.scstatehouse.net
Judicial Website .... http://www.judicial.state.sc.us

South Dakota

Nicknames .... The Mt. Rushmore State
Motto .... Under God the People Rule
Flower .... American Pasque
Bird .... Chinese ring-necked pheasant
Tree .... Black Hills Spruce
Song .... Hail, South Dakota
Entered the Union .... November 2, 1889
Capital .... Pierre

STATISTICS

Land Area (square miles) 75,885
Rank in Nation 16th
Population 796,214
Rank in Nation 46th
Density per square mile 10.5
Capital City .... Pierre
Population 14,032
Rank in State 7th
Largest City .... Sioux Falls
Population 151,505
Number of Representatives in Congress 1
Number of Counties 66
Number of Municipal Governments 308
Number of 2009 Electoral Votes 3
Number of School Districts 176
Number of Special Districts 376

LEGISLATIVE BRANCH

Legislative Body .... Legislature

President of the Senate .... Lt. Gov. Dennis Daugaard
President Pro Tem of the Senate .... Bob Gray
Secretary of the Senate .... Trudy Evenstad

Speaker of the House .... Tim Rave
Speaker Pro Tem of the House .... Val Rausch
Chief Clerk of the House .... Karen Gerdes

2009 Regular Session .... Jan. 13-March 30
Number of Senatorial Districts 35
Number of Representative Districts 35

EXECUTIVE BRANCH

Governor .... Mike Rounds
Lieutenant Governor .... Dennis Daugaard
Secretary of State .... Chris Nelson
Attorney General .... Larry Long
Treasurer .... Vernon L. Larson
Auditor .... Rich Sattgast

Governor's Present Term 1/2003-1/2011
Number of Elected Officials in the Executive Branch 7
Number of Members in the Cabinet 19

JUDICIAL BRANCH

Highest Court .... Supreme Court
Supreme Court Chief Justice .... David E. Gilbertson
Number of Supreme Court Judges 5
Number of Intermediate Appellate Court Judges 0
Number of U.S. Court Districts 1
U.S. Circuit Court .... 8th Circuit

STATE INTERNET ADDRESSES

Official State Website .... http://www.state.sd.us
Governor's Website .... http://www.state.sd.us/governor
Legislative Website .... http://legis.state.sd.us
Judicial Website .... http://www.sdjudicial.com

Tennessee

Nickname .... The Volunteer State
Motto .... Agriculture and Commerce
Flower .... Iris
Bird .... Mockingbird
Tree .... Tulip Poplar
Songs .... When It's Iris Time in Tennessee; The Tennessee Waltz; My Homeland, Tennessee My Tennessee; and Rocky Top
Entered the Union .... June 1, 1796
Capital .... Nashville

STATISTICS

Land Area (square miles) 41,217
Rank in Nation 34th
Population 6,156,719
Rank in Nation 17th
Density per square mile 149.4
Capital City .... Nashville
Population 590,807
Rank in State 2nd
Largest City .... Memphis
Population 674,028
Number of Representatives in Congress 9
Number of Counties 92
Number of Municipal Governments 349
Number of 2009 Electoral Votes 11
Number of School Districts 14
Number of Special Districts 475

LEGISLATIVE BRANCH

Legislative Body .... General Assembly

Speaker of the Senate .... Lt. Gov. Ron Ramsey
Speaker Pro Tem of the Senate .... Jamie Woodson
Chief Clerk of the Senate .... Russell Humphrey

Speaker of the House .... Kent Williams
Speaker Pro Tem of the House .... Lois M. DeBerry
Chief Clerk of the House .... Burney T. Durham

2009 Regular Session .... Jan. 13 - May
Number of Senatorial Districts 33
Number of Representative Districts 99

EXECUTIVE BRANCH

Governor .... Phil Bredesen
Lieutenant Governor .... Ron Ramsey
Secretary of State .... Tre Hargett
Attorney General .... Robert Cooper
Treasurer .... David H. Lillard Jr.
Auditor .... Justin Wilson.
Comptroller of the Treasury .... Jan I. Sylvis

Governor's Present Term 1/2003-1/2011
Number of Elected Officials in the Executive Branch 1
Number of Members in the Cabinet 28

JUDICIAL BRANCH

Highest Court .... Supreme Court
Supreme Court Chief Justice .... Janice M. Holder
Number of Supreme Court Judges 5
Number of Intermediate Appellate Court Judges 24
Number of U.S. Court Districts 3
U.S. Circuit Court .... 6th Circuit

STATE INTERNET ADDRESSES

Official State Website .... http://www.state.tn.us
Governor's Website .... http://www.state.tn.us/governor
Legislative Website .... http://www.legislature.state.tn.us
Judicial Website .... http://www.tsc.state.tn.us

Texas

Nickname ... The Lone Star State
Motto ... Friendship
Flower ... Bluebonnet (Buffalo Clover, Wolf Flower)
Bird ... Mockingbird
Tree ... Pecan
Song ... Texas, Our Texas
Entered the Union ... December 29, 1845
Capital ... Austin

STATISTICS

Land Area (square miles) ... 261,797
Rank in Nation ... 2nd
Population ... 23,904,380
Rank in Nation ... 2nd
Density per square mile ... 91.3
Capital City ... Austin
Population ... 734,074
Rank in State ... 4th
Largest City ... Houston
Population ... 2,208,180
Number of Representatives in Congress ... 32
Number of Counties ... 254
Number of Municipal Governments ... 1,196
Number of 2009 Electoral Votes ... 34
Number of School Districts ... 1,089
Number of Special Districts ... 2,245

LEGISLATIVE BRANCH

Legislative Body ... Legislature

President of the Senate ... Lt. Gov. David Dewhurst
President Pro Tem of the Senate ... Robert Duncan
Secretary of the Senate ... Patsy Spaw

Speaker of the House ... Joe Straus
Speaker Pro Tem of the House ... Sylvester Turner
Chief Clerk of the House ... Robert Haney

2009 Regular Session ... Jan. 13 – Jun. 1
Number of Senatorial Districts ... 31
Number of Representative Districts ... 150

EXECUTIVE BRANCH

Governor ... Rick Perry
Lieutenant Governor ... David Dewhurst
Secretary of State ... Esperanza Andrade
Attorney General ... Greg Abbott
Comptroller of Public Accounts ... Susan Combs
Auditor ... John Keel

Governor's Present Term ... 12/2000-1/2011
Number of Elected Officials in the Executive Branch ... 9
Number of Members in the Cabinet ... No formal cabinet system

JUDICIAL BRANCH

Highest Court ... Supreme Court
Supreme Court Chief Justice ... Wallace B. Jefferson
Number of Supreme Court Judges ... 9
Number of Intermediate Appellate Court Judges ... 80
Number of U.S. Court Districts ... 4
U.S. Circuit Court ... 5th Circuit

STATE INTERNET ADDRESSES

Official State Website ... http://www.state.tx.us
Governor's Website ... http://www.governor.state.tx.us
Legislative Website ... http://www.capitol.state.tx.us
Judicial Website ... http://www.courts.state.tx.us

Utah

Nickname ... The Beehive State
Motto ... Industry
Flower ... Sego Lily
Bird ... California Seagull
Tree ... Blue Spruce
Song ... Utah, We Love Thee
Entered the Union ... January 4, 1896
Capital ... Salt Lake City

STATISTICS

Land Area (square miles) ... 82,144
Rank in Nation ... 12th
Population ... 2,645,330
Rank in Nation ... 34th
Density per square mile ... 32.2
Capital City ... Salt Lake City
Population ... 180,651
Rank in State ... 1st
Largest City ... Salt Lake City
Number of Representatives in Congress ... 3
Number of Counties ... 29
Number of Municipal Governments ... 236
Number of 2009 Electoral Votes ... 5
Number of School Districts ... 40
Number of Special Districts ... 300

LEGISLATIVE BRANCH

Legislative Body ... Legislature

President of the Senate ... Michael G. Waddoups
Secretary of the Senate ... Annette B. Moore

Speaker of the House ... David Clark
Chief Clerk of the House ... Sandy Tenney

2009 Regular Session ... Jan. 26 – March 12
Number of Senatorial Districts ... 29
Number of Representative Districts ... 75

EXECUTIVE BRANCH

Governor ... Jon Huntsman, Jr.
Lieutenant Governor ... Gary R. Herbert
Attorney General ... Mark L. Shurtleff
Treasurer ... Richard Ellis
Auditor ... Auston G. Johnson

Governor's Present Term ... 1/2005-1/2013
Number of Elected Officials in the Executive Branch ... 5
Number of Members in the Cabinet ... 21

JUDICIAL BRANCH

Highest Court ... Supreme Court
Supreme Court Chief Justice ... Christine M. Durham
Number of Supreme Court Judges ... 5
Number of Intermediate Appellate Court Judges ... 7
Number of U.S. Court Districts ... 1
U.S. Circuit Court ... 10th Circuit

STATE INTERNET ADDRESSES

Official State Website ... http://www.utah.gov
Governor's Website ... http://www.utah.gov/governor/
Legislative Website ... http://www.le.state.ut.us
Judicial Website ... http://utcourts.gov

Vermont

Nickname.......The Green Mountain State
Motto.......Freedom and Unity
Flower.......Red Clover
Bird.......Hermit Thrush
Tree.......Sugar Maple
Song.......Hail, Vermont!
Entered the Union.......March 4, 1791
Capital.......Montpelier

STATISTICS

Land Area (square miles).......9,250
Rank in Nation.......43rd
Population.......621,254
Rank in Nation.......49th
Density per square mile.......67.2
Capital City.......Montpelier
Population.......7,806
Rank in State.......13th
Largest City.......Burlington
Population.......38,531
Number of Representatives in Congress.......1
Number of Counties.......14
Number of Municipal Governments.......47
Number of 2009 Electoral Votes.......3
Number of School Districts.......283
Number of Special Districts.......152

LEGISLATIVE BRANCH

Legislative Body.......General Assembly

President of the Senate.......Lt. Gov. Brian Dubie
President Pro Tem of the Senate.......Peter E. Shumlin
Secretary of the Senate.......David A. Gibson

Speaker of the House.......Shap Smith
Clerk of the House.......Donald G. Milne

2009 Regular Session.......Jan. 7 - May
Number of Senatorial Districts.......13
Number of Representative Districts.......106

EXECUTIVE BRANCH

Governor.......James H. Douglas
Lieutenant Governor.......Brian Dubie
Secretary of State.......Deborah Markowitz
Attorney General.......William H. Sorrell
Treasurer.......Jeb Spaulding
Auditor.......Thomas M. Salmon

Governor's Present Term.......1/2003-1/2011
Number of Elected Officials in the Executive Branch.......6
Number of Members in the Cabinet.......7

JUDICIAL BRANCH

Highest Court.......Supreme Court
Supreme Court Chief Justice.......Paul L. Reiber
Number of Supreme Court Judges.......5
Total Number of Appellant Court Judges.......0
Number of U.S. Court Districts.......1
U.S. Circuit Court.......2nd Circuit

STATE INTERNET ADDRESSES

Official State Website.......http://vermont.gov
Governor's Website.......http://www.vermont.gov/governor/
Legislative Website.......http://www.leg.state.vt.us
Judicial Website.......http://www.vermontjudiciary.org

Virginia

Nickname.......The Old Dominion
Motto.......Sic Semper Tyrannis (Thus Always to Tyrants)
Flower.......Dogwood
Bird.......Cardinal
Tree.......Dogwood
Song, emeritus.......Carry Me Back to Old Virginia
Entered the Union.......June 25, 1788
Capital.......Richmond

STATISTICS

Land Area (square miles).......39,594
Rank in Nation.......37th
Population.......7,712,091
Rank in Nation.......12th
Density per square miles.......194.8
Capital City.......Richmond
Population.......200,123
Rank in State.......4th
Largest City.......Virginia Beach
Population.......434,743
Number of Representatives in Congress.......11
Number of Counties.......95
Number of Municipal Governments.......229
Number of 2009 Electoral Votes.......13
Number of School Districts.......132
Number of Special Districts.......196

LEGISLATIVE BRANCH

Legislative Body.......General Assembly

President of the Senate.......Lt. Gov. Bill Bolling
President Pro Tem of the Senate.......Charles J. Colgan
Clerk of the Senate.......Susan Clarke Schaar

Speaker of the House.......William J. Howell
Clerk of the House.......Bruce F. Jamerson

2009 Regular Session.......Jan.14– Feb. 28
Number of Senatorial Districts.......40
Number of Representative Districts.......100

EXECUTIVE BRANCH

Governor.......Timothy M. Kaine
Lieutenant Governor.......William T. Bolling
Secretary of the Commonwealth.......Katherine K. Hanley
Attorney General.......Bill Mims
Treasurer.......Manju Ganeriwala
Auditor.......Walter J. Kucharski
Comptroller.......David Von Moll

Governor's Present Term.......1/2006-1/2010
Number of Elected Officials in the Executive Branch.......3
Number of Members in the Cabinet.......14

JUDICIAL BRANCH

Highest Court.......Supreme Court
Supreme Court Chief Justice.......Leroy R. Hassell Sr.
Number of Supreme Court Judges.......7
Total Number of Appellant Court Judges.......11
Number of U.S. Court Districts.......2
U.S. Circuit Court.......4th Circuit

STATE INTERNET ADDRESSES

Official State Website.......http://www.virginia.gov
Governor's Website..http://www.governor.virginia.gov/MediaRelations/NewsReleases/index.cfm
Legislative Website.......http://legis.state.va.us
Judicial Website.......http://www.courts.state.va.us

Washington

Nickname....The Evergreen State
Motto....Alki (Chinook Indian word meaning By and By)
Flower....Coast Rhododendron
Bird....Willow Goldfinch
Tree....Western Hemlock
Song....Washington, My Home
Entered the Union....November 11, 1889
Capital....Olympia

STATISTICS

Land Area (square miles)....66,544
Rank in Nation....20th
Population....6,468,424
Rank in Nation....13th
Density per square mile....97.2
Capital City....Olympia
Population....44,925
Rank in State....18th
Largest City....Seattle
Population....594,210
Number of Representatives in Congress....9
Number of Counties....39
Number of Municipal Governments....279
Number of 2009 Electoral Votes....11
Number of School Districts....296
Number of Special Districts....1,173

LEGISLATIVE BRANCH

Legislative Body....Legislature

President of the Senate....Lt. Gov. Brad Owen
President Pro Tem of the Senate....Rosa Franklin
Secretary of the Senate....Tom Hoemann

Speaker of the House....Frank Chopp
Speaker Pro Tem of the House....Jeff Morris
Chief Clerk of the House....Barbara Baker

2009 Regular Session....Jan. 12 – Apr. 26
Number of Senatorial Districts....49
Number of Representative Districts....49

EXECUTIVE BRANCH

Governor....Christine O. Gregoire
Lieutenant Governor....Brad Owen
Secretary of State....Sam Reed
Attorney General....Rob McKenna
Treasurer....James McIntire
Auditor....Brian Sonntag
Director of Office of Financial Management....Sadie Rodriguez-Hawkins

Governor's Present Term....1/2005-1/2013
Number of Elected Officials in the Executive Branch....9
Number of Members in the Cabinet....28

JUDICIAL BRANCH

Highest Court....Supreme Court
Supreme Court Chief Justice....Gerry L. Alexander
Number of Supreme Court Judges....9
Total Number of Appellant Court Judges....22
Number of U.S. Court Districts....2
U.S. Circuit Court....9th Circuit

STATE INTERNET ADDRESSES

Official State Website....http://access.wa.gov
Governor's Website....http://www.governor.wa.gov
Legislative Website....http://www.leg.wa.gov
Judicial Website....http://www.courts.wa.gov

West Virginia

Nickname....The Mountain State
Motto....Montani Semper Liberi (Mountaineers Are Always Free)
Flower....Rhododendron
Bird....Cardinal
Tree....Sugar Maple
Songs....West Virginia, My Home Sweet Home; The West Virginia Hills; and This is My West Virginia
Entered the Union....June 20, 1863
Capital....Charleston

STATISTICS

Land Area (square miles)....24,078
Rank in Nation....41st
Population....1,812,035
Rank in Nation....37th
Density per square mile....75.3
Capital City....Charleston
Population....50,478
Rank in State....1st
Largest City....Charleston
Number of Representatives in Congress....3
Number of Counties....55
Number of Municipal Governments....234
Number of 2009 Electoral Votes....5
Number of School Districts....55
Number of Special Districts....342

LEGISLATIVE BRANCH

Legislative Body....Legislature

President of the Senate....Earl Ray Tomblin
President Pro Tem of the Senate....Joseph M. Minard
Clerk of the Senate....Darrell E. Holmes

Speaker of the House of Delegates....Richard Thompson
Speaker Pro Tem of the House of Delegates....Ron Fragale
Clerk of the House of Delegates....Gregory M. Gray

2009 Regular Session....Feb. 11–Apr. 11
Number of Senatorial Districts....17
Number of Representative Districts....58

EXECUTIVE BRANCH

Governor....Joe Manchin III
Lieutenant Governor....Earl Ray Tomblin
Secretary of State....Natalie Tennant
Attorney General....Darrell V. McGraw Jr.
Treasurer....John D. Perdue
Auditor....Glen B. Gainer III

Governor's Present Term....1/2005-1/2013
Number of Elected Officials in the Executive Branch....6
Number of Members in the Cabinet....10

JUDICIAL BRANCH

Highest Court....Supreme Court of Appeals
Supreme Court of Appeals Chief Justice....Brent D. Benjamin
Number of Supreme Court of Appeals Judges....5
Total Number of Appellant Court Judges....0
Number of U.S. Court Districts....2
U.S. Circuit Court....4th Circuit

STATE INTERNET ADDRESSES

Official State Website....http://www.wv.gov/
Governor's Website....http://www.wvgov.org/
Legislative Website....http://www.legis.state.wv.us/
Judicial Website....http://www.state.wv.us/wvsca/

Wisconsin

Nickname* .... The Badger State
Motto .... Forward
Flower .... Wood Violet
Bird .... Robin
Tree .... Sugar Maple
Song .... On, Wisconsin!
Entered the Union .... May 29, 1848
Capitol .... Madison

*unofficial

STATISTICS

Land Area (square miles) 54,310
Rank in Nation 25th
Population 5,601,640
Rank in Nation 20th
Density per square mile 103.1
Capital City .... Madison
Population 228,775
Rank in State 2nd
Largest City .... Milwaukee
Population 602,191
Number of Representatives in Congress 8
Number of Counties 72
Number of Municipal Governments 585
Number of 2009 Electoral Votes 10
Number of School Districts 442
Number of Special Districts 684

LEGISLATIVE BRANCH

Legislative Body .... Legislature

President of the Senate .... Fred A.Risser
President Pro Tem of the Senate .... Pat Kreitlow
Chief Clerk of the Senate .... Robert J. Marchant

Speaker of the Assembly .... Mike Sheridan
Speaker Pro Tem of the Assembly .... Tony Staskunas
Chief Clerk of the Assembly .... Patrick Fuller

2009 Regular Session .... Jan. 13– TBD
Number of Senatorial Districts 33
Number of Representative Districts 99

EXECUTIVE BRANCH

Governor .... James Doyle
Lieutenant Governor .... Barbara Lawton
Secretary of State .... Douglas LaFollette
Attorney General .... J.B. Van Hollen
Treasurer .... Dawn Marie Sass
Auditor .... Janice L. Mueller
Controller .... Steve Censky

Governor's Present Term 1/2003-1/2011
Number of Elected Officials in the Executive Branch 6
Number of Members in the Cabinet 16

JUDICIAL BRANCH

Highest Court .... Supreme Court
Supreme Court Chief Justice .... Shirley S. Abrahamson
Number of Supreme Court Judges 7
Total Number of Appellant Court Judges 16
Number of U.S. Court Districts 2
U.S. Circuit Court .... 7th Circuit

STATE INTERNET ADDRESSES

Official State Website .... http://www.wisconsin.gov
Governor's Website .... http://www.wisgov.state.wi.us
Legislative Website .... http://www.legis.state.wi.us
Judicial Website .... http://www.courts.state.wi.us

Wyoming

Nicknames .... The Equality State and The Cowboy State
Motto .... Equal Rights
Flower .... Indian Paintbrush
Bird .... Western Meadowlark
Tree .... Cottonwood
Song .... Wyoming
Entered the Union .... July 10, 1890
Capital .... Cheyenne

STATISTICS

Land Area (square miles) 97,100
Rank in Nation 9th
Population 522,830
Rank in Nation 50th
Density per square mile 5.4
Capital City .... Cheyenne
Population 55,641
Rank in State 1st
Largest City .... Cheyenne
Number of Representatives in Congress 1
Number of Counties 23
Number of Municipal Governments 98
Number of 2009 Electoral Votes 3
Number of School Districts 55
Number of Special Districts 546

LEGISLATIVE BRANCH

Legislative Body .... Legislature

President of the Senate .... John J. Hines
Vice President of the Senate .... Tony Ross
Chief Clerk of the Senate .... Diane Harvey

Speaker of the House .... Colin M. Simpson
Speaker Pro Tem of the House .... Frank Philp
Chief Clerk of the House .... Patricia Benskin

2009 Regular Session .... Jan. 13 – Mar. 6
Number of Senatorial Districts 30
Number of Representative Districts 60

EXECUTIVE BRANCH

Governor .... Dave Freudenthal
Secretary of State .... Max Maxfield
Attorney General .... Bruce A. Salzburg
Treasurer .... Joseph B. Meyer
Auditor .... Rita Meyer

Governor's Present Term 1/2003-1/2011
Number of Elected Officials in the Executive Branch 5
Number of Members in the Cabinet 20

JUDICIAL BRANCH

Highest Court .... Supreme Court
Supreme Court Chief Justice .... Barton R. Voigt
Number of Supreme Court Judges 5
Total Number of Appellant Court Judges 0
Number of U.S. Court Districts 1
U.S. Circuit Court .... 10th Circuit

STATE INTERNET ADDRESSES

Official State Website .... http://www.state.wy.us
Governor'sWebsite .... http://governor.wy.gov/
Legislative Website .... http://legisweb.state.wy.us
Judicial Website .... http://www.courts.state.wy.us

District of Columbia

Motto .... Justitia Omnibus (Justice to All)
Flower .... American Beauty Rose
Bird .... Wood Thrush
Tree .... Scarlet Oak
Became U.S. Capital .... December 1, 1800

STATISTICS

Land Area (square miles) 61
Population 588,292
Density per square mile 9,581.3
Delegate to Congress* 1
Number of Municipal Governments 1
Number of 2009 Electoral Votes 3
Number of School Districts 2
Number of Special Districts 1

*Committee voting privileges only.

LEGISLATIVE BRANCH

Legislative Body .... Council of the District of Columbia

Chair .... Vincent C. Gray
Chair Pro Tem .... Jack Evans
Secretary to the Council .... Cynthia Brock Smith
2009 Regular Session .... Jan. 6-Dec.31

EXECUTIVE BRANCH

Mayor .... Adrian Fenty
Secretary of the District of Columbia .... Stephanie Scott
Attorney General .... Peter J. Nichols
Chief Financial Officer .... Lasana Mack
Auditor .... Deborah Nichols

Mayor's Present Term 1/2007-1/2011
Number of Elected Officials in the Executive Branch 10
Number of Members in the Cabinet 10

JUDICIAL BRANCH

Highest Court .... D.C. Court of Appeals
Court of Appeals Chief Justice .... Eric Washington
Number of Court of Appeals Judges 9
Number of U.S. Court Districts 1

INTERNET ADDRESSES

Official Website .... http://www.washingtondc.gov
Mayor's Website .... http://dc.gov/mayor/index.shtm
Legislative Website .... http://www.dccouncil.washington.dc.us
Judicial Website .... http://www.dcbar.org

American Samoa

Motto .... Samoa-Maumua le Atua (Samoa, God Is First)
Flower .... Paogo (Ula-fala)
Plant .... Ava
Song .... Amerika Samoa
Became a Territory of the United States 1900
Capital .... Pago Pago

STATISTICS

Land Area (square miles) 77
Population 64,827
Density per square mile 744.0
Capital City .... Pago Pago
Population 4,278
Rank in Territory 3rd
Largest City .... Tafuna
Population 8,409
Delegate to Congress* 1
Number of School Districts 1

*Committee voting privileges only.

LEGISLATIVE BRANCH

Legislative Body .... Legislature

President of the Senate .... Gaoteote P.T. Gaoteote
President Pro Tem of the Senate .... Tulifua Tini Lam Yuen
Secretary of the Senate .... Leo'o V. Ma'o

Speaker of the House .... Savali Talavou Ale
Chief Clerk of the House .... Fialupe Lutu

2009 Regular Session .... Jan. 12 - TBD
Number of Senatorial Districts 12
Number of Representative Districts 17

EXECUTIVE BRANCH

Governor .... Togiola T.A. Tulafono
Lieutenant Governor .... Ipulasi Aito Sunia
Attorney General .... Fepulea'i Afa Ripley Jr.
Treasurer .... Magalei Logovii

Governor's Present Term 4/2003-1/2013
Number of Members in the Cabinet 16

JUDICIAL BRANCH

Highest Court .... High Court
High Court Chief Justice .... F. Michael Kruse
Number of High Court Judges 6

INTERNET ADDRESSES

Official Website .... http://americansamoa.gov/
Governor's Website .... http://www.asg-/gov.com
Legislative Website .... http://www.government.as/legislative.htm
Judicial Website .... http://www.government.as/highcourt.htm

Guam

Nickname .... Hub of the Pacific
Flower .... Puti Tai Nobio (Bougainvillea)
Bird .... Toto (Fruit Dove)
Tree .... Ifit (Intsiabijuga)
Song .... Stand Ye Guamanians
Stone .... Latte
Animal .... Iguana
Ceded to the United States
by Spain .... December 10, 1898
Became a Territory .... August 1, 1950
Request to become a
Commonwealth Plebiscite .... November 1987
Capital .... Hagatna

STATISTICS

Land Area (square miles) 210
Population 175,877
Density per square mile 737.2
Capital .... Hagatna
Population 1,122
Rank in Territory 13th
Largest City .... Tamuning
Population 10,833
Delegate to Congress* 1
Number of School Districts 1

*Committee voting privileges only.

LEGISLATIVE BRANCH

Legislative Body .... Legislature

Speaker .... Judith T. Won Pat
Vice Speaker .... Benjamin J.F. Cruz
Clerk of the Legislature .... Patricia C. Santos

2009 Regular Session .... Jan. 12- TBD
Number of Senatorial Districts 15

EXECUTIVE BRANCH

Governor .... Felix Perez Camacho
Lieutenant Governor .... Michael Cruz
Attorney General .... Alicia Limtiaco
Treasurer .... Y'Asela A. Pereira
Auditor .... Doris Flores Brooks

Governor's Present Term 1/2003-1/2011
Number of Elected Officials in the Executive Branch 10
Number of Members in the Cabinet 55

JUDICIAL BRANCH

Highest Court .... Supreme Court
Supreme Court Chief Justice .... Robert J. Torres Jr.
Number of Supreme Court Judges 3

INTERNET ADDRESSES

Official Website .... http://ns.gov.gu
Governor's Website .... http://ns.gov.gu/webtax/govoff.html
Legislative Website .... http://www.guam.net/gov/senate
Judicial Website .... http://www.justice.gov.gu

Northern Mariana Islands

Flower .... Plumeria
Bird .... Marianas Fruit Dove
Tree .... Flame Tree
Song .... Gi TaloGi Halom Tasi
Administered by the United States
a trusteeship for the United Nations .... July 18, 1947
Voters approved a proposed constitution .... June 1975
U.S. president signed covenant agreeing to commonwealth status for
the islands .... March 24, 1976
Became a self-governing Commonwealth .... January 9, 1978
Capital .... Saipan

STATISTICS

Land Area (square miles) 179
Population 86,616
Density per square mile 386.7
Capital City .... Saipan
Population 62,392
Largest City .... Saipan
Delegate to Congress* 1
Number of School Districts 1

*Committee voting privileges only.

LEGISLATIVE BRANCH

Legislative Body .... Legislature

President of the Senate .... Pete P. Reyes
Vice President of the Senate .... Felix T. Mendiola
Clerk of the Senate .... Doris Bermudes

Speaker of the House .... Arnold I. Palacios
Vice Speaker of the House .... Joseph P. Deleon Guerrero
Clerk of the House .... Evelyn C. Fleming

2009 Regular Session .... Jan. 14 - TBD
Number of Senatorial Districts 9
Number of Representative Districts 18

EXECUTIVE BRANCH

Governor .... Benigno Fitial
Lieutenant Governor .... Timothy Villagomez
Attorney General .... Gregory Baka
Treasurer .... Antoinette S. Calvo

Governor's Present Term 1/2006-1/2010
Number of Elected Officials in the Executive Branch 10
Number of Members in the Cabinet 16

JUDICIAL BRANCH

Highest Court .... Commonwealth Supreme Court
Commonwealth Supreme Court Chief Justice .... Miguel S. Demapan
Number of Commonwealth Supreme Court Judges 3

INTERNET ADDRESSES

Official Website .... www.gksoft.com/govt/en/mp.html
Governor's Website .... http://www.executive.gov.mp/
Legislative Website .... http://www.cnmileg.gov.mp
Judicial Website http://cnmilaw.org/htmlpage/hpg34.htm

Puerto Rico

Nickname .... Island of Enchantment
Motto .... Joannes Est Nomen Ejus
(John is Thy Name)
Flower .... Maga
Bird .... Reinita
Tree .... Ceiba
Song .... La Borinquena
Became a Territory of the
United States .... December 10, 1898
Became a self-governing Commonwealth .... July 25, 1952
Capital .... San Juan

STATISTICS

Land Area (square miles) 3,425
Population 3,942,375
Density per square mile 1,146.8
Capital City .... San Juan
Population 434,374
Largest City .... San Juan
Resident Commissioner in Congress* 1
Number of School Districts 1

*Committee voting privileges only.

LEGISLATIVE BRANCH

Legislative Body .... Legislative Assembly

President of the Senate .... Thomas Rivera Schatz
Vice President of the Senate .... Roberto Arango
Secretary of the Senate .... Manuel A. Torres Nieves

Speaker of the House .... Jenniffer González Colón
Speaker Pro Tem .... Iris Ruiz Class
Clerk of the House .... Brunilda Ortiz-Rodriguez

2009 Regular Session .... Jan. 12- June

Governor .... Luis Fortuño
Secretary of State .... Kenneth McClintock
Attorney General .... Antonio Sagardia
Treasurer .... Juan Carlos Puig

Governor's Present Term 1/2009-12/13
Number of Elected Officials in the Executive Branch 10
Number of Members in the Cabinet 10

JUDICIAL BRANCH

Highest Court .... Supreme Court
Supreme Court Chief Justice .... Frederico Hernandez-Denton
Number of Supreme Court Judges 7

INTERNET ADDRESSES

Official State Website .... http://www.statelocalgov.net/other-pr.htm
Governor's Website .... http://www.fortaleza.gobierno.pr
Senate Website .... http://www.camaradepuertorico.org
House Website .... http://www.camaradepuertorico.org
Judicial Website .... http://www.tribunalpr.org

U.S. Virgin Islands

Nickname .... The American Paradise
Motto .... United in Pride and Hope
Flower .... The Yellow Cedar
Bird .... Yellow Breast or Banana Quit
Song .... Virgin Islands March
Purchased from Denmark .... March 31, 1917
Capital .... Charlotte Amalie, St. Thomas

STATISTICS

Land Area (square miles)* 134
Population 109,840
Density per square mile 810.5
Capital City .... Charlotte Amalie, St. Thomas
Population 18,914
Largest City .... Charlotte Amalie, St. Thomas
Delegate to Congress** 1
Number of School Districts 1

*The U.S. Virgin Islands is comprised of three large islands (St. Croix, St. John, and St. Thomas) and 50 smaller islands and cays.
**Committee voting privileges only.

LEGISLATIVE BRANCH

Legislative Body .... Legislature

President .... Adlah Donastorg Jr.
Vice President .... Michael Thurland
Legislative Secretary of the Senate .... Sammuel Sanes

2009 Regular Session .... Jan.12 – Dec. 31

EXECUTIVE BRANCH

Governor .... John deJongh, Jr.
Lieutenant Governor .... Gregory Francis
Attorney General .... Vincent Frazer
Commissioner of Finance .... Laurel Payne

Governor's Present Term 1/2007-1/2011
Number of Elected Officials in the Executive Branch 10
Number of Members in the Cabinet 21

JUDICIAL BRANCH

Highest Court .... Territorial Court
Territorial Court Chief Justice .... Darryl Dean Donohue
Number of Territorial Court Judges 4
U.S. Circuit Court 3rd

INTERNET ADDRESSES

Official Website .... http://www.statelocalgov.net/other-vi.htm
Governor's Website .... www.governordejongh.com/
Legislative Website .... http://www.senate.gov.vi
Judicial Website .... http://www.vid.uscourts.gov

Index

—A—

—D—

—E—

—G—

—H—

—I—

—J—

—K—

—L—

—M—

—N—

—O—

—P—

—Q—

—R—

—S—

—T—

—U—

—V—

—W—

—X-Y-Z—